AL-AZHAR
ISLAMIC RESEARCH ACADEMY
GENERAL DEPARTMENT
For Research, Writting & Translation

نموذج رقم "١٧"

الأزهـــر
مجمـع البحـوث الإسـلامية
الإدارة العـــامة
للبحـوث والتـأليف والترجمة

السيد/

السلام عليكم ورحمة الله وبركاته- وبعد:

فبناءً على الطلب الخاص بفحص ومراجعة كتاب: The Clear Qur'ān

تأليف: مصطفى علي أمين خطاب

نفيد بأنه ليس بالكتاب ما يمنع من نشره، وبأنه لا مانع من طبعه ونشره على نفقتكم الخاصة.

مع التأكيد على ضرورة العناية التامة بكتابة الآيات القرآنية والأحاديث النبوية الشريفة والالتزام بتسليم (٥) خمس نسخ لمكتبة الأزهر الشريف بعد الطبع.

علمًا بأن هذه الموافقة مقصورة على الطبعة الأولى للكتاب التى أعطيت عنها، وأن هذه الموافقة يزول أثرها، ويتعين تجديدها على أى طبعة جديدة تطبع بخلاف الطبعة الأولى أو بمرور خمس سنوات من تاريخ تصريح تلك الطبعة أيهما أقرب، ومن ثم فإنه لا يجوز إرفاقها بأى طبعة أخرى، التزامًا بأحكام القانون التى يتعين الالتزام بها.

والله تبارك وتعالى من وراء القصد،،،
والسلام عليكم ورحمة الله وبركاته،،،

تحريرًا فى: ٢٩/٧/ ١٤٣٧هـ
الموافق: ٣/ ٥/ ٢٠١٦م

مدير عام
الإدارة العامة للبحوث
والتأليف والترجمة

Surah Index

الجزء	الصّفحة	السّورة	رقمها	الجزء	الصّفحة	السّورة	رقمها
20	386	سورة القصص	28	1	2	سورة الفاتحة	1
20-21	397	سورة العنكبوت	29	1-2-3	3	سورة البقرة	2
21	405	سورة الروم	30	3-4	51	سورة آل عمران	3
21	412	سورة لقمان	31	4-5-6	78	سورة النّساء	4
21	416	سورة السجدة	32	6-7	107	سورة المائدة	5
21-22	419	سورة الْأحزاب	33	7-8	129	سورة الانعام	6
22	429	سورة سبأ	34	8-9	152	سورة الأعراف	7
22	435	سورة فاطر	35	9-10	178	سورة الأنفال	8
22-23	441	سورة يس	36	10-11	188	سورة التوبة	9
23	446	سورة الصافات	37	11	209	سورة يونس	10
23	453	سورة ص	38	11-12	222	سورة هود	11
23-24	459	سورة الزمر	39	12-13	236	سورة يوسف	12
24	468	سورة غافر	40	13	250	سورة الرعد	13
24-25	478	سورة فصلت	41	13	256	سورة إبراهيم	14
25	484	سورة الشورى	42	13-14	262	سورة الحجر	15
25	490	سورة الزخرف	43	14	268	سورة النحل	16
25	496	سورة الدخان	44	15	283	سورة الإسراء	17
25	499	سورة الجاثية	45	15-16	294	سورة الكهف	18
26	503	سورة الْأحقاف	46	16	306	سورة مريم	19
26	507	سورة محمد	47	16	313	سورة طه	20
26	512	سورة الفتح	48	17	323	سورة الأنبياء	21
26	516	سورة الحجرات	49	17	332	سورة الحجّ	22
26	519	سورة ق	50	18	343	سورة المؤمنون	23
26-27	521	سورة الذاريات	51	18	351	سورة النور	24
27	524	سورة الطور	52	18-19	360	سورة الفرقان	25
27	527	سورة النجم	53	19	367	سورة الشعراء	26
27	529	سورة القمر	54	19-20	377	سورة النمل	27

الجز.	الصّفحة	السّورة	رقمها	الجز.	الصّفحة	السّورة	رقمها
30	596	سورة البروج	85	27	532	سورة الرحمن	55
30	597	سورة الطارق	86	27	535	سورة الواقعة	56
30	598	سورة الأعلى	87	27	538	سورة الحديد	57
30	598	سورة الغاشية	88	28	543	سورة المجادلة	58
30	599	سورة الفجر	89	28	546	سورة الحشر	59
30	601	سورة البلد	90	28	550	سورة الممتحنة	60
30	601	سورة الشمس	91	28	552	سورة الصف	61
30	602	سورة اليل	92	28	554	سورة الجمعة	62
30	603	سورة الضحى	93	28	555	سورة المنافقون	63
30	603	سورة الإنشراح	94	28	557	سورة التغابن	64
30	604	سورة التين	95	28	559	سورة الطلاق	65
30	604	سورة العلق	96	28	561	سورة التحريم	66
30	605	سورة القدرِ	97	29	563	سورة الملك	67
30	605	سورة البينة	98	29	565	سورة القلم	68
30	606	سورة الزلزلة	99	29	568	سورة الحآقة	69
30	606	سورة العاديات	100	29	570	سورة المعارج	70
30	607	سورة القارعة	101	29	572	سورة نوح	71
30	607	سورة التكاثر	102	29	574	سورة الجن	72
30	608	سورة العصر	103	29	577	سورة المزمل	73
30	608	سورة الهمزة	104	29	579	سورة المدثر	74
30	608	سورة الفيل	105	29	581	سورة القيامة	75
30	609	سورة قريش	106	29	583	سورة الإنسان	76
30	609	سورة الماعون	107	29	585	سورة المرسلات	77
30	609	سورة الكوثر	108	30	587	سورة النبأ	78
30	609	سورة الكافرون	109	30	588	سورة النازعات	79
30	610	سورة النصر	110	30	590	سورة عبس	80
30	610	سورة اللهب	111	30	591	سورة التكوير	81
30	610	سورة الإخلاص	112	30	592	سورة الإنفطار	82
30	611	سورة الفلق	113	30	593	سورة المطففين	83
30	611	سورة الناس	114	30	595	سورة الإنشقاق	84

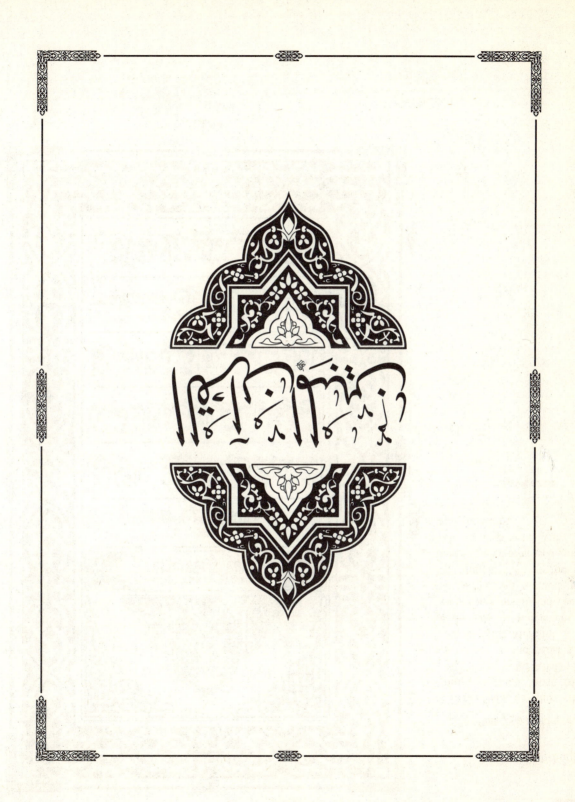

1. Al-Fâtiḥah

1. The Opening (Al-Fâtiḥah)

Prayer for Guidance

1. In the Name of Allah—the Most Compassionate, Most Merciful, 2. All praise is for Allah—Lord of all worlds, 3. the Most Compassionate, Most Merciful, 4. Master of the Day of Judgement. 5. You ˹alone˺ we worship and You ˹alone˺ we ask for help. 6. Guide us along the Straight Path, 7. the Path of those You have blessed—not those You are displeased with, or those who are astray.

2. The Cow (Al-Baqarah)

In the Name of Allah—the Most Compassionate, Most Merciful

Qualities of the Believers

1. *Alif-Lām-Mīm.*[1] **2.** This is the Book! There is no doubt about it[2]— a guide for those mindful ´of Allah´,[3] **3.** who believe in the unseen,[4] establish prayer, and donate from what We have provided for them, **4.** and who believe in what has been revealed to you ´O Prophet´[5] and what was revealed before you, and have sure faith in the Hereafter.

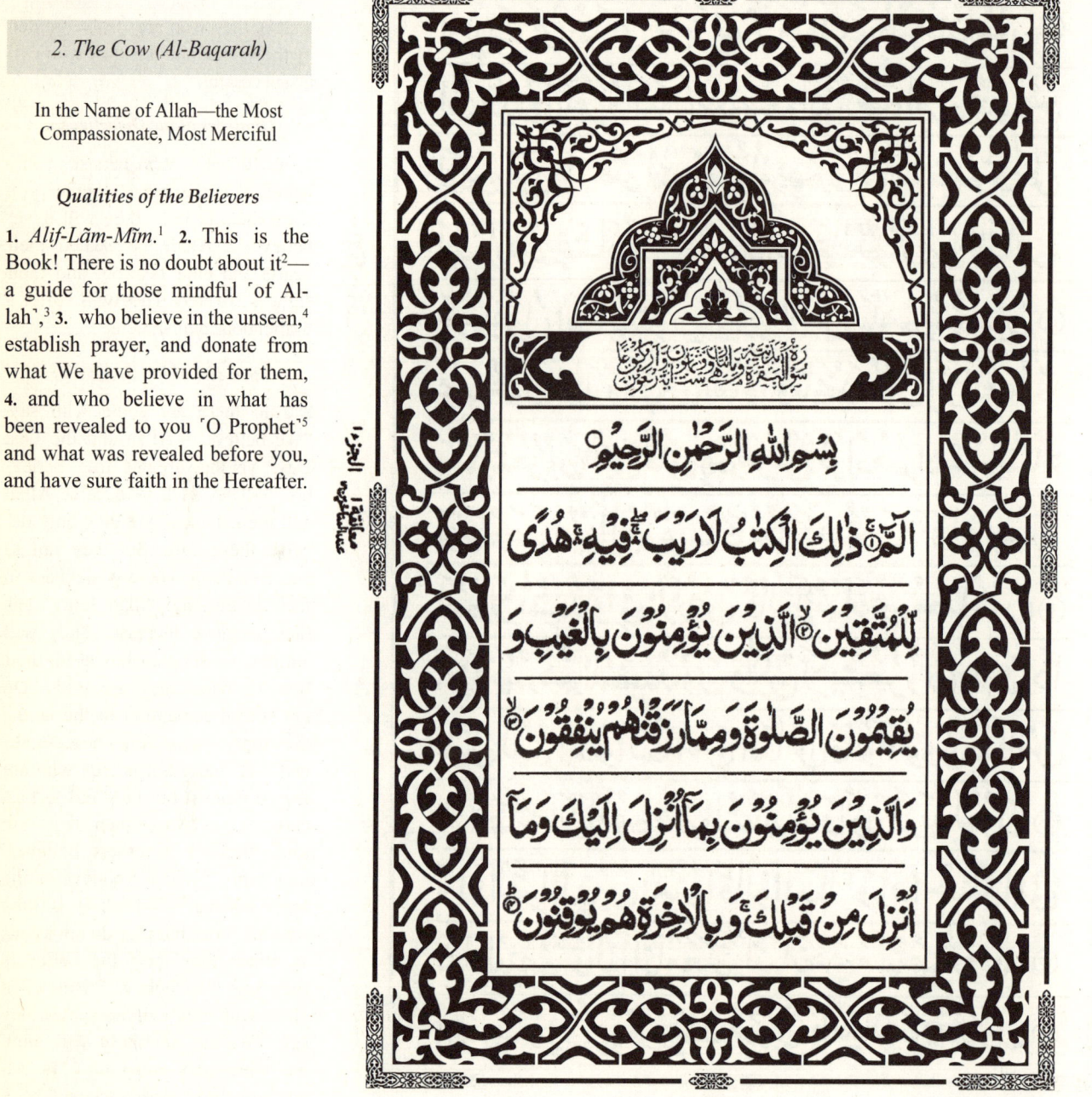

---

1   *See* Stylistic Features for information about these letters.
2   i.e., there is no doubt regarding its authenticity or consistency.
3   The word *muttaqi* (plural *muttaqūn*) can be translated as one who is mindful ´of Allah´, devout, pious, God-fearing, righteous, or God-conscious.
4   i.e., the belief in Allah, the angels, and the Day of Judgment.
5   *See* Notes on Translation for information about the use of ´O Prophet´.

اُولٰٓئِكَ عَلٰى هُدًى مِّنْ رَّبِّهِمْ ۖ وَاُولٰٓئِكَ هُمُ الْمُفْلِحُوْنَ ۝

اِنَّ الَّذِيْنَ كَفَرُوْا سَوَاءٌ عَلَيْهِمْ ءَاَنْذَرْتَهُمْ اَمْ لَمْ تُنْذِرْهُمْ لَا يُؤْمِنُوْنَ ۝ خَتَمَ اللّٰهُ عَلٰى قُلُوْبِهِمْ وَعَلٰى سَمْعِهِمْ ۖ وَعَلٰٓى

اَبْصَارِهِمْ غِشَاوَةٌ ۖ وَّلَهُمْ عَذَابٌ عَظِيْمٌ ۝ وَمِنَ النَّاسِ

مَنْ يَّقُوْلُ اٰمَنَّا بِاللّٰهِ وَبِالْيَوْمِ الْاٰخِرِ وَمَا هُمْ بِمُؤْمِنِيْنَ ۝

يُخٰدِعُوْنَ اللّٰهَ وَالَّذِيْنَ اٰمَنُوْا ۖ وَمَا يَخْدَعُوْنَ اِلَّآ اَنْفُسَهُمْ

وَمَا يَشْعُرُوْنَ ۝ فِيْ قُلُوْبِهِمْ مَّرَضٌ ۙ فَزَادَهُمُ اللّٰهُ مَرَضًا ۖ

وَّلَهُمْ عَذَابٌ اَلِيْمٌ ۢ بِمَا كَانُوْا يَكْذِبُوْنَ ۝ وَاِذَا قِيْلَ

لَهُمْ لَا تُفْسِدُوْا فِى الْاَرْضِ ۙ قَالُوْٓا اِنَّمَا نَحْنُ مُصْلِحُوْنَ ۝

اَلَآ اِنَّهُمْ هُمُ الْمُفْسِدُوْنَ وَلٰكِنْ لَّا يَشْعُرُوْنَ ۝ وَاِذَا

قِيْلَ لَهُمْ اٰمِنُوْا كَمَآ اٰمَنَ النَّاسُ قَالُوْٓا اَنُؤْمِنُ كَمَآ اٰمَنَ

السُّفَهَآءُ ۗ اَلَآ اِنَّهُمْ هُمُ السُّفَهَآءُ وَلٰكِنْ لَّا يَعْلَمُوْنَ ۝

وَاِذَا لَقُوا الَّذِيْنَ اٰمَنُوْا قَالُوْٓا اٰمَنَّا ۖ وَاِذَا خَلَوْا اِلٰى

شَيٰطِيْنِهِمْ ۙ قَالُوْٓا اِنَّا مَعَكُمْ ۙ اِنَّمَا نَحْنُ مُسْتَهْزِءُوْنَ ۝

اَللّٰهُ يَسْتَهْزِئُ بِهِمْ وَيَمُدُّهُمْ فِيْ طُغْيَانِهِمْ يَعْمَهُوْنَ ۝

5. It is they who are ˹truly˺ guided by their Lord, and it is they who will be successful.

Qualities of the Disbelievers

6. As for those who persist in disbelief, it is the same whether you warn them or not—they will never believe. 7. Allah has sealed their hearts and their hearing, and their sight is covered. They will suffer a tremendous punishment.

Qualities of the Hypocrites

8. And there are some who say, "We believe in Allah and the Last Day," yet they are not ˹true˺ believers. 9. They seek to deceive Allah and the believers, yet they only deceive themselves, but they fail to perceive it. 10. There is sickness in their hearts, and Allah ˹only˺ lets their sickness increase. They will suffer a painful punishment for their lies. 11. When they are told, "Do not spread corruption in the land," they reply, "We are only peace-makers!"[6] 12. Indeed, it is they who are the corruptors, but they fail to perceive it. 13. And when they are told, "Believe as others believe," they reply, "Will we believe as the fools believe?" Indeed, it is they who are fools, but they do not know. 14. When they meet the believers they say, "We believe." But when alone with their evil associates they say, "We are definitely with you; we were only mocking." 15. Allah will throw their mockery back at them, leaving them to continue wandering blindly in their defiance.

---

6 When they were criticized for their close association with the pagans who were hostile to Muslims, they would argue that they only wanted to make peace between Muslims and their enemies.

16. They are the ones who trade guidance for misguidance. But this trade is profitless, and they are not ʿrightlyʾ guided.

Hypocrites' Example

17. Their example is that of someone who kindles a fire, but when it lights up all around them, Allah takes away their light, leaving them in complete darkness—unable to see. **18.** They are ʿwilfullyʾ deaf, dumb, and blind, so they will never return ʿto the Right Pathʾ.

Another Example

19. Or ʿthose caught inʾ a rainstorm from the sky with darkness, thunder, and lightning. They press their fingers into their ears at the sound of every thunder-clap for fear of death. And Allah encompasses the disbelievers ʿby His mightʾ. **20.** It is as if the lightning were about to snatch away their sight. Whenever lightning strikes, they walk in its light, but when darkness covers them, they stand still. Had Allah willed, He could have taken away their hearing and sight. Surely Allah is Most Capable of everything.

Order to Worship Allah Alone

21. O humanity! Worship your Lord, Who created you and those before you, so that you may become mindful ʿof Himʾ. **22.** ʿHe is the Oneʾ Who has made the earth a place of settlement for you and the sky a canopy; and sends down rain from the sky, causing fruits to grow as a provision for you. So do not knowingly set up equals to Allah ʿin worshipʾ.

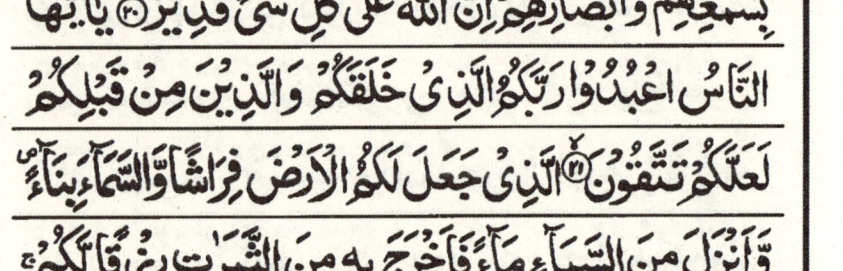

The Challenge of the Quran

23. And if you are in doubt about what We have revealed to Our servant,[7] then produce a *sûrah* like it and call your helpers other than Allah, if what you say is true.

---

7 Muhammad (ﷺ).

بِسْمِ اللَّهِ

Arabic text

فَإِن لَّمْ تَفْعَلُوا وَلَن تَفْعَلُوا فَاتَّقُوا النَّارَ الَّتِي وَقُودُهَا النَّاسُ وَالْحِجَارَةُ أُعِدَّتْ لِلْكَافِرِينَ ۝ وَبَشِّرِ الَّذِينَ آمَنُوا وَعَمِلُوا الصَّالِحَاتِ أَنَّ لَهُمْ جَنَّاتٍ تَجْرِي مِن تَحْتِهَا الْأَنْهَارُ كُلَّمَا رُزِقُوا مِنْهَا مِن ثَمَرَةٍ رِّزْقًا قَالُوا هَٰذَا الَّذِي رُزِقْنَا مِن قَبْلُ وَأُتُوا بِهِ مُتَشَابِهًا وَلَهُمْ فِيهَا أَزْوَاجٌ مُّطَهَّرَةٌ وَهُمْ فِيهَا خَالِدُونَ ۝ إِنَّ اللَّهَ لَا يَسْتَحْيِي أَن يَضْرِبَ مَثَلًا مَّا بَعُوضَةً فَمَا فَوْقَهَا فَأَمَّا الَّذِينَ آمَنُوا فَيَعْلَمُونَ أَنَّهُ الْحَقُّ مِن رَّبِّهِمْ وَأَمَّا الَّذِينَ كَفَرُوا فَيَقُولُونَ مَاذَا أَرَادَ اللَّهُ بِهَٰذَا مَثَلًا يُضِلُّ بِهِ كَثِيرًا وَيَهْدِي بِهِ كَثِيرًا وَمَا يُضِلُّ بِهِ إِلَّا الْفَاسِقِينَ ۝ الَّذِينَ يَنقُضُونَ عَهْدَ اللَّهِ مِن بَعْدِ مِيثَاقِهِ وَيَقْطَعُونَ مَا أَمَرَ اللَّهُ بِهِ أَن يُوصَلَ وَيُفْسِدُونَ فِي الْأَرْضِ أُولَٰئِكَ هُمُ الْخَاسِرُونَ ۝ كَيْفَ تَكْفُرُونَ بِاللَّهِ وَكُنتُمْ أَمْوَاتًا فَأَحْيَاكُمْ ثُمَّ يُمِيتُكُمْ ثُمَّ يُحْيِيكُمْ ثُمَّ إِلَيْهِ تُرْجَعُونَ ۝ هُوَ الَّذِي خَلَقَ لَكُم مَّا فِي الْأَرْضِ جَمِيعًا ثُمَّ اسْتَوَىٰ إِلَى السَّمَاءِ فَسَوَّاهُنَّ سَبْعَ سَمَاوَاتٍ وَهُوَ بِكُلِّ شَيْءٍ عَلِيمٌ ۝

---

24. But if you are unable to do so—and you will never be able to do so—then fear the Fire fuelled with people and stones, which is prepared for the disbelievers.

Reward of the Believers

25. Give good news ˹O Prophet˺ to those who believe and do good that they will have Gardens under which rivers flow. Whenever provided with fruit, they will say, "This is what we were given before," for they will be served fruit that looks similar ˹but tastes different˺. They will have pure spouses,[8] and they will be there forever.

Wisdom Behind Parables

26. Surely Allah does not shy away from using the parable of a mosquito or what is even smaller. As for the believers, they know that it is the truth from their Lord. And as for the disbelievers, they argue, "What does Allah mean by such a parable?" Through this ˹test˺, He leaves many to stray, and guides many. And He leaves none to stray except the rebellious— 27. those who violate Allah's covenant after it has been affirmed, break whatever ˹ties˺ Allah has ordered to be maintained, and spread corruption in the land. It is they who are the ˹true˺ losers.

Allah's Creation

28. How can you deny Allah? You were lifeless and He gave you life, then He will cause you to die and again bring you to life, and then to Him you will ˹all˺ be returned. 29. He is the One Who created everything in the earth for you. Then He turned towards the heaven, forming it into seven heavens. And He has ˹perfect˺ knowledge of all things.

---

8 Residents of Paradise will be in a perfect condition. There will be neither physical impurities such as illness, urination, defecation, or menstruation; nor spiritual blemishes such as jealousy, envy, or hatred.

2. Al-Baqarah

Honouring Adam

30. ˹Remember˺ when your Lord said to the angels, "I am going to place a successive ˹human˺ authority on earth." They asked ˹Allah˺, "Will You place in it someone who will spread corruption there and shed blood while we glorify Your praises and proclaim Your holiness?" Allah responded, "I know what you do not know."[9] 31. He taught Adam the names of all things, then He presented them to the angels and said, "Tell Me the names of these, if what you say is true?" 32. They replied, "Glory be to You! We have no knowledge except what You have taught us. You are truly the All-Knowing, All-Wise." 33. Allah said, "O Adam! Inform them of their names." Then when Adam did, Allah said, "Did I not tell you that I know the secrets of the heavens and the earth, and I know what you reveal and what you conceal?" 34. And ˹remember˺ when We said to the angels, "Prostrate before Adam,"[10] so they all did—but not *Iblîs*,[11] who refused and acted arrogantly,[12] becoming unfaithful.

Temptation and Fall

35. We cautioned, "O Adam! Live with your wife in Paradise and eat as freely as you please, but do not approach this tree, or else you will be wrongdoers." 36. But Satan deceived them—leading to their fall from the ˹blissful˺ state they were in,[13] and We said, "Descend from the heavens ˹to the earth˺ as enemies to each other.[14] You will find in the earth a residence and provision for your appointed stay." 37. Then Adam was inspired with words ˹of prayer˺ by his Lord,[15] so He accepted his repentance. Surely He is the Accepter of Repentance, Most Merciful.

---

9 Allah knew that there would be many righteous people who would do good, make peace, and stand up for justice. Since humans have free choice, whoever chooses to believe and do good is better in the sight of Allah than all other beings, and whoever chooses to disbelieve and do evil is worse than all other beings. See 98:6-8.

10 Prostration in this verse does not mean worship, but an act of respect. A similar occurrence can be found in Sûrah 12, where Jacob (☮), his wife, and his eleven children knelt down before Joseph (☮).

11 Iblîs was the name of Satan before his fall from grace. Iblîs was not an angel, but one of the jinn (see 18:50). Jinn are another creation of Allah, similar to humans in that they—unlike angels—have free will, but are made of smokeless fire and live in another plane of existence.

12 The command to prostrate was a test of obedience. Satan arrogantly refused to comply because he believed he was superior to Adam—arguing that Adam was made of mud while Satan was made of fire (see 7:12).

13 Both Adam and Eve were deceived, both sinned, and both were later forgiven. There is no concept of original sin in Islam.

14 i.e., humans and Satan.

15 The prayer that Adam and Eve were inspired to say is mentioned in 7:23, "Our Lord! We have wronged ourselves. If You do not forgive us and have mercy on us, we will certainly be losers."

38. We said, "Descend all of you! Then when guidance comes to you from Me, whoever follows it, there will be no fear for them, nor will they grieve. **39.** But those who disbelieve and deny Our signs will be the residents of the Fire. They will be there forever."

Advice to the Israelites

40. O children of Israel![16] Remember My favours upon you. Fulfil your covenant and I will fulfil Mine, and stand in awe of Me ˹alone˺. **41.** Believe in My revelations which confirm your Scriptures. Do not be the first to deny them or trade them for a fleeting gain.[17] And be mindful of Me. **42.** Do not mix truth with falsehood or hide the truth knowingly. **43.** Establish prayer, pay alms-tax,[18] and bow down with those who bow down.

More Advice

44. Do you preach righteousness and fail to practice it yourselves, although you read the Scripture? Do you not understand? **45.** And seek help through patience and prayer. Indeed, it is a burden except for the humble— **46.** those who are certain that they will meet their Lord and to Him they will return.

Allah's Favours upon the Israelites
1) Honour

47. O Children of Israel! Remember ˹all˺ the favours I granted you and how I honoured you above the others.[19] **48.** Guard yourselves against the Day on which no soul will be of help to another. No intercession[20] will be accepted, no ransom taken, and no help will be given.

---

16 Israel is another name for Prophet Jacob.

17 Trading Allah's revelations for a fleeting gain is a recurring theme in the first few sûrahs of the Quran. This refers to the practice of some Jewish authorities in Medina who contradicted certain rulings in the Torah by giving people lenient opinions only to please them in exchange for money.

18 The alms-tax (zakâh) is the payment of 2.5% of someone's savings only if the amount is equivalent to or greater than 85 g of gold, if that amount remains untouched for a whole Islamic year—around 355 days.

19 Meaning, I chose you above all peoples of your time.

20 "Intercession" is the act of pleading with Allah on behalf of another person on the Day of Judgment.

2. Al-Baqarah

Favour 2) Ending Persecution

49. ˹Remember˺ how We delivered you from the people of Pharaoh, who afflicted you with dreadful torment, slaughtering your sons and keeping your women. That was a severe test from your Lord.

Favour 3) Parting the Sea

50. And ˹remember˺ when We parted the sea, rescued you, and drowned Pharaoh's people before your very eyes.

Favour 4) Forgiving Calf-Worship

51. And ˹remember˺ when We appointed forty nights for Moses, then you worshipped the calf in his absence, acting wrongfully. 52. Even then We ˹still˺ forgave you so perhaps you would be grateful.

Favour 5) Revealing the Torah

53. And ˹remember˺ when We gave Moses the Scripture—the Decisive Authority that perhaps you would be ˹rightly˺ guided.

Favour 6) The Way to Forgiveness

54. And ˹remember˺ when Moses said to his people, "O my people! Surely you have wronged yourselves by worshipping the calf, so turn in repentance to your Creator and execute ˹the calf-worshippers among˺ yourselves. That is best for you in the sight of your Creator." Then He accepted your repentance. Surely He is the Accepter of Repentance, Most Merciful.

Favour 7) Forgiving the Demand to See Allah

55. And ˹remember˺ when you said, "O Moses! We will never believe you until we see Allah with our own eyes," so a thunderbolt struck you while you were looking on. 56. Then We brought you back to life after your death, so that perhaps you would be grateful.

Favour 8) Food and Shade

57. And ˹remember when˺ We shaded you with clouds and sent down to you manna and quails,[21] ˹saying˺, "Eat from the good things We have provided for you." The evildoers ˹certainly˺ did not wrong Us, but wronged themselves.

---

21 Manna (heavenly bread) and quails (chicken-like birds) sustained the children of Israel in the wilderness after they left Egypt.

2. Al-Baqarah

Favour 9) Permission to Enter Jerusalem

58. And ˹remember˺ when We said, "Enter this city and eat freely from wherever you please; enter the gate with humility, saying, 'Absolve us.' We will forgive your sins and multiply the reward for the good-doers."

59. But the wrongdoers changed the words they were commanded to say. So We sent down a punishment from the heavens upon them for their rebelliousness.

Favour 10) Water for All

60. And ˹remember˺ when Moses prayed for water for his people, We said, "Strike the rock with your staff." Then twelve springs gushed out, ˹and˺ each tribe knew its drinking place. ˹We then said,˺ "Eat and drink of Allah's provisions, and do not go about spreading corruption in the land."

Punishment for Defiance

61. And ˹remember˺ when you said, "O Moses! We cannot endure the same meal ˹every day˺. So ˹just˺ call upon your Lord on our behalf, He will bring forth for us some of what the earth produces of herbs, cucumbers, garlic, lentils, and onions." Moses scolded ˹them˺, "Do you exchange what is better for what is worse? ˹You can˺ go down to any village and you will find what you have asked for." They were stricken with disgrace and misery, and they invited the displeasure of Allah for rejecting Allah's signs and unjustly killing the prophets. This is ˹a fair reward˺ for their disobedience and violations.

2. Al-Baqarah

Reward of the Believers

62. Indeed, the believers, Jews, Christians, and Sabians[22]—whoever 'truly' believes in Allah and the Last Day and does good will have their reward with their Lord. And there will be no fear for them, nor will they grieve.[23]

Allah's Covenant with the Israelites

63. And 'remember' when We took a covenant from you and raised the mountain above you 'saying', "Hold firmly to that 'Scripture' which We have given you and observe its teachings so perhaps you will become mindful 'of Allah'." **64.** Yet you turned away afterwards. Had it not been for Allah's grace and mercy upon you, you would have certainly been of the losers.

Punishment for the Sabbath-Breakers

65. You are already aware of those of you who broke the Sabbath. We said to them, "Be disgraced apes!"[24] **66.** So We made their fate an example to present and future generations, and a lesson to the God-fearing.

Story of the Cow

67. And 'remember' when Moses said to his people, "Allah commands you to sacrifice a cow."[25] They replied, "Are you mocking us?" Moses responded, "I seek refuge in Allah from acting foolishly!" **68.** They said, "Call upon your Lord to clarify for us what type 'of cow' it should be!" He replied, "Allah says, 'The cow should neither be old nor young but in between. So do as you are commanded!'" **69.** They said, "Call upon your Lord to specify for us its colour." He replied, "Allah says, 'It should be a bright yellow cow—pleasant to see.'"

---

22 The Sabians are an indigenous group that believes in a supreme being and lives mostly in Iraq.
23 This verse should be understood in light of 3:19 and 3:85. For more details, see the Introduction.
24 Although many scholars believe that these individuals were turned into real apes, others interpret this verse in a metaphorical sense. This style is not uncommon in the Quran. *See* 62:5 regarding the donkey that carries books and 2:18 regarding the deaf, dumb, and blind.
25 This sûrah is named after the cow in this story, which happened at the time of Moses ( ). A rich man was killed by his nephew, his only heir, and the body was thrown at the door of an innocent man. After a long investigation, no one was identified as the killer. Moses ( ) prayed for guidance and was told that the only way to find the killer was to sacrifice a cow and strike the victim with a piece of it. When this was done, the victim spoke miraculously and said who the killer was.

بِسْمِ قَالُوا ادْعُ لَنَا رَبَّكَ يُبَيِّن لَّنَا مَا هِيَ إِنَّ الْبَقَرَ تَشَٰبَهَ عَلَيْنَا وَإِنَّا إِن شَاءَ اللَّهُ لَمُهْتَدُونَ ۝ قَالَ إِنَّهُ يَقُولُ إِنَّهَا بَقَرَةٌ لَّا ذَلُولٌ تُثِيرُ الْأَرْضَ وَلَا تَسْقِي الْحَرْثَ مُسَلَّمَةٌ لَّا شِيَةَ فِيهَا قَالُوا الْآنَ جِئْتَ بِالْحَقِّ فَذَبَحُوهَا وَمَا كَادُوا يَفْعَلُونَ ۝ وَ إِذْ قَتَلْتُمْ نَفْسًا فَادَّارَأْتُمْ فِيهَا وَاللَّهُ مُخْرِجٌ مَّا كُنتُمْ تَكْتُمُونَ ۝ فَقُلْنَا اضْرِبُوهُ بِبَعْضِهَا كَذَٰلِكَ يُحْيِي اللَّهُ الْمَوْتَىٰ وَيُرِيكُمْ آيَاتِهِ لَعَلَّكُمْ تَعْقِلُونَ ۝ ثُمَّ قَسَتْ قُلُوبُكُم مِّن بَعْدِ ذَٰلِكَ فَهِيَ كَالْحِجَارَةِ أَوْ أَشَدُّ قَسْوَةً وَإِنَّ مِنَ الْحِجَارَةِ لَمَا يَتَفَجَّرُ مِنْهُ الْأَنْهَارُ وَإِنَّ مِنْهَا لَمَا يَشَّقَّقُ فَيَخْرُجُ مِنْهُ الْمَاءُ وَإِنَّ مِنْهَا لَمَا يَهْبِطُ مِنْ خَشْيَةِ اللَّهِ وَمَا اللَّهُ بِغَافِلٍ عَمَّا تَعْمَلُونَ ۝ أَفَتَطْمَعُونَ أَن يُؤْمِنُوا لَكُمْ وَقَدْ كَانَ فَرِيقٌ مِّنْهُمْ يَسْمَعُونَ كَلَامَ اللَّهِ ثُمَّ يُحَرِّفُونَهُ مِن بَعْدِ مَا عَقَلُوهُ وَهُمْ يَعْلَمُونَ ۝ وَإِذَا لَقُوا الَّذِينَ آمَنُوا قَالُوا آمَنَّا وَإِذَا خَلَا بَعْضُهُمْ إِلَىٰ بَعْضٍ قَالُوا أَتُحَدِّثُونَهُم بِمَا فَتَحَ اللَّهُ عَلَيْكُمْ لِيُحَاجُّوكُم بِهِ عِندَ رَبِّكُمْ أَفَلَا تَعْقِلُونَ ۝

---

70. Again they said, "Call upon your Lord so that He may make clear to which cow, for all cows look the same to us. Then, Allah willing, we will be guided ˹to the right one˺." **71.** He replied, "Allah says, 'It should have been used neither to till the soil nor water the fields; wholesome and without blemish.'" They said, "Now you have come with the truth." Yet they still slaughtered it hesitantly! **72.** ˹This is˺ when a man was killed and you disputed who the killer was, but Allah revealed what you concealed. **73.** So We instructed, "Strike the dead body with a piece of the cow." This is how ˹easily˺ Allah brings the dead to life, showing you His signs so that you may understand. **74.** Even then your hearts became hardened like a rock even harder, for some rocks gush rivers; others split, spilling water; while others are humbled in awe of Allah. And Allah is never unaware what you do.

Disobedient Israelites

75. Do you ˹believers still˺ expect them to be true to you, though a group of them would hear the word Allah then knowingly corrupt it after understanding it? **76.** When they meet the believers they say, "We believe." But in private they say ˹to each other˺, "Will you disclose to the believers the knowledge Allah has revealed to you,[26] so that they may use it against you before your Lord? Do you not understand?"

---

26 i.e., verses prophesizing the coming of the Prophet (ﷺ) in the Torah (including Deuteronomy 18:15-18 and 33:2).

13 2. Al-Baqarah

77. Do they not know that Allah is aware of what they conceal and what they reveal? **78.** And among them are the illiterate who know nothing about the Scripture except lies, and ˹so˺ they ˹wishfully˺ speculate. **79.** So woe[27] to those who distort the Scripture with their own hands then say, "This is from Allah"—seeking a fleeting gain! So woe to them for what their hands have written, and woe to them for what they have earned.

Argument and Refutation

80. ˹Some of˺ the Jews claim, "The Fire will not touch us except for a number of days." Say, ˹O Prophet,˺ "Have you taken a pledge from Allah—for Allah never breaks His word—or are you ˹just˺ saying about Allah what you do not know?" **81.** But no! Those who commit evil and are engrossed in sin will be the residents of the Fire. They will be there forever. **82.** And those who believe and do good will be the residents of Paradise. They will be there forever.

The Israelites' Failure to Keep Covenants

83. And ˹remember˺ when We took a covenant from the children of Israel ˹stating˺, "Worship none but Allah; be kind to parents, relatives, orphans and the needy; speak kind to people; establish prayer; and pay alms-tax." But you ˹Israelites˺ turned away—except for a few of you—and were indifferent.

---

27 i.e., warning of a curse or punishment.

2. Al-Baqarah

وَإِذْ أَخَذْنَا مِيثَاقَكُمْ لَا تَسْفِكُونَ دِمَاءَكُمْ وَلَا تُخْرِجُونَ
أَنفُسَكُم مِّن دِيَارِكُمْ ثُمَّ أَقْرَرْتُمْ وَأَنتُمْ تَشْهَدُونَ ۝
ثُمَّ أَنتُمْ هَٰؤُلَاءِ تَقْتُلُونَ أَنفُسَكُمْ وَتُخْرِجُونَ فَرِيقًا مِّنكُم
مِّن دِيَارِهِمْ تَظَاهَرُونَ عَلَيْهِم بِالْإِثْمِ وَالْعُدْوَٰنِ وَإِن
يَأْتُوكُمْ أُسَٰرَىٰ تُفَٰدُوهُمْ وَهُوَ مُحَرَّمٌ عَلَيْكُمْ إِخْرَاجُهُمْ
أَفَتُؤْمِنُونَ بِبَعْضِ الْكِتَٰبِ وَتَكْفُرُونَ بِبَعْضٍ فَمَا جَزَآءُ
مَن يَفْعَلُ ذَٰلِكَ مِنكُمْ إِلَّا خِزْىٌ فِى الْحَيَوٰةِ الدُّنْيَا وَيَوْمَ
الْقِيَٰمَةِ يُرَدُّونَ إِلَىٰ أَشَدِّ الْعَذَابِ وَمَا اللَّهُ بِغَٰفِلٍ عَمَّا
تَعْمَلُونَ ۝ أُوْلَٰئِكَ الَّذِينَ اشْتَرَوُا الْحَيَوٰةَ الدُّنْيَا بِالْأَخِرَةِ
فَلَا يُخَفَّفُ عَنْهُمُ الْعَذَابُ وَلَا هُمْ يُنصَرُونَ ۝ وَ
لَقَدْ ءَاتَيْنَا مُوسَى الْكِتَٰبَ وَقَفَّيْنَا مِنۢ بَعْدِهِ بِالرُّسُلِ
وَءَاتَيْنَا عِيسَى ابْنَ مَرْيَمَ الْبَيِّنَٰتِ وَأَيَّدْنَٰهُ بِرُوحِ الْقُدُسِ
أَفَكُلَّمَا جَآءَكُمْ رَسُولٌۢ بِمَا لَا تَهْوَىٰ أَنفُسُكُمُ اسْتَكْبَرْتُمْ
فَفَرِيقًا كَذَّبْتُمْ وَفَرِيقًا تَقْتُلُونَ ۝ وَقَالُوا قُلُوبُنَا غُلْفٌ
بَل لَّعَنَهُمُ اللَّهُ بِكُفْرِهِمْ فَقَلِيلًا مَّا يُؤْمِنُونَ ۝

84. And ˹remember˺ when We took your covenant that you would neither shed each other's blood nor expel each other from their homes, you gave your pledge and bore witness.
85. But here you are, killing each other and expelling some of your people from their homes, aiding one another in sin and aggression; and when those ˹expelled˺ come to you as captives, you still ransom them—though expelling them was unlawful for you.[28] Do you believe some of the Scripture and reject the rest? Is there any reward for those who do so among you other than disgrace in this worldly life and being subjected to the harshest punishment on the Day of Judgment? For Allah is never unaware of what you do. 86. These are the ones who trade the Hereafter for the life of this world. So their punishment will not be reduced, nor will they be helped.

Denying Allah's Prophets

87. Indeed, We gave Moses the Book and sent after him successive messengers. And We gave Jesus, son of Mary, clear proofs and supported him with the holy spirit.[29] Why is it that every time a messenger comes to you ˹Israelites˺ with something you do not like, you become arrogant, rejecting some and killing others? 88. They say, "Our hearts are unreceptive!"[30] In fact, Allah has condemned them for their disbelief. They have but little faith.

---

28 The indigenous people of Medina were divided into two warring groups: *Al-Aws* and *Al-Khazraj*. Some Jewish tribes were allied with the former and others with the latter, which meant that in times of war each of these Jewish tribes had to fight along with their allies against their enemies, including other Jews. When the Prophet (ﷺ) migrated to Medina, he brought about a lasting peace in the city.
29 The holy spirit is Gabriel, a mighty angel created from light, whose main duty is to communicate Allah's messages to prophets.
30 Their hearts are unreceptive because they claim they have enough knowledge already.

2. Al-Baqarah

Rejecting the Quran

89. Although they used to pray for victory ˹by means of the Prophet˺ over the polytheists,[31] when there came to them a Book from Allah which they recognized,[32] confirming the Scripture they had ˹in their hands˺, they rejected it. So may Allah's condemnation be upon the disbelievers. 90. Miserable is the price they have sold their souls for—denying Allah's revelation and resenting Allah for granting His grace to whoever He wills of His servants! They have earned wrath upon wrath. And such disbelievers will suffer a humiliating punishment.

Excuse for Rejecting the Quran

91. When it is said to them: "Believe in what Allah has revealed," they reply, "We only believe in what was sent down to us," and they deny what came afterwards, though it is the truth confirming their own Scriptures! Ask ˹them, O Prophet˺, "Why then did you kill Allah's prophets before, if you are ˹truly˺ believers?"

Moses Was Defied Too

92. Indeed, Moses came to you with clear proofs, then you worshipped the calf in his absence, acting wrongfully. 93. And when We took your covenant and raised the mountain above you ˹saying˺, "Hold firmly to that ˹Scripture˺ which We have given you and obey," they answered, "We hear and disobey." The love of the calf was rooted in their hearts because of their disbelief. Say, ˹O Prophet,˺ "How evil is what your ˹so-called˺ belief prompts you to do, if you ˹actually˺ believe ˹in the Torah˺!"

---

31 lit., the disbelievers.
32 i.e., the Quran.

قُلْ إِن كَانَتْ لَكُمُ الدَّارُ الْأَخِرَةُ عِندَ اللَّهِ خَالِصَةً مِّن دُونِ النَّاسِ فَتَمَنَّوُا الْمَوْتَ إِن كُنتُمْ صَدِقِينَ ۝ وَلَن يَتَمَنَّوْهُ أَبَدًا بِمَا قَدَّمَتْ أَيْدِيهِمْ ۚ وَاللَّهُ عَلِيمٌ بِالظَّالِمِينَ ۝ وَلَتَجِدَنَّهُمْ أَحْرَصَ النَّاسِ عَلَىٰ حَيَوٰةٍ وَمِنَ الَّذِينَ أَشْرَكُوا ۚ يَوَدُّ أَحَدُهُمْ لَوْ يُعَمَّرُ أَلْفَ سَنَةٍ وَمَا هُوَ بِمُزَحْزِحِهِ مِنَ الْعَذَابِ أَن يُعَمَّرَ ۗ وَاللَّهُ بَصِيرٌ بِمَا يَعْمَلُونَ ۝ قُلْ مَن كَانَ عَدُوًّا لِّجِبْرِيلَ فَإِنَّهُ نَزَّلَهُ عَلَىٰ قَلْبِكَ بِإِذْنِ اللَّهِ مُصَدِّقًا لِّمَا بَيْنَ يَدَيْهِ وَهُدًى وَبُشْرَىٰ لِلْمُؤْمِنِينَ ۝ مَن كَانَ عَدُوًّا لِّلَّهِ وَمَلَٰئِكَتِهِ وَرُسُلِهِ وَجِبْرِيلَ وَمِيكَىٰلَ فَإِنَّ اللَّهَ عَدُوٌّ لِّلْكَٰفِرِينَ ۝ وَلَقَدْ أَنزَلْنَا إِلَيْكَ آيَٰتٍ بَيِّنَٰتٍ ۖ وَمَا يَكْفُرُ بِهَا إِلَّا الْفَٰسِقُونَ ۝ أَوَكُلَّمَا عَٰهَدُوا عَهْدًا نَّبَذَهُ فَرِيقٌ مِّنْهُم ۚ بَلْ أَكْثَرُهُمْ لَا يُؤْمِنُونَ ۝ وَلَمَّا جَآءَهُمْ رَسُولٌ مِّنْ عِندِ اللَّهِ مُصَدِّقٌ لِّمَا مَعَهُمْ نَبَذَ فَرِيقٌ مِّنَ الَّذِينَ أُوتُوا الْكِتَٰبَ كِتَٰبَ اللَّهِ وَرَآءَ ظُهُورِهِمْ كَأَنَّهُمْ لَا يَعْلَمُونَ ۝

2. Al-Baqarah

Clinging to Life

94. Say, ˹O Prophet,˺ "If the ˹eternal˺ Home of the Hereafter with Allah is exclusively for you ˹Israelites˺ out all humanity, then wish for death if what you say is true!" **95.** But they will never wish for that because of what their hands have done.[33] And Allah has ˹perfect˺ knowledge of the wrongdoers. **96.** You will surely find them clinging to life more eagerly than any other people, even more than polytheists. Each one of them wishes to live a thousand years. But even if they were to live that long, it would not save them from the punishment. And Allah is All-Seeing of what they do.

Rejecting the Truth

97. Say, ˹O Prophet,˺ "Whoever is an enemy of Gabriel should know that he revealed this ˹Quran˺ to your heart by Allah's Will, confirming what came before it—a guide and good news for the believers." **98.** Whoever is an enemy of Allah, His angels, His messengers, Gabriel, and Michael, then ˹let them know that˺ Allah is certainly the enemy of the disbelievers. **99.** Indeed, We have sent down to you ˹O Prophet˺ clear revelations. ˹But˺ none will deny them except the rebellious. **100.** Why is it that every time they make a covenant, a group of them casts it aside? In fact, most of them do not believe. **101.** Now, when a messenger from Allah has come to them—confirming their own Scriptures—some of the People of the Book cast the Book of Allah behind their backs as if they did not know.

---

33   i.e., disobeying Allah, killing some of the prophets (including Zachariah and John the Baptist), claiming to have killed Jesus, accusing Mary of adultery, and dealing with usury. *See* 4:153-158.

2. Al-Baqarah

Attachment to Magic

102. They ˹instead˺ followed the magic promoted by the devils during the reign of Solomon. Never did Solomon disbelieve, rather the devils disbelieved. They taught magic to the people, along with what had been revealed to the two angels, Hârût and Mârût, in Babylon.[34] The two angels never taught anyone without saying, "We are only a test ˹for you˺, so do not abandon ˹your˺ faith." Yet people learned ˹magic˺ that caused a rift ˹even˺ between husband and wife; although their magic could not harm anyone except by Allah's Will. They learned what harmed them and did not benefit them—although they already knew that whoever buys into magic would have no share in the Hereafter. Miserable indeed was the price for which they sold their souls, if only they knew! **103.** If only they were faithful and mindful ˹of Allah˺, there would have been a better reward from Allah, if only they knew!

Advice for the Believers

104. O believers! Do not say, "Râ'ina." [Herd us!] But say, "Unzurna," [Tend to us!] and listen ˹attentively˺.[35] And the disbelievers will suffer a painful punishment. **105.** The disbelievers from the People of the Book and the polytheists would not want you to receive any blessing from your Lord, but Allah selects whoever He wills for His mercy. And Allah is the Lord of infinite bounty.

---

34 The two angels, Hârût and Mârût, were sent to enlighten the people in Babylon so they would not confuse magic tricks with miracles. Still some people abused this knowledge, causing mischief in the land. These practices persisted until the time of Solomon, who himself was falsely accused of utilizing magic to run his kingdom, subdue the jinn, and control the wind.

35 Some of the disbelievers used to play with words when they addressed the Prophet (ﷺ) in order to ridicule him. So instead of saying, *râ'ina* "listen to us," they would say, *râ'ina* "our shepherd" or "the foolish among us." They would say loudly, "We listen," then whisper, "but we disobey!" and say, "Hear us," then, "may you never hear!" They used to say to each other, "If he had truly been a prophet of Allah, he would have known that we are mocking him." Therefore, this verse (along with 4:46) was revealed commanding the believers to avoid such words altogether. Better words are recommended.

Obeying the Messenger

106. If We ever abrogate[36] a verse or cause it to be forgotten, We replace it with a better or similar one. Do you not know that Allah is Most Capable of everything? **107.** Do you not know that the kingdom of the heavens and the earth belongs ˹only˺ to Allah, and you have no guardian or helper besides Allah? **108.** Or do you ˹believers˺ intend to ask of your Messenger as Moses was asked before?[37] But whoever trades belief for disbelief has truly strayed from the Right Way.

Adhering to the Straight Path

109. Many among the People of the Book wish they could turn you ˹believers˺ back to disbelief because of their envy, after the truth has been made clear to them. Pardon and bear with them until Allah delivers His decision. Surely Allah is Most Capable of everything. **110.** Establish prayer, and pay alms-tax. Whatever good you send forth for yourselves, you will ˹certainly˺ find ˹its reward˺ with Allah. Surely Allah is All-Seeing of what you do.

Claims and Refutations

111. The Jews and Christians each claim that none will enter Paradise except those of their own faith. These are their desires. Reply, ˹O Prophet,˺ "Show ˹me˺ your proof if what you say is true." **112.** But no! Whoever submits themselves to Allah and does good will have their reward with their Lord. And there will be no fear for them, nor will they grieve.

---

36 The Quran was revealed over a period of twenty-three years. New rules were introduced when the believers were ready to accept and apply them. Replacing a ruling with another is called abrogation (*naskh*). For example, alcohol consumption was forbidden over three stages (*see* 2:219, 4:43, and 5:90, respectively). Some of the Prophet's companions said, "If drinking had been forbidden from day one, no one would have accepted Islam!"

37 i.e., asking to make Allah visible to them and make the angels talk to them.

2. Al-Baqarah

113. The Jews say, "The Christians have nothing to stand on" and the Christians say, "The Jews have nothing to stand on," although both recite the Scriptures. And those ʿpagansʾ who have no knowledge say the same ʿabout people of faithʾ. Surely Allah will judge between them on the Day of Judgment regarding their dispute.

Condemning Attacks on Places of Worship

114. Who does more wrong than those who prevent Allah's Name from being mentioned in His places of worship and strive to destroy them? Such people have no right to enter these places except with fear.[38] For them there is disgrace in this world and they will suffer a tremendous punishment in the Hereafter. 115. To Allah belong the east and the west, so wherever you turn you are facing ʿtowardsʾ Allah.[39] Surely Allah is All-Encompassing,[40] All-Knowing.

Allah is in No Need of Children

116. They say, "Allah has offspring."[41] Glory be to Him! In fact, to Him belongs whatever is in the heavens and the earth—all are subject to His Will. 117. ʿHe isʾ the Originator of the heavens and the earth! When He decrees a matter, He simply tells it, "Be!" And it is!

True Guidance

118. Those who have no knowledge say, "If only Allah would speak to us or a sign would come to us!" The same was said by those who came before. Their hearts are all alike. Indeed, We have made the signs clear for people of sure faith. 119. We have surely sent you with the truth ʿO Prophetʾ as a deliverer of good news and a warner. And you will not be accountable for the residents of the Hellfire.

---

38 Or, "Such people should have never even entered these places except with reverence."
39 lit., wherever you turn, there is the Face of Allah.
40 His mercy and knowledge covers all.
41 Jesus in Christianity, the angels in pagan Arab mythology, etc.

2. Al-Baqarah

120. Never will the Jews or Christians be pleased with you, until you follow their faith. Say, "Allah's guidance is the only ʿtrueʾ guidance." And if you were to follow their desires after ʿallʾ the knowledge that has come to you, there would be none to protect or help you against Allah. **121.** Those We have given the Book follow it as should be followed. It is they who ʿtrulyʾ believe in it. As for those who reject it, it is they who are the losers.

Reminder of Favours upon the Israelites

122. O Children of Israel! Remember My favours upon you and how I honoured you above the others. **123.** And guard yourselves against the Day when no soul will be of any help to another. No ransom will be taken, no intercession accepted, and no help will be given.

Abraham in Mecca

124. ʿRememberʾ when Abraham was tested by his Lord with ʿcertainʾ commandments, which he fulfilled. Allah said, "I will certainly make you into a role model for the people." Abraham asked, "What about my offspring?" Allah replied, "My covenant is not extended to the wrongdoers." **125.** And ʿrememberʾ when We made the Sacred House[42] a centre and a sanctuary for the people ʿsayingʾ, "ʿYou mayʾ take the standing-place of Abraham[43] as a site of prayer." And We entrusted Abraham and Ishmael to purify My House for those who circle it, who meditate in it, and who bow and prostrate themselves ʿin prayerʾ.

Abraham's Prayers

126. And ʿrememberʾ when Abraham said, "My Lord, make this city ʿof Meccaʾ secure and provide fruits to its people—those among them who believe in Allah and the Last Day." He answered, "As for those who disbelieve, I will let them enjoy themselves for a little while, then I will condemn them to the torment of the Fire. What an evil destination!"

---

42 "The Sacred House" (Ka'bah) is a cube-shaped building in Mecca, Islam's holiest sanctuary, which Muslims face when they pray five times a day.
43 "The standing-place of Abraham" is the stone on which Abraham stood while he was building the Ka'bah.

2. Al-Baqarah

Raising the Foundation of the Sacred House

127. And ˹remember˺ when Abraham raised the foundation of the House with Ishmael, ˹both praying,˺ "Our Lord! Accept ˹this˺ from us. You are indeed the All-Hearing, All-Knowing. **128.** Our Lord! Make us both ˹fully˺ submit to You[44] and from our descendants a nation that will submit to you. Show us our rituals, and turn to us in grace. You are truly the Accepter of Repentance, Most Merciful. **129.** Our Lord! Raise from among them a messenger who will recite to them Your revelations, teach them the Book and wisdom, and purify them. Indeed, You ˹alone˺ are the Almighty, All-Wise."

One God

130. And who would reject the faith of Abraham except a fool! We certainly chose him in this life, and in the Hereafter he will surely be among the righteous. **131.** When his Lord ordered him, "Submit ˹to My Will˺," he responded, "I submit to the Lord of all worlds." **132.** This was the advice of Abraham—as well as Jacob—to his children, ˹saying˺, "Indeed, Allah has chosen for you this faith; so do not die except in ˹a state of full˺ submission." **133.** Or did you witness when death came to Jacob? He asked his children, "Who will you worship after my passing?" They replied, "We will ˹continue to˺ worship your God, the God of your forefathers—Abraham, Ishmael, and Isaac—the One God. And to Him we ˹all˺ submit." **134.** That was a community that had already gone before. For them is what they earned and for you is what you have earned. And you will not be accountable for what they have done.

---

44 lit., make both of us Muslims. The word "Muslim" means "one who submits to Allah." All of the prophets submitted to Allah and were, therefore, Muslims.

2. Al-Baqarah

Prophets of Islam

135. The Jews and Christians each say, "Follow our faith to be ʿrightly˺ guided." Say, ʿO Prophet,˺ "No! We follow the faith of Abraham, the upright—who was not a polytheist." **136.** Say, ʿO believers,˺ "We believe in Allah and what has been revealed to us; and what was revealed to Abraham, Ishmael, Isaac, Jacob, and his descendants; and what was given to Moses, Jesus, and other prophets from their Lord. We make no distinction between any of them. And to Allah we all submit." **137.** So if they believe in what you believe, then they will indeed be ʿrightly˺ guided. But if they turn away, they are simply opposed ʿto the truth˺. But Allah will spare you their evil. For He is the All-Hearing, All-Knowing.

Many Messengers; One Message

138. This is the ʿnatural˺ Way of Allah. And who is better than Allah in ordaining a way? And we worship ʿnone but˺ Him. **139.** Say, "Would you dispute with us about Allah, while He is our Lord and your Lord? We are accountable for our deeds and you for yours. And we are devoted to Him ʿalone˺. **140.** Or do you claim that Abraham, Ishmael, Isaac, Jacob, and his descendants were all Jews or Christians?" Say, "Who is more knowledgeable: you or Allah?" Who does more wrong than those who hide the testimony they received from Allah? And Allah is never unaware of what you do. **141.** That was a community that had already gone before. For them is what they earned and for you is what you have earned. And you will not be accountable for what they have done.

2. Al-Baqarah

23

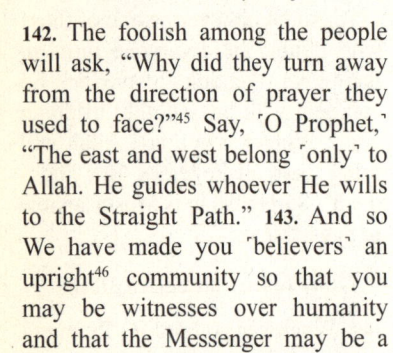

New Direction of Prayer

142. The foolish among the people will ask, "Why did they turn away from the direction of prayer they used to face?"[45] Say, ˹O Prophet,˺ "The east and west belong ˹only˺ to Allah. He guides whoever He wills to the Straight Path." **143.** And so We have made you ˹believers˺ an upright[46] community so that you may be witnesses over humanity and that the Messenger may be a witness over you. We assigned your former direction of prayer only to distinguish those who would remain faithful to the Messenger from those who would lose faith. It was certainly a difficult test except for those ˹rightly˺ guided by Allah. And Allah would never discount your ˹previous acts of˺ faith. Surely Allah is Ever Gracious and Most Merciful to humanity.

Order to Face Mecca in Prayer

144. Indeed, We see you ˹O Prophet˺ turning your face towards heaven. Now We will make you turn towards a direction ˹of prayer˺ that will please you. So turn your face towards the Sacred Mosque ˹in Mecca˺—wherever you are, turn your faces towards it. Those who were given the Scripture certainly know this to be the truth from their Lord. And Allah is never unaware of what they do. **145.** Even if you were to bring every proof to the People of the Book, they would not accept your direction ˹of prayer˺, nor would you accept theirs; nor would any of them accept the direction ˹of prayer˺ of another. And if you were to follow their desires after ˹all˺ the knowledge that has come to you, then you would certainly be one of the wrongdoers.

The Truth About the Prophet

146. Those We have given the Scripture recognize this ˹Prophet˺ as they recognize their own children. Yet a group of them hides the truth knowingly.

---

45 For about sixteen months after daily prayers became obligatory, Muslims used to face towards Jerusalem before the order came to face a new *qiblah* (direction of prayer)—the Sacred Mosque in Mecca.
46 i.e., moderate, balanced, and outstanding.

147. ˹This is˺ the truth from your Lord, so do not ever be one of those who doubt. 148. Everyone turns to their own direction ˹of prayer˺. So compete with one another in doing good. Wherever you are, Allah will bring you all together ˹for judgment˺. Surely Allah is Most Capable of everything.

Order to Face the Sacred Mosque

149. Wherever you are ˹O Prophet˺, turn your face towards the Sacred Mosque. This is certainly the truth from your Lord. And Allah is never unaware of what you ˹all˺ do. 150. Wherever you are ˹O Prophet˺, turn your face towards the Sacred Mosque. And wherever you ˹believers˺ are, face towards it, so that people will have no argument against you, except the wrongdoers among them. Do not fear them; fear Me, so that I may ˹continue to˺ perfect My favour upon you and so you may be ˹rightly˺ guided.

Allah's Favour upon the Believers

151. Since We have sent you a messenger from among yourselves—reciting to you Our revelations, purifying you, teaching you the Book and wisdom, and teaching you what you never knew— 152. remember Me; I will remember you. And thank Me, and never be ungrateful.

Patience in Difficult Times

153. O believers! Seek comfort in patience and prayer. Allah is truly with those who are patient. 154. Never say that those martyred in the cause of Allah are dead—in fact, they are alive! But you do not perceive it. 155. We will certainly test you with a touch of fear and famine and loss of property, life, and crops. Give good news to those who patiently endure— 156. who, when faced with a disaster, say, "Surely to Allah we belong and to Him we will ˹all˺ return."

157. They are the ones who will receive Allah's blessings and mercy. And it is they who are ˹rightly˺ guided.

A Pilgrimage Ritual

158. Indeed, ˹the hills of˺ Ṣafa and Marwah[47] are among the symbols of Allah. So whoever makes the major or minor pilgrimage[48] to the ˹Sacred˺ House, let them walk between ˹the two hills˺. And whoever does good willingly, Allah is truly Appreciative, All-Knowing.

Warning to the Disbelievers

159. Those who hide the clear proofs and guidance that We have revealed—after We made it clear for humanity in the Book—will be condemned by Allah and ˹all˺ those who condemn. **160.** As for those who repent, mend their ways, and let the truth be known, they are the ones to whom I will turn ˹in forgiveness˺, for I am the Accepter of Repentance, Most Merciful. **161.** Surely those who disbelieve and die as disbelievers are condemned by Allah, the angels, and all of humanity. **162.** They will be in Hell forever. Their punishment will not be lightened, nor will they be delayed ˹from it˺.

Allah's Great Signs

163. Your God is ˹only˺ One God. There is no god ˹worthy of worship˺ except Him—the Most Compassionate, Most Merciful. **164.** Indeed, in the creation of the heavens and the earth; the alternation of the day and the night; the ships that sail the sea for the benefit of humanity; the rain sent down by Allah from the skies, reviving the earth after its death; the scattering of all kinds of creatures throughout; the shifting of the winds; and the clouds drifting between the heavens and the earth—˹in all of this˺ are surely signs for people of understanding.

---

47 Ṣafa and Marwah are two hills near the Ka'bah in Mecca.
48 Known as ḥajj and 'umrah respectively, pilgrimage to the Sacred Mosque in Mecca.

وَمِنَ النَّاسِ مَن يَتَّخِذُ مِن دُونِ اللَّهِ أَندَادًا يُحِبُّونَهُمْ كَحُبِّ
اللَّهِ ۖ وَالَّذِينَ آمَنُوا أَشَدُّ حُبًّا لِّلَّهِ ۗ وَلَوْ يَرَى الَّذِينَ ظَلَمُوا إِذْ
يَرَوْنَ الْعَذَابَ أَنَّ الْقُوَّةَ لِلَّهِ جَمِيعًا وَأَنَّ اللَّهَ شَدِيدُ الْعَذَابِ ۝
إِذْ تَبَرَّأَ الَّذِينَ اتُّبِعُوا مِنَ الَّذِينَ اتَّبَعُوا وَرَأَوُا الْعَذَابَ وَ
تَقَطَّعَتْ بِهِمُ الْأَسْبَابُ ۝ وَقَالَ الَّذِينَ اتَّبَعُوا لَوْ أَنَّ لَنَا كَرَّةً
فَنَتَبَرَّأَ مِنْهُمْ كَمَا تَبَرَّءُوا مِنَّا ۗ كَذَٰلِكَ يُرِيهِمُ اللَّهُ أَعْمَالَهُمْ
حَسَرَاتٍ عَلَيْهِمْ ۖ وَمَا هُم بِخَارِجِينَ مِنَ النَّارِ ۝ يَا أَيُّهَا النَّاسُ كُلُوا
مِمَّا فِي الْأَرْضِ حَلَالًا طَيِّبًا وَلَا تَتَّبِعُوا خُطُوَاتِ الشَّيْطَانِ ۚ
إِنَّهُ لَكُمْ عَدُوٌّ مُّبِينٌ ۝ إِنَّمَا يَأْمُرُكُم بِالسُّوءِ وَالْفَحْشَاءِ وَأَن
تَقُولُوا عَلَى اللَّهِ مَا لَا تَعْلَمُونَ ۝ وَإِذَا قِيلَ لَهُمُ اتَّبِعُوا مَا
أَنزَلَ اللَّهُ قَالُوا بَلْ نَتَّبِعُ مَا أَلْفَيْنَا عَلَيْهِ آبَاءَنَا ۗ أَوَلَوْ كَانَ
آبَاؤُهُمْ لَا يَعْقِلُونَ شَيْئًا وَلَا يَهْتَدُونَ ۝ وَمَثَلُ الَّذِينَ كَفَرُوا
كَمَثَلِ الَّذِي يَنْعِقُ بِمَا لَا يَسْمَعُ إِلَّا دُعَاءً وَنِدَاءً ۚ صُمٌّ بُكْمٌ
عُمْيٌ فَهُمْ لَا يَعْقِلُونَ ۝ يَا أَيُّهَا الَّذِينَ آمَنُوا كُلُوا مِن طَيِّبَاتِ
مَا رَزَقْنَاكُمْ وَاشْكُرُوا لِلَّهِ إِن كُنتُمْ إِيَّاهُ تَعْبُدُونَ ۝

Associating Others with Allah

165. Still there are some who take others as Allah's equal—they love them as they should love Allah—but the ˹true˺ believers love Allah even more. If only the wrongdoers could see the ˹horrible˺ punishment ˹awaiting them˺, they would certainly realize that all power belongs to Allah and that Allah is indeed severe in punishment.

Losers Disowning Each Other

166. ˹Consider the Day˺ when those who misled others will disown their followers—when they face the torment—and the bonds that united them will be cut off. **167.** The ˹misled˺ followers will cry, "If only we could have a second chance, we would disown them as they disowned us." And so Allah will make them remorseful of their misdeeds. And they will never ˹be able to˺ leave the Fire.

Warning Against Satan

168. O humanity! Eat from what is lawful and good on the earth and do not follow Satan's footsteps. He is truly your sworn enemy. **169.** He only incites you to commit evil and indecency, and to claim against Allah what you do not know.

Blind Following

170. When it is said to them, "Follow what Allah has revealed," they reply, "No! We ˹only˺ follow what we found our forefathers practicing." ˹Would they still do so,˺ even if their forefathers had ˹absolutely˺ no understanding or guidance?

Example of the Disbelievers

171. The example of the disbelievers ˹not responding to the Messenger's warning˺ is like a flock not comprehending the calls and cries of the shepherd. ˹They are wilfully˺ deaf, dumb and blind so they have no understanding.

Forbidden Foods

172. O believers! Eat from the good things We have provided for you. And give thanks to Allah if you ˹truly˺ worship Him ˹alone˺.

2. Al-Baqarah

173. He has only forbidden you ˹to eat˺ carrion, blood, swine,[49] and what is slaughtered in the name of any other than Allah. But if someone is compelled by necessity—neither driven by desire nor exceeding immediate need—they will not be sinful. Surely Allah is All-Forgiving, Most Merciful.

Hiding the Truth

174. Indeed, those who hide Allah's revelations, trading them for a fleeting gain consume nothing but fire into their bellies. Allah will neither speak to them on the Day of Judgment, nor will He purify them. And they will suffer a painful punishment. **175.** They are the ones who trade guidance for misguidance and forgiveness for punishment. How persistent are they in pursuit of the Fire! **176.** That is because Allah has revealed the Book in truth. And surely those who differ regarding it are totally engrossed in opposition.

True Righteousness

177. Righteousness is not in turning your faces towards the east or the west. Rather, the righteous are those who believe in Allah, the Last Day, the angels, the Books, and the prophets; who give charity out of their cherished wealth to relatives, orphans, the poor, ˹needy˺ travellers, beggars, and for freeing captives; who establish prayer, pay alms-tax, and keep the pledges they make; and who are patient in times of suffering, adversity, and in ˹the heat of˺ battle. It is they who are true ˹in faith˺, and it is they who are mindful ˹of Allah˺.

---

49 Eating pork is forbidden in the Old Testament in Leviticus 11:7-8 and Deuteronomy 14:8.

2. Al-Baqarah

Law of Retaliation[50]

178. O believers! ˹The law of˺ retaliation is set for you in cases of murder—a free man for a free man, a slave for a slave, and a female for a female.[51] But if the offender is pardoned by the victim's guardian,[52] then blood-money should be decided fairly[53] and payment should be made courteously. This is a concession and a mercy from your Lord. But whoever transgresses after that will suffer a painful punishment. **179.** There is ˹security of˺ life for you in ˹the law of˺ retaliation, O people of reason, so that you may become mindful ˹of Allah˺.

Last Will and Bequests

180. It is prescribed that when death approaches any of you—if they leave something of value—a will should be made in favour of parents and immediate family with fairness.[54] ˹This is˺ an obligation on those who are mindful ˹of Allah˺. **181.** But whoever changes the will after hearing it,[55] the blame will only be on those who made the change. Indeed, Allah is All-Hearing, All-Knowing. **182.** Whoever suspects an error or an injustice in the will and brings about a ˹fair˺ settlement among the parties will not be sinful. Surely Allah is All-Forgiving, Most Merciful.

Rules of Fasting

183. O believers! Fasting is prescribed for you—as it was for those before you[56]—so perhaps you will become mindful ˹of Allah˺.

184. ˹Fast a˺ prescribed number of days.[57] But whoever of you is ill or on a journey, then ˹let them fast˺ an equal number of days

---

50 The closest heirs of the victim of an intentional killing have the right to demand the execution of the killer through legal channels. They also have the right to waive the punishment as an act of charity.

51 No one else should be executed in place of the killer. This verse was revealed regarding a particular incident. Nevertheless, the killer is killed regardless of the difference in gender or status, unless the victim's family opts for blood money.

52 The guardian is the victim's closest heir—male or female.

53 Or according to common law.

54 This ruling should be understood in light of the inheritance laws in 4:11-12, which give specific shares to parents and close relatives. Relatives who do not have a share may get a bequest up to one third of the estate.

55 After the death of the one who made the will.

56 i.e., the followers of previous prophets.

57 i.e., the month of Ramaḍân, the 9ᵗʰ month in the Islamic calendar.

'after Ramaḍân'. For those who can only fast with extreme difficulty,[58] compensation can be made by feeding a needy person 'for every day not fasted'. But whoever volunteers to give more, it is better for them. And to fast is better for you, if only you knew.

Excellence of Ramaḍân

185. Ramaḍân is the month in which the Quran was revealed as a guide for humanity with clear proofs of guidance and the Decisive Authority. So whoever is present this month, let them fast. But whoever is ill or on a journey, then 'let them fast' an equal number of days 'after Ramaḍân'. Allah intends ease for you, not hardship, so that you may complete the prescribed period and proclaim the greatness of Allah for guiding you, and perhaps you will be grateful.

Allah Is Always Near

186. When My servants ask you 'O Prophet' about Me: I am truly near. I respond to one's prayer when they call upon Me. So let them respond 'with obedience' to Me and believe in Me, perhaps they will be guided 'to the Right Way'.

Intimacy During the Nights of Ramaḍân

187. It has been made permissible for you to be intimate with your wives during the nights preceding the fast. Your spouses are a garment[59] for you as you are for them. Allah knows that you were deceiving yourselves.[60] So He has accepted your repentance and pardoned you. So now you may be intimate with them and seek what Allah has prescribed for you.[61] 'You may' eat and drink until you see the light of dawn breaking the darkness of night, then complete the fast until nightfall. Do not be intimate with your spouses while you are meditating in the mosques. These are the limits set by Allah, so do not exceed them. This is how Allah makes His revelations clear to people, so they may become mindful 'of Him'.

---

58   In the case of old age or chronic disease.
59   "Garment" (*libâs*) is a metaphor for comfort, chastity, and protection.
60   Initially, intimate relations during the night of Ramaḍân were not permissible. Since some Muslims could not resist not having intercourse with their spouses, this verse was revealed allowing intimacy during the nights preceding the fast.
61   This implies offspring.

بسم الله

Warning Against Injustice

188. Do not consume one another's wealth unjustly, nor deliberately bribe authorities in order to devour a portion of others' property, knowing that it is a sin.

True Righteousness

189. They ask you ˹O Prophet˺ about the phases of the moon. Say, "They are a means for people to determine time and pilgrimage." Righteousness is not in entering your houses from the back doors.[62] Rather, righteousness is to be mindful ˹of Allah˺. So enter your homes through their ˹proper˺ doors, and be mindful of Allah so you may be successful.

Etiquette of Fighting Enemy Combatants

190. Fight in the cause of Allah ˹only˺ against those who wage war against you, but do not exceed the limits.[63] Surely Allah does not like transgressors. **191.** Kill them wherever you come upon them[64] and drive them out of the places from which they have driven you out. For persecution[65] is far worse than killing. And do not fight them at the Sacred Mosque unless they attack you there. If they do so, then fight them—that is the reward of the disbelievers. **192.** But if they cease, then surely Allah is All-Forgiving, Most Merciful.

Resisting Oppression

193. Fight against them ˹if they persecute you˺ until there is no more persecution, and ˹your˺ devotion will be to Allah ˹alone˺. If they stop ˹persecuting you˺, let there be no hostility except against the aggressors.

---

62 Before Islam, there was a superstitious practice for pilgrims to enter their homes through the back door upon returning from the pilgrimage. The verse suggests that being devoted to Allah wholeheartedly is more important than blindly following old traditions.

63 "Do not exceed the limits" refers to Islamic warfare guidelines set by the Prophet. In an authentic saying collected by Abu Dawûd, he (ﷺ) is reported to have instructed the Muslim army, "Depart in the Name of Allah and with His help—following the way of the Messenger of Allah. Do not kill an old man, a child, or a woman. Do not mutilate dead bodies of the enemy. Be gracious and courteous, for Allah loves those who act with grace." The Prophet (ﷺ) also says, "Do not wish to meet your enemy in battle but always pray for well-being. If fighting is a must, then be steadfast."

64 This is probably the most misquoted verse from the Quran. To properly understand the verse, we need to put it into context. Misquoting verses and taking them out of context can be applied to any scripture. For example, in the Bible, Jesus says, "Do not think that I came to bring peace on earth. I did not come to bring peace but a sword!" (Matthew 10:34). He also says, "But as for these enemies of mine who did not want me to be their king—bring them here and slaughter them in my presence!" (Luke 19:27). And Moses says, "The Lord is a man of war, the Lord is his name." (Exodus 15:3). For more details, *see* the Introduction.

65 Persecuting Muslims to abandon their faith.

194. 'There will be retaliation in' a sacred month for 'an offence in' a sacred month,[66] and all violations will bring about retaliation. So, if anyone attacks you, retaliate in the same manner. 'But' be mindful of Allah, and know that Allah is with those mindful 'of Him'. **195.** Spend in the cause of Allah and do not let your own hands throw you into destruction 'by withholding'. And do good, for Allah certainly loves the good-doers.

Some Pilgrimage Rituals

196. Complete the pilgrimage and minor pilgrimage for Allah.[67] But if prevented 'from proceeding', then 'offer' whatever sacrificial animals you can afford. And do not shave your heads until the sacrificial animal reaches its destination. But if any of you is ill or has a scalp ailment 'requiring shaving', then compensate either by fasting, charity, or a sacrificial offering. In times of peace, you may combine the pilgrimage and minor pilgrimage then make the sacrificial offering you can afford. Whoever cannot afford that 'offering', let them fast three days during pilgrimage and seven after returning 'home'—completing ten. These offerings are for those who do not live near the Sacred House. And be mindful of Allah, and know that Allah is severe in punishment.

More Pilgrimage Rituals

197. 'Commitment to' pilgrimage is made in appointed months.[68] Whoever commits to 'performing' pilgrimage, let them stay away from intimate relations, foul language, and arguments during pilgrimage. Whatever good you do, Allah 'fully' knows of it. Take 'necessary' provisions 'for the journey'—surely the best provision is righteousness. And be mindful of Me, O people of reason!

---

66 The sacred months are the 1st, 7th, 11th, and 12th months of the Islamic calendar.
67 *Ḥajj*, the pilgrimage to Mecca, is required at least once in a Muslim's lifetime if they are physically and financially able to. 'Umrah, which is a short version of *ḥajj*, is recommended, but not obligatory.
68 Although pilgrimage is performed over the course of a few days in the 12th month of the Islamic calendar, the intention to perform pilgrimage can be made during the 10th, 11th, and the first half of the 12th months.

2. Al-Baqarah

بِسْمِ اللّٰهِ... (Arabic text)

لَيْسَ عَلَيْكُمْ جُنَاحٌ أَن تَبْتَغُوا فَضْلًا مِّن رَّبِّكُمْ ۚ فَإِذَآ أَفَضْتُم مِّنْ عَرَفَٰتٍ فَاذْكُرُوا اللَّهَ عِندَ الْمَشْعَرِ الْحَرَامِ ۖ وَاذْكُرُوهُ كَمَا هَدَىٰكُمْ وَإِن كُنتُم مِّن قَبْلِهِ لَمِنَ الضَّآلِّينَ ۝ ثُمَّ أَفِيضُوا مِنْ حَيْثُ أَفَاضَ النَّاسُ وَاسْتَغْفِرُوا اللَّهَ ۚ إِنَّ اللَّهَ غَفُورٌ رَّحِيمٌ ۝ فَإِذَا قَضَيْتُم مَّنَاسِكَكُمْ فَاذْكُرُوا اللَّهَ كَذِكْرِكُمْ ءَابَآءَكُمْ أَوْ أَشَدَّ ذِكْرًا ۗ فَمِنَ النَّاسِ مَن يَقُولُ رَبَّنَآ ءَاتِنَا فِي الدُّنْيَا وَمَا لَهُۥ فِي الْءَاخِرَةِ مِنْ خَلَاقٍ ۝ وَمِنْهُم مَّن يَقُولُ رَبَّنَآ ءَاتِنَا فِي الدُّنْيَا حَسَنَةً وَفِي الْءَاخِرَةِ حَسَنَةً وَقِنَا عَذَابَ النَّارِ ۝ أُو۟لَٰٓئِكَ لَهُمْ نَصِيبٌ مِّمَّا كَسَبُوا ۚ وَاللَّهُ سَرِيعُ الْحِسَابِ ۝ وَاذْكُرُوا اللَّهَ فِىٓ أَيَّامٍ مَّعْدُودَٰتٍ ۚ فَمَن تَعَجَّلَ فِى يَوْمَيْنِ فَلَآ إِثْمَ عَلَيْهِ وَمَن تَأَخَّرَ فَلَآ إِثْمَ عَلَيْهِ ۚ لِمَنِ اتَّقَىٰ ۗ وَاتَّقُوا اللَّهَ وَاعْلَمُوٓا أَنَّكُمْ إِلَيْهِ تُحْشَرُونَ ۝

198. There is no blame on you for seeking the bounty of your Lord ˹during this journey˺.[69] When you return from ˹Arafât,[70] praise Allah near the sacred place[71] and praise Him for having guided you, for surely before this ˹guidance˺ you were astray. 199. Then go forth with the rest of the pilgrims. And seek Allah's forgiveness. Surely Allah is All-Forgiving, Most Merciful.

Praying for the Best of Both Worlds

200. When you have fulfilled your sacred rites, praise Allah as you used to praise your forefathers ˹before Islam˺, or even more passionately. There are some who say, "Our Lord! Grant us ˹Your bounties˺ in this world," but they will have no share in the Hereafter. 201. Yet there are others who say, "Our Lord! Grant us the good of this world and the Hereafter, and protect us from the torment of the Fire." 202. It is they who will receive a ˹heavenly˺ reward for the good they have done. Allah is swift in reckoning.[72]

More Pilgrimage Rituals

203. And remember Allah during ˹these˺ appointed days.[73] Whoever departs swiftly on the second day is not sinful, neither are those who stay behind ˹till the third—seeking additional reward˺, so long as they are mindful ˹of their Lord˺. And be mindful of Allah, and know that to Him you will ˹all˺ be gathered.

---

69 By trading during *ḥajj* season.
70 ˹Arafât is a hill in Saudi Arabia, near Mecca, which is visited during pilgrimage.
71 A sacred place called *Muzdalifah*.
72 Swift in reckoning (*sarī'ul-ḥisâb*) means "He is quick in recording the deeds and judging them."
73 The 11ᵗʰ-13ᵗʰ of *Ẕul-Ḥijjah*, the 12ᵗʰ month of the Islamic calendar. These days are part of pilgrimage rituals.

2. Al-Baqarah

Those Who Spread Mischief

204. There are some ʼhypocritesʼ who impress you with their views regarding worldly affairs and openly call upon Allah to witness what is in their hearts, yet they are your worst adversaries. 205. And when they leave ʼyouʼ,[74] they strive throughout the land to spread mischief in it and destroy crops and cattle. Allah does not like mischief. 206. When it is said to them, "Fear Allah," pride carries them off to sin. Hell will be their proper place. What an evil place to rest! 207. And there are those who would dedicate their lives to Allah's pleasure. And Allah is Ever Gracious to ʼHisʼ servants.

Warning Against the Devil

208. O believers! Enter into Islam wholeheartedly and do not follow Satan's footsteps. Surely he is your sworn enemy. 209. If you falter after receiving the clear proofs, then know that Allah is indeed Almighty, All-Wise.

Waiting for Judgment?

210. Are they waiting for Allah ʼHimselfʼ to come to them in the shade of clouds, along with the angels? ʼIf He didʼ, then the matter would be settled ʼat onceʼ. And to Allah ʼallʼ matters will be returned ʼfor judgmentʼ. 211. Ask the Children of Israel how many clear signs We have given them. And whoever trades Allah's favour—after receiving it—ʼfor disbeliefʼ should know that Allah is indeed severe in punishment.

---

74 Another possible translation: "And when they assume authority, they strive …"

بِسْمِ اللَّهِ

زُيِّنَ لِلَّذِينَ كَفَرُوا الْحَيَوٰةُ الدُّنْيَا وَيَسْخَرُونَ مِنَ الَّذِينَ ءَامَنُوا وَالَّذِينَ اتَّقَوْا فَوْقَهُمْ يَوْمَ الْقِيَمَةِ وَاللَّهُ يَرْزُقُ مَن يَشَاءُ بِغَيْرِ حِسَابٍ ۩ كَانَ النَّاسُ أُمَّةً وَٰحِدَةً فَبَعَثَ اللَّهُ النَّبِيِّۦنَ مُبَشِّرِينَ وَمُنذِرِينَ وَأَنزَلَ مَعَهُمُ الْكِتَٰبَ بِالْحَقِّ لِيَحْكُمَ بَيْنَ النَّاسِ فِيمَا اخْتَلَفُوا فِيهِ وَمَا اخْتَلَفَ فِيهِ إِلَّا الَّذِينَ أُوتُوهُ مِنۢ بَعْدِ مَا جَاءَتْهُمُ الْبَيِّنَٰتُ بَغْيًۢا بَيْنَهُمْ فَهَدَى اللَّهُ الَّذِينَ ءَامَنُوا لِمَا اخْتَلَفُوا فِيهِ مِنَ الْحَقِّ بِإِذْنِهِ وَاللَّهُ يَهْدِى مَن يَشَاءُ إِلَىٰ صِرَٰطٍ مُّسْتَقِيمٍ ۩ أَمْ حَسِبْتُمْ أَن تَدْخُلُوا الْجَنَّةَ وَلَمَّا يَأْتِكُم مَّثَلُ الَّذِينَ خَلَوْا مِن قَبْلِكُم مَّسَّتْهُمُ الْبَأْسَاءُ وَالضَّرَّاءُ وَزُلْزِلُوا حَتَّىٰ يَقُولَ الرَّسُولُ وَالَّذِينَ ءَامَنُوا مَعَهُۥ مَتَىٰ نَصْرُ اللَّهِ أَلَا إِنَّ نَصْرَ اللَّهِ قَرِيبٌ ۩ يَسْـَٔلُونَكَ مَاذَا يُنفِقُونَ قُلْ مَا أَنفَقْتُم مِّنْ خَيْرٍ فَلِلْوَٰلِدَيْنِ وَالْأَقْرَبِينَ وَالْيَتَٰمَىٰ وَالْمَسَٰكِينِ وَابْنِ السَّبِيلِ وَمَا تَفْعَلُوا مِنْ خَيْرٍ فَإِنَّ اللَّهَ بِهِۦ عَلِيمٌ ۩

Life as a Test

212. The life of this world has been made appealing to the disbelievers, and they mock the believers. Those who are mindful ˹of Allah˺ will rank above them on the Day of Judgment. And Allah provides for whoever He wills without limit.

Why Prophets Were Sent

213. Humanity had once been one community ˹of believers before they lost faith˺. Then Allah raised prophets as deliverers of good news and as warners, and revealed to them the Scriptures in truth to judge among people regarding their disputes. And no one disputed the Scriptures except the very people who received them after clear proofs had come to them—out of jealousy. Then Allah, by His grace, has guided the believers to the truth regarding those disputes. And Allah guides whoever He wills to the Straight Path.

Faith Reinforced by Affliction

214. Do you think you will be admitted into Paradise without being tested like those before you? They were afflicted with suffering and adversity and were so ˹violently˺ shaken that ˹even˺ the Messenger and the believers with him cried out, "When will Allah's help come?" Indeed, Allah's help is ˹always˺ near.

Charity Begins at Home

215. They ask you ˹O Prophet in˺ what ˹way˺ they should donate. Say, "Whatever donations you give are for parents, relatives, orphans, the poor, and ˹needy˺ travellers. Whatever good you do is certainly well known to Allah."

35   2. Al-Baqarah

Fighting in Self-Defence

216. Fighting has been made obligatory upon you ˹believers˺, though you dislike it. Perhaps you dislike something which is good for you and like something which is bad for you. Allah knows and you do not know.

Fighting in the Sacred Months

217. They[75] ask you ˹O Prophet˺ about fighting in the sacred months.[76] Say, "Fighting during these months is a great sin. But hindering ˹others˺ from the Path of Allah, rejecting Him, and expelling the worshippers from the Sacred Mosque is ˹a˺ greater ˹sin˺ in the sight of Allah. For persecution[77] is far worse than killing. And they will not stop fighting you until they turn you away from your faith—if they can. And whoever among you renounces their own faith and dies a disbeliever, their deeds will become void in this life and in the Hereafter. It is they who will be the residents of the Fire. They will be there forever."[78]

Reward of the Devout

218. Surely those who have believed, emigrated, and struggled in the Way of Allah—they can hope for Allah's mercy. And Allah is All-Forgiving, Most Merciful.

Question About Intoxicants

219. They ask you ˹O Prophet˺ about intoxicants and gambling. Say, "There is great evil in both, as well as some benefit for people—but the evil outweighs the benefit."[79]

---

75 The pagans of Mecca.

76 *See* footnote for 2:194.

77 Persecuting Muslims to abandon their faith.

78 While many traditional scholars maintain that apostates are to be first invited to re-enter the fold of Islam then executed if the invitation is turned down, some traditional and modern scholars (like Sufyân Ath-Thawrî, the late Grand Imâm of Al-Azhar Sheikh Maḥmûd Shaltût, and Dr. Jamal Badawi) are of the opinion that the Quran (2:256) guarantees freedom of religion and (2:217) promises no worldly punishment for leaving Islam. It is reported in a *ḥadîth* collected by Imâm Muslim that a man came to the Prophet (ﷺ) in Medina and retracted the allegiance he had pledged to him (ﷺ)—leaving Islam. The Prophet (ﷺ) did not punish the man. The narrations that command the killing of apostates refer only to those who fight against Muslims—so they are killed for treason, not for apostasy. Other *aḥâdîth* are meant to deter those who conspired to accept Islam then leave it soon after only to shake the faith of early Muslims, as mentioned in 3:72.

79 *See* footnote for 4:43.

Question About Charity

They ˹also˺ ask you ˹O Prophet˺ what they should donate. Say, "Whatever you can spare." This is how Allah makes His revelations clear to you ˹believers˺, so perhaps you may reflect 220. upon this world and the Hereafter.

Question About Orphans

And they ask you ˹O Prophet˺ concerning orphans. Say, "Improving their condition is best. And if you partner with them, they are bonded with you ˹in faith˺.[80] And Allah knows who intends harm and who intends good. Had Allah willed, He could have made it difficult for you.[81] Surely Allah is Almighty, All-Wise."

Marrying Believers

221. Do not marry polytheistic women until they believe; for a believing slave-woman is better than a free polytheist, even though she may look pleasant to you. And do not marry your women to polytheistic men until they believe, for a believing slave-man is better than a free polytheist, even though he may look pleasant to you. They invite ˹you˺ to the Fire while Allah invites ˹you˺ to Paradise and forgiveness by His grace.[82] He makes His revelations clear to the people so perhaps they will be mindful.

Intercourse During Menstruation

222. They ask you ˹O Prophet˺ about menstruation. Say, "Beware of its harm! So keep away, and do not have intercourse with your wives during their monthly cycles until they are purified.[83] When they purify themselves, then you may approach them in the manner specified by Allah. Surely Allah loves those who always turn to Him in repentance and those who purify themselves." **223.** Your wives are like farmland for you,[84] so approach them ˹consensually˺ as you please.[85] And send forth something good for yourselves.[86] Be mindful of Allah, and know that you will meet Him. And give good news to the believers.

---

80 Literal translation, "They are your brothers."
81 By not allowing partnership between you and orphans.
82 lit., "by His permission."
83 Do not have intercourse with them until their menstruation is over and they have taken a full bath.
84 *Harth* means "farmland"—the husband being like a farmer, the wife like productive land, and children like seeds—a metaphor for fertility and growth.
85 It is permissible to have intimate relations in any position, however anal sex is impermissible. Vaginal penetration during monthly cycles, or while bleeding persists after childbirth, up to forty days, is also not permitted.
86 This can either imply "sending forth good deeds that will be rewarded in the next life" or—according to some interpretations—"engaging in foreplay with one's spouse before intercourse."

2. Al-Baqarah

Rules Regarding Oaths

224. Do not use Allah's Name in your oaths as an excuse for not doing good, not guarding against evil, or not making peace between people. And Allah is All-Hearing, All-Knowing. **225.** Allah will not hold you accountable for unintentional oaths, but for what you intended in your hearts. And Allah is All-Forgiving, Most Forbearing.

Vowing Not to Touch One's Own Wife

226. Those who swear not to have intercourse with their wives must wait for four months.[87] If they change their mind, then Allah is certainly All-Forgiving, Most Merciful. **227.** But if they settle on divorce, then Allah is indeed All-Hearing, All-Knowing.

Waiting Period After Divorce

228. Divorced women must wait three monthly cycles ˹before they can re-marry˺. It is not lawful for them to conceal what Allah has created in their wombs,[88] if they ˹truly˺ believe in Allah and the Last Day. And their husbands reserve the right to take them back within that period if they desire reconciliation. Women have rights similar to those of men equitably, although men have a degree ˹of responsibility˺ above them. And Allah is Almighty, All-Wise.

Proper Way to Divorce

229. Divorce may be retracted twice, then the husband must retain ˹his wife˺ with honour or separate ˹from her˺ with grace.[89] It is not lawful for husbands to take back anything of the dowry given to their wives, unless the couple fears not being able to keep within the limits of Allah.[90] So if you fear they will not be able to keep within the

---

87 This ruling is called *ilâ'*. *Ilâ'* means that a husband vows not to be intimate with his wife because of a dispute or any other legitimate reason. The verse here says if it is four months or less and the husband keeps his vow, then he does not have to make up for breaking his vow (by feeding ten poor people, or fasting three days), otherwise he will need to make up for breaking his vow. If the vow is made for over four months, the wife has the right to seek divorce after four months. *Ilâ'* should be avoided altogether since it deprives the wife of her right to sexual satisfaction. Instead, counselling is a better alternative at the time of dispute.

88 This could mean "pregnancy" or "accurate information about monthly cycles."

89 A husband may separate from his wife after each of the first two counts of divorce or at the end of her waiting period (*see* 65:1-5) with dignity. If he chooses to stay with her after the first two counts of divorce then divorces her a third time, the marriage is terminated at the end of her third waiting period. The wife will have to marry and divorce another man before she can be remarried to her ex-husband (*see* 2:230). However, a woman marrying someone with the intention of getting divorced, in order to return to her first husband, is forbidden.

90 The "limits of Allah" implies fidelity to one's spouse according to Allah's commands.

فَإِن طَلَّقَهَا فَلَا تَحِلُّ لَهُۥ مِنۢ بَعْدُ حَتَّىٰ تَنكِحَ زَوْجًا غَيْرَهُۥ ۗ فَإِن طَلَّقَهَا فَلَا جُنَاحَ عَلَيْهِمَآ أَن يَتَرَاجَعَآ إِن ظَنَّآ أَن يُقِيمَا حُدُودَ ٱللَّهِ ۗ وَتِلْكَ حُدُودُ ٱللَّهِ يُبَيِّنُهَا لِقَوْمٍ يَعْلَمُونَ ۝ وَإِذَا طَلَّقْتُمُ ٱلنِّسَآءَ فَبَلَغْنَ أَجَلَهُنَّ فَأَمْسِكُوهُنَّ بِمَعْرُوفٍ أَوْ سَرِّحُوهُنَّ بِمَعْرُوفٍ ۚ وَلَا تُمْسِكُوهُنَّ ضِرَارًا لِّتَعْتَدُوا ۚ وَمَن يَفْعَلْ ذَٰلِكَ فَقَدْ ظَلَمَ نَفْسَهُۥ ۚ وَلَا تَتَّخِذُوٓا ءَايَٰتِ ٱللَّهِ هُزُوًا ۚ وَٱذْكُرُوا نِعْمَتَ ٱللَّهِ عَلَيْكُمْ وَمَآ أَنزَلَ عَلَيْكُم مِّنَ ٱلْكِتَٰبِ وَٱلْحِكْمَةِ يَعِظُكُم بِهِۦ ۚ وَٱتَّقُوا ٱللَّهَ وَٱعْلَمُوٓا أَنَّ ٱللَّهَ بِكُلِّ شَىْءٍ عَلِيمٌ ۝ وَإِذَا طَلَّقْتُمُ ٱلنِّسَآءَ فَبَلَغْنَ أَجَلَهُنَّ فَلَا تَعْضُلُوهُنَّ أَن يَنكِحْنَ أَزْوَٰجَهُنَّ إِذَا تَرَٰضَوْا بَيْنَهُم بِٱلْمَعْرُوفِ ۗ ذَٰلِكَ يُوعَظُ بِهِۦ مَن كَانَ مِنكُمْ يُؤْمِنُ بِٱللَّهِ وَٱلْيَوْمِ ٱلْءَاخِرِ ۗ ذَٰلِكُمْ أَزْكَىٰ لَكُمْ وَأَطْهَرُ ۗ وَٱللَّهُ يَعْلَمُ وَأَنتُمْ لَا تَعْلَمُونَ ۝

limits of Allah, there is no blame if the wife compensates the husband to obtain divorce.[91] These are the limits set by Allah, so do not transgress them. And whoever transgresses the limits of Allah, they are the ˹true˺ wrongdoers.

Husband Remarrying His Ex-Wife

230. So if a husband divorces his wife ˹three times˺, then it is not lawful for him to remarry her until after she has married another man and then is divorced. Then it is permissible for them to reunite, as long as they feel they are able to maintain the limits of Allah. These are the limits set by Allah, which He makes clear for people of knowledge.

Etiquette of Divorce

231. When you divorce women and they have ˹almost˺ reached the end of their waiting period, either retain them honourably or let them go honourably. But do not retain them ˹only˺ to harm them ˹or˺ to take advantage ˹of them˺. Whoever does that surely wrongs his own soul. Do not take Allah's revelations lightly. Remember Allah's favours upon you as well as the Book and wisdom[92] He has sent down for your guidance. Be mindful of Allah, and know that Allah has ˹perfect˺ knowledge of all things.

Remarrying One's Ex-Spouse

232. When you have divorced women and they have reached the end of their waiting period, do not prevent them from re-marrying their ex-husbands if they come to an honourable agreement. This is enjoined on whoever has faith in Allah and the Last Day. This is purer and more dignifying for you. Allah knows and you do not know.

---

91 If the wife does not want to continue in the marriage for legitimate reasons, then she can return the dowry (*mahr*) to the husband in compensation for divorce. This ruling is called *khul'*.
92 "Wisdom" means the "*sunnah*" or the tradition of the Prophet (ﷺ) when it is mentioned along with the Book (i.e., the Quran).

2. Al-Baqarah

Nursing Children After Divorce

233. ˹Divorced˺ mothers will breast-feed their offspring for two whole years, for those who wish to complete the nursing ˹of their child˺. The child's father will provide reasonable maintenance and clothing for the mother ˹during that period˺. No one will be charged with more than they can bear. No mother or father should be made to suffer for their child. The ˹father's˺ heirs are under the same obligation. But if both sides decide—after mutual consultation and consent—to wean a child, then there is no blame on them.

Opting for a Wet-Nurse

If you decide to have your children nursed by a wet-nurse, it is permissible as long as you pay fairly. Be mindful of Allah, and know that Allah is All-Seeing of what you do.

Widows' Waiting Period

234. As for those of you who die and leave widows behind, let them observe a waiting period of four months and ten days. When they have reached the end of this period, then you[93] are not accountable for what they decide for themselves in a reasonable manner. And Allah is All-Aware of what you do.

Proposing to Widowed or Divorced Women

235. There is no blame on you for subtly showing interest in ˹divorced or widowed˺ women[94] or for hiding ˹the intention˺ in your hearts. Allah knows that you are considering them ˹for marriage˺. But do not make a secret commitment with them—you can only show interest in them appropriately. Do not commit to the bond of marriage until the waiting period expires. Know that Allah is aware of what is in your hearts, so beware of Him. And know that Allah is All-Forgiving, Most Forbearing.

---

93 i.e., the guardians.
94 During their waiting periods.

2. Al-Baqarah 40

Divorce Before Consummation

236. There is no blame if you divorce women before the marriage is consummated or the dowry is settled. But give them a ʿsuitableʾ compensation—the rich according to his means and the poor according to his. A reasonable compensation is an obligation on the good-doers. **237.** And if you divorce them before consummating the marriage but after deciding on a dowry, pay half of the dowry, unless the wife graciously waives it or the husband graciously pays in full. Graciousness is closer to righteousness. And do not forget kindness among yourselves. Surely Allah is All-Seeing of what you do.

Observing Prayers[95]

238. Observe the ʿfive obligatoryʾ prayers—especially the middle prayer[96]—and stand in true devotion to Allah. **239.** If you are in danger, pray on foot or while riding. But when you are safe, ʿtake time toʾ remember Allah for teaching you what you did not know.

Widows' Original Waiting Period

240. Those of you who die leaving widows should bequeath for them a year's maintenance without forcing them out.[97] But if they choose to leave, you are not accountable for what they reasonably decide for themselves. And Allah is Almighty, All-Wise.

Care for Divorced Women

241. Reasonable provisions must be made for divorced women—a duty on those mindful ʿof Allahʾ. **242.** This is how Allah makes His revelations clear to you, so perhaps you will understand.

---

95 The passage that discusses prayer falls between the passages that discuss divorce and women's rights after divorce because it serves as a reminder that prayers should motivate spouses to always be mindful of their Lord during their marriage and also after divorce so no one will be wronged in anyway.

96 As mentioned in several authentic sayings of Prophet Muḥammad (ﷺ), the middle prayer is the afternoon prayer, ʿAṣr.

97 This ruling was later replaced by the ruling in 2:234.

2. Al-Baqarah

Sacrifices in Allah's Cause

243. Have you ʿO Prophet̒ not seen those who fled their homes in the thousands for fear of death?[98] Allah said to them, "Die!" then He gave them life. Surely Allah is ever Bountiful to humanity, but most people are ungrateful. **244.** Fight in the cause of Allah, and know that Allah is All-Hearing, All-Knowing. **245.** Who will lend to Allah a good loan which Allah will multiply many times over? It is Allah ʿaloneʾ who decreases and increases ʿwealthʾ. And to Him you will ʿallʾ be returned.

Prophet Samuel

246. Have you not seen those chiefs of the Children of Israel after Moses? They said to one of their prophets, "Appoint for us a king, ʿandʾ we will fight in the cause of Allah." He said, "Are you not going to cower if ordered to fight?" They replied, "How could we refuse to fight in the cause of Allah, while we were driven out of our homes and ʿseparated fromʾ our children?" But when they were ordered to fight, they fled, except for a few of them. And Allah has ʿperfectʾ knowledge of the wrongdoers.

King Saul

247. Their prophet told them, "Allah has appointed Saul[99] to be your king." They protested, "How can he be our king when some of us are more deserving of kingship than he, and he has not been blessed with vast riches?" He replied, "Allah has chosen him over you and blessed him with knowledge and stature. Allah grants kingship to whoever He wills. And Allah is All-Bountiful, All-Knowing."

---

98 They fled in the wake of a plague or an enemy attack.
99 Ṭālūt.

2. Al-Baqarah

248. Their prophet further told them, "The sign of Saul's kingship is that the Ark will come to you—containing reassurance[100] from your Lord and relics of the family of Moses and the family of Aaron,[101] which will be carried by the angels. Surely in this is a sign for you, if you ˹truly˺ believe."

Saul's Victory

249. When Saul marched forth with his army, he cautioned: "Allah will test you with a river. So whoever drinks ˹his fill˺ from it is not with me, and whoever does not taste it—except a sip from the hollow of his hands—is definitely with me." They all drank ˹their fill˺ except for a few! When he and the ˹remaining˺ faithful with him crossed the river, they said, "Now we are no match for Goliath and his warriors." But those ˹believers˺ who were certain they would meet Allah reasoned, "How many times has a small force vanquished a mighty army by the Will of Allah! And Allah is ˹always˺ with the steadfast."

David Kills Goliath

250. When they advanced to face Goliath and his warriors, they prayed, "Our Lord! Shower us with perseverance, make our steps firm, and give us victory over the disbelieving people." **251.** So they defeated them by Allah's Will, and David killed Goliath. And Allah blessed David with kingship and wisdom and taught him what He willed. Had Allah not repelled a group of people by ˹the might of˺ another, corruption would have dominated the earth, but Allah is Gracious to all. **252.** These are Allah's revelations which We recite to you ˹O Prophet˺ in truth. And you are truly one of the messengers.

---

100 Reassurance refers to the Torah.
101 i.e., the staff of Moses and fragments of the Tablets.

2. Al-Baqarah

Some Messengers Raised in Rank

253. We have chosen some of those messengers above others.[102] Allah spoke directly to some, and raised some high in rank. To Jesus, son of Mary, We gave clear proofs and supported him with the holy spirit.[103] If Allah had willed, succeeding generations would not have fought ˹among themselves˺ after receiving the clear proofs. But they differed—some believed while others disbelieved. Yet if Allah had willed, they would not have fought one another. But Allah does what He wills.

Spending in Allah's Way

254. O believers! Donate from what We have provided for you before the arrival of a Day when there will be no bargaining,[104] friendship,[105] or intercession. Those who disbelieve are ˹truly˺ the wrongdoers.

One True Allah

255. Allah! There is no god ˹worthy of worship˺ except Him, the Ever-Living, All-Sustaining. Neither drowsiness nor sleep overtakes Him. To Him belongs whatever is in the heavens and whatever is on the earth. Who could possibly intercede with Him without His permission? He ˹fully˺ knows what is ahead of them and what is behind them, but no one can grasp any of His knowledge—except what He wills ˹to reveal˺. His Seat[106] encompasses the heavens and the earth, and the preservation of both does not tire Him. For He is the Most High, the Greatest.[107]

Free Will in Accepting Islam

256. Let there be no compulsion in religion, for the truth stands out clearly from falsehood.[108] So whoever renounces false gods and believes in Allah has certainly grasped the firmest, unfailing hand-hold. And Allah is All-Hearing, All-Knowing.

---

102 Those messengers mentioned earlier in this sûrah (*see* verse 136).
103 i.e., Gabriel.
104 This implies ransoming one's self.
105 i.e., friendly connections.
106 The Arabic word *kursi* can either mean seat or knowledge. There are some narrations attributed to Prophet Muḥammad (ﷺ) that describe Allah's Throne ('*Arsh*) as being greater than His *Kursi*.
107 According to Muslim belief, this is the greatest verse in the Quran.
108 This verse was revealed when some new Muslims tried to force their Jewish and Christian children to convert to Islam after the Prophet's emigration (*Hijrah*) to Medina. The verse prohibits forced conversion.

2. Al-Baqarah

257. Allah is the Guardian of the believers—He brings them out of darkness and into light. As for the disbelievers, their guardians are false gods who lead them out of light and into darkness. It is they who will be the residents of the Fire. They will be there forever.

Abraham and the Arrogant King

258. Are you ˹O Prophet˺ not aware of the one who argued with Abraham about his Lord because Allah had granted him kingship? ˹Remember˺ when Abraham said, "My Lord is the One Who has power to give life and cause death." He argued, "I too have the power to give life and cause death." Abraham challenged ˹him˺, "Allah causes the sun to rise from the east. So make it rise from the west." And so the disbeliever was dumbstruck. And Allah does not guide the wrongdoing people.

Story of Ezra

259. Or ˹are you not aware of˺ the one who passed by a city which was in ruins. He wondered, "How could Allah bring this back to life after its destruction?" So Allah caused him to die for a hundred years then brought him back life. Allah asked, "How long have you remained ˹in this state˺?" He replied, "Perhaps a day or part of a day." Allah said, "No! You have remained here for hundred years! Just look at your food and drink—they have not spoiled. ˹But now˺ look at ˹the remains of˺ your donkey! And ˹so˺ We have made you into a sign for humanity. And look at the bones ˹of the donkey˺, how We bring them together then clothe them with flesh!"[109] When this was made clear to him, he declared, "˹Now˺ I know that Allah is Most Capable of everything."

---

109 Bringing the donkey back to life.

Abraham Inquiring About Resurrection

260. And ˹remember˺ when Abraham said, "My Lord! Show me how you give life to the dead." Allah responded, "Do you not believe?" Abraham replied, "Yes I do, but just so my heart can be reassured." Allah said, "Then bring four birds, train them to come to you, ˹then cut them into pieces,˺ and scatter them on different hilltops. Then call them back, they will fly to you in haste. And ˹so you will˺ know that Allah Almighty, All-Wise."

Multiplied Rewards for Charity

261. The example of those who spend their wealth in the cause of Allah is that of a grain that sprouts into seven ears, each bearing one hundred grains. And Allah multiplies ˹the reward even more˺ to whoever He wills. For Allah is All-Bountiful, All-Knowing.

Sincere Charity

262. Those who spend their wealth in the cause of Allah and do not follow their charity with reminders of their generosity or hurtful words—they will get their reward from their Lord, and there will be no fear for them, nor will they grieve. **263.** Kind words and forgiveness are better than charity followed by injury. And Allah is Self-Sufficient, Most Forbearing.

Parable for Wasted Charity

264. O believers! Do not waste your charity with reminders ˹of your generosity˺ or hurtful words, like those who donate their wealth just to show off and do not believe in Allah or the Last Day. Their example is that of a hard barren rock covered with a thin layer of soil hit by a strong rain—leaving it just a bare stone. Such people are unable to preserve the reward of their charity. Allah does not guide ˹such˺ disbelieving people.

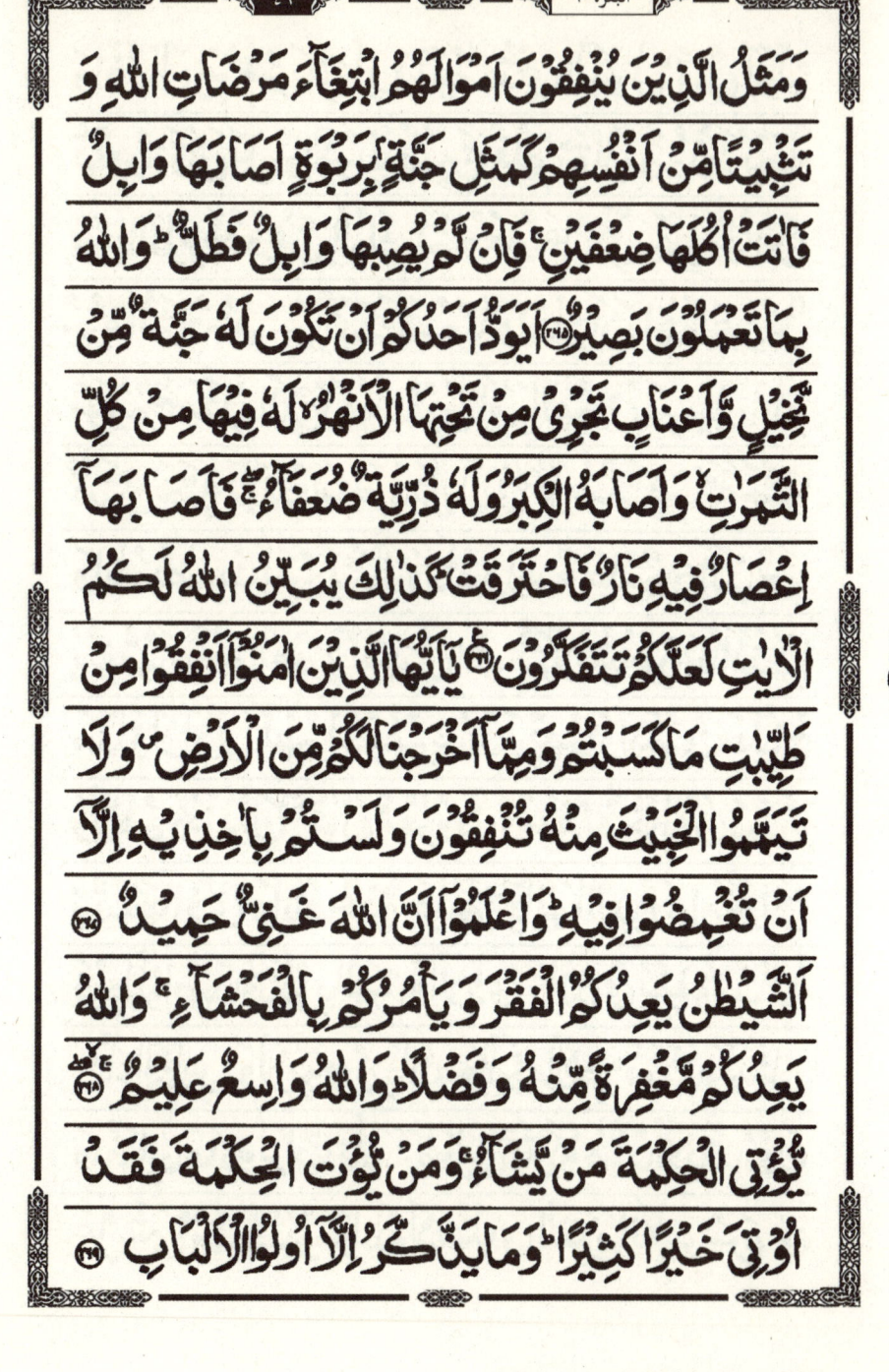

Parable for Accepted Charity

265. And the example of those who donate their wealth, seeking Allah's pleasure and believing the reward is certain,[110] is that of a garden on a fertile hill: when heavy rain falls, it yields up twice its normal produce. If no heavy rain falls, a drizzle is sufficient. And Allah is All-Seeing of what you do.

Wasted Reward

266. Would any of you wish to have a garden with palm trees, grapevines, and all kinds of fruits with rivers flowing underneath and as they grow very old with dependent children, a fiery whirlwind hits the garden, burning it all up? This is how Allah makes His revelations clear to you, so perhaps you will reflect.

Quality Charity

267. O believers! Donate from the best of what you have earned and of what We have produced for you from the earth. Do not pick out worthless things for donation, which you yourselves would only accept with closed eyes. And know that Allah is Self-Sufficient, Praiseworthy.

Devil Discouraging Charity

268. The Devil threatens you with ʿthe prospect ofʾ poverty and bids you to the shameful deed ʿof stinginessʾ, while Allah promises you forgiveness and ʿgreatʾ bounties from Him. And Allah is All-Bountiful, All-Knowing.

Wisdom as a Privilege, Not a Right

269. He grants wisdom to whoever He wills. And whoever is granted wisdom is certainly blessed with a great privilege. But none will be mindful ʿof thisʾ except people of reason.

---

110 It could also mean "... seeking Allah's pleasure and proving their sincerity."

2. Al-Baqarah

Donating Openly and Secretly

270. Whatever charities you give or vows you make are surely known to Allah. And the wrongdoers will have no helpers. **271.** To give charity publicly is good, but to give to the poor privately is better for you, and will absolve you of your sins. And Allah is All-Aware of what you do.[111] **272.** You are not responsible for people's guidance ˹O Prophet˺— it is Allah Who guides whoever He wills. Whatever you ˹believers˺ spend in charity, it is for your own good—as long as you do so seeking the pleasure of Allah.[112] Whatever you donate will be paid back to you in full, and you will not be wronged.

Caring for the Needy

273. ˹Charity is˺ for the needy who are too engaged in the cause of Allah to move about in the land ˹for work˺. Those unfamiliar with their situation will think they are not in need ˹of charity˺ because they do not beg. You can recognize them by their appearance. They do not beg people persistently. Whatever you give in charity is certainly well known to Allah. **274.** Those who spend their wealth in charity day and night, secretly and openly—their reward is with their Lord, and there will be no fear for them, nor will they grieve.

---

111 Donations for a public cause may be done openly to encourage others to donate, whereas it is recommended to give charity to the poor secretly.
112 lit., seeking the Face of Allah.

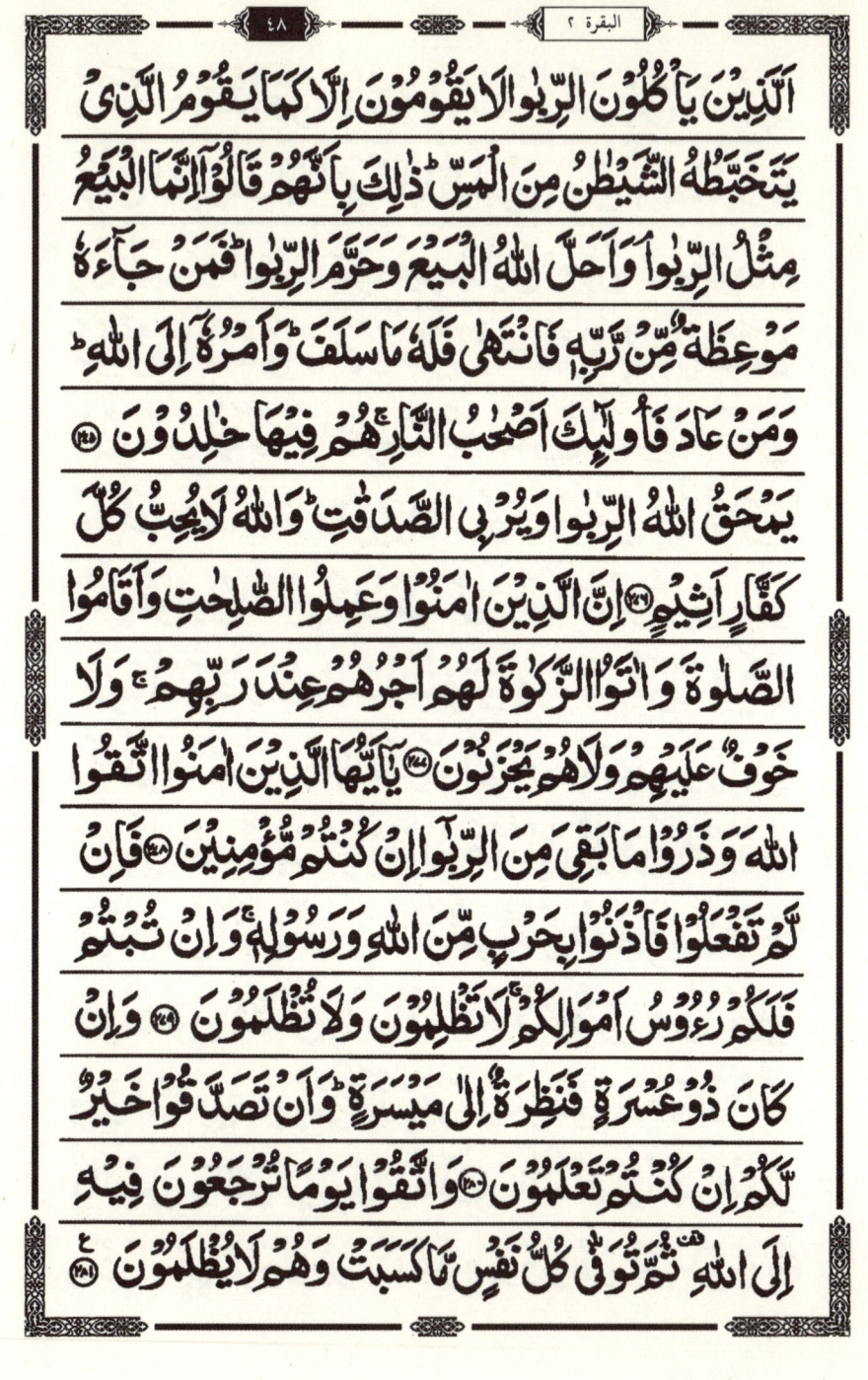

Interest Prohibited

275. Those who consume interest will stand ˹on Judgment Day˺ like those driven to madness by Satan's touch. That is because they say, "Trade is no different than interest." But Allah has permitted trading and forbidden interest. Whoever refrains—after having received warning from their Lord—may keep their previous gains, and their case is left to Allah. As for those who persist, it is they who will be the residents of the Fire. They will be there forever. **276.** Allah has made interest fruitless and charity fruitful. And Allah does not like any ungrateful evildoer.

True Believers

277. Indeed, those who believe, do good, establish prayer, and pay alms-tax will receive their reward from their Lord, and there will be no fear for them, nor will they grieve.

Warning Against Interest

278. O believers! Fear Allah, and give up outstanding interest if you are ˹true˺ believers. **279.** If you do not, then beware of a war with Allah and His Messenger! But if you repent, you may retain your principal—neither inflicting nor suffering harm.

Kindness in Collecting Debts

280. If it is difficult for someone to repay a debt, postpone it until a time of ease. And if you waive it as an act of charity, it will be better for you, if only you knew.

Reminder of Judgment Day

281. Be mindful of the Day when you will ˹all˺ be returned to Allah, then every soul will be paid in full for what it has done, and none will be wronged.[113]

---

113 Verse 281 is believed by many scholars to be the last verse revealed of the Quran.

2. Al-Baqarah

Writing a Debt Contract

282. O believers! When you contract a loan for a fixed period of time, commit it to writing. Let the scribe maintain justice between the parties. The scribe should not refuse to write as Allah has taught them to write. They will write what the debtor dictates, bearing Allah in mind and not defrauding the debt. If the debtor is incompetent, weak, or unable to dictate, let their guardian dictate for them with justice.

Witnessing a Debt Contract

Call upon two of your men to witness. If two men cannot be found, then one man and two women of your choice will witness—so if one of the women forgets the other may remind her.[114] The witnesses must not refuse when they are summoned. You must not be against writing ˹contracts˺ for a fixed period—whether the sum is small or great. This is more just ˹for you˺ in the sight of Allah, and more convenient to establish evidence and remove doubts. However, if you conduct an immediate transaction among yourselves, then there is no need for you to record it, but call upon witnesses when a deal is finalized. Let no harm come to the scribe or witnesses. If you do, then you have gravely exceeded ˹your limits˺. Be mindful of Allah, for Allah ˹is the One Who˺ teaches you. And Allah has ˹perfect˺ knowledge of all things.

---

114 Generally speaking, there is a difference between witnessing and giving testimony before a judge. Verse 2:282 talks about witnessing a debt contract, not giving testimony. To fully understand the context of this verse, we need to keep in mind that 1500 years ago women did not normally participate in business transactions or travel with trading caravans and, therefore, not every woman had the expertise to witness a debt contract. Even if two women were available at the time of signing the contract, perhaps the primary witness might not be able to recall the details of the contract or appear before a judge because of compelling circumstances such as pregnancy or delivery. In any of these cases, the second woman will be a back-up. Some scholars maintain that one woman can be sufficient as a witness so long as she is reliable. As for giving testimony, a ruling can be made based on available testimony, regardless of the number or gender of the witnesses. For example, the beginning of Ramaḍān is usually confirmed by the sighting of the new moon, regardless of the gender of the person who sights the moon. Also the highest form of witness in Islam is for someone to testify they heard a narration (or ḥadīth) from the Prophet (ﷺ). An authentic ḥadīth is accepted by all Muslims regardless of the gender of the narrator. Moreover, if a husband accuses his wife of adultery and he has no witnesses, each spouse must testify five times that they are telling the truth and the other side is lying. Both testimonies are equal (see 24:6-10). In some cases, only women's testimony is accepted while men's testimony is rejected, such as testifying regarding a woman's pregnancy or virginity.

Taking Collateral

283. If you are on a journey and a scribe cannot be found, then a security can be taken. If you trust one another, then ˹there is no need for a security, but˺ the debtor should honour this trust ˹by repaying the debt˺—and let them fear Allah, their Lord. And do not conceal the testimony, for whoever conceals it, their hearts are indeed sinful. And Allah ˹fully˺ knows what you do.

Allah's Might

284. To Allah ˹alone˺ belongs whatever is in the heavens and whatever is on the earth. Whether you reveal what is in your hearts or conceal it, Allah will call you to account for it. He forgives whoever He wills, and punishes whoever He wills. And Allah is Most Capable of everything.

Articles of Faith

285. The Messenger ˹firmly˺ believes in what has been revealed to him from his Lord, and so do the believers. They ˹all˺ believe in Allah, His angels, His Books, and His messengers. ˹They proclaim,˺ "We make no distinction between any of His messengers." And they say, "We hear and obey. ˹We seek˺ Your forgiveness, our Lord! And to You ˹alone˺ is the final return."

Prayer for Grace

286. Allah does not require of any soul more than what it can afford. All good will be for its own benefit, and all evil will be to its own loss. ˹The believers pray,˺ "Our Lord! Do not punish us if we forget or make a mistake. Our Lord! Do not place a burden on us like the one you placed on those before us. Our Lord! Do not burden us with what we cannot bear. Pardon us, forgive us, and have mercy on us. You are our ˹only˺ Guardian. So grant us victory over the disbelieving people."

3. The Family of 'Imrân (Âli-'Imrân)

In the Name of Allah—the Most Compassionate, Most Merciful

Scriptures as a Source of Guidance

1. *Alif-Lãm-Mĩm*. 2. Allah! There is no god ˹worthy of worship˺ except Him—the Ever-Living, All-Sustaining. 3. He has revealed to you ˹O Prophet˺ the Book in truth, confirming what came before it, as He revealed the Torah and the Gospel 4. previously, as a guide for people, and ˹also˺ revealed the Decisive Authority.[115] Surely those who reject Allah's revelations will suffer a severe torment. For Allah is Almighty, capable of punishment.

Allah Almighty

5. Surely nothing on earth or in the heavens is hidden from Allah. 6. He is the One Who shapes you in the wombs of your mothers as He wills. There is no god ˹worthy of worship˺ except Him—the Almighty, All-Wise.

Precise and Elusive Verses

7. He is the One Who has revealed to you ˹O Prophet˺ the Book, of which some verses are precise—they are the foundation of the Book—while others are elusive.[116] Those with deviant hearts follow the elusive verses seeking ˹to spread˺ doubt through their ˹false˺ interpretations—but none grasps their ˹full˺ meaning except Allah.

Prayers of the Knowledgeable

As for those well-grounded in knowledge, they say, "We believe in this ˹Quran˺—it is all from our Lord." But none will be mindful ˹of this˺ except people of reason. 8. ˹They say,˺ "Our Lord! Do not let our hearts deviate after you have guided us. Grant us Your mercy. You are indeed the Giver ˹of all bounties˺.

---

115 The Decisive Authority (*Al-Furqãn*) is one of the names of the Quran.

116 The precise verses are easy to understand and deal mostly with matters of belief and practice, such as the belief in one God (Sûrah 112), forbidden foods (*see* 5:3), and the commandments in 6:151-152 and 17:23-39. As for the elusive verses, their full meaning is known only to Allah, such as the meaning of letter combinations at the beginning of some sûrahs, such as *Alif-Lãm-Mĩm* (*see* Stylistic Features), and how Allah settles Himself on the Throne.

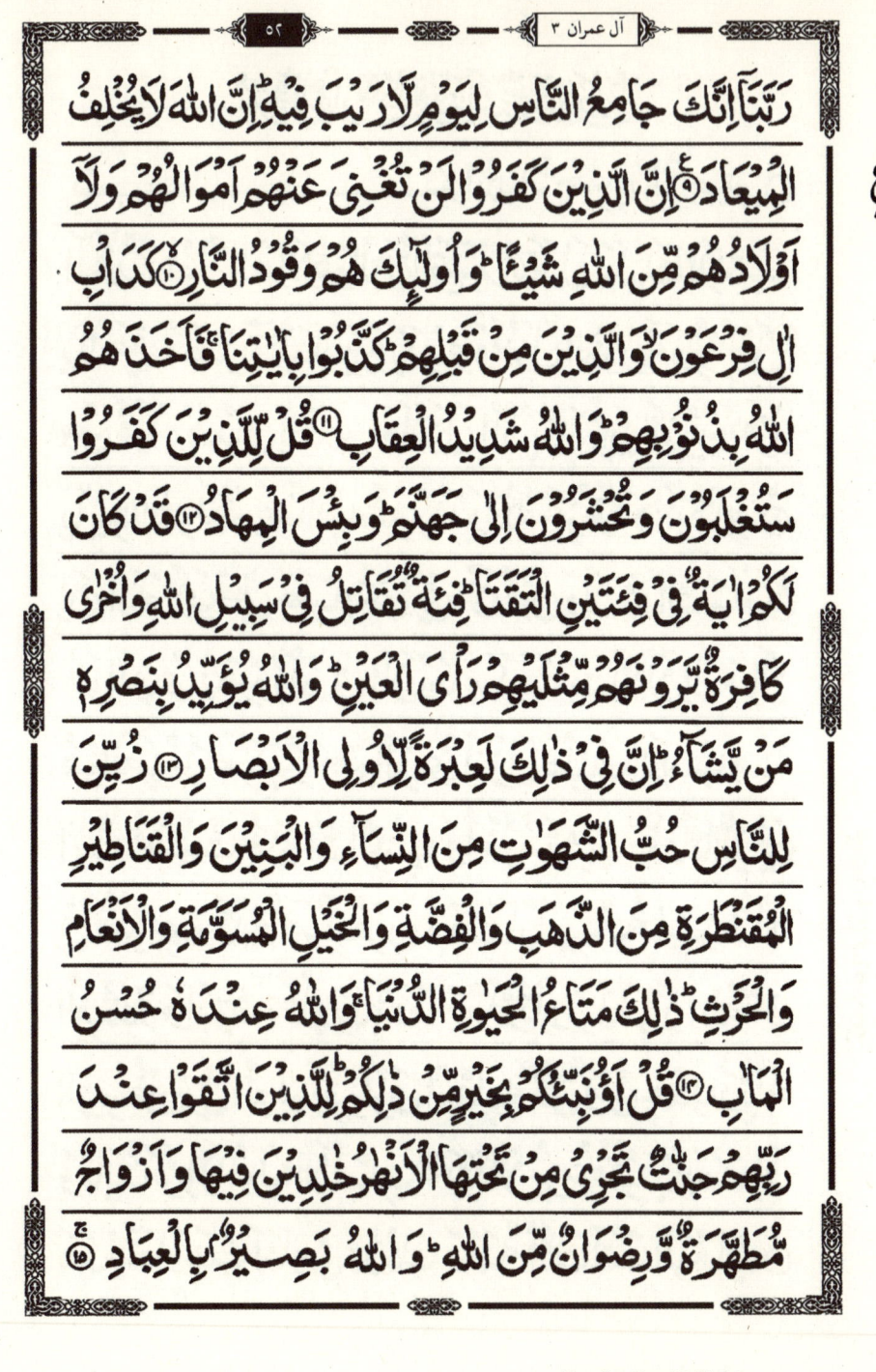

3. Âli-'Imrân — 52

9. Our Lord! You will certainly gather all humanity for the ˹promised˺ Day—about which there is no doubt. Surely Allah does not break His promise."

Punishment of the Disbelievers

10. Indeed, neither the wealth nor children[117] of the disbelievers will be of any benefit to them against Allah—and they will be the fuel for the Fire. 11. Their fate will be like that of the people of Pharaoh and those before them—they all rejected Our signs, so Allah seized them for their sins. And Allah is severe in punishment. 12. ˹O Prophet!˺ Tell the disbelievers, "Soon you will be overpowered and driven to Hell— what an evil place to rest!"

Allah's Help at the Battle of Badr[118]

13. Indeed, there was a sign for you in the two armies that met in battle—one fighting for the cause of Allah and the other in denial. The believers saw their enemy twice their number.[119] But Allah supports with His victory whoever He wills. Surely in this is a lesson for people of insight.

Temporary Pleasures

14. The enjoyment of ˹worldly˺ desires—women, children,[120] treasures of gold and silver, fine horses, cattle, and fertile land—has been made appealing to people. These are the pleasures of this worldly life, but with Allah is the finest destination.

Everlasting Delight

15. Say, ˹O Prophet,˺ "Shall I inform you of what is better than ˹all of˺ this? Those mindful ˹of Allah˺ will have Gardens with their Lord under which rivers flow, to stay there forever, and pure spouses,[121] along with Allah's pleasure." And Allah is All-Seeing of ˹His˺ servants,

---

117 Wealth and children were considered the most important things in pre-Islamic Arabia, and so the frequent mention of these things in the Quran is meant to represent all worldly gains.
118 Badr is the name of the location where the Muslim army and the pagan army of Mecca fought in 2 A.H./624 C.E. The Muslim army was made up of over 300 soldiers whereas the pagan army was over 1000.
119 It can also be understood that the disbelievers were made to think there were twice as many believers in the battlefield.
120 *Banīn* means sons. In the ancient Arab culture, sons were a source of pride for their parents and tribes. This is because they provided for their families and took up arms in defence of their tribes.
121 See footnote for 2:25.

3. Âli-'Imrân

16. who pray, "Our Lord! We have believed, so forgive our sins and protect us from the torment of the Fire." 17. 'It is they' who are patient, sincere, obedient, and charitable, and who pray for forgiveness before dawn.[122]

One God

18. Allah 'Himself' is a Witness that there is no god 'worthy of worship' except Him—and so are the angels and people of knowledge. He is the Maintainer of justice. There is no god 'worthy of worship' except Him—the Almighty, All-Wise.

One Way

19. Certainly, Allah's only Way is Islam.[123] Those who were given the Scripture did not dispute 'among themselves' out of mutual envy until knowledge came to them.[124] Whoever denies Allah's signs, then surely Allah is swift in reckoning. 20. So if they argue with you 'O Prophet', say, "I have submitted myself to Allah, and so have my followers." And ask those who were given the Scripture and the illiterate 'people',[125] "Have you submitted yourselves 'to Allah'?" If they submit, they will be 'rightly' guided. But if they turn away, then your duty is only to deliver 'the message'. And Allah is All-Seeing of 'His' servants.

Reward of the Rebellious

21. Indeed, those who deny Allah's signs, kill the prophets unjustly, and kill people who stand up for justice—give them good news of a painful punishment. 22. They are the ones whose deeds are wasted in this world and the Hereafter. And they will have no helpers.

---

122 Optional prayers before dawn are recommended and are more likely to be accepted.
123 I.e., full submission to the Will of Allah.
124 No community split into believers and disbelievers until they received the knowledge given by their prophet.
125 This refers to the pagans of Arabia before Islam.

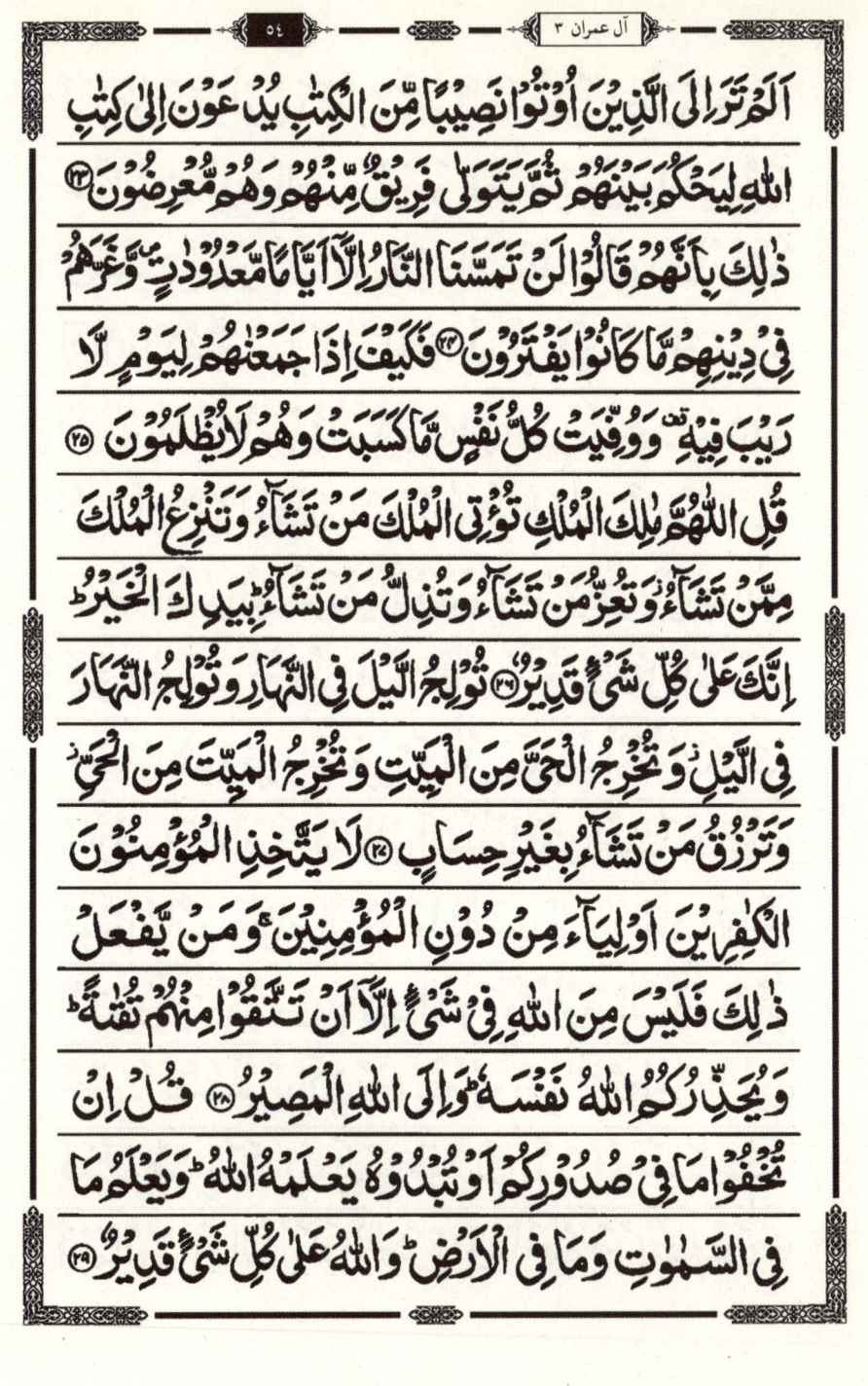

3. Âli-'Imrân

Rejecting Allah's Judgment

23. Have you not seen those who were given a portion of the Scriptures?[126] Yet when they are invited to the Book of Allah to settle their disputes, some of them turn away heedlessly. 24. This is because they say, "The Fire will not touch us except for a few days." They have been deceived in their faith by their wishful lying. 25. But how ˹horrible˺ will it be when We gather them together on the Day about which there is no doubt—when every soul will be paid in full for what it has done, and none will be wronged!

Allah's Infinite Power

26. Say, ˹O Prophet,˺ "O Allah! Lord over all authorities! You give authority to whoever You please and remove it from who You please; You honour whoever You please and disgrace who You please—all good is in Your Hands. Surely You ˹alone˺ are Most Capable of everything. 27. You cause the night to pass into the day and the day into the night. You bring forth the living from the dead and the dead from the living. And You provide for whoever You will without limit."

Taking Disbelievers as Guardians[127]

28. Believers should not take disbelievers as guardians instead of the believers—and whoever does so will have nothing to hope for from Allah—unless it is a precaution against their tyranny. And Allah warns you about Himself. And to Allah is the final return.

Allah's Infinite Knowledge

29. Say, ˹O Prophet,˺ "Whether you conceal what is in your hearts or reveal it, it is known to Allah. For He knows whatever is in the heavens and whatever is on the earth. And Allah is Most Capable of everything."

---

126 i.e., the Torah.
127 Like 4:139 and 4:144, this verse forbids the believers from taking the disbelievers who were at war with Muslims as strategic allies.

3. Âli-'Imrân

Accountability for Good and Evil

30. ʿWatch forʾ the Day when every soul will be presented with whatever good it has done. And it will wish that its misdeeds were far off. And Allah warns you about Himself. And Allah is Ever Gracious to ʿHisʾ servants.

Obeying Allah and His Messenger

31. Say, ʿO Prophet,ʾ "If you ʿsincerelyʾ love Allah, then follow me; Allah will love you and forgive your sins. For Allah is All-Forgiving, Most Merciful." **32.** Say, ʿO Prophet,ʾ "Obey Allah and His Messenger." If they still turn away, then truly Allah does not like the disbelievers.

Blessed People

33. Indeed, Allah chose Adam, Noah, the family of Abraham, and the family of ʾImrân above all people ʿof their timeʾ. **34.** They are descendants of one another. And Allah is All-Hearing, All-Knowing.

Birth of Mary

35. ʿRememberʾ when the wife of ʾImrân said, "My Lord! I dedicate what is in my womb entirely to Your service,[128] so accept it from me. You ʿaloneʾ are truly the All-Hearing, All-Knowing." **36.** When she delivered, she said, "My Lord! I have given birth to a girl,"—and Allah fully knew what she had delivered—"and the male is not like the female.[129] I have named her Mary, and I seek Your protection for her and her offspring from Satan, the accursed."[130] **37.** So her Lord accepted her graciously and blessed her with a pleasant upbringing— entrusting her to the care of Zachariah. Whenever Zachariah visited her in the sanctuary, he found her supplied with provisions. He exclaimed, "O Mary! Where did this come from?" She replied, "It is from Allah. Surely Allah provides for whoever He wills without limit."

---

128 i.e., dedicating the child to service in the temple.

129 Service at the temple was hosted by males only.

130 The prayers of Mary's mother were answered. In a *ḥadīth* collected by Bukhâri and Muslim, the Prophet (ﷺ) says, "Every child is touched by Satan when they are born—and they cry because of this contact—except Jesus and his mother."

3. Âli-'Imrân

هُنَالِكَ دَعَا زَكَرِيَّا رَبَّهُ قَالَ رَبِّ هَبْ لِي مِن لَّدُنكَ ذُرِّيَّةً
طَيِّبَةً إِنَّكَ سَمِيعُ الدُّعَاءِ ۝ فَنَادَتْهُ الْمَلَائِكَةُ وَهُوَ قَائِمٌ
يُصَلِّي فِي الْمِحْرَابِ أَنَّ اللَّهَ يُبَشِّرُكَ بِيَحْيَى مُصَدِّقًا بِكَلِمَةٍ
مِّنَ اللَّهِ وَسَيِّدًا وَحَصُورًا وَنَبِيًّا مِّنَ الصَّالِحِينَ ۝ قَالَ رَبِّ
أَنَّى يَكُونُ لِي غُلَامٌ وَقَدْ بَلَغَنِيَ الْكِبَرُ وَامْرَأَتِي عَاقِرٌ قَالَ
كَذَلِكَ اللَّهُ يَفْعَلُ مَا يَشَاءُ ۝ قَالَ رَبِّ اجْعَل لِّي آيَةً قَالَ
ءَايَتُكَ أَلَّا تُكَلِّمَ النَّاسَ ثَلَاثَةَ أَيَّامٍ إِلَّا رَمْزًا وَاذْكُر رَّبَّكَ
كَثِيرًا وَسَبِّحْ بِالْعَشِيِّ وَالْإِبْكَارِ ۝ وَإِذْ قَالَتِ الْمَلَائِكَةُ
يَمَرْيَمُ إِنَّ اللَّهَ اصْطَفَاكِ وَطَهَّرَكِ وَاصْطَفَاكِ عَلَى
نِسَاءِ الْعَالَمِينَ ۝ يَمَرْيَمُ اقْنُتِي لِرَبِّكِ وَاسْجُدِي وَارْكَعِي
مَعَ الرَّاكِعِينَ ۝ ذَلِكَ مِنْ أَنبَاءِ الْغَيْبِ نُوحِيهِ إِلَيْكَ وَمَا
كُنتَ لَدَيْهِمْ إِذْ يُلْقُونَ أَقْلَامَهُمْ أَيُّهُمْ يَكْفُلُ مَرْيَمَ وَمَا
كُنتَ لَدَيْهِمْ إِذْ يَخْتَصِمُونَ ۝ إِذْ قَالَتِ الْمَلَائِكَةُ يَمَرْيَمُ
إِنَّ اللَّهَ يُبَشِّرُكِ بِكَلِمَةٍ مِّنْهُ اسْمُهُ الْمَسِيحُ عِيسَى ابْنُ مَرْيَمَ
وَجِيهًا فِي الدُّنْيَا وَالْآخِرَةِ وَمِنَ الْمُقَرَّبِينَ ۝

Birth of John the Baptist

38. Then and there Zachariah prayed to his Lord, saying, "My Lord! Grant me—by your grace—righteous offspring. You are certainly the Hearer of ˹all˺ prayers." **39.** So the angels called out to him while he stood praying in the sanctuary, "Allah gives you good news of ˹the birth of˺ John who will confirm the Word of Allah and will be a great leader, chaste, and a prophet among the righteous." **40.** Zachariah exclaimed, "My Lord! How can I have a son when I am very old and my wife is barren?" He replied, "So will it be. Allah does what He wills." **41.** Zachariah said, "My Lord! Grant me a sign." He said, "Your sign is that you will not ˹be able to˺ speak to people for three days except through gestures. Remember your Lord often and glorify ˹Him˺ morning and evening."

Mary Chosen over All Women

42. And ˹remember˺ when the angels said, "O Mary! Surely Allah has selected you, purified you, and chosen you over all women of the world. **43.** O Mary! Be devout to your Lord, prostrate yourself ˹in prayer˺ and bow along with those who bow down." **44.** This is news of the unseen that We reveal to you ˹O Prophet˺. You were not with them when they cast lots to decide who would be Mary's guardian, nor were you there when they argued ˹about it˺.

Birth of Jesus Christ

45. ˹Remember˺ when the angels proclaimed, "O Mary! Allah gives you good news of a Word[131] from Him, his name will be the Messiah,[132] Jesus, son of Mary; honoured in this world and the Hereafter, and he will be one of those nearest ˹to Allah˺.

---

131 In the Quran, Jesus is called the "Word" of Allah since he was created with the word "Be!"
132 Messiah (*Masîḥ*) means the "anointed one." It is used in the Quran exclusively as a title for Jesus Christ.

3. Âli-'Imrân

46. And he will speak to people in ˹his˺ infancy and adulthood and will be one of the righteous." **47.** Mary wondered, "My Lord! How can I have a child when no man has ever touched me?" An angel replied, "So will it be. Allah creates what He wills. When He decrees a matter, He simply tells it, 'Be!' And it is!

The Mission and Miracles of Jesus

48. And Allah will teach him writing and wisdom, the Torah and the Gospel, **49.** and ˹make him˺ a messenger to the Children of Israel ˹to proclaim,˺ "I have come to you with a sign from your Lord: I will make for you a bird from clay, breathe into it, and it will become a ˹real˺ bird—by Allah's Will. I will heal the blind and the leper and raise the dead to life—by Allah's Will. And I will prophesize what you eat and store in your houses. Surely in this is a sign for you if you ˹truly˺ believe. **50.** And I will confirm the Torah revealed before me and legalize some of what had been forbidden to you. I have come to you with a sign from your Lord, so be mindful of Allah and obey me. **51.** Surely Allah is my Lord and your Lord. So worship Him ˹alone˺. This is the Straight Path."

The Disciples

52. When Jesus sensed disbelief from his people, he asked, "Who will stand up with me for Allah?" The disciples replied, "We will stand up for Allah. We believe in Allah, so bear witness that we have submitted." **53.** ˹They prayed to Allah,˺ "Our Lord! We believe in Your revelations and follow the messenger, so count us among those who bear witness."

3. Âli-'Imrân

Conspiracy Against Jesus

54. And the disbelievers made a plan ˹against Jesus˺, but Allah also planned—and Allah is the best of planners. **55.** ˹Remember˺ when Allah said, "O Jesus! I will take you[133] and raise you up to Myself. I will deliver you from those who disbelieve, and elevate your followers above the disbelievers until the Day of Judgment. Then to Me you will ˹all˺ return, and I will settle all your disputes.

Fair Reward

56. "As for those who disbelieve, I will subject them to a severe punishment in this life and the Hereafter, and they will have no helpers. **57.** And as for those who believe and do good, they will be rewarded in full. And Allah does not like the wrongdoers." **58.** We recite ˹all˺ this to you ˹O Prophet˺ as one of the signs[134] and ˹as˺ a wise reminder.

Jesus and Adam

59. Indeed, the example of Jesus in the sight of Allah is like that of Adam. He created him from dust, then said to him, "Be!" And he was! **60.** This is the truth from your Lord, so do not be one of those who doubt.

Disputes over Jesus

61. Now, whoever disputes with you ˹O Prophet˺ concerning Jesus after full knowledge has come to you, say, "Come! Let us gather our children and your children, our women and your women, ourselves and yourselves—then let us sincerely invoke Allah's curse upon the liars."

62. Certainly, this is the true narrative, and there is no god ˹worthy of worship˺ except Allah. And indeed, Allah ˹alone˺ is the Almighty, All-Wise.

---

133 *Mutawaffîka* means literally: "I will make you reach the end of your worldly term." The popular Muslim belief is that a conspiracy was made to kill Jesus. Allah made the main culprit who betrayed Jesus look exactly like Jesus, while the culprit was crucified. Similar to Christians, Muslims believe in the second coming of Jesus (☽).

134 As a testament to your prophethood.

63. If they turn away, then surely Allah has ˹perfect˺ knowledge of the corruptors.

Devotion to Allah Alone

64. Say, ˹O Prophet,˺ "O People of the Book! Let us come to common terms: that we will worship none but Allah, associate none with Him, nor take one another as lords instead of Allah." But if they turn away, then say, "Bear witness that we have submitted ˹to Allah alone˺."

The Truth About Abraham

65. O People of the Book! Why do you argue about Abraham, while the Torah and the Gospel were not revealed until long after him? Do you not understand? **66.** Here you are! You disputed about what you have ˹little˺ knowledge of,[135] but why do you now argue about what you have no knowledge of?[136] Allah knows and you do not know. **67.** Abraham was neither a Jew nor a Christian; he submitted in all uprightness[137] and was not a polytheist. **68.** Indeed, those who have the best claim to Abraham are his followers, this Prophet,[138] and the believers. And Allah is the Guardian of those who believe.

Distorting the Truth

69. Some of the People of the Book wish to mislead you ˹believers˺. They mislead none but themselves, yet they fail to perceive it. **70.** O People of the Book! Why do you reject the signs of Allah while you bear witness ˹to their truth˺?

---

135 The perception of Jesus (ﷺ).
136 Abraham (ﷺ) being Jewish or Christian.
137 Linguistically, "Muslim" means "someone who has submitted themselves to Allah."
138 Muḥammad (ﷺ).

3. Âli-'Imrân • 60

71. O People of the Book! Why do you mix the truth with falsehood and hide the truth knowingly?

Deception Exposed

72. A group among the People of the Book said ˹to one another˺, "Believe in what has been revealed to the believers in the morning and reject it in the evening, so they may abandon their faith. 73. And only believe those who follow your religion." Say, ˹O Prophet,˺ "Surely, ˹the only˺ true guidance is Allah's guidance." ˹They also said,˺ "Do not believe that someone will receive ˹revealed˺ knowledge similar to yours or argue against you before your Lord." Say, ˹O Prophet,˺ "Indeed, all bounty is in the Hands of Allah—He grants it to whoever He wills. And Allah is Ever-Bountiful, All-Knowing." 74. He chooses whoever He wills to receive His mercy. And Allah is the Lord of infinite bounty.

Honouring Trusts

75. There are some among the People of the Book who, if entrusted with a stack of gold, will readily return it. Yet there are others who, if entrusted with a single coin, will not repay it unless you constantly demand it. This is because they say, "We are not accountable for ˹exploiting˺ the Gentiles."[139] And ˹so˺ they attribute lies to Allah knowingly. 76. Absolutely! Those who honour their trusts and shun evil—surely Allah loves those who are mindful ˹of Him˺.

Breaking Allah's Covenant

77. Indeed, those who trade Allah's covenant and their oaths for a fleeting gain will have no share in the Hereafter. Allah will neither speak to them, nor look at them, nor purify them on the Day of Judgment. And they will suffer a painful punishment.

---

139 "Gentiles" here refers to the pagans of Arabia.

3. Âli-'Imrân

Distorting the Scripture

78. There are some among them who distort the Book with their tongues to make you think this ʿdistortionʾ is from the Book—but it is not what the Book says. They say, "It is from Allah"—but it is not from Allah. And ʿsoʾ they attribute lies to Allah knowingly.

Prophets Never Claim Divinity

79. It is not appropriate for someone who Allah has blessed with the Scripture, wisdom, and prophethood to say to people, "Worship me instead of Allah." Rather, he would say, "Be devoted to the worship of your Lord ʿaloneʾ, by virtue of what you read in the Scripture and what you teach." **80.** And he would never ask you to take angels and prophets as lords. Would he ask you to disbelieve after you have submitted?

Allah's Covenant with Prophets

81. ʿRememberʾ when Allah made a covenant with the prophets, ʿsaying,ʾ "Now that I have given you the Book and wisdom, if there comes to you a messenger[140] confirming what you have, you must believe in him and support him." He added, "Do you affirm this covenant and accept this commitment?" They said, "Yes, we do." Allah said, "Then bear witness, and I too am a Witness." **82.** Whoever turns back after this, they will be the rebellious.

Full Submission

83. Do they desire a way other than Allah's—knowing that all those in the heavens and the earth submit to His Will, willingly or unwillingly, and to Him they will ʿallʾ be returned?

---

140 Muḥammad (ﷺ).

بسم الله - Arabic text (Surah Ali-'Imran, verses 84-91)

قُلْ آمَنَّا بِاللَّهِ وَمَا أُنزِلَ عَلَيْنَا وَمَا أُنزِلَ عَلَىٰ إِبْرَاهِيمَ وَإِسْمَاعِيلَ وَإِسْحَاقَ وَيَعْقُوبَ وَالْأَسْبَاطِ وَمَا أُوتِيَ مُوسَىٰ وَعِيسَىٰ وَالنَّبِيُّونَ مِن رَّبِّهِمْ لَا نُفَرِّقُ بَيْنَ أَحَدٍ مِّنْهُمْ وَنَحْنُ لَهُ مُسْلِمُونَ ۝ وَمَن يَبْتَغِ غَيْرَ الْإِسْلَامِ دِينًا فَلَن يُقْبَلَ مِنْهُ وَهُوَ فِي الْآخِرَةِ مِنَ الْخَاسِرِينَ ۝ كَيْفَ يَهْدِي اللَّهُ قَوْمًا كَفَرُوا بَعْدَ إِيمَانِهِمْ وَشَهِدُوا أَنَّ الرَّسُولَ حَقٌّ وَجَاءَهُمُ الْبَيِّنَاتُ وَاللَّهُ لَا يَهْدِي الْقَوْمَ الظَّالِمِينَ ۝ أُولَٰئِكَ جَزَاؤُهُمْ أَنَّ عَلَيْهِمْ لَعْنَةَ اللَّهِ وَالْمَلَائِكَةِ وَالنَّاسِ أَجْمَعِينَ ۝ خَالِدِينَ فِيهَا لَا يُخَفَّفُ عَنْهُمُ الْعَذَابُ وَلَا هُمْ يُنظَرُونَ ۝ إِلَّا الَّذِينَ تَابُوا مِن بَعْدِ ذَٰلِكَ وَأَصْلَحُوا فَإِنَّ اللَّهَ غَفُورٌ رَّحِيمٌ ۝ إِنَّ الَّذِينَ كَفَرُوا بَعْدَ إِيمَانِهِمْ ثُمَّ ازْدَادُوا كُفْرًا لَّن تُقْبَلَ تَوْبَتُهُمْ وَأُولَٰئِكَ هُمُ الضَّالُّونَ ۝ إِنَّ الَّذِينَ كَفَرُوا وَمَاتُوا وَهُمْ كُفَّارٌ فَلَن يُقْبَلَ مِنْ أَحَدِهِم مِّلْءُ الْأَرْضِ ذَهَبًا وَلَوِ افْتَدَىٰ بِهِ أُولَٰئِكَ لَهُمْ عَذَابٌ أَلِيمٌ وَمَا لَهُم مِّن نَّاصِرِينَ ۝

Prophets of Islam

84. Say, ˹O Prophet,˺ "We believe in Allah and what has been revealed to us and what was revealed to Abraham, Ishmael, Isaac, Jacob, and his descendants; and what was given to Moses, Jesus, and other prophets from their Lord—we make no distinction between any of them, and to Him we ˹fully˺ submit."

The Only Way

85. Whoever seeks a way other than Islam,[141] it will never be accepted from them, and in the Hereafter they will be among the losers.

Deviating from the Right Path

86. How will Allah guide a people who chose to disbelieve after they had believed, acknowledged the Messenger to be true, and received clear proofs? For Allah does not guide the wrongdoing people. 87. Their reward is that they will be condemned by Allah, the angels, and all of humanity. 88. They will be in Hell forever. Their punishment will not be lightened, nor will they be delayed ˹from it˺. 89. As for those who repent afterwards and mend their ways, then surely Allah is All-Forgiving, Most Merciful.

Dying in a State of Disbelief

90. Indeed, those who disbelieve after having believed then increase in disbelief, their repentance will never be accepted.[142] It is they who are astray. 91. Indeed, if each of those who disbelieve then die as disbelievers were to offer a ransom of enough gold to fill the whole world, it would never be accepted from them. It is they who will suffer a painful punishment, and they will have no helpers.

---

141 i.e., full submission to the Will of Allah.
142 Their repentance will not be accepted if they die as disbelievers.

3. Âli-'Imrân

Righteous Giving

92. You will never achieve righteousness until you donate some of what you cherish. And whatever you give is certainly well known to Allah.

Jacob's Dietary Restriction

93. All food was lawful for the children of Israel, except what Israel[143] made unlawful for himself before the Torah was revealed.[144] Say, ˹O Prophet,˺ "Bring the Torah and read it, if your claims are true." **94.** Then whoever still fabricates lies about Allah, they will be the ˹true˺ wrongdoers. **95.** Say, ˹O Prophet,˺ "Allah has declared the truth. So follow the Way of Abraham, the upright—who was not a polytheist."

Pilgrimage to the Sacred House in Mecca

96. Surely the first House ˹of worship˺ established for humanity is the one at Bakkah—a blessed sanctuary and a guide for ˹all˺ people. **97.** In it are clear signs and the standing-place of Abraham. Whoever enters it should be safe. Pilgrimage to this House is an obligation by Allah upon whoever is able among the people.[145] And whoever disbelieves, then surely Allah is not in need of ˹any of His˺ creation.

Rejecting the Truth

98. Say, ˹O Prophet,˺ "O People of the Book! Why do you deny the revelations of Allah, when Allah is a Witness to what you do?" **99.** Say, "O People of the Book! Why do you turn the believers away from the Way of Allah—striving to make it ˹appear˺ crooked, while you are witnesses ˹to its truth˺? And Allah is never unaware of what you do."

Warning Against Evil Influence

100. O believers! If you were to yield to a group of those who were given the Scripture, they would turn you back from belief to disbelief.

---

143 Jacob (ﷺ).
144 When Jacob fell sick, he made camel meat unlawful for himself, but not for the rest of his people.
145 Pilgrimage is obligatory on every Muslim at least once in their lifetime if the person is physically and financially able.

وَكَيْفَ تَكْفُرُونَ وَأَنتُمْ تُتْلَىٰ عَلَيْكُمْ ءَايَٰتُ ٱللَّهِ وَفِيكُمْ رَسُولُهُ ۗ وَمَن يَعْتَصِم بِٱللَّهِ فَقَدْ هُدِىَ إِلَىٰ صِرَٰطٍ مُّسْتَقِيمٍ ۝ يَٰٓأَيُّهَا ٱلَّذِينَ ءَامَنُوا۟ ٱتَّقُوا۟ ٱللَّهَ حَقَّ تُقَاتِهِۦ وَلَا تَمُوتُنَّ إِلَّا وَأَنتُم مُّسْلِمُونَ ۝ وَٱعْتَصِمُوا۟ بِحَبْلِ ٱللَّهِ جَمِيعًا وَلَا تَفَرَّقُوا۟ ۚ وَٱذْكُرُوا۟ نِعْمَتَ ٱللَّهِ عَلَيْكُمْ إِذْ كُنتُمْ أَعْدَآءً فَأَلَّفَ بَيْنَ قُلُوبِكُمْ فَأَصْبَحْتُم بِنِعْمَتِهِۦٓ إِخْوَٰنًا وَكُنتُمْ عَلَىٰ شَفَا حُفْرَةٍ مِّنَ ٱلنَّارِ فَأَنقَذَكُم مِّنْهَا ۗ كَذَٰلِكَ يُبَيِّنُ ٱللَّهُ لَكُمْ ءَايَٰتِهِۦ لَعَلَّكُمْ تَهْتَدُونَ ۝ وَلْتَكُن مِّنكُمْ أُمَّةٌ يَدْعُونَ إِلَى ٱلْخَيْرِ وَيَأْمُرُونَ بِٱلْمَعْرُوفِ وَيَنْهَوْنَ عَنِ ٱلْمُنكَرِ ۚ وَأُو۟لَٰٓئِكَ هُمُ ٱلْمُفْلِحُونَ ۝ وَلَا تَكُونُوا۟ كَٱلَّذِينَ تَفَرَّقُوا۟ وَٱخْتَلَفُوا۟ مِنۢ بَعْدِ مَا جَآءَهُمُ ٱلْبَيِّنَٰتُ ۚ وَأُو۟لَٰٓئِكَ لَهُمْ عَذَابٌ عَظِيمٌ ۝ يَوْمَ تَبْيَضُّ وُجُوهٌ وَتَسْوَدُّ وُجُوهٌ ۚ فَأَمَّا ٱلَّذِينَ ٱسْوَدَّتْ وُجُوهُهُمْ أَكَفَرْتُم بَعْدَ إِيمَٰنِكُمْ فَذُوقُوا۟ ٱلْعَذَابَ بِمَا كُنتُمْ تَكْفُرُونَ ۝ وَأَمَّا ٱلَّذِينَ ٱبْيَضَّتْ وُجُوهُهُمْ فَفِى رَحْمَةِ ٱللَّهِ هُمْ فِيهَا خَٰلِدُونَ ۝ تِلْكَ ءَايَٰتُ ٱللَّهِ نَتْلُوهَا عَلَيْكَ بِٱلْحَقِّ ۗ وَمَا ٱللَّهُ يُرِيدُ ظُلْمًا لِّلْعَٰلَمِينَ ۝

101. How can you disbelieve when Allah's revelations are recited to you and His Messenger is in your midst? Whoever holds firmly to Allah is surely guided to the Straight Path.

Warning Against Disunity

102. O believers! Be mindful of Allah in the way He deserves,[146] and do not die except in ˹a state of full˺ submission ˹to Him˺.[147] **103.** And hold firmly together to the rope of Allah[148] and do not be divided. Remember Allah's favour upon you when you were enemies, then He united your hearts, so you—by His grace—became brothers. And you were at the brink of a fiery pit and He saved you from it. This is how Allah makes His revelations clear to you, so that you may be ˹rightly˺ guided. **104.** Let there be a group among you who call ˹others˺ to goodness, encourage what is good, and forbid what is evil—it is they who will be successful. **105.** And do not be like those who split ˹into sects˺ and differed after clear proofs had come to them. It is they who will suffer a tremendous punishment.

The Joyful and the Miserable

106. On that Day some faces will be bright while others gloomy. To the gloomy-faced it will be said, "Did you disbelieve after having believed? So taste the punishment for your disbelief." **107.** As for the bright-faced, they will be in Allah's mercy, where they will remain forever. **108.** These are Allah's revelations We recite to you ˹O Prophet˺ in truth. And Allah desires no injustice to ˹His˺ creation.

---

146 Meaning, always be conscious of Him; obedient and grateful to Him.

147 lit., except as Muslims.

148 i.e., Allah's covenant.

3. Âli-'Imrân

109. To Allah ˹alone˺ belongs whatever is in the heavens and whatever is on the earth. And to Allah ˹all˺ matters will be returned ˹for judgment˺.

Excellence of the Muslim Nation

110. You are the best community ever raised for humanity—you encourage good, forbid evil, and believe in Allah. Had the People of the Book believed, it would have been better for them. Some of them are faithful, but most are rebellious.

Reward of the Rebellious

111. They can never inflict harm on you, except a little annoyance.[149] But if they meet you in battle, they will flee and they will have no helpers. **112.** They will be stricken with disgrace wherever they go, unless they are protected by a covenant with Allah or a treaty with the people. They have invited the displeasure of Allah and have been branded with misery for rejecting Allah's revelations and murdering ˹His˺ prophets unjustly. This is ˹a fair reward˺ for their disobedience and violations.

Upright People of the Book

113. Yet they are not all alike: there are some among the People of the Book who are upright, who recite Allah's revelations throughout the night, prostrating ˹in prayer˺. **114.** They believe in Allah and the Last Day, encourage good and forbid evil, and race with one another in doing good. They are ˹truly˺ among the righteous. **115.** They will never be denied the reward for any good they have done. And Allah has ˹perfect˺ knowledge of those mindful ˹of Him˺.

---

149 i.e., they can only annoy you with their words.

Warning Against Hypocrites

116. Indeed, neither the wealth nor children of the disbelievers will be of any benefit to them against Allah. It is they who will be the residents of the Fire. They will be there forever. 117. The good they do in this worldly life is like the harvest of an evil people struck by a bitter wind, destroying it ˹completely˺. Allah never wronged them, but they wronged themselves.

Association with Hypocrites

118. O believers! Do not associate closely with others who would not miss a chance to harm you. Their only desire is to see you suffer. Their prejudice has become evident from what they say—and what their hearts hide is far worse. We have made Our revelations clear to you, if only you understood. 119. Here you are! You love them but they do not love you, and you believe in all Scriptures. When they meet you they say, "We believe." But when alone, they bite their fingertips in rage. Say, ˹O Prophet,˺ ˹"May you˺ die of your rage!" Surely Allah knows best what is ˹hidden˺ in the heart. 120. When you ˹believers˺ are touched with good, they grieve; but when you are afflicted with evil, they rejoice. ˹Yet,˺ if you are patient and mindful ˹of Allah˺, their schemes will not harm you in the least. Surely Allah is Fully Aware of what they do.

The Battle of Uḥud[150]

121. ˹Remember, O Prophet,˺ when you left your home in the early morning to position the believers in the battlefield. And Allah is All-Hearing, All-Knowing.

---

150 Uḥud is the name of the location where a battle took place in 3 A.H./625 C.E. between 750 Muslims and 3700 Meccans. This battle came only a year after the Meccan army was defeated at the Battle of Badr by the vastly outnumbered Muslim army. Initially, Muslims were winning the second battle. However, events took a different turn when the archers, who had been positioned by the Prophet on the mount of Uḥud, left their strategic position in pursuit of spoils of war—allowing a surprise attack by the Meccan cavalry. Many Muslims were martyred and Prophet Muḥammad himself was injured.

3. Âli-'Imrân

122. 'Remember' when two groups among you 'believers' were about to cower, then Allah reassured them. So in Allah let the believers put their trust.

The Battle of Badr

123. Indeed, Allah made you victorious at Badr when you were 'vastly' outnumbered. So be mindful of Allah, perhaps you will be grateful. 124. 'Remember, O Prophet,' when you said to the believers, "Is it not enough that your Lord will send down a reinforcement of three thousand angels for your aid?" 125. Most certainly, if you 'believers' are firm and mindful 'of Allah' and the enemy launches a sudden attack on you, Allah will reinforce you with five thousand angels designated 'for battle'. 126. Allah ordained this 'reinforcement' only as good news for you and reassurance for your hearts. And victory comes only from Allah—the Almighty, All-Wise— 127. to destroy a group of the disbelievers and humble the rest, causing them to withdraw in disappointment.

Allah Is the Judge

128. You 'O Prophet' have no say in the matter.[151] It is up to Allah to turn to them in mercy or punish them, for indeed they are wrongdoers. 129. To Allah 'alone' belongs whatever is in the heavens and whatever is on the earth. He forgives whoever He wills, and punishes whoever He wills. And Allah is All-Forgiving, Most Merciful.

Warning Against Interest

130. O believers! Do not consume interest, multiplying it many times over. And be mindful of Allah, so you may prosper. 131. Guard yourselves against the Fire prepared for the disbelievers. 132. Obey Allah and the Messenger, so you may be shown mercy.

---

151 When the Prophet (ﷺ) was injured at the Battle of Uḥud, some of his companions suggested that he should pray against the pagans of Mecca. He responded, "I have not come to condemn people, but as a mercy to pray for their guidance." The verse here says that it is not up to the Prophet whether they believe or disbelieve. A prophet's only duty is to convey the message. Eventually, almost all Meccans accepted Islam before the death of the Prophet (ﷺ).

3. Âli-'Imrân

Reward of the Righteous

133. And hasten towards forgiveness from your Lord and a Paradise as vast as the heavens and the earth, prepared for those mindful ˹of Allah˺. **134.** ˹They are˺ those who donate in prosperity and adversity, control their anger, and pardon others. And Allah loves the good-doers. **135.** ˹They are˺ those who, upon committing an evil deed or wronging themselves, remember Allah and seek forgiveness and do not knowingly persist in sin—and who forgives sins except Allah? **136.** Their reward is forgiveness from their Lord and Gardens under which rivers flow, staying there forever. How excellent is the reward for those who work ˹righteousness˺!

Battle Between Good and Evil

137. Similar situations came to pass before you, so travel throughout the land and see the fate of the deniers. **138.** This[152] is an insight to humanity—a guide and a lesson to the God-fearing.

Reassuring the Believers

139. Do not falter or grieve, for you will have the upper hand, if you are ˹true˺ believers. **140.** If you have suffered injuries ˹at Uḥud˺, they suffered similarly ˹at Badr˺. We alternate these days ˹of victory and defeat˺ among people so that Allah may reveal the ˹true˺ believers, choose martyrs from among you—and Allah does not like the wrongdoers—

---

152 "This" either refers to how the forces of evil are ultimately destroyed, or that the Quran is a reminder of the destruction of evildoers.

141. and distinguish the ˈtrueˈ believers and destroy the disbelievers.

Believers Tested

142. Do you think you will enter Paradise without Allah proving which of you ˈtrulyˈ struggled ˈfor His causeˈ and patiently endured? **143.** You certainly wished ˈfor the opportunityˈ for martyrdom before encountering it, now you have seen it with your own eyes.

Believers Disheartened[153]

144. Muḥammad is no more than a messenger; other messengers have gone before him. If he were to die or to be killed, would you regress into disbelief? Those who do so will not harm Allah whatsoever. And Allah will reward those who are grateful. **145.** No soul can ever die without Allah's Will at the destined time. Those who desire worldly gain, We will let them have it, and those who desire heavenly reward, We will grant it to them. And We will reward those who are grateful.

Reward of the Steadfast

146. ˈImagineˈ how many devotees fought along with their prophets and never faltered despite whatever ˈlossesˈ they suffered in the cause of Allah, nor did they weaken or give in! Allah loves those who persevere. **147.** And all they said was, "Our Lord! Forgive our sins and excesses, make our steps firm, and give us victory over the disbelieving people."

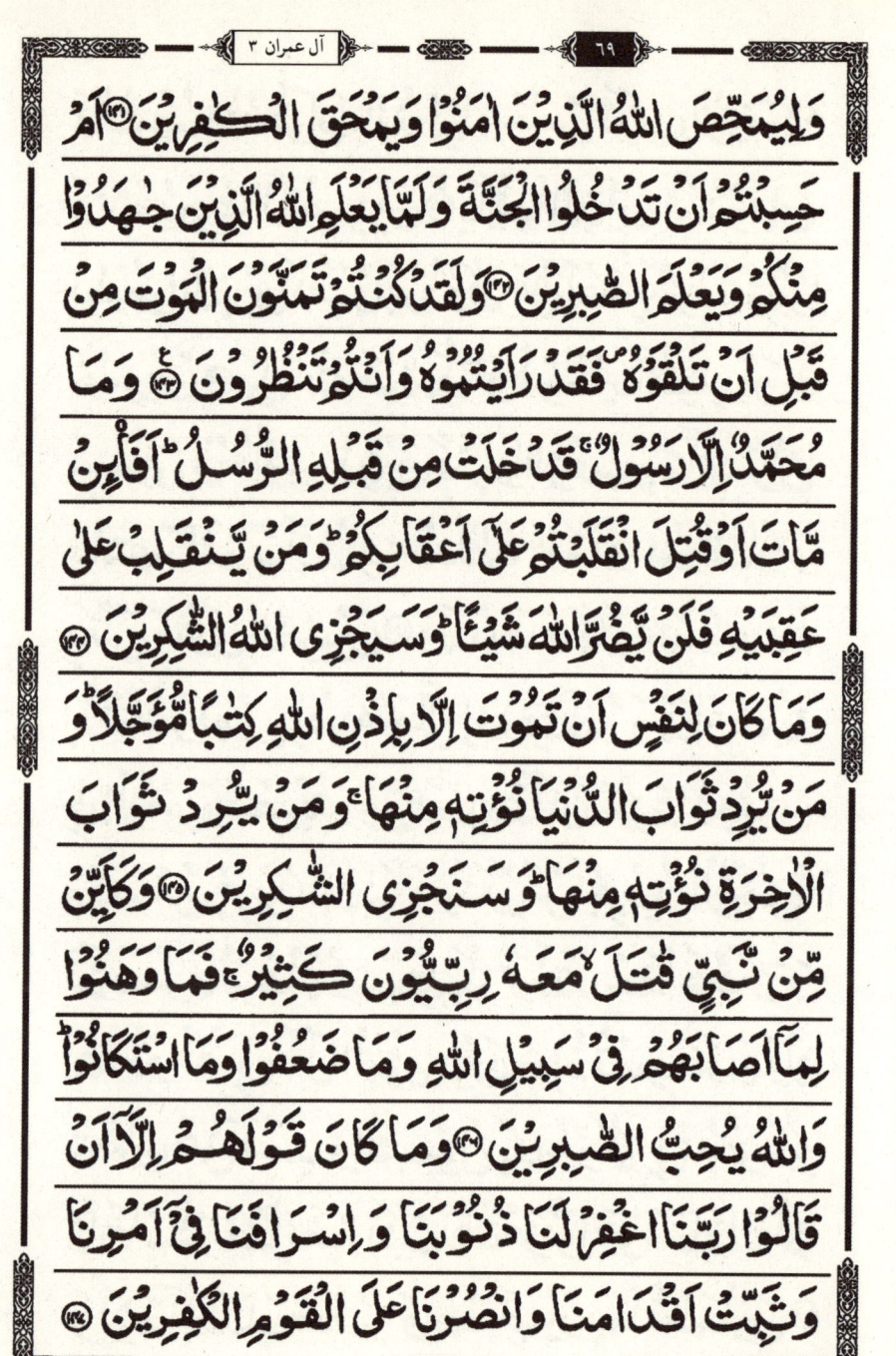

---

153 The faith of many Muslims was shaken when the pagan army spread rumours that Muḥammad (ﷺ) was killed in the Battle of Uḥud.

فَآتَىٰهُمُ ٱللَّهُ ثَوَابَ ٱلدُّنْيَا وَحُسْنَ ثَوَابِ ٱلْآخِرَةِ ۗ وَٱللَّهُ يُحِبُّ ٱلْمُحْسِنِينَ ۝ يَـٰٓأَيُّهَا ٱلَّذِينَ ءَامَنُوٓاْ إِن تُطِيعُواْ ٱلَّذِينَ كَفَرُواْ يَرُدُّوكُمْ عَلَىٰٓ أَعْقَـٰبِكُمْ فَتَنقَلِبُواْ خَـٰسِرِينَ ۝ بَلِ ٱللَّهُ مَوْلَىٰكُمْ ۖ وَهُوَ خَيْرُ ٱلنَّـٰصِرِينَ ۝ سَنُلْقِى فِى قُلُوبِ ٱلَّذِينَ كَفَرُواْ ٱلرُّعْبَ بِمَآ أَشْرَكُواْ بِٱللَّهِ مَا لَمْ يُنَزِّلْ بِهِۦ سُلْطَـٰنًا ۖ وَمَأْوَىٰهُمُ ٱلنَّارُ ۚ وَبِئْسَ مَثْوَى ٱلظَّـٰلِمِينَ ۝ وَلَقَدْ صَدَقَكُمُ ٱللَّهُ وَعْدَهُۥٓ إِذْ تَحُسُّونَهُم بِإِذْنِهِۦ ۖ حَتَّىٰٓ إِذَا فَشِلْتُمْ وَتَنَـٰزَعْتُمْ فِى ٱلْأَمْرِ وَعَصَيْتُم مِّنۢ بَعْدِ مَآ أَرَىٰكُم مَّا تُحِبُّونَ ۚ مِنكُم مَّن يُرِيدُ ٱلدُّنْيَا وَمِنكُم مَّن يُرِيدُ ٱلْآخِرَةَ ۚ ثُمَّ صَرَفَكُمْ عَنْهُمْ لِيَبْتَلِيَكُمْ ۖ وَلَقَدْ عَفَا عَنكُمْ ۗ وَٱللَّهُ ذُو فَضْلٍ عَلَى ٱلْمُؤْمِنِينَ ۝ إِذْ تُصْعِدُونَ وَلَا تَلْوُۥنَ عَلَىٰٓ أَحَدٍ وَٱلرَّسُولُ يَدْعُوكُمْ فِىٓ أُخْرَىٰكُمْ فَأَثَـٰبَكُمْ غَمًّۢا بِغَمٍّ لِّكَيْلَا تَحْزَنُواْ عَلَىٰ مَا فَاتَكُمْ وَلَا مَآ أَصَـٰبَكُمْ ۗ وَٱللَّهُ خَبِيرٌۢ بِمَا تَعْمَلُونَ ۝

148. So Allah gave them the reward of this world and the excellent reward of the Hereafter. For Allah loves the good-doers.

Yielding to the Disbelievers

149. O believers! If you yield to the disbelievers, they will drag you back to disbelief—and you will become losers. 150. But no! Allah is your Guardian, and He is the best Helper. 151. We will cast horror into the hearts of the disbelievers for associating ˹false gods˺ with Allah—a practice He has never authorized. The Fire will be their home—what an evil place for the wrongdoers to stay!

Victory Denied at Uḥud

152. Indeed, Allah fulfilled His promise to you when you ˹initially˺ swept them away by His Will, then your courage weakened and you disputed about the command and disobeyed,[154] after Allah had brought victory within your reach. Some of you were after worldly gain while others desired a heavenly reward. He denied you victory over them as a test, yet He has pardoned you. And Allah is Gracious to the believers.

The Army Retreats

153. ˹Remember˺ when you were running far away ˹in panic˺—not looking at anyone—while the Messenger was calling to you from behind! So Allah rewarded your disobedience with distress upon distress. Now, do not grieve over the victory you were denied or the injury you suffered. And Allah is All-Aware of what you do.

---

154 The archers disputed whether to keep their positions after the initial victory. Eventually, most of them decided to go in pursuit of the spoils of war, disobeying the Prophet's direct orders not to leave their position no matter what happened. Defeat became inevitable.

71   3. Âli-'Imrân

154. Then after distress, He sent down serenity in the form of drowsiness overcoming some of you, while others were disturbed by evil thoughts about Allah—the thoughts of ˹pre-Islamic˺ ignorance. They ask, "Do we have a say in the matter?" Say, ˹O Prophet,˺ "All matters are destined by Allah." They conceal in their hearts what they do not reveal to you. They say ˹to themselves˺, "If we had any say in the matter, none of us would have come to die here." Say, ˹O Prophet,˺ "Even if you were to remain in your homes, those among you who were destined to be killed would have met the same fate." Through this, Allah tests what is within you and purifies what is in your hearts. And Allah knows best what is ˹hidden˺ in the heart.

The Deserters

155. Indeed those ˹believers˺ who fled on the day when the two armies met were made to slip by Satan because of their misdeeds. But Allah has pardoned them. Surely Allah is All-Forgiving, Most Forbearing.

It Is All Destined

156. O believers! Do not be like the unfaithful[155] who say about their brothers who travel throughout the land or engage in battle, "If they had stayed with us, they would not have died or been killed." Allah makes such thinking a cause of agony in their hearts. It is Allah who gives life and causes death. And Allah is All-Seeing of what you do. **157.** Should you be martyred or die in the cause of Allah, then His forgiveness and mercy are far better than whatever ˹wealth˺ those ˹who stay behind˺ accumulate.

---

155 i.e., the hypocrites.

وَلَئِن مُّتُّمْ أَوْ قُتِلْتُمْ لَإِلَى اللَّهِ تُحْشَرُونَ ۝ فَبِمَا رَحْمَةٍ مِّنَ اللَّهِ لِنتَ لَهُمْ ۖ وَلَوْ كُنتَ فَظًّا غَلِيظَ الْقَلْبِ لَانفَضُّوا مِنْ حَوْلِكَ ۖ فَاعْفُ عَنْهُمْ وَاسْتَغْفِرْ لَهُمْ وَشَاوِرْهُمْ فِي الْأَمْرِ ۖ فَإِذَا عَزَمْتَ فَتَوَكَّلْ عَلَى اللَّهِ ۚ إِنَّ اللَّهَ يُحِبُّ الْمُتَوَكِّلِينَ ۝ إِن يَنصُرْكُمُ اللَّهُ فَلَا غَالِبَ لَكُمْ ۖ وَإِن يَخْذُلْكُمْ فَمَن ذَا الَّذِي يَنصُرُكُم مِّن بَعْدِهِ ۗ وَعَلَى اللَّهِ فَلْيَتَوَكَّلِ الْمُؤْمِنُونَ ۝ وَمَا كَانَ لِنَبِيٍّ أَن يَغُلَّ ۚ وَمَن يَغْلُلْ يَأْتِ بِمَا غَلَّ يَوْمَ الْقِيَامَةِ ۚ ثُمَّ تُوَفَّىٰ كُلُّ نَفْسٍ مَّا كَسَبَتْ وَهُمْ لَا يُظْلَمُونَ ۝ أَفَمَنِ اتَّبَعَ رِضْوَانَ اللَّهِ كَمَن بَاءَ بِسَخَطٍ مِّنَ اللَّهِ وَمَأْوَاهُ جَهَنَّمُ ۚ وَبِئْسَ الْمَصِيرُ ۝ هُمْ دَرَجَاتٌ عِندَ اللَّهِ ۗ وَاللَّهُ بَصِيرٌ بِمَا يَعْمَلُونَ ۝ لَقَدْ مَنَّ اللَّهُ عَلَى الْمُؤْمِنِينَ إِذْ بَعَثَ فِيهِمْ رَسُولًا مِّنْ أَنفُسِهِمْ يَتْلُو عَلَيْهِمْ آيَاتِهِ وَيُزَكِّيهِمْ وَيُعَلِّمُهُمُ الْكِتَابَ وَالْحِكْمَةَ وَإِن كَانُوا مِن قَبْلُ لَفِي ضَلَالٍ مُّبِينٍ ۝ أَوَلَمَّا أَصَابَتْكُم مُّصِيبَةٌ قَدْ أَصَبْتُم مِّثْلَيْهَا قُلْتُمْ أَنَّىٰ هَٰذَا ۖ قُلْ هُوَ مِنْ عِندِ أَنفُسِكُمْ ۗ إِنَّ اللَّهَ عَلَىٰ كُلِّ شَيْءٍ قَدِيرٌ ۝

158. Whether you die or are martyred—all of you will be gathered before Allah.

Prophet's Kindness to the Believers

159. It is out of Allah's mercy that you ˹O Prophet˺ have been lenient with them. Had you been cruel or hard-hearted, they would have certainly abandoned you. So pardon them, ask Allah's forgiveness for them, and consult with them in ˹conducting˺ matters. Once you make a decision, put your trust in Allah. Surely Allah loves those who trust in Him.

Victory Is from Allah

160. If Allah helps you, none can defeat you. But if He denies you help, then who else can help you? So in Allah let the believers put their trust.

Spoils of War

161. It is not appropriate for a prophet to illegally withhold spoils of war. And whoever does so, it will be held against them on the Day of Judgment. Then every soul will be paid in full for what it has done, and none will be wronged.

Good-Doers and Wrongdoers

162. Are those who seek Allah's pleasure like those who deserve Allah's wrath? Hell is their home. What an evil destination! 163. They ˹each˺ have varying degrees in the sight of Allah. And Allah is All-Seeing of what they do.

The Prophet as a Blessing

164. Indeed, Allah has done the believers a ˹great˺ favour by raising a messenger from among them—reciting to them His revelations, purifying them, and teaching them the Book and wisdom. For indeed they had previously been clearly astray.

Lessons from the Battle of Uḥud

165. Why is it when you suffered casualties ˹at Uḥud˺—although you had made your enemy suffer twice as much ˹at Badr˺—you protested, "How could this be?"? Say, ˹O Prophet,˺ "It is because of your disobedience." Surely Allah is Most Capable of everything.

166. So what you suffered on the day the two armies met was by Allah's Will, so that He might distinguish the ʿtrueʾ believers **167.** and expose the hypocrites. When it was said to them, "Come fight in the cause of Allah or ʿat leastʾ defend yourselves," they replied, "If we had known there was fighting, we would have definitely gone with you." They were closer to disbelief than to belief on that day—for saying with their mouths what was not in their hearts. Allah is All-Knowing of what they hide. **168.** Those who sat at home, saying about their brothers, "Had they listened to us, they would not have been killed." Say, ʿO Prophet,ʾ "Try not to die[156] if what you say is true!"

Martyrs Honoured

169. Never think of those martyred in the cause of Allah as dead. In fact, they are alive with their Lord, well provided for— **170.** rejoicing in Allah's bounties and being delighted for those yet to join them. There will be no fear for them, nor will they grieve. **171.** They are joyful for receiving Allah's grace and bounty, and that Allah does not deny the reward of the believers.

Reward of the Steadfast

172. ʿAs forʾ those who responded to the call of Allah and His Messenger after their injury,[157] those of them who did good and were mindful ʿof Allahʾ will have a great reward. **173.** Those who were warned, "Your enemies have mobilized their forces against you, so fear them," the warning only made them grow stronger in faith and they replied, "Allah ʿaloneʾ is sufficient ʿas an aidʾ for us and ʿHeʾ is the best Protector."

---

156 i.e., try not to die when your time comes.
157 The Prophet (ﷺ) realized that the city of Medina became vulnerable after the Muslim loss at Uḥud. So on the next day of the battle he decided to lead a small force of his companions—many of whom had been wounded at Uḥud—to chase away the Meccan army which was camping at a place called Ḥamrâ' Al-Asad—not far from Medina. Abu Sufyân, commander of the Meccan army, sent a man to discourage the Muslims from following the Meccans. Although the man falsely claimed that the Meccans were mobilizing to launch a decisive attack on Medina, the Prophet became more determined to chase them away. Eventually, the Meccans decided to flee and not waste their victory after the Prophet sent a revert to Islam—who was friends with Abu Sufyân—to convince him to withdraw; otherwise Muslims were going to avenge their loss at Uḥud.

3. Âli-'Imrân

174. So they returned with Allah's favours and grace, suffering no harm. For they sought to please Allah. And surely Allah is ˹the˺ Lord of infinite bounty. **175.** That ˹warning˺ was only ˹from˺ Satan, trying to prompt you to fear his followers.[158] So do not fear them; fear Me if you are ˹true˺ believers.

Disbelievers' Delusion

176. ˹O Prophet!˺ Do not grieve for those who race to disbelieve—surely they will not harm Allah in the least. It is Allah's Will to disallow them a share in the Hereafter, and they will suffer a tremendous punishment. **177.** Those who trade belief for disbelief will never harm Allah in the least, and they will suffer a painful punishment. **178.** Those who disbelieve should not think that living longer is good for them. They are only given more time to increase in sin, and they will suffer a humiliating punishment.

Sincerity Test

179. Allah would not leave the believers in the condition you were in, until He distinguished the good from the evil ˹among you˺. Nor would Allah ˹directly˺ reveal to you the unseen,[159] but He chooses whoever He wills as a messenger. So believe in Allah and His messengers. And if you are faithful and mindful ˹of Allah˺, you will receive a great reward.

Reward of the Stingy

180. And do not let those who ˹greedily˺ withhold Allah's bounties think it is good for them— in fact, it is bad for them! They will be leashed ˹by their necks˺ on the Day of Judgment with whatever ˹wealth˺ they used to withhold. And Allah is the ˹sole˺ inheritor of the heavens and the earth. And Allah is All-Aware of what you do.

---

158 This refers to the warning mentioned in 3:173.
159 i.e., the distinction between the true believers and hypocrites.

Blasphemy Exposed

181. Indeed, Allah has heard those ˹among the Jews˺ who said, "Allah is poor; we are rich!" We have certainly recorded their slurs and their killing of prophets unjustly. Then We will say, "Taste the torment of burning! 182. This is ˹the reward˺ for what your hands have done. And Allah is never unjust to ˹His˺ creation."

Rejecting Allah's Messengers

183. Those ˹are the same people˺ who say, "Allah has commanded us not to believe in any messenger unless he brings us an offering to be consumed by fire ˹from the sky˺." Say, ˹O Prophet,˺ "Other prophets did in fact come to you[160] before me with clear proofs and ˹even˺ what you demanded—why then did you kill them, if what you say is true?" 184. If you are rejected by them, so too were messengers before you who came with clear proofs, divine Books, and enlightening Scriptures.[161]

Death Is Inevitable

185. Every soul will taste death. And you will only receive your full reward on the Day of Judgment. Whoever is spared from the Fire and is admitted into Paradise will ˹indeed˺ triumph, whereas the life of this world is no more than the delusion of enjoyment.

Patience Tested

186. You ˹believers˺ will surely be tested in your wealth and yourselves,[162] and you will certainly hear many hurtful words from those who were given the Scripture before you and ˹from˺ the polytheists. But if you are patient and mindful ˹of Allah˺—surely this is a resolve to aspire to.

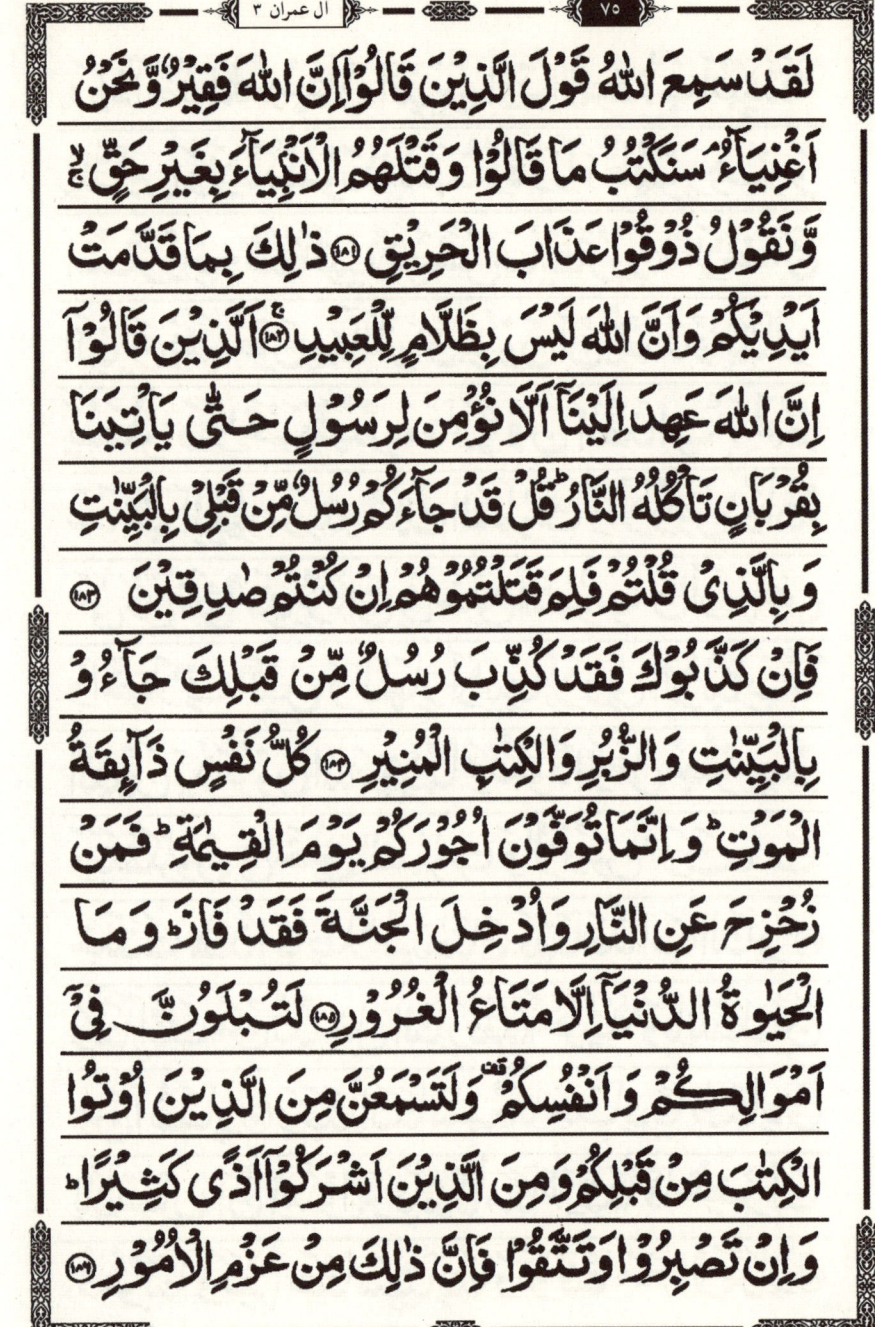

---

160 i.e., your forefathers.
161 i.e., the original Torah of Moses and the Gospel of Jesus.
162 Meaning, a believer is always tested through the loss of wealth as well as sickness, injuries, and the loss of life.

3. Âli-'Imrân

Breaking Allah's Covenant

187. ˹Remember, O Prophet,˺ when Allah took the covenant of those who were given the Scripture to make it known to people and not hide it, yet they cast it behind their backs and traded it for a fleeting gain. What a miserable profit!
188. Do not let those who rejoice in their misdeeds and love to take credit for what they have not done think they will escape torment. They will suffer a painful punishment.

Allah's Signs

189. To Allah ˹alone˺ belongs the kingdom of the heavens and the earth. And Allah is Most Capable of everything. 190. Indeed, in the creation of the heavens and the earth and the alternation of the day and night there are signs for people of reason.

A Prayer of the Righteous

191. ˹They are˺ those who remember Allah while standing, sitting, and lying on their sides, and reflect on the creation of the heavens and the earth ˹and pray˺, "Our Lord! You have not created ˹all of˺ this without purpose. Glory be to You! Protect us from the torment of the Fire. 192. Our Lord! Indeed, those You commit to the Fire will be ˹completely˺ disgraced! And the wrongdoers will have no helpers. 193. Our Lord! We have heard the caller[163] to ˹true˺ belief, ˹proclaiming,˺ 'Believe in your Lord ˹alone,˺' so we believed. Our Lord! Forgive our sins, absolve us of our misdeeds, and join us with the virtuous when we die.

---

163 The caller is Muḥammad (ﷺ).

3. Âli-'Imrân

194. Our Lord! Grant us what You have promised us through Your messengers and do not put us to shame on Judgment Day—for certainly You never fail in Your promise."

Prayers Answered

195. So their Lord responded to them: "I will never deny any of you—male or female—the reward of your deeds. Both are equal in reward. Those who migrated or were expelled from their homes, and were persecuted for My sake and fought and ˹some˺ were martyred—I will certainly forgive their sins and admit them into Gardens under which rivers flow, as a reward from Allah. And with Allah is the finest reward!"

Disbelievers' Brief Enjoyment

196. Do not be deceived by the prosperity of the disbelievers throughout the land. **197.** It is only a brief enjoyment. Then Hell will be their home—what an evil place to rest!

Believers' Everlasting Delight

198. But those who are mindful of their Lord will be in Gardens under which rivers flow, to stay there forever—as an accommodation from Allah. And what is with Allah is best for the virtuous.

Believers Among People of the Book

199. Indeed, there are some among the People of the Book who truly believe in Allah and what has been revealed to you ˹believers˺ and what was revealed to them. They humble themselves before Allah— never trading Allah's revelations for a fleeting gain. Their reward is with their Lord. Surely Allah is swift in reckoning.

Advice for Success

200. O believers! Patiently endure, persevere, stand on guard,[164] and be mindful of Allah, so you may be successful.

❀

---

164 *Râbiṭo* refers to watching over the borders of one's homeland. It can also mean keeping up one's prayers.

4. An-Nisâ'

4. Women (An-Nisâ')

In the Name of Allah—the Most Compassionate, Most Merciful

Commitment to Allah and Kinship Ties

1. O humanity! Be mindful of your Lord Who created you from a single soul, and from it He created its mate,[165] and through both He spread countless men and women. And be mindful of Allah—in Whose Name you appeal to one another—and ˹honour˺ family ties. Surely Allah is ever Watchful over you.

Orphans Given back Their Wealth

2. Give orphans their wealth ˹when they reach maturity˺, and do not exchange your worthless possessions for their valuables, nor cheat them by mixing their wealth with your own. For this would indeed be a great sin.

Bridal Gifts

3. If you fear you might fail to give orphan women their ˹due˺ rights ˹if you were to marry them˺, then marry other women of your choice— two, three, or four. But if you are afraid you will fail to maintain justice, then ˹content yourselves with˺ one[166] or those ˹bondwomen˺ in your possession.[167] This way you are less likely to commit injustice. **4.** Give women ˹you wed˺ their due dowries graciously. But if they waive some of it willingly, then you may enjoy it freely with a clear conscience.

Managing Wealth Responsibly

5. Do not entrust the incapable ˹among your dependants˺ with your wealth which Allah has made a means of support for you—but feed and clothe them from it, and speak to them kindly.

---

165 i.e., Adam and Eve.

166 The Quran is the only scripture that says marry only one. Unlike any previous faith, Islam puts a limit on the number of wives a man can have. Under certain circumstances, a Muslim man may marry up to four wives as long as he is able to provide for them and maintain justice among them—otherwise it is unlawful. With the exception of Jesus Christ and John the Baptist (neither of whom were married), almost all religious figures in the Bible had more than one wife. According to the Bible, Solomon (؉) had 700 wives and 300 concubines (1 Kings 11:3) and his father, David (؉), had many wives and concubines (2 Samuel 5:13).

167 A bondwoman is a female slave that a man owned either through purchase or taking her captive in war—a common ancient practice in many parts of the world. Islam opened the door for ending slavery by making it an act of charity to free slaves. Many sins (such as breaking one's oath, unintentional killing, and intercourse with one's wife during the day of fasting in Ramaḍân) can be atoned by freeing a slave. According to Islamic teachings, no free person can be enslaved. Islam also improved the condition of slaves. It was unlawful to separate a mother from her child. Children born to a slave-master were deemed free, and their mother would gain her freedom upon the death of her master. With regards to slaves, Prophet Muḥammad (؉) says, "Feed them from what you eat, clothe them from what you wear, and do not overwhelm them with work unless you assist them." He (؉) also says, "Whoever kills his slave will be killed and whoever injures his slave will be injured." In recent times, slavery has been outlawed in all countries—including the Muslim world.

Orphans' Wealth

6. Test ʻthe competence ofʼ the orphans until they reach a marriageable age. Then if you feel they are capable of sound judgment, return their wealth to them. And do not consume it wastefully and hastily before they grow up ʻto demand itʼ. If the guardian is well-off, they should not take compensation; but if the guardian is poor, let them take a reasonable provision. When you give orphans back their property, call in witnesses. And sufficient is Allah as a ʻvigilantʼ Reckoner.

Inheritance Law[168] 1)
Males and Females

7. For men there is a share in what their parents and close relatives leave, and for women there is a share in what their parents and close relatives leave—whether it is little or much. ʻThese areʼ obligatory shares.

Acts of Kindness

8. If ʻnon-inheritingʼ relatives, orphans,[169] or the needy are present at the time of distribution, offer them a ʻsmallʼ provision from it and speak to them kindly.

Caring for Orphans

9. Let the guardians be as concerned ʻfor the orphansʼ as they would if they were to ʻdie andʼ leave ʻtheir ownʼ helpless children behind. So let them be mindful of Allah and speak equitably. **10.** Indeed, those who unjustly consume orphans' wealth ʻin factʼ consume nothing but fire into their bellies. And they will be burned in a blazing Hell!

---

168 Inheritance entitlements of immediate family members (children, parents, full- and half-brothers and sisters, and spouses) are given in the following verses: 7, 11-13, 32-33, and 176. Shares are determined mainly according to the closeness of the heir to the deceased (i.e., close relatives get more than distant relatives), age (i.e., those who are young get more than those who are old), and—to a lesser degree—gender.

169 For example, in the case of orphaned children whose grandfather then dies, leaving behind other children, some scholars rule that an obligatory bequest should be made to them despite not having a share in inheritance.

Inheritance Law 2) Offspring and Parents

11. Allah commands you regarding your children: the share of the male will be twice that of the female.[170] If you leave only two ʿor moreʾ females, their share is two-thirds of the estate. But if there is only one female, her share will be one-half. Each parent is entitled to one-sixth if you leave offspring.[171] But if you are childless and your parents are the only heirs, then your mother will receive one-third.[172] But if you leave siblings, then your mother will receive one-sixth[173]—after the fulfilment of bequests and debts.[174] ʿBe fairʾ to your parents and children, as you do not ʿfullyʾ know who is more beneficial to you.[175] ʿThis isʾ an obligation from Allah. Surely Allah is All-Knowing, All-Wise.

Inheritance Law 3) Spouses

12. You will inherit half of what your wives leave if they are childless. But if they have children, then ʿyour share isʾ one-fourth of the estate—after the fulfilment of bequests and debts. And your wives will inherit one-fourth of what you leave if you are childless. But if you have children, then your wives will receive one-eighth of your estate—after the fulfilment of bequests and debts.

Inheritance Law 4) Maternal Siblings

And if a man or a woman leaves neither parents nor children but only a brother or a sister ʿfrom their mother's sideʾ, they will each inherit one-sixth, but if they are more than one, they ʿallʾ will share one-third

---

170 According to Islamic law of inheritance, a female—whether she is a mother, a wife, a sister, a daughter, etc.—gets one of three shares, depending on her closeness to the deceased:
- *Less than a male's share.* If she is a daughter, she will get half of the share of her brother, since he—unlike his sister—has to provide for the family and pay a dowry at the time of his marriage.
- *More than a male's share.* For example, if a man leaves $24 000 and six sons, two brothers, a wife, and a mother. The wife will get one-eighth ($3000), the mother one-sixth ($4000), each of the sons will receive about $2 833 and the two brothers will not get anything.
- *An equal share.* This is in the case of siblings from the mother's side (mentioned in verse 12 of this sûrah).

171 "Offspring" here means any number of children—male or female.

172 And the father will take the rest of the estate.

173 Although the existence of siblings reduces the mother's share from one-third to one-sixth, siblings themselves do not receive a share of inheritance and the rest of the estate goes to the father.

174 Debts as well as any other financial obligations (such as funeral expenses, unfulfilled vows, or unpaid dowry) have to be repaid before the fulfilment of bequests, then the estate can be distributed among the heirs. A person can bequest up to one-third of their estate for charities as well as individuals who are not entitled to a share in inheritance.

175 You do not know who will benefit you by looking after you during your life or doing good deeds on your behalf after your death.

4. An-Nisâ'

of the estate[176]— after the fulfilment of bequests and debts without harm ˹to the heirs˺.[177] ˹This is˺ a commandment from Allah. And Allah is All-Knowing, Most Forbearing.

Compliance with Inheritance Laws

13. These ˹entitlements˺ are the limits set by Allah. Whoever obeys Allah and His Messenger will be admitted into Gardens under which rivers flow, to stay there forever. That is the ultimate triumph! **14.** But whoever disobeys Allah and His Messenger and exceeds their limits will be cast into Hell, to stay there forever. And they will suffer a humiliating punishment.

Illegal Sexual Relationships[178]

15. ˹As for˺ those of your women who commit illegal intercourse— call four witnesses from among yourselves. If they testify, confine the offenders to their homes until they die or Allah ordains a ˹different˺ way for them. **16.** And the two among you who commit this sin—discipline them. If they repent and mend their ways, relieve them. Surely Allah is ever Accepting of Repentance, Most Merciful.

Accepted and Rejected Repentance

17. Allah only accepts the repentance of those who commit evil ignorantly ˹or recklessly˺ then repent soon after[179]—Allah will pardon them. And Allah is All-Knowing, All-Wise. **18.** However, repentance is not accepted from those who knowingly persist in sin until they start dying, and then cry, "Now I repent!" nor those who die as disbelievers. For them We have prepared a painful punishment.

---

176 If there are two or more brothers and sisters from the mother's side, they share one-third equally—the female will receive the same share of the male.

177 Harming the heirs includes giving away more than one-third of the estate as a bequest.

178 The popular interpretation among Muslim scholars is that verses 15 and 16 refer to male and female premarital/extramarital relations, though the punishment was later abrogated by 24:2. A few scholars maintain that these two verses refer to homosexuality. Their argument is that, unlike other verses in the Quran that talk about illegal relations between males and females, each of these two verses specifies a gender—females in the first and males in the second.

179 A person's repentance will be accepted as long as they repent any time before their death. But one should not procrastinate because they do not know when they will die.

بِسْمِ اللَّهِ

يَـٰٓأَيُّهَا الَّذِينَ ءَامَنُوا لَا يَحِلُّ لَكُمْ أَن تَرِثُوا النِّسَآءَ كَرْهًا ۖ وَلَا تَعْضُلُوهُنَّ لِتَذْهَبُوا بِبَعْضِ مَآ ءَاتَيْتُمُوهُنَّ إِلَّآ أَن يَأْتِينَ بِفَـٰحِشَةٍ مُّبَيِّنَةٍ ۚ وَعَاشِرُوهُنَّ بِالْمَعْرُوفِ ۚ فَإِن كَرِهْتُمُوهُنَّ فَعَسَىٰٓ أَن تَكْرَهُوا شَيْـًٔا وَيَجْعَلَ اللَّهُ فِيهِ خَيْرًا كَثِيرًا ۩ وَإِنْ أَرَدتُّمُ اسْتِبْدَالَ زَوْجٍ مَّكَانَ زَوْجٍ وَءَاتَيْتُمْ إِحْدَىٰهُنَّ قِنطَارًا فَلَا تَأْخُذُوا مِنْهُ شَيْـًٔا ۚ أَتَأْخُذُونَهُۥ بُهْتَـٰنًا وَإِثْمًا مُّبِينًا ۩ وَ كَيْفَ تَأْخُذُونَهُۥ وَقَدْ أَفْضَىٰ بَعْضُكُمْ إِلَىٰ بَعْضٍ وَأَخَذْنَ مِنكُم مِّيثَـٰقًا غَلِيظًا ۩ وَلَا تَنكِحُوا مَا نَكَحَ ءَابَآؤُكُم مِّنَ النِّسَآءِ إِلَّا مَا قَدْ سَلَفَ ۚ إِنَّهُۥ كَانَ فَـٰحِشَةً وَمَقْتًا وَسَآءَ سَبِيلًا ۩ حُرِّمَتْ عَلَيْكُمْ أُمَّهَـٰتُكُمْ وَبَنَاتُكُمْ وَأَخَوَٰتُكُمْ وَعَمَّـٰتُكُمْ وَخَـٰلَـٰتُكُمْ وَبَنَاتُ الْأَخِ وَبَنَاتُ الْأُخْتِ وَأُمَّهَـٰتُكُمُ الَّـٰتِىٓ أَرْضَعْنَكُمْ وَأَخَوَٰتُكُم مِّنَ الرَّضَـٰعَةِ وَ أُمَّهَـٰتُ نِسَآئِكُمْ وَرَبَـٰٓئِبُكُمُ الَّـٰتِى فِى حُجُورِكُم مِّن نِّسَآئِكُمُ الَّـٰتِى دَخَلْتُم بِهِنَّ فَإِن لَّمْ تَكُونُوا دَخَلْتُم بِهِنَّ فَلَا جُنَاحَ عَلَيْكُمْ وَحَلَـٰٓئِلُ أَبْنَآئِكُمُ الَّذِينَ مِنْ أَصْلَـٰبِكُمْ وَأَن تَجْمَعُوا بَيْنَ الْأُخْتَيْنِ إِلَّا مَا قَدْ سَلَفَ ۗ إِنَّ اللَّهَ كَانَ غَفُورًا رَّحِيمًا ۩

4. An-Nisâ'   82

Abusing Women Financially

19. O believers! It is not permissible for you to inherit women against their will[180] or mistreat them to make them return some of the dowry ʿas a ransom for divorceʾ—unless they are found guilty of adultery.[181] Treat them fairly. If you happen to dislike them, you may hate something which Allah turns into a great blessing. **20.** If you desire to replace a wife with another and you have given the former ʿevenʾ a stack of gold ʿas a dowryʾ, do not take any of it back. Would you ʿstillʾ take it unjustly and very sinfully? **21.** And how could you take it back after having enjoyed each other intimately and she has taken from you a firm commitment?[182]

Unlawful Women to Marry[183]

22. Do not marry former wives of your fathers—except what was done previously. It was indeed a shameful, despicable, and evil practice. **23.** ʿAlsoʾ forbidden to you for marriage are your mothers, your daughters, your sisters, your paternal and maternal aunts, your brother's daughters, your sister's daughters, your foster-mothers, your foster-sisters, your mothers-in-law, your stepdaughters under your guardianship if you have consummated marriage with their mothers—but if you have not, then you can marry them—nor the wives of your own sons, nor two sisters together at the same time—except what was done previously. Surely Allah is All-Forgiving, Most Merciful.

---

180 For example, a man would prevent a female relative (such as his sister or mother) from getting married so he can secure her estate for himself.
181 lit., blatant misconduct. If someone's wife has been found guilty of adultery, he has the right to ask for his dowry back.
182 i.e., the promise to live with her in kindness or divorce her with dignity.
183 Marriage to any of the listed women became null and void with the revelation of these verses.

24. Also ˹forbidden are˺ married women—except ˹female˺ captives in your possession.[184] This is Allah's commandment to you.

Lawful Women to Marry

Lawful to you are all beyond these—as long as you seek them with your wealth in a legal marriage, not in fornication. Give those you have consummated marriage with their due dowries. It is permissible to be mutually gracious regarding the set dowry. Surely Allah is All-Knowing, All-Wise.

Marrying Bondwomen

25. But if any of you cannot afford to marry a free believing woman, then ˹let him marry˺ a believing bondwoman possessed by one of you. Allah knows best ˹the state of˺ your faith ˹and theirs˺. You are from one another.[185] So marry them with the permission of their owners,[186] giving them their dowry in fairness, if they are chaste, neither promiscuous nor having secret affairs. If they commit indecency after marriage, they receive half the punishment of free women.[187] This is for those of you who fear falling into sin. But if you are patient, it is better for you. And Allah is All-Forgiving, Most Merciful.

Allah's Grace

26. It is Allah's Will to make things clear to you, guide you to the ˹noble˺ ways of those before you, and turn to you in mercy. For Allah is All-Knowing, All-Wise. **27.** And it is Allah's Will to turn to you in grace, but those who follow their desires wish to see you deviate entirely ˹from Allah's Way˺. **28.** And it is Allah's Will to lighten your burdens, for humankind was created weak.

---

184 A man was not allowed to have a relationship with a bondwoman who he had taken captive in war unless he made sure she was not pregnant. This was verified by her having at least one monthly cycle. *See* footnote for 4:3.
185 Do not be ashamed to marry a bondwoman since you are all part of the same human family and Allah knows you are doing so to avoid illegal relationships.
186 A married slave-woman is forbidden from having a relationship with her master.
187 i.e., fifty lashes.

4. An-Nisâ'

Prohibition of Abuse

29. O believers! Do not devour one another's wealth illegally, but rather trade by mutual consent. And do not kill ˹each other or˺ yourselves. Surely Allah is ever Merciful to you. **30.** And whoever does this sinfully and unjustly, We will burn them in the Fire. That is easy for Allah.

Avoiding Major Sins

31. If you avoid the major sins forbidden to you, We will absolve you of your ˹lesser˺ misdeeds and admit you into a place of honour.[188]

Inheritance Law 5) Contentment

32. And do not crave what Allah has given some of you over others. Men will be rewarded according to their deeds and women ˹equally˺ according to theirs. Rather, ask Allah for His bounties. Surely Allah has ˹perfect˺ knowledge of all things. **33.** And We have appointed heirs to what has been left by parents and next of kin. As for those you have made a pledge to, give them their share.[189] Surely Allah is a Witness over all things.

Husbands as Providers and Protectors

34. Men are the caretakers of women, as men have been provisioned by Allah over women and tasked with supporting them financially. And righteous women are devoutly obedient and, when alone, protective of what Allah has entrusted them with.[190] And if you sense ill-conduct from your women, advise them ˹first˺, ˹if they persist,˺ do not share their beds, ˹but if they still persist,˺ then discipline them ˹gently˺.[191] But if they change their ways, do not be unjust to them. Surely Allah is Most High, All-Great.

---

188 i.e., Paradise.
189 This pledge was a common practice before Islam between friends and allies—taking oaths to inherit each other. This practice came to an end with the revelation of verse 8:75 of the Quran. Although friends and allies do not have a share in inheritance anymore, they still can get some of the estate through bequest.
190 i.e., their husbands' honour and wealth.
191 Disciplining one's wife gently is the final resort. The earliest commentators understood that this was to be light enough not to leave a mark, should be done with nothing bigger than a tooth stick, and should not be on the face. Prophet Muhammad (ﷺ) said to his companions "Do not beat the female servants of Allah." He said that honourable husbands do not beat their wives, and he himself never hit a woman or a servant. If a woman feels her husband is ill-behaved, then she can get help from her guardian or seek divorce.

Reconciling Married Couples

35. If you anticipate a split between them, appoint a mediator from his family and another from hers. If they desire reconciliation, Allah will restore harmony between them. Surely Allah is All-Knowing, All-Aware.

The Kind, the Stingy, and the Insincere

36. Worship Allah ˹alone˺ and associate none with Him. And be kind to parents, relatives, orphans, the poor, near and distant neighbours, close friends, ˹needy˺ travellers, and those ˹bondspeople˺ in your possession. Surely Allah does not like whoever is arrogant, boastful— **37.** those who are stingy, promote stinginess among people, and withhold Allah's bounties. We have prepared for the disbelievers a humiliating punishment. **38.** Likewise for those who spend their wealth to show off and do not believe in Allah or the Last Day. And whoever takes Satan as an associate—what an evil associate they have!

Divine Justice

39. What harm could have come to them if they had believed in Allah and the Last Day and donated from what Allah has provided for them? And Allah has ˹perfect˺ knowledge of them. **40.** Indeed, Allah never wrongs ˹anyone˺—even by an atom's weight.[192] And if it is a good deed, He will multiply it many times over and will give a great reward out of His grace.

Witnesses on Judgment Day

41. So how will it be when We bring a witness from every faith-community and bring you ˹O Prophet˺ as a witness against yours?

---

192 lit., the smallest particle of dust (*ẓarrah*).

4. An-Nisâ'

بِسْمِ اللَّهِ

يَوْمَئِذٍ يَوَدُّ الَّذِينَ كَفَرُوا وَعَصَوُا الرَّسُولَ لَوْ تُسَوَّىٰ بِهِمُ الْأَرْضُ وَلَا يَكْتُمُونَ اللَّهَ حَدِيثًا ۞ يَـٰٓأَيُّهَا الَّذِينَ ءَامَنُوا لَا تَقْرَبُوا الصَّلَوٰةَ وَأَنتُمْ سُكَـٰرَىٰ حَتَّىٰ تَعْلَمُوا مَا تَقُولُونَ وَلَا جُنُبًا إِلَّا عَابِرِى سَبِيلٍ حَتَّىٰ تَغْتَسِلُوا ۚ وَإِن كُنتُم مَّرْضَىٰ أَوْ عَلَىٰ سَفَرٍ أَوْ جَآءَ أَحَدٌ مِّنكُم مِّنَ الْغَآئِطِ أَوْ لَـٰمَسْتُمُ النِّسَآءَ فَلَمْ تَجِدُوا مَآءً فَتَيَمَّمُوا صَعِيدًا طَيِّبًا فَامْسَحُوا بِوُجُوهِكُمْ وَأَيْدِيكُمْ ۗ إِنَّ اللَّهَ كَانَ عَفُوًّا غَفُورًا ۞ أَلَمْ تَرَ إِلَى الَّذِينَ أُوتُوا نَصِيبًا مِّنَ الْكِتَـٰبِ يَشْتَرُونَ الضَّلَـٰلَةَ وَيُرِيدُونَ أَن تَضِلُّوا السَّبِيلَ ۞ وَاللَّهُ أَعْلَمُ بِأَعْدَآئِكُمْ ۚ وَكَفَىٰ بِاللَّهِ وَلِيًّا وَكَفَىٰ بِاللَّهِ نَصِيرًا ۞ مِّنَ الَّذِينَ هَادُوا يُحَرِّفُونَ الْكَلِمَ عَن مَّوَاضِعِهِ وَيَقُولُونَ سَمِعْنَا وَعَصَيْنَا وَاسْمَعْ غَيْرَ مُسْمَعٍ وَرَاعِنَا لَيًّا بِأَلْسِنَتِهِمْ وَطَعْنًا فِى الدِّينِ ۚ وَلَوْ أَنَّهُمْ قَالُوا سَمِعْنَا وَأَطَعْنَا وَاسْمَعْ وَانظُرْنَا لَكَانَ خَيْرًا لَّهُمْ وَأَقْوَمَ وَلَـٰكِن لَّعَنَهُمُ اللَّهُ بِكُفْرِهِمْ فَلَا يُؤْمِنُونَ إِلَّا قَلِيلًا ۞

42. On that Day, those who denied ʿAllahʾ and disobeyed the Messenger will wish they were reduced to dust. And they will never be able to hide anything from Allah.[193]

Purification Before Prayers

43. O believers! Do not approach prayer while intoxicated[194] until you are aware of what you say, nor in a state of ʿfullʾ impurity[195]—unless you merely pass through ʿthe mosqueʾ—until you have bathed. But if you are ill, on a journey, or have relieved yourselves, or been intimate with your wives and cannot find water, then purify yourselves with clean earth, wiping your faces and hands.[196] And Allah is Ever-Pardoning, All-Forgiving.

Warning Against Deviance

44. Have you ʿO Prophetʾ not seen those who were given a portion of the Scriptures yet trade it for misguidance and wish to see you deviate from the ʿRightʾ Path? **45.** Allah knows best who your enemies are! And Allah is sufficient as a Guardian, and He is sufficient as a Helper.

Humility with the Prophet[197]

46. Some Jews take words out of context and say, "We listen and we disobey," "Hear! May you never hear," and *"Râ'ina!"*—playing with words and discrediting the faith. Had they said ʿcourteouslyʾ, "We hear and obey," "Listen to us," and *"Unẓurna,"* it would have been better for them and more proper. Allah has condemned them for their disbelief, so they do not believe except for a few.

---

193 Prophet Muḥammad (ﷺ) asked one of his companions, ʾAbdullah ibn Masʿûd, to recite some verses of the Quran for him because he loved to hear it from someone other than himself. ʾAbdullah recited from the beginning of this sûrah until he reached verse 42. When he was told he may stop, ʾAbdullah said he looked at the face of Prophet (ﷺ) and saw tears rolling down his cheeks.

194 Intoxicants were prohibited in the Quran in three stages: 2:219, 4:43, and finally 5:90-91.

195 i.e., after sexual intercourse or a wet dream.

196 This ruling is called *tayammum* or 'dry ablution.' If someone cannot find water or is unable to use it because of illness or cold weather, then they are allowed to touch clean earth, sand, etc. with the palms of their hands once then blow in their hands and wipe over their face and hands.

197 *See* footnote for 2:104.

Reward for Rejecting the Truth

47. O you who were given the Book! Believe in what We have revealed—confirming your own Scriptures—before We wipe out ʿyourʾ faces, turning them backwards, or We condemn the defiant as We did to the Sabbath-breakers.[198] And Allah's command is always executed!

The Only Unforgivable Sin

48. Indeed, Allah does not forgive associating others with Him ʿin worshipʾ,[199] but forgives anything else of whoever He wills. And whoever associates others with Allah has indeed committed a grave sin.

Self-Righteousness

49. Have you ʿO Prophetʾ not seen those who ʿfalselyʾ elevate themselves? It is Allah who elevates whoever He wills. And none will be wronged ʿeven by the width ofʾ the thread of a date stone. **50.** See how they fabricate lies against Allah—this alone is a blatant sin.

False Reassurance

51. Have you ʿO Prophetʾ not seen those who were given a portion of the Scriptures yet believe in idols and false gods and reassure the disbelievers[200] that they are better guided than the believers? **52.** It is they who have been condemned by Allah. And whoever is condemned by Allah will have no helper.

Envy Breeds Disbelief

53. Do they have control over shares of the kingdom? If so, they would not have given anyone so much as the speck on a date stone. **54.** Or do they envy the people for Allah's bounties? Indeed, We have given the descendants of Abraham the Book and wisdom, along with great authority.

---

198 *See* 7:163-165.
199 A person will never be forgiven if they die as a disbeliever. But if they repent before their death and mend their ways, then their repentance will be accepted (*see* 25:68-70).
200 i.e., the polytheists.

55. Yet some believed in him while others turned away from him.[201] Hell is sufficient as a torment!

Punishment of the Disbelievers

56. Surely those who reject Our signs, We will cast them into the Fire. Whenever their skin is burnt completely, We will replace it so they will ˹constantly˺ taste the punishment. Indeed, Allah is Almighty, All-Wise.

Reward of the Believers

57. As for those who believe and do good, We will admit them into Gardens under which rivers flow, to stay there for ever and ever. There they will have pure spouses,[202] and We will place them under a vast shade.

Maintaining Justice

58. Indeed, Allah commands you to return trusts to their rightful owners;[203] and when you judge between people, judge with fairness. What a noble commandment from Allah to you! Surely Allah is All-Hearing, All-Seeing.

Divine Judgment

59. O believers! Obey Allah and obey the Messenger and those in authority among you. Should you disagree on anything, then refer it to Allah and His Messenger, if you ˹truly˺ believe in Allah and the Last Day. This is the best and fairest resolution.

Hypocrites Rejecting Divine Judgment

60. Have you ˹O Prophet˺ not seen those who claim they believe in what has been revealed to you and what was revealed before you? They seek the judgment of false judges, which they were commanded to reject. And Satan ˹only˺ desires to lead them farther away.

---

201 i.e., Abraham (﷽) or Muḥammad (﷽).
202 *See* footnote for 2:25.
203 This verse was revealed right after Mecca had peacefully surrendered to the Muslims. ʿAli ibn Abi Ṭâlib, the Prophet's cousin and son-in-law, took the Ka'bah's key by force from Othmân ibn Ṭalḥa, the non-Muslim keeper of the Ka'bah. The verse was revealed to the Prophet (﷽) inside the Ka'bah with the order to give the key back to its rightful owner. He (﷽) ordered Ali to return the key to the keeper immediately along with an apology. Othmân was also promised that his family would keep the key forever. The keeper was so touched by the Quranic sense of justice that he decided to accept Islam.

89   4. An-Nisâ'

61. When it is said to them, "Come to Allah's revelations and to the Messenger," you see the hypocrites turn away from you stubbornly. **62.** How ˹horrible˺ will it be if a disaster strikes them because of what their hands have done, then they come to you swearing by Allah, "We intended nothing but goodwill and reconciliation." **63.** ˹Only˺ Allah knows what is in their hearts. So turn away from them, caution them, and give them advice that will shake their very souls.

Obeying the Messenger

64. We only sent messengers to be obeyed by Allah's Will. If only those ˹hypocrites˺ came to you ˹O Prophet˺—after wronging themselves—seeking Allah's forgiveness and the Messenger prayed for their forgiveness, they would have certainly found Allah ever Accepting of Repentance, Most Merciful.

Unconditional Obedience

65. But no! By your Lord, they will never be ˹true˺ believers until they accept you ˹O Prophet˺ as the judge in their disputes, and find no resistance within themselves against your decision and submit wholeheartedly. **66.** If We had commanded them to sacrifice themselves or abandon their homes, none would have obeyed except for a few. Had they done what they were advised to do,[204] it would have certainly been far better for them and more reassuring, **67.** and We would have granted them a great reward by Our grace **68.** and guided them to the Straight Path.

---

204   i.e., obeying Allah and His Messenger.

An-Nisâ' 90

وَمَن يُطِعِ اللَّهَ وَالرَّسُولَ فَأُوْلَٰئِكَ مَعَ الَّذِينَ أَنْعَمَ اللَّهُ عَلَيْهِم مِّنَ النَّبِيِّنَ وَالصِّدِّيقِينَ وَالشُّهَدَاءِ وَالصَّالِحِينَ ۚ وَحَسُنَ أُوْلَٰئِكَ رَفِيقًا ۝ ذَٰلِكَ الْفَضْلُ مِنَ اللَّهِ ۚ وَكَفَىٰ بِاللَّهِ عَلِيمًا ۝ يَٰأَيُّهَا الَّذِينَ آمَنُوا خُذُوا حِذْرَكُمْ فَانفِرُوا ثُبَاتٍ أَوِ انفِرُوا جَمِيعًا ۝ وَإِنَّ مِنكُمْ لَمَن لَّيُبَطِّئَنَّ فَإِنْ أَصَابَتْكُم مُّصِيبَةٌ قَالَ قَدْ أَنْعَمَ اللَّهُ عَلَيَّ إِذْ لَمْ أَكُن مَّعَهُمْ شَهِيدًا ۝ وَلَئِنْ أَصَابَكُمْ فَضْلٌ مِّنَ اللَّهِ لَيَقُولَنَّ كَأَن لَّمْ تَكُن بَيْنَكُمْ وَبَيْنَهُ مَوَدَّةٌ يَٰلَيْتَنِي كُنتُ مَعَهُمْ فَأَفُوزَ فَوْزًا عَظِيمًا ۝ فَلْيُقَاتِلْ فِي سَبِيلِ اللَّهِ الَّذِينَ يَشْرُونَ الْحَيَوٰةَ الدُّنْيَا بِالْآخِرَةِ ۚ وَمَن يُقَاتِلْ فِي سَبِيلِ اللَّهِ فَيُقْتَلْ أَوْ يَغْلِبْ فَسَوْفَ نُؤْتِيهِ أَجْرًا عَظِيمًا ۝ وَمَا لَكُمْ لَا تُقَاتِلُونَ فِي سَبِيلِ اللَّهِ وَالْمُسْتَضْعَفِينَ مِنَ الرِّجَالِ وَالنِّسَاءِ وَالْوِلْدَانِ الَّذِينَ يَقُولُونَ رَبَّنَا أَخْرِجْنَا مِنْ هَٰذِهِ الْقَرْيَةِ الظَّالِمِ أَهْلُهَا وَاجْعَل لَّنَا مِن لَّدُنكَ وَلِيًّا وَاجْعَل لَّنَا مِن لَّدُنكَ نَصِيرًا ۝

Reward for Obedience

69. And whoever obeys Allah and the Messenger will be in the company of those blessed by Allah: the prophets, the people of truth, the martyrs, and the righteous—what honourable company! **70.** This is Allah's favour, and Allah fully knows ˹who deserves it˺.

Advice to the Army

71. O believers! Take your precautions and go forth either in groups or together. **72.** There will be some among you who will lag behind so that if you face a disaster, they will say, "Allah has blessed us for not being there among them." **73.** But if you return with Allah's bounties, they will say—as if there had been no bond between you—"We wish we had been there with them to share the great gain!"

Fighting Against Oppression

74. Let those who would sacrifice this life for the Hereafter fight in the cause of Allah. And whoever fights in Allah's cause—whether they achieve martyrdom or victory—We will honour them with a great reward. **75.** And what is it with you? You do not fight in the cause of Allah and for oppressed men, women, and children who cry out, "Our Lord! Deliver us from this land of oppressors! Appoint for us a saviour; appoint for us a helper—all by Your grace."

91 4. An-Nisâ'

Fighting Satan's Allies

76. Believers fight for the cause of Allah, whereas disbelievers fight for the cause of the Devil. So fight against Satan's ˹evil˺ forces. Indeed, Satan's schemes are ever weak.

Those Who Cower

77. Have you ˹O Prophet˺ not seen those who had been told, "Do not fight! Rather, establish prayer and pay alms-tax."? Then once the order came to fight, a group of them feared those ˹hostile˺ people as Allah should be feared—or even more. They said, "Our Lord! Why have You ordered us to fight? If only You had delayed ˹the order for˺ us for a little while!" Say, ˹O Prophet,˺ "The enjoyment of this world is so little, whereas the Hereafter is far better for those mindful ˹of Allah˺. And none of you will be wronged ˹even by the width of˺ the thread of a date stone.

Divine Destiny

78. "Wherever you may be, death will overcome you—even if you were in fortified towers." When something good befalls them, they say, "This is from Allah," but when something evil befalls them, they say, "This is from you." Say, ˹O Prophet,˺ "Both have been destined by Allah." So what is the matter with these people? They can hardly comprehend anything! 79. Whatever good befalls you is from Allah and whatever evil befalls you is from yourself.[205] We have sent you ˹O Prophet˺ as a messenger to ˹all˺ people. And Allah is sufficient as a Witness.

Obeying the Messenger

80. Whoever obeys the Messenger has truly obeyed Allah. But whoever turns away, then ˹know that˺ We have not sent you ˹O Prophet˺ as a keeper over them.

---

205 Both good and evil are destined by Allah. The good comes as Allah's reward for good deeds, whereas the bad comes as Allah's punishment for evil deeds. In some cases, bad things happen to good people to test their faith, or as an atonement for their sins, or as part of a process of replacing something with what is better (e.g., a job or a spouse).

81. And they say, "We obey," but when they leave you, a group of them would spend the night contradicting what they said. Allah records all their schemes. So turn away from them, and put your trust in Allah. And Allah is sufficient as a Trustee of Affairs.

Reflecting on the Quran

82. Do they not then reflect on the Quran? Had it been from anyone other than Allah, they would have certainly found in it many inconsistencies.

Spreading Rumours

83. And when they hear news of security or fear,[206] they publicize it. Had they referred it to the Messenger or their authorities, those with sound judgment among them would have validated it. Had it not been for Allah's grace and mercy, you would have followed Satan—except for a few.

Show of Strength

84. So fight in the cause of Allah ˹O Prophet˺. You are accountable for none but yourself. And motivate the believers ˹to fight˺, so perhaps Allah will curb the disbelievers' might. And Allah is far superior in might and in punishment.

Good and Evil Intercession

85. Whoever intercedes for a good cause will have a share in the reward, and whoever intercedes for an evil cause will have a share in the burden. And Allah is Watchful over all things.

Responding to Greetings

86. And when you are greeted, respond with a better greeting or at least similarly. Surely Allah is a ˹vigilant˺ Reckoner of all things.

Assembly for Judgment Day

87. Allah, there is no god ˹worthy of worship˺ except Him. He will certainly gather ˹all of˺ you together on the Day of Judgment—about which there is no doubt. And whose word is more truthful than Allah's?

---

206 i.e., when they get the news of victory or a threat.

4. An-Nisâ'

Stance on Hypocrites

88. Why are you ˹believers˺ divided into two groups regarding the hypocrites while Allah allowed them to regress ˹to disbelief˺ because of their misdeeds? Do you wish to guide those left by Allah to stray? And whoever Allah leaves to stray, you will never find for them a way. **89.** They wish you would disbelieve as they have disbelieved, so you may all be alike. So do not take them as allies unless they emigrate in the cause of Allah. But if they turn away, then seize them and kill them wherever you find them, and do not take any of them as allies or helpers,[207] **90.** except those who are allies of a people you are bound with in a treaty or those wholeheartedly opposed to fighting either you or their own people. If Allah had willed, He would have empowered them to fight you. So if they refrain from fighting you and offer you peace, then Allah does not permit you to harm them. **91.** You will find others who wish to be safe from you and their own people. Yet they cannot resist the temptation ˹of disbelief or hostility˺. If they do not keep away, offer you peace, or refrain from attacking you, then seize them and kill them wherever you find them. We have given you full permission over such people.

---

207 The verse discusses a group of people who nominally became Muslims and secretly supported the enemies of Muslims. For those hypocrites to prove their loyalty, they were commanded to emigrate and join the ranks of the believers, or they would be considered enemies.

4. An-Nisâ' 94

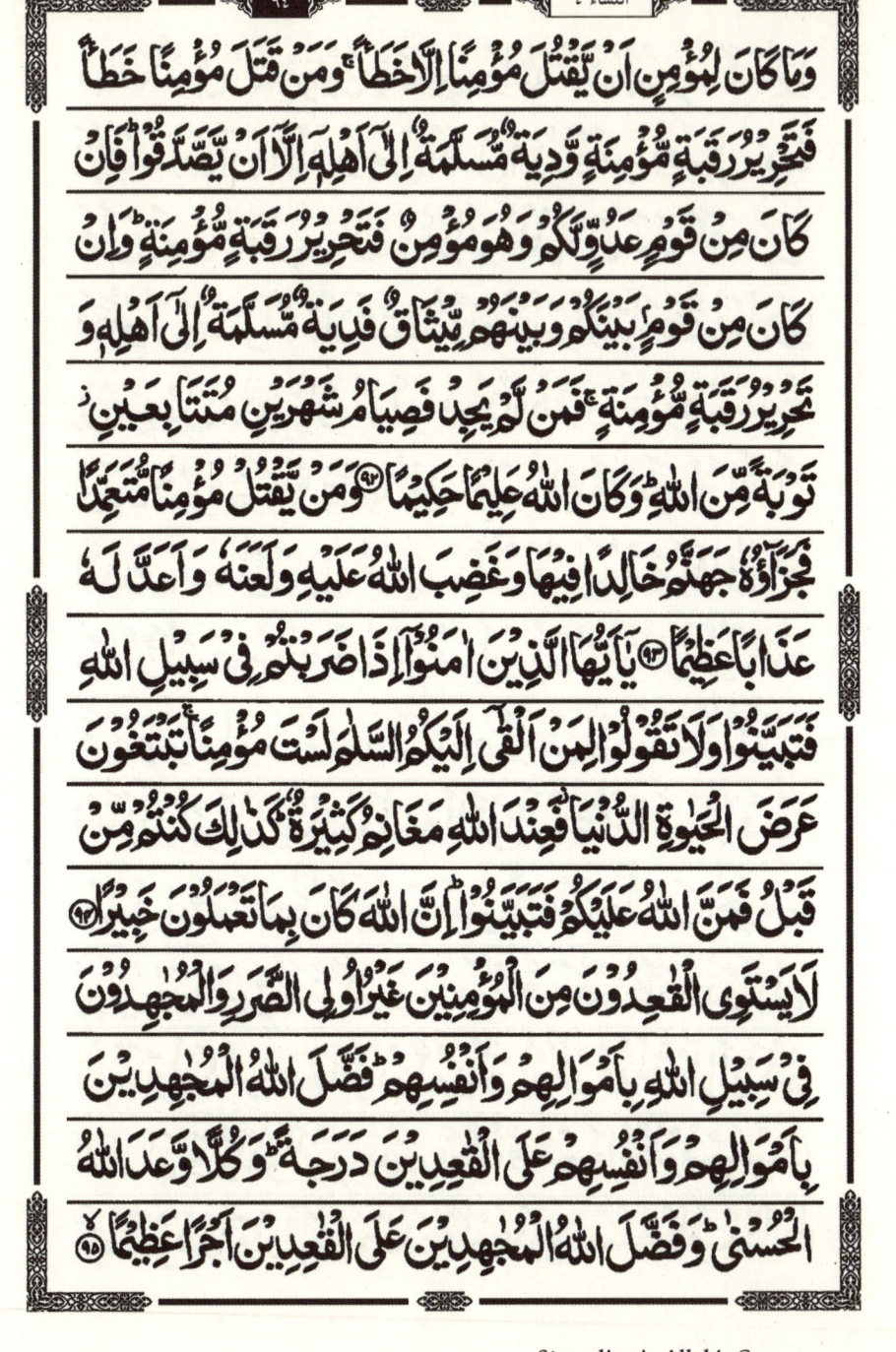

Killing a Believer Unintentionally

92. It is not lawful for a believer to kill another except by mistake. And whoever kills a believer unintentionally must free a believing slave and pay blood-money to the victim's family—unless they waive it charitably. But if the victim is a believer from a hostile people, then a believing slave must be freed. And if the victim is from a people bound with you in a treaty, then blood-money must be paid to the family along with freeing a believing slave. Those who are unable, let them fast two consecutive months—as a means of repentance to Allah. And Allah is All-Knowing, All-Wise.

Killing a Believer Intentionally

93. And whoever kills a believer intentionally, their reward will be Hell—where they will stay indefinitely.[208] Allah will be displeased with them, condemn them, and will prepare for them a tremendous punishment.

Random Fighting

94. O believers! When you struggle in the cause of Allah, be sure of who you fight. And do not say to those who offer you ˹greetings of˺ peace, "You are no believer!"—seeking a fleeting worldly gain.[209] Instead, Allah has infinite bounties ˹in store˺. You were initially like them then Allah blessed you ˹with Islam˺. So be sure! Indeed, Allah is All-Aware of what you do.

Struggling in Allah's Cause

95. Those who stay at home—except those with valid excuses[210]—are not equal to those who strive in the cause of Allah with their wealth and their lives. Allah has elevated in rank those who strive with their wealth and their lives above those who stay behind ˹with valid excuses˺. Allah has promised each a fine reward, but those who strive will receive a far better reward than others—

---

208 If a Muslim commits a major sin (such as intentional killing or adultery) and dies without repenting, they will be punished in Hell according to the severity or magnitude of the sin, then eventually be taken out of Hell. No Muslim will stay in Hell forever.
209 i.e., spoils of war.
210 This includes women, the elderly, the sick, etc.

96. far superior ranks, forgiveness, and mercy from Him. And Allah is All-Forgiving, Most Merciful.

Yielding to Oppression

97. When the angels seize the souls of those who have wronged themselves[211]—scolding them, "What do you think you were doing?" they will reply, "We were oppressed in the land." The angels will respond, "Was Allah's earth not spacious enough for you to emigrate?" It is they who will have Hell as their home—what an evil destination! **98.** Except helpless men, women, and children who cannot afford a way out— **99.** it is right to hope that Allah will pardon them. For Allah is Ever-Pardoning, All-Forgiving.

Migrating in Allah's Cause

100. Whoever emigrates in the cause of Allah will find many safe havens and bountiful resources throughout the earth. Those who leave their homes and die while emigrating to Allah and His Messenger—their reward has already been secured with Allah. And Allah is All-Forgiving, Most Merciful.

Shortening Prayers

101. When you travel through the land, it is permissible for you to shorten the prayer[212]—'especially' if you fear an attack by the disbelievers. Indeed, the disbelievers are your sworn enemies.

---

211 This verse refers to some of those who had accepted Islam secretly in Mecca but refused to emigrate to Medina along with the rest of the believers. Some of them were killed in the Battle of Badr when they were rallied by the Meccans to fight against the Muslims. The verse also applies to any Muslim who accepts abuse and refuses to move to another place where they can live with dignity and practice their faith freely.

212 Generally, it is permissible for Muslims who are travelling a distance of 85 km or more to shorten their prayers. A four-unit prayer is reduced to two.

Praying in a State of Fear

102. When you ˹O Prophet˺ are ˹campaigning˺ with them and you lead them in prayer, let one group of them pray with you—while armed. When they prostrate themselves, let the other group stand guard behind them. Then the group that has not yet prayed will then join you in prayer—and let them be vigilant and armed.[213] The disbelievers would wish to see you neglect your weapons and belongings, so they could launch a sweeping assault on you. But there is no blame if you lay aside your weapons when overcome by heavy rain or illness—but take precaution. Indeed, Allah has prepared a humiliating punishment for the disbelievers. **103.** When the prayers are over, remember Allah—whether you are standing, sitting, or lying down. But when you are secure, establish regular prayers. Indeed, performing prayers is a duty on the believers at the appointed times.

Diligence Against the Enemy

104. Do not falter in pursuit of the enemy—if you are suffering, they too are suffering. But you can hope to receive from Allah what they can never hope for. And Allah is All-Knowing, All-Wise.

Justice to a Jew[214]

105. Indeed, We have sent down the Book to you ˹O Prophet˺ in truth to judge between people by means of what Allah has shown you. So do not be an advocate for the deceitful.

---

213 When the first group prays, the second group stands guard behind them, then the first group withdraws to the back when they finish their prayers and stand guard when the second group moves up to pray.

214 Verses 105-112 were revealed in defence of Zaid ibn As-Samīn, a Jewish man, who was falsely accused of theft. A shield was stolen by a Muslim named Ṭu'mah ibn Obairaq and entrusted to Zaid. Ṭu'mah's family rushed to his defence and accused Zaid of the crime. They also tried to influence Prophet Muḥammad (ﷺ) to make a decision in favour of Ṭu'mah and punish the Jew, but the verses were soon revealed declaring Zaid's innocence.

97   4. An-Nisâ'

106. And seek Allah's forgiveness—indeed, Allah is All-Forgiving, Most Merciful. **107.** Do not advocate for those who wrong themselves.[215] Surely Allah does not like those who are deceitful, sinful. **108.** They try to hide ˹their deception˺ from people, but they can never hide it from Allah—in Whose presence they plot by night what is displeasing to Him. And Allah is Fully Aware of what they do. **109.** Here you are! You ˹believers˺ are advocating for them in this life, but who will ˹dare to˺ advocate for them before Allah on the Day of Judgment? Or who will come to their defence?

After Sin

110. Whoever commits evil or wrongs themselves then seeks Allah's forgiveness will certainly find Allah All-Forgiving, Most Merciful. **111.** And whoever commits a sin—it is only to their own loss. Allah is All-Knowing, All-Wise. **112.** And whoever commits an evil or sinful deed then blames it on an innocent person, they will definitely bear the guilt of slander and blatant sin.

Allah's Grace to the Prophet

113. Had it not been for Allah's grace and mercy, a group of them would have sought to deceive you ˹O Prophet˺. Yet they would deceive none but themselves, nor can they harm you in the least. Allah has revealed to you the Book and wisdom and taught you what you never knew. Great ˹indeed˺ is Allah's favour upon you!

---

215   lit., deceive themselves.

Secret Talks

114. There is no good in most of their secret talks—except those encouraging charity, kindness, or reconciliation between people. And whoever does this seeking Allah's pleasure, We will grant them a great reward.

Opposing the Messenger

115. And whoever defies the Messenger after guidance has become clear to them and follows a path other than that of the believers, We will let them pursue what they have chosen, then burn them in Hell—what an evil end!

Unforgivable Sin

116. Surely Allah does not forgive associating ˹others˺ with Him ˹in worship˺,[216] but forgives anything else of whoever He wills. Indeed, whoever associates ˹others˺ with Allah has clearly gone far astray.

Satan's Allies

117. Instead of Allah, they only invoke female gods[217] and they ˹actually˺ invoke none but a rebellious Satan— 118. cursed by Allah— who said, "I will surely take hold of a certain number of Your servants. 119. I will certainly mislead them and delude them with empty hopes. Also, I will order them and they will slit the ears of cattle[218] and alter Allah's creation." And whoever takes Satan as a guardian instead of Allah has certainly suffered a tremendous loss. 120. Satan only makes them ˹false˺ promises and deludes them with ˹empty˺ hopes. Truly Satan promises them nothing but delusion. 121. It is they who will have Hell as their home, and they will find no escape from it!

---

216 This applies to those who die in a state of disbelief in Allah. But those who repent before their death and mend their ways, their repentance will be accepted (see 25:68-70).
217 The pagans of Arabia used to give their idols feminine forms and names such as Al-Lât, Al-'Uzza, and Manât.
218 Slitting the ears of cattle dedicated to idols was a superstitious practice before Islam.

99   4. An-Nisâ'

Reward of the Believers

122. And those who believe and do good, We will soon admit them into Gardens under which rivers flow, to stay there for ever and ever. Allah's promise is ˹always˺ true. And whose word is more truthful than Allah's?

Doing, Not Wishing

123. ˹Divine grace is˺ neither by your wishes nor those of the People of the Book! Whoever commits evil will be rewarded accordingly, and they will find no protector or helper besides Allah. **124.** But those who do good—whether male or female— and have faith will enter Paradise and will never be wronged ˹even as much as˺ the speck on a date stone.

Abraham's Way

125. And who is better in faith than those who ˹fully˺ submit themselves to Allah, do good, and follow the Way of Abraham, the upright? Allah chose Abraham as a close friend. **126.** To Allah ˹alone˺ belongs whatever is in the heavens and whatever is on the earth. And Allah is Fully Aware of everything.

Caring for Female Orphans

127. They ask you ˹O Prophet˺ regarding women. Say, "It is Allah Who instructs you regarding them. Instruction has ˹already˺ been revealed in the Book[219] concerning the orphan women you deprive of their due rights[220] but still wish to marry, also helpless children, as well as standing up for orphans' rights. And whatever good you do is certainly well known to Allah."

---

219   This refers to verses 2-11 of this sûrah.
220   i.e., their inheritance and dowries.

4. An-Nisâ'

Reconciling Married Couples

128. If a woman fears indifference or neglect from her husband, there is no blame on either of them if they seek ˹fair˺ settlement, which is best. Humans are ever inclined to selfishness.[221] But if you are gracious and mindful ˹of Allah˺, surely Allah is All-Aware of what you do.

Maintaining Justice Among Wives

129. You will never be able to maintain ˹emotional˺ justice between your wives—no matter how keen you are. So do not totally incline towards one leaving the other in suspense.[222] And if you do what is right and are mindful ˹of Allah˺, surely Allah is All-Forgiving, Most Merciful. **130.** But if they choose to separate, Allah will enrich both of them from His bounties. And Allah is Ever-Bountiful, All-Wise.

Allah's Might and Grace

131. To Allah ˹alone˺ belongs whatever is in the heavens and whatever is on the earth. Indeed, We have commanded those given the Scripture before you, as well as you, to be mindful of Allah. But if you disobey, then ˹know that˺ to Allah belongs whatever is in the heavens and the earth. And Allah is Self-Sufficient, Praiseworthy. **132.** To Allah ˹alone˺ belongs whatever is in the heavens and whatever is on the earth. And Allah is sufficient as a Trustee of Affairs. **133.** If it is His Will, He can remove you altogether, O humanity, and replace you with others. And Allah is Most Capable to do so. **134.** Whoever desires the reward of this world, then ˹let them know that˺ with Allah are the rewards of this world and the Hereafter. And Allah is All-Hearing, All-Seeing.

---

221 This implies that many husbands and wives are unwilling to give the other their rights.
222 Do not leave one hanging—not fully enjoying the rights of a married woman and not fully divorced.

Standing up for Justice

135. O believers! Stand firm for justice as witnesses for Allah even if it is against yourselves, your parents, or close relatives. Be they rich or poor, Allah is best to ensure their interests. So do not let your desires cause you to deviate ˹from justice˺. If you distort the testimony or refuse to give it, then ˹know that˺ Allah is certainly All-Aware of what you do.

True Belief

136. O believers! Have faith in Allah, His Messenger, the Book He has revealed to His Messenger, and the Scriptures He revealed before. Indeed, whoever denies Allah, His angels, His Books, His messengers, and the Last Day has clearly gone far astray.

Warning Against Hypocrites

137. Indeed, those who believed then disbelieved, then believed and again disbelieved—˹only˺ increasing in disbelief— Allah will neither forgive them nor guide them to the ˹Right˺ Way. **138.** Give good news of a painful punishment to hypocrites, **139.** who choose disbelievers as allies instead of the believers. Do they seek honour and power through that company? Surely all honour and power belongs to Allah.

Shunning Ridiculers

140. He has already revealed to you in the Book that when you hear Allah's revelations being denied or ridiculed, then do not sit in that company unless they engage in a different topic, or else you will be like them.[223] Surely Allah will gather the hypocrites and disbelievers all together in Hell.

---

223 This refers to 6:68.

الآيات العربية

اِلَّذِيْنَ يَتَرَبَّصُوْنَ بِكُمْ ۚ فَاِنْ كَانَ لَكُمْ فَتْحٌ مِّنَ اللّٰهِ قَالُوْۤا اَلَمْ نَكُنْ مَّعَكُمْ ۖ وَاِنْ كَانَ لِلْكٰفِرِيْنَ نَصِيْبٌ ۙ قَالُوْۤا اَلَمْ نَسْتَحْوِذْ عَلَيْكُمْ وَنَمْنَعْكُمْ مِّنَ الْمُؤْمِنِيْنَ ؕ فَاللّٰهُ يَحْكُمُ بَيْنَكُمْ يَوْمَ الْقِيٰمَةِ ؕ وَلَنْ يَّجْعَلَ اللّٰهُ لِلْكٰفِرِيْنَ عَلَى الْمُؤْمِنِيْنَ سَبِيْلًا ۧ ﴿١٤١﴾ اِنَّ الْمُنٰفِقِيْنَ يُخٰدِعُوْنَ اللّٰهَ وَهُوَ خَادِعُهُمْ ۚ وَاِذَا قَامُوْۤا اِلَى الصَّلٰوةِ قَامُوْا كُسَالٰى ۙ يُرَآءُوْنَ النَّاسَ وَلَا يَذْكُرُوْنَ اللّٰهَ اِلَّا قَلِيْلًا ﴿١٤٢﴾ مُّذَبْذَبِيْنَ بَيْنَ ذٰلِكَ ۖ لَاۤ اِلٰى هٰۤؤُلَآءِ وَلَاۤ اِلٰى هٰۤؤُلَآءِ ؕ وَمَنْ يُّضْلِلِ اللّٰهُ فَلَنْ تَجِدَ لَهٗ سَبِيْلًا ﴿١٤٣﴾ يٰۤاَيُّهَا الَّذِيْنَ اٰمَنُوْا لَا تَتَّخِذُوا الْكٰفِرِيْنَ اَوْلِيَآءَ مِنْ دُوْنِ الْمُؤْمِنِيْنَ ؕ اَتُرِيْدُوْنَ اَنْ تَجْعَلُوْا لِلّٰهِ عَلَيْكُمْ سُلْطٰنًا مُّبِيْنًا ﴿١٤٤﴾ اِنَّ الْمُنٰفِقِيْنَ فِى الدَّرْكِ الْاَسْفَلِ مِنَ النَّارِ ۚ وَلَنْ تَجِدَ لَهُمْ نَصِيْرًا ﴿١٤٥﴾ اِلَّا الَّذِيْنَ تَابُوْا وَاَصْلَحُوْا وَاعْتَصَمُوْا بِاللّٰهِ وَاَخْلَصُوْا دِيْنَهُمْ لِلّٰهِ فَاُولٰٓئِكَ مَعَ الْمُؤْمِنِيْنَ ؕ وَسَوْفَ يُؤْتِ اللّٰهُ الْمُؤْمِنِيْنَ اَجْرًا عَظِيْمًا ﴿١٤٦﴾ مَا يَفْعَلُ اللّٰهُ بِعَذَابِكُمْ اِنْ شَكَرْتُمْ وَاٰمَنْتُمْ ؕ وَكَانَ اللّٰهُ شَاكِرًا عَلِيْمًا ﴿١٤٧﴾

Hypocritical Stance

141. ˹The hypocrites are˺ those who wait to see what happens to you. So if Allah grants you victory, they say ˹to you˺, "Were we not on your side?" But if the disbelievers have a share ˹of victory˺, they say ˹to them˺, "Did we not have the advantage over you, yet we protected you from the believers?" Allah will judge between ˹all of˺ you on the Day of Judgment. And Allah will never grant the disbelievers a way over the believers.

Qualities of the Hypocrites

142. Surely the hypocrites seek to deceive Allah, but He outwits them. When they stand up for prayer, they do it half-heartedly only to be seen by people—hardly remembering Allah at all. 143. Torn between belief and disbelief—belonging neither to these ˹believers˺ nor those ˹disbelievers˺. And whoever Allah leaves to stray, you will never find for them a way.

Unacceptable Guardianship

144. O believers! Do not take disbelievers as allies instead of the believers. Would you like to give Allah solid proof against yourselves?

Reward of Hypocrites

145. Surely the hypocrites will be in the lowest depths of the Fire—and you will never find for them any helper— 146. except those who repent, mend their ways, hold fast to Allah, and are sincere in their devotion to Allah; they will be with the believers. And Allah will grant the believers a great reward. 147. Why should Allah punish you if you are grateful and faithful? Allah is ever Appreciative, All-Knowing.

4. An-Nisâ'

Negativity in Public

148. Allah does not like negative thoughts to be voiced—except by those who have been wronged.[224] Allah is All-Hearing, All-Knowing. **149.** Whether you reveal or conceal a good or pardon an evil—surely Allah is Ever-Pardoning, Most Capable.

Faith in All Prophets

150. Surely those who deny Allah and His messengers and wish to make a distinction between Allah and His messengers,[225] saying, "We believe in some and disbelieve in others," desiring to forge a compromise, **151.** they are indeed the true disbelievers. And We have prepared for the disbelievers a humiliating punishment. **152.** As for those who believe in Allah and His messengers—accepting all; rejecting none—He will surely give them their rewards. And Allah is All-Forgiving, Most Merciful.

Moses and the Children of Israel

153. The People of the Book demand that you ˹O Prophet˺ bring down for them a revelation in writing from heaven.[226] They demanded what is even greater than this from Moses, saying, "Make Allah visible to us!" So a thunderbolt struck them for their wrongdoing. Then they took the calf for worship after receiving clear signs. Still We forgave them for that ˹after their repentance˺ and gave Moses compelling proof. **154.** We raised the Mount over them ˹as a warning˺ for ˹breaking˺ their covenant and said, "Enter the gate ˹of Jerusalem˺ with humility." We also warned them, "Do not break the Sabbath," and took from them a firm covenant.

---

224 i.e., Allah does not like talking about people behind their backs—except when someone who has been wronged seeks counselling or assistance from authorities.
225 By their claim that they believe in Allah but still reject some of His messengers.
226 i.e., they demanded the Quran to be revealed all at once in writing similar to the Tablets of Moses. This demand is refuted in 25:32.

4. An-Nisâ'

فَبِمَا نَقْضِهِم مِّيثَاقَهُمْ وَكُفْرِهِم بِـَٔايَٰتِ ٱللَّهِ وَقَتْلِهِمُ ٱلْأَنۢبِيَآءَ بِغَيْرِ حَقٍّ وَقَوْلِهِمْ قُلُوبُنَا غُلْفٌۢ بَلْ طَبَعَ ٱللَّهُ عَلَيْهَا بِكُفْرِهِمْ فَلَا يُؤْمِنُونَ إِلَّا قَلِيلًا ۝ وَبِكُفْرِهِمْ وَقَوْلِهِمْ عَلَىٰ مَرْيَمَ بُهْتَٰنًا عَظِيمًا ۝ وَقَوْلِهِمْ إِنَّا قَتَلْنَا ٱلْمَسِيحَ عِيسَى ٱبْنَ مَرْيَمَ رَسُولَ ٱللَّهِ وَمَا قَتَلُوهُ وَمَا صَلَبُوهُ وَلَٰكِن شُبِّهَ لَهُمْ وَإِنَّ ٱلَّذِينَ ٱخْتَلَفُوا۟ فِيهِ لَفِى شَكٍّ مِّنْهُ مَا لَهُم بِهِۦ مِنْ عِلْمٍ إِلَّا ٱتِّبَاعَ ٱلظَّنِّ وَمَا قَتَلُوهُ يَقِينًۢا ۝ بَل رَّفَعَهُ ٱللَّهُ إِلَيْهِ وَكَانَ ٱللَّهُ عَزِيزًا حَكِيمًا ۝ وَإِن مِّنْ أَهْلِ ٱلْكِتَٰبِ إِلَّا لَيُؤْمِنَنَّ بِهِۦ قَبْلَ مَوْتِهِۦ وَيَوْمَ ٱلْقِيَٰمَةِ يَكُونُ عَلَيْهِمْ شَهِيدًا ۝ فَبِظُلْمٍ مِّنَ ٱلَّذِينَ هَادُوا۟ حَرَّمْنَا عَلَيْهِمْ طَيِّبَٰتٍ أُحِلَّتْ لَهُمْ وَبِصَدِّهِمْ عَن سَبِيلِ ٱللَّهِ كَثِيرًا ۝ وَأَخْذِهِمُ ٱلرِّبَوٰا۟ وَقَدْ نُهُوا۟ عَنْهُ وَأَكْلِهِمْ أَمْوَٰلَ ٱلنَّاسِ بِٱلْبَٰطِلِ وَأَعْتَدْنَا لِلْكَٰفِرِينَ مِنْهُمْ عَذَابًا أَلِيمًا ۝ لَّٰكِنِ ٱلرَّٰسِخُونَ فِى ٱلْعِلْمِ مِنْهُمْ وَٱلْمُؤْمِنُونَ يُؤْمِنُونَ بِمَآ أُنزِلَ إِلَيْكَ وَمَآ أُنزِلَ مِن قَبْلِكَ وَٱلْمُقِيمِينَ ٱلصَّلَوٰةَ وَٱلْمُؤْتُونَ ٱلزَّكَوٰةَ وَٱلْمُؤْمِنُونَ بِٱللَّهِ وَٱلْيَوْمِ ٱلْءَاخِرِ أُو۟لَٰٓئِكَ سَنُؤْتِيهِمْ أَجْرًا عَظِيمًا ۝

Falsehood About Mary and Jesus

155. ˹They were condemned˺ for breaking their covenant, rejecting Allah's signs, killing the prophets unjustly, and for saying, "Our hearts are unreceptive!"[227]—it is Allah Who has sealed their hearts for their disbelief, so they do not believe except for a few— **156.** and for their denial and outrageous accusation against Mary,[228] **157.** and for boasting, "We killed the Messiah, Jesus, son of Mary, the messenger of Allah." But they neither killed nor crucified him—it was only made to appear so.[229] Even those who argue for this ˹crucifixion˺ are in doubt. They have no knowledge whatsoever—only making assumptions. They certainly did not kill him. **158.** Rather, Allah raised him up to Himself. And Allah is Almighty, All-Wise. **159.** Every one of the People of the Book will definitely believe in him before his death.[230] And on the Day of Judgment Jesus will be a witness against them.

Consequences of Disobedience

160. We forbade the Jews certain foods that had been lawful to them for their wrongdoing, and for hindering many from the Way of Allah, **161.** taking interest despite its prohibition, and consuming people's wealth unjustly. We have prepared for the disbelievers among them a painful punishment. **162.** But those of them well-grounded in knowledge, the faithful ˹who˺ believe in what has been revealed to you ˹O Prophet˺ and what was revealed before you—˹especially˺ those who establish prayer—and those who pay alms-tax and believe in Allah and the Last Day, to these ˹people˺ We will grant a great reward.

---

227 Their hearts are unreceptive because they claim they have enough knowledge already.

228 i.e., they slandered Mary by claiming that she conceived Jesus through an illegal relationship.

229 The popular belief among Muslims is that a conspiracy was made to kill Jesus, Allah made the main culprit who betrayed Jesus look exactly like Jesus, then he was crucified in Jesus' place. Jesus was raised safe and sound to the heavens. Muslims also believe in the second coming of Jesus (ﷺ).

230 Scholars disagree whether Jews and Christians will come to realize that Jesus is a prophet of Allah at the time of their death or before the death of Jesus after his second coming.

4. An-Nisâ'

Messengers of Islam

163. Indeed, We have sent revelation to you ˹O Prophet˺ as We sent revelation to Noah and the prophets after him. We also sent revelation to Abraham, Ishmael, Isaac, Jacob, and his descendants, ˹as well as˺ Jesus, Job, Jonah, Aaron, and Solomon. And to David We gave the Psalms. **164.** There are messengers whose stories We have told you already and others We have not. And to Moses Allah spoke directly. **165.** ˹All were˺ messengers delivering good news and warnings so humanity should have no excuse before Allah after ˹the coming of˺ the messengers. And Allah is Almighty, All-Wise.

Muḥammad's Messengership

166. Yet ˹if you are denied, O Prophet,˺ Allah bears witness to what He has sent down to you—He has sent it with His knowledge. The angels too bear witness. And Allah ˹alone˺ is sufficient as a Witness.

Punishment for Rejecting the Truth

167. Those who disbelieve and hinder ˹others˺ from the Way of Allah have certainly strayed far away. **168.** Those who disbelieve and wrong themselves—surely Allah will neither forgive them nor guide them to any path **169.** except that of Hell, to stay there for ever and ever. And that is easy for Allah.

Universality of Islam

170. O humanity! The Messenger has certainly come to you with the truth from your Lord, so believe for your own good. But if you disbelieve, then ˹know that˺ to Allah belongs whatever is in the heavens and the earth. And Allah is All-Knowing, All-Wise.

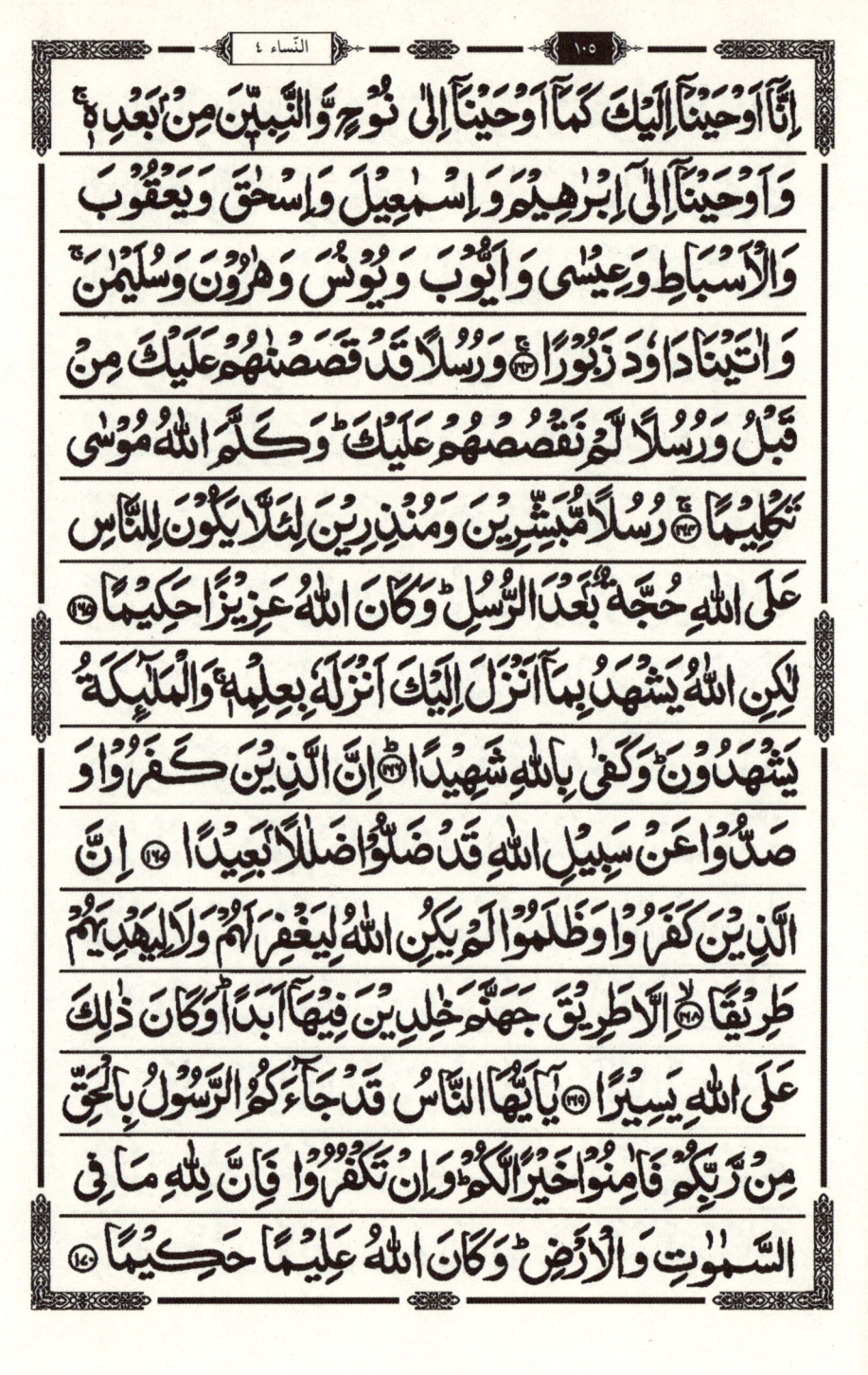

Wake-up Call

171. O People of the Book! Do not go to extremes regarding your faith; say nothing about Allah except the truth.[231] The Messiah, Jesus, son of Mary, was no more than a messenger of Allah and the fulfilment of His Word through Mary and a spirit ʿcreated by a commandʾ from Him.[232] So believe in Allah and His messengers and do not say, "Trinity." Stop!—for your own good. Allah is only One God. Glory be to Him! He is far above having a son! To Him belongs whatever is in the heavens and whatever is on the earth. And Allah is sufficient as a Trustee of Affairs. **172.** The Messiah would never be too proud to be a servant of Allah, nor would the angels nearest to Allah. Those who are too proud and arrogant to worship Him will be brought before Him all together.

The Reward

173. As for those who believe and do good, He will reward them in full and increase them out of His grace. But those who are too proud and arrogant, He will subject them to a painful punishment. And besides Allah they will find no protector or helper.

Universal Call to Islam

174. O humanity! There has come to you conclusive evidence from your Lord. And We have sent down to you a brilliant light. **175.** As for those who believe in Allah and hold fast to Him, He will admit them into His mercy and grace and guide them to Himself through the Straight Path.

---

231 The Jews are warned against denying Jesus as the Messiah, while Christians are warned against calling Jesus Allah.
232 i.e., Jesus was created by Allah's Word "Be!" and he was, and life was breathed into Jesus by the holy spirit (the angel Gabriel) at the command of Allah.

5. Al-Mâ'idah

Inheritance Law 6) Full Siblings[233]

176. They ask you ˹for a ruling, O Prophet˺. Say, "Allah gives you a ruling regarding those who die without children or parents." If a man dies childless and leaves behind a sister, she will inherit one-half of his estate, whereas her brother will inherit all of her estate if she dies childless. If this person leaves behind two sisters, they together will inherit two-thirds of the estate. But if the deceased leaves male and female siblings, a male's share will be equal to that of two females. Allah makes ˹this˺ clear to you so you do not go astray. And Allah has ˹perfect˺ knowledge of all things.[234]

༺❁ ✸ ❁༻

5. The Spread Table (Al-Mâ'idah)

In the Name of Allah—the Most Compassionate, Most Merciful

Honouring Obligations

1. O believers! Honour your obligations. All grazing livestock has been made lawful to you—except what is hereby announced to you and hunting while on pilgrimage. Indeed, Allah commands what He wills.

Allah's Sanctities

2. O believers! Do not violate Allah's rituals ˹of pilgrimage˺, the sacred months, the sacrificial animals, the ˹offerings decorated with˺ garlands, nor those ˹pilgrims˺ on their way to the Sacred House seeking their Lord's bounty and pleasure. When pilgrimage has ended, you are allowed to hunt.

Standing up for What Is Right

Do not let the hatred of a people who once barred you from the Sacred Mosque provoke you to transgress. Cooperate with one another in goodness and righteousness, and do not cooperate in sin and transgression. And be mindful of Allah. Surely Allah is severe in punishment.

---

233 This ruling also applies to brothers and sisters from the father's side—if they are the only heirs.
234 This verse is placed at the end of the sûrah and not with similar verses at the beginning to connect the end of this sûrah with the next one or, according to Al-Fakhr Ar-Râzi, either to tie the end of the sûrah with its beginning for emphasis, as found in 20:2 and 124 as well as 23:1 and 117, or to emphasize Allah's knowledge, just like the first verse emphasizes His power.

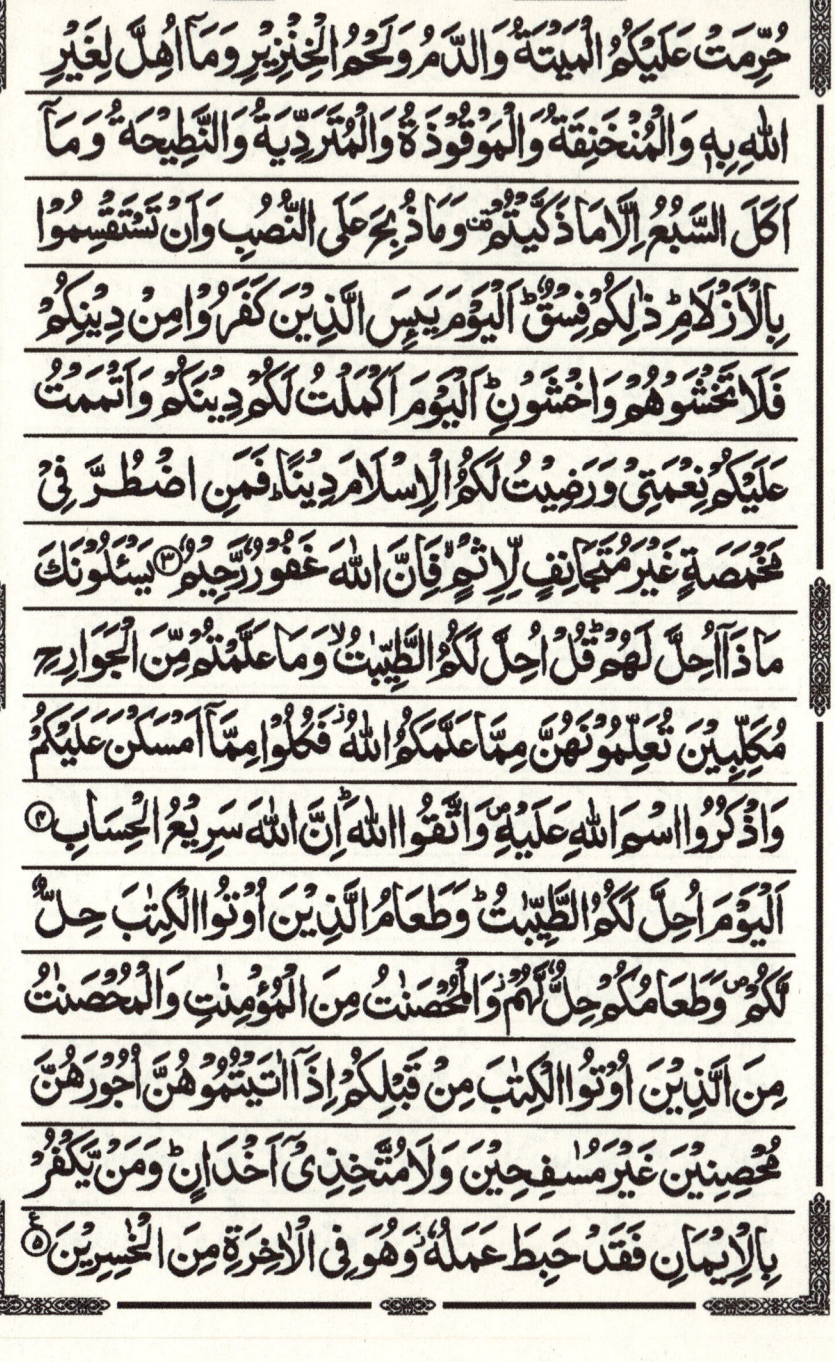

Forbidden Foods

3. Forbidden to you are carrion, blood, and swine; what is slaughtered in the name of any other than Allah; what is killed by strangling, beating, a fall, or by being gored to death; what is partly eaten by a predator unless you slaughter it; and what is sacrificed on altars. You are also forbidden to draw lots for decisions.[235] This is all evil.

Faith Perfected

Today the disbelievers have given up all hope of ˹undermining˺ your faith. So do not fear them; fear Me! Today I have perfected your faith for you, completed My favour upon you, and chosen Islam as your way.

Forbidden Food Allowed by Necessity

But whoever is compelled by extreme hunger—not intending to sin—then surely Allah is All-Forgiving, Most Merciful.

Lawful Foods

4. They ask you, ˹O Prophet,˺ what is permissible for them ˹to eat˺. Say, "What is good and lawful. Also what is caught by your hunting animals and birds of prey which you have trained as instructed by Allah. So eat what they catch for you, but mention the Name of Allah over it ˹first˺." And be mindful of Allah. Surely Allah is swift in reckoning.

What to Eat and Who to Marry

5. Today all good, pure foods have been made lawful for you. Similarly, the food of the People of the Book[236] is permissible for you and yours is permissible for them. And ˹permissible for you in marriage˺ are chaste believing women as well as chaste women of those given the Scripture before you—as long as you pay them their dowries in wedlock, neither fornicating nor taking them as mistresses.

---

235 To make a decision in pre-Islamic Arabia, a person would draw one of three straws: one saying "Do it," the other "Do not do it," and the third was left blank, whereas in Islam there is a special prayer (called *istikhârah*) for guidance when making a decision.

236 "The food of the People of the Book" here means the meat of the animals slaughtered by the Jews and Christians.

5. Al-Mâ'idah

Those Who Reject Islam

And whoever rejects the faith, all their good deeds will be void ˹in this life˺ and in the Hereafter they will be among the losers.

Purification Before Prayer

6. O believers! When you rise up for prayer, wash your faces and your hands up to the elbows, wipe your heads, and wash your feet to the ankles. And if you are in a state of ˹full˺ impurity,[237] then take a full bath. But if you are ill, on a journey, or have relieved yourselves, or have been intimate with your wives and cannot find water, then purify yourselves with clean earth by wiping your faces and hands.[238] It is not Allah's Will to burden you, but to purify you and complete His favour upon you, so perhaps you will be grateful.

Allah's Favour to the Believers

7. Remember Allah's favour upon you and the covenant He made with you when you said, "We hear and obey." And be mindful of Allah. Surely Allah knows best what is ˹hidden˺ in the heart.

Be Just

8. O believers! Stand firm for Allah and bear true testimony. Do not let the hatred of a people lead you to injustice. Be just! That is closer to righteousness. And be mindful of Allah. Surely Allah is All-Aware of what you do.

Reward of Belief and Disbelief

9. Allah has promised those who believe and do good ˹His˺ forgiveness and a great reward.

---

237 For example, following sexual intercourse or a wet dream.
238 This ruling is called *tayammum* or 'dry ablution.' *See* footnote for 4:43.

5. Al-Mâ'idah

10. As for those who disbelieve and deny Our signs, they are the residents of the Hellfire.

Believers Saved from Harm

11. O believers! Remember Allah's favour upon you: when a people sought to harm you, but He held their hands back from you. Be mindful of Allah. And in Allah let the believers put their trust.

Allah's Covenant with the Israelites

12. Allah made a covenant with the Children of Israel and appointed twelve leaders from among them and ˹then˺ said, "I am truly with you. If you establish prayer, pay alms-tax, believe in My messengers, support them, and lend to Allah a good loan, I will certainly forgive your sins and admit you into Gardens under which rivers flow. And whoever among you disbelieves afterwards has truly strayed from the Right Way."

The Covenant Is Broken

13. But for breaking their covenant We condemned them and hardened their hearts. They distorted the words of the Scripture and neglected a portion of what they had been commanded to uphold. You ˹O Prophet˺ will always find deceit on their part, except for a few. But pardon them and bear with them. Indeed, Allah loves the good-doers.

5. Al-Mâ'idah

Covenant with Christians Broken Too

14. And from those who say, "We are Christians," We took their covenant, but they neglected a portion of what they had been commanded to uphold. So We let hostility and enmity arise between them until the Day of Judgment, and soon Allah will inform them of all they have done.

The Prophet's Mission

15. O People of the Book! Now Our Messenger has come to you, revealing much of what you have hidden of the Scriptures and disregarding much. There certainly has come to you from Allah a light and a clear Book **16.** through which Allah guides those who seek His pleasure to the ways of peace, brings them out of darkness and into light by His Will, and guides them to the Straight Path.

Jesus Is Not Allah

17. Indeed, those who say, "Allah is the Messiah, son of Mary," have fallen into disbelief. Say, ˹O Prophet,˺ "Who has the power to prevent Allah if He chose to destroy the Messiah, son of Mary, his mother, and everyone in the world all together?" To Allah ˹alone˺ belongs the kingdom of the heavens and the earth and everything in between. He creates whatever He wills. And Allah is Most Capable of everything.

5. Al-Mâ'idah

Children of Allah?

18. The Jews and the Christians each say, "We are the children of Allah and His most beloved!" Say, ʿO Prophet,ʾ "Why then does He punish you for your sins? No! You are only humans like others of His Own making. He forgives whoever He wills and punishes whoever He wills. To Allah ʿaloneʾ belongs the kingdom of the heavens and the earth and everything in between. And to Him is the final return."

No Excuse

19. O People of the Book! Our Messenger has indeed come to you, making things clear to you after an interval between the messengers so you do not say, "There has never come to us a deliverer of good news or a warner." Now there has come to you a deliverer of good news and a warner. And Allah is Most Capable of everything.

*The Israelites Ordered
to Enter the Holy Land*

20. And ʿrememberʾ when Moses said to his people, "O my people! Remember Allah's favours upon you when He raised prophets from among you, made you sovereign,[239] and gave you what He had never given anyone in the world.[240] **21.** O my people! Enter the Holy Land which Allah has destined for you ʿto enterʾ. And do not turn back or else you will become losers." **22.** They replied, "O Moses! There is an enormously powerful people there, so we will never ʿbe able toʾ enter it until they leave. If they do, then we will enter!" **23.** Two God-fearing men—who had been blessed by Allah—said, "Surprise them through the gate. If you do, you will certainly prevail. Put your trust in Allah if you are ʿtrulyʾ believers."

---

239 He rescued you from Egypt where the Pharaoh treated you like slaves and blessed you with freedom so you can manage your own affairs.
240 i.e., the miracles of splitting the sea, water coming out of the rock, manna and quails, and clouds shading them.

| 113 | 5. Al-Mâ'idah |

24. ˹Yet˺ they said, "O Moses! ˹Still˺ we will never enter as long as they remain there. So go—both you and your Lord—and fight; we are staying right here!"

Forty Years in the Wilderness

25. Moses pleaded, "My Lord! I have no control over anyone except myself and my brother. So set us apart from the rebellious people."
26. Allah replied, "Then this land is forbidden to them for forty years, during which they will wander through the land. So do not grieve for the rebellious people."

Abel and Cain[241]

27. Relate to them in truth ˹O Prophet˺ the story of Adam's two sons— how each offered a sacrifice: Abel's offering was accepted while Cain's was not. So Cain threatened, "I will kill you!" His brother replied, "Allah only accepts ˹the offering˺ of the sincerely devout. **28.** If you raise your hand to kill me, I will not raise mine to kill you, because I fear Allah—the Lord of all worlds. **29.** I want to let you bear your sin against me along with your other sins, then you will be one of those destined to the Fire. And that is the reward of the wrongdoers." **30.** Yet Cain convinced himself to kill his brother, so he killed him—becoming a loser. **31.** Then Allah sent a crow digging ˹a grave˺ in the ground ˹for a dead crow˺, in order to show him how to bury the corpse of his brother. He cried, "Alas! Have I ˹even˺ failed to be like this crow and bury the corpse of my brother?" So he became regretful.[242]

---

241 Hâbîl and Qâbîl, respectively.
242 In Islam, regret for doing something wrong is essential for repentance. But in the case of Cain, his regret was not for killing his brother, but for failing to bury his corpse to hide the evidence of his crime. Therefore, his regret was not intended as a step towards repentance.

5. Al-Mâ'idah

بِسْمِ
اللَّهِ
الرَّحْمَٰنِ

مِنْ أَجْلِ ذَٰلِكَ كَتَبْنَا عَلَىٰ بَنِي إِسْرَآءِيلَ أَنَّهُۥ مَن
قَتَلَ نَفْسًۢا بِغَيْرِ نَفْسٍ أَوْ فَسَادٍ فِي الْأَرْضِ فَكَأَنَّمَا قَتَلَ
النَّاسَ جَمِيعًا ۚ وَمَنْ أَحْيَاهَا فَكَأَنَّمَآ أَحْيَا النَّاسَ جَمِيعًا ۚ
وَلَقَدْ جَآءَتْهُمْ رُسُلُنَا بِالْبَيِّنَٰتِ ثُمَّ إِنَّ كَثِيرًا مِّنْهُم بَعْدَ
ذَٰلِكَ فِي الْأَرْضِ لَمُسْرِفُونَ ۝ إِنَّمَا جَزَٰٓؤُا۟ الَّذِينَ يُحَارِبُونَ
اللَّهَ وَرَسُولَهُۥ وَيَسْعَوْنَ فِي الْأَرْضِ فَسَادًا أَن يُقَتَّلُوٓا۟ أَوْ
يُصَلَّبُوٓا۟ أَوْ تُقَطَّعَ أَيْدِيهِمْ وَأَرْجُلُهُم مِّنْ خِلَٰفٍ أَوْ
يُنفَوْا۟ مِنَ الْأَرْضِ ۚ ذَٰلِكَ لَهُمْ خِزْيٌ فِي الدُّنْيَا ۖ وَ
لَهُمْ فِي الْآخِرَةِ عَذَابٌ عَظِيمٌ ۝ إِلَّا الَّذِينَ تَابُوا۟
مِن قَبْلِ أَن تَقْدِرُوا۟ عَلَيْهِمْ ۖ فَاعْلَمُوٓا۟ أَنَّ اللَّهَ غَفُورٌ
رَّحِيمٌ ۝ يَٰٓأَيُّهَا الَّذِينَ آمَنُوا۟ اتَّقُوا۟ اللَّهَ وَابْتَغُوٓا۟
إِلَيْهِ الْوَسِيلَةَ وَجَٰهِدُوا۟ فِي سَبِيلِهِۦ لَعَلَّكُمْ
تُفْلِحُونَ ۝ إِنَّ الَّذِينَ كَفَرُوا۟ لَوْ أَنَّ لَهُم مَّا فِي
الْأَرْضِ جَمِيعًا وَمِثْلَهُۥ مَعَهُۥ لِيَفْتَدُوا۟ بِهِۦ مِنْ عَذَابِ
يَوْمِ الْقِيَٰمَةِ مَا تُقُبِّلَ مِنْهُمْ ۖ وَلَهُمْ عَذَابٌ أَلِيمٌ ۝

Value of Human Life

32. That is why We ordained for the Children of Israel that whoever takes a life— unless as a punishment for murder or mischief in the land—it will be as if they killed all of humanity; and whoever saves a life, it will be as if they saved all of humanity.[243] ˹Although˺ Our messengers already came to them with clear proofs, many of them still transgressed afterwards through the land.

Anti-Terrorism Law

33. Indeed, the penalty for those who wage war against Allah and His Messenger and spread mischief in the land is death, crucifixion, cutting off their hands and feet on opposite sides, or exile from the land. This ˹penalty˺ is a disgrace for them in this world, and they will suffer a tremendous punishment in the Hereafter.[244] 34. As for those who repent before you seize them, then know that Allah is All-Forgiving, Most Merciful.

Closer to Allah

35. O believers! Be mindful of Allah and seek what brings you closer to Him and struggle in His Way, so you may be successful.

Reward of the Disbelievers

36. As for the disbelievers, even if they were to possess everything in the world twice over ˹and offer it all˺ to ransom themselves from the punishment of the Day of Judgment, it would never be accepted from them. And they will suffer a painful punishment.

---

243 Although this is addressed to the Children of Israel, it is applicable to everyone at all times.
244 This ruling (called *ḥirâbah*) applies to crimes committed by armed individuals or groups against civilians—Muslim or non-Muslim. Different punishments apply depending on the severity of the crime:
- In the case of murder or rape, offenders are to be executed.
- In the case of armed robbery, offenders' right hands and left feet are to be cut off.
- In the case of terrorizing innocent people, offenders are to be jailed in exile.
- Penalties for lesser offences are left for the judge to decide.

37. They will be desperate to get out of the Fire but they will never be able to. And they will suffer an everlasting punishment.

Punishment of Theft

38. As for male and female thieves, cut off their hands for what they have done—a deterrent from Allah. And Allah is Almighty, All-Wise.[245]

39. But whoever repents after their wrongdoing and mends their ways, Allah will surely turn to them in forgiveness. Indeed, Allah is All-Forgiving, Most Merciful.

Allah's Might and Grace

40. Do you not know that the kingdom of the heavens and the earth belongs to Allah ˹alone˺? He punishes whoever He wills and forgives whoever He wills. And Allah is Most Capable of everything.

Do Not Be Disheartened

41. O Messenger! Do not grieve for those who race to disbelieve—those who say, "We believe" with their tongues, but their hearts are in disbelief. Nor those among the Jews who eagerly listen to lies, attentive to those who are too arrogant to come to you. They distort the Scripture, taking rulings out of context, then say, "If this is the ruling you get ˹from Muḥammad˺, accept it. If not, beware!" Whoever Allah allows to be deluded, you can never be of any help to them against Allah. It is not Allah's Will to purify their hearts. For them there is disgrace in this world, and they will suffer a tremendous punishment in the Hereafter.

---

245 In Islam, strict conditions must be met for punishments to be carried out. For example, for someone to be punished for theft, the thief must be a sane adult who knows that theft is forbidden, the crime has to be proven either by confession or the testimony of two reliable eyewitnesses, the stolen item has to be of value and taken secretly from a safe place, and the owner has to claim it. Otherwise, the punishment is not applied. Islamic punishments apply neither in non-Muslim countries nor in Muslim countries where *Sharia* is not fully applied. Moreover, the punishment is only applicable in a society where the needs of the poor are adequately met (i.e., they receive alms-tax, charity, or welfare) and where theft is more out of desire than necessity. It is worth mentioning that 'Umar ibn Al-Khaṭṭāb, Islam's 2nd Caliph, suspended this punishment for one year due to widespread famine.

Fair Judgment

42. They eagerly listen to falsehood and consume forbidden gain.[246] So if they come to you ʿO Prophetʾ, either judge between them or turn away from them. If you turn away from them, they cannot harm you whatsoever. But if you judge between them, then do so with justice. Surely Allah loves those who are just.
43. But why do they come to you for judgment when they ʿalreadyʾ have the Torah containing Allah's judgment, then they turn away after all? They are not ʿtrueʾ believers.

Judging by the Torah

44. Indeed, We revealed the Torah, containing guidance and light, by which the prophets, who submitted themselves to Allah, made judgments for Jews. So too did the rabbis and scholars judge according to Allah's Book, with which they were entrusted and of which they were made keepers. So do not fear the people; fear Me! Nor trade my revelations for a fleeting gain. And those who do not judge by what Allah has revealed are ʿtrulyʾ the disbelievers.

Justice System

45. We ordained for them in the Torah, "A life for a life, an eye for an eye, a nose for a nose, an ear for an ear, a tooth for a tooth—and for wounds equal retaliation." But whoever waives it charitably, it will be atonement for them. And those who do not judge by what Allah has revealed are ʿtrulyʾ the wrongdoers.

---

246 i.e., bribes and interest.

5. Al-Mâ'idah

Judging by the Gospel

46. Then in the footsteps of the prophets, We sent Jesus, son of Mary, confirming the Torah revealed before him. And We gave him the Gospel containing guidance and light and confirming what was revealed in the Torah—a guide and a lesson to the God-fearing. **47.** So let the people of the Gospel judge by what Allah has revealed in it. And those who do not judge by what Allah has revealed are ˹truly˺ the rebellious.

Judging by the Quran

48. We have revealed to you ˹O Prophet˺ this Book with the truth, as a confirmation of previous Scriptures and a supreme authority on them. So judge between them by what Allah has revealed, and do not follow their desires over the truth that has come to you. To each of you We have ordained a code of law and a way of life. If Allah had willed, He would have made you one community, but His Will is to test you with what He has given ˹each of˺ you. So compete with one another in doing good. To Allah you will all return, then He will inform you ˹of the truth˺ regarding your differences.

Allah's Judgment

49. And judge between them ˹O Prophet˺ by what Allah has revealed, and do not follow their desires. And beware, so they do not lure you away from some of what Allah has revealed to you. If they turn away ˹from Allah's judgment˺, then know that it is Allah's Will to repay them for some of their sins, and that many people are indeed rebellious. **50.** Is it the judgment of ˹pre-Islamic˺ ignorance they seek? Who could be a better judge than Allah for people of sure faith?

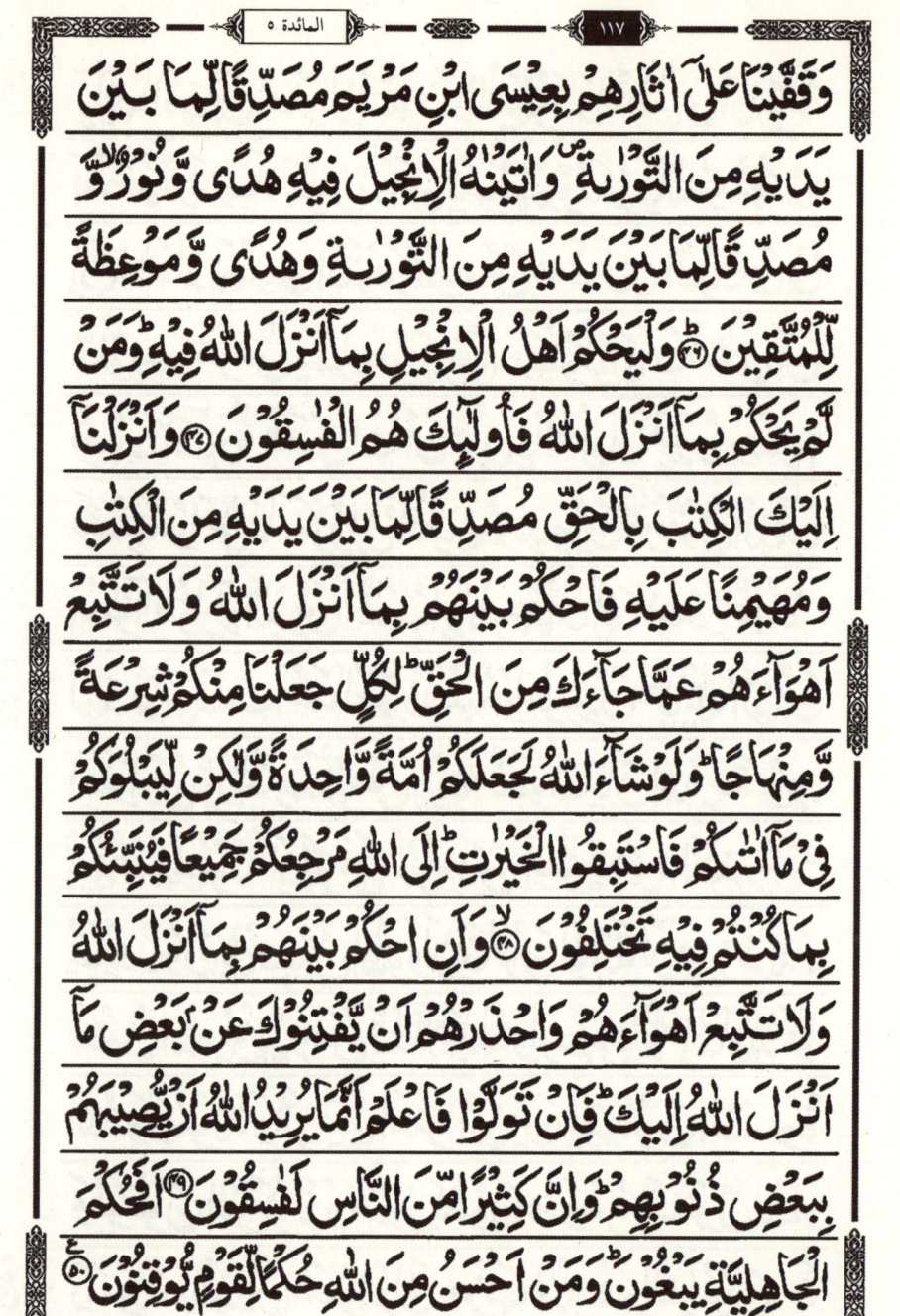

5. Al-Mâ'idah

Hypocrites' Guardians

51. O believers! Take neither Jews nor Christians as guardians—they are guardians of each other.[247] Whoever does so will be counted as one of them. Surely Allah does not guide the wrongdoing people. **52.** You see those with sickness in their hearts racing for their guardianship, saying ˹in justification˺, "We fear a turn of fortune will strike us." But perhaps Allah will bring about ˹your˺ victory or another favour by His command, and they will regret what they have hidden in their hearts. **53.** ˹Only then,˺ the believers will ask ˹one another˺, "Are these the ones who swore solemn oaths by Allah that they were with you?" Their deeds have been in vain, so they have become losers.

True Believers

54. O believers! Whoever among you abandons their faith, Allah will replace them with others who love Him and are loved by Him. They will be humble with the believers but firm towards the disbelievers, struggling in the Way of Allah; fearing no blame from anyone. This is the favour of Allah. He grants it to whoever He wills. And Allah is Ever-Bountiful, All-Knowing.

True Guardianship

55. Your only guardians are Allah, His Messenger, and fellow believers—who establish prayer and pay alms-tax with humility. **56.** Whoever allies themselves with Allah, His Messenger, and fellow believers, then it is certainly Allah's party that will prevail.

---

247 *Wali* means guardian, caretaker, protector, provider, ally, etc. The Prophet (ﷺ) for example says, "A woman should not get married without a *wali*."—that is a guardian such as her father to represent her in the marriage and make sure she receives her full rights. The verse forbids Muslims from allying with the Jews and Christians (or anyone else) conspiring to persecute Muslims. On the other hand, as long as non-Muslims are not at war with Muslims or persecuting them, the Quran (60:8) commands Muslims to be kind and gracious to them.

5. Al-Mâ'idah

Unacceptable Guardianship

57. O believers! Do not seek the guardianship of those given the Scripture before you and the disbelievers who have made your faith a mockery and amusement. And be mindful of Allah if you are ˹truly˺ believers. **58.** When you call to prayer, they mock it in amusement. This is because they are a people without understanding.

Who Deserves Resentment?

59. Say, ˹O Prophet,˺ "O People of the Book! Do you resent us only because we believe in Allah and what has been revealed to us and what was revealed before—while most of you are rebellious?" **60.** Say, ˹O Prophet,˺ "Shall I inform you of those who deserve a worse punishment from Allah ˹than the rebellious˺? It is those who earned Allah's condemnation and displeasure—some being reduced to apes and pigs[248] and worshippers of false gods. These are far worse in rank and farther astray from the Right Way."

Hypocrites Among Jews

61. When they come to you ˹believers˺ they say, "We believe." But they are committed to disbelief when they enter and when they leave. And Allah knows what they hide. **62.** You see many of them racing towards sin, transgression, and consumption of forbidden gain. Evil indeed are their actions! **63.** Why do their rabbis and scholars not forbid them from saying what is sinful and consuming what is unlawful? Evil indeed is their inaction!

---

248 Literally or metaphorically. See footnote for 2:65.

5. Al-Mâ'idah

Allah Is Ever Generous

64. ˹Some among˺ the Jews said, "Allah is tight-fisted."[249] May their fists be tied and they be condemned for what they said. Rather, He is open-handed, giving freely as He pleases. That which has been revealed to you ˹O Prophet˺ from your Lord will only cause many of them to increase in wickedness and disbelief. We have stirred among them hostility and hatred until the Day of Judgment. Whenever they kindle the fire of war, Allah puts it out. And they strive to spread corruption in the land. And Allah does not like corruptors.

Worst of Both Worlds

65. Had the People of the Book only been faithful and mindful ˹of Allah˺, We would have certainly absolved them of their sins and admitted them into the Gardens of Bliss. 66. And had they observed the Torah, the Gospel, and what has been revealed to them from their Lord, they would have been overwhelmed with provisions from above and below. Some among them are upright, yet many do nothing but evil.

A Messenger's Duty Is to Convey

67. O Messenger! Convey everything revealed to you from your Lord. If you do not, then you have not delivered His message. Allah will ˹certainly˺ protect you from the people. Indeed, Allah does not guide the people who disbelieve.

Adherence to Scriptures

68. Say, ˹O Prophet,˺ "O People of the Book! You have nothing to stand on unless you observe the Torah, the Gospel, and what has been revealed to you from your Lord." And your Lord's revelation to you ˹O Prophet˺ will only cause many of them to increase in wickedness and disbelief. So do not grieve for the people who disbelieve.

---

249 lit., Allah's Hand is tied up ˹with greed˺.

True Belief in Allah

69. Indeed, the believers, Jews, Sabians[250] and Christians—whoever ˹truly˺ believes in Allah and the Last Day and does good, there will be no fear for them, nor will they grieve.

The Israelites Rejecting Messengers

70. Indeed, We took a covenant from the Children of Israel and sent them messengers. Whenever a messenger came to them with what they did not desire, they denied some and killed others. 71. They thought there would be no consequences, so they turned a blind eye and a deaf ear. Yet Allah turned to them in forgiveness ˹after their repentance˺, but again many became blind and deaf. And Allah is All-Seeing of what they do.

One God, Not Three

72. Those who say, "Allah is the Messiah, son of Mary," have certainly fallen into disbelief. The Messiah ˹himself˺ said, "O Children of Israel! Worship Allah—my Lord and your Lord." Whoever associates others with Allah ˹in worship˺ will surely be forbidden Paradise by Allah. Their home will be the Fire. And the wrongdoers will have no helpers. 73. Those who say, "Allah is one in a Trinity," have certainly fallen into disbelief. There is only One God. If they do not stop saying this, those who disbelieve among them will be afflicted with a painful punishment.

Still Not Too Late

74. Will they not turn to Allah in repentance and seek His forgiveness? And Allah is All-Forgiving, Most Merciful.

Jesus Was Human, Not Divine

75. The Messiah, son of Mary, was no more than a messenger. ˹Many˺ messengers had ˹come and˺ gone before him. His mother was a woman of truth. They both ate food.[251] See how We make the signs clear to them, yet see how they are deluded ˹from the truth˺!

---

250 See footnote for 2:62.

251 i.e., they were in need of food for nourishment. According to some scholars, this implies that Jesus and his mother had to relieve themselves after the food had been digested. Almighty Allah is far above depending on food or having to go to the restroom.

5. Al-Mâ'idah

Follow the Truth

76. Say, ˹O Prophet,˺ "How can you worship besides Allah those who can neither harm nor benefit you? And Allah ˹alone˺ is the All-Hearing, All-Knowing." 77. Say, "O People of the Book! Do not go to extremes in your faith beyond the truth, nor follow the vain desires of those who went astray before ˹you˺. They misled many and strayed from the Right Way."

Evildoers Among the Israelites

78. The disbelievers among the Children of Israel were condemned in the revelations of David and Jesus, son of Mary. That was for their disobedience and violations. 79. They did not forbid one another from doing evil. Evil indeed was what they did! 80. You see many of them taking the disbelievers[252] as allies. Truly wicked are their misdeeds, which have earned them Allah's wrath. And they will be in everlasting torment. 81. Had they believed in Allah, the Prophet, and what has been revealed to him, they would have never taken those ˹pagans˺ as allies. But most of them are rebellious.

Those Most Gracious Towards Believers

82. You will surely find the most bitter towards the believers to be the Jews and polytheists and the most gracious to be those who call themselves Christian. That is because there are priests and monks among them and because they are not arrogant.

---

252 i.e., the pagans.

5. Al-Mâ'idah

83. When they listen to what has been revealed to the Messenger, you see their eyes overflowing with tears for recognizing the truth. They say, "Our Lord! We believe, so count us among the witnesses. **84.** Why should we not believe in Allah and the truth that has come to us? And we long for our Lord to include us in the company of the righteous." **85.** So Allah will reward them for what they said with Gardens under which rivers flow, to stay there forever. And that is the reward of the good-doers. **86.** As for those who disbelieve and reject Our signs, they will be the residents of the Hellfire.

Be Moderate

87. O believers! Do not forbid the good things which Allah has made lawful for you, and do not transgress. Indeed, Allah does not like transgressors. **88.** Eat of the good, lawful things provided to you by Allah. And be mindful of Allah in Whom you believe.

Broken Oaths

89. Allah will not call you to account for your thoughtless oaths, but He will hold you accountable for deliberate oaths. The penalty for a broken oath is to feed ten poor people from what you normally feed your own family, or to clothe them, or to free a bondsperson. But if none of this is affordable, then you must fast three days. This is the penalty for breaking your oaths. So be mindful of your oaths. This is how Allah makes things clear to you, so perhaps you will be grateful.

5. Al-Mâ'idah — 124

بِسْمِ يَـٰٓأَيُّهَا ٱلَّذِينَ ءَامَنُوٓاْ إِنَّمَا ٱلْخَمْرُ وَٱلْمَيْسِرُ وَٱلْأَنصَابُ وَٱلْأَزْلَـٰمُ

رِجْسٌ مِّنْ عَمَلِ ٱلشَّيْطَـٰنِ فَٱجْتَنِبُوهُ لَعَلَّكُمْ تُفْلِحُونَ ٩٠ إِنَّمَا

يُرِيدُ ٱلشَّيْطَـٰنُ أَن يُوقِعَ بَيْنَكُمُ ٱلْعَدَٰوَةَ وَٱلْبَغْضَآءَ فِى ٱلْخَمْرِ

وَٱلْمَيْسِرِ وَيَصُدَّكُمْ عَن ذِكْرِ ٱللَّهِ وَعَنِ ٱلصَّلَوٰةِ فَهَلْ أَنتُم مُّنتَهُونَ ٩١

وَأَطِيعُواْ ٱللَّهَ وَأَطِيعُواْ ٱلرَّسُولَ وَٱحْذَرُواْ فَإِن تَوَلَّيْتُمْ فَٱعْلَمُوٓاْ أَنَّمَا

عَلَىٰ رَسُولِنَا ٱلْبَلَـٰغُ ٱلْمُبِينُ ٩٢ لَيْسَ عَلَى ٱلَّذِينَ ءَامَنُواْ وَعَمِلُواْ

ٱلصَّـٰلِحَـٰتِ جُنَاحٌ فِيمَا طَعِمُوٓاْ إِذَا مَا ٱتَّقَواْ وَّءَامَنُواْ وَعَمِلُواْ ٱلصَّـٰلِحَـٰتِ

ثُمَّ ٱتَّقَواْ وَّءَامَنُواْ ثُمَّ ٱتَّقَواْ وَّأَحْسَنُواْ وَٱللَّهُ يُحِبُّ ٱلْمُحْسِنِينَ ٩٣ يَـٰٓأَيُّهَا

ٱلَّذِينَ ءَامَنُواْ لَيَبْلُوَنَّكُمُ ٱللَّهُ بِشَىْءٍ مِّنَ ٱلصَّيْدِ تَنَالُهُۥٓ أَيْدِيكُمْ وَ

رِمَاحُكُمْ لِيَعْلَمَ ٱللَّهُ مَن يَخَافُهُۥ بِٱلْغَيْبِ فَمَنِ ٱعْتَدَىٰ بَعْدَ

ذَٰلِكَ فَلَهُۥ عَذَابٌ أَلِيمٌ ٩٤ يَـٰٓأَيُّهَا ٱلَّذِينَ ءَامَنُواْ لَا تَقْتُلُواْ ٱلصَّيْدَ وَأَنتُمْ

حُرُمٌ وَمَن قَتَلَهُۥ مِنكُم مُّتَعَمِّدًا فَجَزَآءٌ مِّثْلُ مَا قَتَلَ مِنَ ٱلنَّعَمِ

يَحْكُمُ بِهِۦ ذَوَا عَدْلٍ مِّنكُمْ هَدْيًۢا بَـٰلِغَ ٱلْكَعْبَةِ أَوْ كَفَّـٰرَةٌ طَعَامُ

مَسَـٰكِينَ أَوْ عَدْلُ ذَٰلِكَ صِيَامًا لِّيَذُوقَ وَبَالَ أَمْرِهِۦ عَفَا ٱللَّهُ

عَمَّا سَلَفَ وَمَنْ عَادَ فَيَنتَقِمُ ٱللَّهُ مِنْهُ وَٱللَّهُ عَزِيزٌ ذُو ٱنتِقَامٍ ٩٥

Forbidden Items

90. O believers! Intoxicants, gambling, idols, and drawing lots for decisions[253] are all evil of Satan's handiwork. So shun them so you may be successful. **91.** Satan's plan is to stir up hostility and hatred between you with intoxicants and gambling and to prevent you from remembering Allah and praying. Will you not then abstain? **92.** Obey Allah and obey the Messenger and beware! But if you turn away, then know that Our Messenger's duty is only to deliver ˹the message˺ clearly.

The Past Is Forgiven

93. There is no blame on those who believe and do good for what they had consumed before ˹the prohibition˺, as long as they fear Allah, have faith, and do what is good; then they believe and act virtuously, then become fully mindful ˹of Allah˺ and do righteous deeds. For Allah loves the good-doers.

Hunting While on Pilgrimage

94. O believers! Allah will surely test you with game within the reach of your hands and spears to distinguish those who fear Him in secret. Whoever transgresses from now on will suffer a painful punishment. **95.** O believers! Do not kill game while on pilgrimage. Whoever kills game intentionally must compensate by offering its equivalence—as judged by two just men among you—to be offered at the Sacred House, or by feeding the needy, or by fasting so that they may taste the consequences of their violations. Allah has forgiven what has been done. But those who persist will be punished by Allah. And Allah is Almighty, capable of punishment.

---

253 *See footnote for 5:3.*

125   5. Al-Mâ'idah

Seafood Is Lawful

96. It is lawful for you to hunt and eat seafood, as a provision for you and for travellers. But hunting on land is forbidden to you while on pilgrimage. Be mindful of Allah to Whom you all will be gathered.

Pilgrimage Symbols

97. Allah has made the Ka'bah—the Sacred House—a sanctuary of well-being for all people, along with the sacred months, the sacrificial animals, and the 'offerings decorated with' garlands. All this so you may know that Allah knows whatever is in the heavens and whatever is on the earth, and that He has 'perfect' knowledge of everything. 98. Know that Allah is severe in punishment and that He is All-Forgiving, Most Merciful. 99. The Messenger's duty is only to deliver 'the message'. And Allah 'fully' knows what you reveal and what you conceal.

Good and Evil Not Equal

100. Say, 'O Prophet,' "Good and evil are not equal, though you may be dazzled by the abundance of evil. So be mindful of Allah, O people of reason, so you may be successful."

Unnecessary Questions[254]

101. O believers! Do not ask about any matter which, if made clear to you, may disturb you. But if you inquire about what is being revealed in the Quran, it will be made clear to you. Allah has forgiven what was done 'in the past'.[255] And Allah is All-Forgiving, Most Forbearing.

102. Some people before you asked such questions then denied their answers.

Camels Dedicated to Idols

103. Allah has never ordained the 'so-called' *baḥîrah*, *sâ'ibah*, *waṣîlah*, and *ḥâm* camels.[256] But the disbelievers[257] just fabricate lies about Allah, and most of them lack understanding. 104. When it is said to them, "Come to Allah's revelations and to the Mes-

---

254 Some Muslims would ask the Prophet (ﷺ) unnecessary and sometimes meaningless questions. For example: who their fathers were, where their lost animals were, what they had in their pockets, etc. Some would even demand new rulings that would probably make things difficult for some Muslims or even themselves.

255 This implies that either these minor details have been overlooked by Allah out of His mercy or that Allah has forgiven them for these unnecessary questions.

256 These camels were allowed by pagan Arabs to pasture freely and were not to be used for labour or transportation after fathering or giving birth to a certain number of male or female camels.

257 i.e., the pagans.

وَإِذَا قِيلَ لَهُمْ تَعَالَوْا إِلَىٰ مَآ أَنزَلَ ٱللَّهُ وَإِلَى ٱلرَّسُولِ قَالُوا۟
حَسْبُنَا مَا وَجَدْنَا عَلَيْهِ ءَابَآءَنَآ أَوَلَوْ كَانَ ءَابَآؤُهُمْ لَا يَعْلَمُونَ
شَيْـًٔا وَلَا يَهْتَدُونَ ۝ يَـٰٓأَيُّهَا ٱلَّذِينَ ءَامَنُوا۟ عَلَيْكُمْ أَنفُسَكُمْ لَا
يَضُرُّكُم مَّن ضَلَّ إِذَا ٱهْتَدَيْتُمْ إِلَى ٱللَّهِ مَرْجِعُكُمْ جَمِيعًا فَيُنَبِّئُكُم
بِمَا كُنتُمْ تَعْمَلُونَ ۝ يَـٰٓأَيُّهَا ٱلَّذِينَ ءَامَنُوا۟ شَهَـٰدَةُ بَيْنِكُمْ إِذَا
حَضَرَ أَحَدَكُمُ ٱلْمَوْتُ حِينَ ٱلْوَصِيَّةِ ٱثْنَانِ ذَوَا عَدْلٍ مِّنكُمْ
أَوْ ءَاخَرَانِ مِنْ غَيْرِكُمْ إِنْ أَنتُمْ ضَرَبْتُمْ فِى ٱلْأَرْضِ فَأَصَـٰبَتْكُم
مُّصِيبَةُ ٱلْمَوْتِ تَحْبِسُونَهُمَا مِنۢ بَعْدِ ٱلصَّلَوٰةِ فَيُقْسِمَانِ بِٱللَّهِ
إِنِ ٱرْتَبْتُمْ لَا نَشْتَرِى بِهِۦ ثَمَنًا وَلَوْ كَانَ ذَا قُرْبَىٰ وَلَا نَكْتُمُ
شَهَـٰدَةَ ٱللَّهِ إِنَّآ إِذًا لَّمِنَ ٱلْـَٔاثِمِينَ ۝ فَإِنْ عُثِرَ عَلَىٰٓ أَنَّهُمَا ٱسْتَحَقَّآ
إِثْمًا فَـَٔاخَرَانِ يَقُومَانِ مَقَامَهُمَا مِنَ ٱلَّذِينَ ٱسْتَحَقَّ عَلَيْهِمُ
ٱلْأَوْلَيَـٰنِ فَيُقْسِمَانِ بِٱللَّهِ لَشَهَـٰدَتُنَآ أَحَقُّ مِن شَهَـٰدَتِهِمَا وَ
مَا ٱعْتَدَيْنَآ إِنَّآ إِذًا لَّمِنَ ٱلظَّـٰلِمِينَ ۝ ذَٰلِكَ أَدْنَىٰٓ أَن يَأْتُوا۟
بِٱلشَّهَـٰدَةِ عَلَىٰ وَجْهِهَآ أَوْ يَخَافُوٓا۟ أَن تُرَدَّ أَيْمَـٰنٌۢ بَعْدَ أَيْمَـٰنِهِمْ
وَٱتَّقُوا۟ ٱللَّهَ وَٱسْمَعُوا۟ وَٱللَّهُ لَا يَهْدِى ٱلْقَوْمَ ٱلْفَـٰسِقِينَ ۝

senger," they reply, "What we found our forefathers practicing is good enough for us." ˹Would they still do so,˺ even if their forefathers had absolutely no knowledge or guidance?

Everyone Accountable for Themselves

105. O believers! You are accountable only for yourselves.[258] It will not harm you if someone chooses to deviate—as long as you are ˹rightly˺ guided. To Allah you will all return, and He will inform you of what you used to do.

Verifying Bequests

106. O believers! When death approaches any of you, call upon two just Muslim men to witness as you make a bequest; otherwise, two non-Muslims if you are afflicted with death while on a journey.[259] If you doubt ˹their testimony˺, keep them after prayer and let them testify under oath ˹saying˺, "By Allah! We would never sell our testimony for any price, even in favour of a close relative, nor withhold the testimony of Allah. Otherwise, we would surely be sinful." **107.** If they are found guilty ˹of false testimony˺, let the deceased's two closest heirs affected by the bequest replace the witnesses and testify under oath ˹saying˺, "By Allah! Our testimony is truer than theirs. We have not transgressed. Otherwise, we would surely be wrongdoers." **108.** In this way it is more likely that witnesses will give true testimony or else fear that their oaths could be refuted by those of the heirs. Be mindful of Allah and obey. For Allah does not guide the rebellious people.

---

258 After fulfilling their obligation of delivering the truth, enjoining what is good, and forbidding what is evil.
259 If no Muslim witnesses can be found.

5. Al-Mâ'idah

Allah Asking the Messengers

109. 'Consider' the Day Allah will gather the messengers and say, "What response did you receive?" They will reply, "We have no knowledge 'compared to You'! You 'alone' are indeed the Knower of all unseen."

Allah's Favours upon Jesus

110. And 'on Judgment Day' Allah will say, "O Jesus, son of Mary! Remember My favour upon you and your mother: how I supported you with the holy spirit[260] so you spoke to people in 'your' infancy and adulthood. How I taught you writing, wisdom, the Torah, and the Gospel. How you moulded a bird from clay—by My Will—and breathed into it and it became a 'real' bird—by My Will. How you healed the blind and the lepers—by My Will. How you brought the dead to life—by My Will. How I prevented the Children of Israel from harming you when you came to them with clear proofs and the disbelievers among them said, "This is nothing but pure magic." 111. And how I inspired the disciples, "Believe in Me and My messenger!" They declared, "We believe and bear witness that we fully submit 'to Allah'."[261]

Miracle of the Table

112. 'Remember' when the disciples asked, "O Jesus, son of Mary! Would your Lord be willing to send down to us a table spread with food from heaven?" Jesus answered, "Fear Allah if you are 'truly' believers." 113. They said, "We 'only' wish to eat from it to reassure our hearts, to verify you are indeed truthful to us, and to become its witnesses."

---

260 i.e., the angel Gabriel.
261 lit., Muslims.

114. Jesus, son of Mary, prayed, "O Allah, our Lord! Send us from heaven a table spread with food as a feast for us—the first and last of us—and as a sign from You. Provide for us! You are indeed the Best Provider." **115.** Allah answered, "I am sending it down to you. But whoever among you denies afterwards will be subjected to a torment I have never inflicted on anyone of My creation."

Jesus Denying Claim to Divinity

116. And ˹on Judgment Day˺ Allah will say, "O Jesus, son of Mary! Did you ever ask the people to worship you and your mother as gods besides Allah?" He will answer, "Glory be to You! How could I ever say what I had no right to say? If I had said such a thing, you would have certainly known it. You know what is ˹hidden˺ within me, but I do not know what is within You. Indeed, You ˹alone˺ are the Knower of all unseen. **117.** I never told them anything except what You ordered me to say: "Worship Allah—my Lord and your Lord!" And I was witness over them as long as I remained among them. But when You took me,[262] You were the Witness over them—and You are a Witness over all things. **118.** If You punish them, they belong to You after all.[263] But if You forgive them, You are surely the Almighty, All-Wise." **119.** Allah will declare, "This is the Day when ˹only˺ the faithful will benefit from their faithfulness. Theirs are Gardens under which rivers flow, to stay there for ever and ever. Allah is pleased with them and they are pleased with Him. That is the ultimate triumph." **120.** To Allah ˹alone˺ belongs the kingdom of the heavens and the earth and everything within. And He is Most Capable of everything.

---

262 This refers to the ascension of Jesus Christ. *See* footnote for 3:54.
263 i.e., as Your creation, they cannot escape the punishment.

6. Cattle (Al-An'âm)

In the Name of Allah—the Most Compassionate, Most Merciful

Rejecting the Almighty

1. All praise is for Allah Who created the heavens and the earth and made darkness and light.[264] Yet the disbelievers set up equals to their Lord ˹in worship˺. 2. He is the One Who created you from clay,[265] then appointed a term ˹for your death˺ and another known only to Him ˹for your resurrection˺—yet you continue to doubt! 3. He is the Only True God in the heavens and the earth. He knows whatever you conceal and whatever you reveal, and knows whatever you do.

Taking Allah's Signs Lightly

4. Whenever a sign comes to them from their Lord, they turn away from it. 5. They have indeed rejected the truth when it came to them, so they will soon face the consequences of their ridicule.

Fate of the Deniers

6. Have they not seen how many ˹disbelieving˺ peoples We destroyed before them? We had made them more established in the land than you. We sent down abundant rain for them and made rivers flow at their feet. Then We destroyed them for their sins and replaced them with other peoples.

Demanding Written Scripture[266]

7. Had We sent down to you ˹O Prophet˺ a revelation in writing and they were to touch it with their own hands, the disbelievers would still have said, "This is nothing but pure magic!"

Demanding to See an Angel

8. They say, "Why has no ˹visible˺ angel come with him?" Had We sent down an angel, the matter would have certainly been settled ˹at once˺,[267] and they would have never been given more time ˹to repent˺.

---

264 "Light" is always used in the Quran in the singular (*nûr*), whereas "darkness" is used in the plural (*ẓulumât*). *Nûr* is usually used in a metaphorical sense to refer to true guidance, whereas *ẓulumât* refers to different forms of misguidance.
265 i.e., created your father, Adam, from clay. Some scholars suggest that if we examine all the minerals found in the earth (potassium, nitrogen, and carbon), we find that these are the same minerals that make up our body. Furthermore when we die, our bodies are absorbed back into the ground. And when we are resurrected, we will be resurrected from the ground (*see* 20:55).
266 Similar to the Tablets of Moses.
267 i.e., they would have been destroyed immediately upon denying the angel.

6. Al-An'âm

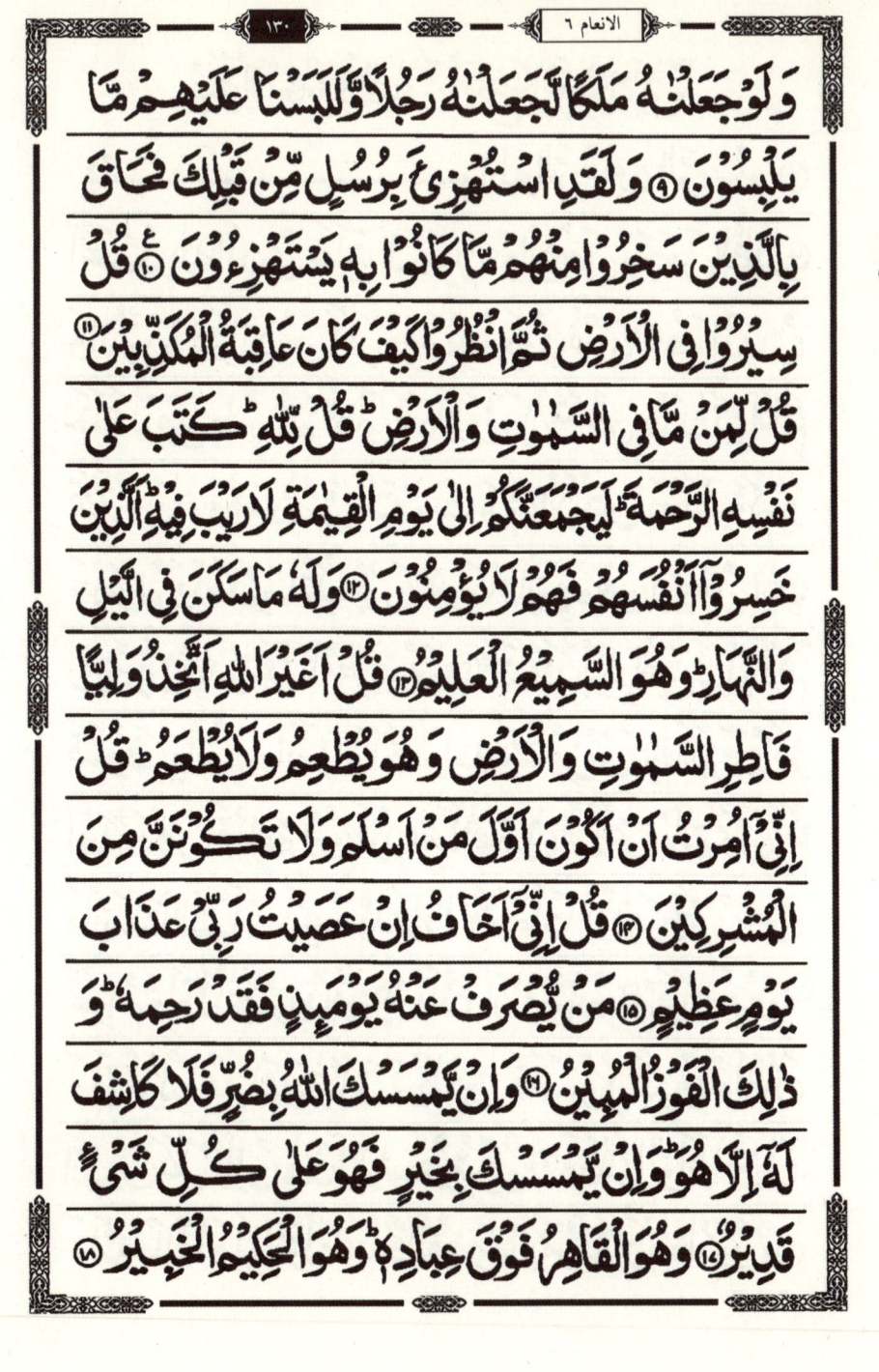

9. And if We had sent an angel, We would have certainly made it ˹assume the form of˺ a man—leaving them more confused than they already are.

Fate of the Ridiculers

10. ˹Other˺ messengers had already been ridiculed before you ˹O Prophet˺, but those who mocked them were overtaken by what they used to ridicule. 11. Say, "Travel throughout the land and see the fate of the deniers."

Allah Almighty

12. Ask ˹them, O Prophet˺, "To whom belongs everything in the heavens and the earth?" Say, "To Allah!" He has taken upon Himself to be Merciful. He will certainly gather ˹all of˺ you together for the Day of Judgment—about which there is no doubt. But those who have ruined themselves will never believe. 13. To Him belongs whatever exists in the day and night. And He is the All-Hearing, All-Knowing.

Allah Is the Guardian

14. Say, ˹O Prophet,˺ "Will I take any guardian other than Allah, the Originator of the heavens and the earth, Who provides for all and is not in need of provision?" Say, "I have been commanded to be the first to submit and not be one of the polytheists." 15. Say, "I truly fear—if I were to disobey my Lord—the torment of a tremendous Day." 16. Whoever is spared the torment of that Day will have certainly been shown Allah's mercy. And that is the absolute triumph.

Allah Reigns Supreme

17. If Allah touches you with harm, none can undo it except Him. And if He touches you with a blessing, He is Most Capable of everything. 18. He reigns supreme over His creation. And He is the All-Wise, All-Aware.

6. Al-An'âm

Allah Is the Best Witness

19. Ask ˹them, O Prophet˺, "Who is the best witness?" Say, "Allah is! He is a Witness between me and you. And this Quran has been revealed to me so that, with it, I may warn you and whoever it reaches. Do you ˹pagans˺ testify that there are other gods besides Allah?" ˹Then˺ say, "I will never testify ˹to this˺!" ˹And˺ say, "There is only One God. And I totally reject whatever ˹idols˺ you associate with Him."

Recognizing the Prophet

20. Those to whom We gave the Scripture recognize him ˹to be a true prophet˺ as they recognize their own children. Those who have ruined themselves will never believe. **21.** Who does more wrong than those who fabricate lies against Allah or deny His signs? Indeed, the wrongdoers will never succeed.

The Polytheists

22. ˹Consider˺ the Day We will gather them all together then ask those who associated others ˹with Allah in worship˺, "Where are those gods you used to claim?" **23.** Their only argument will be: "By Allah, our Lord! We were never polytheists." **24.** See how they will lie about themselves and how those ˹gods˺ they fabricated will fail them!

Disbelievers Turning Away

25. There are some of them who ˹pretend to˺ listen to your recitation ˹of the Quran˺, but We have cast veils over their hearts—leaving them unable to comprehend it—and deafness in their ears. Even if they were to see every sign, they still would not believe in them. The disbelievers would ˹even˺ come to argue with you, saying, "This ˹Quran˺ is nothing but ancient fables!" **26.** They turn others away from the Prophet and distance themselves as well. They ruin none but themselves, yet they fail to perceive it.

6. Al-An'âm

Horrified by the Fire

27. If only you could see when they will be detained before the Fire! They will cry, "Oh! If only we could be sent back, we would never deny the signs of our Lord and we would ˹surely˺ be of the believers." **28.** But no! ˹They only say this˺ because the truth they used to hide will become all too clear to them. Even if they were to be sent back, they would certainly revert to what they were forbidden. Indeed they are liars!

Deniers of the Hereafter

29. They insisted, "There is nothing beyond this worldly life and we will never be resurrected." **30.** But if only you could see when they will be detained before their Lord! He will ask ˹them˺, "Is this ˹Hereafter˺ not the truth?" They will cry, "Absolutely, by our Lord!" He will say, "Then taste the punishment for your disbelief." **31.** Losers indeed are those who deny the meeting with Allah until the Hour takes them by surprise, then they will cry, "Woe to us for having ignored this!" They will bear ˹the burden of˺ their sins on their backs. Evil indeed is their burden!

Fleeting Enjoyment

32. This worldly life is no more than play and amusement, but far better is the ˹eternal˺ Home of the Hereafter for those mindful ˹of Allah˺. Will you not then understand?

Not the First Rejected Prophet

33. We certainly know that what they say grieves you ˹O Prophet˺. It is not your honesty they question—it is Allah's signs that the wrongdoers deny. **34.** Indeed, messengers before you were rejected but patiently endured rejection and persecution until Our help came to them. And Allah's promise ˹to help˺ is never broken. And you have already received some of the narratives of these messengers.

6. Al-An'âm

Disbelievers, No Matter What

35. If you find their denial unbearable, then build—if you can—a tunnel through the earth or stairs to the sky to bring them a ˹more compelling˺ sign. Had Allah so willed, He could have guided them all. So do not be one of those ignorant ˹of this fact˺.

Deaf to the Truth

36. Only the attentive will respond ˹to your call˺. As for the dead, Allah will raise them up, then to Him they will ˹all˺ be returned. **37.** They ask, "Why has no ˹other˺ sign been sent down to him from his Lord?" Say, ˹O Prophet,˺ "Allah certainly has the power to send down a sign"—though most of them do not know.

The Animal Kingdom

38. All living beings roaming the earth and winged birds soaring in the sky are communities like yourselves.[268] We have left nothing out of the Record.[269] Then to their Lord they will be gathered all together.

Guidance Is from Allah Only

39. Those who deny Our signs are ˹wilfully˺ deaf and dumb—lost in darkness. Allah leaves whoever He wills to stray and guides whoever He wills to the Straight Way.

Allah Alone Removes Hardships

40. Ask ˹them, O Prophet˺, "Imagine if you were overwhelmed by Allah's torment or the Hour—would you call upon any other than Allah ˹for help˺? ˹Answer me˺ if your claims are true! **41.** No! He is the only One you would call. And if He willed, He could remove the affliction that made you invoke Him. Only then will you forget whatever you associate with Him ˹in worship˺."

Deniers' Gradual Destruction

42. Indeed, We have sent messengers before you ˹O Prophet˺ to other people who We put through suffering and adversity ˹for their denial˺, so perhaps they would be humbled. **43.** Why did they not humble themselves when We made them suffer? Instead, their

---

268 Allah has created living beings (like animals, birds, and fish) just like He created human beings. He provides for all and is merciful to all. They all belong to communities and have their own systems of living.

269 The Record refers to the Preserved Tablet (*Al-Lawḥ Al-Maḥfûẓ*) in which Allah has written the destiny of His entire creation.

hearts were hardened, and Satan made their misdeeds appealing to them. 44. When they became oblivious to warnings, We showered them with everything they desired. But just as they became prideful of what they were given, We seized them by surprise, then they instantly fell into despair! 45. So the wrongdoers were utterly uprooted. And all praise is for Allah—Lord of all worlds.

Only Allah Can Relieve Affliction

46. Ask ˹them, O Prophet˺, "Imagine if Allah were to take away your hearing or sight, or seal your hearts—who else other than Allah could restore it?" See ˹O Prophet˺ how We vary the signs, yet they still turn away. 47. Ask, "Imagine if Allah's punishment were to overwhelm you with or without warning—who would be destroyed other than the wrongdoers?"

The Messengers' Duty

48. We have sent messengers only as deliverers of good news and as warners. Whoever believes and does good, there will be no fear for them, nor will they grieve. 49. But those who deny Our signs will be afflicted with punishment for their rebelliousness.

No More than a Prophet

50. Say, ˹O Prophet,˺ "I do not say to you that I possess Allah's treasuries or know the unseen, nor do I claim to be an angel. I only follow what is revealed to me." Say, "Are those blind ˹to the truth˺ equal to those who can see? Will you not then reflect?"

The Quran as a Warning

51. Warn with this ˹Quran˺ those who are awed by the prospect of being gathered before their Lord—when they will have no protector or intercessor besides Him—so perhaps they will be mindful ˹of Him˺.

135   6. Al-An'âm

Influential Meccans vs. Poor Believers[270]

52. ˹O Prophet!˺ Do not dismiss those ˹poor believers˺ who invoke their Lord morning and evening, seeking His pleasure.[271] You are not accountable for them whatsoever, nor are they accountable for you. So do not dismiss them, or you will be one of the wrongdoers. 53. In this way We have tested some by means of others, so those ˹disbelievers˺ may say, "Has Allah favoured these ˹poor believers˺ out of all of us?" Does Allah not best recognize the grateful? 54. When the believers in Our revelations come to you, say, "Peace be upon you! Your Lord has taken upon Himself to be Merciful. Whoever among you commits evil ignorantly ˹or recklessly˺ then repents afterwards and mends their ways, then Allah is truly All-Forgiving, Most Merciful." 55. This is how We make Our signs clear, so the way of the wicked may become distinct.

Only One God

56. Say, ˹O Prophet,˺ "I have been forbidden to worship those you invoke besides Allah." Say, "I will not follow your desires, for I then would certainly be astray and not one of those ˹rightly˺ guided."

Desperate to Be Destroyed

57. Say, ˹O Prophet,˺ "Indeed, I stand on a clear proof from my Lord—yet you have denied it. That ˹torment˺ you seek to hasten is not within my power. It is only Allah Who decides ˹its time˺. He declares the truth. And He is the Best of Judges." 58. Say ˹also˺, "If what you seek to hasten were within my power, the matter between us would have already been settled. But Allah knows the wrongdoers best."

---

270 Some of the influential leaders of Mecca asked the Prophet (ﷺ) to send poor Muslims away if he ever wanted these elites to sit and listen to his message. These verses were revealed commanding the Prophet (ﷺ) to keep the company of the poor and not alienate them.
271 lit., seeking His Face.

6. Al-An'âm

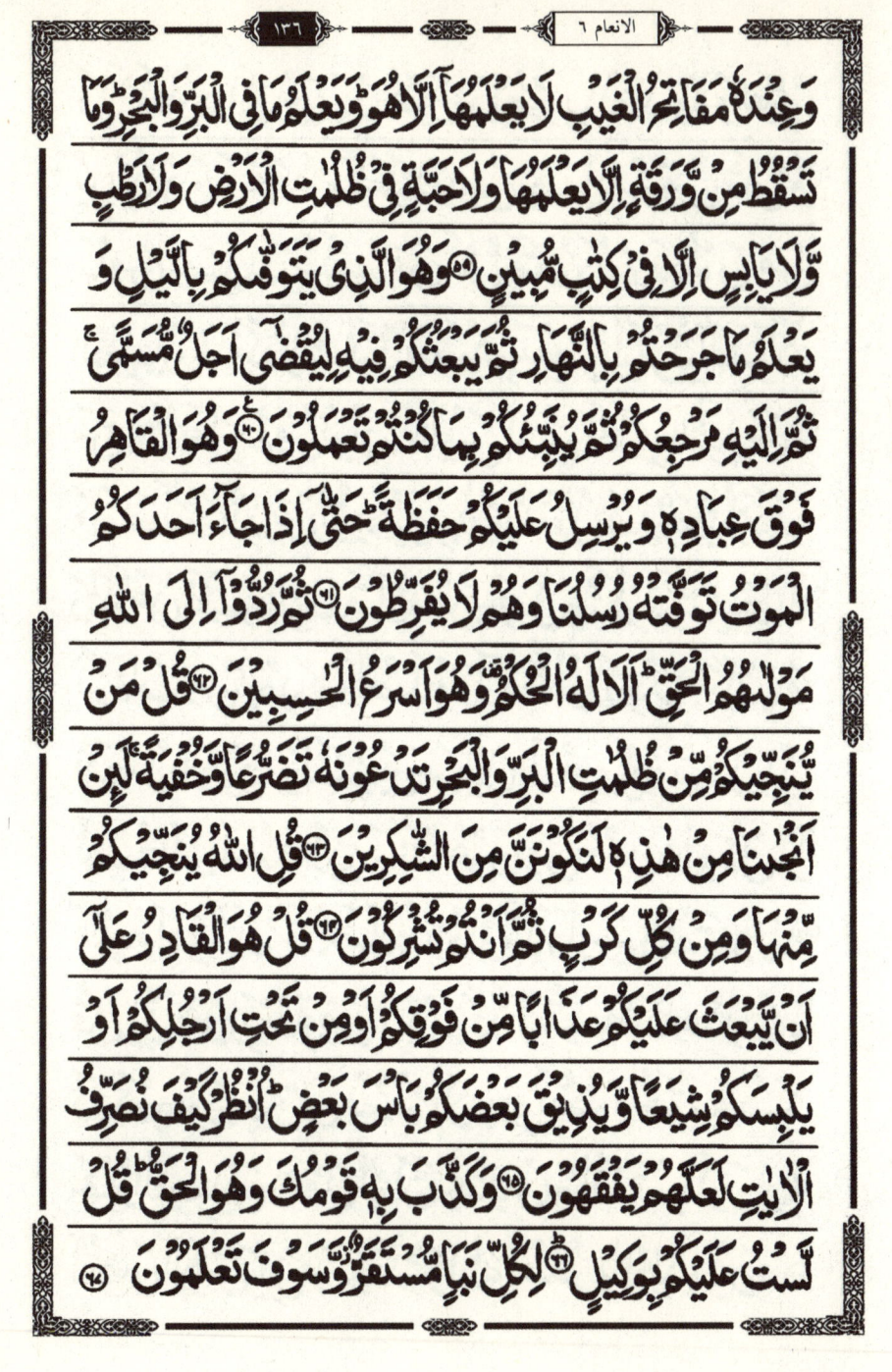

Allah's Infinite Knowledge

59. With Him are the keys of the unseen—no one knows them except Him.[272] And He knows what is in the land and sea. Not even a leaf falls without His knowledge, nor a grain in the darkness of the earth or anything—green or dry—but is ˹written˺ in a perfect Record.[273]

Sleep: The Twin Brother of Death

60. He is the One Who calls back your souls by night and knows what you do by day, then revives you daily to complete your appointed term. To Him is your ˹ultimate˺ return, then He will inform you of what you used to do. **61.** He reigns supreme over all of His creation, and sends recording-angels, watching over you. When death comes to any of you, Our angels take their soul, never neglecting this duty. **62.** Then they are ˹all˺ returned to Allah—their True Master. Judgment is His ˹alone˺. And He is the Swiftest Reckoner.

Allah's Power

63. Say, ˹O Prophet,˺ "Who rescues you from the darkest times on land and at sea? He ˹alone˺ you call upon with humility, openly and secretly: "If You rescue us from this, we will be ever grateful." **64.** Say, "˹Only˺ Allah rescues you from this and any other distress, yet you associate others with Him ˹in worship˺." **65.** Say, "He ˹alone˺ has the power to unleash upon you a torment from above or below you or split you into ˹conflicting˺ factions and make you taste the violence of one another." See how We vary the signs, so perhaps they will comprehend.

Deniers of the Truth

66. Still your people ˹O Prophet˺ have rejected this ˹Quran˺, although it is the truth. Say, "I am not a keeper over you." **67.** Every ˹destined˺ matter has a ˹set˺ time to transpire. And you will soon come to know.

---

272 The five keys of the unseen are mentioned in 31:34.
273 *See* footnote for 6:38.

137   6. Al-An'âm

Mockers of the Quran

68. And when you come across those who ridicule Our revelations, do not sit with them unless they engage in a different topic. Should Satan make you forget, then once you remember, do not ˹continue to˺ sit with the wrongdoing people. **69.** Those mindful ˹of Allah˺ will not be accountable for those ˹who ridicule it˺ whatsoever—their duty is to advise, so perhaps the ridiculers will abstain.

Way to Salvation

70. And leave those who take this[274] faith ˹of Islam˺ as mere play and amusement and are deluded by ˹their˺ worldly life. Yet remind them by this ˹Quran˺, so no one should be ruined for their misdeeds. They will have no protector or intercessor other than Allah. Even if they were to offer every ˹possible˺ ransom, none will be accepted from them. Those are the ones who will be ruined for their misdeeds. They will have a boiling drink and painful punishment for their disbelief.

Almighty Allah

71. Ask ˹them, O Prophet˺, "Should we invoke, other than Allah, those ˹idols˺ which cannot benefit or harm us, and turn back to disbelief after Allah has guided us? ˹If we do so, we will be˺ like those disoriented by devils in the wilderness, while their companions call them to guidance, ˹saying˺, 'Come to us!' Say, ˹O Prophet,˺ "Allah's guidance is the ˹only˺ true guidance. And we are commanded to submit to the Lord of all worlds, **72.** establish prayer, and be mindful of Him. To Him you will all be gathered together. **73.** He is the One Who created the heavens and the earth in truth. On the Day ˹of Judgment˺ He will say, 'Be!' And there will be!

---

274   lit., their faith (which they are supposed to follow).

His command is truth. All authority is His ʿaloneʾ[275] on the Day the Trumpet will be blown.[276] He is the Knower of all—seen or unseen. And He is the All-Wise, All-Aware."

Abraham Corrects His Father

74. And ʿrememberʾ when Abraham said to his father, Âzar, "Do you take idols as gods? It is clear to me that you and your people are entirely misguided."

Abraham Refutes Celestial Worship

75. We also showed Abraham the wonders of the heavens and the earth, so he would be sure in faith. 76. When the night grew dark upon him, he saw a star and said, "This is my Lord!" But when it set, he said, "I do not love things that set." 77. Then when he saw the moon rising, he said, "This one is my Lord!" But when it disappeared, he said, "If my Lord does not guide me, I will certainly be one of the misguided people." 78. Then when he saw the sun shining, he said, "This must be my Lord—it is the greatest!" But again when it set, he declared, "O my people! I totally reject whatever you associate ʿwith Allah in worshipʾ. 79. I have turned my face towards the One Who has originated the heavens and the earth—being upright—and I am not one of the polytheists."

Abraham Debates His People

80. And his people argued with him. He responded, "Are you arguing with me about Allah, while He has guided me? I am not afraid of whatever ʿidolsʾ you associate with Him—ʿnone can harm me,ʾ unless my Lord so wills. My Lord encompasses everything in ʿHisʾ knowledge. Will you not be mindful? 81. And how should I fear your associate-gods, while you have no fear in associating ʿothersʾ with Allah—a practice He has never authorized? Which side has more right to security? ʿTell meʾ if you really know!"

---

275 Allah grants authority to some of His servants in this world, but none will have authority on Judgment Day except Him. *See* 3:26.
276 On the Day of Judgment, the Trumpet will be blown by an angel—causing all to die. When it is blown a second time, everyone will be raised from the dead for judgment (*see* 39:68).

139   6. Al-An'âm

82. It is ʿonlyʾ those who are faithful and do not tarnish their faith with falsehood[277] who are guaranteed security and are ʿrightlyʾ guided. **83.** This was the argument We gave Abraham against his people. We elevate in rank whoever We please. Surely your Lord is All-Wise, All-Knowing.

Abraham and Other Noble Prophets

84. And We blessed him with Isaac and Jacob. We guided them all as We previously guided Noah and those among his descendants: David, Solomon, Job, Joseph, Moses, and Aaron. This is how We reward the good-doers. **85.** Likewise, ʿWe guidedʾ Zachariah, John, Jesus, and Elias, who were all of the righteous. **86.** ʿWe also guidedʾ Ishmael, Elisha, Jonah, and Lot, favouring each over other people ʿof their timeʾ. **87.** And ʿWe favouredʾ some of their forefathers, their descendants, and their brothers. We chose them and guided them to the Straight Path.

Prophetic Guidance

88. This is Allah's guidance with which He guides whoever He wills of His servants. Had they associated others with Him ʿin worshipʾ, their ʿgoodʾ deeds would have been wasted. **89.** Those were the ones to whom We gave the Scripture, wisdom, and prophethood. But if these ʿpagansʾ disbelieve in this ʿmessageʾ, then We have already entrusted it to a people who will never disbelieve in it.[278] **90.** These ʿprophetsʾ were ʿrightlyʾ guided by Allah, so follow their guidance. Say, "I ask no reward of you for this ʿQuranʾ—it is a reminder to the whole world."

---

277 i.e., associating false gods in worship with the Almighty.
278 i.e., the companions of the Prophet (ﷺ).

6. Al-An'âm — 140

بِسْمِ

Scriptures Denied

91. And they[279] have not shown Allah His proper reverence when they said, "Allah has revealed nothing to any human being." Say, ˹O Prophet,˺ "Who then revealed the Book brought forth by Moses as a light and guidance for people, which you split into separate sheets—revealing some and hiding much? You have been taught ˹through this Quran˺ what neither you nor your forefathers knew." Say, ˹O Prophet,˺ "Allah ˹revealed it˺!" Then leave them to amuse themselves with falsehood.

Quran for All

92. This is a blessed Book which We have revealed—confirming what came before it—so you may warn the Mother of Cities[280] and everyone around it. Those who believe in the Hereafter ˹truly˺ believe in it and guard their prayers.

Fate of the Wicked

93. Who does more wrong than the one who fabricates lies against Allah or claims, "I have received revelations!"—although nothing was revealed to them—or the one who says, "I can reveal the like of Allah's revelations!"? If you ˹O Prophet˺ could only see the wrongdoers in the throes of death while the angels are stretching out their hands ˹saying˺, "Give up your souls! Today you will be rewarded with the torment of disgrace for telling lies about Allah and for being arrogant towards His revelations!" **94.** ˹Today˺ you have come back to Us all alone as We created you the first time—leaving behind everything We have provided you with. We do not see your intercessors with you—those you claimed were Allah's partners ˹in worship˺. All your ties have been broken and all your claims have let you down."

---

279 Some Jews.
280 "The Mother of Cities" is an honorary title given to the City of Mecca because of its great religious significance as the home of Allah's first house of worship ever built on earth, and perhaps because of its central location as well.

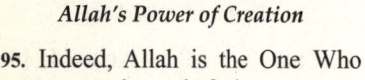

6. Al-An'âm

Allah's Power of Creation

95. Indeed, Allah is the One Who causes seeds and fruit stones to sprout. He brings forth the living from the dead and the dead from the living. That is Allah! How can you then be deluded ˹from the truth˺? **96.** He causes the dawn to break, and has made the night for rest and ˹made˺ the sun and the moon ˹to travel˺ with precision. That is the design of the Almighty, All-Knowing. **97.** And He is the One Who has made the stars as your guide through the darkness of land and sea. We have already made the signs clear for people who know. **98.** And He is the One Who originated you all from a single soul,[281] then assigned you a place to live and another to ˹be laid to˺ rest. We have already made the signs clear for people who comprehend. **99.** And He is the One Who sends down rain from the sky—causing all kinds of plants to grow—producing green stalks from which We bring forth clustered grain. And from palm trees come clusters of dates hanging within reach. ˹There are˺ also gardens of grapevines, olives, and pomegranates, similar ˹in shape˺ but dissimilar ˹in taste˺. Look at their fruit as it yields and ripens! Indeed, in these are signs for people who believe.

Allah Has No Children

100. Yet they associate the jinn[282] with Allah ˹in worship˺, even though He created them, and they falsely attribute to Him sons[283] and daughters[284] out of ignorance. Glorified and Exalted is He above what they claim! **101.** ˹He is˺ the Originator of the heavens and earth. How could He have children when He has no mate? He created all things and has ˹perfect˺ knowledge of everything.

---

281 i.e., Adam (☺).
282 Jinn are another creation of Allah, made of "smokeless fire," and inhabit a realm parallel to our own. Like us, they have free will and can choose guidance or disobedience.
283 i.e., "Jesus" in Christian belief.
284 i.e., "the angels" in pre-Islamic Arab tradition.

6. Al-An'âm

Worship Allah Alone

102. That is Allah—your Lord! There is no god ˹worthy of worship˺ except Him. ˹He is˺ the Creator of all things, so worship Him ˹alone˺. And He is the Maintainer of everything. **103.** No vision can encompass Him, but He encompasses all vision. For He is the Most Subtle, All-Aware.[285]

Call to Humanity

104. Indeed, there have come to you insights from your Lord. So whoever chooses to see, it is for their own good. But whoever chooses to be blind, it is to their own loss. And I am not a keeper over you. **105.** And so We vary our signs to the extent that they will say, "You have studied ˹previous scriptures˺,"[286] and We make this ˹Quran˺ clear for people who know.

Guidance Is from Allah Alone

106. ˹O Prophet!˺ Follow what is revealed to you from your Lord—there is no god ˹worthy of worship˺ except Him—and turn away from the polytheists. **107.** Had Allah willed, they would not have been polytheists. We have not appointed you as their keeper, nor are you their maintainer.

Allah Is the Judge

108. ˹O believers!˺ Do not insult what they invoke besides Allah or they will insult Allah spitefully out of ignorance. This is how We have made each people's deeds appealing to them. Then to their Lord is their return, and He will inform them of what they used to do.

Signs of No Use

109. They swear by Allah their most solemn oaths that if a sign were to come to them, they would certainly believe in it. Say, ˹O Prophet,˺ "Signs are only with Allah." What will make you ˹believers˺ realize that even if a sign were to come to them, they still would not believe? **110.** We turn their hearts and eyes away ˹from the truth˺ as they refused to believe at first, leaving them to wander blindly in their defiance.

---

285 No one is able to see Allah in this world, but there is extensive evidence in the Quran and the teachings of the Prophet (ﷺ) that the believers will be able to see their Lord on the Day of Judgment.

286 Allegations have always been made that the Prophet (ﷺ) copied the Quran from the Bible, mostly because of similar narratives in both Scriptures (such as the stories of Adam, Joseph, Moses, and others). Historically, the Bible was not translated into Arabic until centuries after the Prophet (ﷺ). Even if an Arabic translation of the Bible existed at his time, he (ﷺ) could not have copied it because he could not read or write. From an Islamic point of view, similarities stem from the fact that both scriptures came originally from the same source—divine revelation. For more details, *see* the Introduction.

111. Even if We had sent them the angels, made the dead speak to them, and assembled before their own eyes every sign ʿthey demandedʾ, they still would not have believed—unless Allah so willed. But most of them are ignorant ʿof thisʾ.

The Deception

112. And so We have made for every prophet enemies—devilish humans and jinn—whispering to one another with elegant words of deception. Had it been your Lord's Will, they would not have done such a thing. So leave them and their deceit, **113.** so that the hearts of those who disbelieve in the Hereafter may be receptive to it, be pleased with it, and be persistent in their evil pursuits.

The Perfect Book

114. ʿSay, O Prophet,ʾ "Should I seek a judge other than Allah while He is the One Who has revealed for you the Book ʿwith the truthʾ perfectly explained?" Those who were given the Scripture know that it has been revealed ʿto youʾ from your Lord in truth. So do not be one of those who doubt. **115.** The Word of your Lord has been perfected in truth and justice. None can change His Words. And He is the All-Hearing, All-Knowing.

Most Are Deviant

116. ʿO Prophet!ʾ If you were to obey most of those on earth, they would lead you away from Allah's Way. They follow nothing but assumptions and do nothing but lie. **117.** Indeed, your Lord knows best who has strayed from His Way and who is ʿrightlyʾ guided.

Lawful and Unlawful Meat

118. So eat only of what is slaughtered in Allah's Name if you truly believe in His revelations.

6. Al-An'âm

وَمَا لَكُمْ أَلَّا تَأْكُلُوا مِمَّا ذُكِرَ اسْمُ اللَّهِ عَلَيْهِ وَقَدْ فَصَّلَ لَكُم مَّا حَرَّمَ عَلَيْكُمْ إِلَّا مَا اضْطُرِرْتُمْ إِلَيْهِ ۗ وَإِنَّ كَثِيرًا لَّيُضِلُّونَ بِأَهْوَائِهِم بِغَيْرِ عِلْمٍ ۗ إِنَّ رَبَّكَ هُوَ أَعْلَمُ بِالْمُعْتَدِينَ ۝ وَذَرُوا ظَاهِرَ الْإِثْمِ وَبَاطِنَهُ ۚ إِنَّ الَّذِينَ يَكْسِبُونَ الْإِثْمَ سَيُجْزَوْنَ بِمَا كَانُوا يَقْتَرِفُونَ ۝ وَلَا تَأْكُلُوا مِمَّا لَمْ يُذْكَرِ اسْمُ اللَّهِ عَلَيْهِ وَإِنَّهُ لَفِسْقٌ ۗ وَإِنَّ الشَّيَاطِينَ لَيُوحُونَ إِلَىٰ أَوْلِيَائِهِمْ لِيُجَادِلُوكُمْ ۖ وَإِنْ أَطَعْتُمُوهُمْ إِنَّكُمْ لَمُشْرِكُونَ ۝ أَوَمَن كَانَ مَيْتًا فَأَحْيَيْنَاهُ وَجَعَلْنَا لَهُ نُورًا يَمْشِي بِهِ فِي النَّاسِ كَمَن مَّثَلُهُ فِي الظُّلُمَاتِ لَيْسَ بِخَارِجٍ مِّنْهَا ۚ كَذَٰلِكَ زُيِّنَ لِلْكَافِرِينَ مَا كَانُوا يَعْمَلُونَ ۝ وَكَذَٰلِكَ جَعَلْنَا فِي كُلِّ قَرْيَةٍ أَكَابِرَ مُجْرِمِيهَا لِيَمْكُرُوا فِيهَا ۖ وَمَا يَمْكُرُونَ إِلَّا بِأَنفُسِهِمْ وَمَا يَشْعُرُونَ ۝ وَإِذَا جَاءَتْهُمْ آيَةٌ قَالُوا لَن نُّؤْمِنَ حَتَّىٰ نُؤْتَىٰ مِثْلَ مَا أُوتِيَ رُسُلُ اللَّهِ ۘ اللَّهُ أَعْلَمُ حَيْثُ يَجْعَلُ رِسَالَتَهُ ۗ سَيُصِيبُ الَّذِينَ أَجْرَمُوا صَغَارٌ عِندَ اللَّهِ وَعَذَابٌ شَدِيدٌ بِمَا كَانُوا يَمْكُرُونَ ۝

119. Why should you not eat of what is slaughtered in Allah's Name when He has already explained to you what He has forbidden to you—except when compelled by necessity? Many 'deviants' certainly mislead others by their whims out of ignorance. Surely your Lord knows the transgressors best. 120. Shun all sin—open and secret. Indeed, those who commit sin will be punished for what they earn. 121. Do not eat of what is not slaughtered in Allah's Name. For that would certainly be 'an act of' disobedience. Surely the devils whisper to their 'human' associates to argue with you.[287] If you were to obey them, then you 'too' would be polytheists.

Metaphor for Believers and Disbelievers

122. Can those who had been dead, to whom We gave life and a light with which they can walk among people, be compared to those in complete darkness from which they can never emerge?[288] That is how the misdeeds of the disbelievers have been made appealing to them. 123. And so We have placed in every society the most wicked to conspire in it. Yet they plot only against themselves, but they fail to perceive it.

Craving Prophethood

124. Whenever a sign comes to them, they say, "We will never believe until we receive what Allah's messengers received." Allah knows best where to place His message. The wicked will soon be overwhelmed by humiliation from Allah and a severe punishment for their evil plots.

---

287 Because Muslims are allowed to eat the meat of animals slaughtered properly and not carrion, the pagans of Mecca used to argue, "Why are you only allowed to eat what you yourselves kill but not what Allah causes to die?"

288 The Quran often compares disbelief to death and blindness whereas belief is compared to life and the ability to see.

6. Al-An'âm

Open and Restricted Hearts

125. Whoever Allah wills to guide, He opens their heart to Islam.[289] But whoever He wills to leave astray, He makes their chest tight and constricted as if they were climbing up into the sky. This is how Allah dooms those who disbelieve. **126.** That is your Lord's Path—perfectly straight. We have already made the signs clear to those who are mindful. **127.** They will have the Home of Peace with their Lord, Who will be their Guardian because of what they used to do.

Humans and Jinn on Judgment Day

128. ˹Consider˺ the Day He will gather them ˹all˺ together and say, "O assembly of jinn! You misled humans in great numbers." And their human associates will say, "Our Lord! We benefited from each other's company,[290] but now we have reached the term which You appointed for us." ˹Then˺ He will say, "The Fire is your home, yours to stay in forever, except whoever Allah wills to spare."[291] Surely your Lord is All-Wise, All-Knowing. **129.** This is how We make the wrongdoers ˹destructive˺ allies of one another because of their misdeeds.

Confession of Evil Humans and Jinn

130. ˹Allah will ask,˺ "O assembly of jinn and humans! Did messengers not come from among you, proclaiming My revelations and warning you of the coming of this Day of yours?" They will say, "We confess against ourselves!" For they have been deluded by ˹their˺ worldly life. And they will testify against themselves that they were disbelievers.

---

289 Islam literally means 'submission to the Will of Allah.'
290 For example, the jinn helped humans with magic, while the jinn had a feeling of importance when they had a human following.
291 i.e., disobedient Muslims. They will be punished according to the severity of their sins, but eventually no Muslim will stay in Hell forever.

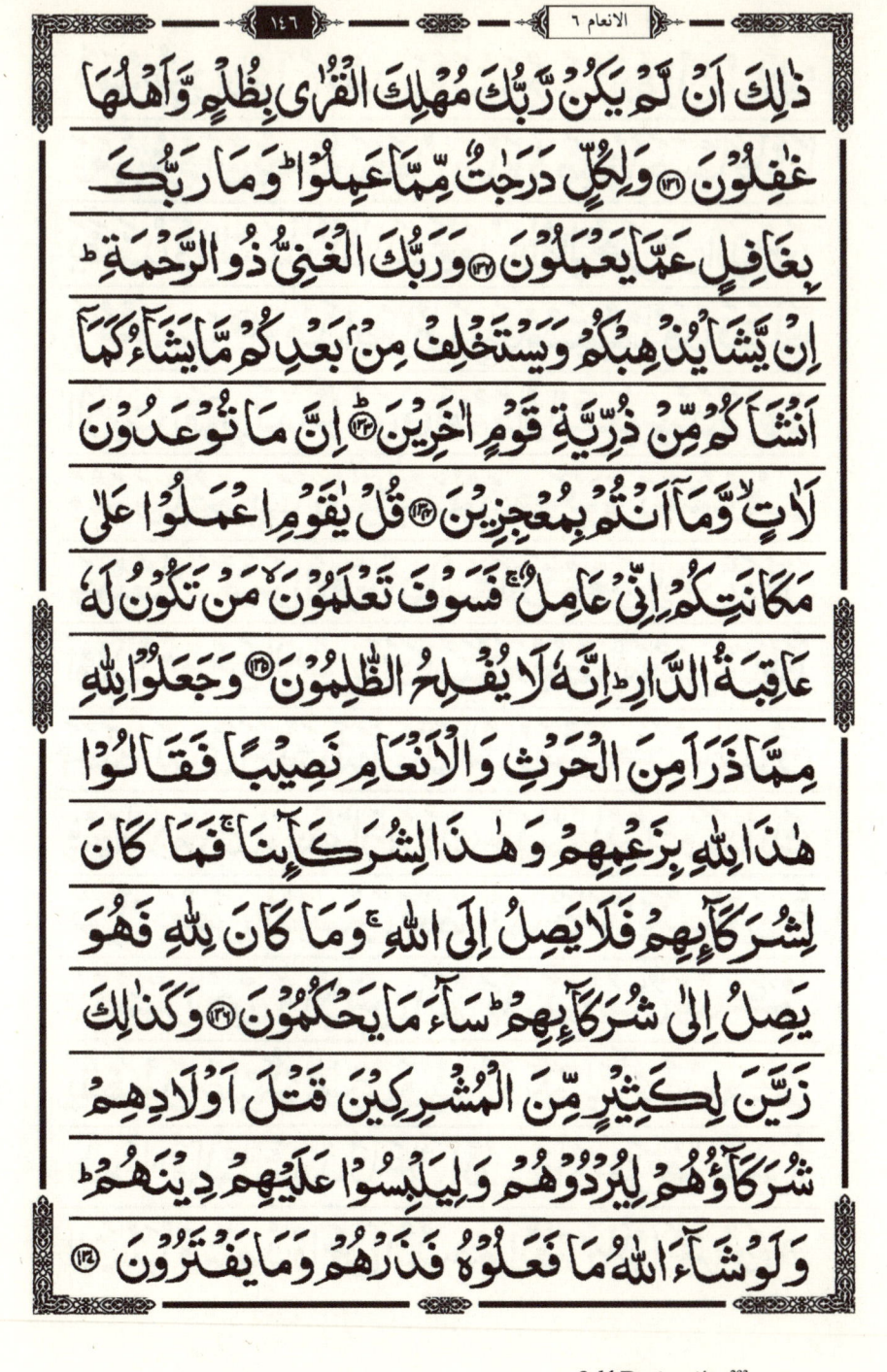

131. This 'sending of the messengers' is because your Lord would never destroy a society for their wrongdoing while its people are unaware 'of the truth'.

The Good and the Evil

132. They will each be assigned ranks according to their deeds. And your Lord is not unaware of what they do.

Allah Is Not in Need of His Creation

133. Your Lord is the Self-Sufficient, Full of Mercy. If He wills, He can do away with you and replace you with whoever He wills, just as He produced you from the offspring of other people. **134.** Indeed, what you have been promised will certainly come to pass. And you will have no escape.

Warning to Meccan Pagans

135. Say, 'O Prophet,' "O my people! Persist in your ways, for I 'too' will persist in mine. You will soon know who will fare best in the end. Indeed, the wrongdoers will never succeed."

Unfair Giving[292]

136. The pagans set aside for Allah a share of the crops and cattle He created, saying, "This 'portion' is for Allah," so they claim, "and this 'one' for our associate-gods." Yet the portion of their associate-gods is not shared with Allah while Allah's portion is shared with their associate-gods. What unfair judgment!

Self-Destruction[293]

137. Likewise, the pagans' evil associates have made it appealing to them to kill their own children— only leading to their destruction as well as confusion in their faith. Had it been Allah's Will, they would not have done such a thing. So leave them and their falsehood.

---

292 The pagans used to assign Allah a share of their property (as a charity to the poor) and another to their idols (as a fee to idol keepers). However, Allah's share always ended up in the pockets of the keepers, whereas the share of false gods was never donated to the poor.

293 Some pagan Arabs used to kill their own children (especially females) for fear of poverty. Others would vow to sacrifice a son if blessed with a certain number of sons.

147   6. Al-An'âm

Idols' Share in Cattle and Crops

138. They say, "These cattle and crops are reserved—none may eat them except those we permit," so they claim. Some other cattle are exempted from labour and others are not slaughtered in Allah's Name—falsely attributing lies to Him. He will repay them for their lies. **139.** They ˹also˺ say, "The offspring of this cattle is reserved for our males and forbidden to our females; but if it is stillborn, they may all share it." He will repay them for their falsehood. Surely He is All-Wise, All-Knowing.

Lost in Ignorance

140. Lost indeed are those who have murdered their own children foolishly out of ignorance and have forbidden what Allah has provided for them—falsely attributing lies to Allah. They have certainly strayed and are not ˹rightly˺ guided.

Allah's Bounties

141. He is the One Who produces gardens— both cultivated and wild[294]—and palm trees, crops of different flavours, olives, and pomegranates—similar ˹in shape˺, but dissimilar ˹in taste˺. Eat from the fruit they bear and pay the dues at harvest, but do not waste. Surely He does not like the wasteful.

Four Pairs of Cattle, Male and Female[295]

142. Some cattle are fit for labour, others are too small.[296] Eat of what Allah has provided for you and do not follow Satan's footsteps. Certainly, he is your sworn enemy.

---

294 Or trellised and untrellised.
295 These four pairs were the main domesticated cattle in Arabia at the time of revelation.
296 Strong cattle like camels and oxen can be used for labour, whereas smaller ones like goats and sheep are not suitable for labour but are good for their meat, milk, hide, etc.

6. Al-An'âm

143. ˹Allah has created˺ four pairs: a pair of sheep and a pair of goats—ask ˹them, O Prophet˺, "Has He forbidden ˹to you˺ the two males or the two females or what is in the wombs of the two females? Tell me with knowledge, if what you say is true."— **144.** and a pair of camels and a pair of oxen. Ask ˹them˺, "Has He forbidden ˹to you˺ the two males or the two females or what is in the wombs of the two females? Or were you present when Allah gave you this commandment?" Who does more wrong than those who fabricate lies against Allah to mislead others without ˹any˺ knowledge? Surely Allah does not guide the wrongdoing people.

Meat Forbidden to Muslims

145. Say, ˹O Prophet,˺ "I do not find in what has been revealed to me anything forbidden to eat except carrion, running blood, swine—which is impure—or a sinful offering in the name of any other than Allah. But if someone is compelled by necessity—neither driven by desire nor exceeding immediate need—then surely your Lord is All-Forgiving, Most Merciful."

Meat Forbidden to Jews

146. For those who are Jewish, We forbade every animal with undivided hoofs and the fat of oxen and sheep except what is joined to their backs or intestines or mixed with bone. In this way We rewarded them for their violations. And We are certainly truthful.

147. But if they deny you ˹O Prophet˺, say, "Your Lord is infinite in mercy, yet His punishment will not be averted from the wicked people."

Free Choice

148. The polytheists will argue, "Had it been Allah's Will, neither we nor our forefathers would have associated others with Him ˹in worship˺ or made anything unlawful." Likewise, those before them rejected the truth until they tasted Our punishment. Ask ˹them, O Prophet˺, "Do you have any knowledge that you can produce for us? Surely you follow nothing but ˹false˺ assumptions and you do nothing but lie."

149. Say, "Allah has the most conclusive argument. Had it been His Will, He would have easily imposed guidance upon all of you." **150.** Say, ˹O Prophet,˺ "Bring your witnesses who can testify that Allah has forbidden this." If they ˹falsely˺ testify, do not testify with them. And do not follow the desires of those who deny Our proofs, disbelieve in the Hereafter, and set up equals with their Lord.

Allah's Commandments

151. Say, ˹O Prophet,˺ "Come! Let me recite to you what your Lord has forbidden to you: do not associate others with Him ˹in worship˺. ˹Do not fail to˺ honour your parents. Do not kill your children for fear of poverty. We provide for you and for them. Do not come near indecencies, openly or secretly. Do not take a ˹human˺ life—made sacred by Allah—except with ˹legal˺ right.[297] This is what He has commanded you, so perhaps you will understand.

---

297 For example, in retaliation for intentional killing through legal channels.

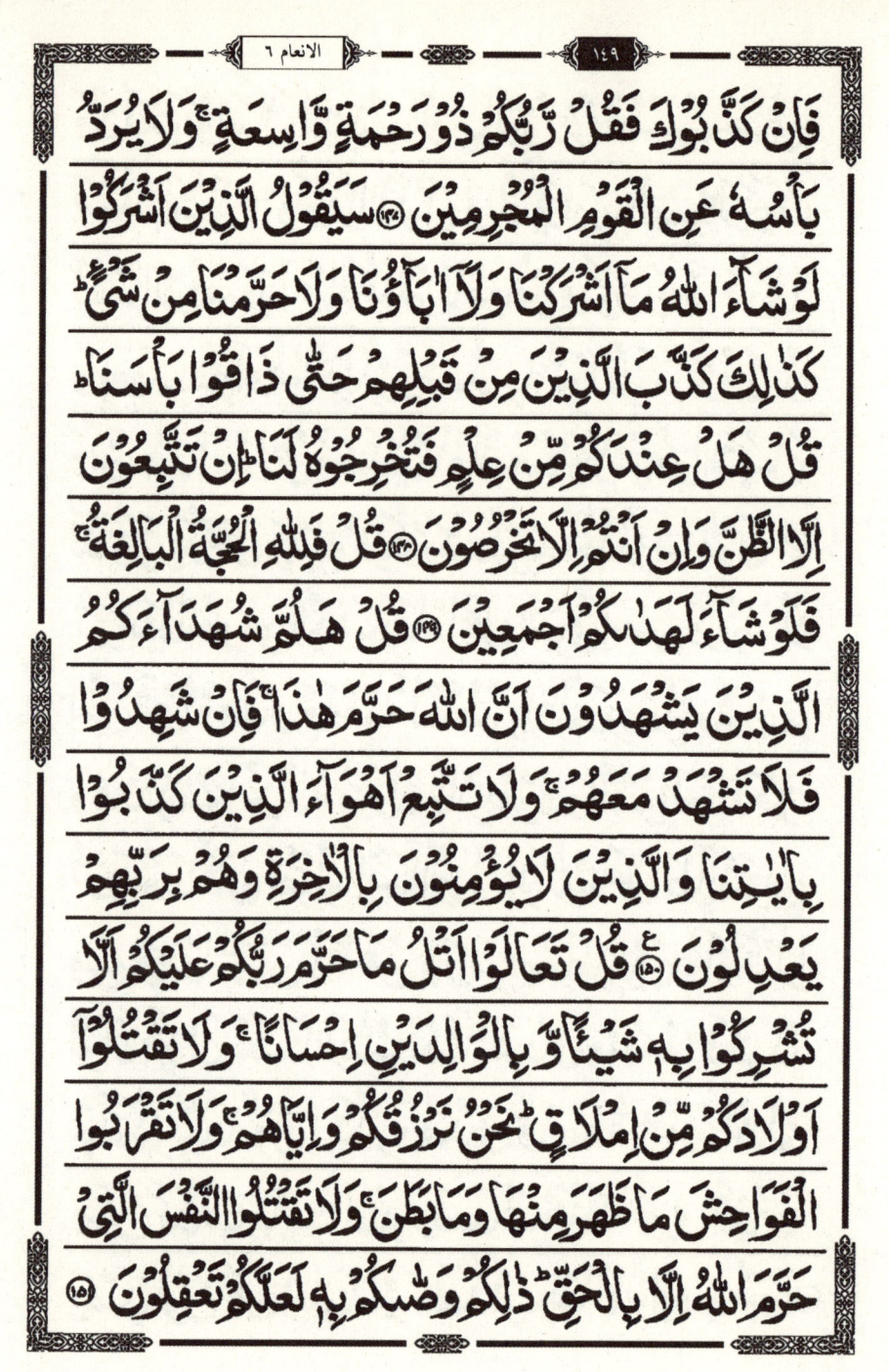

6. Al-An'âm — 150

وَلَا تَقْرَبُوا مَالَ الْيَتِيمِ إِلَّا بِالَّتِي هِيَ أَحْسَنُ حَتَّىٰ يَبْلُغَ أَشُدَّهُ وَأَوْفُوا الْكَيْلَ وَالْمِيزَانَ بِالْقِسْطِ لَا نُكَلِّفُ نَفْسًا إِلَّا وُسْعَهَا وَإِذَا قُلْتُمْ فَاعْدِلُوا وَلَوْ كَانَ ذَا قُرْبَىٰ وَبِعَهْدِ اللَّهِ أَوْفُوا ذَٰلِكُمْ وَصَّاكُم بِهِ لَعَلَّكُمْ تَذَكَّرُونَ ۝

وَأَنَّ هَٰذَا صِرَاطِي مُسْتَقِيمًا فَاتَّبِعُوهُ وَلَا تَتَّبِعُوا السُّبُلَ فَتَفَرَّقَ بِكُمْ عَن سَبِيلِهِ ذَٰلِكُمْ وَصَّاكُم بِهِ لَعَلَّكُمْ تَتَّقُونَ ۝

ثُمَّ آتَيْنَا مُوسَى الْكِتَابَ تَمَامًا عَلَى الَّذِي أَحْسَنَ وَتَفْصِيلًا لِّكُلِّ شَيْءٍ وَهُدًى وَرَحْمَةً لَّعَلَّهُم بِلِقَاءِ رَبِّهِمْ يُؤْمِنُونَ ۝

وَهَٰذَا كِتَابٌ أَنزَلْنَاهُ مُبَارَكٌ فَاتَّبِعُوهُ وَاتَّقُوا لَعَلَّكُمْ تُرْحَمُونَ ۝ أَن تَقُولُوا إِنَّمَا أُنزِلَ الْكِتَابُ عَلَىٰ طَائِفَتَيْنِ مِن قَبْلِنَا وَإِن كُنَّا عَن دِرَاسَتِهِمْ لَغَافِلِينَ ۝ أَوْ تَقُولُوا لَوْ أَنَّا أُنزِلَ عَلَيْنَا الْكِتَابُ لَكُنَّا أَهْدَىٰ مِنْهُمْ فَقَدْ جَاءَكُم بَيِّنَةٌ مِّن رَّبِّكُمْ وَهُدًى وَرَحْمَةٌ فَمَنْ أَظْلَمُ مِمَّن كَذَّبَ بِآيَاتِ اللَّهِ وَصَدَفَ عَنْهَا سَنَجْزِي الَّذِينَ يَصْدِفُونَ عَنْ آيَاتِنَا سُوءَ الْعَذَابِ بِمَا كَانُوا يَصْدِفُونَ ۝

---

152. And do not come near the wealth of the orphan—unless intending to enhance it—until they attain maturity. Give full measure and weigh with justice. We never require of any soul more than what it can afford. Whenever you speak,[298] maintain justice—even regarding a close relative. And fulfil your covenant with Allah. This is what He has commanded you, so perhaps you will be mindful. 153. Indeed, that is My Path—perfectly straight. So follow it and do not follow other ways, for they will lead you away from His Way. This is what He has commanded you, so perhaps you will be conscious ˹of Allah˺."

The Torah

154. Additionally, We gave Moses the Scripture, completing the favour upon those who do good, detailing everything, and as a guide and a mercy, so perhaps they would be certain of the meeting with their Lord.

The Quran

155. This is a blessed Book We have revealed. So follow it and be mindful ˹of Allah˺, so you may be shown mercy. 156. You ˹pagans˺ can no longer say, "Scriptures were only revealed to two groups before us and we were unaware of their teachings." 157. Nor can you say, "If only the Scriptures had been revealed to us, we would have been better guided than they." Now there has come to you from your Lord a clear proof[299]—a guide and mercy. Who then does more wrong than those who deny Allah's revelations and turn away from them? We will reward those who turn away from Our revelations with a dreadful punishment for turning away.

---

298 i.e., when you testify or judge.
299 i.e., the Quran.

151   6. Al-An'âm

Waiting for the Apocalypse?

158. Are they awaiting the coming of the angels, or your Lord ˹Himself˺, or some of your Lord's ˹major˺ signs? On the Day your Lord's signs arrive, belief will not benefit those who did not believe earlier or those who did no good through their faith.[300] Say, "Keep waiting! We too are waiting."

Not Responsible

159. Indeed, you ˹O Prophet˺ are not responsible whatsoever for those who have divided their faith and split into sects. Their judgment rests only with Allah. And He will inform them of what they used to do.

Reward for Good and Evil Deeds

160. Whoever comes with a good deed will be rewarded tenfold. But whoever comes with a bad deed will be punished for only one. None will be wronged.

Way of Life

161. Say, ˹O Prophet,˺ "Surely my Lord has guided me to the Straight Path, a perfect way, the faith of Abraham, the upright, who was not one of the polytheists." **162.** Say, "Surely my prayer, my worship, my life, and my death are all for Allah— Lord of all worlds. **163.** He has no partner. So I am commanded, and so I am the first to submit."

Divine Justice

164. Say, ˹O Prophet,˺ "Should I seek a lord other than Allah while He is the Lord of everything?" No one will reap except what they sow. No soul burdened with sin will bear the burden of another. Then to your Lord is your return, and He will inform you of your differences.

Test of Life

165. He is the One Who has placed you as successors on earth and elevated some of you in rank over others, so He may test you with what He has given you. Surely your Lord is swift in punishment, but He is certainly All-Forgiving, Most Merciful.

❀❁ ❀ ❁❀

---

300   This refers to disobedient believers who neither did any good nor repented before the time of their death or the arrival of the Day of Judgment. This is supported by authentic narrations from the Prophet (ﷺ).

7. Al-A'râf   152

7. The Heights (Al-A'râf)

In the Name of Allah—the Most Compassionate, Most Merciful

Advice to the Prophet

1. *Alif-Lãm-Mĩm-Ṣãd.* **2.** ˹This is˺ a Book sent down to you ˹O Prophet˺—do not let anxiety into your heart regarding it—so with it you may warn ˹the disbelievers˺, and as a reminder to the believers.

Advice to Humanity

3. Follow what has been sent down to you from your Lord, and do not take others as guardians besides Him. How seldom are you mindful! **4.** ˹Imagine˺ how many societies We have destroyed! Our torment took them by surprise ˹while sleeping˺ at night or midday. **5.** Their only cry—when overwhelmed by Our torment—was, "We have indeed been wrongdoers."

Response to Messengers

6. We will surely question those who received messengers and We will question the messengers ˹themselves˺. **7.** Then We will give them a full account with sure knowledge—for We were never absent.

Weighing Deeds on Judgment Day

8. The weighing on that Day will be just. As for those whose scale will be heavy ˹with good deeds˺, ˹only˺ they will be successful. **9.** But those whose scale is light, they have doomed themselves for wrongfully denying Our signs.

Satan's Arrogance

10. We have indeed established you on earth and provided you with a means of livelihood. ˹Yet˺ you seldom give any thanks.
11. Surely We created you,[301] then shaped you, then said to the angels, "Prostrate before Adam," so they all did—but not *Iblîs*,[302] who refused to prostrate with the others.

---

301 i.e., your father, Adam (ﷺ).
302 See footnote for 2:34.

7. Al-A'râf

12. Allah asked, "What prevented you from prostrating when I commanded you?" He replied, "I am better than he is: You created me from fire and him from clay." **13.** Allah said, "Then get down from Paradise! It is not for you to be arrogant here. So get out! You are truly one of the disgraced." **14.** He appealed, "Then delay my end until the Day of their resurrection." **15.** Allah said, "You are delayed ˹until the appointed Day˺."[303] **16.** He said, "For leaving me to stray I will lie in ambush for them on Your Straight Path. **17.** I will approach them from their front, their back, their right, their left, and then You will find most of them ungrateful." **18.** Allah said, "Get out of Paradise! You are disgraced and rejected! I will certainly fill up Hell with you and your followers all together."

Adam and Eve: Temptation and Fall

19. ˹Allah said,˺ "O Adam! Live with your wife in Paradise and eat from wherever you please, but do not approach this tree, or else you will be wrongdoers." **20.** Then Satan tempted them in order to expose what was hidden of their nakedness. He said, "Your Lord has forbidden this tree to you only to prevent you from becoming angels or immortals." **21.** And he swore to them, "I am truly your sincere advisor." **22.** So he brought about their fall through deception. And when they tasted of the tree, their nakedness was exposed to them, prompting them to cover themselves with leaves from Paradise. Then their Lord called out to them, "Did I not forbid you from that tree and ˹did I not˺ tell you that Satan is your sworn enemy?"

---

303 Satan asked to be allowed to live until humans are resurrected in order to escape death at the end of time. He was told he was going to live only until the time appointed by Allah Almighty.

7. Al-A'râf

23. They replied, "Our Lord! We have wronged ourselves. If You do not forgive us and have mercy on us, we will certainly be losers." **24.** Allah said, "Descend as enemies to each other.[304] You will find in the earth a residence and provision for your appointed stay." **25.** He added, "There you will live, there you will die, and from there you will be resurrected."

Best Clothing

26. O children of Adam! We have provided for you clothing to cover your nakedness and as an adornment. However, the best clothing is righteousness. This is one of Allah's bounties, so perhaps you will be mindful.

Warning Against Satan

27. O children of Adam! Do not let Satan deceive you as he tempted your parents out of Paradise and caused their cover to be removed in order to expose their nakedness. Surely he and his soldiers watch you from where you cannot see them. We have made the devils allies of those who disbelieve. **28.** Whenever they commit a shameful deed,[305] they say, "We found our forefathers doing it and Allah has commanded us to do it." Say, "No! Allah never commands what is shameful. How can you attribute to Allah what you do not know?" **29.** Say, 'O Prophet,' "My Lord has commanded uprightness and dedication 'to Him alone' in worship, calling upon Him with sincere devotion. Just as He first brought you into being, you will be brought to life again." **30.** He has guided some, while others are destined to stray. They have taken devils as their masters instead of Allah—thinking they are 'rightly' guided.

---

304 There will be enmity between humans and Satan.
305 It was customary for the pagans of Mecca to circle the Ka'bah while naked. So verses 26-31 of this sûrah were revealed commanding the believers to cover themselves properly when praying to their Lord.

7. Al-A'râf

The Lawful and the Forbidden

31. O Children of Adam! Dress properly whenever you are at worship. Eat and drink, but do not waste. Surely He does not like the wasteful. **32.** Ask, ˹O Prophet,˺ "Who has forbidden the adornments and lawful provisions Allah has brought forth for His servants?" Say, "They are for the enjoyment of the believers in this worldly life, but they will be exclusively theirs on the Day of Judgment.[306] This is how We make Our revelations clear for people of knowledge." **33.** Say, "My Lord has only forbidden open and secret indecencies, sinfulness, unjust aggression, associating ˹others˺ with Allah ˹in worship˺— a practice He has never authorized—and attributing to Allah what you do not know." **34.** For each community there is an appointed term. When their time arrives, they can neither delay it for a moment, nor could they advance it.

Receiving the Truth

35. O children of Adam! When messengers from among yourselves come to you reciting My revelations—whoever shuns evil and mends their ways, there will be no fear for them, nor will they grieve. **36.** But those who receive Our revelations with denial and arrogance will be the residents of the Fire. They will be there forever.

Evil Leaders and Their Followers

37. Who does more wrong than those who fabricate lies against Allah or deny His revelations? They will receive what is destined for them,[307] until Our messenger-angels arrive to take their souls, asking them, "Where are those ˹false gods˺ you used to invoke besides Allah?" They will cry, "They have failed us," and they will confess against themselves that they were indeed disbelievers.

---

306 The pleasures of this worldly life are shared by believers and disbelievers, whereas the pleasures of the Hereafter will be enjoyed exclusively by the believers.
307 i.e., they will receive all provisions and bounties destined for them by their Lord.

7. Al-A'râf

38. Allah will say, "Enter the Fire along with the ˹evil˺ groups of jinn and humans that preceded you." Whenever a group enters Hell, it will curse the preceding one until they are all gathered inside, the followers will say about their leaders, "Our Lord! They have misled us, so multiply their torment in the Fire." He will answer, "It has already been multiplied for all, but you do not know." **39.** Then the leaders will say to their followers, "You were no better than us! So taste the torment for what you used to commit."

Punishment of the Disbelievers

40. Surely those who receive our revelations with denial and arrogance, the gates of heaven will not be opened for them, nor will they enter Paradise until a camel passes through the eye of a needle. This is how We reward the wicked. **41.** Hell will be their bed; flames will be their cover. This is how We reward the wrongdoers.

Reward of the Believers

42. As for those who believe and do good—We never require of any soul more than what it can afford—it is they who will be the residents of Paradise. They will be there forever. **43.** We will remove whatever bitterness they had in their hearts.[308] Rivers will flow under their feet. And they will say, "Praise be to Allah for guiding us to this. We would have never been guided if Allah had not guided us. The messengers of our Lord had certainly come with the truth." It will be announced to them, "This is Paradise awarded to you for what you used to do."

---

308 i.e., the bitterness they had in their hearts towards other believers who wronged them in the worldly life.

7. Al-A'râf

The Lord's Promise

44. The residents of Paradise will call out to the residents of the Fire, "We have certainly found our Lord's promise to be true. Have you too found your Lord's promise to be true?" They will reply, "Yes, we have!" Then a caller will announce to both, "May Allah's condemnation be upon the wrongdoers, 45. those who hindered ˹others˺ from Allah's Way, strived to make it ˹appear˺ crooked, and disbelieved in the Hereafter."

People on the Heights[309]

46. There will be a barrier between Paradise and Hell. And on the heights ˹of that barrier˺ will be people[310] who will recognize ˹the residents of˺ both by their appearance.[311] They will call out to the residents of Paradise, "Peace be upon you!" They will have not yet entered Paradise, but eagerly hope to. 47. When their eyes will turn towards the residents of Hell, they will pray, "Our Lord! Do not join us with the wrongdoing people." 48. Those on the heights will call out to some ˹tyrants in the Fire˺, who they will recognize by their appearance, saying, "Your large numbers and arrogance are of no use ˹today˺! 49. Are these ˹humble believers˺ the ones you swore would never be shown Allah's mercy?" ˹Finally, those on the heights will be told:˺ "Enter Paradise! There is no fear for you, nor will you grieve."

Disbelievers Begging Believers

50. The residents of the Fire will then cry out to the residents of Paradise, "Aid us with some water or any provision Allah has granted you." They will reply, "Allah has forbidden both to the disbelievers, 51. those who took this[312] faith ˹of Islam˺ as mere amusement and play and were deluded by ˹their˺ worldly life." ˹Allah will say,˺ "Today We will ignore them just as they ignored the coming of this Day of theirs and for rejecting Our revelations."

---

309 This is a group of people whose good deeds equal their bad deeds, so they will be held on the heights separating Paradise and Hellfire until their judgment is settled.
310 Although the word "rijâl" generally means "men," some Quran commentators believe that the word "rijâl" here can also mean "people," but they are called men since men make up the majority in the group. In some Arabic dialects, "rijâl" is the plural of "rajul" (man) and "rajulah" (woman).
311 The faces of the residents of Paradise will be bright, whereas those of the residents of Hell will be gloomy.
312 lit., their faith (which they are supposed to follow).

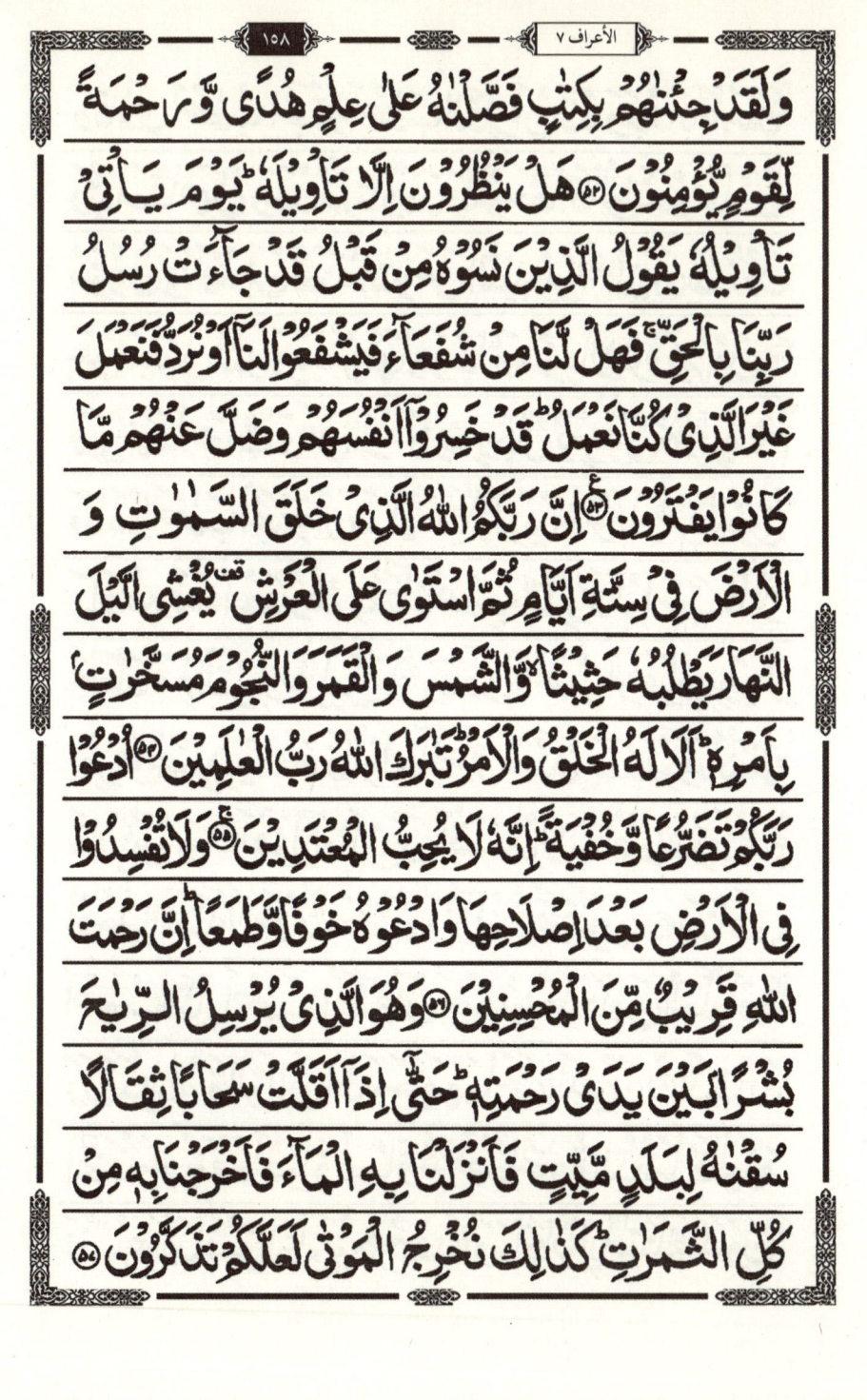

Too Late

52. We have certainly brought them a Book which We explained with knowledge—a guide and mercy for those who believe. **53.** Do they only await the fulfilment ʿof its warningʾ? The Day it will be fulfilled, those who ignored it before will say, "The messengers of our Lord certainly came with the truth. Are there any intercessors who can plead on our behalf? Or can we be sent back so we may do ʿgood,ʾ unlike what we used to do?" They will have certainly ruined themselves, and whatever ʿgodsʾ they fabricated will fail them.

The Almighty Creator

54. Indeed your Lord is Allah Who created the heavens and the earth in six Days,[313] then established Himself on the Throne. He makes the day and night overlap in rapid succession. He created the sun, the moon, and the stars—all subjected by His command. The creation and the command belong to Him ʿaloneʾ. Blessed is Allah—Lord of all worlds! **55.** Call upon your Lord humbly and secretly. Surely He does not like the transgressors. **56.** Do not spread corruption in the land after it has been set in order. And call upon Him with hope and fear. Indeed, Allah's mercy is always close to the good-doers.

Parable of Resurrection

57. He is the One Who sends the winds ushering in His mercy. When they bear heavy clouds, We drive them to a lifeless land and then cause rain to fall, producing every type of fruit. Similarly, We will bring the dead to life, so perhaps you will be mindful.

---

313 The word day is not always used in the Quran to mean a 24-hour period. According to 22:47, a heavenly Day is 1000 years of our time. The Day of Judgment will be 50 000 years of our time (see 70:4). Hence, the six Days of creation refer to six eons of time, known only by Allah.

7. Al-A'râf

Parable of Believers and Disbelievers

58. The fertile land produces abundantly by the Will of its Lord, whereas the infertile land hardly produces anything. This is how We vary ˹Our˺ lessons to those who are thankful.

Prophet Noah

59. Indeed, We sent Noah to his people. He said, "O my people! Worship Allah—you have no other god except Him. I truly fear for you the torment of a tremendous Day."

His People's Response

60. But the chiefs of his people said, "We surely see that you are clearly misguided." **61.** He replied, "O my people! I am not misguided! But I am a messenger from the Lord of all worlds, **62.** conveying to you my Lord's messages and giving you ˹sincere˺ advice. And I know from Allah what you do not know. **63.** Do you find it astonishing that a reminder should come to you from your Lord through one of your own, warning you, so you may beware and perhaps be shown mercy?"

The Fate of His People

64. But they rejected him, so We saved him and those with him in the Ark, and drowned those who rejected Our signs. They were certainly a blind people.

Prophet Hûd

65. And to the people of 'Âd We sent their brother Hûd. He said, "O my people! Worship Allah—you have no other god except Him. Will you not then fear Him?"

His People's Response

66. The disbelieving chiefs of his people responded, "We surely see you as a fool, and we certainly think you are a liar." **67.** Hûd replied, "O my people! I am no fool! But I am a messenger from the Lord of all worlds,

أُبَلِّغُكُمْ رِسَالَاتِ رَبِّي وَأَنَا لَكُمْ نَاصِحٌ أَمِينٌ ۞ أَوَعَجِبْتُمْ أَن جَاءَكُمْ ذِكْرٌ مِّن رَّبِّكُمْ عَلَىٰ رَجُلٍ مِّنكُمْ لِيُنذِرَكُمْ ۚ وَاذْكُرُوا إِذْ جَعَلَكُمْ خُلَفَاءَ مِن بَعْدِ قَوْمِ نُوحٍ وَزَادَكُمْ فِي الْخَلْقِ بَسْطَةً ۖ فَاذْكُرُوا آلَاءَ اللَّهِ لَعَلَّكُمْ تُفْلِحُونَ ۞ قَالُوا أَجِئْتَنَا لِنَعْبُدَ اللَّهَ وَحْدَهُ وَنَذَرَ مَا كَانَ يَعْبُدُ آبَاؤُنَا ۖ فَأْتِنَا بِمَا تَعِدُنَا إِن كُنتَ مِنَ الصَّادِقِينَ ۞ قَالَ قَدْ وَقَعَ عَلَيْكُم مِّن رَّبِّكُمْ رِجْسٌ وَغَضَبٌ ۖ أَتُجَادِلُونَنِي فِي أَسْمَاءٍ سَمَّيْتُمُوهَا أَنتُمْ وَآبَاؤُكُم مَّا نَزَّلَ اللَّهُ بِهَا مِن سُلْطَانٍ ۚ فَانتَظِرُوا إِنِّي مَعَكُم مِّنَ الْمُنتَظِرِينَ ۞ فَأَنجَيْنَاهُ وَالَّذِينَ مَعَهُ بِرَحْمَةٍ مِّنَّا وَقَطَعْنَا دَابِرَ الَّذِينَ كَذَّبُوا بِآيَاتِنَا ۖ وَمَا كَانُوا مُؤْمِنِينَ ۞ وَإِلَىٰ ثَمُودَ أَخَاهُمْ صَالِحًا ۗ قَالَ يَا قَوْمِ اعْبُدُوا اللَّهَ مَا لَكُم مِّنْ إِلَٰهٍ غَيْرُهُ ۖ قَدْ جَاءَتْكُم بَيِّنَةٌ مِّن رَّبِّكُمْ ۖ هَٰذِهِ نَاقَةُ اللَّهِ لَكُمْ آيَةً ۖ فَذَرُوهَا تَأْكُلْ فِي أَرْضِ اللَّهِ ۖ وَلَا تَمَسُّوهَا بِسُوءٍ فَيَأْخُذَكُمْ عَذَابٌ أَلِيمٌ ۞

68. conveying to you my Lord's messages. And I am your sincere advisor. **69.** Do you find it astonishing that a reminder should come to you from your Lord through one of your own so he may warn you? Remember that He made you successors after the people of Noah and increased you greatly in stature. So remember Allah's favours, so you may be successful." **70.** They said, "Have you come to us so that we would worship Allah alone and abandon what our forefathers used to worship? Then bring us what you threaten us with, if what you say is true!" **71.** He said, "You will certainly be subjected to your Lord's torment and wrath. Do you dispute with me regarding the so-called gods which you and your forefathers have made up—a practice Allah has never authorized? Then wait! I too am waiting with you."

The Fate of His People

72. So We saved him and those with him by Our mercy and uprooted those who denied Our signs. They were not believers.

Prophet Ṣâliḥ

73. And to the people of Thamûd We sent their brother Ṣâliḥ. He said, "O my people! Worship Allah—you have no other god except Him. A clear proof has come to you from your Lord: this is Allah's she-camel as a sign to you. So leave her to graze ˹freely˺ on Allah's land and do not harm her, or else you will be overcome by a painful punishment.

74. Remember when He made you successors after 'Âd and established you in the land—'and' you built palaces on its plains and carved homes into mountains. So remember Allah's favours, and do not go about spreading corruption in the land."

His People's Response

75. The arrogant chiefs of his people asked the lowly who believed among them, "Are you certain that Ṣâliḥ has been sent by his Lord?" They replied, "We certainly believe in what he has been sent with." **76.** The arrogant said, "We surely reject what you believe in." **77.** Then they killed the she-camel—defying their Lord's command—and challenged 'Ṣâliḥ', "Bring us what you threaten us with, if you are 'truly' one of the messengers."

The Fate of His People

78. Then an 'overwhelming' earthquake struck them, and they fell lifeless in their homes. **79.** So he turned away from them, saying, "O my people! Surely I conveyed to you my Lord's message and gave you 'sincere' advice, but you do not like 'sincere' advisors."

Prophet Lot

80. And 'remember' when Lot scolded 'the men of' his people, 'saying,' "Do you commit a shameful deed that no man has ever done before? **81.** You lust after men instead of women! You are certainly transgressors."

7. Al-A'râf

بِسْمِ ٱللَّهِ الرَّحْمَٰنِ الرَّحِيمِ

وَمَا كَانَ جَوَابَ قَوْمِهِ إِلَّا أَن قَالُوٓاْ أَخْرِجُوهُم مِّن قَرْيَتِكُمْ إِنَّهُمْ أُنَاسٌ يَتَطَهَّرُونَ ۝ فَأَنجَيْنَاهُ وَأَهْلَهُ إِلَّا ٱمْرَأَتَهُۥ كَانَتْ مِنَ ٱلْغَٰبِرِينَ ۝ وَأَمْطَرْنَا عَلَيْهِم مَّطَرًا ۖ فَٱنظُرْ كَيْفَ كَانَ عَٰقِبَةُ ٱلْمُجْرِمِينَ ۝ وَإِلَىٰ مَدْيَنَ أَخَاهُمْ شُعَيْبًا ۗ قَالَ يَٰقَوْمِ ٱعْبُدُواْ ٱللَّهَ مَا لَكُم مِّنْ إِلَٰهٍ غَيْرُهُۥ ۖ قَدْ جَآءَتْكُم بَيِّنَةٌ مِّن رَّبِّكُمْ ۖ فَأَوْفُواْ ٱلْكَيْلَ وَٱلْمِيزَانَ وَلَا تَبْخَسُواْ ٱلنَّاسَ أَشْيَآءَهُمْ وَلَا تُفْسِدُواْ فِي ٱلْأَرْضِ بَعْدَ إِصْلَٰحِهَا ۚ ذَٰلِكُمْ خَيْرٌ لَّكُمْ إِن كُنتُم مُّؤْمِنِينَ ۝ وَلَا تَقْعُدُواْ بِكُلِّ صِرَٰطٍ تُوعِدُونَ وَتَصُدُّونَ عَن سَبِيلِ ٱللَّهِ مَنْ ءَامَنَ بِهِۦ وَتَبْغُونَهَا عِوَجًا ۚ وَٱذْكُرُوٓاْ إِذْ كُنتُمْ قَلِيلًا فَكَثَّرَكُمْ ۖ وَٱنظُرُواْ كَيْفَ كَانَ عَٰقِبَةُ ٱلْمُفْسِدِينَ ۝ وَإِن كَانَ طَآئِفَةٌ مِّنكُمْ ءَامَنُواْ بِٱلَّذِىٓ أُرْسِلْتُ بِهِۦ وَطَآئِفَةٌ لَّمْ يُؤْمِنُواْ فَٱصْبِرُواْ حَتَّىٰ يَحْكُمَ ٱللَّهُ بَيْنَنَا ۚ وَهُوَ خَيْرُ ٱلْحَٰكِمِينَ ۝

His People's Response

82. But his people's only response was to say, "Expel them from your land! They are a people who wish to remain chaste!"

The Fate of His People

83. So We saved him and his family except his wife, who was one of the doomed. **84.** We poured upon them a rain ˹of brimstone˺. See what was the end of the wicked!

Prophet Shu'aib

85. And to the people of Midian We sent their brother Shu'aib. He said, "O my people! Worship Allah—you have no other god except Him. A clear proof has already come to you from your Lord. So give just measure and weight, do not defraud people of their property, nor spread corruption in the land after it has been set in order. This is for your own good, if you are ˹truly˺ believers. **86.** And do not lie in ambush on every road—threatening and hindering those who believe in Allah from His Path and striving to make it ˹appear˺ crooked. Remember when you were few, then He increased you in number. And consider the fate of the corruptors! **87.** If some of you do believe in what I have been sent with while others do not, then be patient until Allah judges between us. He is the Best of Judges."

7. Al-A'râf

His People's Response

88. The arrogant chiefs of his people threatened, "O Shu'aib! We will certainly expel you and your fellow believers from our land, unless you return to our faith." He replied, "Even if we hate it? 89. We would surely be fabricating a lie against Allah if we were to return to your faith after Allah has saved us from it. It does not befit us to return to it unless it is the Will of Allah, our Lord. Our Lord has encompassed everything in ˹His˺ knowledge. In Allah we trust. Our Lord! Judge between us and our people with truth. You are the best of those who judge."

The Fate of His People

90. The disbelieving chiefs of his people threatened, "If you follow Shu'aib, you will surely be losers!" 91. Then an ˹overwhelming˺ earthquake struck them and they fell lifeless in their homes. 92. Those who rejected Shu'aib were ˹wiped out˺ as if they had never lived there. Those who rejected Shu'aib were the true losers. 93. He turned away from them, saying, "O my people! Indeed, I have delivered to you the messages of my Lord and gave you ˹sincere˺ advice. How can I then grieve for those who chose to disbelieve?"

Destroyed Peoples

94. Whenever We sent a prophet to a society, We afflicted its ˹disbelieving˺ people with suffering and adversity, so perhaps they would be humbled. 95. Then We changed their adversity to prosperity until they flourished and argued ˹falsely˺, "Our forefathers ˹too˺ had been visited by adversity and prosperity."[314] So We seized them by surprise, while they were unaware.

---

314 They argued that life has its ups and downs and, therefore, they did not perceive adversity as a punishment or prosperity as a test—arguing that the same thing happened to their ancestors.

Arabic Text

وَلَوْ أَنَّ أَهْلَ الْقُرَىٰ آمَنُوا وَاتَّقَوْا لَفَتَحْنَا عَلَيْهِم بَرَكَاتٍ مِّنَ السَّمَاءِ وَالْأَرْضِ وَلَٰكِن كَذَّبُوا فَأَخَذْنَاهُم بِمَا كَانُوا يَكْسِبُونَ ۝ أَفَأَمِنَ أَهْلُ الْقُرَىٰ أَن يَأْتِيَهُم بَأْسُنَا بَيَاتًا وَهُمْ نَائِمُونَ ۝ أَوَأَمِنَ أَهْلُ الْقُرَىٰ أَن يَأْتِيَهُم بَأْسُنَا ضُحًى وَهُمْ يَلْعَبُونَ ۝ أَفَأَمِنُوا مَكْرَ اللَّهِ ۚ فَلَا يَأْمَنُ مَكْرَ اللَّهِ إِلَّا الْقَوْمُ الْخَاسِرُونَ ۝ أَوَلَمْ يَهْدِ لِلَّذِينَ يَرِثُونَ الْأَرْضَ مِن بَعْدِ أَهْلِهَا أَن لَّوْ نَشَاءُ أَصَبْنَاهُم بِذُنُوبِهِمْ ۚ وَنَطْبَعُ عَلَىٰ قُلُوبِهِمْ فَهُمْ لَا يَسْمَعُونَ ۝ تِلْكَ الْقُرَىٰ نَقُصُّ عَلَيْكَ مِنْ أَنبَائِهَا ۚ وَلَقَدْ جَاءَتْهُمْ رُسُلُهُم بِالْبَيِّنَاتِ فَمَا كَانُوا لِيُؤْمِنُوا بِمَا كَذَّبُوا مِن قَبْلُ ۚ كَذَٰلِكَ يَطْبَعُ اللَّهُ عَلَىٰ قُلُوبِ الْكَافِرِينَ ۝ وَمَا وَجَدْنَا لِأَكْثَرِهِم مِّنْ عَهْدٍ ۖ وَإِن وَجَدْنَا أَكْثَرَهُمْ لَفَاسِقِينَ ۝ ثُمَّ بَعَثْنَا مِن بَعْدِهِم مُّوسَىٰ بِآيَاتِنَا إِلَىٰ فِرْعَوْنَ وَمَلَئِهِ فَظَلَمُوا بِهَا ۖ فَانظُرْ كَيْفَ كَانَ عَاقِبَةُ الْمُفْسِدِينَ ۝ وَقَالَ مُوسَىٰ يَا فِرْعَوْنُ إِنِّي رَسُولٌ مِّن رَّبِّ الْعَالَمِينَ ۝

English Translation

Learn from History

96. Had the people of those societies been faithful and mindful ˹of Allah˺, We would have overwhelmed them with blessings from heaven and earth. But they disbelieved, so We seized them for what they used to commit. 97. Did the people of those societies feel secure that Our punishment would not come upon them by night while they were asleep? 98. Or did they feel secure that Our punishment would not come upon them by day while they were at play? 99. Did they feel secure against Allah's planning? None would feel secure from Allah's planning except the losers. 100. Is it not clear to those who take over the land after ˹the destruction of˺ its former residents that— if We will—We can punish them ˹too˺ for their sins and seal their hearts so they will not hear ˹the truth˺?

Sealed Hearts

101. We have narrated to you ˹O Prophet˺ some of the stories of those societies. Surely, their messengers came to them with clear proofs, but still they would not believe in what they had already denied. This is how Allah seals the hearts of the disbelievers. 102. We did not find most of them true to their covenant. Rather, We found most of them truly rebellious.

Prophet Moses

103. Then after them We sent Moses with Our signs to Pharaoh and his chiefs, but they wrongfully rejected them. See what was the end of the corruptors! 104. And Moses said, "O Pharaoh! I am truly a messenger from the Lord of all worlds,

165   7. Al-A'râf

105. obliged to say nothing about Allah except the truth. Indeed, I have come to you with clear proof from your Lord, so let the children of Israel go with me." **106.** Pharaoh said, "If you have come with a sign, then bring it if what you say is true." **107.** So Moses threw down his staff and—behold!—it became a real snake. **108.** Then he drew his hand ˹out of his collar˺ and it was ˹shining˺ white for all to see.

Moses vs. Pharaoh's Magicians

109. The chiefs of Pharaoh's people said, "He is indeed a skilled magician, **110.** who seeks to drive you from your land." ˹So Pharaoh asked,˺ "What do you propose?" **111.** They replied, "Let him and his brother wait and send mobilizers to all cities **112.** to bring you every clever magician." **113.** The magicians came to Pharaoh, saying, "Shall we receive a ˹suitable˺ reward if we prevail?" **114.** He replied, "Yes, and you will certainly be among those closest to me." **115.** They asked, "O Moses! Will you cast, or shall we be the first to cast?" **116.** Moses said, "You first." So when they did, they deceived the eyes of the people, stunned them, and made a great display of magic. **117.** Then We inspired Moses, "Throw down your staff," and—behold!—it devoured the objects of their illusion! **118.** So the truth prevailed and their illusions failed.

Magicians Become Believers

119. So Pharaoh and his people were defeated right there and put to shame. **120.** And the magicians fell down, prostrating. **121.** They declared, "We ˹now˺ believe in the Lord of all worlds—

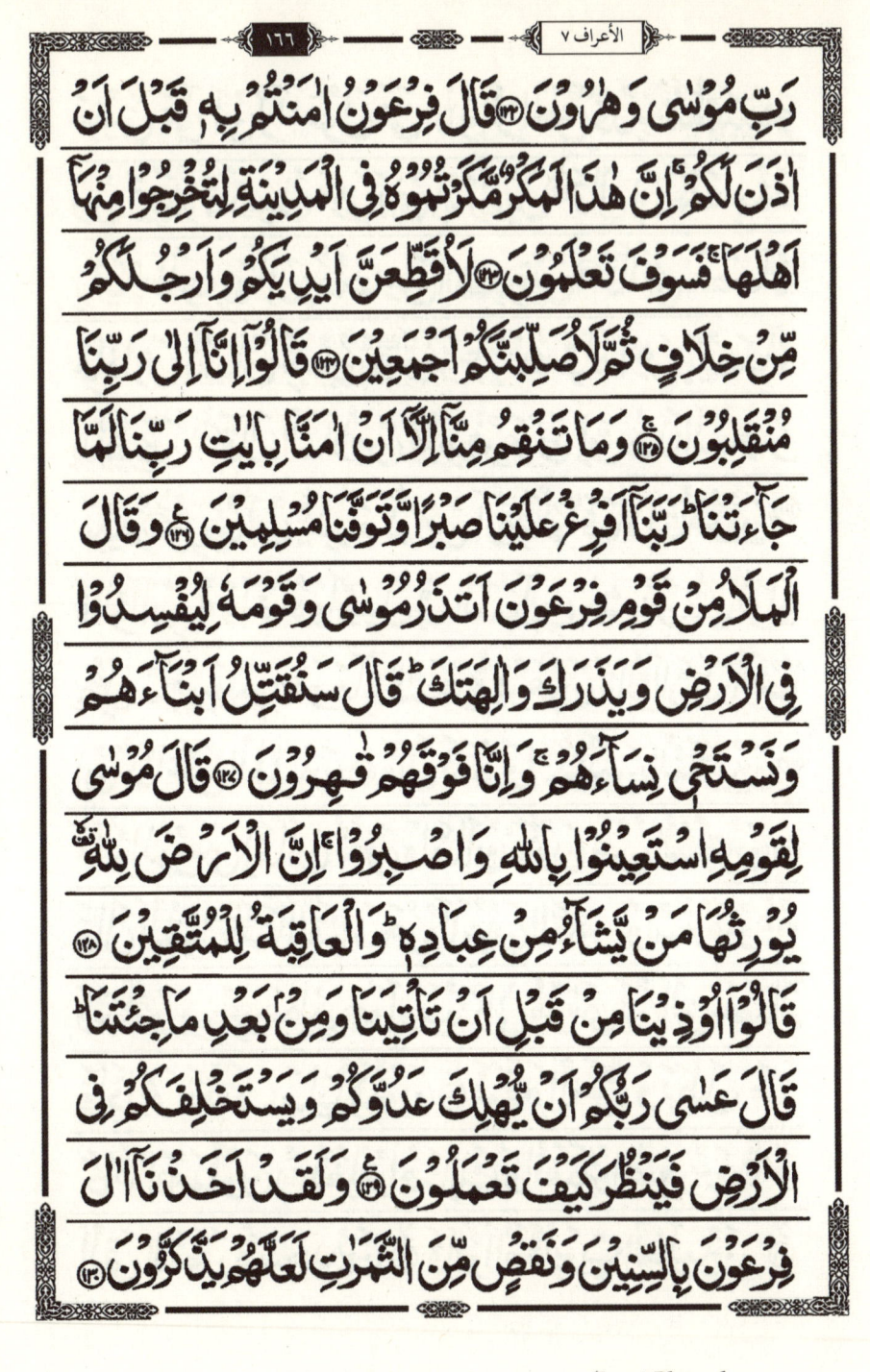

7. Al-A'râf 166

122. the Lord of Moses and Aaron."

123. Pharaoh threatened, "How dare you believe in him before I give you permission? This must be a conspiracy you devised in the city to drive out its people, but soon you will see. 124. I will certainly cut off your hands and feet on opposite sides, then crucify you all." 125. They responded, "Surely to our Lord we will ˹all˺ return. 126. Your rage towards us is only because we believed in the signs of our Lord when they came to us. Our Lord! Shower us with perseverance, and let us die while submitting ˹to You˺."[315]

Pharaoh's Persecution of the Israelites

127. The chiefs of Pharaoh's people protested, "Are you going to leave Moses and his people free to spread corruption in the land and abandon you and your gods?" He responded, "We will kill their sons and keep their women.[316] We will completely dominate them."

Moses Reassures His People

128. Moses reassured his people, "Seek Allah's help and be patient. Indeed, the earth belongs to Allah ˹alone˺. He grants it to whoever He chooses of His servants. The ultimate outcome belongs ˹only˺ to the righteous." 129. They complained, "We have always been oppressed—before and after you came to us ˹with the message˺." He replied, "Perhaps your Lord will destroy your enemy and make you successors in the land to see what you will do."

Egypt Plagued

130. Indeed, We afflicted Pharaoh's people with famine and shortage of crops so they might come back ˹to their senses˺.

---

315 lit., as Muslims.
316 As we did before the birth of Moses.

131. In times of prosperity, they said, "This is what we deserve," but in adversity, they blamed it on Moses and those with him.[317] Surely all is destined by Allah. Yet most of them did not know.

Pharaoh's People in Denial

132. They said, "No matter what sign you may bring to deceive us, we will never believe in you." **133.** So We plagued them with floods, locusts, lice, frogs, and blood—all as clear signs, but they persisted in arrogance and were a wicked people. **134.** When tormented, they pleaded, "O Moses! Pray to your Lord on our behalf, by virtue of the covenant He made with you. If you help remove this torment from us, we will certainly believe in you and let the Children of Israel go with you." **135.** But as soon as We removed the torment from them—until they met their inevitable fate[318]—they broke their promise. **136.** So We inflicted punishment upon them, drowning them in the sea for denying Our signs and being heedless of them. **137.** And ˹so˺ We made the oppressed people successors of the eastern and western lands, which We had showered with blessings. ˹In this way˺ the noble Word of your Lord was fulfilled for the Children of Israel for what they had endured. And We destroyed what Pharaoh and his people constructed and what they established.

---

317 In psychology, this is called self-serving bias and scapegoating.
318 i.e., their drowning in the sea.

7. Al-A'râf

The Israelites Demanding an Idol

138. We brought the Children of Israel across the sea and they came upon a people devoted to idols. They demanded, "O Moses! Make for us a god like their gods." He replied, "Indeed, you are a people acting ignorantly! **139.** What they follow is certainly doomed to destruction and their deeds are in vain." **140.** He added, "Shall I seek for you a god other than Allah, while He has honoured you above the others?" **141.** And ˹remember˺ when We rescued you from the people of Pharaoh, who afflicted you with dreadful torment— killing your sons and keeping your women. That was a severe test from your Lord.

Moses' Appointment with Allah

142. We appointed for Moses thirty nights then added another ten— completing his Lord's term of forty nights. Moses commanded his brother Aaron, "Take my place among my people, do what is right, and do not follow the way of the corruptors." **143.** When Moses came at the appointed time and his Lord spoke to him, he asked, "My Lord! Reveal Yourself to me so I may see You." Allah answered, "You cannot see Me! But look at the mountain. If it remains firm in its place, only then will you see Me." When his Lord appeared to the mountain, He levelled it to dust and Moses collapsed unconscious. When he recovered, he cried, "Glory be to You! I turn to You in repentance and I am the first of the believers."

7. Al-A'râf

144. Allah said, "O Moses! I have ʿalreadyʾ elevated you above all others by My messages and speech.[319] So hold firmly to what I have given you and be grateful."

The Tablets

145. We wrote for him on the Tablets ʿthe fundamentalsʾ of everything; commandments and explanations of all things. ʿWe commanded,ʾ "Hold to this firmly and ask your people to take the best of it.[320] I will soon show ʿall ofʾ you the home of the rebellious.[321] **146.** I will turn away from My signs those who act unjustly with arrogance in the land. And even if they were to see every sign, they still would not believe in them. If they see the Right Path, they will not take it. But if they see a crooked path, they will follow it. This is because they denied Our signs and were heedless of them. **147.** The deeds of those who deny Our signs and the meeting ʿwith Allahʾ in the Hereafter will be in vain. Will they be rewarded except for what they have done?"

The Golden Calf

148. In the absence of Moses, his people made from their ʿgoldenʾ jewellery an idol of a calf that made a lowing sound. Did they not see that it could neither speak to them nor guide them to the ʿRightʾ Path? Still they took it as a god and were wrongdoers. **149.** Later, when they were filled with remorse and realized they had gone astray, they cried, "If our Lord does not have mercy on us and forgive us, we will certainly be losers."

---

319 Allah reminds Moses that even though his request to see Allah was denied, he has already been favoured by Allah over the people of his time through prophethood and direct communication with the Almighty.
320 To follow the commandments that generate more rewards than others, to put grace before justice, etc.
321 This could either mean the ruins of destroyed nations or the Hellfire which is the home of the wicked.

وَلَمَّا رَجَعَ مُوسَىٰ إِلَىٰ قَوْمِهِ غَضْبَانَ أَسِفًا قَالَ بِئْسَمَا خَلَفْتُمُونِي مِنْ بَعْدِي أَعَجِلْتُمْ أَمْرَ رَبِّكُمْ وَأَلْقَى الْأَلْوَاحَ وَأَخَذَ بِرَأْسِ أَخِيهِ يَجُرُّهُ إِلَيْهِ قَالَ ابْنَ أُمَّ إِنَّ الْقَوْمَ اسْتَضْعَفُونِي وَكَادُوا يَقْتُلُونَنِي فَلَا تُشْمِتْ بِيَ الْأَعْدَاءَ وَلَا تَجْعَلْنِي مَعَ الْقَوْمِ الظَّالِمِينَ ۝ قَالَ رَبِّ اغْفِرْ لِي وَلِأَخِي وَأَدْخِلْنَا فِي رَحْمَتِكَ وَأَنْتَ أَرْحَمُ الرَّاحِمِينَ ۝ إِنَّ الَّذِينَ اتَّخَذُوا الْعِجْلَ سَيَنَالُهُمْ غَضَبٌ مِنْ رَبِّهِمْ وَذِلَّةٌ فِي الْحَيَاةِ الدُّنْيَا وَكَذَٰلِكَ نَجْزِي الْمُفْتَرِينَ ۝ وَالَّذِينَ عَمِلُوا السَّيِّئَاتِ ثُمَّ تَابُوا مِنْ بَعْدِهَا وَآمَنُوا إِنَّ رَبَّكَ مِنْ بَعْدِهَا لَغَفُورٌ رَحِيمٌ ۝ وَلَمَّا سَكَتَ عَنْ مُوسَى الْغَضَبُ أَخَذَ الْأَلْوَاحَ وَفِي نُسْخَتِهَا هُدًى وَرَحْمَةٌ لِلَّذِينَ هُمْ لِرَبِّهِمْ يَرْهَبُونَ ۝ وَاخْتَارَ مُوسَىٰ قَوْمَهُ سَبْعِينَ رَجُلًا لِمِيقَاتِنَا فَلَمَّا أَخَذَتْهُمُ الرَّجْفَةُ قَالَ رَبِّ لَوْ شِئْتَ أَهْلَكْتَهُمْ مِنْ قَبْلُ وَإِيَّايَ أَتُهْلِكُنَا بِمَا فَعَلَ السُّفَهَاءُ مِنَّا إِنْ هِيَ إِلَّا فِتْنَتُكَ تُضِلُّ بِهَا مَنْ تَشَاءُ وَتَهْدِي مَنْ تَشَاءُ أَنْتَ وَلِيُّنَا فَاغْفِرْ لَنَا وَارْحَمْنَا وَأَنْتَ خَيْرُ الْغَافِرِينَ ۝

150. Upon Moses' return to his people, ˹totally˺ furious and sorrowful, he said, "What an evil thing you committed in my absence! Did you want to hasten your Lord's torment?" Then he threw down the Tablets and grabbed his brother by the hair, dragging him closer. Aaron pleaded, "O son of my mother! The people overpowered me and were about to kill me. So do not ˹humiliate me and˺ make my enemies rejoice, nor count me among the wrongdoing people."

Moses Prays for Forgiveness

151. Moses prayed, "My Lord! Forgive me and my brother! And admit us into Your mercy. You are the Most Merciful of the merciful." **152.** Those who worshipped the calf will certainly be afflicted with Allah's wrath as well as disgrace in the life of this world. This is how We reward those who invent falsehood. **153.** But those who commit evil, then repent and become ˹true˺ believers, your Lord will certainly be All-Forgiving, Most-Merciful. **154.** When Moses' anger subsided, he took up the Tablets whose text contained guidance and mercy for those who stand in awe of their Lord.

Begging for Allah's Mercy

155. Moses chose seventy men from among his people for Our appointment and, when they were seized by an earthquake,[322] he cried, "My Lord! Had You willed, You could have destroyed them long ago, and me as well. Will You destroy us for what the foolish among us have done? This is only a test from You—by which You allow whoever you will to stray and guide whoever You will. You are our Guardian. So forgive us and have mercy on us. You are the best forgiver.

---

322 For asking Moses to make Allah visible to them.

156. Ordain for us what is good in this life and the next. Indeed, we have turned to You ˹in repentance˺." Allah replied, "I will inflict My torment on whoever I will. But My mercy encompasses everything. I will ordain mercy for those who shun evil, pay alms-tax, and believe in Our revelations.

Prophet Muḥammad in the Bible

157. "˹They are˺ the ones who follow the Messenger, the unlettered Prophet, whose description they find in their Torah and the Gospel.[323] He commands them to do good and forbids them from evil, permits for them what is lawful and forbids to them what is impure, and relieves them from their burdens and the shackles that bound them. ˹Only˺ those who believe in him, honour and support him, and follow the light sent down to him will be successful."

Universality of Islam

158. Say, ˹O Prophet,˺ "O humanity! I am Allah's Messenger to you all. To Him ˹alone˺ belongs the kingdom of the heavens and the earth. There is no god ˹worthy of worship˺ except Him. He gives life and causes death." So believe in Allah and His Messenger, the unlettered Prophet, who believes in Allah and His revelations. And follow him, so you may be ˹rightly˺ guided.

The Israelites Tested

159. There are some among the people of Moses who guide with the truth and establish justice accordingly.

وَاكْتُبْ لَنَا فِى هَـٰذِهِ الدُّنْيَا حَسَنَةً وَفِى الْأَخِرَةِ إِنَّا هُدْنَا إِلَيْكَ قَالَ عَذَابِى أُصِيبُ بِهِ مَنْ أَشَاءُ وَرَحْمَتِى وَسِعَتْ كُلَّ شَىْءٍ فَسَأَكْتُبُهَا لِلَّذِينَ يَتَّقُونَ وَيُؤْتُونَ الزَّكَوٰةَ وَالَّذِينَ هُم بِـَٔايَـٰتِنَا يُؤْمِنُونَ ۝ الَّذِينَ يَتَّبِعُونَ الرَّسُولَ النَّبِىَّ الْأُمِّىَّ الَّذِى يَجِدُونَهُ مَكْتُوبًا عِندَهُمْ فِى التَّوْرَىٰةِ وَالْإِنجِيلِ يَأْمُرُهُم بِالْمَعْرُوفِ وَيَنْهَىٰهُمْ عَنِ الْمُنكَرِ وَيُحِلُّ لَهُمُ الطَّيِّبَـٰتِ وَيُحَرِّمُ عَلَيْهِمُ الْخَبَـٰئِثَ وَيَضَعُ عَنْهُمْ إِصْرَهُمْ وَالْأَغْلَـٰلَ الَّتِى كَانَتْ عَلَيْهِمْ فَالَّذِينَ ءَامَنُوا بِهِ وَعَزَّرُوهُ وَنَصَرُوهُ وَاتَّبَعُوا النُّورَ الَّذِى أُنزِلَ مَعَهُ أُو۟لَـٰئِكَ هُمُ الْمُفْلِحُونَ ۝ قُلْ يَـٰٓأَيُّهَا النَّاسُ إِنِّى رَسُولُ اللَّهِ إِلَيْكُمْ جَمِيعًا الَّذِى لَهُ مُلْكُ السَّمَـٰوَٰتِ وَالْأَرْضِ لَآ إِلَـٰهَ إِلَّا هُوَ يُحْىِۦ وَيُمِيتُ فَـَٔامِنُوا بِاللَّهِ وَرَسُولِهِ النَّبِىِّ الْأُمِّىِّ الَّذِى يُؤْمِنُ بِاللَّهِ وَكَلِمَـٰتِهِ وَاتَّبِعُوهُ لَعَلَّكُمْ تَهْتَدُونَ ۝ وَمِن قَوْمِ مُوسَىٰٓ أُمَّةٌ يَهْدُونَ بِالْحَقِّ وَبِهِ يَعْدِلُونَ ۝

---

323 Some Muslim scholars cite Deuteronomy 18:15-18 and 33:2, Isaiah 42, and John 14:16 as examples of the description of Prophet Muḥammad in the Bible. However, Bible scholars interpret these verses differently. The name of Prophet Muḥammad (ﷺ) appears several times in the Gospel of Barnabas, which is deemed apocryphal by Christian authorities.

160. We divided them into twelve tribes—each as a community. And We revealed to Moses, when his people asked for water, "Strike the rock with your staff." Then twelve springs gushed out. Each tribe knew its drinking place. We shaded them with clouds and sent down to them manna and quails,[324] ˹saying˺, "Eat from the good things We have provided for you." They ˹certainly˺ did not wrong Us, but wronged themselves. **161.** And ˹remember˺ when it was said to them, "Enter this city ˹of Jerusalem˺ and eat from wherever you please. Say, 'Absolve us,' and enter the gate with humility. We will forgive your sins, ˹and˺ We will multiply the reward for the good-doers." **162.** But the wrongdoers among them changed the words they were commanded to say. So We sent down a punishment from the heavens upon them for their wrongdoing.

The Sabbath-Breakers

163. Ask them ˹O Prophet˺ about ˹the people of˺ the town which was by the sea, who broke the Sabbath.[325] During the Sabbath, ˹abundant˺ fish would come to them clearly visible, but on other days the fish were never seen. In this way We tested them for their rebelliousness.

---

324 Manna (heavenly bread) and quails (chicken-like birds) sustained the children of Israel in the wilderness after they left Egypt.

325 The people of Aylah, an ancient town by the Red Sea, were forbidden to catch fish on the Sabbath. However, on Saturdays fish were everywhere, whereas on weekdays no fish were seen. To get around the prohibition, some decided to lay their nets on Fridays and collect the fish caught in their nets on Sundays. Those opposed to this practice were divided into two groups: one group tried to convince the offenders to honour the Sabbath, but soon gave up when their advice was not taken seriously. The second group was persistent in giving advice to the Sabbath-breakers. Eventually, the Sabbath-breakers were punished whereas the other two groups were saved.

164. When some of 'the righteous among' them questioned 'their fellow Sabbath-keepers', "Why do you 'bother to' warn those 'Sabbath-breakers' who will either be destroyed or severely punished by Allah?" They replied, "Just to be free from your Lord's blame, and so perhaps they may abstain." **165.** When they ignored the warning they were given, We rescued those who used to warn against evil and overtook the wrongdoers with a dreadful punishment for their rebelliousness. **166.** But when they stubbornly persisted in violation, We said to them, "Be disgraced apes!"[326]

The Israelites Tested Again

167. And 'remember, O Prophet,' when your Lord declared that He would send against them others who would make them suffer terribly until the Day of Judgment. Indeed, your Lord is swift in punishment, but He is certainly All-Forgiving, Most Merciful. **168.** We dispersed them through the land in groups—some were righteous, others were less so. We tested them with prosperity and adversity, so perhaps they would return 'to the Right Path'.

Their Successors

169. Then they were succeeded by other generations who inherited the Scripture. They indulged in unlawful gains, claiming, "We will be forgiven 'after all'." And if similar gain came their way, they would seize it. Was a covenant not taken from them in the Scripture that they would not say anything about Allah except the truth? And they were already well-versed in its teachings. But the 'eternal' Home of the Hereafter is far better for those mindful 'of Allah'. Will you not then understand? **170.** As for those who firmly abide by the Scripture and establish prayer—surely We never discount the reward of those acting righteously.

---

326 Literally or metaphorically. *See* footnote for 2:65.

7. Al-A'râf 174

Covenant with the Israelites

171. And ˹remember˺ when We raised the mountain over them as if it were a cloud and they thought it would fall on them.[327] ˹We said,˺ "Hold firmly to that ˹Scripture˺ which We have given you and observe its teachings so perhaps you will become mindful ˹of Allah˺."

Covenant with Humanity

172. And ˹remember˺ when your Lord brought forth from the loins of the children of Adam their descendants and had them testify regarding themselves. ˹Allah asked,˺ "Am I not your Lord?" They replied, "Yes, You are! We testify." ˹He cautioned,˺ "Now you have no right to say on Judgment Day, 'We were not aware of this.' **173.** Nor say, 'It was our forefathers who had associated others ˹with Allah in worship˺ and we, as their descendants, followed in their footsteps. Will you then destroy us for the falsehood they invented?'" **174.** This is how We make our signs clear, so perhaps they will return ˹to the Right Path˺.

The Deviant Scholar[328]

175. And relate to them ˹O Prophet˺ the story of the one to whom We gave Our signs, but he abandoned them, so Satan took hold of him, and he became a deviant. **176.** If We had willed, We would have elevated him with Our signs, but he clung to this life— following his evil desires. His example is that of a dog: if you chase it away, it pants, and if you leave it, it ˹still˺ pants. This is the example of the people who deny Our signs.[329] So narrate ˹to them˺ stories ˹of the past˺, so perhaps they will reflect. **177.** What an evil example of those who denied Our signs! They ˹only˺ wronged their own souls.

Guidance from Allah Only

178. Whoever Allah guides is truly guided. And whoever He leaves to stray, they are the ˹true˺ losers.

---

327 The mountain was raised over their heads when Moses came to them with the teachings of the Torah and was met with defiance. So the mountain was raised as a miracle and a display of Allah's infinite power over them.

328 Bal'am ibn Bâ'ûrâ' was a scholar who lived at the time of Moses but later deviated from the truth.

329 Regardless of whether they are warned or not, still they will not believe.

7. Al-A'râf

179. Indeed, We have destined many jinn and humans for Hell. They have hearts they do not understand with, eyes they do not see with, and ears they do not hear with. They are like cattle. In fact, they are even less guided! Such ˹people˺ are ˹entirely˺ heedless.

Allah's Beautiful Names

180. Allah has the Most Beautiful Names. So call upon Him by them, and keep away from those who abuse His Names.[330] They will be punished for what they used to do.

The Guided and the Misguided

181. And among those We created is a group that guides with the truth and establishes justice accordingly. **182.** As for those who deny Our signs, We will gradually draw them to destruction in ways they cannot comprehend. **183.** I ˹only˺ delay their end for a while, but My planning is flawless.

Rejecting the Prophet

184. Have they not ever given it a thought? Their fellow man[331] is not insane. He is only sent with a clear warning. **185.** Have they ever reflected on the wonders of the heavens and the earth, and everything Allah has created, and that perhaps their end is near? So what message after this ˹Quran˺ would they believe in? **186.** Whoever Allah allows to stray, none can guide, leaving them to wander blindly in their defiance.

Time of the Final Hour

187. They ask you ˹O Prophet˺ regarding the Hour, "When will it be?" Say, "That knowledge is only with my Lord. He alone will reveal it when the time comes. It is too tremendous for the heavens and the earth and will only take you by surprise." They ask you as if you had full knowledge of it. Say, "That knowledge is only with Allah, but most people do not know."

---

330 Those who twist Allah's Names then use them to call false gods. For example, *Allât*, a name of one of the idols was derived from *Allah* (the One God), *Al-'Uzza* was derived from *Al-'Azîz* (the Almighty), and *Manât* was derived from *Al-Mannân* (the Bestower).

331 i.e., Muḥammad (ﷺ).

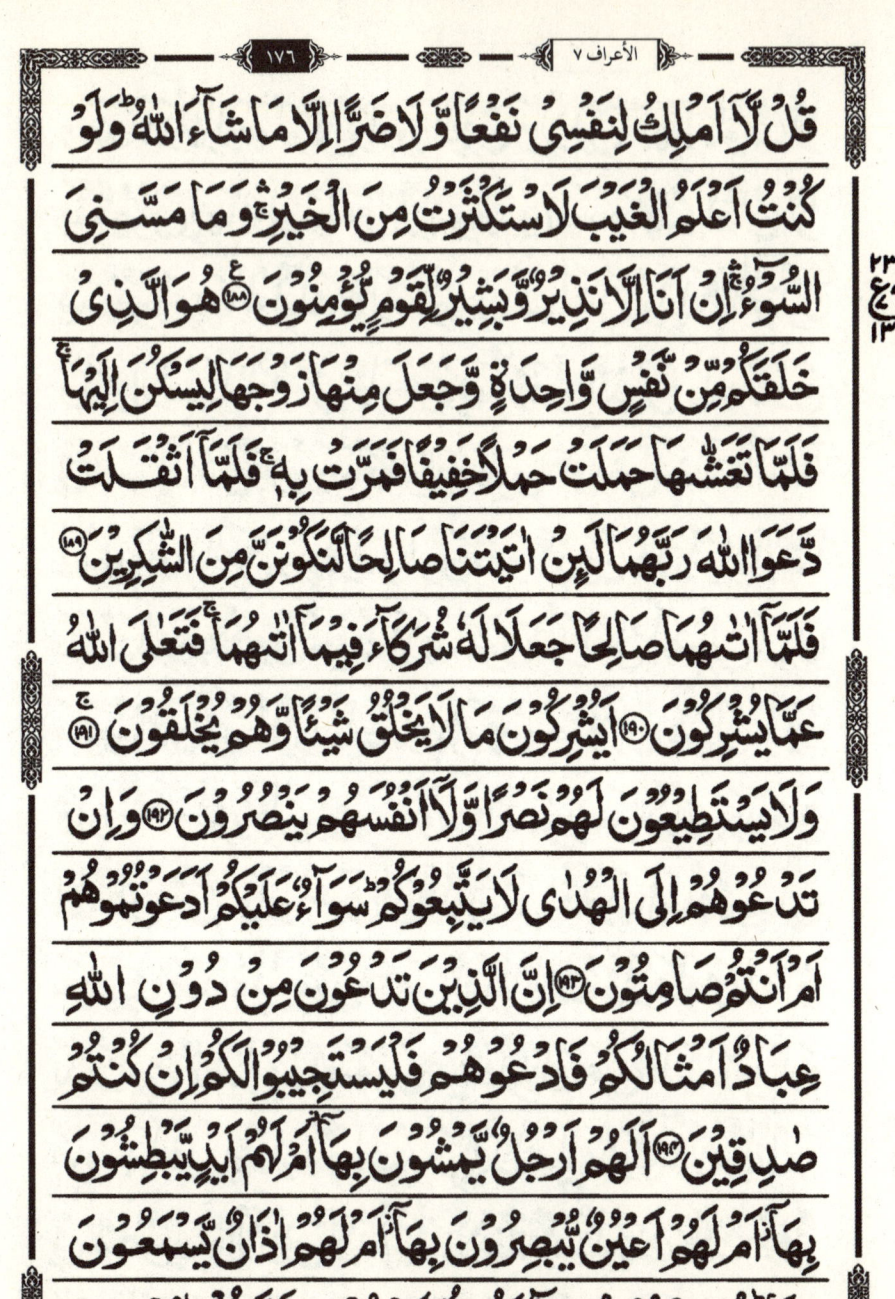

188. Say, "I have no power to benefit or protect myself, except by the Will of Allah. If I had known the unknown, I would have benefited myself enormously, and no harm would have ever touched me. I am only a warner and deliverer of good news for those who believe."

Going Astray

189. He is the One Who created you from a single soul, then from it made its spouse so he may find comfort in her. After he had been united with her, she carried a light burden that developed gradually. When it grew heavy, they prayed to Allah, their Lord, "If you grant us good offspring, we will certainly be grateful." **190.** But when He granted their descendants good offspring, they associated false gods in what He has given them. Exalted is Allah above what they associate ˹with Him˺!

Helpless Gods

191. Do they associate ˹with Allah˺ those ˹idols˺ which cannot create anything, but are in fact created; **192.** which cannot help them, or even help themselves? **193.** And if you ˹idolaters˺ call upon them for guidance, they cannot respond to you. It is all the same whether you call them or remain silent. **194.** Those ˹idols˺ you invoke besides Allah are created beings like yourselves. So call upon them and see if they will answer you, if your claims are true! **195.** Do they have feet to walk with? Or hands to hold with? Or eyes to see with? Or ears to hear with? Say, ˹O Prophet,˺ "Call upon your associate-gods and conspire against me without delay!

7. Al-A'râf

Allah Is the Protector

196. "Indeed, my Protector is Allah Who has revealed this Book. For He ˹alone˺ protects the righteous. **197.** But those ˹false gods˺ you call besides Him can neither help you nor even themselves." **198.** If you ˹idolaters˺ call them to guidance, they cannot hear. And you ˹O Prophet˺ may see them facing towards you, but they cannot see.

Grace and Tolerance

199. Be gracious, enjoin what is right, and turn away from those who act ignorantly.

Evil Impulses

200. If you are tempted by Satan, then seek refuge with Allah. Surely He is All-Hearing, All-Knowing. **201.** Indeed, when Satan whispers to those mindful ˹of Allah˺, they remember ˹their Lord˺ then they start to see ˹things˺ clearly. **202.** But the devils persistently plunge their ˹human˺ associates[332] deeper into wickedness, sparing no effort.

Only a Messenger

203. If you ˹O Prophet˺ do not bring them a sign ˹which they demanded˺, they ask, "Why do you not make it yourself?" Say, "I only follow what is revealed to me from my Lord. This ˹Quran˺ is an insight from your Lord—a guide and a mercy for those who believe."

Honouring the Quran

204. When the Quran is recited, listen to it attentively and be silent, so you may be shown mercy.

Being in Awe of Allah

205. Remember your Lord inwardly with humility and reverence and in a moderate tone of voice, both morning and evening. And do not be one of the heedless. **206.** Surely those ˹angels˺ nearest to your Lord are not too proud to worship Him. They glorify Him. And to Him they prostrate.

---

332 lit., their brothers.

8. Al-Anfâl | 178

8. Spoils of War (Al-Anfâl)

In the Name of Allah—the Most Compassionate, Most Merciful

Distribution of Spoils of War[333]

1. They ask you ˹O Prophet˺ regarding the spoils of war. Say, "Their distribution is decided by Allah and His Messenger. So be mindful of Allah, settle your affairs, and obey Allah and His Messenger if you are ˹true˺ believers."

Qualities of True Believers

2. The ˹true˺ believers are only those whose hearts tremble at the remembrance of Allah, whose faith increases when His revelations are recited to them, and who put their trust in their Lord. **3.** ˹They are˺ those who establish prayer and donate from what We have provided for them. **4.** It is they who are the true believers. They will have elevated ranks, forgiveness, and an honourable provision from their Lord.

Opposition to Fighting

5. Similarly, when your Lord brought you ˹O Prophet˺ out of your home for a just cause, a group of believers was totally against it. **6.** They disputed with you about the truth after it had been made clear, as if they were being driven to death with their eyes wide open.

Establishing the Truth

7. ˹Remember, O believers,˺ when Allah promised ˹to give˺ you the upper hand over either target, you wished to capture the unarmed party.[334] But it was Allah's Will to establish the truth by His Words and uproot the disbelievers; **8.** to firmly establish the truth and wipe out falsehood—even to the dismay of the wicked.

---

333 Following the victory of the Muslims over the Meccan army at Badr, some Muslims disagreed on the way the spoils of war should be distributed, so these verses were revealed.

334 After many years of persecution in Mecca, the Prophet (ﷺ) and many of his early followers decided to emigrate secretly to Medina, about 250 miles to the north, leaving behind their homes and valuables, which were soon taken over by the pagans of Mecca. To avenge this financial loss, the Prophet (ﷺ) decided to capture an unarmed Meccan trade caravan headed by Abu Sufyân, a Meccan chief. Eventually, the caravan escaped, but the Meccans mobilized an army of over 1000 well-armed soldiers, more than three times the size of the Muslim force. Many Muslims had hoped to capture the caravan without having to meet the Meccan army in battle. Although the Muslims were vastly outnumbered and lightly-armed, they still won this decisive battle.

Divine Reinforcement

9. ˹Remember˺ when you cried out to your Lord for help, He answered, "I will reinforce you with a thousand angels—followed by many others."[335] **10.** And Allah made this a sign of victory and reassurance to your hearts. Victory comes only from Allah. Surely Allah is Almighty, All-Wise.

Sense of Serenity

11. ˹Remember˺ when He caused drowsiness to overcome you, giving you serenity.[336] And He sent down rain from the sky to purify you, free you from Satan's whispers, strengthen your hearts, and make ˹your˺ steps firm.

Warning to Meccan Pagans

12. ˹Remember, O Prophet,˺ when your Lord revealed to the angels, "I am with you. So make the believers stand firm. I will cast horror into the hearts of the disbelievers. So strike their necks and strike their fingertips." **13.** This is because they defied Allah and His Messenger. And whoever defies Allah and His Messenger, then ˹know that˺ Allah is surely severe in punishment. **14.** That ˹worldly punishment˺ is yours, so taste it! Then the disbelievers will suffer the torment of the Fire.

Do Not Flee

15. O believers! When you face the disbelievers in battle, never turn your backs to them. **16.** And whoever does so on such an occasion—unless it is a manoeuvre or to join their own troops—will earn the displeasure of Allah, and their home will be Hell. What an evil destination!

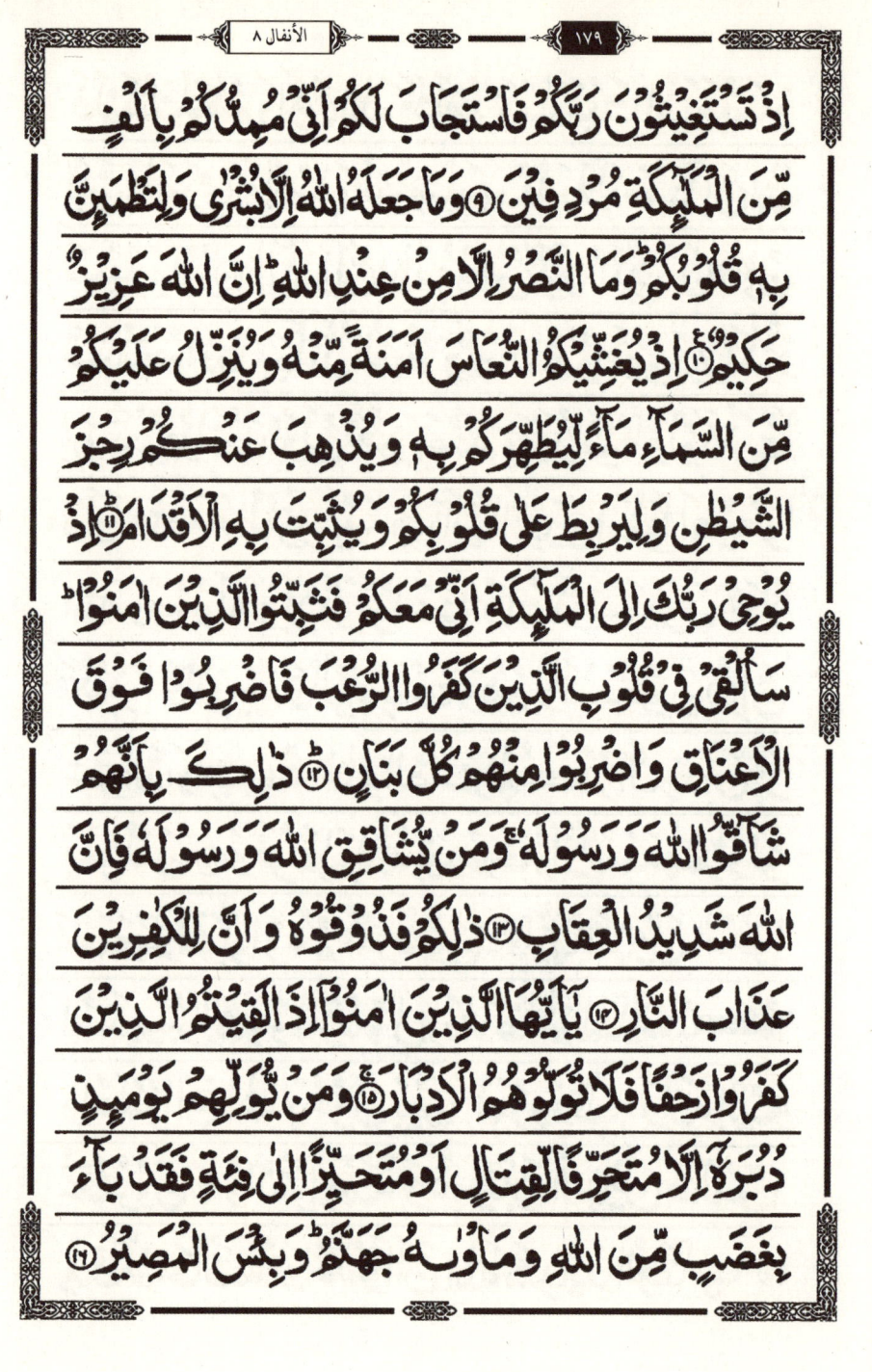

---

335 Five thousand angels in total, as mentioned in 3:125.
336 This happened the night before the battle.

8. Al-Anfâl

Victory from Allah

17. It was not you ˹believers˺ who killed them, but it was Allah Who did so. Nor was it you ˹O Prophet˺ who threw ˹a handful of sand at the disbelievers˺,[337] but it was Allah Who did so, rendering the believers a great favour. Surely Allah is All-Hearing, All-Knowing. **18.** As such, Allah frustrates the evil plans of the disbelievers.

Reasoning with Pagans

19. If you ˹Meccans˺ sought judgment, now it has come to you. And if you cease, it will be for your own good. But if you persist, We will persist. And your forces—no matter how numerous they might be—will not benefit you whatsoever. For Allah is certainly with the believers.

Hearing and Obeying

20. O believers! Obey Allah and His Messenger and do not turn away from him while you hear ˹his call˺. **21.** Do not be like those who say, "We hear," but in fact they are not listening. **22.** Indeed, the worst of all beings in the sight of Allah are the ˹wilfully˺ deaf and dumb, who do not understand.[338] **23.** Had Allah known any goodness in them, He would have certainly made them hear. ˹But˺ even if He had made them hear, they would have surely turned away heedlessly.

Reminder to the Believers

24. O believers! Respond to Allah and His Messenger when he calls you to that which gives you life. And know that Allah stands between a person and their heart, and that to Him you will all be gathered. **25.** Beware of a trial that will not only affect the wrongdoers among you. And know that Allah is severe in punishment.

---

337 Before the battle, the Prophet (ﷺ) threw a handful of sand at the disbelievers and prayed for their defeat.
338 This refers metaphorically to the disbelievers who fail to see and hear the truth.

8. Al-Anfâl

Allah's Help

26. Remember when you had been vastly outnumbered and oppressed in the land,[339] constantly in fear of attacks by your enemy, then He sheltered you, strengthened you with His help, and provided you with good things so perhaps you would be thankful.

Warning to the Believers

27. O believers! Do not betray Allah and the Messenger, nor betray your trusts knowingly. **28.** And know that your wealth and your children are only a test and that with Allah is a great reward.

Reward of the Believers

29. O believers! If you are mindful of Allah, He will grant you a decisive authority, absolve you of your sins, and forgive you. And Allah is the Lord of infinite bounty.

Pagan Conspiracy

30. And ˹remember, O Prophet,˺ when the disbelievers conspired to capture, kill, or exile you. They planned, but Allah also planned. And Allah is the best of planners.

Pagan Challenge

31. Whenever Our revelations are recited to them, they challenge ˹you˺, "We have already heard ˹the recitation˺. If we wanted, we could have easily produced something similar. This ˹Quran˺ is nothing but ancient fables!"

Pagan Denial

32. And ˹remember˺ when they prayed, "O Allah! If this is indeed the truth from You, then rain down stones upon us from the sky or overcome us with a painful punishment." **33.** But Allah would never punish them while you ˹O Prophet˺ were in their midst. Nor would He ever punish them if they prayed for forgiveness.

---

339 i.e., Mecca.

8. Al-Anfâl

Arabic Text

وَمَا لَهُمْ أَلَّا يُعَذِّبَهُمُ اللَّهُ وَهُمْ يَصُدُّونَ عَنِ الْمَسْجِدِ الْحَرَامِ وَمَا كَانُوٓا أَوْلِيَآءَهُۥٓ إِنْ أَوْلِيَآؤُهُۥٓ إِلَّا الْمُتَّقُونَ وَلَٰكِنَّ أَكْثَرَهُمْ لَا يَعْلَمُونَ ۩ وَمَا كَانَ صَلَاتُهُمْ عِندَ الْبَيْتِ إِلَّا مُكَآءً وَتَصْدِيَةً ۚ فَذُوقُوا الْعَذَابَ بِمَا كُنتُمْ تَكْفُرُونَ ۩ إِنَّ الَّذِينَ كَفَرُوا يُنفِقُونَ أَمْوَٰلَهُمْ لِيَصُدُّوا عَن سَبِيلِ اللَّهِ ۚ فَسَيُنفِقُونَهَا ثُمَّ تَكُونُ عَلَيْهِمْ حَسْرَةً ثُمَّ يُغْلَبُونَ ۗ وَالَّذِينَ كَفَرُوٓا إِلَىٰ جَهَنَّمَ يُحْشَرُونَ ۩ لِيَمِيزَ اللَّهُ الْخَبِيثَ مِنَ الطَّيِّبِ وَيَجْعَلَ الْخَبِيثَ بَعْضَهُۥ عَلَىٰ بَعْضٍ فَيَرْكُمَهُۥ جَمِيعًا فَيَجْعَلَهُۥ فِي جَهَنَّمَ ۚ أُو۟لَٰٓئِكَ هُمُ الْخَٰسِرُونَ ۩ قُل لِّلَّذِينَ كَفَرُوٓا إِن يَنتَهُوا يُغْفَرْ لَهُم مَّا قَدْ سَلَفَ وَإِن يَعُودُوا فَقَدْ مَضَتْ سُنَّتُ الْأَوَّلِينَ ۩ وَقَٰتِلُوهُمْ حَتَّىٰ لَا تَكُونَ فِتْنَةٌ وَيَكُونَ الدِّينُ كُلُّهُۥ لِلَّهِ ۚ فَإِنِ انتَهَوْا فَإِنَّ اللَّهَ بِمَا يَعْمَلُونَ بَصِيرٌ ۩ وَإِن تَوَلَّوْا فَاعْلَمُوٓا أَنَّ اللَّهَ مَوْلَىٰكُمْ ۚ نِعْمَ الْمَوْلَىٰ وَنِعْمَ النَّصِيرُ ۩

English Translation

Punishment Deserved

34. And why should Allah not punish them while they hinder pilgrims from the Sacred Mosque, claiming to be its rightful guardians? None has the right to guardianship except those mindful ˹of Allah˺, but most pagans do not know. **35.** Their prayer at the Sacred House was nothing but whistling and clapping. So taste the punishment for your disbelief.

Pagans' Wasted Efforts

36. Surely the disbelievers spend their wealth to hinder others from the Path of Allah. They will continue to spend to the point of regret. Then they will be defeated and the disbelievers will be driven into Hell, **37.** so Allah may separate the evil from the good. He will pile up the evil ones all together and then cast them into Hell. They are the ˹true˺ losers.

Peace Offer

38. Tell the disbelievers that if they desist, their past will be forgiven. But if they persist, then they have an example in those destroyed before them. **39.** Fight against them until there is no more persecution—and ˹your˺ devotion will be entirely to Allah. But if they desist, then surely Allah is All-Seeing of what they do. **40.** And if they do not comply, then know that Allah is your Protector. What an excellent Protector, and what an excellent Helper!

8. Al-Anfâl

Distribution of Spoils of War

41. Know that whatever spoils you take, one-fifth is for Allah and the Messenger, his close relatives, orphans, the poor, and ˹needy˺ travellers, if you ˹truly˺ believe in Allah and what We revealed to Our servant on that decisive day when the two armies met ˹at Badr˺. And Allah is Most Capable of everything. **42.** ˹Remember˺ when you were on the near side of the valley, your enemy on the far side, and the caravan was below you. Even if the two armies had made an appointment ˹to meet˺, both would have certainly missed it.[340] Still it transpired so Allah may establish what He had destined—that those who were to perish and those who were to survive might do so after the truth had been made clear to both. Surely Allah is All-Hearing, All-Knowing.

Vision of Enemy Force

43. ˹Remember, O Prophet,˺ when Allah showed them in your dream as few in number. Had He shown them to you as many, you ˹believers˺ would have certainly faltered and disputed in the matter. But Allah spared you ˹from that˺. Surely He knows best what is ˹hidden˺ in the heart. **44.** Then when your armies met, Allah made them appear as few in your eyes, and made you appear as few in theirs, so Allah may establish what He had destined. And to Allah ˹all˺ matters will be returned ˹for judgment˺.

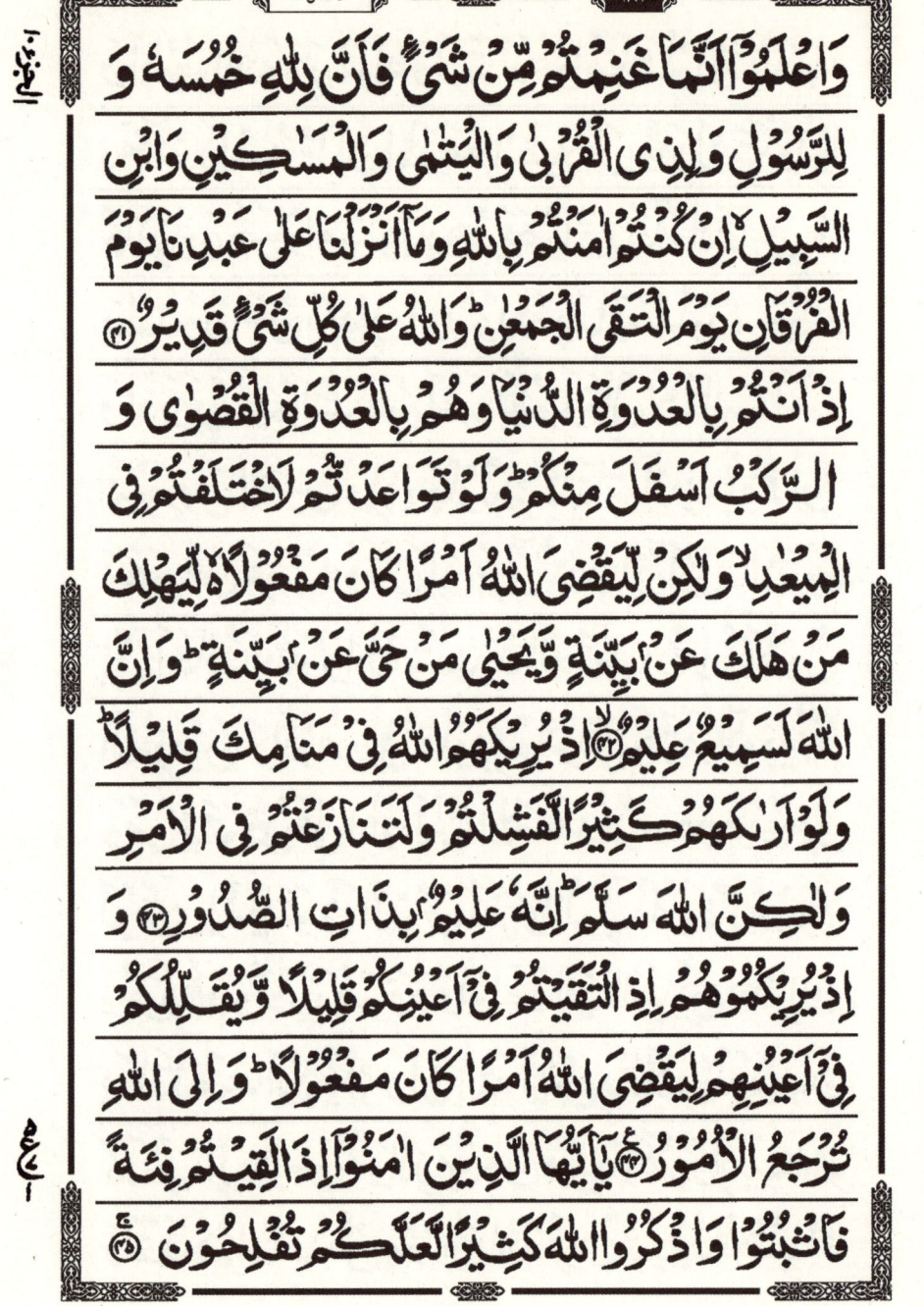

Word of Advice

45. O believers! When you face an enemy, stand firm and remember Allah often so you may triumph.

---

340 The battle was not planned since the Muslim force was after the caravan. Had the two armies made plans to meet in battle at that time and place, they both probably would have missed each other.

8. Al-Anfâl 184

46. Obey Allah and His Messenger and do not dispute with one another, or you would be discouraged and weakened. Persevere! Surely Allah is with those who persevere. **47.** Do not be like those ˹pagans˺ who left their homes arrogantly, only to be seen by people and to hinder others from Allah's Path. And Allah is Fully Aware of what they do.

Satan Tempts the Meccan Pagans

48. And ˹remember˺ when Satan made their ˹evil˺ deeds appealing to them, and said, "No one can overcome you today. I am surely by your side." But when the two forces faced off, he cowered and said, "I have absolutely nothing to do with you. I certainly see what you do not see. I truly fear Allah, for Allah is severe in punishment."

Trust in Allah

49. ˹Remember˺ when the hypocrites and those with sickness in their hearts said, "These ˹believers˺ are deluded by their faith." But whoever puts their trust in Allah, surely Allah is Almighty, All-Wise.

Evil Ending

50. If only you could see when the angels take the souls of the disbelievers, beating their faces and backs, ˹saying,˺ "Taste the torment of burning! **51.** This is ˹the reward˺ for what your hands have done. And Allah is never unjust to ˹His˺ creation."

Fate of the Wicked

52. Their fate is that of the people of Pharaoh and those before them—they all disbelieved in Allah's signs, so Allah seized them for their sins. Indeed, Allah is All-Powerful, severe in punishment.

53. This is because Allah would never discontinue His favour to a people until they discontinue their faith. Surely Allah is All-Hearing, All-Knowing. **54.** That was the case with Pharaoh's people and those before them—they all rejected the signs of their Lord, so We destroyed them for their sins and drowned Pharaoh's people. They were all wrongdoers.

Those Who Violate Peace Treaties

55. Indeed, the worst of all beings in the sight of Allah are those who persist in disbelief, never to have faith— **56.** ˹namely˺ those with whom you ˹O Prophet˺ have entered into treaties, but they violate them every time, not fearing the consequences. **57.** If you ever encounter them in battle, make a fearsome example of them, so perhaps those who would follow them may be deterred.

No Betrayal in Treaties

58. And if you ˹O Prophet˺ see signs of betrayal by a people, respond by openly terminating your treaty with them. Surely Allah does not like those who betray.

Military Deterrence

59. Do not let those disbelievers[341] think they are not within reach. They will have no escape. **60.** Prepare against them what you ˹believers˺ can of ˹military˺ power and cavalry to deter Allah's enemies and your enemies as well as other enemies unknown to you but known to Allah. Whatever you spend in the cause of Allah will be paid to you in full and you will not be wronged.

Advice to the Prophet: Opt for Peace

61. If the enemy is inclined towards peace, make peace with them. And put your trust in Allah. Indeed, He ˹alone˺ is the All-Hearing, All-Knowing.

---

341 Who survived the Battle of Badr.

62. But if their intention is only to deceive you, then Allah is certainly sufficient for you. He is the One Who has supported you with His help and with the believers. 63. He brought their hearts together. Had you spent all the riches in the earth, you could not have united their hearts. But Allah has united them. Indeed, He is Almighty, All-Wise. 64. O Prophet! Allah is sufficient for you and for the believers who follow you.

Readiness to Fight

65. O Prophet! Motivate the believers to fight. If there are twenty steadfast among you, they will overcome two hundred. And if there are one hundred of you, they will overcome one thousand of the disbelievers, for they are a people who do not comprehend. 66. Now Allah has lightened your burden, for He knows that there is weakness in you. So if there are a hundred steadfast among you, they will overcome two hundred. And if there be one thousand, they will overcome two thousand, by Allah's Will. And Allah is with the steadfast.

Decision on Captives

67. It is not fit for a prophet that he should take captives until he has thoroughly subdued the land. You ˹believers˺ settled with the fleeting gains of this world,[342] while Allah's aim ˹for you˺ is the Hereafter. Allah is Almighty, All-Wise. 68. Had it not been for a prior decree from Allah,[343] you would have certainly been disciplined with a tremendous punishment for whatever ˹ransom˺ you have taken. 69. Now enjoy what you have taken, for it is lawful and good. And be mindful of Allah. Surely Allah is All-Forgiving, Most Merciful.

---

342 i.e., ransom.
343 The decree that ransoming captives will be allowed.

8. Al-Anfâl

Ransomed Captives

70. O Prophet! Tell the captives in your custody, "If Allah finds goodness in your hearts, He will give you better than what has been taken from you, and forgive you. For Allah is All-Forgiving, Most Merciful."

71. But if their intention is only to betray you ˹O Prophet˺, they sought to betray Allah before. But He gave you power over them. And Allah is All-Knowing, All-Wise.

Guardianship Among Believers

72. Those who believed, emigrated, and strived with their wealth and lives in the cause of Allah, as well as those who gave them shelter and help—they are truly guardians of one another. As for those who believed but did not emigrate, you have no obligations to them until they emigrate. But if they seek your help ˹against persecution˺ in faith, it is your obligation to help them, except against people bound with you in a treaty. Allah is All-Seeing of what you do.

Guardianship Among Disbelievers

73. As for the disbelievers, they are guardians of one another. And unless you ˹believers˺ act likewise, there will be great oppression and corruption in the land.

True Believers

74. Those who believed, migrated, and struggled in the cause of Allah, and those who gave ˹them˺ shelter and help, they are the true believers. They will have forgiveness and an honourable provision.

Relatives Inherit One Another

75. And those who later believed, migrated, and struggled alongside you, they are also with you. But only blood relatives are now entitled to inherit from one another, as ordained by Allah. Surely Allah has ˹full˺ knowledge of everything.[344]

---

344 This verse ended a previous ruling that allowed inheritance between Muslims from Mecca (Al-Muhâjirûn, the Emigrants) and Muslims from Medina (Al-Anṣâr, the Helpers). Now, only relatives can inherit from one another, whereas non-heirs can receive a share through bequest, up to one third of the estate. See 4:7, 11-13, 32-33, and 176.

9. Repentance (At-Tawbah)

Declaration to the Polytheists[345]

1. ˹This is˺ a discharge from all obligations, by Allah and His Messenger, to the polytheists you ˹believers˺ have entered into treaties with:
2. "You ˹polytheists˺ may travel freely through the land for four months, but know that you will have no escape from Allah, and that Allah will disgrace the disbelievers."
3. A declaration from Allah and His Messenger ˹is made˺ to all people on the day of the greater pilgrimage[346] that Allah and His Messenger are free of the polytheists. So if you ˹pagans˺ repent, it will be better for you. But if you turn away, then know that you will have no escape from Allah. And give good news ˹O Prophet˺ to the disbelievers of a painful punishment.

Exception to the Declaration

4. As for the polytheists who have honoured every term of their treaty with you and have not supported an enemy against you, honour your treaty with them until the end of its term. Surely Allah loves those who are mindful ˹of Him˺.

After the Grace Period

5. But once the Sacred Months have passed, kill the polytheists ˹who violated their treaties˺ wherever you find them,[347] capture them, besiege them, and lie in wait for them on every way. But if they repent, perform prayers, and pay alms-tax, then set them free. Indeed, Allah is All-Forgiving, Most Merciful.

Pagans Seeking Protection

6. And if anyone from the polytheists asks for your protection ˹O Prophet˺, grant it to them so they may hear the Word of Allah, then escort them to a place of safety, for they are a people who have no knowledge.

---

345 This is the only sûrah in the Quran that does not begin with: "In the Name of Allah—the Most Compassionate, Most Merciful." The reason is that this sûrah is considered to be a continuation of the previous one, and that it begins with an open termination of treaties not fully respected by the polytheists. Since this constitutes a declaration of war, it would not be fitting to open with the mention of Allah's compassion and mercy.

346 The 10th of Zul-Ḥijjah, a significant day in the greater pilgrimage (ḥajj). The lesser pilgrimage is known as 'umrah.

347 i.e., inside or outside the sanctuary of the Sacred House in Mecca.

9. At-Tawbah

Treacherous Polytheists

7. How can such polytheists have a treaty with Allah and His Messenger, except those you have made a treaty with at the Sacred Mosque?[348] So, as long as they are true to you, be true to them. Indeed Allah loves those who are mindful ˹of Him˺. **8.** How ˹can they have a treaty˺? If they were to have the upper hand over you, they would have no respect for kinship or treaty. They only flatter you with their tongues, but their hearts are in denial, and most of them are rebellious.

Arab Pagans

9. They chose a fleeting gain over Allah's revelations, hindering ˹others˺ from His Way. Evil indeed is what they have done! **10.** They do not honour the bonds of kinship or treaties with the believers. It is they who are the transgressors. **11.** But if they repent, perform prayer, and pay alms-tax, then they are your brothers in faith. This is how We make the revelations clear for people of knowledge. **12.** But if they break their oaths after making a pledge and attack your faith, then fight the champions of disbelief—who never honour their oaths—so perhaps they will desist.

Order to Fight

13. Will you not fight those who have broken their oaths, conspired to expel the Messenger ˹from Mecca˺, and attacked you first? Do you fear them? Allah is more deserving of your fear, if you are ˹true˺ believers.

---

348 This is known as the Treaty of Ḥudaibiyah, which was signed by the Prophet (ﷺ) and the pagans of Mecca in 6 A.H./628 C.E., diffusing the tension between Muslims and the Meccans and affirming a 10-year peace truce. The treaty was violated by the Meccans in 8 A.H./630 C.E.

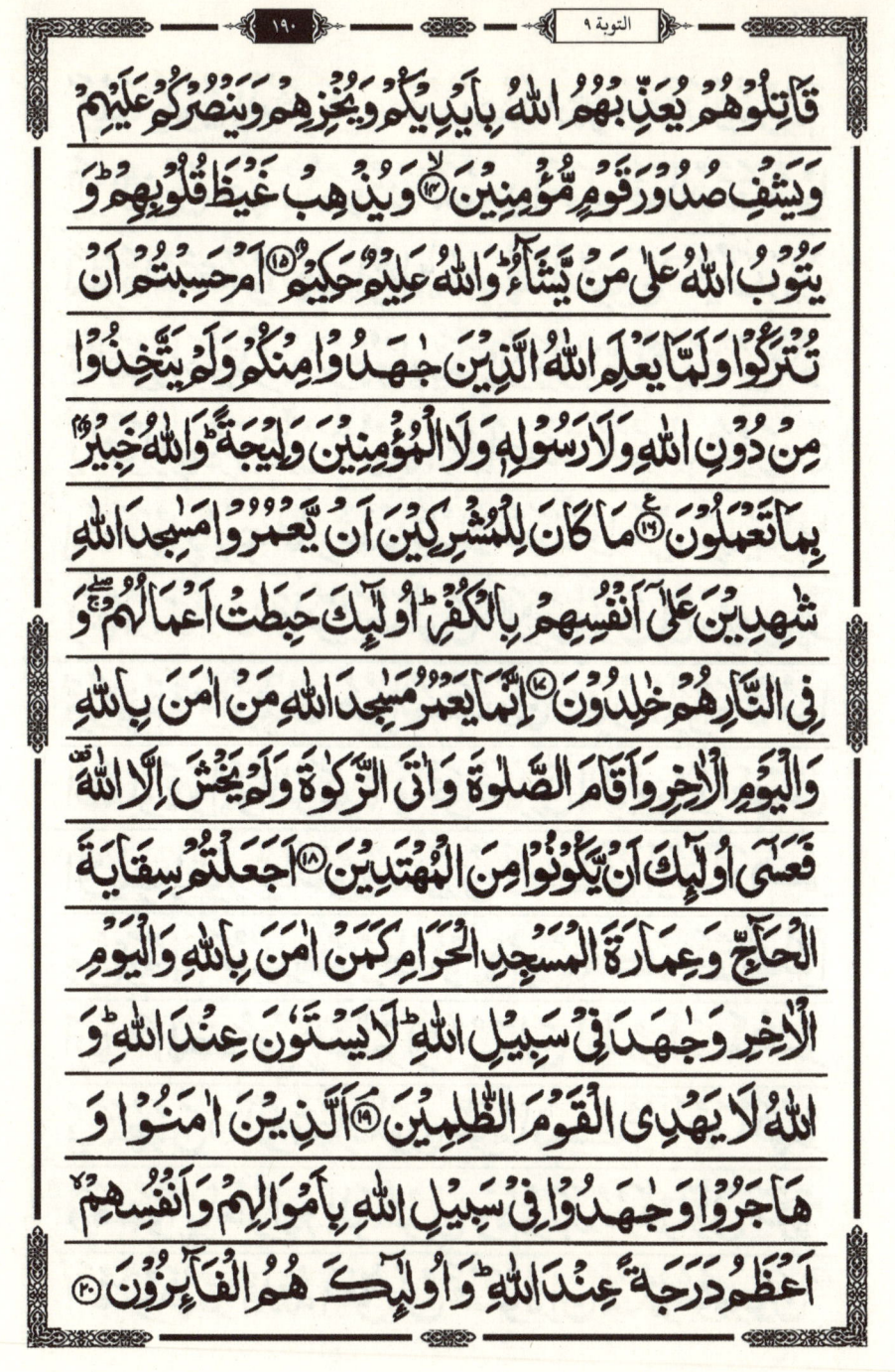

14. ˹So˺ fight them and Allah will punish them at your hands, put them to shame, help you overcome them, and soothe the hearts of the believers— 15. removing rage from their hearts. And Allah pardons whoever He wills. For Allah is All-Knowing, All-Wise.

Wisdom Behind Fighting

16. Do you ˹believers˺ think that you will be left without Allah proving who among you ˹truly˺ struggles ˹in His cause˺ and never takes trusted allies other than Allah, His Messenger, or the believers? And Allah is All-Aware of what you do.

Maintenance of Mosques

17. It is not for the polytheists to maintain the mosques of Allah while they openly profess disbelief. Their deeds are void, and they will be in the Fire forever. 18. The mosques of Allah should only be maintained by those who believe in Allah and the Last Day, establish prayer, pay alms-tax, and fear none but Allah. It is right to hope that they will be among the ˹truly˺ guided.

Not Equal

19. Do you ˹pagans˺ consider providing the pilgrims with water and maintaining the Sacred Mosque as equal to believing in Allah and the Last Day and struggling in the cause of Allah? They are not equal in Allah's sight. And Allah does not guide the wrongdoing people.

Reward of the Believers

20. Those who have believed, emigrated, and strived in the cause of Allah with their wealth and their lives are greater in rank in the sight of Allah. It is they who will triumph.

9. At-Tawbah

21. Their Lord gives them good news of His mercy, pleasure, and Gardens with everlasting bliss, **22.** to stay there for ever and ever. Surely with Allah is a great reward.

Warning to the Believers

23. O believers! Do not take your parents and siblings as trusted allies if they choose disbelief over belief. And whoever of you does so, they are the ˹true˺ wrongdoers. **24.** Say, ˹O Prophet,˺ "If your parents and children and siblings and spouses and extended family and the wealth you have acquired and the trade you fear will decline and the homes you cherish—˹if all these˺ are more beloved to you than Allah and His Messenger and struggling in His Way, then wait until Allah brings about His Will. Allah does not guide the rebellious people."

Victory Is from Allah Alone

25. Indeed Allah has given you ˹believers˺ victory on many battle-fields, even at the Battle of Ḥunain-when you took pride in your great numbers, but they proved of no advantage to you.[349] The earth, despite its vastness, seemed to close in on you, then you turned back in retreat. **26.** Then Allah sent down His reassurance[350] upon His Messenger and the believers, and sent down forces[351] you could not see, and punished those who disbelieved. Such was the reward of the disbelievers.

---

349 After the Muslims' victory in Mecca in 8 A.H/630 C.E., almost all Arab tribes pledged allegiance to the Prophet (ﷺ) except some tribes such as Hawâzin and Thaqîf. Both tribes decided to attack the Muslims, so the Prophet (ﷺ) led an army of 12 000 soldiers to attack the two tribes. Since that was the largest Muslim army ever mobilized, some Muslims expressed their conviction that such an army could not be defeated. However, on the way to battle, the Muslim army was ambushed and most soldiers fled, except for the Prophet (ﷺ) and a few loyalists. Eventually, the Muslims were re-organized and won a decisive battle.

350 lit., tranquility.

351 i.e., angels.

9. At-Tawbah

27. Then afterwards Allah will turn in grace to whoever He wills.[352] And Allah is All-Forgiving, Most Merciful.

No More Idolatry at the Ka'bah

28. O believers! Indeed, the polytheists are ˹spiritually˺ impure,[353] so they should not approach the Sacred Mosque after this year.[354] If you fear poverty, Allah will enrich you out of His bounty, if He wills. Surely, Allah is All-Knowing, All-Wise.

Command to Fight

29. Fight those who do not believe in Allah and the Last Day, nor comply with what Allah and His Messenger have forbidden, nor embrace the religion of truth from among those who were given the Scripture,[355] until they pay the tax,[356] willingly submitting, fully humbled.

Blind Following

30. The Jews say, "Ezra is the son of Allah," while the Christians say, "The Messiah is the son of Allah." Such are their baseless assertions, only parroting the words of earlier disbelievers. May Allah condemn them! How can they be deluded ˹from the truth˺? **31.** They have taken their rabbis and monks as well as the Messiah, son of Mary, as lords besides Allah,[357] even though they were commanded to worship none but One God. There is no god ˹worthy of worship˺ except Him. Glorified is He above what they associate ˹with Him˺!

---

352 i.e., Allah will accept those who embrace Islam. Almost all of Arabia became Muslim before the death of Prophet Muḥammad (ﷺ) in 11 A.H./632 C.E.

353 i.e., impure spiritually because of idolatry, not physically.

354 The 9th year of the Prophet's migration from Mecca to Medina.

355 To fully understand this verse we need to bear in mind that Quranic verses are of two types. General verses talk about belief in Allah, good manners, and acts of worship. Specific verses, such as this verse, were revealed in regards to particular situations. This sûrah came at a time when the pagans of Arabia (and their allies) repeatedly violated treaties they had signed with the Prophet (ﷺ). Muslims had to fight for the survival of their newly established state in Medina. So this verse discusses dealing with those who violated their agreements and attacked the Muslims. Offenders were fought, unless they stopped their aggression. If they chose not to accept Islam, they were obligated to pay Jizya-tax.

356 Taxation systems have existed since ancient times. There are several references in the Old Testament (e.g., Ezra 4:20). In the New Testament, Jesus allows paying taxes to Caesar (Luke 20:25). Under Islamic rule, all individuals had financial obligations—Muslims paid zakâh (2.5% of their savings) and non-Muslims (zimmîs) were required to pay jizyah (tax for protection from foreign enemies). The jizyah was an average of one dinar (4.25 g of gold) annually. Women, children, the elderly, the clergy, the poor, and those who were unable to work were exempt. Those who opted to join the army were also exempt. Poor zimmîs were supported financially by the state. Muslim rulers refunded the jizyah if they failed to protect their non-Muslim subjects.

357 When 'Adi ibn Ḥâtim, a companion of the Prophet (ﷺ), heard this verse, he said, "But the Jews and Christians do not worship their rabbis and monks!" The Prophet (ﷺ) replied, "Do the rabbis and monks not forbid the permissible and permit the forbidden, and they obey them?" 'Adi answered, "Yes, they do." The Prophet (ﷺ) concluded, "This is how they worship them." Collected by at-Tirmizî.

The True Faith

32. They wish to extinguish Allah's light[358] with their mouths, but Allah will only allow His light to be perfected, even to the dismay of the disbelievers. **33.** He is the One Who has sent His Messenger with ˹true˺ guidance and the religion of truth, making it prevail over all others, even to the dismay of the polytheists.

Unlawful Gains

34. O believers! Indeed, many rabbis and monks consume people's wealth wrongfully and hinder ˹others˺ from the Way of Allah. Give good news of a painful torment to those who hoard gold and silver and do not spend it in Allah's cause. **35.** The Day ˹will come˺ when their treasure will be heated up in the Fire of Hell, and their foreheads, sides, and backs branded with it. ˹It will be said to them,˺ "This is the treasure you hoarded for yourselves. Now taste what you hoarded!"

Honouring the Sacred Months

36. Indeed, the number of months ordained by Allah is twelve—in Allah's Record[359] since the day He created the heavens and the earth—of which four are sacred. That is the Right Way. So do not wrong one another during these months. And together fight the polytheists as they fight against you together. And know that Allah is with those mindful ˹of Him˺.

---

358 i.e., religion of truth.
359 i.e., the Preserved Tablet in which everything is written.

9. At-Tawbah

إِنَّمَا النَّسِيءُ زِيَادَةٌ فِي الْكُفْرِ يُضَلُّ بِهِ الَّذِينَ كَفَرُوا يُحِلُّونَهُ عَامًا وَيُحَرِّمُونَهُ عَامًا لِّيُوَاطِئُوا عِدَّةَ مَا حَرَّمَ اللَّهُ فَيُحِلُّوا مَا حَرَّمَ اللَّهُ زُيِّنَ لَهُمْ سُوءُ أَعْمَالِهِمْ وَاللَّهُ لَا يَهْدِي الْقَوْمَ الْكَافِرِينَ ۝ يَا أَيُّهَا الَّذِينَ آمَنُوا مَا لَكُمْ إِذَا قِيلَ لَكُمُ انفِرُوا فِي سَبِيلِ اللَّهِ اثَّاقَلْتُمْ إِلَى الْأَرْضِ أَرَضِيتُم بِالْحَيَاةِ الدُّنْيَا مِنَ الْآخِرَةِ فَمَا مَتَاعُ الْحَيَاةِ الدُّنْيَا فِي الْآخِرَةِ إِلَّا قَلِيلٌ ۝ إِلَّا تَنفِرُوا يُعَذِّبْكُمْ عَذَابًا أَلِيمًا وَيَسْتَبْدِلْ قَوْمًا غَيْرَكُمْ وَلَا تَضُرُّوهُ شَيْئًا وَاللَّهُ عَلَىٰ كُلِّ شَيْءٍ قَدِيرٌ ۝ إِلَّا تَنصُرُوهُ فَقَدْ نَصَرَهُ اللَّهُ إِذْ أَخْرَجَهُ الَّذِينَ كَفَرُوا ثَانِيَ اثْنَيْنِ إِذْ هُمَا فِي الْغَارِ إِذْ يَقُولُ لِصَاحِبِهِ لَا تَحْزَنْ إِنَّ اللَّهَ مَعَنَا فَأَنزَلَ اللَّهُ سَكِينَتَهُ عَلَيْهِ وَأَيَّدَهُ بِجُنُودٍ لَّمْ تَرَوْهَا وَجَعَلَ كَلِمَةَ الَّذِينَ كَفَرُوا السُّفْلَىٰ وَكَلِمَةُ اللَّهِ هِيَ الْعُلْيَا وَاللَّهُ عَزِيزٌ حَكِيمٌ ۝ انفِرُوا خِفَافًا وَثِقَالًا وَجَاهِدُوا بِأَمْوَالِكُمْ وَأَنفُسِكُمْ فِي سَبِيلِ اللَّهِ ذَٰلِكُمْ خَيْرٌ لَّكُمْ إِن كُنتُمْ تَعْلَمُونَ ۝

37. Reallocating the sanctity of ˹these˺ months[360] is an increase in disbelief, by which the disbelievers are led ˹far˺ astray. They adjust the sanctity one year and uphold it in another, only to maintain the number of months sanctified by Allah, violating the very months Allah has made sacred. Their evil deeds have been made appealing to them. And Allah does not guide the disbelieving people.

Clinging to This Life

38. O believers! What is the matter with you that when you are asked to march forth in the cause of Allah, you cling firmly to ˹your˺ land?[361] Do you prefer the life of this world over the Hereafter? The enjoyment of this worldly life is insignificant compared to that of the Hereafter. 39. If you do not march forth, He will afflict you with a painful torment and replace you with other people. You are not harming Him in the least. And Allah is Most Capable of everything.

Supporting the Prophet

40. ˹It does not matter˺ if you ˹believers˺ do not support him, for Allah did in fact support him when the disbelievers drove him out ˹of Mecca˺ and he was only one of two. While they both were in the cave, he reassured his companion,[362] "Do not worry; Allah is certainly with us." So Allah sent down His serenity upon the Prophet, supported him with forces you ˹believers˺ did not see, and made the word of the disbelievers lowest, while the Word of Allah is supreme. And Allah is Almighty, All-Wise.

---

360 The sacred months are the 11th, 12th, 1st, and 7th of the Islamic calendar. Since the polytheists knew that it was forbidden to fight in the sacred months, they used to transfer the sanctity to other months, say for example, the 3rd, 4th, 8th, and 10th as long as they maintained the sanctity of any four months throughout the year.

361 The fast pace of the spread of Islam in Arabia in the 7th century was intimidating to the world's two superpowers of that time: the Romans and Persians. The Prophet (ﷺ) received the news that a Roman army was being mobilized to launch an attack on the newly established Muslim state in Medina, so he announced that he was going to march to Tabūk, located over 700 miles to the north, to meet the Romans in the summer of 9 A.H./631 C.E. It was a time of hardship because of the scorching heat, the long distance, and the financial situation of the Muslims. Although the Prophet (ﷺ) was able to mobilize over 30 000 Muslims for battle, many others did not join the army with or without valid excuses. Eventually, the Roman forces were discouraged from fighting and fled to Damascus and other cities under Roman rule. Therefore, the Prophet (ﷺ) returned to Medina with a feeling of triumph. With a new power now emerging in Arabia, many tribes started to switch their alliances from Caesar to the Prophet (ﷺ).

362 Abu Bakr Aṣ-Ṣiddīq, Islam's first Caliph and a prominent figure in Islamic history. He accompanied the Prophet (ﷺ) during his emigration from Mecca to Medina after years of persecution at the hands of the Meccan pagans.

9. At-Tawbah

41. ˹O believers!˺ March forth whether it is easy or difficult for you, and strive with your wealth and your lives in the cause of Allah. That is best for you, if only you knew.

False Excuse 1) Inability

42. Had the gain been within reach and the journey shorter, they would have followed you, but the distance seemed too long for them. And they will swear by Allah, "Had we been able, we would have certainly joined you." They are ruining themselves. And Allah knows that they are surely lying. **43.** May Allah pardon you ˹O Prophet˺! Why did you give them permission ˹to stay behind˺ before those who told the truth were distinguished from those who were lying?

Exemption from Fighting

44. Those who believe in Allah and the Last Day do not ask for exemption from striving with their wealth and their lives. And Allah has perfect knowledge of those who are mindful ˹of Him˺. **45.** No one would ask for exemption except those who have no faith in Allah or the Last Day, and whose hearts are in doubt, so they are torn by their doubts.

The Trouble-Makers

46. Had they ˹really˺ intended to march forth, they would have made preparations for it. But Allah disliked that they should go, so He let them lag behind, and it was said ˹to them˺, "Stay with those ˹helpless˺ who remain behind." **47.** Had they gone forth with you ˹believers˺, they would have been nothing but trouble for you, and would have scrambled around, seeking to spread discord in your midst. And some of you would have eagerly listened to them. And Allah has ˹perfect˺ knowledge of the wrongdoers.

بِسْمِ اللّٰهِ الرَّحْمٰنِ الرَّحِيمِ

لَقَدِ ابْتَغَوُا الْفِتْنَةَ مِن قَبْلُ وَقَلَّبُوا لَكَ الْأُمُورَ حَتَّىٰ جَآءَ الْحَقُّ وَظَهَرَ أَمْرُ اللّٰهِ وَهُمْ كَٰرِهُونَ ۝ وَمِنْهُم مَّن يَقُولُ ائْذَن لِّى وَلَا تَفْتِنِّىٓ أَلَا فِى الْفِتْنَةِ سَقَطُوا وَإِنَّ جَهَنَّمَ لَمُحِيطَةٌۢ بِالْكَٰفِرِينَ ۝ إِن تُصِبْكَ حَسَنَةٌ تَسُؤْهُمْ وَإِن تُصِبْكَ مُصِيبَةٌ يَقُولُوا قَدْ أَخَذْنَآ أَمْرَنَا مِن قَبْلُ وَيَتَوَلَّوا وَّهُمْ فَرِحُونَ ۝ قُل لَّن يُصِيبَنَآ إِلَّا مَا كَتَبَ اللّٰهُ لَنَا هُوَ مَوْلَىٰنَا وَعَلَى اللّٰهِ فَلْيَتَوَكَّلِ الْمُؤْمِنُونَ ۝ قُلْ هَلْ تَرَبَّصُونَ بِنَآ إِلَّآ إِحْدَى الْحُسْنَيَيْنِ وَنَحْنُ نَتَرَبَّصُ بِكُمْ أَن يُصِيبَكُمُ اللّٰهُ بِعَذَابٍ مِّنْ عِندِهِۦٓ أَوْ بِأَيْدِينَا فَتَرَبَّصُوٓا إِنَّا مَعَكُم مُّتَرَبِّصُونَ ۝ قُلْ أَنفِقُوا طَوْعًا أَوْ كَرْهًا لَّن يُتَقَبَّلَ مِنكُمْ إِنَّكُمْ كُنتُمْ قَوْمًا فَٰسِقِينَ ۝ وَمَا مَنَعَهُمْ أَن تُقْبَلَ مِنْهُمْ نَفَقَٰتُهُمْ إِلَّآ أَنَّهُمْ كَفَرُوا بِاللّٰهِ وَبِرَسُولِهِۦ وَلَا يَأْتُونَ الصَّلَوٰةَ إِلَّا وَهُمْ كُسَالَىٰ وَلَا يُنفِقُونَ إِلَّا وَهُمْ كَٰرِهُونَ ۝

---

48. They had already sought to spread discord before[363] and devised every ˹possible˺ plot against you ˹O Prophet˺, until the truth came and Allah's Will prevailed—much to their dismay.

False Excuse 2) Temptation

49. There are some of them who say, "Exempt me and do not expose me to temptation."[364] They have already fallen into temptation. And Hell will surely engulf the disbelievers.

Those Who Stayed Behind

50. If a blessing befalls you ˹O Prophet˺, they grieve, but if a disaster befalls you, they say, "We took our precaution in advance," and turn away, rejoicing. **51.** Say, "Nothing will ever befall us except what Allah has destined for us. He is our Protector." So in Allah let the believers put their trust. **52.** Say, "Are you awaiting anything to befall us except one of the two best things: ˹victory or martyrdom˺? But We are awaiting Allah to afflict you with torment either from Him or at our hands. So keep waiting! We too are waiting with you."

Unaccepted Contributions

53. Say, ˹O Prophet,˺ "˹Whether you˺ donate willingly or unwillingly, it will never be accepted from you, for you have been a rebellious people." **54.** And what prevented their donations from being accepted is that they have lost faith in Allah and His Messenger, they never come to prayer except half-heartedly, and they never donate except resentfully.

---

363 For example, ˈAbdullâh ibn Ubai ibn Salûl, a chief hypocrite, marched with the Prophet (ﷺ) for the Battle of Uḥud in the outskirts of Medina, then decided not to join the fight and returned to Medina with his followers who made up around one third of the Muslim army.

364 Another hypocrite by the name of Jadd ibn Qais came to the Prophet (ﷺ) asking to be exempt from joining the army because he had a weakness for women and he was afraid that he would be tempted by Roman women.

9. At-Tawbah

55. So let neither their wealth nor children impress you ˹O Prophet˺. Allah only intends to torment them through these things in this worldly life, then their souls will depart while they are disbelievers.

False Oaths

56. They swear by Allah that they are part of you, but they are not. They only say so out of fear. **57.** If only they could find a refuge, or a cave, or any hiding-place, they would rush headlong towards it.

Discontent with Charity

58. There are some of them who are critical of your distribution of alms ˹O Prophet˺. If they are given some of it they are pleased, but if not they are enraged. **59.** If only they had been content with what Allah and His Messenger had given them and said, "Allah is sufficient for us! Allah will grant us out of His bounty, and so will His Messenger. To Allah ˹alone˺ we turn with hope."

Alms-Tax Recipients

60. Alms-tax is only for the poor and the needy, for those employed to administer it, for those whose hearts are attracted ˹to the faith˺, for ˹freeing˺ slaves, for those in debt, for Allah's cause, and for ˹needy˺ travellers. ˹This is˺ an obligation from Allah. And Allah is All-Knowing, All-Wise.

Criticizing the Prophet

61. And there are others who hurt the Prophet by saying, "He listens to anyone." Say, ˹O Prophet,˺ "He listens to what is best for you. He believes in Allah, has faith in the believers, and is a mercy for those who believe among you." Those who hurt Allah's Messenger will suffer a painful punishment.

The Disgrace

62. They swear by Allah to you ˹believers˺ in order to please you, while it is the pleasure of Allah and His Messenger they should seek, if they are ˹true˺ believers. **63.** Do they not know that whoever opposes Allah and His Messenger will be in the Fire of Hell forever? That is the ultimate disgrace.

Blasphemy Exposed

64. The hypocrites fear that a *sûrah* should be revealed about them, exposing what is in their hearts. Say, ˹O Prophet,˺ "Keep mocking! Allah will definitely bring to light what you fear." **65.** If you question them, they will certainly say, "We were only talking idly and joking around." Say, "Was it Allah, His revelations, and His Messenger that you ridiculed?" **66.** Make no excuses! You have lost faith after your belief. If We pardon a group of you,[365] We will punish others for their wickedness.

Punishment of the Hypocrites

67. The hypocrites, both men and women, are all alike: they encourage what is evil, forbid what is good, and withhold ˹what is in˺ their hands. They neglected Allah, so He neglected them. Surely the hypocrites are the rebellious. **68.** Allah has promised the hypocrites, both men and women, and the disbelievers an everlasting stay in the Fire of Hell—it is sufficient for them. Allah has condemned them, and they will suffer a never-ending punishment.

---

365 i.e., those who will repent.

9. At-Tawbah

Fate of the Disbelievers

69. ˹You hypocrites are˺ like those ˹disbelievers˺ before you. They were far superior to you in might and more abundant in wealth and children. They enjoyed their share in this life. You have enjoyed your share, just as they did. And you have engaged in idle talk, just as they did. Their deeds have become void in this world and the Hereafter. And it is they who are the ˹true˺ losers. 70. Have they not received the stories of those ˹destroyed˺ before them: the people of Noah, ˹Âd, and Thamûd, the people of Abraham, the residents of Midian, and the overturned cities ˹of Lot˺?[366] Their messengers came to them with clear proofs. Allah would have never wronged them, but it was they who wronged themselves.

Reward of the Believers

71. The believers, both men and women, are guardians of one another. They encourage good and forbid evil, establish prayer and pay alms-tax, and obey Allah and His Messenger. It is they who will be shown Allah's mercy. Surely Allah is Almighty, All-Wise. 72. Allah has promised the believers, both men and women, Gardens under which rivers flow, to stay there forever, and splendid homes in the Gardens of Eternity, and—above all—the pleasure of Allah. That is ˹truly˺ the ultimate triumph.

---

366 The overturned cities of Sodom and Gomorrah.

9. At-Tawbah

Returning Favour with Ingratitude

73. O Prophet! Struggle against the disbelievers and the hypocrites, and be firm with them. Hell will be their home. What an evil destination! **74.** They swear by Allah that they never said anything ˹blasphemous˺, while they did in fact utter a blasphemy, lost faith after accepting Islam, and plotted what they could not carry out.[367] It is only through resentment that they pay Allah and His Messenger back for enriching them out of His bounty! If they repent, it will be better for them. But if they turn away, Allah will torment them with a painful punishment in this world and the Hereafter, and they will have no one on earth to protect or help them.

The Ungrateful

75. And there are some who had made a vow to Allah: "If He gives us from His bounty, we will surely spend in charity and be of the righteous." **76.** But when He gave them out of His bounty, they withheld it and turned away indifferently. **77.** So He caused hypocrisy to plague their hearts until the Day they will meet Him, for breaking their promise to Allah and for their lies. **78.** Do they not know that Allah ˹fully˺ knows their ˹evil˺ thoughts and secret talks, and that Allah is the Knower of all unseen?

Donations Criticized[368]

79. ˹There are˺ those who slander ˹some of˺ the believers for donating liberally and mock others for giving only the little they can afford. Allah will throw their mockery back at them, and they will suffer a painful punishment.

---

367 i.e., some of them tried to assassinate the Prophet (ﷺ) on the way back from Tabûk.

368 Not only did the hypocrites withhold their wealth, but they were also critical of those who donated. If a rich believer gave generously, the hypocrites would say, "He is showing off," and if a poor believer gave what they could afford, they would say, "This is not good enough."

80. 'It does not matter' whether you 'O Prophet' pray for them to be forgiven or not. Even if you pray for their forgiveness seventy times, Allah will never forgive them. That is because they have lost faith in Allah and His Messenger. And Allah does not guide the rebellious people.

False Excuse 3) Heat

81. Those 'hypocrites' who remained behind rejoiced for doing so in defiance of the Messenger of Allah and hated 'the prospect of' striving with their wealth and their lives in the cause of Allah. They said 'to one another', "Do not march forth in the heat." Say, 'O Prophet,' "The Fire of Hell is far hotter!" If only they could comprehend! **82.** So let them laugh a little—they will weep much as a reward for what they have committed.

Instructions to the Prophet

83. If Allah returns you 'O Prophet' to a group of them and they ask to go forth with you, say, "You will not ever go forth or fight an enemy along with me. You preferred to stay behind the first time, so stay with those 'helpless' who remain behind." **84.** And do not ever offer 'funeral' prayers for any of their dead, nor stand by their grave 'at burial', for they have lost faith in Allah and His Messenger and died rebellious. **85.** And let neither their wealth nor children impress you 'O Prophet'. Allah only intends to torment them through these things in this world, and 'then' their souls will depart while they are disbelievers.

The Unfaithful

86. Whenever a *sûrah* is revealed stating, "Believe in Allah and struggle along with His Messenger," the rich among them would ask to be exempt, saying, "Leave us with those who remain behind."

9. At-Tawbah

87. They preferred to stay behind with the helpless, and their hearts have been sealed so they do not comprehend.

The Faithful

88. But the Messenger and the believers with him strived with their wealth and their lives. They will have all the best, and it is they who will be successful. **89.** Allah has prepared for them Gardens under which rivers flow, to stay there forever. That is the ultimate triumph.

Unfaithful Nomads

90. Some nomadic Arabs ˹also˺ came with excuses, seeking exemption. And those who were untrue to Allah and His Messenger remained behind ˹with no excuse˺. The unfaithful among them will be afflicted with a painful punishment.

Valid Excuses

91. There is no blame on the weak, the sick, or those lacking the means ˹if they stay behind˺, as long as they are true to Allah and His Messenger. There is no blame on the good-doers. And Allah is All-Forgiving, Most Merciful. **92.** Nor ˹is there any blame on˺ those who came to you ˹O Prophet˺ for mounts, then when you said, "I can find no mounts for you," they left with eyes overflowing with tears out of grief that they had nothing to contribute.

Invalid Excuses

93. Blame is only on those who seek exemption from you although they have the means. They preferred to stay behind with the helpless, and Allah has sealed their hearts so they do not realize ˹the consequences˺.

9. At-Tawbah

94. They will make excuses to you ˹believers˺ when you return to them. Say, "Make no excuses, ˹for˺ we will not believe you. Allah has already informed us about your ˹true˺ state ˹of faith˺. Your ˹future˺ deeds will be observed by Allah and His Messenger as well. And you will be returned to the Knower of the seen and unseen, then He will inform you of what you used to do." 95. When you return, they will swear to you by Allah so that you may leave them alone. So leave them alone—they are truly evil. Hell will be their home as a reward for what they have committed. 96. They will swear to you in order to please you. And even if you are pleased with them, Allah will never be pleased with the rebellious people.

Unfaithful Nomads

97. The nomadic Arabs ˹around Medina˺ are far worse in disbelief and hypocrisy, and less likely to know the laws revealed by Allah to His Messenger. And Allah is All-Knowing, All-Wise. 98. And among the nomads are those who consider what they donate to be a loss and await your misfortune. May ill-fortune befall them! And Allah is All-Hearing, All-Knowing.

Faithful Nomads

99. However, among the nomadic Arabs are those who believe in Allah and the Last Day, and consider what they donate as a means of coming closer to Allah and ˹receiving˺ the prayers of the Messenger. It will certainly bring them closer. Allah will admit them into His mercy. Surely Allah is All-Forgiving, Most Merciful.

9. At-Tawbah

The Foremost

100. As for the foremost—the first of the Emigrants[369] and the Helpers[370]—and those who follow them in goodness, Allah is pleased with them and they are pleased with Him. And He has prepared for them Gardens under which rivers flow, to stay there for ever and ever. That is the ultimate triumph.

Master Hypocrites

101. Some of the nomads around you ˹believers˺ are hypocrites, as are some of the people of Medina. They have mastered hypocrisy. They are not known to you ˹O Prophet˺; they are known to Us. We will punish them twice ˹in this world˺,[371] then they will be brought back ˹to their Lord˺ for a tremendous punishment.

Those Who Are Forgiven

102. Some others have confessed their wrongdoing: they have mixed goodness with evil.[372] It is right to hope that Allah will turn to them in mercy. Surely Allah is All-Forgiving, Most Merciful. **103.** Take from their wealth ˹O Prophet˺ charity to purify and bless them, and pray for them—surely your prayer is a source of comfort for them. And Allah is All-Hearing, All-Knowing. **104.** Do they not know that Allah alone accepts the repentance of His servants and receives ˹their˺ charity, and that Allah alone is the Accepter of Repentance, Most Merciful?

A Second Chance

105. Tell ˹them, O Prophet˺, "Do as you will. Your deeds will be observed by Allah, His Messenger, and the believers. And you will be returned to the Knower of the seen and unseen, then He will inform you of what you used to do."

The Three Who Remained Behind[373]

106. And some others are left for Allah's decision, either to punish them or turn to them in mercy. And Allah is All-Knowing,

---

369 i.e., the early Muslims who emigrated from Mecca to Medina, known as *Al-Muhâjirûn*.
370 i.e., those from Medina, known as *Al-Anṣâr*, who accepted Islam and sheltered Muslim emigrants from Mecca.
371 Through disgrace in this world and bad ending of their lives.
372 They have mixed their adherence to Islam with their disobedience to march forth with the Prophet (ﷺ) to Tabûk.
373 This verse refers to Ka'b ibn Mâlik, Murarah ibn Rabi', and Hilâl ibn Umaiyah, the three companions who remained in Medina with no excuse, but were honest about what they did. They were boycotted by the Muslims for about fifty days until verses 118-119 of this sûrah were revealed declaring the acceptance of their repentance.

All-Wise.

The Mosque of Harm

107. There are also those ʿhypocritesʾ who set up a mosque ʿonlyʾ to cause harm, promote disbelief, divide the believers, and as a base for those who had previously fought against Allah and His Messenger.[374] They will definitely swear, "We intended nothing but good," but Allah bears witness that they are surely liars. 108. Do not ʿO Prophetʾ ever pray in it. Certainly, a mosque founded on righteousness from the first day is more worthy of your prayers. In it are men who love to be purified.[375] And Allah loves those who purify themselves. 109. Which is better: those who laid the foundation of their building on the fear and pleasure of Allah, or those who did so on the edge of a crumbling cliff that tumbled down with them into the Fire of Hell? And Allah does not guide the wrongdoing people. 110. The building which they erected will never cease to fuel hypocrisy in their hearts until their hearts are torn apart. And Allah is All-Knowing, All-Wise.

The Finest Bargain

111. Allah has indeed purchased from the believers their lives and wealth in exchange for Paradise. They fight in the cause of Allah and kill or are killed. This is a true promise binding on Him in the Torah, the Gospel, and the Quran. And whose promise is truer than Allah's? So rejoice in the exchange you have made with Him. That is ʿtrulyʾ the ultimate triumph.

---

374 Abu ʿÂmer Ar-Râhib was a monk who fought against the Muslims at the Battle of Badr. He ordered a group of twelve hypocrites to build a mosque near the Mosque of Qubâ', the first mosque built by the Muslims and also where the Prophet (ﷺ) and his companions would pray. The new mosque, commonly referred to as *Masjid Ad-Dirâr* (Mosque of Harm), was intended to attract other hypocrites and reduce the number of Muslims who prayed at Qubâ'. The hypocrites who built the mosque also anticipated the arrival of Abu ʿÂmer with Roman forces to expel the Prophet (ﷺ) and Muslims out of Medina. Upon a request from these hypocrites, the Prophet (ﷺ) had planned to visit the new mosque once he returned from Tabûk, but verses 107-110 of this sûrah were revealed, warning the Prophet (ﷺ) against that mosque. According to some narrations, the Prophet (ﷺ) ordered this mosque to be burned down.

375 *See* footnote for 7:46.

112. ˹It is the believers˺ who repent, who are devoted to worship, who praise ˹their Lord˺, who fast, who bow down and prostrate themselves, who encourage good and forbid evil, and who observe the limits set by Allah. And give good news to the believers.

Praying for the Polytheists

113. It is not ˹proper˺ for the Prophet and the believers to seek forgiveness for the polytheists, even if they were close relatives, after it has become clear to the believers that they are bound for the Hellfire. **114.** As for Abraham's prayer for his father's forgiveness, it was only in fulfilment of a promise he had made to him. But when it became clear to Abraham that his father was an enemy of Allah, he broke ties with him.[376] Abraham was truly tender-hearted, forbearing. **115.** Allah would never consider a people deviant after He has guided them, until He makes clear to them what they must avoid. Surely Allah has ˹full˺ knowledge of everything.

Allah's Might

116. Indeed, to Allah ˹alone˺ belongs the kingdom of the heavens and the earth. He gives life and causes death. And besides Allah you have no guardian or helper.

Allah's Mercy

117. Allah has certainly turned in mercy to the Prophet[377] as well as the Emigrants and the Helpers who stood by him in the time of hardship, after the hearts of a group of them had almost faltered. He then accepted their repentance. Surely He is Ever Gracious and Most Merciful to them.

---

376 Abraham promised to pray for his father's forgiveness in 19:47 and 60:4, but when his father died as a disbeliever he discontinued praying for him.
377 The Prophet (ﷺ) is forgiven for exempting all those who came to him with excuses regardless of their honesty, or for seeking forgiveness for the polytheists.

9. At-Tawbah

The Three[378]

118. And ˹Allah has also turned in mercy to˺ the three who had remained behind, ˹whose guilt distressed them˺ until the earth, despite its vastness, seemed to close in on them, and their souls were torn in anguish. They knew there was no refuge from Allah except in Him. Then He turned to them in mercy so that they might repent. Surely Allah ˹alone˺ is the Accepter of Repentance, Most Merciful. **119.** O believers! Be mindful of Allah and be with the truthful.

A Fine Reward

120. It was not ˹proper˺ for the people of Medina and the nomadic Arabs around them to avoid marching with the Messenger of Allah or to prefer their own lives above his. That is because whenever they suffer from thirst, fatigue, or hunger in the cause of Allah; or tread on a territory, unnerving the disbelievers; or inflict any loss on an enemy— it is written to their credit as a good deed. Surely Allah never discounts the reward of the good-doers. **121.** And whenever they make a donation, small or large, or cross a valley ˹in Allah's cause˺—it is written to their credit, so that Allah may grant them the best reward for what they used to do.

Gaining Knowledge

122. ˹However,˺ it is not necessary for the believers to march forth all at once. Only a party from each group should march forth, leaving the rest to gain religious knowledge then enlighten their people when they return to them, so that they ˹too˺ may beware ˹of evil˺.

---

378 *See footnote for verse 106 of this sûrah.*

9. At-Tawbah

Firmness with the Disbelievers[379]

123. O believers! Fight the disbelievers around you and let them find firmness in you. And know that Allah is with those mindful ˹of Him˺.

Hypocrites Reacting to Revelation

124. Whenever a *sûrah* is revealed, some of them ask ˹mockingly˺, "Which of you has this increased in faith?" As for the believers, it has increased them in faith and they rejoice. **125.** But as for those with sickness in their hearts,[380] it has increased them only in wickedness upon their wickedness, and they die as disbelievers. **126.** Do they not see that they are tried once or twice every year?[381] Yet they neither repent nor do they learn a lesson. **127.** Whenever a *sûrah* is revealed, they look at one another, ˹saying,˺ "Is anyone watching you?" Then they slip away. ˹It is˺ Allah ˹Who˺ has turned their hearts away because they are a people who do not comprehend.

Invitation to All

128. There certainly has come to you a messenger from among yourselves. He is concerned by your suffering, anxious for your well-being, and gracious and merciful to the believers. **129.** But if they turn away, then say, ˹O Prophet,˺ "Allah is sufficient for me. There is no god ˹worthy of worship˺ except Him. In Him I put my trust. And He is the Lord of the Mighty Throne."

---

379 This verse talks exclusively about the disbelievers at war with Muslims. *See* 2:190-193 and 60:8-9.
380 i.e., hypocrites.
381 Their hypocrisy is exposed over and over again.

10. Jonah (Yûnus)

In the Name of Allah—the Most
Compassionate, Most Merciful

Universal Messenger

1. *Alif-Lãm-Ra.* These are the verses of the Book, rich in wisdom.
2. Is it astonishing to people that
We have sent revelation to a man
from among themselves, ʿinstruct-
ing him,ʾ "Warn humanity and give
good news to the believers that they
will have an honourable status with
their Lord."? Yet the disbelievers
said, "Indeed, this ʿmanʾ is clearly
a magician!"

Origin of Creation

3. Surely your Lord is Allah Who
created the heavens and the earth in
six Days,[382] then established Himself on the Throne, conducting every
affair. None can intercede except by
His permission. That is Allah—your
Lord, so worship Him ʿaloneʾ. Will
you not then be mindful? **4.** To Him
is your return all together. Allah's
promise is ʿalwaysʾ true. Indeed, He
originates the creation then resurrects it so that He may justly reward
those who believe and do good. But
those who disbelieve will have a
boiling drink and a painful punishment for their disbelief.

Signs in Allah's Creation

5. He is the One Who made the sun
a radiant source and the moon a reflected light, with precisely ordained
phases, so that you may know the
number of years and calculation ʿof
timeʾ. Allah did not create all this
except for a purpose. He makes the
signs clear for people of knowledge. **6.** Surely in the alternation of the day and the night, and in all that Allah has created in the
heavens and the earth, there are truly signs for those mindful ʿof Himʾ.

---

382 *See footnote for 7:54.*

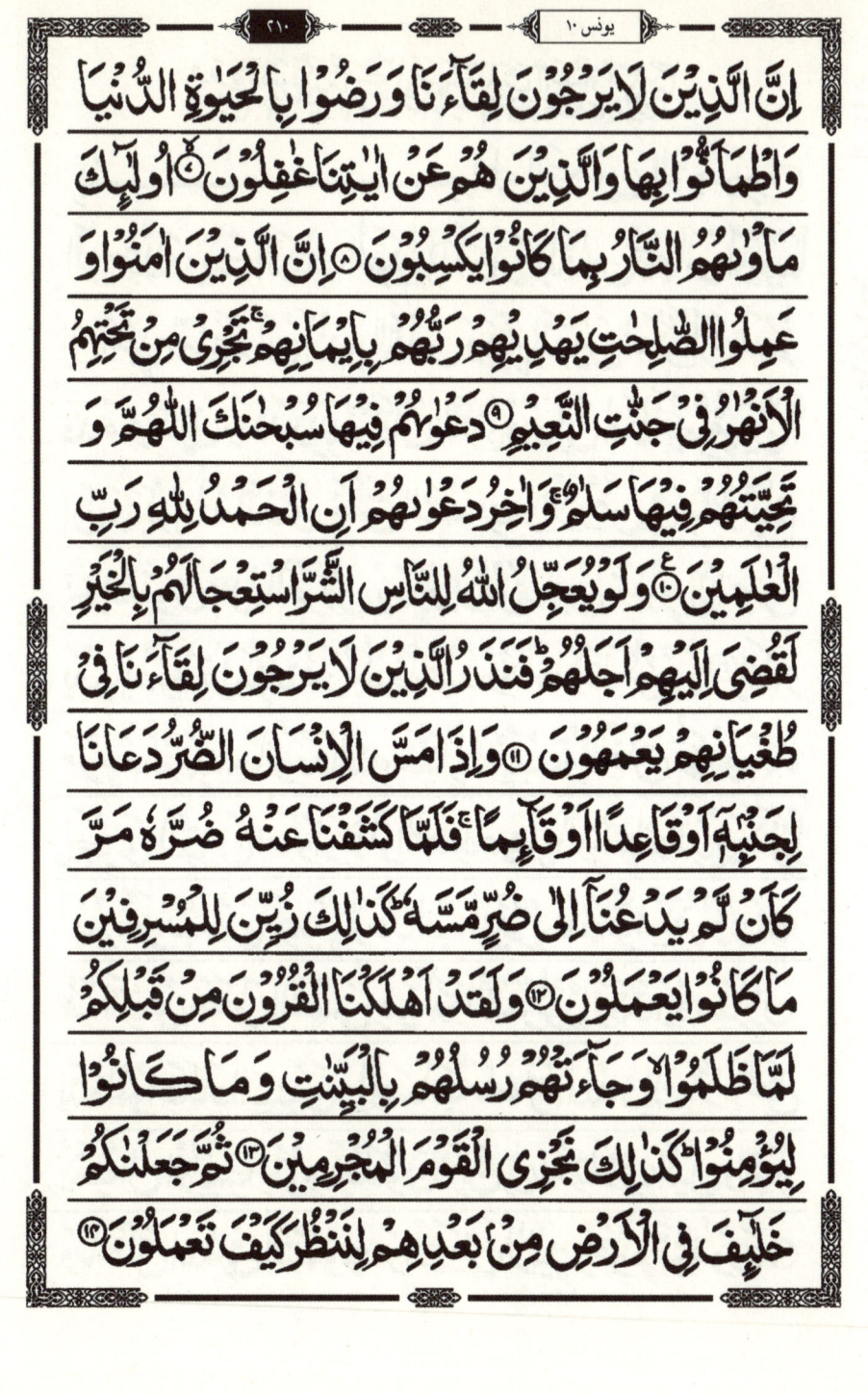

10. Yûnus — 210

Deniers of Resurrection

7. Indeed, those who do not expect to meet Us, being pleased and content with this worldly life, and who are heedless of Our signs, 8. they will have the Fire as a home because of what they have committed.

Guided by Faith

9. Surely those who believe and do good, their Lord will guide them ˹to Paradise˺ through their faith, rivers will flow under their feet in the Gardens of Bliss, 10. in which their prayer will be, "Glory be to You, O Allah!" and their greeting will be, "Peace!" and their closing prayer will be, "All praise is for Allah— Lord of all worlds!"

No Rush for Evil

11. If Allah were to hasten evil for people[383] as they wish to hasten good, they would have certainly been doomed. But We leave those who do not expect to meet Us to wander blindly in their defiance.

The Ungrateful

12. Whenever someone is touched by hardship, they cry out to Us, whether lying on their side, sitting, or standing. But when We relieve their hardship, they return to their old ways as if they had never cried to Us to remove any hardship! This is how the misdeeds of the transgressors have been made appealing to them.

Warning to the Meccan Pagans

13. We surely destroyed ˹other˺ peoples before you when they did wrong, and their messengers came to them with clear proofs but they would not believe! This is how We reward the wicked people. 14. Then We made you their successors in the land to see how you would act.

---

383 When they pray against themselves or their children, or when they demand to be destroyed.

10. Yûnus

The Pagans Demand a New Quran

15. When Our clear revelations are recited to them, those who do not expect to meet Us say ˹to the Prophet˺, "Bring us a different Quran or make some changes in it." Say ˹to them˺, "It is not for me to change it on my own. I only follow what is revealed to me. I fear, if I were to disobey my Lord, the punishment of a tremendous Day." 16. Say, "Had Allah willed, I would not have recited it to you, nor would He have made it known to you. I had lived my whole life among you before this ˹revelation˺. Do you not understand?" 17. Who does more wrong than those who fabricate lies against Allah or deny His revelations? Indeed, the wicked will never succeed.

False Gods

18. They worship besides Allah others who can neither harm nor benefit them, and say, "These are our intercessors with Allah." Ask ˹them, O Prophet˺, "Are you informing Allah of something He does not know in the heavens or the earth? Glorified and Exalted is He above what they associate ˹with Him˺!"

No Longer United by Faith

19. Humanity was once nothing but a single community ˹of believers˺, but then they differed.[384] Had it not been for a prior decree from your Lord,[385] their differences would have been settled ˹at once˺.

Demanding a New Miracle[386]

20. They ask, "Why has no ˹other˺ sign been sent down to him from his Lord?" Say, ˹O Prophet,˺ "˹The knowledge of˺ the unseen is with Allah alone. So wait! I too am waiting with you."

---

384 i.e., they split into believers and disbelievers.
385 That He will delay their judgment until the Hereafter.
386 The pagans of Mecca were not satisfied with the literary miracle of the Quran, so they demanded a tangible miracle such as the staff of Moses.

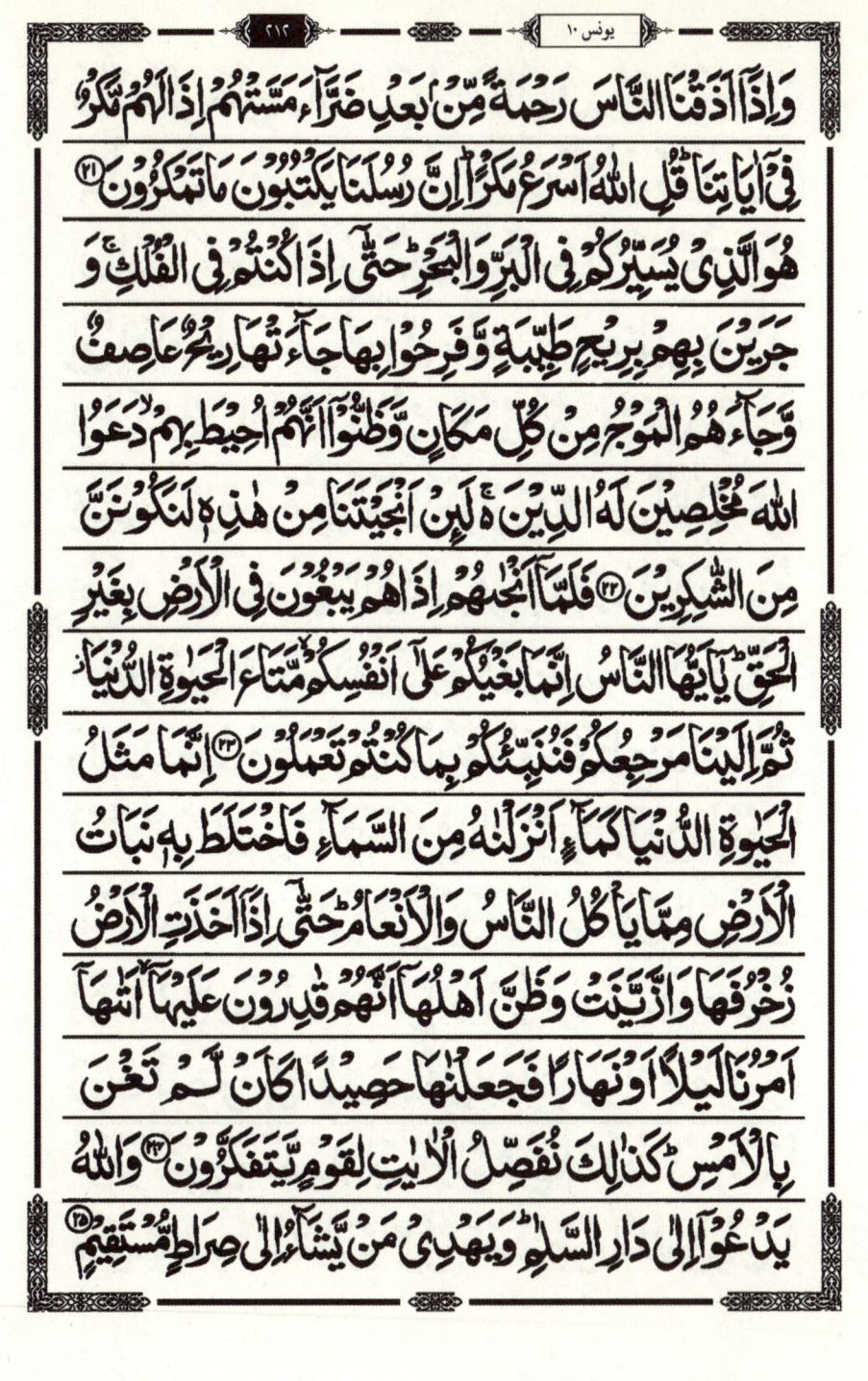

Returning Favour with Denial

21. When We give people a taste of mercy after being afflicted with a hardship, they swiftly devise plots against Our revelations! Say, ˹O Prophet,˺ "Allah is swifter in devising ˹punishment˺. Surely Our messenger-angels record whatever you devise."

Metaphor for Human Ingratitude

22. He is the One Who enables you to travel through land and sea. And it so happens that you are on ships, sailing with a favourable wind, to the passengers' delight. Suddenly, the ships are overcome by a gale wind and those on board are overwhelmed by waves from every side, and they assume they are doomed. They cry out to Allah ˹alone˺ in sincere devotion, "If You save us from this, we will certainly be grateful."
23. But as soon as He rescues them, they transgress in the land unjustly. O humanity! Your transgression is only against your own souls. ˹There is only˺ brief enjoyment in this worldly life, then to Us is your return, and then We will inform you of what you used to do.

This Fleeting Life

24. The life of this world is just like rain We send down from the sky, producing a mixture of plants which humans and animals consume. Then just as the earth looks its best, perfectly beautified, and its people think they have full control over it, there comes to it Our command by night or by day, so We mow it down as if it never flourished yesterday! This is how We make the signs clear for people who reflect.

Invitation to Paradise

25. And Allah invites ˹all˺ to the Home of Peace and guides whoever He wills to the Straight Path.

213   10. Yûnus

26. Those who do good will have the finest reward[387] and ˹even˺ more.[388] Neither gloom nor disgrace will cover their faces. It is they who will be the residents of Paradise. They will be there forever.

Warning Against Hell

27. As for those who commit evil, the reward of an evil deed is its equivalent. Humiliation will cover them—with no one to protect them from Allah—as if their faces were covered with patches of the night's deep darkness. It is they who will be the residents of the Fire. They will be there forever.

False Gods and Their Followers

28. ˹Consider˺ the Day We will gather them all together then say to those who associated others ˹with Allah in worship˺, "Stay in your places—you and your associate-gods." We will separate them from each other, and their associate-gods will say, "It was not us that you worshipped! **29.** Allah is sufficient as a Witness between each of us that we were totally unaware of your worship." **30.** Then and there every soul will face ˹the consequences of˺ what it had done. They all will be returned to Allah—their True Master. And whatever ˹gods˺ they fabricated will fail them.

Questions to Pagans: 1) Who Provides?

31. Ask ˹them, O Prophet˺, "Who provides for you from heaven and earth? Who owns ˹your˺ hearing and sight? Who brings forth the living from the dead and the dead from the living? And who conducts every affair?" They will ˹surely˺ say, "Allah." Say, "Will you not then fear ˹Him˺"? **32.** That is Allah— your True Lord. So what is beyond the truth except falsehood? How can you then be turned away?" **33.** And so your Lord's decree has been proven true against the rebellious—that they will never believe.

---

387 Paradise.
388 Seeing Almighty Allah in the Hereafter.

10. Yûnus | 214

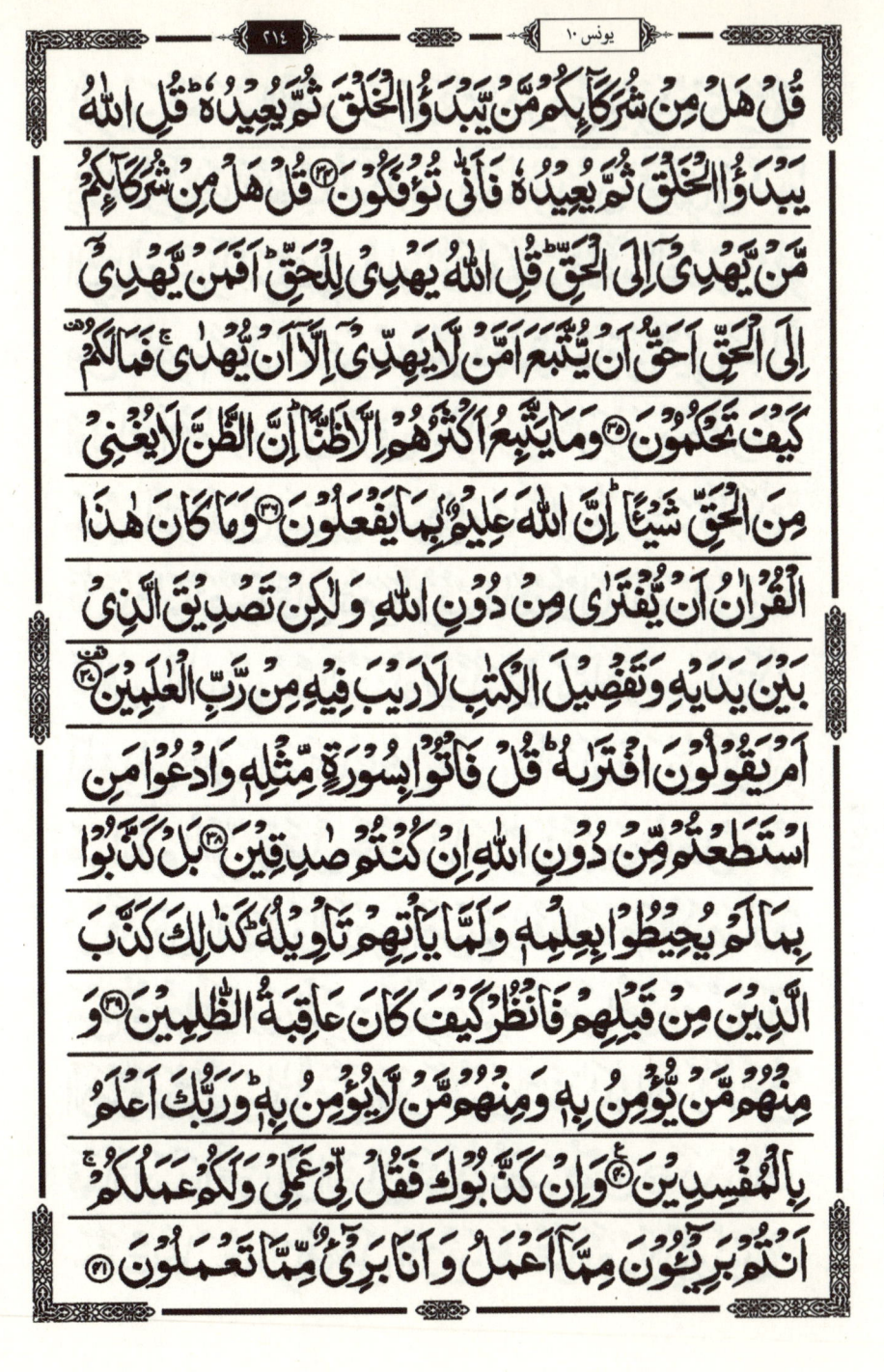

2) Who Creates?

34. Ask ˹them, O Prophet˺, "Can any of your associate-gods originate creation and then resurrect it?" Say, "˹Only˺ Allah originates creation and then resurrects it. How can you then be deluded ˹from the truth˺?"

3) Who Guides?

35. Ask ˹them, O Prophet˺, "Can any of your associate-gods guide to the truth?" Say, "˹Only˺ Allah guides to the truth." Who then is more worthy to be followed: the One Who guides to the truth or those who cannot find the way unless guided? What is the matter with you? How do you judge? **36.** Most of them follow nothing but ˹inherited˺ assumptions. ˹And˺ surely assumptions can in no way replace the truth. Allah is indeed All-Knowing of what they do.

The Challenge of the Quran

37. It is not ˹possible˺ for this Quran to have been produced by anyone other than Allah. In fact, it is a confirmation of what came before, and an explanation of the Scripture. It is, without a doubt, from the Lord of all worlds. **38.** Or do they claim, "He[389] made it up!"? Tell them ˹O Prophet˺, "Produce one *surah* like it then, and seek help from whoever you can—other than Allah—if what you say is true!" **39.** In fact, they ˹hastily˺ rejected the Book without comprehending it and before the fulfilment of its warnings. Similarly, those before them were in denial. See then what was the end of the wrongdoers!

It Is Allah Who Guides

40. Some of them will ˹eventually˺ believe in it; others will not. And your Lord knows best the corruptors. **41.** If they deny you, then say, "My deeds are mine and your deeds are yours. You are free of what I do and I am free of what you do!"

---

389 The Prophet (ﷺ).

10. Yûnus

42. Some of them listen to what you say, but can you make the deaf hear even though they do not understand? **43.** And some of them look at you, but can you guide the blind even though they cannot see?[390] **44.** Indeed, Allah does not wrong people in the least, but it is people who wrong themselves.

Short Life

45. On the Day He will gather them, it will be as if they had not stayed ˹in the world˺ except for an hour of a day,[391] ˹as though they were only˺ getting to know one another. Lost indeed will be those who denied the meeting with Allah, and were not ˹rightly˺ guided!

Warning Before Judgment

46. Whether We show you ˹O Prophet˺ some of what We threaten them with, or cause you to die ˹before that˺, to Us is their return and Allah is a Witness over what they do. **47.** And for every community there is a messenger. After their messenger has come,[392] judgment is passed on them in all fairness, and they are not wronged.

When the Time Comes …

48. They ask ˹the believers˺, "When will this threat come to pass if what you say is true?" **49.** Say, ˹O Prophet,˺ "I have no power to benefit or protect myself, except by the Will of Allah." For each community there is an appointed term. When their time arrives, they cannot delay it for a moment, nor could they advance it.

Allah's Torment

50. Tell them ˹O Prophet˺, "Imagine if His torment were to overcome you by night or day—do the wicked realize what they are ˹really˺ asking Him to hasten? **51.** Will you believe in it only after it has overtaken you? Now? But you always wanted to hasten it!" **52.** Then the wrongdoers will be told, "Taste the torment of eternity! Are you not rewarded except for what you used to commit?"

---

390 This refers metaphorically to the pagans who fail to see and hear the truth.
391 i.e., only for a short period of time.
392 Either in this life to deliver the message or on the Day of Judgment to testify for or against them.

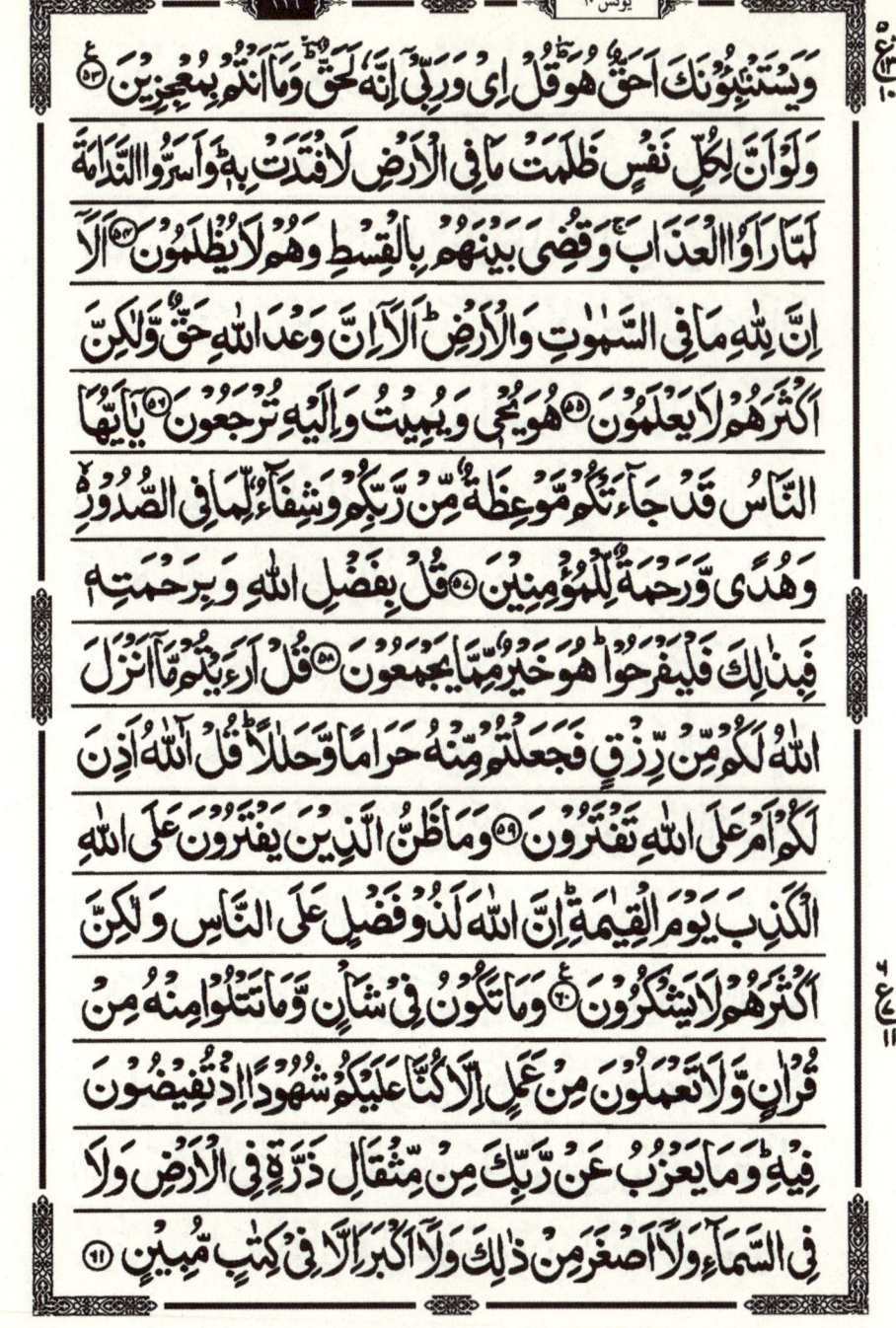

Allah's Promise

53. They ask you ˹O Prophet˺, "Is this true?" Say, "Yes, by my Lord! Most certainly it is true! And you will have no escape." **54.** If every wrongdoer were to possess everything in the world, they would surely ransom themselves with it. They will hide ˹their˺ remorse when they see the torment. And they will be judged in all fairness, and none will be wronged. **55.** Surely to Allah belongs whatever is in the heavens and the earth. Surely Allah's promise is ˹always˺ true, but most of them do not know. **56.** He ˹is the One Who˺ gives life and causes death, and to Him you will ˹all˺ be returned.

Excellence of the Quran

57. O humanity! Indeed, there has come to you a warning from your Lord, a cure for what is in the hearts, a guide, and a mercy for the believers. **58.** Say, ˹O Prophet,˺ "In Allah's grace and mercy let them rejoice. That is far better than whatever ˹wealth˺ they amass."

Allah's Provisions

59. Ask ˹the pagans, O Prophet˺, "Have you seen that which Allah has sent down for you as a provision, of which you have made some lawful and some unlawful?"[393] Say, "Has Allah given you authorization, or are you fabricating lies against Allah?" **60.** What do those who fabricate lies against Allah expect on Judgment Day? Surely Allah is ever Bountiful to humanity,[394] but most of them are ungrateful.

Allah's Knowledge

61. There is no activity you may be engaged in ˹O Prophet˺ or portion of the Quran you may be reciting, nor any deed you ˹all˺ may be doing except that We are a Witness over you while doing it. Not ˹even˺ an atom's weight is hidden from your Lord on earth or in heaven; nor anything smaller or larger than that, but is ˹written˺ in a perfect Record.[395]

---

393 This refers to 6:138-139.
394 By delaying their punishment and allowing them time to repent.
395 The Record refers to the Preserved Tablet (Al-Lawḥ Al-Maḥfûẓ) in which Allah has written the destiny of His entire creation.

10. Yûnus

Allah's Close Servants

62. There will certainly be no fear for the close servants of Allah, nor will they grieve. **63.** ˹They are˺ those who are faithful and are mindful ˹of Him˺. **64.** For them is good news in this worldly life and the Hereafter. There is no change in the promise of Allah. That is ˹truly˺ the ultimate triumph.

The Almighty

65. Do not let their words grieve you ˹O Prophet˺. Surely all honour and power belongs to Allah. He is the All-Hearing, All-Knowing. **66.** Certainly to Allah ˹alone˺ belong all those in the heavens and all those on the earth. And what do those who associate others with Allah really follow? They follow nothing but assumptions and do nothing but lie. **67.** He is the One Who has made the night for you to rest in and the day bright. Surely in this are signs for people who listen.

Allah Has No Children

68. They[396] say, "Allah has offspring."[397] Glory be to Him! He is the Self-Sufficient. To Him belongs whatever is in the heavens and whatever is on the earth. You have no proof of this! Do you say about Allah what you do not know? **69.** Say, ˹O Prophet,˺ "Indeed, those who fabricate lies against Allah will never succeed." **70.** ˹It is only˺ a brief enjoyment in this world, then to Us is their return, then We will make them taste the severe punishment for their disbelief.

---

396 The Christians, pagans, etc.
397 Jesus in Christianity, the angels in pagan Arab mythology, etc.

10. Yûnus

Noah and His People

71. Relate to them ˹O Prophet˺ the story of Noah when he said to his people, "O my People! If my presence and my reminders to you of Allah's signs are unbearable to you, then ˹know that˺ I have put my trust in Allah. So devise a plot along with your associate-gods—and you do not have to be secretive about your plot—then carry it out against me without delay! **72.** And if you turn away, ˹remember˺ I have never demanded a reward from you ˹for delivering the message˺. My reward is only from Allah. And I have been commanded to be one of those who submit ˹to Allah˺." **73.** But they still rejected him, so We saved him and those with him in the Ark and made them successors, and drowned those who rejected Our signs. See then what was the end of those who had been warned!

Messengers After Noah

74. Then after him We sent ˹other˺ messengers to their ˹own˺ people and they came to them with clear proofs. But they would not believe in what they had rejected before. This is how We seal the hearts of the transgressors.

Moses and Aaron

75. Then after these ˹messengers˺ We sent Moses and Aaron to Pharaoh and his chiefs with Our signs. But they behaved arrogantly and were a wicked people. **76.** When the truth came to them from Us, they said, "This is certainly pure magic!" **77.** Moses responded, "Is this what you say about the truth when it has come to you? Is this magic? Magicians will never succeed." **78.** They argued, "Have you come to turn us away from the faith of our forefathers so that the two of you may become supreme in the land? We will never believe in you!"

10. Yûnus

79. Pharaoh demanded, "Bring me every skilled magician." 80. When the magicians came, Moses said to them, "Cast whatever you wish to cast!" 81. When they did, Moses said, "What you have produced is mere magic, Allah will surely make it useless, for Allah certainly does not set right the work of the corruptors. 82. And Allah establishes the truth by His Words—even to the dismay of the wicked."

A Few Believers

83. But no one believed in Moses except a few youths of his people, while fearing that Pharaoh and their own chiefs might persecute them. And certainly Pharaoh was a tyrant in the land, and he was truly a transgressor. 84. Moses said, "O my people! If you do believe in Allah and submit ˹to His Will˺, then put your trust in Him." 85. They replied, "In Allah we trust. Our Lord! Do not subject us to the persecution of the oppressive people, 86. and deliver us by Your mercy from the disbelieving people."

Power of Prayer

87. We revealed to Moses and his brother, "Appoint houses for your people in Egypt. Turn these houses into places of worship, establish prayer, and give good news to the believers!" 88. Moses prayed, "Our Lord! You have granted Pharaoh and his chiefs luxuries and riches in this worldly life, ˹which they abused˺ to lead people astray from Your Way! Our Lord, destroy their riches and harden their hearts so that they will not believe until they see the painful punishment."

10. Yûnus

89. Allah responded ˹to Moses and Aaron˺,[398] "Your prayer is answered! So be steadfast and do not follow the way of those who do not know."

End of Pharaoh

90. We brought the Children of Israel across the sea. Then Pharaoh and his soldiers pursued them unjustly and oppressively. But as Pharaoh was drowning, he cried out, "I believe that there is no god except that in whom the Children of Israel believe, and I am ˹now˺ one of those who submit." **91.** ˹He was told,˺ "Now ˹you believe˺? But you always disobeyed and were one of the corruptors. **92.** Today We will preserve your corpse so that you may become an example[399] for those who come after you. And surely most people are heedless of Our examples!"

Allah's Grace to the Israelites

93. Indeed, We settled the Children of Israel in a blessed land,[400] and granted them good, lawful provisions. They did not differ until knowledge came to them.[401] Surely your Lord will judge between them on the Day of Judgment regarding their differences.

Confirming the Truth

94. If you ˹O Prophet˺ are in doubt about ˹these stories˺ that We have revealed to you, then ask those who read the Scripture before you. The truth has certainly come to you from your Lord, so do not be one of those who doubt, **95.** and do not be one of those who deny Allah's signs or you will be one of the losers.[402]

Jonah's People Spared from Torment

96. Indeed, those against whom Allah's decree ˹of torment˺ is justified will not believe— **97.** even if every sign were to come to them—until they see the painful punishment.

---

398 Moses prayed while Aaron said, "Amen." So it is as if both of them prayed.
399 lit., sign.
400 In Egypt, Jerusalem, and other places.
401 They did not split into believers and disbelievers until they received the knowledge given to their prophets.
402 When these verses were revealed, the Prophet (ﷺ) responded, "I am not in doubt and I will not ask ˹anyone˺."

98. If only there had been a society which believed 'before seeing the torment' and, therefore, benefited from its belief, like the people of Jonah.[403] When they believed, We lifted from them the torment of disgrace in this world and allowed them enjoyment for a while.[404]

Conviction, Not Compulsion

99. Had your Lord so willed 'O Prophet', all 'people' on earth would have certainly believed, every single one of them! Would you then force people to become believers? **100.** It is not for any soul to believe except by Allah's leave, and He will bring His wrath upon those who are unmindful.

Invitation to Think

101. Say, 'O Prophet,' "Consider all that is in the heavens and the earth!" Yet neither signs nor warners are of any benefit to those who refuse to believe. **102.** Are they waiting for 'anything' except the same torments that befell those before them? Say, "Keep waiting then! I too am waiting with you." **103.** Then We saved Our messengers and those who believed. For it is Our duty to save the believers.

True Faith

104. Say, 'O Prophet,' "O humanity! If you are in doubt of my faith, then 'know that' I do not worship those 'idols' you worship instead of Allah. But I worship Allah, Who has the power to cause your death. And I have been commanded, 'Be one of the believers,' **105.** and, 'Be steadfast in faith in all uprightness, and do not be one of the polytheists,' **106.** and 'Do not invoke, instead of Allah, what can neither benefit nor harm you—for if you do, then you will certainly be one of the wrongdoers,'

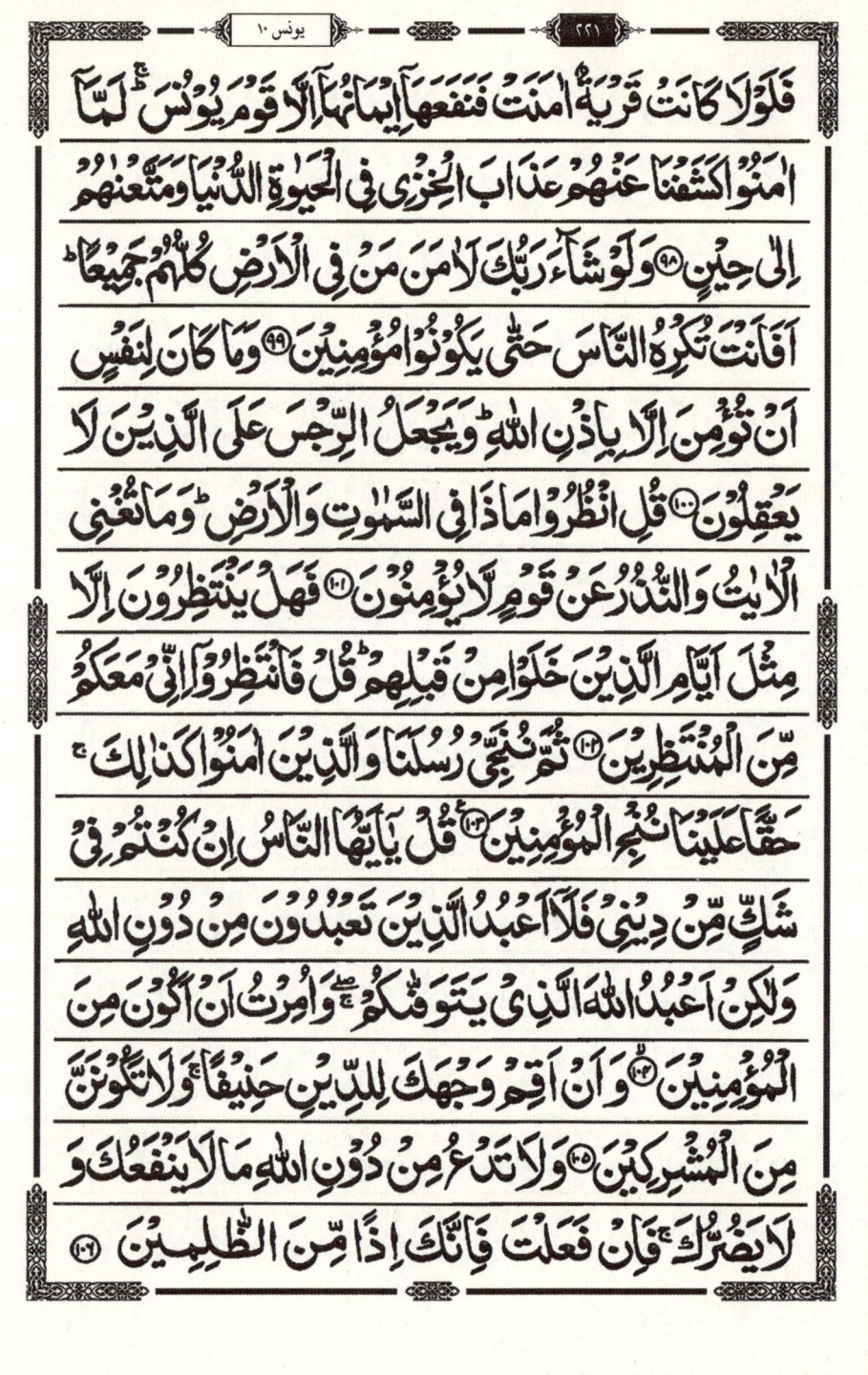

---

403 Initially, the people of Jonah rejected his message. When he was told they would be punished after three days for their defiance, he left his city without Allah's permission before its destruction. Jonah's people became convinced that they were going to be destroyed when he left them and they saw signs of the imminent torment, so they felt remorseful and cried out for forgiveness before the coming of the punishment. Therefore, Allah accepted their repentance and the torment was retracted.

404 i.e., until the end of their term.

11. Hûd — 222

107. and 'If Allah touches you with harm, none can undo it except Him. And if He intends good for you, none can withhold His bounty. He grants it to whoever He wills of His servants. And He is the All-Forgiving, Most Merciful.'"

Call to Humanity

108. Say, ˹O Prophet,˺ "O humanity! The truth has surely come to you from your Lord. So whoever chooses to be guided, it is only for their own good. And whoever chooses to stray, it is only to their own loss. And I am not a keeper over you."

Advice to the Prophet

109. And follow what is revealed to you, and be patient until Allah passes His judgment. For He is the Best of Judges.

೧೮೦ ✳ ೧೮೦

11. Hûd (Hûd)

In the Name of Allah—the Most Compassionate, Most Merciful

Message of the Quran

1. *Alif-Lãm-Ra.* ˹This is˺ a Book whose verses are well perfected and then fully explained. ˹It is˺ from the One ˹Who is˺ All-Wise, All-Aware. 2. ˹Tell them, O Prophet,˺ "Worship none but Allah. Surely I am a warner and deliverer of good news to you from Him. 3. And seek your Lord's forgiveness and turn to Him in repentance. He will grant you a good provision for an appointed term and graciously reward the doers of good. But if you turn away, then I truly fear for you the torment of a formidable Day. 4. To Allah is your return. And He is Most Capable of everything."

Hiding Disbelief

5. Indeed, they[405] enfold ˹what is in˺ their hearts, ˹trying˺ to hide it from Him! But even when they cover themselves with their clothes, He knows what they conceal and what they reveal. Surely He knows best what is ˹hidden˺ in the heart.

---

405 The hypocrites or the disbelievers.

11. Hûd

Allah's Might

6. There is no moving creature on earth whose provision is not guaranteed by Allah. And He knows where it lives and where it is laid to rest. All is ʿwrittenʾ in a perfect Record.[406] **7.** He is the One Who created the heavens and the earth in six Days[407]—and His Throne was upon the waters—in order to test which of you is best in deeds. And if you ʿO Prophetʾ say, "Surely you will ʿallʾ be raised up after death," the disbelievers will certainly say, "That is nothing but pure magic!" **8.** And if We delay their punishment until an appointed time, they will definitely say, "What is holding it back?" Indeed, on the Day it overtakes them, it will not be averted from them, and they will be overwhelmed by what they used to ridicule.

Adversity and Prosperity

9. If We give people a taste of Our mercy then take it away from them, they become utterly desperate, ungrateful. **10.** But if We give them a taste of prosperity after being touched with adversity, they say, "My ills are gone," and become totally prideful and boastful, **11.** except those who patiently endure and do good. It is they who will have forgiveness and a mighty reward.

Pagan Annoyances

12. Perhaps you ʿO Prophetʾ may wish to give up some of what is revealed to you and may be distressed by it because they say, "If only a treasure had been sent down to him, or an angel had come with him!" You are only a warner, and Allah is the Trustee of All Affairs.

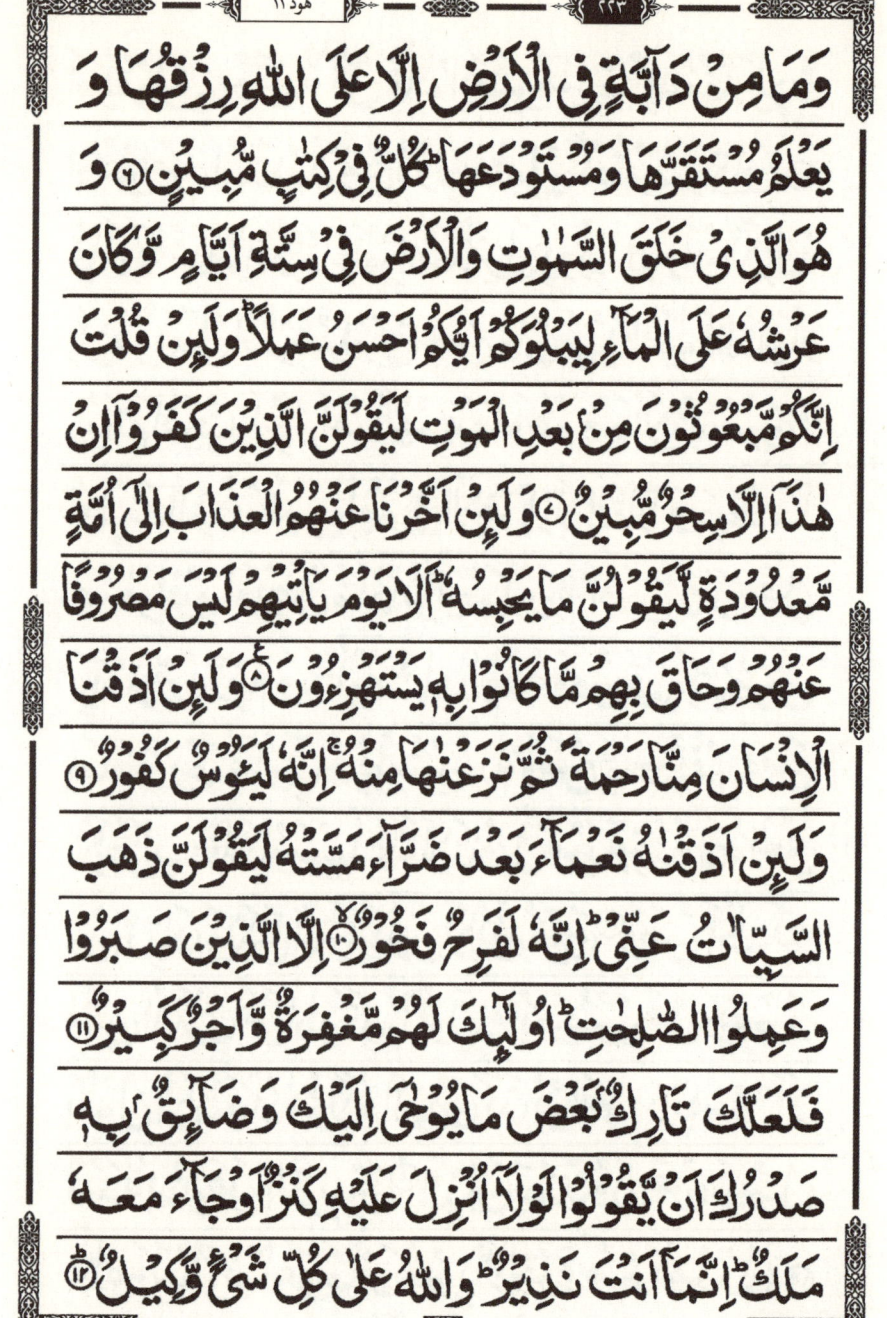

---

406 *See footnote for 10:61.*
407 *See footnote for 7:54.*

11. Hûd

بِسْمِ ٱللَّهِ ٱلرَّحْمَٰنِ ٱلرَّحِيمِ

أَمْ يَقُولُونَ ٱفْتَرَىٰهُ قُلْ فَأْتُوا۟ بِعَشْرِ سُوَرٍ مِّثْلِهِۦ مُفْتَرَيَٰتٍ وَٱدْعُوا۟ مَنِ ٱسْتَطَعْتُم مِّن دُونِ ٱللَّهِ إِن كُنتُمْ صَٰدِقِينَ ۞

فَإِلَّمْ يَسْتَجِيبُوا۟ لَكُمْ فَٱعْلَمُوٓا۟ أَنَّمَآ أُنزِلَ بِعِلْمِ ٱللَّهِ وَأَن لَّآ إِلَٰهَ إِلَّا هُوَ فَهَلْ أَنتُم مُّسْلِمُونَ ۞ مَن كَانَ يُرِيدُ ٱلْحَيَوٰةَ ٱلدُّنْيَا وَ زِينَتَهَا نُوَفِّ إِلَيْهِمْ أَعْمَٰلَهُمْ فِيهَا وَهُمْ فِيهَا لَا يُبْخَسُونَ ۞ أُو۟لَٰٓئِكَ ٱلَّذِينَ لَيْسَ لَهُمْ فِى ٱلْءَاخِرَةِ إِلَّا ٱلنَّارُ وَحَبِطَ مَا صَنَعُوا۟ فِيهَا وَبَٰطِلٌ مَّا كَانُوا۟ يَعْمَلُونَ ۞ أَفَمَن كَانَ عَلَىٰ بَيِّنَةٍ مِّن رَّبِّهِۦ وَيَتْلُوهُ شَاهِدٌ مِّنْهُ وَمِن قَبْلِهِۦ كِتَٰبُ مُوسَىٰٓ إِمَامًا وَرَحْمَةً أُو۟لَٰٓئِكَ يُؤْمِنُونَ بِهِۦ وَمَن يَكْفُرْ بِهِۦ مِنَ ٱلْأَحْزَابِ فَٱلنَّارُ مَوْعِدُهُۥ فَلَا تَكُ فِى مِرْيَةٍ مِّنْهُ إِنَّهُ ٱلْحَقُّ مِن رَّبِّكَ وَلَٰكِنَّ أَكْثَرَ ٱلنَّاسِ لَا يُؤْمِنُونَ ۞ وَمَنْ أَظْلَمُ مِمَّنِ ٱفْتَرَىٰ عَلَى ٱللَّهِ كَذِبًا أُو۟لَٰٓئِكَ يُعْرَضُونَ عَلَىٰ رَبِّهِمْ وَ يَقُولُ ٱلْأَشْهَٰدُ هَٰٓؤُلَآءِ ٱلَّذِينَ كَذَبُوا۟ عَلَىٰ رَبِّهِمْ أَلَا لَعْنَةُ ٱللَّهِ عَلَى ٱلظَّٰلِمِينَ ۞ ٱلَّذِينَ يَصُدُّونَ عَن سَبِيلِ ٱللَّهِ وَيَبْغُونَهَا عِوَجًا وَهُم بِٱلْءَاخِرَةِ هُمْ كَٰفِرُونَ ۞

Challenging the Pagans

13. Or do they say, "He[408] has fabricated this ˹Quran˺!"? Say, ˹O Prophet,˺ "Produce ten fabricated sûrahs like it and seek help from whoever you can—other than Allah—if what you say is true!" **14.** But if your helpers fail you, then know that it has been revealed with the knowledge of Allah, and that there is no god ˹worthy of worship˺ except Him! Will you ˹not˺ then submit ˹to Allah˺?

Fleeting Gain

15. Whoever desires ˹only˺ this worldly life and its luxuries, We will pay them in full for their deeds in this life—nothing will be left out. **16.** It is they who will have nothing in the Hereafter except the Fire. Their efforts in this life will be fruitless and their deeds will be useless.

Everlasting Gain

17. ˹Can these people be compared to˺ those ˹believers˺ who stand on clear proof from their Lord, backed by ˹the Quran as˺ a witness from Him, and preceded by the Book of Moses ˹which was revealed˺ as a guide and mercy? It is those ˹believers˺ who have faith in it. But whoever from the ˹disbelieving˺ groups rejects it, the Fire will be their destiny. So do not be in doubt of it. It is certainly the truth from your Lord, but most people do not believe.

The Losers

18. Who does more wrong than those who fabricate lies against Allah? They will be brought before their Lord, and the witnesses[409] will say, "These are the ones who lied against their Lord." Surely Allah's condemnation is upon the wrongdoers, **19.** who hinder ˹others˺ from Allah's Path, striving to make it ˹appear˺ crooked, and disbelieve in the Hereafter.

---

408 The Prophet (ﷺ).
409 i.e., the angels and the prophets.

20. They will never frustrate Allah on earth, and they will have no protector besides Allah. Their punishment will be multiplied, for they failed to hear or see ˹the truth˺. **21.** It is they who have ruined themselves, and whatever ˹gods˺ they fabricated will fail them. **22.** Without a doubt, they will be the worst losers in the Hereafter.

The Winners

23. Surely those who believe, do good, and humble themselves before their Lord will be the residents of Paradise. They will be there forever.

The Disbelievers and the Believers

24. The example of these two parties is that of the blind and the deaf, compared to the seeing and the hearing. Can the two be equal? Will you not then be mindful?

Prophet Noah

25. Surely We sent Noah to his people. ˹He said,˺ "Indeed, I am sent to you with a clear warning **26.** that you should worship none but Allah. I truly fear for you the torment of a painful Day." **27.** The disbelieving chiefs of his people said, "We see you only as a human being like ourselves, and we see that no one follows you except the lowliest among us, who do so ˹hastily˺ without thinking.[410] We do not see anything that makes ˹all of˺ you any better than us. In fact, we think you are liars."

Noah's Argument

28. He said, "O my people! Consider if I stand on a clear proof from my Lord and He has blessed me with a mercy from Himself,[411] which you fail to see. Should we ˹then˺ force it on you against your will?

---

410 Typically, the poor and the helpless are the first to believe in prophets, taking them as saviours, whereas the rich and powerful are hesitant to believe, perceiving the new faith as a threat to their influence.
411 Mercy here means prophethood.

29. O my people! I do not ask you for a payment for this ˹message˺. My reward is only from Allah. And I will never dismiss the believers, for they will surely meet their Lord. But I can see that you are a people acting ignorantly. **30.** O my people! Who would protect me from Allah if I were to dismiss them? Will you not then be mindful? **31.** I do not say to you that I possess Allah's treasuries or know the unseen, nor do I claim to be an angel, nor do I say that Allah will never grant goodness to those you look down upon. Allah knows best what is ˹hidden˺ within them. ˹If I did,˺ then I would truly be one of the wrongdoers."

His People's Response

32. They protested, "O Noah! You have argued with us far too much, so bring upon us what you threaten us with, if what you say is true." **33.** He responded, "It is Allah Who can bring it upon you if He wills, and then you will have no escape! **34.** My advice will not benefit you—no matter how hard I try—if Allah wills ˹for˺ you to stray. He is your Lord, and to Him you will ˹all˺ be returned."

The Pagans Discredit the Quran

35. Or do they say, "He[412] has fabricated this ˹Quran˺!"? Say, ˹O Prophet,˺ "If I have done so, then I bear the burden of that sin! But I am free from your sinful accusation."

The Ark

36. And it was revealed to Noah, "None of your people will believe except those who already have. So do not be distressed by what they have been doing. **37.** And build the Ark under Our ˹watchful˺ Eyes and directions, and do not plead with Me for those who have done wrong, for they will surely be drowned."

---

412 Muḥammad (ﷺ).

38. So he began to build the Ark, and whenever some of the chiefs of his people passed by, they mocked him. He said, "If you laugh at us, we will ˹soon˺ laugh at you similarly. **39.** You will soon come to know who will be visited by a humiliating torment ˹in this life˺ and overwhelmed by an everlasting punishment ˹in the next˺."

The Flood

40. And when Our command came and the oven burst ˹with water˺,[413] We said ˹to Noah˺, "Take into the Ark a pair from every species along with your family—except those against whom the decree ˹to drown˺ has already been passed—and those who believe." But none believed with him except for a few. **41.** And he said, "Board it! In the Name of Allah it will sail and cast anchor. Surely my Lord is All-Forgiving, Most Merciful."

Noah's Son

42. And ˹so˺ the Ark sailed with them through waves like mountains. Noah called out to his son, who stood apart, "O my dear son! Come aboard with us and do not be with the disbelievers." **43.** He replied, "I will take refuge on a mountain, which will protect me from the water." Noah cried, "Today no one is protected from Allah's decree except those to whom He shows mercy!" And the waves came between them, and his son was among the drowned. **44.** And it was said, "O earth! Swallow up your water. And O sky! Withhold ˹your rain˺." The floodwater receded and the decree was carried out. The Ark rested on Mount Judi, and it was said, "Away with the wrongdoing people!"

Noah Pleading for His Son

45. Noah called out to his Lord, saying, "My Lord! Certainly my son is ˹also˺ of my family, Your promise is surely true, and You are the most just of all judges!"

---

413 Noah was given a signal that once the water gushes out of a particular oven then the Flood is about to begin. It can also be translated as: "The fountains of the earth gushed forth."

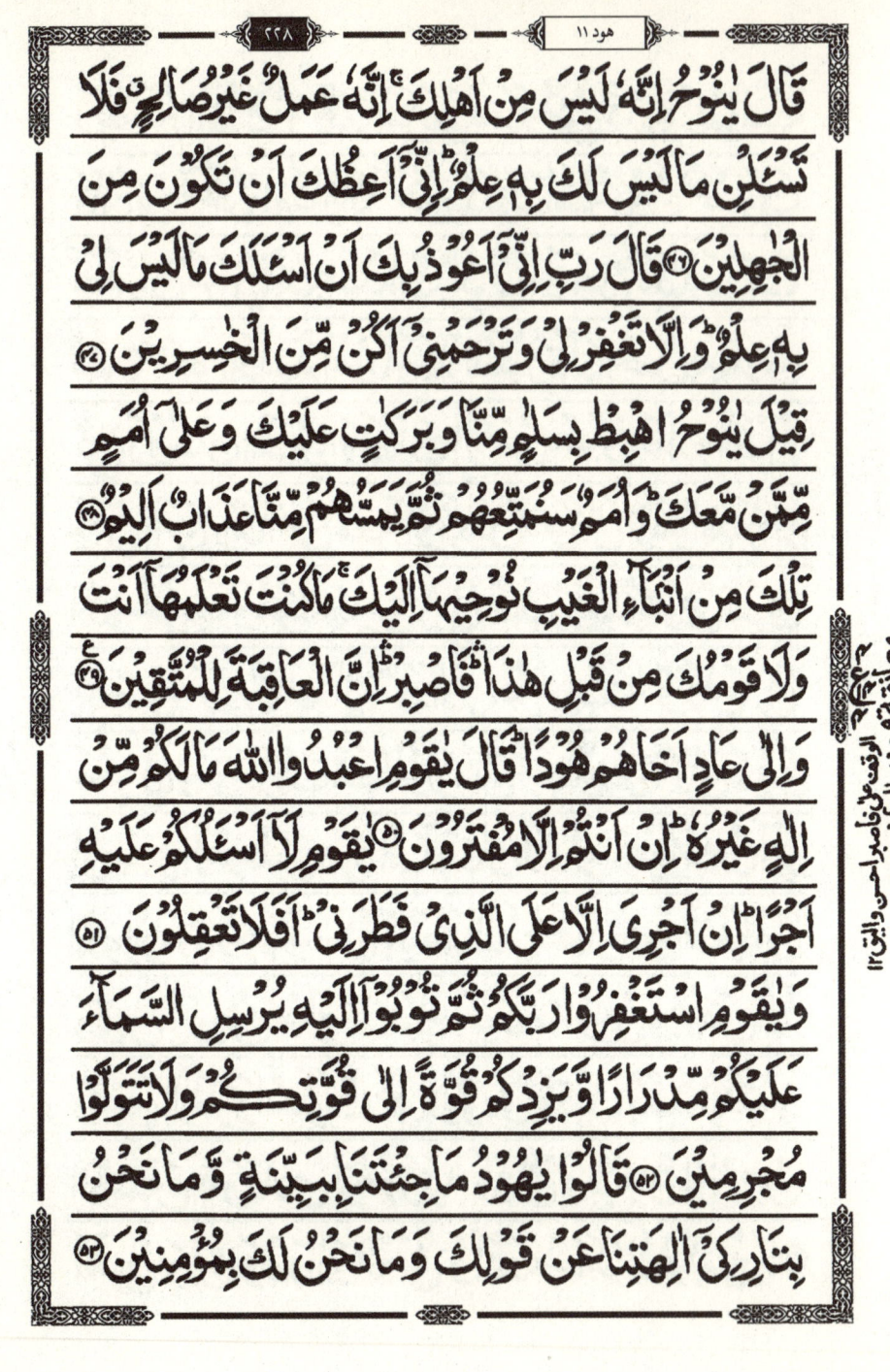

46. Allah replied, "O Noah! He is certainly not of your family—he was entirely of unrighteous conduct. So do not ask Me about what you have no knowledge of! I warn you so you do not fall into ignorance." 47. Noah pleaded, "My Lord, I seek refuge in You from asking You about what I have no knowledge of, and unless You forgive me and have mercy on me, I will be one of the losers." 48. It was said, "O Noah! Disembark with Our peace and blessings on you and some of the descendants of those with you. As for the others, We will allow them ˹a brief˺ enjoyment, then they will be touched with a painful punishment from Us."

Stories of the Past

49. This is one of the stories of the unseen, which we reveal to you ˹O Prophet˺. Neither you nor your people knew it before this. So be patient! Surely the ultimate outcome belongs ˹only˺ to the righteous.

Prophet Hûd

50. And to the people of ˺Âd We sent their brother Hûd. He said, "O my people! Worship Allah. You have no god other than Him. You do nothing but fabricate lies ˹against Allah˺. 51. O my people! I do not ask you for any reward for this ˹message˺. My reward is only from the One Who created me. Will you not then understand? 52. And O my people! Seek your Lord's forgiveness and turn to Him in repentance. He will shower you with rain in abundance, and add strength to your strength. So do not turn away, persisting in wickedness."

His People's Response

53. They argued, "O Hûd! You have not given us any clear proof, and we will never abandon our gods upon your word, nor will we believe in you. 54. All we can say is that some of our gods have possessed you with evil."

Hûd's Argument

He said, "I call Allah to witness, and you too bear witness, that I 'totally' reject whatever you associate
55. with Him 'in worship'. So let all of you plot against me without delay! 56. I have put my trust in Allah—my Lord and your Lord. There is no living creature that is not completely under His control.[414] Surely my Lord's Way is perfect justice.[415]
57. But if you turn away, I have already delivered to you what I have been sent with. My Lord will replace you with others. You are not harming Him in the least. Indeed, my Lord is a 'vigilant' Keeper over all things."

The Torment

58. When Our command came, We rescued Hûd and those who believed with him by a mercy from Us, saving them from a harsh torment.
59. That was 'Âd. They denied the signs of their Lord, disobeyed His messengers, and followed the command of every stubborn tyrant.
60. They were followed by a curse in this world, as they will be on the Day of Judgment. Surely 'Âd denied their Lord. So away with 'Âd, the people of Hûd.

Prophet Ṣâliḥ

61. And to the people of Thamûd We sent their brother Ṣâliḥ. He said, "O my people! Worship Allah. You have no god other than Him. He 'is the One Who' produced you from the earth and settled you on it. So seek His forgiveness and turn to Him in repentance. Surely my Lord is Ever Near, All-Responsive 'to prayers'."

His People's Argument

62. They argued, "O Ṣâliḥ! We truly had high hopes in you before this.[416] How dare you forbid us to worship what our forefathers had worshipped? We are certainly in alarming doubt about what you are inviting us to."

---

414 lit., there is no moving creature that He does not hold by its forelock.
415 lit., my Lord is on the Straight Path.
416 They believed that Ṣâliḥ had the potential to be their future leader.

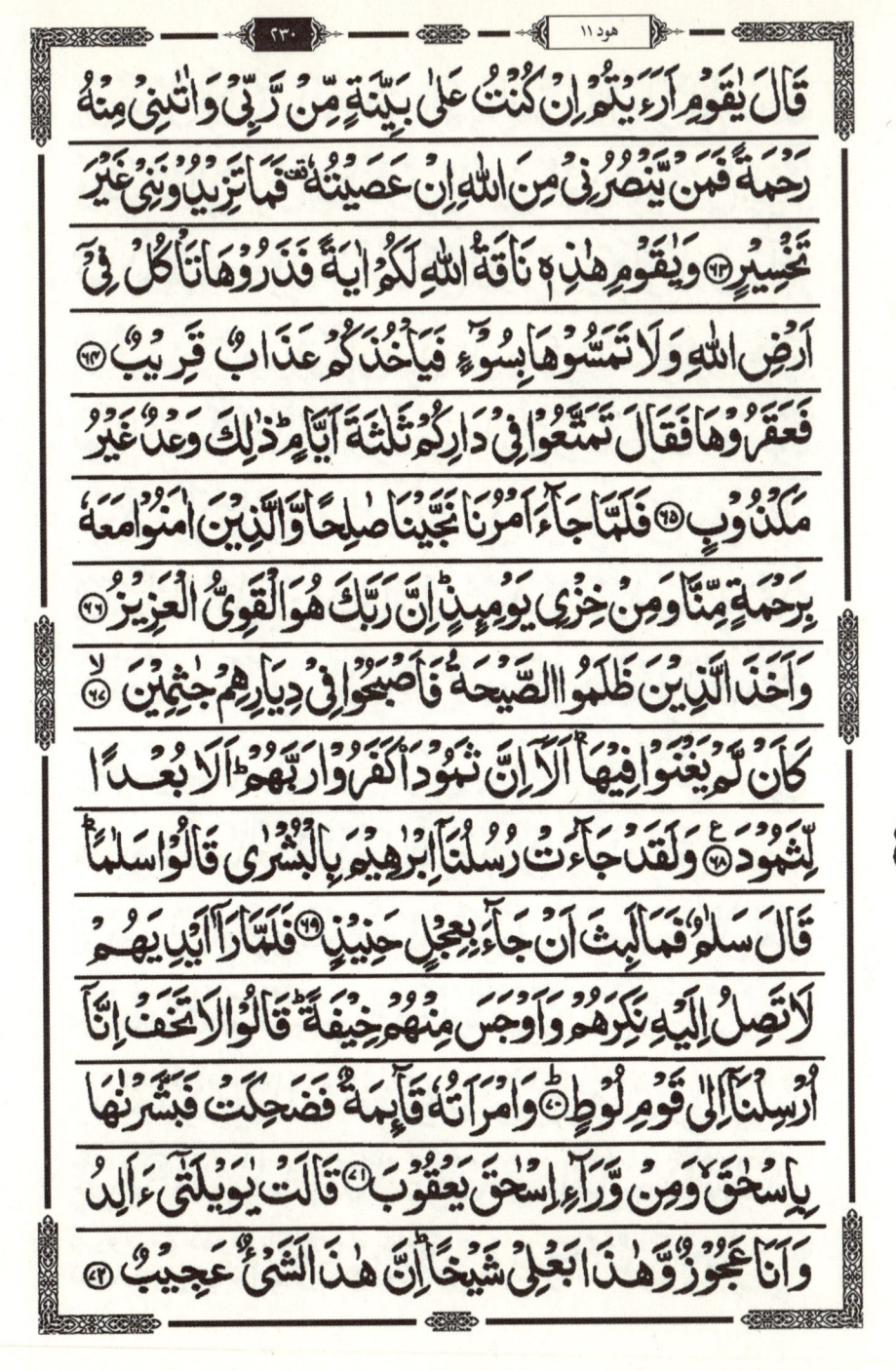

11. Hûd

His Response

63. He responded, "O my people! Consider if I stand on a clear proof from my Lord and He has blessed me with a mercy from Him. Who could help me against Allah if I were to disobey Him? You would only contribute to my doom. **64.** And O my people! This she-camel of Allah is a sign for you.[417] So leave her to graze ˹freely˺ on Allah's earth and do her no harm, or a swift punishment will overtake you!" **65.** But they killed her, so he warned ˹them˺, "You have ˹only˺ three ˹more˺ days to enjoy life in your homes—this is an unfailing promise!"

The Torment

66. When Our command came, We saved Ṣâliḥ and those who believed with him by a mercy from Us and spared them the disgrace of that Day. Surely your Lord ˹alone˺ is the All-Powerful, Almighty. **67.** And the ˹mighty˺ blast overtook the wrongdoers, so they fell lifeless in their homes, **68.** as if they had never lived there. Surely Thamûd denied their Lord, so away with Thamûd!

Abraham Visited by Angels

69. And surely Our messenger-angels came to Abraham with good news ˹of a son˺. They greeted ˹him with˺, "Peace!" And he replied, "Peace ˹be upon you˺!" Then it was not long before he brought ˹them˺ a ˹fat,˺ roasted calf. **70.** And when he saw that their hands did not reach for the food, he became suspicious and fearful of them.[418] They reassured ˹him˺, "Do not be afraid! We are ˹angels˺ sent ˹only˺ against the people of Lot."

Good News to Sarah

71. And his wife was standing by, so she laughed,[419] then We gave her good news of ˹the birth of˺ Isaac, and, after him, Jacob.
72. She wondered, "Oh, my! How can I have a child in this old age, and my husband here is an old man? This is truly an astonishing thing!"

---

417 The she-camel came out of a mountain as a sign for them.
418 In ancient Middle Eastern culture, if a guest refused to eat the food provided by their host, it was a sign of ill-will.
419 She laughed after her husband was assured that the guests intended no harm or when she heard the news of the imminent destruction of the sinful people of Lot.

73. They responded, "Are you astonished by Allah's decree? May Allah's mercy and blessings be upon you, O people of this house. Indeed, He is Praiseworthy, All-Glorious."

Abraham Pleading for Lot's People

74. Then after the fear had left Abraham, and the good news had reached him, he began to plead with Us for the people of Lot. **75.** Truly, Abraham was forbearing, tender-hearted, and ever turning 'to his Lord'. **76.** 'The angels said,' "O Abraham! Plead no more! Your Lord's decree has already come, and they will certainly be afflicted with a punishment that cannot be averted!"

Lot's Handsome Guests

77. When Our messenger-angels came to Lot, he was distressed and worried by their arrival.[420] He said, "This is a terrible day." **78.** And 'the men of' his people—who were used to shameful deeds—came to him rushing. He pleaded, "O my people! Here are my daughters[421] 'for marriage'—they are pure for you. So fear Allah, and do not humiliate me by disrespecting my guests. Is there not 'even' a single right-minded man among you?" **79.** They argued, "You certainly know that we have no need for your daughters. You already know what we desire!" **80.** He responded, "If only I had the strength 'to resist you' or could rely on a strong supporter."

Reassuring Lot

81. The angels said, "O Lot! We are the messengers of your Lord. They will never reach you. So travel with your family in the dark of night, and do not let any of you look back, except your wife. She will certainly suffer the fate of the others.[422] Their appointed time is the morning. Is the morning not near?"

---

420 Since the angels came in the form of handsome men, Lot was worried for the dignity and safety of his guests among his people—not knowing that they were angels.
421 Single women of his community.
422 Lot's wife disbelieved in his message. It is believed that she is the one who informed the people of Lot's handsome guests.

11. Hûd

بِسْمِ اللّٰهِ

فَلَمَّا جَآءَ أَمْرُنَا جَعَلْنَا عَالِيَهَا سَافِلَهَا وَأَمْطَرْنَا عَلَيْهَا حِجَارَةً مِّن سِجِّيلٍ مَّنضُودٍ ۞ مُّسَوَّمَةً عِندَ رَبِّكَ وَمَا هِيَ مِنَ الظَّالِمِينَ بِبَعِيدٍ ۞ وَإِلَىٰ مَدْيَنَ أَخَاهُمْ شُعَيْبًا قَالَ يَاقَوْمِ اعْبُدُوا اللّٰهَ مَا لَكُم مِّنْ إِلَٰهٍ غَيْرُهُ وَلَا تَنقُصُوا الْمِكْيَالَ وَالْمِيزَانَ إِنِّيٓ أَرَاكُم بِخَيْرٍ وَإِنِّيٓ أَخَافُ عَلَيْكُمْ عَذَابَ يَوْمٍ مُّحِيطٍ ۞ وَيَاقَوْمِ أَوْفُوا الْمِكْيَالَ وَالْمِيزَانَ بِالْقِسْطِ وَلَا تَبْخَسُوا النَّاسَ أَشْيَآءَهُمْ وَلَا تَعْثَوْا فِي الْأَرْضِ مُفْسِدِينَ ۞ بَقِيَّتُ اللّٰهِ خَيْرٌ لَّكُمْ إِن كُنتُم مُّؤْمِنِينَ وَمَآ أَنَا۠ عَلَيْكُم بِحَفِيظٍ ۞ قَالُوا يَاشُعَيْبُ أَصَلَاتُكَ تَأْمُرُكَ أَن نَّتْرُكَ مَا يَعْبُدُ ءَابَآؤُنَآ أَوْ أَن نَّفْعَلَ فِيٓ أَمْوَالِنَا مَا نَشَٰٓؤُا۟ إِنَّكَ لَأَنتَ الْحَلِيمُ الرَّشِيدُ ۞ قَالَ يَاقَوْمِ أَرَءَيْتُمْ إِن كُنتُ عَلَىٰ بَيِّنَةٍ مِّن رَّبِّي وَرَزَقَنِي مِنْهُ رِزْقًا حَسَنًا وَمَآ أُرِيدُ أَنْ أُخَالِفَكُمْ إِلَىٰ مَآ أَنْهَاكُمْ عَنْهُ إِنْ أُرِيدُ إِلَّا الْإِصْلَاحَ مَا اسْتَطَعْتُ وَمَا تَوْفِيقِيٓ إِلَّا بِاللّٰهِ عَلَيْهِ تَوَكَّلْتُ وَإِلَيْهِ أُنِيبُ ۞

The Torment

82. When Our command came, We turned the cities upside down and rained down on them clustered stones of baked clay, **83.** marked by your Lord ˹O Prophet˺. And these stones are not far from the ˹pagan˺ wrongdoers!

Prophet Shu'aib

84. And to the people of Midian We sent their brother Shu'aib. He said, "O my people! Worship Allah. You have no god other than Him. And do not give short measure and weight. I do see you in prosperity now, but I truly fear for you the torment of an overwhelming Day. **85.** O my people! Give full measure and weigh with justice. Do not defraud people of their property, nor go about spreading corruption in the land. **86.** What is left ˹as a lawful gain˺ by Allah is far better for you if you are ˹truly˺ believers. And I am not a keeper over you."

His People's Response

87. They asked ˹sarcastically˺, "O Shu'aib! Does your prayer command you that we should abandon what our forefathers worshipped or give up managing our wealth as we please? Indeed, you are such a tolerant, sensible man!"

Shu'aib's Argument

88. He said, "O my people! Consider if I stand on a clear proof from my Lord and He has blessed me with a good provision from Him. I do not want to do what I am forbidding you from. I only intend reform to the best of my ability. My success comes only through Allah. In Him I trust and to Him I turn.

89. O my people! Do not let your opposition to me lead you to a fate similar to that of the people of Noah, or Hûd, or Ṣâliḥ. And the people of Lot are not far from you.[423] **90.** So seek your Lord's forgiveness and turn to Him in repentance. Surely my Lord is Most Merciful, All-Loving."

The Threat

91. They threatened, "O Shuʻaib! We do not comprehend much of what you say, and surely we see you powerless among us. Were it not for your clan, we would have certainly stoned you, for you are nothing to us."

Shuʻaib's Response

92. He said, "O my people! Do you have more regard for my clan than for Allah, turning your back on Him entirely? Surely my Lord is Fully Aware of what you do. **93.** O my people! Persist in your ways, for I ˹too˺ will persist in mine. You will soon come to know who will be visited by a humiliating torment and is a liar! And watch! I too am watching with you!"

The Torment

94. When Our command came, We saved Shuʻaib and those who believed with him by a mercy from Us. And the ˹mighty˺ blast overtook the wrongdoers, so they fell lifeless in their homes, **95.** as if they had never lived there. So away with Midian as it was with Thamûd!

Prophet Moses

96. Indeed, We sent Moses with Our signs and compelling proof **97.** to Pharaoh and his chiefs, but they followed the command of Pharaoh, and Pharaoh's command was not well guided.

---

423 Geographically and chronologically.

98. He will be before his people on the Day of Judgment and will lead them into the Fire. What an evil place to be led into! **99.** They were followed by a curse in this ˹life˺ and ˹will receive another˺ on the Day of Judgment. What an evil gift to receive!

Reward of Wickedness

100. These are accounts, We relate to you ˹O Prophet˺, of the ˹destroyed˺ cities. Some are still standing ˹barren˺, while others have been mowed down. **101.** We did not wrong them, rather they wronged themselves. The gods they invoked beside Allah were of no help at all when the command of your Lord came, and only contributed to their ruin. **102.** Such is the ˹crushing˺ grip of your Lord when He seizes the societies entrenched in wrongdoing. Indeed, His grip is ˹terribly˺ painful and severe.

Judgment Day

103. Surely in this is a sign for those who fear the torment of the Hereafter. That is a Day for which humanity will be gathered and a Day ˹that will be˺ witnessed ˹by all˺. **104.** We only delay it for a fixed term. **105.** When that Day arrives, no one will dare speak except with His permission. Some of them will be miserable, others joyful.

The Miserable

106. As for those bound for misery, they will be in the Fire, where they will be sighing and gasping, **107.** staying there forever, as long as the heavens and the earth will endure, except what your Lord wills.[424] Surely your Lord does what He intends.

The Joyful

108. And as for those destined to joy, they will be in Paradise, staying there forever, as long as the heavens and the earth will endure, except what your Lord wills[425]—a ˹generous˺ giving, without end.

---

424 Sinful believers will eventually be removed from Hell after receiving their punishment.
425 Except the time they spend on earth and in the grave, or except the time the sinful believers spend in Hell before being transferred to Paradise.

235   11. Hûd

Blind Following

109. So do not be in doubt ˹O Prophet˺ about what those ˹pagans˺ worship. They worship nothing except what their forefathers worshipped before ˹them˺. And We will certainly give them their share ˹of punishment˺ in full, without any reduction.

The Torah

110. Indeed, We had given Moses the Scripture, but differences arose regarding it. Had it not been for a prior decree from your Lord,[426] their differences would have been settled ˹at once˺. They are truly in alarming doubt about it. **111.** And surely your Lord will fully pay all for their deeds. He is certainly All-Aware of what they do.

Advice to the Believers

112. So be steadfast as you are commanded ˹O Prophet˺, along with those who turn ˹in submission to Allah˺ with you. And do not transgress. Surely He is All-Seeing of what you ˹believers˺ do. **113.** And do not be inclined to the wrongdoers or you will be touched by the Fire. For then you would have no protectors other than Allah, nor would you be helped. **114.** Establish prayer ˹O Prophet˺ at both ends of the day and in the early part of the night.[427] Surely good deeds wipe out evil deeds. That is a reminder for the mindful. **115.** And be patient! Certainly Allah does not discount the reward of the good-doers.

Speaking out Against Evil

116. If only there had been among the ˹destroyed˺ peoples before you, ˹O believers,˺ virtuous individuals who forbade corruption in the land—other than the few We had saved ˹from the torment˺. But the wrongdoers ˹only˺ pursued their ˹worldly˺ pleasures, becoming wicked. **117.** And your Lord ˹O Prophet˺ would never destroy a society unjustly while its people were acting rightly.

---

426 That He will delay their judgment until the Hereafter.

427 This verse talks about the five daily prayers. The prayers at the two ends of the day are the dawn prayer (*Fajr*) at one end and the afternoon prayers (*Zuhr* and *'Aṣr*) at the other. Prayers in the early part of the night include the sunset (*Maghrib*) and late evening (*'Ishâ*) prayers.

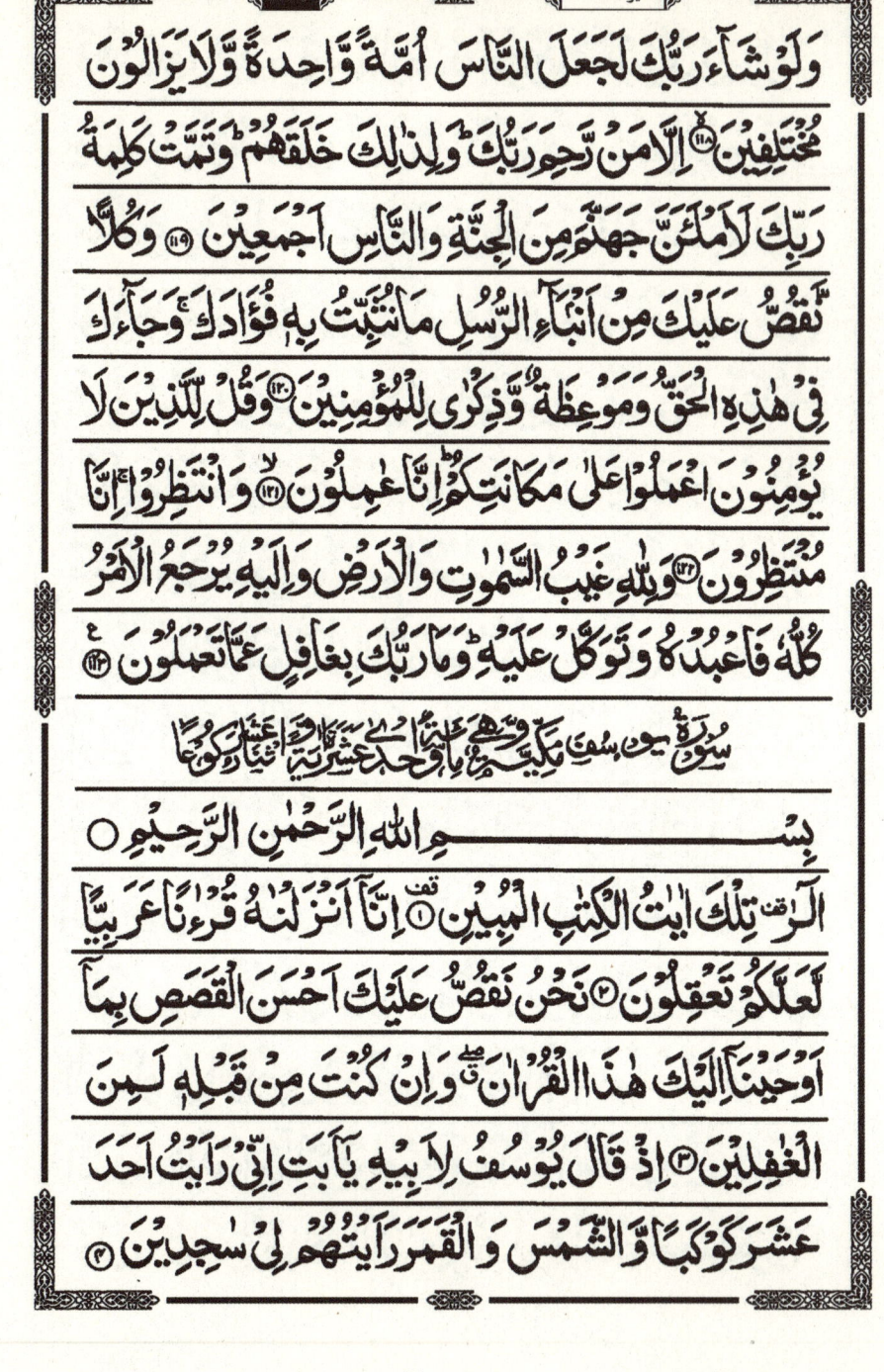

12. Yûsuf — 236

Free Choice

118. Had your Lord so willed, He would have certainly made humanity one single community ˹of believers˺, but they will always ˹choose to˺ differ— **119.** except those shown mercy by your Lord—and so He created them ˹to choose freely˺. And so the Word of your Lord will be fulfilled: "I will surely fill up Hell with jinn and humans all together."

Moral of the Stories

120. And We relate to you ˹O Prophet˺ the stories of the messengers to reassure your heart. And there has come to you in this ˹sûrah˺ the truth, a warning ˹to the disbelievers˺, and a reminder to the believers. **121.** Say to those who disbelieve, "Persist in your ways; we will certainly persist in ours. **122.** And wait! Surely we ˹too˺ are waiting."

Allah Almighty

123. To Allah ˹alone˺ belongs the knowledge of what is hidden in the heavens and the earth. And to Him all matters are returned. So worship Him and put your trust in Him. And your Lord is never unaware of what you do.

❧✽❧

12. Joseph (Yûsuf)

In the Name of Allah—the Most Compassionate, Most Merciful

The Best of Stories

1. *Alif-Lãm-Ra.* These are the verses of the clear Book. **2.** Indeed, We have sent it down as an Arabic Quran[428] so that you may understand.[429] **3.** We relate to you ˹O Prophet˺ the best of stories through Our revelation of this Quran, though before this you were totally unaware ˹of them˺.

Joseph's Dream

4. ˹Remember˺ when Joseph said to his father, "O my dear father! Indeed I dreamt of eleven stars, and the sun, and the moon—I saw them prostrating to me!"[430]

---

428 Quran literally means recitation.
429 The address here is to the Arabs and, by extension, all of humanity.
430 This dream came true at the end of the story (see 12:100).

237   12. Yûsuf

5. He replied, "O my dear son! Do not relate your vision to your brothers, or they will devise a plot against you. Surely Satan is a sworn enemy to humankind. 6. And so will your Lord choose you ˹O Joseph˺, and teach you the interpretation of dreams, and perfect His favour upon you and the descendants of Jacob—˹just˺ as He once perfected it upon your forefathers, Abraham and Isaac. Surely your Lord is All-Knowing, All-Wise."

Conspiracy by Joseph's Brothers

7. Indeed, in the story of Joseph and his brothers there are lessons for all who ask. 8. ˹Remember˺ when they said ˹to one another˺, "Surely Joseph and his brother ˹Benjamin˺ are more beloved to our father than we, even though we are a group of so many.[431] Indeed, our father is clearly mistaken. 9. Kill Joseph or cast him out to some ˹distant˺ land so that our father's attention will be only ours, then after that you may ˹repent and˺ become righteous people!" 10. One of them said, "Do not kill Joseph. But if you must do something, throw him into the bottom of a well so perhaps he may be picked up by some travellers."

Convincing Jacob

11. They said, "O our father! Why do you not trust us with Joseph, although we truly wish him well? 12. Send him out with us tomorrow so that he may enjoy himself and play. And we will really watch over him." 13. He responded, "It would truly sadden me if you took him

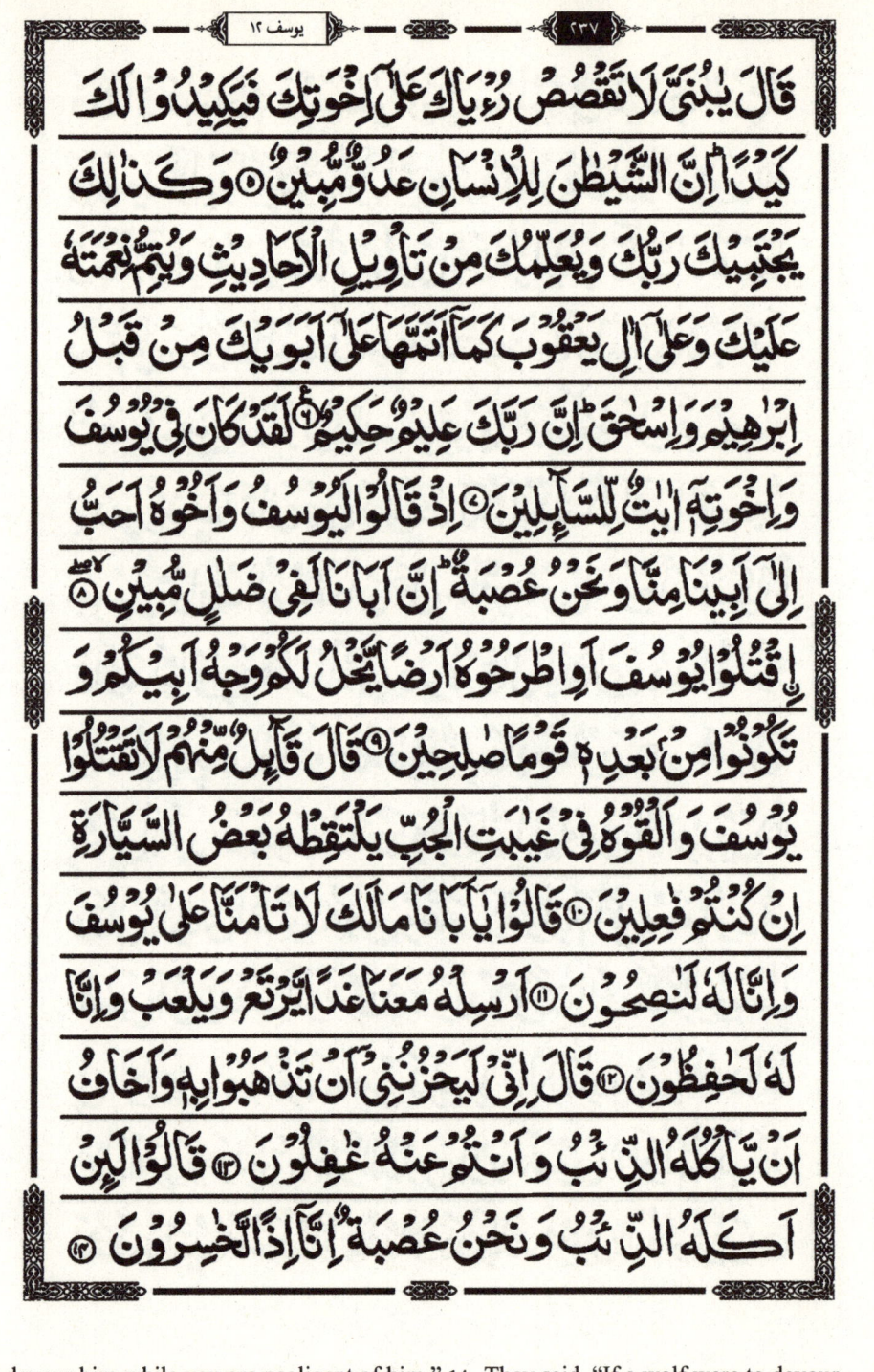

away with you, and I fear that a wolf may devour him while you are negligent of him." 14. They said, "If a wolf were to devour him, despite our strong group, then we would certainly be losers!"

---

431 Unlike Joseph's other brothers, Benjamin was Joseph's full brother. They lost their mother at a young age, so their half-brothers thought that their father loved them more.

12. Yûsuf

15. And so, when they took him away and decided to throw him into the bottom of the well, We inspired him: "˹One day˺ you will remind them of this deed of theirs while they are unaware ˹of who you are˺."

Faking Joseph's Death

16. Then they returned to their father in the evening, weeping. **17.** They cried, "Our father! We went racing and left Joseph with our belongings, and a wolf devoured him! But you will not believe us, no matter how truthful we are." **18.** And they brought his shirt, stained with false blood.[432] He responded, "No! Your souls must have tempted you to do something ˹evil˺. So ˹I can only endure with˺ beautiful patience![433] It is Allah's help that I seek to bear your claims."

Joseph Sold into Slavery

19. And there came some travellers, and they sent their water-boy who let down his bucket into the well. He cried out, "Oh, what a great find! Here is a boy!" And they took him secretly ˹to be sold˺ as merchandise, but Allah is All-Knowing of what they did. **20.** They ˹later˺ sold him for a cheap price, just a few silver coins—only wanting to get rid of him.[434]

Joseph in Egypt

21. The man from Egypt[435] who bought him said to his wife, "Take good care of him, perhaps he may be useful to us or we may adopt him as a son." This is how We established Joseph in the land, so that We might teach him the interpretation of dreams. Allah's Will always prevails, but most people do not know. **22.** And when he reached maturity, We gave him wisdom and knowledge. This is how We reward the good-doers.

---

432 They stained Joseph's shirt with blood from a sheep, but forgot to tear his shirt. So Jacob became suspicious when he saw the intact shirt.

433 i.e., patience without complaining.

434 Other possible translations: 1. "… so little did they value him." 2. "… they had no interest in him." In any case, they wanted to sell him immediately before someone claimed him. According to some Quran commentators, it was Joseph's brothers who sold him to the travellers after he was picked up from the well. The verse states that Joseph was sold for a few worthless coins. Ironically, in 12:88 Joseph's brothers came to him after he became Egypt's Chief Minister, begging for supplies and saying that the only money they could afford was a few worthless coins. This is when Joseph revealed his true identity to them.

435 Potiphar, the Chief Minister of Egypt (Al-'Azîz).

239   12. Yûsuf

The Temptation

23. And the lady, in whose house he lived, tried to seduce him. She locked the doors ˹firmly˺ and said, "Come to me!" He replied, "Allah is my refuge! It is ˹not right to betray˺ my master, who has taken good care of me. Indeed, the wrongdoers never succeed." **24.** She advanced towards him, and he would have done likewise, had he not seen a sign from his Lord.[436] This is how We kept evil and indecency away from him, for he was truly one of Our chosen servants. **25.** They raced for the door and she tore his shirt from the back, only to find her husband at the door. She cried, "What is the penalty for someone who tried to violate your wife, except imprisonment or a painful punishment?"

The Witness

26. Joseph responded, "It was she who tried to seduce me." And a witness from her own family testified: "If his shirt is torn from the front, then she has told the truth and he is a liar. **27.** But if it is torn from the back, then she has lied and he is truthful." **28.** So when her husband saw that Joseph's shirt was torn from the back, he said ˹to her˺, "This must be ˹an example˺ of the cunning of you ˹women˺! Indeed, your cunning is so shrewd! **29.** O Joseph! Forget about this. And you ˹O wife˺! Seek forgiveness for your sin.[437] It certainly has been your fault."

The Women and Joseph's Beauty

30. Some women of the city gossiped, "The Chief Minister's wife is trying to seduce her slave-boy. Love for him has plagued her heart. Indeed, we see that she is clearly mistaken."[438]

---

436 Joseph (☺) received warning against fornication either through divine inspiration or a vision of his father.
437 She was urged to seek forgiveness from her husband.
438 The women's only objection was because the wife of the Chief Minister was in love with someone raised in her house like a son.

12. Yûsuf

240

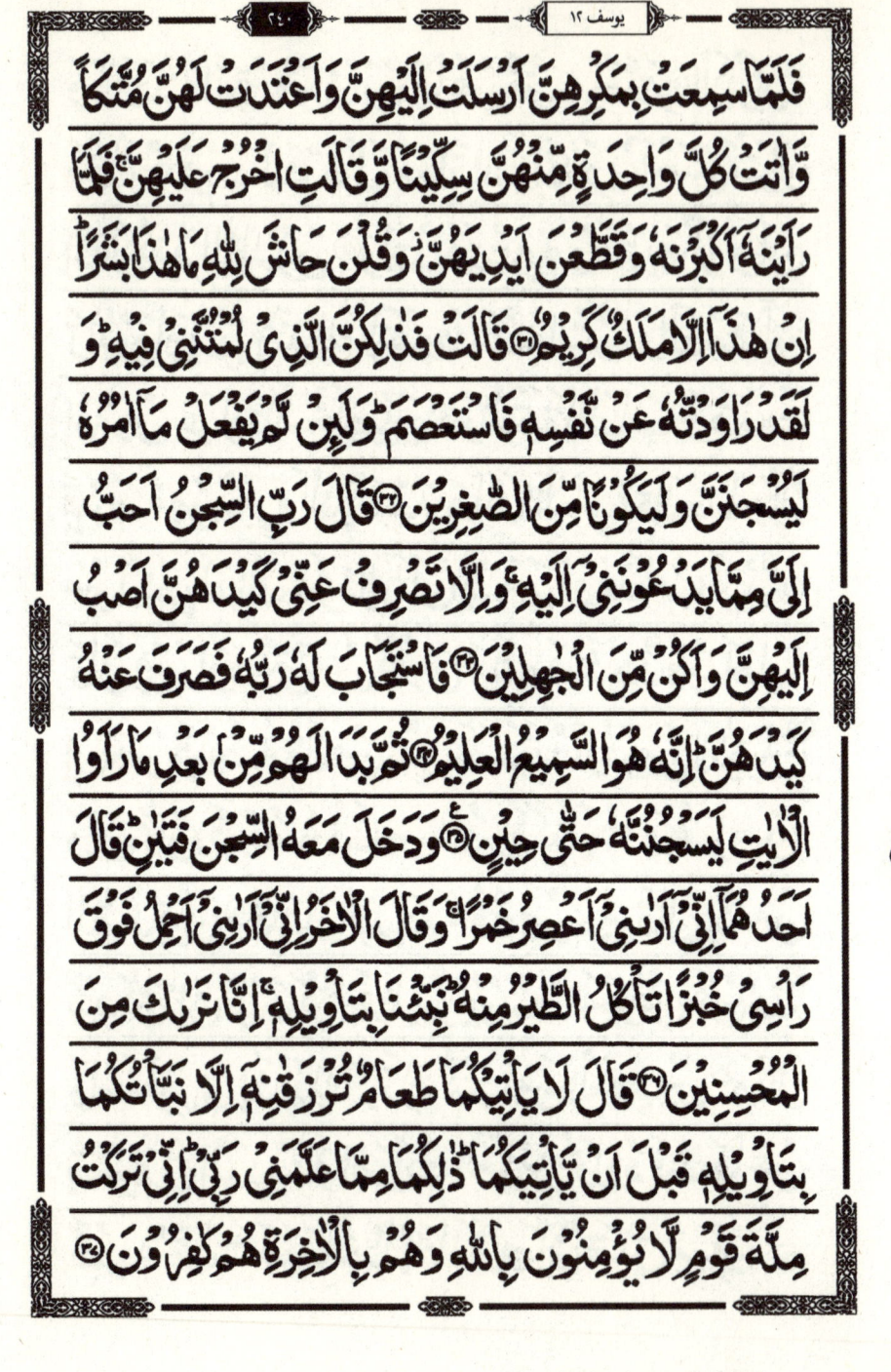

31. When she heard about their gossip,[439] she invited them and set a banquet for them. She gave each one a knife, then said ˹to Joseph˺, "Come out before them." When they saw him, they were so stunned ˹by his beauty˺ that they cut their hands,[440] and exclaimed, "Good God! This cannot be human; this must be a noble angel!" **32.** She said, "This is the one for whose love you criticized me! I did try to seduce him but he ˹firmly˺ refused. And if he does not do what I order him to, he will certainly be imprisoned and ˹fully˺ disgraced."[441]

The Lesser of Two Evils

33. Joseph prayed, "My Lord! I would rather be in jail than do what they invite me to. And if You do not turn their cunning away from me, I might yield to them and fall into ignorance." **34.** So his Lord responded to him, turning their cunning away from him. Surely He is the All-Hearing, All-Knowing. **35.** And so it occurred to those in charge, despite seeing all the proofs ˹of his innocence˺, that he should be imprisoned for a while.[442]

Dreams of the Two Inmates

36. And two other servants went to jail with Joseph. One of them said, "I dreamt I was pressing wine." The other said, "I dreamt I was carrying ˹some˺ bread on my head, from which birds were eating." ˹Then both said,˺ "Tell us their interpretation, for we surely see you as one of the good-doers."

Invitation to the Truth

37. Joseph replied, "I can even tell you what kind of meal you will be served before you receive it. This ˹knowledge˺ is from what my Lord has taught me. I have shunned the faith of a people who disbelieve in Allah and deny the Hereafter.

---

439 lit., 'their cunning' because the women themselves were probably interested in Joseph.
440 The women were cutting fruit, and when Joseph came out they were so impressed by his beauty that they sliced through the fruit and into their hands without knowing.
441 The women tried to convince him to obey the Chief Minister's wife, so Joseph prayed to Allah to keep him away from them.
442 To stop women from being charmed by Joseph's beauty, or to put an end to the rumours, or to keep him away from the Minister's wife.

38. I follow the faith of my fathers: Abraham, Isaac, and Jacob. It is not ˹right˺ for us to associate anything with Allah ˹in worship˺. This is part of Allah's grace upon us and humanity, but most people are not grateful.
39. O my fellow-prisoners! Which is far better: many different lords or Allah—the One, the Supreme?
40. Whatever ˹idols˺ you worship instead of Him are mere names which you and your forefathers have made up[443]—a practice Allah has never authorized. It is only Allah Who decides. He has commanded that you worship none but Him. That is the upright faith, but most people do not know.

Interpretation of the Dreams

41. "O my fellow-prisoners! ˹The first˺ one of you will serve wine to his master, and the other will be crucified and the birds will eat from his head. The matter about which you inquired has been decided."
42. Then he said to the one he knew would survive, "Mention me in the presence of your master.[444]" But Satan made him forget to mention Joseph to his master, so he remained in prison for several years.

The King's Dream

43. And ˹one day˺ the King[445] said, "I dreamt of seven fat cows eaten up by seven skinny ones; and seven green ears of grain and ˹seven˺ others dry. O chiefs! Tell me the meaning of my dream if you can interpret dreams."

---

443 Meaning, "You call them gods while in fact they are not gods."
444 The King of Egypt.
445 In the Bible (the Book of Genesis), this ruler is referred to as a pharaoh, while in the Quran he is referred to as a king. Typically, Egypt was ruled by pharaohs, but there existed a brief period in Egyptian history in which Egypt was ruled by the Hyksos invaders (1700-1550 B.C.E.). Hyksos rulers were called kings, not pharaohs. Joseph entered Egypt during the reign of the Hyksos, who used to appoint some foreigners to prominent positions in Egypt. According to *The Jewish Encyclopedia*, "Those who regard the Joseph stories as historical generally hold that the Pharaoh by whom Joseph was made the practical ruler of Egypt was one of the Hyksos kings." "Joseph," *The Jewish Encyclopedia*, Volume VII (London: Funk and Wagnalls Company, 1916), p. 252.

12. Yûsuf

بِسْمِ ٱللَّهِ ٱلرَّحْمَٰنِ ٱلرَّحِيمِ

قَالُوٓا۟ أَضْغَٰثُ أَحْلَٰمٍۖ وَمَا نَحْنُ بِتَأْوِيلِ ٱلْأَحْلَٰمِ بِعَٰلِمِينَ ۝ وَقَالَ ٱلَّذِى نَجَا مِنْهُمَا وَٱدَّكَرَ بَعْدَ أُمَّةٍ أَنَا۠ أُنَبِّئُكُم بِتَأْوِيلِهِۦ فَأَرْسِلُونِ ۝ يُوسُفُ أَيُّهَا ٱلصِّدِّيقُ أَفْتِنَا فِى سَبْعِ بَقَرَٰتٍ سِمَانٍ يَأْكُلُهُنَّ سَبْعٌ عِجَافٌ وَسَبْعِ سُنۢبُلَٰتٍ خُضْرٍ وَأُخَرَ يَابِسَٰتٍ لَّعَلِّىٓ أَرْجِعُ إِلَى ٱلنَّاسِ لَعَلَّهُمْ يَعْلَمُونَ ۝ قَالَ تَزْرَعُونَ سَبْعَ سِنِينَ دَأَبًا فَمَا حَصَدتُّمْ فَذَرُوهُ فِى سُنۢبُلِهِۦٓ إِلَّا قَلِيلًا مِّمَّا تَأْكُلُونَ ۝ ثُمَّ يَأْتِى مِنۢ بَعْدِ ذَٰلِكَ سَبْعٌ شِدَادٌ يَأْكُلْنَ مَا قَدَّمْتُمْ لَهُنَّ إِلَّا قَلِيلًا مِّمَّا تُحْصِنُونَ ۝ ثُمَّ يَأْتِى مِنۢ بَعْدِ ذَٰلِكَ عَامٌ فِيهِ يُغَاثُ ٱلنَّاسُ وَفِيهِ يَعْصِرُونَ ۝ وَقَالَ ٱلْمَلِكُ ٱئْتُونِى بِهِۦۖ فَلَمَّا جَآءَهُ ٱلرَّسُولُ قَالَ ٱرْجِعْ إِلَىٰ رَبِّكَ فَسْـَٔلْهُ مَا بَالُ ٱلنِّسْوَةِ ٱلَّٰتِى قَطَّعْنَ أَيْدِيَهُنَّۚ إِنَّ رَبِّى بِكَيْدِهِنَّ عَلِيمٌ ۝ قَالَ مَا خَطْبُكُنَّ إِذْ رَٰوَدتُّنَّ يُوسُفَ عَن نَّفْسِهِۦۚ قُلْنَ حَٰشَ لِلَّهِ مَا عَلِمْنَا عَلَيْهِ مِن سُوٓءٍۚ قَالَتِ ٱمْرَأَتُ ٱلْعَزِيزِ ٱلْـَٰٔنَ حَصْحَصَ ٱلْحَقُّ أَنَا۠ رَٰوَدتُّهُۥ عَن نَّفْسِهِۦ وَإِنَّهُۥ لَمِنَ ٱلصَّٰدِقِينَ ۝ ذَٰلِكَ لِيَعْلَمَ أَنِّى لَمْ أَخُنْهُ بِٱلْغَيْبِ وَأَنَّ ٱللَّهَ لَا يَهْدِى كَيْدَ ٱلْخَآئِنِينَ ۝

---

44. They replied, "These are confused visions and we do not know the interpretation of such dreams." 45. ˹Finally,˺ the surviving ex-prisoner remembered ˹Joseph˺ after a long time and said, "I will tell you its interpretation, so send me forth ˹to Joseph˺."

Interpretation of the King's Dream

46. ˹He said,˺ "Joseph, O man of truth! Interpret for us ˹the dream of˺ seven fat cows eaten up by seven skinny ones; and seven green ears of grain and ˹seven˺ others dry, so that I may return to the people and let them know." 47. Joseph replied, "You will plant ˹grain˺ for seven consecutive years, leaving in the ear whatever you will harvest, except for the little you will eat. 48. Then after that will come seven years of great hardship which will consume whatever you have saved, except the little you will store ˹for seed˺. 49. Then after that will come a year in which people will receive abundant rain and they will press ˹oil and wine˺."

Joseph Declared Innocent

50. The King ˹then˺ said, "Bring him to me." When the messenger came to him, Joseph said, "Go back to your master and ask him about the case of the women who cut their hands. Surely my Lord has ˹full˺ knowledge of their cunning." 51. The King asked ˹the women˺, "What did you get when you tried to seduce Joseph?" They replied, "Allah forbid! We know nothing indecent about him." Then the Chief Minister's wife admitted, "Now the truth has come to light. It was I who tried to seduce him, and he is surely truthful. 52. From this, Joseph should know that I did not speak dishonestly about him in his absence, for Allah certainly does not guide the scheming of the dishonest.

53. And I do not seek to free myself from blame, for indeed the soul is ever inclined to evil, except those shown mercy by my Lord. Surely my Lord is All-Forgiving, Most Merciful."

Joseph, the Chief Minister

54. The King said, "Bring him to me. I will employ him exclusively in my service." And when Joseph spoke to him, the King said, "Today you are highly esteemed and fully trusted by us." **55.** Joseph proposed, "Put me in charge of the store-houses of the land, for I am truly reliable and adept." **56.** This is how We established Joseph in the land to settle wherever he pleased. We shower Our mercy on whoever We will, and We never discount the reward of the good-doers. **57.** And the reward of the Hereafter is far better for those who are faithful and are mindful ʿof Allah˼.

Joseph's Brothers Visit Egypt[446]

58. And Joseph's brothers came and entered his presence. He recognized them but they were unaware of who he really was. **59.** When he had provided them with their supplies, he demanded, "Bring me your brother on your father's side.[447] Do you not see that I give full measure and I am the best of hosts? **60.** But if you do not bring him to me ʿnext time˼, I will have no grain for you, nor will you ever come close to me again." **61.** They promised, "We will try to convince his father to let him come. We will certainly do ʿour best˼." **62.** Joseph ordered his servants to put his brothers' money back into their saddlebags so that they would find it when they returned to their family and perhaps they would come back.

The Brothers Return Home

63. When Joseph's brothers returned to their father, they pleaded, "O our father! We have been denied ʿfurther˼ supplies. So send our brother with us so that we may receive our measure, and we will definitely watch over him."

---

446 Joseph's family was affected by famine, so they had to travel to Egypt to buy supplies.
447 i.e., Benjamin. When Joseph hosted his half-brothers, they told him the number of people in their household for future supplies.

12. Yûsuf — 244

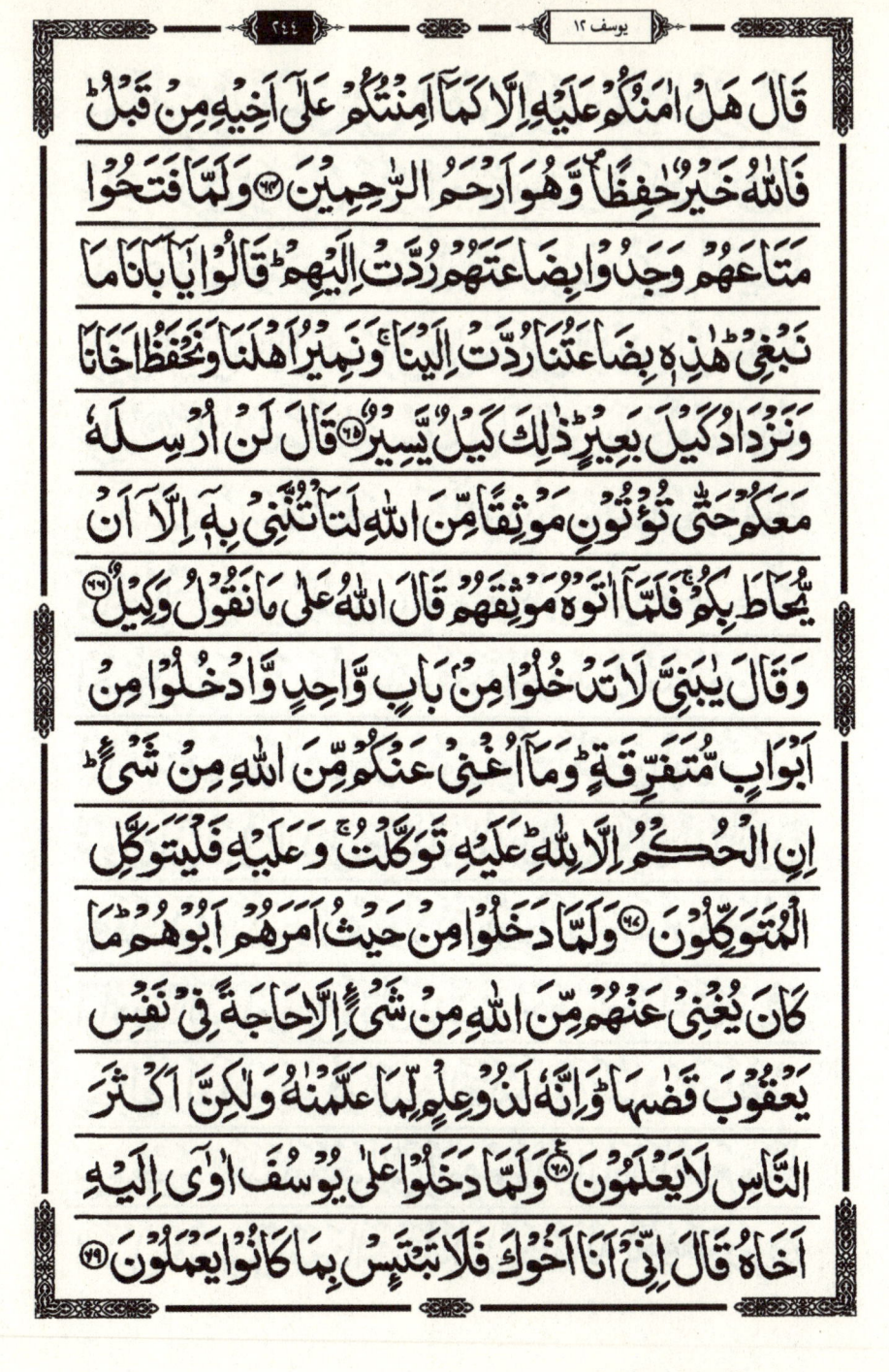

64. He responded, "Should I trust you with him as I once trusted you with his brother ˹Joseph˺? But ˹only˺ Allah is the best Protector, and He is the Most Merciful of the merciful." **65.** When they opened their bags, they discovered that their money had been returned to them. They argued, "O our father! What more can we ask for? Here is our money, fully returned to us. Now we can buy more food for our family. We will watch over our brother, and obtain an extra camel-load of grain. That load can be easily secured."

Jacob's Wisdom

66. Jacob insisted, "I will not send him with you until you give me a solemn oath by Allah that you will certainly bring him back to me, unless you are totally overpowered." Then after they had given him their oaths, he concluded, "Allah is a Witness to what we have said." **67.** He then instructed ˹them˺, "O my sons! Do not enter ˹the city˺ all through one gate, but through separate gates.[448] I cannot help you against ˹what is destined by˺ Allah in the least. It is only Allah Who decides. In Him I put my trust. And in Him let the faithful put their trust." **68.** Then when they entered as their father had instructed them, this did not help them against ˹the Will of˺ Allah whatsoever. It was just a desire in Jacob's heart which he satisfied. He was truly blessed with ˹great˺ knowledge because of what We had taught him, but most people have no knowledge.

The Royal Cup[449]

69. When they entered Joseph's presence, he called his brother ˹Benjamin˺ aside, and confided ˹to him˺, "I am indeed your brother ˹Joseph˺! So do not feel distressed about what they have been doing."

---

448 He told them that every three or four of them should enter through a different gate. His desire was to protect them from envy and harm.
449 The King's cup was also used as the standard measure for grain.

12. Yûsuf

70. When Joseph had provided them with supplies, he slipped the royal cup into his brother's bag. Then a herald cried, "O people of the caravan! You must be thieves!" 71. They asked, turning back, "What have you lost?" 72. The herald ˹along with the guards˺ replied, "We have lost the King's measuring cup. And whoever brings it will be awarded a camel-load ˹of grain˺. I guarantee it." 73. Joseph's brothers replied, "By Allah! You know well that we did not come to cause trouble in the land, nor are we thieves." 74. Joseph's men asked, "What should be the price for theft, if you are lying?" 75. Joseph's brothers responded, "The price will be ˹the enslavement of˺ the one in whose bag the cup is found. That is how we punish the wrongdoers."

Joseph Takes Benjamin

76. Joseph began searching their bags before that of his brother ˹Benjamin˺, then brought it out of Benjamin's bag. This is how We inspired Joseph to plan. He could not have taken his brother under the King's law, but Allah had so willed. We elevate in rank whoever We will. But above those ranking in knowledge is the One All-Knowing. 77. ˹To distance themselves,˺ Joseph's brothers argued, "If he has stolen, so did his ˹full˺ brother before."[450] But Joseph suppressed his outrage—revealing nothing to them—and said ˹to himself˺, "You are in such an evil position,[451] and Allah knows best ˹the truth of˺ what you claim." 78. They appealed, "O Chief Minister! He has a very old father, so take one of us instead. We surely see you as one of the good-doers."

---

450 Joseph was falsely accused of theft when he was young.
451 He meant: I did not steal anything, nor did my brother ˹Benjamin˺. You are the real thieves; you stole me from my father and threw me into the well.

12. Yûsuf — 246

79. Joseph responded, "Allah forbid that we should take other than the one with whom we found our property. Otherwise, we would surely be unjust."

Bad News for Jacob, Again

80. When they lost all hope in him, they spoke privately. The eldest of them said, "Do you not know that your father had taken a solemn oath by Allah from you, nor how you failed him regarding Joseph before? So I am not leaving this land until my father allows me to, or Allah decides for me. For He is the Best of Judges. **81.** Return to your father and say, 'O our father! Your son committed theft. We testify only to what we know. We could not guard against the unforeseen.[452] **82.** Ask ˹the people of˺ the land where we were and the caravan we travelled with. We are certainly telling the truth.'"

Jacob's Grief

83. He cried, "No! Your souls must have tempted you to do something ˹evil˺. So ˹I am left with nothing but˺ beautiful patience![453] I trust Allah will return them all to me. Surely He ˹alone˺ is the All-Knowing, All-Wise." **84.** He turned away from them, lamenting, "Alas, poor Joseph!" And his eyes turned white out of the grief he suppressed.[454] **85.** They said, "By Allah! You will not cease to remember Joseph until you lose your health or ˹even˺ your life." **86.** He replied, "I complain of my anguish and sorrow only to Allah, and I know from Allah what you do not know.

---

452 We did not know when we gave you our solemn oath that our brother was going to steal.

453 i.e., patience without complaining.

454 Jacob (☉) cried for so long that he became very weak-sighted. Some scholars suggest that he lost his sight completely. This does not contradict Jacob's beautiful patience because he did not complain to anyone, but expressed his sorrow only to Allah.

12. Yûsuf

87. O my sons! Go and search ˹diligently˺ for Joseph and his brother. And do not lose hope in the mercy of Allah, for no one loses hope in Allah's mercy except those with no faith."

Joseph Reveals His Identity

88. When they entered Joseph's presence, they pleaded, "O Chief Minister! We and our family have been touched with hardship, and we have brought only a few worthless coins, but ˹please˺ give us our supplies in full and be charitable to us. Indeed, Allah rewards the charitable." **89.** He asked, "Do you remember what you did to Joseph and his brother in your ignorance?" **90.** They replied ˹in shock˺, "Are you really Joseph?" He said, "I am Joseph, and here is my brother ˹Benjamin˺! Allah has truly been gracious to us. Surely whoever is mindful ˹of Allah˺ and patient, then certainly Allah never discounts the reward of the good-doers."

Brothers' Apology Accepted

91. They admitted, "By Allah! Allah has truly preferred you over us, and we have surely been sinful." **92.** Joseph said, "There is no blame on you today. May Allah forgive you! He is the Most Merciful of the merciful! **93.** Go with this shirt of mine and cast it over my father's face, and he will regain his sight. Then come back to me with your whole family."

Jacob Regains His Sight

94. When the caravan departed ˹from Egypt˺, their father said ˹to those around him˺, "You may think I am senile, but I certainly sense the smell of Joseph." **95.** They replied, "By Allah! You are definitely still in your old delusion." **96.** But when the bearer of the good news arrived, he cast the shirt over Jacob's face, so he regained his sight. Jacob then said ˹to his children˺, "Did I not tell you that I truly know from Allah what you do not know?"

12. Yûsuf

97. They begged, "O our father! Pray for the forgiveness of our sins. We have certainly been sinful."
98. He said, "I will pray to my Lord for your forgiveness.[455] He ˹alone˺ is indeed the All-Forgiving, Most Merciful."

Joseph's Dream Comes True

99. When they entered Joseph's presence, he received his parents ˹graciously˺ and said, "Enter Egypt, Allah willing, in security." **100.** Then he raised his parents to the throne, and they all fell down in prostration to Joseph,[456] who then said, "O my dear father! This is the interpretation of my old dream. My Lord has made it come true. He was truly kind to me when He freed me from prison, and brought you all from the desert after Satan had ignited rivalry between me and my siblings.[457] Indeed my Lord is subtle in fulfilling what He wills. Surely He ˹alone˺ is the All-Knowing, All-Wise."

Joseph's Prayer

101. "My Lord! You have surely granted me authority and taught me the interpretation of dreams. ˹O˺ Originator of the heavens and the earth! You are my Guardian in this world and the Hereafter. Allow me to die as one who submits[458] and join me with the righteous."

Reminders to Prophet Muḥammad

102. That is from the stories of the unseen which We reveal to you ˹O Prophet˺. You were not present when they ˹all˺[459] made up their minds, and when they plotted ˹against Joseph˺.

---

455 Jacob (📿) delayed the prayer for his children to be forgiven until pre-dawn, which is a blessed time for supplication.
456 Joseph's parents and his eleven brothers prostrated before him out of respect, not as an act of worship. This was permissible in their tradition, but in Islam, Muslims prostrate only to Allah.
457 Joseph (📿) did not mention how Allah saved him from the well because he did not want to embarrass his brothers after forgiving them.
458 lit., as a Muslim.
459 This includes Joseph's brothers, the travellers who picked him up from the well and sold him into slavery, and the Chief Minister's wife and other women in the city.

103. And most people will not believe—no matter how keen you are— **104.** even though you are not asking them for a reward for this ˹Quran˺. It is only a reminder to the whole world. **105.** How many signs in the heavens and the earth do they pass by with indifference! **106.** And most of them do not believe in Allah without associating others with Him ˹in worship˺. **107.** Do they feel secure that an overwhelming torment from Allah will not overtake them, or that the Hour will not take them by surprise when they least expect ˹it˺?

Invitation with Knowledge and Wisdom

108. Say, ˹O Prophet,˺ "This is my way. I invite to Allah with insight—I and those who follow me. Glory be to Allah, and I am not one of the polytheists."

Allah's Messengers

109. We only sent before you ˹O Prophet˺ men inspired by Us from among the people of each society. Have the deniers not travelled through the land to see what was the end of those ˹destroyed˺ before them? And surely the ˹eternal˺ Home of the Hereafter is far better for those mindful ˹of Allah˺. Will you not then understand? **110.** And when the messengers despaired and their people thought the messengers had been denied help, Our help came to them ˹at last˺. We then saved whoever We willed, and Our punishment is never averted from the wicked people.

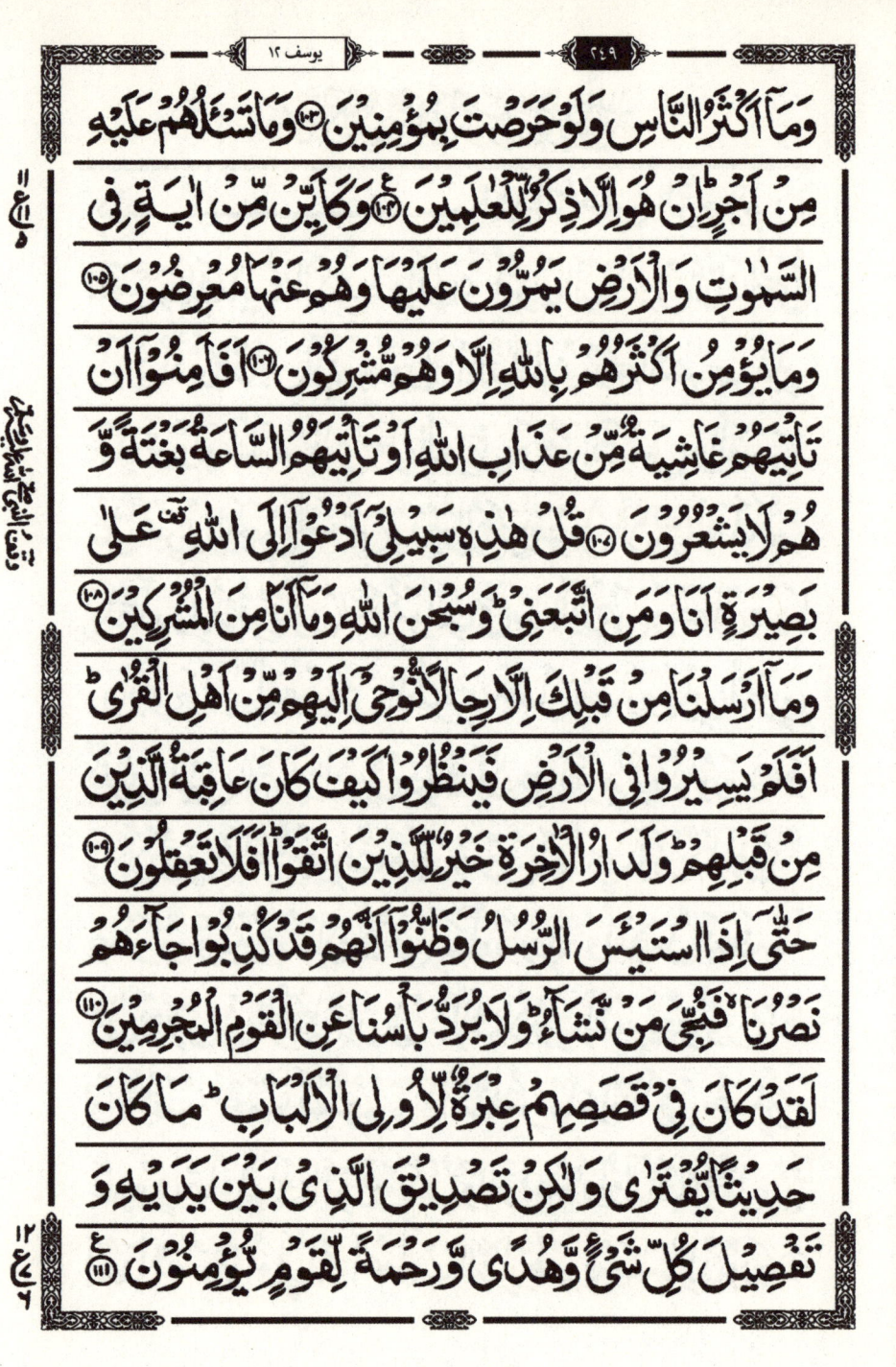

Messengers' Stories in the Quran

111. In their stories there is truly a lesson for people of reason. This message cannot be a fabrication, rather ˹it is˺ a confirmation of previous revelation, a detailed explanation of all things, a guide, and a mercy for people of faith.

13. Ar-Ra'd 250

13. Thunder (Ar-Ra'd)

In the Name of Allah—the Most
Compassionate, Most Merciful

The Truth

1. *Alif-Lām-Mīm-Ra.* These are the
verses of the Book. What has been
revealed to you ˹O Prophet˺ from
your Lord is the truth, but most people do not believe.

Allah's Might

2. It is Allah Who has raised the
heavens without pillars—as you
can see—then established Himself
on the Throne. He has subjected the
sun and the moon, each orbiting for
an appointed term. He conducts the
whole affair. He makes the signs
clear so that you may be certain of
the meeting with your Lord. 3. And
He is the One Who spread out the
earth and placed firm mountains and
rivers upon it, and created fruits of
every kind in pairs.[460] He covers the
day with night. Surely in this are
signs for those who reflect. 4. And
on the earth there are ˹different˺
neighbouring tracts, gardens of
grapevines, ˹various˺ crops, palm
trees—some stemming from the
same root, others standing alone.
They are all irrigated with the same
water, yet We make some taste better than others. Surely in this are
signs for those who understand.

Denying Resurrection

5. ˹Now,˺ if anything should amaze
you ˹O Prophet˺, then it is their
question: "When we are reduced to
dust, will we really be raised as a
new creation?" It is they who have
disbelieved in their Lord. It is they who will have shackles around their necks. And it is they who will be the residents of the Fire.
They will be there forever.

---

460 Males and females, sweet and bitter, etc.

13. Ar-Ra'd

Hastening the Torment

6. They ask you ˹O Prophet˺ to hasten the torment rather than grace, though there have ˹already˺ been ˹many˺ torments before them. Surely your Lord is full of forgiveness for people, despite their wrongdoing, and your Lord is truly severe in punishment.

Demanding a Sign from the Prophet[461]

7. The disbelievers say, "If only a sign could be sent down to him from his Lord." You ˹O Prophet˺ are only a warner. And every people had a guide.

Allah's Knowledge

8. Allah knows what every female bears and what increases and decreases in the wombs.[462] And with Him everything is determined with precision. **9.** ˹He is the˺ Knower of the seen and the unseen—the All-Great, Most Exalted. **10.** It is the same ˹to Him˺ whether any of you speaks secretly or openly, whether one hides in the darkness of night or goes about in broad daylight.

Allah's Power

11. For each one there are successive angels before and behind, protecting them by Allah's command. Indeed, Allah would never change a people's state ˹of favour˺ until they change their own state ˹of faith˺. And if it is Allah's Will to torment a people, it can never be averted, nor can they find a protector other than Him.

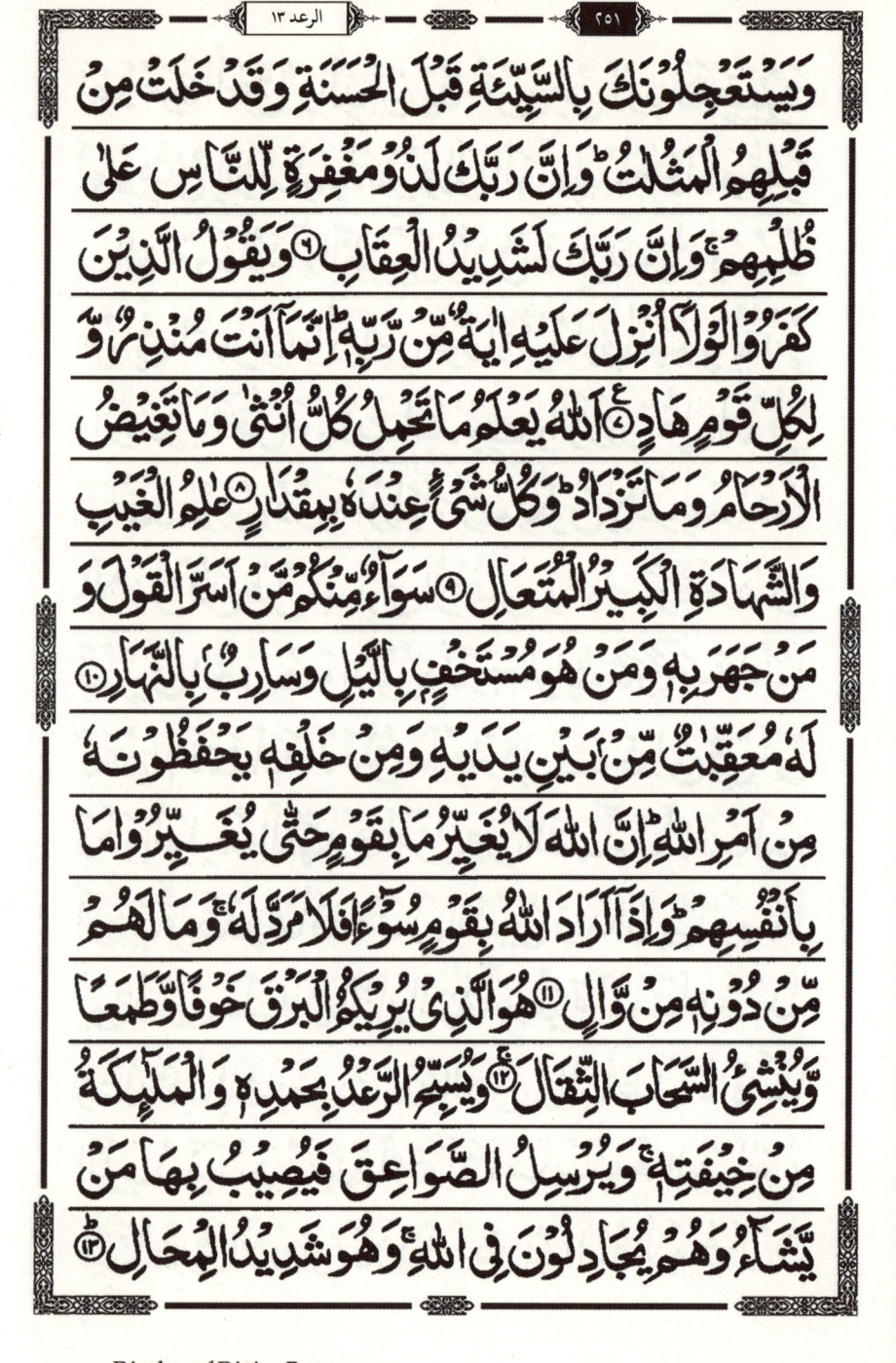

Display of Divine Power

12. He is the One Who shows you lightning, inspiring ˹you with˺ hope and fear,[463] and produces heavy clouds. **13.** The thunder glorifies His praises, as do the angels in awe of Him. He sends thunderbolts, striking with them whoever He wills. Yet they dispute about Allah. And He is tremendous in might.

---

461 Like the staff of Moses.
462 He knows whether the egg will be fertilized or not, whether the baby will be born before or after nine months, whether the pregnancy will end with delivery or miscarriage, and whether there will be one baby or more.
463 Hope of rain and fear of torment.

13. Ar-Ra'd

Useless Idols

14. Calling upon Him ˹alone˺ is the truth. But those ˹idols˺ the pagans invoke besides Him ˹can˺ never respond to them in any way. ˹It is˺ just like someone who stretches out their hands to water, ˹asking it˺ to reach their mouths, but it can never do so. The calls of the disbelievers are only in vain.

The True Lord

15. To Allah ˹alone˺ bow down ˹in submission˺[464] all those in the heavens and the earth—willingly or unwillingly—as do their shadows, morning and evening.

Almighty Allah or Powerless Gods?

16. Ask ˹them, O Prophet˺, "Who is the Lord of the heavens and the earth?" Say, "Allah!" Ask ˹them˺, "Why then have you taken besides Him lords who cannot even benefit or protect themselves?" Say, "Can the blind and the sighted be equal? Or can darkness and light be equal?"[465] Or have they associated with Allah partners who ˹supposedly˺ produced a creation like His, leaving them confused between the two creations? Say, "Allah is the Creator of all things, and He is the One, the Supreme."

Parable of Truth and Falsehood

17. He sends down rain from the sky, causing the valleys to flow, each according to its capacity. The currents then carry along rising foam, similar to the slag produced from metal that people melt in the fire for ornaments or tools. This is how Allah compares truth to falsehood. The ˹worthless˺ residue is then cast away, but what benefits people remains on the earth. This is how Allah sets forth parables.

---

464 lit., prostrate. Meaning, all beings submit to His Will.
465 Blindness and darkness are commonly used as an analogy for disbelief, whereas the ability to see and light refer to true faith in Allah.

253 | 13. Ar-Ra'd

Blindness to the Truth

18. Those who respond to ˹the call of˺ their Lord will have the finest reward. As for those who do not respond to Him, even if they were to possess everything in the world twice over, they would certainly offer it to ransom themselves. They will face strict judgment, and Hell will be their home. What an evil place to rest! **19.** Can the one who knows that your Lord's revelation to you ˹O Prophet˺ is the truth be like the one who is blind? None will be mindful ˹of this˺ except people of reason.

People of Reason

20. ˹They are˺ those who honour God's covenant, never breaking the pledge; **21.** and those who maintain whatever ˹ties˺ Allah has ordered to be maintained, stand in awe of their Lord, and fear strict judgment. **22.** And ˹they are˺ those who endure patiently, seeking their Lord's pleasure,[466] establish prayer, donate from what We have provided for them—secretly and openly—and respond to evil with good. It is they who will have the ultimate abode: **23.** the Gardens of Eternity, which they will enter along with the righteous among their parents, spouses, and descendants. And the angels will enter upon them from every gate, ˹saying,˺ **24.** "Peace be upon you for your perseverance. How excellent is the ultimate abode!"

The Wicked

25. And those who violate Allah's covenant after it has been affirmed, break whatever ˹ties˺ Allah has ordered to be maintained, and spread corruption in the land—it is they who will be condemned and will have the worst abode.[467]

Worldly Delusions

26. Allah gives abundant or limited provisions to whoever He wills. And the disbelievers become prideful of ˹the pleasures of˺ this worldly life. But the life of this world, compared to the Hereafter, is nothing but a fleeting enjoyment.

---

466 lit., seeking their Lord's Face.
467 i.e., the Hellfire.

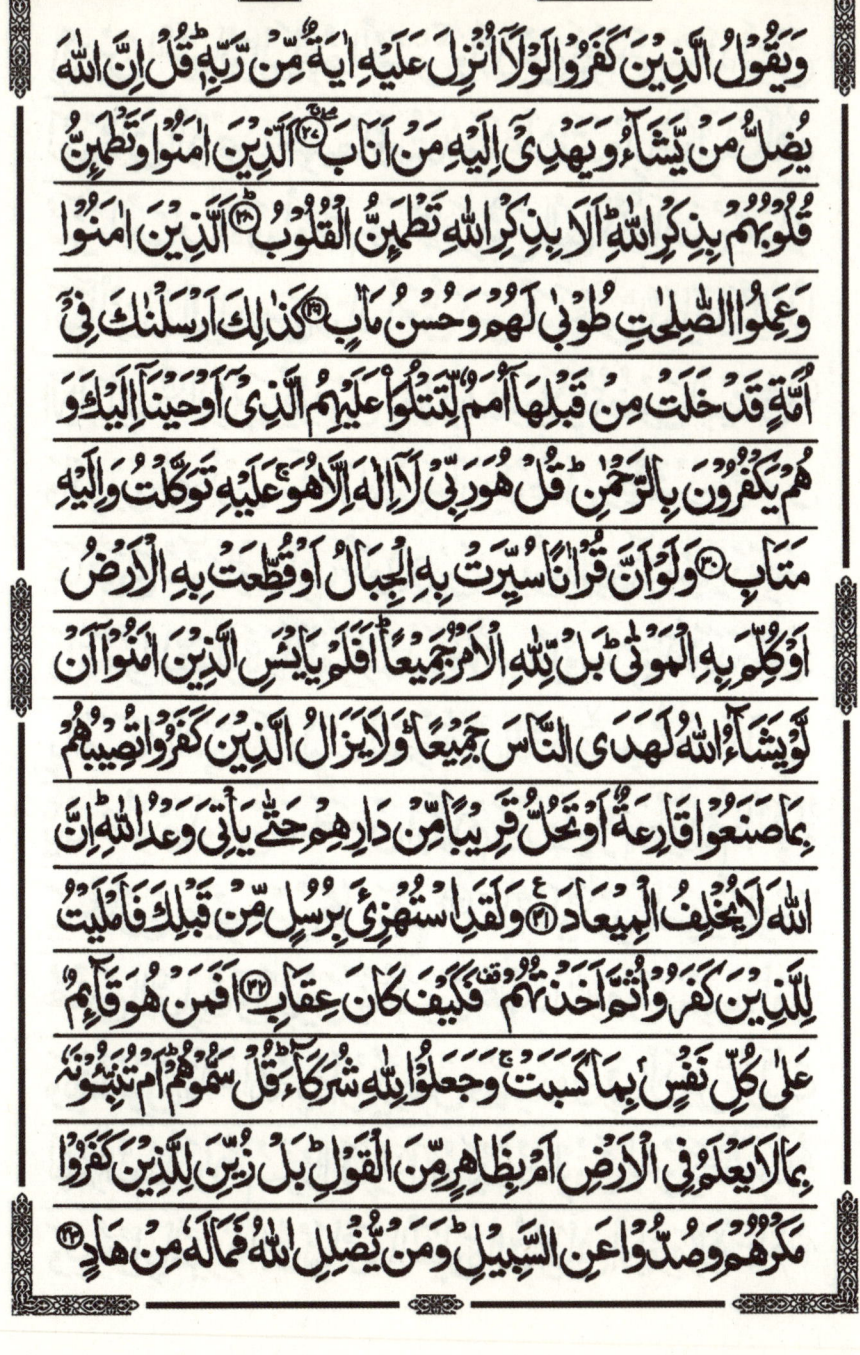

Remembrance of Allah

27. The disbelievers say, "If only a sign could be sent down to him from his Lord."[468] Say, ˹O Prophet,˺ "Indeed, Allah leaves to stray whoever He wills, and guides to Himself whoever turns to Him— 28. those who believe and whose hearts find comfort in the remembrance of Allah. Surely in the remembrance of Allah do hearts find comfort. 29. Those who believe and do good, for them will be bliss and an honourable destination."

Denying the Most Compassionate

30. And so We have sent you ˹O Prophet˺ to a community, like ˹We did with˺ earlier communities, so that you may recite to them what We have revealed to you. Yet they deny the Most Compassionate.[469] Say, "He is my Lord! There is no god ˹worthy of worship˺ except Him. In Him I put my trust, and to Him I turn ˹in repentance˺."

Deniers Will Always Deny

31. If there were a recitation that could cause mountains to move, or the earth to split, or the dead to speak, ˹it would have been this Quran˺. But all matters are by Allah's Will. Have the believers not yet realized that had Allah willed, He could have guided all of humanity? And disasters will continue to afflict the disbelievers or strike close to their homes for their misdeeds, until Allah's promise comes to pass. Surely Allah never fails in His promise. 32. Other messengers had already been ridiculed before you, but I delayed the disbelievers ˹for a while˺ then seized them. And how ˹horrible˺ was My punishment!

Falsehood Made Appealing

33. Is ˹there any equal to˺ the Vigilant One Who knows what every soul commits? Yet the pagans have associated others with Allah ˹in worship˺. Say, ˹O Prophet,˺ "Name them! Or do you ˹mean to˺ inform Him of something He does not know on the earth? Or are these ˹gods˺ just empty words?" In fact, the disbelievers' falsehood has been made so appealing to them that they have been turned away from the Path. And whoever Allah leaves to stray will be left with no guide.

---

468 The disbelievers demanded a tangible miracle such as the staff of Moses.
469 See 17:110 and 25:60.

255 13. Ar-Ra'd

34. For them is punishment in this worldly life, but the punishment of the Hereafter is truly far worse. And none can shield them from Allah.

Paradise Described

35. The description of the Paradise promised to the righteous is that under it rivers flow; eternal is its fruit as well as its shade. That is the ˹ultimate˺ outcome for the righteous. But the outcome for the disbelievers is the Fire!

Embracing the Quran

36. ˹The believers among˺ those who were given the Scripture rejoice at what has been revealed to you ˹O Prophet˺, while some ˹disbelieving˺ factions deny a portion of it. Say, "I have only been commanded to worship Allah, associating none with Him ˹in worship˺. To Him I invite ˹all˺, and to Him is my return."

37. And so We have revealed it as an authority in Arabic. And if you were to follow their desires after ˹all˺ the knowledge that has come to you, there would be none to protect or shield you from Allah.

The Last of Many

38. We have certainly sent messengers before you ˹O Prophet˺ and blessed them with wives and offspring. It was not for any messenger to bring a sign without Allah's permission. Every destined matter has a ˹set˺ time. 39. Allah eliminates and confirms what He wills, and with Him is the Master Record.[470]

Deliver, Not Judge

40. Whether We show you ˹O Prophet˺ some of what We threaten them with, or cause you to die ˹before that˺, your duty is only to deliver ˹the message˺. Judgment is for Us.

Warning to the Pagans

41. Do they not see that We gradually reduce their land from its borders? Allah decides—none can reverse His decision. And He is swift in reckoning.

---

470 This refers to the Preserved Tablet, *Al-Lawḥ Al-Maḥfūẓ*, in which Allah has written the destiny of His entire creation.

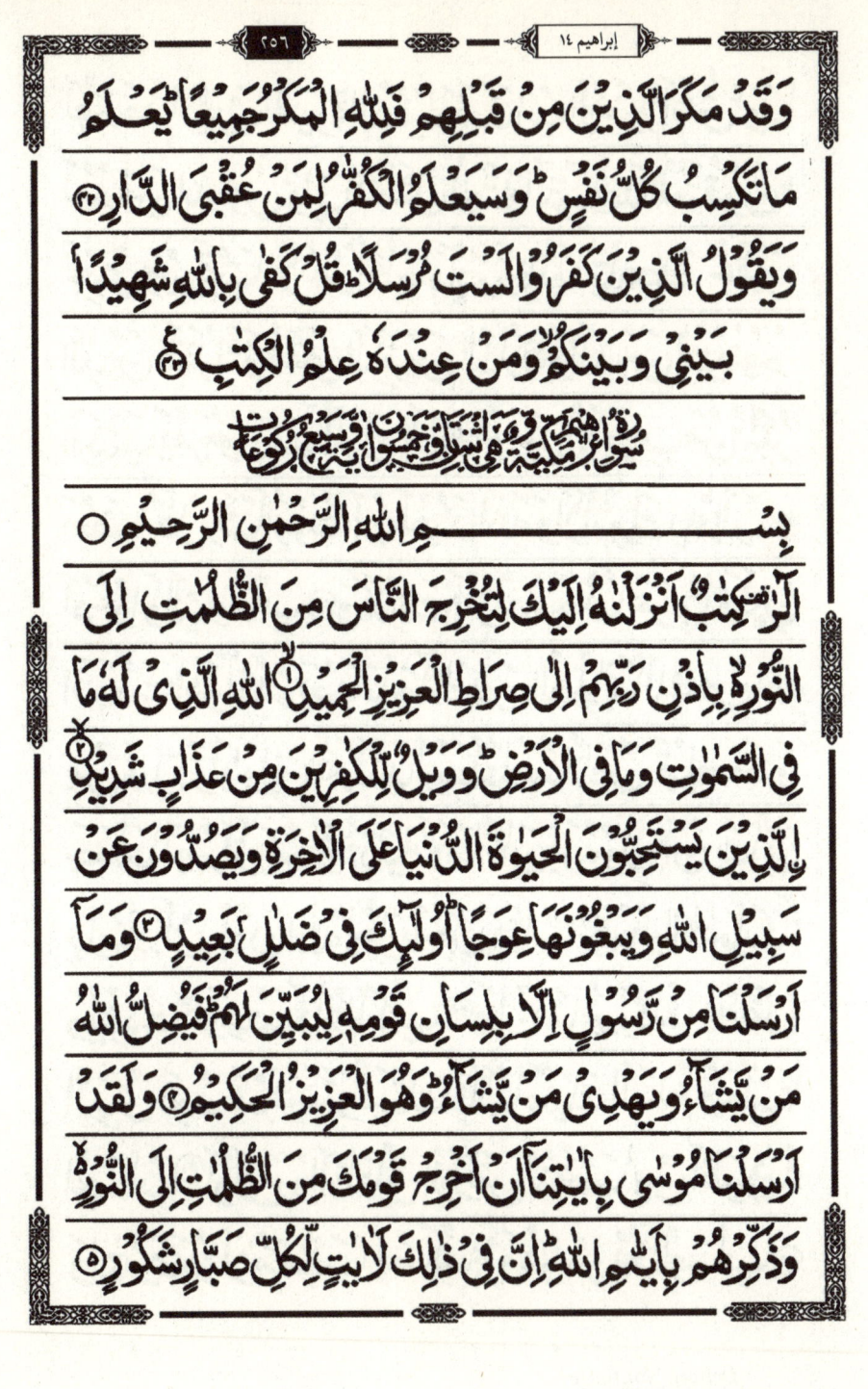

14. Ibrâhîm 256

42. Those ʿdisbelieversʾ before them ʿsecretlyʾ planned, but Allah has the ultimate plan. He knows what every soul commits. And the disbelievers will soon know who will have the ultimate outcome. **43.** The disbelievers say, "You ʿMuḥammadʾ are no messenger." Say, ʿO Prophet,ʾ "Allah is sufficient as a Witness between me and you, as is whoever has knowledge of the Scripture."

ᏉᎬᎾ ✴ ᏉᎬᎾ

14. Abraham (Ibrâhîm)

In the Name of Allah—the Most Compassionate, Most Merciful

Warning to the Disbelievers

1. *Alif-Lãm-Ra.* ʿThis isʾ a Book which We have revealed to you ʿO Prophetʾ so that you may lead people out of darkness and into light, by the Will of their Lord, to the Path of the Almighty, the Praiseworthy— **2.** Allah, to Whom belongs whatever is in the heavens and whatever is on the earth. And woe to the disbelievers because of a severe torment! **3.** ʿThey areʾ the ones who favour the life of this world over the Hereafter and hinder ʿothersʾ from the Way of Allah, striving to make it ʿappearʾ crooked. It is they who have gone far astray.

Delivering the Message

4. We have not sent a messenger except in the language of his people to clarify ʿthe messageʾ for them. Then Allah leaves whoever He wills to stray and guides whoever He wills. And He is the Almighty, All-Wise.

Prophet Moses

5. Indeed, We sent Moses with Our signs, ʿordering him,ʾ "Lead your people out of darkness and into light, and remind them of Allah's days ʿof favourʾ." Surely in this are signs for whoever is steadfast, grateful.

14. Ibrâhîm

6. ˹Consider˺ when Moses said to his people, "Remember Allah's favour upon you when He rescued you from the people of Pharaoh, who afflicted you with dreadful torment—slaughtering your sons and keeping your women. That was a severe test from your Lord. **7.** And ˹remember˺ when your Lord proclaimed, 'If you are grateful, I will certainly give you more. But if you are ungrateful, surely My punishment is severe.'" **8.** Moses said ˹to his people˺, "If you along with everyone on earth were to be ungrateful, then ˹know that˺ Allah is indeed Self-Sufficient, Praiseworthy."

Warning to the Pagans of Mecca

9. Have you not ˹already˺ received the stories of those who were before you: the people of Noah, 'Âd, Thamûd, and those after them? Only Allah knows how many they were. Their messengers came to them with clear proofs, but they put their hands over their mouths[471] and said, "We totally reject what you have been sent with, and we are certainly in alarming doubt about what you are inviting us to."

Disbelievers' Arguments

10. Their messengers asked ˹them˺, "Is there any doubt about Allah, the Originator of the heavens and the earth? He is inviting you in order to forgive your sins, and delay your end until your appointed term."[472] They argued, "You are no more than humans like us! You ˹only˺ wish to turn us away from what our forefathers worshipped. So bring us some compelling proof."

---

471 This can mean that the disbelievers bit their own hands in rage, or they covered their own mouths mockingly, or that they put their hands over their messengers' mouths to silence them.
472 It is out of Allah's mercy that He does not hasten your punishment but delays your death until your destined time.

14. Ibrâhîm   258

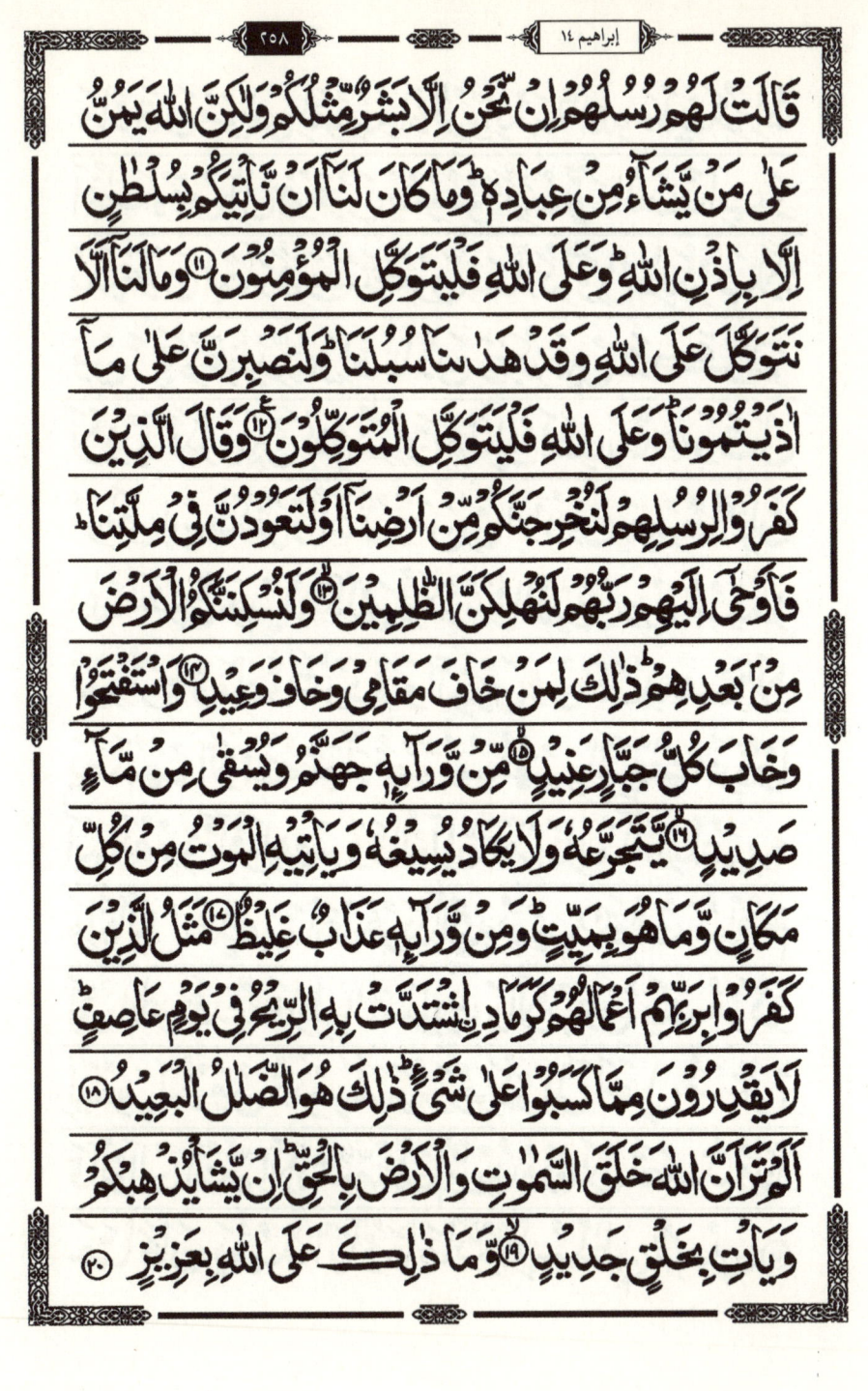

11. Their messengers said to them, "We are ˹indeed˺ only humans like you, but Allah favours whoever He chooses of His servants. It is not for us to bring you any proof without Allah's permission. And in Allah let the believers put their trust. 12. Why should we not put our trust in Allah, when He has truly guided us to ˹the very best of˺ ways? Indeed, we will patiently endure whatever harm you may cause us. And in Allah let the faithful put their trust."

Disbelievers' Fate

13. The disbelievers then threatened their messengers, "We will certainly expel you from our land, unless you return to our faith." So their Lord revealed to them, "We will surely destroy the wrongdoers, 14. and make you reside in the land after them. This is for whoever is in awe of standing before Me and fears My warning." 15. And both sides called for judgment, so every stubborn tyrant was doomed. 16. Awaiting them is Hell, and they will be left to drink oozing pus, 17. which they will sip with difficulty, and can hardly swallow. Death will overwhelm them from every side, yet they will not ˹be able to˺ die. Awaiting them still is harsher torment.

Wasted Deeds

18. The parable of the deeds of those who disbelieve in their Lord is that of ashes fiercely blown away by wind on a stormy day. They will gain nothing from what they have earned. That is ˹truly˺ the farthest one can stray.

A Reminder to Humanity

19. Have you not seen that Allah created the heavens and the earth for a reason? If He wills, He can eliminate you and produce a new creation. 20. And that is not difficult for Allah ˹at all˺.

14. Ibrâhîm

Disbelievers Disowning Each Other

21. They will all appear before Allah, and the lowly ʾfollowersʾ will appeal to the arrogant ʾleadersʾ, "We were your ʾdedicatedʾ followers, so will you ʾthenʾ protect us from Allah's torment in any way?" They will reply, "Had Allah guided us, we would have guided you. ʾNowʾ it is all the same for us whether we suffer patiently or impatiently, there is no escape for us."

Satan's Talk[473]

22. And Satan will say ʾto his followersʾ after the judgment has been passed, "Indeed, Allah has made you a true promise. I too made you a promise, but I failed you. I did not have any authority over you. I only called you, and you responded to me. So do not blame me; blame yourselves. I cannot save you, nor can you save me. Indeed, I denounce your previous association of me with Allah ʾin loyaltyʾ. Surely the wrongdoers will suffer a painful punishment."

Reward of the Believers

23. Those who believe and do good will be admitted into Gardens, under which rivers flow—to stay there forever by the Will of their Lord—where they will be greeted with "Peace!"

Parable of Good and Evil Words

24. Do you not see how Allah compares a good word to a good tree? Its root is firm and its branches reach the sky, 25. ʾalwaysʾ yielding its fruit in every season by the Will of its Lord. This is how Allah sets forth parables for the people, so perhaps they will be mindful. 26. And the parable of an evil word is that of an evil tree, uprooted from the earth, having no stability.

---

473 On the Day of Judgment, when the wicked realize that they are doomed, they will blame Satan for their great loss and will plead to him to do whatever he can to rescue them from the Hellfire. Satan will then stand up and deliver the speech quoted in this verse.

The Firm Word

27. Allah makes the believers steadfast with the firm Word ˹of faith˺[474] in this worldly life and the Hereafter. And Allah leaves the wrongdoers to stray. For Allah does what He wills.

Reward of the Ungrateful

28. Have you not seen those ˹disbelievers˺ who meet Allah's favours with ingratitude and lead their own people to their doom? **29.** In Hell they will burn. What an evil place for settlement. **30.** They set up equals to Allah to mislead ˹others˺ from His Way. Say, ˹O Prophet,˺ "Enjoy yourselves! Surely your destination is the Fire."

Order to the Prophet

31. Tell My believing servants to establish prayer and donate from what We have provided for them—openly and secretly—before the arrival of a Day in which there will be no ransom or friendly connections.

Allah's Favours

32. It is Allah Who created the heavens and the earth and sends down rain from the sky, causing fruits to grow as a provision for you. He has subjected the ships for your service, sailing through the sea by His command, and has subjected the rivers for you. **33.** He has ˹also˺ subjected for you the sun and the moon, both constantly orbiting, and has subjected the day and night for you. **34.** And He has granted you all that you asked Him for. If you tried to count Allah's blessings, you would never be able to number them. Indeed humankind is truly unfair, ˹totally˺ ungrateful.[475]

Abraham's Prayers

35. ˹Remember˺ when Abraham prayed, "My Lord! Make this city ˹of Mecca˺ secure, and keep me and my children away from the worship of idols.

---

474 That there is only one God worthy of worship.
475 In this context, "humankind" refers only to those who deny Allah's favours.

36. My Lord! They have caused many people to go astray. So whoever follows me is with me, and whoever disobeys me—then surely You are ˹still˺ All-Forgiving, Most Merciful. **37.** Our Lord! I have settled some of my offspring in a barren valley, near Your Sacred House, our Lord, so that they may establish prayer. So make the hearts of ˹believing˺ people incline towards them and provide them with fruits, so perhaps they will be thankful. **38.** Our Lord! You certainly know what we conceal and what we reveal. Nothing on earth or in heaven is hidden from Allah. **39.** All praise is for Allah who has blessed me with Ishmael and Isaac in my old age. My Lord is indeed the Hearer of ˹all˺ prayers. **40.** My Lord! Make me and those ˹believers˺ of my descendants keep up prayer. Our Lord! Accept my prayers. **41.** Our Lord! Forgive me, my parents, and the believers on the Day when the judgment will come to pass."

Warning to the Wicked

42. Do not think ˹O Prophet˺ that Allah is unaware of what the wrongdoers do. He only delays them until a Day when ˹their˺ eyes will stare in horror— **43.** rushing forth, heads raised, never blinking, hearts void.

44. And warn the people of the Day when the punishment will overtake ˹the wicked among˺ them, and the wrongdoers will cry, "Our Lord! Delay us for a little while. We will respond to Your call and follow the messengers!" ˹It will be said,˺ "Did you not swear before that you would never be removed ˹to the next life˺?"

45. You passed by the ruins of those ˹destroyed peoples˺ who had wronged themselves.[476] It was made clear to you how We dealt with them, and We gave you ˹many˺ examples. 46. They devised every plot, which was fully known to Allah, but their plotting was not enough to ˹even˺ overpower mountains ˹let alone Allah˺.

Reward of the Wicked

47. So do not think ˹O Prophet˺ that Allah will fail to keep His promise to His messengers. Allah is indeed Almighty, capable of punishment. 48. ˹Watch for˺ the Day ˹when˺ the earth will be changed into a different earth and the heavens as well, and all will appear before Allah—the One, the Supreme. 49. On that Day you will see the wicked bound together in chains, 50. with garments of tar, and their faces covered with flames. 51. As such, Allah will reward every soul for what it has committed. Surely Allah is swift in reckoning.

A Universal Message

52. This ˹Quran˺ is a ˹sufficient˺ message for humanity so that they may take it as a warning and know that there is only One God, and so that people of reason may be mindful.

༄ ❀ ༄

15. The Stone Valley (Al-Ḥijr)

In the Name of Allah—the Most Compassionate, Most Merciful

Warning to the Disbelievers

1. *Alif-Lãm-Ra.* These are the verses of the Book; the clear Quran.

---

476 Arab traders used to pass by the homes of some destroyed nations on their journeys to Syria and Yemen (such as ʿÂd and Thamûd, respectively), stopping shortly for rest.

15. Al-Ḥijr

2. ˹The day will come when˺ the disbelievers will certainly wish they had submitted ˹to Allah˺.[477] **3.** ˹So˺ let them eat and enjoy themselves and be diverted by ˹false˺ hope, for they will soon know. **4.** We have never destroyed a society without a destined term. **5.** No people can advance their doom, nor can they delay it.

The Pagans Mocking the Prophet

6. They say, "O you to whom the Reminder[478] is revealed! You must be insane! **7.** Why do you not bring us the angels, if what you say is true?" **8.** We do not send the angels down except for a just cause, and then ˹the end of˺ the disbelievers will not be delayed. **9.** It is certainly We Who have revealed the Reminder, and it is certainly We Who will preserve it.

Committed to Disbelief

10. Indeed, We sent messengers before you ˹O Prophet˺ among the groups of early peoples, **11.** but no messenger ever came to them without being mocked. **12.** This is how We allow disbelief ˹to steep˺ into the hearts of the wicked. **13.** They would not believe in this ˹Quran˺ despite the ˹many˺ examples of those ˹destroyed˺ before. **14.** And even if We opened for them a gate to heaven, through which they continued to ascend, **15.** still they would say, "Our eyes have truly been dazzled! In fact, we must have been bewitched."

Divine Power

16. Indeed, We have placed constellations in the sky, and adorned it for all to see. **17.** And We protected it from every accursed devil, **18.** except the one eavesdropping, who is then pursued by a visible flare.[479]

---

477 lit., had been Muslims.
478 i.e., the Quran.
479 Some jinn used to eavesdrop on the angels in heaven so they could disclose this information to their human associates. But this practice came to an end when the Prophet (ﷺ) was sent with the message of Islam. *See* 72:8-10.

15. Al-Ḥijr

بِسۡمِ...

وَٱلۡأَرۡضَ مَدَدۡنَٰهَا وَأَلۡقَيۡنَا فِيهَا رَوَٰسِيَ وَأَنۢبَتۡنَا فِيهَا مِن كُلِّ شَىۡءٍ مَّوۡزُونٍ ۝ وَجَعَلۡنَا لَكُمۡ فِيهَا مَعَٰيِشَ وَمَن لَّسۡتُمۡ لَهُۥ بِرَٰزِقِينَ ۝ وَإِن مِّن شَىۡءٍ إِلَّا عِندَنَا خَزَآئِنُهُۥ وَمَا نُنَزِّلُهُۥٓ إِلَّا بِقَدَرٍ مَّعۡلُومٍ ۝ وَأَرۡسَلۡنَا ٱلرِّيَٰحَ لَوَٰقِحَ فَأَنزَلۡنَا مِنَ ٱلسَّمَآءِ مَآءً فَأَسۡقَيۡنَٰكُمُوهُ وَمَآ أَنتُمۡ لَهُۥ بِخَٰزِنِينَ ۝ وَإِنَّا لَنَحۡنُ نُحۡىِۦ وَنُمِيتُ وَنَحۡنُ ٱلۡوَٰرِثُونَ ۝ وَلَقَدۡ عَلِمۡنَا ٱلۡمُسۡتَقۡدِمِينَ مِنكُمۡ وَلَقَدۡ عَلِمۡنَا ٱلۡمُسۡتَـٔۡخِرِينَ ۝ وَإِنَّ رَبَّكَ هُوَ يَحۡشُرُهُمۡ إِنَّهُۥ حَكِيمٌ عَلِيمٌ ۝ وَلَقَدۡ خَلَقۡنَا ٱلۡإِنسَٰنَ مِن صَلۡصَٰلٍ مِّنۡ حَمَإٍ مَّسۡنُونٍ ۝ وَٱلۡجَآنَّ خَلَقۡنَٰهُ مِن قَبۡلُ مِن نَّارِ ٱلسَّمُومِ ۝ وَإِذۡ قَالَ رَبُّكَ لِلۡمَلَٰٓئِكَةِ إِنِّى خَٰلِقٌۢ بَشَرًا مِّن صَلۡصَٰلٍ مِّنۡ حَمَإٍ مَّسۡنُونٍ ۝ فَإِذَا سَوَّيۡتُهُۥ وَنَفَخۡتُ فِيهِ مِن رُّوحِى فَقَعُوا۟ لَهُۥ سَٰجِدِينَ ۝ فَسَجَدَ ٱلۡمَلَٰٓئِكَةُ كُلُّهُمۡ أَجۡمَعُونَ ۝ إِلَّآ إِبۡلِيسَ أَبَىٰٓ أَن يَكُونَ مَعَ ٱلسَّٰجِدِينَ ۝ قَالَ يَٰٓإِبۡلِيسُ مَا لَكَ أَلَّا تَكُونَ مَعَ ٱلسَّٰجِدِينَ ۝ قَالَ لَمۡ أَكُن لِّأَسۡجُدَ لِبَشَرٍ خَلَقۡتَهُۥ مِن صَلۡصَٰلٍ مِّنۡ حَمَإٍ مَّسۡنُونٍ ۝

19. As for the earth, We spread it out and placed upon it firm mountains, and caused everything to grow there in perfect balance. **20.** And We made in it means of sustenance for you and others, who you do not provide for. **21.** There is not any means ˹of sustenance˺ whose reserves We do not hold, only bringing it forth in precise measure. **22.** We send fertilizing winds, and bring down rain from the sky for you to drink. It is not you who hold its reserves. **23.** Surely it is We Who give life and cause death. And We are the ˹Eternal˺ Successor.[480] **24.** We certainly know those who have gone before you and those who will come after ˹you˺. **25.** Surely your Lord ˹alone˺ will gather them together ˹for judgment˺. He is truly All-Wise, All-Knowing.

Creation of Adam

26. Indeed, We created man from sounding clay moulded from black mud. **27.** As for the jinn, We created them earlier from smokeless fire. **28.** ˹Remember, O Prophet˺ when your Lord said to the angels, "I am going to create a human being from sounding clay moulded from black mud.[481] **29.** So when I have fashioned him and had a spirit of My Own ˹creation˺ breathed into him, fall down in prostration to him."

Satan's Defiance

30. So the angels prostrated all together— **31.** but not *Iblîs*,[482] who refused to prostrate with the others. **32.** Allah asked, "O *Iblîs*! What is the matter with you that you did not join others in prostration?" **33.** He replied, "It is not for me to prostrate to a human You created from sounding clay moulded from black mud."

---

480 Allah will remain eternally after all pass away.
481 This does not contradict other verses that say Adam was created out of dust and those that say he was made out of mud. Adam was created in stages: first from dust, which was later turned into mud, then clay. This is similar to saying: I made a loaf of bread out of grain, or flour, or dough.
482 See footnote for 2:34.

265   15. Al-Ḥijr

34. Allah commanded, "Then get out of Paradise, for you are truly cursed. **35.** And surely upon you is condemnation until the Day of Judgment."

Satan's Appeal

36. Satan appealed, "My Lord! Then delay my end until the Day of their resurrection." **37.** Allah said, "You will be delayed **38.** until the appointed Day." **39.** Satan responded, "My Lord! For allowing me to stray I will surely tempt them on earth and mislead them all together, **40.** except Your chosen servants among them." **41.** Allah said, "This is the Way, binding on Me: **42.** you will certainly have no authority over My servants, except the deviant who follow you, **43.** and surely Hell is their destined place, all together. **44.** It has seven gates, to each a group of them is designated."

The Righteous in Paradise

45. Indeed, the righteous will be amid Gardens and springs. **46.** ˹It will be said to them,˺ "Enter in peace and security." **47.** We will remove whatever bitterness they had in their hearts.[483] In a friendly manner, they will be on thrones, facing one another. **48.** No fatigue will touch them there, nor will they ever be asked to leave.

Allah's Grace and Torment

49. Inform My servants ˹O Prophet˺ that I am truly the All-Forgiving, Most Merciful, **50.** and that My torment is indeed the most painful.

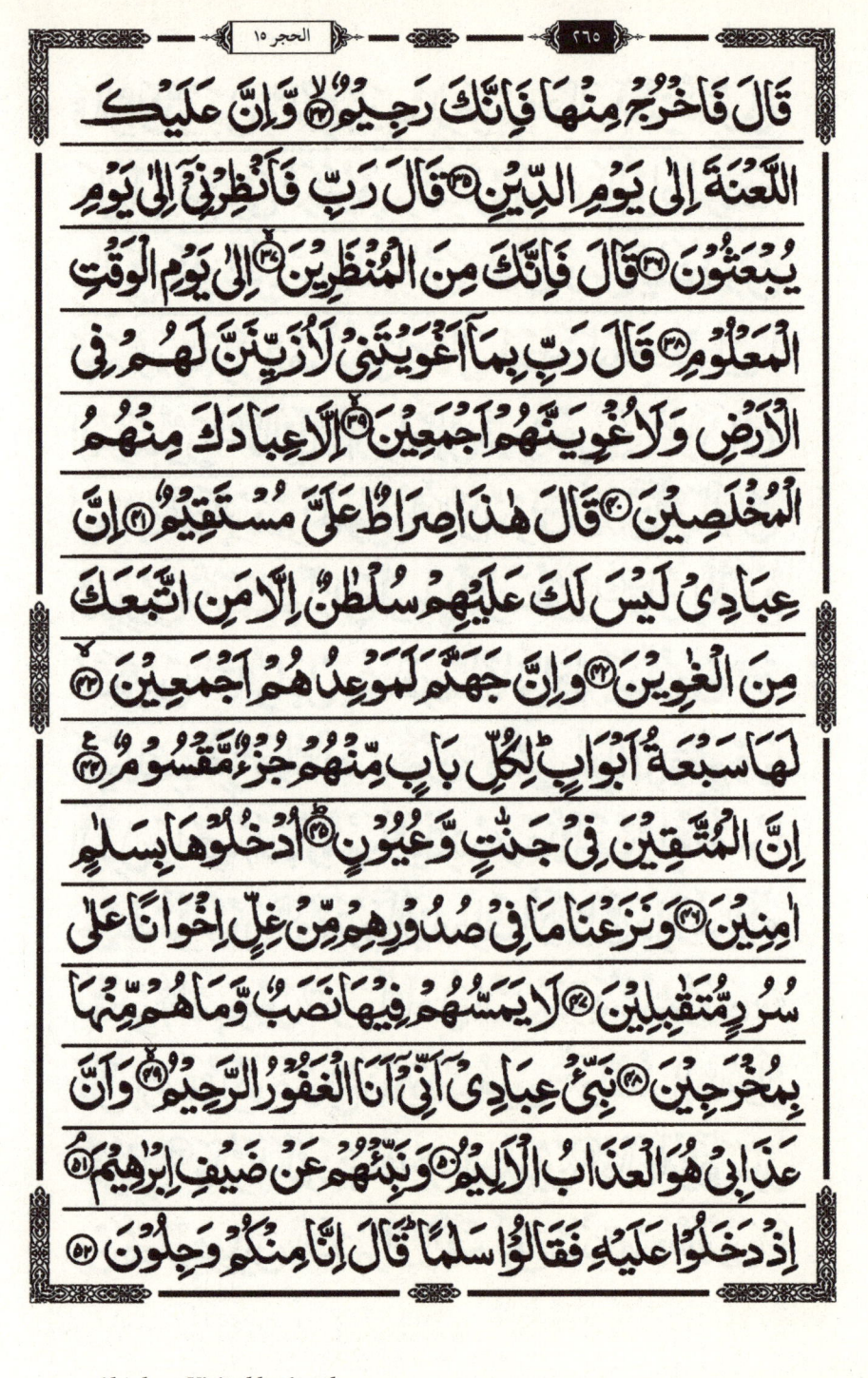

Abraham Visited by Angels

51. And inform them ˹O Prophet˺ about Abraham's guests **52.** who entered upon him and greeted ˹him with˺, "Peace!" He ˹later˺ said, "Surely we are afraid of you."[484]

---

483   i.e., the bitterness they had in their hearts towards other believers who wronged them in the worldly life.
484   As mentioned in 11:69-70, the angels came to Abraham in the form of men and when he offered them food, they did not eat. In ancient Middle Eastern culture, if a guest refused to eat the food provided by their host, it was a sign of ill-will.

15. Al-Ḥijr

53. They reassured ˹him˺, "Do not be afraid! Surely we give you good news of a knowledgeable son." **54.** He wondered, "Do you give me good news despite my old age? What unlikely news!" **55.** They responded, "We give you good news in all truth, so do not be one of those who despair." **56.** He exclaimed, "Who would despair of the mercy of their Lord except the misguided?" **57.** He ˹then˺ added, "What is your mission, O messengers?" **58.** They replied, "We have actually been sent to a wicked people. **59.** As for the family of Lot, we will certainly deliver them all, **60.** except his wife. We have determined that she will be one of the doomed."

Lot Visited by Angels

61. So when the messengers came to the family of Lot, **62.** he said, "You are surely an unfamiliar people!" **63.** They responded, "We have come to you with that ˹torment˺ which they have doubted. **64.** We come to you with the truth, and we are certainly truthful. **65.** So travel with your family in the dark of night, and follow ˹closely˺ behind them. Do not let any of you look back, and go where you are commanded." **66.** We revealed to him this decree: "Those ˹sinners˺ will be uprooted in the morning."

Destruction of the People of Lot

67. And there came the men of the city, rejoicing. **68.** Lot pleaded, "Indeed, these are my guests, so do not embarrass me. **69.** Fear Allah and do not humiliate me." **70.** They responded, "Have we not forbidden you from protecting anyone?" **71.** He said, "O my people! Here are my daughters[485] ˹so marry them˺ if you wish to do so." **72.** By your life ˹O Prophet˺,[486] they certainly wandered blindly, intoxicated ˹by lust˺.

---

485 Single women of his community.
486 This is the only time in the Quran where Allah swears by the life of a human being. Elsewhere Allah swears by the sun, the moon, the stars, and other marvels of His creation.

15. Al-Ḥijr

73. So the ˹mighty˺ blast overtook them at sunrise. **74.** And We turned the cities ˹of Sodom and Gomorrah˺ upside down and rained upon them stones of baked clay. **75.** Surely in this are signs for those who contemplate. **76.** Their ruins still lie along a known route. **77.** Surely in this is a sign for those who believe.

The People of Shuʿaib

78. And the residents of the Forest were truly wrongdoers, **79.** so We inflicted punishment upon them. The ruins of both nations still lie on a well-known road.

The People of Ṣâliḥ

80. Indeed, the residents of the Stone Valley also denied the messengers.[487] **81.** We gave them Our signs, but they turned away from them. **82.** They carved their homes in the mountains, feeling secure. **83.** But the ˹mighty˺ blast overtook them in the morning, **84.** and all they achieved was of no help to them.

Advice to the Prophet

85. We have not created the heavens and the earth and everything in between except for a purpose. And the Hour is certain to come, so forgive graciously. **86.** Surely your Lord is the Master Creator, All-Knowing. **87.** We have certainly granted you the seven often-repeated verses[488] and the great Quran. **88.** Do not let your eyes crave the ˹fleeting˺ pleasures We have provided for some of the disbelievers, nor grieve for them. And be gracious to the believers.

More Advice to the Prophet

89. And say, "I am truly sent with a clear warning"— **90.** ˹a warning˺ similar to what We sent to those who divided ˹the Scriptures˺,

---

487 Denying Ṣâliḥ (ﷺ) was equal to denying all of Allah's messengers.
488 Sûrah 1 of the Quran.

16. An-Nahl — 268

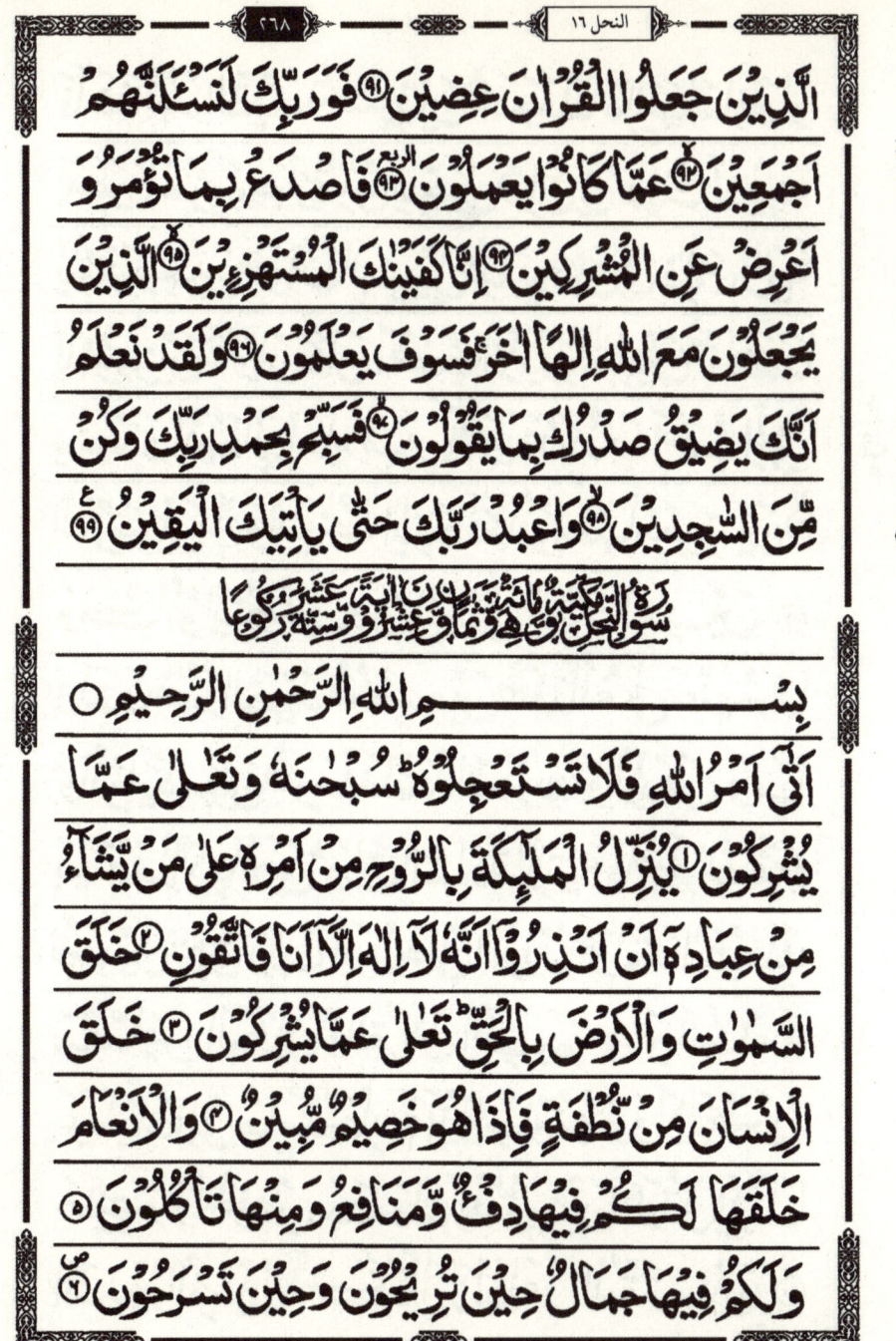

91. who 'now' accept parts of the Quran, rejecting others. 92. So by your Lord! We will certainly question them all 93. about what they used to do. 94. So proclaim what you have been commanded, and turn away from the polytheists. 95. Surely We will be sufficient for you against the mockers, 96. who set up 'other' gods with Allah. They will soon come to know.

Allah Is the Refuge

97. We certainly know that your heart is truly distressed by what they say. 98. So glorify the praises of your Lord and be one of those who 'always' pray, 99. and worship your Lord until the inevitable[489] comes your way.

ﷻﷺﷻ

---

16. Bees (An-Naḥl)

In the Name of Allah—the Most Compassionate, Most Merciful

Warning of Judgment

1. The command of Allah is at hand, so do not hasten it. Glorified and Exalted is He above what they associate 'with Him in worship'!

Allah's Favours: 1) Divine Guidance

2. He sends down the angels with revelation by His command to whoever He wills of His servants, 'stating:' "Warn 'humanity' that there is no god 'worthy of worship' except Me, so be mindful of Me 'alone'."

Favour 2) The Heavens and Earth

3. He created the heavens and the earth for a purpose. Exalted is He above what they associate with Him 'in worship'!

Favour 3) Creation of Humans

4. He created humans from a sperm-drop, then—behold!—they openly challenge 'Him'.

Favour 4) Animals

5. And He created the cattle for you as a source of warmth, food, and 'many other' benefits. 6. They are also pleasing to you when

---

489 i.e., lit., what is certain—death.

16. An-Naḥl

you bring them home and when you take them out to graze. 7. And they carry your loads to ˹distant˺ lands which you could not otherwise reach without great hardship. Surely your Lord is Ever Gracious, Most Merciful. 8. ˹He also created˺ horses, mules, and donkeys for your transportation and adornment. And He creates what you do not know.

Favour 5) The Way of Islam

9. It is upon Allah ˹alone˺ to ˹clearly˺ show the Straight Way. Other ways are deviant. Had He willed, He would have easily imposed guidance upon all of you.

Favour 6) Water

10. He is the One Who sends down rain from the sky, from which you drink and by which plants grow for your cattle to graze. 11. With it He produces for you ˹various˺ crops, olives, palm trees, grapevines, and every type of fruit. Surely in this is a sign for those who reflect.

Favour 7) Celestial Events

12. And He has subjected for your benefit the day and the night, the sun and the moon. And the stars have been subjected by His command. Surely in this are signs for those who understand.

Favour 8) Other Creation

13. And ˹He subjected˺ for you whatever He has created on earth of varying colours.[490] Surely in this is a sign for those who are mindful.

Favour 9) Seas

14. And He is the One Who has subjected the sea, so from it you may eat tender seafood and extract ornaments to wear. And you see the ships ploughing their way through it, so you may seek His bounty and give thanks ˹to Him˺.

---

490 The verse refers to the diverse creatures that have been created for the service of humanity.

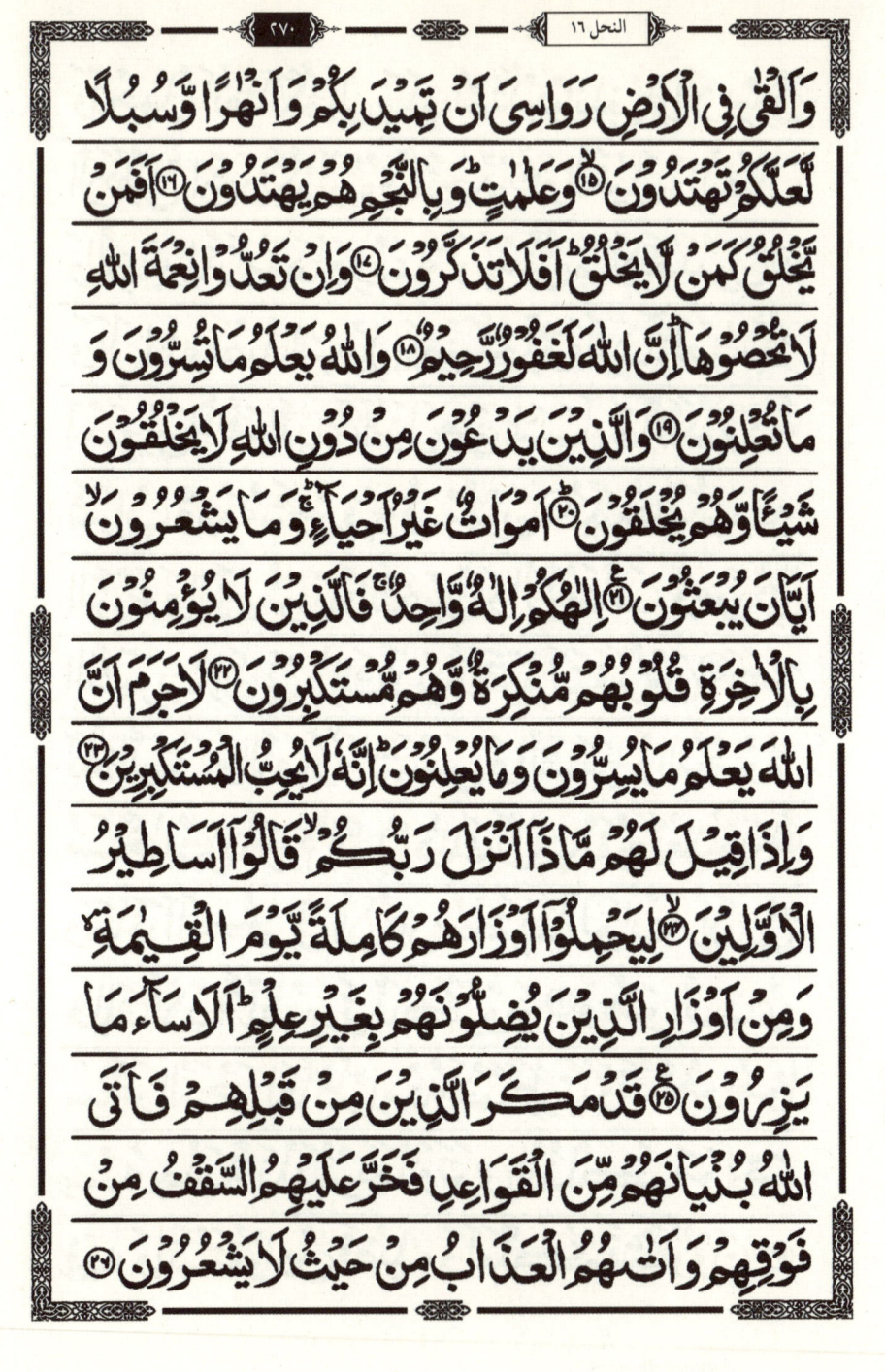

16. An-Naḥl

Favour 10) Natural Marvels

15. He has placed into the earth firm mountains, so it does not shake with you, as well as rivers, and pathways so you may find your way. **16.** Also by landmarks and stars do people find their way.

Almighty Allah or Powerless Gods?

17. Can the One Who creates be equal to those who do not? Will you not then be mindful? **18.** If you tried to count Allah's blessings, you would never be able to number them. Surely Allah is All-Forgiving, Most Merciful. **19.** And Allah knows what you conceal and what you reveal. **20.** But those ˹idols˺ they invoke besides Allah cannot create anything—they themselves are created. **21.** They are dead, not alive—not even knowing when their followers will be resurrected. **22.** Your God is ˹only˺ One God. As for those who do not believe in the Hereafter, their hearts are in denial, and they are too proud. **23.** Without a doubt, Allah knows what they conceal and what they reveal. He certainly does not like those who are too proud.

Reward of the Wicked

24. And when it is said to them, "What has your Lord revealed?" They say, "Ancient fables!" **25.** Let them bear their burdens in full on the Day of Judgment as well as some of the burdens of those they mislead without knowledge. Evil indeed is what they will bear! **26.** Indeed, those before them had plotted, but Allah struck at the ˹very˺ foundation of their structure, so the roof collapsed on top of them, and the torment came upon them from where they did not expect.[491]

---

491 This verse refers to a tyrant king who ordered the building of a tower so he can reach the heavens and fight Allah and the angels. Eventually the tower collapsed, leaving the tyrant crushed.

271 **16. An-Naḥl**

27. Then on the Day of Judgment He will humiliate them and say, "Where are My ˹so-called˺ associate-gods for whose sake you used to oppose ˹the believers˺?" Those gifted with knowledge will say, "Surely disgrace and misery today are upon the disbelievers." **28.** Those whose souls the angels seize while they wrong themselves will then offer ˹full˺ submission ˹and say falsely,˺ "We did not do any evil." ˹The angels will say,˺ "No! Surely Allah fully knows what you used to do. **29.** So enter the gates of Hell, to stay there forever. Indeed, what an evil home for the arrogant!"

Reward of the Righteous

30. And ˹when˺ it is said to those mindful ˹of Allah˺, "What has your Lord revealed?" They say, "All the best!" For those who do good in this world, there is goodness. But far better is the ˹eternal˺ Home of the Hereafter. How excellent indeed is the home of the righteous: **31.** the Gardens of Eternity which they will enter, under which rivers flow. In it they will have whatever they desire. This is how Allah rewards the righteous— **32.** those whose souls the angels take while they are virtuous, saying ˹to them˺, "Peace be upon you! Enter Paradise for what you used to do."

Warning to Pagan Deniers

33. Are they only awaiting the coming of the angels or the command of your Lord ˹O Prophet˺? So were those before them. And Allah never wronged them, but it was they who wronged themselves. **34.** Then the evil ˹consequences˺ of their deeds overtook them, and they were overwhelmed by what they used to ridicule.

Arabic Text

وَقَالَ الَّذِينَ أَشْرَكُوا لَوْ شَاءَ اللَّهُ مَا عَبَدْنَا مِن دُونِهِ مِن شَيْءٍ نَّحْنُ وَلَا آبَاؤُنَا وَلَا حَرَّمْنَا مِن دُونِهِ مِن شَيْءٍ كَذَٰلِكَ فَعَلَ الَّذِينَ مِن قَبْلِهِمْ فَهَلْ عَلَى الرُّسُلِ إِلَّا الْبَلَاغُ الْمُبِينُ ۝ وَلَقَدْ بَعَثْنَا فِي كُلِّ أُمَّةٍ رَّسُولًا أَنِ اعْبُدُوا اللَّهَ وَاجْتَنِبُوا الطَّاغُوتَ فَمِنْهُم مَّنْ هَدَى اللَّهُ وَمِنْهُم مَّنْ حَقَّتْ عَلَيْهِ الضَّلَالَةُ فَسِيرُوا فِي الْأَرْضِ فَانظُرُوا كَيْفَ كَانَ عَاقِبَةُ الْمُكَذِّبِينَ ۝ إِن تَحْرِصْ عَلَىٰ هُدَاهُمْ فَإِنَّ اللَّهَ لَا يَهْدِي مَن يُضِلُّ وَمَا لَهُم مِّن نَّاصِرِينَ ۝ وَأَقْسَمُوا بِاللَّهِ جَهْدَ أَيْمَانِهِمْ لَا يَبْعَثُ اللَّهُ مَن يَمُوتُ بَلَىٰ وَعْدًا عَلَيْهِ حَقًّا وَلَٰكِنَّ أَكْثَرَ النَّاسِ لَا يَعْلَمُونَ ۝ لِيُبَيِّنَ لَهُمُ الَّذِي يَخْتَلِفُونَ فِيهِ وَلِيَعْلَمَ الَّذِينَ كَفَرُوا أَنَّهُمْ كَانُوا كَاذِبِينَ ۝ إِنَّمَا قَوْلُنَا لِشَيْءٍ إِذَا أَرَدْنَاهُ أَن نَّقُولَ لَهُ كُن فَيَكُونُ ۝ وَالَّذِينَ هَاجَرُوا فِي اللَّهِ مِن بَعْدِ مَا ظُلِمُوا لَنُبَوِّئَنَّهُمْ فِي الدُّنْيَا حَسَنَةً وَلَأَجْرُ الْآخِرَةِ أَكْبَرُ لَوْ كَانُوا يَعْلَمُونَ ۝ الَّذِينَ صَبَرُوا وَعَلَىٰ رَبِّهِمْ يَتَوَكَّلُونَ ۝

False Argument

35. The polytheists argue, "Had Allah willed, neither we nor our forefathers would have worshipped anything other than Him, nor prohibited anything without His command." So did those before them. Is not the messengers' duty only to deliver ˹the message˺ clearly?

Same Fate

36. We surely sent a messenger to every community, saying, "Worship Allah and shun false gods." But some of them were guided by Allah, while others were destined to stray. So travel throughout the land and see the fate of the deniers! **37.** Even though you ˹O Prophet˺ are keen on their guidance, Allah certainly does not guide those He leaves to stray, and they will have no helpers.

The Resurrection

38. They swear by Allah their most solemn oaths that Allah will never raise the dead to life. Yes ˹He will˺! It is a true promise binding on Him, but most people do not know. **39.** ˹He will do that˺ to make clear to them what they disagreed on, and for the disbelievers to know that they were liars. **40.** If We ever will something ˹to exist˺, all We say is: "Be!" And it is!

Reward of the Steadfast

41. As for those who emigrated in ˹the cause of˺ Allah after being persecuted, We will surely bless them with a good home in this world. But the reward of the Hereafter is far better, if only they knew. **42.** ˹It is˺ they who have patiently endured, and in their Lord they put their trust.

16. An-Naḥl

273

Messengers Are Not Angels

43. We did not send ˹messengers˺ before you ˹O Prophet˺ except mere men inspired by Us. If you ˹polytheists˺ do not know ˹this already˺, then ask those who have knowledge ˹of the Scriptures˺. **44.** ˹We sent them˺ with clear proofs and divine Books. And We have sent down to you ˹O Prophet˺ the Reminder, so that you may explain to people what has been revealed for them, and perhaps they will reflect.

Warning to the Wicked

45. Do those who devise evil plots feel secure that Allah will not cause the earth to swallow them? Or that the torment will not come upon them in ways they cannot comprehend? **46.** Or that He will not seize them while they go about ˹their day˺, for then they will have no escape? **47.** Or that He will not destroy them gradually? But your Lord is truly Ever Gracious, Most Merciful.

Everything Submits to Allah

48. Have they not considered how the shadows of everything Allah has created incline to the right and the left ˹as the sun moves˺, totally submitting to Allah in all humility? **49.** And to Allah ˹alone˺ bows down ˹in submission˺[492] whatever is in the heavens and whatever is on the earth of living creatures, as do the angels—who are not too proud ˹to do so˺. **50.** They[493] fear their Lord above them, and do whatever they are commanded.

One God Alone

51. And Allah has said, "Do not take two gods. There is only One God. So be in awe of Me ˹alone˺." **52.** To Him belongs whatever is in the heavens and the earth, and to Him ˹alone˺ is the everlasting devotion. Will you then fear any other than Allah?

Ingratitude to Allah

53. Whatever blessings you have are from Allah. Then whenever hardship touches you, to Him ˹alone˺ you cry ˹for help˺. **54.** Then as soon as He removes the hardship from you, a group of you associates ˹others˺ with their Lord ˹in worship˺,

---

492 lit., prostrates.
493 The angels.

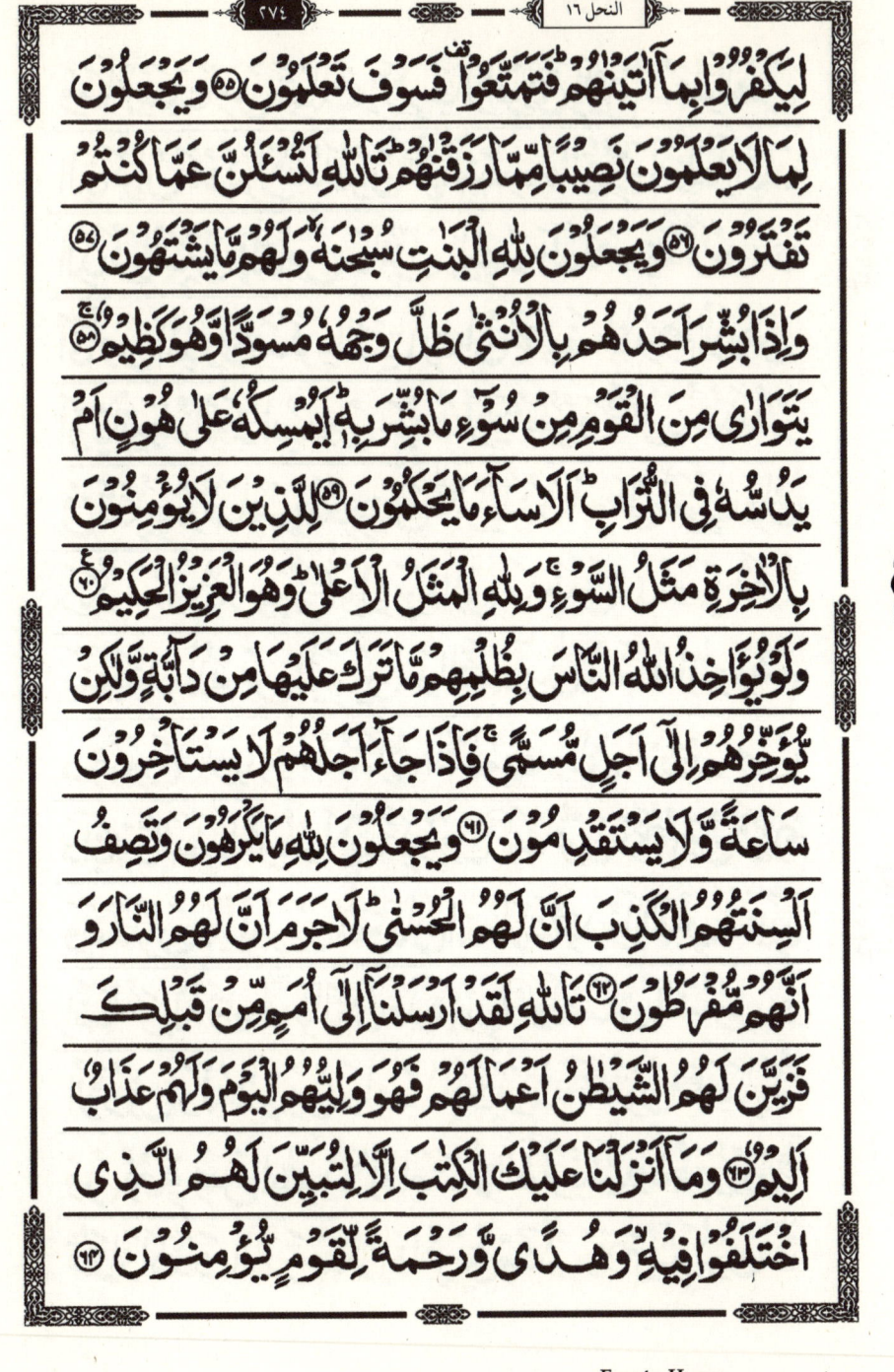

16. An-Naḥl 274

55. only returning Our favours with ingratitude. So enjoy yourselves, for you will soon know.

Offerings to Idols

56. And they ʿevenʾ assign to those ʿidolsʾ—who know nothing—a share of what We have provided for them. By Allah! You will certainly be questioned about whatever ʿliesʾ you used to fabricate ʿagainst Allahʾ.

Allah's Daughters?

57. And they attribute ʿangels asʾ daughters to Allah—glory be to Him!—the opposite of what they desire for themselves. 58. Whenever one of them is given the good news of a baby girl, his face grows gloomy, as he suppresses his rage. 59. He hides himself from the people because of the bad news he has received. Should he keep her in disgrace, or bury her ʿaliveʾ in the ground? Evil indeed is their judgment![494] 60. To those who disbelieve in the Hereafter belong all evil qualities, whereas to Allah belong the finest attributes. And He is the Almighty, All-Wise.

Favour 11)
Allowing Time for Repentance

61. If Allah were to punish people ʿimmediatelyʾ for their wrongdoing, He would not have left a single living being on earth. But He delays them for an appointed term. And when their time arrives, they cannot delay it for a moment, nor could they advance it.

Empty Hopes

62. They attribute to Allah what they hate ʿfor themselvesʾ,[495] and their tongues utter the lie that they will have the finest reward. Without a doubt, for them is the Fire, where they will be abandoned.

Evil Communities

63. By Allah! We have surely sent messengers to communities before you ʿO Prophetʾ, but Satan made their misdeeds appealing to them. So he is their patron today, and they will suffer a painful punishment. 64. We have revealed to you the Book only to clarify for them what they differed about, and as a guide and mercy for those who believe.

---

494 Some pagan Arabs used to bury their infant daughters alive for fear of shame or poverty. This practice was condemned and abolished by Islam. *See* 6:151 and 81:8-9.
495 They say that Allah has daughters (i.e., the angels), although they themselves do not like to have daughters.

16. An-Nahl

Favour 12) Rain

65. And Allah sends down rain from the sky, giving life to the earth after its death. Surely in this is a sign for those who listen.

Favour 13) Cattle and Milk

66. And there is certainly a lesson for you in cattle: We give you to drink of what is in their bellies, from between digested food and blood: pure milk, pleasant to drink.[496]
67. And from the fruits of palm trees and grapevines you derive intoxicants[497] as well as wholesome provision. Surely in this is a sign for those who understand.

Favour 14) Bees and Honey

68. And your Lord inspired the bees: "Make ˹your˺ homes in the mountains, the trees, and in what people construct, **69.** and feed from ˹the flower of˺ any fruit ˹you please˺ and follow the ways your Lord has made easy for you. From their bellies comes forth liquid of varying colours, in which there is healing for people. Surely in this is a sign for those who reflect.

Allah's Power over Humans

70. Allah has created you, and then causes you to die. And some of you are left to reach the most feeble stage of life so that they may know nothing after having known much. Indeed, Allah is All-Knowing, Most Capable.

Favour 15) Provisions

71. And Allah has favoured some of you over others in provision. But those who have been much favoured would not share their wealth with those ˹bondspeople˺ in their possession, making them their equals.[498] Do they then deny Allah's favours?

Favour 16) Spouses and Offspring

72. And Allah has made for you spouses of your own kind, and given you through your spouses children and grandchildren.[499] And He has granted you good, lawful provisions. Are they then faithful to falsehood and ungrateful for Allah's favours?

---

496 lit., pleasant for those who drink.
497 Intoxicants were later prohibited in the Quran in three stages: 2:219, 4:43, and finally 5:90-91.
498 In other words, if the pagan slave-masters are not willing to be equal to their slaves, why would they make anyone equal to Allah—the Supreme Master and Creator of all things?
499 Ḥafadah means grandchildren, but can also mean children-in-law.

16. An-Naḥl

بِسْمِ اللّٰهِ الرَّحْمٰنِ الرَّحِيْمِ

وَيَعْبُدُوْنَ مِنْ دُوْنِ اللّٰهِ مَا لَا يَمْلِكُ لَهُمْ رِزْقًا مِّنَ السَّمٰوٰتِ وَالْاَرْضِ شَيْئًا وَّلَا يَسْتَطِيْعُوْنَۙ ۝ فَلَا تَضْرِبُوْا لِلّٰهِ الْاَمْثَالَ اِنَّ اللّٰهَ يَعْلَمُ وَاَنْتُمْ لَا تَعْلَمُوْنَ ۝ ضَرَبَ اللّٰهُ مَثَلًا عَبْدًا مَّمْلُوْكًا لَّا يَقْدِرُ عَلٰى شَيْءٍ وَّمَنْ رَّزَقْنٰهُ مِنَّا رِزْقًا حَسَنًا فَهُوَ يُنْفِقُ مِنْهُ سِرًّا وَّجَهْرًا هَلْ يَسْتَوٗنَ الْحَمْدُ لِلّٰهِ بَلْ اَكْثَرُهُمْ لَا يَعْلَمُوْنَ ۝ وَضَرَبَ اللّٰهُ مَثَلًا رَّجُلَيْنِ اَحَدُهُمَا اَبْكَمُ لَا يَقْدِرُ عَلٰى شَيْءٍ وَّهُوَ كَلٌّ عَلٰى مَوْلٰىهُ اَيْنَمَا يُوَجِّهْهُّ لَا يَاْتِ بِخَيْرٍ هَلْ يَسْتَوٖيْ هُوَ وَمَنْ يَّاْمُرُ بِالْعَدْلِ وَهُوَ عَلٰى صِرَاطٍ مُّسْتَقِيْمٍ ۝ وَلِلّٰهِ غَيْبُ السَّمٰوٰتِ وَالْاَرْضِ وَمَا اَمْرُ السَّاعَةِ اِلَّا كَلَمْحِ الْبَصَرِ اَوْ هُوَ اَقْرَبُ اِنَّ اللّٰهَ عَلٰى كُلِّ شَيْءٍ قَدِيْرٌ ۝ وَاللّٰهُ اَخْرَجَكُمْ مِّنْ بُطُوْنِ اُمَّهٰتِكُمْ لَا تَعْلَمُوْنَ شَيْئًا وَّجَعَلَ لَكُمُ السَّمْعَ وَالْاَبْصَارَ وَالْاَفْئِدَةَ لَعَلَّكُمْ تَشْكُرُوْنَ ۝ اَلَمْ يَرَوْا اِلَى الطَّيْرِ مُسَخَّرٰتٍ فِيْ جَوِّ السَّمَاءِ مَا يُمْسِكُهُنَّ اِلَّا اللّٰهُ اِنَّ فِيْ ذٰلِكَ لَاٰيٰتٍ لِّقَوْمٍ يُّؤْمِنُوْنَ ۝

Parables for Powerless Gods and Almighty Allah

73. Yet they worship besides Allah those ˹idols˺ who do not afford them any provision from the heavens and the earth, nor do they have the power to. **74.** So do not set up equals to Allah, for Allah certainly knows and you do not know. **75.** Allah sets forth a parable: a slave who lacks all means, compared to a ˹free˺ man to whom We granted a good provision, of which he donates ˹freely,˺ openly and secretly. Are they equal? Praise be to Allah. In fact, most of them do not know. **76.** And Allah sets forth a parable of two men: one of them is dumb, incapable of anything. He is a burden on his master. Wherever he is sent, he brings no good. Can such a person be equal to the one who commands justice and is on the Straight Path?[500]

Allah's Knowledge and Might

77. To Allah ˹alone˺ belongs ˹the knowledge of˺ the unseen in the heavens and the earth. Bringing about the Hour would only take the blink of an eye, or even less. Surely Allah is Most Capable of everything.

Favour 17) Senses

78. And Allah brought you out of the wombs of your mothers while you knew nothing, and gave you hearing, sight, and intellect so perhaps you would be thankful.

Favour 18) Birds

79. Have they not seen the birds glide in the open sky? None holds them up except Allah. Surely in this are signs for those who believe.

---

500 The two parables emphasize that Almighty Allah masterfully conducts the affairs of the heavens and the earth, whereas false gods are incapable of anything. If this is the case, these gods are not His equal and He is the only one worthy of worship.

16. An-Naḥl

Favour 19) Homes

80. And Allah has made your homes a place to rest, and has given you tents from the hide of animals, light to handle when you travel and when you camp. And out of their wool, fur, and hair He has given you furnishings and goods for a while.

Favour 20) Shelters

81. And Allah has provided you shade out of what He created, and has given you shelter in the mountains. He has also provided you with clothes protecting you from the heat ˹and cold˺, and armour shielding you in battle. This is how He perfects His favour upon you, so perhaps you will ˹fully˺ submit ˹to Him˺.

Denying Allah's Favours

82. But if they turn away, then your duty ˹O Prophet˺ is only to deliver ˹the message˺ clearly. 83. They are aware of Allah's favours, but still deny them. And most of them are ˹truly˺ ungrateful.

Fate of the Disbelievers

84. ˹Consider, O Prophet,˺ the Day We will call ˹a prophet as˺ a witness from every faith-community. Then the disbelievers will neither be allowed to plead nor appease ˹their Lord˺. 85. And when the wrongdoers face the punishment, it will not be lightened for them, nor will they be delayed ˹from it˺. 86. And when the polytheists see their associate-gods, they will say, "Our Lord! These are our associate-gods that we used to invoke besides You." Their gods will throw a rebuttal at them, ˹saying,˺ "You are definitely liars." 87. They will offer ˹full˺ submission to Allah on that Day, and whatever ˹gods˺ they fabricated will fail them.

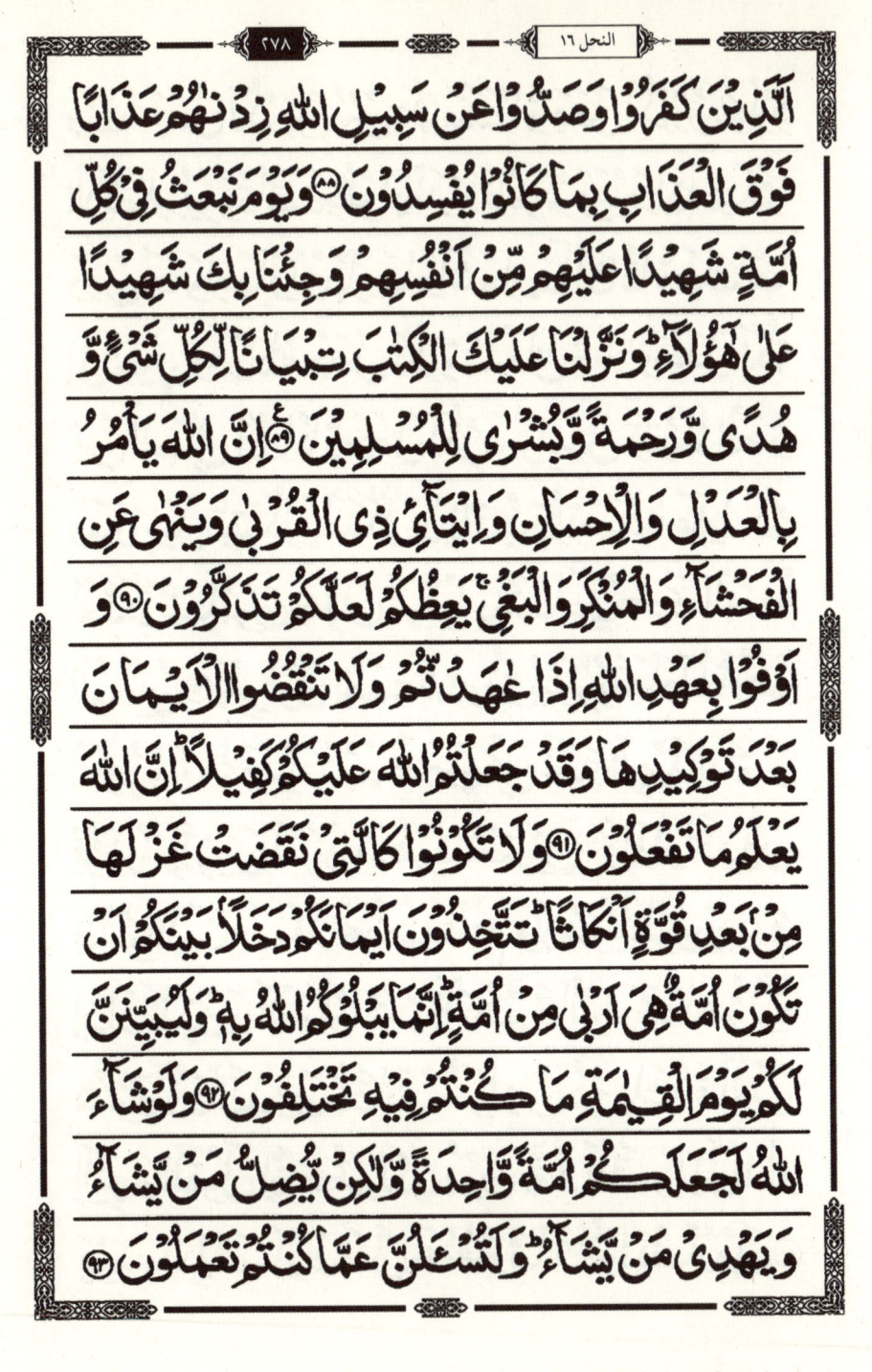

88. For those who disbelieve and hinder ʿothersʾ from the Way of Allah, We will add more punishment to their punishment for all the corruption they spread.

Prophets Witness Against Disbelievers

89. ʿConsider, O Prophet,ʾ the Day We will call against every faith-community a witness of their own. And We will call you to be a witness against these ʿpeople of yoursʾ. We have revealed to you the Book as an explanation of all things, a guide, a mercy, and good news for those who ʿfullyʾ submit.

Allah's Commands and Prohibitions

90. Indeed, Allah commands justice, grace, as well as courtesy to close relatives. He forbids indecency, wickedness, and aggression. He instructs you so perhaps you will be mindful.

Honouring Pledges

91. Honour God's covenant when you make a pledge, and do not break your oaths after confirming them, having made Allah your guarantor. Surely Allah knows all you do.
92. Do not be like the woman who ʿfoolishlyʾ unravels her yarn after it is firmly spun, by taking your oaths as a means of deceiving one another in favour of a stronger group. Surely Allah tests you through this. And on the Day of Judgment He will certainly make your differences clear to you.

Favour 21) Free Choice

93. Had Allah willed, He could have easily made you one community ʿof believersʾ, but He leaves to stray whoever He wills and guides whoever He wills.[501] And you will certainly be questioned about what you used to do.

---

501 He guides those who are sincere in their quest for guidance.

279 16. An-Naḥl

Honouring Agreements

94. And do not take your oaths as a means of deceiving one another or your feet will slip after they have been firm. Then you will taste the evil ˹consequences˺ of hindering ˹others˺ from the Way of Allah, and you will suffer a tremendous punishment. **95.** And do not trade Allah's covenant for a fleeting gain. What is with Allah is certainly far better for you, if only you knew. **96.** Whatever you have will end, but whatever Allah has is everlasting. And We will certainly reward the steadfast according to the best of their deeds.

Reward of the Good-Doers

97. Whoever does good, whether male or female, and is a believer, We will surely bless them with a good life, and We will certainly reward them according to the best of their deeds.

Advice to the Believers

98. When you recite the Quran, seek refuge with Allah from Satan, the accursed. **99.** He certainly has no authority over those who believe and put their trust in their Lord. **100.** His authority is only over those who take him as a patron and who—under his influence—associate ˹others˺ with Allah ˹in worship˺.

Who Is the Fabricator?

101. When We replace a verse with another[502]—and Allah knows best what He reveals—they say, "You ˹Muhammad˺ are just a fabricator." In fact, most of them do not know. **102.** Say, "The holy spirit[503] has brought it down from your Lord with the truth to reassure the believers, and as a guide and good news for those who submit ˹to Allah˺."

---

502 See footnote for 2:106.
503 The angel Gabriel.

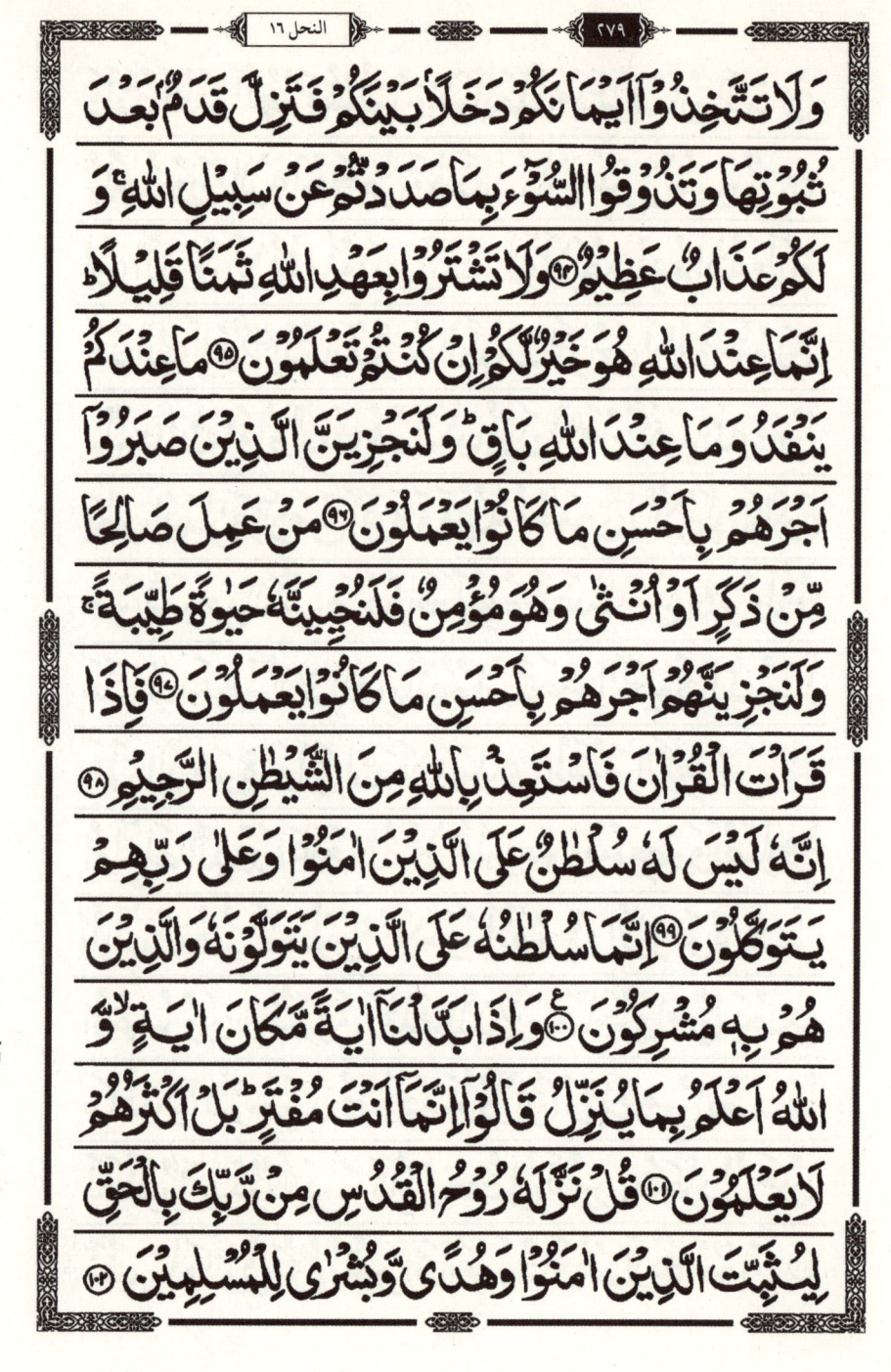

16. An-Nahl — 280

103. And We surely know that they say, "No one is teaching him except a human." But the man they refer to speaks a foreign tongue, whereas this ˹Quran˺ is ˹in˺ eloquent Arabic.[504] 104. Surely those who do not believe in Allah's revelations will never be guided by Allah, and they will suffer a painful punishment. 105. No one fabricates lies except those who disbelieve in Allah's revelations, and it is they who are the ˹true˺ liars.

Abandoning Faith

106. Whoever disbelieves in Allah after their belief—not those who are forced while their hearts are firm in faith,[505] but those who embrace disbelief wholeheartedly—they will be condemned by Allah and suffer a tremendous punishment. 107. This is because they prefer the life of this world over the Hereafter. Surely Allah never guides those who ˹choose to˺ disbelieve. 108. They are the ones whose hearts, ears, and eyes are sealed by Allah, and it is they who are ˹truly˺ heedless. 109. Without a doubt, they will be the losers in the Hereafter. 110. As for those who emigrated after being compelled ˹to renounce Islam˺, then struggled ˹in Allah's cause˺, and persevered, your Lord ˹O Prophet˺ is truly All-Forgiving, Most Merciful after all.

Pay Day

111. ˹Consider˺ the Day ˹when˺ every soul will come pleading for itself, and each will be paid in full for what it did, and none will be wronged.

---

504 Some Meccan pagans claimed that the Prophet (ﷺ) received the Quran from a non-Arab slave owned by an Arab pagan.
505 This refers to ˹Ammâr ibn Yâsser, an early revert to Islam, who was tortured to leave Islam. To save his life, ˹Ammâr pretended to denounce Islam, but his heart was full of faith. When he told the Prophet (ﷺ) about what happened, this verse was revealed, reassuring him that his faith was intact.

16. An-Naḥl

The Ungrateful People

112. And Allah sets forth the example of a society which was safe and at ease, receiving its provision in abundance from all directions. But its people met Allah's favours with ingratitude, so Allah made them taste the clutches of hunger and fear for their misdeeds. **113.** A messenger of their own actually did come to them, but they denied him. So the torment overtook them while they persisted in wrongdoing.

Lawful and Prohibited Foods

114. So eat from the good, lawful things which Allah has provided for you, and be grateful for Allah's favours, if you ˹truly˺ worship Him ˹alone˺. **115.** He has only forbidden you ˹to eat˺ carrion, blood, swine,[506] and what is slaughtered in the name of any other than Allah. But if someone is compelled by necessity—neither driven by desire nor exceeding immediate need—then surely Allah is All-Forgiving, Most Merciful.

Warning to the Polytheists

116. Do not falsely declare with your tongues, "This is lawful, and that is unlawful," ˹only˺ fabricating lies against Allah. Indeed, those who fabricate lies against Allah will never succeed. **117.** ˹It is only˺ a brief enjoyment, then they will suffer a painful punishment.

Prohibited Foods for Jews

118. To the Jews, We have forbidden what We related to you before.[507] We did not wrong them, but it was they who wronged themselves.

---

506 *See* footnote for 2:173.
507 What is mentioned in 6:146.

16. An-Naḥl — 282

Allah Accepts Repentance

119. As for those who commit evil ignorantly ˹or recklessly˺, then repent afterwards and mend their ways, then your Lord is surely All-Forgiving, Most Merciful.

Prophet Abraham

120. Indeed, Abraham was a model of excellence: devoted to Allah, ˹perfectly˺ upright—not a polytheist— **121.** ˹utterly˺ grateful for Allah's favours. ˹So˺ He chose him and guided him to the Straight Path. **122.** We blessed him with all goodness in this world,[508] and in the Hereafter he will certainly be among the righteous. **123.** Then We revealed to you ˹O Prophet, saying˺: "Follow the faith of Abraham, the upright, who was not one of the polytheists." **124.** ˹Honouring˺ the Sabbath was ordained only for those who disputed about Abraham.[509] And surely your Lord will judge between them on the Day of Judgment regarding their disputes.

Inviting to Islam

125. Invite ˹all˺ to the Way of your Lord with wisdom and kind advice, and only debate with them in the best manner. Surely your Lord ˹alone˺ knows best who has strayed from His Way and who is ˹rightly˺ guided.

Grace Is Best

126. If you retaliate, then let it be equivalent to what you have suffered. But if you patiently endure, it is certainly best for those who are patient. **127.** Be patient ˹O Prophet˺, for your patience is only with Allah's help. Do not grieve over those ˹who disbelieve˺, nor be distressed by their schemes. **128.** Surely Allah is with those who shun evil and who do good ˹deeds˺.

---

508 i.e., honourable mention and a righteous family.
509 This verse refers to the Jews who claimed that Abraham was Jewish. *See* 3:65-68.

17. The Night Journey (Al-Isrâ')

In the Name of Allah—the Most Compassionate, Most Merciful

Journey from Mecca to Jerusalem

1. Glory be to the One Who took His servant ˹Muḥammad˺ by night from the Sacred Mosque to the Farthest Mosque whose surroundings We have blessed, so that We may show him some of Our signs.[510] Indeed, He[511] alone is the All-Hearing, All-Seeing. **2.** And We gave Moses the Scripture and made it a guide for the Children of Israel, ˹stating:˺ "Do not take besides Me any other Trustee of Affairs. **3.** ˹O˺ descendants of those We carried with Noah ˹in the Ark˺! He was indeed a grateful servant."

Warning to the Israelites

4. And We warned the Children of Israel in the Scripture, "You will certainly cause corruption in the land twice, and you will become extremely arrogant.

The 1st Corruption

5. "When the first of the two warnings would come to pass, We would send against you some of Our servants of great might, who would ravage your homes. This would be a warning fulfilled. **6.** Then ˹after your repentance˺ We would give you the upper hand over them and aid you with wealth and offspring, causing you to outnumber them. **7.** If you act rightly, it is for your own good, but if you do wrong, it is to your own loss.

The 2nd Corruption

"And when the second warning would come to pass, your enemies would ˹be left to˺ totally disgrace you and enter the Temple ˹of Jerusalem˺ as they entered it the first time, and utterly destroy whatever would fall into their hands.

---

510 *Al-Isrâ'* refers to the Prophet's Night Journey from Mecca to Jerusalem about a year before his emigration (or *Hijrah*) from Mecca to Medina. This journey came as a comfort for the Prophet after several years of hardship and persecution, which included a 3-year siege by Meccan pagans, who drove the Muslims out of the city and forbade anyone from trading, marrying, or feeding them. This was followed by the "Year of Sadness," which included the death of the Prophet's uncle Abu Ṭâlib, the major defender of Muḥammad (ﷺ) despite his disbelief in his message, as well as the death of the Prophet's beloved wife Khadîjah. The Prophet was carried overnight by a noble steed (called *Burâq*) from Mecca to Jerusalem where he met some earlier prophets and led them in prayer. He was later carried to the heavens (this journey is called *Al-Mi'râj*, or the Ascension) where he received direct orders from Allah to observe five daily prayers. The Ascension is referred to in 53:13–18.

511 i.e., Allah.

17. Al-Isrâ' 284

8. Perhaps your Lord will have mercy on you ˹if you repent˺, but if you return ˹to sin˺, We will return ˹to punishment˺. And We have made Hell a ˹permanent˺ confinement for the disbelievers."

The Message of the Quran

9. Surely this Quran guides to what is most upright, and gives good news to the believers—who do good—that they will have a mighty reward. 10. And ˹it warns˺ those who do not believe in the Hereafter ˹that˺ We have prepared for them a painful punishment.

Prayers in Anger

11. And humans ˹swiftly˺ pray for evil[512] as they pray for good. For humankind is ever hasty.

The Day and Night

12. We made the day and night as two signs. So We made the sign of the night devoid of light, and We made the sign of the day ˹perfectly˺ bright, so that you may seek the bounty of your Lord and know the number of years and calculation ˹of time˺. And We have explained everything in detail.

The Record of Deeds

13. We have bound every human's destiny to their neck.[513] And on the Day of Judgment We will bring forth to each ˹person˺ a record which they will find laid open. 14. ˹And it will be said,˺ "Read your record. You ˹alone˺ are sufficient this Day to take account of yourself." 15. Whoever chooses to be guided, it is only for their own good. And whoever chooses to stray, it is only to their own loss. No soul burdened with sin will bear the burden of another. And We would never punish ˹a people˺ until We have sent a messenger ˹to warn them˺.

Punishment of the Wicked

16. Whenever We intend to destroy a society, We command its elite ˹to obey Allah˺ but they act rebelliously in it. So the decree ˹of punishment˺ is justified, and We destroy it utterly. 17. ˹Imagine˺ how many peoples We have destroyed after Noah! And sufficient is your Lord as All-Aware and All-Seeing of the sins of His servants.

---

512 Some people are quick to pray against themselves or others in times of anger and frustration.

513 This refers to the deeds that one is destined to do of their own free will. Out of His infinite knowledge, Allah knows people's choices even before they make them. In the Hereafter, He will raise them from the dead for judgment.

285 17. Al-Isrâ'

This Life or the Next?

18. Whoever desires this fleeting world ʿaloneʾ, We hasten in it whatever We please to whoever We will; then We destine them for Hell, where they will burn, condemned and rejected. 19. But whoever desires the Hereafter and strives for it accordingly, and is a ʿtrueʾ believer, it is they whose striving will be appreciated. 20. We provide both the former and the latter from the bounty of your Lord. And the bounty of your Lord can never be withheld. 21. See how We have favoured some over others ʿin this lifeʾ, but the Hereafter is certainly far greater in rank and in favour.

Commandments: 1) Worship Allah Alone

22. Do not set up any other god with Allah, or you will end up condemned, abandoned. 23. For your Lord has decreed that you worship none but Him.

2) Honour Your Parents

And honour your parents. If one or both of them reach old age in your care, never say to them ʿevenʾ 'ugh,' nor yell at them. Rather, address them respectfully. 24. And be humble with them out of mercy, and pray, "My Lord! Be merciful to them as they raised me when I was young." 25. Your Lord knows best what is within yourselves. If you are righteous, He is certainly All-Forgiving to those who ʿconstantlyʾ turn to Him.

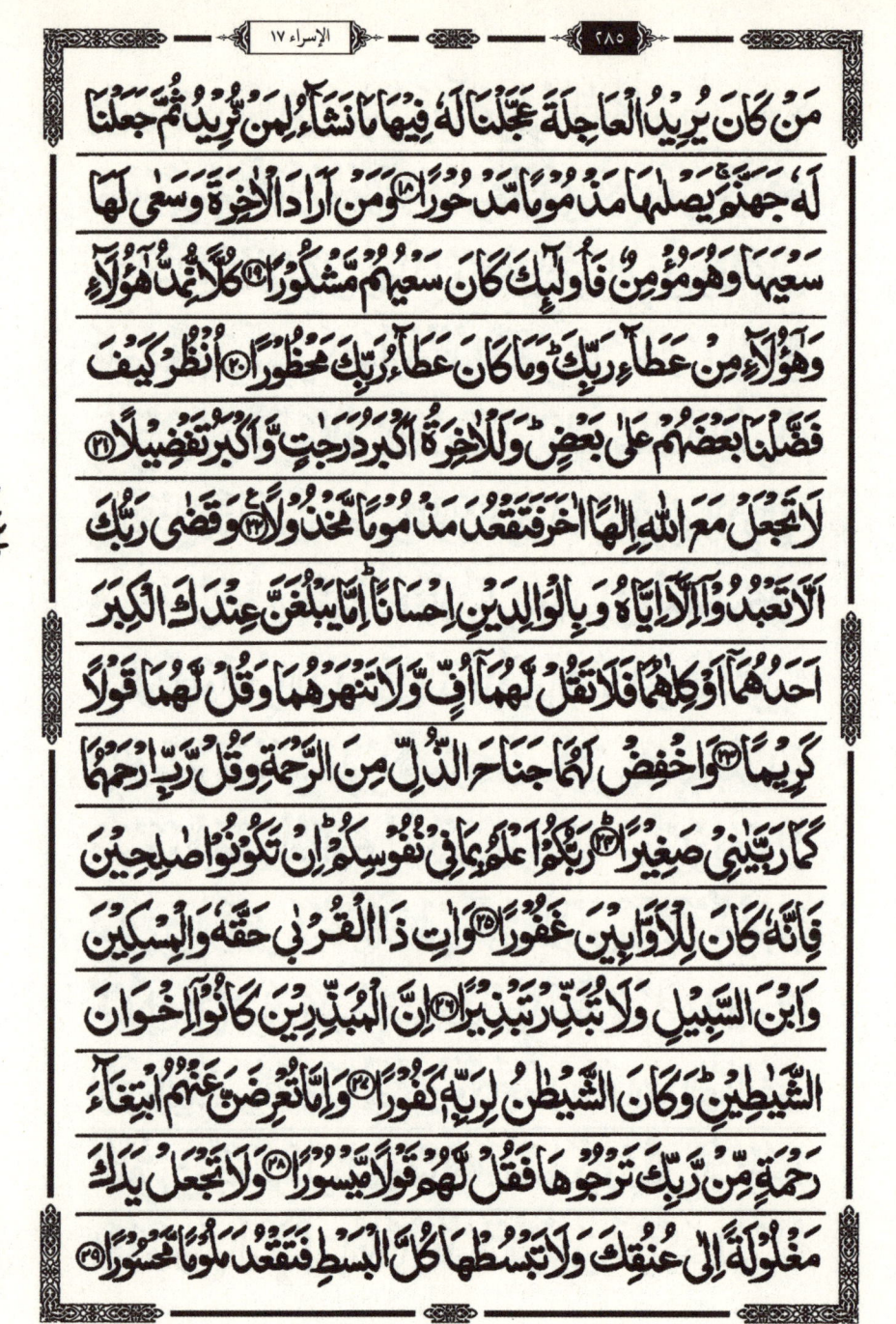

3) Give and 4) Do Not Waste

26. Give to close relatives their due, as well as the poor and ʿneedyʾ travellers. And do not spend wastefully. 27. Surely the wasteful are ʿlikeʾ brothers to the devils. And the Devil is ever ungrateful to his Lord. 28. But if you must turn them down ʿbecause you lack the means to giveʾ—while hoping to receive your Lord's bounty—then ʿat leastʾ give them a kind word.

5) Spend Moderately

29. Do not be so tight-fisted, for you will be blameworthy; nor so open-handed, for you will end up in poverty.

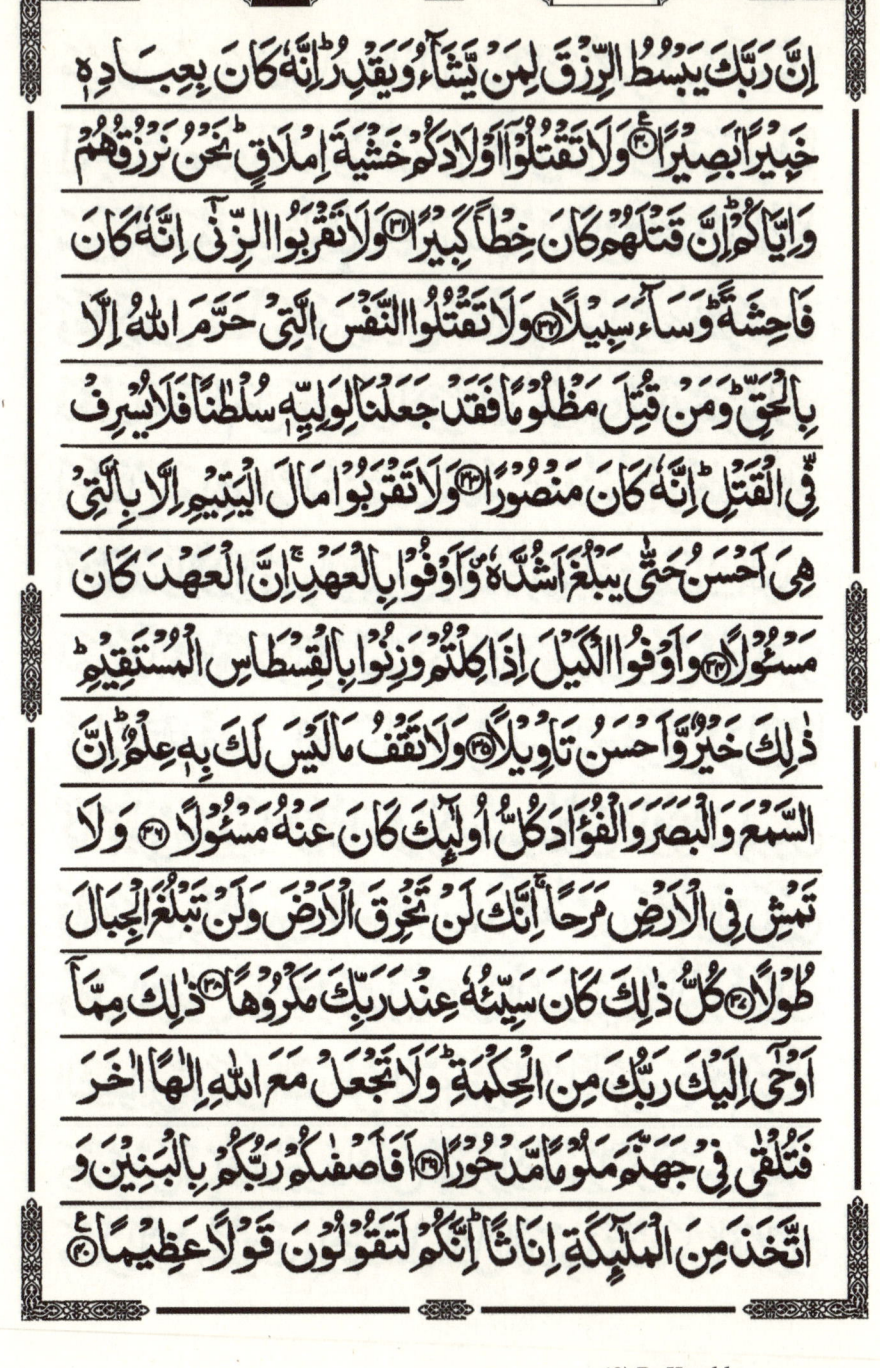

30. Surely your Lord gives abundant or limited provisions to whoever He wills. He is certainly All-Aware, All-Seeing of His servants.

6) Treasure Your Children

31. Do not kill your children for fear of poverty. We provide for them and for you. Surely killing them is a heinous sin.

7) Do Not Commit Adultery

32. Do not go near adultery. It is truly a shameful deed and an evil way.

8) Do Not Kill

33. Do not take a ˹human˺ life—made sacred by Allah—except with ˹legal˺ right.[514] If anyone is killed unjustly, We have given their heirs[515] the authority, but do not let them exceed limits in retaliation,[516] for they are already supported ˹by law˺.

9) Protect Orphans' Wealth

34. Do not come near the wealth of the orphan—unless intending to enhance it—until they attain maturity.

10) Honour Pledges

Honour ˹your˺ pledges, for you will surely be accountable for them.

11) Maintain Fairness

35. Give in full when you measure, and weigh with an even balance. That is fairest and best in the end.

12) Be Sure

36. Do not follow what you have no ˹sure˺ knowledge of. Indeed, all will be called to account for ˹their˺ hearing, sight, and intellect.

13) Be Humble

37. And do not walk on the earth arrogantly. Surely you can neither crack the earth nor stretch to the height of the mountains.

Compliance with the Commandments

38. The violation of any of these ˹commandments˺ is detestable to your Lord. **39.** This is part of the wisdom which your Lord has revealed to you ˹O Prophet˺. And do not set up any other god with Allah ˹O humanity˺, or you will be cast into Hell, blameworthy, rejected.

---

514 For example, in retaliation for intentional killing through legal channels.
515 Here the word *wali*, "heir," actually means *awliyâ'* or "heirs," which includes the closest relatives, both men and women.
516 By killing anyone other than the killer, or killing others with the killer.

17. Al-Isrâ'

Rebuttal to a Pagan Claim

40. Has your Lord favoured you ˹pagans˺ with sons and taken angels as ˹His˺ daughters?[517] You are truly making an outrageous claim. **41.** We have surely varied ˹the signs˺ in this Quran so perhaps they may be mindful, but it only drives them farther away.

Other Gods?

42. Say, ˹O Prophet,˺ "Had there been other gods besides Him—as they claim—then they would have certainly sought a way to ˹challenge˺ the Lord of the Throne. **43.** Glorified and Highly Exalted is He above what they claim! **44.** The seven heavens, the earth, and all those in them glorify Him. There is not a single thing that does not glorify His praises—but you ˹simply˺ cannot comprehend their glorification. He is indeed Most Forbearing, All-Forgiving.

The Pagans Mock the Quran

45. When you ˹O Prophet˺ recite the Quran, We put a hidden barrier between you and those who do not believe in the Hereafter. **46.** We have cast veils over their hearts—leaving them unable to comprehend it—and deafness in their ears. And when you mention your Lord alone in the Quran, they turn their backs in aversion. **47.** We know best how they listen to your recitation and what they say privately—when the wrongdoers say, "You would only be following a bewitched man." **48.** See how they call you names ˹O Prophet˺![518] So they have gone so ˹far˺ astray that they cannot find the ˹Right˺ Way.

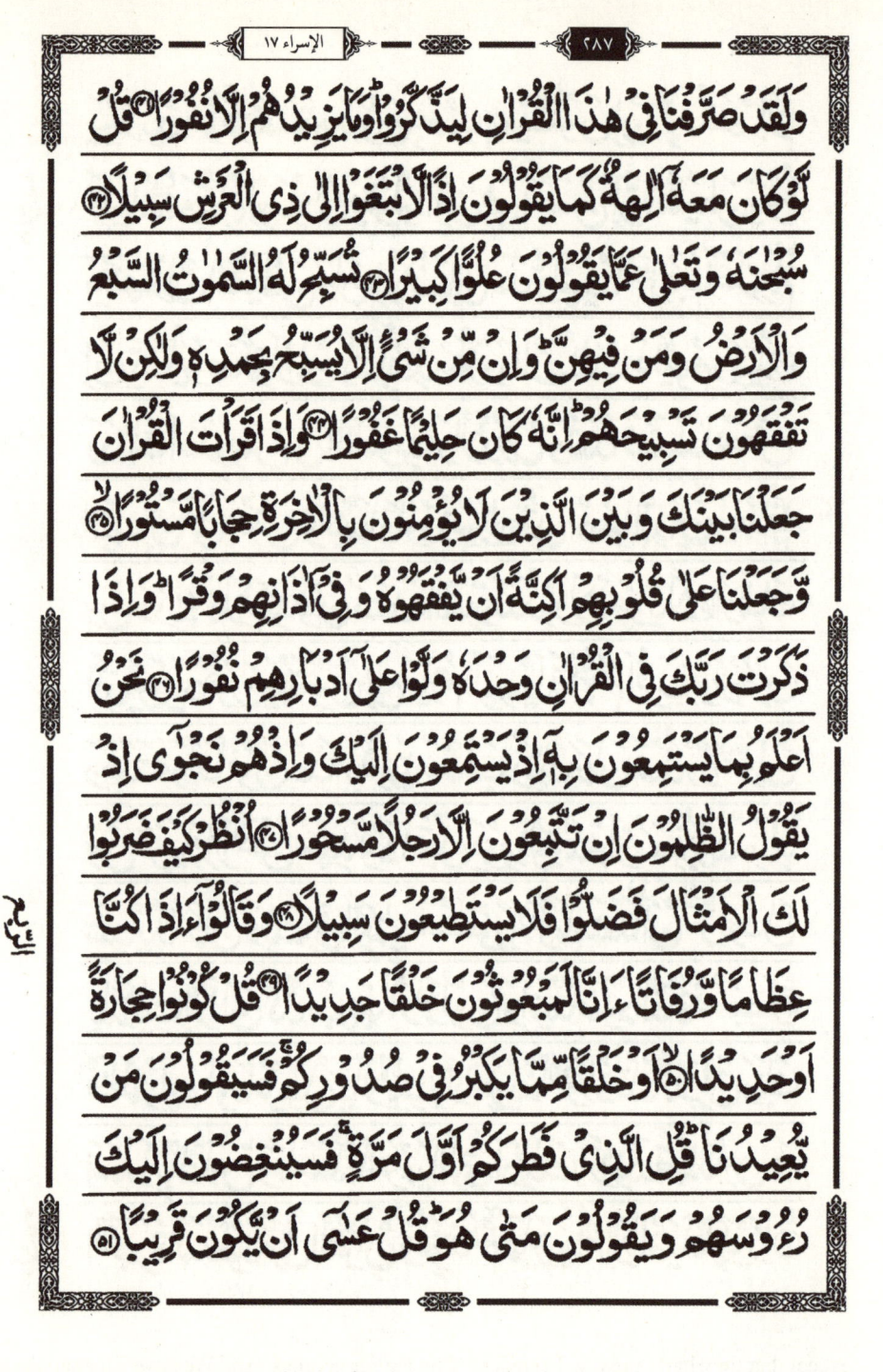

The Resurrection

49. And they say ˹mockingly˺, "When we are reduced to bones and ashes, will we really be raised as a new creation?" **50.** Say, ˹O Prophet,˺ "Yes, even if˺ you become stones, or iron, **51.** or whatever you think is harder to bring to life!" Then they will ask ˹you˺, "Who will bring us back ˹to life˺?" Say, "The One Who created you the first time." They will then shake their heads at you and ask, "When will that be?" Say, "Perhaps it is soon!"

---

517 Some pagans had the belief that the angels are the daughters of Allah.
518 They rejected you as a magician, a poet, a fabricator, and mad man.

52. On the Day He will call you, you will ʿinstantlyʾ respond by praising Him,[519] thinking you had remained ʿin the worldʾ only for a little while.

Advice to the Prophet

53. Tell My ʿbelievingʾ servants to say only what is best. Satan certainly seeks to sow discord among them. Satan is indeed a sworn enemy to humankind.

Invitation to the Disbelievers

54. Your Lord knows you best. He may have mercy on you if He wills, or punish you if He wills. We have not sent you ʿO Prophetʾ as a keeper over them. **55.** Your Lord knows best all those in the heavens and the earth. And We have surely favoured some prophets above others, and to David We gave the Psalms.[520]

Other Gods Besides Allah?

56. Say, ʿO Prophet,ʾ "Invoke those you claim ʿto be divineʾ[521] besides Him—they do not have the power to undo harm from you or transfer it ʿto someone elseʾ." **57.** ʿEvenʾ the closest ʿto Allahʾ of those invoked would be seeking a way to their Lord, hoping for His mercy, and fearing His punishment. Indeed, your Lord's torment is fearsome.

Signs Always Denied

58. There is not a ʿwickedʾ society that We will not destroy or punish with a severe torment before the Day of Judgment. That is written in the Record. **59.** Nothing keeps Us from sending the ʿdemandedʾ signs except that they had ʿalreadyʾ been denied by earlier peoples. And We gave Thamûd the she-camel as a clear sign, but they wrongfully rejected it.[522] We only send the signs as a warning.

Signs as a Test

60. And ʿremember, O Prophetʾ when We told you, "Certainly your Lord encompasses the people." And We have made what We

---

519 When everyone is raised from the dead, they will all praise Allah, regardless of what they had believed in this life.

520 The reason David is singled out here is because some Jewish authorities at the time of the Prophet (ﷺ) claimed that no scripture had been revealed after Moses. So this verse refutes this claim by referring to the Psalms of David.

521 i.e., Jesus, Ezra, and the angels. Idol worship is refuted in other passages such as 7:191-198 and 34:22.

522 Or they did wrong by it.

brought you to see[523] as well as the cursed tree 'mentioned' in the Quran[524] only as a test for the people. We keep warning them, but it only increases them greatly in defiance.

Satan's Defiance

61. And 'remember' when We said to the angels, "Prostrate before Adam," so they all did—but not *Iblîs*,[525] who protested, "Should I prostrate to the one You have created from mud?" 62. Adding, "Do you see this one you honoured above me? If you delay my end until the Day of Judgment, I will certainly take hold of his descendants, except for a few." 63. Allah responded, "Be gone! Whoever of them follows you, Hell will surely be the reward for all of you—an ample reward. 64. And incite whoever you can of them with your voice, mobilize against them all your cavalry and infantry, manipulate them in their wealth and children, and make them promises." But Satan promises them nothing but delusion. 65. 'Allah added,' "You will truly have no authority over My 'faithful' servants." And sufficient is your Lord as a Guardian.

Human Ingratitude

66. It is your Lord Who steers the ships for you through the sea, so that you may seek His bounty. Surely He is ever Merciful to you. 67. When you are touched with hardship at sea, you 'totally' forget all 'the gods' you 'normally' invoke, except Him. But when He delivers you 'safely' to shore, you turn away. Humankind is ever ungrateful.

False Immunity

68. Do you feel secure that He will not cause the land to swallow you up, or unleash upon you a storm of stones? Then you will find none to protect you. 69. Or do you feel secure that He will not send you back to sea once again, and send upon you a violent storm, drowning you for your denial? Then you will find none to avenge you against Us.

---

523 During the Night Journey mentioned in 17:1.
524 The tree of *Zaqqûm* which grows in the depths of Hell as mentioned in 37:62-65. The pagans of Mecca used to make fun of the Prophet (ﷺ) and say, "How can a tree grow in Hell?"
525 See footnote for 2:34.

17. Al-Isrâ'

Allah's Favours to Humanity

70. Indeed, We have dignified the children of Adam, carried them on land and sea, granted them good and lawful provisions, and privileged them far above many of Our creatures.

The Record of Deeds

71. ˹Beware of˺ the Day We will summon every people with their leader.[526] So whoever will be given their record in their right hand will read it ˹happily˺ and will not be wronged ˹even by the width of˺ the thread of a date stone. **72.** But whoever is blind ˹to the truth˺ in this ˹world˺ will be blind in the Hereafter, and ˹even˺ far more astray from the ˹Right˺ Way.

Temptation by Meccan Pagans

73. They definitely ˹thought they˺ were about to lure you away from what We have revealed to you ˹O Prophet˺, hoping that you would attribute something else to Us falsely— and then they would have certainly taken you as a close friend.[527] **74.** Had We not made you steadfast, you probably would have inclined to them a little, **75.** and then We truly would have made you taste double ˹punishment˺ both in this life and after death, and you would have found no helper against Us. **76.** They were about to intimidate you to drive you out of the land ˹of Mecca˺, but then they would not have survived after you ˹had left˺ except for a little while. **77.** ˹This has been˺ Our way with the messengers We sent before you. And you will never find any change in Our way.

Advice to the Prophet

78. Observe the prayer from the decline of the sun until the darkness of the night and the recitation at dawn, for certainly the dawn prayer is witnessed ˹by angels˺.[528] **79.** And rise at ˹the last˺ part of the night, offering additional prayers, so your Lord may raise you to a station of praise.[529] **80.** And say, "My Lord! Grant me an honourable entrance and an honourable exit[530] and give me a

---

526 Other meanings include: with their record of deeds, or their prophet, or their scripture.

527 The pagans of Mecca tried in vain to dissuade the Prophet (ﷺ) from preaching the message of Islam. In some instances they offered to worship his Allah if he agreed to bow to their idols, and some even offered him riches and positions if he just stopped preaching in the city.

528 This verse gives the times of the five daily prayers: the decline of the sun refers to the afternoon and late afternoon prayers, the darkness of night refers to sunset and late evening prayers, then the dawn prayer.

529 This refers to the time when the Prophet (ﷺ) will make intercession (*shafâ'ah*) on the Day of Judgment.

530 This verse was revealed when the Prophet (ﷺ) received the order to emigrate from Mecca to Medina. So here he (ﷺ) is praying to leave Mecca honourably and enter Medina honourably. It can also apply to any worldly activity that a person starts and finishes.

supporting authority from Yourself."
81. And declare, "The truth has come and falsehood has vanished. Indeed, falsehood is bound to vanish."

The Quran as a Healing

82. We send down the Quran as a healing and mercy for the believers, but it only increases the wrongdoers in loss.

Arrogance and Ingratitude

83. When We grant people Our favours, they turn away, acting arrogantly. But when touched with evil, they lose all hope. 84. Say, ˹O Prophet,˺ "Everyone acts in their own way. But your Lord knows best whose way is rightly guided."

Question by Pagans

85. They ask you ˹O Prophet˺ about the spirit. Say, "Its nature is known only to my Lord, and you ˹O humanity˺ have been given but little knowledge."

The Quran as a Favour

86. If We willed, We could have certainly taken away what We have revealed to you ˹O Prophet˺—then you would find none to guarantee its return from Us— 87. had it not been for the mercy of your Lord. Indeed, His favour upon you is immense.

The Quran Challenge

88. Say, ˹O Prophet,˺ "If ˹all˺ humans and jinn were to come together to produce the equivalent of this Quran, they could not produce its equal, no matter how they supported each other."

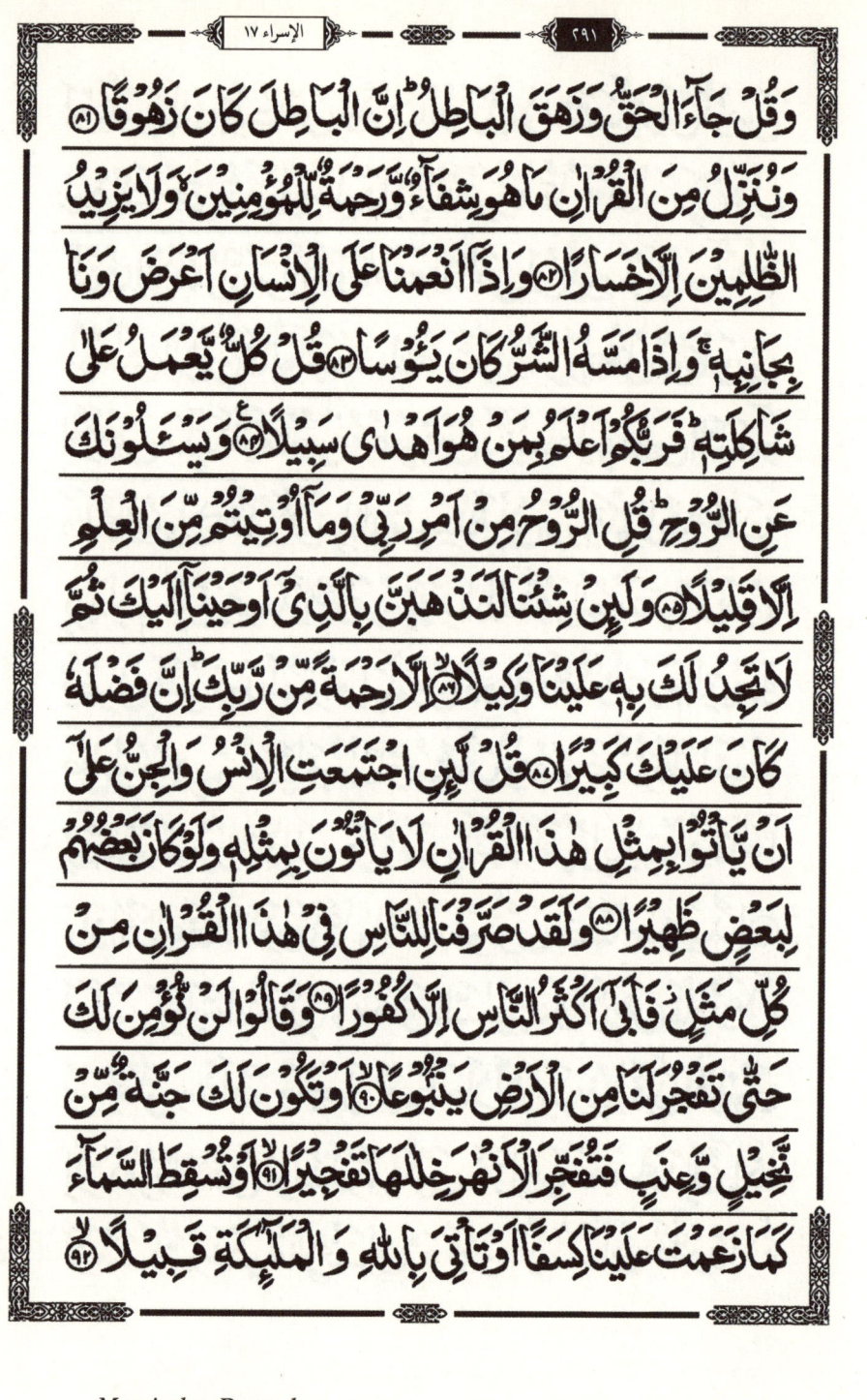

Meaningless Demands

89. And We have truly set forth every ˹kind of˺ lesson for humanity in this Quran, yet most people persist in disbelief. 90. They challenge ˹the Prophet˺, "We will never believe in you until you cause a spring to gush forth from the earth for us, 91. or until you have a garden of palm trees and vineyards, and cause rivers to flow abundantly in it, 92. or cause the sky to fall upon us in pieces, as you have claimed, or bring Allah and the angels before us, face to face,

17. Al-Isrâ' 292

93. or until you have a house of gold, or you ascend into heaven— and even then we will not believe in your ascension until you bring down to us a book that we can read." Say, "Glory be to my Lord! Am I not only a human messenger?"

An Angelic Messenger?

94. And nothing has prevented people from believing when guidance comes to them except their protest: "Has Allah sent a human as a messenger?" **95.** Say, ˹O Prophet,˺ "Had there been angels walking the earth, well settled, We would have surely sent down for them an angel from heaven as a messenger." **96.** Say, "Sufficient is Allah as a Witness between me and you. He is certainly All-Knowing, All-Seeing of His servants."

Reward of the Wicked

97. Whoever Allah guides is truly guided. And whoever He leaves to stray, you will find no guardians for them besides Him. And We will drag them on their faces on the Day of Judgment—deaf, dumb, and blind. Hell will be their home. Whenever it dies down, We will flare it up for them. **98.** That is their reward for rejecting Our signs and asking ˹mockingly˺, "When we are reduced to bones and ashes, will we really be raised as a new creation?" **99.** Have they not realized that Allah, Who created the heavens and the earth, can ˹easily˺ re-create them? He has ˹already˺ set for them a time, about which there is no doubt. But the wrongdoers persist in denial. **100.** Say ˹to them, O Prophet˺, "Even if you were to possess the ˹infinite˺ treasuries of my Lord's mercy, then you would certainly withhold ˹them˺, fearing they would run out—for humankind is ever stingy!"

Pharaoh Challenges Moses

101. We surely gave Moses nine clear signs.[531] ˹You, O Prophet, can˺ ask the Children of Israel. When Moses came to them, Pharaoh said to him, "I really think that you, O Moses, are bewitched."

---

531 The nine signs of Moses are: the staff, the hand (both mentioned in 20:17-22), famine, shortage of crops, floods, locusts, lice, frogs, and blood (all mentioned in 7:130-133). These signs came as proofs for Pharaoh and the Egyptians. Otherwise, Moses had some other signs such water gushing out of the rock after he hit it with his staff, and splitting the sea.

17. Al-Isrâ'

102. Moses replied, "You know well that none has sent these ˹signs˺ down except the Lord of the heavens and the earth as insights. And I really think that you, O Pharaoh, are doomed." 103. So Pharaoh wanted to scare the Israelites out of the land ˹of Egypt˺, but We drowned him and all of those with him. 104. And We said to the Children of Israel after Pharaoh, "Reside in the land, but when the promise of the Hereafter comes to pass,[532] We will bring you all together."

The Noble Quran

105. We have sent down the Quran in truth, and with the truth it has come down. We have sent you ˹O Prophet˺ only as a deliverer of good news and a warner. 106. ˹It is˺ a Quran We have revealed in stages so that you may recite it to people at a deliberate pace. And We have sent it down in successive revelations. 107. Say, ˹O Prophet,˺ "Believe in this ˹Quran˺, or do not. Indeed, when it is recited to those who were gifted with knowledge[533] before it ˹was revealed˺, they fall upon their faces in prostration, 108. and say, 'Glory be to our Lord! Surely the promise of our Lord has been fulfilled.' 109. And they fall down upon their faces weeping, and it increases them in humility."

Advice to the Prophet

110. Say, ˹O Prophet,˺ "Call upon Allah or call upon the Most Compassionate—whichever you call, He has the Most Beautiful Names." Do not recite your prayers too loudly or silently, but seek a way between.

111. And say, "All praise is for Allah, Who has never had ˹any˺ offspring;[534] nor does He have a partner in ˹governing˺ the kingdom;[535] nor is He pathetic, needing a protector.[536] And revere Him immensely."

---

532 This may also refer to the second warning in 17:7.
533 i.e., the faithful among the scholars of the Torah and the Gospel.
534 i.e., Jesus, Ezra, or the angels.
535 i.e., another god equal to Him.
536 i.e., the idols.

18. The Cave (Al-Kahf)

In the Name of Allah—the Most Compassionate, Most Merciful

Message of the Quran

1. All praise is for Allah Who has revealed the Book to His servant,[537] allowing no crookedness in it, 2. ˹making it˺ perfectly upright, to warn ˹the disbelievers˺ of a severe torment from Him; to give good news to the believers—who do good—that they will have a fine reward, 3. in which they will remain forever; 4. and to warn those who claim, "Allah has offspring."[538] 5. They have no knowledge of this, nor did their forefathers. What a terrible claim that comes out of their mouths! They say nothing but lies.

Be Steadfast

6. Now, perhaps you ˹O Prophet˺ will grieve yourself to death over their denial, if they ˹continue to˺ disbelieve in this message. 7. We have indeed made whatever is on earth as an adornment for it, in order to test which of them is best in deeds. 8. And We will certainly reduce whatever is on it to barren ground.

Story 1) The People of the Cave

9. Have you ˹O Prophet˺ thought that the people of the cave and the plaque were ˹the only˺ wonders of Our signs?[539] 10. ˹Remember˺ when those youths took refuge in the cave, and said, "Our Lord! Grant us mercy from Yourself and guide us rightly through our ordeal." 11. So We caused them to fall into a dead sleep[540] in the cave for many years,

---

537 Muḥammad (ﷺ).
538 i.e., Jesus in Christianity and the angels in Arab pagan tradition.
539 *Ar-Raqîm* is the plaque that was placed at the entrance of the cave with the names and story of the People of the Cave. This is the story of a group of Christian youths who hid inside a cave outside the city of Ephesus around 250 C.E., to escape persecution at the hands of pagans during the reign of the Roman emperor Decius. The Quran does not give an exact number of the youths, although many scholars believe there were seven in addition to a dog. The youths slept for 300 years, plus nine (300 solar years equal 309 lunar years).
540 lit., We cast a cover of ˹deep˺ sleep over their ears.

18. Al-Kahf

12. then We raised them so We may show which of the two groups would make a better estimation of the length of their stay.[541]

Standing up for the Truth

13. We relate to you ˹O Prophet˺ their story in truth. They were youths who truly believed in their Lord, and We increased them in guidance. **14.** And We strengthened their hearts when they stood up and declared, "Our Lord is the Lord of the heavens and the earth. We will never call upon any god besides Him, or we would truly be uttering an outrageous lie." **15.** ˹Then they said to one another,˺ "These people of ours have taken gods besides Him. Why do they not produce a clear proof of them? Who then does more wrong than those who fabricate lies against Allah? **16.** Since you have distanced yourselves from them and what they worship besides Allah, take refuge in the cave. Your Lord will extend His mercy to you and accommodate you in your ordeal."

In the Cave

17. And you would have seen the sun, as it rose, inclining away from their cave to the right, and as it set, declining away from them to the left, while they lay in its open space.[542] That is one of the signs of Allah. Whoever Allah guides is truly guided. But whoever He leaves to stray, you will never find for them a guiding mentor. **18.** And you would have thought they were awake,[543] though they were asleep. We turned them over, to the right and left, while their dog stretched his forelegs at the entrance. Had you looked at them, you would have certainly fled away from them, filled with horror.

---

541 The People of the Cave themselves disagreed on how long they had slept in the cave. *See* 18:19.
542 While they slept in the open space of the cave, fresh air blew through the cave, but they were protected from the heat of the sun.
543 This is because, during their long sleep, their eyes were open, their hair grew long, and their bodies rolled over to the right and left to prevent bedsores.

18. Al-Kahf

The Youths Are Awakened

19. And so We awakened them so that they might question one another. One of them exclaimed, "How long have you remained ˹asleep˺?" Some replied, "Perhaps a day, or part of a day." They said ˹to one another˺, "Your Lord knows best how long you have remained. So send one of you with these silver coins of yours to the city, and let him find which food is the purest, and then bring you provisions from it. Let him be ˹exceptionally˺ cautious, and do not let him give you away. 20. For, indeed, if they find out about you, they will stone you ˹to death˺, or force you back into their faith, and then you will never succeed."

The Hideout Is Found

21. That is how We caused them to be discovered so that their people might know that Allah's promise ˹of resurrection˺ is true and that there is no doubt about the Hour.[544] When the people disputed with each other about the case of the youth ˹after their death˺,[545] some proposed, "Build a structure around them. Their Lord knows best about them." Those who prevailed in the matter said, "We will surely build a place of worship over them."

How Many Were They?

22. Some will say, "They were three, their dog was the fourth," while others will say, "They were five, their dog was the sixth," ˹only˺ guessing blindly. And others will say, "They were seven and their dog was the eighth." Say, ˹O Prophet,˺ "My Lord knows best their ˹exact˺ number. Only a few people know as well." So do not argue about them except with sure knowledge,[546] nor consult any of those ˹who debate˺ about them.

---

544 Their antique silver coins gave them away. People rushed to the cave to greet the youths, who finally passed away and were buried in the cave. The King decided to build a place of worship at the cave to commemorate their story.

545 Some pagans suggested that a wall should be built to seal off the cave, whereas the believers decided to build a place of worship at the cave to honour those youths.

546 Based on what has been revealed in the Quran.

Say, "Allah Willing"

23. And never say of anything, "I will definitely do this tomorrow," **24.** without adding, "if Allah so wills!" But if you forget, then remember your Lord, and say, "I trust my Lord will guide me to what is more right than this."

Time Spent in the Cave

25. They had remained in their cave for three hundred years, adding nine.[547] **26.** Say, ˹O Prophet,˺ "Allah knows best how long they stayed. With Him ˹alone˺ is ˹the knowledge of˺ the unseen of the heavens and the earth. How perfectly He hears and sees! They have no guardian besides Him, and He shares His command with none."

Advice to the Prophet

27. Recite what has been revealed to you from the Book of your Lord. None can change His Words, nor can you find any refuge besides Him. **28.** And patiently stick with those who call upon their Lord morning and evening, seeking His pleasure.[548] Do not let your eyes look beyond them, desiring the luxuries of this worldly life. And do not obey those whose hearts We have made heedless of Our remembrance, who follow ˹only˺ their desires and whose state is ˹total˺ loss.

Warning to the Disbelievers

29. And say, ˹O Prophet,˺ "˹This is˺ the truth from your Lord. Whoever wills let them believe, and whoever wills let them disbelieve." Surely We have prepared for the wrongdoers a Fire whose walls will ˹completely˺ surround them. When they cry for aid, they will be aided with water like molten metal, which will burn ˹their˺ faces. What a horrible drink! And what a terrible place to rest!

---

547 Three hundred years in the Gregorian calendar equal three hundred and nine years in the Islamic lunar calendar.
548 lit., seeking His Face.

18. Al-Kahf

Reward of the Believers

30. As for those who believe and do good, We certainly never deny the reward of those who are best in deeds. **31.** It is they who will have the Gardens of Eternity, with rivers flowing under their feet. There they will be adorned with bracelets of gold, and wear green garments of fine silk and rich brocade, reclining there on ˹canopied˺ couches. What a marvellous reward! And what a fabulous place to rest!

Story 2) The Owner of the Two Gardens

32. Give them ˹O Prophet˺ an example of two men. To ˹the disbelieving˺ one We gave two gardens of grapevines, which We surrounded with palm trees and placed ˹various˺ crops in between. **33.** Each garden yielded ˹all˺ its produce, never falling short. And We caused a river to flow between them. **34.** And he had other resources[549] ˹as well˺. So he boasted to a ˹poor˺ companion of his, while conversing with him, "I am greater than you in wealth and superior in manpower." **35.** And he entered his property, while wronging his soul, saying, "I do not think this will ever perish, **36.** nor do I think the Hour will ˹ever˺ come. And if in fact I am returned to my Lord, I will definitely get a far better outcome than ˹all˺ this."

The Rebuttal

37. His ˹believing˺ companion replied, while conversing with him, "Do you disbelieve in the One Who created you from dust,[550] then ˹developed you˺ from a sperm-drop, then formed you into a man? **38.** But as for me: He is Allah, my Lord, and I will never associate anyone with my Lord ˹in worship˺.

---

549 The word *"thamar"* can mean fruits, gold and silver, etc.
550 Created your father, Adam, from dust.

18. Al-Kahf   **299**

39. If only you had said, upon entering your property, 'This is what Allah has willed! There is no power except with Allah!' Even though you see me inferior to you in wealth and offspring, **40.** perhaps my Lord will grant me ˹something˺ better than your garden, and send down upon your garden a thunderbolt from the sky, turning it into a barren waste. **41.** Or its water may sink ˹into the earth˺, and then you will never be able to seek it out."

The Punishment

42. And so all his produce was ˹totally˺ ruined, so he started to wring his hands for all he had spent on it, while it had collapsed on its trellises. He cried, "Alas! I wish I had never associated anyone with my Lord ˹in worship˺!" **43.** And he had no manpower to help him against Allah, nor could he ˹even˺ help himself. **44.** At this time, support comes ˹only˺ from Allah—the True ˹Lord˺. He is best in reward and best in outcome.

Fleeting and Everlasting Gains

45. And give them a parable of this worldly life. ˹It is˺ like the plants of the earth, thriving when sustained by the rain We send down from the sky. Then they ˹soon˺ turn into chaff scattered by the wind. And Allah is fully capable of ˹doing˺ all things. **46.** Wealth and children are the adornment of this worldly life, but the everlasting good deeds are far better with your Lord in reward and in hope.[551]

Judgment Day

47. ˹Beware of˺ the Day We will blow the mountains away, and you will see the earth laid bare. And We will gather all ˹humankind˺, leaving none behind.

---

551 This refers to good deeds that will benefit the believer in the Hereafter such as prayers or praises of Allah such as saying: '*Subḥâna-Allâh*' (Glory be to Allah), '*Alḥamdulillâh*' (Praise be to Allah), '*Lâ ilâha illa-Allâh*' (There is no god ˹worthy of worship˺ except Allah), and '*Allâhu akbar*' (Allah is the Greatest).

18. Al-Kahf — 300

وَعُرِضُوا عَلَىٰ رَبِّكَ صَفًّا لَّقَدْ جِئْتُمُونَا كَمَا خَلَقْنَـٰكُمْ

أَوَّلَ مَرَّةٍ بَلْ زَعَمْتُمْ أَلَّن نَّجْعَلَ لَكُم مَّوْعِدًا ۝ وَوُضِعَ

الْكِتَـٰبُ فَتَرَى الْمُجْرِمِينَ مُشْفِقِينَ مِمَّا فِيهِ وَ

يَقُولُونَ يَـٰوَيْلَتَنَا مَالِ هَـٰذَا الْكِتَـٰبِ لَا يُغَادِرُ صَغِيرَةً

وَلَا كَبِيرَةً إِلَّا أَحْصَىٰهَا وَوَجَدُوا مَا عَمِلُوا حَاضِرًا وَ

لَا يَظْلِمُ رَبُّكَ أَحَدًا ۝ وَإِذْ قُلْنَا لِلْمَلَـٰئِكَةِ اسْجُدُوا

لِـَٔادَمَ فَسَجَدُوا إِلَّا إِبْلِيسَ كَانَ مِنَ الْجِنِّ فَفَسَقَ عَنْ

أَمْرِ رَبِّهِ أَفَتَتَّخِذُونَهُ وَذُرِّيَّتَهُ أَوْلِيَاءَ مِن دُونِي وَهُمْ

لَكُمْ عَدُوٌّ بِئْسَ لِلظَّـٰلِمِينَ بَدَلًا ۝ مَّا أَشْهَدتُّهُمْ خَلْقَ

السَّمَـٰوَٰتِ وَالْأَرْضِ وَلَا خَلْقَ أَنفُسِهِمْ وَمَا كُنتُ مُتَّخِذَ

الْمُضِلِّينَ عَضُدًا ۝ وَيَوْمَ يَقُولُ نَادُوا شُرَكَاءِيَ الَّذِينَ

زَعَمْتُمْ فَدَعَوْهُمْ فَلَمْ يَسْتَجِيبُوا لَهُمْ وَجَعَلْنَا بَيْنَهُم

مَّوْبِقًا ۝ وَرَأَى الْمُجْرِمُونَ النَّارَ فَظَنُّوا أَنَّهُم مُّوَاقِعُوهَا وَ

لَمْ يَجِدُوا عَنْهَا مَصْرِفًا ۝ وَلَقَدْ صَرَّفْنَا فِي هَـٰذَا الْقُرْءَانِ

لِلنَّاسِ مِن كُلِّ مَثَلٍ وَكَانَ الْإِنسَـٰنُ أَكْثَرَ شَيْءٍ جَدَلًا ۝

48. They will be presented before your Lord in rows, ˹and the deniers will be told,˺ "You have surely returned to Us ˹all alone˺ as We created you the first time, although you ˹always˺ claimed that We would never appoint a time for your return." **49.** And the record ˹of deeds˺ will be laid ˹open˺, and you will see the wicked in fear of what is ˹written˺ in it. They will cry, "Woe to us! What kind of record is this that does not leave any sin, small or large, unlisted?" They will find whatever they did present ˹before them˺. And your Lord will never wrong anyone.

Satan and His Followers

50. And ˹remember˺ when We said to the angels, "Prostrate before Adam," so they all did—but not *Iblîs*,[552] who was one of the jinn, but he rebelled against the command of his Lord. Would you then take him and his descendants as patrons instead of Me, although they are your enemy? What an evil alternative for the wrongdoers ˹to choose˺! **51.** I never called them to witness the creation of the heavens and the earth or ˹even˺ their own creation, nor would I take the misleaders as helpers. **52.** And ˹beware of˺ the Day He will say, "Call upon those you claimed were My associate-gods." So they will call them, but will receive no response. And We will make them ˹all˺ share in the same doom. **53.** The wicked will see the Fire and realize that they are bound to fall into it, and will find no way to avoid it.

Denying the Quran

54. We have surely set forth in this Quran every ˹kind of˺ lesson for people, but humankind is the most argumentative of all beings.

---

552 *See footnote for 2:34.*

55. And nothing prevents people from believing when guidance comes to them and from seeking their Lord's forgiveness except ˹their demand˺ to meet the same fate of earlier deniers or that the torment would confront them face to face. **56.** We do not send the messengers except as deliverers of good news and warners. But the disbelievers argue in falsehood, ˹hoping˺ to discredit the truth with it, and make a mockery of My revelations and warnings. **57.** And who does more wrong than those who, when reminded of their Lord's revelations, turn away from them and forget what their own hands have done? We have certainly cast veils over their hearts—leaving them unable to comprehend this ˹Quran˺—and deafness in their ears. And if you ˹O Prophet˺ invite them to ˹true˺ guidance, they will never be ˹rightly˺ guided.

Allah's Forbearance

58. Your Lord is the All-Forgiving, Full of Mercy. If He were to seize them ˹immediately˺ for what they commit, He would have certainly hastened their punishment. But they have an appointed time, from which they will find no refuge. **59.** Those ˹are the˺ societies We destroyed when they persisted in wrong,[553] and We had set a time for their destruction.

Story 3) Moses and Al-Khaḍir

60. And ˹remember˺ when Moses said to his young assistant, "I will never give up until I reach the junction of the two seas, even if I travel for ages."[554] **61.** But when they ˹finally˺ reached the point where the seas met, they forgot their ˹salted˺ fish, and it made its way into the sea, slipping away ˹wondrously˺. **62.** When they had passed further, he said to his assistant, "Bring us our meal! We have certainly been exhausted by today's journey."

---

553 i.e., the peoples of ʿĀd and Thamûd.
554 It is reported in an authentic narration collected by Bukhâri that a man approached Moses after he gave a talk and asked him, "Who is the most knowledgeable person on earth?" Moses responded, "That would be me!" So Allah revealed to Moses that he should not have said this and there was in fact someone who was more knowledgeable than him. Moses was commanded to travel to meet this man, named Al-Khaḍir, at the junction of the two seas (which could be the northern part of Sinai between the Red Sea and the Mediterranean Sea, or the Southern part of Sinai where the Red Sea splits into the Gulf of Suez and the Gulf of Aqaba).

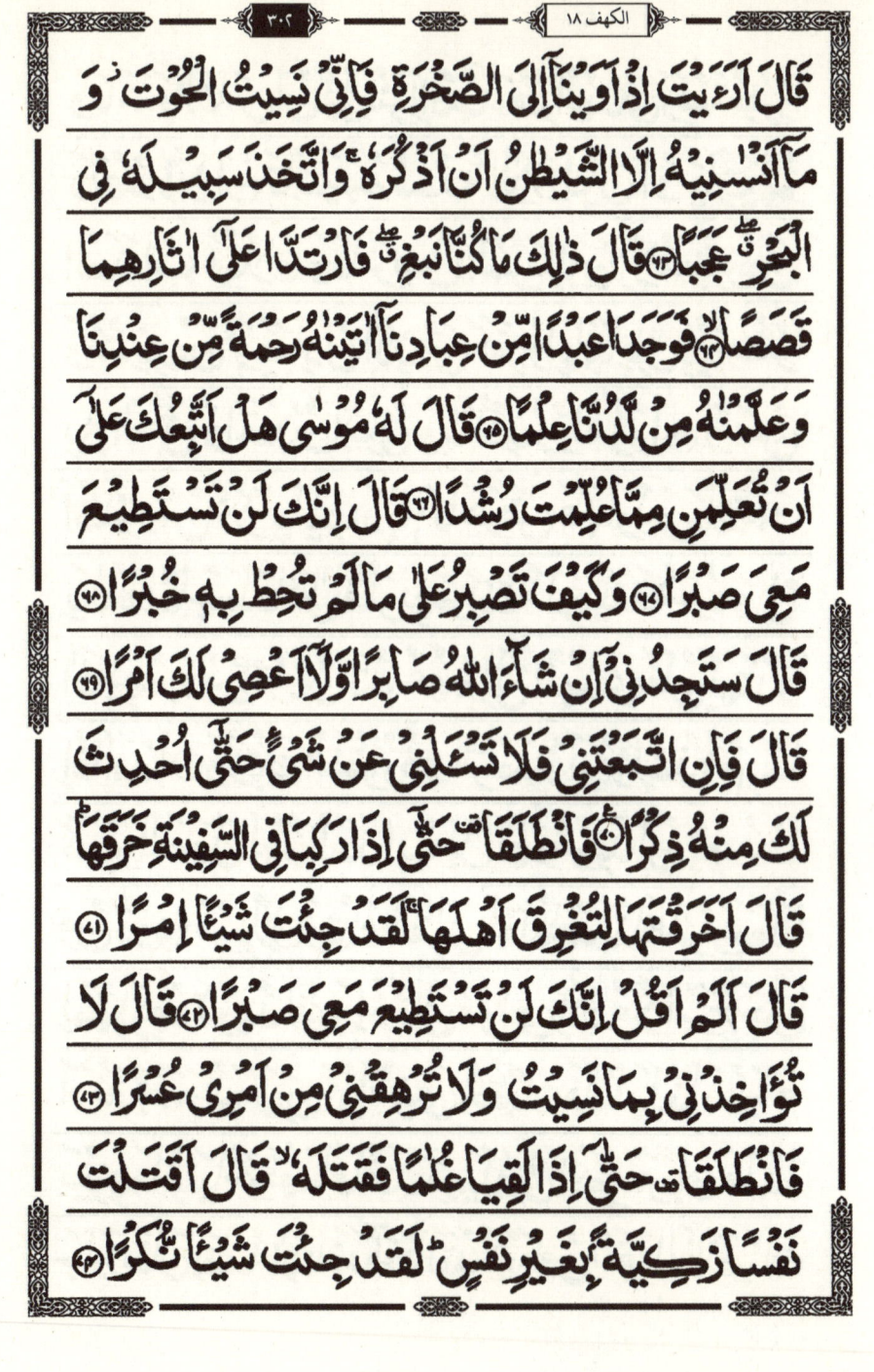

63. He replied, "Do you remember when we rested by the rock? ˹That is when˺ I forgot the fish. None made me forget to mention this except Satan. And the fish made its way into the sea miraculously."555 **64.** Moses responded, "That is ˹exactly˺ what we were looking for."556 So they returned, retracing their footsteps.

The Encounter

65. There they found a servant of Ours, to whom We had granted mercy from Us and enlightened with knowledge of Our Own. **66.** Moses said to him, "May I follow you, provided that you teach me some of the right guidance you have been taught?" **67.** He said, "You certainly cannot be patient ˹enough˺ with me. **68.** And how can you be patient with what is beyond your ˹realm of˺ knowledge?" **69.** Moses assured ˹him˺, "You will find me patient, Allah willing, and I will not disobey any of your orders." **70.** He responded, "Then if you follow me, do not question me about anything until I ˹myself˺ clarify it for you."

The Ship Incident

71. So they set out, but after they had boarded a ship, the man made a hole in it. Moses protested, "Have you done this to drown its people? You have certainly done a terrible thing!" **72.** He replied, "Did I not say that you cannot have patience with me?" **73.** Moses pleaded, "Excuse me for forgetting, and do not be hard on me."

The Boy Incident

74. So they proceeded until they came across a boy, and the man killed him. Moses protested, "Have you killed an innocent soul, who killed no one? You have certainly done a horrible thing."

---

555 Another possible translation: "The ˹salted˺ fish must have made its way into the sea. How strange!"
556 Moses was given a sign: when he and his assistant Joshua (or Yûsha' ibn Nûn) lost their food (a salted fish), this would be the place where they would find the man of knowledge.

75. He answered, "Did I not tell you that you cannot have patience with me?" **76.** Moses replied, "If I ever question you about anything after this, then do not keep me in your company, for by then I would have given you enough of an excuse."

The Wall Incident

77. So they moved on until they came to the people of a town. They asked them for food, but the people refused to give them hospitality. There they found a wall ready to collapse, so the man set it right. Moses protested, "If you wanted, you could have demanded a fee for this." **78.** He replied, "This is the parting of our ways. I will explain to you what you could not bear patiently.

The Ship

79. "As for the ship, it belonged to some poor people, working at sea. So I intended to damage it, for there was a ˹tyrant˺ king ahead of them who seizes every ˹good˺ ship by force.

The Boy

80. "And as for the boy, his parents were ˹true˺ believers, and we[557] feared that he would pressure them into defiance and disbelief. **81.** So we hoped that their Lord would give them another, more virtuous and caring in his place.

The Wall

82. "And as for the wall, it belonged to two orphan boys in the city, and under the wall was a treasure that belonged to them, and their father had been a righteous man. So your Lord willed that these children should come of age and retrieve their treasure, as a mercy from your Lord. I did not do it ˹all˺ on my own. This is the explanation of what you could not bear patiently."[558]

Story 4) *Ẕul-Qarnain*

83. They ask you ˹O Prophet˺ about Ẕul-Qarnain. Say, "I will relate to you something of his narrative."[559]

---

557 This is the royal 'we'.

558 The Prophet (ﷺ) commented on the story, "I wish Moses had been more patient so we can learn more from that wise man."

559 This is the story of a righteous king who travelled far and wide. He is titled Ẕul-Qarnain (lit., the man of the two horns) because of his journeys to the far east and far west (or the two horns/points of sunrise and sunset). Some believe Ẕul-Qarnain was Alexander the Great, but this is not sound since Alexander the Great was a polytheist. Many scholars believe it was Abu Kuraib Al-Ḥamiri, a righteous king from Yemen.

18. Al-Kahf

84. Surely We established him in the land, and gave him the means to all things.

Journey to the West

85. So he travelled a course, **86.** until he reached the setting ˹point˺ of the sun, which appeared to him to be setting in a spring of murky water, where he found some people. We said, "O Zul-Qarnain! Either punish them or treat them kindly." **87.** He responded, "Whoever does wrong will be punished by us, then will be returned to their Lord, Who will punish them with a horrible torment. **88.** As for those who believe and do good, they will have the finest reward, and we will assign them easy commands."

Journey to the East

89. Then he travelled a ˹different˺ course **90.** until he reached the rising ˹point˺ of the sun. He found it rising on a people for whom We had provided no shelter from it.[560] **91.** So it was. And We truly had full knowledge of him.

Another Journey

92. Then he travelled a ˹third˺ course **93.** until he reached ˹a pass˺ between two mountains. He found in front of them a people who could hardly understand ˹his˺ language. **94.** They pleaded, "O Zul-Qarnain! Surely Gog and Magog[561] are spreading corruption throughout the land. Should we pay you tribute, provided that you build a wall between us and them?" **95.** He responded, "What my Lord has provided for me is far better. But assist me with resources, and I will build a barrier between you and them.

96. Bring me blocks of iron!" Then, when he had filled up ˹the gap˺ between the two mountains, he ordered, "Blow!" When the iron became red hot, he said, "Bring me molten copper to pour over it."

---

560 They either had no clothes or homes to protect them from the sun.
561 Gog and Magog are two wild peoples who were sealed off by a barrier built by Zul-Qarnain to stop them from raiding their peaceful neighbours. There are many speculations as to their location, but none is supported by reliable sources. Their coming out is mentioned in 21:96-97 as one of the major signs of the final Hour.

305   18. Al-Kahf

97. And so the enemies could neither scale nor tunnel through it. **98.** He declared, "This is a mercy from my Lord. But when the promise of my Lord comes to pass, He will level it to the ground. And my Lord's promise is ever true." **99.** On that Day, We will let them[562] surge 'like waves' over one another. Later, the Trumpet will be blown,[563] and We will gather all 'people' together.

The Wicked on Judgment Day

100. On that Day We will display Hell clearly for the disbelievers, **101.** those who turned a blind eye to My Reminder[564] and could not stand listening 'to it'. **102.** Do the disbelievers think they can 'simply' take My servants[565] as lords instead of Me? We have surely prepared Hell as an accommodation for the disbelievers.

The Losers

103. Say, 'O Prophet,' "Shall we inform you of who will be the biggest losers of deeds? **104.** 'They are' those whose efforts are in vain in this worldly life, while they think they are doing good!" **105.** It is they who reject the signs of their Lord and their meeting with Him, rendering their deeds void, so We will not give their deeds any weight on Judgment Day. **106.** That is their reward: Hell, for their disbelief and mockery of My signs and messengers.

The Winners

107. Indeed, those who believe and do good will have the Gardens of Paradise[566] as an accommodation, **108.** where they will be forever, never desiring anywhere else.

Recording Allah's Knowledge

109. Say, 'O Prophet,' "If the ocean were ink for 'writing' the Words of my Lord, it would certainly run out before the Words of my Lord were finished, even if We refilled it with its equal."

---

562 Gog and Magog.
563 On the Day of Judgment, the Trumpet will be blown by an angel—causing all to die. When it is blown a second time, everyone will be raised from the dead to be assembled for the Judgment (see 39:68).
564 i.e., the Quran.
565 i.e., Jesus, Ezra, and the angels.
566 Al-Firdaws, the highest place in Paradise.

Have Faith and Do Good

110. Say, ˹O Prophet,˺ "I am only a man like you, ˹but˺ it has been revealed to me that your God is only One God. So whoever hopes for the meeting with their Lord, let them do good deeds and associate none in the worship of their Lord."

৩৯৪ ✷ ৩৯৪

19. Mary (Mariam)

In the Name of Allah—the Most Compassionate, Most Merciful

Zachariah's Prayer

1. *Kãf-Ha-Ya-'Aĩn-Ṣãd.* **2.** ˹This is˺ a reminder of your Lord's mercy to His servant Zachariah, **3.** when he cried out to his Lord privately, **4.** saying, "My Lord! Surely my bones have become brittle, and grey hair has spread across my head, but I have never been disappointed in my prayer to You, my Lord! **5.** And I am concerned about ˹the faith of˺ my relatives after me, since my wife is barren. So grant me, by Your grace, an heir, **6.** who will inherit ˹prophethood˺ from me and the family of Jacob, and make him, O Lord, pleasing ˹to You˺!"

Prayer Answered

7. ˹The angels announced,˺ "O Zachariah! Indeed, We give you the good news of ˹the birth of˺ a son, whose name will be John—a name We have not given to anyone before." **8.** He wondered, "My Lord! How can I have a son when my wife is barren, and I have become extremely old?" **9.** An angel replied, "So will it be! Your Lord says, 'It is easy for Me, just as I created you before, when you were nothing!'" **10.** Zachariah said, "My Lord! Grant me a sign." He responded, "Your sign is that you will not ˹be able to˺ speak to people for three nights, despite being healthy." **11.** So he came out to his people from the sanctuary, signalling to them to glorify ˹Allah˺ morning and evening.

307   19. Mariam

John's Noble Qualities

12. ˹It was later said,˺ "O John! Hold firmly to the Scriptures." And We granted him wisdom while ˹he was still˺ a child, 13. as well as purity and compassion from Us. And he was God-fearing, 14. and kind to his parents. He was neither arrogant nor disobedient. 15. Peace be upon him the day he was born, and the day of his death, and the day he will be raised back to life!

Gabriel Visits Mary

16. And mention in the Book ˹O Prophet, the story of˺ Mary when she withdrew from her family to a place in the east, 17. screening herself off from them. Then We sent to her Our angel, ˹Gabriel,˺ appearing before her as a man, perfectly formed. 18. She appealed, "I truly seek refuge in the Most Compassionate from you! ˹So leave me alone˺ if you are God-fearing." 19. He responded, "I am only a messenger from your Lord, ˹sent˺ to bless you with a pure son." 20. She wondered, "How can I have a son when no man has ever touched me, nor am I unchaste?" 21. He replied, "So will it be! Your Lord says, 'It is easy for Me. And so will We make him a sign for humanity and a mercy from Us.' It is a matter ˹already˺ decreed."

Jesus' Virgin Birth

22. So she conceived him and withdrew with him to a remote place. 23. Then the pains of labour drove her to the trunk of a palm tree. She cried, "Alas! I wish I had died be-

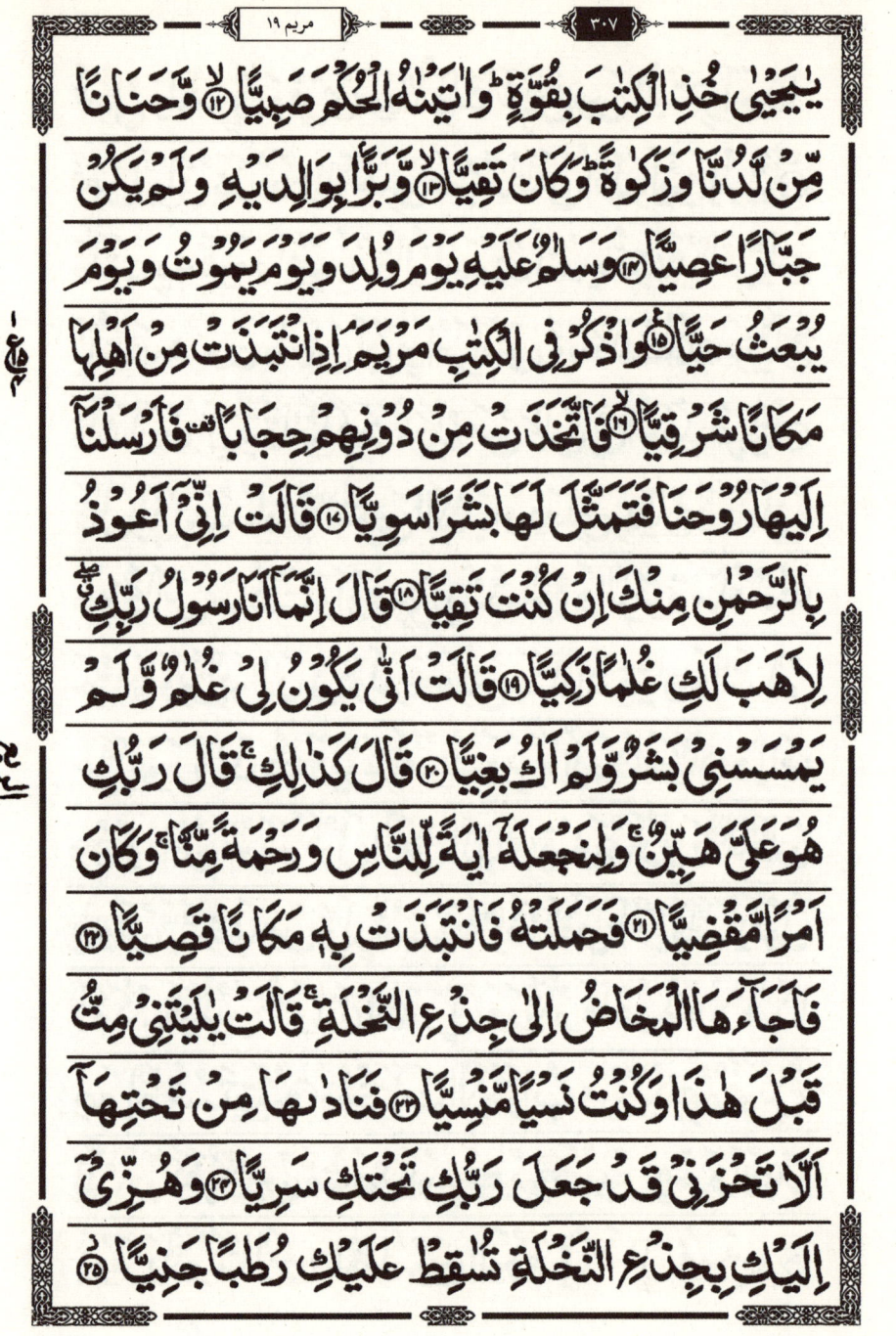

fore this, and was a thing long forgotten!" 24. So a voice[567] reassured her from below her, "Do not grieve! Your Lord has provided a stream at your feet. 25. And shake the trunk of this palm tree towards you, it will drop fresh, ripe dates upon you.

---

567   This was the voice of baby Jesus. Some say it was Gabriel.

26. So eat and drink, and put your heart at ease. But if you see any of the people, say, 'I have vowed silence[568] to the Most Compassionate, so I am not talking to anyone today.'"

Reaction to Baby Jesus

27. Then she returned to her people, carrying him. They said ˹in shock˺, "O Mary! You have certainly done a horrible thing! **28.** O sister of Aaron![569] Your father was not an indecent man, nor was your mother unchaste." **29.** So she pointed to the baby. They exclaimed, "How can we talk to someone who is an infant in the cradle?"

Baby Jesus Talks

30. Jesus declared, "I am truly a servant of Allah. He has destined me to be given the Scripture and to be a prophet. **31.** He has made me a blessing wherever I go, and bid me to establish prayer and give alms-tax as long as I live, **32.** and to be kind to my mother. He has not made me arrogant or defiant. **33.** Peace be upon me the day I was born, the day I die, and the day I will be raised back to life!"

Christians and Jews Differ on Jesus

34. That is Jesus, son of Mary. ˹And this is˺ a word of truth, about which they dispute. **35.** It is not for Allah to take a son! Glory be to Him. When He decrees a matter, He simply tells it, "Be!" And it is! **36.** ˹Jesus also declared,˺ "Surely Allah is my Lord and your Lord, so worship Him ˹alone˺. This is the Straight Path."

37. Yet their ˹various˺ groups have differed among themselves ˹about him˺, so woe to the disbelievers when they face a tremendous Day! **38.** How clearly will they hear and see on the Day they will come to Us! But today the wrongdoers are clearly astray.

---

568 lit., fast ˹from speech˺. Linguistically, *ṣawm* means to abstain from something, such as food, speaking, and playing.
569 i.e., his twin in virtue. They meant that they did not expect her to do something like that because they held her in high esteem like Aaron, Moses' brother (perhaps because she was his descendant).

وَأَنذِرْهُمْ يَوْمَ الْحَسْرَةِ إِذْ قُضِيَ الْأَمْرُ وَهُمْ فِي غَفْلَةٍ وَهُمْ
لَا يُؤْمِنُونَ ﴿٣٩﴾ إِنَّا نَحْنُ نَرِثُ الْأَرْضَ وَمَنْ عَلَيْهَا وَإِلَيْنَا
يُرْجَعُونَ ﴿٤٠﴾ وَاذْكُرْ فِي الْكِتَابِ إِبْرَاهِيمَ إِنَّهُ كَانَ صِدِّيقًا
نَبِيًّا ﴿٤١﴾ إِذْ قَالَ لِأَبِيهِ يَا أَبَتِ لِمَ تَعْبُدُ مَا لَا يَسْمَعُ وَلَا يُبْصِرُ وَ
لَا يُغْنِي عَنكَ شَيْئًا ﴿٤٢﴾ يَا أَبَتِ إِنِّي قَدْ جَاءَنِي مِنَ الْعِلْمِ مَا لَمْ
يَأْتِكَ فَاتَّبِعْنِي أَهْدِكَ صِرَاطًا سَوِيًّا ﴿٤٣﴾ يَا أَبَتِ لَا تَعْبُدِ الشَّيْطَانَ
إِنَّ الشَّيْطَانَ كَانَ لِلرَّحْمَٰنِ عَصِيًّا ﴿٤٤﴾ يَا أَبَتِ إِنِّي أَخَافُ أَن
يَمَسَّكَ عَذَابٌ مِّنَ الرَّحْمَٰنِ فَتَكُونَ لِلشَّيْطَانِ وَلِيًّا ﴿٤٥﴾ قَالَ أَرَاغِبٌ
أَنتَ عَنْ آلِهَتِي يَا إِبْرَاهِيمُ لَئِن لَّمْ تَنتَهِ لَأَرْجُمَنَّكَ وَاهْجُرْنِي مَلِيًّا ﴿٤٦﴾
قَالَ سَلَامٌ عَلَيْكَ سَأَسْتَغْفِرُ لَكَ رَبِّي إِنَّهُ كَانَ بِي حَفِيًّا ﴿٤٧﴾ وَ
أَعْتَزِلُكُمْ وَمَا تَدْعُونَ مِن دُونِ اللَّهِ وَأَدْعُو رَبِّي عَسَىٰ أَلَّا
أَكُونَ بِدُعَاءِ رَبِّي شَقِيًّا ﴿٤٨﴾ فَلَمَّا اعْتَزَلَهُمْ وَمَا يَعْبُدُونَ مِن
دُونِ اللَّهِ وَهَبْنَا لَهُ إِسْحَاقَ وَيَعْقُوبَ وَكُلًّا جَعَلْنَا نَبِيًّا ﴿٤٩﴾
وَوَهَبْنَا لَهُم مِّن رَّحْمَتِنَا وَجَعَلْنَا لَهُمْ لِسَانَ صِدْقٍ عَلِيًّا ﴿٥٠﴾
وَاذْكُرْ فِي الْكِتَابِ مُوسَىٰ إِنَّهُ كَانَ مُخْلَصًا وَكَانَ رَسُولًا نَّبِيًّا ﴿٥١﴾

Warning to the Disbelievers

39. And warn them ˹O Prophet˺ of the Day of Regret, when all matters will be settled, while they are ˹engrossed˺ in heedlessness and disbelief. **40.** Indeed, it is We Who will succeed the earth and whoever is on it. And to Us they will ˹all˺ be returned.

Abraham and His Father, Âzar

41. And mention in the Book ˹O Prophet, the story of˺ Abraham. He was surely a man of truth and a prophet. **42.** ˹Remember˺ when he said to his father, "O dear father! Why do you worship what can neither hear nor see, nor benefit you at all? **43.** O dear father! I have certainly received some knowledge which you have not received, so follow me and I will guide you to the Straight Path. **44.** O dear father! Do not worship Satan. Surely Satan is ever rebellious against the Most Compassionate. **45.** O dear father! I truly fear that you will be touched by a torment from the Most Compassionate, and become Satan's companion ˹in Hell˺."

Âzar's Angry Response

46. He threatened, "How dare you reject my idols, O Abraham! If you do not desist, I will certainly stone you ˹to death˺. So be gone from me for a long time!" **47.** Abraham responded, "Peace be upon you! I will pray to my Lord for your forgiveness. He has truly been Most Gracious to me. **48.** As I distance myself from ˹all of˺ you and from whatever you invoke besides Allah, I will ˹continue to˺ call upon my Lord ˹alone˺, trusting that I will never be disappointed in invoking my Lord." **49.** So after he had left them and what they worshipped besides Allah, We granted him Isaac and Jacob, and made each of them a prophet. **50.** We showered them with Our mercy, and blessed them with honourable mention.[570]

Prophet Moses

51. And mention in the Book ˹O Prophet, the story of˺ Moses. He was truly a chosen man, and was a messenger and a prophet.

570 On a daily basis, Muslims invoke Allah's blessings upon Prophet Muḥammad (ﷺ) and his family and Prophet Abraham (ﷺ) and his family, in both obligatory and optional prayers.

19. Mariam 310

وَنَادَيْنَٰهُ مِن جَانِبِ ٱلطُّورِ ٱلْأَيْمَنِ وَقَرَّبْنَٰهُ نَجِيًّا ۝ وَ
وَهَبْنَا لَهُۥ مِن رَّحْمَتِنَآ أَخَاهُ هَٰرُونَ نَبِيًّا ۝ وَٱذْكُرْ فِى ٱلْكِتَٰبِ
إِسْمَٰعِيلَ ۚ إِنَّهُۥ كَانَ صَادِقَ ٱلْوَعْدِ وَكَانَ رَسُولًا نَّبِيًّا ۝ وَ
كَانَ يَأْمُرُ أَهْلَهُۥ بِٱلصَّلَوٰةِ وَٱلزَّكَوٰةِ وَكَانَ عِندَ رَبِّهِۦ مَرْضِيًّا ۝
وَٱذْكُرْ فِى ٱلْكِتَٰبِ إِدْرِيسَ ۚ إِنَّهُۥ كَانَ صِدِّيقًا نَّبِيًّا ۝ وَرَفَعْنَٰهُ
مَكَانًا عَلِيًّا ۝ أُو۟لَٰٓئِكَ ٱلَّذِينَ أَنْعَمَ ٱللَّهُ عَلَيْهِم مِّنَ ٱلنَّبِيِّۦنَ
مِن ذُرِّيَّةِ ءَادَمَ وَمِمَّنْ حَمَلْنَا مَعَ نُوحٍ وَمِن ذُرِّيَّةِ إِبْرَٰهِيمَ
وَإِسْرَآءِيلَ وَمِمَّنْ هَدَيْنَا وَٱجْتَبَيْنَآ ۚ إِذَا تُتْلَىٰ عَلَيْهِمْ ءَايَٰتُ
ٱلرَّحْمَٰنِ خَرُّوا۟ سُجَّدًا وَبُكِيًّا ۩ ۝ فَخَلَفَ مِنۢ بَعْدِهِمْ خَلْفٌ
أَضَاعُوا۟ ٱلصَّلَوٰةَ وَٱتَّبَعُوا۟ ٱلشَّهَوَٰتِ ۖ فَسَوْفَ يَلْقَوْنَ غَيًّا ۝
إِلَّا مَن تَابَ وَءَامَنَ وَعَمِلَ صَٰلِحًا فَأُو۟لَٰٓئِكَ يَدْخُلُونَ
ٱلْجَنَّةَ وَلَا يُظْلَمُونَ شَيْـًٔا ۝ جَنَّٰتِ عَدْنٍ ٱلَّتِى وَعَدَ
ٱلرَّحْمَٰنُ عِبَادَهُۥ بِٱلْغَيْبِ ۚ إِنَّهُۥ كَانَ وَعْدُهُۥ مَأْتِيًّا ۝ لَّا يَسْمَعُونَ
فِيهَا لَغْوًا إِلَّا سَلَٰمًا ۖ وَلَهُمْ رِزْقُهُمْ فِيهَا بُكْرَةً وَعَشِيًّا ۝
تِلْكَ ٱلْجَنَّةُ ٱلَّتِى نُورِثُ مِنْ عِبَادِنَا مَن كَانَ تَقِيًّا ۝

52. We called him from the right side of Mount Ṭûr, and drew him near, speaking ˹with him˺ directly. **53.** And We appointed for him—out of Our grace—his brother, Aaron, as a prophet.

Prophet Ishmael

54. And mention in the Book ˹O Prophet, the story of˺ Ishmael. He was truly a man of his word, and was a messenger and a prophet. **55.** He used to urge his people to pray and give alms-tax. And his Lord was well pleased with him.

Prophet Enoch

56. And mention in the Book ˹O Prophet, the story of˺ Enoch. He was surely a man of truth and a prophet. **57.** And We elevated him to an honourable status.[571]

Noble Prophets

58. Those were ˹some of˺ the prophets who Allah has blessed from among the descendants of Adam, and of those We carried with Noah ˹in the Ark˺, and of the descendants of Abraham and Israel,[572] and of those We ˹rightly˺ guided and chose. Whenever the revelations of the Most Compassionate were recited to them, they fell down, prostrating and weeping.

Evil Successors

59. But they were succeeded by generations who neglected prayer and followed their lusts and so will soon face the evil consequences.[573] **60.** As for those who repent, believe, and do good, it is they who will be admitted into Paradise, never being denied any reward. **61.** ˹They will be in˺ the Gardens of Eternity, promised in trust by the Most Compassionate to His servants. Surely His promise will be fulfilled. **62.** There they will never hear any idle talk—only ˹greetings of˺ peace. And there they will have their provisions morning and evening.[574] **63.** That is Paradise, which We will grant to whoever is devout among Our servants.

---

571 Prophet Enoch (*Idrîs*) (﷽) is said to be in the fourth heaven.
572 Israel is another name for Jacob (﷽).
573 The word *ghai* can either mean the evil consequences or a valley in Hell where they will be punished.
574 There is no day or night in Paradise, only light. The verse says that the residents of Paradise will either be receiving provisions around these worldly times or without failure. Words such as morning and evening are used to make it easier for the people to understand.

19. Mariam

Gabriel's Response to the Prophet [575]

64. "We only descend by the command of your Lord. To Him belongs whatever is before us, and whatever is behind us, and everything in between. And your Lord is never forgetful. 65. ˹He is the˺ Lord of the heavens, and the earth, and everything in between. So worship Him ˹alone˺, and be steadfast in His worship. Do you know of anyone equal to Him ˹in His attributes˺?"

The Deniers of Resurrection

66. Yet ˹some˺ people ask ˹mockingly˺, "After I die, will I really be raised to life again?" 67. Do ˹such˺ people not remember that We created them before, when they were nothing? 68. By your Lord ˹O Prophet˺! We will surely gather them along with the devils, and then set them around Hell on their knees. 69. Then We will certainly begin by dragging out of every group the ones most defiant to the Most Compassionate. 70. And We truly know best who is most deserving of burning in it. 71. There is none of you who will not pass over it. [576] ˹This is˺ a decree your Lord must fulfil. 72. Then We will deliver those who were devout, leaving the wrongdoers there on their knees.

Arrogant Disbelievers

73. When Our clear revelations are recited to them, the disbelievers ask the believers ˹mockingly˺, "Which of the two of us is better in position and superior in assembly?" 74. ˹Imagine, O Prophet˺ how many peoples We have destroyed before them, who were far better in luxury and splendour! 75. Say, ˹O Prophet,˺ "Whoever is ˹entrenched˺ in misguidance, the Most Compassionate will allow them plenty of time, until—behold!—they face what they are threatened with: either the torment or the Hour. Only then will they realize who is worse in position and inferior in manpower."

---

575 This passage is a response to the Prophet's request to be visited by Gabriel more often.

576 This refers to the bridge (known as Aṣ-Ṣirāṭ) which is extended over Hell. Both the believers and disbelievers will be made to cross that bridge. The believers will cross it safely, each at a different speed according to the strength of their faith, whereas the disbelievers and the hypocrites will plunge into the Fire.

19. Mariam | 312

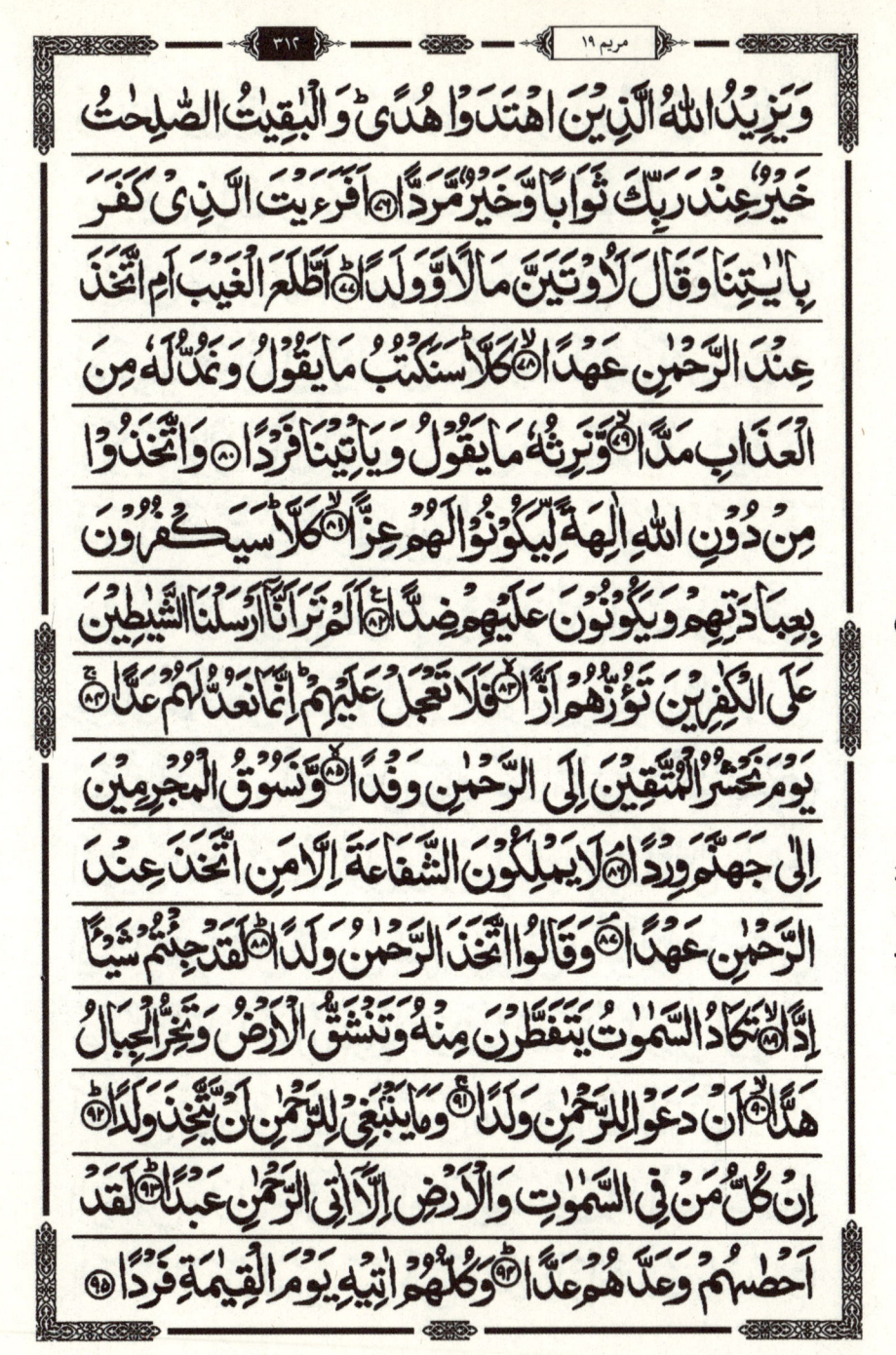

Reward of the Devout

76. And Allah increases in guidance those who are ˹rightly˺ guided. And the everlasting good deeds are far better with your Lord in reward and in outcome.[577]

A Denier of Resurrection

77. Have you seen ˹O Prophet˺ the one[578] who rejects Our revelations yet boasts, "I will definitely be granted ˹plenty of˺ wealth and children ˹if there is an afterlife˺."? 78. Has he looked into the unseen or taken a pledge from the Most Compassionate? 79. Not at all! We certainly record whatever he claims and will increase his punishment extensively. 80. And We will inherit what he boasts of, and he will come before Us all by himself.

Believers and Disbelievers on Judgment Day

81. They have taken other gods, instead of Allah, seeking strength ˹and protection˺ through them. 82. But no! Those ˹gods˺ will deny their worship and turn against them. 83. Do you ˹O Prophet˺ not see that We have sent the devils against the disbelievers, constantly inciting them? 84. So do not be in haste against them, for indeed We are ˹closely˺ counting down their days. 85. ˹Watch for˺ the Day We will gather the righteous before the Most Compassionate as an honoured delegation, 86. and drive the wicked to Hell like a thirsty herd. 87. None will have the right to intercede, except those who have taken a covenant from the Most Compassionate.[579]

Allah's Children?

88. They[580] say, "The Most Compassionate has offspring." 89. You have certainly made an outrageous claim, 90. by which the heavens are about to burst, the earth to split apart, and the mountains to crumble to pieces 91. in protest of attributing children to the Most Compassionate. 92. It does not befit ˹the majesty of˺ the Most Compassionate to have children. 93. There is none in the heavens or the earth who will not return to the Most Compassionate in full submission. 94. Indeed, He fully knows them and has counted them precisely. 95. And each of them will return to Him on the Day of Judgment all alone.

---

577 See footnote for 18:46.
578 This statement was made by Al-ʿÂṣ ibn Wael, a Meccan pagan who staunchly disbelieved in resurrection.
579 No one will be allowed to intercede except those who firmly believe in Almighty Allah.
580 The pagans who claimed that the angels are Allah's daughters, the Christians who claim that Jesus is the son of Allah, etc.

Believers' Love for One Another

96. As for those who believe and do good, the Most Compassionate will ˹certainly˺ bless them with ˹genuine˺ love.

The Message of the Quran

97. Indeed, We have made this ˹Quran˺ easy in your own language ˹O Prophet˺ so with it you may give good news to the righteous and warn those who are contentious. **98.** ˹Imagine˺ how many peoples We have destroyed before them! Do you ˹still˺ see any of them, or ˹even˺ hear from them the slightest sound?

৩৩৩ ✻ ৩৩৩

20. Ṭâ-Hâ (Ṭâ-Hâ)

In the Name of Allah—the Most Compassionate, Most Merciful

Almighty Allah's Revelation

1. *Ṭâ-Hâ.* **2.** We have not revealed the Quran to you ˹O Prophet˺ to cause you distress, **3.** but as a reminder to those in awe ˹of Allah˺. **4.** ˹It is˺ a revelation from the One Who created the earth and the high heavens— **5.** the Most Compassionate, ˹Who is˺ established on the Throne. **6.** To Him belongs whatever is in the heavens and whatever is on the earth and whatever is in between and whatever is underground. **7.** Whether you speak openly ˹or not˺, He certainly knows what is secret and what is even more hidden. **8.** Allah—there is no god ˹worthy of worship˺ except Him. He has the Most Beautiful Names.

Moses' Great Encounter

9. Has the story of Moses reached you ˹O Prophet˺? **10.** When he saw a fire, he said to his family, "Wait here, ˹for˺ I have spotted a fire. Perhaps I can bring you a torch from it, or find some guidance at the fire."[581] **11.** But when he approached it, he was called, "O Moses! **12.** It is truly I. I am your Lord! So take off your sandals, for you are in the sacred valley of Ṭuwa.

---

581 Moses and his family lost their way in the dark while they were travelling from Midian to Egypt.

20. Ṭâ-Ha | 314

وَأَنَا اخْتَرْتُكَ فَاسْتَمِعْ لِمَا يُوحَىٰ ۞ إِنَّنِي أَنَا اللَّهُ لَا إِلَٰهَ إِلَّا
أَنَا فَاعْبُدْنِي وَأَقِمِ الصَّلَاةَ لِذِكْرِي ۞ إِنَّ السَّاعَةَ آتِيَةٌ
أَكَادُ أُخْفِيهَا لِتُجْزَىٰ كُلُّ نَفْسٍ بِمَا تَسْعَىٰ ۞ فَلَا يَصُدَّنَّكَ عَنْهَا
مَن لَّا يُؤْمِنُ بِهَا وَاتَّبَعَ هَوَاهُ فَتَرْدَىٰ ۞ وَمَا تِلْكَ بِيَمِينِكَ يَا مُوسَىٰ ۞
قَالَ هِيَ عَصَايَ أَتَوَكَّؤُا عَلَيْهَا وَأَهُشُّ بِهَا عَلَىٰ غَنَمِي وَلِيَ فِيهَا
مَآرِبُ أُخْرَىٰ ۞ قَالَ أَلْقِهَا يَا مُوسَىٰ ۞ فَأَلْقَاهَا فَإِذَا هِيَ حَيَّةٌ
تَسْعَىٰ ۞ قَالَ خُذْهَا وَلَا تَخَفْ سَنُعِيدُهَا سِيرَتَهَا الْأُولَىٰ ۞
وَاضْمُمْ يَدَكَ إِلَىٰ جَنَاحِكَ تَخْرُجْ بَيْضَاءَ مِنْ غَيْرِ سُوءٍ آيَةً
أُخْرَىٰ ۞ لِنُرِيَكَ مِنْ آيَاتِنَا الْكُبْرَى ۞ اذْهَبْ إِلَىٰ فِرْعَوْنَ إِنَّهُ
طَغَىٰ ۞ قَالَ رَبِّ اشْرَحْ لِي صَدْرِي ۞ وَيَسِّرْ لِي أَمْرِي ۞ وَاحْلُلْ
عُقْدَةً مِّن لِّسَانِي ۞ يَفْقَهُوا قَوْلِي ۞ وَاجْعَل لِّي وَزِيرًا مِّنْ
أَهْلِي ۞ هَارُونَ أَخِي ۞ اشْدُدْ بِهِ أَزْرِي ۞ وَأَشْرِكْهُ فِي أَمْرِي ۞
كَيْ نُسَبِّحَكَ كَثِيرًا ۞ وَنَذْكُرَكَ كَثِيرًا ۞ إِنَّكَ كُنتَ بِنَا
بَصِيرًا ۞ قَالَ قَدْ أُوتِيتَ سُؤْلَكَ يَا مُوسَىٰ ۞ وَلَقَدْ مَنَنَّا
عَلَيْكَ مَرَّةً أُخْرَىٰ ۞ إِذْ أَوْحَيْنَا إِلَىٰ أُمِّكَ مَا يُوحَىٰ ۞

13. I have chosen you, so listen to what is revealed: 14. 'It is truly I. I am Allah! There is no god ˹worthy of worship˺ except Me. So worship Me ˹alone˺, and establish prayer for My remembrance. 15. The Hour is sure to come. My Will is to keep it hidden, so that every soul may be rewarded according to their efforts. 16. So do not let those who disbelieve in it and follow their desires distract you from it, or you will be doomed.'"

Two Signs for Moses

17. ˹Allah added,˺ "And what is that in your right hand, O Moses?" 18. He replied, "It is my staff! I lean on it, and with it I beat down ˹branches˺ for my sheep, and have other uses for it."[582] 19. Allah said, "Throw it down, O Moses!" 20. So he did, then—behold!—it became a serpent, slithering. 21. Allah said, "Take it, and have no fear. We will return it to its former state. 22. And put your hand under your armpit, it will come out ˹shining˺ white, unblemished,[583] as another sign, 23. so that We may show you some of Our greatest signs. 24. Go to Pharaoh, for he has truly transgressed ˹all bounds˺."

Moses Prays for Help

25. Moses prayed, "My Lord! Uplift my heart for me, 26. and make my task easy, 27. and remove the impediment from my tongue 28. so people may understand my speech,[584] 29. and grant me a helper from my family, 30. Aaron, my brother. 31. Strengthen me through him, 32. and let him share my task, 33. so that we may glorify You much 34. and remember You much, 35. for truly You have ˹always˺ been overseeing us." 36. Allah responded, "All that you requested has been granted, O Moses!

Allah's Favours to Young Moses

37. "And surely We had shown You favour before, 38. when We inspired your mother with this:

---

582 Moses could have just said, "A staff." But he volunteered to talk about the uses of the staff, adding that there are many other uses he has not mentioned, with the hope that Allah would ask him about it more. The reason is that Moses wanted to prolong the conversation with Allah as much as he could.

583 Moses, who was dark-skinned, was asked to put his hand under his armpit. When he took it out it was shining white, but not out of a skin condition like melanoma.

584 Moses (ﷺ) put a brand of fire in his mouth, which hindered his speech as he grew up. In this verse, he prays to Allah to help him speak clearly, and his prayer is answered.

315   20. Ṭâ-Hâ

39. 'Put him into a chest, then put it into the river. The river will wash it ashore, and he will be taken by ˹Pharaoh,˺ an enemy of Mine and his.' And I blessed you with lov-ability from Me[585] ˹O Moses˺ so that you would be brought up under My ˹watchful˺ Eye. **40.** ˹Remem-ber˺ when your sister came along and proposed, 'Shall I direct you to someone who will nurse him?'[586] So We reunited you with your moth-er so that her heart would be put at ease, and she would not grieve. ˹Later˺ you killed a man ˹by mis-take˺, but We saved you from sor-row, as well as other tests We put you through. Then you stayed for a number of years among the people of Midian. Then you came here as pre-destined, O Moses! **41.** And I have selected you for My service.

Orders to Moses and Aaron

42. "Go forth, you and your broth-er, with My signs and never falter in remembering Me. **43.** Go, both of you, to Pharaoh, for he has truly transgressed ˹all bounds˺. **44.** Speak to him gently, so perhaps he may be mindful ˹of Me˺ or fearful ˹of My punishment˺." **45.** They both plead-ed, "Our Lord! We fear that he may be quick to harm us or act tyranni-cally." **46.** Allah reassured ˹them˺, "Have no fear! I am with you, hear-ing and seeing. **47.** So go to him and say, 'Indeed we are both messengers from your Lord, so let the Children of Israel go with us, and do not op-press them. We have come to you with a sign from your Lord. And sal-vation will be for whoever follows the ˹right˺ guidance. **48.** It has indeed been revealed to us that the punishment will be upon whoever denies ˹the truth˺ and turns away.'"

Pharaoh's Arrogance

49. Pharaoh asked, "Who then is the Lord of you two, O Moses?" **50.** He answered, "Our Lord is the One Who has given every-thing its ˹distinctive˺ form, then guided ˹it˺." **51.** Pharaoh asked, "And what about previous peoples?"

---

585   In other words, Allah made Moses a likeable person so Pharaoh and his wife would agree to keep him.
586   Moses had refused all wet-nurses that were brought for him.

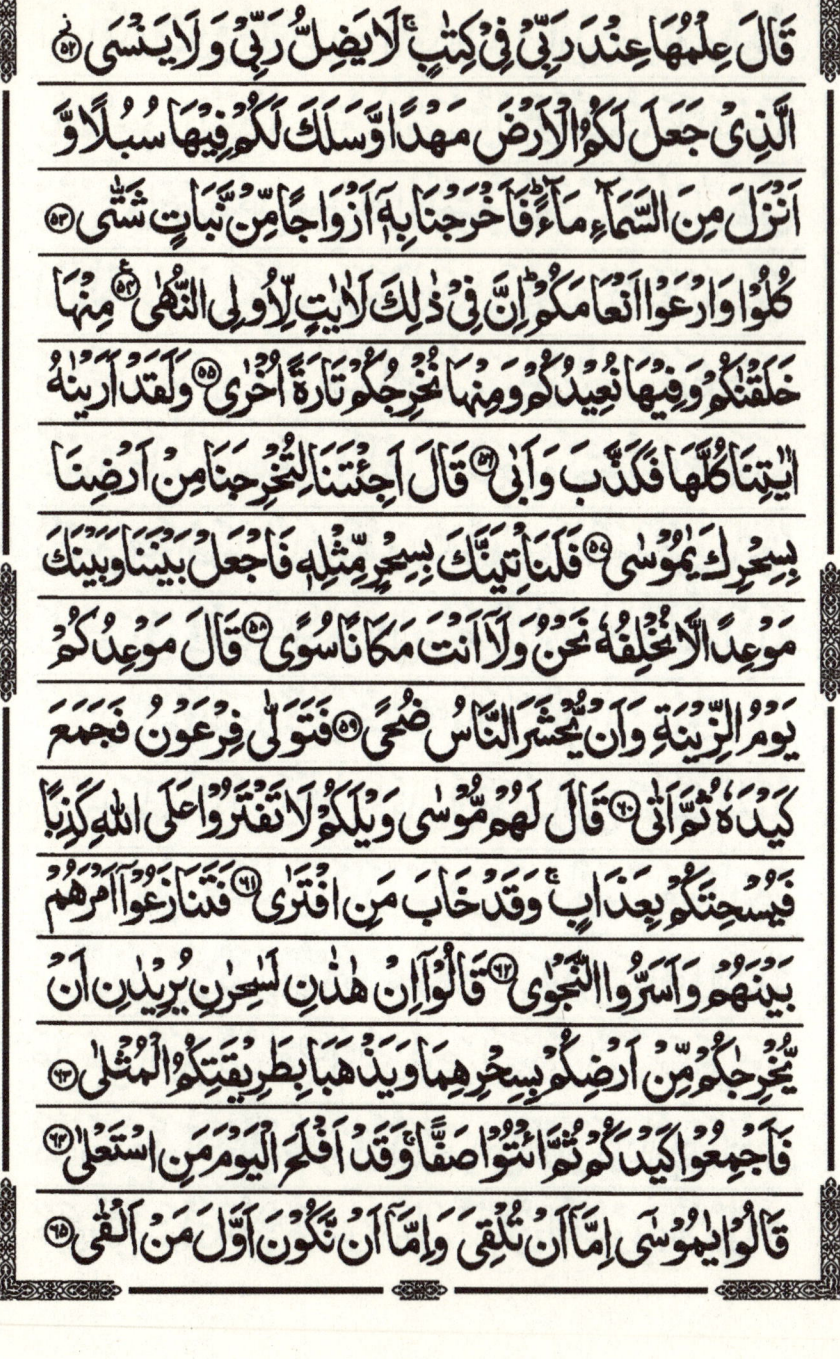

20. Ṭâ-Hâ 316

52. He replied, "That knowledge is with my Lord in a Record. My Lord neither falters nor forgets ˹anything˺." 53. ˹He is the One˺ Who has laid out the earth for ˹all of˺ you, and set in it pathways for you, and sends down rain from the sky, causing various types of plants to grow, 54. ˹so˺ eat and graze your cattle. Surely in this are signs for people of sound judgment. 55. From the earth We created you, and into it We will return you, and from it We will bring you back again.

The Challenge

56. And We certainly showed Pharaoh all of Our signs,[587] but he denied them and refused ˹to believe˺. 57. He said, "Have you come to drive us out of our land with your magic, O Moses? 58. We can surely meet you with similar magic. So set for us an appointment that neither of us will fail to keep, in a central place." 59. Moses said, "Your appointment is on the Day of the Festival, and let the people be gathered mid-morning."

Moses' Warning

60. Pharaoh then withdrew, orchestrated his scheme, then returned. 61. Moses warned the magicians, "Woe to you! Do not fabricate a lie against Allah,[588] or He will wipe you out with a torment. Whoever fabricates ˹lies˺ is bound to fail." 62. So the magicians disputed the matter among themselves, conversing privately. 63. They concluded, "These two are only magicians who want to drive you out of your land with their magic, and do away with your most cherished traditions. 64. So orchestrate your plan, then come forward in ˹perfect˺ ranks. And whoever prevails today will certainly be successful."

Moses Prevails

65. They said, "O Moses! Either you cast, or let us be the first to cast."

---

587 *See* footnote for 17:101.
588 By saying that Moses' miracle is pure magic.

317   **20. Ṭâ-Hâ**

66. Moses responded, "No, you go first." And suddenly their ropes and staffs appeared to him—by their magic—to be slithering. 67. So Moses concealed fear within himself. 68. We reassured ˹him˼, "Do not fear! It is certainly you who will prevail. 69. Cast what is in your right hand, and it will swallow up what they have made, for what they have made is no more than a magic trick. And magicians can never succeed wherever they go."

Magicians Become Believers

70. So the magicians fell down in prostration, declaring, "We believe in the Lord of Aaron and Moses." 71. Pharaoh threatened, "How dare you believe in him before I give you permission? He must be your master who taught you magic. I will certainly cut off your hands and feet on opposite sides, and crucify you on the trunks of palm trees. You will really see whose punishment is more severe and more lasting." 72. They responded, "By the One Who created us! We will never prefer you over the clear proofs that have come to us. So do whatever you want! Your authority only covers the ˹fleeting˼ life of this world. 73. Indeed, we have believed in our Lord so He may forgive our sins and that magic you have forced us to practice. And Allah is far superior ˹in reward˼ and more lasting ˹in punishment˼."

Reward of Disbelievers and Believers

74. Whoever comes to their Lord as an evildoer will certainly have Hell, where they can neither live nor die.

75. But whoever comes to Him as a believer, having done good, they will have the highest ranks: 76. the Gardens of Eternity, under which rivers flow, where they will stay forever. That is the reward of those who purify themselves.

وَلَقَدْ أَوْحَيْنَآ إِلَىٰ مُوسَىٰٓ أَنْ أَسْرِ بِعِبَادِى فَٱضْرِبْ لَهُمْ طَرِيقًا فِى ٱلْبَحْرِ يَبَسًا لَّا تَخَٰفُ دَرَكًا وَلَا تَخْشَىٰ ۝ فَأَتْبَعَهُمْ فِرْعَوْنُ بِجُنُودِهِۦ فَغَشِيَهُم مِّنَ ٱلْيَمِّ مَا غَشِيَهُمْ ۝ وَأَضَلَّ فِرْعَوْنُ قَوْمَهُۥ وَمَا هَدَىٰ ۝ يَٰبَنِىٓ إِسْرَٰٓءِيلَ قَدْ أَنجَيْنَٰكُم مِّنْ عَدُوِّكُمْ وَوَٰعَدْنَٰكُمْ جَانِبَ ٱلطُّورِ ٱلْأَيْمَنَ وَنَزَّلْنَا عَلَيْكُمُ ٱلْمَنَّ وَٱلسَّلْوَىٰ ۝ كُلُوا۟ مِن طَيِّبَٰتِ مَا رَزَقْنَٰكُمْ وَلَا تَطْغَوْا۟ فِيهِ فَيَحِلَّ عَلَيْكُمْ غَضَبِى وَمَن يَحْلِلْ عَلَيْهِ غَضَبِى فَقَدْ هَوَىٰ ۝ وَإِنِّى لَغَفَّارٌ لِّمَن تَابَ وَءَامَنَ وَعَمِلَ صَٰلِحًا ثُمَّ ٱهْتَدَىٰ ۝ وَمَآ أَعْجَلَكَ عَن قَوْمِكَ يَٰمُوسَىٰ ۝ قَالَ هُمْ أُو۟لَآءِ عَلَىٰٓ أَثَرِى وَعَجِلْتُ إِلَيْكَ رَبِّ لِتَرْضَىٰ ۝ قَالَ فَإِنَّا قَدْ فَتَنَّا قَوْمَكَ مِنۢ بَعْدِكَ وَأَضَلَّهُمُ ٱلسَّامِرِىُّ ۝ فَرَجَعَ مُوسَىٰٓ إِلَىٰ قَوْمِهِۦ غَضْبَٰنَ أَسِفًا قَالَ يَٰقَوْمِ أَلَمْ يَعِدْكُمْ رَبُّكُمْ وَعْدًا حَسَنًا أَفَطَالَ عَلَيْكُمُ ٱلْعَهْدُ أَمْ أَرَدتُّمْ أَن يَحِلَّ عَلَيْكُمْ غَضَبٌ مِّن رَّبِّكُمْ فَأَخْلَفْتُم مَّوْعِدِى ۝

Pharaoh's Doom

77. And We surely inspired Moses, ˹saying,˺ "Leave with My servants ˹at night˺ and strike a dry passage for them across the sea. Have no fear of being overtaken, nor be concerned ˹of drowning˺." **78.** Then Pharaoh pursued them with his soldiers—but how overwhelming were the waters that submerged them! **79.** And ˹so˺ Pharaoh led his people astray, and did not guide ˹them rightly˺.

Allah's Favours to the Israelites

80. O Children of Israel! We saved you from your enemy, and made an appointment with you[589] on the right side of Mount Ṭûr, and sent down to you manna and quails,[590] **81.** ˹saying,˺ "Eat from the good things We have provided for you, but do not transgress in them, or My wrath will befall you. And whoever My wrath befalls is certainly doomed. **82.** But I am truly Most Forgiving to whoever repents, believes, and does good, then persists on ˹true˺ guidance."

The Golden Calf

83. ˹Allah asked,˺ "Why have you come with such haste ahead of your people, O Moses?"[591] **84.** He replied, "They are close on my tracks. And I have hastened to You, my Lord, so You will be pleased." **85.** Allah responded, "We have indeed tested your people in your absence, and the Sâmiri[592] has led them astray." **86.** So Moses returned to his people, furious and sorrowful. He said, "O my people! Had your Lord not made you a good promise?[593] Has my absence been too long for you? Or have you wished for wrath from your Lord to befall you, so you broke your promise to me?"[594]

---

589 i.e., your prophet to receive the Tablets for your guidance.
590 Manna (heavenly bread) and quails (chicken-like birds) sustained the children of Israel in the wilderness after they left Egypt.
591 Moses selected a delegation of seventy people from his community to go to Mount Ṭûr where it was appointed for him to receive the Tablets. On the way, he rushed for the appointment with Allah, arriving before the delegation.
592 The Sâmiri, or the man from Samaria, was a hypocrite who led the Children of Israel into idol-worship.
593 To reveal the Torah for their guidance.
594 To worship Allah alone until Moses returned with the Tablets.

The Calf Worshippers

87. They argued, "We did not break our promise to you of our own free will, but we were made to carry the burden of the people's ˹golden˺ jewellery,[595] then we threw it ˹into the fire˺, and so did the Sâmiri." **88.** Then he moulded for them an idol of a calf that made a lowing sound. They said, "This is your god and the god of Moses, but Moses forgot ˹where it was˺!" **89.** Did they not see that it did not respond to them, nor could it protect or benefit them?

Aaron's Stance

90. Aaron had already warned them beforehand, "O my people! You are only being tested by this, for indeed your ˹one true˺ Lord is the Most Compassionate. So follow me and obey my orders." **91.** They replied, "We will not cease to worship it until Moses returns to us." **92.** Moses scolded ˹his brother˺, "O Aaron! What prevented you, when you saw them going astray, **93.** from following after me? How could you disobey my orders?"[596] **94.** Aaron pleaded, "O son of my mother! Do not seize me by my beard or ˹the hair of˺ my head. I really feared that you would say, 'You have caused division among the Children of Israel, and did not observe my word.'"

The Sâmiri's Punishment

95. Moses then asked, "What did you think you were doing, O Sâmiri?" **96.** He said, "I saw what they did not see, so I took a handful ˹of dust˺ from the hoof-prints of ˹the horse of˺ the messenger-angel ˹Gabriel˺ then cast it ˹on the moulded calf˺. This is what my lower-self tempted me into."[597] **97.** Moses said, "Go away then! And for ˹the rest of your˺ life you will surely be crying, 'Do not touch ˹me˺!'[598] Then you will certainly have a fate[599] that you cannot escape. Now look at your god to which you have been devoted: we will burn it up, then scatter it in the sea completely."

---

595 The jewellery they borrowed from their Egyptian neighbours before they fled Egypt.

596 Moses' orders are mentioned in 7:142.

597 This verse could also be translated as follows: "I had an insight which they did not have, then grasped some knowledge from the messenger ˹Moses˺, but ˹later˺ threw it away. This is what my lower-self tempted me to do." According to many Quran commentators, while Moses and the Children of Israel were crossing the sea to escape abuse by Pharaoh and his people, the Sâmiri saw Gabriel on a horse leading the way, and every time the horse touched the ground, it turned green. So the Sâmiri took a handful of dust from the hoof-prints of the horse, and later tossed it at the calf so it started to make a lowing sound.

598 Meaning, alienated in the dessert, away from the people.

599 lit., destined time.

بِسْمِ اللّٰهِ

إِنَّمَآ إِلَٰهُكُمُ اللّٰهُ الَّذِى لَآ إِلَٰهَ إِلَّا هُوَ وَسِعَ كُلَّ شَىْءٍ عِلْمًا ۝ كَذَٰلِكَ نَقُصُّ عَلَيْكَ مِنْ أَنۢبَآءِ مَا قَدْ سَبَقَ ۚ وَقَدْ ءَاتَيْنَٰكَ مِن لَّدُنَّا ذِكْرًا ۝ مَّنْ أَعْرَضَ عَنْهُ فَإِنَّهُۥ يَحْمِلُ يَوْمَ الْقِيَٰمَةِ وِزْرًا ۝ خَٰلِدِينَ فِيهِ ۖ وَسَآءَ لَهُمْ يَوْمَ الْقِيَٰمَةِ حِمْلًا ۝ يَوْمَ يُنفَخُ فِى الصُّورِ ۚ وَنَحْشُرُ الْمُجْرِمِينَ يَوْمَئِذٍ زُرْقًا ۝ يَتَخَٰفَتُونَ بَيْنَهُمْ إِن لَّبِثْتُمْ إِلَّا عَشْرًا ۝ نَّحْنُ أَعْلَمُ بِمَا يَقُولُونَ إِذْ يَقُولُ أَمْثَلُهُمْ طَرِيقَةً إِن لَّبِثْتُمْ إِلَّا يَوْمًا ۝ وَيَسْـَٔلُونَكَ عَنِ الْجِبَالِ فَقُلْ يَنسِفُهَا رَبِّى نَسْفًا ۝ فَيَذَرُهَا قَاعًا صَفْصَفًا ۝ لَّا تَرَىٰ فِيهَا عِوَجًا وَلَآ أَمْتًا ۝ يَوْمَئِذٍ يَتَّبِعُونَ الدَّاعِىَ لَا عِوَجَ لَهُۥ ۖ وَخَشَعَتِ الْأَصْوَاتُ لِلرَّحْمَٰنِ فَلَا تَسْمَعُ إِلَّا هَمْسًا ۝ يَوْمَئِذٍ لَّا تَنفَعُ الشَّفَٰعَةُ إِلَّا مَنْ أَذِنَ لَهُ الرَّحْمَٰنُ وَرَضِىَ لَهُۥ قَوْلًا ۝ يَعْلَمُ مَا بَيْنَ أَيْدِيهِمْ وَمَا خَلْفَهُمْ وَلَا يُحِيطُونَ بِهِۦ عِلْمًا ۝ وَعَنَتِ الْوُجُوهُ لِلْحَىِّ الْقَيُّومِ ۖ وَقَدْ خَابَ مَنْ حَمَلَ ظُلْمًا ۝ وَمَن يَعْمَلْ مِنَ الصَّٰلِحَٰتِ وَهُوَ مُؤْمِنٌ فَلَا يَخَافُ ظُلْمًا وَلَا هَضْمًا ۝ وَكَذَٰلِكَ أَنزَلْنَٰهُ قُرْءَانًا عَرَبِيًّا وَصَرَّفْنَا فِيهِ مِنَ الْوَعِيدِ لَعَلَّهُمْ يَتَّقُونَ أَوْ يُحْدِثُ لَهُمْ ذِكْرًا ۝

98. ˹Then Moses addressed his people,˺ "Your only god is Allah, there is no god ˹worthy of worship˺ except Him. He encompasses everything in ˹His˺ knowledge."

The Deniers of the Quran

99. This is how We relate to you ˹O Prophet˺ some of the stories of the past. And We have certainly granted you a Reminder[600] from Us. **100.** Whoever turns away from it will surely bear the burden ˹of sin˺ on the Day of Judgment, **101.** suffering its consequences forever. What an evil burden they will carry on Judgment Day! **102.** ˹Beware of˺ the Day the Trumpet will be blown,[601] and We will gather the wicked on that Day blue-faced ˹from horror and thirst˺.[602] **103.** They will whisper among themselves, "You stayed no more than ten days ˹on the earth˺." **104.** We know best what they will say—the most reasonable of them will say, "You stayed no more than a day."

Mountains on Judgment Day

105. And ˹if˺ they ask you ˹O Prophet˺ about the mountains, ˹then˺ say, "My Lord will wipe them out completely, **106.** leaving the earth level and bare, **107.** with neither depressions nor elevations to be seen."

People on Judgment Day

108. On that Day all will follow the caller ˹for assembly˺, ˹and˺ none will dare to deviate. All voices will be hushed before the Most Compassionate. Only whispers[603] will be heard. **109.** On that Day no intercession will be of any benefit, except by those granted permission by the Most Compassionate and whose words are agreeable to Him. **110.** He ˹fully˺ knows what is ahead of them and what is behind them,[604] but they cannot encompass Him in ˹their˺ knowledge.[605] **111.** And all faces will be humbled before the Ever-Living, All-Sustaining. And those burdened with wrongdoing will be in loss. **112.** But whoever does good and is a believer will have no fear of being wronged or denied ˹their reward˺.

---

600 The Quran.
601 See footnote for 18:99.
602 This can also mean "blind."
603 This can also mean "footsteps."
604 Allah fully knows what fate awaits them and what they did in the world.
605 Or "... they cannot encompass His knowledge."

The Quran

113. And so We have sent it down as an Arabic Quran and varied the warnings in it, so perhaps they will shun evil or it may cause them to be mindful. **114.** Exalted is Allah, the True King! Do not rush to recite ʿa revelation ofʾ the Quran ʿO Prophetʾ before it is ʿproperlyʾ conveyed to you,[606] and pray, "My Lord! Increase me in knowledge."

Satan vs. Adam

115. And indeed, We once made a covenant with Adam, but he forgot, and ʿsoʾ We did not find determination in him. **116.** And ʿrememberʾ when We said to the angels, "Prostrate before Adam," so they all did—but not *Iblîs*,[607] who refused ʿarrogantlyʾ. **117.** So We cautioned, "O Adam! This is surely an enemy to you and to your wife. So do not let him drive you both out of Paradise, for you ʿO Adamʾ would then suffer ʿhardshipʾ. **118.** Here it is guaranteed that you will never go hungry or unclothed, **119.** nor will you ʿeverʾ suffer from thirst or ʿthe sun'sʾ heat."[608]

The Temptation

120. But Satan whispered to him, saying, "O Adam! Shall I show you the Tree of Immortality and a kingdom that does not fade away?" **121.** So they both ate from the tree and then their nakedness was exposed to them, prompting them to cover themselves with leaves from Paradise. So Adam disobeyed his Lord, and ʿsoʾ lost his way.[609] **122.** Then his Lord chose him ʿfor His graceʾ, accepted his repentance, and guided him ʿrightlyʾ.

The Fall

123. Allah said, "Descend, both of you, from here together ʿwith Satanʾ as enemies to each other. Then when guidance comes to you from Me, whoever follows My guidance will neither go astray ʿin this lifeʾ nor suffer ʿin the nextʾ. **124.** But whoever turns away from My Reminder will certainly have a miserable life,[610] then We will raise them up blind on the Day of Judgment." **125.** They will cry, "My Lord! Why have you raised me up blind, although I used to see?" **126.** Allah will respond, "It is so, just as Our revelations came to you and you neglected them, so Today you are neglected."

---

606 The Prophet (ﷺ) was eager to recite the Quran while it was being revealed to him through the angel Gabriel. So he (ﷺ) was told to take his time to learn it by heart once the verses are properly delivered to him.

607 See footnote for 2:34.

608 There is no sun or cold weather in Paradise, only light. *See* 76:13.

609 Unlike the Bible (Genesis 3), the Quran does not blame Eve for Adam's fall from the Garden.

610 The Reminder is another name for the Quran.

20. Ṭâ-Hâ

بِسْمِ ٱللَّهِ ٱلرَّحْمَٰنِ ٱلرَّحِيمِ

وَكَذَٰلِكَ نَجْزِى مَنْ أَسْرَفَ وَلَمْ يُؤْمِن بِـَٔايَٰتِ رَبِّهِۦ ۚ وَلَعَذَابُ الْأَخِرَةِ أَشَدُّ وَأَبْقَىٰ ۝ أَفَلَمْ يَهْدِ لَهُمْ كَمْ أَهْلَكْنَا قَبْلَهُم مِّنَ الْقُرُونِ يَمْشُونَ فِى مَسَٰكِنِهِمْ ۚ إِنَّ فِى ذَٰلِكَ لَءَايَٰتٍ لِّأُولِى النُّهَىٰ ۝ وَلَوْلَا كَلِمَةٌ سَبَقَتْ مِن رَّبِّكَ لَكَانَ لِزَامًا وَأَجَلٌ مُّسَمًّى ۝ فَاصْبِرْ عَلَىٰ مَا يَقُولُونَ وَسَبِّحْ بِحَمْدِ رَبِّكَ قَبْلَ طُلُوعِ الشَّمْسِ وَقَبْلَ غُرُوبِهَا ۖ وَمِنْ ءَانَآئِ الَّيْلِ فَسَبِّحْ وَأَطْرَافَ النَّهَارِ لَعَلَّكَ تَرْضَىٰ ۝ وَلَا تَمُدَّنَّ عَيْنَيْكَ إِلَىٰ مَا مَتَّعْنَا بِهِۦ أَزْوَٰجًا مِّنْهُمْ زَهْرَةَ الْحَيَوٰةِ الدُّنْيَا لِنَفْتِنَهُمْ فِيهِ ۚ وَرِزْقُ رَبِّكَ خَيْرٌ وَأَبْقَىٰ ۝ وَأْمُرْ أَهْلَكَ بِالصَّلَوٰةِ وَاصْطَبِرْ عَلَيْهَا ۖ لَا نَسْـَٔلُكَ رِزْقًا ۖ نَّحْنُ نَرْزُقُكَ ۗ وَالْعَٰقِبَةُ لِلتَّقْوَىٰ ۝ وَقَالُوا لَوْلَا يَأْتِينَا بِـَٔايَةٍ مِّن رَّبِّهِۦٓ ۚ أَوَلَمْ تَأْتِهِم بَيِّنَةُ مَا فِى الصُّحُفِ الْأُولَىٰ ۝ وَلَوْ أَنَّآ أَهْلَكْنَٰهُم بِعَذَابٍ مِّن قَبْلِهِۦ لَقَالُوا رَبَّنَا لَوْلَآ أَرْسَلْتَ إِلَيْنَا رَسُولًا فَنَتَّبِعَ ءَايَٰتِكَ مِن قَبْلِ أَن نَّذِلَّ وَنَخْزَىٰ ۝ قُلْ كُلٌّ مُّتَرَبِّصٌ فَتَرَبَّصُوا ۖ فَسَتَعْلَمُونَ مَنْ أَصْحَٰبُ الصِّرَٰطِ السَّوِىِّ وَمَنِ اهْتَدَىٰ ۝

127. This is how We reward whoever transgresses and does not believe in the revelations of their Lord. And the punishment of the Hereafter is far more severe and more lasting.

Warning to Meccan Pagans

128. Is it not yet clear to them how many peoples We destroyed before them, whose ruins they still pass by? Surely in this are signs for people of sound judgment. 129. Had it not been for a prior decree from your Lord[611] ˹O Prophet˺ and a term already set, their ˹instant˺ doom would have been inevitable.

Advice to the Prophet

130. So be patient ˹O Prophet˺ with what they say. And glorify the praises of your Lord before sunrise and before sunset, and glorify Him in the hours of the night and at both ends of the day,[612] so that you may be pleased ˹with the reward˺. 131. Do not let your eyes crave what We have allowed some of the disbelievers to enjoy; the ˹fleeting˺ splendour of this worldly life, which We test them with. But your Lord's provision ˹in the Hereafter˺ is far better and more lasting. 132. Bid your people to pray, and be diligent in ˹observing˺ it. We do not ask you to provide. It is We Who provide for you. And the ultimate outcome is ˹only˺ for ˹the people of˺ righteousness.

Warning to the Pagans

133. They demand, "If only he could bring us a sign from his Lord!"[613] Have they not ˹already˺ received a confirmation of what is in earlier Scriptures?[614] 134. Had We destroyed them with a torment before this ˹Prophet came˺, they would have surely argued, "Our Lord! If only You had sent us a messenger, we would have followed Your revelations before being humiliated and put to shame." 135. Say ˹to them, O Prophet˺, "Each ˹of us˺ is waiting, so keep waiting! You will soon know who is on the Straight Path and is ˹rightly˺ guided."

---

611 That He will delay their judgment until the Hereafter.
612 This verse refers to the times of the five daily prayers.
613 The pagans of Mecca were not satisfied with a literary miracle in the form of the Quran, so they asked for a tangible miracle (*see* 17:90-91) similar to the staff of Moses.
614 This either refers to the Biblical stories confirmed by the Quran or the prophecies of Muḥammad (ﷺ) in the Bible. Some Muslim scholars cite Deuteronomy 18:15-18 and 33:2, Isaiah 42, and John 14:16 as examples of the description of Prophet Muḥammad (ﷺ) in the Bible. However, Bible scholars interpret these verses differently.

21. The Prophets (Al-Anbiyâ')

In the Name of Allah—the Most Compassionate, Most Merciful

Indifference to Judgment

1. ˹The time of˺ people's judgment has drawn near, yet they are heedlessly turning away. 2. Whatever new reminder comes to them from their Lord, they only listen to it jokingly, 3. with their hearts ˹totally˺ distracted.

Discrediting the Prophet

The evildoers would converse secretly, ˹saying,˺ "Is this ˹one˺ not human like yourselves? Would you fall for ˹this˺ witchcraft, even though you can ˹clearly˺ see?" 4. The Prophet responded, "My Lord ˹fully˺ knows every word spoken in the heavens and the earth. For He is the All-Hearing, All-Knowing." 5. Yet they say, "This ˹Quran˺ is a set of confused dreams! No, he has fabricated it! No, he must be a poet! So let him bring us a ˹tangible˺ sign like those ˹prophets˺ sent before." 6. Not a ˹single˺ society We destroyed before them ever believed ˹after receiving the signs˺. Will these ˹pagans˺ then believe?

Human, Not Angelic Messengers

7. We did not send ˹messengers˺ before you ˹O Prophet˺ except mere men inspired by Us. If you ˹polytheists˺ do not know ˹this already˺, then ask those who have knowledge ˹of the Scriptures˺. 8. We did not give those messengers ˹supernatural˺ bodies that did not need food, nor were they immortal. 9. Then We fulfilled Our promise to them, saving them along with whoever We willed and destroying the transgressors.

Reasoning with Meccan Pagans

10. We have surely revealed to you a Book, in which there is glory for you. Will you not then understand? 11. ˹Imagine˺ how many societies of wrongdoers We have destroyed, raising up other people after them!

12. When the wrongdoers sensed ˹the arrival of˺ Our torment, they started to run away from their cities. **13.** ˹They were told,˺ "Do not run away! Return to your luxuries and your homes, so you may be questioned ˹about your fate˺." **14.** They cried, "Woe to us! We have surely been wrongdoers." **15.** They kept repeating their cry until We mowed them down, ˹leaving them˺ lifeless.[615]

Divine Amusement?

16. We did not create the heavens and the earth and everything in between for sport. **17.** Had We intended to take ˹some˺ amusement, We could have found it in Our presence, if that had been Our Will. **18.** In fact, We hurl the truth against falsehood, leaving it crushed, and it quickly vanishes. And woe be to you for what you claim![616] **19.** To Him belong all those in the heavens and the earth. And those nearest to Him are not too proud to worship Him, nor do they tire. **20.** They glorify ˹Him˺ day and night, never wavering.

False Gods

21. Or have they taken gods from the earth, who can raise the dead? **22.** Had there been other gods besides Allah in the heavens or the earth, both ˹realms˺ would have surely been corrupted. So Glorified is Allah, Lord of the Throne, far above what they claim. **23.** He cannot be questioned about what He does, but they will ˹all˺ be questioned. **24.** Or have they taken other gods besides Him? Say, ˹O Prophet,˺ "Show ˹me˺ your proof. Here is ˹the Quran,˺ the Reminder for those with me; along with ˹earlier Scriptures,˺ the Reminder for those before me."[617] But most of them do not know the truth, so they turn away.

---

615 lit., extinguished like ashes.

616 That Allah has a partner and children.

617 The Prophet (ﷺ) is ordered to challenge the pagans to produce logical and scriptural proofs for the existence of other gods beside Allah. The verses then argue that if there is more than one god, the different gods would have fought among themselves for domination, and the whole universe would have been ruined. The Quran, the Torah, and the Gospel are all in agreement that there is only One God.

325   21. Al-Anbiyâ'

25. We never sent a messenger before you ʿO Prophetʾ without revealing to him: "There is no god ʿworthy of worshipʾ except Me, so worship Me ʿaloneʾ."

A Pagan Claim

26. And they say, "The Most Compassionate has offspring!"[618] Glory be to Him! In fact, those ʿangelsʾ are only ʿHisʾ honoured servants, 27. who do not speak until He has spoken, ʿonlyʾ acting at His command. 28. He ʿfullyʾ knows what is ahead of them and what is behind them. They do not intercede except for whom He approves, and they tremble in awe of Him. 29. Whoever of them were to say, "I am a god besides Him," they would be rewarded with Hell by Us. This is how We reward the wrongdoers.

Miracles in the Universe

30. Do the disbelievers not realize that the heavens and earth were ʿonceʾ one mass then We split them apart?[619] And We created from water every living thing. Will they not then believe? 31. And We have placed firm mountains upon the earth so it does not shake with them, and made in it broad pathways so they may find their way. 32. And We have made the sky a well-protected canopy, still they turn away from its signs.[620] 33. And He is the One Who created the day and the night, the sun and the moon— each travelling in an orbit.

Fleeting World

34. We have not granted immortality to any human before you ʿO Prophetʾ: so if you die, will they live forever? 35. Every soul will taste death. And We test you ʿO humanityʾ with good and evil as a trial, then to Us you will ʿallʾ be returned.

---

618 Some pagans claimed that the angels are Allah's daughters.

619 This probably refers to the event commonly known as the Big Bang.

620 The signs of the heaven include the galaxies, planets, stars, etc., all of which have an orbit. Our planet orbits the sun, the sun orbits the Milky Way Galaxy, and the Milky Way Galaxy orbits the Virgo Supercluster, etc.

21. Al-Anbiyâ' 326

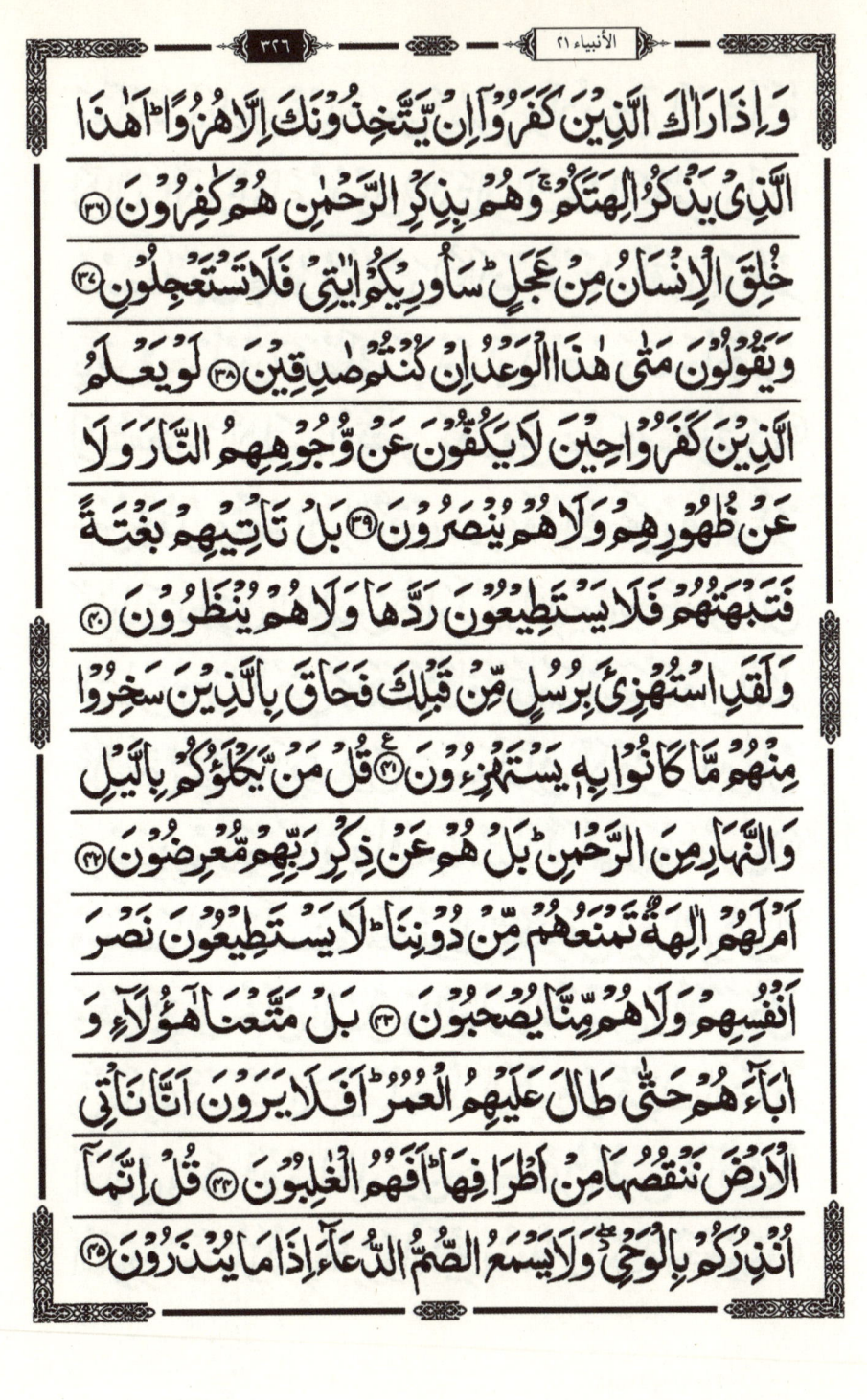

Warning to the Polytheists

36. When the disbelievers see you ˹O Prophet˺, they only make fun of you, ˹saying,˺ "Is this the one who speaks ˹ill˺ of your gods?" while they disbelieve at the mention of the Most Compassionate. **37.** Humankind is made of haste. I will soon show you My signs, so do not ask Me to hasten them. **38.** They ask ˹the believers˺, "When will this threat come to pass if what you say is true?" **39.** If only the disbelievers knew that a time will come when they will not be able to keep the Fire off their faces or backs, nor will they be helped. **40.** In fact, the Hour will take them by surprise, leaving them stunned. So they will not be able to avert it, nor will it be delayed from them. **41.** ˹Other˺ messengers had already been ridiculed before you ˹O Prophet˺, but those who mocked them were overtaken by what they used to ridicule.

Questions to the Pagans

42. Ask ˹them, O Prophet,˺ "Who can defend you by day or by night against the Most Compassionate?" Still they turn away from the remembrance of their Lord. **43.** Or do they have gods—other than Us—that can protect them? They cannot ˹even˺ protect themselves, nor will they be aided against Us. **44.** In fact, We have allowed enjoyment for these ˹Meccans˺ and their forefathers for such a long time ˹that they took it for granted˺. Do they not see that We gradually reduce ˹their˺ land from its borders? Is it they who will then prevail?

Warning of Torment

45. Say, ˹O Prophet,˺ "I warn you only by revelation." But the deaf cannot hear the call when they are warned!

21. Al-Anbiyâ'

46. If they were touched by even a breath of your Lord's torment, they would certainly cry, "Woe to us! We have really been wrongdoers."

Divine Justice

47. We will set up the scales of justice on the Day of Judgment, so no soul will be wronged in the least. And ˹even˺ if a deed is the weight of a mustard seed, We will bring it forth. And sufficient are We as a ˹vigilant˺ Reckoner.

The Torah

48. Indeed, We granted Moses and Aaron the Decisive Authority—a light and a reminder for the righteous, **49.** who are in awe of their Lord without seeing Him,[621] and are fearful of the Hour.

The Quran

50. And this ˹Quran˺ is a blessed reminder which We have revealed. Will you ˹pagans˺ then deny it?

Prophet Abraham

51. And indeed, We had granted Abraham sound judgment early on, for We knew him well ˹to be worthy of it˺. **52.** ˹Remember˺ when he questioned his father and his people, "What are these statues to which you are so devoted?" **53.** They replied, "We found our forefathers worshipping them." **54.** He responded, "Indeed, you and your forefathers have been clearly astray." **55.** They asked, "Have you come to us with the truth, or is this a joke?" **56.** He replied, "In fact, your Lord is the Lord of the heavens and the earth, Who created them ˹both˺. And to that I bear witness." **57.** ˹Then he said to himself,˺ "By Allah! I will surely plot against your idols after you have turned your backs and gone away."

---

621 This can also mean that they are in awe of their Lord as much in private as they are in public.

21. Al-Anbiyâ'

بِسْمِ اللّٰهِ الرَّحْمٰنِ الرَّحِيْمِ

فَجَعَلَهُمْ جُذٰذًا اِلَّا كَبِيْرًا لَّهُمْ لَعَلَّهُمْ اِلَيْهِ يَرْجِعُوْنَ ۝

قَالُوْا مَنْ فَعَلَ هٰذَا بِاٰلِهَتِنَا اِنَّهٗ لَمِنَ الظّٰلِمِيْنَ ۝ قَالُوْا

سَمِعْنَا فَتًى يَّذْكُرُهُمْ يُقَالُ لَهٗۤ اِبْرٰهِيْمُ ۝ قَالُوْا

فَاْتُوْا بِهٖ عَلٰۤى اَعْيُنِ النَّاسِ لَعَلَّهُمْ يَشْهَدُوْنَ ۝ قَالُوْۤا

ءَاَنْتَ فَعَلْتَ هٰذَا بِاٰلِهَتِنَا يٰۤاِبْرٰهِيْمُ ۝ قَالَ بَلْ فَعَلَهٗ

كَبِيْرُهُمْ هٰذَا فَسْـَٔلُوْهُمْ اِنْ كَانُوْا يَنْطِقُوْنَ ۝ فَرَجَعُوْۤا اِلٰۤى

اَنْفُسِهِمْ فَقَالُوْۤا اِنَّكُمْ اَنْتُمُ الظّٰلِمُوْنَ ۝ ثُمَّ نُكِسُوْا عَلٰى

رُءُوْسِهِمْ لَقَدْ عَلِمْتَ مَا هٰۤؤُلَاۤءِ يَنْطِقُوْنَ ۝ قَالَ اَفَتَعْبُدُوْنَ

مِنْ دُوْنِ اللّٰهِ مَا لَا يَنْفَعُكُمْ شَيْـًٔا وَّلَا يَضُرُّكُمْ ۝ اُفٍّ

لَّكُمْ وَلِمَا تَعْبُدُوْنَ مِنْ دُوْنِ اللّٰهِ اَفَلَا تَعْقِلُوْنَ ۝

قَالُوْا حَرِّقُوْهُ وَانْصُرُوْۤا اٰلِهَتَكُمْ اِنْ كُنْتُمْ فٰعِلِيْنَ ۝

قُلْنَا يٰنَارُ كُوْنِيْ بَرْدًا وَّسَلٰمًا عَلٰۤى اِبْرٰهِيْمَ ۝ وَاَرَادُوْا

بِهٖ كَيْدًا فَجَعَلْنٰهُمُ الْاَخْسَرِيْنَ ۝ وَنَجَّيْنٰهُ وَلُوْطًا

اِلَى الْاَرْضِ الَّتِيْ بٰرَكْنَا فِيْهَا لِلْعٰلَمِيْنَ ۝ وَوَهَبْنَا لَهٗۤ

اِسْحٰقَ ۗ وَيَعْقُوْبَ نَافِلَةً ۗ وَكُلًّا جَعَلْنَا صٰلِحِيْنَ ۝

---

58. So he smashed them into pieces, except the biggest of them, so they might turn to it ˹for answers˺.

His People's Reaction

59. They protested, "Who dared do this to our gods? It must be an evil-doer!" **60.** Some said, "We heard a young man, called Abraham, speaking ˹ill˺ of them." **61.** They demanded, "Bring him before the eyes of the people, so that they may witness ˹his trial˺." **62.** They asked, "Was it you who did this to our gods, O Abraham?" **63.** He replied ˹sarcastically˺, "No, this one—the biggest of them—did it! So ask them, if they can talk!" **64.** So they came back to their senses, saying ˹to one another˺, "You yourselves are truly the wrong-doers!" **65.** Then they ˹quickly˺ regressed to their ˹original˺ mind-set, ˹arguing,˺ "You already know that those ˹idols˺ cannot talk." **66.** He rebuked ˹them˺, "Do you then worship—instead of Allah—what can neither benefit nor harm you in any way? **67.** Shame on you and whatever you worship instead of Allah! Do you not have any sense?" **68.** They concluded, "Burn him up to avenge your gods, if you must act."

Abraham Prevails

69. We ordered, "O fire! Be cool and safe for Abraham!"[622] **70.** They had sought to harm him, but We made them the worst losers. **71.** Then We delivered him, along with Lot, to the land We had showered with blessings for all people.[623] **72.** And We blessed him with Isaac ˹as a son˺ and Jacob ˹as a grandson˺, as an additional favour—making all of them righteous.

---

622 It is reported in a *ḥadîth* collected by Bukhâri that Abraham (۞) said, while being thrown into the fire, "Allah ˹alone˺ is sufficient ˹as an aid˺ for us and ˹He˺ is the best Protector."
623 Abraham and his nephew, Lot, migrated from Babel, Iraq to Jerusalem.

329 21. Al-Anbiyâ'

73. We ˹also˺ made them leaders, guiding by Our command, and inspired them to do good deeds, establish prayer, and pay alms-tax. And they were devoted to Our worship.

Prophet Lot

74. And to Lot We gave wisdom and knowledge, and delivered him from the society engrossed in shameful practices. They were certainly an evil, rebellious people. 75. And We admitted him into Our mercy, ˹for˺ he was truly one of the righteous.

Prophet Noah

76. And ˹remember˺ when Noah had cried out to Us earlier, so We responded to him and delivered him and his family[624] from the great distress. 77. And We made him prevail over those who had rejected Our signs. They were truly an evil people, so We drowned them all.

Prophet David and Prophet Solomon

78. And ˹remember˺ when David and Solomon passed judgment regarding the crops ruined ˹at night˺ by someone's sheep, and We were witness to their judgments. 79. We guided ˹young˺ Solomon to a fairer settlement,[625] and granted each of them wisdom and knowledge. We subjected the mountains as well as the birds to hymn ˹Our praises˺ along with David. It is We Who did ˹it all˺. 80. We taught him the art of making body armour to protect you in battle. Will you then be grateful? 81. And to Solomon We subjected the raging winds, blowing by his command to the land We had showered with blessings. It is We Who know everything.

---

624 i.e., the believers in his family.

625 A man's flock of sheep strayed into another man's vineyard, eating and destroying all his produce. When the two men came to David for judgment, he ruled that the shepherd must give his animals to the vineyard owner in compensation for the damage. On their way out, the two men met young Solomon and the shepherd complained to him. Solomon discussed the case with his father, and suggested that the sheep should be kept with the man who lost his produce so he may benefit from their milk and wool, while the shepherd worked on the farm to restore it to its original state. Eventually the farmer would take back his farm in perfect condition, and the sheep would be returned to the shepherd. David was impressed by his son's insight and approved his fair judgment immediately.

21. Al-Anbiyâ'

وَمِنَ الشَّيَـٰطِينِ مَن يَغُوصُونَ لَهُۥ وَيَعْمَلُونَ عَمَلًا دُونَ ذَٰلِكَ ۖ وَكُنَّا لَهُمْ حَـٰفِظِينَ ۞ وَأَيُّوبَ إِذْ نَادَىٰ رَبَّهُۥٓ أَنِّى مَسَّنِىَ الضُّرُّ وَأَنتَ أَرْحَمُ الرَّٰحِمِينَ ۞ فَٱسْتَجَبْنَا لَهُۥ فَكَشَفْنَا مَا بِهِۦ مِن ضُرٍّ ۖ وَءَاتَيْنَـٰهُ أَهْلَهُۥ وَمِثْلَهُم مَّعَهُمْ رَحْمَةً مِّنْ عِندِنَا وَذِكْرَىٰ لِلْعَـٰبِدِينَ ۞ وَإِسْمَـٰعِيلَ وَإِدْرِيسَ وَذَا ٱلْكِفْلِ ۖ كُلٌّ مِّنَ ٱلصَّـٰبِرِينَ ۞ وَأَدْخَلْنَـٰهُمْ فِى رَحْمَتِنَآ ۖ إِنَّهُم مِّنَ ٱلصَّـٰلِحِينَ ۞ وَذَا ٱلنُّونِ إِذ ذَّهَبَ مُغَـٰضِبًا فَظَنَّ أَن لَّن نَّقْدِرَ عَلَيْهِ فَنَادَىٰ فِى ٱلظُّلُمَـٰتِ أَن لَّآ إِلَـٰهَ إِلَّآ أَنتَ سُبْحَـٰنَكَ إِنِّى كُنتُ مِنَ ٱلظَّـٰلِمِينَ ۞ فَٱسْتَجَبْنَا لَهُۥ وَنَجَّيْنَـٰهُ مِنَ ٱلْغَمِّ ۚ وَكَذَٰلِكَ نُـۨجِى ٱلْمُؤْمِنِينَ ۞ وَزَكَرِيَّآ إِذْ نَادَىٰ رَبَّهُۥ رَبِّ لَا تَذَرْنِى فَرْدًا وَأَنتَ خَيْرُ ٱلْوَٰرِثِينَ ۞ فَٱسْتَجَبْنَا لَهُۥ وَوَهَبْنَا لَهُۥ يَحْيَىٰ وَأَصْلَحْنَا لَهُۥ زَوْجَهُۥٓ ۚ إِنَّهُمْ كَانُوا۟ يُسَـٰرِعُونَ فِى ٱلْخَيْرَٰتِ وَيَدْعُونَنَا رَغَبًا وَرَهَبًا ۖ وَكَانُوا۟ لَنَا خَـٰشِعِينَ ۞

82. And ˹We subjected˺ some jinn[626] that dived for him,[627] and performed other duties. It is We Who kept them in check.

Prophet Job

83. And ˹remember˺ when Job cried out to his Lord, "I have been touched with adversity,[628] and You are the Most Merciful of the merciful." 84. So We answered his prayer and removed his adversity, and gave him back his family, twice as many, as a mercy from Us and a lesson for the ˹devoted˺ worshippers.

More Prophets

85. And ˹remember˺ Ishmael, Enoch, and Zul-Kifl.[629] They were all steadfast. 86. We admitted them into Our mercy, for they were truly of the righteous.

Prophet Jonah

87. And ˹remember˺ when the Man of the Whale stormed off ˹from his city˺ in a rage, thinking We would not restrain him.[630] Then in the ˹veils of˺ darkness[631] he cried out, "There is no god ˹worthy of worship˺ except You. Glory be to You! I have certainly done wrong." 88. So We answered his prayer and rescued him from anguish. And so do We save the ˹true˺ believers.

Prophet Zachariah

89. And ˹remember˺ when Zachariah cried out to his Lord, "My Lord! Do not leave me childless, though You are the Best of Successors."[632] 90. So We answered his prayer, granted him John, and made his wife fertile. Indeed, they used to race in doing good, and call upon Us with hope and fear, totally humbling themselves before Us.

---

626 lit., devils.
627 The jinn dived to bring him pearls.
628 This refers to his loss of health, wealth, and children.
629 Scholars are in disagreement as to whether Zul-Kifl was a prophet or just a righteous man. Those who maintain that he was a prophet identify him with various Biblical prophets such as Ezekiel, Isaiah, and Obadiah.
630 Or "thinking We will let him get away with it." Jonah (عليه السلام) had been met with denial for many years. When he sensed the coming of Allah's torment, he abandoned his city without Allah's permission. Eventually, his people repented before the coming of the torment, and Allah accepted their repentance (see 10:98), whereas Jonah ended up in the belly of the whale (see 37:140-148).
631 The darkness of the night, the sea, and the belly of the whale.
632 Meaning, "You will be there for eternity after all pass away."

21. Al-Anbiyâ'

Prophet Jesus and His Mother

91. And ˹remember˺ the one who guarded her chastity, so We breathed into her through Our angel, ˹Gabriel,˺[633] making her and her son a sign for all peoples.

One Way

92. ˹O prophets!˺ Indeed, this religion of yours is ˹only˺ one, and I am your Lord, so worship Me ˹alone˺. **93.** Yet the people have divided it into sects. But to Us they will all return. **94.** So whoever does good and is a believer will never be denied ˹the reward for˺ their striving, for We are recording it all.

The People of Hell

95. It is impossible for a society which We have destroyed to ever rise again, **96.** until ˹after˺ Gog and Magog have broken loose ˹from the barrier˺, swarming down from every hill,[634] **97.** ushering in the True Promise.[635]   Then—behold!—the disbelievers will stare ˹in horror, crying,˺ "Oh, woe to us! We have truly been heedless of this. In fact, we have been wrongdoers." **98.** Certainly you ˹disbelievers˺ and whatever you worship instead of Allah will be the fuel of Hell.[636] You are ˹all˺ bound to enter it. **99.** Had those idols been ˹true˺ gods, they would not have entered it. And they will be there forever. **100.** In it they will groan, and will not be able to hear.

The People of Paradise

101. Surely those for whom We have destined the finest reward will be kept far away from Hell, **102.** not even hearing the slightest hissing from it. And they will delight forever in what their souls desire.

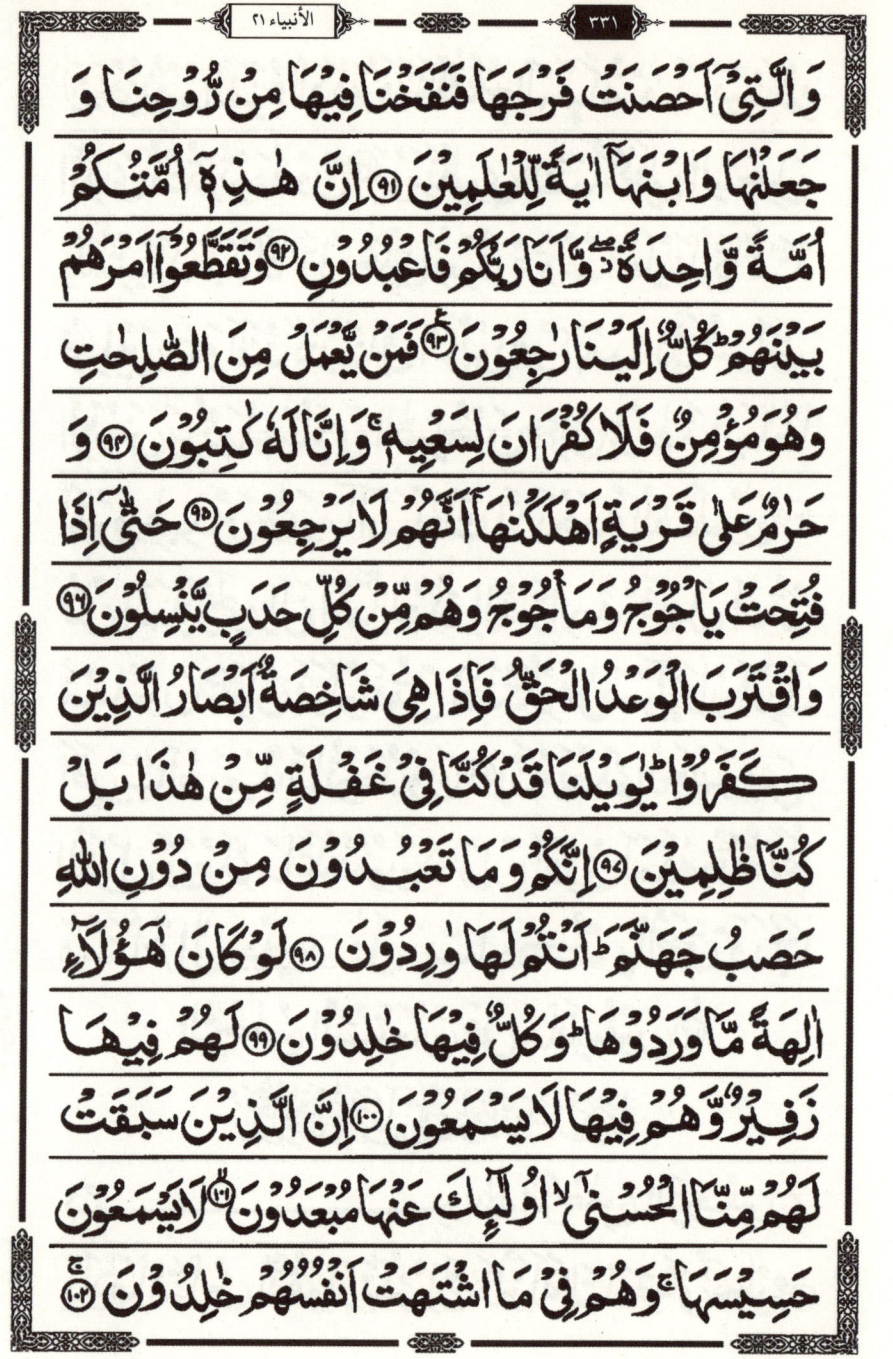

---

633 Gabriel breathed into the sleeves of Mary's garment so she conceived Jesus.
634 *See* 18:93-99.
635 i.e., the Final Hour.
636 *See* footnote for 43:57-58.

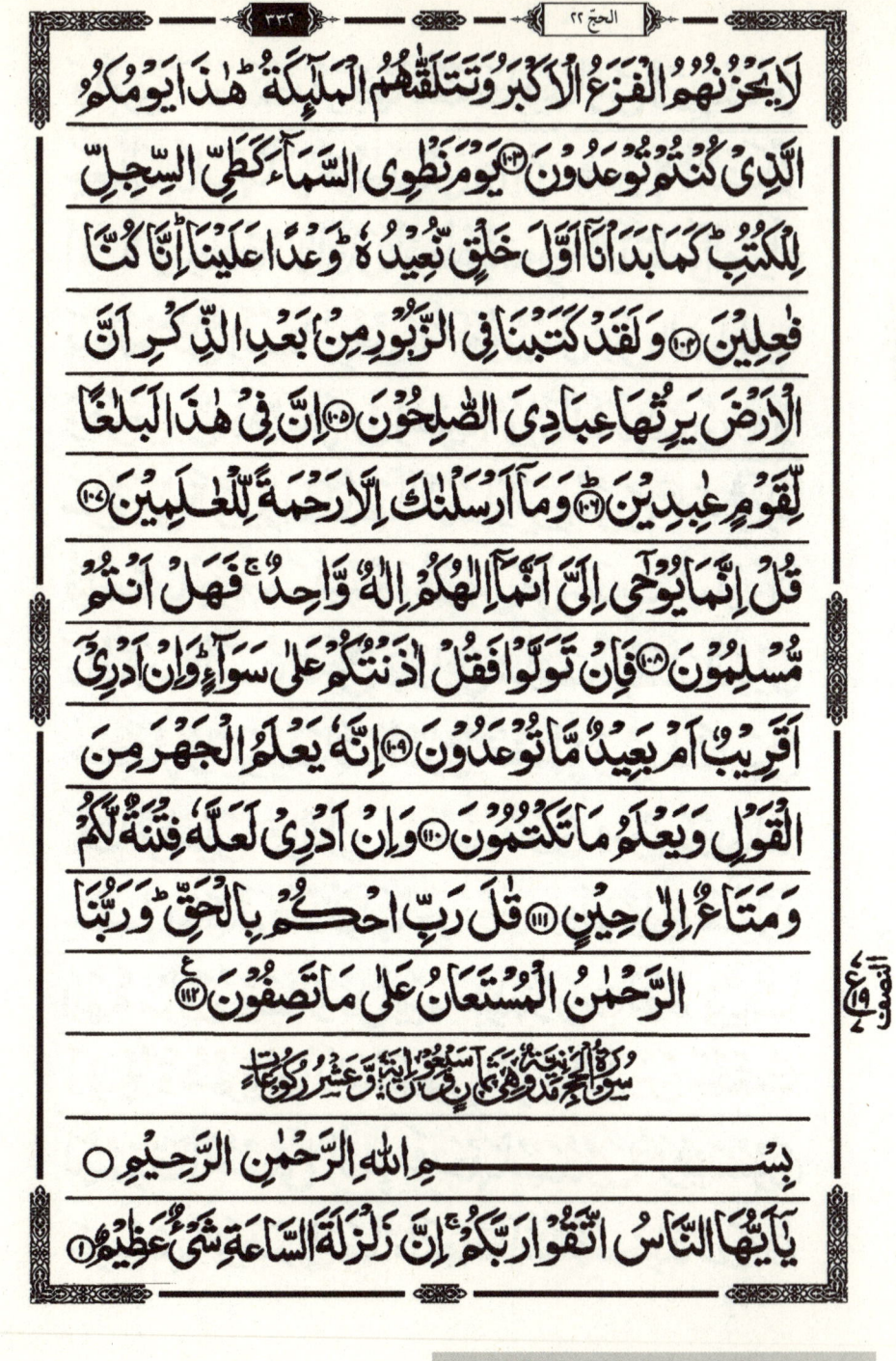

103. The Supreme Horror ˹of that Day˺ will not disturb them, and the angels will greet them, ˹saying,˺ "This is your Day, which you have been promised." **104.** On that Day We will roll up the heavens like a scroll of writings. Just as We produced the first creation, ˹so˺ shall We reproduce it. That is a promise binding on Us. We truly uphold ˹Our promises˺! **105.** Surely, following the ˹heavenly˺ Record, We decreed in the Scriptures: "My righteous servants shall inherit the land."[637]

Advice for the Prophet

106. Surely this ˹Quran˺ is sufficient ˹as a reminder˺ for those devoted to worship. **107.** We have sent you ˹O Prophet˺ only as a mercy for the whole world. **108.** Say, "What has been revealed to me is this: 'Your God is only One God.' Will you then submit?" **109.** If they turn away, then say, "I have warned you all equally. I do not know if what you are threatened with is near or far. **110.** Allah surely knows what you say openly and whatever you hide. **111.** I do not know if this ˹delay˺ is possibly a test for you and an enjoyment for a while." **112.** ˹In the end,˺ the Prophet said, "My Lord! Judge ˹between us˺ in truth. And our Lord is the Most Compassionate, Whose help is sought against what you claim."[638]

৽৽৽ ❈ ৽৽৽

---

22. The Pilgrimage (Al-Ḥajj)

In the Name of Allah—the Most Compassionate, Most Merciful

The Horror of Judgment Day

1. O humanity! Fear your Lord, for the ˹violent˺ quaking at the Hour is surely a dreadful thing.

---

637 This refers to Psalm 37:29: "The righteous shall inherit the land." *See* footnote for 39:47.
638 Meaning, "We seek Allah's help against your claims that He has partners ˹in worship˺."

2. The Day you see it, every nursing mother will abandon what she is nursing, and every pregnant woman will deliver her burden ˹prematurely˺. And you will see people ˹as if they were˺ drunk, though they will not be drunk; but the torment of Allah is ˹terribly˺ severe.

Denying Allah's Might

3. ˹Still˺ there are some who dispute about Allah without knowledge, and follow every rebellious devil. **4.** It has been decreed for such devils that whoever takes them as a guide will be misguided and led by them into the torment of the Blaze.

Allah's Power to Create

5. O humanity! If you are in doubt about the Resurrection, then ˹know that˺ We did create you[639] from dust, then from a sperm-drop,[640] then ˹developed you into˺ a clinging clot ˹of blood˺,[641] then a lump of flesh[642]—fully formed or unformed[643]—in order to demonstrate ˹Our power˺ to you. ˹Then˺ We settle whatever ˹embryo˺ We will in the womb for an appointed term, then bring you forth as infants, so that you may reach your prime. Some of you ˹may˺ die ˹young˺, while others are left to reach the most feeble stage of life so that they may know nothing after having known much. And you see the earth lifeless, but as soon as We send down rain upon it, it begins to stir ˹to life˺ and swell, producing every type of pleasant plant. **6.** That is because Allah ˹alone˺ is the Truth, He ˹alone˺ gives life to the dead, and He ˹alone˺ is Most Capable of everything.

---

639 Your father, Adam.
640 *Nuṭfah* refers to the union of male and female gametes (sperm and egg) which results in the zygote after fertilization.
641 *'Alaqah*, meaning the embryo resembles a leech.
642 *Muḍghah*, meaning it resembles a chewed morsel.
643 Fully formed or defected, evolving into a healthy embryo or ending in miscarriage.

22. Al-Ḥajj

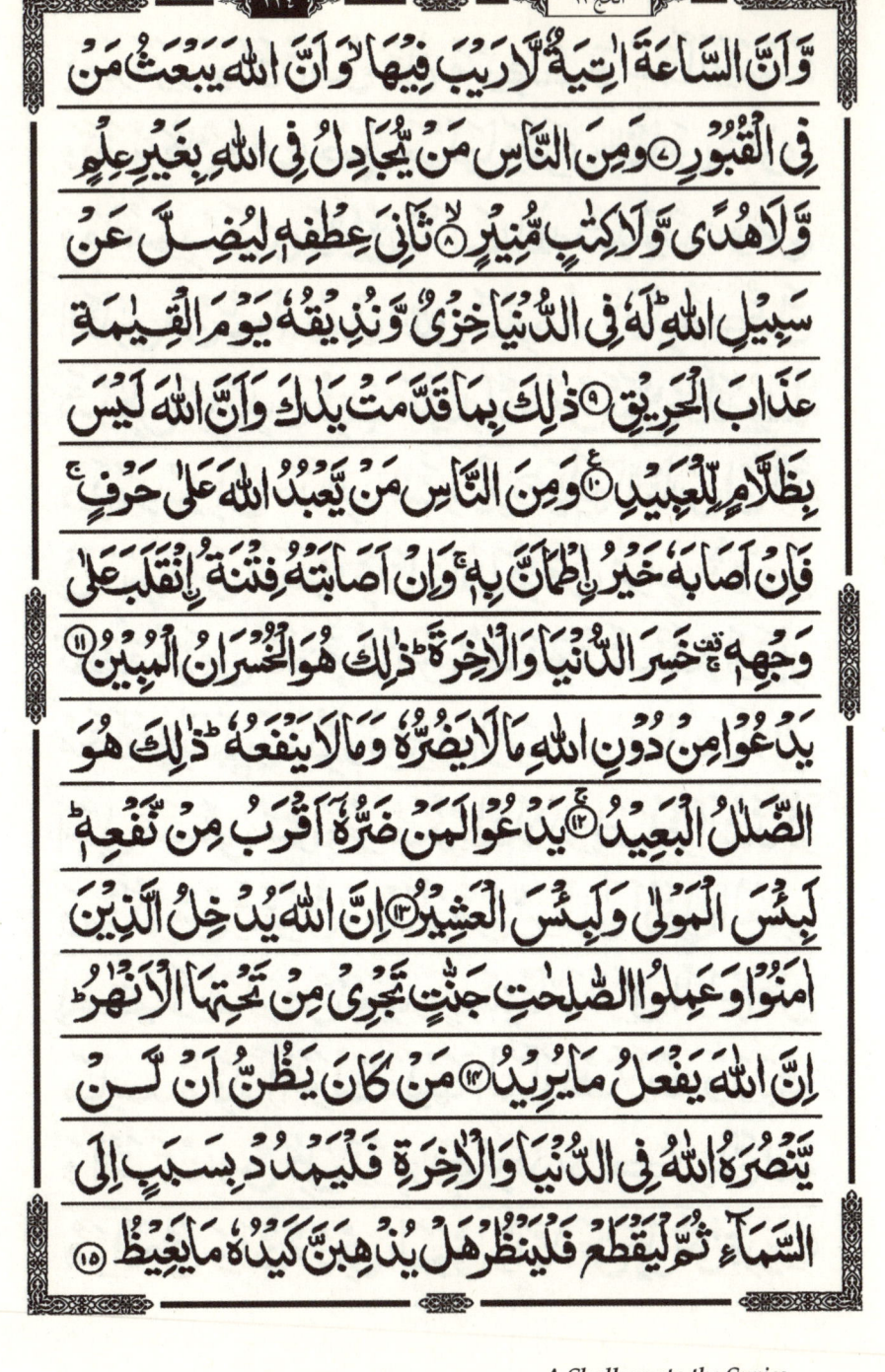

7. And certainly the Hour is coming, there is no doubt about it. And Allah will surely resurrect those in the graves.

Punishment of the Wicked

8. ˹Still˺ there are some who dispute about Allah without knowledge, guidance, or an enlightening scripture, 9. turning away ˹in pride˺ to lead ˹others˺ astray from Allah's Way. They will suffer disgrace in this world, and on the Day of Judgment We will make them taste the torment of burning. 10. ˹They will be told,˺ "This is ˹the reward˺ for what your hands have done. And Allah is never unjust to ˹His˺ creation."

Half-Hearted Worship

11. And there are some who worship Allah on the verge ˹of faith˺: if they are blessed with something good, they are content with it; but if they are afflicted with a trial, they relapse ˹into disbelief˺,[644] losing this world and the Hereafter. That is ˹truly˺ the clearest loss. 12. They call besides Allah what can neither harm nor benefit them. That is ˹truly˺ the farthest one can stray. 13. They invoke those whose worship leads to harm, not benefit. What an evil patron and what an evil associate!

Reward of True Believers

14. Indeed, Allah will admit those who believe and do good into Gardens, under which rivers flow. Surely Allah does what He wills.

A Challenge to the Cynics

15. Whoever thinks that Allah will not help His Prophet in this world and the Hereafter, let them stretch out a rope to the ceiling and strangle themselves, then let them see if this plan will do away with ˹the cause of˺ their rage.[645]

---

644 lit., they tumble on their faces.
645 Meaning, no matter what the deniers do, Allah will never stop supporting His Prophet (ﷺ).

The Sole Guide and Judge

16. And so We revealed this ˹Quran˺ as clear verses. And Allah certainly guides whoever He wills. 17. Indeed, the believers, Jews, Sabians,[646] Christians, Magi,[647] and the polytheists—Allah will judge between them ˹all˺ on Judgment Day. Surely Allah is a Witness over all things.

Submission to the Almighty

18. Do you not see that to Allah bow down ˹in submission˺[648] all those in the heavens and all those in the earth, as well as the sun, the moon, the stars, the mountains, the trees, and ˹all˺ living beings, as well as many humans, while many are deserving of punishment. And whoever Allah disgraces, none can honour. Surely Allah does what He wills.

The Believers and Disbelievers

19. These are two opposing groups that disagree about their Lord: as for the disbelievers, garments of Fire will be cut out for them and boiling water will be poured over their heads, 20. melting whatever is in their bellies, along with their skin. 21. And awaiting them are maces of iron. 22. Whenever they try to escape from Hell—out of anguish—they will be forced back into it, ˹and will be told,˺ "Taste the torment of burning!" 23. ˹But˺ Allah will surely admit those who believe and do good into Gardens, under which rivers flow, where they will be adorned with bracelets of gold and pearls, and their clothing will be silk,

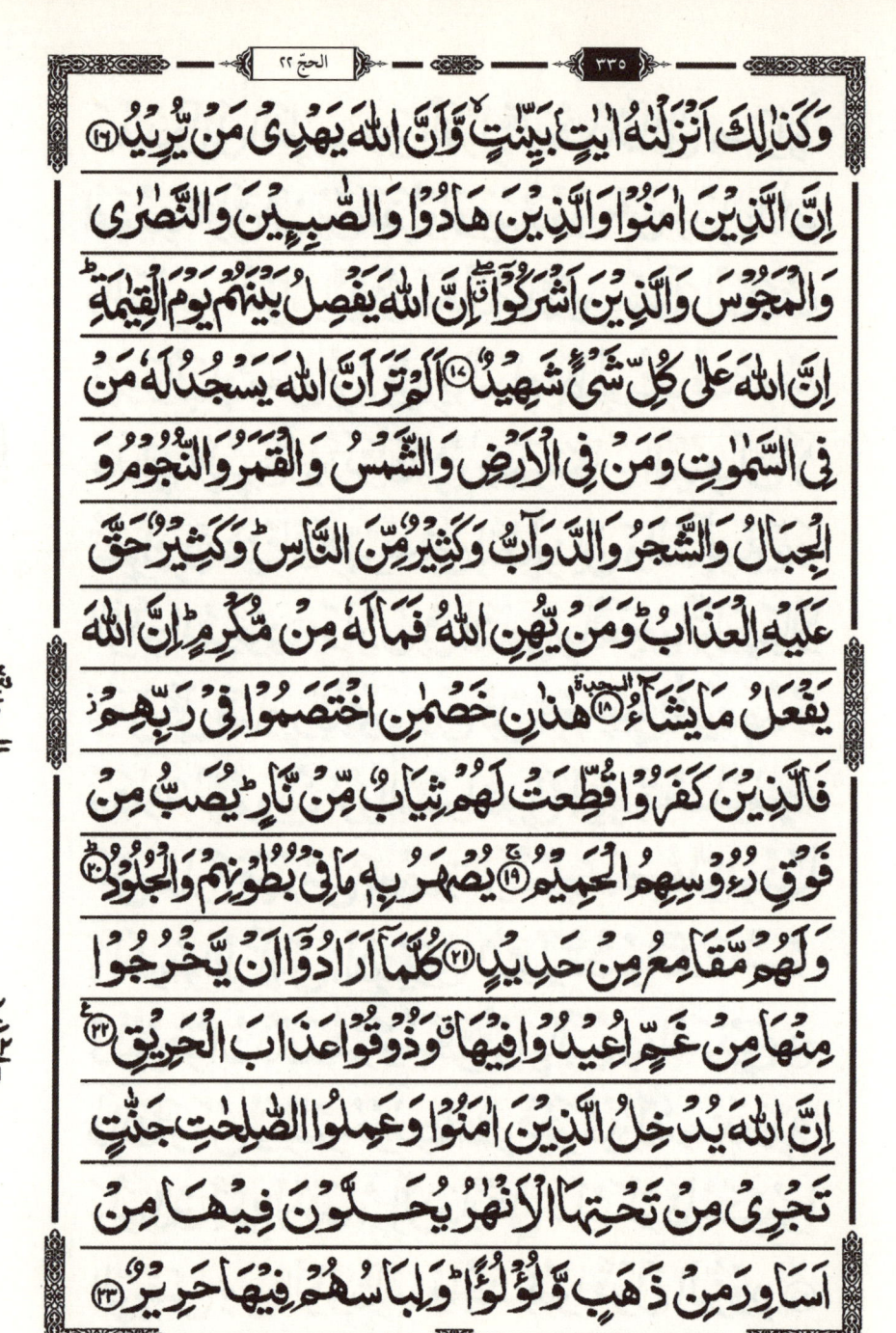

---

646 See footnote for 2:62.
647 Magi (singular: magus): Zoroastrians; fire-worshippers.
648 lit., prostrate. Meaning, all beings submit to His Will.

22. Al-Ḥajj

وَهُدُوٓاْ إِلَى ٱلطَّيِّبِ مِنَ ٱلْقَوْلِ وَهُدُوٓاْ إِلَىٰ صِرَٰطِ ٱلْحَمِيدِ ٢٤ إِنَّ ٱلَّذِينَ كَفَرُواْ وَيَصُدُّونَ عَن سَبِيلِ ٱللَّهِ وَٱلْمَسْجِدِ ٱلْحَرَامِ ٱلَّذِى جَعَلْنَٰهُ لِلنَّاسِ سَوَآءً ٱلْعَٰكِفُ فِيهِ وَٱلْبَادِ وَمَن يُرِدْ فِيهِ بِإِلْحَادٍ بِظُلْمٍ نُّذِقْهُ مِنْ عَذَابٍ أَلِيمٍ ٢٥ وَإِذْ بَوَّأْنَا لِإِبْرَٰهِيمَ مَكَانَ ٱلْبَيْتِ أَن لَّا تُشْرِكْ بِى شَيْـًٔا وَطَهِّرْ بَيْتِىَ لِلطَّآئِفِينَ وَٱلْقَآئِمِينَ وَٱلرُّكَّعِ ٱلسُّجُودِ ٢٦ وَأَذِّن فِى ٱلنَّاسِ بِٱلْحَجِّ يَأْتُوكَ رِجَالًا وَعَلَىٰ كُلِّ ضَامِرٍ يَأْتِينَ مِن كُلِّ فَجٍّ عَمِيقٍ ٢٧ لِّيَشْهَدُواْ مَنَٰفِعَ لَهُمْ وَيَذْكُرُواْ ٱسْمَ ٱللَّهِ فِىٓ أَيَّامٍ مَّعْلُومَٰتٍ عَلَىٰ مَا رَزَقَهُم مِّنۢ بَهِيمَةِ ٱلْأَنْعَٰمِ فَكُلُواْ مِنْهَا وَأَطْعِمُواْ ٱلْبَآئِسَ ٱلْفَقِيرَ ٢٨ ثُمَّ لْيَقْضُواْ تَفَثَهُمْ وَلْيُوفُواْ نُذُورَهُمْ وَلْيَطَّوَّفُواْ بِٱلْبَيْتِ ٱلْعَتِيقِ ٢٩ ذَٰلِكَ وَمَن يُعَظِّمْ حُرُمَٰتِ ٱللَّهِ فَهُوَ خَيْرٌ لَّهُۥ عِندَ رَبِّهِۦ وَأُحِلَّتْ لَكُمُ ٱلْأَنْعَٰمُ إِلَّا مَا يُتْلَىٰ عَلَيْكُمْ فَٱجْتَنِبُواْ ٱلرِّجْسَ مِنَ ٱلْأَوْثَٰنِ وَٱجْتَنِبُواْ قَوْلَ ٱلزُّورِ ٣٠

24. for they have been guided to the best of speech, and they have been guided to the Commendable Path.[649]

Violating the Sacred Mosque[650]

25. Indeed, those who persist in disbelief and hinder ʿothersʾ from the Way of Allah and from the Sacred Mosque[651]—which We have appointed for all people, residents and visitors alike—along with whoever intends to deviate by doing wrong in it,[652] We will cause them to taste a painful punishment.

The Pilgrimage

26. And ʿrememberʾ when We assigned to Abraham the site of the House, ʿsaying,ʾ "Do not associate anything with Me ʿin worshipʾ and purify My House for those who circle ʿthe Kaʾbahʾ, stand ʿin prayerʾ, and bow and prostrate themselves. **27.** Call ʿallʾ people to the pilgrimage.[653] They will come to you on foot and on every lean camel from every distant path, **28.** so they may obtain the benefits ʿin storeʾ for them,[654] and pronounce the Name of Allah on appointed days over the sacrificial animals He has provided for them. So eat from their meat and feed the desperately poor. **29.** Then let them groom themselves,[655] fulfil their vows, and circle the Ancient House.

Total Devotion to Allah

30. That is so. And whoever honours the rituals of Allah, it is best for them in the sight of their Lord. The ʿmeat ofʾ cattle has been made lawful for you, except what has ʿalready' been recited to you.[656] So shun the impurity of idolatry, and shun words of falsehood.

---

649 Another possible translation: "… and they have been guided to the Path of the Praiseworthy ʿAllahʾ."

650 This was revealed after the pagans of Mecca had refused to let the Prophet (ﷺ) and his companions proceed to the Sacred Mosque to perform the minor pilgrimage (ʿumrah), although they came all the way from Medina. Eventually, an agreement was made, stipulating that the Muslims return to Medina and come back the following year for ʿumrah.

651 The Sacred Mosque is in Mecca.

652 Generally, intending to do wrong does not necessitate a punishment, unless the person acts upon it. But the Sacred Mosque is unique in that intending to sin in it is sufficient to bring punishment from Allah, unless the person repents.

653 According to Ibn Kathîr, Abraham (ﷺ) said to Allah, "But my voice cannot reach all peoples." Allah responded, "You make the call, and We will deliver the invitation to all."

654 Spiritual benefits such as prayers, pilgrimage, and forgiveness of sins, as well as worldly benefits such as meeting Muslims from everywhere and trading.

655 Shaving their hair, clipping nails, and taking a shower.

656 See 5:3.

31. Be upright ˹in devotion˺ to Allah, associating none with Him ˹in worship˺. For whoever associates ˹others˺ with Allah is like someone who has fallen from the sky and is either snatched away by birds or swept by the wind to a remote place. **32.** That is so. And whoever honours the symbols of Allah, it is certainly out of the piety of the heart. **33.** You may benefit from sacrificial animals for an appointed term,[657] then their place of sacrifice is at the Ancient House.

Good News for the Humble

34. For every community We appointed a rite of sacrifice so that they may pronounce the Name of Allah over the sacrificial animals He has provided for them. For your God is only One God, so submit yourselves to Him ˹alone˺. And give good news ˹O Prophet˺ to the humble: **35.** those whose hearts tremble at the remembrance of Allah, who patiently endure whatever may befall them, and who establish prayer and donate from what We have provided for them.

Purpose of Sacrificial Animals

36. We have made sacrificial camels ˹and cattle˺ among the symbols of Allah, in which there is ˹much˺ good for you. So pronounce the Name of Allah over them when they are lined up ˹for sacrifice˺. Once they have fallen ˹lifeless˺ on their sides, you may eat from their meat, and feed the needy—those who do not beg, and those who do. In this way We have subjected these ˹animals˺ to you so that you may be grateful. **37.** Neither their meat nor blood reaches Allah. Rather, it is your piety that reaches Him. This is how He has subjected them to you so that you may proclaim the greatness of Allah for what He has guided you to, and give good news to the good-doers.

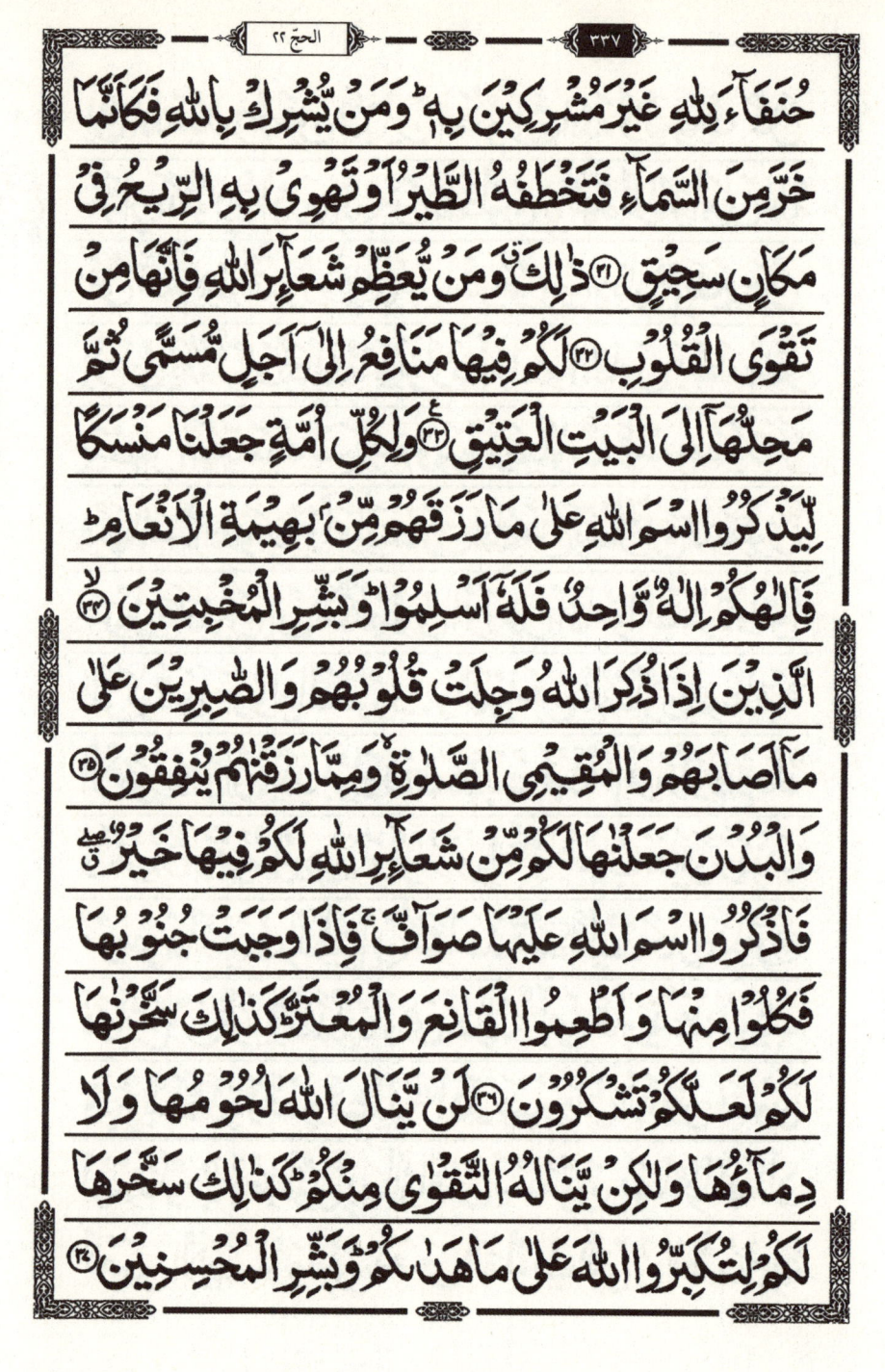

---

657 Milking or riding them until the time for sacrifice.

22. Al-Ḥajj

Permission to Fight in Self-Defence

38. Indeed, Allah defends those who believe. Surely Allah does not like whoever is deceitful, ungrateful. **39.** Permission ˹to fight back˺ is ˹hereby˺ granted to those being fought, for they have been wronged.[658] And Allah is truly Most Capable of helping them ˹prevail˺. **40.** ˹They are˺ those who have been expelled from their homes for no reason other than proclaiming: "Our Lord is Allah." Had Allah not repelled ˹the aggression of˺ some people by means of others, destruction would have surely claimed monasteries, churches, synagogues, and mosques in which Allah's Name is often mentioned. Allah will certainly help those who stand up for Him. Allah is truly All-Powerful, Almighty. **41.** ˹They are˺ those who, if established in the land by Us, would perform prayer, pay alms-tax, encourage what is good, and forbid what is evil. And with Allah rests the outcome of all affairs.

Warning to Meccan Pagans

42. If they deny you ˹O Prophet˺, so did the people of Noah before them, as well as ˹the tribes of˺ 'Âd and Thamûd, **43.** the people of Abraham, the people of Lot, **44.** and the residents of Midian. And Moses was denied ˹too˺. But I delayed ˹the fate of˺ the disbelievers ˹until their appointed time˺ then seized them. And how severe was My response! **45.** Many are the societies We have destroyed for persisting in wrongdoing, leaving them in total ruin. ˹Many are˺ also the abandoned wells and lofty palaces! **46.** Have they not travelled throughout the land so their hearts may reason, and their ears may listen? Indeed, it is not the eyes that are blind, but it is the hearts in the chests that grow blind.

---

658 For over thirteen years, Muslims had not been allowed to fight back against the brutality of the Meccan pagans, leading to the emigration of the Prophet and many of his companions to Medina. As the hostilities continued, this verse was later revealed allowing Muslims to fight back in self-defence.

22. Al-Ḥajj

47. They challenge you ˹O Prophet˺ to hasten the torment. And Allah will never fail in His promise. But a day with your Lord is indeed like a thousand years by your counting. **48.** Many are the societies whose end We delayed while they did wrong, then seized them. And to Me is the final return.

The Prophet's Duty

49. Say, ˹O Prophet,˺ "O humanity! I am only sent to you with a clear warning. **50.** So those who believe and do good will have forgiveness and an honourable provision. **51.** But those who strive to discredit Our revelations, they will be the residents of the Hellfire."

Satan's Influence

52. Whenever We sent a messenger or a prophet before you ˹O Prophet˺ and he recited ˹Our revelations˺, Satan would influence ˹people's understanding of˺ his recitation. But ˹eventually˺ Allah would eliminate Satan's influence. Then Allah would ˹firmly˺ establish His revelations. And Allah is All-Knowing, All-Wise. **53.** All that so He may make Satan's influence a trial for those ˹hypocrites˺ whose hearts are sick and those ˹disbelievers˺ whose hearts are hardened. Surely the wrongdoers are totally engrossed in opposition. **54.** ˹This is˺ also so that those gifted with knowledge would know that this ˹revelation˺ is the truth from your Lord, so they have faith in it, and so their hearts would submit humbly to it. And Allah surely guides the believers to the Straight Path. **55.** Yet the disbelievers will persist in doubt about this ˹revelation˺ until the Hour takes them by surprise, or the torment of a terminating[659] Day comes to them.

---

659 The Day ˹of Judgment˺ is described as *'aqîm* (lit., barren) because it will terminate all forms of life on earth and no new day will be born.

22. Al-Ḥajj

Justice on Judgment Day

56. All authority on that Day is for Allah ˹alone˺.[660] He will judge between them. So those who believe and do good will be in the Gardens of Bliss. **57.** But those who disbelieve and deny Our revelations, it is they who will suffer a humiliating punishment. **58.** As for those who emigrate in the cause of Allah and then are martyred or die, Allah will indeed grant them a good provision. Surely Allah is the Best Provider. **59.** He will certainly admit them into a place they will be pleased with. For Allah is truly All-Knowing, Most Forbearing.

Divine Justice

60. That is so. And whoever retaliates in equivalence to the injury they have received, and then are wronged ˹again˺, Allah will certainly help them. Surely Allah is Ever-Pardoning, All-Forgiving.

Allah's Power

61. That is because Allah causes the night to merge into the day, and the day into the night. Indeed, Allah is All-Hearing, All-Seeing. **62.** That is because Allah ˹alone˺ is the Truth and what they invoke besides Him is falsehood, and Allah ˹alone˺ is truly the Most High, All-Great. **63.** Do you not see that Allah sends down rain from the sky, then the earth becomes green? Surely Allah is Most Subtle, All-Aware. **64.** To Him belongs whatever is in the heavens and whatever is on the earth. Allah ˹alone˺ is truly the Self-Sufficient, Praiseworthy.

---

660 Allah grants authority to some of His servants in this world, but none will have authority on Judgment Day except Him. *See* 3:26.

22. Al-Ḥajj

Allah's Grace

65. Do you not see that Allah has subjected to you[661] whatever is in the earth as well as the ships ˹that˺ sail through the sea by His command? He keeps the sky from falling down on the earth except by His permission. Surely Allah is Ever Gracious and Most Merciful to humanity. **66.** And He is the One Who gave you life, then will cause you to die, and then will bring you back to life. ˹But˺ surely humankind is ever ungrateful.

One Message, Different Laws

67. For every community We appointed a code[662] of life to follow.[663] So do not let them dispute with you ˹O Prophet˺ in this matter. And invite ˹all˺ to your Lord, for you are truly on the Right Guidance. **68.** But if they argue with you, then say, "Allah knows best what you do." **69.** Allah will judge between you ˹all˺ on Judgment Day regarding your differences. **70.** Do you not know that Allah ˹fully˺ knows whatever is in the heavens and the earth? Surely it is all ˹written˺ in a Record. That is certainly easy for Allah.

Almighty Allah or False Gods?

71. Yet they worship besides Allah that for which He has sent down no authority, and of which they have no knowledge. The wrongdoers will have no helper. **72.** Whenever Our clear revelations are recited to them, you ˹O Prophet˺ recognize rage on the faces of the disbelievers, as if they are going to snap at those who recite Our revelations to them. Say, "Shall I inform you of something far more enraging than that? ˹It is˺ the Fire with which Allah has threatened those who disbelieve. What an evil destination!"

---

661 For your service.
662 All prophets came with the same message: have faith in one God and do good. But each faith-community had their own law.
663 The Muslim code of life is called *Sharia*, which means a "path." For more information, *see* the Introduction.

22. Al-Ḥajj | 342

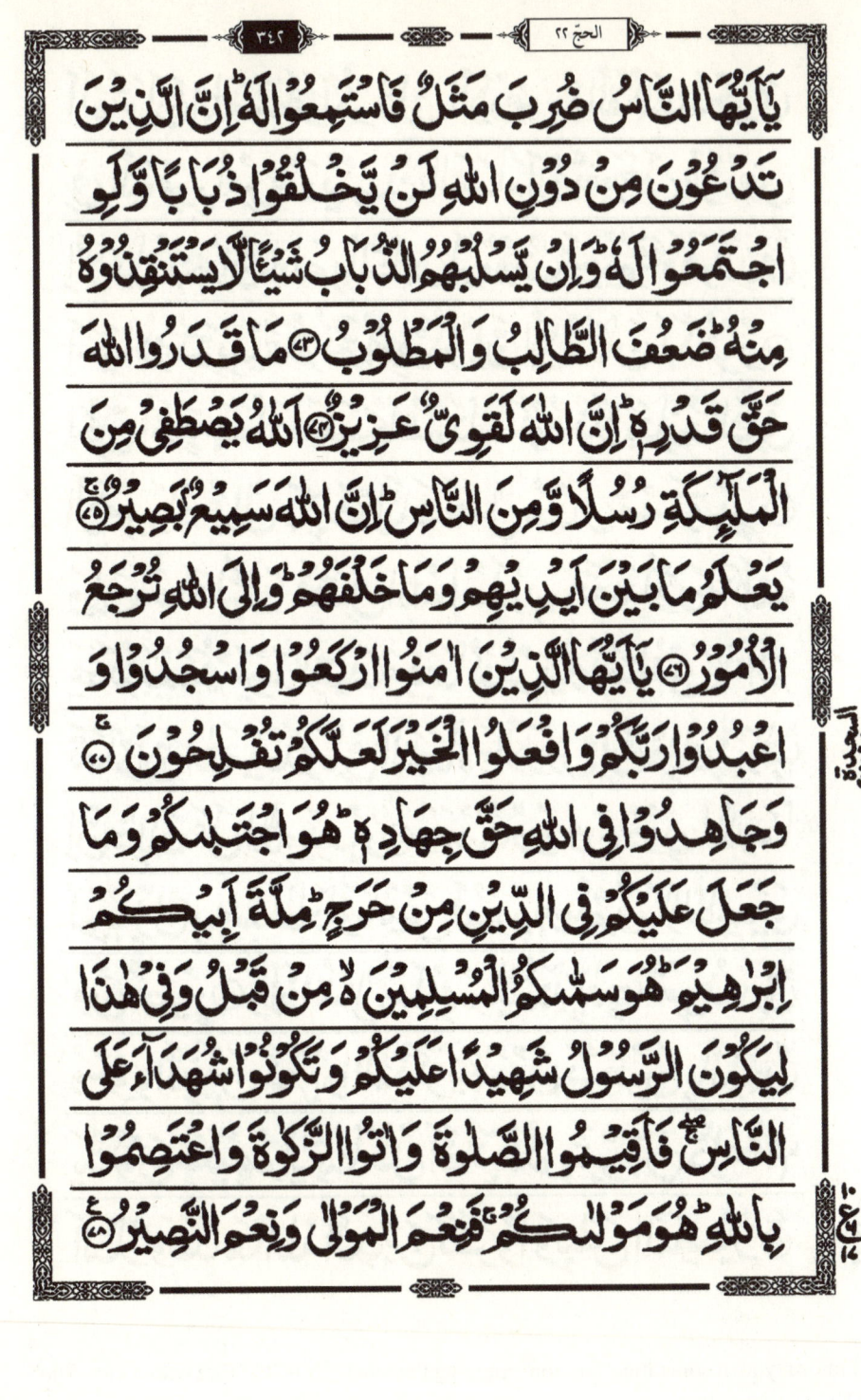

The Fly Challenge

73. O humanity! A lesson is set forth, so listen to it ˹carefully˺: those ˹idols˺ you invoke besides Allah can never create ˹so much as˺ a fly, even if they ˹all˺ were to come together for that. And if a fly were to snatch anything away from them, they cannot ˹even˺ retrieve it from the fly. How powerless are those who invoke and those invoked![664] **74.** They have not shown Allah the reverence He deserves. Surely Allah is All-Powerful, Almighty.

Divine Choice

75. Allah selects messengers from both angels and people, for Allah is truly All-Hearing, All-Seeing. **76.** He knows what is ahead of them and what is behind them. And to Allah ˹all˺ matters will be returned ˹for judgment˺.

Advice to the Believers

77. O believers! Bow down, prostrate yourselves, worship your Lord, and do ˹what is˺ good so that you may be successful. **78.** Strive for ˹the cause of˺ Allah in the way He deserves, for ˹it is˺ He ˹Who˺ has chosen you, and laid upon you no hardship in the religion—the way of your forefather Abraham. ˹It is Allah˺ Who named you 'the ones who submit'[665] ˹in the˺ earlier ˹Scriptures˺ and in this ˹Quran˺, so that the Messenger may be a witness over you, and that you may be witnesses over humanity. So establish prayer, pay alms-tax, and hold fast to Allah. He ˹alone˺ is your Guardian. What an excellent Guardian, and what an excellent Helper!

---

664 Another possible translation: "How weak are the seekers (i.e., the idols) and the sought (i.e., the fly)!"
665 i.e., Muslims.

الجزء ١٨

سُورَةُ المُؤْمِنُونَ مَكِّيَّةٌ وَهِيَ مِائَةٌ وَثَمَانِ عَشْرَةَ آيَةً وَسِتُّ رُكُوعَاتٍ

بِسْمِ اللَّهِ الرَّحْمَٰنِ الرَّحِيمِ ○
قَدْ أَفْلَحَ الْمُؤْمِنُونَ ① الَّذِينَ هُمْ فِي صَلَاتِهِمْ
خَاشِعُونَ ② وَالَّذِينَ هُمْ عَنِ اللَّغْوِ مُعْرِضُونَ ③ وَالَّذِينَ
هُمْ لِلزَّكَاةِ فَاعِلُونَ ④ وَالَّذِينَ هُمْ لِفُرُوجِهِمْ حَافِظُونَ ⑤ إِلَّا
عَلَىٰ أَزْوَاجِهِمْ أَوْ مَا مَلَكَتْ أَيْمَانُهُمْ فَإِنَّهُمْ غَيْرُ مَلُومِينَ ⑥ فَمَنِ
ابْتَغَىٰ وَرَاءَ ذَٰلِكَ فَأُولَٰئِكَ هُمُ الْعَادُونَ ⑦ وَالَّذِينَ هُمْ
لِأَمَانَاتِهِمْ وَعَهْدِهِمْ رَاعُونَ ⑧ وَالَّذِينَ هُمْ عَلَىٰ صَلَوَاتِهِمْ يُحَافِظُونَ ⑨
أُولَٰئِكَ هُمُ الْوَارِثُونَ ⑩ الَّذِينَ يَرِثُونَ الْفِرْدَوْسَ هُمْ فِيهَا
خَالِدُونَ ⑪ وَلَقَدْ خَلَقْنَا الْإِنْسَانَ مِنْ سُلَالَةٍ مِنْ طِينٍ ⑫
ثُمَّ جَعَلْنَاهُ نُطْفَةً فِي قَرَارٍ مَكِينٍ ⑬ ثُمَّ خَلَقْنَا النُّطْفَةَ عَلَقَةً
فَخَلَقْنَا الْعَلَقَةَ مُضْغَةً فَخَلَقْنَا الْمُضْغَةَ عِظَامًا فَكَسَوْنَا الْعِظَامَ
لَحْمًا ثُمَّ أَنْشَأْنَاهُ خَلْقًا آخَرَ ۚ فَتَبَارَكَ اللَّهُ أَحْسَنُ الْخَالِقِينَ ⑭
ثُمَّ إِنَّكُمْ بَعْدَ ذَٰلِكَ لَمَيِّتُونَ ⑮ ثُمَّ إِنَّكُمْ يَوْمَ الْقِيَامَةِ تُبْعَثُونَ ⑯
وَلَقَدْ خَلَقْنَا فَوْقَكُمْ سَبْعَ طَرَائِقَ وَمَا كُنَّا عَنِ الْخَلْقِ غَافِلِينَ ⑰

23. The Believers (Al-Mu'minûn)

In the Name of Allah—the Most Compassionate, Most Merciful

The True Believers

1. Successful indeed are the believers: **2.** those who humble themselves in prayer; **3.** those who avoid idle talk; **4.** those who pay alms-tax;[666] **5.** those who guard their chastity[667] **6.** except with their wives or those ˹bondwomen˺ in their possession,[668] for then they are free from blame, **7.** but whoever seeks beyond that are the transgressors; **8.** ˹the believers are also˺ those who are true to their trusts and covenants; **9.** and those who are ˹properly˺ observant of their prayers. **10.** These are the ones who will be awarded **11.** Paradise as their own.[669] They will be there forever.

The Creation of Humans

12. And indeed, We created humankind[670] from an extract of clay, **13.** then placed each ˹human˺ as a sperm-drop[671] in a secure place, **14.** then We developed the drop into a clinging clot ˹of blood˺, then developed the clot into a lump ˹of flesh˺, then developed the lump into bones, then clothed the bones with flesh, then We brought it into being as a new creation.[672] So Blessed is Allah, the Best of Creators. **15.** After that you will surely die, **16.** then on the Day of Judgment you will be resurrected.

Allah's Power

17. And indeed, We created above you seven levels ˹of heaven˺. We are never unmindful of ˹Our˺ creation.

---

666 *Zakâh* means purification and growth. Paying alms-tax and charity are forms of purifying one's wealth.
667 lit., private parts.
668 *See* footnote for 4:3.
669 *Al-Firdaws*, the highest place in Paradise.
670 Adam (ﷺ).
671 *See* footnote for 22:5.
672 This happens when the spirit is breathed into the embryo.

18. We send down rain from the sky in perfect measure, causing it to soak into the earth. And We are surely able to take it away. **19.** With it We produce for you gardens of palm trees and grapevines, in which there are abundant fruits, and from which you may eat, **20.** as well as ˹olive˺ trees which grow at Mount Sinai, providing oil and a condiment to eat. **21.** And there is certainly a lesson for you in cattle, from whose bellies We give you ˹milk˺ to drink, and in them are many other benefits for you, and from them you may eat. **22.** And you are carried upon ˹some of˺ them and upon ships.

Prophet Noah

23. Indeed, We sent Noah to his people. He declared, "O my people! Worship Allah ˹alone˺. You have no god other than Him. Will you not then fear ˹Him˺?" **24.** But the disbelieving chiefs of his people said ˹to the masses˺, "This is only a human like you, who wants to be superior to you. Had Allah willed, He could have easily ˹sent down angels ˹instead˺. We have never heard of this in ˹the history of˺ our forefathers. **25.** He is simply insane, so bear with him for a while."[673]

The Flood

26. Noah prayed, "My Lord! Help me, because they have denied ˹me˺." **27.** So We inspired him: "Build the Ark under Our ˹watchful˺ Eyes and directions. Then when Our command comes and the oven bursts ˹with water˺,[674] take on board a pair from every species along with your family—except those against whom the decree ˹to drown˺ has already been passed. And do not plead with Me for those who have done wrong, for they will surely be drowned."

---

673 So he may recover from his "madness" or die.

674 Noah was given a signal that once the water gushes out of a particular oven then the Flood is about to begin. It can also be translated as: "The fountains of the earth gushed forth."

345   23. Al-Mu'minûn

28. Then when you and those with you have settled in the Ark, say, "All praise is for Allah, Who saved us from the wrongdoing people."
29. And pray, "My Lord! Allow me a blessed landing, for You are the best accommodator." 30. Surely in this are lessons.[675] And We ˹always˺ put ˹people˺ to the test.

Prophet Hûd[676]

31. Then We raised another generation after them, 32. and sent to them a messenger from among themselves, ˹declaring,˺ "Worship Allah ˹alone˺. You have no god other than Him. Will you not then fear ˹Him˺?"
33. But the chiefs of his people—who disbelieved, denied the meeting ˹with Allah˺ in the Hereafter, and were spoiled by the worldly luxuries We had provided for them—said ˹to the masses˺, "This is only a human like you. He eats what you eat, and drinks what you drink. 34. And if you ˹ever˺ obey a human like yourselves, then you would certainly be losers. 35. Does he promise you that once you are dead and reduced to dust and bones, you will be brought forth ˹alive˺? 36. Impossible, simply impossible is what you are promised! 37. There is nothing beyond our worldly life. We die, others are born, and none will be resurrected. 38. He is no more than a man who has fabricated a lie about Allah, and we will never believe in him."

The Blast

39. The messenger prayed, "My Lord! Help me, because they have denied ˹me˺." 40. Allah responded, "Soon they will be truly regretful." 41. Then the ˹mighty˺ blast overtook them with justice, and We reduced them to rubble. So away with the wrongdoing people!

More Prophets

42. Then We raised other generations after them.

---

675 lit., signs.
676 Some scholars believe this passage refers to Prophet Ṣâliḥ (﷽).

23. Al-Mu'minûn — 346

ما تَسْبِقُ مِنْ أُمَّةٍ أَجَلَهَا وَمَا يَسْتَأْخِرُونَ ۝ ثُمَّ أَرْسَلْنَا رُسُلَنَا تَتْرَا ۖ كُلَّ مَا جَاءَ أُمَّةً رَّسُولُهَا كَذَّبُوهُ ۚ فَأَتْبَعْنَا بَعْضَهُم بَعْضًا وَجَعَلْنَاهُمْ أَحَادِيثَ ۚ فَبُعْدًا لِّقَوْمٍ لَّا يُؤْمِنُونَ ۝ ثُمَّ أَرْسَلْنَا مُوسَىٰ وَأَخَاهُ هَارُونَ بِآيَاتِنَا وَسُلْطَانٍ مُّبِينٍ ۝ إِلَىٰ فِرْعَوْنَ وَمَلَئِهِ فَاسْتَكْبَرُوا وَكَانُوا قَوْمًا عَالِينَ ۝ فَقَالُوا أَنُؤْمِنُ لِبَشَرَيْنِ مِثْلِنَا وَقَوْمُهُمَا لَنَا عَابِدُونَ ۝ فَكَذَّبُوهُمَا فَكَانُوا مِنَ الْمُهْلَكِينَ ۝ وَلَقَدْ آتَيْنَا مُوسَى الْكِتَابَ لَعَلَّهُمْ يَهْتَدُونَ ۝ وَجَعَلْنَا ابْنَ مَرْيَمَ وَأُمَّهُ آيَةً وَآوَيْنَاهُمَا إِلَىٰ رَبْوَةٍ ذَاتِ قَرَارٍ وَمَعِينٍ ۝ يَا أَيُّهَا الرُّسُلُ كُلُوا مِنَ الطَّيِّبَاتِ وَاعْمَلُوا صَالِحًا ۖ إِنِّي بِمَا تَعْمَلُونَ عَلِيمٌ ۝ وَإِنَّ هَٰذِهِ أُمَّتُكُمْ أُمَّةً وَاحِدَةً وَأَنَا رَبُّكُمْ فَاتَّقُونِ ۝ فَتَقَطَّعُوا أَمْرَهُم بَيْنَهُمْ زُبُرًا ۖ كُلُّ حِزْبٍ بِمَا لَدَيْهِمْ فَرِحُونَ ۝ فَذَرْهُمْ فِي غَمْرَتِهِمْ حَتَّىٰ حِينٍ ۝ أَيَحْسَبُونَ أَنَّمَا نُمِدُّهُم بِهِ مِن مَّالٍ وَبَنِينَ ۝ نُسَارِعُ لَهُمْ فِي الْخَيْرَاتِ ۚ بَل لَّا يَشْعُرُونَ ۝ إِنَّ الَّذِينَ هُم مِّنْ خَشْيَةِ رَبِّهِم مُّشْفِقُونَ ۝ وَالَّذِينَ هُم بِآيَاتِ رَبِّهِمْ يُؤْمِنُونَ ۝

43. No people can advance their doom, nor can they delay it.
44. Then We sent Our messengers in succession: whenever a messenger came to his people, they denied him. So We destroyed them, one after the other, reducing them to ˹cautionary˺ tales. So away with the people who refuse to believe!

Prophet Moses and Prophet Aaron

45. Then We sent Moses and his brother Aaron with Our signs[677] and compelling proof 46. to Pharaoh and his chiefs, but they behaved arrogantly and were a tyrannical people. 47. They argued, "Will we believe in two humans, like ourselves, whose people are slaves to us?" 48. So they rejected them both, and ˹so˺ were among those destroyed. 49. And We certainly gave Moses the Scripture, so perhaps his people would be ˹rightly˺ guided.

Prophet Jesus and His Mother

50. And We made the son of Mary and his mother a sign, and gave them refuge on high ground—a ˹suitable˺ place for rest with flowing water.

One Way

51. O messengers! Eat from what is good and lawful, and act righteously. Indeed, I fully know what you do. 52. Surely this religion of yours is ˹only˺ one, and I am your Lord, so fear Me ˹alone˺. 53. Yet the people have divided it into different sects, each rejoicing in what they have. 54. So leave them ˹O Prophet˺ in their heedlessness for a while. 55. Do they think, since We provide them with wealth and children, 56. that We hasten to ˹honour˺ them ˹with˺ all kinds of good? No! They are not aware.

The True Believers

57. Surely those who tremble in awe of their Lord, 58. and who believe in the revelations of their Lord,

---

677 The nine signs are: the staff, the hand (both mentioned in 20:17-22), famine, shortage of crops, floods, locusts, lice, frogs, and blood (all mentioned in 7:130-133).

23. Al-Mu'minûn

59. and who associate none with their Lord, 60. and who do whatever ˹good˺ they do with their hearts fearful, ˹knowing˺ that they will return to their Lord[678]— 61. it is they who race to do good deeds, always taking the lead. 62. We never require of any soul more than what it can afford. And with Us is a record which speaks the truth. None will be wronged.

The Disbelievers

63. But the hearts of those ˹who disbelieve˺ are oblivious to ˹all of˺ this,[679] and they have other ˹evil˺ deeds, opposite to this, in which they are engrossed. 64. But as soon as We seize their elite with torment, they start to cry for help. 65. ˹They will be told,˺ "Do not cry for help today. Surely you will never be saved from Us. 66. Indeed, My revelations were recited to you, but you used to back away ˹in disgust˺, 67. boasting of the Sacred House, and babbling ˹nonsense about the Quran˺ by night."

Why the Denial?

68. Is it because they have never contemplated the Word ˹of Allah˺? Or ˹because˺ there has come to them something that did not come to their forefathers? 69. Or ˹because˺ they failed to recognize their Messenger, and so they denied him? 70. Or ˹because˺ they say, "He is insane?" In fact, he has come to them with the truth, but most of them are resentful of the truth. 71. Had the truth followed their desires,[680] the heavens, the earth, and all those in them would have certainly been corrupted. In fact, We have brought them ˹the means to˺ their glory, but they turn away from it. 72. Or ˹is it because˺ you ˹O Prophet˺ are asking them for tribute? But the reward of your Lord is best, for He is the Best Provider. 73. And surely you are calling them to the Straight Path, 74. but those who disbelieve in the Hereafter are certainly deviating from that Path.

---

678 It is reported in an authentic narration collected by At-Tirmizi that 'Âishah, the Prophet's wife, asked him (ﷺ) if this verse refers to those who steal or drink ˹alcohol˺. The Prophet (ﷺ) answered, "No, it refers to those who pray, fast, and donate, but are afraid that their deeds are rejected because they are not good enough." Then he (ﷺ) recited the last part of the verse: "It is they who race to do good deeds, always taking the lead."

679 This refers to the believers' good deeds mentioned in 23:57-62.

680 Their desire that the universe has more than one God. See 21:22.

23. Al-Mu'minûn

Those Persisting in Denial

75. ˹Even˺ if We had mercy on them and removed their affliction,[681] they would still persist in their transgression, wandering blindly. **76.** And We have already seized them with torment, but they never humbled themselves to their Lord, nor did they ˹submissively˺ appeal ˹to Him˺. **77.** But as soon as We open for them a gate of severe punishment, they will be utterly desperate.

Ingratitude to the Almighty

78. He is the One Who created for you hearing, sight, and intellect. ˹Yet˺ you hardly give any thanks. **79.** And He is the One Who has dispersed you ˹all˺ over the earth, and to Him you will ˹all˺ be gathered. **80.** And He is the One Who gives life and causes death, and to Him belongs the alternation of the day and night. Will you not then understand? **81.** But they ˹just˺ say what their predecessors said. **82.** They said, "Once we are dead and reduced to dust and bones, will we really be resurrected? **83.** We have already been promised this, as well as our forefathers earlier. This is nothing but ancient fables!"

Almighty Allah

84. Ask ˹them, O Prophet˺, "To whom belong the earth and all those on it, if you ˹really˺ know?" **85.** They will reply, "To Allah!" Say, "Why are you not then mindful?" **86.** ˹And˺ ask ˹them˺, "Who is the Lord of the seven heavens and the Lord of the Mighty Throne?"

87. They will reply, "Allah." Say, "Will you not then fear ˹Him˺?" **88.** Ask ˹them also,˺ "In Whose Hands is the authority over all things, protecting ˹all˺ while none can protect against Him, if you ˹really˺ know?" **89.** They will reply, "Allah." Say, "How are you then so deluded?"

---

681 This refers to famine which affected the pagans of Mecca.

349 | *23. Al-Mu'minûn*

90. In fact, We have brought them the truth, and they are certainly liars.

One True Allah

91. Allah has never had ʿanyʾ offspring, nor is there any god besides Him. Otherwise, each god would have taken away what he created, and they would have tried to dominate one another. Glorified is Allah above what they claim! **92.** ʿHe is theʾ Knower of the seen and unseen. Exalted is He above what they associate ʿwith Himʾ.

Advice to the Prophet

93. Say, ʿO Prophet,ʾ "My Lord! Should You show me what they[682] are threatened with, **94.** then, my Lord, do not count me among the wrongdoing people." **95.** We are indeed able to show you what We have threatened them with. **96.** Respond to evil with what is best. We know well what they claim.[683] **97.** And say, "My Lord! I seek refuge in You from the temptations of the devils. **98.** And I seek refuge in You, my Lord, that they ʿevenʾ come near me."

Too Late for the Wicked

99. When death approaches any of them, they cry, "My Lord! Let me go back, **100.** so I may do good in what I left behind." Never! It is only a ʿuselessʾ appeal they make. And there is a barrier behind them until the Day they are resurrected.[684]

Judgment Day

101. Then, when the Trumpet will be blown,[685] there will be no kinship between them on that Day, nor will they ʿeven care toʾ ask about one another.[686]

The Successful Ones

102. As for those whose scale is heavy ʿwith good deedsʾ, it is they who will be successful.

---

682 The Meccan pagans.
683 Their claims that there are many gods, and that the Prophet is a liar, a poet, etc.
684 Meaning, once they are dead, they will never return to the world.
685 On the Day of Judgment, the Trumpet will be blown by an angel—causing all to die. When it is blown a second time, everyone will be raised from the dead for judgment (*see* 39:68).
686 Everyone will be busy with their own situation.

The Losers

103. But those whose scale is light, they will have doomed themselves, staying in Hell forever. **104.** The Fire will burn their faces, leaving them deformed. **105.** ˹It will be said,˺ "Were My revelations not recited to you, but you used to deny them?" **106.** They will cry, "Our Lord! Our ill-fate took hold of us, so we became a misguided people. **107.** Our Lord! Take us out of this ˹Fire˺. Then if we ever return ˹to denial˺, we will truly be wrongdoers." **108.** Allah will respond, "Be despised in there! Do not ˹ever˺ plead with Me ˹again˺! **109.** Indeed, there was a group of My servants who used to pray, 'Our Lord! We have believed, so forgive us and have mercy on us, for You are the best of those who show mercy,' **110.** but you were ˹so busy˺ making fun of them that it made you forget My remembrance. And you used to laugh at them. **111.** Today I have indeed rewarded them for their perseverance: they are certainly the triumphant."

Fleeting World

112. He will ask ˹them˺, "How many years did you remain on earth?" **113.** They will reply, "We remained ˹only˺ a day or part of a day.[687] But ask those who kept count." **114.** He will say, "You only remained for a little while, if only you knew. **115.** Did you then think that We had created you without purpose, and that you would never be returned to Us?"

One God Only

116. Exalted is Allah, the True King! There is no god ˹worthy of worship˺ except Him, the Lord of the Honourable Throne. **117.** Whoever invokes, besides Allah, another god—for which they can have no proof—they will surely find their penalty with their Lord. Indeed, the disbelievers will never succeed.

Advice to the Prophet

118. Say, ˹O Prophet,˺ "My Lord! Forgive and have mercy, for You are the best of those who show mercy."

---

687 Compared to the length and misery of their stay in the grave and Hell, their worldly life will seem very short to them.

24. The Light (An-Nûr)

In the Name of Allah—the Most Compassionate, Most Merciful

The Introduction

1. ˹This is˺ a *sûrah* which We have revealed and made ˹its rulings˺ obligatory, and revealed in it clear commandments so that you may be mindful.

Punishment for Fornication

2. As for female and male fornicators, give each of them one hundred lashes,[688] and do not let pity for them make you lenient in ˹enforcing˺ the law of Allah, if you ˹truly˺ believe in Allah and the Last Day. And let a number of believers witness their punishment.

Like for Like

3. A male fornicator would only marry a female fornicator or idolatress. And a female fornicator would only be married to a fornicator or idolater. This is ˹all˺ forbidden to the believers.[689]

Unsupported Accusations

4. Those who accuse chaste women ˹of adultery˺ and fail to produce four witnesses, give them eighty lashes ˹each˺. And do not ever accept any testimony from them—for they are indeed the rebellious— 5. except those who repent afterwards and mend their ways, then surely Allah is All-Forgiving, Most Merciful.

Accusation to One's Wife

6. And those who accuse their wives ˹of adultery˺ but have no witness except themselves, the accuser must testify,[690] swearing four times by Allah that he is telling the truth, 7. and a fifth oath that Allah may condemn him if he is lying.

---

688 The address here is to legal authorities. Adultery has to be proven either by confession or the testimony of four reliable witnesses.
689 It is reported in a *ḥadîth* collected by At-Tirmizi that Marthad ibn Abi Marthad, a companion of the Prophet (ﷺ), asked if he could marry 'Anâq, a pagan prostitute he befriended in Mecca before he accepted Islam. So this verse was revealed. However, if someone committed a sin then later repented genuinely, they will be accepted by Allah and the rest of the believers.
690 In order to be spared the punishment for false accusation.

24. An-Nûr

8. For her to be spared the punishment, she must swear four times by Allah that he is telling a lie, **9.** and a fifth oath that Allah may be displeased with her if he is telling the truth.[691] **10.** ˹You would have suffered,˺ had it not been for Allah's grace and mercy upon you, and had Allah not been Accepting of Repentance, All-Wise.

Those Who Slandered the Prophet's Wife[692]

11. Indeed, those who came up with that ˹outrageous˺ slander are a group of you. Do not think this is bad for you. Rather, it is good for you.[693] They will be punished, each according to their share of the sin. As for their mastermind,[694] he will suffer a tremendous punishment.

How the Believers Should Have Reacted

12. If only the believing men and women had thought well of one another, when you heard this ˹rumour˺, and said, "This is clearly ˹an outrageous˺ slander!" **13.** Why did they not produce four witnesses? Now, since they have failed to produce witnesses, they are ˹truly˺ liars in the sight of Allah. **14.** Had it not been for Allah's grace and mercy upon you in this world and the Hereafter, you would have certainly been touched with a tremendous punishment for what you plunged into— **15.** when you passed it from one tongue to the other, and said with your mouths what you had no knowledge of, taking it lightly while it is ˹extremely˺ serious in the sight of Allah. **16.** If only you had said upon hearing it, "How can we speak about such a thing! Glory be to You ˹O Lord˺! This is a heinous slander!" **17.** Allah forbids you from ever doing something like this again, if you are ˹true˺ believers. **18.** And Allah makes ˹His˺ commandments clear to you, for Allah is All-Knowing, All-Wise.

---

691 This ruling is called *li'ân* in Islamic legal system. Once the husband and the wife swear each five times, as specified in 24:6-9, the marriage is terminated forever—which means that they can never be remarried.

692 This is referring to an incident where the Prophet's wife, 'Âishah, was accused of adultery. She was part of a caravan, and when she lost her necklace and went looking for it, the caravan moved on without her. She waited until a man named Ṣafwân ibn Al-Mu'aṭṭal found her and escorted her to the caravan. When they returned, the hypocrites began accusing her of adultery. The rumour spread, and 'Âishah defended her innocence, saying "If I told you now I had not done this, you would not believe me. And if I told you that I had done it, you would believe me. I now say what Jacob had once said. He said (12:18): "I can only endure˺ beautiful patience! It is Allah's help that I seek to bear your claims."' Right after she said this, these verses were revealed to the Prophet (ﷺ), proclaiming her innocence.

693 Because now you can tell who is a true believer and who is a hypocrite.

694 This refers to 'Abdullâh ibn Ubai, the leader of the hypocrites in Medina.

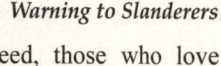

24. An-Nûr

Warning to Slanderers

19. Indeed, those who love to see indecency spread among the believers will suffer a painful punishment in this life and the Hereafter. Allah knows and you do not know. **20.** ˹You would have suffered,˺ had it not been for Allah's grace and mercy upon you, and had Allah not been Ever Gracious, Most Merciful.

Warning Against Satan

21. O believers! Do not follow the footsteps of Satan. Whoever follows Satan's footsteps, then ˹let them know that˺ he surely bids ˹all to˺ immorality and wickedness. Had it not been for Allah's grace and mercy upon you, none of you would have ever been purified. But Allah purifies whoever He wills. And Allah is All-Hearing, All-Knowing.

Uninterrupted Kindness

22. Do not let the people of virtue and affluence among you swear to suspend donations to their relatives, the needy, and the emigrants in the cause of Allah. Let them pardon and forgive. Do you not love to be forgiven by Allah? And Allah is All-Forgiving, Most Merciful.[695]

Punishment of the Slanderers

23. Surely those who accuse chaste, unsuspecting,[696] believing women are cursed in this life and the Hereafter. And they will suffer a tremendous punishment **24.** on the Day their tongues, hands, and feet will testify against them for what they used to do. **25.** On that Day, Allah will give them their just penalty in full, and they will ˹come to˺ know that Allah ˹alone˺ is the Ultimate Truth.

Birds of a Feather ...

26. Wicked women are for wicked men, and wicked men are for wicked women. And virtuous women are for virtuous men, and virtuous men are for virtuous women. The virtuous are innocent of what the wicked say. They will have forgiveness and an honourable provision.[697]

---

695 This verse was revealed when Abu Bakr Aṣ-Ṣiddîq, ʾÂishah's father, swore to end his financial assistance to his poor cousin, Misṭaḥ ibn Athathah, for taking part in the rumours against ʾÂishah. Once the verse was revealed, Abu Bakr resumed his assistance to Misṭaḥ.

696 Immoral thoughts never cross the minds of these chaste women and, therefore, they never expect slander.

697 This passage declares the innocence of ʾÂishah, the Prophet's wife.

24. An-Nûr

Entering People's Homes

27. O believers! Do not enter any house other than your own until you have asked for permission and greeted its occupants. This is best for you, so perhaps you will be mindful. **28.** If you find no one at home, do not enter it until you have been given permission. And if you are asked to leave, then leave. That is purer for you. And Allah has ˹perfect˺ knowledge of what you do.

Entering Public Places

29. There is no blame on you if you enter public places[698] where there is something of benefit for you. And Allah knows what you reveal and what you conceal.

Advice to Muslim Men

30. ˹O Prophet!˺ Tell the believing men to lower their gaze and guard their chastity. That is purer for them. Surely Allah is All-Aware of what they do.

Advice to Muslim Women

31. And tell the believing women to lower their gaze and guard their chastity, and not to reveal their adornments[699] except what normally appears.[700] Let them draw their veils over their chests, and not reveal their ˹hidden˺ adornments[701] except to their husbands, their fathers, their fathers-in-law, their sons, their step-sons, their brothers, their brothers' sons or sisters' sons, their fellow women, those ˹bondwomen˺ in their possession, male attendants with no desire, or children who are still un-

aware of women's nakedness. Let them not stomp their feet, drawing attention to their hidden adornments. Turn to Allah in repentance all together, O believers, so that you may be successful.

---

698 lit., non-residential buildings.
699 i.e., hair, body shape, and underclothes.
700 i.e., the face, hands, outer clothes, rings, kohl, and henna.
701 i.e., hair, arms, and legs.

24. An-Nûr

Helping Singles to Marry

32. Marry off the ˹free˺ singles among you, as well as the righteous of your bondmen and bondwomen. If they are poor, Allah will enrich them out of His bounty. For Allah is All-Bountiful, All-Knowing. **33.** And let those who do not have the means to marry keep themselves chaste until Allah enriches them out of His bounty.

Slaves Buying Their Freedom

And if any of those ˹bondspeople˺ in your possession desires a deed of emancipation, make it possible for them, if you find goodness in them. And give them some of Allah's wealth which He has granted you.

Forced Prostitution[702]

Do not force your ˹slave˺ girls into prostitution for your own worldly gains while they wish to remain chaste. And if someone coerces them, then after such a coercion Allah is certainly All-Forgiving, Most Merciful ˹to them˺.

Examples and Lessons[703]

34. Indeed, We have sent down to you clear revelations, along with examples of those who had gone before you, and a lesson to the God-fearing.

Parable for the Believer's Heart

35. Allah is the Light of the heavens and the earth. His light[704] is like a niche in which there is a lamp, the lamp is in a crystal, the crystal is like a shining star, lit from ˹the oil of˺ a blessed olive tree, ˹located˺ neither to the east nor the west,[705] whose oil would almost glow, even without being touched by fire. Light upon light! Allah guides whoever He wills to His light. And Allah sets forth parables for humanity. For Allah has ˹perfect˺ knowledge of all things.

True Believers

36. ˹That light shines˺ through houses ˹of worship˺ which Allah has ordered to be raised, and where His Name is mentioned. He is glorified there morning and evening

---

702 Some slave-masters used to force their slave-women into prostitution before Islam. In Islam, wilful prostitution is a sin, as is forcing others into prostitution. Victims of this crime are not held accountable.
703 Before 'Âishah, Mary and Prophet Joseph had each been falsely accused of fornication, but Almighty Allah declared their innocence.
704 This is a metaphor for the light of guidance in the heart of the believer.
705 Meaning, the olive tree is wholesome because it is located in a central place, so it is hit by sunrays all day-long, and, therefore, the oil is of a premium quality.

37. by men[706] who are not distracted—either by buying or selling—from Allah's remembrance, or performing prayer, or paying alms-tax. They fear a Day when hearts and eyes will tremble, **38.** ˹hoping˺ that Allah may reward them according to the best of their deeds, and increase them out of His grace. And Allah provides for whoever He wills without limit.

Parable for the Disbelievers

39. As for the disbelievers, their deeds are like a mirage in a desert, which the thirsty perceive as water, but when they approach it, they find it to be nothing. Instead, they find Allah there ˹in the Hereafter, ready˺ to settle their account. And Allah is swift in reckoning.

Another Parable

40. Or ˹their deeds are˺ like the darkness in a deep sea, covered by waves upon waves,[707] topped by ˹dark˺ clouds. Darkness upon darkness! If one stretches out their hand, they can hardly see it. And whoever Allah does not bless with light will have no light!

Submission to Allah

41. Do you not see that Allah is glorified by all those in the heavens and the earth, even the birds as they soar? Each ˹instinctively˺ knows their manner of prayer and glorification. And Allah has ˹perfect˺ knowledge of all they do. **42.** To Allah ˹alone˺ belongs the kingdom of the heavens and the earth. And to Allah is the final return.

The Miracle of Rain

43. Do you not see that Allah gently drives the clouds, then joins them together, piling them up into masses, from which you see raindrops come forth? And He sends down from the sky mountains ˹of clouds˺ loaded with hail, pouring it on whoever He wills and averting it from whoever He wills. The flash of the clouds' lightning nearly takes away eyesight.

---

706 *See* footnote for 7:46.
707 This is another scientific fact mentioned in the Quran: the existence of underwater waves, like layers.

44. Allah alternates the day and night. Surely in this is a lesson for people of insight.

The Miracle of Creation

45. And Allah has created from water every living creature. Some of them crawl on their bellies, some walk on two legs, and some walk on four. Allah creates whatever He wills. Surely Allah is Most Capable of everything.

The Hypocrites and Judgment

46. We have indeed sent down revelations clarifying ˹the truth˺. But Allah ˹only˺ guides whoever He wills to the Straight Path. **47.** And the hypocrites say, "We believe in Allah and the Messenger, and we obey." Then a group of them turns away soon after that. These are not ˹true˺ believers. **48.** And as soon as they are called to Allah and His Messenger so he may judge between them, a group of them[708] turns away. **49.** But if the truth is in their favour, they come to him, fully submitting. **50.** Is there a sickness in their hearts? Or are they in doubt? Or do they fear that Allah and His Messenger will be unjust to them? In fact, it is they who are the ˹true˺ wrongdoers.

The Believers and Judgment

51. The only response of the ˹true˺ believers, when they are called to Allah and His Messenger so he may judge between them, is to say, "We hear and obey." It is they who will ˹truly˺ succeed. **52.** For whoever obeys Allah and His Messenger, and fears Allah and is mindful of Him, then it is they who will ˹truly˺ triumph.

Hypocrites' Lip Service

53. They swear by Allah their most solemn oaths that if you ˹O Prophet˺ were to command them, they would certainly march forth ˹in Allah's cause˺. Say, "˹You˺ do not ˹have to˺ swear; your obedience is well known!"[709] Surely Allah is All-Aware of what you do."

---

708 Those at fault.
709 This is used in a sarcastic way. It means, "Save your oaths! Everyone knows you are only bluffing. It is actions that matter, not words."

54. Say, "Obey Allah and obey the Messenger. But if you turn away, then he is only responsible for his duty[710] and you are responsible for yours.[711] And if you obey him, you will be ˹rightly˺ guided. The Messenger's duty is only to deliver ˹the message˺ clearly."

Allah's Promise to the Believers

55. Allah has promised those of you who believe and do good that He will certainly make them successors in the land, as He did with those before them; and will surely establish for them their faith which He has chosen for them; and will indeed change their fear into security—˹provided that˺ they worship Me, associating nothing with Me. But whoever disbelieves after this ˹promise˺, it is they who will be the rebellious. **56.** Moreover, establish prayer, pay alms-tax, and obey the Messenger, so you may be shown mercy. **57.** Do not think ˹O Prophet˺ that the disbelievers can escape in the land. The Fire will be their home. Indeed, what an evil destination!

Permission at Three Times

58. O believers! Let those ˹bondspeople˺ in your possession and those of you who are still under age ask for your permission ˹to come in˺ at three times: before dawn prayer, when you take off your ˹outer˺ clothes at noon, and after the late evening prayer. ˹These are˺ three times of privacy for you. Other than these times, there is no blame on you or them to move freely, attending to one another. This is how Allah makes the revelations clear to you, for Allah is All-Knowing, All-Wise.

---

710 The Prophet's only duty is to deliver the message.
711 Their only duty is to obey the Prophet (ﷺ) by submitting to Allah.

359   24. An-Nûr

Permission at All Times

59. And when your children reach the age of puberty, let them seek permission ʿto come inʾ, as their seniors do. This is how Allah makes His revelations clear to you, for Allah is All-Knowing, All-Wise.

Modesty for Elderly Women

60. As for elderly women past the age of marriage, there is no blame on them if they take off their ʿouterʾ garments, without revealing their adornments. But it is better for them if they avoid this ʿaltogetherʾ. And Allah is All-Hearing, All-Knowing.

No Restrictions

61. There is no restriction on the blind, or the disabled, or the sick.[712] Nor on yourselves if you eat from your homes,[713] or the homes of your fathers, or your mothers, or your brothers, or your sisters, or your paternal uncles, or your paternal aunts, or your maternal uncles, or your maternal aunts, or from the homes in your trust, or ʿthe homes ofʾ your friends. There is no blame on you eating together or separately. However, when you enter houses, greet one another with a greeting ʿof peaceʾ from Allah, blessed and good.[714] This is how Allah makes His revelations clear to you, so perhaps you will understand.

---

712 There is no blame on any of the three if they do not march forth in Allah's cause. Moreover, some Muslims would give the keys of their homes to one of those who could not march forth (namely the blind, the disabled, or the sick) or their own relatives and ask them to enter their houses and eat at will but these people were shy to do that.

713 i.e., the home of your spouse or children.

714 If someone is in the house, greet them by saying, 'As-salâmu 'alaikum' (peace be upon you)." But if there is no one there, you greet yourselves by saying, 'Asalâmu 'alaina wa 'ala 'ibâd-illâhi aṣ-ṣâliḥîn' (peace be upon us and all righteous servants of Allah)."

25. Al-Furqân

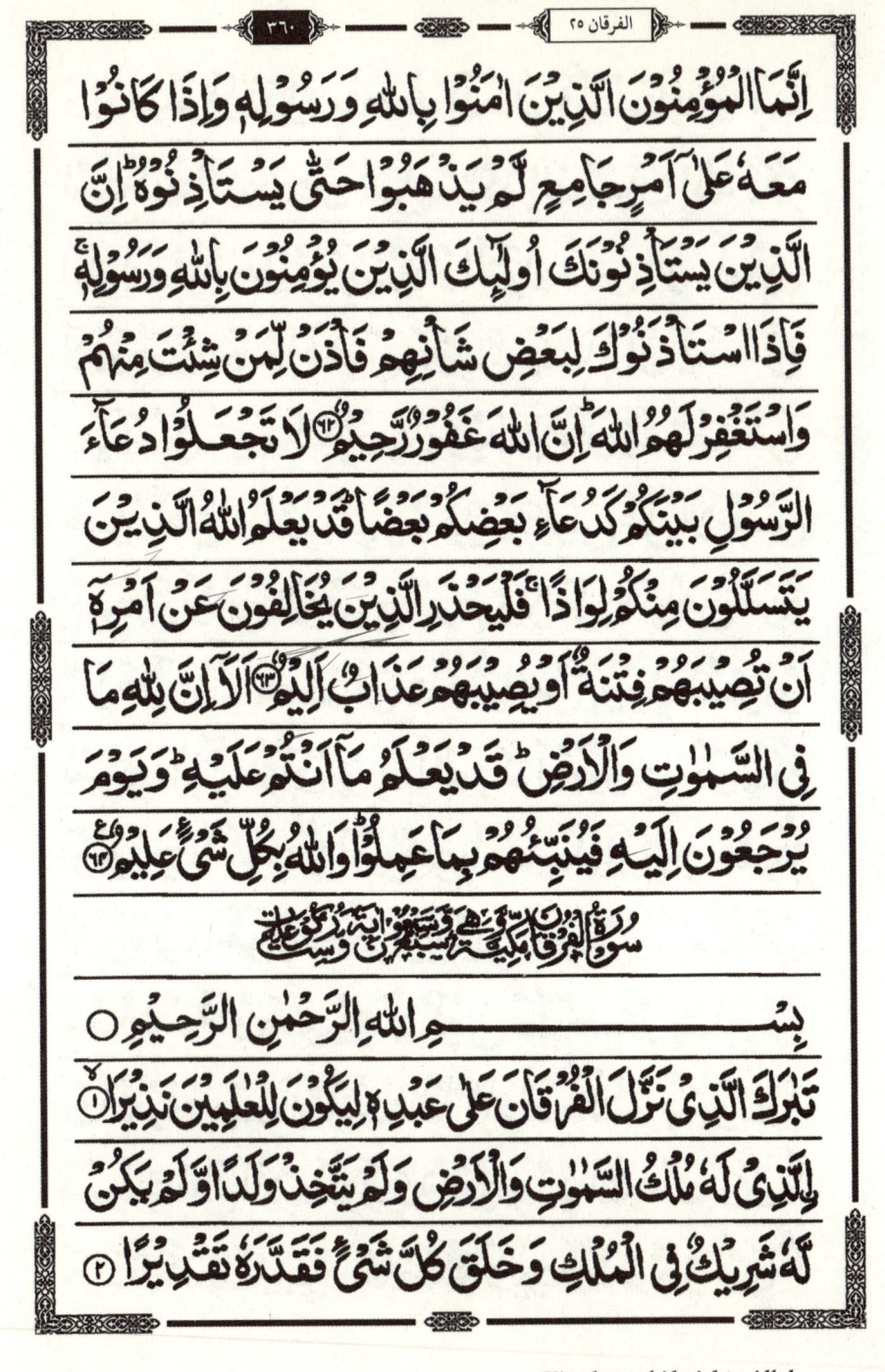

Sticking with the Prophet

62. The ˹true˺ believers are only those who believe in Allah and His Messenger, and when they are with him on a public matter, they do not leave without his permission. Indeed, those who ask your permission ˹O Prophet˺ are the ones who ˹truly˺ believe in Allah and His Messenger. So when they ask your permission for a private matter, grant permission to whoever you wish and ask Allah's forgiveness for them. Surely Allah is All-Forgiving, Most Merciful. **63.** Do not treat the Messenger's summons to you ˹as lightly˺ as your summons to one another.[715] Allah certainly knows those of you who slip away, hiding behind others.[716] So let those who disobey his orders beware, for an affliction may befall them, or a painful torment may overtake them.

Allah Knows Everything

64. Surely to Allah belongs whatever is in the heavens and the earth. He knows well what you stand for. And ˹on˺ the Day all will be returned to Him, He will inform them of what they did. For Allah has ˹perfect˺ knowledge of all things.

ೞ๏๏ ✸ ೞ๏๏

25. The Decisive Authority (Al-Furqân)

In the Name of Allah—the Most Compassionate, Most Merciful

Kingdom of Almighty Allah

1. Blessed is the One Who sent down the Decisive Authority[717] to His servant,[718] so that he may be a warner to the whole world.[719]

2. ˹Allah is˺ the One to Whom belongs the kingdom of the heavens and the earth, Who has never had ˹any˺ offspring, nor does He have a partner in ˹governing˺ the kingdom. He has created everything, ordaining it precisely.

---

715 There is also a different interpretation: "Do not call the Messenger ˹by his name˺ as you call one another." In other words, Do not say, 'O Muḥammad.' Rather, say, 'O Prophet.'
716 Some hypocrites used to sneak out while the Prophet (ﷺ) was talking.
717 Al-Furqân, which is one of names of the Quran, means "the Decisive Authority."
718 Prophet Muḥammad (ﷺ).
719 For both humans and jinn.

25. Al-Furqân

The Polytheists

3. Yet they have taken besides Him gods who cannot create anything but are themselves created. Nor can they protect or benefit themselves. Nor can they control life, death, or resurrection.

Denying the Quran

4. The disbelievers say, "This ˹Quran˺ is nothing but a fabrication which he[720] made up with the help of others." Their claim is totally unjustified and untrue! 5. And they say, "˹These revelations are only˺ ancient fables which he has had written down, and they are rehearsed to him morning and evening."[721] 6. Say, ˹O Prophet,˺ "This ˹Quran˺ has been revealed by the One Who knows the secrets of the heavens and the earth. Surely He is All-Forgiving, Most Merciful."[722]

Denying the Prophet

7. And they say ˹mockingly˺, "What kind of messenger is this who eats food and goes about in market-places ˹for a living˺? If only an angel had been sent down with him to be his co-warner, 8. or a treasure had been cast down to him, or he had had a garden from which he may eat!" And the wrongdoers say ˹to the believers˺, "You are only following a bewitched man." 9. See ˹O Prophet˺ how they call you names![723] So they have gone so ˹far˺ astray that they cannot find the ˹Right˺ Way. 10. Blessed is the One Who—if He wills—can give you far better than ˹all˺ that: gardens under which rivers flow, and palaces as well.

Torment for the Deniers

11. In fact, they deny the Hour.[724] And for the deniers of the Hour, We have prepared a blazing Fire.

---

720 The Prophet (ﷺ).
721 Some Arab pagans claimed that the Prophet (ﷺ) had been taught the Bible by some non-Arab Christians. The Quran itself (16:103) refutes this claim by arguing that a non-Arab could not come up with an eloquent Arabic scripture like the Quran when eloquent Arabs failed to produce something like it. For more details, *see* the Introduction.
722 He forgives those who repent, and gives a grace period to those who do not.
723 i.e., a magician, a poet, a fabricator, and a mad man.
724 What they have said about you are only excuses to justify their denial of the Hereafter.

25. Al-Furqân 362

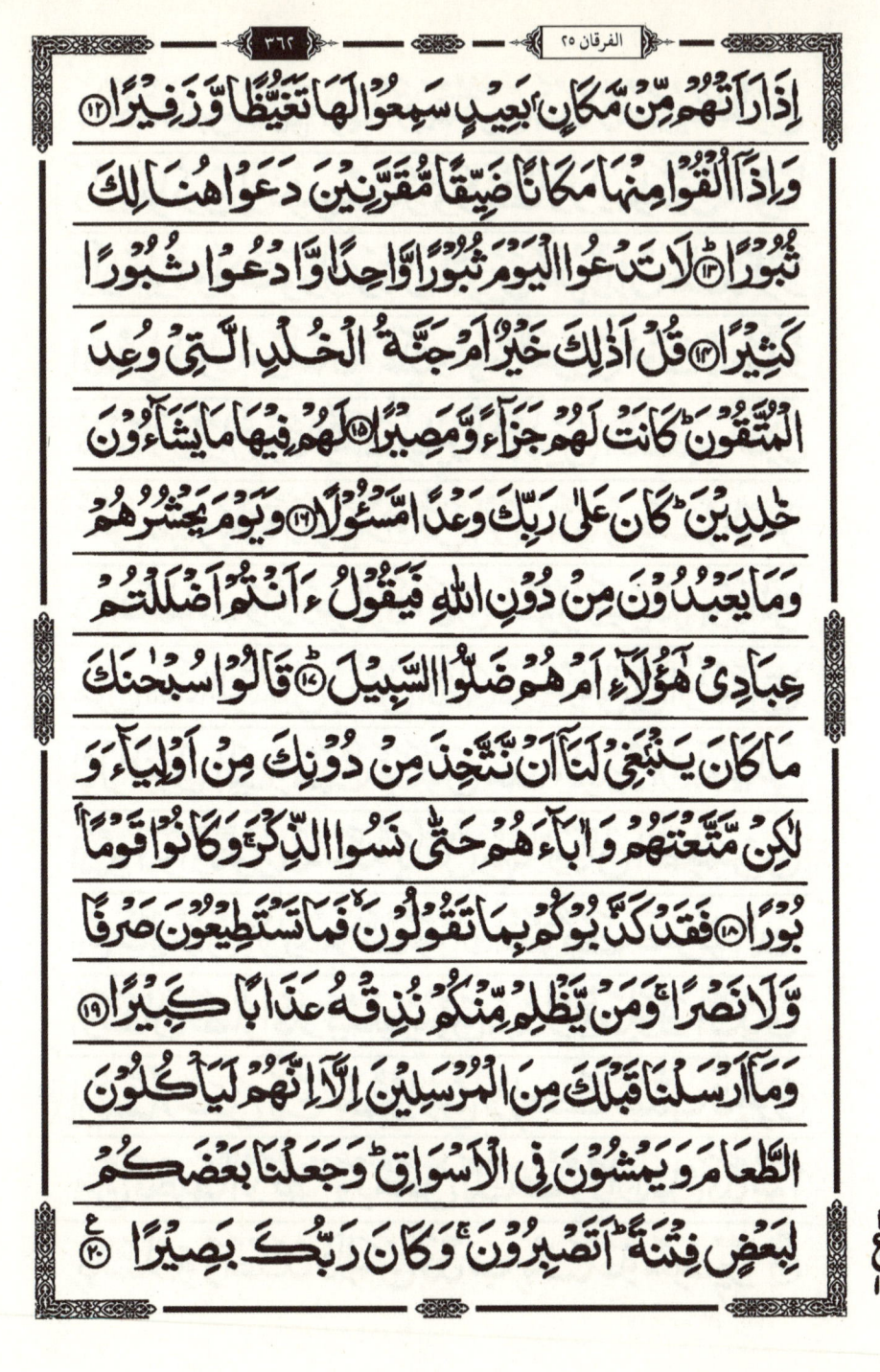

12. Once it sees them from a distance, they will hear it fuming and growling. **13.** And when they are tossed into a narrow place inside ˹Hell˺, chained together, then and there they will cry out for ˹instant˺ destruction. **14.** ˹They will be told,˺ "Do not cry only once for destruction, but cry many times over!"

Reward of the Righteous

15. Say, ˹O Prophet,˺ "Is this better or the Garden of Eternity which the righteous have been promised, as a reward and ˹an ultimate˺ destination? **16.** There they will have whatever they wish for, forever. That is a promise ˹to be sought after˺, binding on your Lord.

The Disavowal

17. ˹Watch for˺ the Day He will gather them along with what they used to worship besides Allah, and ask ˹the objects of worship˺,[725] "Was it you who misled these servants of Mine, or did they stray from the Way ˹on their own˺?" **18.** They will say, "Glory be to You! It was not right for ˹others like˺ us to take any lords besides You,[726] but You allowed enjoyment for them and their forefathers ˹for so long˺ that they forgot ˹Your˺ remembrance and became a doomed people." **19.** ˹The doomed will be told˺, "Your gods have clearly denied your claims. So now you can neither ward off ˹the punishment˺ nor get any help." And whoever of you does wrong, We will make them taste a horrible punishment.

Messengers Are Human

20. We never sent any messenger before you ˹O Prophet˺, who did not eat food and go about in market-places. We have made some of you a trial for others. Will you ˹not then˺ be patient? And your Lord is All-Seeing.

---

725 e.g., Jesus and the angels.
726 Another possible translation: "They will say, 'Glory be to You! We would not dare to take other lords besides You ˹so how can we claim to be lords?˺'"

25. Al-Furqân

Desperate to Meet the Angels

21. Those who do not expect to meet Us say, "If only the angels were sent down to us, or we could see our Lord!" They have certainly been carried away by their arrogance and have entirely exceeded all limits.
22. ˹But˺ on the Day they will see the angels, there will be no good news for the wicked, who will cry, "Keep away! Away ˹from us˺!"[727]
23. Then We will turn to whatever ˹good˺ deeds they did, reducing them to scattered dust.[728] 24. ˹But˺ on that Day the residents of Paradise will have the best settlement and the finest place to rest.

Judgment Day

25. ˹Watch for˺ the Day the heavens will burst with clouds, and the angels will be sent down in successive ranks. 26. True authority on that Day will belong ˹only˺ to the Most Compassionate.[729] And it will be a hard day for the disbelievers.

Useless Remorse[730]

27. And ˹beware of˺ the Day the wrongdoer will bite his nails ˹in regret˺ and say, "Oh! I wish I had followed the Way along with the Messenger! 28. Woe to me! I wish I had never taken so-and-so as a close friend. 29. It was he who truly made me stray from the Reminder after it had reached me." And Satan has always betrayed humanity.

Pagans' Neglect of the Quran

30. The Messenger has cried, "O my Lord! My people have indeed received this Quran with neglect."

31. Similarly, We made enemies for every prophet from among the wicked, but sufficient is your Lord as a Guide and Helper.
32. The disbelievers say, "If only the Quran had been sent down to him all at once!" ˹We have sent it˺ as such ˹in stages˺ so We may reassure your heart with it. And We have revealed it at a deliberate pace.

---

727 Another possible translation: "And the angels will say, 'All good is forbidden to you!'"
728 The good deeds of the disbelievers (like charity) will have no weight on Judgment Day.
729 Some people (like kings and rulers) have some sort of authority in this world. But on Judgment Day Allah will be the sole authority.
730 This passage refers to ʿOqba ibn Abi-Muʿaiṭ who had initially become Muslim, but later left Islam only to please his close friend, Ubai ibn Khalaf.

33. Whenever they bring you an argument, We come to you with the right refutation and the best explanation. **34.** Those who will be dragged into Hell on their faces will be in the worst place, and are ˹now˺ farthest from the ˹Right˺ Way.

Destruction of Pharaoh's People

35. We certainly gave Moses the Book and appointed his brother Aaron as his helper. **36.** We had ordered ˹them˺, "Go to the people who would deny Our signs." Then We annihilated the deniers entirely.

Destruction of Noah's People

37. And when the people of Noah rejected the messengers,[731] We drowned them, making them an example to humanity. And We have prepared a painful punishment for the wrongdoers.

Destruction of Other Peoples

38. Also ˹We destroyed˺ 'Âd, Thamûd, and the people of the Water-pit,[732] as well as many peoples in between. **39.** For each We set forth ˹various˺ lessons, and We ultimately destroyed each.

Warning to Meccan Pagans

40. They have certainly passed by the city ˹of Sodom˺, which had been showered with a dreadful rain ˹of stones˺. Have they not seen its ruins? But they do not expect to be resurrected. **41.** When they see you ˹O Prophet˺, they only make fun of you, ˹saying,˺ "Is this the one that Allah has sent as a messenger? **42.** He would have almost tricked us away from our gods, had we not been so devoted to them." ˹But˺ soon they will know, when they face the punishment, who is far astray from the ˹Right˺ Way. **43.** Have you seen ˹O Prophet˺ the one who has taken their own desires as their god? Will you then be a keeper over them? **44.** Or do you think that most of them listen or understand?[733] They are only like cattle—no, more than that, they are astray from the ˹Right˺ Way![734]

---

731 Denying Noah was equal to denying all of Allah's messengers.
732 *Ar-Rass* means "well" or "water-pit". This refers to a pagan people, along with Midian, to whom Allah sent Prophet Shu'aib.
733 They neither pay attention, nor think for themselves. They only follow others blindly.
734 Generally, animals are obedient and loyal to their masters who care for them and they seem to know their way, whereas Meccan pagans are disobedient and ungrateful to their Lord and Sustainer, choosing to stray from the right path.

25. Al-Furqân

Allah's Power: 1) The Sun and Shade

45. Have you not seen how your Lord extends the shade—He could have simply made it ʿremainʾ still if He so willed—then We make the sun its guide, 46. causing the shade to retreat gradually?[735]

2) The Day and Night

47. He is the One Who has made the night for you as a cover, and ʿmadeʾ sleep for resting, and the day for rising.

3) The Rain

48. And He is the One Who sends the winds ushering in His mercy, and We send down pure rain from the sky, 49. giving life to a lifeless land, and providing water for countless animals and humans of Our Own creation. 50. We certainly disperse it among them so they may be mindful, but most people persist in ungratefulness.

One Universal Messenger

51. Had We willed, We could have easily sent a warner to every society. 52. So do not yield to the disbelievers, but strive diligently against them with this ʿQuranʾ.

4) Fresh and Salt Water

53. And He is the One Who merges the two bodies of water: one fresh and palatable and the other salty and bitter, placing between them a barrier they cannot cross.[736]

5) Creation of Humans

54. And He is the One Who creates human beings from a ʿhumbleʾ liquid,[737] then establishes for them bonds of kinship and marriage. For your Lord is Most Capable.

Powerless Gods

55. Yet they worship besides Allah what can neither benefit nor harm them. And the disbeliever always collaborates against their Lord.

---

735 This means that one of the great miracles of Allah is that He allows the sun to rise in the morning, causing darkness to retreat. He could have stopped the sun and the earth from rotating, so half of the world would be engulfed in complete darkness, leading to an imbalance in the earth's eco-systems and endangering life on the planet.

736 This refers to estuaries where salt and fresh waters meet forming brackish water. Although both waters mix together, each still keeps its distinctive qualities.

737 The mixture of sperm and egg.

25. Al-Furqân

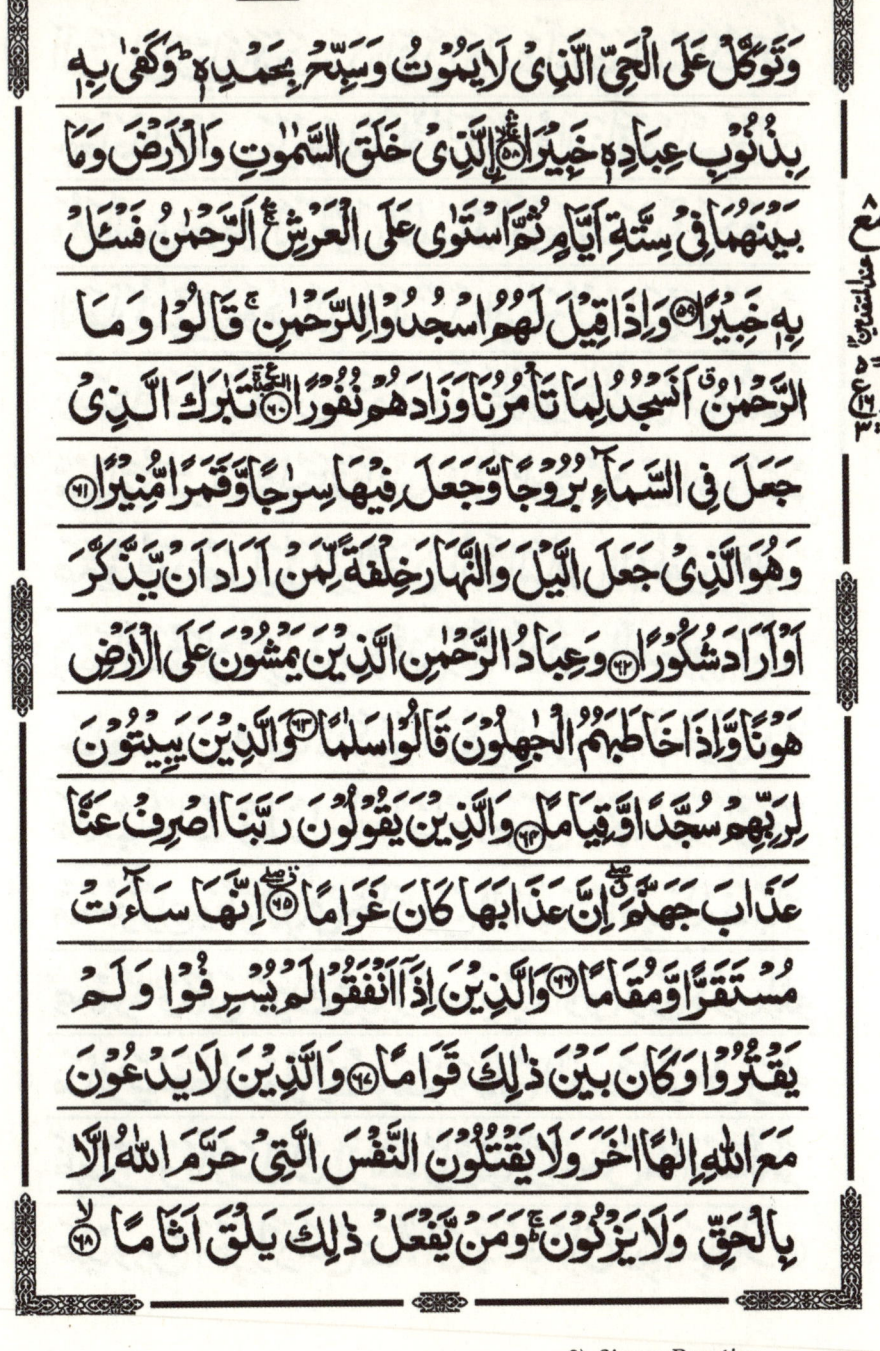

Advice to the Prophet: Trust in Allah

56. And We have sent you ʿO Prophetʾ only as a deliverer of good news and a warner. **57.** Say, "I do not ask you for any reward for this ʿmessageʾ, but whoever wishes, let them pursue the Way to their Lord." **58.** Put your trust in the Ever-Living, Who never dies, and glorify His praises. Sufficient is He as All-Aware of the sins of His servants. **59.** ʿHe isʾ the One Who created the heavens and the earth and everything in between in six Days,[738] then established Himself on the Throne. ʿHe isʾ the Most Compassionate! Ask ʿnone other thanʾ the All-Knowledgeable about Himself.

Denying Allah

60. When it is said to them, "Prostrate to the Most Compassionate," they ask ʿin disgustʾ, "What is 'the Most Compassionate'? Will we prostrate to whatever you order us to?" And it only drives them farther away.

Allah Almighty

61. Blessed is the One Who has placed constellations in the sky, as well as a ʿradiantʾ lamp[739] and a luminous moon. **62.** And He is the One Who causes the day and the night to alternate, ʿas a signʾ for whoever desires to be mindful or to be grateful.

Qualities of the Righteous: 1) Humility

63. The ʿtrueʾ servants of the Most Compassionate are those who walk on the earth humbly, and when the foolish address them ʿimproperlyʾ, they only respond with peace.

2) Sincere Devotion

64. ʿThey areʾ those who spend ʿa good portion ofʾ the night, prostrating themselves and standing before their Lord.

3) ʿHope andʾ Fear

65. ʿThey areʾ those who pray, "Our Lord! Keep the punishment of Hell away from us, for its punishment is indeed unrelenting. **66.** It is certainly an evil place to settle and reside."

4) Moderate Spending

67. ʿThey areʾ those who spend neither wastefully nor stingily, but moderately in between.

---

738 See footnote for 7:54.
739 The sun.

5) Avoiding Major Sins

68. ˹They are˺ those who do not invoke any other god besides Allah, nor take a ˹human˺ life—made sacred by Allah—except with ˹legal˺ right,[740] nor commit fornication. And whoever does ˹any of˺ this will face the penalty. 69. Their punishment will be multiplied on the Day of Judgment, and they will remain in it forever, in disgrace. 70. As for those who repent, believe, and do good deeds, they are the ones whose evil deeds Allah will change into good deeds. For Allah is All-Forgiving, Most Merciful. 71. And whoever repents and does good has truly turned to Allah properly.

6) Avoiding Falsehood

72. ˹They are˺ those who do not bear false witness, and when they come across falsehood, they pass ˹it˺ by with dignity.

7) Full Submission

73. ˹They are˺ those who, when reminded of the revelation of their Lord, do not turn a blind eye or a deaf ear to it.

8) Righteous Company

74. ˹They are˺ those who pray, "Our Lord! Bless us with ˹pious˺ spouses and offspring who will be the joy of our hearts, and make us models for the righteous."

Reward of the Righteous

75. It is they who will be rewarded with ˹elevated˺ mansions ˹in Paradise˺ for their perseverance, and will be received with salutations and ˹greetings of˺ peace, 76. staying there forever. What an excellent place to settle and reside!

Call to Humanity

77. Say, ˹O Prophet,˺ "You ˹all˺ would not ˹even˺ matter to my Lord were it not for your faith ˹in Him˺. But now you ˹disbelievers˺ have denied ˹the truth˺, so the torment is bound to come."

---

26. The Poets (Ash-Shu'arâ')

In the Name of Allah—the Most Compassionate, Most Merciful

---

740 For example, in retaliation for intentional killing through legal channels.

26. Ash-Shu'arâ' | **368**

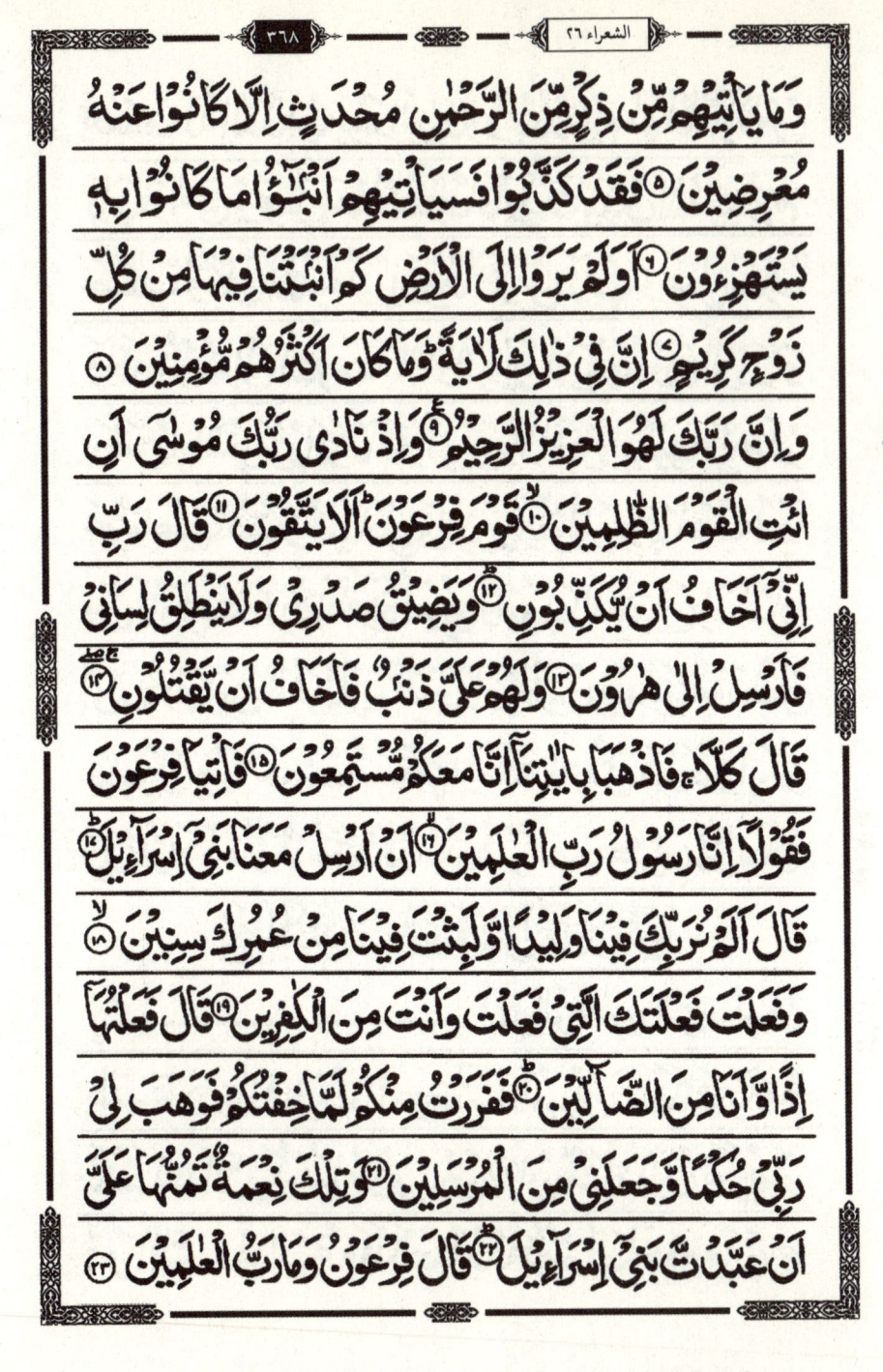

Warning to the Disbelievers

1. *Ṭâ-Sîn-Mîm.* 2. These are the verses of the clear Book. 3. Perhaps you ˹O Prophet˺ will grieve yourself to death over their disbelief. 4. If We willed, We could send down upon them a ˹compelling˺ sign from the heavens, leaving their necks bent in ˹utter˺ submission to it. 5. Whatever new reminder comes to them from the Most Compassionate, they always turn away from it. 6. They have certainly denied ˹the truth˺, so they will soon face the consequences of their ridicule. 7. Have they failed to look at the earth, ˹to see˺ how many types of fine plants We have caused to grow in it? 8. Surely in this is a sign. Yet most of them would not believe. 9. And your Lord is certainly the Almighty, Most Merciful.

Prophet Moses

10. ˹Remember˺ when your Lord called out to Moses, "Go to the wrongdoing people— 11. the people of Pharaoh. Will they not fear ˹Allah˺?" 12. He replied, "My Lord! I fear that they will reject me. 13. And ˹so˺ my heart will be broken and my tongue will be tied. So send Aaron along ˹as a messenger˺. 14. Also, they have a charge against me,[741] so I fear they may kill me." 15. Allah responded, "Certainly not! So go, both of you, with Our signs. We will be with you, listening. 16. Go to Pharaoh and say, 'We are messengers from the Lord of all worlds, 17. ˹commanded to say:˺ 'Let the Children of Israel go with us.'"

Moses vs. Pharaoh

18. Pharaoh protested, "Did we not raise you among us as a child, and you stayed several years of your life in our care? 19. Then you did what you did,[742] being ˹utterly˺ ungrateful!" 20. Moses replied, "I did it then, lacking guidance. 21. So I fled from you when I feared you. Then my Lord granted me wisdom and made me one of the messengers. 22. How can that be a 'favour,' of which you remind me, when ˹it was only because˺ you ˹have˺ enslaved the Children of Israel?" 23. Pharaoh asked, "And what is ˹the Lord of all worlds˺?"

---

741 For killing an Egyptian by mistake before prophethood. See 28:15-17.
742 *See* previous footnote.

24. Moses replied, "'He is' the Lord of the heavens and the earth and everything in between, if only you had sure faith." **25.** Pharaoh said to those around him, "Did you hear 'what he said'?" **26.** Moses added, "'He is' your Lord and the Lord of your forefathers." **27.** Pharaoh said 'mockingly', "Your messenger, who has been sent to you, must be insane." **28.** Moses responded: "'He is' the Lord of the east and west, and everything in between, if only you had any sense."

The Challenge

29. Pharaoh threatened, "If you take any other god besides me, I will certainly have you imprisoned." **30.** Moses responded, "Even if I bring you a clear proof?" **31.** Pharaoh demanded, "Bring it then, if what you say is true." **32.** So he threw down his staff and—behold!—it became a real snake. **33.** Then he drew his hand 'out of his collar' and it was 'shining' white for all to see. **34.** Pharaoh said to the chiefs around him, "He is indeed a skilled magician, **35.** who seeks to drive you from your land by his magic. So what do you propose?" **36.** They replied, "Let him and his brother wait and dispatch mobilizers to all cities **37.** to bring you every skilled magician." **38.** So the magicians were assembled at the set time on the appointed day. **39.** And the people were asked, "Will you join the gathering, **40.** so that we may follow the magicians if they prevail?"

Moses and the Magicians Face off

41. When the magicians came, they asked Pharaoh, "Shall we have a 'suitable' reward if we prevail?" **42.** He replied, "Yes, and you will then certainly be among those closest to me." **43.** Moses said to them, "Cast whatever you wish to cast."

26. Ash-Shu'arâ'

44. So they cast down their ropes and staffs, saying, "By Pharaoh's might, it is we who will surely prevail." **45.** Then Moses threw down his staff, and—behold!—it devoured the objects of their illusion!

Magicians Become Believers

46. So the magicians fell down, prostrating. **47.** They declared, "We ˹now˺ believe in the Lord of all worlds— **48.** the Lord of Moses and Aaron." **49.** Pharaoh threatened, "How dare you believe in him before I give you permission? He must be your master who taught you magic, but soon you will see. I will certainly cut off your hands and feet on opposite sides, then crucify you all." **50.** They responded, "˹That would be˺ no harm! Surely to our Lord we will ˹all˺ return. **51.** We really hope that our Lord will forgive our sins, as we are the first to believe."

Pharaoh Chases the Israelites

52. And We inspired Moses, ˹saying,˺ "Leave with My servants at night, for you will surely be pursued." **53.** Then Pharaoh sent mobilizers to all cities, **54.** ˹and said,˺ "These ˹outcasts˺ are just a handful of people, **55.** who have really enraged us, **56.** but we are all on the alert." **57.** So We lured the tyrants[743] out of ˹their˺ gardens, springs, **58.** treasures, and splendid residences. **59.** So it was. And We awarded it ˹all˺ to the Children of Israel.

The End of Pharaoh

60. And so they pursued them at sunrise. **61.** When the two groups came face to face, the companions of Moses cried out, "We are overtaken for sure." **62.** Moses reassured ˹them˺, "Absolutely not! My Lord is certainly with me—He will guide me." **63.** So We inspired Moses: "Strike the sea with your staff," and the sea was split, each part was like a huge mountain. **64.** We drew the pursuers to that place,

---

743 Pharaoh and his soldiers.

371 26. Ash-Shu'arâ'

65. and delivered Moses and those with him all together. 66. Then We drowned the others. 67. Surely in this is a sign. Yet most of them would not believe. 68. And your Lord is certainly the Almighty, Most Merciful.

Prophet Abraham

69. Relate to them ˹O Prophet˺ the story of Abraham, 70. when he questioned his father and his people, "What is that you worship ˹besides Allah˺?" 71. They replied, "We worship idols, to which we are fully devoted." 72. Abraham asked, "Can they hear you when you call upon them? 73. Or can they benefit or harm you?" 74. They replied, "No! But we found our forefathers doing the same." 75. Abraham responded, "Have you ˹really˺ considered what you have been worshipping— 76. you and your ancestors? 77. They are ˹all˺ enemies to me, except the Lord of all worlds. 78. ˹He is˺ the One Who created me, and He ˹alone˺ guides me. 79. ˹He is˺ the One Who provides me with food and drink. 80. And He ˹alone˺ heals me when I am sick. 81. And He ˹is the One Who˺ will cause me to die, and then bring me back to life. 82. And He is ˹the One˺ Who, I hope, will forgive my flaws[744] on Judgment Day."

Abraham's Prayer

83. "My Lord! Grant me wisdom, and join me with the righteous. 84. Bless me with honourable mention among later generations.[745] 85. Make me one of those awarded the Garden of Bliss. 86. Forgive my father, for he is certainly one of the misguided. 87. And do not disgrace me on the Day all will be resurrected— 88. the Day when neither wealth nor children will be of any benefit. 89. Only those who come before Allah with a pure heart ˹will be saved˺."[746]

Judgment Day

90. ˹On that Day˺ Paradise will be brought near to the God-fearing,

---

744 It is reported in an authentic narration collected by At-Tirmizi that Prophet Muḥammad (ﷺ) said that Abraham (ﷺ) did not tell the full truth only on three different occasions: when he justified his absence from the pagan festival by saying 'I am really sick' (see 37:89), and when he destroyed the idols and blamed it on the biggest one (see 21:63), and when he said that Sarah was his sister to save her from a tyrant ruler.

745 On a daily basis, Muslims invoke Allah's blessings upon Prophet Muḥammad (ﷺ) and his family and Prophet Abraham (ﷺ) and his family, in both obligatory and optional prayers.

746 A pure and sound heart is that of the believer, compared to that of the disbeliever and the hypocrite.

26. Ash-Shu'ara'   372

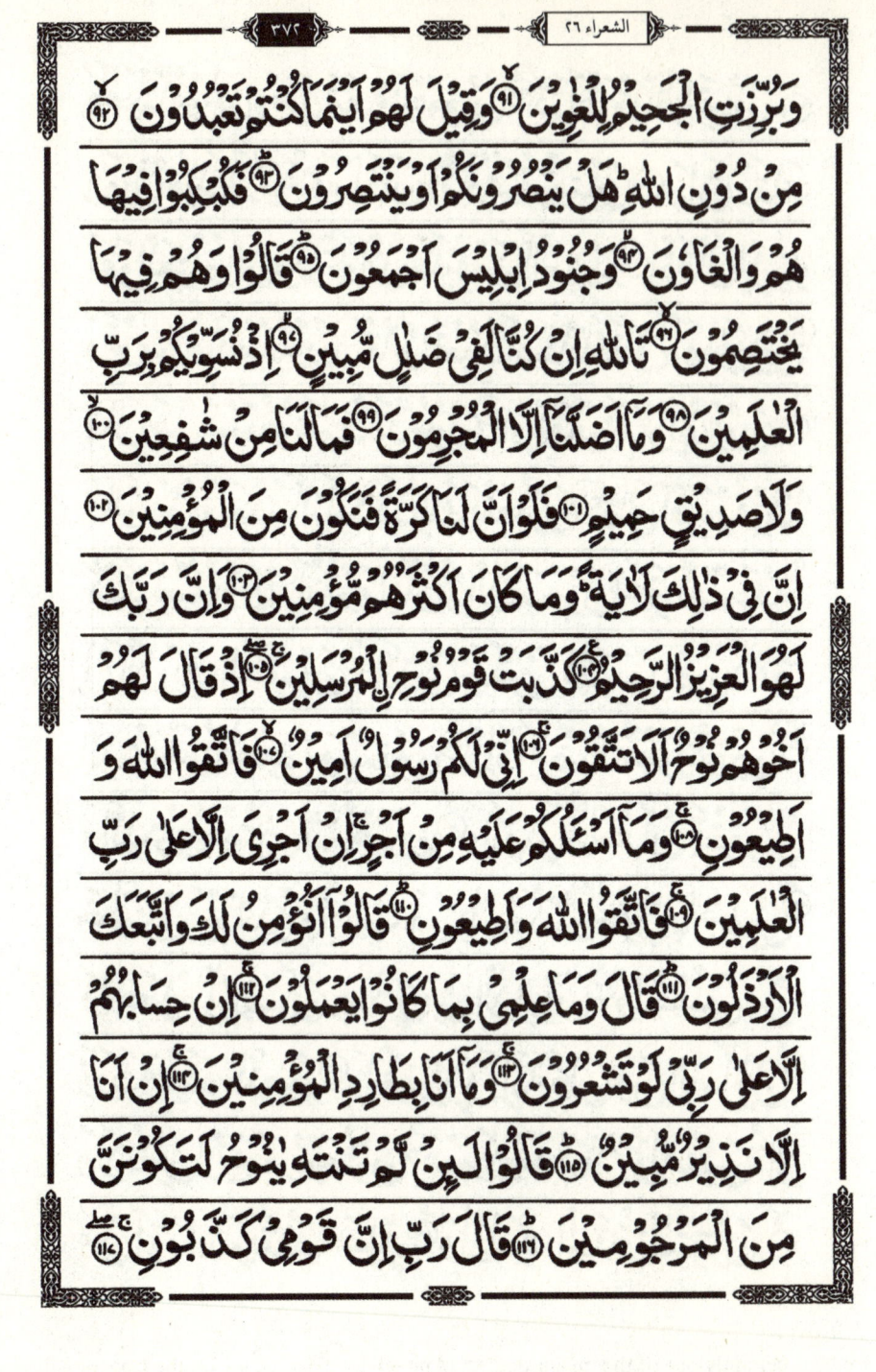

91. and the Hellfire will be displayed to the deviant. 92. And it will be said to them, "Where are those you used to worship 93. besides Allah? Can they help you or even help themselves?" 94. Then the idols will be hurled headlong into Hell, along with the deviant 95. and the soldiers of *Iblîs*,[747] all together. 96. There the deviant will cry while disputing with their idols, 97. "By Allah! We were clearly mistaken, 98. when we made you equal to the Lord of all worlds. 99. And none led us astray other than the wicked. 100. Now we have none to intercede for us, 101. nor a close friend. 102. If only we could have a second chance, then we would be believers." 103. Surely in this is a sign. Yet most of them would not believe. 104. And your Lord is certainly the Almighty, Most Merciful.

Prophet Noah

105. The people of Noah rejected the messengers[748] 106. when their brother Noah said to them, "Will you not fear ˹Allah˺? 107. I am truly a trustworthy messenger to you. 108. So fear Allah, and obey me. 109. I do not ask you for any reward for this ˹message˺. My reward is only from the Lord of all worlds. 110. So fear Allah, and obey me." 111. They argued, "How can we believe in you, when you are followed ˹only˺ by the lowest of the low?"[749] 112. He responded, "And what knowledge do I have of what they do? 113. Their judgment is with my Lord, if you had any sense! 114. I am not going to expel the believers. 115. I am only sent with a clear warning."

Noah's People Destroyed

116. They threatened, "If you do not desist, O Noah, you will surely be stoned ˹to death˺." 117. Noah prayed, "My Lord! My people have truly rejected me.

---

747 *Iblîs* was the name of Satan before his fall from grace. *See* footnote for 2:34.
748 Denying Noah (۝) was equal to denying all of Allah's messengers.
749 The pagans were accusing the impoverished believers of following Noah (۝) only for personal gain, not out of sincere faith.

26. Ash-Shu'arâ'

118. So judge between me and them decisively, and save me and the believers with me." 119. So We saved him and those with him in the fully loaded Ark. 120. Then afterwards We drowned the rest. 121. Surely in this is a sign. Yet most of them would not believe. 122. And your Lord is certainly the Almighty, Most Merciful.

Prophet Hûd

123. The people of 'Âd rejected the messenger s124. when their brother Hûd said to them, "Will you not fear ˹Allah˺? 125. I am truly a trustworthy messenger to you. 126. So fear Allah, and obey me. 127. I do not ask you for any reward for this ˹message˺. My reward is only from the Lord of all worlds. 128. ˹Why˺ do you build a landmark on every high place in vanity, 129. and construct castles, as if you are going to live forever, 130. and act so viciously when you attack ˹others˺? 131. So fear Allah, and obey me. 132. Fear the One Who has provided you with ˹the good˺ things you know: 133. He provided you with cattle, and children, 134. and gardens, and springs. 135. I truly fear for you the torment of a tremendous day."

Hûd's People Destroyed

136. They responded, "It is all the same to us whether you warn ˹us˺ or not. 137. This is simply the tradition of our predecessors. 138. And we will never be punished." 139. So they rejected him, and ˹so˺ We destroyed them. Surely in this is a sign. Yet most of them would not believe. 140. And your Lord is certainly the Almighty, Most Merciful.

Prophet Şâliḥ

141. The people of Thamûd rejected the messengers 142. when their brother Şâliḥ said to them, "Will you not fear ˹Allah˺?

26. Ash-Shu'arâ' | 374

إِنِّي لَكُمْ رَسُولٌ أَمِينٌ ۝ فَاتَّقُوا اللَّهَ وَأَطِيعُونِ ۝ وَمَآ أَسْـَٔلُكُمْ عَلَيْهِ مِنْ أَجْرٍ إِنْ أَجْرِيَ إِلَّا عَلَىٰ رَبِّ الْعَٰلَمِينَ ۝ أَتُتْرَكُونَ فِي مَا هَٰهُنَآ ءَامِنِينَ ۝ فِي جَنَّٰتٍ وَعُيُونٍ ۝ وَزُرُوعٍ وَنَخْلٍ طَلْعُهَا هَضِيمٌ ۝ وَتَنْحِتُونَ مِنَ الْجِبَالِ بُيُوتًا فَٰرِهِينَ ۝ فَاتَّقُوا اللَّهَ وَأَطِيعُونِ ۝ وَلَا تُطِيعُوٓا أَمْرَ الْمُسْرِفِينَ ۝ الَّذِينَ يُفْسِدُونَ فِي الْأَرْضِ وَلَا يُصْلِحُونَ ۝ قَالُوٓا إِنَّمَآ أَنتَ مِنَ الْمُسَحَّرِينَ ۝ مَآ أَنتَ إِلَّا بَشَرٌ مِّثْلُنَا فَأْتِ بِـَٔايَةٍ إِن كُنتَ مِنَ الصَّٰدِقِينَ ۝ قَالَ هَٰذِهِۦ نَاقَةٌ لَّهَا شِرْبٌ وَلَكُمْ شِرْبُ يَوْمٍ مَّعْلُومٍ ۝ وَلَا تَمَسُّوهَا بِسُوٓءٍ فَيَأْخُذَكُمْ عَذَابُ يَوْمٍ عَظِيمٍ ۝ فَعَقَرُوهَا فَأَصْبَحُوا نَٰدِمِينَ ۝ فَأَخَذَهُمُ الْعَذَابُ إِنَّ فِي ذَٰلِكَ لَـَٔايَةً وَمَا كَانَ أَكْثَرُهُم مُّؤْمِنِينَ ۝ وَإِنَّ رَبَّكَ لَهُوَ الْعَزِيزُ الرَّحِيمُ ۝ كَذَّبَتْ قَوْمُ لُوطٍ الْمُرْسَلِينَ ۝ إِذْ قَالَ لَهُمْ أَخُوهُمْ لُوطٌ أَلَا تَتَّقُونَ ۝ إِنِّي لَكُمْ رَسُولٌ أَمِينٌ ۝ فَاتَّقُوا اللَّهَ وَأَطِيعُونِ ۝ وَمَآ أَسْـَٔلُكُمْ عَلَيْهِ مِنْ أَجْرٍ إِنْ أَجْرِيَ إِلَّا عَلَىٰ رَبِّ الْعَٰلَمِينَ ۝ أَتَأْتُونَ الذُّكْرَانَ مِنَ الْعَٰلَمِينَ ۝ وَتَذَرُونَ مَا خَلَقَ لَكُمْ رَبُّكُم مِّنْ أَزْوَٰجِكُم بَلْ أَنتُمْ قَوْمٌ عَادُونَ ۝

143. I am truly a trustworthy messenger to you. 144. So fear Allah, and obey me. 145. I do not ask you for any reward for this ˹message˺. My reward is only from the Lord of all worlds. 146. Do you think you will be ˹forever˺ left secure in what you have here: 147. amid gardens and springs, 148. and ˹various˺ crops, and palm trees ˹loaded˺ with tender fruit; 149. to carve homes in the mountains with great skill? 150. So fear Allah, and obey me. 151. And do not follow the command of the transgressors, 152. who spread corruption throughout the land, never setting things right."

Ṣâliḥ's People Destroyed

153. They replied, "You are simply bewitched! 154. You are only a human being like us, so bring forth a sign if what you say is true." 155. Ṣâliḥ said, "Here is a camel. She will have her turn to drink as you have yours, each on an appointed day. 156. And do not ever touch her with harm, or you will be overtaken by the torment of a tremendous day." 157. But they killed her, becoming regretful. 158. So the punishment overtook them. Surely in this is a sign. Yet most of them would not believe. 159. And your Lord is certainly the Almighty, Most Merciful.

Prophet Lot

160. The people of Lot rejected the messengers 161. when their brother Lot said to them, "Will you not fear ˹Allah˺? 162. I am truly a trustworthy messenger to you. 163. So fear Allah, and obey me. 164. I do not ask you for any reward for this ˹message˺. My reward is only from the Lord of all worlds. 165. Why do you ˹men˺ lust after fellow men,[750] 166. leaving the wives that your Lord has created for you? In fact, you are a transgressing people."

---
750 lit., men of the world.

26. Ash-Shu'arâ'

Lot's People Destroyed

167. They threatened, "If you do not desist, O Lot, you will surely be expelled." 168. Lot responded, "I am truly one of those who despise your ˹shameful˺ practice. 169. My Lord! Save me and my family from ˹the consequences of˺ what they do." 170. So We saved him and all of his family, 171. except an old woman,[751] who was one of the doomed. 172. Then We utterly destroyed the rest, 173. pouring upon them a rain ˹of brimstone˺. How evil was the rain of those who had been warned! 174. Surely in this is a sign. Yet most of them would not believe. 175. And your Lord is certainly the Almighty, Most Merciful.

Prophet Shu'aib

176. The residents of the Forest rejected the messengers 177. when Shu'aib said to them,[752] "Will you not fear ˹Allah˺? 178. I am truly a trustworthy messenger to you. 179. So fear Allah, and obey me. 180. I do not ask you for any reward for this ˹message˺. My reward is only from the Lord of all worlds. 181. Give full measure, and cause no loss ˹to others˺. 182. Weigh with an even balance, 183. and do not defraud people of their property. Nor go about spreading corruption in the land. 184. And fear the One Who created you and ˹all˺ earlier peoples."

Shu'aib's People Destroyed

185. They replied, "You are simply bewitched! 186. Also, you are only a human being like us, and we think you are indeed a liar. 187. So cause ˹deadly˺ pieces of the sky to fall upon us, if what you say is true." 188. Shu'aib responded, "My Lord knows best whatever you do." 189. So they rejected him, and ˹so˺ were overtaken by the torment of the day of the ˹deadly˺ cloud.[753] That was really a torment of a tremendous day.

---

751 Lot's wife, who betrayed her husband.

752 Unlike other prophets in this sûrah who are identified as the brothers of fellow tribesmen, Shu'aib is not identified as the brother of the people of the *Aykah* (which is the name of the forest where they used to worship a particular tree) because they are identified by faith, rather than a tribal connection.

753 They were targeted by scorching heat, so they did not know where to go. Finally, a soothing cloud appeared in the sky, so they rushed to it for shade, then the cloud rained torment upon them, as they had requested.

26. Ash-Shu'arâ' 376

190. Surely in this is a sign. Yet most of them would not believe. 191. And your Lord is certainly the Almighty, Most Merciful.

The Quran

192. This is certainly a revelation from the Lord of all worlds, 193. which the trustworthy spirit ˹Gabriel˺ brought down 194. into your heart ˹O Prophet˺—so that you may be one of the warners— 195. in a clear Arabic tongue. 196. And it has indeed been ˹foretold˺ in the Scriptures of those before. 197. Was it not sufficient proof for the deniers that it has been recognized by the knowledgeable among the Children of Israel?[754] 198. Had We revealed it to a non-Arab, 199. who would then recite it to the deniers ˹in fluent Arabic˺, still they would not have believed in it! 200. This is how We allow denial ˹to steep˺ into the hearts of the wicked. 201. They will not believe in it until they see the painful punishment, 202. which will take them by surprise when they least expect ˹it˺. 203. Then they will cry, "Can we be allowed more time?"

Warning to the Meccan Pagans

204. Do they ˹really˺ seek to hasten Our torment? 205. Imagine ˹O Prophet˺ if We allowed them enjoyment for years, 206. then there came to them what they had been threatened with: 207. would that enjoyment be of any benefit to them ˹at all˺? 208. We have never destroyed a society without warners 209. to remind ˹them˺, for We would never wrong ˹anyone˺.

The Quran Is Allah's Word

210. It was not the devils who brought this ˹Quran˺ down: 211. it is not for them ˹to do so˺, nor can they, 212. for they are strictly barred from ˹even˺ overhearing ˹it˺.[755]

Advice to the Prophet

213. So do not ever call upon any other god besides Allah, or you will be one of the punished. 214. And warn ˹all, starting with˺ your closest relatives, 215. and be gracious to the believers who follow you. 216. But if they disobey you, say, "I am certainly free

---

754 i.e., 'Abdullâh ibn Salâm, a Jewish authority, who accepted Islam during the time of the Prophet (ﷺ).
755 The devils can no longer eavesdrop on heaven. *See* 72:8-10.

27. An-Naml

of what you do." **217.** Put your trust in the Almighty, Most Merciful, **218.** Who sees you when you rise ˹for prayer at night˺, **219.** as well as your movements ˹in prayer˺ along with ˹fellow˺ worshippers. **220.** He ˹alone˺ is indeed the All-Hearing, All-Knowing.

The Devils

221. Shall I inform you of whom the devils ˹actually˺ descend upon? **222.** They descend upon every sinful liar, **223.** who gives an ˹attentive˺ ear ˹to half-truths˺, mostly passing on sheer lies.[756]

The Poets

224. As for poets, they are followed ˹merely˺ by deviants. **225.** Do you not see how they rant in every field,[757] **226.** only saying what they never do? **227.** Except those who believe, do good, remember Allah often, and ˹poetically˺ avenge ˹the believers˺ after being wrongfully slandered. The wrongdoers will come to know what ˹evil˺ end they will meet.

 মকল✻মকল

27. The Ants (An-Naml)

In the Name of Allah—the Most Compassionate, Most Merciful

Qualities of the Believers

1. *Ṭâ-Sîn.* These are the verses of the Quran; the clear Book. **2.** ˹It is˺ a guide and good news for the believers: **3.** ˹those˺ who establish prayer, pay alms-tax, and have sure faith in the Hereafter.

Qualities of the Disbelievers

4. As for those who do not believe in the Hereafter, We have certainly made their ˹evil˺ deeds appealing to them, so they wander blindly. **5.** It is they who will suffer a dreadful torment, and in the Hereafter they will ˹truly˺ be the greatest losers.

---

756 This refers to fortune-tellers who listen to Satanic whispers, adding more lies as they pass on the information to people.
757 lit., roam aimlessly in every valley.

27. An-Naml

6. And indeed, you ˹O Prophet˺ are receiving the Quran from the One ˹Who is˺ All-Wise, All-Knowing.

Moses and the Nine Signs

7. ˹Remember˺ when Moses said to his family, "I have spotted a fire. I will either bring you some directions[758] from there, or a burning torch so you may warm yourselves."
8. But when he came to it, he was called ˹by Allah˺, "Blessed is the one at the fire, and whoever is around it![759] Glory be to Allah, the Lord of all worlds. 9. O Moses! It is truly I. I am Allah—the Almighty, All-Wise.
10. Now, throw down your staff!" But when he saw it slithering like a snake, he ran away without looking back. ˹Allah reassured him,˺ "O Moses! Do not be afraid! Messengers should have no fear in My presence. 11. ˹Fear is˺ only for those who do wrong. But if they later mend ˹their˺ evil ˹ways˺ with good, then I am certainly All-Forgiving, Most Merciful. 12. Now put your hand through ˹the opening of˺ your collar, it will come out ˹shining˺ white, unblemished.[760] ˹These are two˺ of nine signs for Pharaoh and his people.[761] They have truly been a rebellious people." 13. But when Our enlightening signs came to them, they said, "This is pure magic." 14. And, although their hearts were convinced the signs were true, they still denied them wrongfully and arrogantly. See then what was the end of the corruptors!

David and Solomon

15. Indeed, We granted knowledge to David and Solomon. And they said ˹in acknowledgment˺, "All praise is for Allah Who has privileged us over many of His faithful servants."[762] 16. And David was succeeded by Solomon, who said, "O people! We have been taught the language of birds, and been given everything ˹we need˺. This is indeed a great privilege."

---

758 lit., information. Moses and his family lost their way in the dark while they were travelling from Midian to Egypt.
759 This refers to the angels who were present around the light.
760 See footnote for 20:22.
761 *See* footnote for 23:45.
762 The privilege was their ability to communicate with members of the animal kingdom, control the wind, utilize the jinn for their service, etc.

27. An-Naml

Solomon and the Ant

17. Solomon's forces of jinn, humans, and birds were rallied for him, perfectly organized. **18.** And when they came across a valley of ants, an ant warned, "O ants! Go quickly into your homes so Solomon and his armies do not crush you, unknowingly." **19.** So Solomon smiled in amusement at her words, and prayed, "My Lord! Inspire me to ˹always˺ be thankful for Your favours which You have blessed me and my parents with, and to do good deeds that please you. Admit me, by Your mercy, into ˹the company of˺ Your righteous servants."

Solomon and the Hoopoe

20. ˹One day˺ he inspected the birds, and wondered, "Why is it that I cannot see the hoopoe? Or could he be absent? **21.** I will surely subject him to a severe punishment, or ˹even˺ slaughter him, unless he brings me a compelling excuse." **22.** It was not long before the bird came and said, "I have found out something you do not know. I have just come to you from Sheba with sure news. **23.** Indeed, I found a woman ruling over them,[763] who has been given everything ˹she needs˺, and who has a magnificent throne. **24.** I found her and her people prostrating to the sun instead of Allah. For Satan has made their deeds appealing to them—hindering them from the ˹Right˺ Way and leaving them unguided— **25.** so they do not prostrate to Allah, Who brings forth what is hidden in the heavens and the earth, and knows what you ˹all˺ conceal and what you reveal. **26.** ˹He is˺ Allah! There is no god ˹worthy of worship˺ except Him, the Lord of the Mighty Throne."

---

763 The Queen of Sheba is known in Islamic tradition as Bilkis.

27. An-Naml 380

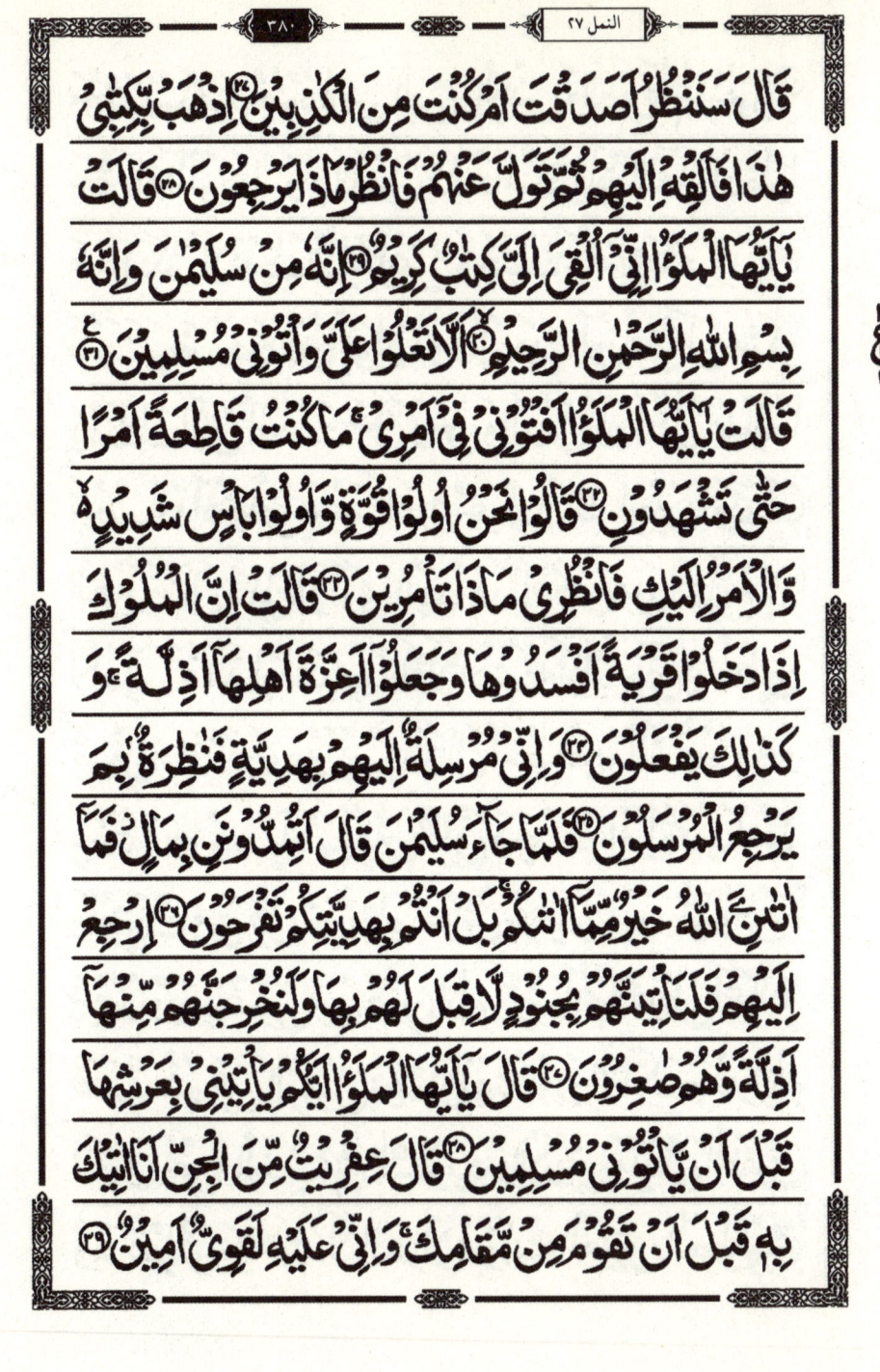

Solomon's Letter

27. Solomon said, "We will see whether you are telling the truth or lying. **28.** Go with this letter of mine and deliver it to them, then stand aside and see how they will respond." **29.** The Queen ˹later˺ announced, "O chiefs! Indeed, a noble letter has been delivered to me. **30.** It is from Solomon, and it reads: 'In the Name of Allah—the Most Compassionate, Most Merciful. **31.** Do not be arrogant with me, but come to me, fully submitting ˹to Allah˺.'"

The Queen's Response

32. She said, "O chiefs! Advise me in this matter of mine, for I would never make any decision without you." **33.** They responded, "We are a people of strength and great ˹military˺ might, but the decision is yours, so decide what you will command." **34.** She reasoned, "Indeed, when kings invade a land, they ruin it and debase its nobles. They really do so! **35.** But I will certainly send him a gift, and see what ˹response˺ my envoys will return with."[764]

Solomon's Response

36. When the chief-envoy came to him, Solomon said, "Do you offer me wealth? What Allah has granted me is far greater than what He has granted you. No! It is you who rejoice in ˹receiving˺ gifts. **37.** Go back to them, for we will certainly mobilize against them forces which they can never resist, and we will drive them out from there in disgrace, fully humbled."[765]

The Queen's Throne

38. Solomon asked, "O chiefs! Which of you can bring me her throne before they come to me in ˹full˺ submission?"[766] **39.** One mighty jinn responded, "I can bring it to you before you rise from this council of yours. And I am quite strong and trustworthy for this ˹task˺."

---

764 She wanted to test Solomon (☾) to see if he was only a king (so he would be satisfied with a tribute) or a prophet (who would only settle with submission to the True God).

765 If they refuse to submit.

766 To explain why Prophet Solomon brought the Queen's magnificent throne and built the marvellous palace, many traditional commentators cite some folkloric or legendary stories. However, none of these stories is supported by reliable Islamic sources.

40. But the one who had knowledge of the Scripture said,[767] "I can bring it to you in the blink of an eye." So when Solomon saw it placed before him, he exclaimed, "This is by the grace of my Lord to test me whether I am grateful or ungrateful. And whoever is grateful, it is only for their own good. But whoever is ungrateful, surely my Lord is Self-Sufficient, Most Generous." **41.** ˹Then˺ Solomon said, "Disguise her throne for her so we may see whether she will recognize ˹it˺ or she will not be able to." **42.** So when she arrived, it was said ˹to her˺, "Is your throne like this?" She replied, "It looks to be the same. We have ˹already˺ received knowledge ˹of Solomon's prophethood˺[768] before this ˹miracle˺,[769] and have submitted ˹to Allah˺." **43.** But she had been hindered by what she used to worship instead of Allah, for she was indeed from a disbelieving people.

Solomon's Palace

44. Then she was told, "Enter the palace." But when she saw the hall, she thought it was a body of water, so she bared her legs. Solomon said. "It is just a palace paved with crystal." ˹At last˺ she declared, "My Lord! I have certainly wronged my soul. Now I ˹fully˺ submit myself along with Solomon to Allah, the Lord of all worlds."

Prophet Ṣâliḥ and His People

45. And We certainly sent to the people of Thamûd their brother Ṣâliḥ, proclaiming, "Worship Allah," but they suddenly split into two opposing groups.[770] **46.** He urged ˹the disbelieving group˺, "O my people! Why do you ˹seek to˺ hasten the torment[771] rather than grace?[772] If only you sought Allah's forgiveness so you may be shown mercy!"

---

767 This refers to 'Aṣif ibn Barkhiya, a knowledgeable and righteous assistant of Solomon.
768 Because he had refused her tribute.
769 Bringing her well-guarded, mighty throne all the way from Sheba, Yemen.
770 i.e., believers and disbelievers.
771 lit., the evil
772 lit., the good

27. An-Naml

47. They replied, "You and your followers are a bad omen for us."[773] He responded, "Your omens are destined by Allah. In fact, you are ˹only˺ a people being tested."

An Attempt on Ṣâliḥ's Life

48. And there were in the city nine ˹elite˺ men who spread corruption in the land, never doing what is right. **49.** They vowed, "Let us swear by Allah that we will take him and his family down by night. Then we will certainly say to his ˹closest˺ heirs, 'We did not witness the murder of his family. We are definitely telling the truth.'" **50.** And ˹so˺ they made a plan, but We too made a plan, while they were unaware. **51.** See then what the consequences of their plan were: We ˹utterly˺ destroyed them and their people all together. **52.** So their homes are there, ˹but completely˺ ruined because of their wrongdoing. Surely in this is a lesson for people of knowledge. **53.** And We delivered those who were faithful and were mindful ˹of Allah˺.

Prophet Lot and His People

54. And ˹remember˺ Lot, when he rebuked ˹the men of˺ his people, "Do you commit that shameful deed while you can see ˹one another˺? **55.** Do you really lust after men instead of women? In fact, you are ˹only˺ a people acting ignorantly." **56.** But his people's only response was to say, "Expel Lot's followers from your land! They are a people who wish to remain chaste!" **57.** So We delivered him and his family, except his wife. We had destined her to be one of the doomed. **58.** And We poured upon them a rain ˹of brimstone˺. How evil was the rain of those who had been warned!

Questions to the Pagans: 1) Who Is the Creator?

59. Say, ˹O Prophet,˺ "Praise be to Allah, and peace be upon the servants He has chosen." ˹Ask the disbelievers,˺ "Which is better: Allah or whatever ˹gods˺ they associate ˹with Him˺?"

---

773 They were struck with famine, which they blamed on Ṣâliḥ and his followers.

383   27. An-Naml

60. Or ˹ask them,˺ "Who created the heavens and the earth, and sends down rain for you from the sky, by which We cause delightful gardens to grow? You could never cause their trees to grow. Was it another god besides Allah? Absolutely not!" But they are a people who set up equals ˹to Allah˺! **61.** Or ˹ask them,˺ "Who made the earth a place of settlement, caused rivers to flow through it, placed firm mountains upon it, and set a barrier between ˹fresh and salt˺ bodies of water?[774] Was it another god besides Allah? Absolutely not!" But most of them do not know.

2) Who Is the Most Gracious?

62. Or ˹ask them,˺ "Who responds to the distressed when they cry to Him, relieving ˹their˺ affliction, and ˹Who˺ makes you successors in the earth? Is it another god besides Allah? Yet you are hardly mindful!" **63.** Or ˹ask them,˺ "Who guides you in the darkness of the land and sea,[775] and sends the winds ushering in His mercy?[776] Is it another god besides Allah? Exalted is Allah above what they associate ˹with Him˺! **64.** Or ˹ask them,˺ "Who originates the creation then resurrects it, and gives you provisions from the heavens and the earth? Is it another god besides Allah?" Say, ˹O Prophet,˺ "Show ˹me˺ your proof, if what you say is true."

Only Allah Knows the Unseen[777]

65. Say, ˹O Prophet,˺ "None in the heavens and the earth has knowledge of the unseen except Allah. Nor do they know when they will be resurrected. **66.** No! Their knowledge of the Hereafter amounts to ignorance. In fact, they are in doubt about it. In truth, they are ˹totally˺ blind to it.

---

774 *See* footnote for 25:53.
775 Via the stars and constellations.
776 In the form of rain.
777 This passage was revealed when the polytheists asked the Prophet (ﷺ) about the time of the Final Hour.

27. An-Naml

Denying Resurrection

67. The disbelievers ask, "When we and our fathers are reduced to dust, will we really be brought forth ˹alive˺? **68.** We have already been promised this, as well as our forefathers earlier. This is nothing but ancient fables!" **69.** Say, ˹O Prophet,˺ "Travel throughout the land and see the fate of the wicked." **70.** Do not grieve for them, nor be distressed by their schemes.

Ridiculing Punishment

71. They ask ˹the believers˺, "When will this threat come to pass, if what you say is true?" **72.** Say, ˹O Prophet,˺ "Perhaps some of what you seek to hasten is close at hand." **73.** Surely your Lord is ever Bountiful to humanity,[778] but most of them are ungrateful. **74.** And surely your Lord knows what their hearts conceal and what they reveal.[779] **75.** For there is nothing hidden in the heavens or the earth without being ˹written˺ in a perfect Record.[780]

Advice to the Prophet

76. Indeed, this Quran clarifies for the Children of Israel most of what they differ over. **77.** And it is truly a guide and mercy for the believers. **78.** Your Lord will certainly judge between them by His justice, for He is the Almighty, All-Knowing. **79.** So put your trust in Allah, for you are surely upon the ˹Path of˺ clear truth.

---

778 By delaying their punishment and allowing them time to repent.
779 Through their tongues or actions.
780 The Record refers to the Preserved Tablet (*Al-Lawḥ Al-Maḥfûz*) in which Allah has written the destiny of His entire creation.

80. You certainly cannot make the dead hear ˹the truth˺. Nor can you make the deaf hear the call when they turn their backs and walk away. **81.** Nor can you lead the blind out of their misguidance. You can make none hear ˹the truth˺ except those who believe in Our revelations, ˹fully˺ submitting ˹to Allah˺.

The Apocalypse

82. And when the decree ˹of the Hour˺ comes to pass against them, We will bring forth for them a beast from the earth,[781] telling them that the people had no sure faith in Our revelations. **83.** ˹Watch for˺ the Day We will gather from every faith-community a group of those who denied Our revelations, and they will be driven in ranks. **84.** When they ˹finally˺ come before their Lord, He will ask ˹them˺, "Did you deny My revelations without ˹even˺ comprehending them? Or what ˹exactly˺ did you do?" **85.** And the decree ˹of torment˺ will be justified against them for their wrongdoing, leaving them speechless.

Allah's Power 1) The Day and Night

86. Do they not see that We made the night for them to rest in and the day bright?[782] Surely in this are signs for those who believe.

The Apocalypse

87. And ˹beware of˺ the Day the Trumpet will be blown, and all those in the heavens and all those on the earth will be horrified ˹to the point of death˺,[783] except those Allah wills ˹to spare˺. And all will come before Him, fully humbled.

Allah's Power 2) Earth's Rotation

88. Now you see the mountains, thinking they are firmly fixed, but they are travelling ˹just˺ like clouds. ˹That is˺ the design of Allah, Who has perfected everything. Surely He is All-Aware of what you do.

---

781 The beast is believed to be one of the major signs of the Day of Judgment. No further details are given in reliable resources about this beast.

782 To demonstrate His ability to bring people back to life, Allah usually refers to some wonders of His creation, such as the planets, the alternation of the day and night, the mountains, and the development of the human embryo.

783 The Trumpet will be blown at two different occasions, signalling the beginning of Judgment Day. The first blow will cause all creation to die, except whoever Allah spares, and the second one will cause them to be raised from the dead.

28. Al-Qaşaş

Judgment Day

89. Whoever comes with a good deed will be rewarded with what is better, and they will be secure from the horror on that Day. 90. And whoever comes with an evil deed will be hurled face-first into the Fire. Are you rewarded except for what you used to do?

Advice to the Prophet

91. Say, ˹O Prophet,˺ "I have only been commanded to worship the Lord of this city ˹of Mecca˺, Who has made it sacred, and to Him belongs everything. And I am commanded to be one of those who ˹fully˺ submit ˹to Him˺, 92. and to recite the Quran." Then whoever chooses to be guided, it is only for their own good. But whoever chooses to stray, say, ˹O Prophet,˺ "I am only a warner." 93. And say, "All praise is for Allah! He will show you His signs, and you will recognize them. And your Lord is never unaware of what you do."

❦✳❦

28. The Whole Story (Al-Qaşaş)

In the Name of Allah—the Most Compassionate, Most Merciful

Pharaoh's Tyranny

1. Ţâ-Sîn-Mîm. 2. These are the verses of the clear Book. 3. We narrate to you ˹O Prophet˺ part of the story of Moses and Pharaoh in truth for people who believe. 4. Indeed, Pharaoh ˹arrogantly˺ elevated himself in the land and divided its people into ˹subservient˺ groups, one of which he persecuted, slaughtering their sons and keeping their women. He was truly one of the corruptors. 5. But it was Our Will to favour those who were oppressed in the land, making them models ˹of faith˺ as well as successors;

387 28. Al-Qaṣaṣ

6. and to establish them in the land; and through them show Pharaoh, Hamân,[784] and their soldiers ʿthe fulfilment ofʾ what they feared.[785]

Baby Moses in the Nile

7. We inspired the mother of Moses: "Nurse him, but when you fear for him, put him then into the river, and do not fear or grieve. We will certainly return him to you, and make him one of the messengers." 8. And ʿit so happened thatʾ Pharaoh's people picked him up, only to become their enemy and source of grief. Surely Pharaoh, Hamân, and their soldiers were sinful.

Moses in the Palace

9. Pharaoh's wife said ʿto himʾ, "ʿThis baby isʾ a source of joy for me and you. Do not kill him. Perhaps he may be useful to us or we may adopt him as a son." They were unaware ʿof what was to comeʾ. 10. And the heart of Moses' mother ached so much that she almost gave away his identity, had We not reassured her heart in order for her to have faith ʿin Allah's promiseʾ. 11. And she said to his sister, "Keep track of him!" So she watched him from a distance, while they were unaware. 12. And We had caused him to refuse all wet-nurses at first, so his sister suggested, "Shall I direct you to a family who will bring him up for you and take good care of him?" 13. This is how We returned him to his mother so that her heart would be put at ease, and not grieve, and that she would know that Allah's promise is ʿalwaysʾ true. But most people do not know.

---

784 It is commonly believed that Hamân was in charge of architecture during the reign of Pharaoh at the time of Moses (☘).
785 The fulfilment of the Pharaoh's old dream that his reign would come to an end at the hands of a boy from the Children of Israel.

28. Al-Qaṣaṣ 388

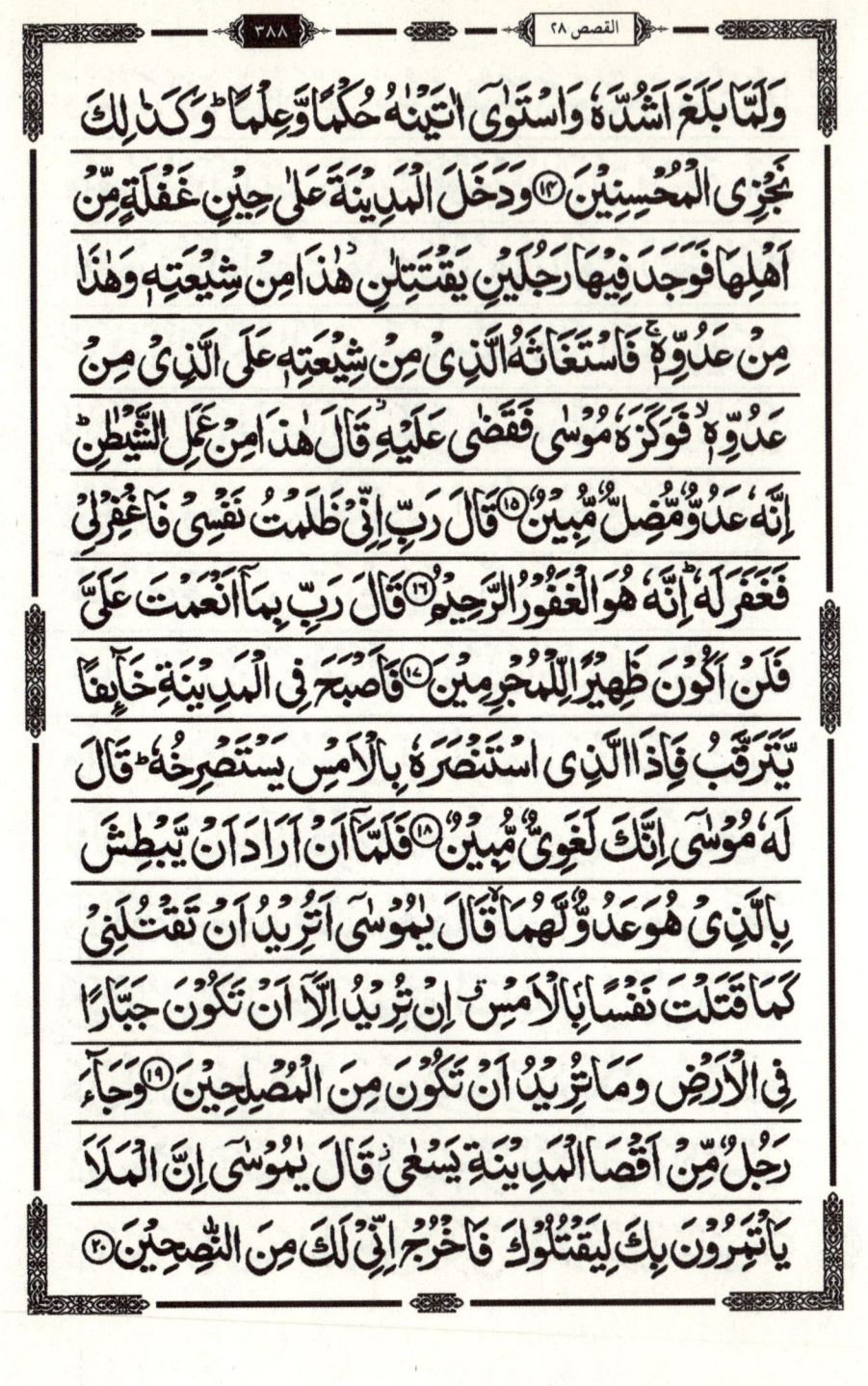

14. And when he reached full strength and maturity, We gave him wisdom and knowledge. This is how We reward the good-doers.

Unintentional Killing

15. ˹One day˺ he entered the city unnoticed by its people.[786] There he found two men fighting: one of his own people, and the other of his enemies. The man from his people called to him for help against his foe. So Moses punched him, causing his death. Moses cried, "This is from Satan's handiwork. He is certainly a sworn, misleading enemy." **16.** He pleaded, "My Lord! I have definitely wronged my soul, so forgive me." So He forgave him, ˹for˺ He is indeed the All-Forgiving, Most Merciful. **17.** Moses pledged, "My Lord! For all Your favours upon me, I will never side with the wicked."

The Incident Comes to Light

18. And so Moses became fearful, watching out in the city, when suddenly the one who sought his help the day before cried out to him again for help. Moses rebuked him, "Indeed, you are clearly a trouble-maker." **19.** Then when Moses was about to lay his hands on their foe,[787] the enemy said, "O Moses! Do you intend to kill me as you killed a man yesterday? You only want to be a tyrant in the land. You do not intend to make peace!"

Moses Escapes to Midian

20. And there came a man, rushing from the farthest end of the city. He said, "O Moses! The chiefs are actually conspiring against you to put you to death, so leave ˹the city˺. I really advise you ˹to do so˺."

---

786 In his adulthood, Moses and Pharaoh's people were not on good terms because he started to question their evil practices.
787 The man assumed that Moses was going to hit him.

28. Al-Qaṣaṣ

21. So Moses left the city in a state of fear and caution, praying, "My Lord! Deliver me from the wrongdoing people." 22. And as he made his way towards Midian, he said, "I trust my Lord will guide me to the right way."

Moses Helps Two Women

23. When he arrived at the well of Midian, he found a group of people watering ˹their herds˺. Apart from them, he noticed two women holding back ˹their herd˺. He asked ˹them˺, "What is the problem?" They replied, "We cannot water ˹our animals˺ until the ˹other˺ shepherds are done, for our father is a very old man." 24. So he watered ˹their herd˺ for them, then withdrew to the shade and prayed, "My Lord! I am truly in ˹desperate˺ need of whatever provision You may have in store for me."[788]

Moses Gets Married

25. Then one of the two women came to him, walking bashfully. She said, "My father is inviting you so he may reward you for watering ˹our animals˺ for us." When Moses came to him and told him his whole story, the old man said, "Have no fear! You are ˹now˺ safe from the wrongdoing people." 26. One of the two daughters suggested, "O my dear father! Hire him. The best man for employment is definitely the strong and trustworthy ˹one˺." 27. The old man proposed, "I wish to marry one of these two daughters of mine to you, provided that you stay in my service for eight years. If you complete ten, it will be ˹a favour˺ from you, but I do not wish to make it difficult for you. Allah willing, you will find me an agreeable man." 28. Moses responded, "˹Then˺ it is ˹settled˺ between you and I. Whichever term I fulfill, there will be no ˹further˺ obligation on me. And Allah is a Witness to what we say."

---

788 Moses left Egypt with no food, money, or even shoes. He was completely worn out by the time he arrived in Midian. After he prayed for help, Allah gave him a wife, a job, and a home on the same day.

القصص ٢٨

فَلَمَّا قَضَىٰ مُوسَى الْأَجَلَ وَسَارَ بِأَهْلِهِ ءَانَسَ مِن جَانِبِ الطُّورِ نَارًا قَالَ لِأَهْلِهِ امْكُثُوٓا إِنِّىٓ ءَانَسْتُ نَارًا لَّعَلِّىٓ ءَاتِيكُم مِّنْهَا بِخَبَرٍ أَوْ جَذْوَةٍ مِّنَ النَّارِ لَعَلَّكُمْ تَصْطَلُونَ ۝ فَلَمَّآ أَتَىٰهَا نُودِىَ مِن شَاطِئِ الْوَادِ الْأَيْمَنِ فِى الْبُقْعَةِ الْمُبَٰرَكَةِ مِنَ الشَّجَرَةِ أَن يَٰمُوسَىٰٓ إِنِّىٓ أَنَا اللَّهُ رَبُّ الْعَٰلَمِينَ ۝ وَأَنْ أَلْقِ عَصَاكَ فَلَمَّا رَءَاهَا تَهْتَزُّ كَأَنَّهَا جَآنٌّ وَلَّىٰ مُدْبِرًا وَلَمْ يُعَقِّبْ يَٰمُوسَىٰٓ أَقْبِلْ وَلَا تَخَفْ إِنَّكَ مِنَ الْءَامِنِينَ ۝ اسْلُكْ يَدَكَ فِى جَيْبِكَ تَخْرُجْ بَيْضَآءَ مِنْ غَيْرِ سُوٓءٍ وَاضْمُمْ إِلَيْكَ جَنَاحَكَ مِنَ الرَّهْبِ فَذَٰنِكَ بُرْهَٰنَانِ مِن رَّبِّكَ إِلَىٰ فِرْعَوْنَ وَمَلَإِيْهِ إِنَّهُمْ كَانُوا قَوْمًا فَٰسِقِينَ ۝ قَالَ رَبِّ إِنِّى قَتَلْتُ مِنْهُمْ نَفْسًا فَأَخَافُ أَن يَقْتُلُونِ ۝ وَأَخِى هَٰرُونُ هُوَ أَفْصَحُ مِنِّى لِسَانًا فَأَرْسِلْهُ مَعِىَ رِدْءًا يُصَدِّقُنِىٓ إِنِّىٓ أَخَافُ أَن يُكَذِّبُونِ ۝ قَالَ سَنَشُدُّ عَضُدَكَ بِأَخِيكَ وَنَجْعَلُ لَكُمَا سُلْطَٰنًا فَلَا يَصِلُونَ إِلَيْكُمَا بِ‍َٔايَٰتِنَآ أَنتُمَا وَمَنِ اتَّبَعَكُمَا الْغَٰلِبُونَ ۝

The Fateful Encounter

29. When Moses had completed the term and was travelling with his family, he spotted a fire on the side of Mount Ṭûr. He said to his family, "Stay here, ˹for˺ I have spotted a fire. Perhaps from there I can bring you some directions[789] or a torch from the fire so you may warm yourselves." **30.** But when he came to it, he was called from the bush in the sacred ground to the right side of the valley: "O Moses! It is truly I. I am Allah—the Lord of all worlds. **31.** Now, throw down your staff!" But when he saw it slithering like a snake, he ran away without looking back. ˹Allah reassured him,˺ "O Moses! Draw near, and have no fear. You are perfectly secure. **32.** Now put your hand through ˹the opening of˺ your collar, it will come out ˹shining˺ white, unblemished.[790] And cross your arms tightly to calm your fears.[791] These are two proofs from your Lord to Pharaoh and his chiefs. They have truly been a rebellious people."

Moses Asks Allah for Help

33. Moses appealed, "My Lord! I have indeed killed a man from them, so I fear they may kill me. **34.** And my brother Aaron is more eloquent than I, so send him with me as a helper to support what I say, for I truly fear they may reject me." **35.** Allah responded, "We will assist you with your brother and grant you both authority, so they cannot harm you. With Our signs, you and those who follow you will ˹certainly˺ prevail."

---

789 information. Moses and his family lost their way in the dark while they were travelling from Midian to Egypt.
790 See footnote for 20:22.
791 When Moses put his arm through the opening in his collar again, his hand returned to its original colour.

28. Al-Qaṣaṣ

Pharaoh's Response

36. But when Moses came to them with Our clear signs, they said ˹arrogantly˺, "This is nothing but conjured magic ˹tricks˺. We have never heard of this in ˹the history of˺ our forefathers." 37. Moses responded, "My Lord knows best who has come with ˹true˺ guidance from Him and will fare best in the end. Indeed, the wrongdoers will never succeed." 38. Pharaoh declared, "O chiefs! I know of no other god for you but myself. So bake bricks out of clay for me, O Hamân, and build a high tower so I may look at the God of Moses, although I am sure he is a liar."

End of Pharaoh

39. And so he and his soldiers behaved arrogantly in the land with no right, thinking they would never be returned to Us. 40. So We seized him and his soldiers, casting them into the sea. See then what was the end of the wrongdoers! 41. We made them leaders inviting ˹others˺ to the Fire. And on the Day of Judgment they will not be helped. 42. We caused a curse to follow them in this world. And on the Day of Judgment they will be among the outcasts.

Excellence of the Torah

43. Indeed, We gave Moses the Scripture—after destroying earlier nations—as an insight for the people, a guide, and mercy so perhaps they would be mindful.

Revealed Stories

44. You were not there ˹O Prophet˺ on the western side of the mountain when We entrusted the Commandments to Moses, nor were you present ˹in his time˺.[792]

---

792 The pagans are reminded repeatedly in the Quran that the Prophet (ﷺ) did not witness any of these events that happened centuries before he was born. For example, the conspiracies that were made against Joseph (12:102), the dispute on who should be the guardian of young Mary (3:44), and the drowning of Noah's son in the Flood (11:49). These details were not known to Arabs before the revelation of the Quran. So the only logical way that the Prophet (ﷺ) knew about these stories is through divine revelation.

وَمَا كُنتَ بِجَانِبِ الْغَرْبِيِّ إِذْ قَضَيْنَآ إِلَىٰ مُوسَى الْأَمْرَ وَمَا كُنتَ مِنَ الشَّٰهِدِينَ ۝ وَلَٰكِنَّآ أَنشَأْنَا قُرُونًا فَتَطَاوَلَ عَلَيْهِمُ الْعُمُرُ ۚ وَمَا كُنتَ ثَاوِيًا فِىٓ أَهْلِ مَدْيَنَ تَتْلُوا۟ عَلَيْهِمْ ءَايَٰتِنَا وَلَٰكِنَّا كُنَّا مُرْسِلِينَ ۝ وَمَا كُنتَ بِجَانِبِ الطُّورِ إِذْ نَادَيْنَا وَلَٰكِن رَّحْمَةً مِّن رَّبِّكَ لِتُنذِرَ قَوْمًا مَّآ أَتَىٰهُم مِّن نَّذِيرٍ مِّن قَبْلِكَ لَعَلَّهُمْ يَتَذَكَّرُونَ ۝ وَلَوْلَآ أَن تُصِيبَهُم مُّصِيبَةٌۢ بِمَا قَدَّمَتْ أَيْدِيهِمْ فَيَقُولُوا۟ رَبَّنَا لَوْلَآ أَرْسَلْتَ إِلَيْنَا رَسُولًا فَنَتَّبِعَ ءَايَٰتِكَ وَنَكُونَ مِنَ الْمُؤْمِنِينَ ۝ فَلَمَّا جَآءَهُمُ الْحَقُّ مِنْ عِندِنَا قَالُوا۟ لَوْلَآ أُوتِىَ مِثْلَ مَآ أُوتِىَ مُوسَىٰٓ ۚ أَوَلَمْ يَكْفُرُوا۟ بِمَآ أُوتِىَ مُوسَىٰ مِن قَبْلُ ۖ قَالُوا۟ سِحْرَانِ تَظَٰهَرَا وَقَالُوٓا۟ إِنَّا بِكُلٍّ كَٰفِرُونَ ۝ قُلْ فَأْتُوا۟ بِكِتَٰبٍ مِّنْ عِندِ اللَّهِ هُوَ أَهْدَىٰ مِنْهُمَآ أَتَّبِعْهُ إِن كُنتُمْ صَٰدِقِينَ ۝ فَإِن لَّمْ يَسْتَجِيبُوا۟ لَكَ فَاعْلَمْ أَنَّمَا يَتَّبِعُونَ أَهْوَآءَهُمْ ۚ وَمَنْ أَضَلُّ مِمَّنِ اتَّبَعَ هَوَىٰهُ بِغَيْرِ هُدًى مِّنَ اللَّهِ ۚ إِنَّ اللَّهَ لَا يَهْدِى الْقَوْمَ الظَّٰلِمِينَ ۝

45. But We ˹later˺ raised ˹several˺ generations, and the ages took their toll on them.[793] Nor were you living among the people of Midian, rehearsing Our revelations with them. But it is We Who have sent ˹this revelation to you˺. 46. And you were not at the side of Mount Ṭûr when We called out ˹to Moses˺. But ˹you have been sent˺ as a mercy from your Lord to warn a people to whom no warner has come before you, so perhaps they may be mindful. 47. Also so they would not say, if struck by an affliction for what their hands have done: "Our Lord! If only You had sent us a messenger, we would have followed Your revelations and become believers."

Pagan Response to the Quran

48. But when the truth came to them from Us, they said, "If only he was given the like of what Moses had been given."[794] Did they not deny what had been given to Moses earlier? They claimed, "Both ˹Scriptures˺ are works of magic, supporting each other!"[795] Adding, "We truly deny both." 49. Say, ˹O Prophet,˺ "Bring then a scripture from Allah which is a better guide than these two so I may follow it, if your claim is true." 50. So if they fail to respond to you, then know that they only follow their desires. And who could be more astray than those who follow their desires with no guidance from Allah? Surely Allah does not guide the wrongdoing people.

---

793 So they neglected the Commandments over time.
794 The pagans of Mecca demanded that the Quran should have been revealed all at once like the Torah, and the Prophet (ﷺ) should have had some tangible signs like the staff of Moses.
795 Some Meccan pagans approached some Jewish authorities to inquire about the Prophet's message and they were told that there are references of him in the Torah. So the pagans immediately rejected both the Torah and the Quran as two works of magic.

28. Al-Qaşaş

The Doubly Rewarded

51. Indeed, We have steadily delivered the Word ˹of Allah˺ to the people so they may be mindful. 52. ˹As for˺ those ˹faithful˺ to whom We had given the Scripture before this ˹Quran˺, they do believe in it. 53. When it is recited to them, they declare, "We believe in it. This is definitely the truth from our Lord. We had already submitted[796] ˹even˺ before this." 54. These ˹believers˺ will be given a double reward for their perseverance, responding to evil with good, and for donating from what We have provided for them. 55. When they hear slanderous talk, they turn away from it, saying, "We are accountable for our deeds and you for yours. Peace ˹is our only response˺ to you! We want nothing to do with those who act ignorantly."

Guidance Is from Allah Alone

56. You surely cannot guide whoever you like ˹O Prophet˺, but it is Allah Who guides whoever He wills, and He knows best who are ˹fit to be˺ guided.

Pagan Excuses

57. They say ˹to the Prophet˺, "If we were to follow ˹true˺ guidance with you, we would certainly be snatched away from our land." Have We not established for them a safe haven ˹in Mecca˺ to which fruits of all kinds are brought as a provision from Us? But most of them do not know ˹this favour˺. 58. ˹Imagine˺ how many societies We have destroyed that had been spoiled by their ˹comfortable˺ living! Those are their residences, never inhabited after them except passingly.[797] And We ˹alone˺ were the Successor. 59. Your Lord would never destroy a society until He had sent to its capital a messenger, reciting Our revelations to them. Nor would We ever destroy a society unless its people persisted in wrongdoing.

---

796 lit., 'We had already been Muslims.'
797 By travellers such as the Meccan pagans.

28. Al-Qasas   394

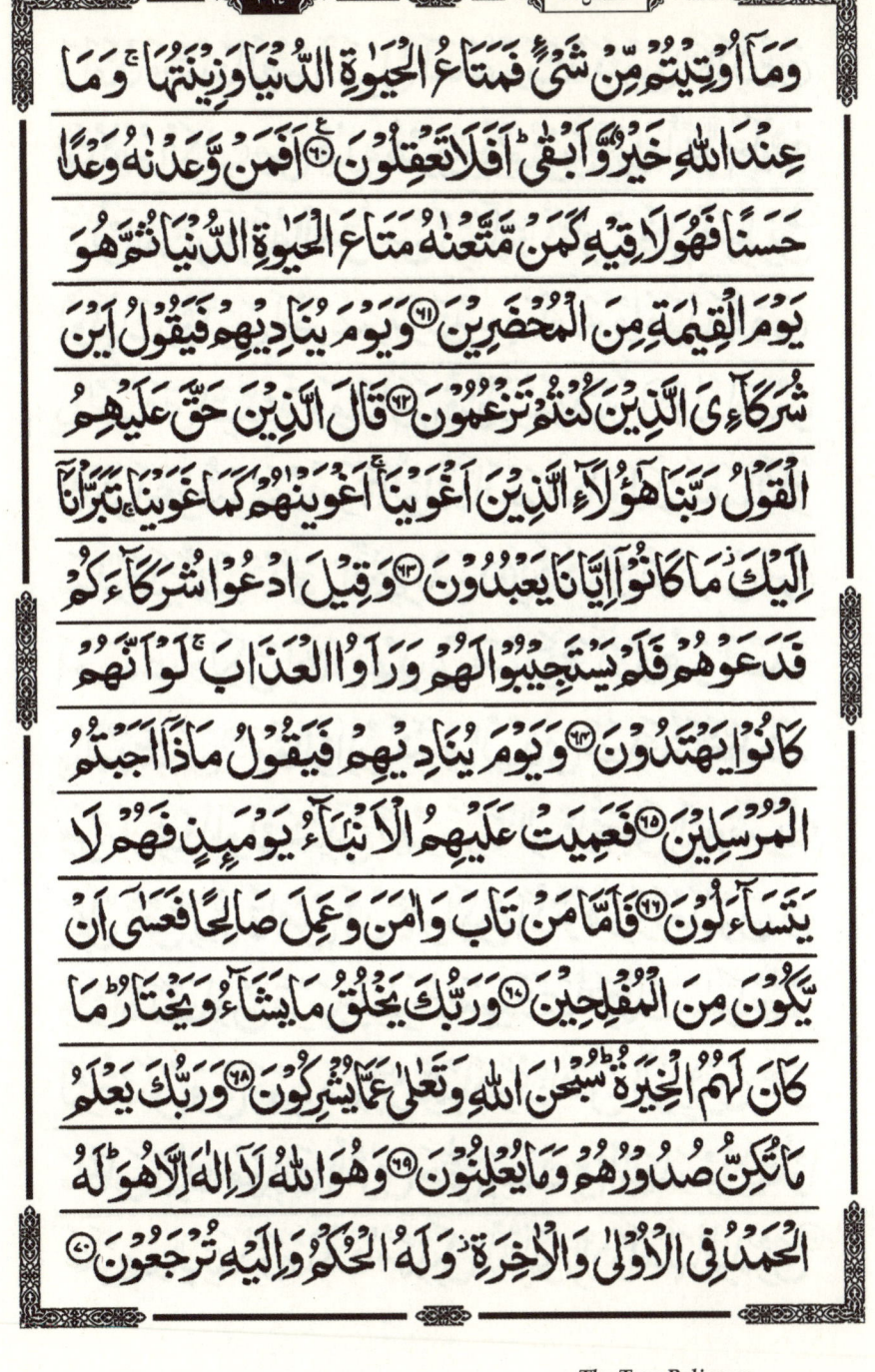

This World or the Hereafter?

60. Whatever ˹pleasure˺ you have been given is no more than ˹a fleeting˺ enjoyment and adornment of this worldly life. But what is with Allah is far better and more lasting. Will you not then understand? 61. Can those to whom We have made a fine promise—which they will see fulfilled—be like those who We have allowed to enjoy the pleasures of this worldly life, but on the Day of Judgment will be brought ˹for punishment˺?

The Misleaders and the Misled

62. ˹Watch for˺ the Day He will call to them, "Where are those you claimed were My associate-gods?" 63. Those ˹misleaders˺ against whom the decree ˹of torment˺ is justified will cry, "Our Lord! These ˹followers˺ are the ones we caused to deviate. We led them into deviance, for we ourselves were deviant. We disassociate ourselves ˹from them˺ before You. It was not us that they used to worship." 64. It will be said ˹to the disbelievers˺, "Call upon your associate-gods ˹for help˺." So they will call them, but will receive no response. And they will face the punishment, wishing they had been ˹rightly˺ guided!

A Question to the Disbelievers

65. And ˹watch for˺ the Day He will call to them, asking, "What response did you give to the messengers?" 66. They will be too dumbstruck on that Day to ask one another ˹for answers˺.

The True Believers

67. As for those who repent, believe, and do good ˹in this world˺, it is right to hope that they will be among the successful.

Allah Almighty

68. Your Lord creates and chooses whatever He wills—the choice is not theirs. Glorified and Exalted is Allah above what they associate ˹with Him˺! 69. And your Lord knows what their hearts conceal and what they reveal. 70. He is Allah. There is no god ˹worthy of worship˺ except Him. All praise belongs to Him in this life and the next. All authority is His. And to Him you will ˹all˺ be returned.

28. Al-Qaṣaṣ

Allah's Might and Grace

71. Ask ˹them, O Prophet˺, "Imagine if Allah were to make the night perpetual for you until the Day of Judgment, which god other than Allah could bring you sunlight? Will you not then listen?" **72.** Ask ˹them also˺, "Imagine if Allah were to make the day perpetual for you until the Day of Judgment, which god other than Allah could bring you night to rest in? Will you not then see?" **73.** It is out of His mercy that He has made for you the day and night so that you may rest ˹in the latter˺ and seek His bounty ˹in the former˺, and perhaps you will be grateful.

Polytheists Rebuked Again

74. And ˹watch for˺ the Day He will call to them, "Where are those you claimed were My associate-gods?" **75.** And We will bring forth a witness[798] from every faith-community and ask ˹the polytheists˺, "Show ˹Us˺ your proof." Then they will ˹come to˺ know that the truth is with Allah ˹alone˺. And whatever ˹gods˺ they fabricated will fail them."

Korah's Arrogance

76. Indeed, Korah[799] was from the people of Moses, but he behaved arrogantly towards them. We had granted him such treasures that even their keys would burden a group of strong men. ˹Some of˺ his people advised him, "Do not be prideful! Surely Allah does not like the prideful. **77.** Rather, seek the ˹reward˺ of the Hereafter by means of what Allah has granted you, without forgetting your share of this world. And be good ˹to others˺ as Allah has been good to you. Do not seek to spread corruption in the land, for Allah certainly does not like the corruptors."

---

798 A prophet.

799 Korah was the cousin of Moses. Because of Korah's close association with Pharaoh, he became very rich and started to behave arrogantly towards his own people. When he was asked repeatedly by Moses (۩) to pay his alms-tax to help poor Israelites, Korah refused and eventually conspired with a prostitute to damage the reputation of Moses, but Moses was cleared of any wrongdoing.

28. Al-Qaṣaṣ

Korah's Response

78. He replied, "I have been granted all this because of some knowledge I have."[800] Did he not know that Allah had already destroyed some from the generations before him who were far superior to him in power and greater in accumulating ˹wealth˺? There will be no need for the wicked to be asked about their sins.[801]

Debate on Korah

79. Then he came out before his people in all his glamour. Those who desired the life of this world wished, "If only we could have something like what Korah has been given. He is truly a man of great fortune!" **80.** But those gifted with knowledge said, "Shame on you! Allah's reward is far better for those who believe and do good. But none will attain this except the steadfast."

Korah's End

81. Then We caused the earth to swallow him up, along with his home. There was no one to help him against Allah, nor could he even help himself. **82.** And those who had craved his position the previous day began to say, "Ah! It is certainly Allah Who gives abundant or limited provisions to whoever He wills of His servants. Had it not been for the grace of Allah, He could have surely caused the earth to swallow us up! Oh, indeed! The disbelievers will never succeed."

Pay Day

83. That ˹eternal˺ Home in the Hereafter We reserve ˹only˺ for those who seek neither tyranny nor corruption on the earth. The ultimate outcome belongs ˹only˺ to the righteous. **84.** Whoever comes with a good deed will be rewarded with what is better. And whoever comes with an evil deed, then the evildoers will only be rewarded for what they used to do.

Advice to the Prophet

85. Most certainly, the One Who has ordained the Quran for you will ˹ultimately˺ bring you back home ˹to Mecca˺.[802] Say, "My Lord

---

800 Or: "I have been granted all this because I know that Allah knows I deserve it."
801 Since their sins are already known to Allah and written in perfect records, they will only be interrogated as a form of punishment.
802 This verse was revealed while the Prophet (ﷺ) was on the way to Medina, emigrating from Mecca after years of persecution. Eventually the Prophet (ﷺ) returned to Mecca and the majority of its people accepted Islam.

knows best who has come with ˹true˺ guidance and who is clearly astray." **86.** You never expected this Book to be revealed to you, but ˹it came˺ only ˹as˺ a mercy from your Lord. So never side with the disbelievers ˹in their disbelief˺. **87.** Do not let them turn you away from the revelations of Allah after they have been sent down to you. Rather, invite ˹all˺ to ˹the Way of˺ your Lord, and never be one of the polytheists. **88.** And do not invoke any other god with Allah. There is no god ˹worthy of worship˺ except Him. Everything is bound to perish except He Himself.[803] All authority belongs to Him. And to Him you will ˹all˺ be returned.

୧෴෴෴

29. The Spider (Al-'Ankabût)

In the Name of Allah—the Most Compassionate, Most Merciful

The Test

1. *Alif-Lãm-Mĩm.* **2.** Do people think once they say, "We believe," that they will be left without being put to the test? **3.** We certainly tested those before them. And ˹in this way˺ Allah will clearly distinguish between those who are truthful and those who are liars. **4.** Or do the evildoers ˹simply˺ think that they will escape Us? How wrong is their judgment!

The True Believers

5. Whoever hopes for the meeting with Allah, ˹let them know that˺ Allah's appointed time is sure to come. He is the All-Hearing, All-Knowing.

---

803 lit., except His Face.

29. Al-'Ankabût

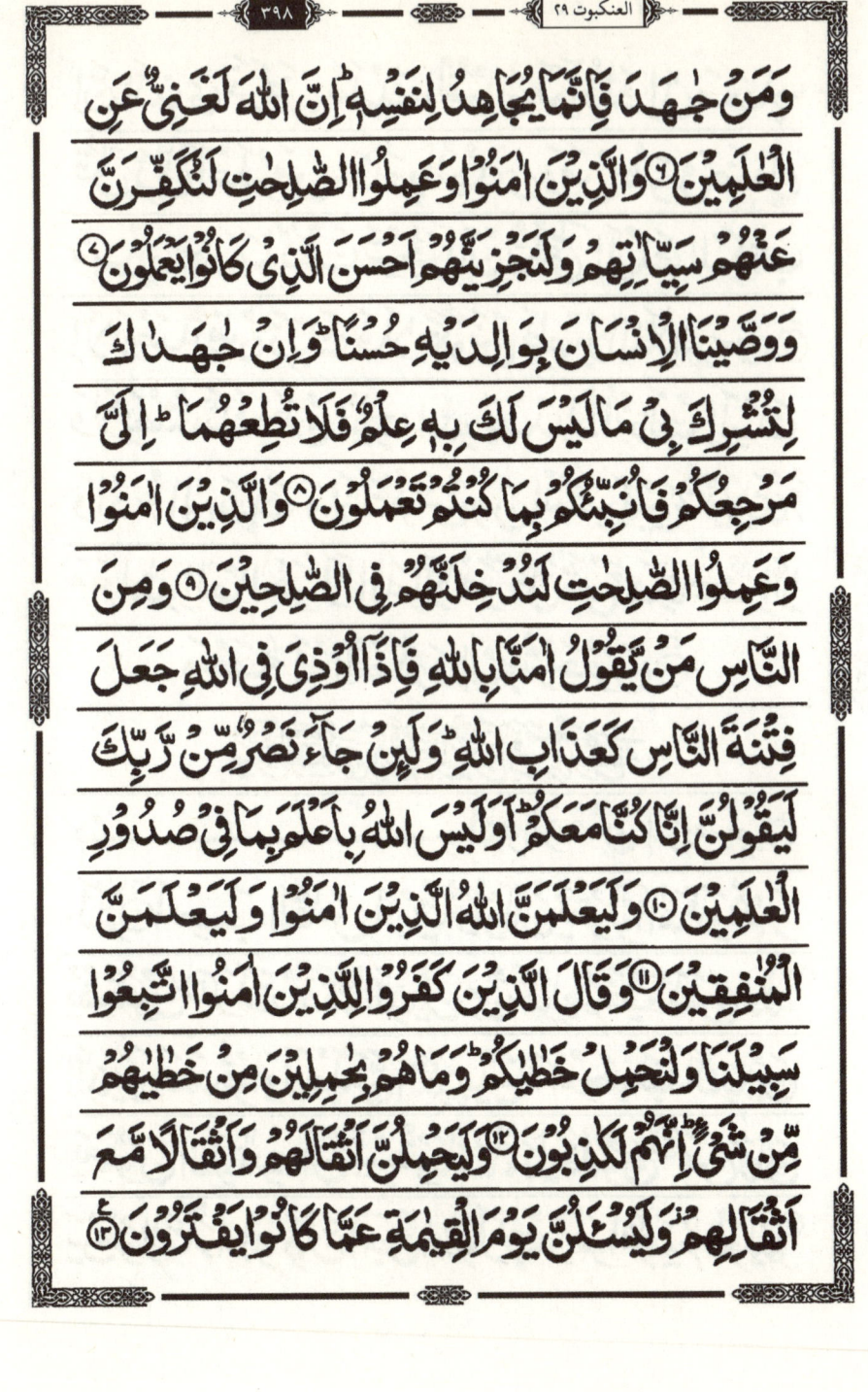

6. And whoever strives ˹in Allah's cause˺, only does so for their own good. Surely Allah is not in need of ˹any of˺ His creation. 7. As for those who believe and do good, We will certainly absolve them of their sins, and reward them according to the best of what they used to do. 8. We have commanded people to honour their parents. But if they urge you to associate with Me what you have no knowledge of,[804] then do not obey them. To Me you will ˹all˺ return, and then I will inform you of what you used to do. 9. Those who believe and do good will surely be admitted by Us into ˹the company of˺ the righteous.

The Hypocrites

10. There are some who say, "We believe in Allah," but when they suffer in the cause of Allah, they mistake ˹this˺ persecution at the hands of people for the punishment of Allah. But when victory comes from your Lord, they surely say ˹to the believers˺, "We have always been with you." Does Allah not know best what is in the hearts of all beings? 11. Allah will certainly distinguish between those who have ˹sure˺ faith and the hypocrites.

False Promise

12. The disbelievers say to the believers, "˹Just˺ follow our way, and we will bear ˹the burden of˺ your sins." But they would never ˹want to˺ bear any of the believers' sins. They are simply lying. 13. Yet they will certainly ˹be made to˺ carry their own burdens, as well as other burdens along with their own.[805] And they will surely be questioned on Judgment Day about what they used to fabricate.

---

804 Other gods.
805 The burdens of those they misled.

Noah's People Destroyed

14. Indeed, We sent Noah to his people, and he remained among them for a thousand years, less fifty. Then the Flood overtook them, while they persisted in wrongdoing. 15. But We delivered him and those in the Ark, making it a sign for all people.

The People of Abraham

16. And ˹remember˺ when Abraham said to his people, "Worship Allah, and fear Him. This is better for you, if only you knew. 17. You worship besides Allah nothing but idols, simply creating lies ˹about them˺. Those you worship besides Allah certainly cannot give you any provision. So seek provision from Allah ˹alone˺, worship Him, and be grateful to Him. To Him you will ˹all˺ be returned.

Warning to Meccan Pagans

18. If you persist in denial, so did ˹many˺ communities before you. The Messenger's duty is only to deliver ˹the message˺ clearly." 19. Have they not seen how Allah originates the creation then resurrects it? That is certainly easy for Allah. 20. Say, ˹O Prophet,˺ "Travel throughout the land and see how He originated the creation, then Allah will bring it into being one more time. Surely Allah is Most Capable of everything. 21. He punishes whoever He wills, and shows mercy to whoever He wills. And you will ˹all˺ be returned to Him.

29. Al-'Ankabût

22. And you cannot escape Him on earth or in heaven. Nor have you any protector or helper besides Allah." **23.** As for those who disbelieve in Allah's signs and the meeting with Him, it is they who will have no hope in His mercy.[806] And it is they who will suffer a painful punishment.

Abraham Prevails

24. But the only response of Abraham's people was to say: "Kill him or burn him!" But Allah saved him from the fire.[807] Surely in this are signs for people who believe. **25.** He said ˹to his people˺, "You have taken idols ˹for worship˺ instead of Allah, only to keep ˹the bond of˺ harmony among yourselves in this worldly life. But on the Day of Judgment you will disown and curse one another. Your home will be the Fire, and you will have no helper!" **26.** So Lot believed in him. And Abraham said, "I am emigrating ˹in obedience˺ to my Lord. He ˹alone˺ is indeed the Almighty, All-Wise." **27.** We blessed him with Isaac and ˹later˺ Jacob, and reserved prophethood and revelation for his descendants. We gave him his reward in this life,[808] and in the Hereafter he will certainly be among the righteous.

The People of Lot

28. And ˹remember˺ when Lot rebuked ˹the men of˺ his people: "You certainly commit a shameful deed that no man has ever done before you.

---

806 lit., My mercy.
807 The idolaters tried to burn Abraham because he smashed their idols. *See* 21:51-71 for the full story.
808 Through honourable mention, righteous family, etc.

401   29. Al-'Ankabût

29. Do you really lust after ˹other˺ men, abuse the travellers, and practice immorality ˹openly˺ in your gatherings?" His people's only response was to say ˹mockingly˺: "Bring Allah's punishment upon us, if what you say is true." 30. Lot prayed, "My Lord! Help me against the people of corruption."

Abraham Visited by Angels

31. When Our messenger-angels came to Abraham with the good news ˹of the birth of Isaac˺, they said, "We are going to destroy the people of this city ˹of Sodom˺, for its people have persisted in wrong-doing." 32. He said, "But Lot is there!" They responded, "We know best who is there. We will certainly save him and his family—except his wife, who is one of the doomed."

The People of Lot Destroyed

33. And when Our messenger-angels came to Lot, he was distressed and worried by their arrival.[809] They reassured ˹him˺, "Do not fear, nor grieve. We will surely deliver you and your family—except your wife, who is one of the doomed. 34. We are certainly bringing down a punishment from heaven upon the people of this city for their rebelliousness." 35. And We did leave ˹some of˺ its ruins as a clear lesson for people of understanding.

Shu'aib's People Destroyed

36. And to the people of Midian ˹We sent˺ their brother Shu'aib. He said, "O my people! Worship Allah, and hope for ˹the reward of˺ the Last Day. And do not go about spreading corruption in the land."

---

809 Since the angels came in the form of handsome men, Lot was worried for the dignity and safety of his guests among his people—not knowing that they were angels.

29. Al-'Ankabût 402

فَكَذَّبُوهُ فَأَخَذَتْهُمُ الرَّجْفَةُ فَأَصْبَحُوا فِي دَارِهِمْ جَٰثِمِينَ ۝ وَعَادًا وَثَمُودَا۟ وَقَد تَّبَيَّنَ لَكُم مِّن مَّسَٰكِنِهِمْ وَزَيَّنَ لَهُمُ الشَّيْطَٰنُ أَعْمَٰلَهُمْ فَصَدَّهُمْ عَنِ السَّبِيلِ وَكَانُوا۟ مُسْتَبْصِرِينَ ۝ وَقَٰرُونَ وَفِرْعَوْنَ وَهَٰمَٰنَ وَلَقَدْ جَآءَهُم مُّوسَىٰ بِالْبَيِّنَٰتِ فَاسْتَكْبَرُوا۟ فِي الْأَرْضِ وَمَا كَانُوا۟ سَٰبِقِينَ ۝ فَكُلًّا أَخَذْنَا بِذَنۢبِهِۦ فَمِنْهُم مَّنْ أَرْسَلْنَا عَلَيْهِ حَاصِبًا وَمِنْهُم مَّنْ أَخَذَتْهُ الصَّيْحَةُ وَمِنْهُم مَّنْ خَسَفْنَا بِهِ الْأَرْضَ وَمِنْهُم مَّنْ أَغْرَقْنَا وَمَا كَانَ اللَّهُ لِيَظْلِمَهُمْ وَلَٰكِن كَانُوٓا۟ أَنفُسَهُمْ يَظْلِمُونَ ۝ مَثَلُ الَّذِينَ اتَّخَذُوا۟ مِن دُونِ اللَّهِ أَوْلِيَآءَ كَمَثَلِ الْعَنكَبُوتِ اتَّخَذَتْ بَيْتًا وَإِنَّ أَوْهَنَ الْبُيُوتِ لَبَيْتُ الْعَنكَبُوتِ لَوْ كَانُوا۟ يَعْلَمُونَ ۝ إِنَّ اللَّهَ يَعْلَمُ مَا يَدْعُونَ مِن دُونِهِۦ مِن شَىْءٍ وَهُوَ الْعَزِيزُ الْحَكِيمُ ۝ وَتِلْكَ الْأَمْثَٰلُ نَضْرِبُهَا لِلنَّاسِ وَمَا يَعْقِلُهَآ إِلَّا الْعَٰلِمُونَ ۝ خَلَقَ اللَّهُ السَّمَٰوَٰتِ وَالْأَرْضَ بِالْحَقِّ إِنَّ فِي ذَٰلِكَ لَءَايَةً لِّلْمُؤْمِنِينَ ۝

37. But they rejected him, so an ˹overwhelming˺ earthquake struck them and they fell lifeless in their homes.

Previously Destroyed Nations

38. And the people of 'Âd and Thamûd ˹met a similar fate˺, which must be clear to you ˹Meccans˺ from their ruins.[810] Satan made their ˹evil˺ deeds appealing to them, hindering them from the ˹Right˺ Way, although they were capable of reasoning. **39.** ˹We˺ also ˹destroyed˺ Korah, Pharaoh, and Hamân. Indeed, Moses had come to them with clear proofs, but they behaved arrogantly in the land. Yet they could not escape ˹Us˺. **40.** So We seized each ˹people˺ for their sin: against some of them We sent a storm of stones, some were overtaken by a ˹mighty˺ blast, some We caused the earth to swallow, and some We drowned. Allah would not have wronged them, but it was they who wronged themselves.

Allah Is the Mighty Protector

41. The parable of those who take protectors other than Allah is that of a spider spinning a shelter. And the flimsiest of all shelters is certainly that of a spider, if only they knew. **42.** Allah surely knows that whatever ˹gods˺ they invoke besides Him are ˹simply˺ nothing. For He is the Almighty, All-Wise. **43.** These are the parables We set forth for humanity, but none will understand them except the people of knowledge. **44.** Allah created the heavens and the earth for a purpose. Surely in this is a sign for the people of faith.

---

810 Meccan caravans always passed by these ruins on the way to Yemen and Syria for business.

29. Al-'Ankabût

Advice to the Prophet

45. Recite what has been revealed to you of the Book and establish prayer. Indeed, ˹genuine˺ prayer should deter ˹one˺ from indecency and wickedness. The remembrance of Allah is ˹an˺ even greater ˹deterrent˺. And Allah ˹fully˺ knows what you ˹all˺ do.

Arguing with the People of the Book

46. Do not argue with the People of the Book unless gracefully, except with those of them who act wrongfully. And say, "We believe in what has been revealed to us and what was revealed to you. Our Allah and your God is ˹only˺ One. And to Him we ˹fully˺ submit."

One Last Revelation

47. Similarly ˹to earlier messengers˺, We have revealed to you a Book ˹O Prophet˺. ˹The faithful of˺ those to whom We gave the Scriptures believe in it, as do some of these ˹pagan Arabs˺. And none denies Our revelations except the ˹stubborn˺ disbelievers. **48.** You ˹O Prophet˺ could not read any writing ˹even˺ before this ˹revelation˺, nor could you write at all. Otherwise, the people of falsehood would have been suspicious. **49.** But this ˹Quran˺ is ˹a set of˺ clear revelations ˹preserved˺ in the hearts of those gifted with knowledge. And none denies Our revelations except the ˹stubborn˺ wrongdoers.

The Pagans Demand Signs[811]

50. They say, "If only ˹some˺ signs had been sent down to him from his Lord!" Say, ˹O Prophet,˺ "Signs are only with Allah. And I am only sent with a clear warning." **51.** Is it not enough for them that We have sent down to you the Book, ˹which is˺ recited to them. Surely in this ˹Quran˺ is a mercy and reminder for people who believe. **52.** Say, ˹O Prophet,˺ "Sufficient is Allah as a Witness between me and you. He ˹fully˺ knows whatever is in the heavens and the earth. And those who believe in falsehood and disbelieve in Allah, it is they who are the ˹true˺ losers."

---

811 They were not convinced of the Quran's literary miracle and, therefore, asked for tangible signs similar to the staff of Moses.

29. Al-'Ankabût

وَيَسْتَعْجِلُونَكَ بِالْعَذَابِ وَلَوْلَا أَجَلٌ مُّسَمًّى لَّجَاءَهُمُ الْعَذَابُ وَلَيَأْتِيَنَّهُم بَغْتَةً وَهُمْ لَا يَشْعُرُونَ ۝ يَسْتَعْجِلُونَكَ بِالْعَذَابِ وَإِنَّ جَهَنَّمَ لَمُحِيطَةٌ بِالْكَافِرِينَ ۝ يَوْمَ يَغْشَاهُمُ الْعَذَابُ مِن فَوْقِهِمْ وَمِن تَحْتِ أَرْجُلِهِمْ وَيَقُولُ ذُوقُوا مَا كُنتُمْ تَعْمَلُونَ ۝ يَا عِبَادِيَ الَّذِينَ آمَنُوا إِنَّ أَرْضِي وَاسِعَةٌ فَإِيَّايَ فَاعْبُدُونِ ۝ كُلُّ نَفْسٍ ذَائِقَةُ الْمَوْتِ ثُمَّ إِلَيْنَا تُرْجَعُونَ ۝ وَالَّذِينَ آمَنُوا وَعَمِلُوا الصَّالِحَاتِ لَنُبَوِّئَنَّهُم مِّنَ الْجَنَّةِ غُرَفًا تَجْرِي مِن تَحْتِهَا الْأَنْهَارُ خَالِدِينَ فِيهَا نِعْمَ أَجْرُ الْعَامِلِينَ ۝ الَّذِينَ صَبَرُوا وَعَلَى رَبِّهِمْ يَتَوَكَّلُونَ ۝ وَكَأَيِّن مِّن دَابَّةٍ لَّا تَحْمِلُ رِزْقَهَا اللَّهُ يَرْزُقُهَا وَإِيَّاكُمْ وَهُوَ السَّمِيعُ الْعَلِيمُ ۝ وَلَئِن سَأَلْتَهُم مَّنْ خَلَقَ السَّمَاوَاتِ وَالْأَرْضَ وَسَخَّرَ الشَّمْسَ وَالْقَمَرَ لَيَقُولُنَّ اللَّهُ فَأَنَّى يُؤْفَكُونَ ۝ اللَّهُ يَبْسُطُ الرِّزْقَ لِمَن يَشَاءُ مِنْ عِبَادِهِ وَيَقْدِرُ لَهُ إِنَّ اللَّهَ بِكُلِّ شَيْءٍ عَلِيمٌ ۝ وَلَئِن سَأَلْتَهُم مَّن نَّزَّلَ مِنَ السَّمَاءِ مَاءً فَأَحْيَا بِهِ الْأَرْضَ مِن بَعْدِ مَوْتِهَا لَيَقُولُنَّ اللَّهُ قُلِ الْحَمْدُ لِلَّهِ بَلْ أَكْثَرُهُمْ لَا يَعْقِلُونَ ۝

Hastening the Punishment

53. They challenge you ˹O Prophet˺ to hasten the punishment. Had it not been for a time already set, the punishment would have certainly come to them ˹at once˺. But it will definitely take them by surprise when they least expect it. **54.** They urge you to hasten the punishment. And Hell will certainly encompass the disbelievers **55.** on the Day the punishment will overwhelm them from above them and from below their feet. And it will be said, "Reap what you sowed."

Advice to Persecuted Believers[812]

56. O My believing servants! My earth is truly spacious, so worship Me ˹alone˺. **57.** Every soul will taste death, then to Us you will ˹all˺ be returned. **58.** ˹As for˺ those who believe and do good, We will certainly house them in ˹elevated˺ mansions in Paradise, under which rivers flow, to stay there forever. How excellent is the reward for those who work ˹righteousness!˺— **59.** those who patiently endure, and put their trust in their Lord! **60.** How many are the creatures that cannot secure their provisions! ˹It is˺ Allah ˹Who˺ provides for them and you ˹as well˺. He is indeed the All-Hearing, All-Knowing.

Questions to the Polytheists

61. If you ask them ˹O Prophet˺ who created the heavens and the earth and subjected the sun and the moon ˹for your benefit˺, they will certainly say, "Allah!" How can they then be deluded ˹from the truth˺? **62.** Allah gives abundant or limited provisions to whoever He wills of His servants. Surely Allah has ˹full˺ knowledge of everything. **63.** And if you ask them who sends down rain from the sky, giving life to the earth after its death, they will surely say, "Allah!" Say, "Praise be to Allah!" In fact, most of them do not understand.

---

812 This passage addresses poor Muslims who were subject to persecution in Mecca and had to move elsewhere. Some of them were worried that they would not find provisions if they moved to a new place.

64. This worldly life is no more than play and amusement. But the Hereafter is indeed the real life, if only they knew.

The Disbelievers' Ingratitude

65. If they happen to be aboard a ship ˹caught in a storm˺, they cry out to Allah ˹alone˺ in sincere devotion. But as soon as He delivers them ˹safely˺ to shore, they associate ˹others with Him once again˺. **66.** So let them be ungrateful for all We have given them, and ˹let them˺ enjoy themselves ˹for now˺! For they will soon know.

Warning to Meccan Pagans

67. Have they not seen how We have made ˹Mecca˺ a safe haven, whereas people ˹all˺ around them are snatched away?[813] How can they then believe in falsehood[814] and deny Allah's favours? **68.** And who does more wrong than those who fabricate lies against Allah or reject the truth after it has reached them? Is Hell not a ˹fitting˺ home for the disbelievers?

The Faithful Reassured

69. As for those who struggle in Our cause, We will surely guide them along Our Way. And Allah is certainly with the good-doers.

༺❀༻

30. The Romans (Ar-Rûm)

In the Name of Allah—the Most Compassionate, Most Merciful

From Defeat to Victory

1. *Alif-Lãm-Mĩm.* **2.** The Romans have been defeated **3.** in a nearby land. Yet following their defeat, they will triumph **4.** within three to nine years. The ˹whole˺ matter rests with Allah before and after ˹victory˺. And on that day the believers will rejoice **5.** at the victory willed by Allah. He gives victory to whoever He wills. For He is the Almighty, Most Merciful.

---

813 Mecca was considered as a sanctuary. Therefore, fighting was not allowed there, and whoever entered Mecca (especially in the neighbourhood of the Ka'bah) was safe—a privilege that other cities in Arabia did not have.
814 i.e., the false gods and idols.

30. Ar-Rûm

وَعْدَ اللَّهِ ۖ لَا يُخْلِفُ اللَّهُ وَعْدَهُ وَلَٰكِنَّ أَكْثَرَ النَّاسِ لَا يَعْلَمُونَ ۝ يَعْلَمُونَ ظَاهِرًا مِّنَ الْحَيَاةِ الدُّنْيَا وَهُمْ عَنِ الْآخِرَةِ هُمْ غَافِلُونَ ۝ أَوَلَمْ يَتَفَكَّرُوا فِي أَنفُسِهِم ۗ مَّا خَلَقَ اللَّهُ السَّمَاوَاتِ وَالْأَرْضَ وَمَا بَيْنَهُمَا إِلَّا بِالْحَقِّ وَأَجَلٍ مُّسَمًّى ۗ وَإِنَّ كَثِيرًا مِّنَ النَّاسِ بِلِقَاءِ رَبِّهِمْ لَكَافِرُونَ ۝ أَوَلَمْ يَسِيرُوا فِي الْأَرْضِ فَيَنظُرُوا كَيْفَ كَانَ عَاقِبَةُ الَّذِينَ مِن قَبْلِهِمْ ۚ كَانُوا أَشَدَّ مِنْهُمْ قُوَّةً وَأَثَارُوا الْأَرْضَ وَعَمَرُوهَا أَكْثَرَ مِمَّا عَمَرُوهَا وَجَاءَتْهُمْ رُسُلُهُم بِالْبَيِّنَاتِ ۖ فَمَا كَانَ اللَّهُ لِيَظْلِمَهُمْ وَلَٰكِن كَانُوا أَنفُسَهُمْ يَظْلِمُونَ ۝ ثُمَّ كَانَ عَاقِبَةَ الَّذِينَ أَسَاءُوا السُّوأَىٰ أَن كَذَّبُوا بِآيَاتِ اللَّهِ وَكَانُوا بِهَا يَسْتَهْزِئُونَ ۝ اللَّهُ يَبْدَأُ الْخَلْقَ ثُمَّ يُعِيدُهُ ثُمَّ إِلَيْهِ تُرْجَعُونَ ۝ وَيَوْمَ تَقُومُ السَّاعَةُ يُبْلِسُ الْمُجْرِمُونَ ۝ وَلَمْ يَكُن لَّهُم مِّن شُرَكَائِهِمْ شُفَعَاءُ وَكَانُوا بِشُرَكَائِهِمْ كَافِرِينَ ۝ وَيَوْمَ تَقُومُ السَّاعَةُ يَوْمَئِذٍ يَتَفَرَّقُونَ ۝ فَأَمَّا الَّذِينَ آمَنُوا وَعَمِلُوا الصَّالِحَاتِ فَهُمْ فِي رَوْضَةٍ يُحْبَرُونَ ۝

6. ˹This is˺ the promise of Allah. ˹And˺ Allah never fails in His promise. But most people do not know. 7. They ˹only˺ know the worldly affairs of this life, but are ˹totally˺ oblivious to the Hereafter.

Wake-up Call to the Disbelievers

8. Have they not reflected upon their own being? Allah only created the heavens and the earth and everything in between for a purpose and an appointed term. Yet most people are truly in denial of the meeting with their Lord! 9. Have they not travelled throughout the land to see what was the end of those ˹destroyed˺ before them? They were far superior in might; they cultivated the land and developed it more than these ˹Meccans˺ ever have. Their messengers came to them with clear proofs. Allah would have never wronged them, but it was they who wronged themselves. 10. Then most evil was the end of the evildoers for denying and mocking the signs of Allah.

The Wicked on Judgment Day

11. It is Allah Who originates the creation, and will resurrect it. And then to Him you will ˹all˺ be returned. 12. On the Day the Hour will arrive, the wicked will be dumbstruck. 13. There will be no intercessors for them from among their associate-gods, and they will ˹totally˺ deny their associate-gods.

The Blessed and the Doomed

14. And on the Day the Hour will arrive, the people will then be split ˹into two groups˺. 15. As for those who believed and did good, they will be rejoicing in a Garden.

407 30. Ar-Rûm

16. And as for those who disbelieved, and denied Our signs and the meeting ˹with Allah˺ in the Hereafter, they will be confined in punishment.

Keeping up Prayers

17. So glorify Allah in the evening and in the morning— **18.** all praise is for Him in the heavens and the earth—as well as in the afternoon, and at noon.[815]

Allah's Power over Life and Death

19. He brings forth the living from the dead and the dead from the living. And He gives life to the earth after its death. And so will you be brought forth ˹from the grave˺.

Allah's Signs 1) Creation of Humankind

20. One of His signs is that He created you from dust, then—behold!—you are human beings spreading over ˹the earth˺.

Allah's Signs 2) Spouses

21. And one of His signs is that He created for you spouses from among yourselves so that you may find comfort in them. And He has placed between you compassion and mercy. Surely in this are signs for people who reflect.

Allah's Signs 3) Diversity

22. And one of His signs is the creation of the heavens and the earth, and the diversity of your languages and colours. Surely in this are signs for those of ˹sound˺ knowledge.

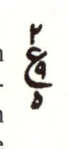

Allah's Signs 4) Sleep and Work

23. And one of His signs is your sleep by night and by day ˹for rest˺ as well as your seeking His bounty ˹in both˺. Surely in this are signs for people who listen.

Allah's Signs 5) Lightning

24. And one of His signs is that He shows you lightning, inspiring ˹you with˺ hope and fear.[816] And He sends down rain from the sky, reviving the earth after its death. Surely in this are signs for people who understand.

---

815 This verse outlines the times of the five daily prayers. The evening refers to *Maghrib* and *'Ishâ'* prayers, the morning refers to *Fajr*, the afternoon refers to *'Aṣr*, and noon refers to *Ẓuhr*.
816 Hope of rain and fear of torment.

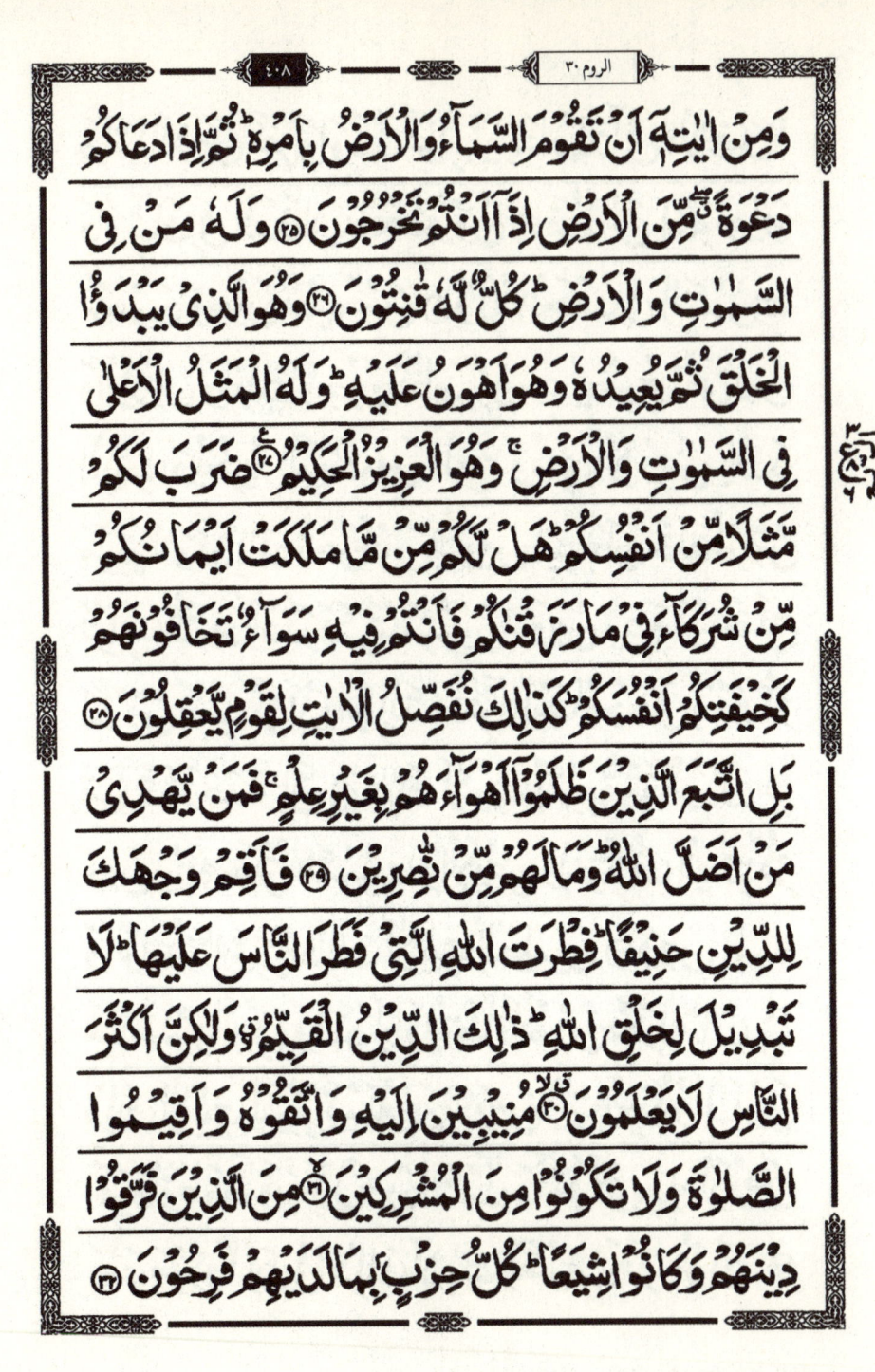

Allah's Signs 6) The Universe

25. And one of His signs is that the heavens and the earth persist by His command. Then when He calls you out of the earth just once, you will instantly come forth. 26. And to Him belong all those in the heavens and the earth—all are subject to His Will.[817] 27. And He is the One Who originates the creation then will resurrect it—which is even easier for Him.[818] To Him belong the finest attributes in the heavens and the earth. And He is the Almighty, All-Wise.

An Example for the Polytheists

28. He sets forth for you an example ˹drawn˺ from your own lives: would you allow some of those ˹bondspeople˺ in your possession to be your equal partners in whatever ˹wealth˺ We have provided you, keeping them in mind as you are mindful of your peers?[819] This is how We make the signs clear for people who understand. 29. In fact, the wrongdoers merely follow their desires with no knowledge. Who then can guide those Allah has left to stray? They will have no helpers.

Hold Firmly to Faith

30. So be steadfast in faith in all uprightness ˹O Prophet˺—the natural Way of Allah which He has instilled in ˹all˺ people. Let there be no change in this creation of Allah. That is the Straight Way, but most people do not know. 31. ˹O believers!˺ Always turn to Him ˹in repentance˺, be mindful of Him, and establish prayers. And do not be polytheists— 32. ˹like˺ those who have divided their faith and split into sects, each rejoicing in what they have.

---

817 lit., to Him.
818 This is from a human perspective. Otherwise, both the creation of the universe and the resurrection of humans are easy for Allah.
819 The passage says that since humans would not allow those who are inferior to them to become their partners in wealth, how can they set up helpless partners with Allah in His kingdom?

409   30. Ar-Rûm

Human Ingratitude

33. When people are touched with hardship, they cry out to their Lord, turning to Him ˹alone˺. But as soon as He gives them a taste of His mercy, a group of them associates ˹others˺ with their Lord ˹in worship˺, 34. becoming ungrateful for whatever ˹favours˺ We have given them. So enjoy yourselves, for soon you will know. 35. Or have We sent down to them an authority which attests to what they associate ˹with Him˺?

Human Impatience

36. If We give people a taste of mercy, they become prideful ˹because˺ of it. But if they are afflicted with an evil for what their hands have done, they instantly fall into despair.

Interest vs. Charity

37. Have they not seen that Allah gives abundant or limited provisions to whoever He wills? Surely in this are signs for people who believe. 38. So give your close relatives their due, as well as the poor and the ˹needy˺ traveller. That is best for those who seek the pleasure of Allah,[820] and it is they who will be successful. 39. Whatever loans you give, ˹only˺ seeking interest at the expense of people's wealth[821] will not increase with Allah. But whatever charity you give, ˹only˺ seeking the pleasure of Allah—it is they whose reward will be multiplied.

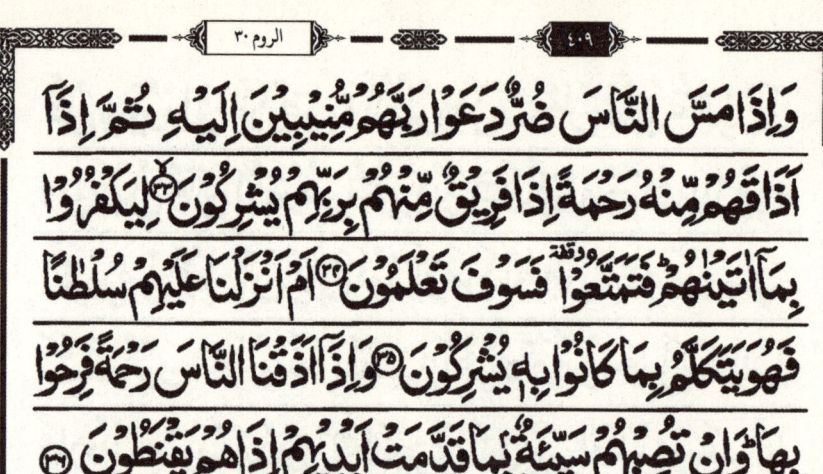

Allah's Might

40. It is Allah Who created you, then gives you provisions, then will cause you to die, and then will bring you back to life. Can any of your associate-gods do any of this? Glorified and Exalted is He above what they associate with Him ˹in worship˺!

The Spread of Corruption

41. Corruption has spread on land and sea as a result of what people's hands have done, so that Allah may cause them to taste ˹the consequences of˺ some of their deeds and perhaps they might return ˹to the Right Path˺.

---

820 lit., seek the Face of Allah.
821 Another meaning is the gift given to someone with the intention of getting a more expensive gift in return—a common ancient practice.

30. Ar-Rûm

Arabic text

قُلْ سِيرُوا فِى الْأَرْضِ فَانظُرُوا كَيْفَ كَانَ عَاقِبَةُ الَّذِينَ مِن قَبْلُ كَانَ أَكْثَرُهُم مُّشْرِكِينَ ۞ فَأَقِمْ وَجْهَكَ لِلدِّينِ الْقَيِّمِ مِن قَبْلِ أَن يَأْتِيَ يَوْمٌ لَّا مَرَدَّ لَهُ مِنَ اللَّهِ يَوْمَئِذٍ يَصَّدَّعُونَ ۞ مَن كَفَرَ فَعَلَيْهِ كُفْرُهُ وَمَنْ عَمِلَ صَالِحًا فَلِأَنفُسِهِمْ يَمْهَدُونَ ۞ لِيَجْزِيَ الَّذِينَ آمَنُوا وَعَمِلُوا الصَّالِحَاتِ مِن فَضْلِهِ إِنَّهُ لَا يُحِبُّ الْكَافِرِينَ ۞ وَمِنْ آيَاتِهِ أَن يُرْسِلَ الرِّيَاحَ مُبَشِّرَاتٍ وَلِيُذِيقَكُم مِّن رَّحْمَتِهِ وَلِتَجْرِيَ الْفُلْكُ بِأَمْرِهِ وَلِتَبْتَغُوا مِن فَضْلِهِ وَلَعَلَّكُمْ تَشْكُرُونَ ۞ وَلَقَدْ أَرْسَلْنَا مِن قَبْلِكَ رُسُلًا إِلَىٰ قَوْمِهِمْ فَجَاءُوهُم بِالْبَيِّنَاتِ فَانتَقَمْنَا مِنَ الَّذِينَ أَجْرَمُوا وَكَانَ حَقًّا عَلَيْنَا نَصْرُ الْمُؤْمِنِينَ ۞ اللَّهُ الَّذِي يُرْسِلُ الرِّيَاحَ فَتُثِيرُ سَحَابًا فَيَبْسُطُهُ فِى السَّمَاءِ كَيْفَ يَشَاءُ وَيَجْعَلُهُ كِسَفًا فَتَرَى الْوَدْقَ يَخْرُجُ مِنْ خِلَالِهِ فَإِذَا أَصَابَ بِهِ مَن يَشَاءُ مِنْ عِبَادِهِ إِذَا هُمْ يَسْتَبْشِرُونَ ۞ وَإِن كَانُوا مِن قَبْلِ أَن يُنَزَّلَ عَلَيْهِم مِّن قَبْلِهِ لَمُبْلِسِينَ ۞

---

42. Say, ˹O Prophet,˺ "Travel throughout the land and see what was the end of those ˹destroyed˺ before ˹you˺—most of them were polytheists."

The Successful and the Losers

43. So be steadfast in the Upright Faith ˹O Prophet˺, before the coming of a Day from Allah that cannot be averted. On that Day the people will be divided: **44.** those who disbelieved will bear ˹the burden of˺ their own disbelief; and those who did good will have prepared for themselves ˹eternal homes˺, **45.** so that He may ˹generously˺ reward those who believe and do good, out of His grace. He truly does not like the disbelievers.

Allah's Signs 7) The Wind

46. And one of His signs is that He sends the winds, ushering in good news ˹of rain˺ so that He may give you a taste of His mercy, and that ships may sail by His command, and that you may seek His bounty, and perhaps you will be grateful.

Warning to the Disbelievers

47. Indeed, We sent before you ˹O Prophet˺ messengers, each to their own people, and they came to them with clear proofs. Then We inflicted punishment upon those who persisted in wickedness. For it is Our duty to help the believers.

Allah's Signs 8) Rain

48. It is Allah Who sends the winds, which then stir up ˹vapour, forming˺ clouds, which He then spreads out in the sky or piles up into masses as He wills, from which you see rain come forth. Then as soon as He causes it to fall on whoever He wills of His servants, they rejoice, **49.** although they had utterly lost hope just before it was sent down to them.

411　30. Ar-Rûm

50. See then the impact of Allah's mercy: how He gives life to the earth after its death! Surely That 'same God' can raise the dead. For He is Most Capable of everything. **51.** Then if We send a 'harsh' wind which they see withering 'their' crops, they will definitely deny 'old favours' right after.

The Dead, Deaf, and Blind

52. So you 'O Prophet' certainly cannot make the dead hear 'the truth'. Nor can you make the deaf hear the call when they turn their backs and walk away. **53.** Nor can you lead the blind out of their misguidance. You can make none hear 'the truth' except those who believe in Our revelations, 'fully' submitting 'to Allah'.

Allah's Power of Creation

54. It is Allah Who created you in a state of weakness, then developed 'your' weakness into strength, then developed 'your' strength into weakness and old age.[822] He creates whatever He wills. For He is the All-Knowing, Most Capable.

Fleeting Life

55. And on the Day the Hour will arrive, the wicked will swear that they did not stay 'in this world' more than an hour. In this way they were always deluded 'in the world'. **56.** But those gifted with knowledge and faith will say 'to them', "You did actually stay—as destined by Allah—until the Day of Resurrection. So here is the Day of Resurrection 'which you denied'! But you did not know 'it was true'." **57.** So on that Day the wrongdoers' excuses will not benefit them, nor will they be allowed to appease 'their Lord'.

Advice to the Prophet

58. We have certainly set forth every 'kind of' lesson for people in this Quran. And no matter what sign you bring to them 'O Prophet', the disbelievers will definitely say 'to the believers', "You are only a people of falsehood."

---

822 lit., grey hair.

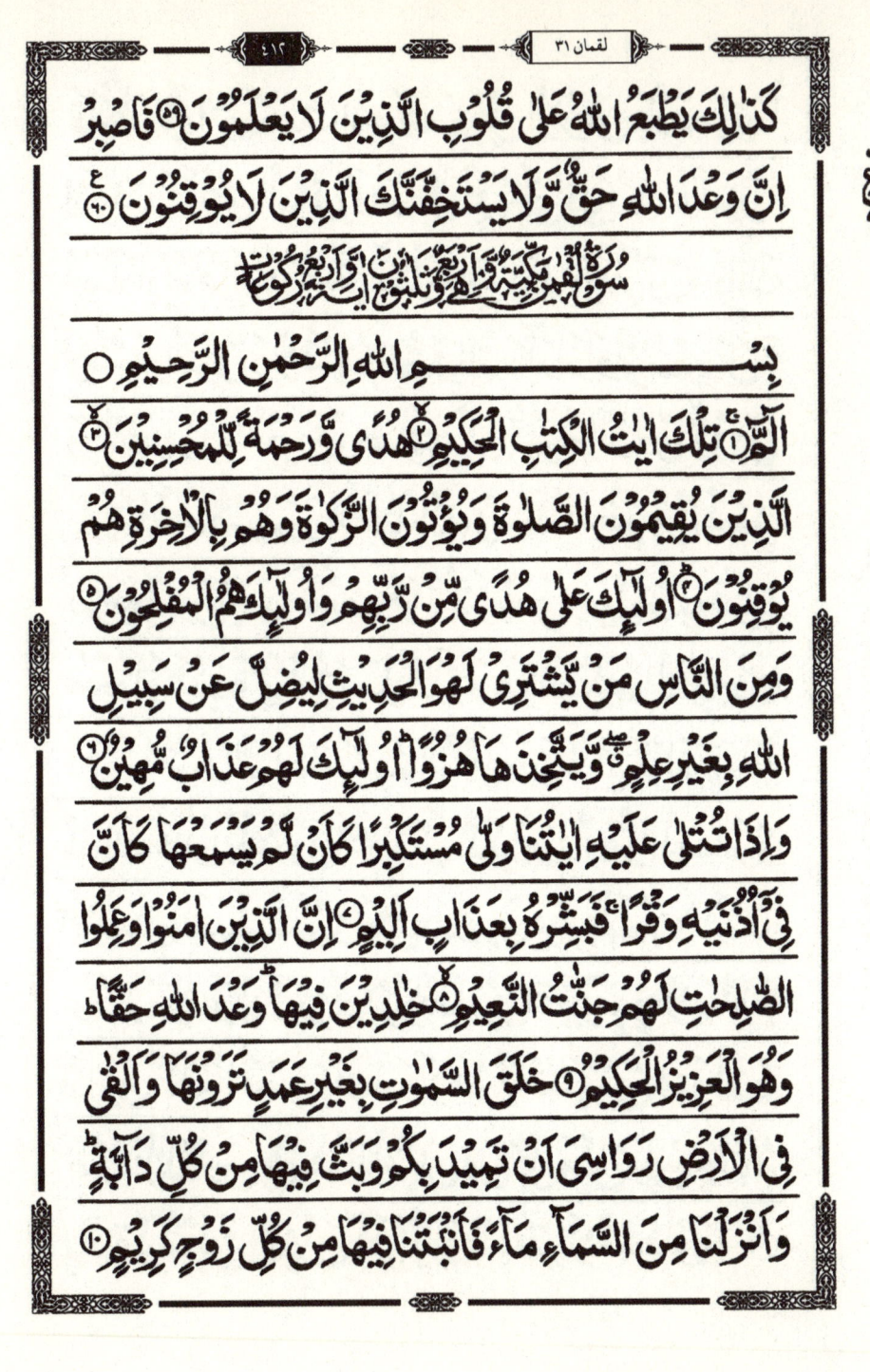

59. This is how Allah seals the hearts of those unwilling to know ˹the truth˺. **60.** So be patient, for the promise of Allah certainly is true. And do not be disturbed by those who have no sure faith.

❀

31. Luqmân (Luqmân)

In the Name of Allah—the Most Compassionate, Most Merciful

Qualities of True Believers

1. *Alif-Lãm-Mĩm.* **2.** These are the verses of the Book, rich in wisdom. **3.** ˹It is˺ a guide and mercy for the good-doers— **4.** those who establish prayer, pay alms-tax, and have sure faith in the Hereafter. **5.** It is they who are ˹truly˺ guided by their Lord, and it is they who will be successful.

Distracting People from the Truth

6. But there are some who employ theatrics,[823] only to lead others away from Allah's Way—without any knowledge—and to make a mockery of it. They will suffer a humiliating punishment. **7.** Whenever Our revelations are recited to them, they turn away in arrogance as if they did not hear them, as if there is deafness in their ears. So give them good news ˹O Prophet˺ of a painful punishment.

Reward of the Believers

8. Surely those who believe and do good will have the Gardens of Bliss, **9.** staying there forever. Allah's promise is true. And He is the Almighty, All-Wise.

Allah's Creation

10. He created the heavens without pillars—as you can see—and placed firm mountains upon the earth so it does not shake with you, and scattered throughout it all types of creatures. And We send down rain from the sky, causing every type of fine plant to grow on earth.

---

823 Some pagan Arabs used to utilize singing, dancing, chanting, etc. to distract people's attention from listening to the recitation of the Quran.

11. This is Allah's creation. Now show Me what those ˹gods˺ other than Him have created. In fact, the wrongdoers are clearly astray.

Luqmân's Advice: 1)
Worship Allah Alone

12. Indeed, We blessed Luqmân with wisdom, ˹saying˺, "Be grateful to Allah, for whoever is grateful, it is only for their own good. And whoever is ungrateful, then surely Allah is Self-Sufficient, Praiseworthy."[824]

13. And ˹remember˺ when Luqmân said to his son, while advising him, "O my dear son! Never associate ˹anything˺ with Allah ˹in worship˺, for associating ˹others with Him˺ is truly the worst of all wrongs."

2) Honour Your Parents[825]

14. And We have commanded people to ˹honour˺ their parents. Their mothers bore them through hardship upon hardship, and their weaning takes two years. So be grateful to Me and your parents. To Me is the final return. **15.** But if they pressure you to associate with Me what you have no knowledge of,[826] do not obey them. Still keep their company in this world courteously, and follow the way of those who turn to Me ˹in devotion˺. Then to Me you will ˹all˺ return, and then I will inform you of what you used to do.

3) Know That Allah
Will Judge All Deeds

16. ˹Luqmân added,˺ "O my dear son! ˹Even˺ if a deed were the weight of a mustard seed—be it ˹hidden˺ in a rock or in the heavens or the earth—Allah will bring it forth. Surely Allah is Most Subtle, All-Aware.

4) Fulfil Your Duty to Allah

17. "O my dear son! Establish prayer, encourage what is good and forbid what is evil, and endure patiently whatever befalls you. Surely this is a resolve to aspire to.

---

824 Luqmân is believed to have been a righteous, wise man who lived around the time of Prophet David (☝).
825 The Quran usually combines the command to worship Allah with the order to honour one's parents (*see* 6:151 and 17:23). This is why this passage interjects Luqmân's advice to his son. In some instances, the Quran follows the order to be kind to parents with emphasizing the role of the mother. This is because some of the mother's sacrifices take place before the child is born and when they are too young. So the Quran brings these sacrifices to the children's attention.
826 Other gods.

5) Be Humble

18. "And do not turn your nose up to people, nor walk pridefully upon the earth. Surely Allah does not like whoever is arrogant, boastful. **19.** Be moderate in your pace. And lower your voice, for the ugliest of all voices is certainly the braying of donkeys."

Allah's Favours

20. Have you not seen that Allah has subjected for you whatever is in the heavens and whatever is on the earth, and has lavished His favours upon you, both seen and unseen? ˹Still˺ there are some who dispute about Allah without knowledge, or guidance, or an enlightening scripture. **21.** When it is said to them, "Follow what Allah has revealed," they reply, "No! We ˹only˺ follow what we found our forefathers practicing." ˹Would they still do so˺ even if Satan is inviting them to the torment of the Blaze?

The Believers and the Disbelievers

22. Whoever fully submits themselves to Allah and is a good-doer, they have certainly grasped the firmest hand-hold. And with Allah rests the outcome of ˹all˺ affairs. **23.** But whoever disbelieves, do not let their disbelief grieve you ˹O Prophet˺. To Us is their return, and We will inform them of all they did. Surely Allah knows best what is ˹hidden˺ in the heart. **24.** We allow them enjoyment for a little while, then ˹in time˺ We will force them into a harsh torment. **25.** And if you ask them who created the heavens and the earth, they will definitely say, "Allah!" Say, "Praise be to Allah!" In fact, most of them do not know.

Allah's Infinite Knowledge

26. To Allah belongs whatever is in the heavens and the earth. Allah is truly the Self-Sufficient, Praiseworthy. **27.** If all the trees on earth were pens and the ocean ˹were ink˺, refilled by seven other oceans, the Words of Allah would not be exhausted. Surely Allah is Almighty, All-Wise.

31. Luqmân

Allah's Infinite Power

28. The creation and resurrection of you ˹all˺ is as simple ˹for Him˺ as that of a single soul. Surely Allah is All-Hearing, All-Seeing. **29.** Do you not see that Allah causes the night to merge into the day and the day into the night, and has subjected the sun and the moon, each orbiting for an appointed term, and that Allah is All-Aware of what you do? **30.** That is because Allah ˹alone˺ is the Truth and what they invoke besides Him is falsehood, and ˹because˺ Allah ˹alone˺ is the Most High, All-Great.

Human Ingratitude

31. Do you not see that the ships sail ˹smoothly˺ through the sea by the grace of Allah so that He may show you some of His signs? Surely in this are signs for whoever is steadfast, grateful. **32.** And as soon as they are overwhelmed by waves like mountains, they cry out to Allah ˹alone˺ in sincere devotion. But when He delivers them ˹safely˺ to shore, only some become relatively grateful. And none rejects Our signs except whoever is deceitful, ungrateful.

Warning of Judgment Day

33. O humanity! Be mindful of your Lord, and beware of a Day when no parent will be of any benefit to their child, nor will a child be of any benefit to their parent. Surely Allah's promise is true. So do not let the life of this world deceive you, nor let the Chief Deceiver[827] deceive you about Allah.

The Five Keys of the Unseen[828]

34. Indeed, Allah ˹alone˺ has the knowledge of the Hour. He sends down the rain,[829] and knows what is in the wombs.[830] No soul knows what it will earn for tomorrow, and no soul knows in what land it will die. Surely Allah is All-Knowing, All-Aware.

༺ ❈ ༻

---

827 Satan.

828 See footnote for 6:59.

829 He knows precisely when, where, and how much rain falls, and whether it is going to be drunk by people and animals or used for irrigation, or absorbed by the earth, etc.

830 The Prophet (ﷺ) was reported in a *ḥadîth* collected by Bukhāri and Muslim to have said, "Indeed, the creation of each one of you is brought together in the womb of one's mother as a drop of ˹male and female˺ discharges for forty days, then one becomes a clinging clot of blood for a similar period, then a lump of flesh for a similar period. Then an angel is sent to blow the breath of life into the embryo. The angel is then commanded to write four things: one's destined provisions, lifespan, actions, and whether one will be happy or miserable ˹in the Hereafter˺."

32. As-Sajdah | 416

32. The Prostration (As-Sajdah)

In the Name of Allah—the Most Compassionate, Most Merciful

Reassuring the Prophet

1. Alif-Lãm-Mĩm. 2. The revelation of this Book is—beyond doubt—from the Lord of all worlds. 3. Or do they say, "He has fabricated it!"? No! It is the truth from your Lord in order for you to warn a people to whom no warner has come before you, so they may be ˹rightly˺ guided.

Allah's Power of Creation

4. It is Allah Who has created the heavens and the earth and everything in between in six Days,[831] then established Himself on the Throne. You have no protector or intercessor besides Him. Will you not then be mindful? 5. He conducts every affair from the heavens to the earth, then it all ascends to Him on a Day whose length is a thousand years by your counting. 6. That is the Knower of the seen and unseen—the Almighty, Most Merciful, 7. Who has perfected everything He created. And He originated the creation of humankind from clay.[832] 8. Then He made his descendants from an extract of a humble fluid, 9. then He fashioned them and had a spirit of His Own ˹creation˺ breathed into them. And He gave you hearing, sight, and intellect. ˹Yet˺ you hardly give any thanks.

The Deniers of Resurrection

10. ˹Still˺ they ask ˹mockingly˺, "When we are disintegrated into the earth, will we really be raised as a new creation?" In fact, they are in denial of the meeting with their Lord.

---

831 *See* footnote for 7:54.
832 Adam (🙏).

32. As-Sajdah

11. Say, ˹O Prophet,˺ "Your soul will be taken by the Angel of Death, who is in charge of you. Then to your Lord you will ˹all˺ be returned."
12. If only you could see the wicked hanging their heads ˹in shame˺ before their Lord, ˹crying:˺ "Our Lord! We have now seen and heard, so send us back and we will do good. We truly have sure faith ˹now˺!"
13. Had We willed, We could have easily imposed guidance on every soul. But My Word will come to pass: I will surely fill up Hell with jinn and humans all together. 14. So taste ˹the punishment˺ for neglecting the meeting of this Day of yours. We ˹too˺ will certainly neglect you. And taste the torment of eternity for what you used to do!

Qualities of the Believers

15. The only ˹true˺ believers in Our revelation are those who—when it is recited to them—fall into prostration and glorify the praises of their Lord and are not too proud. 16. They abandon their beds, invoking their Lord with hope and fear, and donate from what We have provided for them. 17. No soul can imagine what delights are kept in store for them as a reward for what they used to do.

The Faithful and the Rebellious

18. Is the one who is a believer equal ˹before Allah˺ to the one who is rebellious? They are not equal!
19. As for those who believe and do good, they will have the Gardens of ˹Eternal˺ Residence—as an accommodation for what they used to do.
20. But as for those who are rebellious, the Fire will be their home. Whenever they try to escape from it, they will be forced back into it, and will be told, "Taste the Fire's torment, which you used to deny."

قُلْ يَتَوَفَّىٰكُم مَّلَكُ الْمَوْتِ الَّذِي وُكِّلَ بِكُمْ ثُمَّ إِلَىٰ رَبِّكُمْ تُرْجَعُونَ ۝ وَلَوْ تَرَىٰ إِذِ الْمُجْرِمُونَ نَاكِسُوا رُءُوسِهِمْ عِندَ رَبِّهِمْ رَبَّنَا أَبْصَرْنَا وَسَمِعْنَا فَارْجِعْنَا نَعْمَلْ صَالِحًا إِنَّا مُوقِنُونَ ۝ وَلَوْ شِئْنَا لَآتَيْنَا كُلَّ نَفْسٍ هُدَاهَا وَلَٰكِنْ حَقَّ الْقَوْلُ مِنِّي لَأَمْلَأَنَّ جَهَنَّمَ مِنَ الْجِنَّةِ وَالنَّاسِ أَجْمَعِينَ ۝ فَذُوقُوا بِمَا نَسِيتُمْ لِقَاءَ يَوْمِكُمْ هَٰذَا إِنَّا نَسِينَاكُمْ وَذُوقُوا عَذَابَ الْخُلْدِ بِمَا كُنتُمْ تَعْمَلُونَ ۝ إِنَّمَا يُؤْمِنُ بِآيَاتِنَا الَّذِينَ إِذَا ذُكِّرُوا بِهَا خَرُّوا سُجَّدًا وَسَبَّحُوا بِحَمْدِ رَبِّهِمْ وَهُمْ لَا يَسْتَكْبِرُونَ ۩ تَتَجَافَىٰ جُنُوبُهُمْ عَنِ الْمَضَاجِعِ يَدْعُونَ رَبَّهُمْ خَوْفًا وَطَمَعًا وَمِمَّا رَزَقْنَاهُمْ يُنفِقُونَ ۝ فَلَا تَعْلَمُ نَفْسٌ مَّا أُخْفِيَ لَهُم مِّن قُرَّةِ أَعْيُنٍ جَزَاءً بِمَا كَانُوا يَعْمَلُونَ ۝ أَفَمَن كَانَ مُؤْمِنًا كَمَن كَانَ فَاسِقًا لَا يَسْتَوُونَ ۝ أَمَّا الَّذِينَ آمَنُوا وَعَمِلُوا الصَّالِحَاتِ فَلَهُمْ جَنَّاتُ الْمَأْوَىٰ نُزُلًا بِمَا كَانُوا يَعْمَلُونَ ۝ وَأَمَّا الَّذِينَ فَسَقُوا فَمَأْوَاهُمُ النَّارُ كُلَّمَا أَرَادُوا أَن يَخْرُجُوا مِنْهَا أُعِيدُوا فِيهَا وَقِيلَ لَهُمْ ذُوقُوا عَذَابَ النَّارِ الَّذِي كُنتُم بِهِ تُكَذِّبُونَ ۝

32. As-Sajdah

21. We will certainly make them taste some of the minor torment ˹in this life˺ before the major torment ˹of the Hereafter˺, so perhaps they will return ˹to the Right Path˺. **22.** And who does more wrong than the one who is reminded of Allah's revelations then turns away from them? We will surely inflict punishment upon the wicked.

Divine Revelations

23. Indeed, We gave the Scripture to Moses—so let there be no doubt ˹O Prophet˺ that you ˹too˺ are receiving revelations—[833] and We made it a guide for the Children of Israel. **24.** We raised from among them leaders,[834] guiding by Our command, when they patiently endured and firmly believed in Our signs. **25.** Indeed, your Lord will decide between them on the Day of Judgment regarding their differences.

Warning to the Disbelievers

26. Is it not yet clear to them how many peoples We destroyed before them, whose ruins they still pass by? Surely in this are signs. Will they not then listen? **27.** Do they not see how We drive rain to parched land, producing ˹various˺ crops from which they and their cattle eat? Will they not then see?

The Deniers of Judgment

28. They ask ˹mockingly˺, "When is this ˹Day of final˺ Decision, if what you say is true?" **29.** Say, ˹O Prophet,˺ "On the Day of Decision it will not benefit the disbelievers to believe then, nor will they be delayed ˹from punishment˺." **30.** So turn away from them, and wait! They too are waiting.

---

833 Other possible translations: 1. "Do not be in doubt that Moses received it." 2. "Do not be in doubt of your meeting with Moses."
834 i.e., prophets.

33. The Enemy Alliance (Al-Aḥzâb)

In the Name of Allah—the Most Compassionate, Most Merciful

Orders to the Prophet

1. O Prophet! ˹Always˺ be mindful of Allah, and do not yield to the disbelievers and the hypocrites. Indeed, Allah is All-Knowing, All-Wise. **2.** Follow what is revealed to you from your Lord. Surely Allah is All-Aware of what you ˹all˺ do. **3.** And put your trust in Allah, for Allah is sufficient as a Trustee of Affairs.

Rules on Divorce and Adoption[835]

4. Allah does not place two hearts in any person's chest. Nor does He regard your wives as ˹unlawful for you like˺ your real mothers, ˹even˺ if you say they are.[836] Nor does He regard your adopted children as your real children.[837] These are only your baseless assertions. But Allah declares the truth, and He ˹alone˺ guides to the ˹Right˺ Way. **5.** Let your adopted children keep their family names. That is more just in the sight of Allah. But if you do not know their fathers, then they are ˹simply˺ your fellow believers and close associates. There is no blame on you for what you do by mistake, but ˹only˺ for what you do intentionally. And Allah is All-Forgiving, Most Merciful.

Guidelines for the Believers

6. The Prophet has a stronger affinity to the believers than they do themselves. And his wives are their mothers. As ordained by Allah, blood relatives are more entitled ˹to inheritance˺ than ˹other˺ believers and immigrants, unless you ˹want to˺ show kindness to your ˹close˺ associates ˹through bequest˺.[838] This is decreed in the Record.[839]

---

835 The passage says that as a person cannot have two hearts, similarly, a man cannot have two real mothers, nor can a child have two real fathers.

836 This divorce (called *ẓihâr*) was commonly practiced in Arabia before the Prophet (ﷺ). If a man declared his wife as unlawful for him as the *ẓahr* (back) of his mother, his wife would be divorced. Islam abolished this type of divorce (see 58:3-4).

837 The following distinction should be made:
- Sponsorship (which is permissible): a person can sponsor a child or host them in their home and care for them as they care for their own children, except for legal matters. For example, adopted children keep their last names, are allowed to marry the children of their adopted parent, adopted and biological children of the opposite sex should dress modestly in front of each other, and do not have a share in the estate of their adopted parents, but can get a share of inheritance (up to one-third of the estate) through bequest (*waṣiyah*).
- Adoption: a person is not allowed to take an orphan and give them his/her last name, give them a share of inheritance similar to their own children, etc.

838 This verse confirms a ruling mentioned in 8:75 which ended a previous ruling that allowed inheritance between Muslims from Mecca (*Al-Muhâjirûn*, the Emigrants) and Muslims from Medina (*Al-Anṣâr*, the Helpers). Now, only relatives can inherit from one another, whereas non-heirs can receive a share through bequest, up to one third of the estate. See 4:7, 11-13, 32-33, and 176.

839 The Record refers to the Preserved Tablet (*Al-Lawḥ Al-Maḥfûẓ*) in which Allah has written the destiny of His entire creation.

Covenant to Deliver the Truth

7. And ˹remember˺ when We took a covenant from the prophets, as well as from you ˹O Prophet˺, and from Noah, Abraham, Moses, and Jesus, son of Mary. We did take a solemn covenant from ˹all of˺ them 8. so that He may question these men of truth about their ˹delivery of the˺ truth. And He has prepared a painful punishment for the disbelievers.

The Battle of the Trench

9. O believers! Remember Allah's favour upon you when ˹enemy˺ forces came to ˹besiege˺ you ˹in Medina˺,[840] so We sent against them a ˹bitter˺ wind and forces you could not see.[841] And Allah is All-Seeing of what you do. 10. ˹Remember˺ when they came at you from east and west,[842] when your eyes grew wild ˹in horror˺ and your hearts jumped into your throats, and you entertained ˹conflicting˺ thoughts about Allah.[843] 11. Then and there the believers were put to the test, and were violently shaken.

Stance of the Hypocrites

12. And ˹remember˺ when the hypocrites and those with sickness in their hearts said, "Allah and His Messenger have promised us nothing but delusion!" 13. And ˹remember˺ when a group of them said, "O people of Yathrib![844] There is no point in you staying ˹here˺, so retreat!" Another group of them asked the Prophet's permission ˹to leave˺, saying, "Our homes are vulnerable," while ˹in fact˺ they were not vulnerable. They only wished to flee. 14. Had their city been sacked from all sides and they had been asked to abandon faith, they would have done so with little hesitation.

Warning to the Hypocrites

15. They had already pledged to Allah earlier never to turn their backs ˹in retreat˺. And a pledge to Allah must be answered for.

---

840 In 5 A.H./627 C.E., the Meccan pagans along with some Arab and Jewish tribes (totalling around 10 000 soldiers) laid a siege around Medina, where the Prophet (ﷺ) was positioned with 3000 soldiers. The Prophet (ﷺ) had anticipated the offence and, upon an advice from one of his companions, dug a trench around the city to protect it from invaders. After several unsuccessful attempts to cross the trench, the allied enemies quickly lost morale, and were forced to end the siege due to severe weather conditions. This encounter is commonly known as the Battle of the Trench or the Enemy Alliance.

841 The angels.

842 lit., from above and below you.

843 The believers were reassured while the doubts of the hypocrites grew more fierce.

844 Yathrib was the name of Medina before the arrival of the Prophet (ﷺ) and Muslim emigrants.

16. Say, ˹O Prophet,˺ "Fleeing will not benefit you if you ˹try to˺ escape a natural or violent death. ˹If it is not your time,˺ you will only be allowed enjoyment for a little while."[845]

17. Ask ˹them, O Prophet˺, "Who can put you out of Allah's reach if He intends to harm you or show you mercy?" They can never find any protector or helper besides Allah.

Hypocritical Tactics

18. Allah knows well those among you who discourage ˹others from fighting˺, saying ˹secretly˺ to their brothers, "Stay with us," and who themselves hardly take part in fighting. **19.** ˹They are˺ totally unwilling to assist you. When danger comes, you see them staring at you with their eyes rolling like someone in the throes of death. But once the danger is over, they slash you with razor-sharp tongues, ravenous for ˹worldly˺ gains. Such people have not ˹truly˺ believed, so Allah has rendered their deeds void. And that is easy for Allah.

Hypocrites Paranoid

20. They ˹still˺ think that the enemy alliance has not ˹yet˺ withdrawn. And if the allies were to come ˹again˺, the hypocrites would wish to be away in the desert among nomadic Arabs, ˹only˺ asking for news about you ˹believers˺. And if the hypocrites were in your midst, they would hardly take part in the fight.

The Prophet as a Role Model

21. Indeed, in the Messenger of Allah you have an excellent example for whoever has hope in Allah and the Last Day, and remembers Allah often.

Stance of the Believers

22. When the believers saw the enemy alliance, they said, "This is what Allah and His Messenger had promised us. The promise of Allah and His Messenger has come true." And this only increased them in faith and submission.

---

845 Until the end of your short life on earth.

33. Al-Aḥzâb

23. Among the believers are men who have proven true to what they pledged to Allah.[846] Some of them have fulfilled their pledge ʿwith their livesʾ, others are waiting ʿtheir turnʾ. They have never changed ʿtheir commitmentʾ in the least. **24.** ʿIt all happenedʾ so Allah may reward the faithful for their faithfulness, and punish the hypocrites if He wills or turn to them ʿin mercyʾ. Surely Allah is All-Forgiving, Most Merciful.

Defeat of the Enemy Alliance

25. And Allah drove back the disbelievers in their rage, totally empty-handed. And Allah spared the believers from fighting. For Allah is All-Powerful, Almighty. **26.** And He brought down those from the People of the Book[847] who supported the enemy alliance from their own strongholds, and cast horror into their hearts. You ʿbelieversʾ killed some, and took others captive. **27.** He has also caused you to take over their lands, homes, and wealth, as well as lands you have not yet set foot on. And Allah is Most Capable of everything.

Advice to the Prophet's Wives: Your Choice

28. O Prophet! Say to your wives, "If you desire the life of this world and its luxury, then come, I will give you a ʿsuitableʾ compensation ʿfor divorceʾ and let you go graciously. **29.** But if you desire Allah and His Messenger and the ʿeverlastingʾ Home of the Hereafter, then surely Allah has prepared a great reward for those of you who do good."

More Advice: Your Reward

30. O wives of the Prophet! If any of you were to commit a blatant misconduct, the punishment would be doubled for her. And that is easy for Allah.

---

846 *See* footnote for 7:46.
847 The Jews of Banu Quraiẓah who had violated their treaty with the Muslims and sided with the enemy alliance. The Prophet (ﷺ) asked how they wished to be judged, and they chose to be judged by their book, the Torah—in which the penalty for treason is death.

31. And whoever of you devoutly obeys Allah and His Messenger and does good, We will grant her double the reward, and We have prepared for her an honourable provision.

More Advice: Your Modesty

32. O wives of the Prophet! You are not like any other women: if you are mindful ˹of Allah˺, then do not be overly effeminate in speech ˹with men˺ or those with sickness in their hearts may be tempted, but speak in a moderate tone. **33.** Settle in your homes, and do not display yourselves as women did in the days of ˹pre-Islamic˺ ignorance. Establish prayer, pay alms-tax, and obey Allah and His Messenger. Allah only intends to keep ˹the causes of˺ evil away from you and purify you completely, O members of the ˹Prophet's˺ family! **34.** ˹Always˺ remember what is recited in your homes of Allah's revelations and ˹prophetic˺ wisdom.[848] Surely Allah is Most Subtle, All-Aware.

Reward of the Righteous

35. Surely ˹for˺ Muslim men and women, believing men and women,[849] devout men and women, truthful men and women, patient men and women, humble men and women, charitable men and women, fasting men and women, men and women who guard their chastity, and men and women who remember Allah often—for ˹all of˺ them Allah has prepared forgiveness and a great reward.

---

848 Allah's revelations refers to verses of the Quran whereas prophetic wisdom refers to the sayings and teachings of the Prophet (ﷺ), known collectively as *ḥadîth*.

849 Though Islam and *Îmân* are sometimes used interchangeably in the Quran, *Îmân* is a higher state of Islam. A Muslim is someone who observes the five pillars of Islam, but a believer is someone with strong faith, who does everything purely for the sake of Allah, and is mindful of Allah in everything they say or do. Every *Mu'min* (believer/faithful) is a Muslim, but not every Muslim is a *Mu'min*. *See* 49:14.

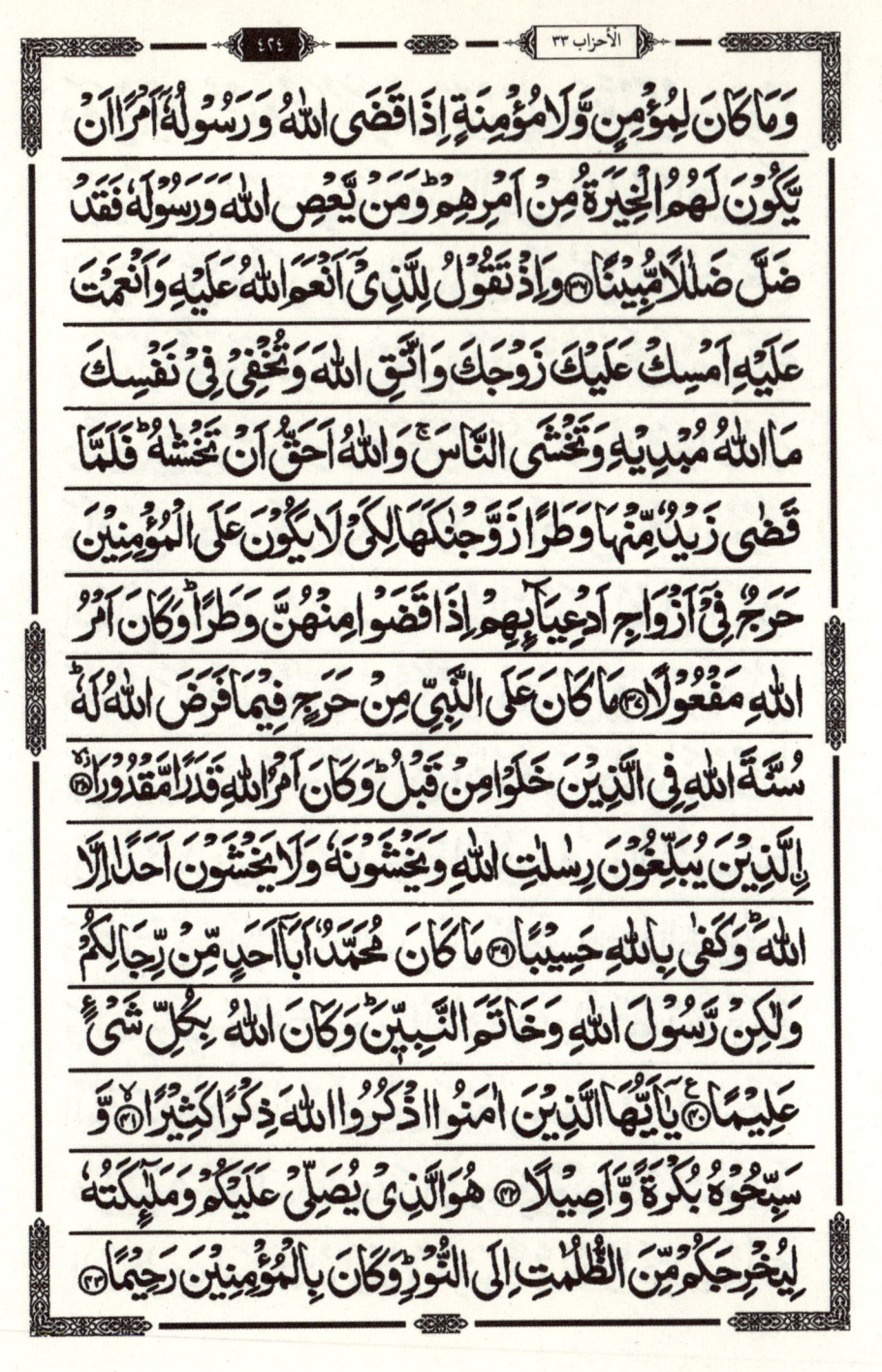

Unconditional Obedience

36. It is not for a believing man or woman—when Allah and His Messenger decree a matter—to have any other choice in that matter.[850] Indeed, whoever disobeys Allah and His Messenger has clearly gone ˹far˺ astray.

The Case of Zaid

37. And ˹remember, O Prophet,˺ when you said to the one[851] for whom Allah has done a favour and you ˹too˺ have done a favour,[852] "Keep your wife and fear Allah," while concealing within yourself what Allah was going to reveal. And ˹so˺ you were considering the people, whereas Allah was more worthy of your consideration. So when Zaid totally lost interest in ˹keeping˺ his wife, We gave her to you in marriage, so that there would be no blame on the believers for marrying the ex-wives of their adopted sons after their divorce. And Allah's command is totally binding. **38.** There is no blame on the Prophet for doing what Allah has ordained for him. That has been the way of Allah with those ˹prophets˺ who had gone before. And Allah's command has been firmly decreed. **39.** ˹That is His way with˺ those ˹prophets˺ who deliver the messages of Allah, and consider Him and none but Allah. And sufficient is Allah as a ˹vigilant˺ Reckoner. **40.** Muḥammad is not the father of any of your men,[853] but is the Messenger of Allah and the seal of the prophets. And Allah has ˹perfect˺ knowledge of all things.

Reward of the Believers

41. O believers! Always remember Allah often, **42.** and glorify Him morning and evening. **43.** He is the One Who showers His blessings upon you—and His angels pray for you—so that He may bring you out of darkness and into light. For He is ever Merciful to the believers.

---

850 Meaning, if Allah makes a ruling in the Quran or the Prophet (ﷺ) makes a ruling, then a Muslim is not allowed to seek judgment from anyone else, nor follow their own desires.

851 This refers to Zaid ibn Ḥârithah, the Prophet's adopted son before adoption was made unlawful. His wife, Zainab bint Jaḥsh was from a prestigious family. Because Zaid and Zainab came from two different social classes, the marriage was not successful. Eventually, Zaid insisted on divorcing his wife, despite several appeals from the Prophet (ﷺ). Since one's adopted son was no longer considered to be one's own son, the Prophet (ﷺ) was later allowed to marry Zainab.

852 Allah's favour to Zaid was to guide him to Islam, and the Prophet's favour was to free him from slavery.

853 He (ﷺ) is not the father of Zaid (mentioned in 33:37) or any other man. The Prophet (ﷺ) had three biological sons, who all died in childhood.

44. Their greeting on the Day they meet Him will be, "Peace!" And He has prepared for them an honourable reward.

Excellence of the Prophet

45. O Prophet! We have sent you as a witness, and a deliverer of good news, and a warner, **46.** and a caller to ʿthe Way of˺ Allah by His command, and a beacon of light. **47.** Give good news to the believers that they will have a great bounty from Allah. **48.** Do not yield to the disbelievers and the hypocrites. Overlook their annoyances, and put your trust in Allah. For Allah is sufficient as a Trustee of Affairs.

Divorce Before Consummation

49. O believers! If you marry believing women and then divorce them before you touch them,[854] they will have no waiting period for you to count,[855] so give them a ʿsuitable˺ compensation, and let them go graciously.

Women Lawful to the Prophet

50. O Prophet! We have made lawful for you your wives to whom you have paid their ʿfull˺ dowries as well as those ʿbondwomen˺ in your possession, whom Allah has granted you.[856] And ʿyou are allowed to marry˺ the daughters of your paternal uncles and aunts, and the daughters of your maternal uncles and aunts, who have emigrated like you. Also ʿallowed for marriage˺ is a believing woman who offers herself to the Prophet ʿwithout dowry˺ if he is interested in marrying her—ʿthis is˺ exclusively for you, not for the rest of the believers.[857] We know well what ʿrulings˺ We have ordained for the believers in relation to their wives and those ʿbondwomen˺ in their possession. As such, there would be no blame on you. And Allah is All-Forgiving, Most Merciful.

---

854 Before the marriage is consummated.

855 If divorce is pronounced after the consummation of marriage, a waiting period of three months is observed to give the couple a chance to get back together and to see if the wife is pregnant (*see* 65:4). But if the divorce happens before the marriage is consummated, then there is no waiting period.

856 *See* footnote for 4:3.

857 This ruling was exclusively for the Prophet (which he never took advantage of), but Muslims have to pay a dowry to their wives. Some women did offer themselves to the Prophet (ﷺ) in marriage, but he declined.

Prophet's Visitation to His Wives

51. It is up to you ˹O Prophet˺ to delay or receive whoever you please of your wives. There is no blame on you if you call back any of those you have set aside.[858] That is more likely that they will be content, not grieved, and satisfied with what you offer them all. Allah ˹fully˺ knows what is in your hearts. And Allah is All-Knowing, Most Forbearing.

No Future Marriages

52. It is not lawful for you ˹O Prophet˺ to marry more women after this, nor can you replace any of your present wives with another, even if her beauty may attract you—except those ˹bondwomen˺ in your possession. And Allah is ever Watchful over all things.

On Visiting the Prophet

53. O believers! Do not enter the homes of the Prophet without permission ˹and if invited˺ for a meal, do not ˹come too early and˺ linger until the meal is ready. But if you are invited, then enter ˹on time˺. Once you have eaten, then go on your way, and do not stay for casual talk. Such behaviour is truly annoying to the Prophet, yet he is too shy to ask you to leave. But Allah is never shy of the truth.

Interacting with the Prophet's Wives

And when you ˹believers˺ ask his wives for something, ask them from behind a barrier. This is purer for your hearts and theirs. And it is not right for you to annoy the Messenger of Allah, nor ever marry his wives after him. This would certainly be a major offence in the sight of Allah. **54.** Whether you reveal something or conceal it, surely Allah has ˹perfect˺ knowledge of all things.

---

858 The Prophet's married life can be classified as follows:
- Until the age of 25: he was single.
- Age 25–50: he was married only to Khadījah.
- Age 50–52: he was single after Khadījah's death.
- Age 53–his death at the age of 63: he had a total of ten wives. Many of these marriages were to widows (who had been left with their children without a provider) and in some cases to foster stronger ties with some of his companions and neighbouring tribes. Of all the women he married, ˹Āishah was the only virgin.

55. There is no blame on the Prophet's wives 'if they appear unveiled' before their fathers,[859] their sons, their brothers, their brothers' sons, their sisters' sons, their fellow 'Muslim' women, and those 'bondspeople' in their possession. And be mindful of Allah 'O wives of the Prophet!' Surely Allah is a Witness over all things.

Blessings on the Prophet

56. Indeed, Allah showers His blessings upon the Prophet, and His angels pray for him. O believers! Invoke Allah's blessings upon him, and salute him with worthy greetings of peace.

Offending Allah, His Messenger, and the Believers

57. Surely those who offend Allah[860] and His Messenger[861] are condemned by Allah in this world and the Hereafter. And He has prepared for them a humiliating punishment. **58.** As for those who abuse believing men and women[862] unjustifiably, they will definitely bear the guilt of slander and blatant sin.

The Veil

59. O Prophet! Ask your wives, daughters, and believing women to draw their cloaks over their bodies. In this way it is more likely that they will be recognized 'as virtuous' and not be harassed. And Allah is All-Forgiving, Most Merciful.[863]

Reward of the Wicked

60. If the hypocrites, and those with sickness in their hearts, and rumour-mongers in Medina do not desist, We will certainly incite you 'O Prophet' against them, and then they will not be your neighbours there any longer. **61.** 'They deserve to be' condemned. 'If they were to persist,' they would get themselves seized and killed relentlessly wherever they are found![864] **62.** That was Allah's way with those 'hypocrites' who have gone before. And you will find no change in Allah's way.

---

859 Paternal and maternal uncles are similar to the fathers.
860 By attributing children to Him or associating gods with Him in worship.
861 By calling him a liar or speaking ill of him and his family.
862 By harming them physically or accusing them falsely.
863 He has forgiven what Muslim women did in the past because they were not obligated to cover up.
864 This verse is intended to deter the hypocrites. The Prophet (ﷺ) never killed any hypocrite as long as they did not join the enemy to attack and kill Muslims.

33. Al-Aḥzâb

When Is the Hour?

63. People ask you ˹O Prophet˺ about the Hour. Say, "That knowledge is only with Allah. You never know, perhaps the Hour is near."

The Doomed

64. Surely Allah condemns the disbelievers, and has prepared for them a blazing Fire, **65.** to stay there for ever and ever—never will they find any protector or helper. **66.** On the Day their faces are ˹constantly˺ flipped in the Fire, they will cry, "Oh! If only we had obeyed Allah and obeyed the Messenger!" **67.** And they will say, "Our Lord! We obeyed our leaders and elite, but they led us astray from the ˹Right˺ Way. **68.** Our Lord! Give them double ˹our˺ punishment, and condemn them tremendously."

Advice to the Believers

69. O believers! Do not be like those who slandered Moses, but Allah cleared him of what they said. And he was honourable in the sight of Allah.[865] **70.** O believers! Be mindful of Allah, and say what is right. **71.** He will bless your deeds for you, and forgive your sins. And whoever obeys Allah and His Messenger, has truly achieved a great triumph.

The Trust[866]

72. Indeed, We offered the trust to the heavens and the earth and the mountains, but they ˹all˺ declined to bear it, being fearful of it. But humanity assumed it, ˹for˺ they are truly wrongful ˹to themselves˺ and ignorant ˹of the consequences˺, **73.** so that Allah will punish hypocrite men and women and polytheistic men and women, and Allah will turn in mercy to believing men and women. For Allah is All-Forgiving, Most Merciful.[867]

---

865 The Quran does not specify how Moses was slandered by some of his people. Some narrations suggest that he was either falsely accused of adultery (*see* footnote for 28:76), killing his brother Aaron (who died a natural death), or having a skin disease since he, unlike others, used to bathe with his clothes on.

866 This refers to free choice in shouldering religious commandments. The great majority of Allah's creation (like angels and animals) do not have free will. Therefore, they are inherently submissive to Allah. As for humans, they rely on their intelligence, and are free to choose between guidance and misguidance, and either to adhere to divine obligations and prohibitions or not.

867 This is a guarantee from Allah that if the hypocrites and polytheists ever turn to Him in repentance, He is always willing to forgive them.

34. Sheba (Saba')

In the Name of Allah—the Most Compassionate, Most Merciful

Praises to the Almighty

1. All praise is for Allah, to Whom belongs whatever is in the heavens and whatever is on the earth. And praise be to Him in the Hereafter. He is the All-Wise, All-Aware. **2.** He knows whatever goes into the earth and whatever comes out of it, and whatever descends from the sky and whatever ascends into it. And He is the Most Merciful, All-Forgiving.

Denying the Hour

3. The disbelievers say, "The Hour will never come to us." Say, ʿO Prophet,ʾ "Yes—by my Lord, the Knower of the unseen—it will certainly come to you! Not ʿevenʾ an atom's weight is hidden from Him in the heavens or the earth; nor anything smaller or larger than that, but is ʿwrittenʾ in a perfect Record.[868] **4.** So He may reward those who believe and do good. It is they who will have forgiveness and an honourable provision. **5.** As for those who strive to discredit Our revelations, it is they who will suffer the ʿworstʾ torment of agonizing pain. **6.** Those gifted with knowledge ʿclearlyʾ see that what has been revealed to you from your Lord ʿO Prophetʾ is the truth, and that it guides to the Path of the Almighty, the Praiseworthy.

Warning to the Deniers

7. The disbelievers say ʿmockingly to one anotherʾ, "Shall we show you a man who claims that when you have been utterly disintegrated you will be raised as a new creation?

---

868 *See footnote for 33:6.*

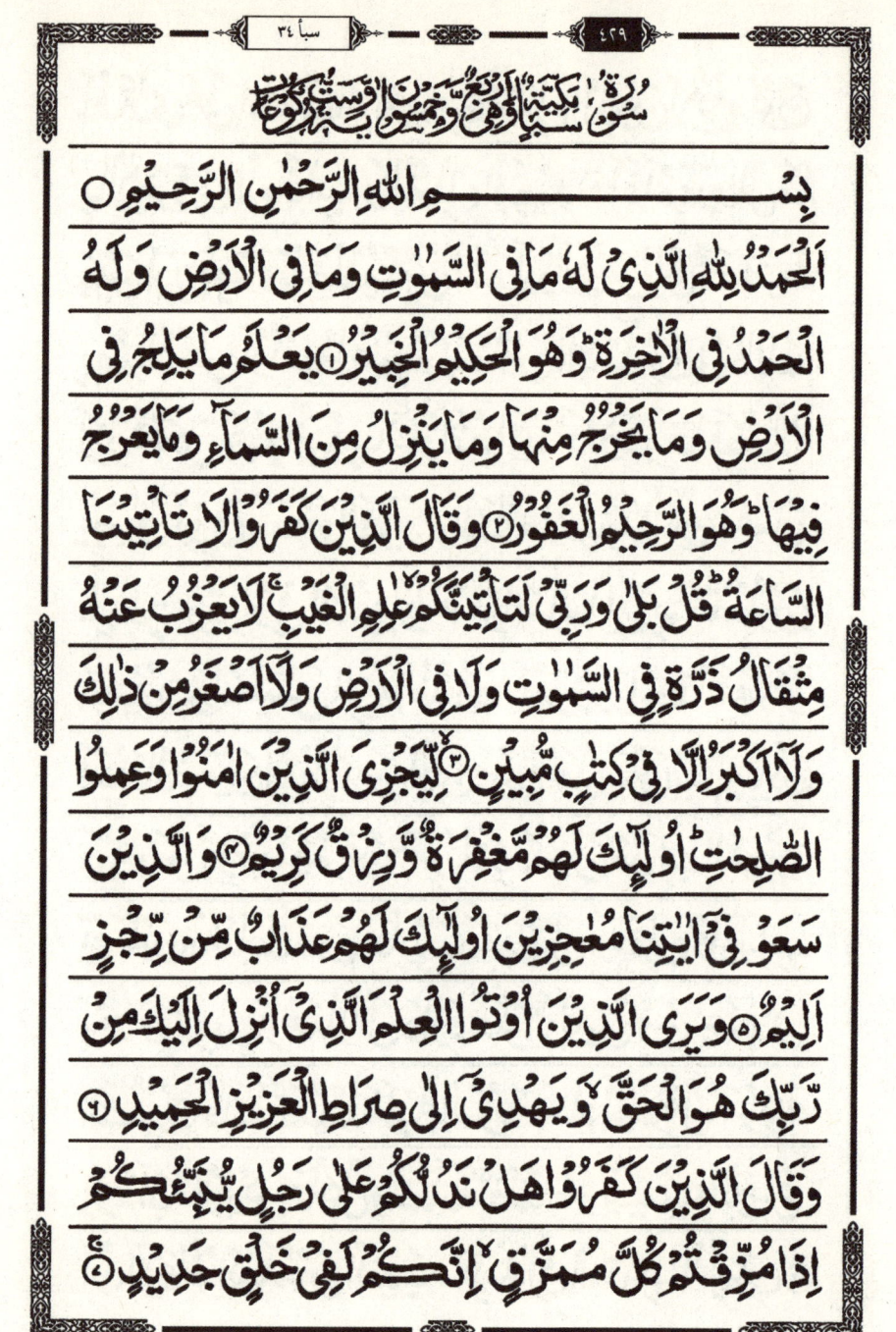

34. Saba' 430

﷽

8. Has he fabricated a lie against Allah or is he insane?" In fact, those who do not believe in the Hereafter are bound for torment and have strayed farthest ˹from the truth˺.

9. Have they not then seen all that surrounds them of the heavens and the earth? If We willed, We could cause the earth to swallow them up, or cause ˹deadly˺ pieces of the sky to fall upon them. Surely in this is a sign for every servant who turns ˹to Allah˺.

Allah's Favours to David

10. Indeed, We granted David a ˹great˺ privilege from Us, ˹commanding:˺ "O mountains! Echo his hymns! And the birds as well." We made iron mouldable for him,

11. instructing: "Make full-length armour, ˹perfectly˺ balancing the links. And work righteousness ˹O family of David!˺. Indeed, I am All-Seeing of what you do."

Allah's Favours to Solomon

12. And to Solomon ˹We subjected˺ the wind: its morning stride was a month's journey and so was its evening stride. And We caused a stream of molten copper to flow for him, and ˹We subjected˺ some of the jinn to work under him by his Lord's Will. And whoever of them deviated from Our command, We made them taste the torment of the blaze.

13. They made for him whatever he desired of sanctuaries, statues,[869] basins as large as reservoirs, and cooking pots fixed ˹into the ground˺. ˹We ordered:˺ "Work gratefully, O family of David!" ˹Only˺ a few of My servants are ˹truly˺ grateful.

14. When We decreed Solomon's death, nothing indicated to the ˹subjected˺ jinn that he was dead except the termites eating away his staff.[870] So when he collapsed, the jinn realized that if they had ˹really˺ known the unseen, they would not have remained in ˹such˺ humiliating servitude.

---

869 Which was permissible at the time of Solomon (ﷺ).
870 Which he died while leaning on.

34. Saba'

Allah's Favours to Sheba 1) Provision

15. Indeed, there was a sign for ˹the tribe of˺ Sheba in their homeland: two orchards—one to the right and the other to the left. ˹They were told:˺ "Eat from the provision of your Lord, and be grateful to Him. ˹Yours is˺ a good land and a forgiving Lord." **16.** But they turned away. So We sent against them a devastating flood, and replaced their orchards with two others producing bitter fruit, fruitless bushes,[871] and a few ˹sparse˺ thorny trees.[872] **17.** This is how We rewarded them for their ingratitude. Would We ever punish ˹anyone in such a way˺ except the ungrateful?

Allah's Favours to Sheba 2) Safe Travel

18. We had also placed between them and the cities[873] We showered with blessings ˹many small˺ towns within sight of one another. And We set moderate travel distances in between, ˹saying,˺ "Travel between them by day and night safely." **19.** But they said, "Our Lord! Make ˹the distances of˺ our journeys longer," wronging themselves.[874] So We reduced them to ˹cautionary˺ tales, and scattered them utterly. Surely in this are lessons for whoever is steadfast, grateful.

Satan's Vow Regarding Humans

20. Indeed, *Iblîs'* assumption about them has come true,[875] so they ˹all˺ follow him, except a group of ˹true˺ believers. **21.** He does not have any authority over them, but ˹Our Will is˺ only to distinguish those who believe in the Hereafter from those who are in doubt about it. And your Lord is a ˹vigilant˺ Keeper over all things."

Helpless Idols

22. Say, ˹O Prophet,˺ "Call upon those you claim ˹to be divine˺ besides Allah. They do not possess ˹even˺ an atom's weight either

---

871 lit., tamarisks.
872 lit., lote trees.
873 i.e., Mecca and Jerusalem.
874 They became bored of living comfortably and traveling easily. A similar example can be found in 2:61, where the Children of Israel became bored with the manna and quails and wanted to eat other things such as onions and garlic.
875 *Iblîs* was the name of Satan before his fall from grace (*see* footnote for 2:33). His assumption (or vow) was that he could easily mislead the majority of people (*see* 7:16-17, 15:39-40, and 38:82-83).

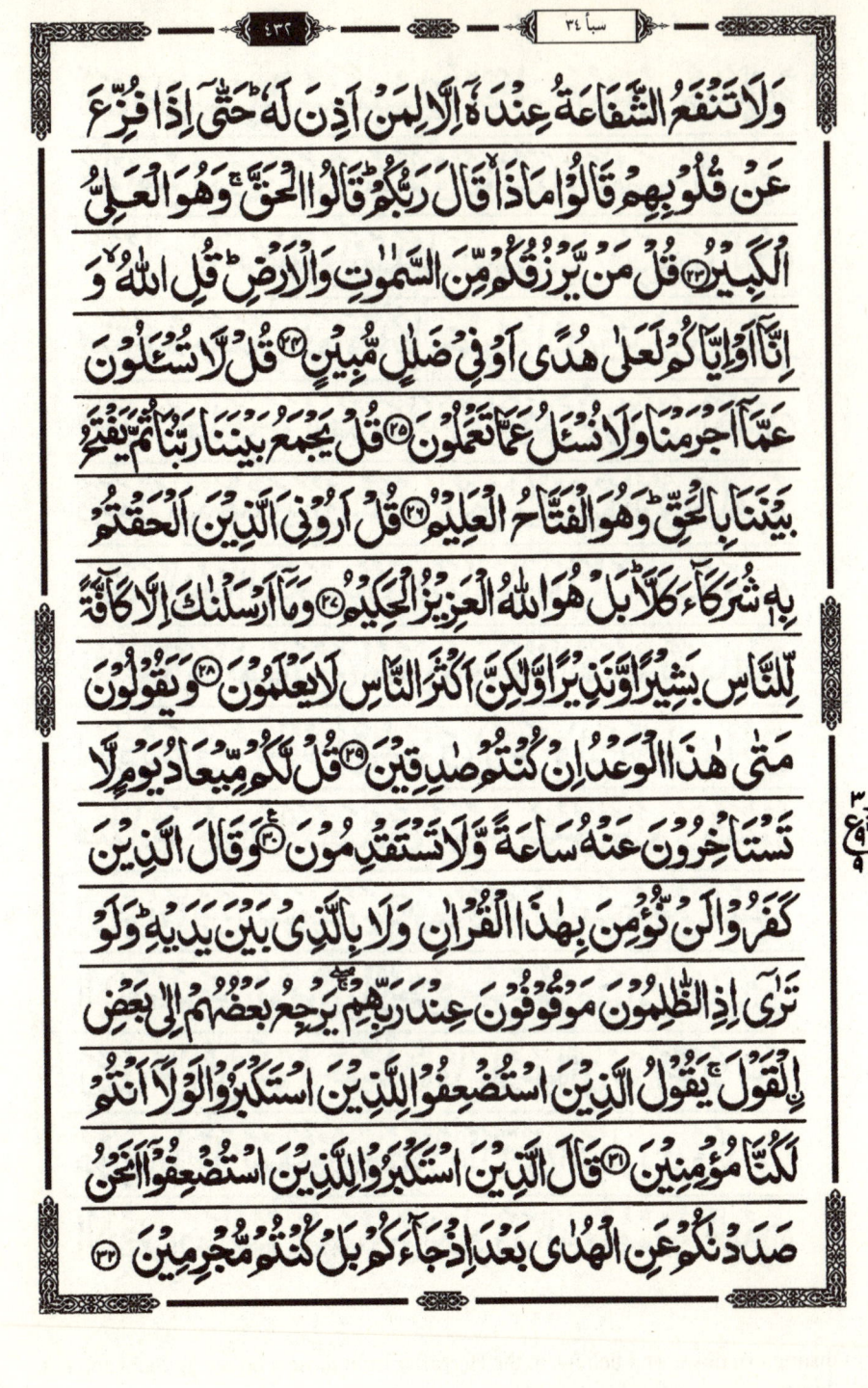

in the heavens or the earth, nor do they have any share in ˹governing˺ them. Nor is any of them a helper to Him." **23.** No intercession will be of any benefit with Him, except by those granted permission by Him. ˹At last,˺ when the dread ˹of Judgment Day˺ is relieved from their hearts ˹because they are permitted to intercede˺, they will ˹excitedly˺ ask ˹the angels˺, "What has your Lord ˹just˺ said?" The angels will reply, "The truth! And He is the Most High, All-Great."

Message to the Polytheists

24. Ask ˹them, O Prophet˺, "Who provides for you from the heavens and the earth?" Say, "Allah! Now, certainly one of our two groups[876] is ˹rightly˺ guided; the other is clearly astray." **25.** Say, "You will not be accountable for our misdeeds, nor will we be accountable for your deeds." **26.** Say, "Our Lord will gather us together, then He will judge between us with the truth. For He is the All-Knowing Judge." **27.** Say, "Show me those ˹idols˺ you have joined with Him as partners. No! In fact, He ˹alone˺ is Allah—the Almighty, All-Wise."

Warning of the Hour

28. We have sent you ˹O Prophet˺ only as a deliverer of good news and a warner to all of humanity, but most people do not know. **29.** And they ask ˹the believers˺, "When will this threat come to pass, if what you say is true?" **30.** Say, ˹O Prophet,˺ "A Day has ˹already˺ been appointed for you, which you can neither delay nor advance by a ˹single˺ moment."

The Misleaders and the Misled

31. The disbelievers vow, "We will never believe in this Quran, nor in those ˹Scriptures˺ before it." If only you could see when the wrongdoers will be detained before their Lord, throwing blame at each other! The lowly ˹followers˺ will say to the arrogant ˹leaders˺, "Had it not been for you, we would certainly have been believers." **32.** The arrogant will respond to the lowly, "Did we ever hinder you from guidance after it came to you? In fact, you were wicked ˹on your own˺."

---

876 The believers and polytheists.

433   **34. Saba'**

33. The lowly will say to the arrogant, "No! It was your plotting by day and night—when you ordered us to disbelieve in Allah and to set up equals with Him." They will ˹all˺ hide ˹their˺ remorse when they see the torment. And We will put shackles around the necks of the disbelievers. Will they be rewarded except for what they used to do?

Spoiled Elite

34. Whenever We sent a warner to a society, its elite would say, "We truly reject what you have been sent with." 35. Adding, "We are far superior ˹to the believers˺ in wealth and children, and we will never be punished." 36. Say, ˹O Prophet,˺ "Surely ˹it is˺ my Lord ˹Who˺ gives abundant or limited provisions to whoever He wills. But most people do not know." 37. It is not your wealth or children that bring you closer to Us. But those who believe and do good—it is they who will have a multiplied reward for what they did, and they will be secure in ˹elevated˺ mansions. 38. As for those who strive to discredit Our revelations, it is they who will be confined in punishment. 39. Say, ˹O Prophet,˺ "Surely ˹it is˺ my Lord ˹Who˺ gives abundant or limited provisions to whoever He wills of His servants. And whatever you spend in charity, He will compensate ˹you˺ for it. For He is the Best Provider."

The Worshippers and the Worshipped

40. And ˹consider˺ the Day He will gather them all together, and then ask the angels, "Was it you that these ˹polytheists˺ used to worship?"

41. They will say, "Glory be to You! Our loyalty is to You, not them. In fact, they ˹only˺ followed the ˹temptations of evil˺ jinn,[877] in whom most of them had faith." **42.** So Today neither of you can benefit or protect each other. And We will say to the wrongdoers, "Taste the torment of the Fire, which you used to deny."

Response of the Polytheists

43. When Our clear revelations are recited to them, they say, "This is only a man who wishes to hinder you from what your forefathers used to worship." They also say, "This ˹Quran˺ is no more than a fabricated lie." And the disbelievers say of the truth when it has come to them, "This is nothing but pure magic." **44.** ˹They say so even though˺ We had never given them any scriptures to study, nor did We ever send them a warner before you ˹O Prophet˺. **45.** Those ˹destroyed˺ before them denied as well—and these ˹Meccans˺ have not attained even one-tenth of what We had given their predecessors.[878] Yet ˹when˺ they denied My messengers, how severe was My response!

Advice to Meccan Pagans

46. Say, ˹O Prophet,˺ "I advise you to do ˹only˺ one thing: stand up for ˹the sake of˺ Allah—individually or in pairs—then reflect. Your fellow man[879] is not insane. He is only a warner to you before ˹the coming of˺ a severe punishment." **47.** Say, "If I had ever asked you for a reward, you could keep it. My reward is only from Allah. And He is a Witness over all things." **48.** Say, "Surely my Lord hurls the truth ˹against falsehood˺. ˹He is˺ the Knower of all unseen."

---

877 i.e., the devils.
878 Like the people of Pharaoh, ʿĀd, and Thamûd.
879 i.e., Muḥammad (ﷺ).

49. Say, "The truth has come, and falsehood will vanish, never to return." **50.** Say, "If I am astray, the loss is only mine. And if I am guided, it is ˹only˺ because of what my Lord reveals to me. He is indeed All-Hearing, Ever Near."

Too Late for the Deniers

51. If only you could see when they will be horrified with no escape ˹on Judgment Day˺! And they will be seized from a nearby place.[880] **52.** They will ˹then˺ cry, "We do ˹now˺ believe in it ˹all˺." But how could they ˹possibly˺ attain faith from a place so far-off ˹from the world˺,[881] **53.** while they had already rejected it before, guessing blindly from a place ˹equally˺ far-away ˹from the Hereafter˺? **54.** They will be sealed off from whatever they desire, as was done to their counterparts before. Indeed, they were ˹all˺ in alarming doubt.

☙❀❧

35. The Originator (Fâṭir)

In the Name of Allah—the Most Compassionate, Most Merciful

Allah's Power 1) Creation and Mercy

1. All praise is for Allah, the Originator of the heavens and the earth, Who made angels ˹as His˺ messengers with wings—two, three, or four. He increases in creation whatever He wills. Surely Allah is Most Capable of everything. **2.** Whatever mercy Allah opens up for people, none can withhold it. And whatever He withholds, none but Him can release it. For He is the Almighty, All-Wise.

One God Only

3. O humanity! Remember Allah's favours upon you. Is there any creator other than Allah who provides for you from the heavens and the earth? There is no god ˹worthy of worship˺ except Him. How can you then be deluded ˹from the truth˺?

---

880 From the place of Judgment to Hell.
881 When it is already too late.

35. Fâṭir

Reassuring the Prophet

4. If you are rejected by them, so too were messengers before you. And to Allah ˹all˺ matters will be returned ˹for judgment˺.

Warning Against Satan

5. O humanity! Indeed, Allah's promise is true. So do not let the life of this world deceive you, nor let the Chief Deceiver[882] deceive you about Allah. 6. Surely Satan is an enemy to you, so take him as an enemy. He only invites his followers to become inmates of the Blaze.

The Evildoers and the Good-Doers

7. Those who disbelieve will have a severe punishment. But those who believe and do good will have forgiveness and a great reward. 8. Are those whose evil-doing is made so appealing to them that they deem it good ˹like those who are rightly guided˺? ˹It is˺ certainly Allah ˹Who˺ leaves to stray whoever He wills, and guides whoever He wills. So do not grieve yourself to death over them ˹O Prophet˺. Surely Allah is All-Knowing of what they do.

Allah's Power 2) The Wind

9. And it is Allah Who sends the winds, which then stir up ˹vapour, forming˺ clouds, and then We drive them to a lifeless land, giving life to the earth after its death. Similar is the Resurrection.

All Honour and Power Belongs to Allah

10. Whoever seeks honour and power, then ˹let them know that˺ all honour and power belongs to Allah. To Him ˹alone˺ good words ascend, and righteous deeds are raised up by Him. As for those who plot evil, they will suffer a severe punishment. And the plotting of such ˹people˺ is doomed ˹to fail˺.

Allah's Power 3) Creation of Humans

11. And ˹it is˺ Allah ˹Who˺ created you from dust,[883] then ˹developed you˺ from a sperm-drop, then made you into pairs.[884] No female ever

---

882 Satan.
883 Created your father, Adam, from dust.
884 Males and females.

conceives or delivers without His knowledge. And no one's life is made long or cut short but is ˹written˺ in a Record.[885] That is certainly easy for Allah.

Allah's Power 4)
Fresh and Salt Water

12. The two bodies of water are not alike: one is fresh, palatable, and pleasant to drink and the other is salty and bitter. Yet from them both you eat tender seafood and extract ornaments to wear. And you see the ships ploughing their way through both, so you may seek His bounty and give thanks ˹to Him˺.

Allah's Power 5)
Alternation of Day and Night

13. He merges the night into the day and the day into the night, and has subjected the sun and the moon, each orbiting for an appointed term.

Allah or Powerless Gods?

That is Allah—your Lord! All authority belongs to Him. But ˹those˺ ˹idols˺ you invoke besides Him do not possess even the skin of a date stone. **14.** If you call upon them, they cannot hear your calls. And if they were to hear, they could not respond to you. On the Day of Judgment they will disown your worship ˹of them˺. And no one can inform you ˹O Prophet˺ like the All-Knowledgeable.

Allah's Power 6) *Sustenance*

15. O humanity! It is you who stand in need of Allah, but Allah ˹alone˺ is the Self-Sufficient, Praiseworthy.

16. If He willed, He could eliminate you and produce a new creation. **17.** And that is not difficult for Allah ˹at all˺.

Everyone Is Accountable for Themselves

18. No soul burdened with sin will bear the burden of another. And if a sin-burdened soul cries for help with its burden, none of it will be carried—even by a close relative. You ˹O Prophet˺ can only warn those who stand in awe of their Lord without seeing Him[886] and establish prayer. Whoever purifies themselves, they only do so for their own good. And to Allah is the final return.

---

885 *See* footnote for 33:6.
886 This can also mean that they are in awe of their Lord as much in private as they are in public.

35. Fâṭir

Guidance vs. Misguidance

19. Those blind ˹to the truth˺ and those who can see are not equal, **20.** nor are the darkness and the light, **21.** nor the ˹scorching˺ heat and the ˹cool˺ shade.[887] **22.** Nor are the dead and the living equal. Indeed, Allah ˹alone˺ makes whoever He wills hear, but you ˹O Prophet˺ can never make those in the graves hear ˹your call˺.

Reassuring the Prophet

23. You are only a warner. **24.** We have surely sent you with the truth as a deliverer of good news and a warner. There is no community that has not had a warner.[888] **25.** If they deny you, so did those before them. Their messengers came to them with clear proofs, divine Books, and enlightening Scriptures.[889] **26.** Then I seized those who persisted in disbelief. How severe was My response!

Allah's Power 7) Diversity

27. Do you not see that Allah sends down rain from the sky with which We bring forth fruits of different colours? And in the mountains are streaks of varying shades of white, red, and raven black; **28.** just as people, living beings, and cattle are of various colours as well. Of all of Allah's servants, only the knowledgeable ˹of His might˺ are ˹truly˺ in awe of Him. Allah is indeed Almighty, All-Forgiving.

The Everlasting Reward

29. Surely those who recite the Book of Allah, establish prayer, and donate from what We have provided for them—secretly and openly—˹can˺ hope for an exchange that will never fail, **30.** so that He will reward them in full and increase them out of His grace. He is truly All-Forgiving, Most Appreciative.

---

887 This implies Hell and Paradise.
888 According to a Prophetic narration collected by Ibn Ḥibbân, the total number of prophets sent around the world, from Adam (﷽) to Muḥammad (﷽), is 124 000—of which only twenty-five are mentioned in the Quran.
889 i.e., the Torah, the Gospel, and Psalms.

35. Fâtir

Three Types of Believers

31. The Book We have revealed to you ʿO Prophetʾ is the truth, confirming what came before it.[890] Surely Allah is All-Aware, All-Seeing of His servants. **32.** Then We granted the Book to those We have chosen from Our servants. Some of them wrong themselves, some follow a middle course, and some are foremost in good deeds by Allah's Will. That is ʿtrulyʾ the greatest bounty.

Reward of the Believers

33. They will enter the Gardens of Eternity, where they will be adorned with bracelets of gold and pearls, and their clothing will be silk. **34.** And they will say, "Praise be to Allah, Who has kept away from us all ʿcauses ofʾ sorrow. Our Lord is indeed All-Forgiving, Most Appreciative. **35.** ʿHe is the Oneʾ Who—out of His grace—has settled us in the Home of Everlasting Stay, where we will be touched by neither fatigue nor weariness."

Punishment of the Disbelievers

36. As for the disbelievers, they will have the Fire of Hell, where they will not be ʿallowed to beʾ finished by death, nor will its torment be lightened for them. This is how We reward every ʿstubbornʾ disbeliever. **37.** There they will be ʿferventlyʾ screaming, "Our Lord! Take us out ʿand send us backʾ. We will do good, unlike what we used to do." ʿThey will be told,ʾ "Did We not give you lives long enough so that whoever wanted to be mindful could have done so? And the warner came to you. So taste ʿthe punishmentʾ, for the wrongdoers have no helper."

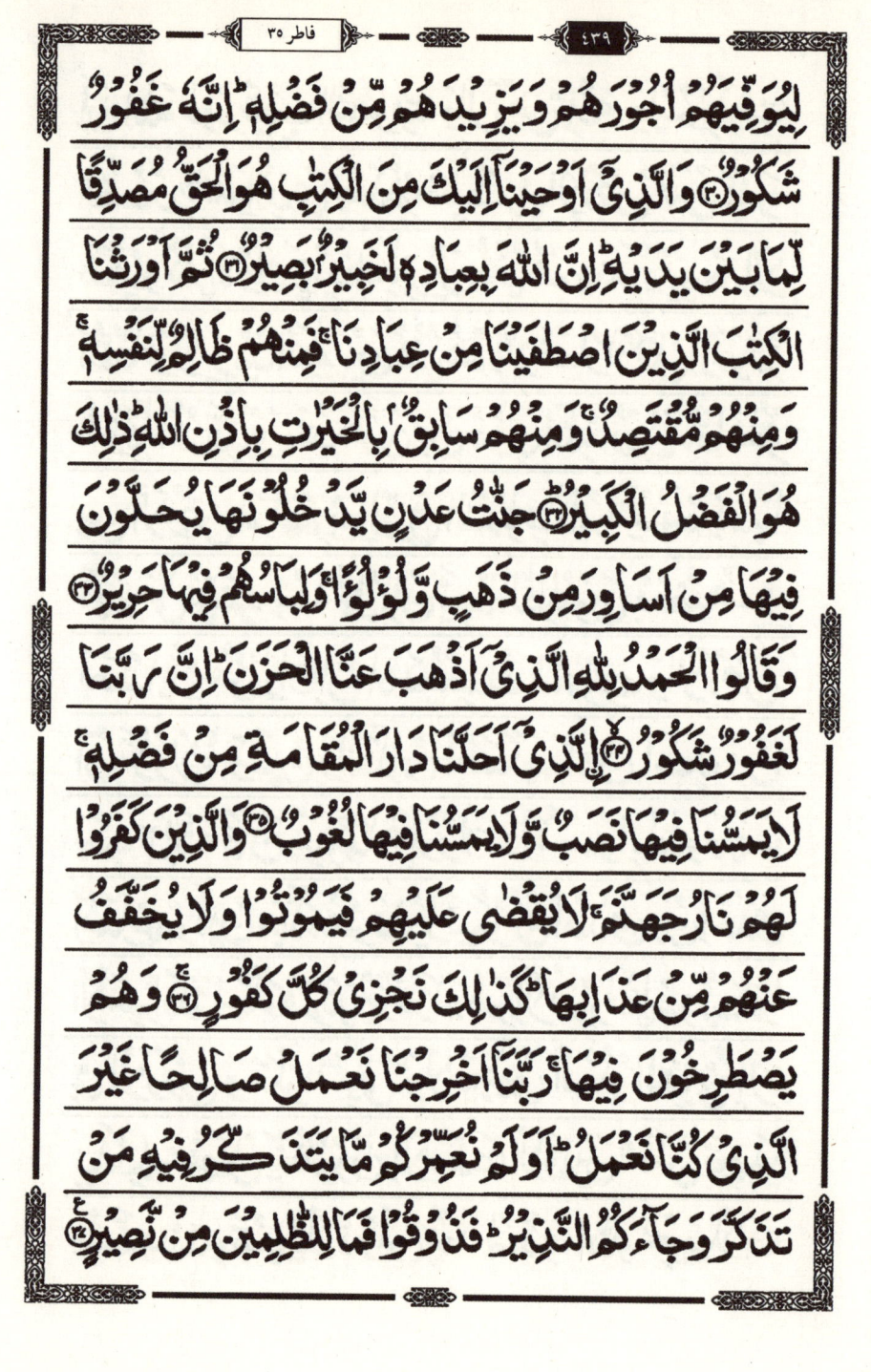

---

890 *See previous footnote.*

بِسْمِ اللَّهِ عَلِمُ غَيْبِ السَّمَوَتِ وَالْأَرْضِ إِنَّهُ عَلِيمٌ بِذَاتِ الصُّدُورِ ۞ هُوَ الَّذِى جَعَلَكُمْ خَلَائِفَ فِى الْأَرْضِ فَمَن كَفَرَ فَعَلَيْهِ كُفْرُهُ وَلَا يَزِيدُ الْكَافِرِينَ كُفْرُهُمْ عِندَ رَبِّهِمْ إِلَّا مَقْتًا وَلَا يَزِيدُ الْكَافِرِينَ كُفْرُهُمْ إِلَّا خَسَارًا ۞ قُلْ أَرَءَيْتُمْ شُرَكَاءَكُمُ الَّذِينَ تَدْعُونَ مِن دُونِ اللَّهِ أَرُونِى مَاذَا خَلَقُوا مِنَ الْأَرْضِ أَمْ لَهُمْ شِرْكٌ فِى السَّمَوَتِ أَمْ ءَاتَيْنَهُمْ كِتَبًا فَهُمْ عَلَى بَيِّنَتٍ مِّنْهُ بَلْ إِن يَعِدُ الظَّالِمُونَ بَعْضُهُم بَعْضًا إِلَّا غُرُورًا ۞ إِنَّ اللَّهَ يُمْسِكُ السَّمَوَتِ وَالْأَرْضَ أَن تَزُولَا وَلَئِن زَالَتَا إِنْ أَمْسَكَهُمَا مِنْ أَحَدٍ مِّنْ بَعْدِهِ إِنَّهُ كَانَ حَلِيمًا غَفُورًا ۞ وَأَقْسَمُوا بِاللَّهِ جَهْدَ أَيْمَنِهِمْ لَئِن جَاءَهُمْ نَذِيرٌ لَّيَكُونُنَّ أَهْدَى مِنْ إِحْدَى الْأُمَمِ فَلَمَّا جَاءَهُمْ نَذِيرٌ مَّا زَادَهُمْ إِلَّا نُفُورًا ۞ اسْتِكْبَارًا فِى الْأَرْضِ وَمَكْرَ السَّيِّئِ وَلَا يَحِيقُ الْمَكْرُ السَّيِّئُ إِلَّا بِأَهْلِهِ فَهَلْ يَنظُرُونَ إِلَّا سُنَّتَ الْأَوَّلِينَ فَلَن تَجِدَ لِسُنَّتِ اللَّهِ تَبْدِيلًا وَلَن تَجِدَ لِسُنَّتِ اللَّهِ تَحْوِيلًا ۞

Denying the Almighty

38. Indeed, Allah is the Knower of the unseen of the heavens and the earth. He surely knows best what is ʿhiddenʾ in the heart. **39.** He is the One Who has placed you as successors on earth. So whoever disbelieves will bear ʿthe burden ofʾ their own disbelief. The disbelievers' denial only increases them in contempt in the sight of their Lord, and it will only contribute to their loss.

Useless Idols

40. Ask ʿthem, O Prophetʾ, "Have you considered your associate-gods which you invoke besides Allah? Show me what they have created on earth! Or do they have a share in ʿthe creation ofʾ the heavens? Or have We given the polytheists a Book, which serves as a clear proof for them? In fact, the wrongdoers promise each other nothing but delusion."

Allah's Power 8)
Maintaining the Universe

41. Indeed, Allah ʿaloneʾ keeps the heavens and the earth from falling apart. If they were to fall apart, none but Him could hold them up. He is truly Most Forbearing, All-Forgiving.

Warning to the Disbelievers

42. They swore by Allah their most solemn oaths that if a warner were to come to them, they would certainly be better guided than any other community. Yet when a warner did come to them, it only drove them farther away— **43.** behaving arrogantly in the land and plotting evil. But evil plotting only backfires on those who plot. Are they awaiting anything but the fate of those ʿdestroyedʾ before? You will find no change in the way of Allah, nor will you find it diverted ʿto someone elseʾ.

44. Have they not travelled throughout the land to see what was the end of those ˹destroyed˺ before them? They were far superior in might. But there is nothing that can escape Allah in the heavens or the earth. He is certainly All-Knowing, Most Capable.

Allowing Time for Repentance

45. If Allah were to punish people ˹immediately˺ for what they have committed, He would not have left a single living being on earth. But He delays them for an appointed term. And when their time arrives, then surely Allah is All-Seeing of His servants.

۞

36. Yâ-Sîn (Yâ-Sîn)

In the Name of Allah—the Most Compassionate, Most Merciful

Wake-up Call

1. *Yâ-Sîn.* **2.** By the Quran, rich in wisdom! **3.** You ˹O Prophet˺ are truly one of the messengers **4.** upon the Straight Path. **5.** ˹This is˺ a revelation from the Almighty, Most Merciful, **6.** so that you may warn a people whose forefathers were not warned, and so are heedless. **7.** The decree ˹of torment˺ has already been justified against most of them, for they will never believe. **8.** ˹It is as if˺ We have put shackles around their necks up to their chins, so their heads are forced up, **9.** and have placed a barrier before them and a barrier behind them and covered them ˹all˺ up, so they fail to see ˹the truth˺.

أَوَلَمْ يَسِيرُوا۟ فِى ٱلْأَرْضِ فَيَنظُرُوا۟ كَيْفَ كَانَ عَٰقِبَةُ ٱلَّذِينَ مِن قَبْلِهِمْ وَكَانُوٓا۟ أَشَدَّ مِنْهُمْ قُوَّةً ۚ وَمَا كَانَ ٱللَّهُ لِيُعْجِزَهُۥ مِن شَىْءٍ فِى ٱلسَّمَٰوَٰتِ وَلَا فِى ٱلْأَرْضِ ۚ إِنَّهُۥ كَانَ عَلِيمًا قَدِيرًا ۝ وَلَوْ يُؤَاخِذُ ٱللَّهُ ٱلنَّاسَ بِمَا كَسَبُوا۟ مَا تَرَكَ عَلَىٰ ظَهْرِهَا مِن دَآبَّةٍ وَلَٰكِن يُؤَخِّرُهُمْ إِلَىٰٓ أَجَلٍ مُّسَمًّى ۖ فَإِذَا جَآءَ أَجَلُهُمْ فَإِنَّ ٱللَّهَ كَانَ بِعِبَادِهِۦ بَصِيرًا ۝

بِسْمِ ٱللَّهِ ٱلرَّحْمَٰنِ ٱلرَّحِيمِ ۝

يسٓ ۝ وَٱلْقُرْءَانِ ٱلْحَكِيمِ ۝ إِنَّكَ لَمِنَ ٱلْمُرْسَلِينَ ۝ عَلَىٰ صِرَٰطٍ مُّسْتَقِيمٍ ۝ تَنزِيلَ ٱلْعَزِيزِ ٱلرَّحِيمِ ۝ لِتُنذِرَ قَوْمًا مَّآ أُنذِرَ ءَابَآؤُهُمْ فَهُمْ غَٰفِلُونَ ۝ لَقَدْ حَقَّ ٱلْقَوْلُ عَلَىٰٓ أَكْثَرِهِمْ فَهُمْ لَا يُؤْمِنُونَ ۝ إِنَّا جَعَلْنَا فِىٓ أَعْنَٰقِهِمْ أَغْلَٰلًا فَهِىَ إِلَى ٱلْأَذْقَانِ فَهُم مُّقْمَحُونَ ۝ وَجَعَلْنَا مِنۢ بَيْنِ أَيْدِيهِمْ سَدًّا وَمِنْ خَلْفِهِمْ سَدًّا فَأَغْشَيْنَٰهُمْ فَهُمْ لَا يُبْصِرُونَ ۝

36. Yâ-Sîn

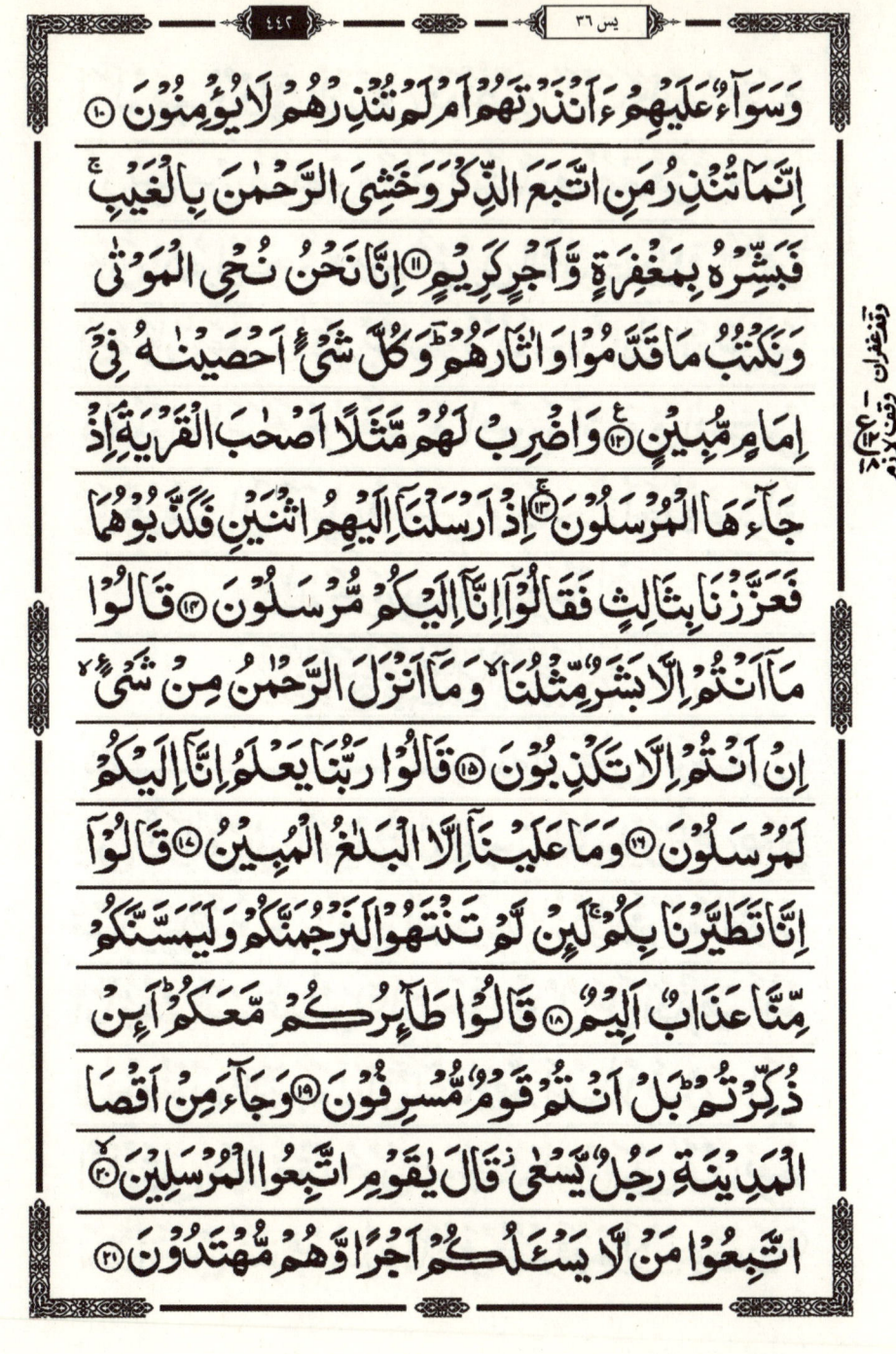

Who Benefits from Reminders

10. It is the same whether you warn them or not—they will never believe. **11.** You can only warn those who follow the Reminder[891] and are in awe of the Most Compassionate without seeing Him.[892] So give them good news of forgiveness and an honourable reward. **12.** It is certainly We Who resurrect the dead, and write what they send forth and what they leave behind. Everything is listed by Us in a perfect Record.[893]

The Three Messengers

13. Give them an example ˹O Prophet˺ of the residents of a town, when the messengers came to them. **14.** We sent them two messengers, but they rejected both. So We reinforced ˹the two˺ with a third, and they declared, "We have indeed been sent to you ˹as messengers˺." **15.** The people replied, "You are only humans like us, and the Most Compassionate has not revealed anything. You are simply lying!" **16.** The messengers responded, "Our Lord knows that we have truly been sent to you. **17.** And our duty is only to deliver ˹the message˺ clearly." **18.** The people replied, "We definitely see you as a bad omen for us. If you do not desist, we will certainly stone you ˹to death˺ and you will be touched with a painful punishment from us." **19.** The messengers said, "Your bad omen lies within yourselves. Are you saying this because you are reminded ˹of the truth˺? In fact, you are a transgressing people."

An Advocate of the Truth

20. Then from the farthest end of the city a man came, rushing. He advised, "O my people! Follow the messengers. **21.** Follow those who ask no reward of you, and are ˹rightly˺ guided.

---

891 The Reminder is another name for the Quran.
892 See footnote for 35:18.
893 *See* footnote for 35:11.

36. Yâ-Sîn

22. And why should I not worship the One Who has originated me, and to Whom you will be returned. 23. How could I take besides Him other gods whose intercession would not be of any benefit to me, nor could they save me if the Most Compassionate intended to harm me? 24. Indeed, I would then be clearly astray. 25. I do believe in your Lord, so listen to me." 26. ˹But they killed him, then˺ he was told ˹by the angels˺, "Enter Paradise!" He said, "If only my people knew 27. of how my Lord has forgiven me, and made me one of the honourable."

The Wicked Destroyed

28. We did not send any soldiers from the heavens against his people after his death, nor did We need to. 29. All it took was one ˹mighty˺ blast, and they were extinguished at once. 30. Oh pity, such beings! No messenger ever came to them without being mocked. 31. Have the deniers not considered how many peoples We destroyed before them who never came back to life again? 32. Yet they will all be brought before Us.

Allah's Signs 1) the Earth

33. There is a sign for them in the dead earth: We give it life, producing grain from it for them to eat. 34. And We have placed in it gardens of palm trees and grapevines, and caused springs to gush forth in it, 35. so that they may eat from its fruit, which they had no hand in making. Will they not then give thanks? 36. Glory be to the One Who created all ˹things in˺ pairs—˹be it˺ what the earth produces, their genders, or what they do not know!

Allah's Signs 2) Night

37. There is also a sign for them in the night: We strip from it daylight, then—behold!—they are in darkness.

Allah's Signs 3) the Sun and the Moon

38. The sun travels for its fixed term. That is the design of the Almighty, All-Knowing. **39.** As for the moon, We have ordained ˹precise˺ phases for it, until it ends up like an old, curved palm stalk. **40.** It is not for the sun to catch up with the moon,[894] nor does the night outrun the day. Each is travelling in an orbit of their own.

Allah's Signs 4) Mercy at Sea

41. Another sign for them is that We carried their ancestors ˹with Noah˺ in the fully loaded Ark, **42.** and created for them similar things to ride in. **43.** If We willed, We could drown them: then no one would respond to their cries, nor would they be rescued— **44.** except by mercy from Us, allowing them enjoyment for a ˹little˺ while.

Stance of the Polytheists

45. ˹Still they turn away˺ when it is said to them, "Beware of what is ahead of you ˹in the Hereafter˺ and what is behind you ˹of destroyed nations˺ so you may be shown mercy." **46.** Whenever a sign comes to them from their Lord, they turn away from it. **47.** And when it is said to them, "Donate from what Allah has provided for you," the disbelievers say to the believers, "Why should we feed those whom Allah could have fed if He wanted to? You are clearly astray!"

Too Late for the Deniers

48. And they ask ˹the believers˺, "When will this threat come to pass, if what you say is true?" **49.** They must be awaiting a single Blast,[895] which will seize them while they are ˹entrenched˺ in ˹worldly˺ disputes. **50.** Then they will not be able to make a ˹last˺ will, nor can they return to their own people. **51.** The Trumpet will be blown ˹a second time˺, then—behold!—they will rush from the graves to their Lord. **52.** They will cry, "Woe to us! Who has raised us up from our place of rest? This must be what the Most Compassionate warned us of; the messengers told the truth!"

---

894 The moon completes a cycle every month (waxing and waning), while the sun takes a whole year to complete its cycle (resulting in the spring, summer, fall, and winter seasons).
895 On the Day of Judgment, the Trumpet will be blown by an angel—causing all to die. When it is blown a second time, everyone will be raised from the dead for judgment (see 39:68).

36. Yâ-Sîn

53. It will only take one Blast, then at once they will all be brought before Us. 54. On that Day no soul will be wronged in the least, nor will you be rewarded except for what you used to do.

Reward of the Believers

55. Indeed, on that Day the residents of Paradise will be busy enjoying themselves. 56. They and their spouses will be in ˹cool˺ shade, reclining on ˹canopied˺ couches. 57. There they will have fruits and whatever they desire. 58. And "Peace!" will be ˹their˺ greeting from the Merciful Lord.

Reward of the Disbelievers

59. ˹Then the disbelievers will be told,˺ "Step away ˹from the believers˺ this Day, O wicked ones! 60. Did I not command you, O Children of Adam, not to follow Satan, for he is truly your sworn enemy, 61. but to worship Me ˹alone˺? This is the Straight Path. 62. Yet he already misled great multitudes of you. Did you not have any sense? 63. This is the Hell you were warned of. 64. Burn in it Today for your disbelief." 65. On this Day We will seal their mouths, their hands will speak to Us, and their feet will testify to what they used to commit.

Allah's Power over the Deniers

66. Had We willed, We could have easily blinded their eyes, so they would struggle to find their way. How then could they see? 67. And had We willed, We could have transfigured them on the spot,[896] so they could neither progress forward nor turn back. 68. And whoever We grant a long life, We reverse them in development.[897] Will they not then understand?

The Prophet Is Not a Poet

69. We have not taught him poetry, nor is it fitting for him. This ˹Book˺ is only a Reminder and a clear Quran 70. to warn whoever is ˹truly˺ alive and fulfil the decree ˹of torment˺ against the disbelievers.

---

896 Meaning, We have the ability to turn them into stone or any other inanimate object.
897 Human beings are born weak, then they reach their prime, then they grow weak after a certain age. See 30:54.

Allah's Signs 5) Domesticated Animals

71. Do they not see that We single-handedly[898] created for them, among other things, cattle which are under their control? **72.** And We have subjected these ˹animals˺ to them, so they may ride some and eat others. **73.** And they derive from them other benefits and drinks. Will they not then give thanks?

Ingratitude of the Deniers

74. Still they have taken other gods besides Allah, hoping to be helped ˹by them˺. **75.** They cannot help the pagans, even though they serve the idols as dedicated guards.[899] **76.** So do not let their words grieve you ˹O Prophet˺. Indeed, We ˹fully˺ know what they conceal and what they reveal.

Allah's Power to Resurrect

77. Do people not see that We have created them from a sperm-drop, then—behold!—they openly challenge ˹Us˺? **78.** And they argue with Us—forgetting they were created—saying, "Who will give life to decayed bones?" **79.** Say, ˹O Prophet,˺ "They will be revived by the One Who produced them the first time, for He has ˹perfect˺ knowledge of every created being. **80.** ˹He is the One˺ Who gives you fire from green trees, and—behold!—you kindle ˹fire˺ from them.[900] **81.** Can the One Who created the heavens and the earth not ˹easily˺ resurrect these ˹deniers˺?" Yes ˹He can˺! For He is the Master Creator, All-Knowing. **82.** All it takes, when He wills something ˹to be˺, is simply to say to it: "Be!" And it is! **83.** So glory be to the One in Whose Hands is the authority over all things, and to Whom ˹alone˺ you will ˹all˺ be returned.

❧ ✻ ☙

---

37. Those ˹Angels˺ Lined up in Ranks (Aṣ-Ṣâffât)

In the Name of Allah—the Most Compassionate, Most Merciful

---

898 lit., 'what Our Own Hands have created.'
899 Another meaning is that those idols will be assembled to witness the torment of their worshippers on Judgment Day.
900 The verse refers to two types of Arabian trees, *markh* and *'afâr*, which produce fire when their green branches are rubbed together.

37. Aṣ-Ṣâffât

One God Only

1. By those ˹angels˺ lined up in ranks, 2. and those who diligently drive ˹the clouds˺, 3. and those who recite the Reminder! 4. Surely your God is One! 5. ˹He is˺ the Lord of the heavens and the earth and everything in between, and the Lord of all points of sunrise.

The Heavens Decorated and Protected

6. Indeed, We have adorned the lowest heaven with the stars for decoration 7. and ˹for˺ protection from every rebellious devil. 8. They cannot listen to the highest assembly ˹of angels˺ for they are pelted from every side, 9. ˹fiercely˺ driven away. And they will suffer an everlasting torment. 10. But whoever manages to stealthily eavesdrop is ˹instantly˺ pursued by a piercing flare.

A Question to Resurrection Deniers

11. So ask them ˹O Prophet˺, which is harder to create: them or other marvels of Our creation?[901] Indeed, We created them from a sticky clay.[902] 12. In fact, you are astonished ˹by their denial˺, while they ridicule ˹you˺. 13. When they are reminded, they are never mindful. 14. And whenever they see a sign, they make fun of it, 15. saying, "This is nothing but pure magic. 16. When we are dead and reduced to dust and bones, will we really be resurrected? 17. And our forefathers as well?" 18. Say, "Yes! And you will be fully humbled."

The Deniers After Resurrection

19. It will only take one Blast,[903] then at once they will see ˹it all˺. 20. They will cry, "Oh, woe to us! This is the Day of Judgment!" 21. ˹They will be told,˺ "This is the Day of ˹Final˺ Decision which you used to deny." 22. ˹Allah will say to the angels,˺ "Gather ˹all˺ the wrongdoers along with their peers, and whatever they used to worship 23. instead of Allah, then lead them ˹all˺ to the path of Hell. 24. And detain them, for they must be questioned." 25. ˹Then they will be asked,˺ "What is the matter with you that you can no longer help each other?" 26. In fact, on that Day they will be ˹fully˺ submissive.

---

901 i.e., the angels, the sun, the moon, the stars, and the mountains.
902 Their father Adam (☘).
903 This is when the Trumpet will be blown the second time.

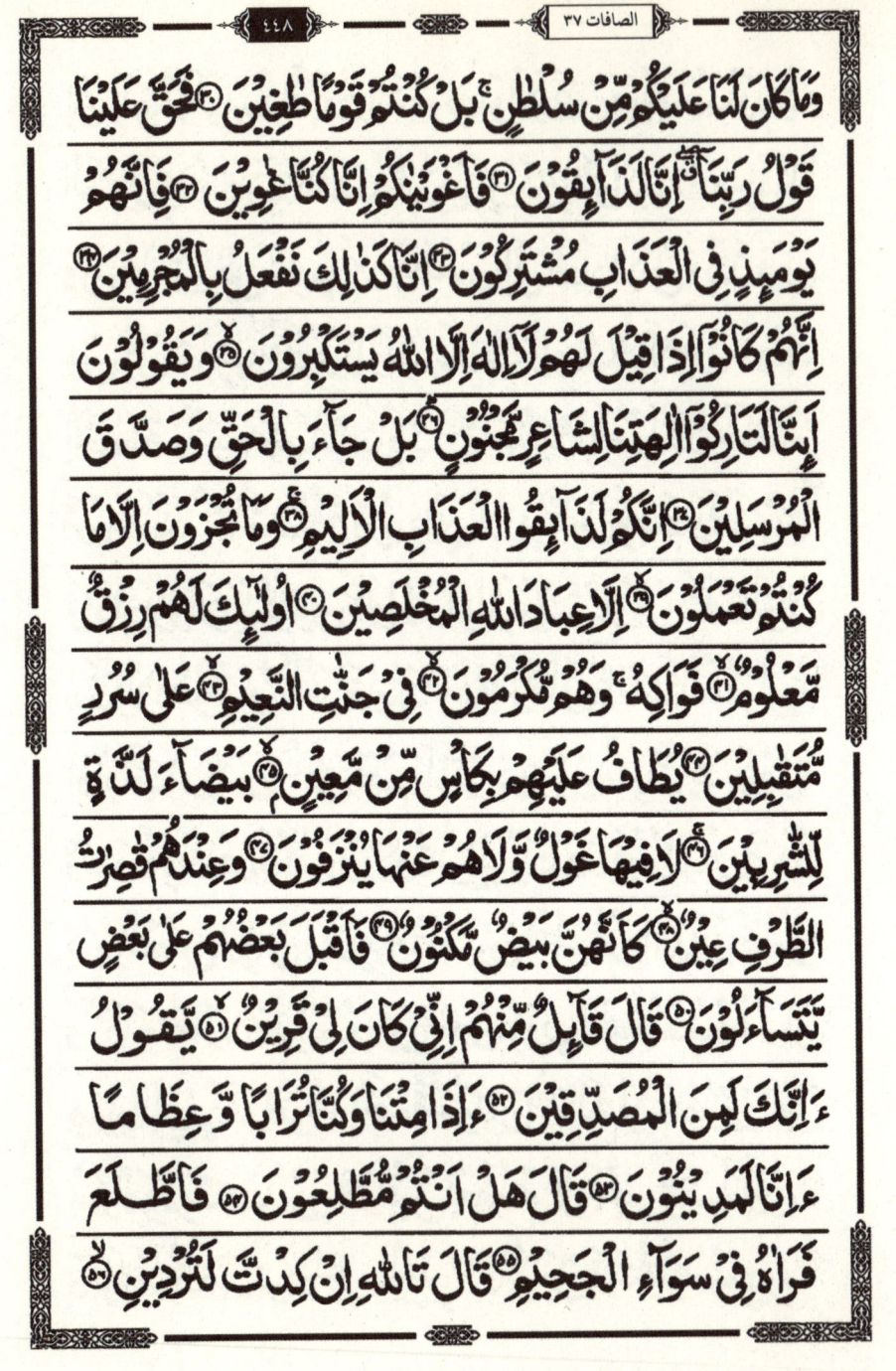

The Misleaders vs. the Misled

27. They will turn on each other, throwing blame. 28. The misled will say, "It was you who deluded us away from what is right."[904] 29. The misleaders will reply, "No! You disbelieved on your own. 30. We had no authority over you. In fact, you yourselves were a transgressing people. 31. The decree of our Lord has come to pass against us ˹all˺: we will certainly taste ˹the punishment˺. 32. We caused you to deviate, for we ourselves were deviant." 33. Surely on that Day they will ˹all˺ share in the punishment.

Warning to Arab Pagans

34. That is certainly how We deal with the wicked. 35. For whenever it was said to them ˹in the world˺, "There is no god ˹worthy of worship˺ except Allah," they acted arrogantly 36. and argued, "Should we really abandon our gods for a mad poet?" 37. In fact, he came with the truth, confirming ˹earlier˺ messengers. 38. You will certainly taste the painful torment, 39. and will only be rewarded for what you used to do.

Reward of the Devout

40. But not the chosen servants of Allah. 41. They will have a known provision: 42. fruits ˹of every type˺.[905] And they will be honoured 43. in the Gardens of Bliss, 44. facing each other on thrones.[906] 45. A drink ˹of pure wine˺ will be passed around to them from a flowing stream: 46. crystal-white, delicious to drink. 47. It will neither harm ˹them˺, nor will they be intoxicated by it. 48. And with them will be maidens of modest gaze and gorgeous eyes, 49. as if they were pristine pearls.[907]

The People of Paradise Chatting

50. Then they will turn to one another inquisitively.[908] 51. One of them will say, "I once had a companion ˹in the world˺ 52. who used to ask ˹me˺, 'Do you actually believe ˹in resurrection˺? 53. When we are dead and reduced to dust and bones, will we really be brought to judgment?'" 54. He will ˹then˺ ask, "Would you care to see ˹his fate˺?" 55. Then he ˹and the others˺ will

---

904 Other possible translations: 1. "It was you who used to pressure us." 2. "It was you who tricked us in the name of the truth." 3. "It was you who dissuaded us from doing good." 4. "It was you who deceived us with false oaths."
905 This implies all sorts of delicacies, not just fruits.
906 Facing each other implies that no one will have anything in their hearts against others.
907 ˹Baiḍun maknûn˺ can also mean spotless eggs.
908 It is assumed that they will ask each other about their lives in the world and what led them to Paradise.

449   37. Aş-Şâffât

look and spot him in the midst of the Hellfire. **56.** He will ˹then˺ say, "By Allah! You nearly ruined me. **57.** Had it not been for the grace of my Lord, I ˹too˺ would have certainly been among those brought ˹to Hell˺." **58.** ˹Then he will ask his fellow believers,˺ "Can you imagine that we will never die, **59.** except our first death, nor be ˹punished like the others˺?" **60.** This is truly the ultimate triumph. **61.** For such ˹honour˺ all should strive.

Hospitality for the People of Hell

62. Is this ˹bliss˺ a better accommodation or the tree of *Zaqqûm*?[909] **63.** We have surely made it a test for the wrongdoers. **64.** Indeed, it is a tree that grows in the depths of Hell, **65.** bearing fruit like devils' heads. **66.** The evildoers will certainly ˹be left to˺ eat from it, filling up their bellies with it. **67.** Then on top of that they will be given a blend of boiling drink. **68.** Then they will ultimately return to ˹their place in˺ Hell.

Blind Following

69. Indeed, they found their forefathers astray, **70.** so they rushed in their footsteps! **71.** And surely most of the earlier generations had strayed before them, **72.** although We had certainly sent warners among them. **73.** See then what was the end of those who had been warned. **74.** But not the chosen servants of Allah.

Prophet Noah

75. Indeed, Noah cried out to Us, and how excellent are We in responding! **76.** We delivered him and his family[910] from the great distress, **77.** and made his descendants the sole survivors.[911] **78.** And We blessed him ˹with honourable mention˺ among later generations: **79.** "Peace be upon Noah among all peoples." **80.** Indeed, this is how We reward the good-doers. **81.** ˹For˺ he was truly one of Our faithful servants. **82.** Then We drowned the others.

---

909 The pagans of Mecca used to make fun of the Prophet (ﷺ) when he warned them of this tree. They asked, "How can a tree grow in Hell?" So Allah revealed this verse in response.
910 i.e., the believers in his family.
911 Noah's sons: Shem, Ham, and Japheth.

Prophet Abraham

83. And indeed, one of those who followed his way was Abraham. **84.** ˹Remember˺ when he came to his Lord with a pure heart, **85.** and said to his father and his people, "What are you worshipping? **86.** Is it false gods that you desire instead of Allah? **87.** What then do you expect from the Lord of all worlds?" **88.** He later looked up to the stars ˹in contemplation˺,[912] **89.** then said, "I am really sick."[913] **90.** So they turned their backs on him and went away. **91.** Then he ˹stealthily˺ advanced towards their gods, and said ˹mockingly˺, "Will you not eat ˹your offerings˺? **92.** What is wrong with you that you cannot speak?" **93.** Then he swiftly turned on them, striking ˹them˺ with his right hand. **94.** Later, his people came rushing towards him ˹furiously˺. **95.** He argued, "How can you worship what you carve ˹with your own hands˺, **96.** when it is Allah Who created you and whatever you do?" **97.** They said ˹to one another˺, "Build him a furnace and cast him into the blazing fire." **98.** And so they sought to harm him, but We made them inferior.

Abraham, Ishmael and the Sacrifice

99. He later said, "I am leaving ˹in obedience˺ to my Lord. He will guide me. **100.** My Lord! Bless me with righteous offspring." **101.** So We gave him good news of a forbearing son. **102.** Then when the boy reached the age to work with him, Abraham said, "O my dear son! I have seen in a dream that I ˹must˺ sacrifice you. So tell me what you think." He replied, "O my dear father! Do as you are commanded. Allah willing, you will find me steadfast." **103.** Then when they submitted ˹to Allah's Will˺, and Abraham laid him on the side of his forehead ˹for sacrifice˺, **104.** We called out to him, "O Abraham! **105.** You have already fulfilled the vision." Indeed, this is how We reward the good-doers. **106.** That was truly a revealing test. **107.** And We ransomed his son with a great sacrifice,[914]

---

912 His people reportedly made decisions based on constellations, so Abraham (ﷺ) pretended to do the same to convince them he was not able to join them at their pagan feast.
913 *See* footnote for 26:82.
914 Allah sent a ram to be sacrificed in place of Ishmael.

451 37. Aṣ-Ṣâffât

108. and blessed Abraham ˹with honourable mention˺ among later generations: **109.** "Peace be upon Abraham." **110.** This is how We reward the good-doers. **111.** He was truly one of Our faithful servants. **112.** We ˹later˺ gave him good news of Isaac—a prophet, and one of the righteous.[915] **113.** We blessed him[916] and Isaac as well. Some of their descendants did good, while others clearly wronged themselves.

Prophet Moses and Prophet Aaron

114. And We certainly showed favour to Moses and Aaron, **115.** and delivered them and their people from the great distress. **116.** We helped them so it was they who prevailed. **117.** We gave them the clear Scripture, **118.** and guided them to the Straight Path. **119.** And We blessed them ˹with honourable mention˺ among later generations: **120.** "Peace be upon Moses and Aaron." **121.** Indeed, this is how We reward the good-doers. **122.** They were truly ˹two˺ of Our faithful servants.

Prophet Elias

123. And Elias was indeed one of the messengers. **124.** ˹Remember˺ when he said to his people, "Will you not fear ˹Allah˺? **125.** Do you call upon ˹the idol of˺ Ba'l and abandon the Best of Creators— **126.** Allah, your Lord and the Lord of your forefathers?" **127.** But they rejected him, so they will certainly be brought ˹for punishment˺. **128.** But not the chosen servants of Allah. **129.** We blessed him ˹with honourable mention˺ among later generations:

130. "Peace be upon Elias." **131.** Indeed, this is how We reward the good-doers. **132.** He was truly one of Our faithful servants.

---

915 The birth of Isaac is announced after the story of sacrifice. So this is a proof that the son who was going to be sacrificed was Ishmael, not Isaac. This is also supported by 11:71, where Sarah is told that she would give birth to Isaac, who would (reach adulthood and) have a son by the name of Jacob.
916 Abraham or Ishmael.

37. Aṣ-Ṣâffât

Prophet Lot

133. And Lot was indeed one of the messengers. **134.** ˹Remember˺ when We delivered him and all of his family, **135.** except an old woman,[917] who was one of the doomed. **136.** Then We ˹utterly˺ destroyed the rest. **137.** You ˹Meccans˺ certainly pass by their ruins day **138.** and night. Will you not then understand?

Prophet Jonah

139. And Jonah was indeed one of the messengers. **140.** ˹Remember˺ when he fled to the overloaded ship. **141.** Then ˹to save it from sinking,˺ he drew straws ˹with other passengers˺. He lost ˹and was thrown overboard˺. **142.** Then the whale engulfed him up while he was blameworthy.[918] **143.** Had he not ˹constantly˺ glorified ˹Allah˺,[919] **144.** he would have certainly remained in its belly until the Day of Resurrection.[920] **145.** But We cast him onto the open ˹shore˺, ˹totally˺ worn out, **146.** and caused a squash plant to grow over him.[921] **147.** We ˹later˺ sent him ˹back˺ to ˹his city of˺ at least one hundred thousand people, **148.** who then believed ˹in him˺, so We allowed them enjoyment for a while.

Questions to Arab Pagans

149. Ask them ˹O Prophet˺ if your Lord has daughters,[922] while the pagans ˹prefer to˺ have sons. **150.** Or ˹ask them˺ if We created the angels as females right before their eyes. **151.** Indeed, it is one of their ˹outrageous˺ fabrications to say, **152.** "Allah has children." They are simply liars. **153.** Has He chosen daughters over sons?[923] **154.** What is the matter with you? How do you judge? **155.** Will you not then be mindful? **156.** Or do you have ˹any˺ compelling proof? **157.** Then bring ˹us˺ your scripture, if what you say is true! **158.** They have also established a ˹marital˺ relationship between Him and the jinn. Yet the jinn ˹themselves˺ know well that such people will certainly be brought ˹for punishment˺.[924] **159.** Glorified is Allah far above what they claim! **160.** But not the chosen servants of Allah.

---

917 Lot's wife.
918 For abandoning his city without Allah's permission.
919 Before being swallowed and while inside the whale (see 21:87). The lesson is: good deeds are of great help during difficult times.
920 The belly of the whale would have become his grave.
921 The squash plant provided Jonah with shade and repelled harmful insects.
922 Some pagan Arabs believed that the angels were Allah's daughters. Some of them were ashamed to have daughters and took pride in their own sons.
923 Both sexes are equal before Allah, so the verse questions pagan chauvinism.
924 Or "Yet the jinn know well that they themselves will be brought ˹for judgment˺." This is based on the claim of some pagan Arabs that the angels are Allah's daughters through female jinn.

453   38. Ṣād

161. Surely you ˹pagans˺ and whatever ˹idols˺ you worship **162.** can never lure ˹anyone˺ away from Him **163.** except those ˹destined˺ to burn in Hell.

Angels' Response

164. ˹The angels respond,˺ "There is not one of us without an assigned station ˹of worship˺. **165.** We are indeed the ones lined up in ranks ˹for Allah˺. **166.** And we are indeed the ones ˹constantly˺ glorifying ˹His praise˺."

The Pagans Before the Quran

167. They certainly used to say, **168.** "If only we had a Reminder like ˹those of˺ earlier peoples,[925] **1649.** we would have truly been Allah's devoted servants." **170.** But ˹now˺ they reject it, so they will soon know.

Reassuring the Prophet

171. Our Word has already gone forth to Our servants, the messengers, **172.** that they would surely be helped, **173.** and that Our forces will certainly prevail. **174.** So turn away from the deniers for a while ˹O Prophet˺. **175.** You will see ˹what will happen to˺ them, and they too will see! **176.** Do they ˹really˺ wish to hasten Our punishment? **177.** Yet when it descends upon them:[926] how evil will that morning be for those who had been warned! **178.** And turn away from them for a while. **179.** You will see, and they too will see!

The Conclusion

180. Glorified is your Lord—the Lord of Honour and Power—above what they claim! **181.** Peace be upon the messengers. **182.** And praise be to Allah—Lord of all worlds.

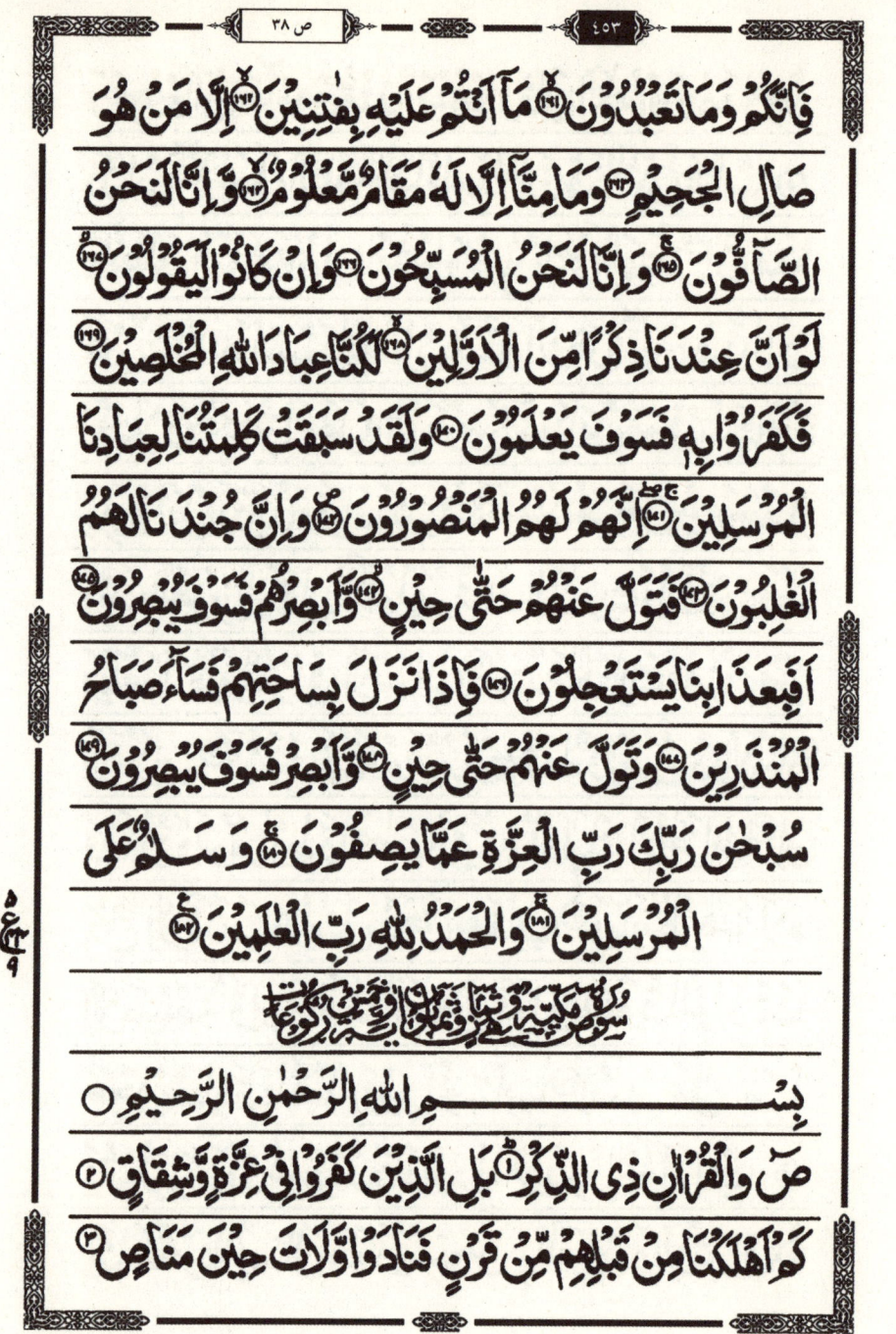

---

38. Ṣād (Ṣād)

In the Name of Allah—the Most Compassionate, Most Merciful

Arab Deniers

1. Ṣād. By the Quran, full of reminders! **2.** ˹This is the truth,˺ yet the disbelievers are ˹entrenched˺ in arrogance and opposition. **3.** ˹Imagine˺ how many peoples We destroyed before them, and they cried out when it was too late to escape.

---

925 The "Reminder" mentioned here refers to Scriptures such as the Torah and the Gospel. It is commonly used in the Quran as another name for Islam's holy book.
926 lit., when it lands in their courtyards.

38. Ṣād

4. Now, the pagans are astonished that a warner has come to them from among themselves.[927] And the disbelievers say, "This is a magician, a total liar! **5.** Has he reduced ˹all˺ the gods to One God? Indeed, this is something totally astonishing."

Chief Deniers

6. The chiefs among them went forth saying, "Carry on, and stand firm in devotion to your gods. Certainly this is just a scheme ˹for power˺.[928] **7.** We have never heard of this in the previous faith.[929] This is nothing but a fabrication. **8.** Has the Reminder been revealed ˹only˺ to him out of ˹all of˺ us?" In fact, they are ˹only˺ in doubt of My ˹revealed˺ Reminder.[930] In fact, ˹they do so because˺ they have not yet tasted My punishment. **9.** Or ˹is it because˺ they possess the treasuries of the mercy of your Lord—the Almighty, the Giver ˹of all bounties˺. **10.** Or ˹is it because˺ the kingdom of the heavens and the earth and everything in between belongs to them? Let them then climb their way ˹to heaven, if their claim is true˺.

Warning to the Deniers

11. This is just another ˹enemy˺ force bound for defeat out there.[931] **12.** Before them, the people of Noah denied ˹the truth˺, as did ʿÂd, Pharaoh of the mighty structures,[932] **13.** Thamûd, the people of Lot, and the residents of the Forest.[933] These were ˹all˺ enemy forces. **14.** Each rejected their messenger, so My punishment was justified. **15.** These ˹pagans˺ are awaiting nothing but a single Blast that cannot be stopped. **16.** They say ˹mockingly˺, "Our Lord! Hasten for us our share ˹of the punishment˺ before the Day of Reckoning."

---

927 The pagans demanded an angel to deliver the message, not a human being like themselves.
928 They meant that the Prophet (ﷺ) is not concerned with their guidance, and that he only wants to gain dominance over them.
929 This refers either to the concept of the Trinity in Christianity or Arab polytheistic beliefs.
930 In other words, they do not question the honesty of the Prophet (ﷺ), but question the Quran itself. This verse is similar to 6:33.
931 This verse alludes to the defeat of the Meccan pagans later at Badr.
932 i.e., pyramids and obelisks.
933 i.e., the people of Shuʿaib (ﷺ).

38. Ṣād

Prophet David

17. Be patient ˹O Prophet˺ with what they say. And remember Our servant, David, the man of strength. Indeed, he ˹constantly˺ turned ˹to Allah˺. 18. We truly subjected the mountains to hymn ˹Our praises˺ along with him in the evening and after sunrise. 19. And ˹We subjected˺ the birds, flocking together. All turned to him ˹echoing his hymns˺. 20. We strengthened his kingship, and gave him wisdom and sound judgment.

David and the Disputing Partners

21. Has the story of the two plaintiffs, who scaled the ˹wall of David's˺ sanctuary, reached you ˹O Prophet˺? 22. When they came into David's presence, he was startled by them. They said, "Have no fear. ˹We are merely˺ two in a dispute: one of us has wronged the other. So judge between us with truth—do not go beyond ˹it˺—and guide us to the right way. 23. This is my brother.[934] He has ninety-nine sheep while I have ˹only˺ one. ˹Still˺ he asked me to give it up to him, overwhelming me with ˹his˺ argument." 24. David ˹eventually˺ ruled, "He has definitely wronged you in demanding ˹to add˺ your sheep to his. And certainly many partners wrong each other, except those who believe and do good—but how few are they!"

David Prays for Forgiveness[935]

Then David realized that We had tested him so he asked for his Lord's forgiveness, fell down in prostration, and turned ˹to Him in repentance˺. 25. So We forgave that for him. And he will indeed have ˹a status of˺ closeness to Us and an honourable destination! 26. ˹We instructed him:˺ "O David! We have surely made you an authority in the land, so judge between people with truth. And do not follow ˹your˺ desires or they will lead you astray from Allah's Way. Surely those who go astray from Allah's Way will suffer a severe punishment for neglecting the Day of Reckoning."

Allah Is Just

27. We have not created the heavens and earth and everything in between without purpose—as the disbelievers think. So woe to the disbelievers because of the Fire!

---

934 Brother in faith or business partner.
935 The verses do not offer a reason why David (ﷺ) asked for Allah's forgiveness. He either did so because he did not make himself available to judge between people or because he entertained some evil thoughts about the two men, thinking they actually came to assassinate him. Still he listened to both of them and made a fair judgment.

28. Or should We treat those who believe and do good like those who make mischief throughout the land? Or should We treat the righteous like the wicked?

The Purpose of the Quran

29. ˹This is˺ a blessed Book which We have revealed to you ˹O Prophet˺ so that they may contemplate its verses, and people of reason may be mindful.

Solomon's Love for Fine Horses

30. And We blessed David with Solomon—what an excellent servant ˹he was˺! Indeed, he ˹constantly˺ turned ˹to Allah˺. **31.** ˹Remember˺ when the well-trained, swift horses were paraded before him in the evening. **32.** He then proclaimed, "I am truly in love with ˹these˺ fine things out of remembrance for my Lord," until they went out of sight. **33.** ˹He ordered,˺ "Bring them back to me!" Then he began to rub down their legs and necks.[936]

Solomon's Authority

34. And indeed, We tested Solomon, placing a ˹deformed˺ body on his throne,[937] then he turned ˹to Allah in repentance˺. **35.** He prayed, "My Lord! Forgive me, and grant me an authority that will never be matched by anyone after me. You are indeed the Giver ˹of all bounties˺." **36.** So We subjected to him the wind, blowing gently at his command to wherever he pleased. **37.** And ˹We subjected to him˺ every builder and diver[938] of the jinn, **38.** and others bound together in chains. **39.** ˹Allah said,˺ "This is Our gift, so give or withhold ˹as you wish˺, never to be called to account." **40.** And he will indeed have ˹a status of˺ closeness to Us and an honourable destination!

Prophet Job

41. And remember Our servant Job, when he cried out to his Lord, "Satan has afflicted me with distress and suffering." **42.** ˹We responded,˺ "Stomp your foot: ˹now˺ here is a cool ˹and refreshing˺ spring for washing and drinking." **43.** And We gave him

---

936 Some commentators have a different interpretation, which is not supported by reliable sources. They maintain that Solomon kept watching these fine horses until the sun set, then he realized that he had missed the noon prayer because of his love for horses, so he killed them, striking at their legs and necks.

937 It is reported in a *ḥadīth* collected by Bukhāri that one night Solomon said that each of his wives would conceive a boy who would struggle in Allah's cause. He forgot to say 'Allah willing,' so only one of them gave birth to a deformed, dead baby. So Solomon prayed to Allah for forgiveness.

938 The jinn dived to bring him pearls.

38. Ṣād

back his family, twice as many, as a mercy from Us and a lesson for people of reason. 44. ˹And We said to him,˺ "Take in your hand a bundle of grass, and strike ˹your wife˺ with it, and do not break your oath."[939] We truly found him patient. What an excellent servant ˹he was˺! Indeed, he ˹constantly˺ turned ˹to Allah˺.

Other Mighty Prophets

45. And remember Our servants: Abraham, Isaac, and Jacob—the men of strength and insight. 46. We truly chose them for the honour of proclaiming the Hereafter. 47. And in Our sight they are truly among the chosen and the finest. 48. Also remember Ishmael, Elisha, and Ẓul-Kifl.[940] All are among the best.

Reward of the Righteous

49. This is ˹all˺ a reminder. And the righteous will certainly have an honourable destination: 50. the Gardens of Eternity, whose gates will be open for them. 51. There they will recline, calling for abundant fruit and drink. 52. And with them will be maidens of modest gaze and equal age. 53. This is what you are promised for the Day of Reckoning. 54. This is indeed Our provision that will never end.

Reward of the Wicked

55. That is that. And the transgressors will certainly have the worst destination: 56. Hell, where they will burn. What an evil place to rest! 57. Let them then taste this: boiling water and ˹oozing˺ pus, 58. and other torments of the same sort!

Disputes of the Wicked

59. ˹The misleaders will say to one another,˺ "Here is a crowd ˹of followers˺ being thrown in with us. They are not welcome, ˹for˺ they ˹too˺ will burn in the Fire."[941] 60. The followers will respond, "No! You are not welcome! You brought this upon us. What an evil place for settlement!" 61. Adding, "Our Lord! Whoever brought this upon us, double their punishment in the Fire." 62. The tyrants will ask ˹one another˺, "But why do we not see those we considered to be lowly?

---

939 Job was afflicted with losing his children, community, and with a long illness. Only his wife stayed with him. He once became angry with his wife and vowed to give her one hundred lashes if he recovered. When Job's affliction was lifted, he became remorseful at what he had said. To help Job fulfil his vow without harming his wife, Allah ordered him to strike her with a bundle of one hundred blades of grass.

940 Scholars are in disagreement as to whether Ẓul-Kifl was a prophet or just a righteous man. Those who maintain that he was a prophet identify him with various Biblical prophets such as Ezekiel, Isaiah, and Obadiah.

941 Meaning, they are not welcome since their presence in Hell with us will not benefit us in anyway.

38. Ṣād 458

63. Were we wrong in mocking them ˹in the world˺?[942] Or do our eyes ˹just˺ fail to see them ˹in the Fire˺?" 64. This dispute between the residents of the Fire will certainly come to pass.

The Messenger and His Message

65. Say, ˹O Prophet,˺ "I am only a warner. And there is no god ˹worthy of worship˺ except Allah—the One, the Supreme. 66. ˹He is the˺ Lord of the heavens and the earth and everything in between—the Almighty, Most Forgiving." 67. Say, "This ˹Quran˺ is momentous news, 68. from which you ˹pagans˺ are turning away." 69. ˹And say,˺ "I had no knowledge of the highest assembly ˹in heaven˺ when they differed ˹concerning Adam˺.[943] 70. What is revealed to me is that I am only sent with a clear warning."

Satan's Arrogance

71. ˹Remember, O Prophet˺ when your Lord said to the angels, "I am going to create a human being from clay. 72. So when I have fashioned him and had a spirit of My Own ˹creation˺ breathed into him, fall down in prostration to him." 73. So the angels prostrated all together— 74. but not *Iblîs*,[944] who acted arrogantly,[945] becoming unfaithful. 75. Allah asked, "O *Iblîs*! What prevented you from prostrating to what I created with My Own Hands? Did you ˹just˺ become proud? Or have you always been arrogant? 76. He replied, "I am better than he is: You created me from fire and him from clay." 77. Allah commanded, "Then get out of Paradise, for you are truly cursed. 78. And surely upon you is My condemnation until the Day of Judgment." 79. Satan appealed, "My Lord! Then delay my end until the Day of their resurrection." 80. Allah said, "You will be delayed 81. until the appointed Day." 82. Satan said, "By Your Glory! I will certainly mislead them all,

---

942 In other words, did we underestimate them?
943 When the angels obeyed Allah's orders to prostrate before Adam, whereas Satan refused to comply.
944 See footnote for 2:34.
945 The command to bow down was a test of obedience. Satan arrogantly refused to comply because he believed he was superior to Adam (؉).

83. except Your chosen servants among them." **84.** Allah concluded, "The truth is—and I ˹only˺ say the truth—: **85.** I will surely fill up Hell with you and whoever follows you from among them, all together."

Message to the Deniers

86. Say, ˹O Prophet,˺ "I do not ask you for any reward for this ˹Quran˺, nor do I pretend to be someone I am not. **87.** It is only a reminder to the whole world. **88.** And you will certainly know its truth before long."

39. The ˹Successive˺ Groups (Az-Zumar)

In the Name of Allah—the Most Compassionate, Most Merciful

Worship Allah Alone

1. The revelation of this Book is from Allah—the Almighty, All-Wise. **2.** Indeed, We have sent down the Book to you ˹O Prophet˺ in truth, so worship Allah ˹alone˺, being sincerely devoted to Him. **3.** Indeed, sincere devotion is due ˹only˺ to Allah. As for those who take other lords besides Him, ˹saying,˺ "We worship them only so they may bring us closer to Allah," surely Allah will judge between all[946] regarding what they differed about. Allah certainly does not guide whoever persists in lying and disbelief.

Allah's Power of Creation

4. Had it been Allah's Will to have offspring, He could have chosen whatever He willed of His creation. Glory be to Him! He is Allah—the One, the Supreme. **5.** He created the heavens and the earth for a purpose. He wraps the night around the day, and wraps the day around the night. And He has subjected the sun and the moon, each orbiting for an appointed term. He is truly the Almighty, Most Forgiving.

---

946 Those who are devoted to Allah alone and those who associate other gods with Him.

6. He created you ˹all˺ from a single soul,[947] then from it He made its mate.[948] And He produced for you four pairs of cattle.[949] He creates you in the wombs of your mothers ˹in stages˺, one development after another, in three layers of darkness.[950] That is Allah—your Lord! All authority belongs to Him. There is no god ˹worthy of worship˺ except Him. How can you then be turned away?

Belief and Disbelief

7. If you disbelieve, then ˹know that˺ Allah is truly not in need of you, nor does He approve of disbelief from His servants. But if you become grateful ˹through faith˺, He will appreciate that from you. No soul burdened with sin will bear the burden of another. Then to your Lord is your return, and He will inform you of what you used to do. He certainly knows best what is ˹hidden˺ in the heart.

Disbelievers' Ingratitude

8. When one is touched with hardship, they cry out to their Lord, turning to Him ˹alone˺. But as soon as He showers them with blessings from Him, they ˹totally˺ forget the One they had cried to earlier, and set up equals to Allah to mislead ˹others˺ from His Way. Say, ˹O Prophet,˺ "Enjoy your disbelief for a little while! You will certainly be one of the inmates of the Fire." **9.** ˹Are they better˺ or those who worship ˹their Lord˺ devoutly in the hours of the night, prostrating and standing, fearing the Hereafter and hoping for the mercy of their Lord? Say, ˹O Prophet,˺ "Are those who know equal to those who do not know?" None will be mindful ˹of this˺ except people of reason.

Orders to the Prophet

10. Say ˹O Prophet, that Allah says˺, "O My servants who believe! Be mindful of your Lord. Those who do good in this world will have a good reward. And Allah's earth is spacious. Only those who endure patiently will be given their reward without limit."

---

947 i.e., Adam (ﷺ).
948 i.e., Eve.
949 The four pairs (males and females), as listed in 6:143-144, are: a pair of sheep, a pair of goats, a pair of camels, and a pair of oxen.
950 The three layers of darkness are: the belly, the womb, and the amniotic sac.

11. Say, "I am commanded to worship Allah, being sincerely devoted to Him ˹alone˺. 12. And I am commanded to be the first of those who submit ˹to His Will˺." 13. Say, "I truly fear—if I were to disobey my Lord—the torment of a tremendous Day." 14. Say, "It is ˹only˺ Allah that I worship, being sincere in my devotion to Him. 15. Worship then whatever ˹gods˺ you want instead of Him." Say, "The ˹true˺ losers are those who will lose themselves and their families on Judgment Day. That is indeed the clearest loss." 16. They will have layers of fire above and below them. That is what Allah warns His servants with. So fear Me, O My servants!

The Faithful and the Unfaithful

17. And those who shun the worship of false gods, turning to Allah ˹alone˺, will have good news. So give good news to My servants ˹O Prophet˺— 18. those who listen to what is said and follow the best of it.[951] These are the ones ˹rightly˺ guided by Allah, and these are ˹truly˺ the people of reason. 19. What about those against whom the decree of torment has been justified? Is it you ˹O Prophet˺ who will then save those bound for the Fire? 20. But those mindful of their Lord will have ˹elevated˺ mansions, built one above the other, under which rivers flow. ˹That is˺ the promise of Allah. ˹And˺ Allah never fails in ˹His˺ promise.

Parable for This Fleeting Life

21. Do you not see that Allah sends down rain from the sky—channelling it through streams in the earth—then produces with it crops of various colours, then they dry up and you see them wither, and then He reduces them to chaff? Surely in this is a reminder for people of reason.

---

951 This verse can apply to anything that a person listens to, and it can also apply specifically to the Quran—meaning, for example, those who read verses about retaliation and other verses about forgiveness, then they opt for forgiveness.

39. Az-Zumar

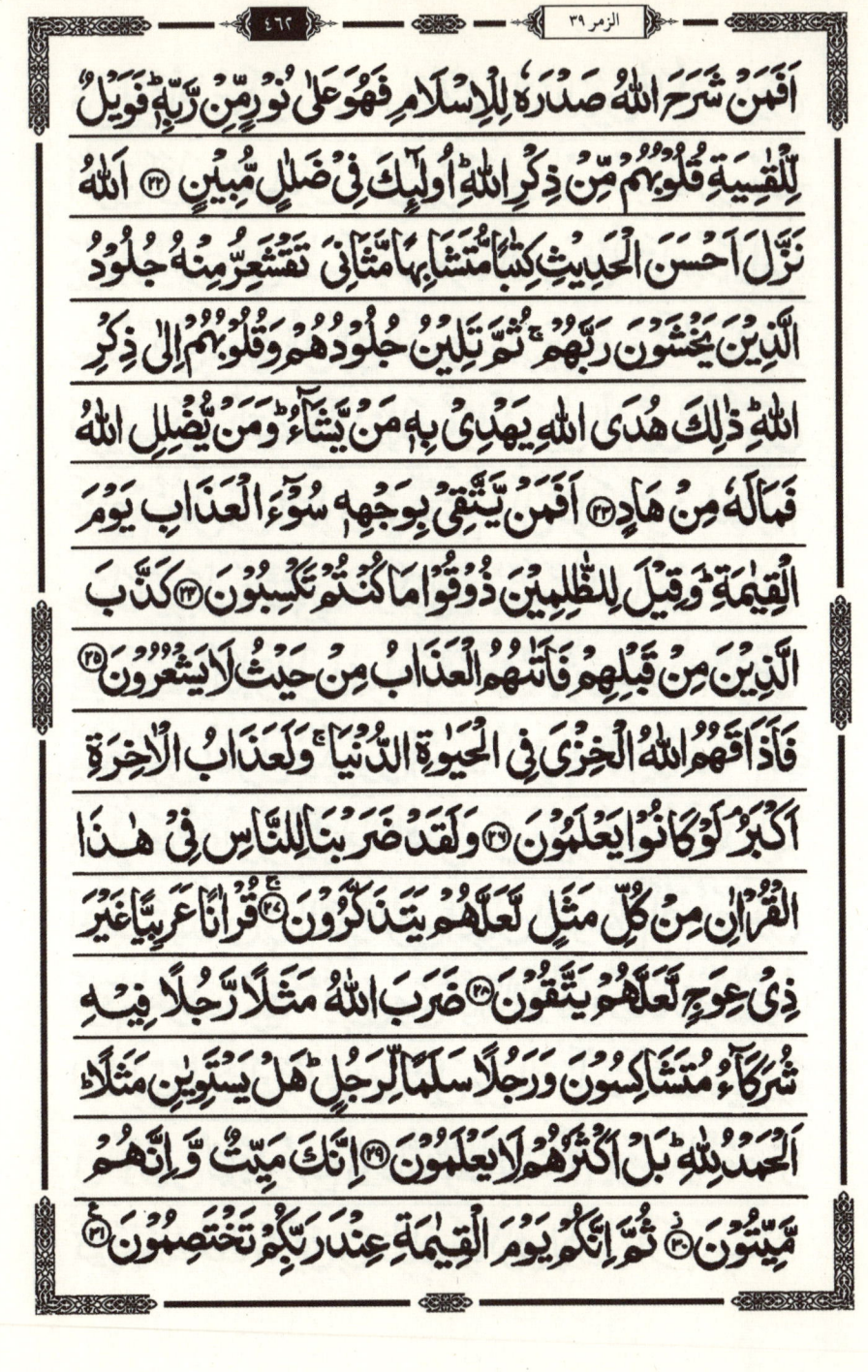

The Believers and the Disbelievers

22. Can ˹the misguided be like˺ those whose hearts Allah has opened to Islam, so they are enlightened by their Lord? So woe to those whose hearts are hardened at the remembrance of Allah! It is they who are clearly astray.

Excellence of the Quran

23. ˹It is˺ Allah ˹Who˺ has sent down the best message—a Book of perfect consistency and repeated lessons—which causes the skin ˹and hearts˺ of those who fear their Lord to tremble, then their skin and hearts soften at the mention of ˹the mercy of˺ Allah. That is the guidance of Allah, through which He guides whoever He wills. But whoever Allah leaves to stray will be left with no guide. **24.** Are those who will only have their ˹bare˺ faces to shield themselves from the awful torment on Judgment Day ˹better than those in Paradise˺? It will ˹then˺ be said to the wrongdoers: "Reap what you sowed!"

Rejection Leads to Punishment

25. Those before them ˹also˺ rejected ˹the truth˺, then the torment came upon them from where they least expected. **26.** So Allah made them taste humiliation in this worldly life, but far worse is the punishment of the Hereafter, if only they knew.

Perfection of the Quran

27. We have certainly set forth every ˹kind of˺ lesson for people in this Quran, so perhaps they will be mindful. **28.** ˹It is˺ a Quran ˹revealed˺ in Arabic without any crookedness, so perhaps they will be conscious ˹of Allah˺.

Parable for a Polytheist and a Monotheist

29. Allah sets forth the parable of a slave owned by several quarrelsome masters, and a slave owned by only one master. Are they equal in condition?[952] Praise be to Allah! In fact, most of them do not know.

---

952 The slave owned by several quarrelsome masters will always be confused because their masters will always give them conflicting orders—similarly, one who worships multiple gods will never find peace between them. This parable is a logical argument against the existence of multiple gods, since each god would try to covet what it created. *See* 23:91 for a similar argument.

39. Az-Zumar

All Will Die

30. You 'O Prophet' will certainly die, and they will die too. 31. Then on the Day of Judgment you will 'all settle your' dispute before your Lord.

Reward of the Believers and Disbelievers

32. Who then does more wrong than those who lie about Allah and reject the truth after it has reached them? Is Hell not a 'fitting' home for the disbelievers? 33. And the one who has brought the truth and those who embrace it—it is they who are the righteous. 34. They will have whatever they desire with their Lord. That is the reward of the good-doers. 35. As such, Allah will absolve them of 'even' the worst of what they did and reward them according to the best of what they used to do.

Allah Protects His Messenger

36. Is Allah not sufficient for His servant? Yet they threaten you with other 'powerless' gods besides Him! Whoever Allah leaves to stray will be left with no guide. 37. And whoever Allah guides, none can lead astray. Is Allah not Almighty, capable of punishment?

Almighty Allah or Powerless Gods

38. If you ask them 'O Prophet' who created the heavens and the earth, they will certainly say, "Allah!" Ask 'them', "Consider then whatever 'idols' you invoke besides Allah: if it was Allah's Will to harm me, could they undo that harm? Or if He willed 'some' mercy for me, could they withhold His mercy?" Say, "Allah is sufficient for me. In Him 'alone' the faithful put their trust."

Warning to the Pagans

39. Say, 'O Prophet,' "O my people! Persist in your ways, for I 'too' will persist in mine. You will soon come to know 40. who will be visited by a humiliating torment 'in this life' and overwhelmed by an everlasting punishment 'in the next'."

39. Az-Zumar

Free Choice

41. Surely We have revealed to you the Book ˹O Prophet˺ with the truth for humanity. So whoever chooses to be guided, it is for their own good. And whoever chooses to stray, it is only to their own loss. You are not a keeper over them.

Sleep: The Twin Brother of Death

42. ˹It is˺ Allah ˹Who˺ calls back the souls ˹of people˺ upon their death as well as ˹the souls˺ of the living during their sleep. Then He keeps those for whom He has ordained death, and releases the others until ˹their˺ appointed time. Surely in this are signs for people who reflect.

Allah or the Idols

43. Or have they taken others besides Allah as intercessors? Say, ˹O Prophet,˺ "˹Would they do so,˺ even though those ˹idols˺ have neither authority nor intelligence?" **44.** Say, "All intercession belongs to Allah ˹alone˺. To Him belongs the kingdom of the heavens and the earth. Then to Him you will ˹all˺ be returned." **45.** Yet when Allah alone is mentioned, the hearts of those who disbelieve in the Hereafter are filled with disgust. But as soon as those ˹gods˺ other than Him are mentioned, they are filled with joy.

Allah Is the Judge

46. Say, ˹O Prophet,˺ "O Allah—Originator of the heavens and the earth, Knower of the seen and unseen! You will judge between Your servants regarding their differences." **47.** Even if the wrongdoers were to possess everything in the world twice over, they would certainly offer it to ransom themselves from the horrible punishment on Judgment Day, for they will see from Allah what they had never expected.

48. And the evil ʿconsequencesʾ of their deeds will unfold before them, and they will be overwhelmed by what they used to ridicule.

Human Ingratitude

49. When one is touched with hardship, they cry out to Us ʿaloneʾ. Then when We shower Our blessings upon them, they say, "I have been granted all this only because of ʿmyʾ knowledge." Not at all! It is ʿno more thanʾ a test. But most of them do not know. **50.** The same had already been said by those ʿdestroyedʾ before them,[953] but their ʿworldlyʾ gains were of no benefit to them. **51.** So the evil ʿconsequencesʾ of their deeds overtook them. And the wrongdoers among these ʿpagansʾ will be overtaken by the evil ʿconsequencesʾ of their deeds. And they will have no escape. **52.** Do they not know that Allah gives abundant or limited provisions to whoever He wills? Surely in this are signs for people who believe.

Allah Forgives All Sins

53. Say, ʿO Prophet, that Allah says,ʾ "O My servants who have exceeded the limits against their souls! Do not lose hope in Allah's mercy, for Allah certainly forgives all sins.[954] He is indeed the All-Forgiving, Most Merciful. **54.** Turn to your Lord ʿin repentanceʾ, and ʿfullyʾ submit to Him before the punishment reaches you, ʿforʾ then you will not be helped. **55.** Follow ʿthe Quran,ʾ the best of what has been revealed to you from your Lord, before the punishment takes you by surprise while you are unaware, **56.** so that no ʿsinfulʾ soul will say ʿon Judgment Dayʾ, 'Woe to me for neglecting ʿmy duties towardsʾ Allah, while ridiculing ʿthe truthʾ.'

---

953 Like Korah (*see* 28:76-81).
954 No matter how big someone's sins are, they cannot be bigger than Allah's mercy. Based on 4:48, the only unforgivable sin in Islam is if someone dies while disbelieving in Allah or associating others with Him in worship. In an authentic narration collected by At-Tirmizi, the Prophet (ﷺ) reports that Almighty Allah says, "O children of Adam! As long as you call upon Me, putting your hope in Me, I will forgive you for what you have done, and I will not mind. O children of Adam! If your sins were to reach the clouds of the sky and then you sought My forgiveness, I would ʿstillʾ forgive you. O children of Adam! If you were to come to Me with sins filling the whole world and then you came to Me without associating other gods with Me, I would certainly match your sins with forgiveness."

39. Az-Zumar

57. Or ʿa soul will' say, 'If only Allah had guided me, I would have certainly been one of the righteous.'
58. Or say, upon seeing the torment, 'If only I had a second chance, I would have been one of the good-doers.'
59. Not at all! My revelations had already come to you, but you rejected them, acted arrogantly, and were one of the disbelievers."

Judgment Day

60. On the Day of Judgment you will see those who lied about Allah with their faces gloomy. Is Hell not a ʿfitting' home for the arrogant?
61. And Allah will deliver those who were mindful ʿof Him' to their place of ʿultimate' triumph. No evil will touch them, nor will they grieve.
62. Allah is the Creator of all things, and He is the Maintainer of everything.
63. To Him belong the keys ʿof the treasuries' of the heavens and the earth. As for those who rejected the signs of Allah, it is they who will be the ʿtrue' losers.

One God Alone

64. Say, ʿO Prophet,' "Are you urging me to worship ʿanyone' other than Allah, O ignorant ones?"
65. It has already been revealed to you—and to those ʿprophets' before you—that if you associate others ʿwith Allah', your deeds will certainly be void and you will truly be one of the losers.
66. Rather, worship Allah ʿalone' and be one of the grateful.

Beginning of the End

67. They have not shown Allah His proper reverence—when on the Day of Judgment the ʿwhole' earth will be in His Grip, and the heavens will be rolled up in His Right Hand. Glorified and Exalted is He above what they associate ʿwith Him'!

68. The Trumpet will be blown and all those in the heavens and all those on the earth will fall dead, except those Allah wills ʿto spareʾ. Then it will be blown again and they will rise up at once, looking on ʿin anticipationʾ.

Divine Justice

69. The earth[955] will shine with the light of its Lord, the record ʿof deedsʾ will be laid ʿopenʾ, the prophets and the witnesses will be brought forward—and judgment will be passed on all with fairness. None will be wronged. **70.** Every soul will be paid in full for its deeds, for Allah knows best what they have done.

Reward of the Wicked

71. Those who disbelieved will be driven to Hell in ʿsuccessiveʾ groups. When they arrive there, its gates will be opened and its keepers will ask them: "Did messengers not come to you from among yourselves, reciting to you the revelations of your Lord and warning you of the coming of this Day of yours?" The disbelievers will cry, "Yes ʿindeedʾ"! But the decree of torment has come to pass against the disbelievers." **72.** It will be said to them, "Enter the gates of Hell, to stay there forever." What an evil home for the arrogant!

Reward of the Righteous

73. And those who were mindful of their Lord will be led to Paradise in ʿsuccessiveʾ groups. When they arrive at its ʿalreadyʾ open gates, its keepers will say, "Peace be upon you! You have done well, so come in, to stay forever." **74.** The righteous will say, "Praise be to Allah Who has fulfilled His promise to us, and made us inherit the ʿeverlastingʾ land[956] to settle in Paradise wherever we please." How excellent is the reward of those who work ʿrighteousnessʾ!

---

955 This refers to the place where the judgment will be held. The Prophet (ﷺ) is reported in a *ḥadīth* collected by Aṭ-Ṭabarâni to have said, "The Judgment will be passed on an earth where neither blood has been shed nor any sin committed."

956 This is emphasized in 21:105. The meaning is that Allah will award Paradise to the believers to be its residents forever. Some commentators say that the word "inherit" is used because of the understanding that when Allah created Paradise and Hell, He made places for all of humanity in both. Those who will go to Paradise will inherit the spots of the disbelievers who chose misguidance (which leads to Hell), and those who will go to Hell will inherit the spots of those who chose guidance (which leads to Paradise).

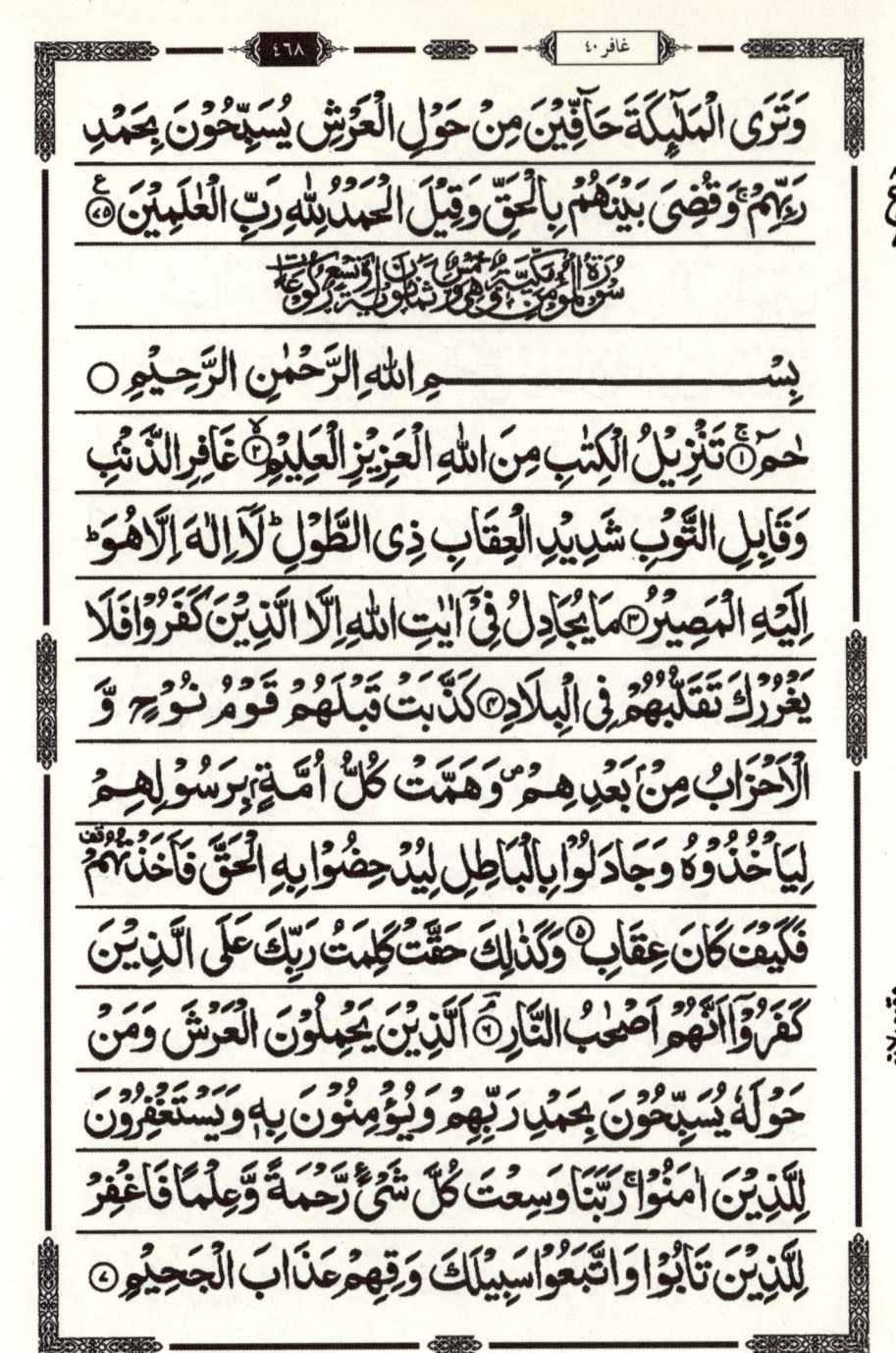

Praising Allah's Grace and Justice

75. You will see the angels all around the Throne, glorifying the praises of their Lord, for judgment will have been passed on all with fairness. And it will be said,[957] "Praise be to Allah—Lord of all worlds!"

❁❈❁

40. The Forgiver (Ghâfir)

In the Name of Allah—the Most Compassionate, Most Merciful

The Quran Is from the Almighty

1. *Ḥâ-Mīm.* **2.** The revelation of this Book is from Allah—the Almighty, All-Knowing, **3.** the Forgiver of sin and Accepter of repentance, the Severe in punishment, and Infinite in bounty. There is no god ˹worthy of worship˺ except Him. To Him ˹alone˺ is the final return.

Warning to the Disbelievers

4. None disputes the signs of Allah except the disbelievers, so do not be deceived by their prosperity throughout the land. **5.** Before them, the people of Noah denied ˹the truth˺, as did ˹other˺ enemy forces afterwards. Every community plotted against its prophet to seize him, and argued in falsehood, ˹hoping˺ to discredit the truth with it. So I seized them. And how ˹horrible˺ was My punishment! **6.** And so your Lord's decree has been proven true against the disbelievers—that they will be the inmates of the Fire.

Angels Pray for the Believers

7. Those ˹angels˺ who carry the Throne and those around it glorify the praises of their Lord, have faith in Him, and seek forgiveness for the believers, ˹praying:˺ "Our Lord! You encompass everything in ˹Your˺ mercy and knowledge. So forgive those who repent and follow Your Way, and protect them from the torment of the Hellfire.

---

957 The believers will praise Him for His grace, and the disbelievers will praise Him for His justice.

8. Our Lord! Admit them into the Gardens of Eternity which You have promised them, along with the righteous among their parents, spouses, and descendants. You ˹alone˺ are truly the Almighty, All-Wise. **9.** And protect them from ˹the consequences of their˺ evil deeds. For whoever You protect from the evil of their deeds on that Day will have been shown Your mercy. That is ˹truly˺ the ultimate triumph."

The Inmates of Hell

10. Indeed, it will be announced to the disbelievers, "Allah's contempt for you—as you disbelieved when invited to belief—was far worse than your contempt for one another ˹Today˺." **11.** They will plead, "Our Lord! You made us lifeless twice, and gave us life twice.[958] Now we confess our sins. So is there any way out?" **12.** ˹They will be told,˺ "˹No!˺ This is because when Allah alone was invoked, you ˹staunchly˺ disbelieved. But when others were associated with Him ˹in worship˺, you ˹readily˺ believed. So ˹Today˺ judgment belongs to Allah ˹alone˺—the Most High, All-Great."

Allah's Might in Both Worlds

13. He is the One Who shows you His signs and sends down ˹rain as˺ a provision for you from the sky. ˹But˺ none will be mindful except those who turn ˹to Him˺. **14.** So call upon Allah with sincere devotion, even to the dismay of the disbelievers. **15.** ˹He is˺ Highly Exalted in rank, Lord of the Throne. He sends down the revelation by His command to whoever He wills of His servants to warn ˹all˺ of the Day of Meeting— **16.** the Day all will appear ˹before Allah˺. Nothing about them will be hidden from Him. ˹He will ask,˺ "Who does all authority belong to this Day? To Allah—the One, the Supreme![959]

---

958 You created us from nothing, then gave us life in the wombs of our mothers, then caused us to die at the end of our worldly lives, and finally resurrected us after our death (*see* 2:28).

959 It is reported in a *ḥadīth* collected by Imâm Muslim that everyone and everything that has ever existed will die on that Day, except for Allah—the Eternal. He will then ask, "Who does all authority belong to this Day? Where are the kings of the world? I am the King." Since no one will be there to answer, Allah will answer Himself, "˹All authority belongs˺ to Allah—the One, the Supreme!"

17. Today every soul will be rewarded for what it has done. No injustice Today! Surely Allah is swift in reckoning."

Horrors of Judgment Day

18. Warn them ˹O Prophet˺ of the approaching Day when the hearts will jump into the throats, suppressing distress. The wrongdoers will have neither a close friend nor intercessor to be heard. **19.** Allah ˹even˺ knows the sly glances of the eyes and whatever the hearts conceal. **20.** And Allah judges with the truth, while those ˹idols˺ they invoke besides Him cannot judge at all. Indeed, Allah ˹alone˺ is the All-Hearing, All-Seeing.

Fate of the Deniers

21. Have they not travelled throughout the land to see what was the end of those ˹destroyed˺ before them? They were far superior in might and ˹richer in˺ monuments throughout the land. But Allah seized them for their sins, and they had no protector from Allah. **22.** That was because their messengers used to come to them with clear proofs, but they persisted in disbelief. So Allah seized them. Surely He is All-Powerful, severe in punishment.

Moses Denied in Egypt

23. Indeed, We sent Moses with Our signs and compelling proof **24.** to Pharaoh, Hamân, and Korah. But they responded: "Magician! Total liar!" **25.** Then, when he came to them with the truth from Us, they said, "Kill the sons of those who believe with him and keep their women." But the plotting of the disbelievers was only in vain.

471 **40. Ghâfir**

26. And Pharaoh said, "Let me kill Moses, and let him call upon his Lord! I truly fear that he may change your traditions or cause mischief in the land." **27.** Moses replied, "I seek refuge in my Lord and your Lord from every arrogant person who does not believe in the Day of Reckoning."

The Believer's Advice: 1)
Do Not Persecute for Belief

28. A believing man from Pharaoh's people, who was hiding his faith, argued, "Will you kill a man[960] 'only' for saying: 'My Lord is Allah,' while he has in fact come to you with clear proofs from your Lord? If he is a liar, it will be to his own loss. But if he is truthful, then you will be afflicted with some of what he is threatening you with. Surely Allah does not guide whoever is a transgressor, a total liar. **29.** O my people! Authority belongs to you today, reigning supreme in the land. But who would help us against the torment of Allah, if it were to befall us?"

Pharaoh's Response

Pharaoh assured 'his people', "I am telling you only what I believe, and I am leading you only to the way of guidance."

Advice 2) Learn from History

30. And the man who believed cautioned, "O my people! I truly fear for you the doom of 'earlier' enemy forces— **31.** like the fate of the people of Noah, 'Âd, Thamûd, and those after them. For Allah would never will to wrong 'His' servants. **32.** O my people! I truly fear for you the Day all will be crying out 'to each other'—

---

960 i.e., Moses (ﷺ).

40. Ghâfir

وَمَ تُوَلُّونَ مُدْبِرِينَ مَا لَكُم مِّنَ ٱللَّهِ مِنْ عَاصِمٍ وَمَن يُضْلِلِ ٱللَّهُ فَمَا لَهُۥ مِنْ هَادٍ ۝ وَلَقَدْ جَآءَكُمْ يُوسُفُ مِن قَبْلُ بِٱلْبَيِّنَٰتِ فَمَا زِلْتُمْ فِى شَكٍّ مِّمَّا جَآءَكُم بِهِۦ حَتَّىٰٓ إِذَا هَلَكَ قُلْتُمْ لَن يَبْعَثَ ٱللَّهُ مِنۢ بَعْدِهِۦ رَسُولًا كَذَٰلِكَ يُضِلُّ ٱللَّهُ مَنْ هُوَ مُسْرِفٌ مُّرْتَابٌ ۝ ٱلَّذِينَ يُجَٰدِلُونَ فِىٓ ءَايَٰتِ ٱللَّهِ بِغَيْرِ سُلْطَٰنٍ أَتَىٰهُمْ كَبُرَ مَقْتًا عِندَ ٱللَّهِ وَعِندَ ٱلَّذِينَ ءَامَنُوا كَذَٰلِكَ يَطْبَعُ ٱللَّهُ عَلَىٰ كُلِّ قَلْبِ مُتَكَبِّرٍ جَبَّارٍ ۝ وَقَالَ فِرْعَوْنُ يَٰهَٰمَٰنُ ٱبْنِ لِى صَرْحًا لَّعَلِّىٓ أَبْلُغُ ٱلْأَسْبَٰبَ ۝ أَسْبَٰبَ ٱلسَّمَٰوَٰتِ فَأَطَّلِعَ إِلَىٰٓ إِلَٰهِ مُوسَىٰ وَإِنِّى لَأَظُنُّهُۥ كَٰذِبًا وَكَذَٰلِكَ زُيِّنَ لِفِرْعَوْنَ سُوٓءُ عَمَلِهِۦ وَصُدَّ عَنِ ٱلسَّبِيلِ وَمَا كَيْدُ فِرْعَوْنَ إِلَّا فِى تَبَابٍ ۝ وَقَالَ ٱلَّذِىٓ ءَامَنَ يَٰقَوْمِ ٱتَّبِعُونِ أَهْدِكُمْ سَبِيلَ ٱلرَّشَادِ ۝ يَٰقَوْمِ إِنَّمَا هَٰذِهِ ٱلْحَيَوٰةُ ٱلدُّنْيَا مَتَٰعٌ وَإِنَّ ٱلْءَاخِرَةَ هِىَ دَارُ ٱلْقَرَارِ ۝ مَنْ عَمِلَ سَيِّئَةً فَلَا يُجْزَىٰٓ إِلَّا مِثْلَهَا وَمَنْ عَمِلَ صَٰلِحًا مِّن ذَكَرٍ أَوْ أُنثَىٰ وَهُوَ مُؤْمِنٌ فَأُو۟لَٰٓئِكَ يَدْخُلُونَ ٱلْجَنَّةَ يُرْزَقُونَ فِيهَا بِغَيْرِ حِسَابٍ ۝

33. the Day you will ˹try in vain to˺ turn your backs and run away, with no one to protect you from Allah. And whoever Allah leaves to stray will be left with no guide. 34. Joseph already came to you[961] earlier with clear proofs, yet you never ceased to doubt what he came to you with. When he died you said, 'Allah will never send a messenger after him.' This is how Allah leaves every transgressor and doubter to stray— 35. those who dispute Allah's signs with no proof given to them. How despicable is that for Allah and the believers! This is how Allah seals the heart of every arrogant tyrant."

Pharaoh's Response

36. Pharaoh ordered, "O Hamân! Build me a high tower so I may reach the pathways 37. leading up to the heavens and look for the God of Moses, although I am sure he is a liar."[962] And so Pharaoh's evil deeds were made so appealing to him that he was hindered from the ˹Right˺ Way. But the plotting of Pharaoh was only in vain.

Advice 3) Mend Your Ways

38. And the man who believed urged, "O my people! Follow me, ˹and˺ I will lead you to the Way of Guidance. 39. O my people! This worldly life is only ˹a fleeting˺ enjoyment, whereas the Hereafter is truly the home of settlement. 40. Whoever does an evil deed will only be paid back with its equivalent. And whoever does good, whether male or female, and is a believer, they will enter Paradise, where they will be provided for without limit.

---

961 Meaning, your ancestors, because Joseph (﷽) died over 400 hundred years before Moses (﷽).
962 See 28:38.

40. Ghâfir

41. O my people! How is it that I invite you to salvation, while you invite me to the Fire! **42.** You invite me to disbelieve in Allah and associate with Him what I have no knowledge of, while I invite you to the Almighty, Most Forgiving. **43.** There is no doubt that whatever ˹idols˺ you invite me to ˹worship˺ are not worthy to be invoked either in this world or the Hereafter.[963] ˹Undoubtedly,˺ our return is to Allah, and the transgressors will be the inmates of the Fire. **44.** You will remember what I say to you, and I entrust my affairs to Allah. Surely Allah is All-Seeing of all ˹His˺ servants."

Allah's Response

45. So Allah protected him from the evil of their schemes. And Pharaoh's people were overwhelmed by an evil punishment: **46.** they are exposed to the Fire ˹in their graves˺ morning and evening. And on the Day the Hour will be established ˹it will be said˺, "Admit Pharaoh's people into the harshest punishment ˹of Hell˺."

Disputes Among Hell's Inmates

47. ˹Consider the Day˺ when they will dispute in the Fire, and the lowly ˹followers˺ will appeal to the arrogant ˹leaders˺, "We were your ˹dedicated˺ followers, will you then shield us from a portion of the Fire?" **48.** The arrogant will say, "We are all in it! ˹For˺ Allah has already passed judgment over ˹His˺ servants."

Appeals from Hell

49. And those in the Fire will cry out to the keepers of Hell,[964] "Pray to your Lord to lighten the torment for us ˹even˺ for one day!"

---

963 Another possible translation: "Without a doubt, whatever ˹gods˺ you are calling me to ˹worship˺ have no claim ˹to divinity˺ in this world or the Hereafter."

964 The verse does not say "Those in the Fire will cry out to its keepers," simply because there are levels in the Fire: those in higher levels will plead to the keepers of the depths of Hell to appeal to Allah to lighten the punishment even for one day, since they think they are better than those at the bottom.

40. Ghâfir 474

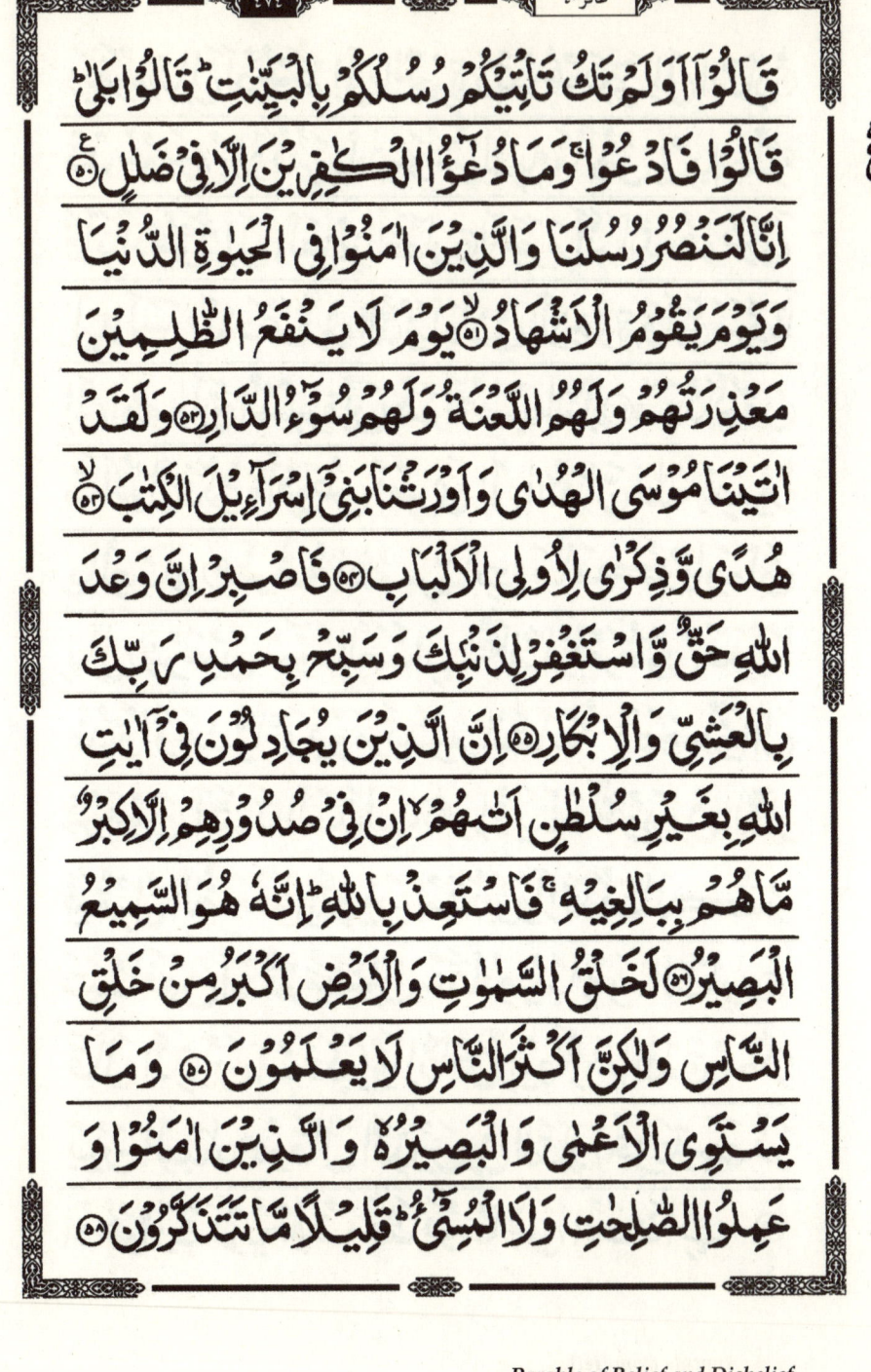

50. The keepers will reply, "Did your messengers not ˹constantly˺ come to you with clear proofs?" They will say, "Yes ˹they did˺." The keepers will say, "Then pray! Though the prayer of the disbelievers is only in vain."

Allah's Help for the Believers

51. We certainly help Our messengers and the believers, ˹both˺ in this worldly life and on the Day the witnesses will stand forth ˹for testimony˺— **52.** the Day the wrongdoers' excuses will be of no benefit to them. They will be condemned, and will have the worst outcome.[965]

Reassuring the Prophet

53. And indeed, We gave Moses ˹true˺ guidance, and made the Children of Israel inherit the Scripture— **54.** a guide and a reminder to people of reason. **55.** So be patient ˹O Prophet˺, ˹for˺ Allah's promise is certainly true. Seek forgiveness for your shortcomings.[966] And glorify the praises of your Lord morning and evening. **56.** Surely those who dispute Allah's signs—with no proof given to them—have nothing in their hearts but greed for dominance, which they will never attain. So seek refuge in Allah. Indeed, He alone is the All-Hearing, All-Seeing.

Greater Creation

57. The creation of the heavens and the earth is certainly greater than the re-creation of humankind, but most people do not know.

Parable of Belief and Disbelief

58. Those blind ˹to the truth˺ and those who can see are not equal, nor are those who believe and do good ˹equal˺ to those who do evil. Yet you are hardly mindful.

---

965 i.e., the Hellfire.
966 Like other prophets, Muḥammad (ﷺ) was infallible of sin. The verse here refers to misjudgments, such as the Prophet's response to the blind man (80:1-10), Jonah's departure from his city without Allah's permission (21:87-88), and David's suspicions of the two men who scaled the wall of his sanctuary (38:21-25). If the Prophet (ﷺ) himself is urged to seek forgiveness, then the believers are even more in need of praying for Allah's forgiveness.

59. The Hour is certainly coming, there is no doubt about it. But most people do not believe.

Allah Answers Prayers

60. Your Lord has proclaimed, "Call upon Me, I will respond to you. Surely those who are too proud to worship Me will enter Hell, fully humbled."

Allah Is Merciful to His Creation

61. It is Allah Who has made the night for you to rest in and the day bright. Surely Allah is ever Bountiful to humanity, but most people are ungrateful. **62.** That is Allah, your Lord, the Creator of all things. There is no god ˹worthy of worship˺ except Him. How can you then be deluded ˹from the truth˺? **63.** This is how those who used to reject Allah's signs were ˹also˺ deluded.

Allah Provides for All

64. It is Allah Who made the earth a place of settlement for you and the sky a canopy. He shaped you ˹in the womb˺, perfecting your form. And He has provided you with what is good and lawful. That is Allah—your Lord. So Blessed is Allah, Lord of all worlds. **65.** He is the Ever-Living. There is no god ˹worthy of worship˺ except Him. So call upon Him with sincere devotion, ˹saying,˺ "All praise is for Allah—Lord of all worlds."

Allah Has Power over Life and Death

66. Say, ˹O Prophet,˺ "I have been forbidden to worship those ˹idols˺ you worship besides Allah, since clear proofs have come to me from my Lord. And I have been commanded to ˹fully˺ submit to the Lord of all worlds."

40. Ghâfir

67. He is the One Who created you[967] from dust, then from a sperm-drop,[968] then ˹developed you into˺ a clinging clot ˹of blood˺,[969] then He brings you forth as infants, so that you may reach your prime, and become old—though some of you ˹may˺ die sooner—reaching an appointed time, so perhaps you may understand ˹Allah's power˺. **68.** He is the One Who gives life and causes death. When He decrees a matter, He simply tells it, "Be!" And it is!

Punishment of the Deniers

69. Have you not seen how those who dispute Allah's signs are turned away? **70.** ˹They are˺ the ones who reject this Book and all ˹scriptures˺ We sent Our messengers with. So they will know ˹the consequences˺ **71.** when shackles will be around their necks and chains ˹on their legs˺. They will be dragged **72.** through boiling water, then burned in the Fire ˹as fuel˺. **73.** Then they will be asked, "Where are those ˹idols˺ you used to associate **74.** with Allah?" They will cry, "They have ˹all˺ failed us. In fact, we did not invoke anything ˹real˺ before." This is how Allah leaves the disbelievers to stray. **75.** ˹They will be told,˺ "This ˹punishment˺ is for being prideful on earth unjustly and for acting arrogantly. **76.** Enter the gates of Hell, to stay there forever. What an evil home for the arrogant!"

Advice to the Prophet

77. So be patient ˹O Prophet˺. Surely Allah's promise is true. Whether We show you some of what We threaten them with, or cause you to die ˹before that˺, to Us they will ˹all˺ be returned.

---

967 Your father, Adam.
968 *Nutfah* refers to the union of male and female gametes (sperm and egg) which results in the zygote after fertilization.
969 *'Alaqah*, meaning the embryo resembles a leech.

78. We already sent messengers before you. We have told you the stories of some of them, while others We have not. It was not for any messenger to bring a sign without Allah's permission. But when Allah's decree comes, judgment will be passed with fairness, and the people of falsehood will then be in ˹total˺ loss.

Some of Allah's Favours

79. It is Allah Who made cattle for you so that you may ride some and eat others. **80.** Also, you find in them ˹other˺ benefits.[970] And by means of them you may reach destinations you desire. And you are carried upon ˹some of˺ them and upon ships. **81.** And He shows you His signs. Now which of Allah's signs will you deny?

More Warning to the Deniers

82. Have they not travelled throughout the land to see what was the end of those who were ˹destroyed˺ before them? They were far superior in number and might and ˹richer in˺ monuments throughout the land, but their ˹worldly˺ gains were of no benefit to them. **83.** When their messengers came to them with clear proofs, they were prideful in whatever ˹worldly˺ knowledge they had,[971] and were ˹ultimately˺ overwhelmed by what they used to ridicule. **84.** When they saw Our punishment, they cried, "˹Now˺ we believe in Allah alone and reject what we had been associating with Him!" **85.** But their faith was of no benefit to them when they saw Our torment. This has ˹always˺ been Allah's way ˹of dealing˺ with His ˹wicked˺ servants. Then and there the disbelievers were in ˹total˺ loss.

---

970 i.e., milk, wool, and hide.
971 And ridiculed the divine knowledge brought to them by their messengers.

41. 'Verses' Perfectly Explained (Fuṣṣilat)

In the Name of Allah—the Most Compassionate, Most Merciful

The Deniers of the Truth

1. *Ḥâ-Mîm.* **2.** 'This is' a revelation from the Most Compassionate, Most Merciful. **3.** 'It is' a Book whose verses are perfectly explained—a Quran in Arabic for people who know, **4.** delivering good news and warning. Yet most of them turn away, so they do not hear. **5.** They say, "Our hearts are veiled against what you are calling us to, there is deafness in our ears, and there is a barrier between us and you. So do 'whatever you want' and so shall we!"

A Message to the Deniers

6. Say, 'O Prophet,' "I am only a man like you, 'but' it has been revealed to me that your God is only One God. So take the Straight Way towards Him, and seek His forgiveness. And woe to the polytheists— **7.** those who do not pay alms-tax and are in denial of the Hereafter. **8.** 'But' those who believe and do good will certainly have a never-ending reward.

A Question to the Deniers

9. Ask 'them, O Prophet', "How can you disbelieve in the One Who created the earth in two Days? How can you set up equals with Him? That is the Lord of all worlds. **10.** He placed on the earth firm mountains, standing high, showered His blessings upon it, and ordained 'all' its means of sustenance—totaling four Days exactly[972]—for all who ask. **11.** Then He turned towards the heaven when it was 'still like' smoke, saying to it and to the earth, 'Submit, willingly or unwillingly.' They both responded, 'We submit willingly.'

---

972 These four Days include the first two, so the total period of creation is six heavenly Days.

12. So He formed the heaven into seven heavens in two Days, assigning to each its mandate. And We adorned the lowest heaven with ˹stars like˺ lamps ˹for beauty˺ and for protection. That is the design of the Almighty, All-Knowing."[973]

The Fate of 'Ãd and Thamûd

13. If they turn away, then say, ˹O Prophet,˺ "I warn you of a ˹mighty˺ blast, like the one that befell 'Ãd and Thamûd." **14.** The messengers had come to them from all angles, ˹proclaiming,˺ "Worship none but Allah." They responded, "Had our Lord willed, He could have easily sent down angels ˹instead˺. So we totally reject what you have been sent with." **15.** As for 'Ãd, they acted arrogantly throughout the land with no right, boasting, "Who is superior to us in might?" Did they not see that Allah ˹Himself˺, Who created them, was far superior to them in might? Still they persisted in denying Our signs. **16.** So We sent against them a furious wind,[974] for ˹several˺ miserable days, to make them taste a humiliating punishment in this worldly life. But far more humiliating will be the punishment of the Hereafter. And they will not be helped. **17.** As for Thamûd, We showed them guidance, but they preferred blindness over guidance. So the blast of a disgracing punishment overtook them for what they used to commit. **18.** And We delivered those who were faithful and were mindful ˹of Allah˺.

Testimony of Organs

19. ˹Consider˺ the Day ˹when˺ the enemies of Allah will be gathered for the Fire, all driven in ranks. **20.** When they reach it, their ears, eyes, and skin will testify against what they used to do.[975]

---

973 *See* footnote for 7:54.
974 lit., a bitter and screaming wind.
975 It is reported in Ibn Kathîr's commentary that, on the Day of Judgment, the wicked will deny the evil deeds in their records—as a desperate attempt to escape the horrible punishment in Hell. They will be asked if they accept Allah, the angels, or even their own families and neighbours as witnesses, but they will refuse. So Allah will make their organs testify against them.

21. They will ask their skin ˹furiously˺, "Why have you testified against us?" It will say, "We have been made to speak by Allah, Who causes all things to speak. He ˹is the One Who˺ created you the first time, and to Him you were bound to return. **22.** You did not ˹bother to˺ hide yourselves from your ears, eyes, and skin to prevent them from testifying against you. Rather, you assumed that Allah did not know much of what you used to do. **23.** It was that ˹false˺ assumption you entertained about your Lord that has brought about your doom, so you have become losers." **24.** Even if they endure patiently, the Fire will ˹always˺ be their home. And if they ˹beg to˺ appease ˹their Lord˺, they will never be allowed to.

What Caused That Fate

25. We placed at their disposal ˹evil˺ associates who made their past and future ˹misdeeds˺ appealing to them.[976] ˹So˺ the fate of earlier communities of jinn and humans has been justified against them ˹as well˺, ˹for˺ they were truly losers. **26.** The disbelievers advised ˹one another˺, "Do not listen to this Quran but drown it out so that you may prevail." **27.** So We will certainly make the disbelievers taste a severe punishment, and We will surely repay them according to the worst of their deeds. **28.** That is the reward of Allah's enemies: the Fire, which will be their eternal home— a ˹fitting˺ reward for their denial of Our revelations.

---

976 i.e., associating others with Allah in worship and denying the Hereafter. *See* 43:36-37.

29. The disbelievers will ˹then˺ cry, "Our Lord! Show us those jinn and humans who led us astray: we will put them under our feet so that they will be among the lowest ˹in Hell˺."

Reward of the Devout

30. Surely those who say, "Our Lord is Allah," and then remain steadfast, the angels descend upon them,[977] ˹saying,˺ "Do not fear, nor grieve. Rather, rejoice in the good news of Paradise, which you have been promised. **31.** We are your supporters in this worldly life and in the Hereafter. There you will have whatever your souls desire, and there you will have whatever you ask for: **32.** an accommodation from the All-Forgiving, Most Merciful ˹Lord˺."

Qualities of True Believers

33. And whose words are better than someone who calls ˹others˺ to Allah, does good, and says, "I am truly one of those who submit."?[978] **34.** Good and evil cannot be equal. Respond ˹to evil˺ with what is best, then the one you are in a feud with will be like a close friend. **35.** But this cannot be attained except by those who are patient and who are truly fortunate. **36.** And if you are tempted by Satan, then seek refuge with Allah. Indeed, He ˹alone˺ is the All-Hearing, All-Knowing.

Worship the Creator, Marvel at Creation

37. Among His signs are the day and the night, the sun and the moon. Do not prostrate to the sun or the moon, but prostrate to Allah, Who created them ˹all˺, if you ˹truly˺ worship Him ˹alone˺. **38.** But if the pagans are too proud, then ˹let them know that˺ those ˹angels˺ nearest to your Lord glorify Him day and night, and never grow weary.

---

977 Especially at the time of their death.
978 lit., Muslims.

39. And among His signs is that you see the earth devoid of life, but as soon as We send down rain upon it, it begins to stir ˹to life˺ and swell. Indeed, the One Who revives it can easily revive the dead. He is certainly Most Capable of everything.

Warning to the Quran Deniers

40. Indeed, those who abuse Our revelations[979] are not hidden from Us. Who is better: the one who will be cast into the Fire or the one who will be secure on Judgment Day? Do whatever you want. He is certainly All-Seeing of what you do. **41.** Indeed, those who deny the Reminder[980] after it has come to them ˹are doomed˺, for it is truly a mighty Book. **42.** It cannot be proven false from any angle. ˹It is˺ a revelation from the ˹One Who is˺ All-Wise, Praiseworthy. **43.** ˹O Prophet!˺ Nothing is said to you ˹by the deniers˺ except what was already said to the messengers before you. Surely your Lord is ˹the Lord˺ of forgiveness and painful punishment.

Response to Demanding Non-Arabic Quran

44. Had We revealed it as a non-Arabic Quran, they would have certainly argued, "If only its verses were made clear ˹in our language˺. What! A non-Arabic revelation for an Arab audience!" Say, ˹O Prophet,˺ "It is a guide and a healing to the believers. As for those who disbelieve, there is deafness in their ears and blindness to it ˹in their hearts˺. It is as if they are being called from a faraway place."[981]

Moses Was Denied Too

45. Indeed, We had given Moses the Scripture, but differences arose regarding it. Had it not been for a prior decree from your Lord,[982] their differences would have been settled ˹at once˺. They are truly in alarming doubt about it.

The Good and the Wicked

46. Whoever does good, it is to their own benefit. And whoever does evil, it is to their own loss. Your Lord is never unjust to ˹His˺ creation.

---

979 This refers to the noise the disbelievers used to make when the Quran was recited (see 41:26), or those who twist the meaning of Quranic passages and take them out of context.
980 The Reminder is one of the names of the Quran.
981 So they neither hear nor understand the call.
982 That He will delay their judgment until the Hereafter.

Allah's Infinite Knowledge

47. With Him ʿaloneʾ is the knowledge of the Hour. No fruit comes out of its husk, nor does a female conceive or deliver without His knowledge.

Polytheists on Judgment Day

And ʿconsiderʾ the Day He will call to them, "Where are My ʿso-calledʾ associate-gods?" They will cry, "We declare before you that none of us testifies to that ʿany longerʾ." **48.** Whatever ʿidolsʾ they used to invoke besides Allah will fail them. And they will realize that they will have no escape.

Ingratitude of the Deniers

49. One never tires of praying for good. And if touched with evil, they become desperate and hopeless. **50.** And if We let them taste a mercy from Us after being touched with adversity, they will certainly say, "This is what I deserve. I do not think the Hour will ʿeverʾ come. And if in fact I am returned to my Lord, the finest reward with Him will definitely be mine." But We will surely inform the disbelievers of what they used to do. And We will certainly make them taste a harsh torment. **51.** When We show favour to someone, they turn away, acting arrogantly. And when touched with evil, they make endless prayers ʿfor goodʾ.

Denying Allah's Revelation

52. Ask ʿthem, O Prophetʾ, "Imagine if this ʿQuranʾ is ʿtrulyʾ from Allah and you deny it: who can be more astray than those who have gone too far in opposition ʿto the truthʾ?"

Creation Testifies to the Truth

53. We will show them Our signs in the universe and within themselves until it becomes clear to them that this ʿQuranʾ is the truth. Is it not enough that your Lord is a Witness over all things? **54.** They are truly in doubt of the meeting with their Lord! ʿButʾ He is indeed Fully Aware of everything.

42. Ash-Shûra

42. Consultation (Ash-Shûra)

In the Name of Allah—the Most Compassionate, Most Merciful

Allah Almighty

1. Ḥâ-Mîm. 2. 'Aĩn-Sĩn-Qâf. 3. And so you ˹O Prophet˺ are sent revelation, just like those before you, by Allah—the Almighty, All-Wise. 4. To Him belongs whatever is in the heavens and whatever is on the earth. And He is the Most High, the Greatest. 5. The heavens nearly burst, one above the other, ˹in awe of Him˺. And the angels glorify the praises of their Lord, and seek forgiveness for those on earth. Surely Allah alone is the All-Forgiving, Most Merciful.

Allah Is the Protector

6. As for those who take other protectors besides Him, Allah is Watchful over them. And you ˹O Prophet˺ are not a keeper over them. 7. And so We have revealed to you a Quran in Arabic, so you may warn the Mother of Cities[983] and everyone around it, and warn of the Day of Gathering—about which there is no doubt—˹when˺ a group will be in Paradise and another in the Blaze. 8. Had Allah willed, He could have easily made all ˹humanity˺ into a single community ˹of believers˺. But He admits into His mercy whoever He wills. And the wrongdoers will have no protector or helper. 9. How can they take protectors besides Him? Allah alone is the Protector. He ˹alone˺ gives life to the dead. And He ˹alone˺ is Most Capable of everything.

Advice to the Believers

10. ˹Say to the believers, O Prophet,˺ "Whatever you may differ about, its judgment rests with Allah. That is Allah—my Lord. In Him I put my trust, and to Him I ˹always˺ turn."

---

983 "The Mother of Cities" is an honorary title given to the City of Mecca because of its great religious significance as the home of Allah's first house of worship ever built on earth, and perhaps because of its central location as well.

42. Ash-Shûra

Allah Is the Creator and Provider

11. ˹He is˺ the Originator of the heavens and the earth. He has made for you spouses from among yourselves, and ˹made˺ mates for cattle ˹as well˺—multiplying you ˹both˺. There is nothing like Him, for He ˹alone˺ is the All-Hearing, All-Seeing. 12. To Him belong the keys ˹of the treasuries˺ of the heavens and the earth. He gives abundant or limited provisions to whoever He wills. Indeed, He has ˹perfect˺ knowledge of all things.

One Message, Different Laws[984]

13. He has ordained for you ˹believers˺ the Way which He decreed for Noah, and what We have revealed to you ˹O Prophet˺ and what We decreed for Abraham, Moses, and Jesus,[985] ˹commanding:˺ "Uphold the faith, and make no divisions in it." What you call the polytheists to is unbearable for them. Allah chooses for Himself whoever He wills, and guides to Himself whoever turns ˹to Him˺. 14. They did not split ˹into sects˺ out of mutual envy until knowledge came to them.[986] Had it not been for a prior decree from your Lord for an appointed term,[987] the matter would have certainly been settled between them ˹at once˺. And surely those who were made to inherit the Scripture[988] after them are truly in alarming doubt about this ˹Quran˺.

Call to the People of the Book

15. Because of that, you ˹O Prophet˺ will invite ˹all˺. Be steadfast as you are commanded, and do not follow their desires. And say, "I believe in every Scripture Allah has revealed. And I am commanded to judge fairly among you. Allah is our Lord and your Lord. We will be accountable for our deeds and you for yours. There is no ˹need for˺ contention between us. Allah will gather us together ˹for judgment˺. And to Him is the final return."

---

984 All prophets came with the same message: have faith in one God and do good. But each faith-community had their own law.
985 Like 33:7, this verse names the five greatest prophets of Islam: Noah, Abraham, Moses, Jesus, and Muḥammad (ﷺ).
986 No community split into believers and disbelievers until they received the knowledge given by their prophet.
987 That He will delay their judgment until the Hereafter.
988 i.e., the Jews and Christians.

وَٱلَّذِينَ يُحَآجُّونَ فِى ٱللَّهِ مِنۢ بَعْدِ مَا ٱسْتُجِيبَ لَهُۥ حُجَّتُهُمْ دَاحِضَةٌ عِندَ رَبِّهِمْ وَعَلَيْهِمْ غَضَبٌ وَلَهُمْ عَذَابٌ شَدِيدٌ ۝

ٱللَّهُ ٱلَّذِىٓ أَنزَلَ ٱلْكِتَٰبَ بِٱلْحَقِّ وَٱلْمِيزَانَ وَمَا يُدْرِيكَ لَعَلَّ ٱلسَّاعَةَ قَرِيبٌ ۝ يَسْتَعْجِلُ بِهَا ٱلَّذِينَ لَا يُؤْمِنُونَ بِهَا وَٱلَّذِينَ ءَامَنُوا۟ مُشْفِقُونَ مِنْهَا وَيَعْلَمُونَ أَنَّهَا ٱلْحَقُّ أَلَآ إِنَّ ٱلَّذِينَ يُمَارُونَ فِى ٱلسَّاعَةِ لَفِى ضَلَٰلٍۭ بَعِيدٍ ۝

ٱللَّهُ لَطِيفٌۢ بِعِبَادِهِۦ يَرْزُقُ مَن يَشَآءُ وَهُوَ ٱلْقَوِىُّ ٱلْعَزِيزُ ۝

مَن كَانَ يُرِيدُ حَرْثَ ٱلْءَاخِرَةِ نَزِدْ لَهُۥ فِى حَرْثِهِۦ وَمَن كَانَ يُرِيدُ حَرْثَ ٱلدُّنْيَا نُؤْتِهِۦ مِنْهَا وَمَا لَهُۥ فِى ٱلْءَاخِرَةِ مِن نَّصِيبٍ ۝ أَمْ لَهُمْ شُرَكَٰٓؤُا۟ شَرَعُوا۟ لَهُم مِّنَ ٱلدِّينِ مَا لَمْ يَأْذَنۢ بِهِ ٱللَّهُ وَلَوْلَا كَلِمَةُ ٱلْفَصْلِ لَقُضِىَ بَيْنَهُمْ وَإِنَّ ٱلظَّٰلِمِينَ لَهُمْ عَذَابٌ أَلِيمٌ ۝ تَرَى ٱلظَّٰلِمِينَ مُشْفِقِينَ مِمَّا كَسَبُوا۟ وَهُوَ وَاقِعٌۢ بِهِمْ وَٱلَّذِينَ ءَامَنُوا۟ وَعَمِلُوا۟ ٱلصَّٰلِحَٰتِ فِى رَوْضَاتِ ٱلْجَنَّاتِ لَهُم مَّا يَشَآءُونَ عِندَ رَبِّهِمْ ذَٰلِكَ هُوَ ٱلْفَضْلُ ٱلْكَبِيرُ ۝

16. As for those who dispute about Allah after He is ʿalreadyʾ acknowledged ʿby manyʾ, their argument is futile in the sight of their Lord. Upon them is wrath, and they will suffer a severe punishment.

A Reminder of the Hour

17. It is Allah Who has revealed the Book with the truth and the balance ʿof justiceʾ. You never know, perhaps the Hour is near.
18. Those who disbelieve in it ʿask toʾ hasten it ʿmockinglyʾ. But the believers are fearful of it, knowing that it is the truth. Surely those who dispute about the Hour have gone far astray.

Allah's Graciousness

19. Allah is Ever Kind to His servants. He provides ʿabundantlyʾ to whoever He wills. And He is the All-Powerful, Almighty.

Worldly Gains and Heavenly Rewards

20. Whoever desires the harvest of the Hereafter, We will increase their harvest. And whoever desires ʿonlyʾ the harvest of this world, We will give them some of it, but they will have no share in the Hereafter.

Reward of the Believers and Polytheists

21. Or do they have associate-gods who have ordained for them some ʿpolytheisticʾ beliefs, which Allah has not authorized? Had it not been for ʿpriorʾ decree on Judgment, the matter would have certainly been settled between them ʿat onceʾ. And surely the wrongdoers will suffer a painful punishment. **22.** You will see the wrongdoers fearful ʿof the punishmentʾ for what they committed but it will be inevitable for them, whereas those who believe and do good will be in the lush Gardens of Paradise. They will have whatever they desire from their Lord. That is ʿtrulyʾ the greatest bounty.

487   42. Ash-Shûra

23. That ʿreward˺ is the good news which Allah gives to His servants who believe and do good.

Appeal to Meccan Pagans

Say, ʿO Prophet,˺ "I do not ask you for a reward for this ʿmessage˺—only honour for ʿour˺ kinship."[989] Whoever earns a good deed, We will increase it in goodness for them. Surely Allah is All-Forgiving, Most Appreciative.

The Quran Fabricated?

24. Or do they say, "He has fabricated a lie about Allah!"? ʿIf you had,˺ Allah would have sealed your heart, if He willed. And Allah wipes out falsehood and establishes the truth by His Words. He certainly knows best what is ʿhidden˺ in the heart.

Allah's Grace and Might

25. He is the One Who accepts repentance from His servants and pardons ʿtheir˺ sins. And He knows whatever you do. **26.** He responds to those who believe and do good, and increases their reward out of His grace. As for the disbelievers, they will suffer a severe punishment.

Allah's Mercy: Provisions and Rain

27. Had Allah given abundant provisions to ʿall˺ His servants, they would have certainly transgressed throughout the land. But He sends down whatever He wills in perfect measure. He is truly All-Aware, All-Seeing of His servants. **28.** He is the One Who sends down rain after people have given up hope, spreading out His mercy. He is the Guardian, the Praiseworthy.

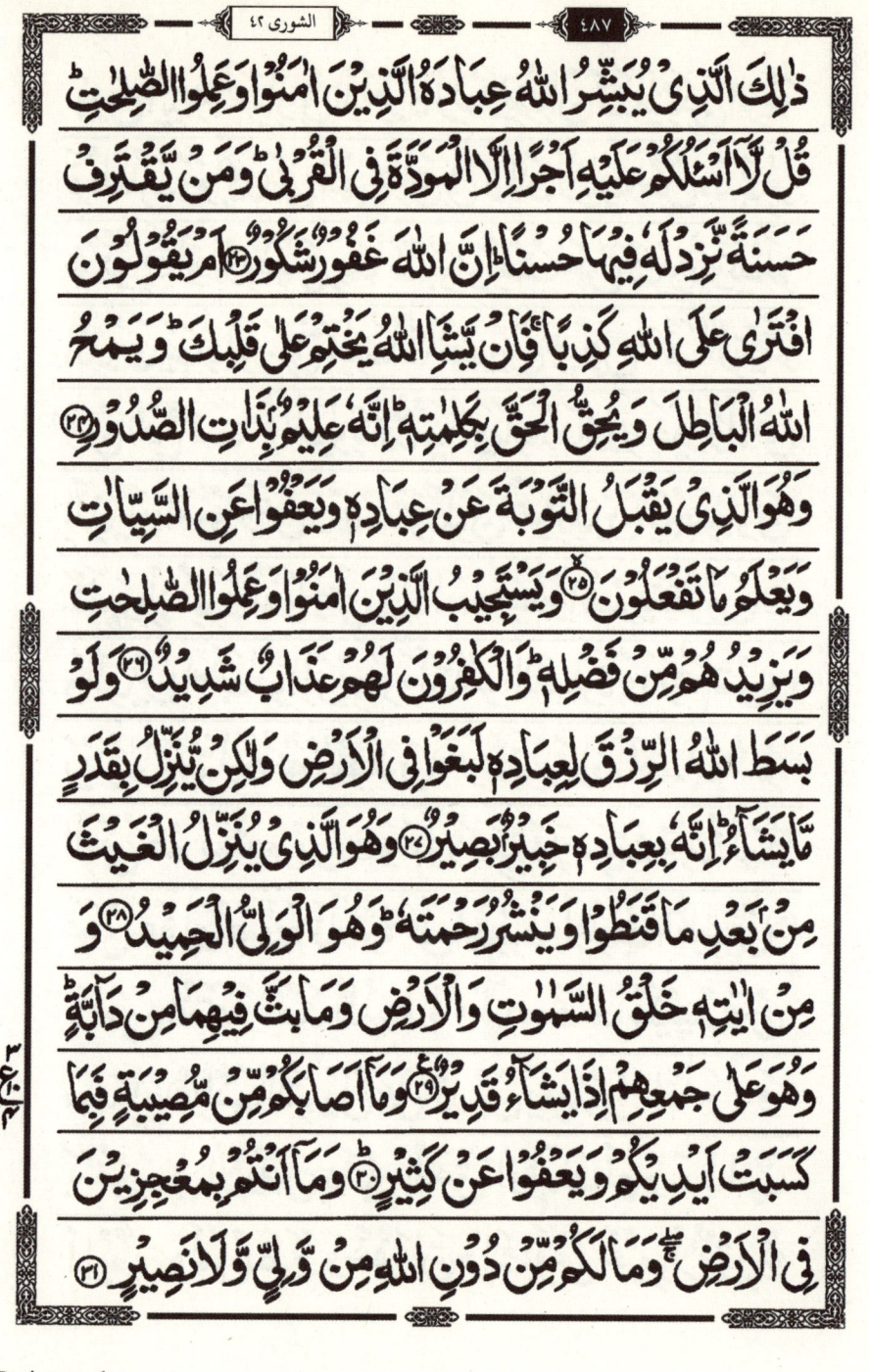

Allah's Mercy: The Universe

29. And among His signs is the creation of the heavens and the earth, and all living beings He dispersed throughout both. And He is Most Capable of bringing all together whenever He wills. **30.** Whatever affliction befalls you is because of what your own hands have committed. And He pardons much. **31.** You can never escape ʿHim˺ on earth, nor do you have any protector or helper besides Allah.

---

989 This could also be a call to all believers to love and respect the immediate family of the Prophet (☙).

42. Ash-Shûra

Allah's Mercy: Sailing Ships

32. And among His signs are the ships like mountains ˹sailing˺ in the sea. **33.** If He wills, He can calm the wind, leaving the ships motionless on the water. Surely in this are signs for whoever is steadfast, grateful. **34.** Or He can wreck the ships for what the people have committed—though He forgives much— **35.** so those who dispute about Our signs may know that they have no refuge.

Qualities of the Devout

36. Whatever ˹pleasure˺ you have been given is ˹no more than a fleeting˺ enjoyment of this worldly life. But what is with Allah is far better and more lasting for those who believe and put their trust in their Lord; **37.** who avoid major sins and shameful deeds, and forgive when angered; **38.** who respond to their Lord, establish prayer, conduct their affairs by mutual consultation, and donate from what We have provided for them; **39.** and who enforce justice when wronged. **40.** The reward of an evil deed is its equivalent. But whoever pardons and seeks reconciliation, then their reward is with Allah. He certainly does not like the wrongdoers. **41.** There is no blame on those who enforce justice after being wronged. **42.** Blame is only on those who wrong people and transgress in the land unjustly. It is they who will suffer a painful punishment. **43.** And whoever endures patiently and forgives—surely this is a resolve to aspire to.

42. Ash-Shûra

The Wicked on Judgment Day

44. And whoever Allah leaves to stray will have no guide after Him. You will see the wrongdoers, when they face the torment, pleading, "Is there any way back ˹to the world˺?"
45. And you will see them exposed to the Fire, fully humbled out of disgrace, stealing glances ˹at it˺. And the believers will say, "The ˹true˺ losers are those who have lost themselves and their families on Judgment Day." The wrongdoers will certainly be in everlasting torment.
46. They will have no protectors to help them against Allah. And whoever Allah leaves to stray, for them there is no way.

Warning to the Disbelievers

47. Respond to your Lord before the coming of a Day from Allah that cannot be averted. There will be no refuge for you then, nor ˹grounds for˺ denial ˹of sins˺.[990] **48.** But if they turn away, We have not sent you ˹O Prophet˺ as a keeper over them. Your duty is only to deliver ˹the message˺.

Ungrateful Disbelievers

And indeed, when We let someone taste a mercy from Us, they become prideful ˹because˺ of it. But when afflicted with evil because of what their hands have done, then one becomes totally ungrateful.[991]

Allah's Gift of Children

49. To Allah ˹alone˺ belongs the kingdom of the heavens and the earth. He creates whatever He wills.

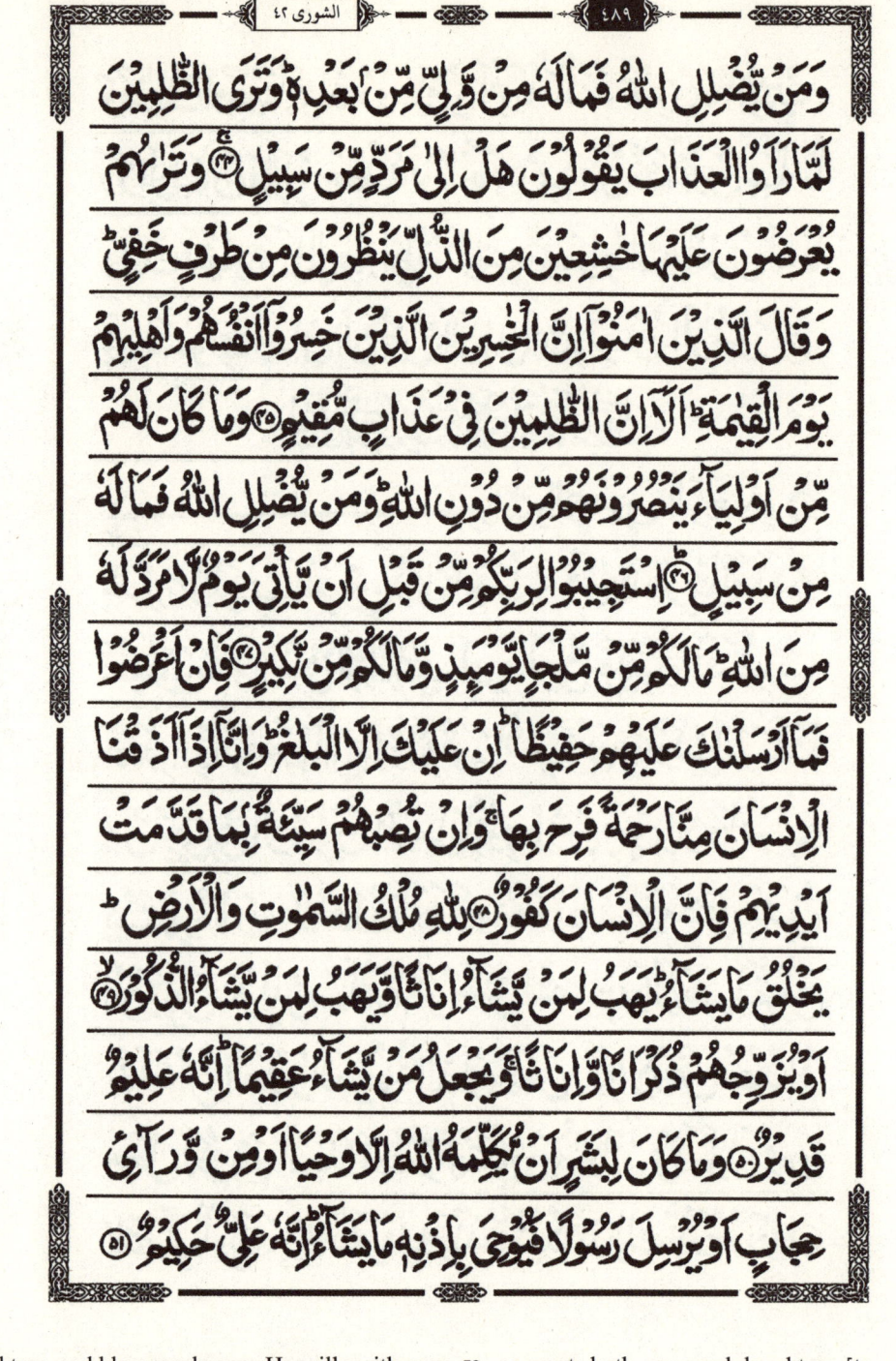

He blesses whoever He wills with daughters, and blesses whoever He wills with sons, **50.** or grants both, sons and daughters, ˹to whoever He wills˺, and leaves whoever He wills infertile. He is indeed All-Knowing, Most Capable.

Forms of Divine Communication

51. It is not ˹possible˺ for a human being to have Allah communicate with them, except through inspiration, or from behind a veil, or by sending a messenger-angel to reveal whatever He wills by His permission. He is surely Most High, All-Wise.

---

990 Other possible translations: 1. "You will have no refuge then, nor will you have an advocate ˹against punishment˺." 2. "You will have no refuge then, nor ˹grounds˺ to protest ˹the torment˺."
991 They totally deny previous favours.

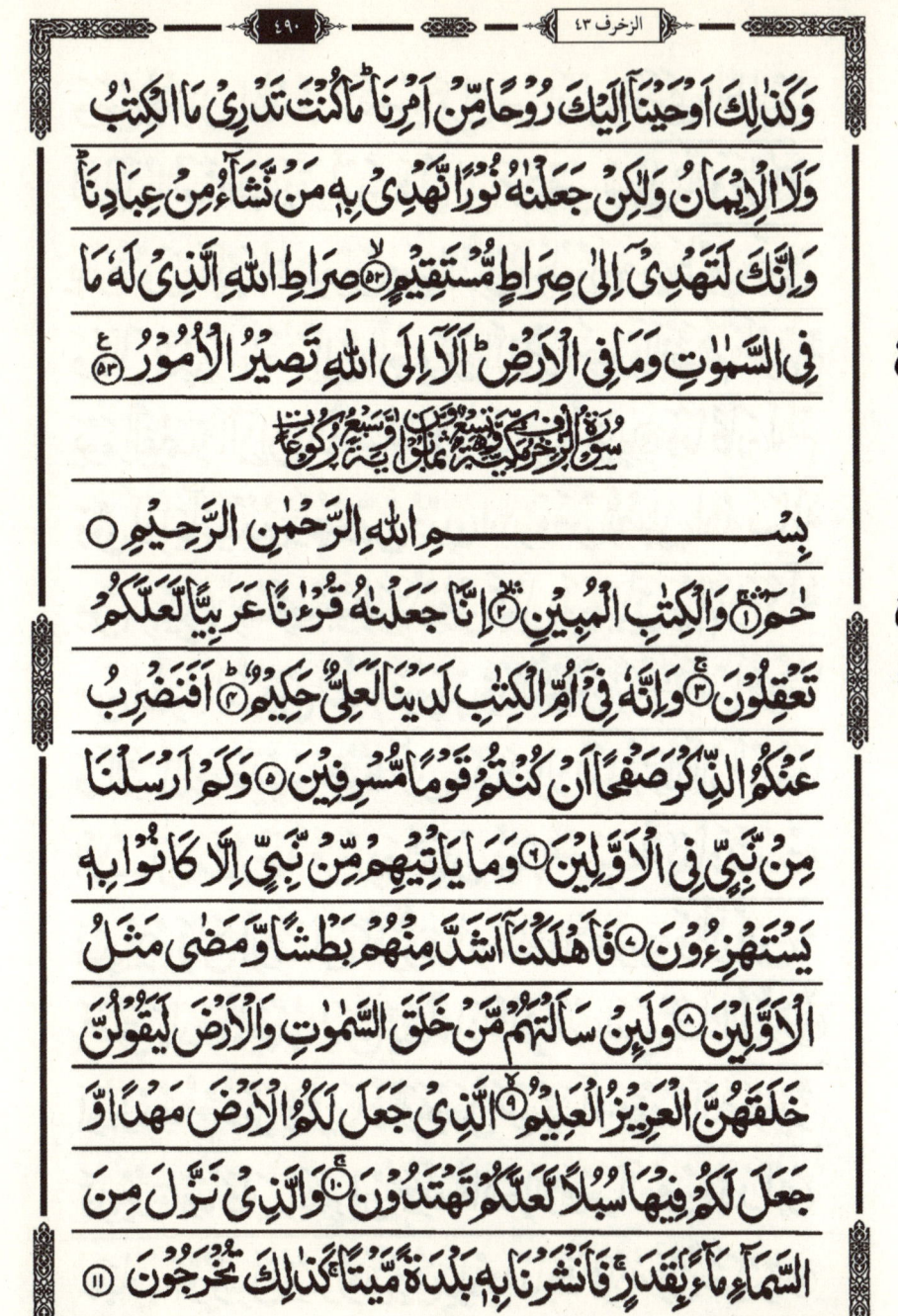

The Light of the Quran

52. And so We have sent to you ˹O Prophet˺ a revelation by Our command. You did not know of ˹this˺ Book and faith ˹before˺. But We have made it a light, by which We guide whoever We will of Our servants. And you are truly leading ˹all˺ to the Straight Path— 53. the Path of Allah, to Whom belongs whatever is in the heavens and whatever is on the earth. Surely to Allah all matters will return ˹for judgment˺.

43. Ornaments (Az-Zukhruf)

In the Name of Allah—the Most Compassionate, Most Merciful

Excellence of the Quran

1. *Ḥâ-Mîm.* 2. By the clear Book! 3. Certainly, We have made it a Quran in Arabic so perhaps you will understand. 4. And indeed, it is—in the Master Record[992] with Us—highly esteemed, rich in wisdom.

Warning to the Deniers

5. Should We then turn the ˹Quranic˺ Reminder away from you ˹simply˺ because you have been a transgressing people? 6. ˹Imagine˺ how many prophets We sent to those ˹destroyed˺ before! 7. But no prophet ever came to them without being mocked. 8. So We destroyed those who were far mightier than these ˹Meccans˺. The examples of ˹their˺ predecessors have ˹already˺ been related.[993]

Allah Is the Creator

9. If you ask them ˹O Prophet˺ who created the heavens and the earth, they will certainly say, "The Almighty, All-Knowing did." 10. ˹He is the One˺ Who has laid out the earth for you, and set in it pathways for you so that you may find your way. 11. And ˹He is the One˺ Who sends down rain from the sky in perfect measure, with which We give life to a lifeless land. And so will you be brought forth ˹from the grave˺.

---

992 This refers to the Preserved Tablet, *Al-Lawḥ Al-Maḥfûẓ*, in which Allah has written the destiny of His entire creation.
993 For example, in the stories of the people of Noah, Lot, Shu'aib and other nations that were destroyed, found throughout the Quran.

12. And ˹He is the One˺ Who created all ˹things in˺ pairs,[994] and made for you ships and animals to ride **13.** so that you may sit firmly on their backs, and remember your Lord's blessings once you are settled on them, saying, "Glory be to the One Who has subjected these for us, for we could have never done so ˹on our own˺. **14.** And surely to our Lord we will ˹all˺ return."

Allah's Daughters?

15. Still the pagans have made some of His creation out to be a part of Him.[995] Indeed, humankind is clearly ungrateful. **16.** Has He taken ˹angels as His˺ daughters from what He created, and favoured you ˹O pagans˺ with sons? **17.** Whenever one of them is given the good news of what they attribute to the Most Compassionate,[996] his face grows gloomy, as he suppresses his rage. **18.** ˹Do they attribute to Him˺ those who are brought up in fineries and are not commanding in disputes? **19.** Still they have labelled the angels, who are servants of the Most Compassionate, as female. Did they witness their creation? Their statement will be recorded, and they will be questioned!

Blind Following

20. And they argue, "Had the Most Compassionate willed, we would have never worshipped them." They have no knowledge ˹in support˺ of this ˹claim˺. They do nothing but lie. **21.** Or have We given them a Book ˹for proof˺, before this ˹Quran˺, to which they are holding firm? **22.** In fact, they say, "We found our forefathers following a ˹particular˺ way, and we are following in their footsteps." **23.** Similarly, whenever We sent a warner to a society before you ˹O Prophet˺, its ˹spoiled˺ elite would say, "We found our forefathers following a ˹particular˺ way, and we are walking in their footsteps."

---

994 For example, male and female, sweet and bitter, day and night, plains and mountains, heat and cold, light and darkness.
995 See footnote for 37:149.
996 i.e., the birth of a baby girl.

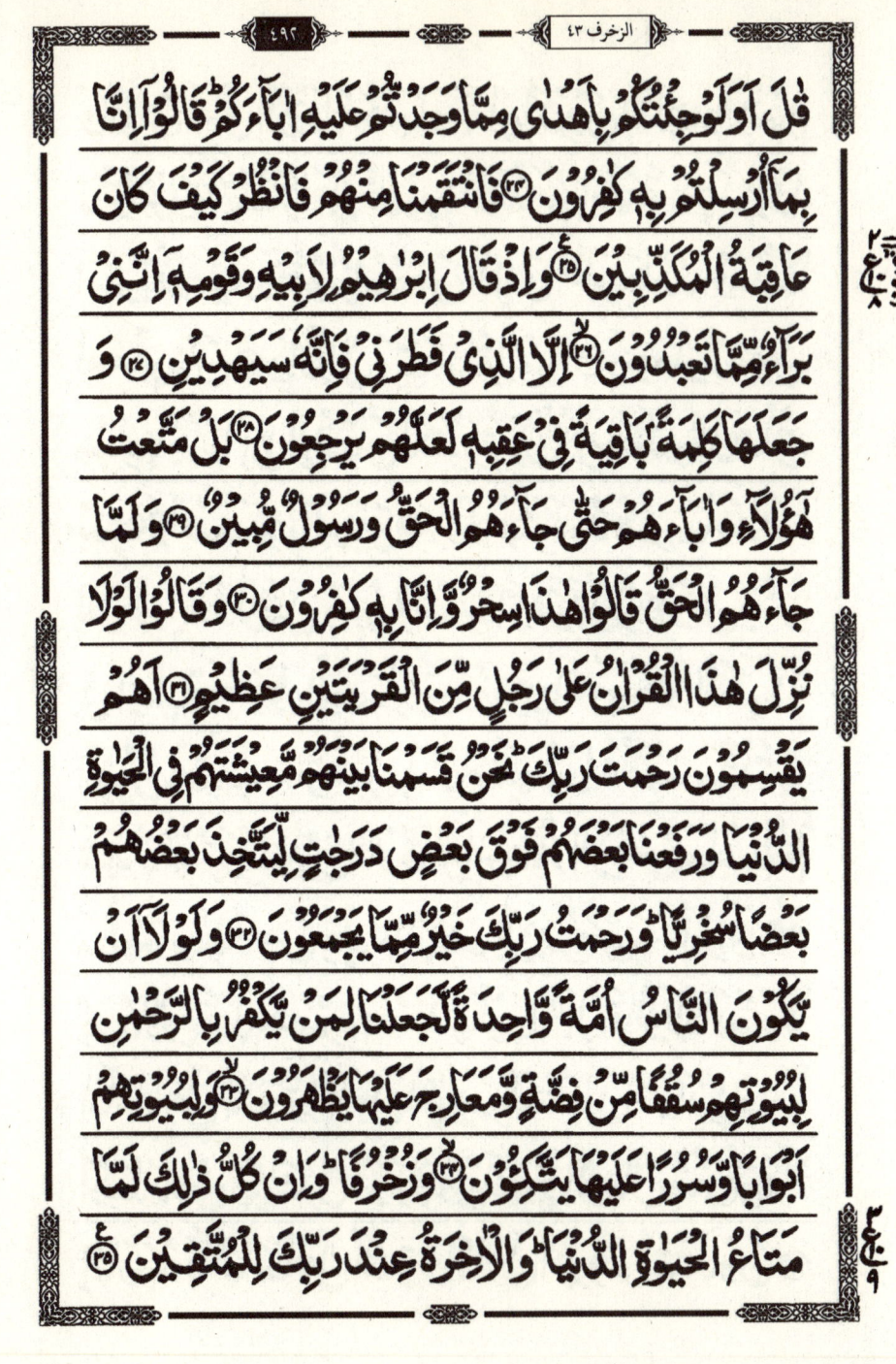

24. Each ˹warner˺ asked, "Even if what I brought you is better guidance than what you found your forefathers practicing?" They replied, "We totally reject whatever you have been sent with." **25.** So We inflicted punishment upon them. See then what was the fate of the deniers!

The Case of Abraham's People

26. ˹Remember, O Prophet˺ when Abraham declared to his father and his people, "I am totally free of whatever ˹gods˺ you worship, **27.** except the One Who originated me, and He will surely guide me." **28.** And he left this enduring declaration among his descendants, so they may ˹always˺ turn back ˹to Allah˺.[997]

The Case of Meccan Pagans

29. In fact, I had allowed enjoyment for these ˹Meccans˺ and their forefathers, until the truth came to them along with a messenger making things clear. **30.** ˹But˺ when the truth came to them, they said, "This is magic, and we totally reject it." **31.** And they exclaimed, "If only this Quran was revealed to a great man from ˹one of˺ the two cities!"[998] **32.** Is it they who distribute your Lord's mercy? We ˹alone˺ have distributed their ˹very˺ livelihood among them in this worldly life and raised some of them in rank above others so that some may employ others in service. ˹But˺ your Lord's mercy is far better than whatever ˹wealth˺ they amass.

Worthlessness of Material Wealth

33. Were it not that people might ˹be tempted to˺ become one community ˹of disbelievers˺, We would have supplied the homes of ˹only˺ those who disbelieve in the Most Compassionate with silver roofs and ˹silver˺ stairways to ascend, **34.** as well as ˹silver˺ gates and thrones to recline on, **35.** and ornaments ˹of gold˺. Yet all this is no more than a ˹fleeting˺ enjoyment in this worldly life. ˹But˺ the Hereafter with your Lord is ˹only˺ for those mindful ˹of Him˺.

---

997 *See* 2:130-132.
1000 This refers to Mecca and Ṭâif, two cities in Arabia, around 100 km apart.

43. Az-Zukhruf

Devilish Associates

36. And whoever turns a blind eye to the Reminder of the Most Compassionate, We place at the disposal of each a devilish one as their close associate, **37.** who will certainly hinder them from the ˹Right˺ Way while they think they are ˹rightly˺ guided. **38.** But when such a person comes to Us, one will say ˹to their associate˺, "I wish you were as distant from me as the east is from the west! What an evil associate ˹you were˺!" **39.** ˹It will be said to both,˺ "Since you all did wrong, sharing in the punishment will be of no benefit to you this Day."[999]

Advice to the Prophet

40. Can you make the deaf hear, or guide the blind or those clearly astray? **41.** Even if We take you away ˹from this world˺, We will surely inflict punishment upon them. **42.** Or if We show you what We threaten them with, We certainly have full power over them. **43.** So hold firmly to what has been revealed to you ˹O Prophet˺. You are truly on the Straight Path. **44.** Surely this ˹Quran˺ is a glory for you and your people. And you will ˹all˺ be questioned ˹about it˺. **45.** Ask ˹the followers of˺ the messengers that We already sent before you if We ˹ever˺ appointed ˹other˺ gods to be worshipped besides the Most Compassionate.

The Case of Pharaoh's People

46. Indeed, We sent Moses with Our signs to Pharaoh and his chiefs, and he said: "I am a messenger of the Lord of all worlds." **47.** But as soon as he came to them with Our signs, they laughed at them, **48.** although every sign We showed them was greater than the one before.[1000] Ultimately, We seized them with torments so that they might return ˹to the Right Path˺.[1001] **49.** ˹Then˺ they pleaded, "O ˹mighty˺ magician! Pray to your Lord on our behalf, by virtue of the covenant He made with you.[1002] We will certainly accept guidance."

---

999 From a worldly perspective, many people are comforted when they hear of others who went through similar trials as them. But this will not be the case on Judgment Day. Everyone will be desperate to save themselves from the punishment, regardless of others.
1000 i.e., the hand and the staff (see 20:17-22).
1001 The torments were: famine, shortage of crops, floods, locusts, lice, frogs, and blood (see 7:130-133).
1002 See 7:134.

50. But as soon as We removed the torments from them, they broke their promise.

Pharaoh's Arrogance

51. And Pharaoh called out to his people, boasting, "O my people! Am I not sovereign over Egypt as well as ˹all˺ these streams[1003] flowing at my feet? Can you not see? **52.** Am I not better than this nobody who can hardly express himself?[1004] **53.** Why then have no golden bracelets ˹of kingship˺ been granted to him or angels come with him as escorts!" **54.** And so he fooled his people, and they obeyed him. They were truly a rebellious people. **55.** So when they enraged Us, We inflicted punishment upon them, drowning them all. **56.** And We made them an example and a lesson for those after them.

All Objects of Worship in Hell?

57. When the son of Mary was cited as an example ˹in argument˺, your people ˹O Prophet˺ broke into ˹joyful˺ applause.[1005] **58.** They exclaimed, "Which is better: our gods or Jesus?" They cite him only to argue. In fact, they are a people prone to dispute. **59.** He was only a servant We showed favour to, and made as an example for the Children of Israel. **60.** Had We willed, We could have easily replaced you ˹all˺ with angels,[1006] succeeding one another on earth. **61.** And his ˹second˺ coming is truly a sign for the Hour. So have no doubt about it, and follow me. This is the Straight Path. **62.** And do not let Satan hinder you, ˹for˺ he is certainly your sworn enemy.

The Truth About Jesus

63. When Jesus came with clear proofs, he declared, "I have come to you with wisdom, and to clarify to you some of what you differ about. So fear Allah, and obey me.

1003 Branches of the Nile.
1004 Moses used to have a speech impediment. But when he became a prophet he prayed to Allah to help him speak clearly, and his prayer was answered (*see* 20:25-36).
1005 When 21:98 was revealed, warning the polytheists that all false gods will be in Hell, 'Abdullâh ibn Az-Ziba'ra, a poet who always attacked Islam, argued with the Prophet (ﷺ) that if what the verse says is true, then Jesus will be in Hell as well! The polytheists, who were present, laughed in agreement with this argument. The Prophet (ﷺ) replied that the verse was talking exclusively about idols, adding that Jesus himself did not ask anyone to worship him. Verse 21:101 was later revealed in support of the Prophet's argument. Eventually, 'Abdullâh accepted Islam.
1006 Or "We could have easily produced angels from you …"

64. Surely Allah ˹alone˺ is my Lord and your Lord, so worship Him ˹alone˺. This is the Straight Path." **65.** Yet their ˹various˺ groups have differed among themselves ˹about him˺, so woe to the wrongdoers when they face the torment of a painful Day! **66.** Are they waiting for the Hour to take them by surprise when they least expect ˹it˺?

Reward of the Righteous

67. Close friends will be enemies to one another on that Day, except the righteous, **68.** ˹who will be told,˺ "O My servants! There is no fear for you Today, nor will you grieve— **69.** ˹those˺ who believed in Our signs and ˹fully˺ submitted ˹to Us˺. **70.** Enter Paradise, you and your spouses, rejoicing." **71.** Golden trays and cups will be passed around to them. There will be whatever the souls desire and the eyes delight in. And you will be there forever. **72.** That is the Paradise which you will be awarded for what you used to do. **73.** There you will have abundant fruit[1007] to eat from.

Reward of the Wicked

74. Indeed, the wicked will be in the torment of Hell forever. **75.** It will never be lightened for them, and there they will be overwhelmed with despair. **76.** We did not wrong them, but it was they who were the wrongdoers. **77.** They will cry, "O Mâlik![1008] Let your Lord finish us off." He will answer, "You are definitely here to stay." **78.** We certainly brought the truth to you, but most of you were resentful of the truth.

Warning to the Polytheists

79. Or have they mastered some ˹evil˺ plan? Then We ˹too˺ are surely planning.

1007 Fruit also implies delicacies.
1008 Angel Mâlik is the chief keeper of Hell.

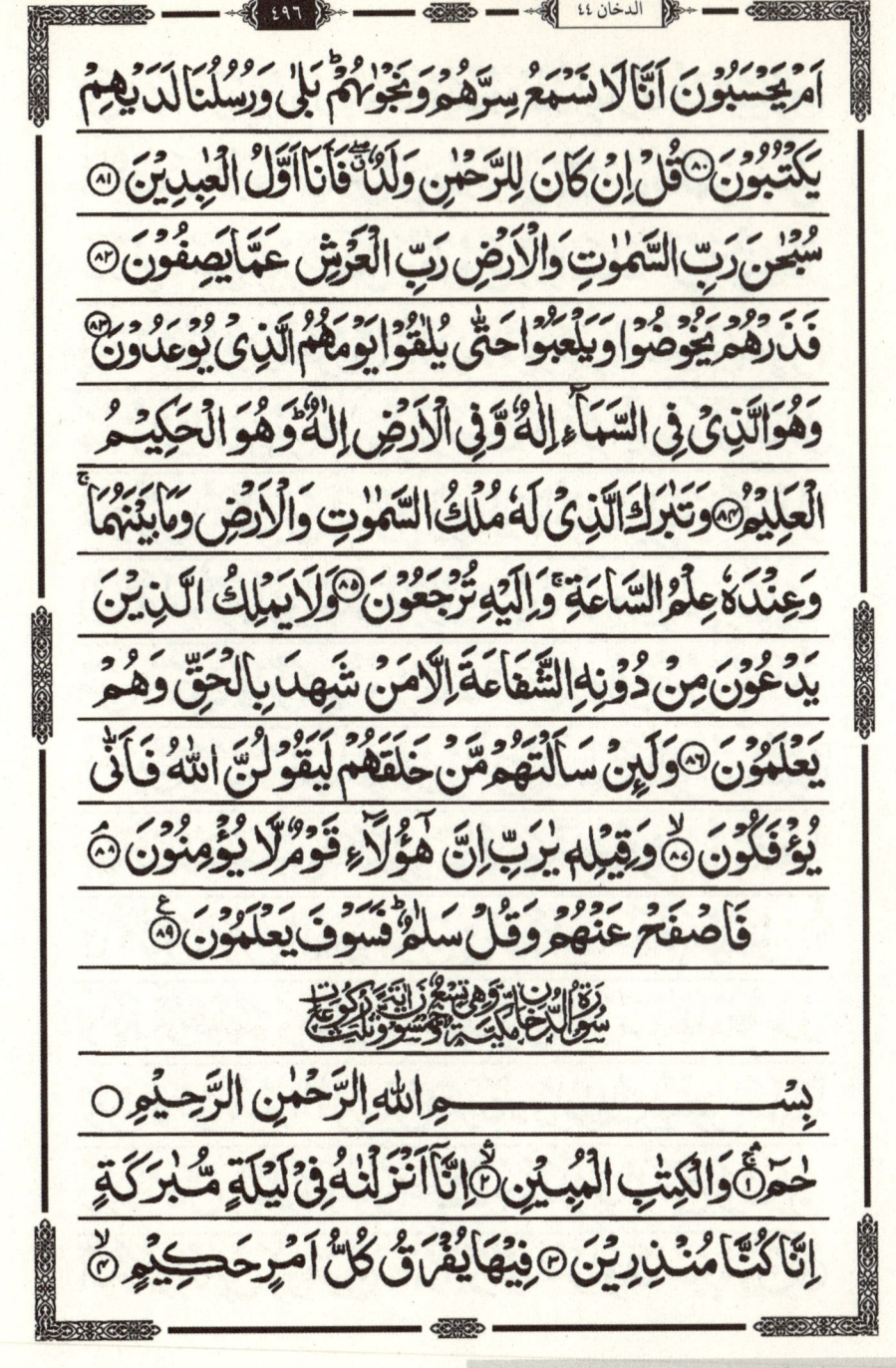

80. Or do they think that We do not hear their ˹evil˺ thoughts and secret talks? Yes ˹We do˺! And Our messenger-angels are in their presence, recording ˹it all˺. **81.** Say, ˹O Prophet,˺ "If the Most Compassionate ˹really˺ had offspring, I would be the first worshipper." **82.** Glorified is the Lord of the heavens and the earth, the Lord of the Throne, far above what they claim. **83.** So let them indulge ˹in falsehood˺ and amuse ˹themselves˺ until they face their Day, which they have been warned of.

The Only God Worthy of Worship

84. It is He Who is ˹the only˺ Allah in the heavens and ˹the only˺ Allah on the earth. For He is the All-Wise, All-Knowing. **85.** And Blessed is the One to Whom belongs the kingdom of the heavens and the earth and everything in between! With Him ˹alone˺ is the knowledge of the Hour. And to Him you will ˹all˺ be returned.

Call to the Worshippers of False Gods

86. ˹But˺ those ˹objects of worship˺ they invoke besides Him have no power to intercede, except those who testify to the truth knowingly.[1009] **87.** If you ask them ˹O Prophet˺ who created them, they will certainly say, "Allah!" How can they then be deluded ˹from the truth˺? **88.** ˹Allah is Aware of˺ the Prophet's cry: "O my Lord! Indeed, these are a people who persist in disbelief." **89.** So bear with them and respond with peace. They will soon come to know.

---

44. The Haze (Ad-Dukhân)

In the Name of Allah—the Most Compassionate, Most Merciful

The Quran as a Mercy

1. *Ḥâ-Mîm.* **2.** By the clear Book! **3.** Indeed, We sent it down on a blessed night,[1010] for We always warn ˹against evil˺. **4.** On that night every matter of wisdom is ordained

---

1009 i.e., Jesus, Ezra, and the angels.
1010 The revelation of the Quran started on the 27th night of Ramaḍân—the 9th month of the Islamic calendar (*see* 97:1 and 2:185)

497   44. Ad-Dukhân

5. by a command from Us, for We have always sent ˹messengers˺ 6. as a mercy from your Lord. He ˹alone˺ is truly the All-Hearing, All-Knowing— 7. the Lord of the heavens and the earth and everything in between, if only you had sure faith. 8. There is no god ˹worthy of worship˺ except Him. He ˹alone˺ gives life and causes death. ˹He is˺ your Lord, and the Lord of your forefathers.

Meccans Warned of Famine[1011]

9. In fact, they are in doubt, amusing themselves. 10. Wait then ˹O Prophet˺ for the day ˹when˺ the sky will be veiled in haze,[1012] clearly visible, 11. overwhelming the people. ˹They will cry,˺ "This is a painful torment. 12. Our Lord! Remove ˹this˺ torment from us, ˹and˺ we will certainly believe." 13. How can they be reminded when a messenger has already come to them, making things clear, 14. then they turned away from him, saying, "A madman, taught by others!"? 15. Indeed, We will remove ˹that˺ torment for a while, and you ˹Meccans˺ will return ˹to disbelief˺. 16. ˹Then˺ on the Day We will deal ˹you˺ the fiercest blow, We will surely inflict punishment.

Moses and Pharaoh's People

17. Indeed, before them We tested Pharaoh's people: a noble messenger came to them, 18. ˹proclaiming,˺ "Hand over the servants of Allah to me.[1013] I am truly a trustworthy messenger to you. 19. And do not be arrogant with Allah. I have certainly come to you with a compelling proof.

20. And indeed, I seek refuge with my Lord and your Lord so you do not stone me ˹to death˺. 21. ˹But˺ if you do not believe me, then let me be." 22. Ultimately, he cried out to his Lord, "These are a wicked people!"

Tyrants Destroyed

23. ˹Allah responded,˺ "Leave with My servants at night, for you will surely be pursued. 24. And leave the sea parted, for they are certainly an army bound to drown." 25. ˹Imagine˺ how many gardens and springs the tyrants[1014] left behind, 26. as well as ˹various˺

1011 One of the major signs of the Day of Judgment, according to authentic narrations from the Prophet (ﷺ), is overwhelming smoke. Some scholars cite 44:10-11 in support of this apocalyptic sign. However, 44:15 supports the understanding of this passage as referring to a drought, simply because once major apocalyptic signs arrive, no second chances will be given.

1012 This refers to the drought that affected the Meccan pagans so badly that they came to the Prophet (ﷺ), begging him to pray to Allah to remove the affliction from them.

1013 Meaning, let my people go.

1014 i.e., Pharaoh and his soldiers.

44. Ad-Dukhân

وَنَعْمَةٍ كَانُوا فِيهَا فَاكِهِينَ ۝ كَذَٰلِكَ ۖ وَأَوْرَثْنَاهَا قَوْمًا آخَرِينَ ۝ فَمَا بَكَتْ عَلَيْهِمُ السَّمَاءُ وَالْأَرْضُ وَمَا كَانُوا مُنْظَرِينَ ۝ وَلَقَدْ نَجَّيْنَا بَنِي إِسْرَائِيلَ مِنَ الْعَذَابِ الْمُهِينِ ۝ مِنْ فِرْعَوْنَ ۚ إِنَّهُ كَانَ عَالِيًا مِنَ الْمُسْرِفِينَ ۝ وَلَقَدِ اخْتَرْنَاهُمْ عَلَىٰ عِلْمٍ عَلَى الْعَالَمِينَ ۝ وَآتَيْنَاهُم مِّنَ الْآيَاتِ مَا فِيهِ بَلَاءٌ مُّبِينٌ ۝ إِنَّ هَٰؤُلَاءِ لَيَقُولُونَ ۝ إِنْ هِيَ إِلَّا مَوْتَتُنَا الْأُولَىٰ وَمَا نَحْنُ بِمُنْشَرِينَ ۝ فَأْتُوا بِآبَائِنَا إِن كُنتُمْ صَادِقِينَ ۝ أَهُمْ خَيْرٌ أَمْ قَوْمُ تُبَّعٍ وَالَّذِينَ مِن قَبْلِهِمْ ۚ أَهْلَكْنَاهُمْ ۖ إِنَّهُمْ كَانُوا مُجْرِمِينَ ۝ وَمَا خَلَقْنَا السَّمَاوَاتِ وَالْأَرْضَ وَمَا بَيْنَهُمَا لَاعِبِينَ ۝ مَا خَلَقْنَاهُمَا إِلَّا بِالْحَقِّ وَلَٰكِنَّ أَكْثَرَهُمْ لَا يَعْلَمُونَ ۝ إِنَّ يَوْمَ الْفَصْلِ مِيقَاتُهُمْ أَجْمَعِينَ ۝ يَوْمَ لَا يُغْنِي مَوْلًى عَن مَّوْلًى شَيْئًا وَلَا هُمْ يُنصَرُونَ ۝ إِلَّا مَن رَّحِمَ اللَّهُ ۚ إِنَّهُ هُوَ الْعَزِيزُ الرَّحِيمُ ۝ إِنَّ شَجَرَتَ الزَّقُّومِ ۝ طَعَامُ الْأَثِيمِ ۝ كَالْمُهْلِ يَغْلِي فِي الْبُطُونِ ۝ كَغَلْيِ الْحَمِيمِ ۝ خُذُوهُ فَاعْتِلُوهُ إِلَىٰ سَوَاءِ الْجَحِيمِ ۝ ثُمَّ صُبُّوا فَوْقَ رَأْسِهِ مِنْ عَذَابِ الْحَمِيمِ ۝

crops and splendid residences, **27.** and luxuries which they fully enjoyed. **28.** So it was. And We awarded it ˹all˺ to another people. **29.** Neither heaven nor earth wept over them, nor was their fate delayed. **30.** And We certainly delivered the Children of Israel from the humiliating torment **31.** of Pharaoh. He was truly a tyrant, a transgressor. **32.** And indeed, We chose the Israelites knowingly above the others. **33.** And We showed them signs in which there was a clear test.

Warning to Deniers of Resurrection

34. Indeed, these ˹Meccans˺ say, **35.** "There is nothing beyond our first death, and we will never be resurrected. **36.** Bring ˹back˺ our forefathers, if what you say is true." **37.** Are they superior to the people of Tubba'[1015] and those before them? We destroyed them ˹all˺, ˹for˺ they were truly wicked. **38.** We did not create the heavens and the earth and everything in between for sport. **39.** We only created them for a purpose, but most of these ˹pagans˺ do not know. **40.** Surely the Day of ˹Final˺ Decision is the time appointed for all— **41.** the Day no kith or kin will be of benefit to another whatsoever, nor will they be helped, **42.** except those shown mercy by Allah. He is truly the Almighty, Most Merciful.

The Tree of Hell

43. Surely ˹the fruit of˺ the tree of *Zaqqûm*[1016] **44.** will be the food of the evildoer. **45.** Like molten metal, it will boil in the bellies **46.** like the boiling of hot water. **47.** ˹It will be said,˺ "Seize them and drag them into the depths of the Hellfire. **48.** Then pour over their heads the torment of boiling water."

1015 Tubba' Al-Ḥimiari was an ancient righteous Yemeni king whose people persisted in disbelief and were destroyed, although they were superior to Meccans in strength and manpower.
1016 *Zaqqûm* is a tree that grows in the depths of Hell as mentioned in 37:62-65. The pagans of Mecca used to make fun of the Prophet and say, "How can a tree grow in Hell?"

499 45. Al-Jâthiyah

49. 'The wicked will be told,' "Taste this. You mighty, noble one![1017] **50.** This is truly what you 'all' used to doubt."

The Pleasures of Paradise

51. Indeed, the righteous will be in a secure place, **52.** amid Gardens and springs, **53.** dressed in fine silk and rich brocade, facing one another. **54.** So it will be. And We will pair them to maidens with gorgeous eyes. **55.** There they will call for every fruit in serenity. **56.** There they will never taste death, beyond the first death. And He will protect them from the punishment of the Hellfire— **57.** as 'an act of' grace from your Lord. That is 'truly' the ultimate triumph.

The Quran Is Easy

58. Indeed, We have made this 'Quran' easy in your own language 'O Prophet' so perhaps they will be mindful. **59.** Wait then! They too are certainly waiting.

❦❧ ✽ ❦❧

45. The Kneeling (Al-Jâthiyah)

In the Name of Allah—the Most Compassionate, Most Merciful

Allah's Signs

1. Ḥâ-Mîm. **2.** The revelation of this Book is from Allah—the Almighty, All-Wise. **3.** Surely in 'the creation of' the heavens and the earth are signs for the believers. **4.** And in your own creation, and whatever living beings He dispersed, are signs for people of sure faith. **5.** And 'in' the alternation of the day and the night, the provision[1018] sent down from the skies by Allah—reviving the earth after its death—and the shifting of the winds, are signs for people of understanding. **6.** These are Allah's revelations which We recite to you 'O Prophet' in truth. So what message will they believe in after 'denying' Allah and His revelations?

1017 Abu Jahl, a Meccan pagan leader, met the warning of punishment in the Hereafter by exclaiming, "How can I be punished when I am the mighty, noble one!"
1018 i.e., rain.

45. Al-Jâthiyah | 500

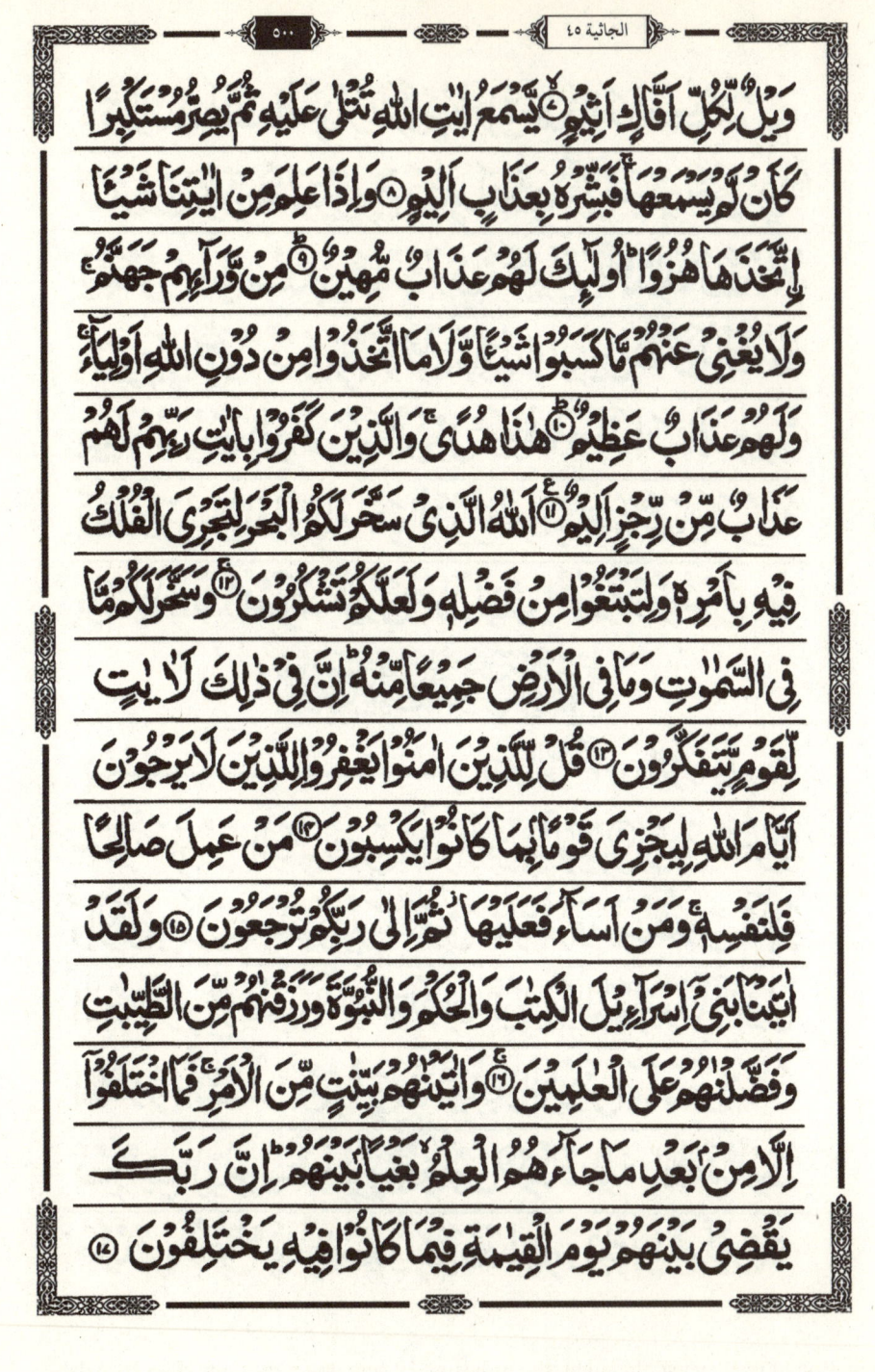

Warning to the Deniers

7. Woe to every sinful liar. 8. They hear Allah's revelations recited to them, then persist ˹in denial˺ arrogantly as if they did not hear them. So give them good news of a painful punishment. 9. And whenever they learn anything of Our revelations, they make a mockery of it. It is they who will suffer a humiliating punishment. 10. Awaiting them is Hell. Their ˹worldly˺ gains will not be of any benefit to them whatsoever, nor will those protectors they have taken besides Allah. And they will suffer a tremendous punishment. 11. This ˹Quran˺ is ˹true˺ guidance. And those who deny their Lord's revelations will suffer the ˹worst˺ torment of agonizing pain.

Allah's Favours to Humanity

12. Allah is the One Who has subjected the sea for you so that ships may sail upon it by His command, and that you may seek His bounty, and that perhaps you will be grateful. 13. He ˹also˺ subjected for you whatever is in the heavens and whatever is on the earth—all by His grace. Surely in this are signs for people who reflect.

Advice to the Believers

14. ˹O Prophet!˺ Tell the believers to forgive those who do not fear Allah's days ˹of torment˺, so that He will reward each group for what they used to commit. 15. Whoever does good, it is to their own benefit. And whoever does evil, it is to their own loss. Then to your Lord you will ˹all˺ be returned.

Differences Among the Israelites

16. Indeed, We gave the Children of Israel the Scripture, wisdom, and prophethood; granted them good, lawful provisions; and favoured them above the others.[1019] 17. We ˹also˺ gave them clear commandments regarding ˹their˺ faith. But it was not until knowledge came to them that they differed out of mutual envy.[1020] Surely your Lord will judge between them on the Day of Judgment regarding their differences.

1019 By sending many prophets, and showing them unique miracles such as the splitting of the sea.
1020 No community split into believers and disbelievers until they received the knowledge given by their prophet.

Advice to the Prophet

18. Now We have set you ˹O Prophet˺ on the ˹clear˺ Way of faith. So follow it, and do not follow the desires of those who do not know ˹the truth˺. **19.** They certainly can be of no benefit to you against Allah whatsoever. Surely the wrongdoers are patrons of each other, whereas Allah is the Patron of the righteous. **20.** This ˹Quran˺ is an insight for humanity—a guide and mercy for people of sure faith.

Good and Evil Are Not Equal

21. Or do those who commit evil deeds ˹simply˺ think that We will make them equal—in their life and after their death—to those who believe and do good? How wrong is their judgment! **22.** For Allah created the heavens and the earth for a purpose, so that every soul may be paid back for what it has committed. And none will be wronged.

Those Led by Desire

23. Have you seen ˹O Prophet˺ those who have taken their own desires as their god? ˹And so˺ Allah left them to stray knowingly, sealed their hearing and hearts, and placed a cover on their sight. Who then can guide them after Allah? Will you ˹all˺ not then be mindful?

Arguments of the Deniers of Resurrection

24. And they argue, "There is nothing beyond our worldly life. We die; others are born. And nothing destroys us but ˹the passage of˺ time." Yet they have no knowledge ˹in support˺ of this ˹claim˺. They only speculate. **25.** And whenever Our clear revelations are recited to them, their only argument is to say: "Bring our forefathers back, if what you say is true!" **26.** Say, ˹O Prophet,˺ "˹It is˺ Allah ˹Who˺ gives you life, then causes you to die, then will gather you ˹all˺ on the Day of Judgment, about which there is no doubt. But most people do not know."

45. Al-Jâthiyah

The Judgment

27. To Allah ˹alone˺ belongs the kingdom of the heavens and the earth. On the Day the Hour will be established, the people of falsehood will then be in ˹total˺ loss. **28.** And you will see every faith-community on its knees. Every community will be summoned to its record ˹of deeds˺. ˹They all will be told,˺ "This Day you will be rewarded for what you used to do. **29.** This record of Ours speaks the truth about you. Indeed, We always had your deeds recorded ˹by the angels˺."

Reward of the Believers

30. As for those who believed and did good, their Lord will admit them into His mercy. That is ˹truly˺ the absolute triumph.

Punishment of the Disbelievers

31. And as for those who disbelieved, ˹they will be told,˺ "Were My revelations not recited to you, yet you acted arrogantly and were a wicked people? **32.** And whenever it was said ˹to you˺, 'Surely Allah's promise ˹of judgment˺ is true and there is no doubt about the Hour,' you said ˹mockingly˺, 'We do not know what the Hour is! We think it is no more than speculation, and we are not convinced ˹that it will ever come˺.'" **33.** And the evil ˹consequences˺ of their deeds will unfold before them, and they will be overwhelmed by what they used to ridicule. **34.** It will be said, "This Day We will neglect you as you neglected the meeting of this Day of yours! Your home will be the Fire, and you will have no helpers. **35.** This is because you made a mockery of Allah's revelations, and were deluded by ˹your˺ worldly life." So ˹from˺ that Day ˹on˺ they will not be taken out of the Fire, nor will they be allowed to appease ˹their Lord˺.

Praises to the Almighty

36. So all praise is for Allah—Lord of the heavens and Lord of the earth, Lord of all worlds. **37.** To Him belongs ˹all˺ Majesty in the heavens and the earth. And He is the Almighty, All-Wise.

46. The Sand-Hills (Al-Ahqâf)

In the Name of Allah—the Most Compassionate, Most Merciful

A Message to Idolaters

1. Ḥâ-Mîm. 2. The revelation of this Book is from Allah—the Almighty, All-Wise. 3. We only created the heavens and the earth and everything in between for a purpose and an appointed term. Yet the disbelievers are turning away from what they have been warned about. 4. Ask ˹them, O Prophet˺, "Have you considered whatever ˹idols˺ you invoke besides Allah? Show me what they have created on earth! Or do they have a share in ˹the creation of˺ the heavens? Bring me a scripture ˹revealed˺ before this ˹Quran˺ or a shred of knowledge, if what you say is true." 5. And who could be more astray than those who call upon others besides Allah—˹others˺ that cannot respond to them until the Day of Judgment, and are ˹even˺ unaware of their calls? 6. And when ˹such˺ people will be gathered together, those ˹gods˺ will be their enemies and will disown their worship.

Pagan Denial of the Quran

7. Whenever Our clear revelations are recited to them, the disbelievers say of the truth when it has come to them, "This is pure magic." 8. Or do they say, "He[1021] has fabricated this ˹Quran˺!"? Say, ˹O Prophet,˺ "If I have done so, then there is nothing whatsoever you can do to save me from Allah. He knows best what ˹slurs˺ you indulge about it. Sufficient is He as a Witness between you and me. And He is the All-Forgiving, Most Merciful."

1021 Muḥammad (ﷺ).

46. Al-Aḥqâf   504

9. Say, "I am not the first messenger ever sent, nor do I know what will happen to me or you. I only follow what is revealed to me. And I am only sent with a clear warning."

Pagan Arrogance Towards Allah

10. Ask ˹them, O Prophet˺, "Consider if this ˹Quran˺ is ˹truly˺ from Allah and you deny it, and a witness from the Children of Israel attests to it and then believes,[1022] whereas you act arrogantly. Surely Allah does not guide the wrongdoing people."

Belittling the Quran

11. The disbelievers say of the believers, "Had it been ˹something˺ good, they[1023] would not have beaten us to it." Now since they reject its guidance, they will say, "˹This is˺ an ancient fabrication!" **12.** And before this ˹Quran˺ the Book of Moses was ˹revealed as˺ a guide and mercy. And this Book is a confirmation, in the Arabic tongue, to warn those who do wrong, and as good news to those who do good.

Reward of the Devout

13. Surely those who say, "Our Lord is Allah," and then remain steadfast—there will be no fear for them, nor will they grieve. **14.** It is they who will be the residents of Paradise, staying there forever, as a reward for what they used to do.

Stance of the Faithful

15. We have commanded people to honour their parents. Their mothers bore them in hardship and delivered them in hardship. Their ˹period of˺ bearing and weaning is thirty months. In time, when the child reaches their prime at the age of forty, they pray, "My Lord! Inspire me to ˹always˺ be thankful for Your favours which You blessed me and my parents with, and to do good deeds that please You. And instil righteousness in my offspring. I truly repent to You, and I truly submit ˹to Your Will˺."

1022 This refers to ʿAbdullâh ibn Salâm, a Jewish scholar, who embraced Islam when the Prophet (ﷺ) emigrated to Medina.
1023 Poor and powerless Muslims.

505   46. Al-Aḥqâf

16. It is from these ˹people˺ that We will accept the good they did, and overlook their misdeeds—along with the residents of Paradise, ˹in fulfilment of˺ the true promise they have been given.

Stance of the Deniers

17. But some scold their parents, "Enough with you! Are you warning me that I will be brought forth ˹from the grave˺, while many generations had already perished before me ˹for good˺?" The parents cry to Allah for help, ˹and warn their child,˺ "Pity you. Have faith! Surely Allah's promise is true." But the deniers insist, "This is nothing but ancient fables." **18.** These are the ones against whom the fate of earlier communities of jinn and humans has been justified, ˹for˺ they were truly losers.

Reward of the Faithful and the Deniers

19. Each ˹of the two groups˺ will be ranked according to what they have done so He may fully reward all. And none will be wronged. **20.** ˹Watch for˺ the Day ˹when˺ the disbelievers will be exposed to the Fire. ˹They will be told,˺ "You ˹already˺ exhausted your ˹share of˺ pleasures during your worldly life, and ˹fully˺ enjoyed them. So Today you will be rewarded with the torment of disgrace for your arrogance throughout the land with no right, and for your rebelliousness."

Prophet Hûd

21. And remember the brother of 'Âd, when he warned his people, who inhabited the sand-hills[1024]—there were certainly warners before and after him—˹saying,˺ "Worship none but Allah. I truly fear for you the torment of a tremendous day." **22.** They argued, "Have you come to turn us away from our gods? Bring us then whatever you threaten us with, if what you say is true."

1024   The people of 'Âd were the residents of the hills in the southern part of the Arabian Peninsula.

46. Al-Aḥqâf

23. He responded, "The knowledge ˹of its time˺ is only with Allah. I only convey to you what I have been sent with. But I can see that you are a people acting ignorantly." **24.** Then when they saw the torment as a ˹dense˺ cloud approaching their valleys, they said ˹happily˺, "This is a cloud bringing us rain." ˹But Hûd replied,˺ "No, it is what you sought to hasten: a ˹fierce˺ wind carrying a painful punishment! **25.** It destroyed everything by the command of its Lord, leaving nothing visible except their ruins. This is how We reward the wicked people.

Warning to Meccan Pagans

26. Indeed, We had established them[1025] in a way We have not established you ˹Meccans˺. And We gave them hearing, sight, and intellect. But neither their hearing, sight, nor intellect were of any benefit to them whatsoever, since they persisted in denying Allah's signs. And ˹so˺ they were overwhelmed by what they used to ridicule. **27.** We certainly destroyed the societies around you after having varied the signs so perhaps they would return ˹to the Right Path˺. **28.** Why then did those ˹idols˺ they took as gods—hoping to get closer ˹to Him˺—not come to their aid? Instead, they failed them. That is ˹the result of˺ their lies and their fabrications.

The Jinn Listen to the Quran

29. ˹Remember, O Prophet,˺ when We sent a group of jinn your way to listen to the Quran. Then, upon hearing it, they said ˹to one another˺, "Listen quietly!" Then when it was over, they returned to their fellow jinn as warners.

1025 The people of Hûd.

507   47. Muḥammad

30. They declared, "O our fellow jinn! We have truly heard a scripture revealed after Moses, confirming what came before it. It guides to the truth and the Straight Way. **31.** O our fellow jinn! Respond to the caller of Allah and believe in him, He will forgive your sins and protect you from a painful punishment. **32.** And whoever does not respond to the caller of Allah will have no escape on earth, nor will they have any protectors against Him. It is they who are clearly astray."

Warning to Deniers of Resurrection

33. Do they not realize that Allah, Who created the heavens and the earth and did not tire in creating them,[1026] is able to give life to the dead? Yes ˹indeed˺! He is certainly Most Capable of everything. **34.** And on the Day the disbelievers will be exposed to the Fire, ˹they will be asked,˺ "Is this ˹Hereafter˺ not the truth?" They will cry, "Absolutely, by our Lord!" It will be said, "Then taste the punishment for your disbelief."

Advice to the Prophet

35. So endure patiently, as did the Messengers of Firm Resolve.[1027] And do not ˹seek to˺ hasten ˹the torment˺ for the deniers. On the Day they see what they have been threatened with, it will be as if they had only stayed ˹in this world˺ for an hour of a day.[1028] ˹This is˺ a ˹sufficient˺ warning! Then, will anyone be destroyed except the rebellious people?

ﷺ ✿ ﷺ

---

47. Muḥammad (Muḥammad)

In the Name of Allah—the Most Compassionate, Most Merciful

Reward of the Believers and Disbelievers

1. Those who disbelieve and hinder ˹others˺ from the Way of Allah, He will render their deeds void.

1026 Or never failed in creating them.
1027 Noah, Abraham, Moses, Jesus, and Muḥammad (ﷺ) are called the Messengers of Firm Resolve.
1028 i.e., only for a very short period of time.

47. Muḥammad

بِسْمِ اللّٰهِ الرَّحْمٰنِ الرَّحِيْمِ

وَالَّذِيْنَ اٰمَنُوْا وَعَمِلُوا الصّٰلِحٰتِ وَاٰمَنُوْا بِمَا نُزِّلَ عَلٰى مُحَمَّدٍ وَهُوَ الْحَقُّ مِنْ رَّبِّهِمْ كَفَّرَ عَنْهُمْ سَيِّاٰتِهِمْ وَاَصْلَحَ بَالَهُمْ ۝

ذٰلِكَ بِاَنَّ الَّذِيْنَ كَفَرُوا اتَّبَعُوا الْبَاطِلَ وَاَنَّ الَّذِيْنَ اٰمَنُوا اتَّبَعُوا الْحَقَّ مِنْ رَّبِّهِمْ كَذٰلِكَ يَضْرِبُ اللّٰهُ لِلنَّاسِ اَمْثَالَهُمْ ۝

فَاِذَا لَقِيْتُمُ الَّذِيْنَ كَفَرُوْا فَضَرْبَ الرِّقَابِ حَتّٰى اِذَآ اَثْخَنْتُمُوْهُمْ فَشُدُّوا الْوَثَاقَ فَاِمَّا مَنًّا بَعْدُ وَاِمَّا فِدَآءً حَتّٰى تَضَعَ الْحَرْبُ اَوْزَارَهَا ذٰلِكَ وَلَوْ يَشَآءُ اللّٰهُ لَانْتَصَرَ مِنْهُمْ وَلٰكِنْ لِّيَبْلُوَا بَعْضَكُمْ بِبَعْضٍ وَالَّذِيْنَ قُتِلُوْا فِيْ سَبِيْلِ اللّٰهِ فَلَنْ يُّضِلَّ اَعْمَالَهُمْ ۝

سَيَهْدِيْهِمْ وَيُصْلِحُ بَالَهُمْ ۝ وَيُدْخِلُهُمُ الْجَنَّةَ عَرَّفَهَا لَهُمْ ۝

يٰٓاَيُّهَا الَّذِيْنَ اٰمَنُوْا اِنْ تَنْصُرُوا اللّٰهَ يَنْصُرْكُمْ وَيُثَبِّتْ اَقْدَامَكُمْ ۝ وَالَّذِيْنَ كَفَرُوْا فَتَعْسًا لَّهُمْ وَاَضَلَّ اَعْمَالَهُمْ ۝

ذٰلِكَ بِاَنَّهُمْ كَرِهُوْا مَآ اَنْزَلَ اللّٰهُ فَاَحْبَطَ اَعْمَالَهُمْ ۝

اَفَلَمْ يَسِيْرُوْا فِي الْاَرْضِ فَيَنْظُرُوْا كَيْفَ كَانَ عَاقِبَةُ الَّذِيْنَ مِنْ قَبْلِهِمْ دَمَّرَ اللّٰهُ عَلَيْهِمْ وَلِلْكٰفِرِيْنَ اَمْثَالُهَا ۝ ذٰلِكَ بِاَنَّ اللّٰهَ مَوْلَى الَّذِيْنَ اٰمَنُوْا وَاَنَّ الْكٰفِرِيْنَ لَا مَوْلٰى لَهُمْ ۝

---

2. As for those who believe, do good, and have faith in what has been revealed to Muḥammad—which is the truth from their Lord—He will absolve them of their sins and improve their condition. 3. This is because the disbelievers follow falsehood, while the believers follow the truth from their Lord. This is how Allah shows people their true state ˹of faith˺.

Rules of Engagement[1029]

4. So when you meet the disbelievers ˹in battle˺, strike ˹their˺ necks until you have thoroughly subdued them, then bind them firmly. Later ˹free them either as˺ an act of grace or by ransom until the war comes to an end. So will it be. Had Allah willed, He ˹Himself˺ could have inflicted punishment on them. But He does ˹this only to˺ test some of you by means of others. And those who are martyred in the cause of Allah,[1030] He will never render their deeds void. 5. He will guide them ˹to their reward˺, improve their condition, 6. and admit them into Paradise, having made it known to them.[1031]

Warning to the Deniers

7. O believers! If you stand up for Allah, He will help you and make your steps firm. 8. As for the disbelievers, may they be doomed and may He render their deeds void. 9. That is because they detest what Allah has revealed, so He has rendered their deeds void. 10. Have they not travelled throughout the land to see what was the end of those before them? Allah annihilated them, and a similar fate awaits the disbelievers. 11. This is because Allah is the Patron of the believers while the disbelievers have no patron.

1029 This passage discusses armed combat in the battlefield only.
1030 Another possible interpretation: "And those who fight in the cause of Allah."
1031 Once in Paradise, the believers will recognize their mansions just like they recognized their homes in the world.

47. Muḥammad

The Final Destination

12. Surely Allah will admit those who believe and do good into Gardens under which rivers flow. As for the disbelievers, they enjoy themselves and feed like cattle.[1032] But the Fire will be their home.

Evil Fate

13. ˹Imagine, O Prophet,˺ how many societies We destroyed that were far superior in might than your society—which drove you out— and there was none to help them! **14.** Can those ˹believers˺ who stand on clear proof from their Lord be like those whose evil deeds are made appealing to them and ˹only˺ follow their desires?

Delights of Paradise

15. The description of the Paradise promised to the righteous is that in it are rivers of fresh water, rivers of milk that never changes in taste, rivers of wine delicious to drink, and rivers of pure honey. There they will ˹also˺ have all kinds of fruit, and forgiveness from their Lord. ˹Can they be˺ like those who will stay in the Fire forever, left to drink boiling water that will tear apart their insides?

Qualities of the Hypocrites
1) Mockery

16. There are some of them who listen to you ˹O Prophet˺, but when they depart from you, they say ˹mockingly˺ to those ˹believers˺ gifted with knowledge, "What did he just say?" These are the ones whose hearts Allah has sealed and who ˹only˺ follow their desires.

17. As for those who are ˹rightly˺ guided, He increases them in guidance and blesses them with righteousness. **18.** Are they only waiting for the Hour to take them by surprise? Yet ˹some of˺ its signs have already come.[1033] Once it actually befalls them, will it not be too late to be mindful?

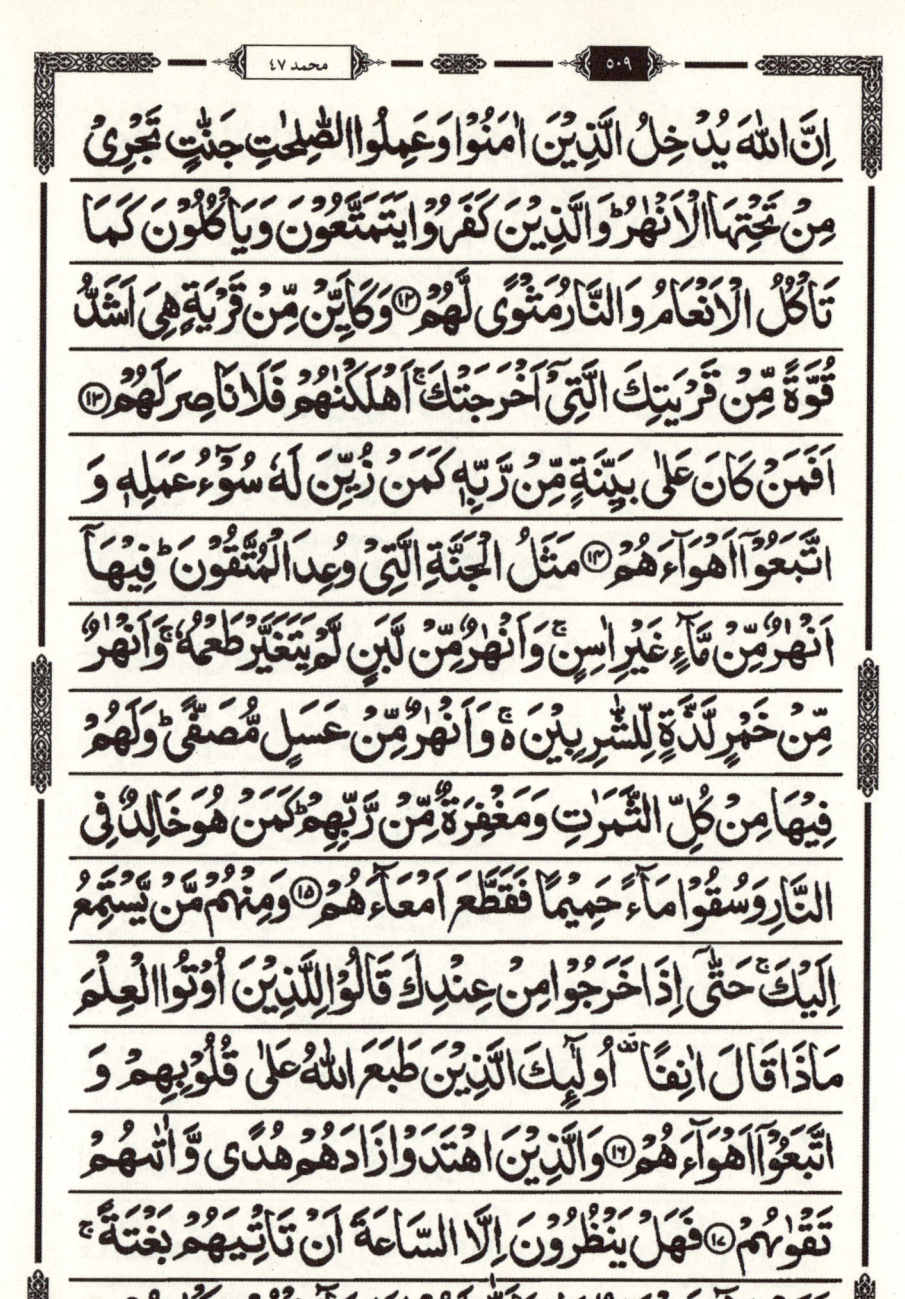

1032 Meaning, the disbelievers enjoy their life to the fullest while they are heedless of what will happen to them in the Hereafter, just like the cattle that graze in the pasture are unaware that they will probably end up in the slaughter house.

1033 The coming of Muḥammad (ﷺ) is one of the signs of the Hour.

47. Muḥammad **510**

Advice to the Prophet

19. So, know ˹well, O Prophet,˺ that there is no god ˹worthy of worship˺ except Allah. And seek forgiveness for your shortcomings[1034] and for ˹the sins of˺ the believing men and women. For Allah ˹fully˺ knows your movements and places of rest ˹O people˺.

Qualities of the Hypocrites
2) Cowardice

20. And the believers say, "If only a *sûrah* was revealed ˹allowing self-defence˺!" Yet when a precise *sûrah* is revealed, in which fighting is ˹explicitly˺ mentioned, you see those with sickness in their hearts staring at you like someone in the throes of death. It would have been better for them **21.** to obey and speak rightly. Then when fighting was ordained, it surely would have been better for them if they were true to Allah. **22.** Now if you ˹hypocrites˺ turn away, perhaps you would then spread corruption throughout the land and sever your ˹ties of˺ kinship![1035] **23.** These are the ones who Allah has condemned, deafening them and blinding their eyes. **24.** Do they not then reflect on the Quran? Or are there locks upon their hearts?

Warning to Hypocrites

25. Indeed, those who relapse ˹into disbelief˺ after ˹true˺ guidance has become clear to them, ˹it is˺ Satan ˹that˺ has tempted them, luring them with false hopes. **26.** That is because they said ˹privately˺ to those who ˹also˺ detest what Allah has revealed, "We will obey you in some matters."[1036] But Allah ˹fully˺ knows what they are hiding. **27.** Then how ˹horrible˺ will it be when the angels take their souls, beating their faces and backs! **28.** This is because they follow whatever displeases Allah and hate whatever pleases Him, so He has rendered their deeds void.

Another Warning to Hypocrites

29. Or do those with sickness in their hearts think that Allah will not ˹be able to˺ expose their malice?

1034 Like other prophets, Muḥammad (ﷺ) was infallible of sin. The verse here refers to misjudgments, such as the example given in 80:1-10. If the Prophet (ﷺ) himself is urged to seek forgiveness, then the believers are even more in need of praying for Allah's forgiveness.

1035 As you did before Islam.

1036 i.e., your opposition to the Prophet (ﷺ).

47. Muḥammad

30. Had We willed, We could have truly shown them to you ˹O Prophet˺, and you would have certainly recognized them by their appearance. But you will surely recognize them by their tone of speech. And Allah ˹fully˺ knows your doings ˹O people˺.

Wisdom Behind the Test

31. We will certainly test you ˹believers˺ until We prove those of you who ˹truly˺ struggle ˹in Allah's cause˺ and remain steadfast, and reveal how you conduct yourselves.

Reward of the Disbelievers

32. Indeed, those who disbelieve, hinder ˹others˺ from the Way of Allah, and defy the Messenger after ˹true˺ guidance has become clear to them; they will not harm Allah in the least, but He will render their deeds void.

Advice to the Believers

33. O believers! Obey Allah and obey the Messenger, and do not let your deeds be in vain. **34.** Surely those who disbelieve, hinder ˹others˺ from the Way of Allah, and then die as disbelievers; Allah will never forgive them. **35.** So do not falter or cry for peace, for you will have the upper hand and Allah is with you. And He will never let your deeds go to waste.

Test of Faith

36. This worldly life is no more than play and amusement. But if you are faithful and mindful ˹of Allah˺, He will grant you your ˹full˺ reward, and will not ask you ˹to donate all˺ your wealth. **37.** If He were to do so and pressure you, you would withhold and He would bring out your resentment. **38.** Here you are, being invited to donate ˹a little˺ in the cause of Allah. Still some of you withhold. And whoever does so, it is only to their own loss. For Allah is the Self-Sufficient, whereas you stand in need ˹of Him˺. If you ˹still˺ turn away, He will replace you with another people. And they will not be like you.

48. Al-Faṭḥ | 512

48. The Triumph (Al-Fatḥ)

In the Name of Allah—the Most Compassionate, Most Merciful

Treaty of Ḥudaibiyah

1. Indeed, We have granted you a clear triumph ˹O Prophet˺ 2. so that Allah may forgive you for your past and future shortcomings,[1037] perfect His favour upon you, guide you along the Straight Path, 3. and so that Allah will help you tremendously. 4. He is the One Who sent down serenity upon the hearts of the believers so that they may increase even more in their faith. To Allah ˹alone˺ belong the forces of the heavens and the earth. And Allah is All-Knowing, All-Wise. 5. So He may admit believing men and women into Gardens under which rivers flow—to stay there forever—and absolve them of their sins. And that is a supreme achievement in the sight of Allah. 6. Also ˹so that˺ He may punish hypocrite men and women and polytheistic men and women, who harbour evil thoughts of Allah.[1038] May ill-fate befall them! Allah is displeased with them. He has condemned them and prepared for them Hell. What an evil destination! 7. To Allah ˹alone˺ belong the forces of the heavens and the earth. And Allah is Almighty, All-Wise.

The Prophet's Duty

8. Indeed, ˹O Prophet,˺ We have sent you as a witness, a deliverer of good news, and a warner, 9. so that you ˹believers˺ may have faith in Allah and His Messenger, support and honour him, and glorify Allah morning and evening.[1039]

1037 See footnote for 47:19.
1038 i.e., that Allah will not support His Prophet (ﷺ) and that misfortune will befall the believers.
1039 Another possible translation: "… so that you ˹all˺ may believe in Allah and His Messenger, support ˹His cause˺, revere, and glorify Him morning and evening."

48. Al-Fatḥ

Allegiance Under the Tree[1040]

10. Surely those who pledge allegiance to you ˹O Prophet˺ are actually pledging allegiance to Allah. Allah's Hand is over theirs. Whoever breaks their pledge, it will only be to their own loss. And whoever fulfils their pledge to Allah, He will grant them a great reward.

Fake Excuses for Not Travelling to Mecca

11. The nomadic Arabs, who stayed behind, will say to you ˹O Prophet˺, "We were preoccupied with our wealth and families, so ask for forgiveness for us." They say with their tongues what is not in their hearts. Say, "Who then can stand between you and Allah in any way, if He intends harm or benefit for you? In fact, Allah is All-Aware of what you do. **12.** The truth is: you thought that the Messenger and the believers would never return to their families again. And that was made appealing in your hearts. You harboured evil thoughts ˹about Allah˺, and ˹so˺ became a doomed people." **13.** And whoever does not believe in Allah and His Messenger, then We surely have prepared for the disbelievers a blazing Fire. **14.** To Allah ˹alone˺ belongs the kingdom of the heavens and the earth. He forgives whoever He wills, and punishes whoever He wills. And Allah is All-Forgiving, Most Merciful.

Shares in the Spoils of War

15. Those who stayed behind will say, when you ˹believers˺ set out to take the spoils of war, "Let us accompany you." They wish to change Allah's promise.[1041] Say, ˹O Prophet,˺ "You will not accompany us. This is what Allah has said before." They will then say, "In fact, you are driven by jealousy against us!"[1042] The truth is: they can hardly comprehend.

1040 *See* the introduction for this sûrah.
1041 Those who pledged allegiance at Ḥudaibiyah were promised by Allah that the spoils of war obtained from the Tribe of Khaibar would be exclusively theirs.
1042 Meaning, you only say so to deprive us of our share.

48. Al-Fatḥ

A Second Chance

16. Say to nomadic Arabs, who stayed behind, "You will be called ˹to fight˺ against a people of great might,[1043] who you will fight unless they submit. If you then obey, Allah will grant you a fine reward. But if you turn away as you did before, He will inflict upon you a painful punishment."

Those Exempted from Fighting

17. There is no blame on the blind, or the disabled, or the sick ˹for staying behind˺. And whoever obeys Allah and His Messenger will be admitted by Him into Gardens under which rivers flow. But whoever turns away will be subjected by Him to a painful punishment.

Allegiance of the Faithful

18. Indeed, Allah was pleased with the believers when they pledged allegiance to you ˹O Prophet˺ under the tree. He knew what was in their hearts, so He sent down serenity upon them and rewarded them with a victory at hand,[1044] **19.** and many spoils of war they will gain. For Allah is Almighty, All-Wise. **20.** Allah has promised you ˹believers˺ abundant spoils, which you will gain, so He hastened this ˹truce˺[1045] for you. And He has held people's hands back from ˹harming˺ you, so it may be a sign for the believers, and so He may guide you along the Straight Path. **21.** And ˹there are˺ other gains which are beyond your reach that Allah is keeping in store ˹for you˺. For Allah is Most Capable of everything.

The Believers Will Prevail

22. If the disbelievers were to fight you, they would certainly flee.[1046] Then they would never find any protector or helper.
23. ˹This is˺ Allah's way, already long established ˹in the past˺. And you will find no change in Allah's way.

1043 This refers to Hawâzin and Thaqîf, two pagan Arab tribes.
1044 The conquest of Khaibar in 7 A.H./628 C.E.
1045 Or the spoils of Khaibar.
1046 lit., turn their backs.

48. Al-Fatḥ

Wisdom Behind the Truce

24. He is the One Who held back their hands from you and your hands from them in the valley of ˹Ḥudai-biyah, near˺ Mecca, after giving you the upper hand over ˹a group of˺ them.[1047] And Allah is All-Seeing of what you do. **25.** They are the ones who persisted in disbelief and hindered you from the Sacred Mosque, preventing the sacrificial animals from reaching their destination.[1048] ˹We would have let you march through Mecca,˺ had there not been believing men and women, unknown to you. You might have trampled them underfoot, incurring guilt for ˹what you did to˺ them unknowingly. That was so Allah may admit into His mercy whoever He wills.[1049] Had those ˹unknown˺ believers stood apart, We would have certainly inflicted a painful punishment on the disbelievers.

Meccan Arrogance

26. ˹Remember˺ when the disbelievers had filled their hearts with pride—the pride of ˹pre-Islamic˺ ignorance[1050]—then Allah sent down His serenity upon His Messenger and the believers, inspiring them to uphold the declaration of faith,[1051] for they were better entitled and more worthy of it. And Allah has ˹perfect˺ knowledge of all things.

The Prophet's Vision[1052]

27. Indeed, Allah will fulfil His Messenger's vision in all truth: Allah willing, you will surely enter the Sacred Mosque, in securi-

ty—˹some with˺ heads shaved and ˹others with˺ hair shortened—without fear.[1053] He knew what you did not know, so He first granted you the triumph at hand.[1054] **28.** He is the One Who has sent His Messenger with ˹right˺ guidance and the religion of truth, making it prevail over all others. And sufficient is Allah as a Witness.

1047 A group of Meccans wanted to attack the Muslims on their way to Mecca, but were taken captive by the Muslims, then were released.
1048 The animals that the Muslims had brought along to be sacrificed after completing the rituals of the minor pilgrimage (ʿumrah).
1049 By doing so, the Meccan Muslims who were unknown to their fellow believers were safe, along with the pagans who later accepted Islam.
1050 This is when the pagans prevented the Prophet (ﷺ) and the believers from entering the Sacred House for ʿumrah and the arrogance they showed when drafting the peace agreement.
1051 The declaration of faith that there is only one God to be worshipped and that Muḥammad (ﷺ) is His Messenger.
1052 The Prophet (ﷺ) had a dream that he and his companions were going to enter the Sacred Mosque in peace.
1053 Pilgrims are required to shave or trim their hair upon successfully completing the rituals of pilgrimage.
1054 This refers to the Treaty of Ḥudaibiyah and/or the gains of Khaibar before the fulfilment of the Prophet's vision to enter Mecca for ʿumrah.

Believers' Description in the Torah

29. Muḥammad is the Messenger of Allah. And those with him are firm with the disbelievers[1055] and compassionate with one another. You see them bowing and prostrating[1056] ˹in prayer˺, seeking Allah's bounty and pleasure. The sign ˹of brightness can be seen˺ on their faces from the trace of prostrating ˹in prayer˺. This is their description in the Torah.[1057]

Believers' Description in the Gospel

And their parable in the Gospel is that of a seed that sprouts its ˹tiny˺ branches, making it strong. Then it becomes thick, standing firmly on its stem, to the delight of the planters[1058]—in this way Allah makes the believers a source of dismay for the disbelievers.[1059] To those of them who believe and do good, Allah has promised forgiveness and a great reward.

༺☼༻

49. The Private Quarters (Al-Ḥujurât)

In the Name of Allah—the Most Compassionate, Most Merciful

Manners with the Prophet 1)
Respect Authority

1. O believers! Do not proceed ˹in any matter˺ before ˹a decree from˺ Allah and His Messenger. And fear Allah. Surely Allah is All-Hearing, All-Knowing.

Manners with the Prophet 2)
Watch Your Tongue

2. O believers! Do not raise your voices above the voice of the Prophet, nor speak loudly to him as you do to one another,[1060] or your deeds will become void while you are unaware. **3.** Indeed, those who lower their voices in the presence of Allah's Messenger are the ones whose hearts Allah has refined for righteousness. They will have forgiveness and a great reward.

1055 This passage and the next should be understood in their historical context. The Muslims were urged to be firm with the Arab pagans and their allies who were at war with the Muslims at that time. Otherwise, Islam encourages Muslims to treat peaceful non-Muslims with kindness and fairness. *See* 60:8-9.

1056 Prostration means lying down on one's face (i.e., touching the ground with the forehead and nose while resting on knees and flat palms of both hands) as an act of prayer and submission to Allah.

1057 In Deuteronomy 33:1-3, ˹Moses proclaimed:˺ "The Lord came from Sinai. Rising from Seir upon us, he shone forth from Mount Paran, accompanied by a myriad of his holy ones, with flaming fire from his right hand for them. Indeed, lover of people, all of his holy ones are in your control. They gather at your feet to do as you have instructed. [*sic*]" Paran is a mountain in Mecca.

1058 In Matthew 13:3-9, "˹Jesus˺ spoke many things to them in parables, saying, "Behold, the sower went out to sow. ... ˹A seed˺ fell on the good soil and yielded a crop, some a hundredfold, some sixty, and some thirty. He who has ears, let him hear."" Or the parable of the growing seed in Mark 4:26-28.

1059 *See* the first footnote for 48:29.

1060 There is also a different interpretation: "... nor call him ˹by his name˺ as you call one another." In other words, Do not say, 'O Muḥammad.' Rather, say, 'O Prophet.'

Manners with the Prophet 3) Respect Privacy

4. Indeed, most of those who call out to you ˹O Prophet˺ from outside ˹your˺ private quarters have no understanding ˹of manners˺.[1061] **5.** Had they been patient until you could come out to them, it would have certainly been better for them. And Allah is All-Forgiving, Most Merciful.

Social Etiquette 1) Verifying News

6. O believers, if an evildoer brings you any news, verify ˹it˺ so you do not harm people unknowingly, becoming regretful for what you have done.[1062] **7.** And keep in mind that Allah's Messenger is ˹still˺ in your midst. If he were to yield to you in many matters, you would surely suffer ˹the consequences˺.[1063] But Allah has endeared faith to you, making it appealing in your hearts. And He has made disbelief, rebelliousness, and disobedience detestable to you. Those are the ones rightly guided. **8.** ˹This is˺ a bounty and a blessing from Allah. And Allah is All-Knowing, All-Wise.

Social Etiquette 2) Sense of Brotherhood

9. And if two groups of believers fight each other, then make peace between them. But if one of them transgresses against the other, then fight against the transgressing group until they ˹are willing to˺ submit to the rule of Allah. If they do so, then make peace between both ˹groups˺ in all fairness and act justly. Surely Allah loves those who uphold justice. **10.** The believers are but one brotherhood, so make peace between your brothers. And be mindful of Allah so you may be shown mercy.

Social Etiquette 3) Respect for All

11. O believers! Do not let some ˹men˺ ridicule others, they may be better than them, nor let ˹some˺ women ridicule other women, they may be better than them. Do not defame one another, nor call each other by offensive nicknames. How evil it is to act rebelliously after having faith! And whoever does not repent, it is they who are the ˹true˺ wrongdoers.

1061 A group from the tribe of Bani Tamīm came to see the Prophet (ﷺ) while he was taking a nap in the afternoon. They stood outside the homes of his wives and started calling him out loud.

1062 Al-Walīd ibn 'Uqbah ibn Abi Mu'aiṭ was sent by the Prophet (ﷺ) to collect alms-tax from Bani Al-Muṣṭaliq. They went out to receive Al-Walīd but he assumed they wanted to harm him. Therefore, he quickly returned to the Prophet (ﷺ) with the bad news so he would punish them. Shortly after, a delegation from Bani Al-Muṣṭaliq came to clarify the misunderstanding.

1063 Or things would have been difficult for you.

12. O believers! Avoid many suspicions, ˹for˺ indeed, some suspicions are sinful. And do not spy, nor backbite one another. Would any of you like to eat the flesh of their dead brother? You would despise that![1064] And fear Allah. Surely Allah is ˹the˺ Accepter of Repentance, Most Merciful.

Social Etiquette 4) Equality

13. O humanity! Indeed, We created you from a male and a female, and made you into peoples and tribes so that you may ˹get to˺ know one another. Surely the most noble of you in the sight of Allah is the most righteous among you. Allah is truly All-Knowing, All-Aware.[1065]

Actions Speak Louder than Words

14. ˹Some of˺ the nomadic Arabs say, "We believe." Say, ˹O Prophet,˺ "You have not believed. But say, 'We have submitted,' for faith has not yet entered your hearts.[1066] But if you obey Allah and His Messenger ˹wholeheartedly˺, He will not discount anything from ˹the reward of˺ your deeds. Allah is truly All-Forgiving, Most Merciful." **15.** The ˹true˺ believers are only those who believe in Allah and His Messenger—never doubting—and strive with their wealth and their lives in the cause of Allah. They are the ones true in faith. **16.** Say, "Do you inform Allah of your faith, when Allah ˹already˺ knows whatever is in the heavens and whatever is on the earth? And Allah has ˹perfect˺ knowledge of all things." **17.** They regard their acceptance of Islam as a favour to you. Tell ˹them, O Prophet˺, "Do not regard your Islam as a favour to me. Rather, it is Allah Who has done you a favour by guiding you to the faith, if ˹indeed˺ you are faithful. **18.** Surely Allah knows the unseen of the heavens and earth. And Allah is All-Seeing of what you do."

1064 Backbiting people is likened to eating their dead bodies. So if eating someone's flesh is detestable, then backbiting them is no different.

1065 The Prophet (ﷺ) is reported in a *ḥadîth* collected by Imâm Aḥmed to have said, "O humanity! Your Lord is one, and your ancestry is one. No Arab is superior to a non-Arab, nor is any non-Arab superior to any Arab. No white is superior to any black, nor is any black superior to any white except on account of their righteousness."

1066 The verse makes a distinction between *Islam* (the declaration of accepting the faith, then performing Islamic duties such as prayers and fasting) and *Îmân* (a higher state of Islam, which means to embrace the faith wholeheartedly). This distinction is very clear in a famous narration from the Prophet (ﷺ), commonly known as the *Ḥadîth* of Gabriel.

50. Qãf (Qãf)

In the Name of Allah—the Most Compassionate, Most Merciful

Pagan Denial of Resurrection

1. **Qãf.** By the glorious Quran! 2. ´All will be resurrected,` yet the deniers are astonished that a warner has come to them from among themselves ´warning of resurrection`. So the disbelievers say, "This is an astonishing thing! 3. ´Will we be returned to life,` when we are dead and reduced to dust? Such a return is impossible." 4. We certainly know what the earth consumes of them ´after their death`, and with us is a well-preserved Record.[1067] 5. In fact, they reject the truth when it has come to them, so they are in a confused state.[1068]

Allah's Power to Create

6. Have they not then looked at the sky above them: how We built it and adorned it ´with stars`, leaving it flawless? 7. As for the earth, We spread it out and placed upon it firm mountains, and produced in it every type of pleasant plant— 8. ´all as` an insight and a reminder to every servant who turns ´to Allah`. 9. And We send down blessed rain from the sky, bringing forth gardens and grains for harvest, 10. and towering palm trees ´loaded` with clustered fruit, 11. ´as` a provision for ´Our` servants. And with this ´rain` We revive a lifeless land. Similar is the emergence ´from the graves`.

Deniers Before Arab Pagans

12. Before them, the people of Noah denied ´the truth,` as did the people of the Water-pit,[1069] Thamûd, 13. 'Âd, Pharaoh, the kinfolk of Lot, 14. the residents of the Forest,[1070] and the people of Tubba'.[1071] Each rejected ´their` messenger, so My warning was fulfilled.

Allah's Power to Resurrect and Know All

15. Were We incapable of creating ´them` the first time? In fact, they are in doubt about ´their` re-creation.

1067 Or a Record preserving ´everything`.
1068 Meaning, they are confused about the Prophet (ﷺ): some say he is a poet, some say he is a fabricator, while others say he is insane. They also rejected the Quran as poetry, magic, or ancient fables.
1069 Ar-Rass means "well" or "water-pit". This refers to a pagan people, along with Midian, to whom Allah sent Prophet Shu'aib (ﷺ).
1070 The people of Shu'aib (ﷺ).
1071 Tubba' Al-Ḥimiari was an ancient righteous Yemeni king whose people persisted in disbelief and were destroyed, although they were superior to the Meccans in strength and manpower.

50. Qāf

وَلَقَدْ خَلَقْنَا الْإِنسَانَ وَنَعْلَمُ مَا تُوَسْوِسُ بِهِ نَفْسُهُ ۖ وَنَحْنُ أَقْرَبُ إِلَيْهِ مِنْ حَبْلِ الْوَرِيدِ ﴿١٦﴾ إِذْ يَتَلَقَّى الْمُتَلَقِّيَانِ عَنِ الْيَمِينِ وَعَنِ الشِّمَالِ قَعِيدٌ ﴿١٧﴾ مَّا يَلْفِظُ مِن قَوْلٍ إِلَّا لَدَيْهِ رَقِيبٌ عَتِيدٌ ﴿١٨﴾ وَجَاءَتْ سَكْرَةُ الْمَوْتِ بِالْحَقِّ ۖ ذَٰلِكَ مَا كُنتَ مِنْهُ تَحِيدُ ﴿١٩﴾ وَنُفِخَ فِي الصُّورِ ۚ ذَٰلِكَ يَوْمُ الْوَعِيدِ ﴿٢٠﴾ وَجَاءَتْ كُلُّ نَفْسٍ مَّعَهَا سَائِقٌ وَشَهِيدٌ ﴿٢١﴾ لَّقَدْ كُنتَ فِي غَفْلَةٍ مِّنْ هَٰذَا فَكَشَفْنَا عَنكَ غِطَاءَكَ فَبَصَرُكَ الْيَوْمَ حَدِيدٌ ﴿٢٢﴾ وَقَالَ قَرِينُهُ هَٰذَا مَا لَدَيَّ عَتِيدٌ ﴿٢٣﴾ أَلْقِيَا فِي جَهَنَّمَ كُلَّ كَفَّارٍ عَنِيدٍ ﴿٢٤﴾ مَّنَّاعٍ لِّلْخَيْرِ مُعْتَدٍ مُّرِيبٍ ﴿٢٥﴾ الَّذِي جَعَلَ مَعَ اللَّهِ إِلَٰهًا آخَرَ فَأَلْقِيَاهُ فِي الْعَذَابِ الشَّدِيدِ ﴿٢٦﴾ قَالَ قَرِينُهُ رَبَّنَا مَا أَطْغَيْتُهُ وَلَٰكِن كَانَ فِي ضَلَالٍ بَعِيدٍ ﴿٢٧﴾ قَالَ لَا تَخْتَصِمُوا لَدَيَّ وَقَدْ قَدَّمْتُ إِلَيْكُم بِالْوَعِيدِ ﴿٢٨﴾ مَا يُبَدَّلُ الْقَوْلُ لَدَيَّ وَمَا أَنَا بِظَلَّامٍ لِّلْعَبِيدِ ﴿٢٩﴾ يَوْمَ نَقُولُ لِجَهَنَّمَ هَلِ امْتَلَأْتِ وَتَقُولُ هَلْ مِن مَّزِيدٍ ﴿٣٠﴾ وَأُزْلِفَتِ الْجَنَّةُ لِلْمُتَّقِينَ غَيْرَ بَعِيدٍ ﴿٣١﴾ هَٰذَا مَا تُوعَدُونَ لِكُلِّ أَوَّابٍ حَفِيظٍ ﴿٣٢﴾ مَّنْ خَشِيَ الرَّحْمَٰنَ بِالْغَيْبِ وَجَاءَ بِقَلْبٍ مُّنِيبٍ ﴿٣٣﴾ ادْخُلُوهَا بِسَلَامٍ ۖ ذَٰلِكَ يَوْمُ الْخُلُودِ ﴿٣٤﴾

16. Indeed, ˹it is˺ We ˹Who˺ created humankind and ˹fully˺ know what their souls whisper to them, and We are closer to them than ˹their˺ jugular vein. **17.** As the two recording-angels—˹one˺ sitting to the right, and ˹the other to˺ the left—note ˹everything˺, **18.** not a word does a person utter without having a ˹vigilant˺ observer ready ˹to write it down˺.[1072]

Bad News for the Deniers

19. ˹Ultimately,˺ with the throes of death will come the truth.[1073] This is what you were trying to escape! **20.** And the Trumpet will be blown.[1074] This is the Day ˹you were˺ warned of. **21.** Each soul will come forth with an angel to drive it and another to testify. **22.** ˹It will be said to the denier,˺ "You were totally heedless of this. Now We have lifted this veil of yours, so Today your sight is sharp!" **23.** And one's accompanying-angel will say, "Here is the record ready with me." **24.** ˹It will be said to both angels,˺ "Throw into Hell every stubborn disbeliever, **25.** withholder of good, transgressor, and doubter, **26.** who set up another god with Allah. So cast them into the severe punishment."

The Misleaders and the Misled

27. One's ˹devilish˺ associate will say, "Our Lord! I did not make them transgress. Rather, they were far astray ˹on their own˺." **28.** Allah will respond, "Do not dispute in My presence, since I had already given you a warning. **29.** My Word cannot be changed,[1075] nor am I unjust to ˹My˺ creation." **30.** ˹Beware of˺ the Day We will ask Hell, "Are you full ˹yet˺?" And it will respond, "Are there any more?"

Good News for the Righteous

31. And Paradise will be brought near to the righteous, not far off. **32.** ˹And it will be said to them,˺ "This is what you were promised, for whoever ˹constantly˺ turned ˹to Allah˺ and kept up ˹His commandments˺— **33.** who were in awe of the Most Compassionate without seeing ˹Him˺,[1076] and have come with a heart turning ˹only to Him˺. **34.** Enter it in peace. This is the Day of eternal life!" **35.** There they will have whatever they desire, and with Us is ˹even˺ more.[1077]

1072 The angel to the right records the good deeds of each person, while the one to the left records every evil deed. They always accompany the person at all times, except when one uses the toilet or is intimate with their spouse.

1073 When a denier dies, they will realize that resurrection, judgment, Paradise, and Hell are all true.

1074 This is the second blow which will cause all to come back to life for judgment.

1075 Meaning, the decree to punish wicked humans and jinn (see 11:119 and 32:13).

1076 This can also mean that they are in awe of their Lord as much in private as they are in public.

1077 i.e., looking at the Face of the Almighty (see 10:26 and 75:22-23).

521   51. Az-Zâriyât

Warning to Meccan Pagans

36. ´Imagine´ how many peoples We destroyed before them, who were far mightier than them. Then ´when the torment came,´ they ´desperately´ sought refuge in the land. ´But´ was there any escape? **37.** Surely in this is a reminder for whoever has a ´mindful´ heart and lends an attentive ear.

Did Allah Get Tired?

38. Indeed, We created the heavens and the earth and everything in between in six Days,[1078] and We were not ´even´ touched with fatigue.[1079] **39.** So be patient ´O Prophet´ with what they say. And glorify the praises of your Lord before sunrise and before sunset. **40.** And glorify Him during part of the night[1080] and after the prayers.

Reassuring the Prophet

41. And listen! On the Day the caller will call out from a near place, **42.** the Day all will hear the ´mighty´ Blast in ´all´ truth,[1081] that will be the Day of emergence ´from the graves´. **43.** It is certainly We Who give life and cause death. And to Us is the final return. **44.** ´Beware of´ the Day the earth will split open, letting them rush forth. That will be an easy gathering for Us. **45.** We know best what they say. And you ´O Prophet´ are not ´there´ to compel them ´to believe´. So remind with the Qur-an ´only´ those who fear My warning.

༺❈༻

51. Scattering Winds (Aẓ-Ẕâriyât)

In the Name of Allah—the Most Compassionate, Most Merciful

Judgment Is Inevitable

1. By the winds scattering ´dust´, **2.** and ´the clouds´ loaded with rain, **3.** and ´the ships´ gliding with ease, **4.** and ´the angels´ administering affairs by ´Allah's´ command! **5.** Indeed, what you are promised is true. **6.** And the Judgment will certainly come to pass.

1078   *See* footnote for 7:54.
1079   Some scholars believe this verse comes in response to Exodus 31:17, which says, "The Lord made the heavens and the earth in six days, but on the seventh day He rested and was refreshed."
1080   This verse refers to the times of the five daily prayers.
1081   See footnote for 50:20.

Warning to the Deniers

7. ˹And˺ by the heavens in their marvellous design![1082] 8. Surely you are ˹lost˺ in conflicting views ˹regarding the truth˺.[1083] 9. Only those ˹destined to be˺ deluded are turned away from it.[1084] 10. Condemned are the liars— 11. those who are ˹steeped˺ in ignorance, totally heedless. 12. They ask ˹mockingly˺, "When is this Day of Judgment?" 13. ˹It is˺ the Day they will be tormented over the Fire. 14. ˹They will be told,˺ "Taste your torment! This is what you sought to hasten."

Good News for the Devout

15. Indeed, the righteous will be amid Gardens and springs, 16. ˹joyfully˺ receiving what their Lord will grant them. Before this ˹reward˺ they were truly good-doers ˹in the world˺: 17. they used to sleep only little in the night, 18. and pray for forgiveness before dawn.[1085] 19. And in their wealth there was a rightful share ˹fulfilled˺ for the beggar and the poor.

Allah's Signs in Creation

20. There are ˹countless˺ signs on earth for those with sure faith, 21. as there are within yourselves. Can you not see? 22. In heaven is your sustenance and whatever you are promised. 23. Then by the Lord of heaven and earth! ˹All˺ this is certainly as true as ˹the fact that˺ you can speak!

Abraham Visited by Angels

24. Has the story of Abraham's honoured guests reached you ˹O Prophet˺? 25. ˹Remember˺ when they entered his presence and greeted ˹him with˺, "Peace!" He replied, "Peace ˹be upon you˺!" ˹Then he said to himself,˺ "˹These are˺ an unfamiliar people." 26. Then he slipped off to his family and brought a fat ˹roasted˺ calf,[1086] 27. and placed it before them, asking, "Will you not eat?" 28. ˹They did not eat,˺ so he grew fearful of them.[1087] They reassured ˹him,˺ "Do not be afraid," and gave him good news of a knowledgeable son.[1088] 29. Then his wife came forward with a cry, clasping her forehead ˹in astonishment˺, exclaiming, "˹A baby from˺ a barren, old woman!" 30. They replied, "Such has your Lord decreed. He is truly the All-Wise, All-Knowing."

1082 Or "By the heavens with their marvellous orbits."
1083 *See* footnote for 50:5.
1084 Other possible translations: 1. "… by which the deluded are turned away." 2. "Whoever is turned away from it is ˹truly˺ deluded."
1085 Optional prayers before dawn are recommended, and are more likely to be accepted.
1086 Abraham (☬) did not want his guests to know that he was going to prepare a meal for them so they would not ask him not to.
1087 As mentioned in 11:69-70, the angels came to Abraham in the form of men and when he offered them food, they did not eat. In ancient Middle Eastern culture, if a guest refused to eat the food provided by their host, it was a sign of ill-will.
1088 Prophet Isaac (☬).

51. Az-Zâriyât

Destruction of the People of Lot

31. ˹Later,˺ Abraham asked, "What is your mission, O messenger-angels?" **32.** They replied, "We have actually been sent to a wicked people, **33.** to send upon them stones of ˹baked˺ clay, **34.** marked by your Lord for the transgressors." **35.** Then ˹before the torment˺ We evacuated the believers from the city. **36.** But We only found one family that had submitted ˹to Allah˺.[1089] **37.** And We have left a sign there[1090] ˹as a lesson˺ for those who fear the painful punishment.

Destruction of Pharaoh's People

38. And in ˹the story of˺ Moses ˹was another lesson,˺ when We sent him to Pharaoh with compelling proof, **39.** but Pharaoh was carried away by his power, saying ˹of Moses˺, "A magician or a madman!" **40.** So We seized him and his soldiers, casting them into the sea while he was blameworthy.[1091]

Destruction of the People of Hûd

41. And in ˹the story of˺ 'Âd ˹was another lesson,˺ when We sent against them the devastating wind.[1092] **42.** There was nothing it came upon that it did not reduce to ashes.

Destruction of the People of Ṣâliḥ

43. And in ˹the story of˺ Thamûd ˹was another lesson,˺ when they were told, "Enjoy yourselves ˹only˺ for a ˹short˺ while."[1093] **44.** Still they persisted in defying the commands of their Lord, so they were overtaken by a ˹mighty˺ blast while they were looking on. **45.** Then they were not able to rise up, nor were they helped.

Destruction of the People of Noah

46. And the people of Noah ˹had also been destroyed˺ earlier. They were truly a rebellious people.

Allah's Power of Creation

47. We built the universe with ˹great˺ might, and We are certainly expanding ˹it˺. **48.** As for the earth, We spread it out. How superbly did We smooth it out![1094] **49.** And We created pairs of all things[1095] so perhaps you would be mindful.

1089 Lot (﷽) and his two daughters.
1090 The ruins of Sodom.
1091 Because of his arrogance and disbelief.
1092 lit., 'a barren wind,' since the wind was not productive—it did not carry rain or fertilize trees.
1093 Meaning, you have only three days to live. *See* 11:65.
1094 The globe was spread out to accommodate Allah's creation. The spherical shape of the earth is expressed in 39:5.
1095 For example, male and female, sweet and bitter, day and night, plains and mountains, heat and cold, light and darkness.

52. Aṭ-Ṭûr | 524

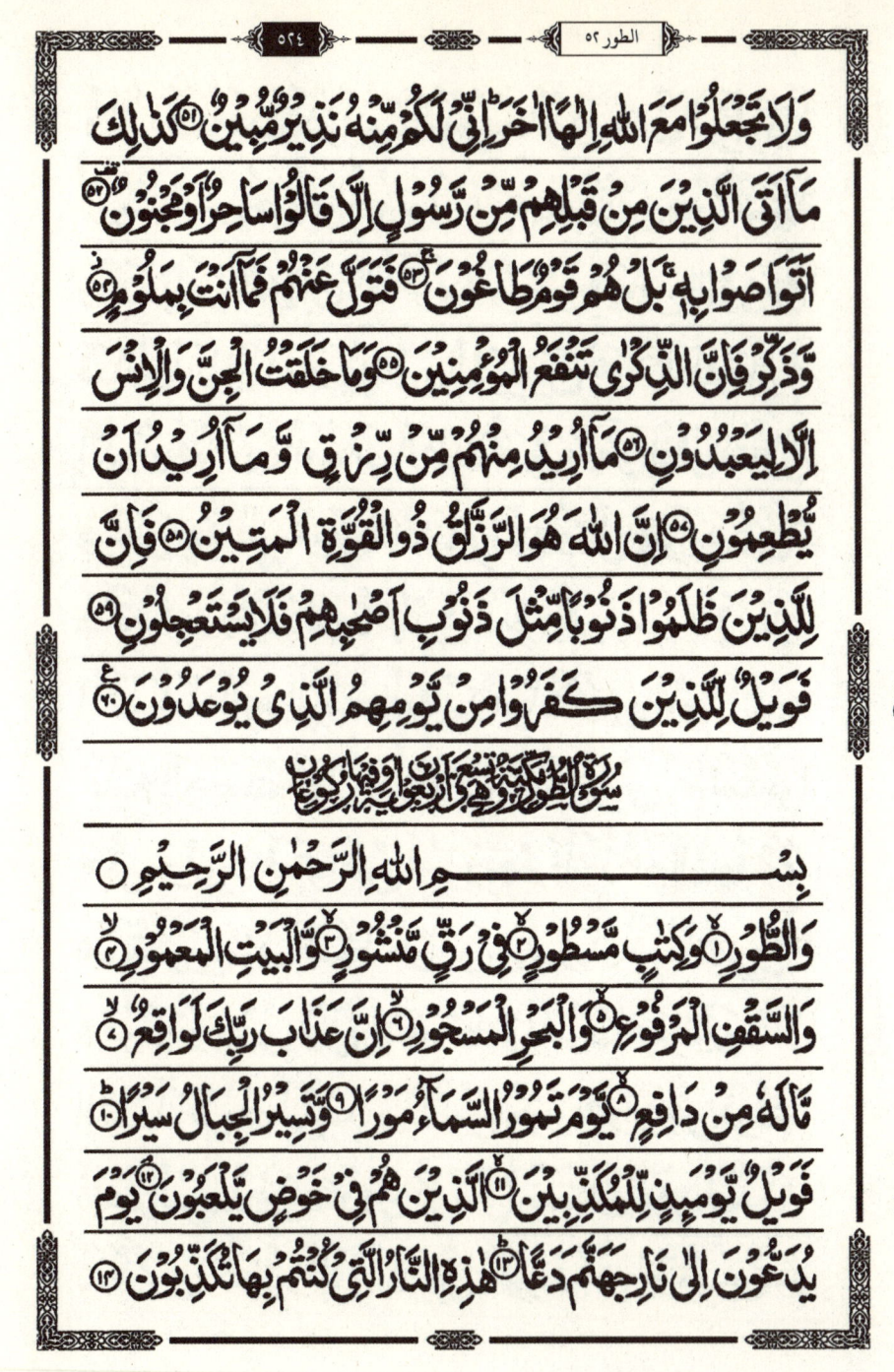

Wake-up Call to the Deniers

50. So ˹proclaim, O Prophet˺: "Flee to Allah! I am truly sent by Him with a clear warning to you. **51.** And do not set up another god with Allah. I am truly sent by Him with a clear warning to you."

Earlier Deniers

52. Similarly, no messenger came to those before them without being told: "A magician or a madman!" **53.** Have they passed this ˹cliché˺ down to one another? In fact, they have ˹all˺ been a transgressing people. **54.** So ˹now˺ turn away from them ˹O Prophet˺, for you will not be blamed.[1096] **55.** But ˹continue to˺ remind. For certainly reminders benefit the believers.

The Purpose of Life

56. I did not create jinn and humans except to worship Me. **57.** I seek no provision from them, nor do I need them to feed Me. **58.** Indeed, Allah ˹alone˺ is the Supreme Provider—Lord of all Power, Ever Mighty.

Warning to the Deniers

59. The wrongdoers will certainly have a share ˹of the torment˺ like that of their predecessors. So do not let them ask Me to hasten ˹it˺. **60.** Woe then to the disbelievers when they face their Day which they are warned of!

❀ ✻ ❀

52. Mount Ṭûr (Aṭ-Ṭûr)

In the Name of Allah—the Most Compassionate, Most Merciful

Judgment Is the Truth

1. By Mount Ṭûr![1097] **2.** And by the Book written **3.** on open pages ˹for all to read˺![1098] **4.** And by the ˹Sacred˺ House frequently visited![1099] **5.** And by the canopy raised ˹high˺! **6.** And by the seas set on fire![1100] **7.** Indeed, the punishment of your Lord will come to pass— **8.** none will avert it— **9.** on the Day the heavens will be shaken violently, **10.** and the mountains will be blown away entirely.

1096 Since you have already delivered the message clearly.
1097 Where Moses (☮) communicated with Allah.
1098 i.e., the Quran.
1099 This is either the Sacred House in Mecca, which is frequented by pilgrims, or a sanctuary in Heaven, which is frequented by angels.
1100 The seas and oceans will be on fire on Judgment Day.

525   **52. Aṭ-Ṭûr**

Horrors Awaiting the Deniers

11. Then woe on that Day to the de-niers— **12.** those who amuse them-selves with falsehood! **13.** ˹It is˺ the Day they will be fiercely shoved into the Fire of Hell. **14.** ˹They will be told,˺ "This is the Fire which you used to deny. **15.** Is this magic, or do you not see? **16.** Burn in it! It is the same whether you endure ˹it˺ patient-ly or not.[1101] You are only rewarded for what you used to do."

Pleasures Awaiting the Faithful

17. Indeed, the righteous will be in Gardens and bliss, **18.** enjoying what-ever their Lord will have granted them. And their Lord will have protected them from the torment of the Hellfire. **19.** ˹They will be told,˺ "Eat and drink happily for what you used to do." **20.** They will be reclining on thrones, ˹neatly˺ lined up ˹facing each other˺. And We will pair them to maidens with gorgeous eyes. **21.** As for those who believe and whose descendants follow them in faith, We will elevate their descendants to their rank, never discounting anything ˹of the reward˺ of their deeds. Every person will reap only what they sowed.[1102] **22.** And We will ˹continually˺ provide them with whatever fruit or meat they desire. **23.** They will pass around to each oth-er a drink ˹of pure wine,˺ which leads to no idle talk or sinfulness. **24.** And they will be waited on by their youth-ful servants like spotless pearls.

Remembering Past Lives in Paradise

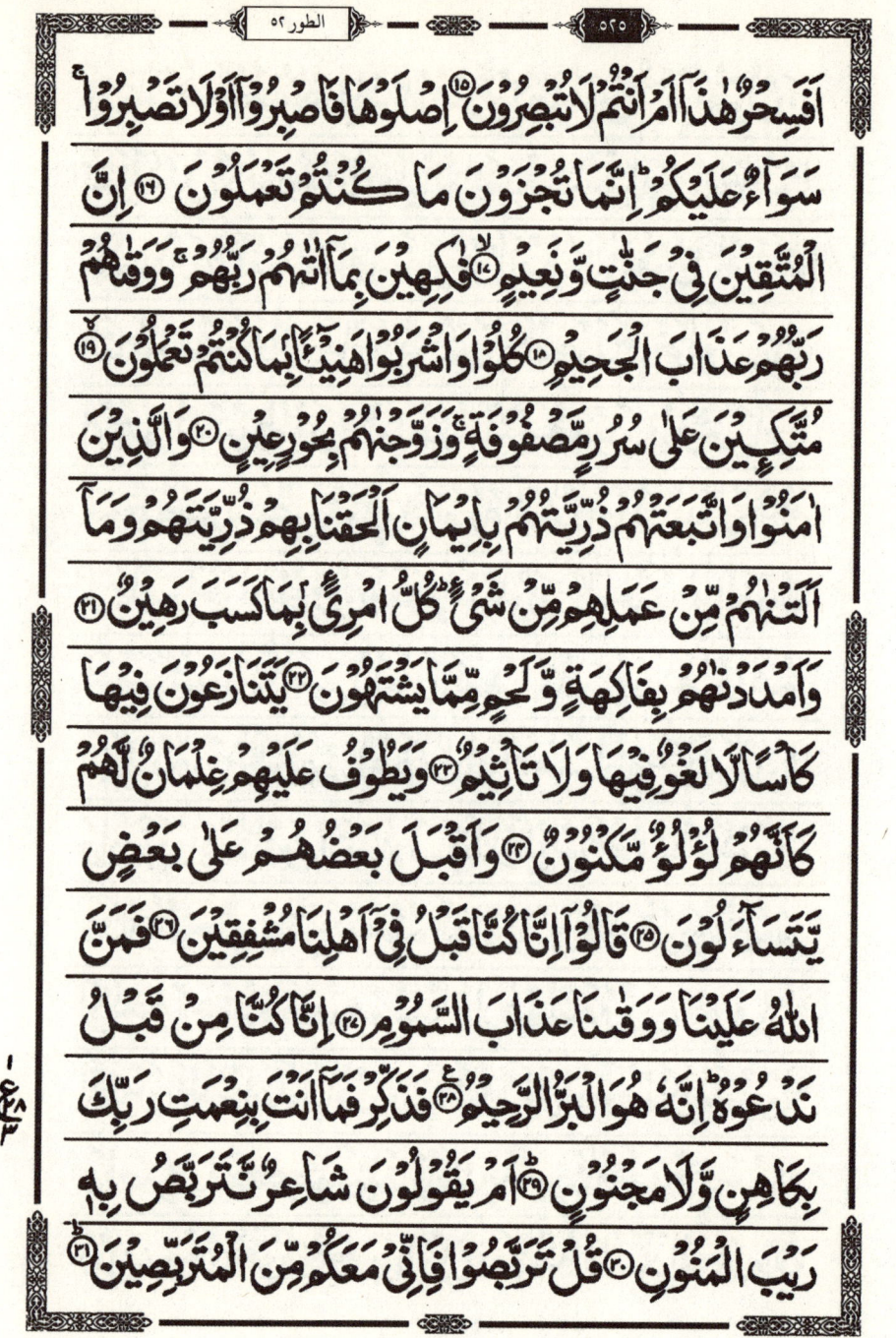

25. They will turn to one another in-quisitively.[1103] **26.** They will say, "Before ˹this reward˺ we used to be in awe ˹of Allah˺ in the midst of our people. **27.** So Allah has graced us and protected us from the torment of ˹Hell's˺ scorching heat. **28.** Indeed, we used to call upon Him ˹alone˺ before. He is truly the Most Kind, Most Merciful."

Why Do Meccans Deny the Truth?

29. So ˹continue to˺ remind ˹all, O Prophet˺. For you, by the grace of your Lord, are not a fortune-teller or a madman. **30.** Or do they say, "˹He is˺ a poet, for whom we ˹eagerly˺ await an ill-fate"? **31.** Say, "Keep waiting! I too am waiting with you."

1101 One gets the reward for being patient in difficult times in this world. As for the Hereafter, those who suffer patiently in Hell will not be rewarded for their patience.
1102 Meaning, no one will carry the burden of another's sins.
1103 It is assumed that they will ask each other about their lives in the world and what led them to Paradise.

52. Aṭ-Ṭûr

32. Or do their ˹intelligent˺ minds prompt them to this ˹paradox˺?[1104] Or are they ˹just˺ a transgressing people? **33.** Or do they say, "He made this ˹Quran˺ up!"? In fact, they have no faith. **34.** Let them then produce something like it, if what they say is true![1105] **35.** Or were they created by nothing, or are they ˹their own˺ creators? **36.** Or did they create the heavens and the earth? In fact, they have no firm belief ˹in Allah˺. **37.** Or do they possess the treasuries of your Lord, or are they in control ˹of everything˺? **38.** Or do they have a stairway, by which they eavesdrop ˹on the heavens˺? Then let those who do so bring a compelling proof. **39.** Or does He have daughters ˹as you claim˺, while you ˹prefer to˺ have sons?[1106] **40.** Or are you ˹O Prophet˺ asking them for a reward ˹for the message˺ so that they are overburdened by debt? **41.** Or do they have access to ˹the Record in˺ the unseen, so they copy it ˹for all to see˺? **42.** Or do they intend to scheme ˹against the Prophet˺? Then it is the disbelievers who will fall victim to ˹their˺ schemes. **43.** Or do they have a god other than Allah? Glorified is Allah far above what they associate ˹with Him˺!

Reassuring the Prophet

44. If they were to see a ˹deadly˺ piece of the sky fall down ˹upon them˺, still they would say, "˹This is just˺ a pile of clouds." **45.** So leave them until they face their Day in which they will be struck dead— **46.** the Day their scheming will be of no benefit to them whatsoever, nor will they be helped. **47.** Also, the wrongdoers will certainly have another torment before that ˹Day˺, but most of them do not know.[1107] **48.** So be patient with your Lord's decree, for you are truly under Our ˹watchful˺ Eyes. And glorify the praises of your Lord when you rise. **49.** And glorify Him during part of the night and at the fading of the stars.

1104 The pagan leaders claimed to be Mecca's most intelligent minds. So this verse questions their intelligence, arguing that the Prophet (ﷺ) cannot be a madman and a poet at the same time.
1105 Arab pagans were challenged in the Quran to produce its equivalent (52:34), or ten sûrahs (11:13), or at least one sûrah (2:23), but the challenge has never been met.
1106 *See* footnote for 37:149.
1107 i.e., famine, droughts, or the defeat at the Battle of Badr (*see* 32:21). The Battle of Badr took place in the 15ᵗʰ year of the Prophet's mission. The previous passage poses fifteen questions to the Meccan pagans before warning them in this passage.

53. The Stars (An-Najm)

In the Name of Allah—the Most Compassionate, Most Merciful

The Prophet's Encounter with Gabriel

1. By the stars when they fade away!
2. Your fellow man[1108] is neither misguided nor astray.
3. Nor does he speak of his own whims.
4. It is only a revelation sent down ˹to him˺.
5. He has been taught by one ˹angel˺ of mighty power[1109]
6. and great perfection, who once rose to ˹his˺ true form[1110]
7. while on the highest point above the horizon,
8. then he approached ˹the Prophet˺, coming so close
9. that he was only two arms-lengths away or even less.[1111]
10. Then Allah revealed to His servant what He revealed ˹through Gabriel˺.
11. The ˹Prophet's˺ heart did not doubt what he saw.
12. How can you ˹O pagans˺ then dispute with him regarding what he saw?
13. And he certainly saw that ˹angel descend˺ a second time
14. at the Lote Tree of the most extreme limit ˹in the seventh heaven˺—
15. near which is the Garden of ˹Eternal˺ Residence—
16. while the Lote Tree was overwhelmed with ˹heavenly˺ splendours!
17. The ˹Prophet's˺ sight never wandered, nor did it overreach.
18. He certainly saw some of his Lord's greatest signs.[1112]

Wake-up Call to Pagans

19. Now, have you considered ˹the idols of˺ *Lât* and *'Uzza*,
20. and the third one, *Manât*, as well?
21. Do you ˹prefer to˺ have sons while ˹you attribute˺ to Him daughters?[1113]
22. Then this is ˹truly˺ a biased distribution!
23. These ˹idols˺ are mere names that you and your forefathers have made up[1114]—a practice Allah has never authorized. They follow nothing but ˹inherited˺ assumptions and whatever ˹their˺ souls desire, although ˹true˺ guidance has already come to them from their Lord.
24. Or should every person ˹simply˺ have whatever ˹intercessors˺ they desire?[1115]
25. In fact, to Allah ˹alone˺ belongs this world and the next.

1108 Muḥammad (ﷺ).
1109 The angel Gabriel.
1110 Gabriel used to come to the Prophet in a human form. But he appeared to him (ﷺ) twice in his angelic form: once at the beginning of the Prophet's mission (when the angel manifested himself, filling the horizon, the Prophet (ﷺ) lost his consciousness), and another time during the Prophet's Night Journey to the seventh heaven to receive the order to pray directly from Allah (see 17:1).
1111 lit., he was only two bow-draws away.
1112 The Prophet was taken to heaven to see some of Allah's magnificent signs. He only saw what he was told to see.
1113 See footnote for 52:39.
1114 Meaning, "You call them gods while in fact they are not gods."
1115 Arab pagans took these idols as intermediaries to intercede for them on the Day of Judgment (see 39:3)

53. An-Najm

26. ˹Imagine˺ how many ˹noble˺ angels are in the heavens! ˹Even˺ their intercession would be of no benefit whatsoever, until Allah gives permission to whoever He wills and ˹only for the people He˺ approves.

Are Angels Allah's Daughters?

27. Indeed, those who do not believe in the Hereafter label angels as female, 28. although they have no knowledge ˹in support˺ of this. They follow nothing but ˹inherited˺ assumptions. And surely assumptions can in no way replace the truth. 29. So turn away ˹O Prophet˺ from whoever has shunned Our Reminder,[1116] only seeking the ˹fleeting˺ life of this world. 30. This is the extent of their knowledge. Surely your Lord knows best who has strayed from His Way and who is ˹rightly˺ guided.

Allah Knows Who Is Righteous

31. To Allah ˹alone˺ belongs whatever is in the heavens and whatever is on the earth so that He may reward the evildoers according to what they did, and reward the good-doers with the finest reward[1117]— 32. those who avoid major sins and shameful deeds, despite ˹stumbling on˺ minor sins. Surely your Lord is infinite in forgiveness. He knew well what would become of you as He created you from the earth[1118] and while you were ˹still˺ fetuses in the wombs of your mothers.[1119] So do not ˹falsely˺ elevate yourselves. He knows best who is ˹truly˺ righteous.

The One Who Returned to Disbelief[1120]

33. Have you seen the one who turned away ˹from Islam,˺ 34. and ˹initially˺ paid a little ˹for his salvation˺, and then stopped? 35. Does he have the knowledge of the unseen so that he sees ˹the Hereafter˺? 36. Or has he not been informed of what is in the Scripture of Moses, 37. and ˹that of˺ Abraham, who ˹perfectly˺ fulfilled ˹his covenant˺? 38. ˹They state˺ that no soul burdened with sin will bear the burden of another, 39. and that each person will only have what they endeavoured towards,

---

1116 i.e., the Quran.
1117 i.e., Paradise.
1118 i.e., your father, Adam.
1119 See footnote for 31:34.
1120 This passage refers to Al-Walîd ibn Al-Mughîrah who initially accepted Islam, and then a man persuaded him to leave Islam, promising to be punished in his place in the Hereafter for a small fee in this world. Initially, Al-Walîd paid him some of the amount they had agreed upon then refused to pay the rest.

40. and that ˹the outcome of˺ their endeavours will be seen ˹in their record˺,
41. then they will be fully rewarded,
42. and that to your Lord ˹alone˺ is the ultimate return ˹of all things˺.

It Is All in Allah's Hands

43. Moreover, He is the One Who brings about joy and sadness.[1121] **44.** And He is the One Who gives life and causes death. **45.** And He created the pairs—males and females— **46.** from a sperm-drop when it is emitted. **47.** And it is upon Him to bring about re-creation. **48.** And He is the One Who enriches and impoverishes. **49.** And He alone is the Lord of Sirius.[1122] **50.** And He destroyed the first ˹people of˺ 'Ȃd, **51.** and ˹then˺ Thamûd,[1123] sparing no one. **52.** And before ˹that He destroyed˺ the people of Noah, who were truly far worse in wrongdoing and transgression. **53.** And ˹it was˺ He ˹Who˺ turned the cities ˹of Sodom and Gomorrah˺ upside down. **54.** How overwhelming was what covered ˹them˺![1124] **55.** Now, which of your Lord's favours will you dispute?

Warning to Arab Pagans

56. This ˹Prophet˺ is a warner like earlier ones. **57.** The approaching ˹Hour˺ has drawn near. **58.** None but Allah can disclose it. **59.** Do you find this revelation astonishing, **60.** laughing ˹at it˺ and not weeping ˹in awe˺, **61.** while persisting in heedlessness? **62.** Instead, prostrate to Allah and worship ˹Him alone˺!

୧୨୧୭ ✹ ୧୨୧୭

54. The Moon (Al-Qamar)

In the Name of Allah—the Most Compassionate, Most Merciful

Warning to Meccan Deniers

1. The Hour has drawn near and the moon was split ˹in two˺.[1125] **2.** Yet, whenever they see a sign, they turn away,[1126] saying, "Same old magic!" **3.** They rejected ˹the truth˺ and followed their own desires—and every matter will be settled—

1121 lit., laughter and weeping.
1122 A star worshipped by some ancient pagans.
1123 Also known as the second 'Ȃd.
1124 The stones of baked clay that were rained upon them (*see* 11:82-83).
1125 The Meccan pagans challenged the Prophet (ﷺ) to have the moon split in two if he wanted them to believe in him. The moon was split, and then re-joined, as reported by several eyewitnesses, but still the pagans refused to believe, calling this miracle "sheer magic."
1126 A miracle (usually referred to as a 'sign' in the Quran) can be defined as an extraordinary event manifesting divine intervention in human affairs. Every prophet was given miracles to prove he was commissioned by Allah. Moses (ﷺ) was given the miracle of the staff and many others. Jesus (ﷺ) gave life to the dead and healed the blind and the leper. And Muḥammad (ﷺ) received the Quran, a literary miracle, to challenge the masters of Arabic eloquence. The Prophet (ﷺ) performed some other miracles such as splitting the moon, multiplying food and water, and healing some of his companions.

54. Al-Qamar

4. even though the stories ʿof destroyed nations’ that have already come to them are a sufficient deterrent. 5. ʿThis Quran is’ profound ʿin’ wisdom, but warnings are of no benefit ʿto them’. 6. So turn away from them ʿO Prophet’. ʿAnd wait for’ the Day ʿwhen’ the caller[1127] will summon ʿthem’ for something horrifying.[1128] 7. With eyes downcast, they will come forth from the graves as if they were swarming locusts, 8. rushing towards the caller. The disbelievers will cry, “This is a difficult Day!”

The People of Noah

9. Before them, the people of Noah denied ʿthe truth’ and rejected Our servant, calling ʿhim’ insane. And he was intimidated. 10. So he cried out to his Lord, “I am helpless, so help ʿme’!” 11. So We opened the gates of the sky with pouring rain, 12. and caused the earth to burst with springs, so the waters met for a fate already set. 13. We carried him on that ʿArk made’ of planks and nails, 14. sailing under Our ʿwatchful’ Eyes—a ʿfair’ punishment on behalf of the one ʿthey’ denied. 15. We certainly left this[1129] as a sign. So is there anyone who will be mindful? 16. Then how ʿdreadful’ were My punishment and warnings! 17. And We have certainly made the Quran easy to remember. So is there anyone who will be mindful?

The People of Hûd

18. ʾÂd ʿalso’ rejected ʿthe truth’. Then how ʿdreadful’ were My punishment and warnings! 19. Indeed, We sent against them a furious wind,[1130] on a day of unrelenting misery, 20. that snatched people up, leaving them like trunks of uprooted palm trees. 21. Then how ʿdreadful’ were My punishment and warnings! 22. And We have certainly made the Quran easy to remember. So is there anyone who will be mindful?

The People of Ṣâliḥ

23. Thamûd rejected the warnings ʿas well’, 24. arguing, “How can we follow one ʿaverage’ human being from among us? We would then truly be misguided and insane.

1127 Angel Isrâfîl will blow the Trumpet, causing all to be raised from the dead for judgment.
1128 i.e., the Judgment.
1129 The Flood or the Ark.
1130 lit., a bitter and screaming wind.

531   **54. Al-Qamar**

25. Has the revelation been sent down ˹only˺ to him out of ˹all of˺ us? In fact, he is a boastful liar." 26. ˹It was revealed to Ṣâliḥ,˺ "They will soon know who the boastful liar is. 27. We are sending the she-camel as a test for them. So watch them ˹closely˺, and have patience. 28. And tell them that the ˹drinking˺ water must be divided between them ˹and her˺, each taking a turn to drink ˹every other day˺. 29. But they roused a companion of theirs, so he dared to kill ˹her˺. 30. Then how ˹dreadful˺ were My punishment and warnings! 31. Indeed, We sent against them ˹only˺ one ˹mighty˺ blast, leaving them like the twigs of fence-builders. 32. And We have certainly made the Quran easy to remember. So is there anyone who will be mindful?

The People of Lot

33. The people of Lot ˹also˺ rejected the warnings. 34. We unleashed upon them a storm of stones. As for ˹the believers of˺ Lot's family, We delivered them before dawn 35. as a blessing from Us. This is how We reward whoever gives thanks. 36. He had already warned them of Our ˹crushing˺ blow but they disputed the warnings. 37. And they even demanded his angel-guests from him,[1131] so We blinded their eyes. ˹And they were told,˺ "Taste then My punishment and warnings!" 38. And indeed, by the early morning they were overwhelmed by an unrelenting torment. 39. ˹Again they were told,˺ "Taste now My punishment and warnings!" 40. And We have certainly made the Quran easy to remember. So is there anyone who will be mindful?

The People of Pharaoh

41. And indeed, the warnings ˹also˺ came to the people of Pharaoh. 42. ˹But˺ they rejected all of Our signs, so We seized them with the ˹crushing˺ grip of the Almighty, Most Powerful.

Warning to Pagan Deniers

43. Now, are you ˹Meccan˺ disbelievers superior to those ˹destroyed peoples˺? Or have you ˹been granted˺ immunity ˹from punishment˺ in divine Books? 44. Or do they say, "We are all ˹a˺ united ˹front˺, bound to prevail."?

1131 Who came in the form of handsome men.

45. ˹Soon˺ their united front will be defeated and ˹forced to˺ flee.[1132] **46.** Better yet, the Hour is their appointed time—and the Hour will be most catastrophic and most bitter. **47.** Indeed, the wicked are ˹entrenched˺ in misguidance, and ˹are bound for˺ blazes. **48.** On the Day they will be dragged into the Fire on their faces, ˹they will be told,˺ "Taste the touch of Hell!"[1133] **49.** Indeed, We have created everything, perfectly preordained. **50.** Our command[1134] is but a single word,[1135] done in the blink of an eye. **51.** We have already destroyed the likes of you. So will any ˹of you˺ be mindful? **52.** Everything they have done is ˹listed˺ in ˹their˺ records. **53.** Every matter, small and large, is written ˹precisely˺.

Reward of the Righteous

54. Indeed, the righteous will be amid Gardens and rivers,[1136] **55.** at the Seat of Honour in the presence of the Most Powerful Sovereign.

⌘❋⌘

55. The Most Compassionate (Ar-Raḥmân)

In the Name of Allah—the Most Compassionate, Most Merciful

Allah's Favours: 1) Speech

1. The Most Compassionate **2.** taught the Quran, **3.** created humanity, **4.** ˹and˺ taught them speech.

Favour 2) The Universe

5. The sun and the moon ˹travel˺ with precision. **6.** The stars and the trees bow down ˹in submission˺.[1137] **7.** As for the sky, He raised it ˹high˺, and set the balance ˹of justice˺ **8.** so that you do not defraud the scales. **9.** Weigh with justice, and do not give short measure.

Favour 3) Provisions

10. He laid out the earth for all beings. **11.** In it are fruit, palm trees with date stalks, **12.** and grain with husks, and aromatic plants.

1132 This was later fulfilled in the Battle of Badr.
1133 *Saqar* is one of the names of Hell.
1134 To bring anything into being.
1135 "Be!" And it is!
1136 Rivers of water, milk, honey, and wine. *See* 47:15.
1137 lit., prostrate.

55. Ar-Raḥmân

13. Then which of your Lord's favours will you ˹humans and jinn˺ both deny?[1138]

Favour 4) Humans and Jinn

14. He created humankind from ˹sounding˺ clay like pottery, **15.** and created jinn from a ˹smokeless˺ flame of fire. **16.** Then which of your Lord's favours will you both deny?

Favour 5) Natural Marvels

17. ˹He is˺ Lord of the two easts and the two wests.[1139] **18.** Then which of your Lord's favours will you both deny? **19.** He merges the two bodies of ˹fresh and salt˺ water, **20.** yet between them is a barrier they never cross.[1140] **21.** Then which of your Lord's favours will you both deny? **22.** Out of both ˹waters˺ come forth pearls and coral. **23.** Then which of your Lord's favours will you both deny? **24.** To Him belong the ships with raised sails, sailing through the seas like mountains. **25.** Then which of your Lord's favours will you both deny?

Only Allah Is Eternal

26. Every being on earth is bound to perish. **27.** Only your Lord Himself,[1141] full of Majesty and Honour, will remain ˹forever˺.[1142] **28.** Then which of your Lord's favours will you both deny?

All Stand In Need of Allah

29. All those in the heavens and the earth are dependent on Him. Day in and day out He has something to bring about.[1143] **30.** Then which of your Lord's favours will you both deny?

Punishment of the People of the Left[1144]

31. We will soon attend to you ˹for judgment˺, O two multitudes ˹of jinn and humans˺! **32.** Then which of your Lord's favours will you both deny? **33.** O assembly of jinn and humans! If you can penetrate beyond the realms of the heavens and the earth, then do so. ˹But˺ you cannot do that without ˹Our˺ authority. **34.** Then which of your Lord's favours will you both deny? **35.** Flames

---

1138 This question is repeated thirty-one times in this sûrah: eight times after reminders of Allah's favours, seven times in the passage talking about the punishment of the deniers of judgment (which is the number of the gates of Hell), and eight times in each of the two following passages talking about Paradise, which has eight gates.

1139 The two points of sunrise and sunset in the summer and the winter.

1140 *See* footnote for 25:53.

1141 lit., your Lord's Face.

1142 Death is listed as one of Allah's favours since it puts an end to tyrants, ends the suffering of the oppressed, makes all people equal, ushers in judgment and the enforcement of justice, and leads the believers to eternal joy and peace in Paradise.

1143 Giving life and causing death, making some rich and others poor, elevating some and debasing others, etc.

1144 According to the next three passages (as well as the next sûrah), people will be divided into three groups on Judgment Day: the foremost, the righteous who are always ahead of others in faith and goodness; the people of the right, the average believers who will receive their records of deeds with their right hands; and the people of the left, the disbelievers who will receive their records with their left hands.

of fire and ˹molten˺ copper will be sent against you, and you will not be able to defend one another. 36. Then which of your Lord's favours will you both deny? 37. ˹How horrible will it be˺ when the heavens will split apart, becoming rose-red like ˹burnt˺ oil! 38. Then which of your Lord's favours will you both deny? 39. On that Day there will be no need for any human or jinn to be asked about their sins.[1145] 40. Then which of your Lord's favours will you both deny? 41. The wicked will be recognized by their appearance, then will be seized by ˹their˺ forelocks and feet. 42. Then which of your Lord's favours will you both deny? 43. ˹They will be told,˺ "This is the Hell which the wicked denied." 44. They will alternate between its flames and scalding water. 45. Then which of your Lord's favours will you both deny?[1148]

Reward of the Foremost Believers

46. And whoever is in awe of standing before their Lord will have two Gardens. 47. Then which of your Lord's favours will you both deny? 48. ˹Both will be˺ with lush branches. 49. Then which of your Lord's favours will you both deny? 50. In each ˹Garden˺ will be two flowing springs. 51. Then which of your Lord's favours will you both deny? 52. In each will be two types of every fruit. 53. Then which of your Lord's favours will you both deny? 54. Those ˹believers˺ will recline on furnishings lined with rich brocade. And the fruit of both Gardens will hang within reach. 55. Then which of your Lord's favours will you both deny? 56. In both ˹Gardens˺ will be maidens of modest gaze, who no human or jinn has ever touched before. 57. Then which of your Lord's favours will you both deny? 58. Those ˹maidens˺ will be ˹as elegant˺ as rubies and coral. 59. Then which of your Lord's favours will you both deny? 60. Is there any reward for goodness except goodness? 61. Then which of your Lord's favours will you both deny?

Reward of the People of the Right

62. And below these two ˹Gardens˺ will be two others. 63. Then which of your Lord's favours will you both deny? 64. Both will be dark green. 65. Then which of your Lord's favours will you both deny? 66. In each will be two gushing springs.

1145 Since their sins are already known to Allah and written in perfect records, they will only be interrogated as a form of punishment.

535   56. Al-Wâqi'ah

67. Then which of your Lord's favours will you both deny? 68. In both will be fruit, palm trees, and pomegranates. 69. Then which of your Lord's favours will you both deny? 70. In all Gardens will be noble, pleasant mates. 71. Then which of your Lord's favours will you both deny? 72. ˹They will be˺ maidens with gorgeous eyes, reserved in pavilions. 73. Then which of your Lord's favours will you both deny? 74. No human or jinn has ever touched these ˹maidens˺ before.[1146] 75. Then which of your Lord's favours will you both deny? 76. All ˹believers˺ will be reclining on green cushions and splendid carpets. 77. Then which of your Lord's favours will you both deny? 78. Blessed is the Name of your Lord, full of Majesty and Honour.

ি⚛⚛

56. The Inevitable Event
(Al-Wâqi'ah)

In the Name of Allah—the Most Compassionate, Most Merciful

The Three Groups
on Judgment Day[1147]

1. When the Inevitable Event takes place, 2. then no one can deny it has come. 3. It will debase ˹some˺ and elevate ˹others˺.[1148] 4. When the earth will be violently shaken, 5. and the mountains will be crushed to pieces, 6. becoming scattered ˹particles of˺ dust, 7. you will ˹all˺ be ˹divided into˺ three groups: 8. the people of the right, how ˹blessed˺ will they be; 9. the people of the left, how ˹miserable˺ will they be;

10. and the foremost ˹in faith˺ will be the foremost ˹in Paradise˺.

1) The Foremost

11. They are the ones nearest ˹to Allah˺, 12. in the Gardens of Bliss. 13. ˹They will be˺ a multitude from earlier generations 14. and a few from later generations. 15. ˹All will be˺ on jewelled thrones, 16. reclining face to face.

1146 Before these righteous servants in Paradise.
1147 *See* footnote for verses 31-45 in the previous sûrah.
1148 Unlike this world of sheer injustice, the Hereafter will put everyone in their right place. The righteous will be elevated in Paradise, while the wicked will be humiliated in Hell.

56. Al-Wâqi'ah

17. They will be waited on by eternal youths 18. with cups, pitchers, and a drink ˹of pure wine˺ from a flowing stream, 19. that will cause them neither headache nor intoxication. 20. ˹They will also be served˺ any fruit they choose 21. and meat from any bird they desire. 22. And ˹they will have˺ maidens with gorgeous eyes, 23. like pristine pearls, 24. ˹all˺ as a reward for what they used to do. 25. There they will never hear any idle or sinful talk— 26. only good and virtuous speech.[1149]

2) People of the Right

27. And the people of the right—how ˹blessed˺ will they be! 28. ˹They will be˺ amid thornless lote trees, 29. clusters of bananas, 30. extended shade, 31. flowing water, 32. abundant fruit— 33. never out of season nor forbidden— 34. and elevated furnishings. 35. Indeed, We will have perfectly created their mates, 36. making them virgins, 37. loving and of equal age, 38. for the people of the right, 39. ˹who will be˺ a multitude from earlier generations 40. and a multitude from later generations.

3) People of the Left

41. And the people of the left—how ˹miserable˺ will they be! 42. ˹They will be˺ in scorching heat and boiling water, 43. in the shade of black smoke, 44. neither cool nor refreshing. 45. Indeed, before this ˹torment˺ they were spoiled by luxury, 46. and persisted in the worst of sin.[1150] 47. They used to ask ˹mockingly˺, "When we are dead and reduced to dust and bones, will we really be resurrected? 48. And our forefathers as well?" 49. Say, ˹O Prophet,˺ "Most certainly, earlier and later generations 50. will surely be gathered ˹together˺ for the appointed Day. 51. Then you, O misguided deniers,

---

1149 Another possible translation: "only exchanging greetings of peace."
1150 i.e., associating others with Allah in worship and denying the resurrection and judgment.

56. Al-Wâqi'ah

52. will certainly eat from ˹the fruit of˺ the trees of *Zaqqûm*,[1151] 53. filling up ˹your˺ bellies with it. 54. Then on top of that you will drink boiling water— 55. and you will drink ˹it˺ like thirsty camels do." 56. This will be their accommodation on the Day of Judgment.

Allah's Power: 1) Creating Humans

57. It is We Who created you. Will you not then believe ˹in resurrection˺? 58. Have you considered what you ejaculate? 59. Is it you who create ˹a child out of˺ it, or is it We Who do so? 60. We have ordained death for ˹all of˺ you, and We cannot be prevented 61. from transforming and recreating you in forms unknown to you. 62. You already know how you were first created. Will you not then be mindful?

2) Causing Plants to Grow

63. Have you considered what you sow? 64. Is it you who cause it to grow, or is it We Who do so? 65. If We willed, We could simply reduce this ˹harvest˺ to chaff, leaving you to lament, 66. "We have truly suffered a ˹great˺ loss. 67. In fact, we have been deprived ˹of our livelihood˺."

3) Bringing Rain down

68. Have you considered the water you drink? 69. Is it you who bring it down from the clouds, or is it We Who do so? 70. If We willed, We could make it salty. Will you not then give thanks?

4) Producing Fire from Trees

71. Have you considered the fire you kindle?[1152] 72. Is it you who produce its trees, or is it We Who do so? 73. We have made it ˹as˺ a reminder ˹of the Hellfire˺ and a provision for the travellers. 74. So glorify the Name of your Lord, the Greatest.

Message to Quran Deniers

75. So I do swear by the positions of the stars— 76. and this, if only you knew, is indeed a great oath—

1151 See footnote for 44:43.
1152 This verse refers to two types of Arabian trees, *markh* and *'afâr*, which produce fire when their green branches are rubbed together.

57. Al-Ḥadîd 538

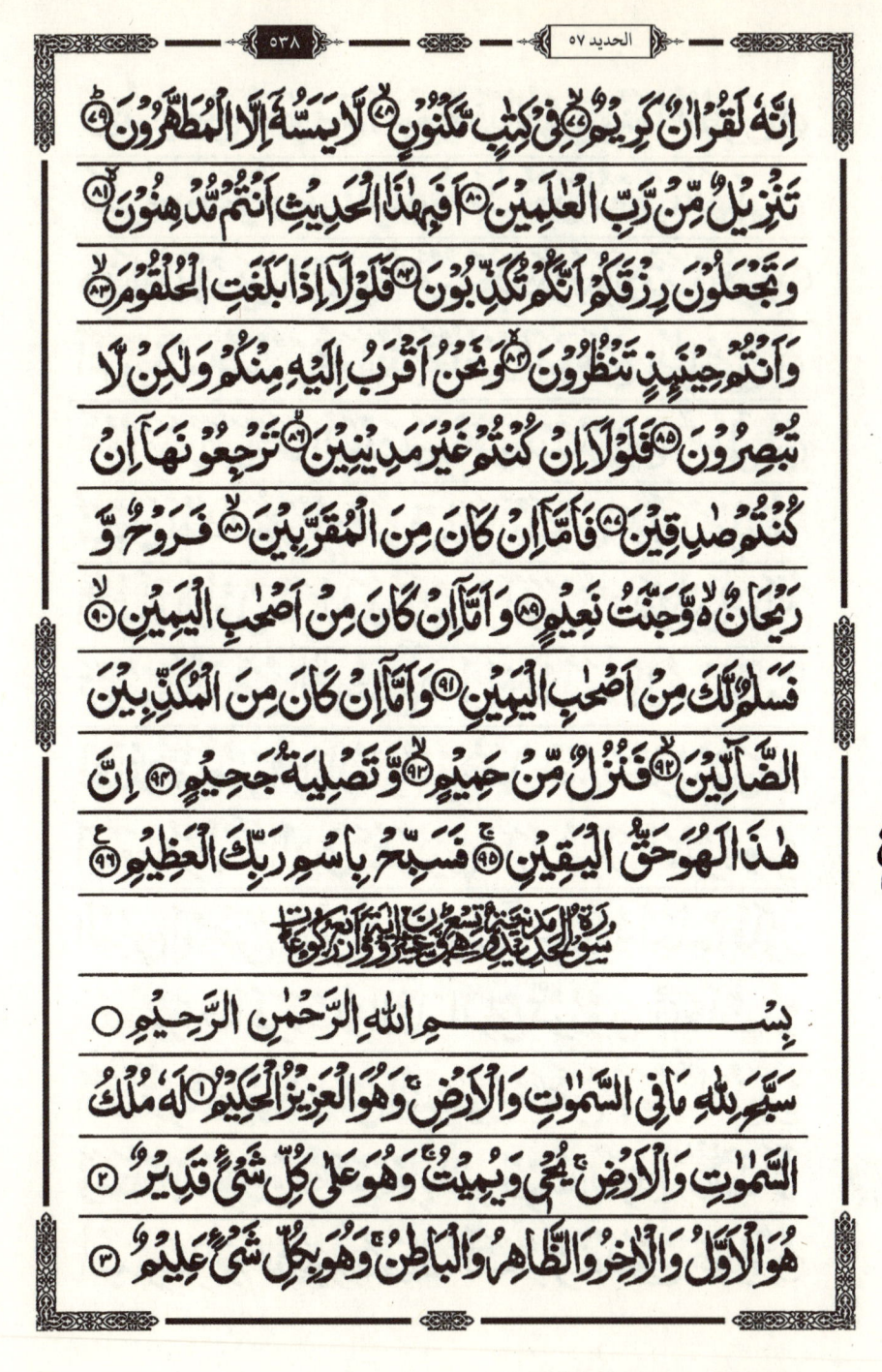

77. that this is truly a noble Quran, 78. in a well-preserved Record,[1153] 79. touched by none except the purified ˹angels˺.[1154] 80. ˹It is˺ a revelation from the Lord of all worlds. 81. How can you then take this message lightly, 82. and repay ˹Allah for˺ your provisions with denial?[1155]

A Challenge to Deniers of the Hereafter

83. Why then ˹are you helpless˺ when the soul ˹of a dying person˺ reaches ˹their˺ throat, 84. while you are looking on? 85. And We are nearer to such a person than you, but you cannot see. 86. Now, if you are not subject to Our Will ˹as you claim˺, 87. bring that soul back, if what you say is true.

Which of the Three Will You Be?

88. So, if the deceased is one of those brought near ˹to Us˺, 89. then ˹such a person will have˺ serenity, fragrance,[1156] and a Garden of Bliss. 90. And if the deceased is one of the people of the right, 91. then ˹they will be told,˺ "Greetings to you from the people of the right." 92. But if such person is one of the misguided deniers, 93. then their accommodation will be boiling water ˹to drink˺ 94. and burning in Hellfire. 95. Indeed, this is the absolute truth. 96. So glorify the Name of your Lord, the Greatest.

ൟ ✶ ൟ

57. Iron (Al-Ḥadîd)

In the Name of Allah—the Most Compassionate, Most Merciful

Allah's Knowledge and Might

1. Whatever is in the heavens and the earth glorifies Allah, for He is the Almighty, All-Wise. 2. To Him belongs the kingdom of the heavens and the earth. He gives life and causes death. And He is Most Capable of everything. 3. He is the First and the Last, the Most High and Most Near,[1157] and He has ˹perfect˺ knowledge of all things.

1153 See 43:4.
1154 This verse refutes the pagan claim that the Quran was sent down by devils (see 26:210-212). Based on this verse, many jurists maintain that a Muslim should perform ablutions before reading the Quran.
1155 Some pagans believed that rain was caused by some stars.
1156 lit., fragrant basil. Throughout the Quran, Paradise is described as being pleasant to the eye, the heart, and the ear. This verse emphasizes the scent as well.
1157 Another possible translation: "the Manifest ˹through His signs˺ and the Hidden ˹from His creation˺."

4. He is the One Who created the heavens and the earth in six Days,[1158] then established Himself on the Throne. He knows whatever goes into the earth and whatever comes out of it, and whatever descends from the sky and whatever ascends into it. And He is with you wherever you are.[1159] For Allah is All-Seeing of what you do. **5.** To Him belongs the kingdom of the heavens and the earth. And to Allah all matters are returned. **6.** He merges the night into day and the day into night. And He knows best what is ˹hidden˺ in the heart.

Believe and Support Allah's Cause

7. Believe in Allah and His Messenger, and donate from what He has entrusted you with. So those of you who believe and donate will have a mighty reward.

Why Do You Not Believe?

8. Why do you not believe in Allah while the Messenger is inviting you to have faith in your Lord, although He has already taken your covenant,[1160] if you will ever believe. **9.** He is the One Who sends down clear revelations to His servant to bring you out of darkness and into light. For indeed Allah is Ever Gracious and Most Merciful to you.

Why Do You Not Donate?

10. And why should you not spend in the cause of Allah, while Allah is the ˹sole˺ inheritor of the heavens and the earth? Those of you who donated and fought before the victory ˹over Mecca˺ are unparalleled. They are far greater in rank than those who donated and fought afterwards.[1161] Yet Allah has promised each a fine reward. And Allah is All-Aware of what you do.

1158 *See* footnote for 7:54.
1159 By His knowledge.
1160 See 7:172.
1161 Prior to the victory over Mecca, Muslims were outnumbered and perceived as weak. Once Mecca surrendered to the Muslims, many tribes either accepted Islam or made peace agreements with the Muslim victors. Therefore, the believers who donated and strived at the time of hardship and weakness deserve more rewards than those who did so at the time of ease and prominence.

57. Al-Ḥadîd   540

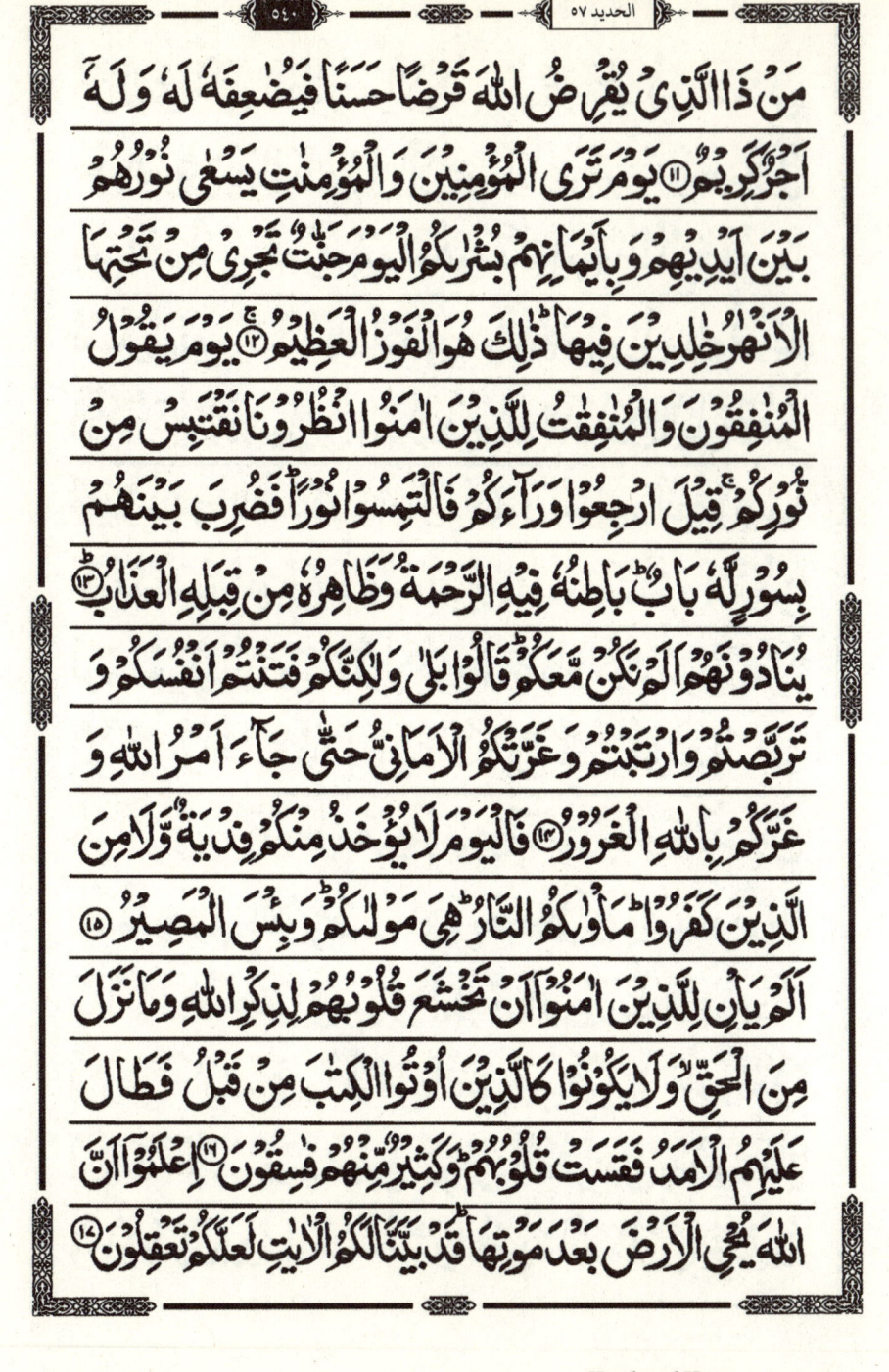

A Generous Reward for the Generous

11. Who is it that will lend to Allah a good loan which Allah will multiply ˹many times over˺ for them, and they will have an honourable reward?[1162] **12.** On that Day you will see believing men and women with their light shining ahead of them and on their right. ˹They will be told,˺ "Today you have good news of Gardens, under which rivers flow, ˹for you˺ to stay in forever. This is ˹truly˺ the ultimate triumph."

The Hypocrites Entrenched in Darkness

13. On that Day hypocrite men and women will beg the believers, "Wait for us so that we may have some of your light." It will be said ˹mockingly˺, "Go back ˹to the world˺ and seek a light ˹there˺!" Then a ˹separating˺ wall with a gate will be erected between them. On the near side will be grace and on the far side will be torment.[1163] **14.** The tormented will cry out to those graced, "Were we not with you?" They will reply, "Yes ˹you were˺. But you chose to be tempted ˹by hypocrisy˺, ˹eagerly˺ awaited ˹our demise˺, doubted ˹the truth˺, and were deluded by false hopes until Allah's decree ˹of your death˺ came to pass. And ˹so˺ the Chief Deceiver[1164] deceived you about Allah. **15.** So Today no ransom will be accepted from you ˹hypocrites˺, nor from the disbelievers. Your home is the Fire—it is the ˹only˺ fitting place for you. What an evil destination!"

Hardened Hearts

16. Has the time not yet come for believers' hearts to be humbled at the remembrance of Allah and what has been revealed of the truth, and not be like those given the Scripture before—˹those˺ who were spoiled for so long that their hearts became hardened. And many of them are ˹still˺ rebellious. **17.** Know that Allah revives the earth after its death.[1165] We have certainly made the signs clear for you so perhaps you will understand.

1162 i.e., Paradise.
1163 This wall is said to be the barrier of *Al-A'râf* (or the heights) between Paradise and Hell. *See* 7:46-49.
1164 Satan.
1165 So it is easy for Him to soften your hearts as well.

Reward of the Faithful

18. Indeed, those men and women who give in charity and lend to Allah a good loan will have it multiplied for them, and they will have an honourable reward.[1166] **19.** ʿAs forʾ those who believe in Allah and His messengers, it is they who are ʿtrulyʾ the people of truth. And the martyrs, with their Lord, will have their reward and their light. But ʿas forʾ those who disbelieve and reject Our signs, it is they who will be the residents of the Hellfire.

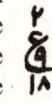

Fleeting Life vs. Eternal Life

20. Know that this worldly life is no more than play, amusement, luxury, mutual boasting, and competition in wealth and children. This is like rain that causes plants to grow, to the delight of the planters. But later the plants dry up and you see them wither, then they are reduced to chaff. And in the Hereafter there will be either severe punishment or forgiveness and pleasure of Allah, whereas the life of this world is no more than the delusion of enjoyment. **21.** ʿSoʾ compete with one another for forgiveness from your Lord and a Paradise as vast as the heavens and the earth, prepared for those who believe in Allah and His messengers. This is the favour of Allah. He grants it to whoever He wills. And Allah is the Lord of infinite bounty.

Everything Is Destined

22. No calamity ʿor blessingʾ occurs on earth or in yourselves without being ʿwrittenʾ in a Record before We bring it into being. This is certainly easy for Allah. **23.** ʿWe let you know thisʾ so that you neither grieve over what you have missed nor boast over what He has granted you. For Allah does not like whoever is arrogant, boastful— **24.** those who are stingy and promote stinginess among people. And whoever turns away ʿshould know thatʾ Allah ʿaloneʾ is truly the Self-Sufficient, Praiseworthy.

1166 i.e., Paradise.

57. Al-Ḥadîd

Prophets and Justice

25. Indeed, We sent Our messengers with clear proofs, and with them We sent down the Scripture and the balance ˹of justice˺ so that people may administer justice. And We sent down iron with its great might, benefits for humanity, and means for Allah to prove who ˹is willing to˺ stand up for Him and His messengers without seeing Him. Surely Allah is All-Powerful, Almighty.

Noah and Abraham

26. And indeed, We sent Noah and Abraham and reserved prophethood and revelation for their descendants. Some of them are ˹rightly˺ guided, while most are rebellious.

Jesus and His Followers

27. Then in the footsteps of these ˹prophets˺, We sent Our messengers, and ˹after them˺ We sent Jesus, son of Mary, and granted him the Gospel, and instilled compassion and mercy into the hearts of his followers. As for monasticism, they made it up— We never ordained it for them—only seeking to please Allah, yet they did not ˹even˺ observe it strictly. So We rewarded those of them who were faithful. But most of them are rebellious.

An Appeal to Jews and Christians

28. O people of faith! Fear Allah and believe in His Messenger. ˹And˺ He will grant you a double share of His mercy, provide you with a light to walk in ˹on Judgment Day˺, and forgive you. For Allah is All-Forgiving, Most Merciful. **29.** ˹This is so˺ that the People of the Book ˹who deny the Prophet˺ may know that they do not have any control over Allah's grace, and that all grace is in Allah's Hands. He grants it to whoever He wills. For Allah is the Lord of infinite bounty.

58. The Pleading Woman (Al-Mujâdilah)

In the Name of Allah—the Most Compassionate, Most Merciful

The Case of Khawlah

1. Indeed, Allah has heard the argument of the woman who pleaded with you ˹O Prophet˺ concerning her husband, and appealed to Allah. Allah has heard your exchange. Surely Allah is All-Hearing, All-Seeing.

The Ruling on Ẓihâr

2. Those of you who ˹sinfully˺ divorce their wives by comparing them to their mothers ˹should know that˺ their wives are in no way their mothers. None can be their mothers except those who gave birth to them. What they say is certainly detestable and false. Yet Allah is truly Ever-Pardoning, All-Forgiving.
3. Those who divorce their wives in this manner, then ˹wish to˺ retract what they said, must free a slave before they touch each other. This ˹penalty˺ is meant to deter you. And Allah is All-Aware of what you do.
4. But if the husband cannot afford this, let him then fast two consecutive months before the couple touch each other. But if he is unable ˹to fast˺, then let him feed sixty poor people. This is to re-affirm your faith in Allah and His Messenger. These are the limits set by Allah. And the disbelievers will suffer a painful punishment.

Fate of the Defiant

5. Indeed, those who defy Allah and His Messenger will be debased, just like those before them. We have certainly sent down clear revelations. And the disbelievers will suffer a humiliating punishment.
6. On the Day Allah resurrects them all together, He will then inform them of what they have done. Allah has kept account of it all, while they have forgotten it. For Allah is a Witness over all things.

58. Al-Mujâdilah 544

Allah's Infinite Knowledge

7. Do you not see that Allah knows whatever is in the heavens and whatever is on the earth? If three converse privately, He is their fourth. If five, He is their sixth. Whether fewer or more, He is with them[1167] wherever they may be. Then, on the Day of Judgment, He will inform them of what they have done. Surely Allah has ˹perfect˺ knowledge of all things.

Evil, Secret Talks

8. Have you not seen those who were forbidden from secret talks, yet they ˹always˺ return to what they were forbidden from, conspiring in sin, aggression, and disobedience to the Messenger? And when they come to you ˹O Prophet˺, they greet you not as Allah greets you,[1168] and say to one another, "Why does Allah not punish us for what we say?" Hell is enough for them—they will burn in it. And what an evil destination!

Guidelines for Secret Talks

9. O believers! When you converse privately, let it not be for sin, aggression, or disobedience to the Messenger, but let it be for goodness and righteousness. And fear Allah, to Whom you will ˹all˺ be gathered.
10. Secret talks are only inspired by Satan to grieve the believers. Yet he cannot harm them whatsoever except by Allah's Will. So in Allah let the believers put their trust.

Etiquette of Gatherings

11. O believers! When you are told to make room in gatherings, then do so. Allah will make room for you ˹in His grace˺. And if you are told to rise, then do so. Allah will elevate those of you who are faithful, and ˹raise˺ those gifted with knowledge in rank. And Allah is All-Aware of what you do.

1167 i.e., by His knowledge.
1168 Some Jews used to play with words when they addressed the Prophet to ridicule him, saying for example 'Asâmu 'alaikum' (death be upon you) instead of 'Asalâmu 'alaikum' (peace be upon you)—which is the greeting of Islam, inspired by Allah.

58. Al-Mujâdilah

Charity Before Consulting the Prophet[1169]

12. O believers! When you consult the Messenger privately, give something in charity before your consultation. That is better and purer for you. But if you lack the means, then Allah is truly All-Forgiving, Most Merciful.
13. Are you afraid of spending in charity before your private consultations ˹with him˺? Since you are unable to do so, and Allah has turned to you in mercy, then ˹continue to˺ establish prayer, pay alms-tax, and obey Allah and His Messenger. And Allah is All-Aware of what you do.

Satan's Party

14. Have you not seen those ˹hypocrites˺ who ally themselves with a people with whom Allah is displeased? They are neither with you nor with them. And they swear to lies knowingly. 15. Allah has prepared for them a severe punishment. Evil indeed is what they do. 16. They have made their ˹false˺ oaths as a shield, hindering ˹others˺ from the cause of Allah. So they will suffer a humiliating punishment. 17. Neither their wealth nor children will be of any help to them against Allah whatsoever. It is they who will be the residents of the Fire. They will be there forever. 18. On the Day Allah resurrects them all, they will ˹falsely˺ swear to Him as they swear to you, thinking they have something to stand on. Indeed, it is they who are the ˹total˺ liars. 19. Satan has taken hold of them, causing them to forget the remembrance of Allah. They are the party of Satan. Surely Satan's party is bound to lose.

Allah's Party

20. ˹As for˺ those who defy Allah and His Messenger, they will definately be among the most debased.

1169 Some companions used to ask the Prophet (ﷺ) unnecessary and sometimes meaningless questions. For example: who their fathers were, where their lost animals were, and what they had in their pockets. Some would ask for new rulings that would probably make things difficult for some Muslims or even themselves. So this verse was revealed to cut down such practice. Eventually, the ruling was lifted in order not to make it difficult for people with good questions, who could not afford to give a charity.

59. Al-Ḥashr   546

21. Allah has decreed, "I and My messengers will certainly prevail." Surely Allah is All-Powerful, Almighty. 22. You will never find a people who ˹truly˺ believe in Allah and the Last Day loyal to those who defy Allah and His Messenger, even if they were their parents, children, siblings, or extended family. For those ˹believers˺, Allah has instilled faith in their hearts and strengthened them with a spirit from Him.[1170] He will admit them into Gardens under which rivers flow, to stay there forever. Allah is pleased with them and they are pleased with Him. They are the party of Allah. Indeed, Allah's party is bound to succeed.

ঙ৯০ ✸ ঙ৯০

59. The Banishment (Al-Ḥashr)

In the Name of Allah—the Most Compassionate, Most Merciful

Banu An-Naḍîr Exiled

1. Whatever is in the heavens and whatever is on the earth glorifies Allah. For He is the Almighty, All-Wise. 2. He is the One Who expelled the disbelievers of the People of the Book from their homes for ˹their˺ first banishment ˹ever˺. You never thought they would go. And they thought their strongholds would put them out of Allah's reach. But ˹the decree of˺ Allah came upon them from where they never expected. And He cast horror into their hearts so they destroyed their houses with their own hands and the hands of the believers.[1171] So take a lesson ˹from this˺, O people of insight! 3. Had Allah not decreed exile for them, He would have certainly punished them in this world. And in the Hereafter they will suffer the punishment of the Fire.

1170 Spirit here can mean revelation, light, or help.
1171 The Prophet (ﷺ) allowed Banu An-Naḍîr to carry whatever they could on their camels, so they removed the wooden pillars of their homes, causing them to collapse.

4. This is because they defied Allah and His Messenger. And whoever defies Allah, then Allah is truly severe in punishment.

Ruling on Palm Trees and Gains

5. Whatever palm trees you ˹believers˺ cut down or left standing intact, it was ˹all˺ by Allah's Will, so that He might disgrace the rebellious.[1172]
6. As for the gains Allah has turned over to His Messenger from them—you did not ˹even˺ spur on any horse or camel for such gains. But Allah gives authority to His messengers over whoever He wills. For Allah is Most Capable of everything.

Distribution of Future Gains[1173]

7. As for gains granted by Allah to His Messenger from the people of ˹other˺ lands, they are for Allah and the Messenger, his close relatives, orphans, the poor, and ˹needy˺ travellers so that wealth may not merely circulate among your rich. Whatever the Messenger gives you, take it. And whatever he forbids you from, leave it. And fear Allah. Surely Allah is severe in punishment. **8.** ˹Some of the gains will be˺ for poor emigrants who were driven out of their homes and wealth, seeking Allah's bounty and pleasure, and standing up for Allah and His Messenger. They are the ones true in faith.

Excellence of the People of Medina[1174]

9. As for those who had settled in the city and ˹embraced˺ the faith before ˹the arrival of˺ the emigrants, they love whoever immigrates to them, never having a desire in their

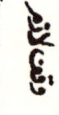

hearts for whatever ˹of the gains˺ is given to the emigrants. They give ˹the emigrants˺ preference over themselves even though they may be in need. And whoever is saved from the selfishness of their own souls, it is they who are ˹truly˺ successful.

1172 The Prophet (ﷺ) had instructed the Muslim army not to cut down trees, but some soldiers had to remove some palm trees to be able to enter the fort, to the dismay of Banu An-Naḍîr. When Muslims disagreed on that act, this verse was revealed.
1173 The verses here talk about the distribution of gains acquired without fighting. These gains are mostly distributed among the poor and the needy. As for the spoils of war, four-fifths of the spoils are distributed among the fighters. See 8:41.
1174 Commonly known as *Al-Anṣâr* (or the Helpers).

59. Al-Ḥashr

Later Believers

10. And those who come after them will pray, "Our Lord! Forgive us and our fellow believers who preceded us in faith, and do not allow bitterness into our hearts towards those who believe. Our Lord! Indeed, You are Ever Gracious, Most Merciful."

The Hypocrites and Banu An-Naḍîr

11. Have you ˹O Prophet˺ not seen the hypocrites who say to their fellow disbelievers from the People of the Book,[1175] "If you are expelled, we will certainly leave with you, and We will never obey anyone against you. And if you are fought against, we will surely help you."? But Allah bears witness that they are truly liars. **12.** Indeed, if they are expelled, the hypocrites will never leave with them. And if they are fought against, the hypocrites will never help them. And even if the hypocrites did so, they would certainly flee, then the disbelievers would be left with no help.

Cowardice of Both Groups

13. Indeed, there is more fear in their hearts for you ˹believers˺ than for Allah. That is because they are a people who do not comprehend. **14.** Even united, they would not ˹dare˺ fight against you except ˹from˺ within fortified strongholds or from behind walls. Their malice for each other is intense: you think they are united, yet their hearts are divided. That is because they are a people with no ˹real˺ understanding. **15.** They are ˹both just˺ like those who recently went down before them:[1176] they tasted the evil consequences of their doings. And they will suffer a painful punishment.

The Hypocrites Luring the Disbelievers

16. ˹They are˺ like Satan when he lures someone to disbelieve. Then after they have done so, he will say ˹on Judgment Day˺, "I have absolutely nothing to do with you. I truly fear Allah—the Lord of all worlds."[1177]

1175 Meaning, Banu An-Naḍîr.
1176 This refers to the pagans of Mecca and the Jews of Banu Qainuqâ' who were defeated a few months earlier at the Battle of Badr.
1177 *See* 14:22.

549   59. Al-Ḥashr

17. So they will both end up in the Fire, staying there forever. That is the reward of the wrongdoers.

Judge Yourselves Before Judgment Day

18. O believers! Be mindful of Allah and let every soul look to what ˹deeds˺ it has sent forth for tomorrow.[1178] And fear Allah, ˹for˺ certainly Allah is All-Aware of what you do. **19.** And do not be like those who forgot Allah, so He made them forget themselves. It is they who are ˹truly˺ rebellious. **20.** The residents of the Fire cannot be equal to the residents of Paradise. ˹Only˺ the residents of Paradise will be successful.

Impact of the Quran

21. Had We sent down this Quran upon a mountain, you would have certainly seen it humbled and torn apart in awe of Allah. We set forth such comparisons for people, ˹so˺ perhaps they may reflect.[1179]

Allah's Beautiful Names

22. He is Allah—there is no god ˹worthy of worship˺ except Him: Knower of the seen and unseen. He is the Most Compassionate, Most Merciful. **23.** He is Allah—there is no god except Him: the King, the Most Holy, the All-Perfect, the Source of Serenity, the Watcher ˹of all˺, the Almighty, the Supreme in Might,[1180] the Majestic. Glorified is Allah far above what they associate with Him ˹in worship˺! **24.** He is Allah: the Creator, the Inventor, the Shaper. He ˹alone˺ has the Most Beautiful Names. Whatever is in the heavens and the earth ˹constantly˺ glorifies Him. And He is the Almighty, All-Wise.

1178 i.e., the Hereafter.
1179 Meaning, that the hearts of the disbelievers are harder than the mountains concerning the Quran.
1180 *Jabbār* comes from the root word *ja-ba-ra* which means to impose, support, or console. For example, *Jabīrah* means the cast that supports a broken bone. Hence, Allah is the One Whose Will cannot be resisted, and Who comforts those who are broken or oppressed.

60. The Test of Faith
(Al-Mumtaḥanah)

In the Name of Allah—the Most Compassionate, Most Merciful

Allying with the Enemy

1. O believers! Do not take My enemies and yours as trusted allies, showing them affection even though they deny what has come to you of the truth. They drove the Messenger and yourselves out ˹of Mecca˺, simply for your belief in Allah, your Lord. If you ˹truly˺ emigrated[1181] to struggle in My cause and seek My pleasure, ˹then do not take them as allies,˺ disclosing secrets ˹of the believers˺ to the pagans out of affection for them, when I know best whatever you conceal and whatever you reveal. And whoever of you does this has truly strayed from the Right Way. 2. If they gain the upper hand over you, they would be your ˹open˺ enemies, unleashing their hands and tongues to harm you, and wishing that you would abandon faith. 3. Neither your relatives nor children will benefit you on Judgment Day—He will decide between you ˹all˺. For Allah is All-Seeing of what you do.

The Example of Abraham and His Followers

4. You already have an excellent example in Abraham and those with him, when they said to their people, "We totally dissociate ourselves from you and ˹shun˺ whatever ˹idols˺ you worship besides Allah. We reject you. The enmity and hatred that has arisen between us and you will last until you believe in Allah alone." The only exception is when Abraham said to his father, "I will seek forgiveness for you,˺" adding, "˹but˺ I cannot protect you from Allah at all." ˹The believers prayed,˺ "Our Lord! In You we trust. And to You we ˹always˺ turn. And to You is the final return.

1181 lit., come out ˹of Mecca˺.

5. Our Lord! Do not subject us to the persecution of the disbelievers. Forgive us, our Lord! You ˹alone˺ are truly the Almighty, All-Wise."

6. You certainly have an excellent example in them for whoever has hope in Allah and the Last Day. But whoever turns away, then surely Allah ˹alone˺ is the Self-Sufficient, Praiseworthy.

Yesterday's Enemies, Tomorrow's Friends

7. ˹In time,˺ Allah may bring about goodwill between you and those of them you ˹now˺ hold as enemies. For Allah is Most Capable. And Allah is All-Forgiving, Most Merciful.

Kindness to Non-Muslims

8. Allah does not forbid you from dealing kindly and fairly with those who have neither fought nor driven you out of your homes. Surely Allah loves those who are fair. **9.** Allah only forbids you from befriending those who have fought you for ˹your˺ faith, driven you out of your homes, or supported ˹others˺ in doing so. And whoever takes them as friends, then it is they who are the ˹true˺ wrongdoers.

Marriage of Female Emigrants

10. O believers! When the believing women come to you as emigrants,[1182] test their intentions—their faith is best known to Allah—and if you find them to be believers, then do not send them back to the disbelievers. These ˹women˺ are not lawful ˹wives˺ for the disbelievers, nor are the disbelievers lawful ˹husbands˺ for them. ˹But˺ repay the disbelievers whatever ˹dowries˺ they had paid. And there is no blame on you if you marry these ˹women˺ as long as you pay them their dowries. And do not hold on to marriage with polytheistic women.[1183] ˹But˺ demand ˹repayment of˺ whatever ˹dowries˺ you had paid, and let the disbelievers do the same. That is the judgment of Allah—He judges between you. And Allah is All-Knowing, All-Wise.

1182 According to the Treaty of Ḥudaibiyah (*see* footnote for 48:1-3), Muslims who chose to move to Mecca would not be returned to Muslims in Medina, and Meccan pagans who accepted Islam and chose to move to Medina would be returned to Mecca (except for women).
1183 Those who moved to Mecca to marry pagans.

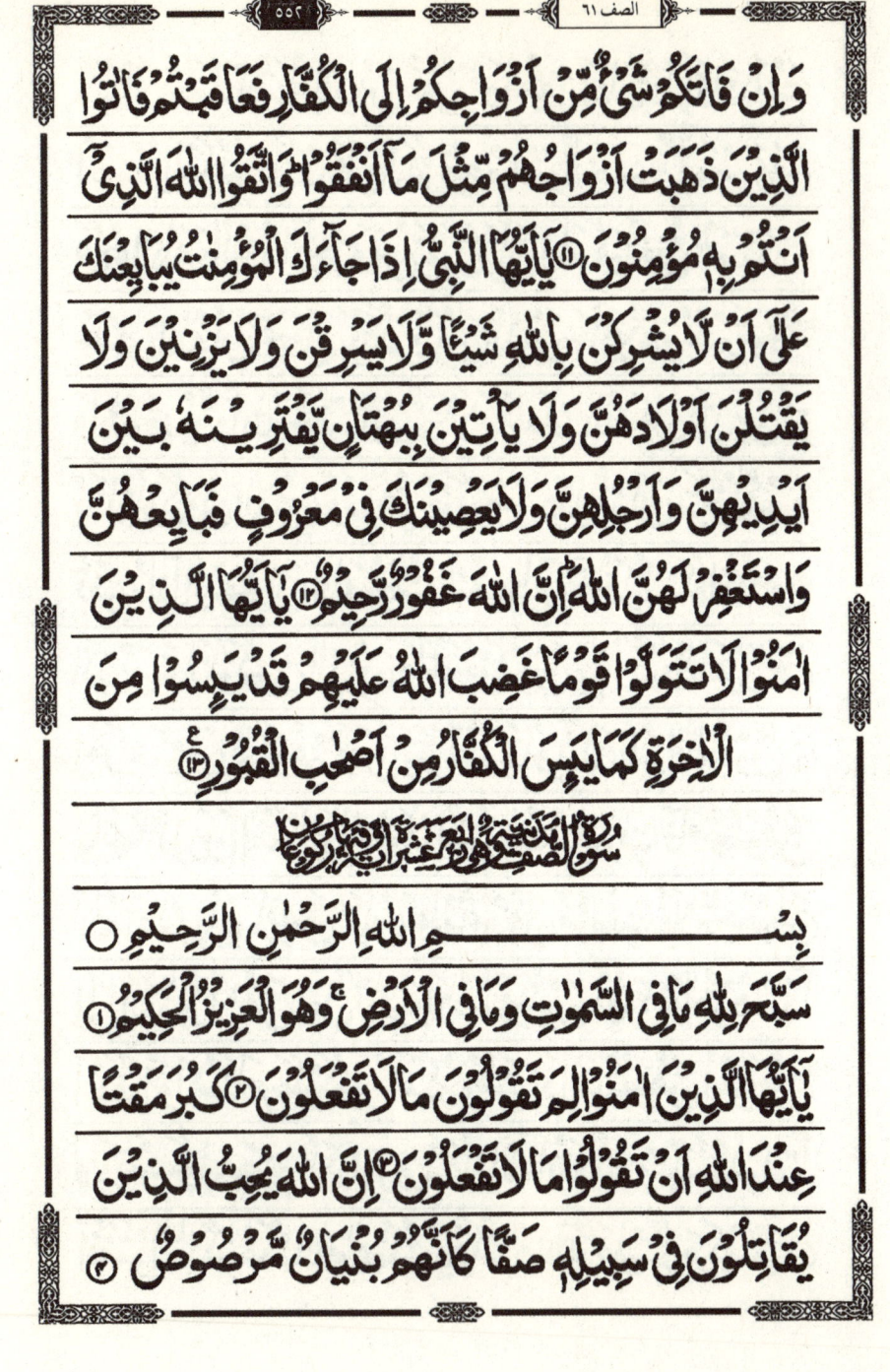

When Dowry Is Not Repaid to Muslims

11. And if any of your wives desert you to the disbelievers, and later you take spoils from them, then pay those whose wives have gone, the equivalent of whatever ˹dowry˺ they had paid. And be mindful of Allah, in Whom you believe.

Women Pledge Allegiance

12. O Prophet! When the believing women come to you, pledging to you that they will neither associate anything with Allah ˹in worship˺, nor steal, nor fornicate, nor kill their children, nor falsely attribute ˹illegitimate˺ children to their husbands,[1184] nor disobey you in what is right, then accept their pledge, and ask Allah to forgive them. Surely Allah is All-Forgiving, Most Merciful.

Do Not Ally with the Enemy

13. O believers! Do not ally yourselves with a people Allah is displeased with. They already have no hope for the Hereafter, just like the disbelievers lying in ˹their˺ graves.

༺⊰✻⊱༻

61. The ˹Solid˺ Ranks (Aṣ-Ṣaff)

In the Name of Allah—the Most Compassionate, Most Merciful

Allah Is Glorified by All

1. Whatever is in the heavens and whatever is on the earth glorifies Allah. For He ˹alone˺ is the Almighty, All-Wise.

Do What You Say[1185]

2. O believers! Why do you say what you do not do? **3.** How despicable it is in the sight of Allah that you say what you do not do! **4.** Surely Allah loves those who fight in His cause in ˹solid˺ ranks as if they were one concrete structure.

1184 lit., nor come up with a falsehood they have forged between their own hands and legs.
1185 Some companions desperately asked the Prophet (ﷺ) about the best deeds. When he told them that one of the best deeds is to fight in self-defence, they pledged to do so. But when the order came to fight the Meccan pagans, some either did not comply or fled in battle like Uḥud

61. Aṣ-Ṣaff

Moses and His People

5. ˹Remember, O Prophet,˺ when Moses said to his people, "O my people! Why do you hurt me when you already know I am Allah's messenger to you?" So when they ˹persistently˺ deviated, Allah caused their hearts to deviate. For Allah does not guide the rebellious people.

Jesus and the Israelites

6. And ˹remember˺ when Jesus, son of Mary, said, "O children of Israel! I am truly Allah's messenger to you, confirming the Torah which came before me, and giving good news of a messenger after me whose name will be Aḥmad."[1186] Yet when the Prophet came to them with clear proofs, they said, "This is pure magic."

Rejecting Islam

7. Who does more wrong than the one who fabricates lies about Allah when invited to submit ˹to Him˺?[1187] For Allah does not guide the wrongdoing people. **8.** They wish to extinguish Allah's light with their mouths, but Allah will ˹certainly˺ perfect His light, even to the dismay of the disbelievers. **9.** He is the One Who has sent His Messenger with ˹true˺ guidance and the religion of truth, making it prevail over all others, even to the dismay of the polytheists.

A Profitable Bargain

10. O believers! Shall I guide you to an exchange that will save you from a painful punishment? **11.** ˹It is to˺ have faith in Allah and His Messen-

ger, and strive in the cause of Allah with your wealth and your lives. That is best for you, if only you knew. **12.** He will forgive your sins, and admit you into Gardens under which rivers flow, and ˹house you in˺ splendid homes in the Gardens of Eternity. That is the ultimate triumph. **13.** ˹He will also give you˺ another favour that you long for: help from Allah and an imminent victory. ˹So˺ give good news ˹O Prophet˺ to the believers.

1186 Aḥmad is another name for Prophet Muḥammad (ﷺ). Both are derived from *ḥa-ma-da* which means 'praise.' Some Muslim scholars believe this verse refers to John 14:16, where Jesus says: "And I will ask the Father, and he will give you another *periklytos*, to be with you forever." *Periklytos* is a Greek word that means 'the praised one.' The name of Prophet Muḥammad (ﷺ) appears several times in the Gospel of Barnabas, which is deemed apocryphal by Christian authorities.
1187 Submission to Allah means 'Islam' in Arabic.

62. Al-Jumu'ah   554

Jesus and the Disciples

14. O believers! Stand up for Allah, as Jesus, son of Mary, asked the disciples, "Who will stand up with me for Allah?" The disciples replied, "We will stand up for Allah." Then a group from the Children of Israel believed while another disbelieved. We then supported the believers against their enemies, so they prevailed.

❦✵❦

62. Friday Congregation (Al-Jumu'ah)

In the Name of Allah—the Most Compassionate, Most Merciful

Allah's Favour to the Believers

1. Whatever is in the heavens and whatever is on the earth ˹constantly˺ glorifies Allah—the King, the Most Holy, the Almighty, the All-Wise. **2.** He is the One Who raised for the illiterate ˹people˺ a messenger from among themselves—reciting to them His revelations, purifying them, and teaching them the Book and wisdom, for indeed they had previously been clearly astray— **3.** along with others of them who have not yet joined them ˹in faith˺. For He is the Almighty, All-Wise. **4.** This is the favour of Allah. He grants it to whoever He wills. And Allah is the Lord of infinite bounty.

Unutilized Knowledge[1188]

5. The example of those who were entrusted with ˹observing˺ the Torah but failed to do so, is that of a donkey carrying books.[1189] How evil is the example of those who reject Allah's signs! For Allah does not guide the wrongdoing people.

Challenge to the Israelites

6. Say, ˹O Prophet,˺ "O Jews! If you claim to be Allah's chosen ˹people˺ out of all humanity, then wish for death, if what you say is true."

1188 Some Jews used to boast that they were Allah's most beloved and that they had been favoured with the Torah and the Sabbath, so the three following passages came in response:
- What is the benefit of the Torah if it is not followed properly (62:5)?
- If you are truly Allah's favourite servants then you should wish to meet Him (62:-6-8).
- Muslims have been blessed with Friday, equivalent to the Sabbath (62:9-10).

1189 Meaning, they can carry the physical burden of the books, but not understand a word of them.

63. Al-Munâfiqûn

7. But they will never wish for that because of what their hands have done.[1190] And Allah has ˹perfect˺ knowledge of the wrongdoers. 8. Say, "The death you are running away from will inevitably come to you. Then you will be returned to the Knower of the seen and unseen, and He will inform you of what you used to do."

Attending Friday Congregation

9. O believers! When the call to prayer is made on Friday, then proceed ˹diligently˺ to the remembrance of Allah and leave off ˹your˺ business. That is best for you, if only you knew. 10. Once the prayer is over, disperse throughout the land and seek the bounty of Allah. And remember Allah often so you may be successful.

Leaving the Sermon

11. When they saw the fanfare along with the caravan, they ˹almost all˺ flocked to it, leaving you ˹O Prophet˺ standing ˹on the pulpit˺. Say, "What is with Allah is far better than amusement and merchandise. And Allah is the Best Provider."[1191]

❦✻❦

63. The Hypocrites
(Al-Munâfiqûn)

In the Name of Allah—the Most Compassionate, Most Merciful

The Hypocrites Have No Faith

1. When the hypocrites come to you ˹O Prophet˺, they say, "We bear witness that you are certainly the Messenger of Allah"—and surely Allah knows that you are His Messenger—but Allah bears witness that the hypocrites are truly liars. 2. They have made their ˹false˺ oaths as a shield, hindering ˹others˺ from the Way of Allah. Evil indeed is what they do! 3. This is because they believed and then abandoned faith. Therefore, their hearts have been sealed, so they do not comprehend.

1190 i.e., disobeying Allah, killing some of the prophets (including Zachariah and John the Baptist), claiming to have killed Jesus, accusing Mary of adultery, and dealing with usury. See 4:153-158.
1191 Initially, the Friday congregational prayer was performed first, followed by the sermon. On one occasion, a caravan of food arrived in Medina during a time of hardship while the Prophet (ﷺ) was on the pulpit. Following ancient traditions, the caravan was received with drum-beats. Most congregants rushed to receive the caravan, leaving the Prophet (ﷺ) in the middle of the sermon. Henceforth, the sermon was given first so everyone would stay for the prayer.

63. Al-Munâfiqûn — 556

بِسْمِ اللّٰهِ الرَّحْمٰنِ الرَّحِيمِ

وَإِذَا رَأَيْتَهُمْ تُعْجِبُكَ أَجْسَامُهُمْ ۖ وَإِن يَقُولُوا تَسْمَعْ لِقَوْلِهِمْ ۖ كَأَنَّهُمْ خُشُبٌ مُّسَنَّدَةٌ ۖ يَحْسَبُونَ كُلَّ صَيْحَةٍ عَلَيْهِمْ ۚ هُمُ الْعَدُوُّ فَاحْذَرْهُمْ ۚ قَاتَلَهُمُ اللّٰهُ ۖ أَنَّىٰ يُؤْفَكُونَ ۝ وَإِذَا قِيلَ لَهُمْ تَعَالَوْا يَسْتَغْفِرْ لَكُمْ رَسُولُ اللّٰهِ لَوَّوْا رُءُوسَهُمْ وَرَأَيْتَهُمْ يَصُدُّونَ وَهُم مُّسْتَكْبِرُونَ ۝ سَوَاءٌ عَلَيْهِمْ أَسْتَغْفَرْتَ لَهُمْ أَمْ لَمْ تَسْتَغْفِرْ لَهُمْ لَن يَغْفِرَ اللّٰهُ لَهُمْ ۚ إِنَّ اللّٰهَ لَا يَهْدِي الْقَوْمَ الْفَاسِقِينَ ۝ هُمُ الَّذِينَ يَقُولُونَ لَا تُنفِقُوا عَلَىٰ مَنْ عِندَ رَسُولِ اللّٰهِ حَتَّىٰ يَنفَضُّوا ۗ وَلِلّٰهِ خَزَائِنُ السَّمَاوَاتِ وَالْأَرْضِ وَلَٰكِنَّ الْمُنَافِقِينَ لَا يَفْقَهُونَ ۝ يَقُولُونَ لَئِن رَّجَعْنَا إِلَى الْمَدِينَةِ لَيُخْرِجَنَّ الْأَعَزُّ مِنْهَا الْأَذَلَّ ۚ وَلِلّٰهِ الْعِزَّةُ وَلِرَسُولِهِ وَلِلْمُؤْمِنِينَ وَلَٰكِنَّ الْمُنَافِقِينَ لَا يَعْلَمُونَ ۝ يَا أَيُّهَا الَّذِينَ آمَنُوا لَا تُلْهِكُمْ أَمْوَالُكُمْ وَلَا أَوْلَادُكُمْ عَن ذِكْرِ اللّٰهِ ۚ وَمَن يَفْعَلْ ذَٰلِكَ فَأُولَٰئِكَ هُمُ الْخَاسِرُونَ ۝ وَأَنفِقُوا مِن مَّا رَزَقْنَاكُم مِّن قَبْلِ أَن يَأْتِيَ أَحَدَكُمُ الْمَوْتُ فَيَقُولَ رَبِّ لَوْلَا أَخَّرْتَنِي إِلَىٰ أَجَلٍ قَرِيبٍ فَأَصَّدَّقَ وَأَكُن مِّنَ الصَّالِحِينَ ۝ وَلَن يُؤَخِّرَ اللّٰهُ نَفْسًا إِذَا جَاءَ أَجَلُهَا ۚ وَاللّٰهُ خَبِيرٌ بِمَا تَعْمَلُونَ ۝

All That Glitters Is Not Gold

4. When you see them, their appearance impresses you. And when they speak, you listen to their ˹impressive˺ speech. But they are ˹just˺ like ˹worthless˺ planks of wood leaned ˹against a wall˺. They think every cry is against them. They are the enemy, so beware of them. May Allah condemn them! How can they be deluded ˹from the truth˺?

Hypocrites' Unwillingness to Repent[1192]

5. When it is said to them, "Come! The Messenger of Allah will pray for you to be forgiven," they turn their heads ˹in disgust˺, and you see them ˹O Prophet˺ turn away in arrogance. 6. It is the same whether you pray for their forgiveness or not, Allah will not forgive them. Surely Allah does not guide the rebellious people.

Hypocrites' Contempt for the Believers

7. They are the ones who say ˹to one another˺, "Do not spend ˹anything˺ on those ˹emigrants˺ with the Messenger of Allah so that they will break away ˹from him˺." But to Allah ˹alone˺ belong the treasuries of the heavens and the earth, yet the hypocrites do not comprehend. 8. They say, "If we return to Medina, the honourable will definitely expel the inferior." But all honour and power belongs to Allah, His Messenger, and the believers, yet the hypocrites do not know.

Be Faithful and Charitable

9. O believers! Do not let your wealth or your children divert you from the remembrance of Allah. For whoever does so, it is they who are the ˹true˺ losers. 10. And donate from what We have provided for you before death comes to one of you, and you cry, "My Lord! If only You delayed me for a short while, I would give in charity and be one of the righteous." 11. But Allah never delays a soul when its appointed time comes. And Allah is All-Aware of what you do.

1192 This passage and the next refer to ˹Abdullâh ibn Ubai, the chief hypocrite in Medina.

64. Mutual Loss and Gain
(At-Taghâbun)

In the Name of Allah—the Most Compassionate, Most Merciful

Allah's Infinite Power and Knowledge

1. Whatever is in the heavens and whatever is on the earth ˹constantly˺ glorifies Allah. The kingdom is His, and all praise is for Him. For He is Most Capable of everything. 2. He is the One Who created you, yet some of you are disbelievers while some are believers. And Allah is All-Seeing of what you do. 3. He created the heavens and the earth for a purpose. He shaped you ˹in the womb˺, perfecting your form. And to Him is the final return. 4. He knows whatever is in the heavens and the earth. And He knows whatever you conceal and whatever you reveal. For Allah knows best what is ˹hidden˺ in the heart.

Earlier Deniers

5. Have the stories of those who disbelieved before not reached you ˹pagans˺? They tasted the evil consequences of their doings, and they will suffer a painful punishment. 6. That was because their messengers used to come to them with clear proofs, but they said ˹mockingly˺, "How can humans be our guides?" So they disbelieved and turned away. And Allah was not in need ˹of their faith˺. For Allah is Self-Sufficient, Praiseworthy.

A Message to Present Deniers

7. The disbelievers claim they will not be resurrected. Say, ˹O Prophet,˺ "Yes, by my Lord, you will surely be resurrected, then you will certainly be informed of what you have done. And that is easy for Allah." 8. So believe in Allah and His Messenger and in the Light[1193] We have revealed. And Allah is All-Aware of what you do.

1193 i.e., the Quran.

يَوْمَ يَجْمَعُكُمْ لِيَوْمِ الْجَمْعِ ذٰلِكَ يَوْمُ التَّغَابُنِ ۗ وَمَنْ يُّؤْمِنْ بِاللّٰهِ
وَيَعْمَلْ صَالِحًا يُّكَفِّرْ عَنْهُ سَيِّاٰتِهٖ وَيُدْخِلْهُ جَنّٰتٍ تَجْرِيْ
مِنْ تَحْتِهَا الْاَنْهٰرُ خٰلِدِيْنَ فِيْهَآ اَبَدًا ۗ ذٰلِكَ الْفَوْزُ الْعَظِيْمُ ﴿٩﴾ وَ
الَّذِيْنَ كَفَرُوْا وَكَذَّبُوْا بِاٰيٰتِنَآ اُولٰٓئِكَ اَصْحٰبُ النَّارِ خٰلِدِيْنَ فِيْهَا ۖ
وَبِئْسَ الْمَصِيْرُ ﴿١٠﴾ مَآ اَصَابَ مِنْ مُّصِيْبَةٍ اِلَّا بِاِذْنِ اللّٰهِ ۗ وَمَنْ
يُّؤْمِنْ بِاللّٰهِ يَهْدِ قَلْبَهٗ ۗ وَاللّٰهُ بِكُلِّ شَيْءٍ عَلِيْمٌ ﴿١١﴾ وَاَطِيْعُوا اللّٰهَ وَ
اَطِيْعُوا الرَّسُوْلَ ۚ فَاِنْ تَوَلَّيْتُمْ فَاِنَّمَا عَلٰى رَسُوْلِنَا الْبَلٰغُ الْمُبِيْنُ ﴿١٢﴾
اَللّٰهُ لَآ اِلٰهَ اِلَّا هُوَ ۗ وَعَلَى اللّٰهِ فَلْيَتَوَكَّلِ الْمُؤْمِنُوْنَ ﴿١٣﴾ يٰٓاَيُّهَا الَّذِيْنَ
اٰمَنُوْٓا اِنَّ مِنْ اَزْوَاجِكُمْ وَاَوْلَادِكُمْ عَدُوًّا لَّكُمْ فَاحْذَرُوْهُمْ ۚ
وَاِنْ تَعْفُوْا وَتَصْفَحُوْا وَتَغْفِرُوْا فَاِنَّ اللّٰهَ غَفُوْرٌ رَّحِيْمٌ ﴿١٤﴾ اِنَّمَآ
اَمْوَالُكُمْ وَاَوْلَادُكُمْ فِتْنَةٌ ۗ وَاللّٰهُ عِنْدَهٗٓ اَجْرٌ عَظِيْمٌ ﴿١٥﴾ فَاتَّقُوا
اللّٰهَ مَا اسْتَطَعْتُمْ وَاسْمَعُوْا وَاَطِيْعُوْا وَاَنْفِقُوْا خَيْرًا لِّاَنْفُسِكُمْ ۗ
وَمَنْ يُّوْقَ شُحَّ نَفْسِهٖ فَاُولٰٓئِكَ هُمُ الْمُفْلِحُوْنَ ﴿١٦﴾ اِنْ
تُقْرِضُوا اللّٰهَ قَرْضًا حَسَنًا يُّضٰعِفْهُ لَكُمْ وَيَغْفِرْ لَكُمْ ۗ وَاللّٰهُ
شَكُوْرٌ حَلِيْمٌ ﴿١٧﴾ عٰلِمُ الْغَيْبِ وَالشَّهَادَةِ الْعَزِيْزُ الْحَكِيْمُ ﴿١٨﴾

9. ˹Consider˺ the Day He will gather you ˹all˺ for the Day of Gathering—that will be the Day of mutual loss and gain. So whoever believes in Allah and does good, He will absolve them of their sins and admit them into Gardens under which rivers flow, to stay there for ever and ever. That is the ultimate triumph. **10.** As for those who disbelieve and reject Our signs, they will be the residents of the Fire, staying there forever. What an evil destination!

Reassuring the Believers

11. No calamity befalls ˹anyone˺ except by Allah's Will. And whoever has faith in Allah, He will ˹rightly˺ guide their hearts ˹through adversity˺. And Allah has ˹perfect˺ knowledge of all things. **12.** Obey Allah and obey the Messenger! But if you turn away, then Our Messenger's duty is only to deliver ˹the message˺ clearly. **13.** Allah—there is no god ˹worthy of worship˺ except Him. So in Allah let the believers put their trust.

The Test of Family and Wealth

14. O believers! Indeed, some of your spouses and children are enemies to you,[1194] so beware of them. But if you pardon, overlook, and forgive ˹their faults˺, then Allah is truly All-Forgiving, Most Merciful. **15.** Your wealth and children are only a test, but Allah ˹alone˺ has a great reward. **16.** So be mindful of Allah to the best of your ability, hear and obey, and spend in charity—that will be best for you. And whoever is saved from the selfishness of their own souls, it is they who are ˹truly˺ successful. **17.** If you lend to Allah a good loan, He will multiply it for you and forgive you. For Allah is Most Appreciative, Most Forbearing. **18.** ˹He is the˺ Knower of the seen and unseen—the Almighty, All-Wise.

1194 This verse was revealed when some early Muslims were prevented from emigrating to Medina by their own spouses and children, so they could not join the Prophet (ﷺ) and the rest of the believers to practice their faith freely.

65. Divorce (Aṭ-Ṭalâq)

In the Name of Allah—the Most Compassionate, Most Merciful

Proper Divorce

1. O Prophet! ˹Instruct the believers:˺ When you ˹intend to˺ divorce women, then divorce them with concern for their waiting period,[1195] and count it accurately. And fear Allah, your Lord.

Divorced Women During the Waiting Period

Do not force them out of their homes, nor should they leave—unless they commit a blatant misconduct. These are the limits set by Allah. And whoever transgresses Allah's limits has truly wronged his own soul. You never know, perhaps Allah will bring about a change ˹of heart˺ later.[1196]

Divorced Women After the Waiting Period

2. Then when they have ˹almost˺ reached the end of their waiting period, either retain them honourably or separate from them honourably.[1197] And call two of your reliable men to witness ˹either way˺—and ˹let the witnesses˺ bear true testimony for ˹the sake of˺ Allah. This is enjoined on whoever has faith in Allah and the Last Day. And whoever is mindful of Allah, He will make a way out for them, 3. and provide for them from sources they could never imagine. And whoever puts their trust in Allah, then He ˹alone˺ is sufficient for them. Certainly Allah achieves His Will. Allah has already set a destiny for everything.

Waiting Periods for Divorced Women

4. As for your women past the age of menstruation, in case you do not know, their waiting period is three months, and those who have not menstruated as well. As for those who are pregnant, their waiting period ends with delivery.[1198] And whoever is mindful of

---

1195 Meaning, when a husband intends to divorce his wife—after the consummation of marriage—he should divorce her outside her monthly cycle, provided that he has not touched her after her period. This makes it easy for the wife to observe her *'iddah* (waiting period for around three months, see 65:4). Otherwise, things will be complicated for her. For example, if divorce happens after sexual intercourse, she might get pregnant, which delays the end of *'iddah* until the end of her pregnancy. If divorce happens during a monthly cycle, scholars are in disagreement as to whether the divorce counts or not. If it does not, she has to wait until her menstruation is over to see if her husband still wants to divorce her.

1196 Perhaps the husband who has divorced his wife may change his mind and restore the marriage before the end of her waiting period (after the first or second count of divorce).

1197 A husband may separate from his wife after each of the first two counts of divorce or at the end of her waiting period with dignity. If he chooses to stay with her after the first two counts of divorce then divorces her a third time, the marriage is terminated at the end of her third waiting period. The wife will have to marry and divorce another man before she can be remarried to her ex-husband (see 2:230). However, a woman marrying someone with the intention of getting divorced, in order to return to her first husband, is forbidden.

1198 This applies to pregnant women who are divorced or widowed.

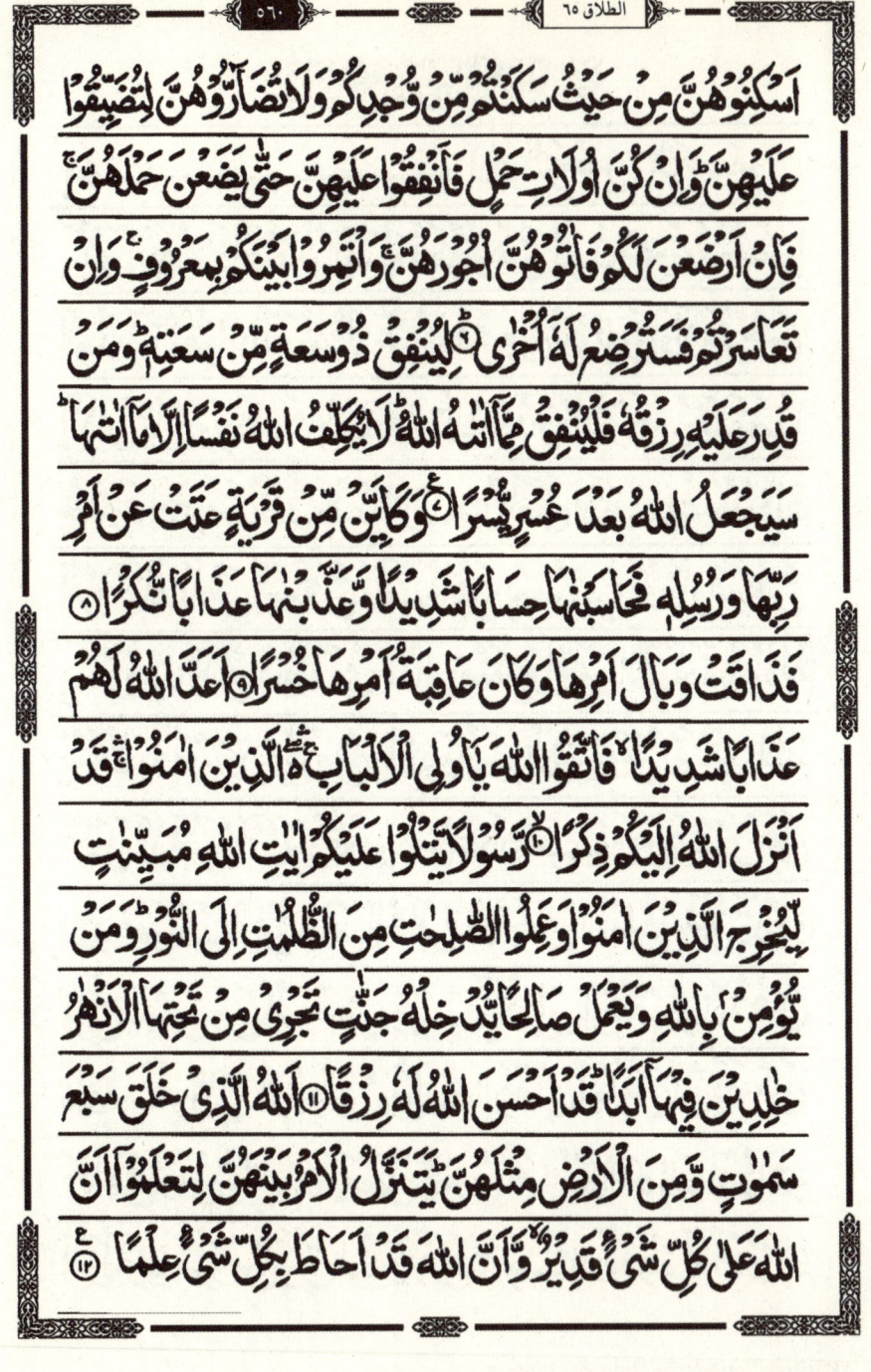

Allah, He will make their matters easy for them. 5. This is the commandment of Allah, which He has revealed to you. And whoever is mindful of Allah, He will absolve them of their sins and reward them immensely.

Housing for Divorced Women

6. Let them live where you live ˹during their waiting period˺, according to your means. And do not harass them to make their stay unbearable. If they are pregnant, then maintain them until they deliver. And if they nurse your child,[1199] compensate them, and consult together courteously. But if you fail to reach an agreement, then another woman will nurse ˹the child˺ for the father. 7. Let the man of wealth provide according to his means. As for the one with limited resources, let him provide according to whatever Allah has given him. Allah does not require of any soul beyond what He has given it. After hardship, Allah will bring about ease.

An Invitation to True Faith

8. ˹Imagine˺ how many societies rebelled against the commandments of their Lord and His messengers, so We called each ˹society˺ to a severe account and subjected them to a horrible punishment. 9. So they tasted the evil consequences of their doings, and the outcome of their doings was ˹total˺ loss. 10. Allah has ˹also˺ prepared for them a severe punishment. So fear Allah, O people of reason and faith. Allah has indeed revealed to you a Reminder,[1200] 11. ˹and sent˺ a messenger reciting to you Allah's revelations, making things clear so that He may bring those who believe and do good out of darkness and into light. And whoever believes in Allah and does good will be admitted by Him into Gardens under which rivers flow, to stay there for ever and ever. Allah will have indeed granted them an excellent provision.

Allah's Infinite Power and Knowledge

12. Allah is the One Who created seven heavens ˹in layers˺, and likewise for the earth. The ˹divine˺ command descends between them so you may know that Allah is Most Capable of everything and that Allah certainly encompasses all things in ˹His˺ knowledge.

1199 After the divorce is finalized.
1200 This is one of the names of the Quran.

66. The Prohibition (At-Taḥrîm)

In the Name of Allah—the Most Compassionate, Most Merciful

A Lesson to the Prophet's Wives

1. O Prophet! Why do you prohibit ˹yourself˺ from what Allah has made lawful to you, seeking to please your wives? And Allah is All-Forgiving, Most Merciful. 2. Allah has already ordained for you ˹believers˺ the way to absolve yourselves from your oaths.[1201] For Allah is your Guardian. And He is the All-Knowing, All-Wise. 3. ˹Remember˺ when the Prophet had ˹once˺ confided something to one of his wives, then when she disclosed it ˹to another wife˺ and Allah made it known to him, he presented ˹to her˺ part of what was disclosed and overlooked a part. So when he informed her of it, she exclaimed, "Who told you this?" He replied, "I was informed by the All-Knowing, All-Aware." 4. ˹It will be better˺ if you ˹wives˺ both turn to Allah in repentance, for your hearts have certainly faltered. But if you ˹continue to˺ collaborate against him, then ˹know that˺ Allah Himself is his Guardian. And Gabriel, the righteous believers, and the angels are ˹all˺ his supporters as well. 5. Perhaps, if he were to divorce you ˹all˺, his Lord would replace you with better wives who are submissive ˹to Allah˺, faithful ˹to Him˺, devout, repentant, dedicated to worship and fasting— previously married or virgins.

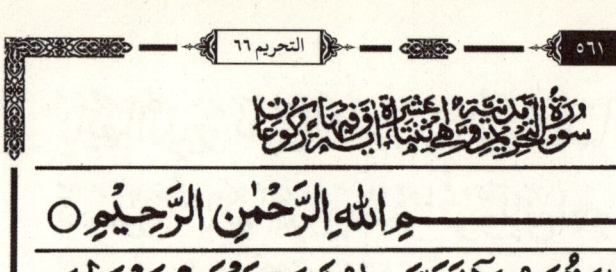

Warning of Judgment Day

6. O believers! Protect yourselves and your families from a Fire whose fuel is people and stones, overseen by formidable and severe angels, who never disobey whatever Allah orders—always doing as commanded.

1201 See 5:89.

7. ˹The deniers will then be told,˺ "O disbelievers! Make no excuses this Day! You are only rewarded for what you used to do."

Reward of Sincere Repentance

8. O believers! Turn to Allah in sincere repentance, so your Lord may absolve you of your sins and admit you into Gardens, under which rivers flow, on the Day Allah will not disgrace the Prophet or the believers with him. Their light will shine ahead of them and on their right, ˹and˺ they will say, "Our Lord! Perfect our light for us, and forgive us. ˹For˺ You are truly Most Capable of everything."

Responding to Evildoers

9. O Prophet! Struggle against the disbelievers and the hypocrites, and be firm with them. Hell will be their home. What an evil destination!

Two Examples for the Disbelievers

10. Allah sets forth an example for the disbelievers: the wife of Noah and the wife of Lot. Each was married to one of Our righteous servants, yet betrayed them.[1202] So their husbands were of no benefit to them against Allah whatsoever. Both were told, "Enter the Fire, along with the others!"

Two Examples for the Believers

11. And Allah sets forth an example for the believers: the wife of Pharaoh, who prayed, "My Lord! Build me a house in Paradise near You, deliver me from Pharaoh and his ˹evil˺ doing, and save me from the wrongdoing people." **12.** ˹There is˺ also ˹the example of˺ Mary, the daughter of 'Imrân, who guarded her chastity, so We breathed into her ˹womb˺ through Our angel ˹Gabriel˺.[1203] She testified to the words of her Lord and His Scriptures, and was one of the ˹sincerely˺ devout.

1202 Both wives were disbelievers. Noah's wife used to give away the identity of the new believers so the disbelievers could persecute them. And Lot's wife used to tell the men about her husband's handsome male visitors so they could approach them.
1203 Gabriel breathed into the sleeves of Mary's garment so she conceived Jesus.

67. All Authority (Al-Mulk)

In the Name of Allah—the Most Compassionate, Most Merciful

Life Is a Test

1. Blessed is the One in Whose Hands rests all authority. And He is Most Capable of everything. 2. ˹He is the One˼ Who created death and life in order to test which of you is best in deeds. And He is the Almighty, All-Forgiving.

Allah's Perfect Creation

3. ˹He is the One˼ Who created seven heavens, one above the other. You will never see any imperfection in the creation of the Most Compassionate.[1204] So look again: do you see any flaws? 4. Then look again and again—your sight will return frustrated and weary. 5. And indeed, We adorned the lowest heaven with ˹stars like˼ lamps, and made them ˹as missiles˼ for stoning ˹eavesdropping˼ devils, for whom We have also prepared the torment of the Blaze.[1205]

Reward of the Disbelievers

6. Those who disbelieve in their Lord will suffer the punishment of Hell. What an evil destination! 7. When they are tossed into it, they will hear its roaring as it boils over, 8. almost bursting in fury. Every time a group is cast into it, its keepers will ask them, "Did a warner not come to you?" 9. They will reply, "Yes, a warner did come to us, but we denied and said, 'Allah has revealed nothing. You are extremely astray.'" 10. And they will lament, "If only we had listened and reasoned, we would not be among the residents of the Blaze!"

1204 Some may point to birth defects, genetic mutations, etc. and say these are flaws. This verse means that, in the grand scheme of creation, everything created has its place, form, and purpose, and that it does exactly what Allah ordained for it.

1205 *See* 72:8-10.

67. Al-Mulk

11. And so they will confess their sins. So away with the residents of the Blaze!

Reward of the Believers

12. Indeed, those in awe of their Lord without seeing Him[1206] will have forgiveness and a mighty reward.

Question 1) Does Allah Not Know His Creation?

13. Whether you speak secretly or openly—He surely knows best what is ˹hidden˺ in the heart. **14.** How could He not know His Own creation? For He ˹alone˺ is the Most Subtle, All-Aware. **15.** He is the One Who smoothed out the earth for you, so move about in its regions and eat from His provisions. And to Him is the resurrection ˹of all˺.

Question 2) Are You out of Allah's Reach?

16. Do you feel secure that the One Who is in heaven will not cause the earth to swallow you up as it quakes violently? **17.** Or do you feel secure that the One Who is in heaven will not unleash upon you a storm of stones. Only then would you know how ˹serious˺ My warning was! **18.** And certainly those before them denied ˹as well˺, then how severe was My response!

Question 3) Do You Not See Allah's Power?

19. Have they not seen the birds above them, spreading and folding their wings? None holds them up except the Most Compassionate. Indeed, He is All-Seeing of everything. **20.** Also, which ˹powerless˺ force will come to your help instead of the Most Compassionate? Indeed, the disbelievers are only ˹lost˺ in delusion. **21.** Or who is it that will provide for you if He withholds His provision? In fact, they persist in arrogance and aversion ˹to the truth˺.

Question 4) Are Believers and Disbelievers Equal?

22. Who is ˹rightly˺ guided: the one who crawls facedown or the one who walks upright on the Straight Path?

1206 This can also mean that they are in awe of their Lord as much in private as they are in public.

68. Al-Qalam

Question 5) Who Created You?

23. Say, ˹O Prophet,˺ "He is the One Who brought you into being and gave you hearing, sight, and intellect. ˹Yet˺ you hardly give any thanks."
24. ˹Also˺ say, "He is the One Who has dispersed you ˹all˺ over the earth, and to Him you will ˹all˺ be gathered."

Question 6) Do You Still Deny the Hour?

25. ˹Still˺ they ask ˹the believers˺, "When will this threat come to pass, if what you say is true?" 26. Say, ˹O Prophet,˺ "That knowledge is with Allah alone, and I am only sent with a clear warning." 27. Then when they see the torment drawing near, the faces of the disbelievers will become gloomy, and it will be said ˹to them˺, "This is what you claimed would never come."[1207]

Question 7) Who Else Can Aid You?

28. Say, ˹O Prophet,˺ "Consider this: whether Allah causes me and those with me to die or shows us mercy, who will save the disbelievers from a painful punishment?"[1208] 29. Say, "He is the Most Compassionate—in Him ˹alone˺ we believe, and in Him ˹alone˺ we trust. You will soon know who is clearly astray." 30. Say, "Consider this: if your water were to sink ˹into the earth˺, then who ˹else˺ could bring you flowing water?"

ೲ ✾ ೲ

68. The Pen (Al-Qalam)

In the Name of Allah—the Most Compassionate, Most Merciful

Excellence of the Prophet

1. *Nūn.* By the pen and what everyone writes! 2. By the grace of your Lord, you ˹O Prophet˺ are not insane. 3. You will certainly have a never-ending reward. 4. And you are truly ˹a man˺ of outstanding character. 5. Soon you and the pagans will see, 6. which of you is mad.

1207 Another possible translation: "This is what you were calling for."
1208 Meaning, whether Allah takes our lives (as you wish) or grants us a long life, it is all good for us. But who will protect you from Allah if you disbelieve in Him.

68. Al-Qalam

إِنَّ رَبَّكَ هُوَ أَعْلَمُ بِمَن ضَلَّ عَن سَبِيلِهِ وَهُوَ أَعْلَمُ بِالْمُهْتَدِينَ ۞ فَلَا تُطِعِ الْمُكَذِّبِينَ ۞ وَدُّوا لَوْ تُدْهِنُ فَيُدْهِنُونَ ۞ وَلَا تُطِعْ كُلَّ حَلَّافٍ مَّهِينٍ ۞ هَمَّازٍ مَّشَّاءِ بِنَمِيمٍ ۞ مَّنَّاعٍ لِّلْخَيْرِ مُعْتَدٍ أَثِيمٍ ۞ عُتُلٍّ بَعْدَ ذَٰلِكَ زَنِيمٍ ۞ أَن كَانَ ذَا مَالٍ وَبَنِينَ ۞ إِذَا تُتْلَىٰ عَلَيْهِ ءَايَٰتُنَا قَالَ أَسَٰطِيرُ الْأَوَّلِينَ ۞ سَنَسِمُهُ عَلَى الْخُرْطُومِ ۞ إِنَّا بَلَوْنَٰهُمْ كَمَا بَلَوْنَآ أَصْحَٰبَ الْجَنَّةِ إِذْ أَقْسَمُوا لَيَصْرِمُنَّهَا مُصْبِحِينَ ۞ وَلَا يَسْتَثْنُونَ ۞ فَطَافَ عَلَيْهَا طَآئِفٌ مِّن رَّبِّكَ وَهُمْ نَآئِمُونَ ۞ فَأَصْبَحَتْ كَالصَّرِيمِ ۞ فَتَنَادَوْا مُصْبِحِينَ ۞ أَنِ اغْدُوا عَلَىٰ حَرْثِكُمْ إِن كُنتُمْ صَٰرِمِينَ ۞ فَانطَلَقُوا وَهُمْ يَتَخَٰفَتُونَ ۞ أَن لَّا يَدْخُلَنَّهَا الْيَوْمَ عَلَيْكُم مِّسْكِينٌ ۞ وَغَدَوْا عَلَىٰ حَرْدٍ قَٰدِرِينَ ۞ فَلَمَّا رَأَوْهَا قَالُوٓا إِنَّا لَضَآلُّونَ ۞ بَلْ نَحْنُ مَحْرُومُونَ ۞ قَالَ أَوْسَطُهُمْ أَلَمْ أَقُل لَّكُمْ لَوْلَا تُسَبِّحُونَ ۞ قَالُوا سُبْحَٰنَ رَبِّنَآ إِنَّا كُنَّا ظَٰلِمِينَ ۞ فَأَقْبَلَ بَعْضُهُمْ عَلَىٰ بَعْضٍ يَتَلَٰوَمُونَ ۞ قَالُوا يَٰوَيْلَنَآ إِنَّا كُنَّا طَٰغِينَ ۞

---

7. Surely your Lord ʿaloneʾ knows best who has strayed from His Way and who is ʿrightlyʾ guided.

Warning the Prophet About the Deniers

8. So do not give in to the deniers. **9.** They wish you would compromise so they would yield ʿto youʾ. **10.** And do not obey the despicable, vain oath-taker, **11.** slanderer, gossip-monger, **12.** withholder of good, transgressor, evildoer, **13.** brute, and—on top of all that—an illegitimate child. **14.** Now, ʿsimplyʾ because he has been blessed with ʿabundantʾ wealth and children, **15.** whenever Our revelations are recited to him, he says, "Ancient fables!" **16.** We will soon mark his snout.[1209]

The Test of the Garden Owners[1210]

17. Indeed, We have tested those ʿMeccansʾ as We tested the owners of the garden—when they swore they would surely harvest ʿallʾ its fruit in the early morning, **18.** leaving no thought for Allah's Will.[1211] **19.** Then it was struck by a torment from your Lord while they slept, **20.** so it was reduced to ashes. **21.** Then by daybreak they called out to each other, **22.** ʿsaying,ʾ "Go early to your harvest, if you want to pick ʿallʾ the fruit." **23.** So they went off, whispering to one another, **24.** "Do not let any poor person enter your garden today." **25.** And they proceeded early, totally fixated on their purpose. **26.** But when they saw it ʿdevastatedʾ, they cried, "We must have lost ʿourʾ way! **27.** In fact, we have been deprived ʿof our livelihoodʾ." **28.** The most sensible of them said, "Did I not urge you to say, 'Allah willing.'?? **29.** They replied, "Glory be to our Lord! We have truly been wrongdoers." **30.** Then they turned on each other, throwing blame. **31.** They said, "Woe to us! We have certainly been transgressors.

1209 Like 53:33-35 and 74:11-26, these verses refer to Al-Walîd ibn Al-Mughîrah, a leader of the Meccan opposition against Islam. He rejected the Prophet (ﷺ) as a madman, so the Quran responded by listing ten of his qualities—two of which were unknown to him: the fact that he was born out of wedlock and that his nose would be chopped off several years later at the Battle of Badr. At least three of his ten sons accepted Islam—including Khâlid ibn Al-Walîd.

1210 This is the story of a righteous man who owned a garden and used to give a share of the harvest to the poor. Following his death, his children decided to keep all the produce for themselves and give nothing to the poor.

1211 Another possible translation: "without leaving some for the poor."

568   **68. Al-Qalam**

32. We trust our Lord will give us a better garden than this, ˹for˺ we are indeed turning to our Lord with hope."[1212] 33. That is the ˹way of Our˺ punishment ˹in this world˺. But the punishment of the Hereafter is certainly far worse, if only they knew.[1213]

Questions to the Pagans

34. Indeed, the righteous will have the Gardens of Bliss with their Lord. 35. Should We then treat those who have submitted like the wicked? 36. What is the matter with you? How do you judge? 37. Or do you have a scripture, in which you read 38. that you will have whatever you choose? 39. Or do you have oaths binding on Us until the Day of Judgment that you will have whatever you decide? 40. Ask them ˹O Prophet˺ which of them can guarantee all that. 41. Or do they have associate-gods ˹supporting this claim˺? Then let them bring forth their associate-gods, if what they say is true.

Warning of Judgment Day

42. ˹Beware of˺ the Day the Shin ˹of Allah˺ will be bared,[1214] and the wicked will be asked to prostrate, but they will not be able to do so, 43. with eyes downcast, totally covered with disgrace. For they were ˹always˺ called to prostrate ˹in the world˺ when they were fully capable ˹but they chose not to˺. 44. So leave to Me ˹O Prophet˺ those who reject this message. We will gradually draw them to destruction in ways they cannot comprehend. 45. I ˹only˺ delay their end for a while, but My planning is flawless. 46. Or are you asking them for a reward ˹for the message˺ so that they are overburdened by debt? 47. Or do they have access to ˹the Record in˺ the unseen, so they copy it ˹for all to see˺?

A Lesson to the Prophet

48. So be patient with your Lord's decree, and do not be like ˹Jonah,˺ the Man of the Whale, who cried out ˹to Allah˺, in total dis-

---

1212   It is believed that Allah accepted their repentance and replaced their garden with a better one.

1213   i.e., if only the Meccan pagans knew.

1214   Like the Face and the Hands, the Shin is believed by many to be one of the qualities of Allah, in a way befitting His Majesty and Greatness. Since baring the shin in the Arab culture is associated with the heat of battle, some interpret the verse metaphorically, so the meaning would be: "˹Beware of˺ the Day when horror sets in."

69. Al-Ḥâqqah — 568

بِسۡمِ ٱللَّهِ ٱلرَّحۡمَٰنِ ٱلرَّحِيمِ

لَوۡلَآ أَن تَدَٰرَكَهُۥ نِعۡمَةٌ مِّن رَّبِّهِۦ لَنُبِذَ بِٱلۡعَرَآءِ وَهُوَ مَذۡمُومٌ ۝ فَٱجۡتَبَٰهُ رَبُّهُۥ فَجَعَلَهُۥ مِنَ ٱلصَّٰلِحِينَ ۝ وَإِن يَكَادُ ٱلَّذِينَ كَفَرُواْ لَيُزۡلِقُونَكَ بِأَبۡصَٰرِهِمۡ لَمَّا سَمِعُواْ ٱلذِّكۡرَ وَيَقُولُونَ إِنَّهُۥ لَمَجۡنُونٌ ۝ وَمَا هُوَ إِلَّا ذِكۡرٌ لِّلۡعَٰلَمِينَ ۝

سُورَةُ ٱلۡحَآقَّةِ مَكِّيَّةٌ وَهِيَ ٱثۡنَانِ وَخَمۡسُونَ آيَةً

بِسۡمِ ٱللَّهِ ٱلرَّحۡمَٰنِ ٱلرَّحِيمِ

ٱلۡحَآقَّةُ ۝ مَا ٱلۡحَآقَّةُ ۝ وَمَآ أَدۡرَىٰكَ مَا ٱلۡحَآقَّةُ ۝ كَذَّبَتۡ ثَمُودُ وَعَادُۢ بِٱلۡقَارِعَةِ ۝ فَأَمَّا ثَمُودُ فَأُهۡلِكُواْ بِٱلطَّاغِيَةِ ۝ وَأَمَّا عَادٌ فَأُهۡلِكُواْ بِرِيحٍ صَرۡصَرٍ عَاتِيَةٍ ۝ سَخَّرَهَا عَلَيۡهِمۡ سَبۡعَ لَيَالٍ وَثَمَٰنِيَةَ أَيَّامٍ حُسُومًا فَتَرَى ٱلۡقَوۡمَ فِيهَا صَرۡعَىٰ كَأَنَّهُمۡ أَعۡجَازُ نَخۡلٍ خَاوِيَةٍ ۝ فَهَلۡ تَرَىٰ لَهُم مِّنۢ بَاقِيَةٍ ۝ وَجَآءَ فِرۡعَوۡنُ وَمَن قَبۡلَهُۥ وَٱلۡمُؤۡتَفِكَٰتُ بِٱلۡخَاطِئَةِ ۝ فَعَصَوۡاْ رَسُولَ رَبِّهِمۡ فَأَخَذَهُمۡ أَخۡذَةً رَّابِيَةً ۝ إِنَّا لَمَّا طَغَا ٱلۡمَآءُ حَمَلۡنَٰكُمۡ فِي ٱلۡجَارِيَةِ ۝ لِنَجۡعَلَهَا لَكُمۡ تَذۡكِرَةً وَتَعِيَهَآ أُذُنٌ وَٰعِيَةٌ ۝

---

tress.[1215] **49.** Had he not been shown grace by his Lord, he would have certainly been cast onto the open ˹shore˺, still blameworthy. **50.** Then his Lord chose him, making him one of the righteous. **51.** The disbelievers would almost cut you down with their eyes when they hear ˹you recite˺ the Reminder,[1216] and say, "He is certainly a madman." **52.** But it is simply a reminder to the whole world.

❀

69. The Inevitable Hour (Al-Ḥâqqah)

In the Name of Allah—the Most Compassionate, Most Merciful

The Final Hour

1. The Inevitable Hour! **2.** What is Inevitable Hour? **3.** And what will make you realize what the Inevitable Hour is?

Examples of Destroyed Peoples

4. ˹Both˺ Thamûd and ʾÂd denied the Striking Disaster.[1217] **5.** As for Thamûd, they were destroyed by an overwhelming blast. **6.** And as for ʾÂd, they were destroyed by a furious, bitter wind **7.** which Allah unleashed on them non-stop for seven nights and eight days, so that you would have seen its people lying dead like trunks of uprooted palm trees. **8.** Do you see any of them left alive? **9.** Also, Pharaoh and those before him, and ˹the people of˺ the overturned cities ˹of Lot˺ indulged in sin, **10.** each disobeying their Lord's messenger, so He seized them with a crushing grip. **11.** Indeed, when the floodwater had overflowed, We carried you[1218] in the floating Ark ˹with Noah˺, **12.** so that We may make this a reminder to you, and that attentive ears may grasp it.

1215 While inside the whale. *See* 21:87 and 37:139-148.
1216 This is one of the names of the Quran.
1217 The Striking Disaster is another name for the Day of Judgment.
1218 i.e., your ancestors.

69. Al-Ḥâqqah

Horrors of Judgment Day

13. At last, when the Trumpet will be blown with one blast, 14. and the earth and mountains will be lifted up and crushed with one blow, 15. on that Day the Inevitable Event will have come to pass. 16. The sky will then be so torn that it will be frail, 17. with the angels on its sides. On that Day eight ˹mighty angels˼ will bear the Throne of your Lord above them. 18. You will then be presented ˹to Him for judgment˼, and none of your secrets will stay hidden.

The Winners

19. As for those given their records in their right hand, they will cry ˹happily˼, "Here ˹everyone˼! Read my record! 20. I surely knew I would face my reckoning." 21. They will be in a life of bliss, 22. in an elevated Garden, 23. whose fruit will hang within reach. 24. ˹They will be told,˼ "Eat and drink joyfully for what you did in the days gone by."

The Losers

25. And as for those given their record in their left hand, they will cry ˹bitterly˼, "I wish I had not been given my record, 26. nor known anything of my reckoning! 27. I wish death was the end! 28. My wealth has not benefited me! 29. My authority has been stripped from me." 30. ˹It will be said,˼ "Seize and shackle them, 31. then burn them in Hell, 32. then tie them up with chains seventy arms long. 33. For they never had faith in Allah, the Greatest, 34. nor encouraged the feeding of the poor.

70. Al-Ma'ârij

35. So this Day they will have no close friend here, **36.** nor any food except 'oozing' pus, **37.** which none will eat except the evildoers."

The Quran Is Allah's Word

38. Now, I do swear by whatever you see, **39.** and whatever you cannot see! **40.** Indeed, this 'Quran' is the recitation of a noble Messenger. **41.** It is not the prose of a poet 'as you claim', 'yet' you hardly have any faith. **42.** Nor is it the mumbling of a fortune-teller, 'yet' you are hardly mindful. **43.** 'It is' a revelation from the Lord of all worlds.

The Quran Is Not a Fabrication

44. Had the Messenger made up something in Our Name, **45.** We would have certainly seized him by his right hand, **46.** then severed his aorta, **47.** and none of you could have shielded him 'from Us'!

The Quran Is the Absolute Truth

48. Indeed, this 'Quran' is a reminder to those mindful 'of Allah'. **49.** And We certainly know that some of you will persist in denial, **50.** and it will surely be a source of regret for the disbelievers. **51.** And indeed, this 'Quran' is the absolute truth. **52.** So glorify the Name of your Lord, the Greatest.

ონდა ❊ ონდა

70. Pathways of 'Heavenly' Ascent (Al-Ma'ârij)

In the Name of Allah—the Most Compassionate, Most Merciful

A Mocker Asks for Judgment Day

1. A challenger[1219] has demanded a punishment bound to come **2.** for the disbelievers—to be averted by none— **3.** from Allah, Lord of pathways of 'heavenly' ascent, **4.** 'through which' the angels and the 'holy' spirit[1220] will ascend to Him on a Day fifty thousand years in length.[1221]

1219 According to 8:32, An-Naḍr ibn Al-Ḥârith challenged Allah, saying, "If this is indeed the truth from You, then rain down stones upon us from the sky or overcome us with a painful punishment."
1220 The holy spirit is the angel Gabriel.
1221 Judgment Day will seem like 50 000 years for a disbeliever, but it will seem like a very short period for a believer. The Prophet (ﷺ) is reported in a ḥadîth collected by Imâm Aḥmed to have said that, for the believer, this long period will be like the time they took to perform a single prayer in the world.

70. Al-Ma'ârij

5. So endure ˹this denial, O Prophet,˺ with beautiful patience. 6. They truly see this ˹Day˺ as impossible, 7. but We see it as inevitable.

Horrors of Judgment Day

8. On that Day the sky will be like molten brass 9. and the mountains like ˹tufts of˺ wool. 10. And no close friend will ask ˹about˺ their friends, 11. ˹although˺ they will be made to see each other. The wicked will wish to ransom themselves from the punishment of that Day by their children, 12. their spouses, their siblings, 13. their clan that sheltered them, 14. and everyone on earth altogether, just to save themselves. 15. But no! There will certainly be a raging Flame 16. ripping off scalps. 17. It will summon whoever turned their backs ˹on Allah˺ and turned away ˹from the truth˺, 18. and gathered and hoarded ˹wealth˺.

Excellence of the Faithful

19. Indeed, humankind was created impatient: 20. distressed when touched with evil, 21. and withholding when touched with good— 22. except those who pray, 23. consistently performing their prayers; 24. and who give the rightful share of their wealth 25. to the beggar and the poor; 26. and who ˹firmly˺ believe in the Day of Judgment; 27. and those who fear the punishment of their Lord— 28. ˹knowing that˺ none should feel secure from their Lord's punishment— 29. and those who guard their chastity[1222] 30. except with their wives or those ˹bondwomen˺ in their possession,[1223] for then they are free from blame, 31. but whoever seeks beyond that are the transgressors.

1222 lit., private parts.
1223 *See* footnote for 4:3.

71. Nûh

32. ˹The faithful are˺ also those who are true to their trusts and covenants; **33.** and who are honest in their testimony; **34.** and who are ˹properly˺ observant of their prayers. **35.** These will be in Gardens, held in honour.

Warning to the Mockers

36. So what is the matter with the disbelievers that they rush ˹head-long˺ towards you ˹O Prophet˺, **37.** from the right and the left, in groups ˹to mock you˺?[1224] **38.** Does every one of them expect to be admitted into a Garden of Bliss? **39.** But no! Indeed, they ˹already˺ know what We created them from.[1225] **40.** So, I do swear by the Lord of ˹all˺ the points of sunrise and sunset[1226] that We are truly capable **41.** of replacing them with ˹others˺ better than them, and We cannot be prevented ˹from doing so˺. **42.** So let them indulge ˹in falsehood˺ and amuse ˹themselves˺ until they face their Day, which they have been threatened with— **43.** the Day they will come forth from the graves swiftly, as if racing to an idol ˹for a blessing˺,[1227] **44.** with eyes downcast, utterly covered with disgrace. That is the Day they have ˹always˺ been warned of.

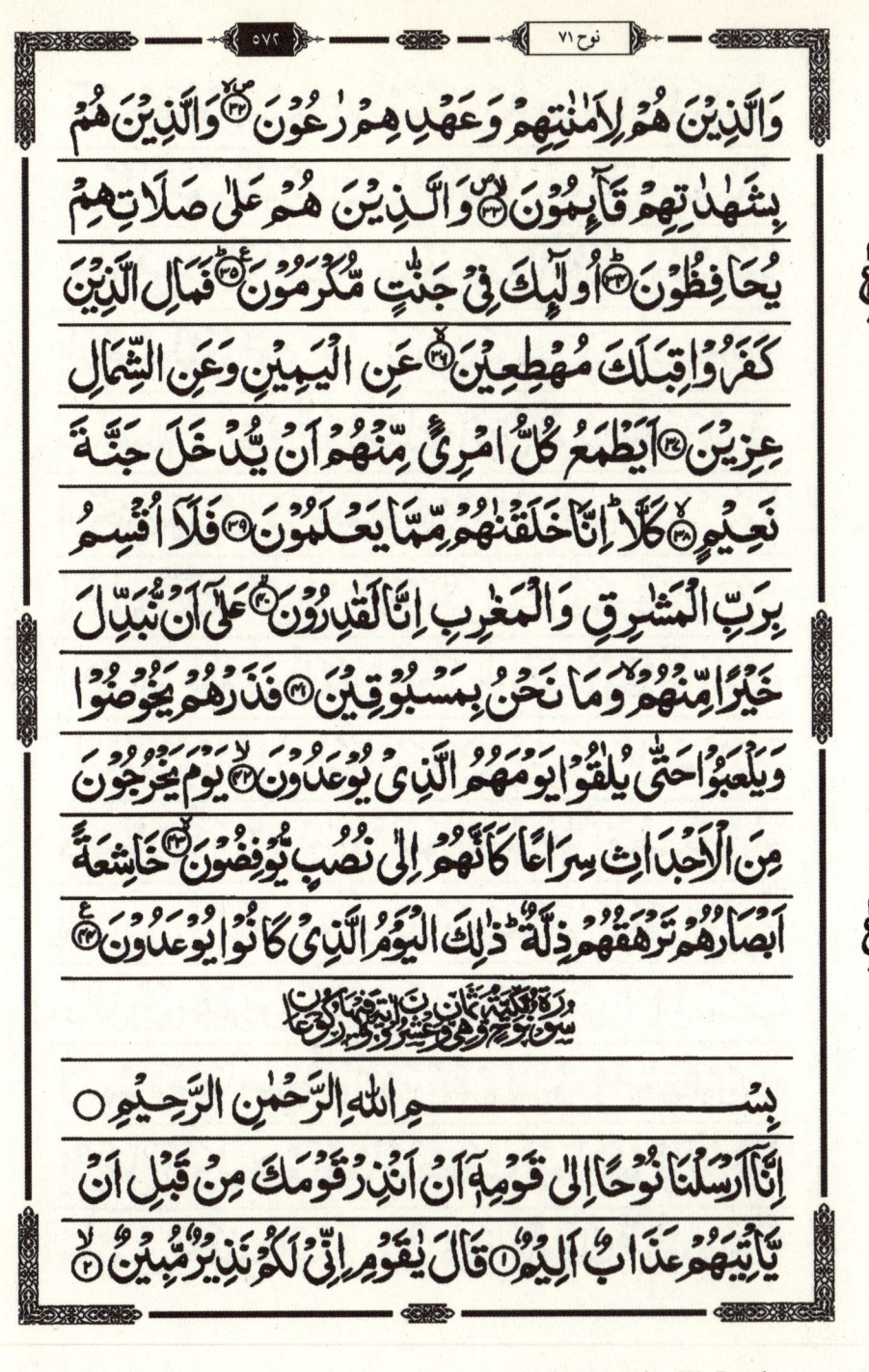

71. Noah (Nûh)

In the Name of Allah—the Most Compassionate, Most Merciful

Noah's Appeal to His People

1. Indeed, We sent Noah to his people ˹saying to him˺, "Warn your people before a painful punishment comes to them." **2.** Noah proclaimed, "O my people! I am truly sent to you with a clear warning:

1224 Some Meccan pagans used to gather around the Prophet (ﷺ) to mock him and the believers, saying that if there is in fact a Hereafter, they are better entitled to Paradise than poor believers.
1225 i.e., from a humble fluid. *See* 32:8.
1226 The daily points of sunrise and sunset, caused by the earth's rotation around its own axis.
1227 Or "as if rushing towards a target."

3. worship Allah ʿaloneʾ, fear Him, and obey me. **4.** He will forgive your sins, and delay your end until the appointed time.[1228] Indeed, when the time set by Allah comes, it cannot be delayed, if only you knew!"

950 Years of Preaching

5. He cried, "My Lord! I have surely called my people day and night, **6.** but my calls only made them run farther away. **7.** And whenever I invite them to be forgiven by You, they press their fingers into their ears, cover themselves with their clothes, persist ʿin denialʾ, and act very arrogantly. **8.** Then I certainly called them openly, **9.** then I surely preached to them publicly and privately, **10.** saying, "Seek your Lord's forgiveness, ʿforʾ He is truly Most Forgiving. **11.** He will shower you with abundant rain, **12.** supply you with wealth and children, and give you gardens as well as rivers. **13.** What is the matter with you that you are not in awe of the Majesty of Allah, **14.** when He truly created you in stages ʿof developmentʾ?[1229] **15.** Do you not see how Allah created seven heavens, one above the other, **16.** placing the moon within them as a ʿreflectedʾ light, and the sun as a ʿradiantʾ lamp? **17.** Allah ʿaloneʾ caused you[1230] to grow from the earth like a plant. **18.** Then He will return you to it, and then simply bring you forth ʿagainʾ.

1228 Meaning, it is out of Allah's mercy that He does not hasten your punishment but delays your death until your destined time.
1229 See 22:5 and 23:12-14.
1230 i.e., your father Adam, who was created from clay.

72. Al-Jinn | 574

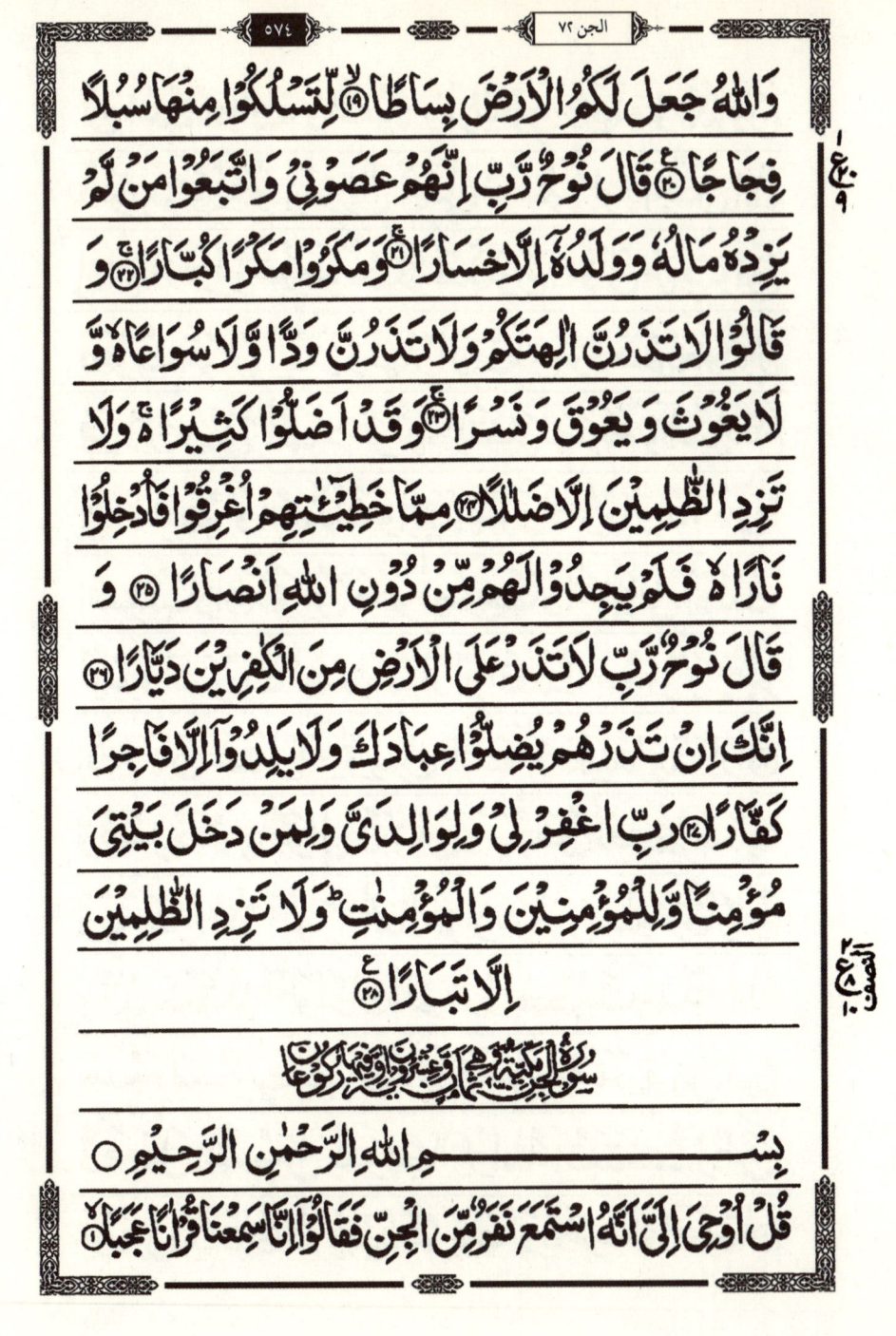

19. And Allah ʿaloneʾ spread out the earth for you 20. to walk along its spacious pathways."

The Flood

21. ʿEventually,ʾ Noah cried, "My Lord! They have certainly persisted in disobeying me, and followed ʿinsteadʾ those ʿeliteʾ whose ʿabundantʾ wealth and children only increase them in loss, 22. and who have devised a tremendous plot, 23. urging ʿtheir followersʾ, 'Do not abandon your idols—especially *Wadd, Suwâ', Yaghûth, Ya'ûq*, and *Nasr*.'[1231] 24. Those ʿeliteʾ have already led many astray. So ʿO Lordʾ, only allow the wrongdoers to stray farther away." 25. So because of their sins, they were drowned, then admitted into the Fire. And they found none to help them against Allah.

Noah's Prayer Before the Flood[1232]

26. Noah had prayed, "My Lord! Do not leave a single disbeliever on earth. 27. For if You spare ʿany ofʾ them, they will certainly mislead Your servants, and give birth only to ʿwickedʾ sinners, staunch disbelievers. 28. My Lord! Forgive me, my parents, and whoever enters my house in faith, and ʿallʾ believing men and women. And increase the wrongdoers only in destruction."

72. The Jinn (Al-Jinn)

In the Name of Allah—the Most Compassionate, Most Merciful

Some Jinn Embrace Islam

1. Say, ʿO Prophet,ʾ "It has been revealed to me that a group of jinn listened ʿto the Quran,ʾ and said ʿto their fellow jinnʾ: 'Indeed, we have heard a wondrous recitation.

1231 These are the names of their main idols. Initially, these idols had been erected to commemorate some righteous people before the time of Noah. After many generations, however, the idols were taken as objects of worship.

1232 Noah (☸) prayed for his people's destruction after Allah revealed to him that no one else was going to believe. *See* 11:36.

72. Al-Jinn

2. It leads to Right Guidance so we believed in it, and we will never associate anyone with our Lord ˹in worship˺. **3.** ˹Now, we believe that˺ our Lord—Exalted is His Majesty—has neither taken a mate nor offspring, **4.** and that the foolish of us used to utter ˹outrageous˺ falsehoods about Allah.[1233] **5.** We certainly thought that humans and jinn would never speak lies about Allah. **6.** And some men used to seek refuge with some jinn—so they increased each other in wickedness.[1234] **7.** And those ˹humans˺ thought, just like you ˹jinn˺, that Allah would not resurrect anyone ˹for judgment˺.

No More Eavesdropping on Heaven

8. ˹Earlier˺ we tried to reach heaven ˹for news˺, only to find it filled with stern guards and shooting stars.[1235] **9.** We used to take up positions there for eavesdropping, but whoever dares eavesdrop now will find a flare lying in wait for them. **10.** Now, we have no clue whether evil is intended for those on earth, or their Lord intends for them what is right.

Righteous and Deviant Jinn

11. Among us are those who are righteous and those who are less so. We have been of different factions. **12.** ˹Now,˺ we truly know that we cannot frustrate Allah on earth, nor can we escape from Him ˹into heaven˺. **13.** When we heard the guidance ˹of the Quran˺, we ˹readily˺ believed in it. For whoever believes in their Lord will have no fear of being denied ˹a reward˺ or wronged.

14. And among us are those who have submitted ˹to Allah˺ and those who are deviant. So ˹as for˺ those who submitted, it is they who have attained Right Guidance.

1233 Meaning, evil jinn tempted some pagan Arabs to believe that the angels are Allah's daughters through female jinn.
1234 *See* footnote for 6:128.
1235 Some jinn used to eavesdrop on the heaven, then pass on what they heard to fortune-tellers. But this practice came to an end once Muḥammad (ﷺ) was sent as a messenger with the Quran.

72. Al-Jinn

15. And as for the deviant, they will be fuel for Hell.'"

A Message to the Deniers

16. Had the deniers followed the Right Way, We would have certainly granted them abundant rain to drink— 17. as a test for them.[1236] And whoever turns away from the remembrance of their Lord will be admitted by Him into an overwhelming punishment.

Worship Allah Alone

18. The places of worship are ˹only˺ for Allah, so do not invoke anyone besides Him. 19. Yet when the servant of Allah[1237] stood up calling upon Him, the pagans almost swarmed over him. 20. Say, ˹O Prophet,˺ "I call only upon my Lord, associating none with Him ˹in worship˺." 21. Say, "It is not in my power to harm or benefit you." 22. Say, "No one can protect me from Allah ˹if I were to disobey Him˺, nor can I find any refuge other than Him. 23. ˹My duty is˺ only to convey ˹the truth˺ from Allah and ˹deliver˺ His messages." And whoever disobeys Allah and His Messenger will certainly be in the Fire of Hell, to stay there for ever and ever.

Warning to Pagan Deniers

24. Only when they see what they have been threatened with will they know who is weaker in helpers and inferior in manpower. 25. Say, "I do not know if what you are promised is near or my Lord has set a distant time for it. 26. ˹He is the˺ Knower of the unseen, disclosing none of it to anyone, 27. except messengers of His choice. Then He appoints angel-guards before and behind them

---

1236 Meaning, to see if they will be grateful to Allah for rain and other provisions.
1237 i.e., Muḥammad (ﷺ).

577 73. Al-Muzzammil

28. to ensure that the messengers fully deliver the messages of their Lord— though He ˹already˺ knows all about them, and keeps account of everything."

❧ ✻ ❧

73. The Wrapped One (Al-Muzzammil)

In the Name of Allah—the Most Compassionate, Most Merciful

Empowering the Prophet Through Prayer

1. O you wrapped ˹in your clothes˺!
2. Stand all night ˹in prayer˺ except a little— 3. ˹pray˺ half the night, or a little less, 4. or a little more— and recite the Quran ˹properly˺ in a measured way. 5. ˹For˺ We will soon send upon you a weighty revelation. 6. Indeed, worship in the night is more impactful and suitable for recitation. 7. For during the day you are over-occupied ˹with worldly duties˺. 8. ˹Always˺ remember the Name of your Lord, and devote yourself to Him wholeheartedly. 9. ˹He is the˺ Lord of the east and the west. There is no god ˹worthy of worship˺ except Him, so take Him ˹alone˺ as a Trustee of Affairs.

Reassuring the Prophet

10. Be patient ˹O Prophet˺ with what they say, and depart from them courteously. 11. And leave to Me the deniers—the people of luxury—and bear with them for a little while. 12. ˹For˺ We certainly have shackles, a ˹raging˺ Fire, 13. choking food, and a painful punishment ˹in store for them˺ 14. on the Day the earth and mountains will shake ˹violently˺, and mountains will be ˹reduced to˺ dunes of shifting sand.

A Warning to the Polytheists

15. Indeed, We have sent to you a messenger as a witness over you, just as We sent a messenger to Pharaoh.

73. Al-Muzzammil

16. But Pharaoh disobeyed the messenger, so We seized him with a stern grip. 17. If you ˹pagans˺ persist in disbelief, then how will you guard yourselves against ˹the horrors of˺ a Day which will turn children's hair grey? 18. It will ˹even˺ cause the sky to split apart. His promise ˹of judgment˺ must be fulfilled. 19. Surely this is a reminder. So let whoever wills take the ˹Right˺ Way to their Lord.

Night Prayers Eased

20. Surely your Lord knows that you ˹O Prophet˺ stand ˹in prayer˺ for nearly two-thirds of the night, or ˹sometimes˺ half of it, or a third, as do some of those with you. Allah ˹alone˺ keeps a ˹precise˺ measure of the day and night. He knows that you ˹believers˺ are unable to endure this, and has turned to you in mercy.[1238] So recite ˹in prayer˺ whatever you can from the Quran. He knows that some of you will be sick, some will be travelling throughout the land seeking Allah's bounty, and some fighting in the cause of Allah. So recite whatever you can from it. And ˹continue to˺ perform ˹regular˺ prayers, pay alms-tax, and lend to Allah a good loan.[1239] Whatever good you send forth for yourselves, you will find it with Allah far better and more rewarding.[1240] And seek Allah's forgiveness. Surely Allah is All-Forgiving, Most Merciful.

༄❀༄

1238 This passage lightens the ruling mentioned in 73:2-4. So from now on, the believers do not have to stick to any of the portions specified at the beginning of this sûrah. Rather, they can pray whatever they can at night.

1239 i.e., giving for charity and good causes.

1240 The reward for your charity will be far better than what you left behind or what you have given in charity because it will be rewarded ten-fold, or even 700-fold, and Allah gives more to whoever He wills. See 2:261.

74. The One Covered up (Al-Muddaththir)

In the Name of Allah—the Most Compassionate, Most Merciful

A Message to the Prophet

1. O you covered up ˹in your clothes˺! 2. Arise and warn ˹all˺. 3. Revere your Lord ˹alone˺. 4. Purify your garments. 5. ˹Continue to˺ shun idols. 6. Do not do a favour expecting more ˹in return˺.[1241] 7. And persevere for ˹the sake of˺ your Lord. 8. ˹For˺ when the Trumpet will be sounded,[1242] 9. that will ˹truly˺ be a difficult Day— 10. far from easy for the disbelievers.

The Fate of a Denier[1243]

11. And leave to me ˹O Prophet˺ the one I created all by Myself, 12. and granted him abundant wealth, 13. and children always by his side, 14. and made life very easy for him. 15. Yet he is hungry for more. 16. But no! ˹For˺ he has been truly stubborn with Our revelations. 17. I will make his fate unbearable, 18. for he contemplated and determined ˹a degrading label for the Quran˺. 19. May he be condemned! How evil was what he determined! 20. May he be condemned even more! How evil was what he determined! 21. Then he re-contemplated ˹in frustration˺, 22. then frowned and scowled, 23. then turned his back ˹on the truth˺ and acted arrogantly, 24. saying, "This ˹Quran˺ is nothing but magic from the ancients. 25. This is no more than the word of a man." 26. Soon I will burn him in Hell! 27. And what will make you realize what Hell is? 28. It does not let anyone live or die,[1244] 29. scorching the skin. 30. It is overseen by nineteen ˹keepers˺.

1241 It was a common practice to give someone a gift, hoping to receive a more valuable gift in return. This practice is disliked in Islam.
1242 This is when the Trumpet will be blown for the second time, causing everyone to rise from the dead for judgment. *See* 39:68.
1243 This refers to Al-Walîd ibn Al-Mughîrah, a leader of Meccan opposition against Islam. *See* footnote for 64:10-16.
1244 Another possible translation: "It spares none and leaves nothing."

74. Al-Muddaththir 580

The Nineteen Keepers of Hell

31. We have appointed only ˹stern˺ angels as wardens of the Fire. And We have made their number only as a test for the disbelievers,[1245] so that the People of the Book will be certain, and the believers will increase in faith, and neither the People of the Book nor the believers will have any doubts, and so that those ˹hypocrites˺ with sickness in their hearts and the disbelievers will argue, "What does Allah mean by such a number?" In this way Allah leaves whoever He wills to stray and guides whoever He wills. And none knows the forces of your Lord except He. And this ˹description of Hell˺ is only a reminder to humanity.

Warning of Hell

32. But no! By the moon, **33.** and the night as it retreats, **34.** and the day as it breaks! **35.** Surely Hell is one of the mightiest catastrophes— **36.** a warning to humankind, **37.** to whichever of you chooses to take the lead or lag behind.

What Leads the Wicked to Hell

38. Every soul will be detained for what it has done, **39.** except the people of the right, **40.** who will be in Gardens, asking one another **41.** about the wicked ˹who will then be asked˺: **42.** "What has landed you in Hell?" **43.** They will reply, "We were not of those who prayed, **44.** nor did we feed the poor. **45.** We used to indulge ˹in falsehood˺ along with others, **46.** and deny the Day of Judgment, **47.** until the inevitable came to us." **48.** So the pleas of intercessors will be of no benefit to them.

Warning to Pagan Deniers

49. Now, what is the matter with them that they are turning away from the reminder,

---

1245 Some pagans made fun of the Prophet (ﷺ) when they were told that the keepers of Hell are nineteen angels. One of them said mockingly to other pagans, "You take care of two angels and I will vanquish the rest all by myself."

581 75. Al-Qiyamah

50. as if they were spooked zebras
51. fleeing from a lion? 52. In fact,
each one of them wishes to be given
a ʿpersonalʾ letter ʿfrom Allahʾ
for all ʿto readʾ.[1246] 53. But no! In
fact, they do not fear the Hereafter.
54. Enough! Surely this ʿQuranʾ is a
reminder. 55. So let whoever wills
be mindful of it. 56. But they cannot
do so unless Allah wills. He ʿaloneʾ
is worthy to be feared and entitled
to forgive.

❀

75. The ʿRising forʾ Judgment (Al-Qiyamah)

In the Name of Allah—the Most
Compassionate, Most Merciful

Warning to Deniers of Resurrection

1. I do swear by the Day of Judgment!
2. And I do swear by the self-reproaching
soul! 3. Do people think
We cannot reassemble their bones?
4. Yes ʿindeedʾ! We are ʿmostʾ capable
of restoring ʿevenʾ their very
fingertips.[1247] 5. Still people want to
deny what is yet to come, 6. asking
ʿmockinglyʾ, "When is this Day of
Judgment?" 7. But when the sight is
stunned, 8. and the moon is dimmed,
9. and the sun and the moon are
brought together,[1248] 10. on that Day
one will cry, "Where is the escape?"
11. But no! There will be no refuge.
12. On that Day all will end up before
your Lord. 13. All will then be
informed of what they have sent
forth and left behind. 14. In fact,
people will testify against their own
souls,[1249] 15. despite the excuses
they come up with.

1246 Another possible translation: "In fact, each of them wishes to be given a scripture open ʿfor all to readʾ." See 6:124.
1247 This refers to the fact that every human has a unique set of fingerprints.
1248 They both will rise from the west and lose their light.
1249 Their organs will testify against them. See 41:19-24.

75. Al-Qiyamah   582

The Prophet's Rush to Memorize the Quran

16. Do not rush your tongue trying to memorize ˹a revelation of˺ the Quran. 17. It is certainly upon Us to ˹make you˺ memorize and recite it. 18. So once We have recited a revelation ˹through Gabriel˺, follow its recitation ˹closely˺. 19. Then it is surely upon Us to make it clear ˹to you˺.

Another Warning to the Deniers

20. But no! In fact, you love this fleeting world, 21. and neglect the Hereafter. 22. On that Day ˹some˺ faces will be bright, 23. looking at their Lord. 24. And ˹other˺ faces will be gloomy, 25. anticipating something devastating to befall them.

Death of a Denier

26. But no! ˹Beware of the day˺ when the soul reaches the collar bone ˹as it leaves˺, 27. and it will be said, "Is there any healer ˹who can save this life˺?" 28. And the dying person realizes it is ˹their˺ time to depart, 29. and ˹then˺ their feet are tied together ˹in a shroud˺. 30. On that day they will be driven to your Lord ˹alone˺. 31. This denier neither believed nor prayed, 32. but persisted in denial and turned away, 33. then went to their own people, walking boastfully. 34. Woe to you, and more woe! 35. Again, woe to you, and even more woe!

Allah's Ability to Create and Resurrect

36. Do people think they will be left without purpose? 37. Were they not ˹once˺ a sperm-drop emitted? 38. Then they became a clinging clot ˹of blood˺,[1250] then He developed and perfected their form, 39. producing from it both sexes, male and female. 40. Is such ˹a Creator˺ unable to bring the dead back to life?

1250 'Alaqah, meaning the embryo resembles a leech.

76. Humans (Al-Insân)

In the Name of Allah—the Most Compassionate, Most Merciful

Free Choice

1. Is there not a period of time when each human is nothing yet worth mentioning?[1251] 2. ˹For˺ indeed, We ˹alone˺ created humans from a drop of mixed fluids,[1252] ˹in order˺ to test them, so We made them hear and see. 3. We already showed them the Way, whether they ˹choose to˺ be grateful or ungrateful.

Reward of the Ungrateful

4. Indeed, We have prepared for the disbelievers chains, shackles, and a blazing Fire.

Reward of the Grateful

5. Indeed, the virtuous will have a drink ˹of pure wine˺—flavoured with camphor— 6. ˹from˺ a spring where Allah's servants will drink, flowing at their will. 7. They ˹are those who˺ fulfil ˹their˺ vows and fear a Day of sweeping horror, 8. and give food—despite their desire for it—to the poor, the orphan, and the captive, 9. ˹saying to themselves,˺ "We feed you only for the sake of Allah, seeking neither reward nor thanks from you. 10. We fear from our Lord a horribly distressful Day." 11. So Allah will deliver them from the horror of that Day, and grant them radiance and joy, 12. and reward them for their perseverance with a Garden ˹in Paradise˺ and ˹garments of˺ silk.

Pleasures in Paradise

13. There they will be reclining on ˹canopied˺ couches, never seeing scorching heat or bitter cold.[1253] 14. The Garden's shade will be right above them, and its fruit will be made very easy to reach.

1251   This is the time before a human comes into being and as an embryo.
1252   The mixture of male and female gametes (sperm and egg) which form the zygote after fertilization.
1253   There will be no day or night, sun or moon, winter or summer in Paradise. It will always be bright and temperate.

15. They will be waited on with silver vessels and cups of crystal— 16. crystalline silver filled precisely as desired. 17. And they will be given a drink ˹of pure wine˺ flavoured with ginger 18. from a spring there, called *Salsabîl*. 19. They will be waited on by eternal youths. If you saw them, you would think they were scattered pearls. 20. And if you looked around, you would see ˹indescribable˺ bliss and a vast kingdom. 21. The virtuous will be ˹dressed˺ in garments of fine green silk and rich brocade, and adorned with bracelets of silver, and their Lord will give them a purifying drink.[1254] 22. ˹And they will be told,˺ "All this is surely a reward for you. Your striving has been appreciated."

Reassuring the Prophet

23. Indeed, it is We Who have revealed the Quran to you ˹O Prophet˺ in stages. 24. So be patient with your Lord's decree, and do not yield to any evildoer or ˹staunch˺ disbeliever from among them. 25. ˹Always˺ remember the Name of your Lord morning and evening, 26. and prostrate before Him during part of the night,[1255] and glorify Him long at night.[1256]

A Message to the Deniers

27. Surely those ˹pagans˺ love this fleeting world, ˹totally˺ neglecting a weighty Day ahead of them. 28. It is We Who created them and perfected their ˹physical˺ form. But if We will, We can easily replace them with others. 29. Surely this is a reminder. So let whoever wills take the ˹Right˺ Way to their Lord. 30. But you cannot will ˹to do so˺ unless Allah wills. Allah is truly All-Knowing, All-Wise.

1254 The word *ṭahûr* implies that once the believers take that pure drink, there will be no bad feelings in their hearts or ailments in their bodies.
1255 This verse refers to the five daily prayers: the dawn prayer, then noon and afternoon prayers, then sunset and late evening prayers, respectively.
1256 Extra prayers offered at night. *See* 73:20.

585   77. Al-Mursalât

31. He admits whoever He wills into His mercy. As for the wrongdoers, He has prepared for them a painful punishment

77. Those ´Winds´ Sent Forth (Al-Mursalât)

In the Name of Allah—the Most Compassionate, Most Merciful

Judgment Day Is Inevitable

1. By those ´winds´ sent forth successively, **2.** and those blowing violently, **3.** and those scattering ´rainclouds´ widely! **4.** And ´by´ those ´angels´ fully distinguishing ´truth from falsehood´, **5.** and those delivering revelation, **6.** ending excuses and giving warnings. **7.** Surely, what you are promised will come to pass.

Horrors of Judgment Day

8. So when the stars are put out, **9.** and the sky is torn apart, **10.** and the mountains are blown away, **11.** and the messengers' time ´to testify´ comes up— **12.** for which Day has all this been set? **13.** For the Day of ´Final´ Decision! **14.** And what will make you realize what the Day of Decision is? **15.** Woe on that Day to the deniers!

Allah's Infinite Power

16. Did We not destroy earlier disbelievers? **17.** And We will make the later disbelievers follow them. **18.** This is how We deal with the wicked. **19.** Woe on that Day to the deniers! **20.** Did We not create you from a humble fluid, **21.** placing it in a secure place **22.** until an appointed time?[1257] **23.** We ´perfectly´ ordained ´its development´. How excellent are We in doing so! **24.** Woe on that Day to the deniers! **25.** Have We not made the earth a lodging

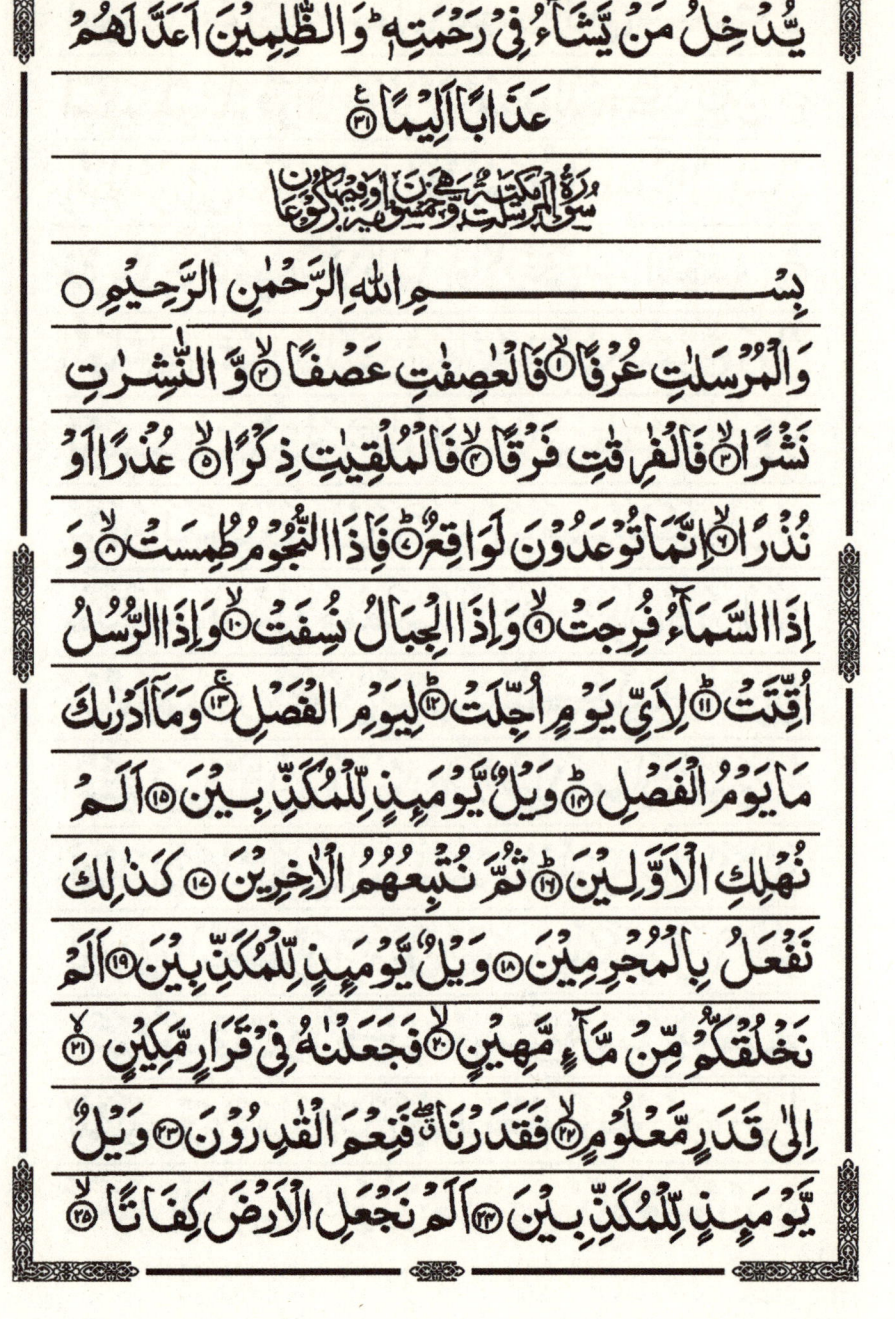

1257 *See* 23:12-14 and 22:5.

77. Al-Mursalât

26. for the living and the dead, **27.** and placed upon it towering, firm mountains, and given you fresh water to drink? **28.** Woe on that Day to the deniers!

Bad News to the Deniers of Hell

29. ˹The disbelievers will be told,˺ "Proceed into that ˹Fire˺ which you used to deny! **30.** Proceed into the shade ˹of smoke˺ which rises in three columns, **31.** providing neither coolness nor shelter from the flames. **32.** Indeed, it hurls sparks ˹as big˺ as huge castles, **33.** and ˹as dark˺ as black camels."[1258] **34.** Woe on that Day to the deniers! **35.** On that Day they will not ˹be in a position to˺ speak, **36.** nor will they be permitted to offer excuses. **37.** Woe on that Day to the deniers! **38.** ˹They will be told by Allah,˺ "This is the Day of ˹Final˺ Decision: We have gathered you along with earlier disbelievers ˹for punishment˺. **39.** So if you have a scheme ˹to save yourselves˺, then use it against Me." **40.** Woe on that Day to the deniers!

Good News for the Believers

41. Indeed, the righteous will be amid ˹cool˺ shade and springs **42.** and any fruit they desire. **43.** ˹They will be told,˺ "Eat and drink happily for what you used to do." **44.** Surely this is how We reward the good-doers. **45.** ˹But˺ woe on that Day to the deniers!

Warning to the Deniers

46. "Eat and enjoy yourselves for a little while, ˹for˺ you are truly wicked." **47.** Woe on that Day to the deniers! **48.** When it is said to them, "Bow down ˹before Allah," they do not bow. **49.** Woe on that Day to the deniers! **50.** So what message after this ˹Quran˺ would they believe in?

1258 lit., yellow camels. Black camels' hair glistens yellow in sunlight.

78. The Momentous News (An-Naba')

In the Name of Allah—the Most Compassionate, Most Merciful

Pagans Mock the Truth

1. What are they asking one another about? 2. About the momentous news, 3. over which they disagree.[1259] 4. But no! They will come to know. 5. Again, no! They will come to know.

Miracle of Allah's Creation

6. Have We not smoothed out the earth ˹like a bed˺, 7. and ˹made˺ the mountains as ˹its˺ pegs,[1260] 8. and created you in pairs, 9. and made your sleep for rest, 10. and made the night as a cover, 11. and made the day for livelihood, 12. and built above you seven mighty ˹heavens˺, 13. and placed in them a shining lamp, 14. and sent down from rainclouds pouring water, 15. producing by it grain and ˹various˺ plants, 16. and dense orchards?

Horrors of Judgment Day

17. Indeed, the Day of ˹Final˺ Decision is an appointed time— 18. ˹it is˺ the Day the Trumpet will be blown, and you will ˹all˺ come forth in crowds. 19. The sky will be ˹split˺ open, becoming ˹many˺ gates, 20. and the mountains will be blown away, becoming ˹like˺ a mirage.

Punishment of the Disbelievers

21. Indeed, Hell is lying in ambush 22. as a home for the transgressors, 23. where they will remain for ˹endless˺ ages. 24. There they will not taste any coolness or drink, 25. except boiling water and ˹oozing˺ pus— 26. a fitting reward. 27. For they never expected any reckoning,

---

1259 The pagans used to mock the teachings of the Quran (e.g., resurrection and judgment). They disagreed whether the Quran was magic, poetry, or fortune-telling.
1260 Just like tent pegs and icebergs, mountains go deep below the surface, slowing tectonic movement.

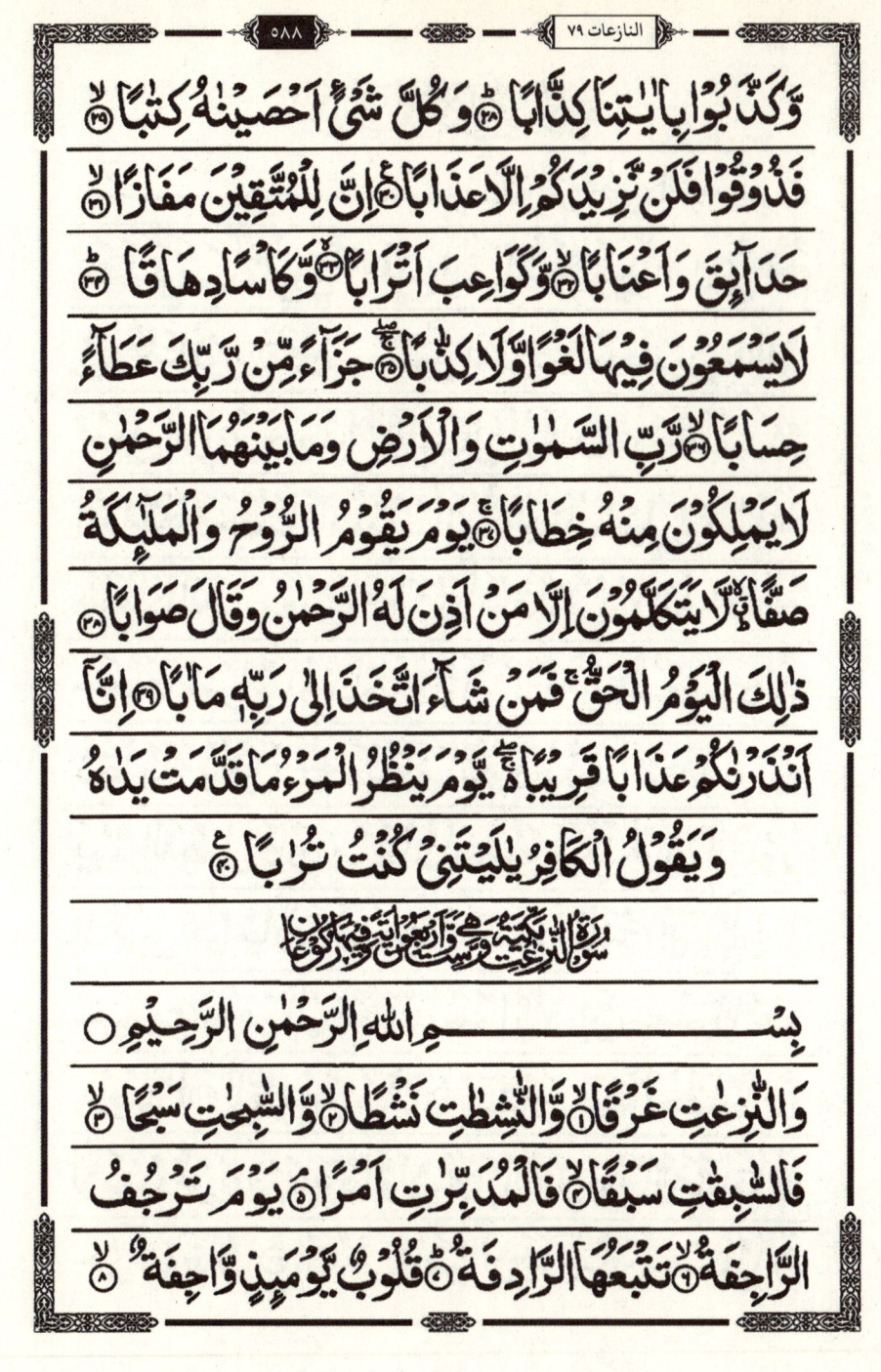

79. An-Nâzi'ât   588

28. and totally rejected Our signs.
29. And We have everything recorded precisely. 30. 'So the deniers will be told,' "Taste 'the punishment', for all you will get from Us is more torment."

Reward of the Believers

31. Indeed, the righteous will have salvation— 32. Gardens, vineyards, 33. and full-bosomed maidens of equal age, 34. and full cups 'of pure wine', 35. never to hear any idle talk or lying therein— 36. a 'fitting' reward as a generous gift from your Lord, 37. the Lord of the heavens and the earth and everything in between, the Most Compassionate. No one will dare speak to Him 38. on the Day the 'holy' spirit[1261] and the angels will stand in ranks. None will talk, except those granted permission by the Most Compassionate and whose words are true. 39. That Day is the 'ultimate' truth. So let whoever wills take the path leading back to their Lord.

Wake-up Call to Humanity

40. Indeed, We have warned you of an imminent punishment—the Day every person will see 'the consequences of' what their hands have done, and the disbelievers will cry, "I wish I were dust."

৽৵৵ ❋ ৽৵৵

79. Those 'Angels' Stripping out 'Souls' (An-Nâzi'ât)

In the Name of Allah—the Most Compassionate, Most Merciful

The Hereafter Is Inevitable

1. By those 'angels' stripping out 'evil souls' harshly, 2. and those pulling out 'good souls' gently, 3. and those gliding 'through heavens' swiftly, 4. and those taking the lead vigorously, 5. and those conducting affairs 'obediently'! 6. 'Consider' the Day 'when' the quaking Blast will come to pass,[1262] 7. followed by a second Blast. 8. 'The deniers'' hearts on that Day will be trembling 'in horror',

---

1261 i.e., the angel Gabriel.
1262 The first Blast will cause everyone to die except those spared by Allah. Then the second one will cause the dead to come to life for judgment. See 39:68.

79. An-Nâzi'ât

9. with their eyes downcast. 10. 'But now' they ask 'mockingly', "Will we really be restored to our former state, 11. even after we have been reduced to decayed bones?" 12. They add, "Then such a return would be a 'total' loss 'for us'!" 13. But indeed, it will take only one 'mighty' Blast, 14. and at once they will be above ground.

Pharaoh Destroyed for Denial

15. Has the story of Moses reached you 'O Prophet'? 16. His Lord called him in the sacred valley of Ṭuwa, 17. 'commanding,' "Go to Pharaoh, for he has truly transgressed 'all bounds'. 18. And say, 'Would you 'be willing to' purify yourself, 19. and let me guide you to your Lord so that you will be in awe 'of Him'?'" 20. Then Moses showed him the great sign,[1263] 21. but he denied and disobeyed 'Allah', 22. then turned his back, striving 'against the truth'. 23. Then he summoned 'his people' and called out, 24. saying, "I am your lord, the most high!" 25. So Allah overtook him, making him an example in this life and the next. 26. Surely in this is a lesson for whoever stands in awe of 'Allah'.

Resurrection Is Easier than Creation

27. Which is harder to create: you or the sky?[1264] He built it, 28. raising it high and forming it flawlessly. 29. He dimmed its night, and brought forth its daylight. 30. As for the earth, He spread it out as well,[1265] 31. bringing forth its water and pastures 32. and setting the mountains firmly 'upon it'— 33. all as 'a means of' sustenance for you and your animals.

Horrors of Judgment Day

34. But, when the Supreme Disaster[1266] comes to pass— 35. the Day every person will remember all 'their' striving, 36. and the Hellfire will be displayed for all to see— 37. then as for those who transgressed 38. and preferred the 'fleeting' life of this world,

---

1263 The staff turning into a snake. *See* 20:17-23.

1264 This is from a human perspective. Otherwise, both the creation of the universe and the resurrection of humans are easy for Allah.

1265 The Arabic verb *daḥa* also suggests that the earth is egg-shaped. The noun form *diḥya* is still used in some Arab dialects to mean an egg. Based on 2:29, 41:9-12, and 79:27-33, Allah ordained both realms, then formed the earth and created its provisions, then formed the heaven into seven heavens—all in six 'heavenly' Days. *See* footnote for 7:54.

1266 This is the second Blast which will cause the dead to come to life for judgment. *See* 39:68.

80. 'Abasa

39. the Hellfire will certainly be ˹their˺ home. **40.** And as for those who were in awe of standing before their Lord and restrained themselves from ˹evil˺ desires, **41.** Paradise will certainly be ˹their˺ home.

The Deniers' Mocking Question

42. They ask you ˹O Prophet˺ regarding the Hour, "When will it be?" **43.** But it is not for you to tell its time.[1267] **44.** That knowledge rests with your Lord ˹alone˺. **45.** Your duty is only to warn whoever is in awe of it. **46.** On the Day they see it, it will be as if they had stayed ˹in the world˺ no more than one evening or its morning.

༺⁕༻

80. He Frowned ('Abasa)

In the Name of Allah—the Most Compassionate, Most Merciful

A Lesson to the Prophet[1268]

1. He frowned and turned ˹his attention˺ away, **2.** ˹simply˺ because the blind man came to him ˹interrupting˺. **3.** You never know ˹O Prophet˺, perhaps he may be purified, **4.** or he may be mindful, benefitting from the reminder. **5.** As for the one who was indifferent, **6.** you gave him your ˹undivided˺ attention, **7.** even though you are not to blame if he would not be purified. **8.** But as for the one who came to you, eager ˹to learn˺, **9.** being in awe ˹of Allah˺, **10.** you were inattentive to him. **11.** But no! This ˹revelation˺ is truly a reminder. **12.** So let whoever wills be mindful of it. **13.** It is ˹written˺ on pages held in honour— **14.** highly esteemed, purified— **15.** by the hands of angel-scribes, **16.** honourable and virtuous.

A Reminder to Resurrection Deniers

17. Condemned are ˹disbelieving˺ humans! How ungrateful they are ˹to Allah˺! **18.** From what substance did He create them? **19.** He created them from a sperm-drop, and ordained their development. **20.** Then He makes the way easy for them,[1269]

1267 Another possible translation: "What is this question? You ˹O Prophet˺ are one of its signs." It is believed—based on authentic narrations from the Prophet—that he (ﷺ) is one of the signs of the Day of Judgment.

1268 This passage, along with others that are critical of some things the Prophet (ﷺ) did (such as 66:1), proves that the Prophet (ﷺ) delivered the revelations in all honesty.

1269 The way to true guidance or the way out of their mothers' wombs.

591   81. At-Takwîr

21. then causes them to die and be buried.[1270] 22. Then when He wills, He will resurrect them. 23. But no! They have failed to comply with what He ordered. 24. Let people then consider their food: 25. how We pour down rain in abundance 26. and meticulously split the earth open ˹for sprouts˺, 27. causing grain to grow in it, 28. as well as grapes and greens, 29. and olives and palm trees, 30. and dense orchards, 31. and fruit and fodder— 32. all as ˹a means of˺ sustenance for you and your animals.

The Overwhelming Day

33. Then, when the Deafening Blast[1271] comes to pass— 34. on that Day every person will flee from their own siblings, 35. and ˹even˺ their mother and father, 36. and ˹even˺ their spouse and children. 37. For then everyone will have enough concern of their own. 38. On that Day ˹some˺ faces will be bright, 39. laughing and rejoicing, 40. while ˹other˺ faces will be dusty, 41. cast in gloom— 42. those are the disbelievers, the ˹wicked˺ sinners.

81. Putting out ˹the Sun˺ (At-Takwîr)

In the Name of Allah—the Most Compassionate, Most Merciful

Horrors of the Apocalypse

1. When the sun is put out, 2. and when the stars fall down, 3. and when the mountains are blown away, 4. and when pregnant camels are left untended,[1272] 5. and when wild beasts are gathered together,[1273] 6. and when the seas are set on fire,[1274] 7. and when the souls ˹and their bodies˺ are paired ˹once more˺,

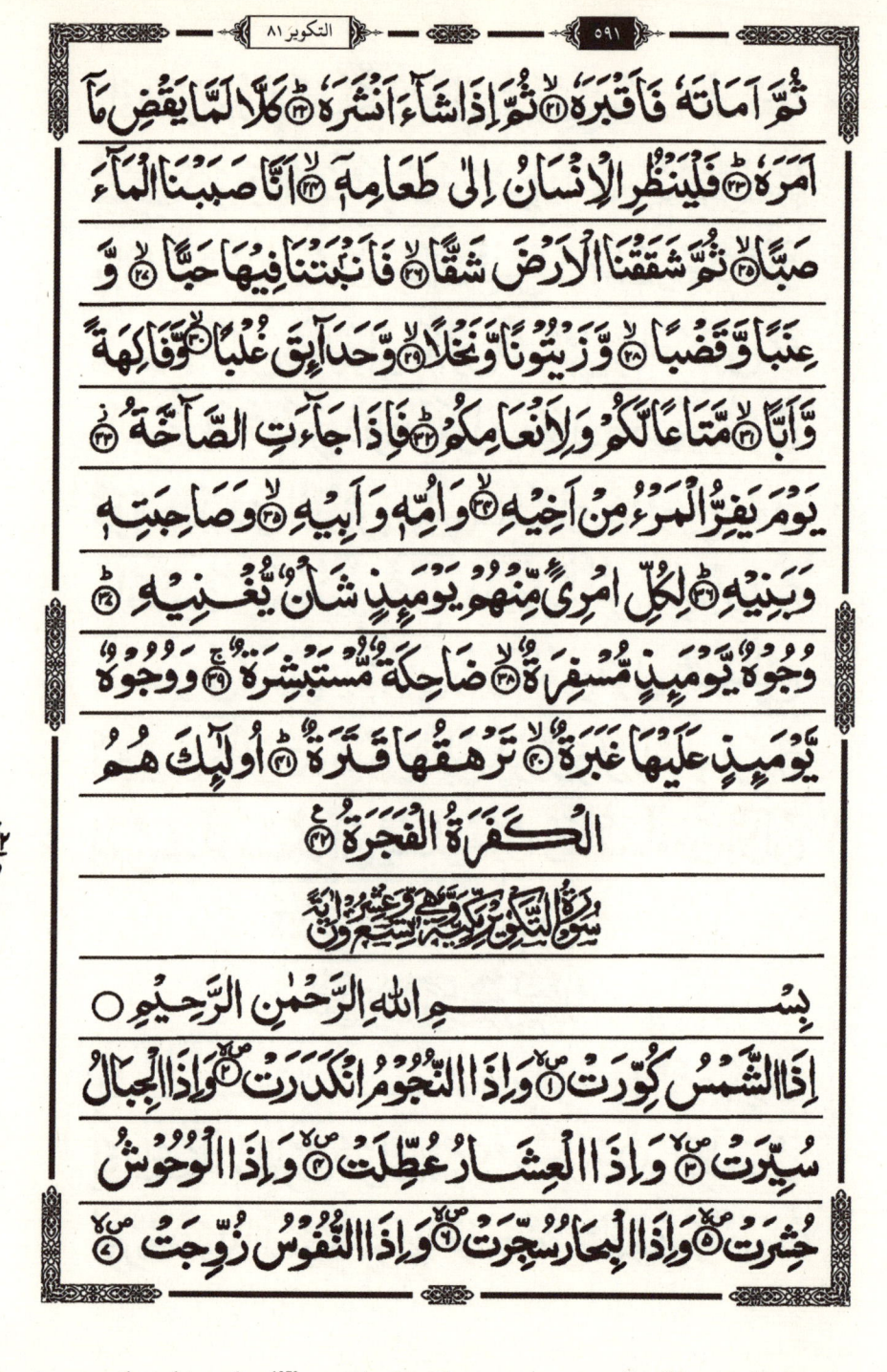

1270   Burial is perceived as a way of honouring human beings after their death.
1271   This is the second Blast which will cause the dead to come to life for judgment. *See* 39:68.
1272   Ten-month pregnant camels were the most precious thing for nomadic Arabs, who cared for and treasured them.
1273   All animals will be brought together for judgment and then they will be reduced to dust.
1274   On the Day of Judgment the oceans and seas will be on fire.

82. Al-Infiṭâr

8. and when baby girls, buried alive, are asked 9. for what crime they were put to death,[1275] 10. and when the records ʿof deedsʾ are laid open, 11. and when the sky is stripped away, 12. and when the Hellfire is fiercely flared up, 13. and when Paradise is brought near— 14. ʿon that Dayʾ each soul will know what ʿdeedsʾ it has brought along.

A Message to the Deniers

15. I do swear by the receding stars 16. which travel and hide,[1276] 17. and the night as it falls 18. and the day as it breaks![1277] 19. Indeed, this ʿQuranʾ is the Word of ʿAllah delivered by Gabriel,ʾ a noble messenger-angel, 20. full of power, held in honour by the Lord of the Throne, 21. obeyed there ʿin heavenʾ, and trustworthy. 22. And your fellow man[1278] is not insane. 23. And he did see that ʿangelʾ on the clear horizon,[1279] 24. and he does not withhold ʿwhat is revealed to him ofʾ the unseen. 25. And this ʿQuranʾ is not the word of an outcast devil.[1280] 26. So what ʿotherʾ path would you take? 27. Surely this ʿQuranʾ is only a reminder to the whole world— 28. to whoever of you wills to take the Straight Way. 29. But you cannot will ʿto do soʾ, except by the Will of Allah, the Lord of all worlds.

ﷺ

82. The ʿSkyʾ Splitting Open (Al-Infiṭâr)

In the Name of Allah—the Most Compassionate, Most Merciful

Horrors of the Final Hour

1. When the sky splits open, 2. and when the stars fall away, 3. and when the seas burst forth, 4. and when the graves spill out, 5. ʿthenʾ each soul will know what it has sent forth or left behind.

1275 Some pagan Arabs used to bury their infant daughters alive for fear of shame or poverty. This practice was condemned and abolished by Islam. *See* 16:58-59.
1276 This probably refers to black holes. *Kanasa* means to sweep or hide. *Miknasah* is derived from this, and is the standard word for a vacuum cleaner.
1277 lit., the day as it takes its first breath.
1278 i.e., Muḥammad ﷺ.
1279 This is first time the Prophet ﷺ saw Gabriel in his angelic form. He saw him a second time in heaven during the Night Journey. *See* 53:5-15.
1280 See 26:210-212.

Human Ingratitude

6. O humanity! What has emboldened you against your Lord, the Most Generous, 7. Who created you, fashioned you, and perfected your design, 8. moulding you in whatever form He willed? 9. But no! In fact, you deny the ʾfinalʿ Judgment, 10. while you are certainly observed by vigilant, 11. honourable angels, recording ʾeverythingʿ. 12. They know whatever you do.

Warning of Judgment Day

13. Indeed, the virtuous will be in bliss, 14. and the wicked will be in Hell, 15. burning in it on Judgment Day, 16. and they will have no escape from it. 17. What will make you realize what Judgment Day is? 18. Again, what will make you realize what Judgment Day is? 19. ʾIt isʿ the Day no soul will be of ʾanyʿ benefit to another whatsoever, for all authority on that Day belongs to Allah ʾentirelyʿ.

83. Defrauders (Al-Muṭaffifīn)

In the Name of Allah—the Most Compassionate, Most Merciful

Warning to Those Who Cheat Others

1. Woe to the defrauders! 2. Those who take full measure ʾwhen they buyʿ from people, 3. but give less when they measure or weigh for buyers. 4. Do such people not think that they will be resurrected 5. for a tremendous Day— 6. the Day ʾallʿ people will stand before the Lord of all worlds?

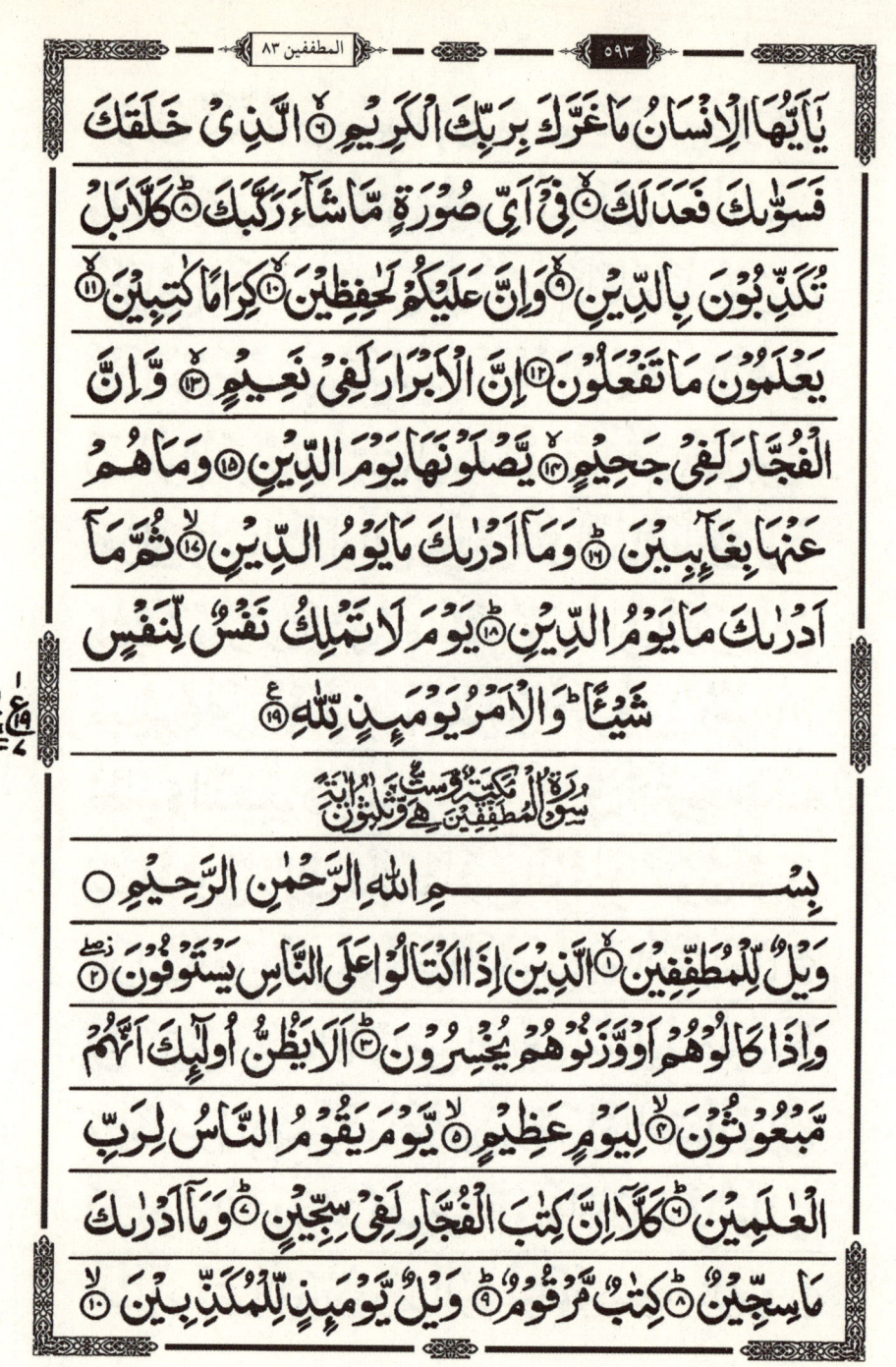

Fate of the Wicked

7. But no! The wicked are certainly bound for *Sijjīn*[1281] ʾin the depths of Hellʿ— 8. and what will make you realize what *Sijjīn* is?— 9. a fate ʾalreadyʿ sealed.[1282] 10. Woe on that Day to the deniers—

1281 *Sijjīn* is the name of place (such as a confinement) in the depths of Hell.
1282 This is based on the commentary of Ibn Kathīr.

الَّذِينَ يُكَذِّبُونَ بِيَوْمِ الدِّينِ ۞ وَمَا يُكَذِّبُ بِهِ إِلَّا كُلُّ
مُعْتَدٍ أَثِيمٍ ۞ إِذَا تُتْلَىٰ عَلَيْهِ ءَايَٰتُنَا قَالَ أَسَٰطِيرُ
الْأَوَّلِينَ ۞ كَلَّا ۖ بَلْ ۜ رَانَ عَلَىٰ قُلُوبِهِم مَّا كَانُوا يَكْسِبُونَ ۞
كَلَّا إِنَّهُمْ عَن رَّبِّهِمْ يَوْمَئِذٍ لَّمَحْجُوبُونَ ۞ ثُمَّ إِنَّهُمْ
لَصَالُوا الْجَحِيمِ ۞ ثُمَّ يُقَالُ هَٰذَا الَّذِي كُنتُم بِهِ تُكَذِّبُونَ ۞
كَلَّا إِنَّ كِتَٰبَ الْأَبْرَارِ لَفِي عِلِّيِّينَ ۞ وَمَا أَدْرَىٰكَ مَا عِلِّيُّونَ ۞
كِتَٰبٌ مَّرْقُومٌ ۞ يَشْهَدُهُ الْمُقَرَّبُونَ ۞ إِنَّ الْأَبْرَارَ لَفِي
نَعِيمٍ ۞ عَلَى الْأَرَائِكِ يَنظُرُونَ ۞ تَعْرِفُ فِي وُجُوهِهِمْ
نَضْرَةَ النَّعِيمِ ۞ يُسْقَوْنَ مِن رَّحِيقٍ مَّخْتُومٍ ۞ خِتَٰمُهُۥ
مِسْكٌ ۚ وَفِي ذَٰلِكَ فَلْيَتَنَافَسِ الْمُتَنَافِسُونَ ۞ وَ
مِزَاجُهُۥ مِن تَسْنِيمٍ ۞ عَيْنًا يَشْرَبُ بِهَا الْمُقَرَّبُونَ ۞
إِنَّ الَّذِينَ أَجْرَمُوا كَانُوا مِنَ الَّذِينَ ءَامَنُوا يَضْحَكُونَ ۞
وَإِذَا مَرُّوا بِهِمْ يَتَغَامَزُونَ ۞ وَإِذَا انقَلَبُوا إِلَىٰ
أَهْلِهِمُ انقَلَبُوا فَكِهِينَ ۞ وَإِذَا رَأَوْهُمْ قَالُوا إِنَّ
هَٰؤُلَاءِ لَضَالُّونَ ۞ وَمَا أُرْسِلُوا عَلَيْهِمْ حَٰفِظِينَ ۞

11. those who deny Judgment Day! 12. None would deny it except every evildoing transgressor. 13. Whenever Our revelations are recited to them, they say, "Ancient fables!" 14. But no! In fact, their hearts have been stained by all ˹the evil˺ they used to commit! 15. Undoubtedly, they will be sealed off from their Lord on that Day. 16. Moreover, they will surely burn in Hell, 17. and then be told, "This is what you used to deny."

Fate of the Virtuous

18. But no! The virtuous are certainly bound for ˹Illiyûn[1283] ˺ in elevated Gardens˺— 19. and what will make you realize what ˹Illiyûn is?— 20. a fate ˹already˺ sealed, 21. witnessed by those nearest ˹to Allah˺. 22. Surely the virtuous will be in bliss, 23. ˹seated˺ on ˹canopied˺ couches, gazing around. 24. You will recognize on their faces the glow of delight. 25. They will be given a drink of sealed, pure wine, 26. whose last sip will smell like musk. So let whoever aspires to this strive ˹diligently˺. 27. And this drink's flavour will come from Tasnîm— 28. a spring from which those nearest ˹to Allah˺ will drink.

The Last Laugh

29. Indeed, the wicked used to laugh at the believers, 30. wink to one another whenever they passed by, 31. and muse ˹over these exploits˺ upon returning to their own people. 32. And when they saw the faithful, they would say, "These ˹people˺ are truly astray," 33. even though they were not sent as keepers over the believers.

1283 ˹Illiyûn is an elevated place in Paradise.

595   84. Al-Inshiqâq

34. But on that Day the believers will be laughing at the disbelievers, 35. as they sit on ˹canopied˺ couches, looking on. 36. ˹The believers will be asked,˺ "Have the disbelievers ˹not˺ been paid back for what they used to do?"

৩০৯০ ✻ ৩০৯০

84. The ˹Sky˺ Bursting Open (Al-Inshiqâq)

In the Name of Allah—the Most Compassionate, Most Merciful

Horrors of Judgment Day

1. When the sky bursts open, 2. obeying its Lord as it must, 3. and when the earth is flattened out, 4. and ejects ˹all˺ its contents[1284] and becomes empty, 5. obeying its Lord as it must, ˹surely you will all be judged˺.

Fate of the Faithful and the Wicked

6. O humanity! Indeed, you are labouring restlessly towards your Lord, and will ˹eventually˺ meet the consequences. 7. As for those who are given their record in their right hand, 8. they will have an easy reckoning, 9. and will return to their people joyfully. 10. And as for those who are given their record ˹in their left hand˺ from behind their backs, 11. they will cry for ˹instant˺ destruction, 12. and will burn in the blazing Fire. 13. For they used to be prideful among their people, 14. thinking they would never return ˹to Allah˺. 15. Yes ˹they would˺! Surely their Lord has always been All-Seeing of them.

Invitation to Believe

16. So, I do swear by the twilight! 17. And by the night and whatever it envelops! 18. And by the moon when it waxes full! 19. You will certainly pass from one state to another.[1285] 20. So what is the matter with them that they do not believe, 21. and when the Quran is recited to them, they do not bow down ˹in submission˺?[1286]

1284   i.e., treasures and dead bodies.
1285   You will pass from life to death and from death to resurrection, from well-being to sickness and from sickness to well-being, from poverty to richness and from richness to poverty, etc.
1286   lit., they do not prostrate.

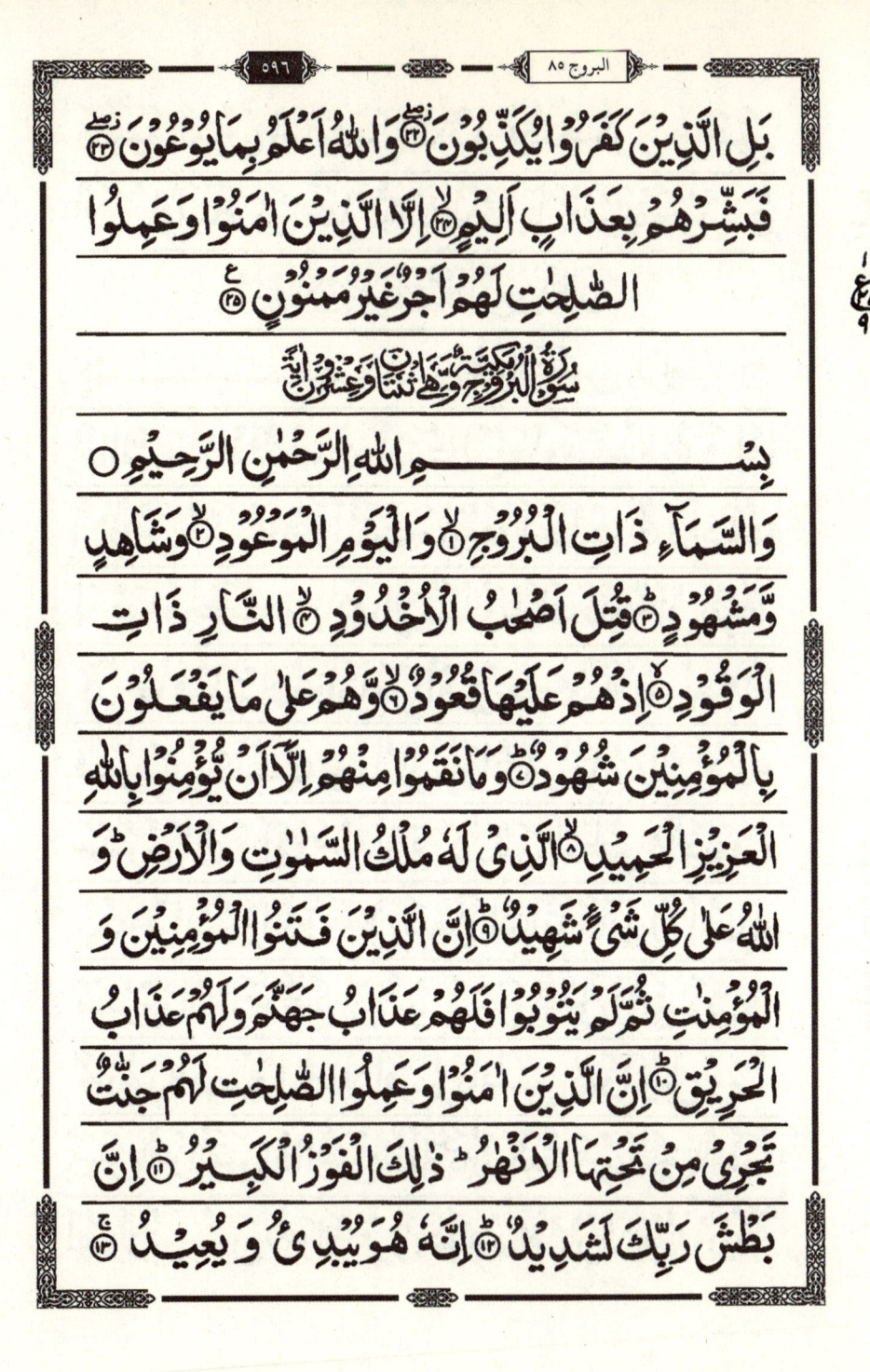

85. Constellations (Al-Burûj)

In the Name of Allah—the Most Compassionate, Most Merciful

The People of the Fire Pit

1. By the sky full of constellations, 2. and the promised Day ˹of Judgment˺, 3. and the witness and what is witnessed![1287] 4. Condemned are the makers of the ditch— 5. the fire ˹pit˺, filled with fuel— 6. when they sat around it, 7. watching what they had ˹ordered to be˺ done to the believers, 8. who they resented for no reason other than belief in Allah—the Almighty, the Praiseworthy— 9. ˹the One˺ to Whom belongs the kingdom of the heavens and earth. And Allah is a Witness over all things. 10. Those who persecute the believing men and women and then do not repent will certainly suffer the punishment of Hell and the torment of burning. 11. Surely those who believe and do good will have Gardens under which rivers flow. That is the greatest triumph.

Warning to Arab Pagans

12. Indeed, the ˹crushing˺ grip of your Lord is severe. 13. ˹For˺ He is certainly the One Who originates and resurrects ˹all˺.

22. In fact, the disbelievers persist in denial. 23. But Allah knows best whatever they hide. 24. So give them good news of a painful punishment. 25. But those who believe and do good will have a never-ending reward.

1287 The witness can be Allah, the angels, or the prophets, and the witnessed can be the people standing for judgment or the overwhelming events of Judgment Day.

86. Aṭ-Ṭâriq

14. And He is the All-Forgiving, All-Loving— 15. Lord of the Throne, the All-Glorious, 16. Doer of whatever He wills. 17. Has the story of the ˹destroyed˺ forces reached you ˹O Prophet˺— 18. ˹the forces of˺ Pharaoh and Thamûd? 19. Yet the disbelievers ˹still˺ persist in denial. 20. But Allah encompasses them from all sides. 21. In fact, this is a glorious Quran, 22. ˹recorded˺ in a Preserved Tablet.

෴ ❈ ෴

86. The Nightly Star (Aṭ-Ṭâriq)

In the Name of Allah—the Most Compassionate, Most Merciful

Allah's Power to Create and Resurrect

1. By the heaven and the nightly star! 2. And what will make you realize what the nightly star is? 3. ˹It is˺ the star of piercing brightness. 4. There is no soul without a vigilant angel ˹recording everything˺. 5. Let people then consider what they were created from! 6. ˹They were˺ created from a spurting fluid, 7. stemming from between the backbone and the ribcage.[1288] 8. Surely He is fully capable of bringing them back ˹to life˺— 9. on the Day all secrets will be disclosed. 10. Then one will have neither power nor ˹any˺ helper.

Warning to Arab Pagans

11. By the sky with its recurring cycles, 12. and the earth with its sprouting plants! 13. Surely this ˹Quran˺ is a decisive word, 14. and is not to be taken lightly. 15. They are certainly devising ˹evil˺ plans, 16. but I too am planning. 17. So bear with the disbelievers ˹O Prophet˺. Let them be for ˹just˺ a little while.

෴ ❈ ෴

1288 Testes and ovaries are formed in the abdomen of the fetus during the first weeks of pregnancy, before descending to their permanent place in the pelvis. Both are sustained by arteries originating between the backbone and the ribcage.

87. Al-A'la | 598

87. The Most High (Al-A'la)

In the Name of Allah—the Most Compassionate, Most Merciful

The Master Creator

1. Glorify the Name of your Lord, the Most High, **2.** Who created and ˹perfectly˺ fashioned ˹all˺, **3.** and Who ordained precisely and inspired accordingly, **4.** and Who brings forth ˹green˺ pasture, **5.** then reduces it to withered chaff.

The Quran and the Way of Ease

6. We will have you recite ˹the Quran, O Prophet,˺ so you will not forget ˹any of it˺, **7.** unless Allah wills otherwise.[1289] He surely knows what is open and what is hidden. **8.** We will facilitate for you the Way of Ease.[1290] **9.** So ˹always˺ remind ˹with the Quran˺—˹even˺ if the reminder is beneficial ˹only to some˺. **10.** Those in awe ˹of Allah˺ will be mindful ˹of it˺. **11.** But it will be shunned by the most wretched, **12.** who will burn in the greatest Fire, **13.** where they will not ˹be able to˺ live or die.

The Way to Success

14. Successful indeed are those who purify themselves, **15.** remember the Name of their Lord, and pray. **16.** But you ˹deniers only˺ prefer the life of this world, **17.** even though the Hereafter is far better and more lasting. **18.** This is certainly ˹mentioned˺ in the earlier Scriptures— **19.** the Scriptures of Abraham and Moses.

88. The Overwhelming Event (Al-Ghâshiyah)

In the Name of Allah—the Most Compassionate, Most Merciful

The People of Hell

1. Has the news of the Overwhelming Event reached you ˹O Prophet˺? **2.** On that Day ˹some˺ faces will be downcast, **3.** ˹totally˺ overburdened, exhausted, **4.** burning in a scorching Fire, **5.** left to drink from a scalding spring. **6.** They will have no food except a foul, thorny shrub, **7.** neither nourishing nor satisfying hunger.

1289 Meaning, We will have you memorize the revelations and apply the rulings contained in them, unless one ruling is replaced by another.
1290 The Islamic way of life which brings about ease in this life and salvation in the next.

The People of Paradise

8. On that Day ˹other˺ faces will be glowing with bliss, 9. ˹fully˺ pleased with their striving, 10. in an elevated Garden, 11. where no idle talk will be heard. 12. In it will be a running spring, 13. along with thrones raised high, 14. and cups set at hand, 15. and ˹fine˺ cushions lined up, 16. and ˹splendid˺ carpets spread out.

A Message to the Deniers

17. Do they not ever reflect on camels—how they were ˹masterfully˺ created;[1291] 18. and the sky—how it was raised ˹high˺; 19. and the mountains—how they were firmly set up; 20. and the earth—how it was levelled out? 21. So, ˹continue to˺ remind ˹them, O Prophet˺, for your duty is only to remind. 22. You are not ˹there˺ to compel them ˹to believe˺. 23. But whoever turns away, persisting in disbelief, 24. then Allah will inflict upon them the major punishment.[1292] 25. Surely to Us is their return, 26. then surely with Us is their reckoning.

৵৵৶ ✻ ৵৵৶

89. Dawn (Al-Fajr)

In the Name of Allah—the Most Compassionate, Most Merciful

Fate of the Deniers

1. By the dawn,[1293] 2. and the ten nights,[1294] 3. and the even and the odd, 4. and the night when it passes! 5. Is all this ˹not˺ a sufficient oath for those who have sense? 6. Did you not see how your Lord dealt with ’Âd— 7. ˹the people˺ of Iram—with ˹their˺ great stature, 8. unmatched in any other land; 9. and Thamûd who carved ˹their homes into˺ the rocks in the ˹Stone˺ Valley;

1291 Another possible translation: "Do they not ever reflect on rainclouds—how they are formed?"
1292 The Hellfire is the major punishment. The minor punishment includes disasters in this life as well as torments in the grave. *See* 32:21.
1293 Like many sûrahs, this one begins with an oath from Allah. He has the right to swear by any object of His creation (i.e., the sun, the moon, the stars, the dawn, or the angels). As for us, we are only allowed to swear by Allah alone.
1294 This refers to the first ten days of the month of Ẓul-Ḥijjah, in which the rituals of pilgrimage are performed.

89. Al-Fajr

10. and the Pharaoh of mighty structures?[1295] 11. They all transgressed throughout the land, 12. spreading much corruption there. 13. So your Lord unleashed on them a scourge of punishment.[1296] 14. ˹For˺ your Lord is truly vigilant.

Bad News for the Deniers

15. Now, whenever a human being is tested by their Lord through ˹His˺ generosity and blessings, they boast, "My Lord has ˹deservedly˺ honoured me!" 16. But when He tests them by limiting their provision, they protest, "My Lord has ˹undeservedly˺ humiliated me!" 17. Absolutely not! In fact, you are not ˹even˺ gracious to the orphan, 18. nor do you urge one another to feed the poor. 19. And you devour ˹others'˺ inheritance greedily,[1297] 20. and love wealth fervently. 21. Enough! When the earth is entirely crushed over and over, 22. and your Lord comes ˹to judge˺ with angels, rank upon rank, 23. and Hell is brought forth on that Day—this is when every ˹disbelieving˺ person will remember ˹their own sins˺. But what is the use of remembering then? 24. They will cry, "I wish I had sent forth ˹something good˺ for my ˹true˺ life." 25. On that Day He will punish ˹them˺ severely, like no other, 26. and bind ˹them˺ tightly, like no other.[1298]

Good News for the Faithful

27. ˹Allah will say to the righteous,˺ "O tranquil soul! 28. Return to your Lord, well pleased ˹with Him˺ and well pleasing ˹to Him˺. 29. So join My servants, 30. and enter My Paradise."

1295 i.e., pyramids and obelisks.
1296 lit., so your Lord poured on them a whip of punishment.
1297 They take over the inheritance of orphans and women.
1298 Another possible translation: "None has ever punished the way He will punish on that Day, nor has anyone bound the way He will bind."

90. The City (Al-Balad)

In the Name of Allah—the Most Compassionate, Most Merciful

Ungrateful Disbelievers

1. I do swear by this city ˹of Mecca˺— 2. even though you ˹O Prophet˺ are subject to abuse in this city— 3. and by every parent and ˹their˺ child! 4. Indeed, We have created humankind in ˹constant˺ struggle. 5. Do they think that no one has power over them, 6. boasting, "I have wasted enormous wealth!"? 7. Do they think that no one sees them? 8. Have We not given them two eyes, 9. a tongue, and two lips; 10. and shown them the two ways ˹of right and wrong˺?

The Challenging Path of Good

11. If only they had attempted the challenging path ˹of goodness instead˺! 12. And what will make you realize what ˹attempting˺ the challenging path is? 13. It is to free a slave; 14. or to give food in times of famine 15. to an orphaned relative 16. or to a poor person in distress; 17. and—above all—to be one of those who have faith and urge each other to perseverance and urge each other to compassion. 18. These are the people of the right. 19. As for those who deny Our signs, they are the people of the left.[1299] 20. The Fire will be sealed over them.

❀

91. The Sun (Ash-Shams)

In the Name of Allah—the Most Compassionate, Most Merciful

Purifying and Corrupting the Soul

1. By the sun and its brightness, 2. and the moon as it follows it,[1300] 3. and the day as it unveils it, 4. and the night as it conceals it! 5. And by heaven and ˹the One˺ Who built it,

---

1299 Other sûrahs describing the people of the right and the people of the left include 56 and 69.
1300 Or "when it reflects the sun's light."

92. Al-Layl

6. and the earth and ˹the One˺ Who spread it! **7.** And by the soul and ˹the One˺ Who fashioned it, **8.** then with ˹the knowledge of˺ right and wrong inspired it. **9.** Successful indeed is the one who purifies their soul, **10.** and doomed is the one who corrupts it!

Destruction of the People of Ṣâliḥ

11. Thamûd rejected ˹the truth˺ out of arrogance, **12.** when the most wicked of them was roused ˹to kill the she-camel˺. **13.** But the messenger of Allah warned them, "˹Do not disturb˺ Allah's camel and her ˹turn to˺ drink!" **14.** Still they defied him and slaughtered her. So their Lord crushed them for their crime, levelling all to the ground.[1301] **15.** He has no fear of consequences.

❁ ✳ ❁

92. The Night (Al-Layl)

In the Name of Allah—the Most Compassionate, Most Merciful

The Faithful and the Faithless

1. By the night when it covers, **2.** and the day when it shines! **3.** And by ˹the One˺ Who created male and female! **4.** Surely the ends you strive for are diverse. **5.** As for the one who is charitable, mindful ˹of Allah˺, **6.** and ˹firmly˺ believes in the finest reward, **7.** We will facilitate for them the Way of Ease. **8.** And as for the one who is stingy, indifferent ˹to Allah˺, **9.** and ˹staunchly˺ denies the finest reward, **10.** We will facilitate for them the path of hardship. **11.** And their wealth will be of no benefit to them when they tumble ˹into Hell˺.

Reward of the Righteous and the Wicked

12. It is certainly upon Us ˹alone˺ to show ˹the way to˺ guidance. **13.** And surely to Us ˹alone˺ belong this life and the next. **14.** And so I have warned you of a raging Fire, **15.** in which none will burn except the most wretched— **16.** who deny and turn away. **17.** But the righteous will be spared from it— **18.** who donate ˹some of˺ their wealth only to purify themselves,

---

1301 It is true that while Qudâr ibn Sâlif was the individual who killed the camel, the rest of the people were supportive of what he did, so they were all punished collectively.

603   94. Ash-Sharḥ

19. not in return for someone's favours, 20. but seeking the pleasure of their Lord, the Most High. 21. They will certainly be pleased.

❦ ✼ ❦

93. The Morning Sunlight (Aḍ-Ḍuḥa)

In the Name of Allah—the Most Compassionate, Most Merciful

Reassuring the Prophet

1. By the morning sunlight, 2. and the night when it falls still! 3. Your Lord ˹O Prophet˺ has not abandoned you, nor has He become hateful ˹of you˺. 4. And the next life is certainly far better for you than this one. 5. And ˹surely˺ your Lord will give so much to you that you will be pleased. 6. Did He not find you as an orphan then sheltered you? 7. Did He not find you unguided then guided you? 8. And did He not find you needy then satisfied your needs? 9. So do not oppress the orphan, 10. nor repulse the beggar.[1302] 11. And proclaim the blessings of your Lord.

❦ ✼ ❦

94. Uplifting the Heart (Ash-Sharḥ)

In the Name of Allah—the Most Compassionate, Most Merciful

More Reassurance to the Prophet

1. Have We not uplifted your heart for you ˹O Prophet˺, 2. relieved you of the burden 3. which weighed so heavily on your back, 4. and elevated your renown for you?[1303] 5. So, surely with hardship comes ease. 6. Surely with ˹that˺ hardship comes ˹more˺ ease.[1304] 7. So once you have fulfilled ˹your duty˺, strive ˹in devotion˺, 8. turning to your Lord ˹alone˺ with hope.

❦ ✼ ❦

1302 And, by extension, anyone asking for help.

1303 The Prophet's name is always mentioned in the call to prayer, along with Allah's Name. Close to the end of each of the five daily prayers, worshippers invoke Allah's blessings upon the Prophet (ﷺ) and his family. When someone reverts to Islam, they testify that Allah is their Lord and Muḥammad is His Messenger. Muslims, even those who are not practicing, love the Prophet (ﷺ) and many name their children after him.

1304 If a definite noun is repeated in Arabic, it means that we are referring to the same thing. For example, "I met the man and I gave the man some money." But if an indefinite noun is repeated, it means we are referring to two different things. For example, "I met a man and I gave a man some money." With this in mind, we realize that 94:5-6 refers to one hardship (a definite noun) and two different eases (an indefinite noun). Hence, the Arabic saying: "Two eases cannot be overcome by one hardship."

بِسْمِ اللّٰهِ الرَّحْمٰنِ الرَّحِيْمِ ۝

وَالتِّيْنِ وَالزَّيْتُوْنِ ۝ وَطُوْرِ سِيْنِيْنَ ۝ وَهٰذَا الْبَلَدِ الْاَمِيْنِ ۝

لَقَدْ خَلَقْنَا الْاِنْسَانَ فِيْ اَحْسَنِ تَقْوِيْمٍ ۝ ثُمَّ رَدَدْنٰهُ اَسْفَلَ

سَافِلِيْنَ ۝ اِلَّا الَّذِيْنَ اٰمَنُوْا وَعَمِلُوا الصّٰلِحٰتِ فَلَهُمْ اَجْرٌ غَيْرُ مَمْنُوْنٍ ۝

فَمَا يُكَذِّبُكَ بَعْدُ بِالدِّيْنِ ۝ اَلَيْسَ اللّٰهُ بِاَحْكَمِ الْحٰكِمِيْنَ ۝

بِسْمِ اللّٰهِ الرَّحْمٰنِ الرَّحِيْمِ ۝

اِقْرَأْ بِاسْمِ رَبِّكَ الَّذِيْ خَلَقَ ۝ خَلَقَ الْاِنْسَانَ مِنْ عَلَقٍ ۝

اِقْرَأْ وَرَبُّكَ الْاَكْرَمُ ۝ الَّذِيْ عَلَّمَ بِالْقَلَمِ ۝ عَلَّمَ الْاِنْسَانَ مَا

لَمْ يَعْلَمْ ۝ كَلَّا اِنَّ الْاِنْسَانَ لَيَطْغٰى ۝ اَنْ رَّاٰهُ اسْتَغْنٰى ۝ اِنَّ

اِلٰى رَبِّكَ الرُّجْعٰى ۝ اَرَءَيْتَ الَّذِيْ يَنْهٰى ۝ عَبْدًا اِذَا صَلّٰى ۝

اَرَءَيْتَ اِنْ كَانَ عَلَى الْهُدٰى ۝ اَوْ اَمَرَ بِالتَّقْوٰى ۝ اَرَءَيْتَ اِنْ

كَذَّبَ وَتَوَلّٰى ۝ اَلَمْ يَعْلَمْ بِاَنَّ اللّٰهَ يَرٰى ۝ كَلَّا لَئِنْ لَّمْ يَنْتَهِ

لَنَسْفَعًا بِالنَّاصِيَةِ ۝ نَاصِيَةٍ كَاذِبَةٍ خَاطِئَةٍ ۝ فَلْيَدْعُ نَادِيَهٗ ۝

---

96. Al-'Alaq 604

95. The Fig (At-Tîn)

In the Name of Allah—the Most Compassionate, Most Merciful

Reward of Ungrateful Deniers

1. By the fig and the olive ˹of Jerusalem˺, 2. and Mount Sinai, 3. and this secure city ˹of Mecca˺![1305] 4. Indeed, We created humans in the best form. 5. But We will reduce them to the lowest of the low ˹in Hell˺, 6. except those who believe and do good—they will have a never-ending reward. 7. Now, what makes you deny the ˹final˺ Judgment? 8. Is Allah not the most just of all judges?

༺❁༻

96. The Clinging Clot ˹of Blood˺ (Al-'Alaq)

In the Name of Allah—the Most Compassionate, Most Merciful

The First Revelation

1. Read, ˹O Prophet,˺ in the Name of your Lord Who created— 2. created humans from a clinging clot.[1306] 3. Read! And your Lord is the Most Generous, 4. Who taught by the pen— 5. taught humanity what they knew not.

The Man Who Abused the Prophet

6. Most certainly, one exceeds all bounds 7. once they think they are self-sufficient. 8. ˹But˺ surely to your Lord is the return ˹of all˺. 9. Have you seen the man who prevents 10. a servant ˹of Ours˺ from praying?[1307] 11. What if this ˹servant˺ is ˹rightly˺ guided, 12. or encourages righteousness? 13. What if that ˹man˺ persists in denial and turns away? 14. Does he not know that Allah sees ˹all˺? 15. But no! If he does not desist, We will certainly drag him by the forelock— 16. a lying, sinful forelock.[1308] 17. So let him call his associates.

1305 This passage refers to the land of figs and olives where Jesus (﷽) lived, Mount Sinai where Moses (﷽) communicated with Allah, and the City of Mecca where the Prophet (﷽) started his mission. A similar reference can be found in Deuteronomy 33:1, ˹Moses proclaimed:˺ "The Lord came from Sinai. Rising from Seir upon us, he [sic] shone forth from Mount Paran." Seir is a mountain near Jerusalem, and Paran is a mountain near Mecca.

1306 'Alaq, meaning the embryo resembles a leech.

1307 Abu Jahl was a staunch leader of the Meccan opposition to Islam. There are many authentic stories of his abuse of the Prophet (﷽).

1308 This refers to the frontal lobe of the brain, where reasoning is processed.

605 · 98. Al-Bayyinah

18. We will call the wardens of Hell.
19. Again, no! Never obey him ˹O Prophet˺! Rather, ˹continue to˺ prostrate and draw near ˹to Allah˺.

❀ ✲ ❀

97. The Night of Glory (Al-Qadr)

In the Name of Allah—the Most Compassionate, Most Merciful

The Night the Quran Was Revealed

1. Indeed, ˹it is˺ We ˹Who˺ sent this ˹Quran˺ down on the Night of Glory.[1309] 2. And what will make you realize what the Night of Glory is? 3. The Night of Glory is better than a thousand months. 4. That night the angels and the ˹holy˺ spirit[1310] descend, by the permission of their Lord, for every ˹decreed˺ matter. 5. It is all peace until the break of dawn.

❀ ✲ ❀

98. The Clear Proof (Al-Bayyinah)

In the Name of Allah—the Most Compassionate, Most Merciful

The Prophet Is the Clear Proof

1. The disbelievers from the People of the Book and the polytheists were not going to desist ˹from disbelief˺ until the clear proof came to them: 2. a messenger from Allah, reciting scrolls of ˹utmost˺ purity, 3. containing upright commandments. 4. It was not until this clear proof came to the People of the Book that they became divided ˹about his prophethood˺— 5. even though they were only commanded to worship Allah ˹alone˺ with sincere devotion to Him in all uprightness, establish prayer, and pay alms-tax. That is the upright Way.

Fate of the Deniers

6. Indeed, those who disbelieve from the People of the Book and the polytheists will be in the Fire of Hell, to stay there forever. They are the worst of ˹all˺ beings.

1309 It is also believed that the angels descend with all decreed matters for the whole year during that night (al-qadr also means ordainment or destiny).
1310 i.e., the angel Gabriel.

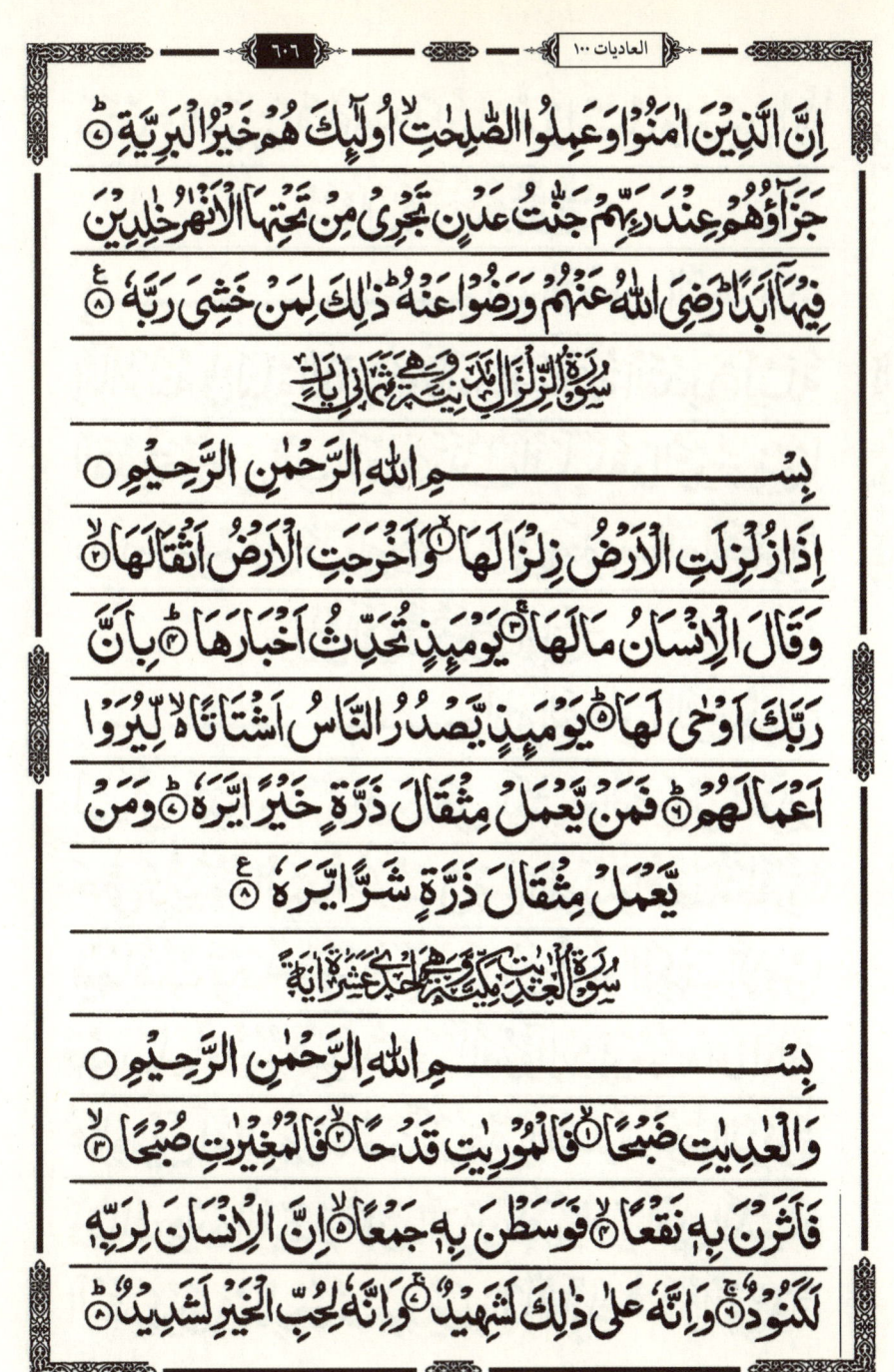

Fate of the Believers

7. Indeed, those who believe and do good—they are the best of ˹all˺ beings. **8.** Their reward with their Lord will be Gardens of Eternity, under which rivers flow, to stay there for ever and ever. Allah is pleased with them and they are pleased with Him. This is ˹only˺ for those in awe of their Lord.

❁ ✳ ❁

99. The ˹Ultimate˺ Quake (Az-Zalzalah)

In the Name of Allah—the Most Compassionate, Most Merciful

Horrors of Judgment Day

1. When the earth is shaken ˹in˺ its ultimate quaking, **2.** and when the earth throws out ˹all˺ its contents,[1311] **3.** and humanity cries, "What is wrong with it?"— **4.** on that Day the earth will recount everything, **5.** having been inspired by your Lord ˹to do so˺. **6.** On that Day people will proceed in separate groups[1312] to be shown ˹the consequences of˺ their deeds. **7.** So whoever does an atom's weight of good will see it. **8.** And whoever does an atom's weight of evil will see it.

❁ ✳ ❁

100. The Galloping ˹Horses˺ (Al-ʾÂdiyât)

In the Name of Allah—the Most Compassionate, Most Merciful

Human Ingratitude

1. By the galloping, panting horses, **2.** striking sparks of fire ˹with their hoofs˺, **3.** launching raids at dawn, **4.** stirring up ˹clouds of˺ dust, **5.** and penetrating into the heart of enemy lines! **6.** Surely humankind is ungrateful to their Lord— **7.** and they certainly attest to this— **8.** and they are truly extreme in their love of ˹worldly˺ gains. **9.** Do they not know that when the contents of the graves will be spilled out,

---

1311 lit., burdens (i.e., treasures and dead bodies).
1312 The believers will head to Paradise and the disbelievers will head to Hell.

10. and the secrets of the hearts will be laid bare— 11. surely their Lord is All-Aware of them on that Day.

❦ ✹ ❦

101. The Striking Disaster (Al-Qâri'ah)

In the Name of Allah—the Most Compassionate, Most Merciful

Fate of the Righteous and the Wicked

1. The Striking Disaster! 2. What is the Striking Disaster? 3. And what will make you realize what the Striking Disaster is? 4. ˹It is˺ the Day people will be like scattered moths, 5. and the mountains will be like carded wool. 6. So as for those whose scale is heavy ˹with good deeds˺, 7. they will be in a life of bliss. 8. And as for those whose scale is light, 9. their home will be the abyss. 10. And what will make you realize what that is? 11. ˹It is˺ a scorching Fire.

❦ ✹ ❦

102. Competition for More ˹Gains˺ (At-Takâthur)

In the Name of Allah—the Most Compassionate, Most Merciful

Wasted Lives

1. Competition for more ˹gains˺ diverts you ˹from Allah˺, 2. until you end up in ˹your˺ graves. 3. But no! You will soon come to know. 4. Again, no! You will soon come to know. 5. Indeed, if you were to know ˹your fate˺ with certainty, ˹you would have acted differently˺. 6. ˹But˺ you will surely see the Hellfire. 7. Again, you will surely see it with the eye of certainty. 8. Then, on that Day, you will definitely be questioned about ˹your worldly˺ pleasures.

❦ ✹ ❦

103. The ˹Passage of˺ Time (Al-ˁAṣr)

In the Name of Allah—the Most Compassionate, Most Merciful

Wake-up Call to Humanity

1. By the ˹passage of˺ time! 2. Surely humanity is in ˹grave˺ loss, 3. except those who have faith, do good, and urge each other to the truth, and urge each other to perseverance.

❀ ✳ ❀

104. The Backbiters (Al-Humazah)

In the Name of Allah—the Most Compassionate, Most Merciful

Warning to Defamers

1. Woe to every backbiter, slanderer, 2. who amasses wealth ˹greedily˺ and counts it ˹repeatedly˺, 3. thinking that their wealth will make them immortal! 4. Not at all! Such a person will certainly be tossed into the Crusher. 5. And what will make you realize what the Crusher is? 6. ˹It is˺ Allah's kindled Fire, 7. which rages over the hearts. 8. It will be sealed over them, 9. ˹tightly secured˺ with long braces.[1313]

❀ ✳ ❀

105. The Elephant (Al-Fîl)

In the Name of Allah—the Most Compassionate, Most Merciful

Allah's Protection of the Ka'bah

1. Have you not seen ˹O Prophet˺ how your Lord dealt with the Army of the Elephant? 2. Did He not frustrate their scheme? 3. For He sent against them flocks of birds, 4. that pelted them with stones of baked clay, 5. leaving them like chewed up straw.[1314]

❀ ✳ ❀

1313 Other possible translations: 1. "The Fire will be in towering columns." 2. "They will be tied to long pillars."
1314 Or worm-eaten leaves.

106. ˹The People of˺ Quraysh (Quraysh)

In the Name of Allah—the Most Compassionate, Most Merciful

Allah's Major Favour to the Meccans[1315]

1. ˹At least˺ for ˹the favour of˺ making Quraysh habitually secure— 2. secure in their trading caravan ˹to Yemen˺ in the winter and ˹Syria˺ in the summer— 3. let them worship the Lord of this ˹Sacred˺ House, 4. Who has fed them against hunger and made them secure against fear.[1316]

ᏘᏇᎧ ❊ ᏘᏇᎧ

107. ˹Simplest˺ Aid (Al-Mâ'ûn)

In the Name of Allah—the Most Compassionate, Most Merciful

Qualities of Judgment Deniers

1. Have you seen the one who denies the ˹final˺ Judgment? 2. That is the one who repulses the orphan, 3. and does not encourage the feeding of the poor. 4. So woe to those ˹hypocrites˺ who pray 5. yet are unmindful of their prayers; 6. those who ˹only˺ show off, 7. and refuse to give ˹even the simplest˺ aid.[1317]

ᏘᏇᎧ ❊ ᏘᏇᎧ

108. Abundant Goodness (Al-Kawthar)

In the Name of Allah—the Most Compassionate, Most Merciful

Good News to the Prophet

1. Indeed, We have granted you ˹O Prophet˺ abundant goodness.[1318] 2. So pray and sacrifice to your Lord ˹alone˺. 3. Only the one who hates you is truly cut off ˹from any goodness˺.

ᏘᏇᎧ ❊ ᏘᏇᎧ

109. The Disbelievers (Al-Kâfirûn)

In the Name of Allah—the Most Compassionate, Most Merciful

1315 Quraysh is another name for the people of Mecca.
1316 Blessing the people of Quraysh with provision and security is probably the answer to Abraham's prayer in 14:35-37.
1317 They refuse to help others with small things like salt or water, let alone alms-tax.
1318 This includes a heavenly river as well other favours in both worlds.

112. Al-Ikhlâs

*No Compromise
in Worshipping Allah*

1. Say, ˹O Prophet,˺ "O you disbeliev-ers! **2.** I do not worship what you wor-ship, **3.** nor do you worship what I wor-ship. **4.** I will never worship what you worship, **5.** nor will you ever worship what I worship. **6.** You have your way, and I have my Way."

❧ ✶ ❧

110. The ˹Ultimate˺ Help (An-Naṣr)

In the Name of Allah—the Most Compassionate, Most Merciful

Nearing the Journey's End

1. When Allah's help comes and the victory ˹over Mecca is achieved˺, **2.** and you ˹O Prophet˺ see the peo-ple embracing Allah's Way in crowds, **3.** then glorify the praises of your Lord and seek His forgiveness, for certainly He is ever Accepting of Repentance.

❧ ✶ ❧

111. The Palm-Fibre Rope (Al-Masad)

In the Name of Allah—the Most Compassionate, Most Merciful

The Fate of an Evil Couple

1. May the hands of Abu Lahab per-ish, and he ˹himself˺ perish! **2.** Nei-ther his wealth nor ˹worldly˺ gains will benefit him. **3.** He will burn in a flaming Fire, **4.** and ˹so will˺ his wife, the carrier of ˹thorny˺ kindling,[1319] **5.** around her neck will be a rope of palm-fibre.[1320]

❧ ✶ ❧

112. Purity of Faith (Al-Ikhlâs)

In the Name of Allah—the Most Compassionate, Most Merciful

Allah's Absolute Oneness

1. Say, ˹O Prophet,˺ "He is Allah—One ˹and Indivisible˺; **2.** Allah—the Sustainer ˹needed by all˺. **3.** He has never had offspring,

---

1319 Since she used to carry thorny branches and throw them in the way of the Prophet (ﷺ), she will be carrying firewood in Hell.
1323 This was one of the earliest sûrahs revealed of the Quran. Paradoxically, for Abu Lahab to disprove the Quran, all he had to do was accept Islam because this verse condemns him to Hell.

nor was He born. **4.** And there is none comparable to Him."[1321]

⊰✾⊱

113. *The Daybreak (Al-Falaq)*

In the Name of Allah—the Most Compassionate, Most Merciful

Seeking Protection Against All Evil

1. Say, ˹O Prophet,˺ "I seek refuge in the Lord of the daybreak **2.** from the evil of whatever He has created, **3.** and from the evil of the night when it grows dark, **4.** and from the evil of those ˹witches casting spells by˺ blowing onto knots, **5.** and from the evil of an envier when they envy."

⊰✾⊱

114. *Humankind (An-Nâs)*

In the Name of Allah—the Most Compassionate, Most Merciful

Seeking Protection Against Evil Whispers

1. Say, ˹O Prophet,˺ "I seek refuge in the Lord of humankind, **2.** the Master of humankind, **3.** the God of humankind, **4.** from the evil of the lurking whisperer— **5.** who whispers into the hearts of humankind— **6.** from among jinn and humankind."

⊰✾⊱

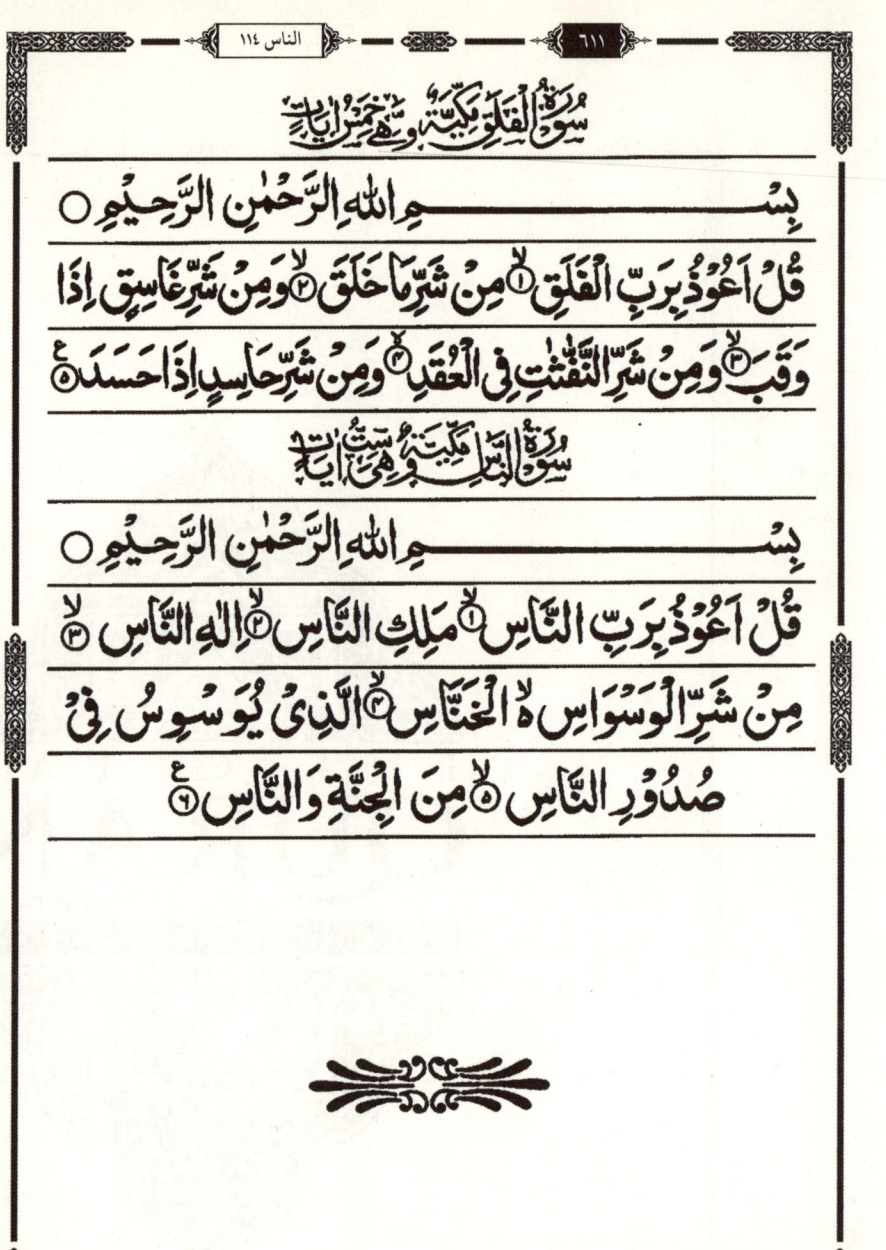

1321 As mentioned in the Introduction, the Quran has three main themes: 1. Stories, 2. Muslim teachings, 3. And belief in the unseen. Since Sûrah 112 covers the third theme, the Prophet (ﷺ) says in a *ḥadīth* collected by Bukhâri and Muslim that reading this sûrah equals reading one third of the Quran.

THE CLEAR QURAN® Series

WITH ARABIC TEXT

BODY OF THE TEXT IS IN THE ARABIC ORIENTATION.
TURN BOOK OVER TO BEGIN FROM THE OTHER SIDE.

☼	76.	Humans (*Al-Insân*)	الإنسان
☼	77.	Those ˹Winds˺ Sent Forth (*Al-Mursalât*)	المرسلات
☼	78.	The Momentous News (*An-Naba'*)	النبأ
☒☼	79.	Those ˹Angels˺ Stripping out ˹Souls˺ (*An-Nâzi'ât*)	النازعات
☾☼	80.	He Frowned (*'Abasa*)	عبس
☼	81.	Putting out ˹the Sun˺ (*At-Takwîr*)	التكوير
☼	82.	The ˹Sky˺ Splitting Open (*Al-Infiṭâr*)	الإنفطار
☾☼	83.	Defrauders (*Al-Muṭaffifîn*)	المطففين
☼	84.	The ˹Sky˺ Bursting Open (*Al-Inshiqâq*)	الإنشقاق
☒☼	85.	Constellations (*Al-Burûj*)	البروج
☼	86.	The Nightly Star (*Aṭ-Ṭâriq*)	الطارق
☾☼	87.	The Most High (*Al-A'la*)	الأعلى
☼	88.	The Overwhelming Event (*Al-Ghâshiyah*)	الغاشية
☼	89.	Dawn (*Al-Fajr*)	الفجر
☾☼	90.	The City (*Al-Balad*)	البلد
☒☼	91.	The Sun (*Ash-Shams*)	الشمس
☾☼	92.	The Night (*Al-Layl*)	الليل
☾	93.	The Morning Sunlight (*Aḍ-Ḍuha*)	الضحى
☾	94.	Uplifting the Heart (*Ash-Sharḥ*)	الشرح
☼	95.	The Fig (*At-Tîn*)	التين
☒☼	96.	The Clinging Clot ˹of Blood˺ (*Al-'Alaq*)	العلق
☼	97.	The Night of Glory (*Al-Qadr*)	القدر
☼	98.	The Clear Proof (*Al-Bayyinah*)	البينة
☼	99.	The ˹Ultimate˺ Quake (*Az-Zalzalah*)	الزلزلة
☼	100.	The Galloping ˹Horses˺ (*Al-'Âdiyât*)	العاديات
☼	101.	The Striking Disaster (*Al-Qâri'ah*)	القارعة
☼	102.	Competition for More ˹Gains˺ (*At-Takâthur*)	التكاثر
☾	103.	The ˹Passage of˺ Time (*Al-'Aṣr*)	العصر
☼	104.	The Backbiters (*Al-Humazah*)	الهمزة
☒	105.	The Elephant (*Al-Fîl*)	الفيل
☼	106.	˹The People of˺ Quraysh (*Quraysh*)	قريش
☾	107.	˹Simplest˺ Aid (*Al-Mâ'ûn*)	الماعون
☼	108.	Abundant Goodness (*Al-Kawthar*)	الكوثر
☾	109.	The Disbelievers (*Al-Kâfirûn*)	الكافرون
☾	110.	The ˹Ultimate˺ Help (*An-Naṣr*)	النصر
☼	111.	The Palm-Fibre Rope (*Al-Masad*)	المسد
☼	112.	Purity of Faith (*Al-Ikhlâṣ*)	الإخلاص
☾	113.	The Daybreak (*Al-Falaq*)	الفلق
☾	114.	Humankind (*An-Nâs*)	الناس

☾☀ 31. Luqmân (*Luqmân*)	لقمان
☀ 32. The Prostration (*As-Sajdah*)	السّجدة
☾☀ 33. The Enemy Alliance (*Al-Aḥzâb*)	الأحزاب
⧖☀ 34. Sheba (*Saba'*)	سبأ
☀ 35. The Originator (*Fâṭir*)	فاطر
⧖☀ 36. Yâ-Sîn (*Yâ-Sîn*)	يس
⧖☀ 37. Those ˹Angels˺ Lined up in Ranks (*Aṣ-Ṣâffât*)	الصّافّات
⧖☀ 38. Ṣâd (*Ṣâd*)	ص
☀ 39. The ˹Successive˺ Groups (*Az-Zumar*)	الزّمر
⧖☀ 40. The Forgiver (*Ghâfir*)	غافر
⧖☀ 41. ˹Verses˺ Perfectly Explained (*Fuṣṣilat*)	فصّلت
☾☀ 42. Consultation (*Ash-Shûra*)	الشّورى
⧖☀ 43. Ornaments (*Az-Zukhruf*)	الزّخرف
⧖☀ 44. The Haze (*Ad-Dukhân*)	الدّخان
☀ 45. The Kneeling (*Al-Jâthiyah*)	الجاثية
⧖☀ 46. The Sand-Hills (*Al-Aḥqâf*)	الأحقاف
☾☀ 47. Muḥammad (*Muḥammad*)	محمّد
☾☀ 48. The Triumph (*Al-Fatḥ*)	الفتح
☾ 49. The Private Quarters (*Al-Ḥujurât*)	الحجرات
☀ 50. Qãf (*Qãf*)	ق
⧖☀ 51. Scattering Winds (*Aẓ-Ẓâriyât*)	الذّاريات
☀ 52. Mount Ṭûr (*Aṭ-Ṭûr*)	الطّور
☀ 53. The Stars (*An-Najm*)	النّجم
⧖☀ 54. The Moon (*Al-Qamar*)	القمر
☀ 55. The Most Compassionate (*Ar-Raḥmân*)	الرّحمن
☀ 56. The Inevitable Event (*Al-Wâqi'ah*)	الواقعة
☾☀ 57. Iron (*Al-Ḥadîd*)	الحديد
☾ 58. The Pleading Woman (*Al-Mujâdilah*)	المجادلة
☾☀ 59. The Banishment (*Al-Ḥashr*)	الحشر
☾ 60. The Test of Faith (*Al-Mumtaḥanah*)	الممتحنة
☾ 61. The ˹Solid˺ Ranks (*Aṣ-Ṣaff*)	الصّفّ
☾ 62. Friday Congregation (*Al-Jumu'ah*)	الجمعة
☾ 63. The Hypocrites (*Al-Munâfiqûn*)	المنافقون
☾☀ 64. Mutual Loss and Gain (*At-Taghâbun*)	التّغابن
☾☀ 65. Divorce (*Aṭ-Ṭalâq*)	الطّلاق
☾☀ 66. The Prohibition (*At-Taḥrîm*)	التّحريم
☀ 67. All Authority (*Al-Mulk*)	الملك
⧖☾ 68. The Pen (*Al-Qalam*)	القلم
⧖☀ 69. The Inevitable Hour (*Al-Ḥâqqah*)	الحاقّة
☾☀ 70. Pathways of ˹Heavenly˺ Ascent (*Al-Ma'ârij*)	المعارج
⧖ 71. Noah (*Nûḥ*)	نوح
☀ 72. The Jinn (*Al-Jinn*)	الجنّ
☾☀ 73. The Wrapped One (*Al-Muzzammil*)	المزّمّل
☀ 74. The One Covered up (*Al-Muddaththir*)	المدّثر
☀ 75. The ˹Rising for˺ Judgment (*Al-Qiyamah*)	القيامة

SÛRAHS BY THEMES

The Quran has three main themes:

☽ **Doctrine** (e.g., acts of worship, human interactions, family relations, and business transactions), which focuses mainly on a Muslim's relationship with Allah, other people, and the rest of Allah's creation.

⧗ **Stories** (e.g., the story of Moses, Noah, and Ṣâliḥ), which served two purposes: to reassure the Prophet's heart, as he (ﷺ) was met with rejection in Mecca, and as cautionary tales for the pagans (*see* 11:120-123). Other stories (e.g., Joseph and Job) focus on moral lessons.

☼ **The Unseen** (e.g., the belief in Allah and His qualities, as well as angels, resurrection, judgment, etc.), which reaffirms one's faith in the divine through one's heart, not eyes.

Some *sûrah*s contain more than one theme, and some individual verses may touch on a theme not presented here, but the following table represents the general themes covered in the body of the text.

☼	1. The Opening (*Al-Fâtiḥah*)	الفاتحة
⧗☽☼	2. The Cow (*Al-Baqarah*)	البقرة
⧗☽☼	3. The Family of 'Imrân (*Âli-'Imrân*)	آل عمران
☽☼	4. Women (*An-Nisâ'*)	النّساء
⧗☽☼	5. The Spread Table (*Al-Mâ'idah*)	المائدة
⧗☽☼	6. Cattle (*Al-An'âm*)	الأنعام
⧗☽☼	7. The Heights (*Al-A'râf*)	الأعراف
☽	8. Spoils of War (*Al-Anfâl*)	الأنفال
☽	9. Repentance (*At-Tawbah*)	التوبة
⧗☼	10. Jonah (*Yûnus*)	يونس
⧗☼	11. Hûd (*Hûd*)	هود
⧗	12. Joseph (*Yûsuf*)	يوسف
☼	13. Thunder (*Ar-Ra'd*)	الرّعد
⧗☼	14. Abraham (*Ibrâhîm*)	إبراهيم
⧗☼	15. The Stone Valley (*Al-Ḥijr*)	الحجر
☽☼	16. Bees (*An-Naḥl*)	النّحل
☽☼	17. The Night Journey (*Al-Isrâ'*)	الإسراء
⧗☼	18. The Cave (*Al-Kahf*)	الكهف
⧗☼	19. Mary (*Mariam*)	مريم
⧗☼	20. Ṭâ-Hâ (*Ṭâ-Hâ*)	طه
⧗☼	21. The Prophets (*Al-Anbiyâ'*)	الأنبياء
☽☼	22. The Pilgrimage (*Al-Ḥajj*)	الحجّ
⧗☽☼	23. The Believers (*Al-Mu'minûn*)	المؤمنون
☽☼	24. The Light (*An-Nûr*)	النّور
☽☼	25. The Decisive Authority (*Al-Furqân*)	الفرقان
⧗☼	26. The Poets (*Ash-Shu'arâ'*)	الشّعراء
⧗☼	27. The Ants (*An-Naml*)	النّمل
⧗☼	28. The Whole Story (*Al-Qaṣaṣ*)	القصص
⧗☽☼	29. The Spider (*Al-'Ankabût*)	العنكبوت
☽☼	30. The Romans (*Ar-Rûm*)	الرّوم

109. The Disbelievers
(Al-Kâfirûn)

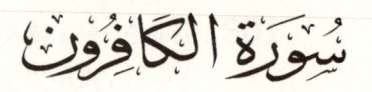

It is reported that the pagans offered to worship Allah alone for one year, provided that the Prophet (ﷺ) worshipped their multiple gods for a year. So this Meccan sûrah was revealed, telling them that he (ﷺ) will be dedicated only to the worship of Allah until the last breath of his life, which is the highlight of the next sûrah.

110. The ˹Ultimate˺ Help
(An-Naṣr)

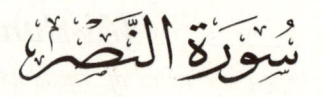

This Medinian sûrah was revealed close to the end of the Prophet's life, instructing him that once his mission is complete and his message is embraced by many, he (ﷺ) should be ready to meet his Creator. A deterring example of those who rejected his message is given in the next sûrah.

111. The Palm-Fibre Rope
(Al-Masad)

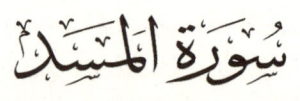

This Meccan sûrah is a warning to Abu Lahab (lit., the Father of Flames), who was an uncle of the Prophet (ﷺ). Both Abu Lahab and his wife Um Jamîl used to abuse the Prophet (ﷺ) and deny the One True God, Who is described in the next sûrah.

112. Purity of Faith
(Al-Ikhlâṣ)

This Meccan sûrah refutes the Trinity, idolatry, atheism, and polytheism and calls for full devotion to the only God, Who is worthy to be worshipped and Whose protection is to be sought, according to the next two sûrahs.

113. The Daybreak
(Al-Falaq)

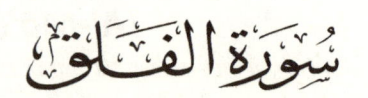

This Medinian sûrah is recited as a supplication to the Almighty against any kind of evil.

114. Humankind
(An-Nâs)

Like the previous sûrah, this Medinian sûrah is a supplication against the evil of humans and jinn. This final sûrah emphasizes the fact that Allah is the Lord and Master of all and that He is the only One to be called upon for help, which connects full circle with the central theme of the first sûrah of the Quran.

103. The ˹Passage of˺ Time (Al-'Aṣr)

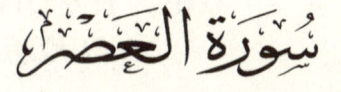

This Meccan sûrah emphasizes that, unlike the evildoers mentioned in the next sûrah, only those who take advantage of this fleeting life by doing good will be successful in the eternal life to come.

104. The Backbiters (Al-Humazah)

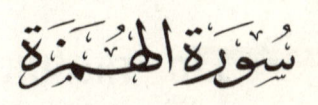

This Meccan sûrah is critical of those who slander others and withhold Allah's bounties. It is made clear that their punishment in Hell is as easy for Allah as the destruction of the evil force mentioned in the next sûrah.

105. The Elephant (Al-Fîl)

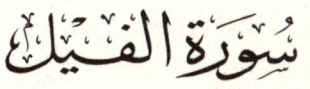

This Meccan sûrah recounts the story of Abraha Al-Ḥabashi (lit., the Abyssinian), who led a large army of men and elephants to demolish the Ka'bah in 570 C.E. so pilgrims would visit the cathedral he had built in Yemen instead. However, the army was destroyed before reaching Mecca. It is commonly believed that the Prophet (ﷺ) was born the same year.

106. ˹The People of˺ Quraysh (Quraysh)

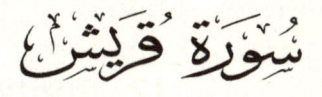

This Meccan sûrah is viewed as a continuation of the previous one. The general idea is that the Meccan pagans must be grateful and devoted to Allah alone for saving the Ka'bah from the Army of the Elephant. Those who are unfaithful to Allah and unkind to the helpless are criticized in the next sûrah.

107. ˹Simplest˺ Aid (Al-Mâ'ûn)

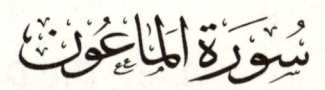

This Meccan sûrah, which takes its name from verse 7, condemns the deniers of the Hereafter for their lack of devotion to Allah and lack of compassion towards the needy. In the next sûrah, the Prophet (ﷺ) is ordered to be devoted to Allah alone and share the meat of his sacrificial animals with those in need.

108. Abundant Goodness (Al-Kawthar)

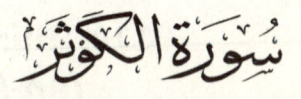

This Meccan sûrah was revealed to reassure the Prophet (ﷺ). Since the Prophet's sons died in childhood, Al-'Âṣ ibn Wâ'il, an infamous Meccan pagan, used to say that Muḥammad (ﷺ) would be forgotten because he had no son to carry his name. Today, 'Muḥammad' is the most common name in the world, whereas the name of Al-'Âṣ is barely mentioned. The Prophet (ﷺ) is ordered to be devoted to Allah alone, which is the underlying theme of the next sûrah.

97. The Night of Glory
(Al-Qadr)

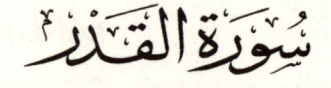

Since the previous sûrah commemorates the first revelation, this Meccan sûrah celebrates the glorious night the Quran was revealed, which is believed to be the night of Ramaḍân 27, 610 C.E. The reason why the Prophet (ﷺ) was sent with the Quran is spelled out in the next sûrah.

98. The Clear Proof
(Al-Bayyinah)

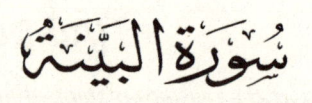

According to this Medinian sûrah, the Prophet (ﷺ) was sent so the disbelievers may change their ways and devote their worship to Allah alone. Those who believe are promised a great reward, whereas those who persist in disbelief are warned of a horrible punishment. The judgment of the believers and disbelievers is the highlight of the next sûrah.

99. The ˹Ultimate˺ Quake
(Az-Zalzalah)

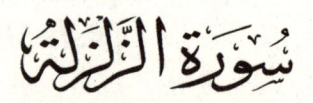

This Medinian sûrah states that all deeds will be brought to light and accounted for on Judgment Day, which is also emphasized in the next sûrah.

100. The Galloping ˹Horses˺
(Al-’Âdiyât)

This Meccan sûrah stresses the fact that people will be accountable on Judgment Day for their ingratitude to their Lord. The scene of the people emerging from their graves (verse 9) is elaborated upon in the next sûrah.

101. The Striking Disaster
(Al-Qâri’ah)

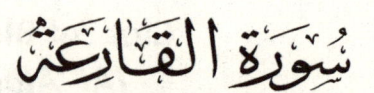

This Meccan sûrah describes the Resurrection and the weighing of deeds in the Hereafter, followed by the final destination to either Paradise or Hell. The reason why many people will end up in the Fire is given in the next sûrah.

102. Competition
for More ˹Gains˺
(At-Takâthur)

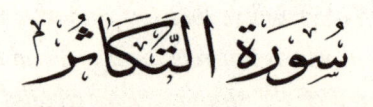

In this Meccan sûrah and the next, the disbelievers are criticized for wasting their lives doing things that do not matter in the Hereafter, most importantly hoarding wealth.

92. The Night
(Al-Layl)

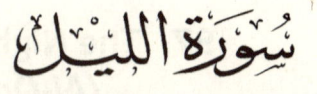

This Meccan sûrah emphasizes Allah's power to create and show the Way, the people's ability to choose between good and evil, and the consequences of each route. The fact that the believers will be rewarded to their satisfaction is highlighted in this sûrah (verse 21) and the next (93:5).

93. The Morning Sunlight
(Aḍ-Ḍuḥa)

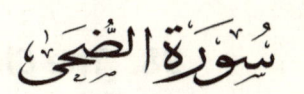

It is reported that the revelation stopped for a while after the initial sûrahs of the Quran, so some Meccan pagans started to mock the Prophet (ﷺ), saying that Allah has become neglectful and hateful of him (ﷺ). Therefore, this Meccan sûrah was revealed to refute their false allegations and remind the Prophet (ﷺ) of some of Allah's favours.

94. Uplifting the Heart
(Ash-Sharḥ)

Like the previous sûrah, this sûrah reminds the Prophet (ﷺ) of more blessings to reassure him of Allah's continued support in the city of Mecca, which is mentioned in the next sûrah.

95. The Fig
(At-Tîn)

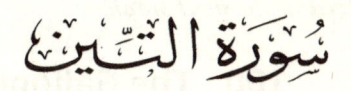

This Meccan sûrah emphasizes that Allah honours humans but many of them debase themselves by denying the meeting with Him in the Hereafter. Abu Jahl, one of the most notorious deniers is referred to in the next sûrah.

96. The Clinging
Clot ˹of Blood˺
(Al-'Alaq)

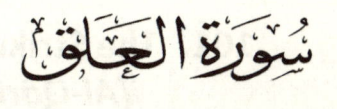

Verses 1-5 are known to be the first ever revealed of the Quran. The Prophet (ﷺ) was retreating at a cave in the outskirts of Mecca when the angel Gabriel appeared to him, squeezing him tightly and ordering him to read. Since the Prophet (ﷺ) was unlettered, he responded, "I cannot read." Ultimately, Gabriel taught him: "Read in the Name of your Lord …" Some scholars believe that this encounter is the fulfilment of Isaiah 29:12, which states, "Then the book will be given to the one who is illiterate, saying, 'Read this.' And he will say, 'I cannot read.'" (The New American Standard Bible). The rest of the sûrah was later revealed to deter Abu Jahl, a Meccan pagan elite, from abusing the Prophet (ﷺ).

87. The Most High
(Al-A'la)

Unlike the wicked who plot against Allah (according to the end of the previous sûrah), the Prophet (ﷺ) is ordered at the beginning of this Meccan sûrah to glorify his Lord. This fleeting world is compared to the short life of plants (verses 4-5). The Prophet (ﷺ) is reassured of Allah's support, and the wicked are warned of burning in Hell. This warning is emphasized in the next sûrah.

88. The Overwhelming
Event
(Al-Ghâshiyah)

This Meccan sûrah compares the fate of the evildoers in the Hereafter to that of the good-doers. Those who disbelieve in Allah's might are criticized for failing to reflect on the wonders of His creation, and are warned of the fate of some destroyed disbelievers mentioned at the beginning of the next sûrah.

89. Dawn
(Al-Fajr)

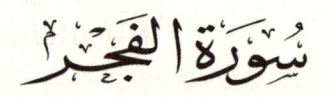

The Prophet (ﷺ) is reassured in this Meccan sûrah that the Arab pagans are not immune to the torments that befell 'Âd, Thamûd, and Pharaoh. A reference is made to the wicked who fail to be grateful in prosperity and patient in adversity. The evildoers will be regretful on Judgment Day, whereas the righteous will be honoured. Those who withhold Allah's bounties are criticized in this sûrah (verses 17-20) and the next (90:11-16).

90. The City
(Al-Balad)

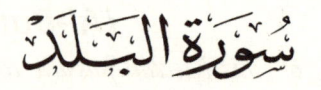

The underlying theme of this Meccan sûrah is that human beings are equipped with the necessary faculties to choose between right and wrong. The good-doers are promised Paradise and the evildoers are promised Hell. This theme is emphasized in the next sûrah.

91. The Sun
(Ash-Shams)

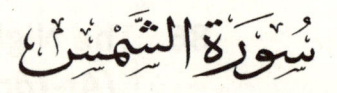

This Meccan sûrah states that people have free choice to purify or corrupt their souls. Those who choose purity will be successful, and those who choose corruption will be destroyed like the people of Thamûd. Free choice is the highlight of the next sûrah as well.

82. The ˹Sky˺ Splitting Open
(Al-Infiṭâr)

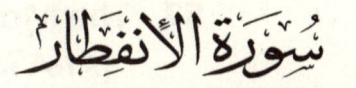

Like the previous sûrah, this Meccan sûrah describes some of the horrors of the Day of Judgment. The disbelievers are criticized for being ungrateful to their Creator. Everyone—including the cheaters mentioned in the next sûrah—will be held accountable for their deeds, which are perfectly recorded by vigilant angels.

83. Defrauders
(Al-Muṭaffifîn)

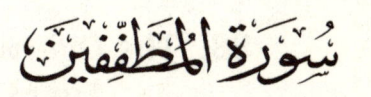

This Meccan sûrah begins with a warning to those who defraud scales about the horrible Day ahead, where the wicked will be severely punished and the virtuous will be richly rewarded. The sûrah closes by stating that the disbelievers will be paid back for making fun of the believers.

84. The ˹Sky˺ Bursting Open
(Al-Inshiqâq)

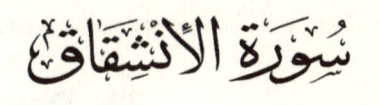

As a follow-up to the previous sûrahs, this Meccan sûrah elaborates upon what to expect on Judgment Day. The believers will receive their records of deeds in their right hands and rejoice after an easy judgment, whereas the disbelievers will receive their records in their left hands and cry for instant destruction. The disbelievers are criticized for failing to submit to Allah, contrasted with the full submission of the sky and the earth in verses 1-5. More warnings to the evildoers appear in the next sûrah.

85. Constellations
(Al-Burûj)

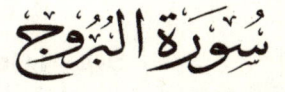

The beginning of this Meccan passage condemns the persecution of the Christians of Najrân (a city on the border of Yemen and Saudi Arabia) at the hands of the pagans around 524 C.E. The tyrants are warned of the torment of burning, whereas the believers are promised a great reward in Paradise. Both this sûrah and the next swear by the towering sky, emphasize Allah's infinite power, pose a warning to the evildoers, and stress the divinity of the Quran.

86. The Nightly Star
(Aṭ-Ṭâriq)

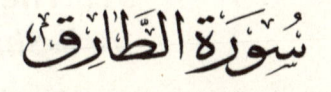

In this Meccan sûrah, an oath is made that whatever a person does is recorded by vigilant angels and that the Resurrection is as easy for Allah as the first creation. Another oath is made that the Quran is a decisive message, and a warning is given to those who plot against Allah.

77. Those ˹Winds˺ Sent Forth (Al-Mursalât)

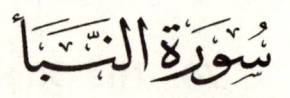

Like the two previous sûrahs and the next two sûrahs, this Meccan sûrah makes it clear that Allah's power to create should be taken as a proof of His ability to bring the dead back to life for judgment. The horrors of the Hour and the punishment of the wicked are stated in strong terms.

78. The Momentous News (An-Naba')

This Meccan sûrah thoroughly refutes the arguments of those who deny the Hereafter by citing some of the marvels of Allah's creation to prove His ability to raise the dead to life and reward everyone according to their deeds.

79. Those ˹Angels˺ Stripping out ˹Souls˺ (An-Nâzi'ât)

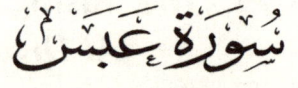

This Meccan sûrah emphasizes that the Day of Judgment is inevitable and its time is known only to Allah. The destruction of Pharaoh is cited as a deterrent to the disbelievers.

80. He Frowned ('Abasa)

In a ḥadîth collected by At-Tirmizi, a blind man by the name of 'Abdullâh ibn um Maktûm, an early Muslim, came to the Prophet (ﷺ) seeking to learn more about the faith, while the Prophet (ﷺ) was in the middle of a discussion with an elite Meccan pagan, trying to convince him to abandon his idols and believe in the One True God. 'Abdullâh was so impatient that he interrupted the discussion several times. The Prophet (ﷺ) frowned and turned all his attention to the man he was already talking to. This Meccan sûrah was later revealed, telling the Prophet (ﷺ) that he should have tended to the faithful man who was eager to learn. After this sûrah was revealed, the Prophet (ﷺ) would honour 'Abdullâh, calling him 'the man for whom my Lord rebuked me.' He (ﷺ) even appointed him several times as his deputy over Medina. The sûrah calls upon the ungrateful disbelievers to reflect on how Allah produces plants out of the earth to realize how He can bring the dead out of their graves. The description of the horrors of the apocalypse is carried over to the next sûrah.

81. Putting out ˹the Sun˺ (At-Takwîr)

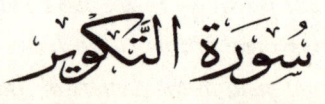

This Meccan sûrah describes some of the apocalyptic events leading up to the Day of Judgment, stating that everyone will meet the consequences of their deeds. The sûrah closes by emphasizing that the Quran is Allah's revealed Word and that the Prophet (ﷺ) is not insane, as the pagans claim.

73. The Wrapped One
(Al-Muzzammil)

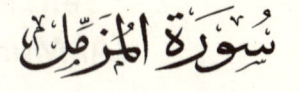

This early Meccan sûrah prepares the Prophet (ﷺ) for the commandments yet to be revealed and the challenges ahead. The Prophet (ﷺ) is advised, both in this sûrah and the next, to seek comfort in patience and prayer, whereas the arrogant disbelievers are warned of a horrible punishment in Hell.

74. The One Covered up
(Al-Muddaththir)

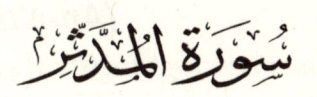

Following his first encounter with the angel Gabriel at a cave in the outskirts of Mecca, the Prophet (ﷺ) rushed to his house in total shock, asking his wife to cover him up with his cloak. Later, this Meccan sûrah was revealed, urging him (ﷺ) to shoulder the responsibility of delivering the message. Allah promises to deal with the pagan tyrants who oppose the truth, defame the Quran, and ridicule warnings of Hell. The pagan denial of the Hereafter is dealt with in the next sûrah.

75. The ˹Rising for˺ Judgment
(Al-Qiyamah)

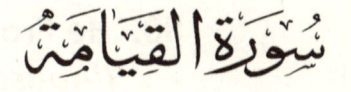

This Meccan sûrah refutes the pagan denial of resurrection and judgment. The sûrah makes it clear that death and judgment are inescapable. The fact that Allah created humans from humble fluids and is able to bring all to account is detailed in the next sûrah.

76. Humans
(Al-Insân)

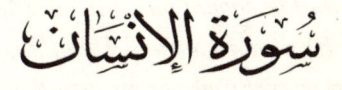

This Meccan sûrah reminds the human beings of how Allah created them, equipped them with different faculties, showed them the Way, and gave them free choice. The reward of those who choose to believe is mentioned at length in this sûrah but passingly in the next sûrah (77:41-44), whereas the reward of those who choose to disbelieve is mentioned passingly in this sûrah (verse 4) but in great detail in the next. The Prophet (ﷺ) is advised to be steadfast and not yield to the deniers of Judgment Day.

69. The Inevitable Hour
(Al-Ḥâqqah)

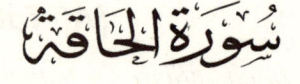

This Meccan sûrah refers to the destruction of the peoples of 'Âd, Thamûd, Pharaoh, and Lot (☀) for denying the Hereafter. A reference is made to the apocalypse, followed by a touching description of the reward of the believers and the punishment of the disbelievers (verses 18-37). The pagan arguments against the Prophet (☀) and the Quran are thoroughly refuted (verses 38-52). The horrors of the apocalypse are further described in the next sûrah.

70. Pathways of ⌜Heavenly⌝ Ascent
(Al-Ma'ârij)

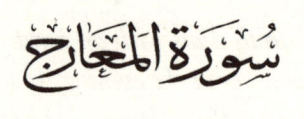

This Meccan sûrah, which takes its name from verse 3, condemns the pagans for ridiculing the Day of Judgment (verses 1-2) and the Prophet (verses 36-37). The truth of the Hour is reaffirmed, along with the horrors that will ensue. The qualities of the people of Hell and the people of Paradise are described (verses 16-35). The Prophet (☀) is reassured, while the pagans are warned—both themes are embedded in the story of Noah (☀) in the next sûrah.

71. Noah
(Nûḥ)

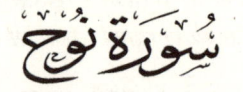

This Meccan sûrah describes how Noah (☀) strived to deliver the message to his people for 950 years (corresponding to the total number of Arabic letters in this sûrah). He called them to the truth secretly and publically, using logical arguments to prove the mercy and oneness of Allah. But his people persisted in denial, only to perish in the Flood. The stubbornness of the Arab pagans in the previous sûrah and the long denial of the people of Noah in this sûrah are contrasted with how some jinn instantly believed once they heard the truth in the next sûrah.

72. The Jinn
(Al-Jinn)

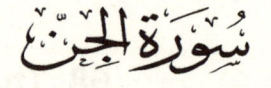

This Meccan sûrah gives an account of a group of jinn who fully submitted to the One True God as soon as they heard the Prophet's recitation of the Quran. In comparison, the Arab pagans are criticized for their polytheistic beliefs. The pagans are told that the Prophet's duty is only to deliver the message. Bringing about the punishment, which the pagans demanded, is only within the power of Allah. The next sûrah provides more warning to the pagans and reassurance to the Prophet (☀).

65. Divorce
(Aṭ-Ṭalâq)

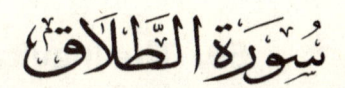

This Medinian sûrah outlines the manner of divorce and accommodation of divorced women and their young children (verses 1-7). Those who comply with Allah's commands are promised a great reward, whereas those who defy Him are warned of the fate of those who were destroyed before. Complying with Allah's orders is elaborated upon in the next sûrah.

66. The Prohibition
(At-Taḥrîm)

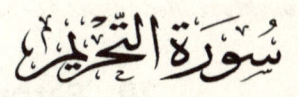

This Medinian sûrah deals with an incident that happened within the Prophet's household. The Prophet (ﷺ) used to visit all of his wives in the evening. It so happened that he stayed longer than usual at the home of Zainab bint Jaḥsh, where he was offered honey—something he liked very much. Out of jealousy, two other wives (Ḥafṣah and 'Âishah) agreed between themselves to tell the Prophet (ﷺ), when he visited each of them, that his mouth gave off a bad smell, knowing that he (ﷺ) did not like bad smells. Eventually, the Prophet made an oath that he would never eat honey again, and told Ḥafṣah not to tell anyone about this. But she told 'Âishah that their plan worked. Both wives are subtly advised to learn from the example of the two believing women mentioned at the end of the sûrah— Mary and Âsiyah, the wife of Pharaoh—and take a lesson from the fate of the wives of Noah and Lot, who were both destroyed despite being wives of prophets. The believers are urged in this sûrah to mend their ways and genuinely repent to Allah in order to win His eternal reward, whereas the disbelievers are warned of a horrible fate. The fate of the disbelievers is elaborated upon in the next sûrah.

67. All Authority
(Al-Mulk)

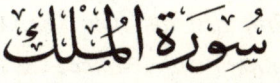

This Meccan sûrah stresses that Allah's infinite power is manifested through His perfect creation. Those who disbelieve in Allah and deny the Resurrection will be regretful in Hell, whereas those in awe of their Lord will be richly rewarded in Paradise. Allah's absolute authority is contrasted with the powerlessness of false gods. The fact that there is no protection from Allah's torment is emphasized in this sûrah (verses 20, 21, and 30) and the next (68:17-33).

68. The Pen
(Al-Qalam)

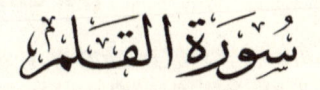

In this Meccan sûrah, the Prophet's heart is reassured and his character is highly praised. He (ﷺ) is advised to be steadfast and not to yield to the pagans who reject his message and call him insane. The pagans are warned of an evil fate in this world and the Hereafter. To deter the pagans, the fate of some earlier disbelievers is cited in the next sûrah.

61. The ˹Solid˺ Ranks
(Aṣ-Ṣaff)

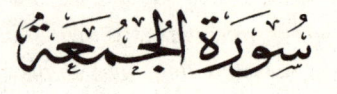

The believers are instructed to strive in Allah's cause in solid battle formations (verse 4), hence the name of this Medinian sûrah. The disciples of Jesus, who stood up for Allah, are cited as an example for the believers to emulate. The believers are reassured that the truth will prevail despite the disbelievers' unrelenting plots against it. Those who stand up for Allah are promised great rewards in both worlds. The next sûrah provides more instructions to the believers.

62. Friday Congregation
(Al-Jumu'ah)

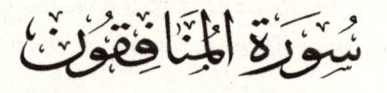

This sûrah and the previous one have much in common. Both start by praising Allah. Those among the Jews who harmed Moses (☝), according to the previous sûrah (61:5), are criticized here for not upholding the Torah (verse 5). Since the disciples of Jesus (☝) are commended in the previous sûrah (61:14), the companions of Muḥammad (☝) are honoured in this sûrah (verses 2-4). The Prophet (☝) is foretold by Jesus (☝) in the previous sûrah (61:6) and is presented in this sûrah as Allah's favour to the believers. Similar to the previous sûrah, some instructions are given to the believers—this time, regarding the Friday congregation (verse 9), which gives this Medinian sûrah its name.

63. The Hypocrites
(Al-Munâfiqûn)

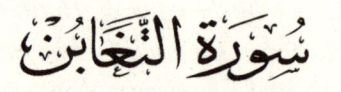

Similar to the two previous sûrahs, this Medinian sûrah closes by offering more advice to the believers. The hypocrites are rebuked for hindering others from the path of Allah and discouraging people from donating in His cause. In contrast, the believers are advised to donate before they are overtaken by death—a reality that can come at any time.

64. Mutual Loss and Gain
(At-Taghâbun)

This Medinian sûrah takes its name from the reference to the Day of Judgment in verse 9, where people are divided into winners and losers. Since the last sûrah closes by urging the believers to donate before they are overtaken by death, this sûrah opens by emphasizing Allah's power to create and His ability to bring the dead back to life for judgment. The sûrah concludes by bidding the believers to spend in the cause of Allah, and not be discouraged by concerns for their spouses and children. The rights of spouses and children after divorce are laid out in the next sûrah.

58. The Pleading Woman
(Al-Mujâdilah)

A companion named Khawlah bint Thaʿlabah had a disagreement with her husband, Aws ibn Aṣ-Ṣâmit, who then told her that she was as unlawful for him as the ẓahr (back) of his mother. This statement had been considered to be a form of divorce (known as ẓihâr) in Arabia. Khawlah came to the Prophet (ﷺ) to ask for his opinion. He (ﷺ) told her that he had not received any revelation in this regard, and that, based on tradition, she was divorced. She argued that she and her husband had children together who would suffer if their parents were separated. Then she started to plead to Allah as the Prophet (ﷺ) repeated the same answer. Eventually, this Medinian sûrah was revealed in response to her pleas, thereby abolishing this ancient practice. The sûrah emphasizes Allah's infinite knowledge and overwhelming power, and makes it clear that those who ally themselves with Allah and comply with His orders are bound to prevail, whereas those who challenge Him and ally themselves with His enemies will be debased and vanquished. This concept is elaborated upon in the next sûrah (verses 59:1-4 and 11-17).

59. The Banishment
(Al-Ḥashr)

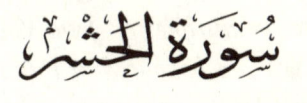

This Medinian sûrah takes its name from verse 2, which refers to the exile of the Jewish tribe of Banu An-Naḍîr from Medina for conspiring with the Meccan pagans to violate peace agreements with the Muslims. The hypocrites are condemned for their secret alliance with Banu An-Naḍîr. Some instructions are given regarding the distribution of the spoils of war. The sûrah closes by stressing unwavering obedience to Almighty Allah, which is further emphasized at the beginning of the next sûrah.

60. The Test of Faith
(Al-Mumtaḥanah)

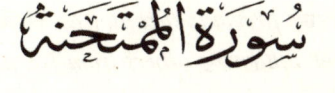

This Medinian sûrah was revealed prior to the Prophet's conquest of Mecca following the pagans' violation of the peace treaty they had signed with the Muslims at Ḥudaibiyah. Despite the Prophet's orders to keep this plan secret, a companion by the name of Ḥâṭib ibn Abi Baltaʿah sent a warning letter to the Meccans, hoping that in turn they would protect his family—who were still in Mecca—in case the Muslims failed to enter the city. Soon the Prophet (ﷺ) received a revelation about what Ḥâṭib did. The letter was intercepted, and Ḥâṭib was later forgiven. Mecca surrendered peacefully to the Muslims, and its residents were pardoned by the Prophet (ﷺ). Muslims are instructed to be loyal to Allah and fellow believers, following the example of Prophet Abraham (ﷺ) (verses 4-6). The believers are not forbidden from courtesy to non-Muslim as long as they are not persecuting Muslims (verses 8-9). This sûrah takes its name from testing the faith of women fleeing Mecca by asking them, for example, if they have emigrated for Islam or only to be separated from their pagan husbands (verse 10). Other instructions to the believers are given at the end of this sûrah and the beginning of the next sûrah.

54. The Moon
(Al-Qamar)

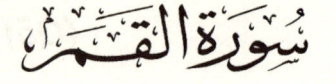

This Meccan sûrah, which takes its name from the splitting of the moon mentioned in verse 1, criticizes the disbelievers for rejecting warnings of the fast-approaching Hour. The pagans are warned of a dreadful fate similar to that of earlier disbelievers, who were mentioned passingly in the previous sûrah (53:50-54). The sûrah concludes by announcing that the righteous will be honoured in the presence of the Almighty, which is the highlight of the next sûrah.

55. The Most Compassionate
(Ar-Raḥmân)

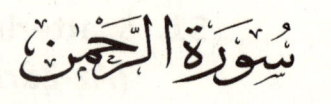

This Meccan sûrah is a call to humans and jinn to acknowledge Allah's infinite blessings, hence the recurring question: "Then which of your Lord's favours will you both deny?" which is repeated thirty-one times. Life on earth will come to an end, ushering in the Day of Judgment, where people will be classified into three groups based on their deeds and consequent rewards: the disbelievers (verses 31-45), the best of the believers (verses 46-61), and the average believers (verses 62-78).

56. The Inevitable Event
(Al-Wâqi'ah)

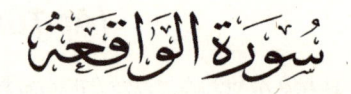

This Meccan sûrah is identical to the previous one in classifying people into three groups on Judgment Day and discussing how Allah's blessings are taken for granted. These blessings should be seen as a proof of His ability to raise the dead for judgment. Moreover, references are made to the creation of the human race, the divine nature of the Quran, and the horrors of the apocalypse. Allah is glorified in the last verse of this sûrah and the first verse of the next sûrah.

57. Iron
(Al-Ḥadîd)

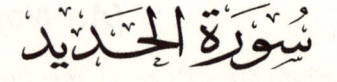

This Medinian sûrah, which takes its name from the reference to iron in verse 25, is an invitation to strive in Allah's cause and spend in His Way. Similar to the next sûrah, a strong emphasis is placed on Allah's knowledge and power. It is made clear that Allah is able to revive faith in the hearts of the believers just as He can revive the earth after its death. The believers are advised regarding destiny and the life of this world, while the hypocrites are warned of the evil fate awaiting them. Some prophets are mentioned passingly before making a final invitation to the People of the Book to believe in Allah and His Prophet (ﷺ).

50. Qãf
(Qãf)

Since the previous sûrah primarily addresses the believers, this sûrah mainly talks about the disbelievers—particularly the deniers of resurrection. References are made to earlier destroyed deniers and Allah's infinite power to prove His ability to create and resurrect. The deniers of resurrection are told what to expect after death and judgment. The Prophet (ﷺ) is urged to be steadfast. The certainty of the Hereafter is emphasized both at the end of this sûrah and the beginning of the next.

51. Scattering Winds
(Az-Zâriyât)

Like the previous sûrah, this Meccan sûrah makes the case for the Resurrection, citing some of Allah's natural signs in the universe to prove His ability to bring the dead back life. Several examples are given of the deniers of judgment who were destroyed, which contrast with the reward of the believers. The Prophet (ﷺ) is urged to carry on reminding. Both the end of this sûrah and the beginning of the next pose a warning of the Day of Judgment.

52. Mount Ṭûr
(Aṭ-Ṭûr)

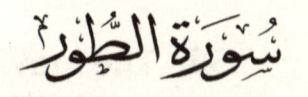

This Meccan sûrah takes its name from verse 1, where Allah swears by Mount Ṭûr, among other things, that the Day of Judgment is inevitable. The punishment of those skeptical of judgment is described, followed by a detailed description of the reward of the believers along with their offspring (verses17-28). Atheism is also rejected (verses 25-36). The Prophet (ﷺ) is reassured of Allah's support, while the pagan beliefs and arguments are refuted both in this sûrah and the next.

53. The Stars
(An-Najm)

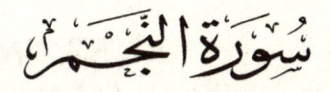

This Meccan sûrah takes its name from the reference to the fading of the stars in the first verse (as well as the last verse of the previous sûrah). The divine source of the Prophet's message is emphasized, followed by reference to his ascension to heaven during the Night Journey (see the introduction to Sûrah 17). The pagans are condemned for associating idols with Allah in worship and for claiming that the angels are Allah's daughters. Manifestations of Allah's infinite power are cited to prove His ability to resurrect. Both the end of this sûrah and the beginning of the next stress the imminence of the Hour.

47. Muḥammad
(Muḥammad)

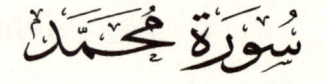

This Medinian sûrah, which takes its title from the Prophet's name in verse 2, discusses the etiquette of fighting in the battlefield. The faithful believers are promised different types of rivers and fruits in Paradise, whereas the disbelievers and the hypocrites are warned of an evil fate. To preserve the reward of their good deeds, the believers are urged to strive in the Way of Allah and donate in His cause, culminating in the clear triumph in the next sûrah.

48. The Triumph
(Al-Fatḥ)

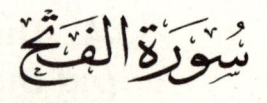

This Medinian sûrah takes its name from the clear triumph (i.e., Treaty of Ḥudaibiyah) in verse 1. The Prophet (ﷺ) and 1400 of his companions travelled to Mecca to perform the minor pilgrimage ('umrah) in 6 A.H./628 C.E. He (ﷺ) sent 'Uthmân ibn 'Affân to let the Meccans know that the Muslims had come in peace, only to visit the Sacred House. When the Meccans delayed 'Uthmân, the Prophet (ﷺ) thought they might have killed his envoy. So he (ﷺ) called upon the faithful to pledge allegiance to him under a tree at Ḥudaibiyah in the outskirts of Mecca. Shortly after, 'Uthmân returned safely and a peace agreement was signed by the Muslims and Meccan pagans, stating in part that the Muslims would have to return to Medina and come back next year for 'umrah. The Treaty of Ḥudaibiyah is described as a clear triumph since it established peace, temporarily diffused the tension between the Muslims and the Meccan pagans, and gave the Muslims plenty of time to spread awareness and understanding of their faith. Thousands from different tribes accepted Islam during that truce. The sûrah commends the believers for proving true to Allah and His Messenger, criticizes the hypocrites for not marching forth with the Prophet (ﷺ), and condemns the pagans for denying the believers access to the Sacred House. The description of the true believers both in the Torah and the Gospel is given at the end of the sûrah, followed by instructions on proper conduct with the Prophet (ﷺ) and other believers in the next sûrah.

49. The Private Quarters
(Al-Ḥujurât)

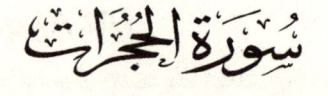

This Medinian sûrah, which takes its name from the reference to the Prophet's private quarters in verse 4, instructs the believers on the proper conduct towards the Prophet (verses 1-5) and the social etiquette of dealing with other believers (verses 6-12) and the rest of humanity (verse 13). At the end of the sûrah, the nomadic Arabs are taught that true faith is proven by action not only words.

43. Ornaments
(Az-Zukhruf)

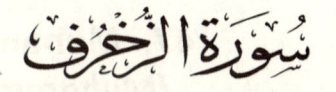

This Meccan sûrah takes its name from the ornaments mentioned in verse 35. The pagans are scorned for following their forefathers blindly, labelling the angels as Allah's daughters, claiming that Muḥammad (ﷺ) is not worthy to receive revelations because he is not rich, and for associating idols with Allah in worship, although they admit that He is the sole Creator of the heavens and the earth. Similar to the next sûrah, the pagans are warned of a horrifying punishment in Hell and the believers are promised a great reward in Paradise.

44. The Haze
(Ad-Dukhân)

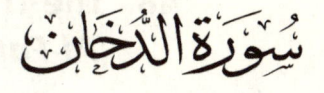

This Meccan sûrah takes its name from the haze (caused by drought), which is mentioned in verse 10. Similar to the previous sûrah, the Meccan pagans are equated with Pharaoh's people for going back on their promise of full submission to Allah once the plague is removed from them. The Quran is said to have been revealed on a blessed night for the guidance of humanity. Those who embrace its guidance will be honoured in Paradise and those who reject it will be debased in Hell. This fate is the underlying theme in the next sûrah.

45. The Kneeling
(Al-Jâthiyah)

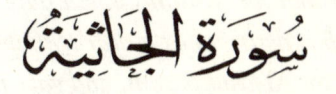

This Meccan sûrah, which takes its name from the kneeling of every faith-community on Judgment Day mentioned in verse 28, is critical of those who turn away from Allah's revelations, deny the Resurrection, ridicule the truth, and fail to appreciate Allah's countless favours and marvels of creation. The dreadful judgment of these deniers is featured in the last part of the sûrah. All these themes are emphasized in the next sûrah as well.

46. The Sand-Hills
(Al-Aḥqâf)

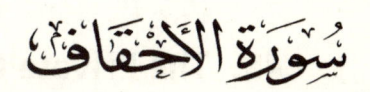

This Meccan sûrah takes its name from the sand-hills mentioned in verse 21 in the story of the people of Hûd (ﷺ) who were destroyed for their disbelief, even though they were far superior to the Arab pagans (verses 21-28). Again, Allah's infinite power is contrasted with the powerlessness of the idols. The pagan arguments against the Quran and the Resurrection are refuted, and reference is made to a group of jinn who readily embraced the truth once they heard the Prophet's recitation of the Quran. The Prophet (ﷺ) is urged to be patient, and reminded of the fate awaiting those who challenge the truth at the end of this sûrah and the beginning of the next.

those descendants choose to be faithful and grateful to their Creator, while others choose not to. Eventually, following a fair judgment, the former will be led to their places in Paradise and the latter to their places in Hell—each in successive groups (hence the sûrah's name). Allah's willingness to forgive sins is highly emphasized in the last part of this sûrah and the beginning of the next.

40. The Forgiver
(Ghâfir)

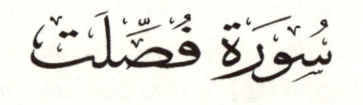

In essence, this Meccan sûrah emphasizes the main concepts highlighted both in the previous and following sûrahs—namely Allah being infinite in mercy and severe in punishment, and humanity being either grateful or ungrateful to their Lord along with the reward that ensues. All this is embodied in the story of Moses (verses 23-54)—with Pharaoh as the ungrateful disbeliever and an unidentified man from Pharaoh's people as the grateful believer. The Prophet (ﷺ) is repeatedly advised to be patient, keeping in mind that Allah never lets His prophets down (verses 51 and 77).

41. ⌈Verses⌉
Perfectly Explained
(Fuṣṣilat)

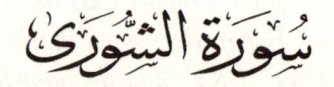

This Meccan sûrah, which takes its name from the description of the Quran in verse 3, rebukes the pagans for turning away from the truth; abusing the Quran; and for denying Allah, the sole Creator of the heavens and the earth. The deniers are warned that their own bodily organs will testify against them on Judgment Day, landing them in Hell forever. Reference to the destruction of the arrogant, ungrateful peoples of 'Âd and Thamûd is made because the pagan Arabs used to pass by their ruins on their journeys to Syria and Yemen, respectively. A profound description of the righteous is given in verses 30-36. The truth of the Quran is emphasized at the end of this sûrah and the beginning of the next.

42. Consultation
(Ash-Shûra)

This Meccan sûrah takes its name from verse 38 which talks about conducting affairs by mutual consultation as one of the qualities of the true believers. The sûrah emphasizes that Allah has decreed for Muslims the same religion ordained for all the previous prophets. The believers are commanded to resort to Allah's judgment if disagreement arises. Allah's oneness, power, and wisdom are emphasized as the pagans' faith in powerless idols is condemned. Both the end of this sûrah and the beginning of the next stress the fact that the Quran has been revealed by Allah.

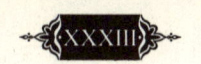

36. Yâ-Sîn
(Yâ-Sîn)

سُورَةُ يسٓ

This Meccan sûrah emphasizes the divine nature and purpose of the Quran. The Arab pagans are reminded of the fate of earlier disbelievers and condemned for following Satan, denying the Resurrection, discrediting the Quran, and rejecting the Prophet (ﷺ) as 'a poet.' Similar to the next sûrah, some examples of Allah's wonders of creation are cited to prove His ability to bring the dead back to life.

37. Those ˹Angels˺
Lined up in Ranks
(Aṣ-Ṣâffât)

سُورَةُ الصَّافَاتِ

For the most part, this Meccan sûrah explains verse 31 from the previous sûrah: "Have the deniers not considered how many peoples We destroyed before them …?". Hence, several examples of destroyed disbelievers are cited here, including the peoples of Noah, Lot, and Elias (ﷺ). Some basic truths are emphasized, including the oneness of Allah, the Resurrection, and the prophethood of Muḥammad (ﷺ). The pagans are criticized for calling the Prophet (ﷺ) 'a mad poet' and for claiming that the angels are Allah's daughters. This sûrah provides more details on the punishment of the disbelievers and the reward of the believers in the Hereafter (verses 19-68). In conclusion, the Prophet (ﷺ) is reassured that Allah's messengers always prevail.

38. Ṣâd
(Ṣâd)

سُورَةُ صٓ

This sûrah is perceived as a continuation of the previous sûrah since it mentions some prophets that are not mentioned there—such as David, Solomon, and Job (ﷺ). Again, the pagans are condemned for denying the oneness of Allah, rejecting the Prophet (ﷺ) as 'a magician, a total liar,' and for claiming that the world was created without purpose. Reference is made to the creation of Adam (ﷺ) and the enmity Satan has for him and his descendants (verses 71-85), and the punishment awaiting the misleaders and their followers (verses 55-64), contrasted with the bliss in store for the righteous (verses 49-54). The end of this sûrah emphasizes the universality of the Quran whereas the beginning of the next speaks of its divine nature.

39. The ˹Successive˺ Groups
(Az-Zumar)

سُورَةُ الزُّمَرِ

This Meccan sûrah builds on the story of the creation of Adam in the previous sûrah by referring to the creation of Adam's spouse, and how their descendants were created in the womb, developing in successive stages. Some of

32. The Prostration
(As-Sajdah)

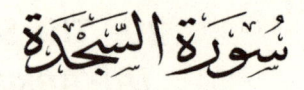

This Meccan sûrah, which takes its name from the prostrations of the believers in worship mentioned in verse 15, makes it clear that the Quran is a divine revelation and that Almighty Allah is the sole Creator, most capable of resurrection. Similar to the previous sûrah, a reference is made to the qualities of the believers and the disbelievers and the reward awaiting each. Both the end of this sûrah and the beginning of the next urge the Prophet (ﷺ) to turn away from the deniers and not yield to them.

33. The Enemy Alliance
(Al-Aḥzâb)

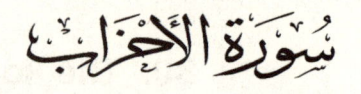

This Medinian sûrah takes its name from the enemy alliance (mentioned in verses 9–27) which laid a siege around Medina during the Battle of the Trench in 5 A.H./627 C.E. While the believers are reminded of Allah's aid against the enemy alliance, the hypocrites are condemned repeatedly. The sûrah provides social guidelines regarding adoption, divorce, modesty, and the etiquette of dealing with the Prophet (ﷺ) and his wives. In view of Allah's favours to the believers (including His forgiveness and generous reward at the end of the sûrah), the next sûrah starts off with praises to Allah.

34. Sheba
(Saba')

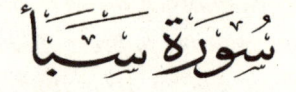

This Meccan sûrah takes its name from the reference to the people of Sheba (verses 15-20) who were punished for meeting Allah's favours with ingratitude. Both David (ﷺ) and Solomon (ﷺ) are cited as grateful servants of Allah. The Meccan pagans are reminded that only faith can bring them closer to Allah, not their wealth. They are criticized for calling the Prophet (ﷺ) 'insane' and are warned of punishment in this life and the next. Both the last part of this sûrah (verses 40-41) and the beginning of the next (verse 1) reaffirm the angels as Allah's faithful servants.

35. The Originator
(Fâṭir)

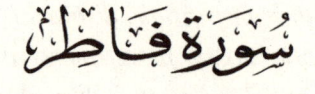

This Meccan sûrah demonstrates Allah's infinite power through the marvels of His creation, in contrast with the powerlessness of the pagan idols. The Prophet (ﷺ) is consoled by the fact that many prophets were denied before him. The believers are promised of a great reward in Paradise (verses 31-35), while the disbelievers are warned of a scathing punishment in Hell (verses 36-39). All these themes are echoed in the next sûrah.

29. The Spider
(Al-'Ankabût)

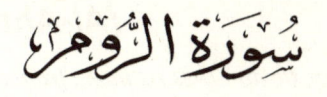

This Meccan sûrah takes its name from the parable of the spider in verse 41. The beginning of the sûrah emphasizes the role of trials and tribulations in revealing those who are truly steadfast and those who are not. Noah, Abraham, Lot, and Shu'aib (﷽) are noted for their perseverance. References are made to various peoples and the different ways they were destroyed for their denial of the truth (verse 40). The pagan arguments against the Prophet and the Quran are thoroughly refuted. The sûrah concludes by commending those who put their trust in Allah and strive in His cause. This conclusion paves the way for the opening of the next sûrah.

30. The Romans
(Ar-Rûm)

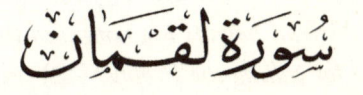

This Meccan sûrah takes its name from the reference to the Romans in verse 2. The world's superpowers in the early 7ᵗʰ century were the Roman Byzantine and Persian Empires. When they went to war in 614 C.E., the Romans suffered a devastating defeat. The Meccan pagans rejoiced at the defeat of the Roman Christians at the hands of the Persian pagans. Soon verses 30:1-5 were revealed, stating that the Romans would be victorious in three to nine years. Eight years later, the Romans won a decisive battle against the Persians, reportedly on the same day the Muslims vanquished the Meccan army at the Battle of Badr. As the sûrah progresses, several blessings and natural signs are cited to prove Allah's infinite mercy and power, coupled with condemnations to the pagans for their ingratitude and for associating powerless idols with Allah in worship. The sûrah closes by bidding the Prophet (ﷺ) not to be disheartened by what the deniers say.

31. Luqmân
(Luqmân)

This Meccan sûrah is named after Luqmân, a wise African man who is quoted giving pieces of advice to his son (verses 12–19) on one's relationship with Allah and the people. While the believers are praised, the pagans are condemned for their ingratitude, distracting others from the Way of Allah, and for setting up idols as His equals. Similar to the previous sûrah, references are made to Allah's natural marvels, challenging the deniers to point out anything their gods have created. The sûrah concludes by warning humanity of the Day of Judgment, ushering in the next sûrah.

25. The Decisive Authority
(Al-Furqân)

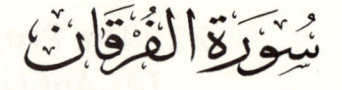

This Meccan sûrah takes its name from verses 1-6, which refute the pagan claims that the Quran was fabricated and plagiarized from earlier scriptures. Other passages condemn polytheism, denial of resurrection, and mocking the Prophet (ﷺ). Allah's power, manifested in the marvels of creation and rain, is emphasized in this sûrah and the previous one. The qualities of the righteous servants of Allah are beautifully laid out in verses 63-76.

26. The Poets
(Ash-Shu'arâ')

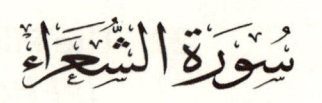

This Meccan sûrah takes its name from the reference to poets in verses 224-226. Since the previous sûrah ends with a warning to the deniers of the truth, this sûrah recounts several cautionary tales of destroyed deniers such as Pharaoh and the peoples of Noah, Shu'aib, Lot, and Ṣâliḥ (ﷺ). The divine origin of the Quran is emphasized at both ends of the sûrah. The qualities of the believers mentioned in the last verse (227) are elaborated upon at the beginning of the next sûrah.

27. The Ants
(An-Naml)

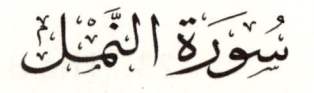

This Meccan sûrah narrates the encounters of Solomon (ﷺ) with ants (hence the sûrah's name), a hoopoe, and the Queen of Sheba—which do not appear in any other sûrah. Allah's power to create and provide is contrasted with the powerlessness of the idols. Some deterring examples are given to the pagans, along with a warning of the horrors of the apocalypse. The Prophet (ﷺ) is reassured of the truth of the Quran and told that his duty is only to deliver the message. Judgment rests with Allah alone.

28. The Whole Story
(Al-Qaṣaṣ)

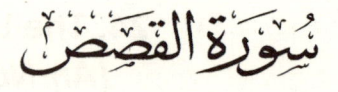

In 26:18-19, Pharaoh reminds Moses (ﷺ) of his up-bringing in the care of Pharaoh and how Moses (ﷺ) killed an Egyptian (accidentally). Unlike the previous sûrah, this Meccan sûrah focuses on these two aspects of Moses' life in Egypt, along with his escape to Median where he met his future wife. Another aspect is the story of Korah, one of the people of Moses, who behaved arrogantly, leading to his own destruction. Just like the previous sûrah, it reaffirms Allah's power and the authenticity of the Quran. Again, the Prophet (ﷺ) is reminded that his duty is not to convert, but to convey. After criticizing the polytheists (verses 45-75), the sûrah concludes by bidding the Prophet (ﷺ) to be steadfast. The next sûrah starts off by talking about steadfastness.

21. The Prophets
(Al-Anbiyâ')

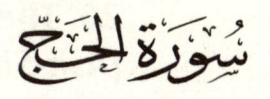

Like the previous sûrah, this is another Meccan sûrah that aims at reassuring the Prophet (ﷺ) by reminding him of Allah's grace and support to His prophets, including Abraham, Job, Jonah, Zachariah, and Jesus (ﷺ). The Prophet (ﷺ) is said to be sent as a mercy to the whole world (verse 107). Warnings of the horrors of Judgment Day are dispersed throughout the sûrah and are carried over to the next sûrah.

22. The Pilgrimage
(Al-Ḥajj)

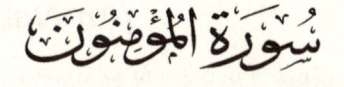

This Medinian sûrah takes its name from the passage that talks about pilgrimage rituals (verses 25-37), along with condemnations to the pagans for hindering the believers from reaching the Sacred House in Mecca. After fifteen years of persecution, here the believers receive the permission to fight back in self-defence (verse 39). Idolatry is condemned and the idols are rejected as pathetic, incapable of even creating a fly. In conclusion, the believers are told that they can achieve success through prayer and good deeds—a theme which extends to the beginning of the next sûrah.

23. The Believers
(Al-Mu'minûn)

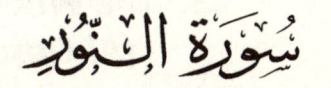

This Meccan sûrah emphasizes that the believers are guaranteed success (verse 1), whereas the disbelievers are bound to fail (verse 117). Like the previous sûrah, it makes the case for Allah's oneness as well as His power to create and resurrect. The last part is dedicated to the judgment of the believers and the disbelievers, focusing on the fate of the wicked who abuse the believers. This theme extends to the next sûrah.

24. The Light
(An-Nûr)

This Medinian sûrah takes its name from the divine light mentioned in verses 35-36. A large portion of this sûrah deals with the issue of sexual misconduct hinted at in the previous sûrah (23:7). The sûrah also offers some guidelines to the believers on how they should have reacted to false rumours against 'Âishah, the Prophet's wife. Other issues are discussed, including modesty, entering people's homes, forced prostitution, hypocrisy, and false accusations of adultery. Allah's power, compliance with His judgment, and obedience to the Prophet (ﷺ) are highly emphasized.

18. The Cave
(Al-Kahf)

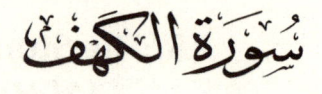

This Meccan sûrah takes its name from the story of the people of the cave in verses 9-26. According to Ibn 'Abbâs, the Prophet (ﷺ) was asked about the youths who hid in a cave, a king who dominated large parts of the world, and about the spirit, so 18:9-26, 18:83-99, and 17:85 were revealed. The Prophet (ﷺ) says in an authentic narration collected by At-Tirmizi, "No one's feet will move on Judgment Day until they are asked about four things: 1) What they did in their youth. 2) How they earned and spent their wealth. 3) What they did with their knowledge. 4) And how they spent their lives." Interestingly, these four questions correspond to the four stories mentioned in this sûrah: 1) The story of the youths and the cave. 2) The story of the wealthy man with two gardens. 3) The story of Moses and the man of knowledge. 4) And finally the story of Zul-Qarnain and his life and travels in the service of Allah. The four stories are interjected by warnings to the disbelievers and good news to the believers. Like the story of the people of the cave, some miraculous stories appear in the next sûrah.

19. Mary
(Mariam)

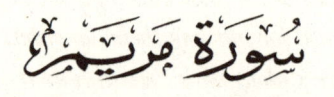

This Meccan sûrah recounts the miraculous stories of the birth of Jesus by the virgin Mary (after whom the sûrah is named) and the birth of John the Baptist to old Zachariah and his elderly, barren wife. Other prophets are cited as recipients of Allah's favour and grace. Attributing children to Allah (verses 88-95) and denial of resurrection (verses 66-70) are rejected as outrageous and blasphemous. Both the end of this sûrah and the beginning of the next one talk about the purpose of revealing the Quran.

20. Ṭâ-Hâ
(Ṭâ-Hâ)

Since Moses (ﷺ) and Adam (ﷺ) are mentioned passingly in the previous sûrah, their stories are recounted here in great detail. This Meccan sûrah reassures the Prophet (ﷺ) that the truth always prevails even against the most tyrannical opposition (in the form of Pharaoh) and that Allah is able to open even the hardest of hearts (in the form of Pharaoh's magicians). Both the beginning and the end of the sûrah emphasize the divine nature of the Quran as a source of guidance and eternal bliss. Those who turn away from the Quranic reminder are warned of misery in this world and horrifying punishment on the Day of Judgment. The Prophet (ﷺ) is advised to seek comfort in patience and prayer against pagan denial, which is detailed at the beginning of the next sûrah.

15. The Stone Valley
(Al-Ḥijr)

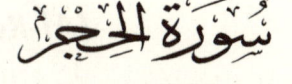

This Meccan sûrah takes its name from the place mentioned in 80-84, where the people of Ṣâliḥ once lived. Other destroyed peoples are mentioned as a warning to Arab deniers, who are also warned at the beginning of the next sûrah. Satan's arrogance towards Allah and enmity towards humanity are emphasized. The Prophet (ﷺ) is urged to exercise patience and seek comfort in worship.

16. Bees
(An-Naḥl)

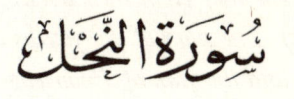

This Meccan sûrah, also known as the Sûrah of Blessings (Sûratu An-Ni'am), takes its name from the bees mentioned in verses 68-69, which are described as one of Allah's numerous favours to humanity. Instead of showing gratitude to Allah for all these blessings, the pagans wilfully set up idols, associating them with Allah in worship. They are also condemned for burying their daughters alive (verses 58-59). References are made to grateful believers and ungrateful disbelievers along with the ultimate reward for each group. Abraham (ﷺ) is cited close to the end of the sûrah as a grateful servant of Allah, whose example should be emulated by all believers. The sûrah concludes by instructing the Prophet (ﷺ) to endure patiently and invite all to the Way of Allah with wisdom and grace.

17. The Night Journey
(Al-Isrâ')

Since Abraham (ﷺ) is praised in the last verses of the previous sûrah as a role model for the world, this Meccan sûrah speaks of how the Prophet (ﷺ) is honoured in this world through the Night Journey from Mecca to Jerusalem then to the heavens and back to Mecca—all in one night (verses 1 and 60). He (ﷺ) will also be honoured on the Day of Judgment through the station of praise where he will make intercession (verse 79). The children of Israel are referred to passingly at the end of the previous sûrah, but more insights are given about them both at the beginning and the end of this sûrah. The key to success in this life and salvation in the next is encapsulated in a set of divine commandments (verses 22-39), along with a warning against Satan and his whispers (verses 61-65). The sûrah is critical of the pagan arguments against resurrection and their ridiculous demands (verses 89-93). Criticism of attributing partners and children to Allah is carried over to the next sûrah.

12. Joseph
(Yûsuf)

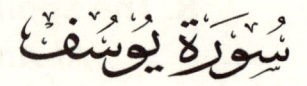

Rightfully called 'the best of stories,' this uplifting Meccan sûrah was revealed along with the two previous sûrahs at a critical time in the life of the Prophet (ﷺ) following the death of his wife Khadîjah and his uncle Abu Ṭâlib, his two main supporters, shortly after a 3-year boycott by the Meccan pagans to suppress the believers. This is the story of Joseph (ﷺ) whose half-brothers were driven by jealousy, conspiring to distance him from his father Jacob (ﷺ). Joseph was sold into slavery in Egypt, falsely accused, and imprisoned for several years, only to become Egypt's Chief Minister. Just like Joseph (ﷺ), the Prophet (ﷺ) had to live away from his hometown, was faced with false allegations and abused by his own people, but ultimately became Arabia's undisputed leader. When the Prophet (ﷺ) triumphed over Mecca after many years of persecution, he treated the very people who abused him with grace, recalling the words of Joseph when his brothers begged for mercy in verse 92, "There is no blame on you today. May Allah forgive you! He is the Most Merciful of the merciful!"

13. Thunder
(Ar-Ra'd)

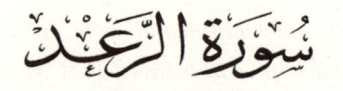

This sûrah, which takes its name from the thunder in verse 13, elaborates upon the last verses of the previous sûrah (starting with 105) relating to Allah's magnificent signs in the heavens and earth which are met with neglect by the deniers; Allah's knowledge, might, and unwavering support for His prophets; the authenticity of the Quran; and warnings to the disbelievers. The sûrah touches on the qualities of the believers and the disbelievers and the reward for each. All these themes are reiterated in the next two sûrahs.

14. Abraham
(Ibrâhîm)

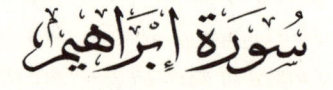

This Meccan sûrah is named after Prophet Abraham (ﷺ) who, upon settling his wife Hagar and his son Ismael in what later became the city of Mecca, invokes Allah to protect his descendants from idol-worship, a practice that Meccans were entrenched in at the time of this revelation (verses 35-41). The sûrah also refers to some of Allah's favours, which are met with ingratitude and denial. A sizable portion reveals how the disbelievers will be let down by Satan and tormented in Hell, wishing they had believed, according to the next sûrah (15:2).

8. The Spoils of War
(Al-Anfâl)

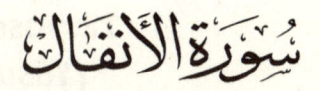

This sûrah was revealed in Medina to explain how the spoils of war should be distributed following the believers' victory over the Meccan pagans at Badr in 2 A.H./624 C.E. The sûrah urges the believers to be true to Allah and His Messenger, reminding them of how they were outnumbered but Allah sent down angels for their aid. It is made clear that although victory comes only from Allah, the believers should always be ready to defend themselves and be open for peace. The pagans are warned that their plots to hinder others from Allah's Way and oppose the truth will only end in failure—a theme emphasized in both the previous and the following sûrahs.

9. Repentance
(At-Tawbah)

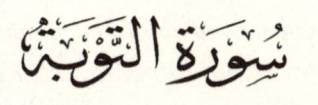

This sûrah, which is perceived as a continuation of the previous sûrah, begins by openly terminating the peace treaties constantly violated by the pagans. The believers are urged to march forth with the Prophet (ﷺ) for the Battle of Tabûk in the summer of 9 A.H./631 C.E. Hypocrites are exposed and their false excuses are refuted. Muslims are reminded of how Allah turned the believers' initial defeat into sweeping victory at the Battle of Ḥunain and how Allah saved His Messenger (ﷺ) from the pagans during his migration to Medina. Allah's acceptance of repentance is echoed throughout the sûrah, hence its title.

10. Jonah
(Yûnus)

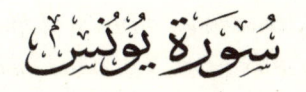

Similar to the previous sûrah, this Meccan sûrah emphasizes Allah's acceptance of repentance, most notably in the case of the people of Jonah (verse 98). The pagan claims against the Quran are refuted both in this sûrah and the next. The short span of this worldly life and people's ingratitude to their Creator are elaborated upon. The Prophet (ﷺ) is urged to exercise patience in the face of denial. The stories of Noah's people and Pharaoh's people are cited as cautionary tales to the Meccan deniers, setting the stage for more elaborate warnings in the next sûrah.

11. Hûd
(Hûd)

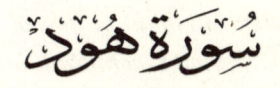

This Meccan sûrah is named after Prophet Hûd (ﷺ), whose story is mentioned in verses 50-60. More details are given about Noah (ﷺ) in this sûrah than the previous sûrah and Sûrah 7. Just like the previous sûrah, the stories of destroyed disbelievers are meant to deter Arab pagans and reassure the Prophet (ﷺ) of his ultimate triumph, and a reference is made to the reward of the believers and the punishment of the disbelievers in the Hereafter.

the relationship between Muslims and the People of the Book, culminating in a rebuttal to the claims about the crucifixion and divinity of Jesus (☻). Like the previous and the next sûrahs, this sûrah also deals with the issue of hypocrisy—a common theme in many other Medinian sûrahs.

5. The Spread Table
(Al-Mâ'idah)

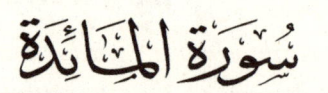

This Medinian sûrah takes its name from the story of the table mentioned in verses 112-115. Several rulings are laid out, including permissible and prohibited foods, hunting while on pilgrimage, and making a bequest while travelling. A reference is made to Allah's covenants with the Jews and Christians and how those covenants were repeatedly violated. The believers are urged to comply with Allah's judgment as communicated by the Prophet (☻). Some topics that have been touched on in the previous sûrahs are detailed here, including making up for a broken oath, the sanctity of the human life, and the humanity of Jesus (☻).

6. Cattle
(Al-An'âm)

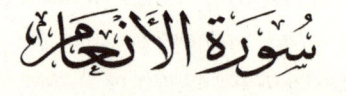

Like the previous sûrah, this Meccan sûrah masterfully demonstrates Allah's power and knowledge, and thoroughly refutes pagan beliefs and unfounded practices, including animal offerings to the idols. Permissible and prohibited foods are explained in more detail than in the previous sûrah. The nature of prophethood is defined, making it clear that messengers cannot do anything without the Will of Allah. This sûrah begins by highlighting Allah's authority, just like the ending of the previous sûrah, and concludes by emphasizing accountability for one's deeds, just like the beginning of the next sûrah.

7. The Heights
(Al-A'râf)

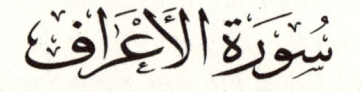

This sûrah takes its name from the heights mentioned in verse 46. Like many other Meccan sûrahs, it recounts the stories of earlier prophets who were denied by their own people and how the deniers were eventually destroyed. As mentioned in the previous sûrah (6:10-11), these stories are meant to reassure the Prophet (☻) and warn his people of Allah's torment. The story of Satan's arrogance and Adam's temptation and fall are detailed, along with lessons for the believers to beware of Satan's whispers. Details about Paradise and Hell (verses 36-53) here are unmatched by any previous sûrah. The powerlessness of idols is further emphasized. Full obedience to Allah and His prophets is stressed in this sûrah and the next.

Sûrah **Introductions**

1. The Opening
(Al-Fâtiḥah)

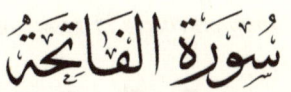

This Meccan sûrah, which is recited a total of seventeen times in the five daily prayers, serves as the cornerstone of the Quran. It sums up the relationship between the Creator and His creation, Allah's undisputed authority in this world and the Hereafter, and humanity's constant dependence on Him for guidance and assistance. The underlying theme is to acknowledge that He is the only god worthy of worship—a simple truth which the disbelievers fail to grasp. All fundamental principles encapsulated in this sûrah are spelled out in the rest of the Quran.

2. The Cow
(Al-Baqarah)

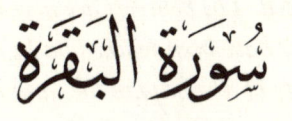

This Medinian sûrah, which takes its name from the story of the cow in verses 67–73, details the main concepts of the previous sûrah, with emphasis on the qualities of the believers, disbelievers, and hypocrites; Allah's power to create and resurrect; the enmity of Satan towards Adam (ﷺ) and his descendants; as well as Allah's covenant with Moses (ﷺ) and the Children of Israel. Several rulings are given in regards to marital relationships, bequest, jihad, fasting, pilgrimage, donations, debts, and interest. Unlike the next sûrah, which focuses on the Christian perception of Jesus, this sûrah dedicates a sizable portion to Jewish attitudes and practices.

3. The Family of 'Imrân
(Âli-'Imrân)

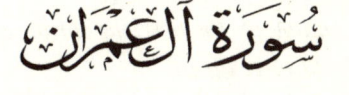

This Medinian sûrah takes its name from the Family of 'Imrân mentioned in verse 33. Like the previous sûrah, it reiterates the fact that Allah is the source of divine revelation and affirms the belief in Allah as the only Lord and Islam as His only accepted religion. The story of the birth of Mary, John the Baptist, and Jesus is mentioned, along with a challenge to the Christian perception of Jesus (ﷺ). The sûrah also touches on early battles against the Meccan pagans with emphasis on the lessons to be drawn from the Muslims' defeat at the Battle of Uḥud, which took place in 3 A.H./625 C.E. The virtue of being mindful of Allah is highlighted at the end of this sûrah and the beginning of the next one.

4. Women
(An-Nisâ')

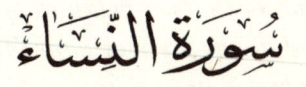

This sûrah focuses on the rights of women (hence the sûrah's name), the law of inheritance, care for orphans, lawful and unlawful women to marry, and standing for justice (see the remarkable example of justice to a Jew in verses 105-112). As the sûrah progresses, the focus shifts to the etiquette of striving in the cause of Allah and

6:73, 23:101, 39:68.

Resurrection 2:28, 16:38, 22:5-7, 23:16, 31:28, 41:39, 64:7; example in the story of Ezra 2:259, Abraham (🕊) 2:260, people of the cave 18:9-26; warning to resurrection deniers 17:49-52, 17:97-100, 19:66-72, 37:11-27, 50:1-15, 80:17-42.

Day of Judgment, *see* DOCTRINE

Paradise, as vast as the heavens and the earth 3:133, 57:21; running water, cool shade, delicacies, and pure mates 2:25, 4:57, 36:55-58, 37:40-49, 38:50-54, 44:51-57, 52:17-24, 69:19-24; 76:5-22; reward of the believers 55:46-78, 56:10-40; rivers of honey, milk, water, and wine 47:15; prayers and greetings 10:9-10, 39:73-74; saluted with greetings of peace 13:23-24, 14:32; everlasting stay in Bliss 11:108; never asked to leave 15:45-48; light shining ahead of them and on their right 57:12; no heat or cold 76:13; all wishes granted 16:30-32, 41:31-32; bracelets of gold and clothes of fine silk 18:30-31, 22:23-24, 44:51-53; trays of golden cups 43:67-73; silver vessels and fruits hanging within reach 76:14-16; reclining on thrones 15:47, 37:44, 52:20; believers will see their Lord 75:22-23.

Hell, burning and boiling water 22:19-22, 23:103-104; pus 14:14-17, 38:55-58, 69:35-37; tree of *Zaqqûm* 37:62-70, 44:43-50, 56:41-56; residents' inability to live or die 87:13; blame throwing 26:91-101, 34:31-33; calls for instant destruction 25:13-14, 43:74-78; fervent cries 35:36-37; Fire growling and roaring 25:11-12, 67:6-11; roasted skins replaced with new ones 4:56; shackles and clothes of tar 14:48-50; maces of iron 22:19-22; chains 13:5; keepers of Hell 39:71, 40:49-50, 43:77, 66:6, 67:8, 74:30-31, 96:18; no ransom accepted 5:36-37; intercession denied 6:94, 26:100, 30:13, 74:48.

Regrets, not following the Prophet 25:27; not obeying Allah and His Messenger 4:41-42, 33:64-68; taking evil friends 25:28-29, 26:96-102, 43:36-39; denying Allah's signs 6:27-30; not working for the Hereafter 89:23-24.

Desperate pleas, begging for return to the world 2:167, 6:27-28, 32:12-14, 42:44; for a second chance 35:36-37; to be removed from the Fire 40:10-12; for food and water 7:51-52; for intercessors 7:52-53; to be leveled to dust 4:41-42, 78:40; for death 43:74-78.

Road to the Hereafter:

Qualities of the righteous, observing the rights of the Creator and His creation 3:133-136, 4:36, 4:69-70, 6:151-154, 8:2-4, 13:19-24, 17:23-39, 18:107-108, 23:1-11, 25:63-76, 42:36-43.

Qualities of the wicked, ungrateful 14:34; stingy 17:100; hasty 21:37; remember Allah only in difficult times 10:12, 41:51; impatient 70:19; argumentative 18:54.

Major Sins, associating others with Allah in worship (*shirk*) 4:48, 4:116, 5:72, 6:19, 31:13; abusing one's own parents 4:36, 6:151, 17:23; neglecting obligatory prayers 19:59-60; not paying alms-tax 41:6-7; murder 6:151, 17:33; killing a believer intentionally 4:93; theft 5:38; fraud 7:85, 11:85, 26:182-183, 83:1-6; lying 2:10, 9:77, 39:60; lying about Allah 6:93, 29:68, 61:7; prohibited sexual relations 2:222, 17:32, 24:2, 25:68, 29:28-30; false accusations of adultery 24:4-5; apostasy 2:217, 5:54; eating swine and other forbidden foods (carrion, blood, etc.) 5:3, 6:145; alcohol and gambling 5:90-91; backbiting 49:11; false testimony 22:30; magic 2:102, 10:77, 20:69.

Doors to forgiveness wide open 4:110, 5:74, 39:53; evil deeds changed into good deeds 25:68-71.

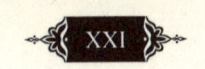

Shu'aib (☀) with his people 7:85-93, 11:84-95, 26:176-191.

Solomon (☀): helps his father David (☀) reach a fairer judgment 21:78-82; story with the ant 27:15-19; story with the hoopoe 27:20-28; story with the Queen of Sheba 27:22-44; Allah's favours upon him 34:12-14, 38:34-40; his love for fine horses 38:30-33.

Zachariah (☀) praying for a child 3:37-41, 19:2-12, 21:89-90.

Zul-Kifl (☀) (mentioned passingly) 21:85, 38:48.

2.   Other stories

Abel and Cain 5:27-31; Al-Khaḍir and Moses (☀) 18:60-82; Army of the Elephant 105:1-4; the believer from Pharaoh's people 40:28-46; birth of Mary 3:35-36; Cow of the Children of Israel 2:67-74; Ezra 2:259; garden owners 68:17-32; Hârût and Mârût 2:102; Korah 28:76:82; Luqmân's advice to his son 31:12-19; owner of the two gardens 18:32-44; people of Sheba 34:15-19; people of the cave 18:9-26; people of the trench 85:1-8; Sabbath-breakers 7:163-165; Sâmiri and the Golden Calf 20:83-97; Saul and Samuel 2:247-251; Zul-Qarnain 18:83-98.

3.   Parables

Accepted charity 2:265; Allah vs. false gods 13:14, 16:76; associating others with Allah in worship 22:31; believers and disbelievers 6:122, 7:58, 11:24, 40:58; believer's heart 24:35; believers' example in the Torah and Gospel 48:29; charity and grain 2:261; deeds of the disbelievers 3:117, 14:18, 24:39; evil word 14:26; good word 14:24-25; fleeting world 10:24, 18:45, 39:21, 57:20; hardened hearts 57:16-17; hypocrites 2:17-20; misguided scholar 7:175-176; monotheist vs. polytheist 39:29; resurrection 7:57, 22:5; 41:39; shepherd and sheep 2:171; spider 29:41; truth vs. falsehood 13:17; unbeneficial knowledge 62:5; wasted charity 2:264, 2:266; wasting the reward of good deeds 16:91-92.

☼

The Unseen

Allah, *see* Doctrine

Angels, *see* Doctrine

Jinn, created from fire 15:25, 55:15; believing and disbelieving jinn 72:1-15; some believed in the message of the Quran 46:29-32; humans and jinn created for a purpose 51:56-58. **Satan** (*Iblîs*), arrogance 2:34, 7:11-27, 15:26-43, 17:61-65, 38:73-85; a jinn 18:50-51; Adam's temptation and fall 7:20-23, 20:116-121; has no authority over the believers 16:98-100; his goal 35:6-8; a sworn enemy to humanity 12:5, 17:53; his party 53:14-19; his handiwork 5:90-91; discourages good deeds 2:268; believers seek refuge in Allah from him 7:200-202; his schemes are weak 4:76; lets his followers down 8:48; talk to his followers in Hell 14:22. **Devils** 2:102, 6:71, 6:112, 6:121, 7:27, 7:30, 17:27, 19:68, 19:83, 22:3-4, 23:97-98, 26:210, 37:7-10, 38:37-38, 67:5; devilish humans and jinn 6:112, 114:6; heaven protected against devils 15:16-18.

Death 3:185, 4:78, 6:61, 6:93, 21:35, 23:99-108, 31:34, 32:11, 44:56, 47:27, 50:19-20, 56:60-62, 56:83-96, 75:26-35; cannot be stopped or delayed 63:10-11; twin brother of sleep 6:60, 39:42; believers and disbelievers at the time of death 8:50, 16:27-32, 41:30; punishment in the grave 40:46.

Final Hour, signs 21:96, 27:82, 43:61, 47:18, 54:1-2; names 1:3, 2:4, 3:55, 19:39, 30:56, 37:21, 40:15, 41:47, 42:7, 50:20, 56:1, 64:9, 69:1, 79:34, 80:33, 88:1, 101:1-3; time known only to Allah 7:187, 31:34, 33:63, 79:42-46; fast approaching 54:1; will take people by surprise 6:31, 7:187; Trumpet will be blown

85; forgiven by Allah 2:37, 20:122.

David (🕊): kills Goliath 2:251; passes a judgment 21:78-79; inherits prophethood 27:15-16; mountains and birds join him in praising Allah 34:10, 38:17-20; judges between two people 38:21-26.

Elias (🕊) with his people 37:123-130.

Elisha (🕊) (mentioned passingly) 6:86, 38:48.

Enoch (🕊) (mentioned passingly) 19:56-57.

Hûd (🕊) with his people 7:65-72, 11:50-60, 26:124-140, 46:21-25.

Isaac (🕊) birth and prophethood 2:136, 3:84, 4:163, 6:84, 11:71, 12:6, 37:112-113.

Ishmael (🕊): raises foundations of the Ka'bah with his father 2:125-140; story of the sacrifice 37:100-113.

Jacob (Israel) (🕊): as a prophet 3:84, 3:93, 4:163, 6:84; in the story of his son Joseph 12:4-100.

Jesus (🕊): his virgin birth, message, and miracles 3:45-51, 19:16-38; reminded of Allah's favours 5:110-115; no more than a messenger 4:171-172, 5:75, 19:30; created by a word from Allah like Adam (🕊) 3:59; honoured in this world and the Hereafter 3:45-46; his mother chosen over all women of the world 3:42; denies being divine 5:116-120; Christians asked not to deify him 4:171; neither killed nor crucified 4:157; his second coming 43:61; his disciples stand up for Allah 3:52, 61:14; compassion and grace in the hearts of his followers 5:82, 57:27.

Job (🕊) tested then rewarded 21:83, 38:41-44.

John the Baptist (🕊) birth and prophethood 3:38-41, 19:7-15, 21:90.

Jonah (🕊) swallowed by whale then saved 10:98, 21:87, 37:139-148, 68:48-50.

Joseph (🕊): best of stories 12:1-3; young Yusuf's dream 12:4-6; conspiracy by his brothers 12:7-18; sold into slavery 12:19-20; raised in Egypt's Chief Minister's house 12:21-22; Chief Minster's wife tries to seduce him 12:23-29; banquet incident 12:30-32; goes to jail 12:33-35; the two inmates 12:36-42; King's dream 12:43-53; becomes Chief Minister 12:54-57; brothers come to him for supplies 12:58-68; takes his brother Benjamin 12:69-82; his father's renewed grief 12:83-87; reveals his true identity 12:88-98; old dream comes true 12:99-100; concluding prayer 12:101.

Lot (🕊) with his people 7:80-84, 11:77-83, 15:61-74, 21:71-75, 26:160-175, 29:28-35, 37:133-138, 54:33-39.

Moses (🕊): childhood 20:38-40; 28:7-13; fateful encounter at the burning bush 20:9-36, 27:7-14; 28:29-35; story with Pharaoh 7:103-137, 10:75-92, 11:96-99, 26:10-68; nine signs for Pharaoh and his people 7:130-133, 20:17-22, 17:101; defeats Pharaoh's magicians 20:70-73, 26:46-52; kills an Egyptian by mistake 28:14-21; escape to Midian and marriage 28:22-28; receives the Tablets 7:142-154, asks to see Allah on the Mount 7:142-145; honoured by Allah 33:69; Allah's favours to Israelites 2:47-61; rebukes his people for calf-worship 7:148-156, 20:83-99; Israelites refuse to enter Jerusalem 5:20-26.

Muḥammad (🕋), *see* DOCTRINE

Noah (🕊): mocked 11:38; the Ark and the Flood 7:59-64, 11:25-48, 23:23-31, 26:105-122, 71:1-28; his son drowned 11:42-48.

Sâliḥ (🕊) with his people 7:73-79, 11:61-68, 26:142-158, 27:45-53, 91:11-15.

Decency: 7:26, 16:81; the veil 24:31; lowering the gaze 24:30-31.

Divorce: arbitration and reconciliation 4:35, 4:128; etiquette of divorce 2:229-231, 65:1-2; dowry and waiting period 2:226-241, 4:19-21, 33:49, 65:1-7; husband not to take back anything of the dowry 4:20; wife not be harassed 65:6; wife to be supported financially during pregnancy 65:6; during her waiting period 65:6; if she nurses ex-husband's child, 65:6; no parent should suffer because of their child 2:233; opting for wet-nurse 65:6.

Encouraging good and forbidding evil 3:104, 3:110, 7:157, 9:71-72, 31:17.

Equality of human beings: 49:13; equality between men and women before Allah and the law, 3:195, 4:124, 5:38, 16:97, 24:2, 40:40; men have a degree of responsibility above women 2:228.

Feeding the poor, orphans, and captives 76:8-9.

Forgiveness and anger control 3:134, 42:40.

Freeing slaves and helping them 4:92, 5:89, 9:60, 24:33, 58:3, 90:13.

Honouring one's own **parents** 4:36, 17:23-25, 31:14-15.

Humility 17:37, 31:18-19.

Interpretation of dreams: of Abraham (🕊) 37:102; Joseph (🕊) 12:4, 12:36, 12:43; Muḥammad (🕊) 8:43, 48:27.

Kindness to non-Muslims 60:8.

Marriage: 4:3, 4:129, 16:72, 30:21; lawful and unlawful women to marry 4:22-24; etiquette of intimacy 2:222-223; pregnancy and nursing 2:233, 31:4, 46:15, 65:6; remarrying one's own ex-wife 2:230; helping singles to marry 24:32; subtly showing interest during the waiting period 2:235.

Oaths: 2:224-225, 16:91-92, 16:94; making up for a broken oath 5:89.

Patience in difficult times 2:45, 2:153-157, 3:186, 12:18, 12:83, 16:127-128, 70:5.

Permission: to enter 24:58-60; entering people's homes 24:27-28; entering public places 24:29.

Social etiquette: verifying news 4:83, 49:6; respect for all 49:11-12; etiquette of gatherings 58:11; private talks 4:114, 58:9.

Vows 2:270, 9:75-77, 22:29, 76:7.

Wasting and stinginess 7:31, 17:29, 25:67.

STORIES

1. **Prophets** (twenty-five mentioned by name)

Aaron (🕊): with his brother Moses (🕊) as messengers to Pharaoh and his people 7:122-172, 10:75, 20:30-92, 21:48, 23:45, 25:35, 26:12-48, 28:34, 37:114-120.

Abraham (🕊): raises the foundations of the Ka'bah 2:124-129; calls his people to the worship of the One True God 2:130-132, 26:69-89, 29:16, 29:24-27; debates arrogant king 2:258, inquires about resurrection 2:260; neither Jew nor Christian 3:65-68; refutes celestial worship 6:74-87; receives news of the birth of Isaac 11:69-76, 51:24-30; his prayer at the Ka'bah 14:35-41; visited by angels 15:51-56; a role model 16:123; calls his father to the truth 19:41-50; destroys idols and is saved from the fire 21:51-73, 37:83-113; calls all to the pilgrimage 22:26.

Adam (🕊): honoured by Allah, tempted by Satan 2:30-38, 7:11-25, 17:61-65, 18:50, 20:115-123, 38:71-

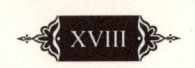

(*shafâ'ah*) 2:48, 2:255, 6:51, 6:70, 10:3, 21:28, 32:4, 36:23, 39:43-44, 43:86, 53:26, 74:48.

Records of deeds: 17:13, 18:49; believers receive their record with their right hand 69:19-24, 84:7-9; disbelievers receive their record with their left hand 69:25-37, 84:10-15; nothing will be hidden from Allah 21:47, 40:16; weighing of deeds 7:8, 23:102-104, 101:1-11; testimony of bodily organs 41:19-24, 24:24; reward for good and evil deeds 6:160, 27:89-90, 28:84.

Types of people: believers 18:107-108; disbelievers 4:167-169; hypocrites 4:145, 57:13-15; residents of Paradise (foremost believers 55:46-61, 56:10-26; people of the right 55:62-78, 56:27-40); residents of Hell (people of the left 55:31-45, 56:41-56); people on the heights 7:46-49.

2.   RELATIONSHIP WITH PEOPLE

A.   **Financial**

Business guidelines 2:188, 2:275, 2:282-283, 4:29, 4:58, 6:152, 17:34-35, 24:36-37, 26:182, 30:39, 55:7-9, 62:9.

Bequests: optional bequests to non-heirs 2:180-183, 4:11-12; before death while on a journey 5:106-108.

Bribery 2:188.

Debts: kindness in collecting debts 2:280; writing and witnessing a debt contract 2:282; taking collateral 2:283.

Inheritance: guidelines 4:7, 4:32-33, 8:75; shares of offspring and parents 4:11; spouses and maternal siblings 4:12; full siblings 4:176; warning to those who don't comply 4:13-14.

Interest: prohibition and warning 2:275-281, 3:130-132; rendered profitless 30:39.

B.   **Legal**

Anti-terrorism law (*hirâbah*) 5:33-34.

Justice: standing up for justice 4:135, 5:8, 16:90-91; standing up for the rights of orphans and women 4:127; justice to a Jew 4:105-112; justice to a pagan 4:58; fairness with non-Muslims 60:8-9.

Retaliation through legal channels (with the option to forgive), 2:178-179, 5:45, 16:126, 17:33, 42:37-43.

Separation between husband and wife: *khul'* 2:229; *li'ân* 24:6-10.

C.   **Political**

Conducting affairs by consultation (*shûra*), 3:159, 42:38.

Fighting in self-defence (*jihad*): etiquette 2:190-192, 2:216, 22:38-40; not to attack indiscriminately 4:94; fighting for oppressed men, women, and children 4:75; protecting places of worship 22:37; reward of martyrs 2:154, 3:169-171, 9:111, 57:19; military might deters potential enemies 8:60; opting for peace 2:192, 8:61.

Making peace between parties, 49:9-10.

Prisoners of war, treatment 8:70, 47:4, 76:8.

D.   **Social**

Adoption 33:4-5.

Caring for orphans 2:220, 4:2-10, 4:127, 6: 152, 17:34.

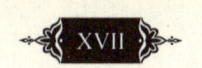

Objects of worship: angels (among some pagan Arabs) 34:40; *Al-Aykah* (among the people of Shu'aib ﷺ) 26:176; Ba'l (among the people of Elias ﷺ) 37:125; Jesus (in Christianity) 5:17; idols (among the people of Abraham ﷺ) 21:52-53; the idols of *Lât, 'Uzza,* and *Manât* (among Arab pagans) 53:19-20; the idols of *Wadd, Suwâ', Yaghûth, Ya'ûq,* and *Nasr* (among the people of Noah ﷺ) 71:23; the sun (the people of Sheba) 27:24; Sirius (among some pagan Arabs) 53:49; Pharaoh (in ancient Egypt) 26:29, 28:38, 79:24; desires 25:43-44, 45:23; belief in multiple gods refuted 17:42-43, 21:21-24, 25:3.

Places of worship: mosques 9:18; churches, synagogues, and monasteries 22:40; sanctuary 3:39, 38:21; temple 17:7.

Religious titles, priests, monks, and rabbis 5:44, 5:63, 5:82, 9:31-34.

2)   **Angels**

Inquire about the creation of Adam 2:30-34, never disobey Allah 21:26-27, 66:6; are not the daughters of Allah 21:26, 43:16-19; guarding angels 13:11; two recording angels 50:16-18, 82:10-12; eight carrying Allah's Throne on Judgment Day 69:17; nineteen keepers of Hell 74:26-31; Angels of Death 6:93, 16:28, 32:11; Gabriel 2:97, 66:4, 26:192-195, 53:1-14; Michael 2:98; Mâlik 43:77.

3)   **Messengers** (*see* Prophets under STORIES),

From among angels and humans 22:75; Messengers of Firm Resolve (Abraham, Noah, Moses, Jesus, and Muḥammad ﷺ) 33:7, 42:13, 46:35.

4)   **Scriptures**

Quran: a revelation from Allah 12:2-3, 20:2-4, 26:192-195, 32:2-3; a reminder to the whole world 68:51-52; guides to the most upright way of life 17:9; revelation started in the month of Ramaḍân 2:185; on a blessed night 44:3, 97:1-5; revealed in stages 17:105-106; made easy to remember 54:17; confirms the truth in previous revelations 3:3-4; a supreme authority on earlier scriptures 5:48; no doubt in it 2:2, 10:37; no contradictions 4:82; not fabricated 10:37-39; not copied from the Bible 25:4-6; not revealed by devils 26:210-212; no one can produce something like it 17:88, 2:23-24,10:13-14, 11:13; protected from corruption 15:9; protected in the Preserved Tablet 56:75-80; cannot be proven false 41:42; foretells future events 30:1-7, 48:27; moves the believers to tears 5:83, 17:107-109; touches hearts 39:23; brilliant light 4:174, 42:52; healing and mercy for the believers 17:82.

Torah 3:3, 3:93, 5:46, 5:66-68, 5:110, 7:157, 9:111, 48:29, 61:6, 62:5.

Gospel 3:3, 3:48, 5:46-47, 5:66-68, 5:77, 5:110, 7:157, 9:111, 48:29, 57:27.

Psalms 4:163, 17:55.

Scrolls of Abraham (ﷺ) 53:36-44, 87:14-19.

5)   **Fate and destiny**

3:145, 9:51, 10:107, 11:6, 54:49, 67:30; free choice 6:148-150, 11:118-119, 16:93, 33:72-73, 39:41, 76:1-3, 91:1-10.

6)   **Day of Judgment**

No injustice 2:281, 18:49, 40:17; horrors of the apocalypse 22:1-2, 27:82-84, 27:87, 40:18, 52:11-16, 69:13-18, 70:8-18, 73:17-18, 75:7-15, 77:8-15, 78:17-20, 79:34-36, 80:33-42, 81:1-14, 82:1-5, 84:1-5, 87:17-40, 99:1-8, 101:1-11; the righteous and the wicked on that Day 11:105-108, 16:27,33, 16:84-89, 18:52-53, 20:100-111, 25:24-29, 30:12-16, 33:63-68, 39:68-75, 50:20-35, 55:37-41, 83:4-36; intercession

Supplications (*du'â'*): of Abraham (﷩) 2:126-129, 14:35-41, 26:83-89; Adam and Eve (﷩) 7:23; Jesus (﷩) 5:114; Job (﷩) 21:83; Jonah (﷩) 21:87; Joseph (﷩) 12:33, 12:101; Moses (﷩) 10:88-89, 20:25-35; Muḥammad (ﷺ) 17:80, 20:114; Noah (﷩) 23:26, 26:117-118, 54:9-10, 71:26, 71:28; Solomon (﷩) 38:35; Shu'aib (﷩) 7:89; Zachariah (﷩) 3:38, 19:2-6, 21:89-90; angels 40:8-9; Mary's mother 3:35-36; Pharaoh's wife 66:11; Pharaoh's magicians 7:126; King Saul and the believers with him 2:250; the believers of the Children of Israel 10:85-86; the people of the cave 18:10; the righteous 2:285-286, 3:8-9, 3:16, 3:147, 3:191-194, 25:74, 59:10; the oppressed 4:75.

Prostration verses (*sajadât*, pl. of *sajdah*, *see* Stylistic Features in the Introduction) 7:206, 13:15, 16:49, 17:109, 19:58, 22:18, 22:77, 25:60, 27:26, 32:15, 38:24, 41:37, 53:62, 84:21, 96:19.

3)   **Alms-tax** (*zakâh*)

Importance of alms-tax: as an obligation 2:110, 2:177, 2:277, 6:141; one of the qualities of the believers 22:41, 23:4, 51:19; recipients 9:60.

Charity (*ṣadaqah*) 2:177, 2:261-263, 2:267-274, 3:92, 63:10.

Warning to those who withhold 3:180, 9:34, 47:38.

4)   **Fasting** (*ṣawm*)

Importance of Fasting: in Ramaḍân 2:183-185; hours of fasting 2:187; exemptions 2:184-185; intimate relations during the night preceding the fast 2:187; fasting during pilgrimage 2:196.

5)   **Pilgrimage** (*ḥajj*)

Importance of pilgirmage: an obligation one those who can afford it 3:97; rituals and rulings 2:158, 2:189, 2:196-203, 5:2, 22:26-37; sacrificial offerings 2:196, 22:36-37; prohibition of hunting on land while on pilgrimage 5:1, 5:94-95; permissibility of hunting at sea 5:96.

Minor pilgrimage (*'umrah*) 2:158, 2:196.

B.   **The Six Articles of Faith**

1)   **Devotion to the One True God**, *see* Allah under Doctrine

Faith-communities: Muslims 2:132-136, 3:64, 3:84, 5:111, 22:77-78, 33:35, 41:33, 43:67-70, 72:14-15; guardians of one another 3:28, 9:71; Christians 2:62, 2:111-140, 4:171-172, 5:14-19, 5:82-86, 5:116-120, 9:30-31, 22:17; Jews 2:62, 2:111-140, 5:44-45, 6:146, 22:17, 62:6-8; Children of Israel 2:40-103, 2:122-123, 2:246-251, 3:49, 3:93-94, 5:12-13, 5:20-26, 5:32, 5:70-71, 5:78-81, 7:137-141, 7:148-153, 7:159-171, 10:83-93, 14:5-8, 17:2-8, 17:104, 20:80-98, 26:52-67, 26:197, 27:76, 44:23-33, 45:16-17, 46:10, 61:5-6; People of the Book (mainly Jews and Christians) 2:109, 3:64-115, 3:199, 4:123-172, 5:15-77, 6:20-21, 13:36, 28:52-55, 29:46-47, 57:16, 57:28-29, 74:31, 98:1-5; Muslims can eat from animals sacrificed by them and marry their women 5:5; foods forbidden to Jews 6:146; Sabians 2:62, 22:17; Magi 22:17; polytheists (pagans, idol worshippers) 3:186, 6:148, 9:6, 9:17, 10:28, 16:86, 22:17, 53:19-30; pagan superstitious practices 2:189, 5:103; 6:138-144; atheists 52:35-36.

Pagan practices abolished: burying daughters alive 16:58-59, 81:8-9; killing children for fear of poverty 6:137, 6:151, 17:31; whistling and clapping around the Ka'bah 8:35; dedicating camels to idols 5:103, 6:136; sacrificing in the name of idols 6:121; *ẓihâr*-divorce 33:4, 58:2-4; *ilâ'* (for more than four months) 2:226-227; drawing lots for decisions 5:3; circling the Ka'bah while naked 7:26-28; entering homes from backdoors after pilgrimage 2:189.

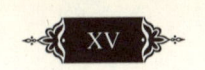

the sun as a radiant source and the moon as a reflected light 10:5; moon splitting 54:1; sky as a well-protected canopy 21:32; all beings created from water 21:30, 24:45; ants communicate 27:17-19; internal waves 24: 40; preservation of Pharaoh's body 10:90-92.

Living beings: angels 39:75; humans (an authority on earth) 2:30, 6:165, 16:4; jinn 72:1-15; animals belong to communities like humans 6:38 (calf 11:69, camel 7:40, dog 18:22, elephant 105:1, horses, mules, and donkeys 16:8, lion and zebras 74:50-51, monkeys 2:65, pigs 2:173, she-camel 7:73, sheep and goats 6:143, wolf 12:17); amphibians (frogs 7:133, snake 7:107); birds 24:41 (crow 5:31, hoopoe 27:20, quails 2:57); sea animals (fish 18:61, whale 37:142); insects (ants 27:18, bees 16:68, mosquito 2:26, fly 22:73, lice and locusts 7:133, spider 29:41); others unknown to us 16:8.

Plants and fruits: 6:99, 13:4, 16:11, 36:33-35 bananas 56:29, dates 19:25, herbs, cucumbers, garlic, lentils, and onions 2:61, grapes 80:28, olives 6:99, fig 95:1, pomegranates 55:68, squash 37:146.

Belief in Muḥammad (ﷺ) 3:144, 33:40, 47:2, 48:29.

Qualities of the Prophet: only a prophet 3:144, 6:50, 7:188, 18:110; to deliver the truth 2:119, 35:24, 42:48; seal of prophets 33:40; noble character 3:159, 68:4; a role model 33:21; as a favour to the believers 3:164; a mercy to the whole world 21:107; a universal messenger 4:170, 7:157-158, 34:28; leads to the Straight Path 42:52-53; cares about people 9:129; as a witness on Judgment Day 4:42, 16:89; unlettered prophet 7:157-158, 29:48, 62:2; prophesied in the Torah and Gospel 7:157; foretold by Jesus (ﷺ) 61:6.

Challenges faced by the Prophet: pagans' meaningless demands 8:32, 15:7, 17:89-93, 25: 7-8; false accusations 10:2, 11:13, 21:5, 24:11-26, 25:4-6, 37:36, 38:4, 52:29-30; attempts on his life 8:30, 9:74; warning to those who harm or oppose him 4:115, 8:13, 9:61, 15:95, 33:57, 47:32, 96:9-19; ordered to respond to denial with patience 20:130, 30:60, 46:35, 70:5; ordered to seek comfort in prayer 15:97-99; reassured by Allah 5:67, 93:1-11, 94:1-8.

Lessons from the Prophet: from his emigration (*hijrah*) to Medina 9:40; Battle of Badr 3:121-129, 8:42-44, 8:65-71; Battle of Uḥud 3:151-180; Battle of the Trench 33:9-27; Battle of Ḥunain 9:25-27; Tabûk 9:38-123; Banu An-Naḍîr 59:2-6; Ḥamrâ' Al-Asad 3:172-175; Truce of Ḥudaibiyah 48:1-7, 48:10-29.

Honours bestowed on the Prophet: Allah and His angels bless him 33:56; night journey from Mecca to Jerusalem 17:1; journey to the heavens 53:1-18; honoured in this life and the next 17:79, 66:8, 108:1; obedience to him is obedience to Allah 4:80; reward of obedience to Allah and His Messenger 4:69; his family purified 33:33-34; sees Gabriel in his true form 53:1-18; believers ordered to obey him 59:7; etiquette of speaking to him 49:1-5; etiquette of visiting him 33:53; etiquette of dealing with his wives 33:53; Allah is pleased with him and his companions 9:100, 9:117; excellence of his faith-community 2:143, 3:110.

2)   **Prayer** (*ṣalâh*)

Importance of Prayer: 2:45, 9:103, 51:18, 70:22-23, 75:31, 96:10, 108:2; Friday congregation 62:9; direction of prayer (*qiblah*) 2:144, 2:149-150; should deter one from evil deeds 29:45; times 11:114, 17:78, 17:79, 20:130, 24:36, 24:58, 30:17-18, 32:16, 38:18, 50:39-40, 51:17, 52:48-49, 73:2-4, 76:25-26; while in danger or on a journey 2:239, 4:101-102; warning to those who neglect prayers 19:59, 74:38-47, 107:5-7; hypocrites' prayers 4:142, 9:54.

Purification: ablution (*wuḍû'*) 5:6; full bath (*ghusl*) 2:222, 4:43; dry ablution (*tayammum*) 4:43, 5:6.

THEMATIC INDEX

☾

DOCTRINE

Basic tennets: Faith perfected 5:3; only Way accepted by Allah 3:19, 3:85; no compulsion in accepting Islam 2:256; one religion with different faiths and codes of law 5:48, 22:67-70, 42:13-14; prophets of Islam 2:135-136, 3:84, 4:163-165; commandments (have faith in Allah and do good) 4:36, 6:151-154, 17:23-39, 18:107-108; five objectives of *Sharia*: protecting faith 5:54; protecting life 5:32, 6:151; protecting wealth 5:38; protecting honour 5:5, 24:4; protecting one's ability to think 5:90.

1. RELATIONSHIP WITH ALLAH
A. **The Five Pillars of Islam**
1) **Belief in Allah and the Prophet (☬)**

Divine qualities of Allah: Beautiful Names 57:1-6, 59:22-24, 85:13-16, 112:1-4; only god worthy of worship 1:1-4, 2:285, 6:3, 43:84; all authority belongs to Him 3:26; His Throne (*'Arsh*) 7:54, 11:7; His Seat (*Kursi*) 2:255; countless favours upon humanity 14:32-34, 2:164, 16:2-93, 31:20, 55:1-25; gives life and causes death 44:8, 53:44, 57:2, 67:2; brings about joy and sadness 53:43; gives abundant or limited provisions 13:26, 17:30, 29:62; Best of all judges 95:8; Most Merciful of the merciful 12:92; All-Loving 85:14; Full of Forgiveness and severe in punishment 13:6, 40:3; the First and Last 57:3; all honour and power belongs to Him 35:10; knows the unknown and sees the unseen 6:59, 6:73, 9:94, 9:105, 13:8-10, 31:34, 32:6, 34:48, 35:38, 39:46, 49:18, 59:22, 62:8, 64:18, 72:26, 74:31, 87:7; knows best what is hidden in the heart 5:7, 11:5, 31:23; knows what happened and what yet to come 2:255; wrote everything in the Record (or the Preserved Tablet) 6:38, 13:39, 36:12; able to do anything 2:117, 3:189, 8:41, 9:116, 11:4, 16:40, 40:68, 41:39, 42:49, 57:2; His infinite power 3:26-27, 24:45, 31:28-30; created the heavens and earth in six Days and never got tired 46:33, 50:38; creates with the word 'Be!' 36:81-83; never unjust to His creation 3:108, 4:40, 17:71, 21:47, 22:10, 26:209, 40:31, 41:46, 45:22, 50:29, 64:11, 78:6-16; everything submits to His Will 3:83, 22:18, 30:26; all stand in need of Him 11:6, 35:15, 55:29; trust in Him 10:84-85, 12:67, 25:58; forms of divine communication 42:51; worthy to be mindful of 2:21, 3:102, 4:1, 33:70-71, 59:18; wisdom is a gift from Him 2:269; He is not in need of any one 3:97, 6:133, 112:2; not one in a Trinity 4:171; has no mate 6:101; has no children 10:68, 19:35, 43:81, 72:3, 112:3; has no partners or associate-gods 6:94, 7:191-195, 46:4-5; nothing like Him 42:11, 112:4.

Order to reflect on the marvels of His creation 3:190, 6:99, 10:5-6, 13:3-4, 16:10-16, 88:17-20.

Signs in creation 2:164, 6:95-99, 7:57-58, 10:5-6, 13:2-4, 16:10-13, 16:65-69, 16:79, 23:27-30, 27:60-65, 30:19-25, 50:6-11; created everything for a purpose 10:5-6, 15:85, 16:3, 23:115, 29:44, 30:8, 38:27, 44:38-39, 75:36; universe perfected 67:3-4; merges day into night 3:27; diversity 30:22, 35:27-28; honey 16:68-69; milk 16:66; gift of children 42:49-50; planets and orbits 21:33, 36:38-44; constellations 25:61, 85:1; stars 37:6-7, 67:5; clouds 7:57, 30:48; earthquake 7:78, 7:155; landslide 28:81, 29:40; storm 10:22; drizzle, hail, and rain 2:265, 6:99, 24:43, 50:9-11; thunder and lightning 13:12-13.

Scientific references: humans created from male and female gametes 76:2; formation and developmental phases of an embryo 22:5, 23:12-14; fetus in three layers of darkness 39:6; earth's rotation 27:88; constant expansion of the universe 51:47-48; spherical shape of the earth 39:5, 79:30; the Big Bang 21:30; black holes 81:15-16; brackish water 25:53-54, 35:12, 55:19-20; wind pollination 15:22; fingerprints 75:3-4; air pressure 6:125; mountains as pegs 78:7; iron sent down 57:25; pain receptors 4:56;

whereas a direct translation of the conversation would be rendered as a monologue in English. The same can be said of other pronouns such as 'they.'

THE QURANIC CHALLENGE

Unlike any other scripture, the Quran poses a falsification test to those who challenge its authenticity which, over time, was made easier and easier. The first challenge was to produce a similar book in Arabic (17:88). Next, the challenge was reduced to only ten *sûrahs* (11:13). Finally, the challenge was to only produce one *sûrah* similar to it (10:38), and despite the shortest *sûrah* being only ten words (*Sûrah* 108), none have been able to match it. The Quran also challenges readers to find contradictions (4:82). Some have attempted these challenges, only to prove their inability to match the elegance and eloquence of the divine revelation or their ignorance of the nuances of Arabic syntax and grammar.

was not going to befall you, and what has befallen you was not going to pass you by. And know that victory comes with perserverence, relief with affliction, and ease with hardship."

Generalizations are also common in the Quran, where "the people," or "the Jews," etc., actually refers to a small group that said or did something that was not challenged by the larger group (*see* 5:64).

With some exceptions, the Quran does not dwell on the names of persons, places, or times (*see* for example 2:255 and 18:9-26). Rather, attention is usually focused on the moral of the story, making it valid for every people, time, and place.

To express the greatness and magnitude of a definite noun (such as *the* Straight Path, *the* Merciful Lord, etc.), the Quran often uses that name in an indefinite form (*a* Straight Path, *a* Merciful Lord, etc.), but this translation uses the definite form in these instances in order to maintain the true meaning in English.

The Quran states that the pleasures which Allah has prepared for the believers in Paradise are beyond human comprehension (*see* 32:17). Hence, generic terms (e.g., rivers, gardens, fruits, garments of silk, bracelets of gold, etc.) are often used to describe these pleasures in an appealing way, bringing it down to our level of understanding, whereas the realities of Paradise are far beyond these descriptions. These terms are no different than those one would have used in 1876 C.E. to describe a cutting-edge smartphone to Alexander Graham Bell, the inventor of the telephone.

LETTERS AND PRONOUNS

Of the twenty-nine letters of the Arabic alphabet, only fourteen appear in various combinations at the beginning of twenty-nine *sûrah*s of the Quran. These letters are: *Nũn, Ṣãd, Ḥa, Kãf, Ya, Mĩm, Qãf, Alif, Ṭa, 'Aĩn, Lãm, Ha, Sĩn*, and *Ra*. According to Ibn Kathîr, a renowned Quran commentator, in his explanation of 2:1, these letters can be arranged into an Arabic sentence that reads نَصٌّ حَكِيمٌ قَاطِعٌ لَهُ سِرّ which roughly translates to: "A wise, decisive text, full of wonders." Although several theories have been suggested by scholars regarding the meaning of these letters, it is commonly believed that these letters are among the miracles of the Quran and, as such, no one knows their actual meaning except Allah.

Unlike other conjunctions like *fa* ف (then/right after) and *thumma* ثمّ (then/later), *wa* و (and) does not signify an order of events. The subjects of 'and' clauses have sometimes been rearranged for better flow in English, such as 'day and night' instead of 'night and day,' 'seen and unseen' instead of 'unseen and seen,' etc. (*see* 35:19-22).

One of the first things that strikes novice readers of the Quran is that the word 'We' is frequently used when Allah speaks (*see* 15:9-23). This plural form, known as the royal we, is employed to indicate reverence and not number. Almost always, 'Allah,' 'I,' or 'He' is mentioned either before or after to emphasize Allah's oneness.

Another visible stylistic feature is the 'rotation of pronouns' (*iltifât*) found throughout the Quran, alternating between first person, second person, and third person (*see* 17:1). If rendered verbatim into English this rhetorical device becomes entirely meaningless, as it is rarely found in any Indo-European language at all, and almost never in English.

A similar feature is found in the referential nature of pronouns in either language. In Classical Arabic, especially in the Quran, the repeated use of a single pronoun (such as 'he') rotates in reference, which is to say it first speaks of the first speaker, then the next use speaks of the second speaker, then back to the first, all using the same pronoun (*see* 26:24-31). In this way, repeatedly using "he said" would indicate a dialogue,

The Quran contains some fascinating numerical patterns. For example, 'Paradise' and 'Hell' are each repeated 77 times, 'angels' and 'devils' 88 times, 'world' and 'Hereafter' 115 times, 'prayers' (ṣalawât) 5 times (the exact number of daily prayers), 'punishment' 117 times, whereas 'forgiveness' is repeated double that number, 234 times. 'Day' is repeated 365 times (the average number of days in the year), 'days' 30 times (the average number of days in the month), and 'month' 12 times (the number of months in the year).

Sarcasm is another common feature of the Quran, especially when it talks about the fate of those who ridicule the truth (*see* 24:53 and 44:49). So readers can expect to see a warning such as: "Give them good news of a painful punishment." This style aims at paying the ridiculers back in kind as well as adding more intensity to the warning.

Many passages in the Quran utilize a preferential style called *tafḍîl*—that is to say, two things share a certain quality but one of them supersedes the other. For example, the Quran says repeatedly that the people of Pharaoh were more powerful and resourceful than the people of Mecca. However, some structures look like *tafḍîl* but do not actually signify a comparison in quality. The assumption that both sides share the same quality but one is greater than the other is what causes confusion in most translations of the Quran. For example, when 12:33 suggests that going to prison is dearer to Joseph (۩) than committing adultery, this does not mean that either option is dear to him. Similarly, 17:84 suggests that the believers' Way is better in guidance than that of the pagans, but in truth the latter is not guided at all. Furthermore, 11:78 suggests that Lot (۩) instructs men that the single women of his nation are purer for marriage than other men, when other men are not pure for marriage in the first place.

EMPHASIS

Emphasis is commonplace in the Quran, especially where a concept is likely to be challenged by the skeptics. Sometimes one or more emphasis words are used, such as 'surely,' 'indeed,' and 'certainly' (*see* 15:9). The repetition of a sentence two consecutive times is also used as emphasis, such as 102:3-4: "But no! You will soon come to know. Again, no! You will soon come to know." The repetition of a verb in its noun form can also be used to similar effect. If translated literally, 56:4 will read, "When the earth will be shaken with a shaking," whereas the meaning is: "When the earth will be violently shaken." Lastly, an oath is one of the most common forms of emphasis. Allah has the right to swear by any of His creation, such as the sun and the moon, the day and night, the heaven and earth (91:1-6). However, a Muslim can only swear by Allah.

PERSONS, TIME, AND PLACE

To prove its divine nature, the Quran often refers to past events that were not known to anyone at the time of the revelation (*see* 12:25-42 and 27:17-28), constantly reminding the Prophet (۩) that, since he was not an eyewitness to these events, it was through divine revelation that he came to know about them (*see* 12:102). The Quran also foretells future events that were later proven true (*see* 30:1-6 and 48:27).

Unlike English, the Arabic language has only three tenses: past, present, and future. The Quran is unique in using the past tense to refer to future events, particularly when it describes the Day of Judgment (*see* 39:68-75). In addition to reminding us that Allah is not bound by the limits of time, the aim is to give the impression that these events are so certain to happen that it is as if they have already happened. However, when these sentences are translated into English (or any other language for that matter), the future tense is used.

Although the Quran is not arranged chronologically, the *sûrah*s are perfectly interrelated. Some of the stories or themes that are touched on passingly in one *sûrah* are explained in detail in the next *sûrah* (*see* 12:105 and 13:1-17). In some cases, both the end of a *sûrah* and the beginning of the next *sûrah* cover the same subject (*see* 53:57-62 and 54:1-5). One *sûrah* might give some stories and the next will continue the narrative by adding more stories (*see sûrah*s 37 and 38). Additionally, two consecutive *sûrah*s might cover the exact same themes, but in a different order (*see sûrah*s 55 and 56).

Quranic *sûrah*s have diverse themes, with main overarching subjects (e.g., verses 2:221-242), interjected by secondary subjects (e.g., verses 2:238-239). In essence, all themes have a common denominator: one's relationship with their Creator and the rest of His creation. Assuming that not everyone will read the Quran in its entirety, readers will run into this common denominator at any given *sûrah*.

STYLE

With the word 'Quran' (lit., recitation) repeated about seventy times, the Quran is unique in that it actually speaks about itself, its Revealer, its purpose, its devotees, and its detractors. The author of this profound book is nowhere to be found on the cover; rather He reveals Himself on every page, speaking with authority, offering compelling proofs, giving commandments to prophets, believers, and all of humanity.

Perhaps one of the most visible stylistic features of the Quran is repetition, which comes in three different forms:

1) **Repetitive phrases** such as "Then which of your Lord's favours will you both deny?" which appears a total of thirty-one times in *Sûrah* 55 and "Woe on that Day to the deniers!" which appears ten times in *Sûrah* 77. Far from redundancy, the purpose of repetition in these two instances is to create an impact by reinforcing the point being made—to acknowledge Allah's many blessings in the former and deter people from denying Allah in the latter. This rhetorical device is still employed by many modern orators. One of the most notable examples is the repetition of "I have a dream" and "Let freedom ring" in Martin Luther King's 1963 famous speech.

2) **Repetitive themes** such as the arguments for Allah's oneness, uniqueness, and power in *sûrah*s 16, 35, and 112; the comparison between Paradise and Hell in *sûrah*s 37, 39, 40, and 41; and the horrors of Judgment Day in *sûrah*s 77, 78, 79, 80, and 81. The purpose is to emphasize a recurring theme (e.g., the reward of the believers and disbelievers) or present more details (e.g., the testimony of bodily organs in 41:19-24 and the fruit of the *Zaqqûm* tree in 37:62-68).

3) **Repetitive stories** such as the story of Moses (﷾) in *sûrah*s 7, 18, 26, and 28 and Abraham (﷾) in *sûrah*s 2, 6, 19, and 37. The purpose is to reassure the Prophet (﷾) and focus on a different aspect of the life of these prophets. For example, the highlights of the story of Moses (﷾) in *Sûrah* 7 are the arrogance of Pharaoh, the defeat of the magicians, and the suffering of the Children of Israel. In *Sûrah* 26, the focus shifts to Moses' childhood, his unintentional killing of an Egyptian man, as well as his escape to Midian and his marriage.

The fact that these repetitive themes and stories are perfectly consistent, despite having been revealed over the course of two decades to an unlettered prophet, is yet another proof of the divine source of the Quran.

STYLISTIC FEATURES OF THE QURAN

The Quran was revealed in 7th century Arabia, where people took so much pride in their mastery of Arabic that literary fairs were commonly held and prized poems were inscribed in gold for all to see. The Quran, which is believed to be Allah's inimitable Word, is a literary miracle, unmatched by any other work of Arabic literature. While Arabic has served as the medium for communicating the Quranic message, the Quran has forever changed the landscape of Arabic literary tradition, promoting Arabic to a leading world language and influencing other languages including Farsi, Urdu, Swahili, Turkish, Spanish, and many others. Several sciences have emerged to serve the Quran such as *tafsîr* (Quranic commentary), *tawḥîd* (theology), *fiqh* (jurisprudence), *tajwîd* (phonetic rules of recitation), *qirâ'ât* (styles of recitation), *naḥw* and *ṣarf* (grammar and morphology), *balâghah* (rhetoric), and *khaṭṭ* (calligraphy). Algebra was also developed in part to solve issues related to the distribution of inheritance shares laid out in *Sûrah* 4. Together with the *Sunnah* or the example of the Prophet (ﷺ), the Quran is the bedrock of Muslim civilization and the main source of Islamic law and practice. The following are some of the distinctive stylistic features of the Quran in its original Arabic form.

STRUCTURE

The body of the Quran is made up of 6236 verses (or *âyât*, plural of *âyah*, which literally means sign, proof, or miracle), composed of 114 *sûrah*s in more than 600 pages. A *sûrah* usually takes its name from the main theme, a story, or a distinctive word within it. With the exception of *Sûrah* 9, all *sûrah*s begin with the *basmalah*: "In the Name of Allah—the Most Compassionate, Most Merciful." Depending on their respective *sûrah*, verses typically rhyme and vary in length—some are long (2:282 is the longest at fifteen lines long), while others are short (20:1 is the shortest at only two Arabic letters). The Quran is divided into 30 parts (or *ajzâ'*, plural of *juz'*), each with 8 subparts (or *arbâ'*, plural of *rub'*, which are marked with ⚙), making it convenient for reading and memorization.

This symbol 🕌 signifies one of fifteen proſtrations (or *sajadât*, plural of *sajdah*) in the Quran. When proſtrating, one should say, "My face proſtrates to the One Who created and fashioned it, and brought forth its ʿfaculties ofʾ hearing and sight with His power and might. So blessed is Allah, the Beſt of Creators," ﴿سَجَدَ وَجْهِيَ لِلَّذِي خَلَقَهُ وَصَوَّرَهُ وَشَقَّ سَمْعَهُ وَبَصَرَهُ بِحَوْلِهِ وَقُوَّتِهِ فَتَبَارَكَ اللَّهُ أَحْسَنُ الْخَالِقِينَ﴾ as the Prophet (ﷺ) is reported to have said in a narration collected by Al-Ḥâkim. Otherwise, one can juſt say, "Glory be to my Lord, the Moſt High." ﴿سُبْحَانَ رَبِّيَ الأَعْلَى﴾

Of the Quran's 114 *sûrah*s, eighty-six are classified as Meccan because they were revealed before the Prophet's emigration to Medina. These *sûrah*s focus mainly on restoring the belief in the One True God. The other twenty-eight *sûrah*s are categorized as Medinian since they were revealed after the Prophet's emigration from Mecca with an emphasis on the commandments regarding a Muslim's relationship with their Lord, their fellow humans, and the rest of Allah's creation. Some Meccan *sûrah*s may have Medinian verses and vice versa. *Sûrah*s and passages were revealed over a period of twenty-three years to address issues facing the Muslim community. As instructed by Allah through the angel Gabriel, the Prophet (ﷺ) ordered his scribes to arrange *sûrah*s mostly according to their lengths, with the longest *sûrah*s first, not chronologically.

The name "Muḥammad" appears only four times in the Quran. In some cases, words such as "Prophet" and "Messenger" are used to address him. But moſt of the time, the Prophet is addressed in the second person "you," this is when "O Prophet" will be used between half brackets ⸢ ⸣ to indicate that "you" is referring to Muḥammad (ﷺ) and not to the believers or anyone else.

ﷺ and ﵊ are calligraphic contractions of Arabic phrases meaning 'peace be upon him,' and 'peace be upon them' respectively. They are used respectfully after the mention of prophets outside the text of the Quran.

"The Day of Judgment" and "Judgment Day" are equivalent and used interchangably based on the flow in English.

Abbreviations used in this translation:
A.H. After *Hijrah*
B.C.E. Before Common Era
C.E. Common Era
e.g., exempli gratia, 'for example'
i.e., id eſt, 'that is to say'
lit., literally

TRANSLITERATION TABLE

Arabic	IPA	Trans.	Example	Arabic	IPA	Trans.	Example	Arabic	IPA	Trans.	Example
ا	a:	â	Fâtiḥah	ظ	ðˤ	ẓ	Ẓihâr	هـ	h	h	Humazah
ء	ʔ	'	Nisâ'	ع	ʕ	'	An'âm	و	w	w	Wâqi'ah
ب	b	b	Baqarah	غ	ɣ	gh	Ghâfir	ـُو	u:	û	Burûj
ت	t	t	Tîn	ف	f	f	Furqân	ى	j	y	Yâ-Sîn
ث	θ	th	Kawthar	ق	q	q	Qalam	ـِـى	i:	î	Ibrâhîm
ج	dʒ	j	Fajr	ك	k	k	Kahf	ـَ	a	a	Shams
ح	ħ	ḥ	Ḥajj	ل	l	l	'Alaq	ـِ	ɪ	i	Jinn
خ	x	kh	Ikhlâṣ	م	m	m	Mariam	ـُ	ʊ	u	Mulk
د	d	d	Balad	ن	n	n	Nûḥ				

English translation. For example, the word 'corn' is no longer used to describe all forms of grain, yet many translations still use this word to describe the fields in the dream of the King in the story of Joseph (12:43 and 46). When Yusuf Ali first wrote this in 1934, it may have been acceptable to refer to wheat as a kind of corn, but in modern vocabulary this is totally unheard of, yet many translations simply erroneously copy that word into their own works.

It is clear that the modern age demands not only a great scholar of Arabic and the Quran to come to the table, but also a modern, adaptable scholar of the English language, as well as someone with native fluency who knows how the translation will be received.

The reception of the Quran by English audiences now indicates a third stage in the historical development of Quran translation. At first it was an academic exercise, a curious study of the 'other.' Next, Muslims translated the Quran as a matter of love or pride, and they shared it among themselves. With this long history and background, and a team of experts in the Quran and in the English language, the struggle we now face is transmitting the real beauty and message of the Quran to Muslims and non-Muslims alike who are interested in it and who also know and love English.

The Alcoran of Ross was the first small step forward, and Yusuf Ali's *The Holy Qur'an* was a turning point in the history of the Quran in English. The next step is to overcome the obstacles outlined here and to deliver Allah's Final Testament to English speaking audiences like never before. The next step is *The Clear Quran*®.

NOTES ON TRANSLATION

Allah's names and attributes are capitalized as well as pronouns used to reference Him.

Proper nouns referring to events and cosmology are also capitalized, such as the Day of Judgment, the Day, the Hour, the Hereafter, Paradise, and Hell.

In some cases, the use of a pronoun would be confusing or misleading, so it has been replaced with the corresponding noun for clarity. Similarly, in some places where the 'rotation of pronouns' (*iltifât*) is found in the Arabic, pronouns have been altered in English to maintain pronoun agreement.

Gendered pronouns have been replaced with 'they' where the meaning is neutral, except in the case of Allah, Who is referred to as 'He' despite being gender-neutral in order to preserve the use of a singular pronoun, while avoiding the use of 'it.'

Unless otherwise indicated, Biblical quotations are from *The Holy Bible: International Standard Version*, copyright © the ISV Foundation, 1996-2012.

Half brackets ⌐ ⌐ indicate words inserted into the English which do not directly correspond to Arabic words in the original text.

The most frequently used speech verb in the Quran is "said," especially in conversation. To enrich conversations in English, several speech verbs are used in this translation (such as replied, cried, protested, pleaded, and threatened), depending on the meaning (*see* 18:71-73).

with translating the Quran value language density, and the religious and scholarly traditions of the English language assume a correlation between complexity of language and truth. This correlation has been carried over into translations of the Quran despite complexity, density, and inaccessibility being tenets far from Islamic scholarly tradition. What we are left with are translations that, though they may be technically correct, miss the simplicity, vigour, or eloquence of the original in favour of a contrived sense of divinity.

Two striking examples of overinflated, though accurate, English translations come to mind. First, M.M. Pickthall writes, "Be modest in thy bearing and subdue thy voice. Lo! the harshest of all voices is the voice of the ass." (31:19) In today's English, this can only be read as a rather vulgar statement, especially by non-academic readers and should instead be rendered, "Be moderate in your pace and lower your voice, for the ugliest of all voices is certainly the braying of donkeys." Second, T.B. Irving writes of 44:16, "Some day We will kidnap everyone in the greatest operation; We shall be Avenged!" Giving Allah a distinctly immature, vindictive, and even rueful voice where a more appropriate translation is, "ʿOnʾ the Day We will deal ʿyouʾ the fiercest blow, We will surely inflict punishment."

The tone of the Quran, as a revelation for all humanity, relies heavily on a number of emotions as well, and a poor understanding of English can lead even great scholars of Arabic into error with translation. There are numerous instances in the Quran of sarcasm and wit, which are often lost entirely in complicated and fragile grammar structures. Elegance and prose are also usually cast out of translations, especially when scholars use a rigid word-for-word replacement technique to encode Arabic into a mock-English cypher that sometimes gives the opposite meaning of what is intended in the verse. The problem with undervaluing the subtleties and intricacies of human language can be underlined by examining the work of Dr. M. Mahmoud Ghali. He translates 4:105, "and do not be a constant adversary of the treacherous." The true translation of this verse is, "so do not be an advocate for the deceitful." A similar example can be found in his translation of 100:8, "And surely he is indeed constantly (passionate) in his love for charity," where "love for charity" in fact refers to "greed for ʿworldlyʾ gains."

In respecting the order and particulars of the Arabic words being used, the meaning of dozens of idioms are lost in translation, hundreds of sentences become a tangled mess of improper grammar, and the flow and ease of reading is entirely lost. It is better to respect the meaning and power of the Quran than the language it happened to be revealed in, otherwise one might end up with the near blasphemous statement found in the Ṣaḥeeḥ International translation, "They have forgotten Allah, so He has forgotten them." (9:67) Surely Allah does not 'forget' anything or anyone. Google Translate might give up a similar translation, but the meaning is poetic, it is much closer to 'neglect.' Both parties are aware of each other, but when humans neglect their duties to Allah, He neglects them in the Fire: "They neglected Allah, so He neglected them."

Aside from these more theologically problematic translation issues, there are dozens of simple grammar structures in the Quran that are easy, clear, or beautiful in Arabic, but entirely untranslatable. Rather than try to fit the English structures and words into a foreign context, it is much better to accept English for what it has to offer and use its own native poetry and balance to create a translation that carries the real meaning and power of the Perfect Book.

With grammar and the particularities of translating aside, a considerable understanding of the context of the Quranic revelation itself as well as the stories found within is needed in order to render a proper

INTRODUCTION

The first translation of the Quran into English was done in 1649 by Alexander Ross. Since that first translation, many more attempts have been made to penetrate the work from an outside, academic point of view, but it wasn't until the early 20th century that it was translated by a Muslim. In 1934, Yusuf Ali would produce one of the most widely circulated versions to date.

Aside from concerns about academia and orientalism, translating the Quran can be an enormous task even for the sincere of heart. Arabic, as a Semitic language, has words that have meanings and shades of meanings which do not easily move over into English, and total mastery of both languages is needed before any truly satisfactory translation can be put forward. Translators also struggle to render what they believe to be the right meaning into a foreign language—knowing that it is almost impossible to reflect the Arabic style, rhythms, and figures of speech, while also struggling with different interpretations of the original Arabic words.

The development of linguistics, current events, and the gradual drift of the English language puts us in an important time to move forward in Quranic translations. For the most part, a lack of understanding Arabic can be seen in older, less popular works from European scholars, however mistakes and errors are persistent in more modern copies, and blunders can even be found in the likes of Yusuf Ali when he writes, "those who believe not in the hereafter name the angels with female names." (53:27) A brief survey of names such as Gabriel, Michael, and Mâlik offers no female names whatsoever. Keeping in mind that some pagan Arabs believed that the angels were Allah's daughters, the true translation can be rendered, "those who do not believe in the Hereafter label the angels as female."

The failure to understand the complex forms of Classical Arabic found in the Quran, and sometimes found only in the Quran, can be a stumbling block for many scholars, but even those with a strong understanding of Arabic need to have their intelligence backed with the wisdom found in a sound theological background. Without understanding the religious context of the Quran, such mistakes can be made as when Muhsin Khan & Muhammad al-Hilali write, "Allah will never lead a people astray after He has guided them until He makes clear to them as to what they should avoid." (9:115)

In context, the verse is instructing the Prophet (ﷺ) and his companions that they should no longer pray to Allah for the forgiveness of polytheists after their death. As pointed out by Ibn Kathîr, drawing on the understanding of Aṭ-Ṭabari, the meaning is clearly "Allah would never consider a people deviant after He has guided them, until He makes clear to them what they must avoid."

For these reasons it is clear that any translation of the Quran must be led by scholars with a profound understanding of the theological context of the Quran, as well as a native understanding of Arabic, but also considerable training in the meaning of the Classical Arabic particular to the Quran. These three things enable a scholar to truly understand the Quran, and a profound understanding is the first step towards a good translation.

Of course, a firm understanding of Arabic is not all that is needed in order to translate the Quran effectively. The Quran states repeatedly that it is accessible, clear, and easy to understand, so it would be an error to translate it into dense or inaccessible language. Naturally, the academic traditions that first dealt

TRANSLATOR'S NOTES

It was a summer day in Toronto and I had just finished leading the Friday congregation at a downtown mosque. On the way home I had an unlikely encounter, since all my cab-drivers in Toronto had been Muslims so far. That day my driver was non-Muslim, so he was able to identify me as Muslim simply because of my traditional Arab garb. Out of nowhere, he commented, "I think Muslims are good, but Islam is evil!" Taken aback by this Fox News style rhetoric, I responded, "Well, first of all thanks for the compliment about Muslims, but why do you think Islam is bad?" He replied, "Because your holy book calls me an animal." In astonishment, I answered, "I know the whole Quran by heart and I don't think it says that anywhere!" He cited 8:55, and I responded by telling him that the word *dâbbah* in Arabic does not mean an animal but a living being (*see* 24:45). He persisted, saying that his translation says so. I later checked many popular translations by Muslims and non-Muslims and realized that the man was right. This fateful encounter opened my eyes to the rampant mistranslations and misrepresentations of the Quran.

The Quran was revealed to Prophet Muḥammad (ﷺ) in the 7th century and was not translated into English by a Muslim until the 20th century. Many Muslims had long believed that the Quran should only be read in Arabic, the original language of revelation. This led to many inaccurate, ill-willed translations by missionaries and orientalists—which explains why we still see some words like 'holy war' and 'infidels' as well as many theological inaccuracies in some existing translations. All this leads to endless false assumptions about Islam and Muslims. Some Muslim translators are no better off than their non-Muslim counterparts because they are not well-versed in Arabic, or English, or Islamic studies, or translation, or all of the above. Looking up words in an Arabic-English dictionary or copying earlier translations when frustrated does not always guarantee accuracy in translation. There are some noteworthy modern translations like that of Dr. Ahmad Zaki Hammad (2007) and Dr. M.A.S. Abdel Haleem (2004), but many others are either overtranslated, making it difficult for laypeople to understand, or undertranslated, doing a great disservice to the Quran. This is why I saw a need for an accurate, smooth, and accessible translation.

To achieve accuracy, I have made use of the greatest and most celebrated works of old and modern *tafsîr* (Quran commentaries), and shared the work with several Imams in North America for feedback and insight. For clarity, every effort has been made to select easy to understand words and phrases that reflect the beauty and power of the original text. Along with informative footnotes, verses have been grouped and titled based on their themes for a better understanding of the *sûrah*s, their main concepts, and internal coherence.

Thanks to our editing and proofreading teams led by Abu-Isa Webb, I believe that what you are holding in your hands now is the most accurate and eloquent translation of the Final Revelation: *The Clear Quran*®.

Mustafa Khattab

ACKNOWLEDGMENTS

First I thank the Almighty for His guidance and assistance. I am eternally indebted to Dr. Muhammad M. Abu-Laylah, Dr. Esam Fayez, Dr. Ahmed Shafik Elkhatib, Dr. Reda Bedeir, Dr. Hassan M. Wageih, Dr. Rasha Al-Disuqi, Dr. Saeed Attia, Dr. Salah Nefeily, Dr. Ahmad Ezabi, and all my professors and colleagues at Al-Azhar University. I am thankful to Imam Refaat Mohamed, Imam Sherif Ayoup, Imam Amr Dabour, Dr. Arafat Elashi, Imam Muhammad Mustafa, Imam Muhammad Abuelezz, Imam Goma'a Makhlouf, Imam Mohamed Masloh, and Imam Ahmad Seddeeq for their valuable feedback.

My thanks go to the chief editors, particularly Abu-Isa Webb for his help with editing, styling, and formatting the work and co-authoring the introduction, as well as Aaron Wannamaker and Hisham Sharif, along with the following sub-editors:

- Sarah Halabi   - Harris Sheikh   - Akber Ali
- Yasmeen Mezil   - Celine Dean   - Jason Gowrie

I also would like to express my deepest gratitude to the following brothers and sisters for proofreading some parts of this work:

Aayesha Bonnie Kalicak	Desmond Sequeira	Misbah Shaikh
Abdullah Al-Hassan	Fahim Khan	Mohammed Halabi
Abubakr Elghul	Faisal Hejazi	Muhamad M. Abutaha
Ahmed Ahmed	Habib Abdul-Habib	Nayrah Islamovic
Ahmed Mezil	Hanan Awadh	Nicole Cathcart
Ahmed Qassem	Jana Bataineh	Osama Fadel
Ala Qubaja	Janette Bramley	Salum 'Zanjibar' Mshoka
Ali Al-Harazi	Kaalyn Thomson	Sulaiman El-Salah
Ali Younes	Karim Ismail	Syed Shafqat
Anthony Stehouwer	Kevin Ruffle	Taher Shayeb
Aqib Nakhooda	Khairija Stehouwer	Tamer Fadaly
Bilkis Al Haddad	Kolton Uitbeyerse	Yageen El-Haj
Brenda Hyde	Logaina Satti	Yahya Ianiri
Carol Dohn	Mahabba Ahmed	Yasin Cetin
Charmaine Kissmann	Malik Watson	Yusuf Al-Harazi
Dana Younes	Meshari Al-Otaibi	Yusuf Fattore

Thanks are also due to Hemen Mahmoudi and Nasir Dowlatkhahi for technical support.

This translation could not have been done without the generous support of the Niagara Pakistani community, with a special thanks to the Islamic Society of St. Catharines, Ontario, Canada and notably Dr. Tareq Omar Azabi.

I am grateful to my parents, my wife Dr. Fawziyah Abdelqadir, and my children (Yasmin, Ziyad, Noura, and Omar) for their patience and support throughout this journey.

Whatever good is in this work is from Allah. Only the mistakes are mine.

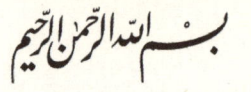

In the Name of Allah—the Most Compassionate, Most Merciful

Published by

Furqaan Institute of Quranic Education (FIQE)
A division of Al-Furqaan Foundation
444 E. Roosevelt Rd., Suite 173, Lombard, IL 60148 USA
Tel: +1 (888-273-2755) or +1 (630) 914-5015
Email: ClearQuran@fiqe.org

© Copyright 2016, Dr. Mustafa Khattab (Translator)
(First Edition, 15 Lines Majeedi Script Edition)

All Rights Reserved. No part of this publication may be reproduced, stored in a retrieval system or transmitted in any form or by any means – electronic, mechanical, photocopying, recording or otherwise – without the written permission from the Publisher.

Translation Approval:

AL-AZHAR (see Letter of Approval):
Islamic Research Academy - General Department for Research, Writing & Translation
For more information about the translation, references, and other approvals, visit: TheClearQuran.org

ISBN: 978-1-949505-02-3 *Regular*
ISBN: 978-1-949505-04-7 *Gift*

Printed in Turkey

Dr. Mustafa Khattab is a Canadian-Egyptian authority on interpreting the Quran. He was a member of the first team that translated the Ramadan night prayers (*Tarawîḥ*) live from the Sacred Mosque in Makkah and the Prophet's Mosque in Madînah (2002-2005). Dr. Khattab memorized the entire Quran at a young age and later obtained a professional *ijâzah* in the *Ḥafṣ* style of recitation with a chain of narrators going all the way to Prophet Muḥammad ﷺ. He received his Ph.D., M.A., and B.A. in Islamic Studies in English with Honours from Al-Azhar University's Faculty of Languages & Translation. He lectured on Islam at Clemson University (OLLI Program, 2009-2010), held the position of Lecturer at Al-Azhar University for over a decade starting in 2003, and served as the Muslim Chaplain at Brock University and the University of Toronto (Mississauga). He is a member of the Canadian Council of Imams and a Fulbright Interfaith Scholar. He has served as an Imam in the U.S. and Canada since 2007 and is the author of *The Clear Quran® Dictionary* (2021), *The Clear Quran® for Kids* (2020), *Shukran* (an illustrated story for children, 2020), *Outfoxing Fox News* (2017), and *The Nation of Islam* (2011), and contributor to the *Encyclopedia of Muslim American History* (2010).

A THEMATIC ENGLISH TRANSLATION

THE CLEAR QURAN®
Series

WITH ARABIC TEXT

TRANSLATOR
DR. MUSTAFA KHATTAB

CHIEF EDITORS
ABU-ISA WEBB
AARON WANNAMAKER
HISHAM SHARIF